DATE DUE

			PRINTED IN U.S.A.

Poetry
Criticism

Guide to Gale Literary Criticism Series

For criticism on	Consult these Gale series
Authors now living or who died after December 31, 1959	*CONTEMPORARY LITERARY CRITICISM (CLC)*
Authors who died between 1900 and 1959	*TWENTIETH-CENTURY LITERARY CRITICISM (TCLC)*
Authors who died between 1800 and 1899	*NINETEENTH-CENTURY LITERATURE CRITICISM (NCLC)*
Authors who died between1400 and 1799	*LITERATURE CRITICISM FROM 1400 TO 1800 (LC)* *SHAKESPEAREAN CRITICISM (SC)*
Authors who died before 1400	*CLASSICAL AND MEDIEVAL LITERATURE CRITICISM (CMLC)*
Black writers of the past two hundred years	*BLACK LITERATURE CRITICISM (BLC) AND BLACK LITERATURE CRITICISM SUPPLEMENT (BLCS)*
Authors of books for children and young adults	*CHILDREN'S LITERATURE REVIEW (CLR)*
Dramatists	*DRAMA CRITICISM (DC)*
Hispanic writers of the late nineteenth and twentieth centuries	*HISPANIC LITERATURE CRITICISM (HLC)*
Native North American writers and orators of the eighteenth, nineteenth, and twentieth centuries	*NATIVE NORTH AMERICAN LITERATURE (NNAL)*
Poets	*POETRY CRITICISM (PC)*
Short story writers	*SHORT STORY CRITICISM (SSC)*
Major authors from the Renaissance to the present	*WORLD LITERATURE CRITICISM, 1500 TO THE PRESENT (WLC)*
Major authors and works from the Bible to the present	*WORLD LITERATURE CRITICISM SUPPLEMENT (WLCS)*

ISSN 1052-4851

R

Poetry Criticism

Excerpts from Criticism of the Works of the Most Significant and Widely Studied Poets of World Literature

VOLUME 24

Laura A. Wisner-Broyles
Editor

GALE

DETROIT · LONDON

STAFF

Laura A. Wisner-Broyles, *Editor*

Anna Sheets Nesbitt, Lawrence J. Trudeau, *Associate Editors*

Lynn U. Koch, Susan Salas, Debra A. Wells, *Assistant Editors*

Kimberly F. Smilay, *Permissions Specialist*
Sarah Chesney, *Permissions Associate*
Stephen Cusack, Sandra K. Gore, Kelly Quin, *Permissions Assistants*

Victoria B. Cariappa, *Research Manager*
Michele P. LaMeau, *Research Specialist*
Julie C. Daniel, Tamara C. Nott, Tracie A. Richardson,
Cheryl L. Warnock, *Research Associates*

Mary Beth Trimper, *Production Director*
Cindy Range, *Production Assistant*

C. J. Jonik, *Desktop Publisher*
Randy Bassett, *Image Database Supervisor*
Michael Ansari, Robert Duncan, *Scanner Operator*
Pamela Reed, Barbara Yarrow, *Photography Coordinators*

Library of Congress Catalog Card Number 91-118494
ISBN 0-7876-2015-7
ISSN 1052-4851

Printed in the United States of America

10 9 8 7 6 5 4 3 2 1

Contents

Preface vii

Acknowledgments xi

Preface

A Comprehensive Information Source on World Poetry

*P*oetry Criticism (PC) provides substantial critical excerpts and biographical information on poets throughout the world who are most frequently studied in high school and undergraduate college courses. Each *PC* entry is supplemented by biographical and bibliographical material to help guide the user to a fuller understanding of the genre and its creators. Although major poets and literary movements are covered in such Gale Literary Criticism Series as *Contemporary Literary Criticism (CLC)*, *Twentieth-Century Literary Criticism (TCLC)*, *Nineteenth-Century Literature Criticism (NCLC)*, *Literature Criticism from 1400 to 1800 (LC)*, and *Classical and Medieval Literature Criticism (CMLC)*, *PC* offers more focused attention on poetry than is possible in the broader, survey-oriented entries on writers in these Gale series. Students, teachers, librarians, and researchers will find that the generous excerpts and supplementary material provided by *PC* supply them with the vital information needed to write a term paper on poetic technique, to examine a poet's most prominent themes, or to lead a poetry discussion group.

Coverage

In order to reflect the influence of tradition as well as innovation, poets of various nationalities, eras, and movements are represented in every volume of *PC*. Each author entry presents a historical survey of the critical response to that author's work; the length of an entry reflects the amount of critical attention that the author has received from critics writing in English and from foreign critics in translation. Since many poets have inspired a prodigious amount of critical explication, *PC* is necessarily selective, and the editors have chosen the most significant published criticism to aid readers and students in their research. In order to provide these important critical pieces, the editors will sometimes reprint essays that have appeared in previous volumes of Gale's Literary Criticism Series. Such duplication, however, never exceeds fifteen percent of a *PC* volume.

Organization

Each *PC* author entry consists of the following components:

- **Author Heading:** the name under which the author wrote appears at the beginning of the entry, followed by birth and death dates. If the author wrote consistently under a pseudonym, the pseudonym will be listed in the author heading and his or her legal name given in parentheses in the lines immediately preceding the Introduction. Uncertainty as to birth or death dates is indicated by question marks.

- **Introduction:** a biographical and critical essay introduces readers to the author and the critical discussions surrounding his or her work.

- **Author Portrait:** a photograph or illustration of the author is included when available.

- **Principal Works:** the author's most important works are identified in a list ordered chronologically by first publication dates. The first section comprises poetry collections and book-length poems. The second section gives information on other major works by the author. For foreign authors, original foreign-language publication information is provided, as well as the best and most complete English-language editions of their works.

- **Criticism:** critical excerpts chronologically arranged in each author entry provide perspective on changes in critical evaluation over the years. All individual titles of poems and poetry collections by the author featured in the entry are printed in boldface type to enable a reader to ascertain without difficulty the works under discussion. For purposes of easy identification, the critic's name and the publication date of the essay are given at the beginning of each piece of criticism. Unsigned criticism is preceded by the title of the journal in which it originally appeared. Publication information (such as publisher names and book prices) and parenthetical numerical references (such as footnotes or page and line references to specific editions of a work) have been deleted at the editor's discretion to enable smoother reading of the text.

- **Explanatory Notes:** introductory comments preface each critical excerpt, providing several types of useful information, including: the reputation of a critic, the importance of a work of criticism, and the specific type of criticism (biographical, psychoanalytic, historical, etc.).

- **Author Commentary:** insightful comments from the authors themselves and excerpts from author interviews are included when available.

- **Bibliographical Citations:** information preceding each piece of criticism guides the interested reader to the original essay or book.

- **Further Reading:** bibliographic references accompanied by descriptive notes at the end of each entry suggest additional materials for study of the author. Boxed material following the Further Reading provides references to other biographical and critical series published by Gale.

Other Features

- **Cumulative Author Index:** comprises all authors who have appeared in Gale's Literary Criticism Series, along with cross-references to such Gale biographical series as *Contemporary Authors* and *Dictionary of Literary Biography*. This cumulated index enables the user to locate an author within the various series.

- **Cumulative Nationality Index:** includes all authors featured in *PC,* arranged alphabetically under their respective nationalities.

- **Cumulative Title Index:** lists in alphabetical order all individual poems, book-length poems, and collection titles contained in the *PC* series. Titles of poetry collections and separately published poems are printed in italics, while titles of individual poems are printed in roman type with quotation marks. Each title is followed by the author's name and the volume and page number corresponding to the location of commentary on specific works. English-language translations of original foreign-language titles are cross-referenced to the foreign titles so that all references to discussion of a work are combined in one listing.

Citing *Poetry Criticism*

When writing papers, students who quote directly from any volume in the Literary Criticism Series may use the following general formats to footnote reprinted criticism. The first example pertains to material drawn from periodicals, the second to material reprinted from books:

[1]David Daiches, "W. H. Auden: The Search for a Public," *Poetry* LIV (June 1939), 148-56; excerpted and reprinted in *Poetry Criticism*, Vol. 1, ed. Robyn V. Young (Detroit: Gale Research, 1990), pp. 7-9.

[2]Pamela J. Annas, *A Disturbance in Mirrors: The Poetry of Sylvia Plath* (Greenwood Press, 1988); excerpted and reprinted in *Poetry Criticism*, Vol. 1, ed. Robyn V. Young (Detroit: Gale Research, 1990), pp. 410-14.

Comments Are Welcome

Readers who wish to suggest authors to appear in future volumes, or who have other suggestions, are cordially invited to contact the editors.

Acknowledgments

The editors wish to thank the copyright holders of the excerpted criticism included in this volume and the permissions managers of many book and magazine publishing companies for assisting us in securing reproduction rights. We are also grateful to the staffs of the Detroit Public Library, the Library of Congress, the University of Detroit Mercy Library, Wayne State University Purdy/Kresge Library Complex, and the University of Michigan Libraries for making their resources available to us. Following is a list of the copyright holders who have granted us permission to reproduce material in this volume of **PC.** Every effort has been made to trace copyright, but if omissions have been made, please let us know.

COPYRIGHTED EXCERPTS IN *PC,* VOLUME 24, WERE REPRODUCED FROM THE FOLLOWING PERIODICALS:

American Poetry, v. 4, Winter, 1987. Reproduced by permission.—*American Poetry Review,* v. 5, January-February, 1976 for "Saying the Life of Things" by Julia Randall. Copyright © 1976 by World Poetry, Inc. Reproduced by permission of the author.—*Ariel,* v. 13, October, 1982 for "The Song of the Caged Bird: Contemporary African Prison Poetry" by Chikwenye Okonjo Ogunyemi. Copyright © 1982 The Board of Governors, The University of Calgary. Reproduced by permission of the publisher and the author.—*Black Academy River,* v. 2, Spring-Summer, 1971.—*Black American Literature Forum,* v. 23, Fall, 1989 for a review of "Airs and Tributes" by Amiri Baraka. Copyright © 1989 by the author. Reproduced by permission of Sterling Lord Literistic, Inc.—*Books and Bookmen,* v. 20, April, 1975 for "How Bad Was Rupert Brooke?" by Derek Stanford; v. 20, April, 1975 for "How Bad Was Rupert Brooke? Part 2" by Derek Stanford. © copyright the author 1975. Both reproduced by permission of the author.—*Bulletin of Hispanic Studies,* v. LXXII, January, 1995. © copyright 1995 Liverpool University Press. Reproduced by permission.—*The Canadian Forum,* v. VII, September, 1927. Reproduced by permission.—*The Centennial Review,* v. XXXII, Spring, 1988 for "Howard Nemerov and the Tyranny of Shakespeare" By Ejner J. Jensen. © 1988 by The Centennial Review. Reproduced by permission of the publisher and the author.—*The Chesterton Review,* v. IV, Spring-Summer, 1978 for "Different Worlds in Verse" by Gertrude M. White; v. XII, May, 1986 for "The Manuscript Poetry of Hilaire Belloc" by Michael H. Markel. © 1978, 1986 *The Chesterton Review.* Both reproduced by permission of the respective authors.—*CLA Journal,* v. XXIX, September, 1985; v. XXXVI, September, 1992. Copyright, 1985, 1992 by The College Language Association. Both used by permission of The College Language Association.—*Colonial Latin American Review,* v. 4, 1995. Reproduced by permission of Carafax Publishing Limited, P.O. Box 25, Abingdon, OX14 3UE, United Kingdom.—*Critical Survey,* v. 2, 1990. Reproduced by permission.—*Cultural Events in Africa,* n. 26, January, 1967. Reproduced by permission.—*English Literature in Transition 1880-1920,* v. 32, 1989. Copyright © 1989 English Literature in Transition: 1880-1920. Reproduced by permission.—*Hispanic Journal,* v. 8, Fall, 1986; v. 13, Fall, 1991. © copyright, 1986, 1991 IUP Indiana University of Pennsylvania. Both reproduced by permission.—*The Journal of Negro History,* v. LII, April, 1967. Reproduced by permission.—*Literary Onomastics Studies,* v. IX, 1982 for "Onomastic Devices in the Poetry of Rupert Brooke" by Allen Walker Read. Reproduced by permission.—*Mester,* v. XX, Fall, 1991. Copyright © 1991 by The Regents of the University of California. Reproduced by permission.—*The Mississippi Quarterly,* v. XXVIII, Fall, 1975. Copyright 1975 Mississippi State University. Reproduced by permission.—*MLN,* v. 106, March, 1991. © copyright 1991 by The Johns Hopkins University Press. All rights reserved. Reproduced by permission.—*Mosaic,* v. 23, Fall, 1990. © Mosaic 1990. Acknowledgment of previous publication is herewith made.—*Neophilologus,* v. LXXV, July, 1991 for "Georgian Poetry's False Dawn" by Paul Moeyes. © 1991 by H. D. Tjeenk Willink. Reproduced by permission of the publisher and the author.—*The New Criterion,* v. 6, January, 1988 for "Death and the Poet" by Robert Richman. Copyright © 1988 by The Foundation for Cultural Review. Reproduced by permission of the author.—*PHYLON: The Atlanta University of Race and Culture,* v. 32, Winter, 1971. Copyright, 1971, by Atlanta University. Reproduced by permission of *PHYLON.*—*Poetry,* v. LXXI, November, 1947 for "Question of Strategy" by F. C. Golffing; v. XCIII, December, 1958 for "Nemerov: The Middle of the Journey" by Carolyn Kizer; v. CII, September, 1963 for "Interim Report" by Hayden Carruth. Copyright 1947, renewed 1974; © 1958, renewed 1986; © 1963, renewed 1991 by the Modern Poetry Association. All reproduced by permission of the Editor of *Poetry* and the respective authors./ v. LXXVI, September, 1950. Copyright 1950, renewed 1974 by the Modern Poetry Association. Reproduced by permission of the Editor of *Poetry.*—*RLA: Romance Languages Annual,* v. 1, 1989.

COPYRIGHTED EXCERPTS IN *PC*, VOLUME 24, WERE REPRODUCED FROM THE FOLLOWING BOOKS:

of Simon & Schuster Macmillan.—Lent, John. From "Turning Stones to Trees: The Transformation of Political Experience in Dennis Brutus' 'Strains'" in *Critical Perspectives on Dennis Brutus.* Edited by Craig W. McLuckie and Patrick J. Colbert. Three Continents Press, 1995. Copyright © Three Continents Press 1995. All rights reserved. Reproduced by permission of the author.—Markel, Michael H. From *Hilaire Belloc.* Twayne Publishers, 1982. Copyright © 1982 by G. K. Hall & Company. All rights reserved. Reproduced by permission of the author.—Meinke, Peter. From "Twenty Years of Accomplishment" in *The Critical Reception of Howard Nemerov: A Selection of Essays and a Bibliography.* Edited by Bowie Duncan. The Scarecrow Press, 1971. Copyright 1971 By Bowie Duncan. Reproduced by permission of the author.—Mills, William. From *The Stillness In Moving Things: The World of Howard Nemerov.* Memphis State University Press, 1975. Copyright © 1975 by Memphis State University Press. All rights reserved. Reproduced by permission.—Olsen, Douglas H. From *Imagination and the Spirit: Essays in Literature and the Christian Faith Presented to Clyde S. Kilby.* Edited by Charles A. Huttar. William B. Eerdmans Publishing Company, 1971. Copyright © 1971 by William B. Eerdmans Publishing Company. All rights reserved. Reproduced by permission.—Paz, Octavio. From *Sor Juana, or, the Traps of Faith.* Translated by Margaret Sayers Peden. Cambridge, Mass.: Harvard University Press, 1988. Copyright © 1988 by the President and Fellows of Harvard College. All rights reserved. Reproduced by permission.—Paz, Octavio. From *The Siren & The Seashell, and Other Essays on Poets and Poetry.* Translated by Lysander Kemp and Margaret Sayers Peden. University of Texas Press, 1976. Translation copyright © 1976 by Octavio Paz. All rights reserved. Reproduced by permission.—Plaver. From *Palaver: Interviews with Five African Writers in Texas.* Bernth Lindfors, Ian Munro, Richard Priebe, Reinhard Sander, eds. African and Afro-American Research Institute, 1972. Reproduced by permission.—Richardson, James. From *Vanishing Lives: Style and Self in Tennyson, D. G. Rossetti, Swinburne, and Yeats.* University Press of Virginia, 1988. Copyright © 1988 by the Rector and Visitors of the University of Virginia. Reproduced by permission.—Riede, David G. From *Swinburne: A Study of Romantic Mythmaking.* University Press of Virginia, 1978. Copyright © 1978 by the Rector and Visitors of the University of Virginia. Reproduced by permission.—Sabat-Rivers, Georgina. From "A Feminist Rereading of Sor Juana's Dream" in *Feminist Perspectives on Sor Juana Inés de la Cruz.* Edited by Stephanie Merrim. Wayne State University Press, 1991. Copyright © 1991 by Wayne State University Press. All rights reserved. Reproduced by permission of the publisher and the author.—Terry, Arthur. From *Studies in Spanish Literature of the Golden Age.* Tamesis Books, 1973. © Copyright. All rights reserved. Reproduced by permission.—Wagner, Jean. From *Black Poets of the United States: From Paul Laurence Dunbar to Langston Hughes.* Translated by Kenneth Douglas. University of Illinois Press, 1973. © 1973 by The Board of Trustees of the University of Illinois. Reproduced by permission.—Wilson, A. N. From *Belloc.* Atheneum, 1984. Copyright © 1984 by A. N. Wilson. All rights reserved. Reproduced by permission of Sterling Lord Literistic, Inc.—Wilson, A. N. From the introduction to *Complete Verse.* By Hilaire Belloc. Pimlico, 1991. Introduction © A. N. Wilson 1991. Reproduced by permission.

PHOTOGRAPHS AND ILLUSTRATIONS APPEARING IN *PC*, VOLUME 24, WERE RECEIVED FROM THE FOLLOWING SOURCES:

Belloc, Hilaire, photograph. The Library of Congress.

Brooke, Rupert, photograph. Hulton-Deutsch Collection/Corbis-Bettmann. Reproduced by permission.

Brutus, Dennis, photograph. AP/Wide World Photos. Reproduced by permission.

Johnson, James Weldon, photograph. The Library of Congress.

Juana Inez de la Cruz, painting. Philadelphia Museum of Art/Corbis-Bettmann. Reproduced by permission.

Nemerov, Howard, photograph. Oscar White/Corbis-Bettmann. Reproduced by permission.

Swinburne, Algernon Charles, engraving. Archive Photos, Inc. Reproduced by permission.

Hilaire Belloc
1870-1953

(Full name Joseph Hilaire Pierre Sébastien Réné Swanton Belloc) English poet, essayist, travel writer, biographer, critic, historian, and novelist.

INTRODUCTION

At the turn of the century Belloc was considered one of England's most provocative essayists and a talented poet. In fact, Belloc and his long-time friend and collaborator G. K. Chesterton have been lauded by W. H. Auden as the best light-verse writers of their era, with Belloc's *Cautionary Tales* considered by some his most successful work in the genre.

Biographical Information

The son of a French father and English mother, Belloc was born in St. Cloud, France, but raised in England, studying at the best private schools. From his studies and his travels between England and France, he acquired cosmopolitan interests in history, polemics, and literature. After brief service in the French military and a brilliant stint at Oxford's Balliol College, Belloc began writing for various London newspapers and magazines. His first book, *Verses and Sonnets,* appeared in 1896, followed by *The Bad Child's Book of Beasts,* which satirized moralistic light verse. Illustrated with superb complementary effect by his friend Basil T. Blackwood, *The Bad Child's Book of Beasts,* according to critics, contains much of the author's best light verse, as do such later collections as *More Beasts (for Worse Children), The Modern Traveller,* and *Cautionary Tales.* But Belloc perceived his primary role as that of polemicist and reformer, whose work must reflect his desire for Europe's spiritual, social, and political return to its monarchist, Roman Catholic heritage.

The period between the century's turn and the mid-1920s was the time of Belloc's widest fame and influence. Throughout these years his name and reputation were frequently linked in the public mind with G. K. Chesterton, whom Belloc had met around 1900 when each was a contributor to the radical journal the *Speaker.* In Chesterton, Belloc found a talented illustrator of his books, a friend, and a man who shared and publicly advocated many of his own religious and political views. They published their political ideas in the *Eye Witness,* a weekly political and literary journal edited by Belloc, which became one of the most widely read periodicals in pre-war England. By the 1930s, Belloc's writings lost popularity on account of his strong anti-Semitic and pro-Catholic viewpoints. Embittered that his opinions were no longer taken seriously and that his creative gifts were diminish-

ing, Belloc spent the last years of his career writing histories and biographies. In the early 1940s, after authoring over 150 books, he was forced into retirement by age and a series of strokes. He spent the last ten years of his life in quiet retirement at his longtime home in rural Sussex, dying in 1953.

Major Works

In his widely known verse for children, Belloc assumed the perspective of a ridiculously stuffy and pedantic adult lecturing children on the inevitable catastrophes that result from improper behavior. Among his outstanding verses of this type are "Maria Who Made Faces and a Deplorable Marriage," "Godolphin Horne, Who Was Cursed with the Sin of Pride, and Became a Bootblack," and "Algernon, Who Played with a Loaded Gun, and, on Missing his Sister, Was Reprimanded by His Father." Like his children's verse, Belloc's satiric light verse is characterized by its jaunty, heavily rhythmic cadences and by the author's keen sense of the absurd, as reflected in "East and West" and in "Lines to a Don." In addition to writing light verse, Belloc also wrote many serious poems and sonnets, which are commonly concerned with the human struggle against the idea of mortality. Of these, "Heroic Song in Praise of Wine" and "The Prophet Lost in the Hills at Evening" are among the most acclaimed of his poems.

Critical Reception

Belloc has received the most critical praise for his amusing verse for children, in particular *The Bad Child's Book of Beasts* and *Cautionary Tales.* Commentators laud his sharp mockery of human pretensions and his rhythmic language, and compare these books to the works of Lewis Carroll and Edward Lear. This simple, humorous verse was commercially and critically popular, as was his other light verse that incorporated more mature themes and situations. Belloc's other poetry, collected in such volumes as *Sonnets and Verses,* garnered mixed assessments from reviewers. Some viewed the verse as superficial and mechanical, yet many critics considered the poetry charming and straightforward.

PRINCIPAL WORKS

Poetry

The Bad Child's Book of Beasts 1896
Verses and Sonnets 1896
More Beasts—For Worse Children 1897
The Modern Traveller 1898
Cautionary Tales 1907
New Cautionary Tales 1930
The Verse of Hilaire Belloc 1954
Collected Verses 1958

Other Major Works

Danton (biography) 1899
Lambkin's Remains (fictional biography) 1900
Robespierre (biography) 1901
The Path to Rome (travel sketches) 1902
Caliban's Guide to Letters (satirical essays) 1903
Avril (essays) 1904
Emmanuel Burden (novel) 1904
On Nothing (essays) 1908
Marie Antoinette (biography) 1909
On Everything (essays) 1909
The French Revolution (history) 1911
The Four Men (travel sketches) 1912
The Servile State (essay) 1912
The Jews (essay) 1922
The Cruise of the "Nona" (travel sketches) 1925
A Companion to Mr. Wells's "Outline of History" (criticism) 1926
Many Cities (travel sketches) 1928
Milton (biography) 1935
Elizabethan Commentary (history) 1942
Selected Essays (essays) 1948

CRITICISM

Joyce Kilmer (essay date 1918)

SOURCE: "The Poetry of Hilaire Belloc," in *Joyce Kilmer. Volume Two: The Prose Works,* edited by Robert Cortes Holliday, Kennikat Press, 1918, pp. 62-77.

[*In the following essay, Kilmer terms Belloc as a natural poet better known for his prose.*]

Far from the poets being astray in prose-writing (said Francis Thompson), it might plausibly be contended that English prose, as an art, is but a secondary stream of the Pierian fount, and owes its very origin to the poets. The first writer one remembers with whom prose became an art was Sir Philip Sidney. And Sidney was a poet.

This quotation is relevant to a consideration of Hilaire Belloc, because Belloc is a poet who happens to be known chiefly for his prose. His *Danton* and *Robespierre* have been read by every intelligent student of French history, his *Path to Rome,* that most high-spirited and engaging of travel books, has passed through many editions, his political writings are known to all lovers—and many foes—of democracy, his whimsically imaginative novels have their large and appreciative audience, and his exquisite brief essays are contemporary classics. And since the unforgetable month of August of the unforgetable year 1914, Hilaire Belloc has added to the number of his friends many thousands who care little for *belles lettres* and less for the French Revolution—he has become certainly the most popular, and by general opinion the shrewdest and best informed, of all chroniclers and critics of the Great War.

There is nothing, it may be said, about these achievements to indicate the poet. How can this most public of publicists woo the shy and exacting Muse? His superabundant energy may now and again overflow in little lyrical rivulets, but how can he find time to turn it into the deep channels of song?

Well, what is the difference between a poet who writes prose and a prose-writer who writes verse? The difference is easy to see but hard to describe. Mr. Thomas Hardy is a prose writer. He has forsaken the novel, of which he was so distinguished a master, to make cynical little sonnet portraits and to pour the acid wine of his philosophy—a sort of perverted Presbyterianism—into the graceful amphora of poetic drama. But he is not a poet. Thackeray was a prose-writer, in spite of his delicious light verse. Every novelist writes or has written verse, but not all of them are poets.

Of course, Sir Walter Scott was first of all a poet—the greatest poet who ever wrote a novel. And no one who has read *Love in the Valley* can hesitate to give Meredith his proper title. Was Macaulay a poet? I think so—but perhaps I am in a hopeless minority in my belief that the author of *The Battle of Naseby* and *The Lays of Ancient Rome* was the last of the great English ballad makers.

But this general truth cannot, I think, honestly be denied; there have been many great poets who have devoted most of their lives to writing prose. Some of them have died without discovering their neglected talent. I think that Walter Pater was one of these; much that is annoyingly subtle or annoyingly elaborate in his essays needs only rhyme and rhythm—the lovely accidents of poetry—to become graceful and appropriate. His famous description of the Mona Lisa is worthless if considered as a piece of serious æsthetic criticism. But it would make an admirable sonnet. And it is significant that Walter Pater's two greatest pupils—Lionel Johnson and Father Gerard Hopkins, S.J.,—found expression for their genius not in prose, the chosen medium of their "unforgetably most gracious friend," but in verse.

From Walter Pater, that exquisite of letters, to the robust Hilaire Belloc may seem a long journey. But there is, I insist, this similarity between these contrasting writers, both are poets, and both are known to fame by their prose.

For proof that Walter Pater was a poet, it is necessary only to read his *Renaissance Studies* or his interpretations—unsound but fascinating—of the soul of ancient Greece. Often his essays, too delicately accurate in phrasing or too heavily laden with golden rhetoric, seem almost to cry aloud for the relief of rhyme and rhythm.

Now, Hilaire Belloc suggests in many of his prose sketches that he is not using his true medium. I remember a brief essay on sleep which appeared in *The New Witness*—or, as it was then called, *The Eye Witness*—several years ago, which was not so much a complete work in itself as it was a draft for a poem. It had the economy of phrase, the concentration of idea, which is proper to poetry.

But it is not necessary in the case of Hilaire Belloc, as it is in that of Walter Pater, to search pages of prose for proof that their author is a poet. Now and then—all too seldom—the idea in this man's brain has insisted on its right, has scorned the proffered dress of prose, however fine of warp and woof, however stiff with rich verbal embroidery, and has demanded its rhymed and rhythmed wedding garments. Therefore, for proof that Hilaire Belloc is a poet it is necessary only to read his poetry.

II

Hilaire Belloc is a poet. Also he is a Frenchman, an Englishman, an Oxford man, a Roman Catholic, a country gentleman, a soldier, a democrat, and a practical journalist. He is always all these things.

One sign that he is naturally a poet is that he is never deliberately a poet. No one can imagine him writing a poem to order—even to his own order. The poems knock at the door of his brain and demand to be let out. And he lets them out, carelessly enough, setting them confortably down on paper simply because that is the treatment they

desire. And this happens to be the way all real poetry is made.

Not that all verse makers work that way. There are men who come upon a waterfall or mountain or an emotion and say: "Aha! here is something out of which I can extract a poem!" And they sit down in front of that waterfall or mountain or an emotion and think up clever things to say about it. These things they put into metrical form, and the result they fondly call a poem.

There's no harm in that. It's good exercise for the mind, and of it comes much interesting verse. But it is not the way in which the sum of the world's literature is increased.

Could anything, for example, be less studied, be more clearly marked with the stigmata of that noble spontaneity we call inspiration, than the passionate, rushing, irresistible lines **"To the Balliol Men Still in Africa"**? Like Gilbert K. Chesterton and many another English democrat, Hilaire Belloc deeply resented his country's war upon the Boers. Yet his heart went out to the friends of his university days who were fighting in Africa. They were fighting, he thought, in an unjust cause; but they were his friends and they were, at any rate, fighting. And so he made something that seems (like all great writing) an utterance rather than a composition; he put his love of war in general and his hatred of this war in particular, his devotion to Balliol and to the friends of his youth into one of the very few pieces of genuine poetry which the Boer War produced. Nor has any of Oxford's much-sung colleges known praise more fit than this

> House that armours a man
>   With the eyes of a boy and the heart of a ranger,
> And a laughing way in the teeth of the world,
>   And a holy hunger and thirst for danger.

But perhaps a more typical example of Hilaire Belloc's wanton genius is to be found not among those poems which are, throughout, the beautiful expressions of beautiful impressions, but among those which are careless, whimsical, colloquial. There is that delightful, but somewhat exasperating **"Dedicatory Ode."** Hilaire Belloc is talking—charmingly, as is his custom—to some of his friends, who had belonged, in their university days, to a youthful revolutionary organisation called the Republican Club. He happens to be talking in verse, for no particular reason except that it amuses him to talk in verse. He makes a number of excellent jokes, and enjoys them very much; his Pegasus is cantering down the road at a jolly gait, when suddenly, to the amazement of the spectators, it spreads out great golden wings and flashes like a meteor across the vault of heaven! We have been laughing at the droll tragedy of the opium-smoking Uncle Paul; we have been enjoying the humorous spectacle of the contemplative freshman—and suddenly we come upon a bit of astonishingly fine poetry. Who would expect, in all this whimsical and jovial writing, to find this really great stanza?

> From quiet homes and first beginning
>   Out to the undiscovered ends,

> There's nothing worth the wear of winning
> But laughter and the love of friends.

Who having read these four lines, can forget them? And who but a poet could write them? But Hilaire Belloc has not forced himself into this high mood, nor does he bother to maintain it. He gaily passes on to another verse of drollery, and then, not because he wishes to bring the poem to an effective climax, but merely because it happens to be his mood, he ends the escapade he calls an Ode with eight or ten stanzas of nobly beautiful poetry.

There is something almost uncanny about the flashes of inspiration which dart out at the astonished reader of Hilaire Belloc's most frivolous verses. Let me alter a famous epigram and call his light verse a circus illuminated by lightning. There is that monumental burlesque, the New-digate Poem—**"A Prize Poem Submitted by Mr. Lambkin of Burford to the Examiners of the University of Oxford on the Prescribed Poetic Theme Set by Them in 1893, 'The Benefits of the Electric Light.'"** It is a tremendous joke; with every line the reader echoes the author's laughter. But without the slightest warning Hilaire Belloc passes from rollicking burlesque to shrewd satire; he has been merrily jesting with a bladder on a stick, he suddenly draws a gleaming rapier and thrusts it into the heart of error. He makes Mr. Lambkin say:

> Life is a veil, its paths are dark and rough
> Only because we do not know enough:
> When Science has discovered something more
> We shall be happier than we were before.

Here we find the directness and restraint which belong to really great satire. This is the materialistic theory, the religion of Science, not burlesqued, not parodied, but merely stated nakedly, without the verbal frills and furbe-lows with which our forward-looking leaders of popular thought are accustomed to cover its obscene absurdity. Almost these very words have been uttered in a dozen "rationalistic" pulpits I could mention, pulpits occupied by robustuous practical gentlemen with very large eyes, great favourites with the women's clubs. Their pet doctrine, their only and most offensive dogma, is not attacked, is not ridiculed; it is merely stated for them, in all kindness and simplicity. They cannot answer it, they cannot deny that it is a mercilessly fair statement of the "philosophy" that is their stock in trade. I hope that many of them will read it.

III

Hilaire Belloc was born July 27, 1870. He was educated at the Oratory School, Edgbaston, and at Balliol College, Oxford. After leaving school he served as a driver in the Eighth Regiment of French Artillery at Toul Meurthe-et-Moselle, being at that time a French citizen. Later he was naturalised as a British subject, and entered the House of Commons in 1906 as Liberal Member for South Salford. British politicians will not soon forget the motion which Hilaire Belloc introduced one day in the early Spring of 1908, the motion that the Party funds, hitherto secretly

administered, be publicly audited. His vigorous and persistent campaign against the party system has placed him, with Cecil Chesterton, in the very front ranks of those to whom the democrats of Great Britain must look for leadership and inspiration. He was always a keen student of military affairs; he prophesied, long before the event, the present international conflict, describing with astonishing accuracy the details of the German invasion of Belgium and the resistance of Liège. Now he occupies a unique position among the journalists who comment upon the War, having tremendously increased the circulation of *Land and Water,* the periodical for which he writes regularly, and lecturing to a huge audience once a week on the events of the War in one of the largest of London's concert halls—Queen's Hall, where the same vast crowds that listen to the War lectures used to gather to hear the works of the foremost German composers.

IV

Hilaire Belloc, as I have said, is a Frenchman, an Englishman, an Oxford man, a country gentleman, a soldier, a democrat, and a practical journalist. In all these characters he utters his poetry. As a Frenchman, he is vivacious and gallant and quick. He has the noble English frankness, and that broad irresistible English mirthfulness which is so much more inclusive than that narrow possession, a sense of humour. Democrat though he is, there is about him something of the atmosphere of the country squire of some generations ago; it is in his heartiness, his jovial dignity, his deep love of the land. The author of *The South Country* and *Courtesy* has made Sussex his inalienable possession; he owns Sussex, as Dickens owns London, and Blackmore owns Devonshire. And he is thoroughly a soldier, a happy warrior, as brave and dexterous, no one can doubt, with a sword of steel as with a sword of words.

He has taken the most severe risk which a poet can take: he has written poems about childhood. What happened when the late Algernon Charles Swinburne bent his energies to the task of celebrating this theme? As the result of his solemn meditation on the mystery of childhood, he arrived at two conclusions, which he melodiously announced to the world. They were, first, that the face of a baby wearing a plush cap looks like a moss-rose bud in its soft sheath, and, second, that "astrolabe" rhymes with "babe." Very charming, of course, but certainly unworthy of a great poet. And upon this the obvious comment is that Swinburne was not a great poet. He took a theme terribly great and terribly simple, and about it he wrote . . . something rather pretty.

Now, when a really great poet—Francis Thompson, for example—has before him such a theme as childhood, he does not spend his time making far-fetched comparisons with moss-rose buds, or hunting for words that rhyme with "babe." Childhood suggests Him Who made childhood sacred, so the poet writes *Ex Ore Infantium* or such a poem as that which ends with the line:

> Look for me in the nurseries of Heaven.

A poet may write pleasingly about mountains, and cyclones and battles, and the love of woman, but if he is at all timid about the verdict of posterity he should avoid the theme of childhood as he would avoid the plague. For only great poets can write about childhood poems worthy to be printed.

The poems knock at the door of Belloc's brain and demand to be let out. And he lets them out, carelessly enough, setting them comfortably down on paper simply because that is the treatment they desire. And this happens to be the way all real poetry is made.

—Joyce Kilmer

Hilaire Belloc has written poems about children, and they are worthy to be printed. He is never ironic when he thinks about childhood; he is gay, whimsical, with a slight suggestion of elfin cynicism, but he is direct, as a child is direct. He has written two dedicatory poems for books to be given to children; they are slight things, but they are a revelation of their author's power to do what only a very few poets can do, that is, to enter into the heart and mind of the child, following that advice which has its literary as well as moral significance, to "become as a little child."

And in many of Hilaire Belloc's poems by no means intended for childish audiences there is an appealing simplicity that is genuinely and beautifully childish, something quite different from the adult and highly artificial simplicity of Professor A. E. Housman's *A Shropshire Lad*. Take that quatrain **"The Early Morning."** It is as clear and cool as the time it celebrates; it is absolutely destitute of rhetorical indulgence, poetical inversions or "literary" phrasing. It is, in fact, conversation—inspired conversation, which is poetry. It might have been written by a Wordsworth not painfully self-conscious, or by a Blake whose brain was not as yet muddled with impressionistic metaphysics.

And his Christmas carols—they are fit to be sung by a chorus of children. Can any songs of the sort receive higher praise than that? Children, too, appreciate **"The Birds"** and **"Our Lord and Our Lady."** Nor is that wonderful prayer rather flatly called **"In a Boat"** beyond the reach of their intelligence.

Naturally enough, Hilaire Belloc is strongly drawn to the almost violent simplicity of the ballad. Bishop Percy would not have enjoyed the theological and political atmosphere of **"The Little Serving Maid,"** but he would have acknowledged its irresistible charm. There is that wholly delightful poem **"The Death and Last Confession of Wandering Peter"**—a most Bellocian vagabond. "He wan-

dered everywhere he would: and all that he approved was sung, and most of what he saw was good." Says Peter:

> If all that I have loved and seen
> Be with me on the Judgment Day,
> I shall be saved the crowd between
> From Satan and his foul array.

Hilaire Belloc has seen much and loved much. He has sung lustily the things he approved—with what hearty hatred has he sung the things he disapproved!

V

Hilaire Belloc is not the man to spend much time in analysing his own emotions; he is not, thank God, a poetical psychologist. Love songs, drinking songs, battle songs—it is with these primitive and democratic things that he is chiefly concerned.

But there is something more democratic than wine or love or war. That thing is Faith. And Hilaire Belloc's part in increasing the sum of the world's beauty would not be the considerable thing that it is were it not for his Faith. It is not that (like Dante Gabriel Rossetti) he is attracted by the Church's pageantry and wealth of legend. To Hilaire Belloc the pageantry is only incidental, the essential thing is his Catholic Faith. He writes convincingly about Our Lady and Saint Joseph and the Child Jesus because he himself is convinced. He does not delve into mediæval tradition in quest of picturesque incidents, he merely writes what he knows to be true. His Faith furnishes him with the theme for those of his poems which are most likely to endure; his Faith gives him the "rapture of an inspiration." His Faith enables him, as it has enabled many another poet, to see "in the lamp that is beauty, the light that is God."

And therein is Hilaire Belloc most thoroughly and consistently a democrat. For in this twentieth century it happens that there is on earth only one genuine democratic institution. And that institution is the Catholic Church.

The Times Literary Supplement **(essay date 1923)**

SOURCE: "Mr. Belloc's Verses," in *The Times Literary Supplement,* November 8, 1923, p. 744.

[In the following essay, the critic offers a mixed review of the poems comprising Sonnets and Verses.*]*

Mr. Belloc, who has been of our times one of the most copious writers in prose, has issued, apart from skits and books for children, only three volumes of verse. The first, which soon disappeared, handed on some pieces to the second; the second is now superseded by this third, which includes it and some new poems. Therefore he, agod fifty-three, presents to us as a lifetime's work in verse, some hundred and sixty pages and a hundred odd pieces, many of which are very short. It is obvious, however, that is not a mere pastime for him, but something which he takes with great seriousness, as well as with much exuberance of spirit. One is moved to see what he has written in prose on the subject. He makes one of the characters in *The Four Men* deliver a comic tirade on the excellence and wholesomeness of well-made verse. He writes more soberly in an essay on José Maria de Heredia:—

> A man determined to produce the greatest things in verse takes up by nature exact and thoughtful words and finds that their rhythm, their combination, and their sound turn under his hand to something greater than he himself at first intended; he becomes a creator, and his name is linked with the name of a masterpiece. The material in which he has worked is hard; the price he has paid is an exceeding effort; the reward he has earned is permanence.

and, of the same poet:—

> He worked upon verse as men work upon the harder metals; all that he did was chiselled very finely, then sawn to an exact configuration, and at last inlaid, for when he published his completed volume it is true to say that every piece fitted in with the sound of one before and of one after. He was careful in the heroic degree.

From these pronouncements something may be deduced about Mr. Belloc's attitude towards his own verse, and this is confirmed by the evidence. It will be noted that he chooses the word which lays most emphasis on workmanship and least on inspiration. He talks of verse, a thing which can be grasped, handled, and materially examined inch by inch, not of poetry, which must be discussed in other terms. It is not for him primarily a medium by means of which he can propagate this or that philosophy, nor yet primarily an outlet for his own feelings. It is a material with which he can create beautiful, worthy, and enduring things. His poems will be, if he succeeds with them, objects like statues or pictures or pieces of jewel-work. They will be detached from the life in which he found them, just as are the sonnets of Heredia. And because this is (today at any rate) an unusual attitude, as well as an unusually definite one, these poems, the results of a lifetime's work in a respected medium, command our attention whether we decide that he is successful in them or not.

Because he has an altogether unmodern contempt for mere self-expression, it follows that he is without the modern anxiety to create a style entirely for himself. He would rather have a good old style, proved by experience suitable for certain uses, than a gimcrack one, indubitably his own but uncertain in its application. And he does not stray far from the periods in which, as it seems to him, the execution of verse was most sedulously attended to, the periods of the Pléiade and of Dryden and his successors. Sometimes he comes near to giving the effect of pastiche, as in "Strephon's Song". . . :

> This morning you kissed me,
> By noon you dismissed me
> As though such great things were the jest of

> one hour,
> And you left me still wondering
> If I were not too blundering
> To deal with that delicate, delicate flower:
> 'Tis such a delicate, delicate, delicate flower!

The line between a pastiche and a belated masterpiece is not an easy one to draw. Knowledge of the facts confuses the judgment; but Sir Francis Palgrave, without that knowledge, went rather astray over what now seems an obvious pastiche by George Darley. In the present instance each reader may be left to decide without suggestion where the line ought to be drawn.

But there are other poems by Mr. Belloc, not markedly individual in style, not certainly of this or of any other period in particular, which cannot be described as pastiches. Many of his sonnets might *almost* have been written by an extra member of the Pléiade—if that extra member had ehanced to think in English:—

> When you to Acheron's ugly water come
> Where darkness is and formless mourners brood
> And down the shelves of that distasteful flood
> Survey the human rank in order dumb.
> When the pale dead go forward, tortured more
> By nothingness and longing than by fire,
> Which bear their hands in suppliance with desire,
> With stretched desire for the ulterior shore.
>
> Then go before them like a royal ghost
> And tread like Egypt or like Carthage crowned;
> Because in your Mortality the most
> Of all we may inherit has been found—
> Children for memory: the Faith for pride,
> Good land to leave: and young Love satisfied.

That is at any rate nearer to Ronsard and Du Bellay than were the elaborate and scholarly compositions of Jean Moréas and Maurice du Plessis, during the short existence of the Ecole Romane. It conveys, too, a suggestion, somewhat peculiar in these days, though it would hardly have been thought odd by the writers or in the times which Mr. Belloc most admires, that a good style instead of revealing the individual may achieve a sort of impersonality. The man who wrote that sonnet may be speaking out of his own personal feelings, but he clearly believes that such feelings are common in humanity. The feelings of humanity are his theme; considered and careful versification is his material. Thus provided, he makes a beautiful thing; he is not concerned to express himself as a unique being.

The carefulness of structure is to be noted. The epithets are not magic, but they are exactly chosen, and leave the mind satisfied. The balance of the parts of the sonnet and its sweep upward to the conclusion are perfect, but not with a wild, instinctive perfection—rather with that which is arrived at by long and hard thought. This is, one may say, a solid and satisfactory piece of work. So it is, too, when Mr. Belloc seems at first sight to move less deliberately:—

Sally is gone that was so kindly,
  Sally is gone from Ha'nacker Hill.
And the Briar grows ever since then so blindly
  And ever since then the clapper is still,
  And the sweeps have fallen from Ha'nacker
    Mill.

Ha'nacker Hill is in Desolation:
  Ruin a-top and a field unploughed.
And Spirits that call on a fallen nation,
  Spirits that loved her calling aloud:
  Spirits abroad in a windy cloud.

Spirits that call and no one answers:
  Ha'nacker's down and England's done.
Wind and Thistle for pipe and dancers
  And never a ploughinan under the Sun.
  Never a ploughman. Never a one.

Again, not, for all its light grace of movement, an instinctive, unconsidered piece. It has obviously been worked on until each word is proper in its place and everything uncontributory has been stripped away.

Good verse has always, and rightly, been considered indispensable for satirical or comic poetry, and in these branches of the art Mr. Belloc notoriously excels. The manner of his invective is well known:—

It serves no purpose to protest,
  It isn't manners to halloo
About the way the thing was messed—
  Or vaguely call a man a Jew.

It serves no purpose, indeed, unless your halloo is delivered from resonant lungs and your protest neat, pointed and well constructed. It is because Mr. Belloc, having strong and truculent opinions, brings to their expression a craft of verse which has discarded everything weak or slipshod, that, whatever we think of his opinions, he must rank as one of the best satirical poets of our time. These are, indeed, among the most successful of his work; and their strength and solidity will probably carry them on after the perishing of whatever in them may be transitory. But there is nothing transitory in the address of the poor man to the rich man, or in the story of the man who kept his word; nor, indeed, in the robust joke of such an epigram as—

When I am dead, I hope it may be said:
"His sins were scarlet, but his books were read."

But these pieces are for certain moods and do not compel their own. So too are many of the mere rollicking pieces in the collection. **"The Chaunty of the Nona"** is a pastiche, though, being a chaunty imaginable as being sung at sea, almost unique among pastiches. There are also drinking songs (one of them very famous) and lusty, high-spirited eulogies of the author's religion. There are pseudomedieval pieces, many of them also in praise of this religion, the archaic simplicity of which seems often a little forced. All of these are readable, enjoyable, and even

memorable, and not one is carelessly done. But they are not first-rate; they make only a background.

The first-rate pieces are few in number, but when one reads them they compel their own moods and assure Mr. Belloc's survival as a poet. Two of them have already been quoted. To these certain of the sonnets must be added: not all—for in many of them Mr. Belloc affects a sort of Shakespearian pregnancy and packedness, which colours unfortunately the impersonality of his style. The **"Dedicatory Ode"** passes from ingenious rhymed fooling without a jar into a passage as beautiful as any in the book, and thence to half-serious but very effective bluster. But perhaps the type of these pieces is **"Tarantella,"** which begins:—

Do you remember an Inn,
Miranda?
Do you remember an Inn?
And the tedding and the spreading
Of the straw for a bedding,
And the fleas that tease in the High Pyrenees,
And the wine that tasted of the tar?

and which ends:—

Never more;
Miranda,
Never more.
Only the high peaks boar:
And Aragon a torrent at the door.
No sound
In the walls of the Halls where falls
The tread
Of the feet of the dead to the ground
No sound:
But the boom
Of the far Waterfall like Doom.

The intricacy and rightness of the versification are extraordinary; the effect they produce is undeniable. There are, as we have said, not many of these pieces of the first rank in the volume. It is therefore a pity that Mr. Belloc should have omitted not only the songs for shouting which stud the pages of *The Four Men,* but also the lovely poem "He does not die that can bequeath," which comes towards the end of that book.

There are not many; and, in so far as copiousness is a virtue, Mr. Belloc fails. He himself would certainly not regard it as a vice, for he once praised Ronsard for having "that power which our anæmic age can hardly comprehend, of writing, writing, writing, without fear of exhaustion, without irritability or self-criticism, without danger of comparing the better with the worse." Beside Ronsard's great mass of work Mr. Belloc's little volume makes a puny figure. But what can be said of it without hesitation is that the best things in it are as good of their sort as can be. It must also be said that his peculiar and independent attitude towards the art of poetry has a considerable interest for our time. It may be suspected that we have now several writers of talent who do no more than excite and then disappoint our attention, because, obsessed with self-expression and the supposed necessity of creating a new style, they will not sedulously devote themselves to what they could well do—namely, the writing of a few (or many) pieces of beautiful and solid verse.

Richard Pennington (essay date 1930)

SOURCE: "Hilaire Belloc as Poet," in *The Bookman,* Vol. LXXIX, No. 469, October, 1930, pp. 22-3.

[*In the following essay, Pennington provides a positive assessment of Belloc's verse.*]

A critic has recently reminded us that Mr. Belloc has just turned sixty. A good age, and well employed, when we consider the fruits of Mr. Belloc's thirty-five years of writing. For no man surely can look back with more pride upon work that has always been honest and well done, loyal to a constant ideal, courageous and sincere, and not infrequently of a high degree of beauty. This was a happy reminder of an anniversary if it sends a few more readers to a good writer and a clear thinker, and a man who, though in a few things wide of the mark and partisan, is yet worth a dozen of his more popular contemporaries.

To speak of Mr. Belloc here as a poet simply may seem strange to some to whom he is memorable chiefly for the excellent prose of his essays or for such exhilarating books as *The Four Men* and *The Path to Rome.* There have moreover been other manifestations of his protean spirit; there are the political novels, the biographical studies, the military histories—and how well Mr. Belloc can describe a campaign in its essentials, and what a suggestive book is *Warfare in England!*—there are the children's books, and finally a most entertaining *History of England,* though it strays to dubious conclusions at times. But these things are more or less of the present day and ephemeral. What is more certain of enduring fame and likely to carry Mr. Belloc's name to posterity is the poetry; yet it is probably true that this has received the least recognition of all his work.

Why this should be so it is difficult to say. His poetry is not obscure or esoteric or "new" in any unpopular way. It has on the contrary the happy characteristics of closeness to tradition and a firm basis upon logical thought. It has also a certainty of utterance and a clarity of form that are admirable, and with these, a lovely rhythm all its own, and that power of intense suggestion that great poetry alone possesses. Some, remembering his partly French descent, have found foreign influences in his work. It may be that the frequent perfection of form—too often not an English trait—suggests the French clarity of mind. But his poetry, the best of it, is essentially English.

Of the immortality of some of the poems there is no doubt. Again and again, scanning one's shelves of modern poets, one takes down the tall blue volume of *Poems and Sonnets* to find the beauty of some of these pieces assuring,

in this age when so much in poetry is unsatisfying. The epigrams for example have the perfection of Landor's finest work; some of the sonnets have a lovely vehemence that Brooke momentarily captured and Wordsworth at his best achieved; while there are lyrics as pure in melody and exquisite in execution as those of the Elizabethan and the Caroline poets. And there is too a satiric humour that plays over some of the pages and gives us a kind of verse too rare in England, yet poetry in spite of the fierce intent.

Several of the poems have become too well known in anthologies to need quotation, such as **"The South Country," "The Birds," "Ha'nacker Mill."** But the fine sonnets are generally not anthologised and go the more widely unknown therefore; for as Mr. Graves complained in his sparkling petard with which he sought to destroy the popular anthology ("A Pamphlet against Anthologies"), when a little of a man's work is put into an anthology the reading public generally content themselves with that and do not search out his other writings. Here however is one sonnet that has not to my knowledge been bagged by the compilers:

> But oh! not lovely Helen, nor the pride
> Of that most ancient Ilium matched with doom.
> Men murdered Priam in his royal room
> And Troy was burned with fire and Hector died.
> For even Hector's dreadful day was more
> Than all his breathing courage dared defend.
> The armoured light and bulwark of the war
> Trailed his great glory to the accustomed end.
>
> He was the city's buttress, Priam's son,
> The soldier born in bivouac praises great
> And horns in double front of battle won.
> Yet down he went: when unremembering fate
> Felled him at last with all his armour on.
> Hector: the horseman: in the Scæan Gate.

There are other lovely ones: the sonnet on frozen winter; on Rome; that one on Sleep, with its lulling sestet:

> Above the surf-line, into the night breeze;
> Eastward above the ever-whispering seas;
> Through the warm airs with no more watch to keep.
> My day's run out and all its dooms are graven.
> O dear forerunner of Death and promise of Haven.
> O my companion, O my sister Sleep.

Simple; perhaps not pleasing to those strict fanatics of the sonnet to whom anything not Miltonic is not worthy of the name; but how lovely, how accomplished! Of this graceful and finished verse Mr. Belloc is a master. There are those stanzas in the **"Dedicatory Ode"** that begin, in an abrupt change from the humour of

> And One (myself I mean—no less),
> Ah!—will Posterity
>   believe it—
> Not only don't deserve
>   success,
> But hasn't managed to

achieve it,

with the lines:

> I will not try the reach
>   again,
> I will not set my sail
>   alone,
> To moor a boat bereft of
>   men
> At Yarnton's tiny docks
>   of stone. . . .

Finally there are the epigrams, that may prove the most enduring of all his work. Landor wrote much, but "Gebir" is forgotten and few read the "Imaginary Conversations": but his epigrams have lasted and are remembered by men the world over. So it may be Posterity will forget the political novels, the history and much of the essays—though some of these are worthy of preservation—and cherish a few lyrics and such epigrams as these:

"On a Sleeping Friend"

> Lady, when your lovely head
> Droops to sink among the Dead,
> And the quiet places keep
> You that so divinely sleep;
> Then the dead shall blessed be
> With a new solemnity,
> For such Beauty, so descending,
> Pledges them that Death is ending.
> Sleep your fill—but when you wake
> Dawn shall over Lethe break.

"The Statue"

> When we are dead, some Hunting-boy will pass
> And find a stone half-hidden in tall grass
> And grey with age; but having seen that stone
> (Which was your image), ride more slowly on.

We may end with another:

> When I am dead, I hope it may be said:
> "His sins were scarlet, but his books were read."

He need have no fear for his poems: they always will be.

Reginald Jebb (essay date 1954)

SOURCE: An introduction to *Sonnets & Verses,* Gerald Duckworth & Co., 1954, pp. xiii-xxiii.

[*In the following essay, Jebb explores the autobiographical aspects of Belloc's poetry.*]

In the latter years of his life Belloc often repeated that what he would wish to be remembered by was his verse. He was a firm believer in the Muse—that influence out-side himself that inspires the poet—and so he treated his verse almost as though it had been written by someone else.

But though the Muse may inspire, the content and form of a man's verse is his own, dictated to him by his vision, his ideals, and the events of his life; for poetry is the spokesman of the soul. That is certainly true of Belloc. His poetry reflects the amazing diversity of his life, and so it may not be out of place in this Introduction to give an outline of some of those events and experiences that find an echo in his poems. This relationship between his writings and his life is, of course, also evident in his prose works, and when critics remark upon—sometimes even complain of—his versatility and the staggering variety of his output, what they are really noting is the scope of his experience accurately recorded by a mind alive with creative power.

Obviously there will be some episodes in such a life which have left a deeper impression than others, and though all must have had a part in the making of the whole man, some will be found to have left little or no significant trace in his writings. Others seemingly are more fitted for representation in prose than in verse. For example, the impact upon him of America, seen for the first time so vividly through the eyes of a young man of nineteen, has been strikingly recorded in prose—notably in "The Contrast"—but there is almost no reference to it in his verse, despite the fact that he was married there and considered the possibility of making it his home for life.

Nor is there any mention in his verse of that formative period, the first eight years of his life, passed at La Celle St. Cloud, on the outskirts of Paris. For the few lyrics he wrote which touch upon childhood are clearly addressed to children he knew in later life. They tell us nothing of himself. It was here at La Celle that he was born, of a French father and an English mother, in that momentous year 1870, and here that he lived, with periodical visits to his mother's house in Wimpole Street (his French father died when he was still a baby), until he was eight years old. He was christened Hilaire after his grandfather, a celebrated French painter, and under this name most of his works were published, but once he had definitely settled in England he adopted the English form Hilary, and it was by this name that he was known to his friends. There are only scanty records of this part of his life, but so far as they go they give the impression of a small boy in many respects the father of the man. Despite the frailness of his body (for his strong shoulders and stocky frame developed later) he appears to have possessed much of the vigour and self-will of later years. In this connection it is perhaps significant that one of his earliest and most sharply defined memories was the delight he experienced in watching the dust rise from a drawing-room cushion when he beat it with a stick. This delight was probably not shared by his mother and devoted nurse (a Bible Christian of Wesleyan upbringing), who may have found their hands over-full in looking after him. But there were other sides of him developing at the same time. Very early he began to take a keen interest in politics, and at the age of seven he produced a poem which showed at least some signs of that structural excellence of which later he was to become a master.

In 1878 Madame Belloc, his mother, who the year before had lost the greater part of her modest fortune through the recklessness or actual knavery of her trusted lawyer, took a house, the Grange, in Slindon, at the foot of the Sussex Downs; and though she retained possession of the French house, this was let and she passed most of her time in England. Here, at this impressionable age, the little Hilary began to drink in the beauties of Sussex, which remained ever after a major influence in his life. In the years between 1878 and 1882 those pictures were taking shape in his mind and those affections were being nourished which later inspired such poems as **"The South Country," "Gumber"** and **"Duncton Hill,"** besides many prose works.

At the beginning of 1882 his life changed again. He was sent as a boarder to the Oratory School at Edgbaston. This step on the part of his mother was no doubt due to the advice of Cardinal Newman, who had founded the school, and whose friendship she enjoyed. He remained there until the summer of 1887, but this is another period of his life of which he has nothing to say in his writings. That may be because he was never very happy at school. The restraints of enforced discipline irked him, and his swiftly developing mind and character found school routine unsatisfying. In later life he always declared himself in favour of day schools as against those where boys were away from their homes for whole terms on end. Yet he made at least one life-long friend, Charles Somers-Cocks, while he was at the Oratory, and he always spoke with deep respect of his headmaster, Father John Norris. As might be expected, he excelled in the subjects taught in the school, winning the Norfolk Prize in his last year and acquiring a sound foundation in the classics, which stood him in good stead throughout his life. What is more surprising, seeing that he never acted after he left school, is that he won considerable distinction for the parts he took in Latin plays performed at the end of each year.

As soon as he left the Oratory in 1887 the interests which were to be so marked in his life and were reflected in his writings developed rapidly. The next four years were crowded with activity. His mother, whose financial position was causing her considerable anxiety, was eager that he should settle down in some permanent employment and earn his living. With this in view she apprenticed him to a farmer whose land was near her home at Slindon. But the young Belloc did not find this life congenial and the experiment soon came to an end. Yet even during this short interlude his mind was maturing fast and his overmastering love of Sussex becoming still more engrained in him. It was at this time, lying on the turf of the Downs above the Amberley chalk pits, that he discovered the beauty of Shakespeare's sonnets, whose rhythms were later to influence his own; and it may well have been at this time, too, that he first experienced the joy of sailing the boat,

> That brought my boyhood to its first encounter
> And taught me the wide sea.

But life on the land—or rather life as an apprentice at the beck and call of a farmer whom he disliked—was far from satisfying him. He was soon immersed in journalism, where there was some scope for expression of the ideas and opinions brimming over in his mind and some opportunity for developing his talent for drawing little pictures of the things he loved best—boats and hills and woods and fragments of architecture. W. T. Stead, evidently recognizing the promise of brilliance, gave him his first work, and later on we find him editing a weekly paper called *The Lamp,* in which appear a few of his early poems, such as the sonnet beginning **"As one who hath sent forth on bold emprise"** and a short piece entitled (surprisingly, seeing that he was but twenty-one when he wrote it) **"Ehcu Fugaces . . ."**

But though these activities helped to relieve a mind bursting to express itself, they were by no means its principal occupation during these four years. In 1889 an event happened which was not merely to influence, but largely to shape the whole of his future life. He fell in love. Elodie Hogan and her sister Elizabeth, whose grandparents had emigrated to California from Ireland at the time of the famine, were on a visit to Europe and had had an introduction to Madame Belloc from their mutual friend, Stead. It was in the drawing-room of Madame Belloc's London house that Hilary first met Elodie. He proposed to her the same year in his "darling valley" in the Downs, but it was seven years before they were married. This long delay had a number of causes, but from that moment in 1889 the die was cast. Belloc was not a man to waver in any decision, least of all in his determination to marry Elodie.

The Hogan sisters finished their visit and returned to California at the end of the year. In 1890 Belloc made up his mind to follow in their wake. With little money in his pocket he crossed the Atlantic steerage, and made his way largely on foot across the United States, selling sketches he had made to earn him lodging and food on the journey. He eventually arrived at Napa, the home town of the Hogans, but was received with some disfavour by Mrs Hogan as a suitor for her daughter's hand. There was an additional difficulty: Elodie had half made up her mind to become a nun. However, the engagement was not broken off, and Elodie persuaded him to return to Europe and go through the military training that was incumbent upon all French citizens, pointing out that though his home was now in England he would never be well received in his native country if he had evaded its laws.

So the following year, in November 1891, we find him presenting himself as a recruit to the 3rd Battery of the 8th Regiment of Artillery, stationed at Toul. In the little service book that all conscripts possessed there is recorded an official description of his appearance at that time. His hair and eyebrows are noted as "châtain claire," his forehead as "haut," his nose "fort," his mouth "petite," his chin "rond," his eyes "bleus," and his face "ovale." His height was exactly measured—1.74 metres. There are some other interesting entries in this book and in the good-conduct certificate that he received at the end of his training. We learn, for example, that he obtained a second class for revolver shooting and for fencing, but only a third for gymnastics. However, it was recorded of him that he "sait lire, écrire, et compter" and that he was "très bon nageur," while against punishments received was written the single word "néant."

Though his service with the French Gunners was short (it was over by August 1892), its effect upon his life and writings was most marked. It was during this year that he acquired that semi-military attitude that was characteristic of him all through his life; here developed his intense love and admiration of the French Army and his detestation of Prussia; here, too, the strong republicanism of his early life gathered force. From 1892 onwards he had French Gunners' boots made for him and wore them, reaching half-way up his shins, under his trousers; and his repertoire of French marching songs, which he constantly sang in his fine tenor voice, seemed unending. Apart from his numerous works of military history, of which his service in the Army must have sown the seeds, there are scattered through his prose and verse many traces of the influence that year with the colours had upon him. There is, for example, that fine prose poem **"The Reveillon"**; and in this volume such poems as **"I from my window where the Meuse is wide," "The Ballad of Val-ès-Dunes," "The Leader,"** etc., owe much of their realism and vigour to the fierce comradeship and disciplined idealism that characterized the French Army of that time.

After his year of service he returned to England, and a completely new phase of his life began which was, like his military service, to leave a lasting impression on him. In October of 1892 he went up to Balliol with a history scholarship. During his three years as an undergraduate he won many distinctions, carrying off the Brackenbury Prize for history, becoming President of the Union, walking from Oxford to London in record time, and getting a brilliant first in his schools. He was also the centre of a circle of friends almost all of whom became famous in after years. Jowett, who was Master of Balliol until Belloc's last year as an undergraduate, had a high opinion of him and foretold his future in glowing terms. He was to start by becoming a fellow of his college, and thereafter the Bar was foreshadowed and a successful political career. But the first item in the prophecy never happened. After considerable delay he realized that he was not, after all, to be admitted to a fellowship, and the disappointment left him with a feeling of injustice which continued all through his life. The bitterness he felt at this refusal was greatly increased, because the year before he had married Elodie in full expectation of a settled income.

During the seven years since they had become engaged they had corresponded regularly. Elodie had tried her vocation at a convent in Baltimore, but after a year in the novitiate had decided that she was not meant to be a nun. From that time onwards their marriage was decided upon and was to take place as soon as he had taken his degree and entered upon a profession. In 1896, thinking that his future was secure, he travelled again to California and was married at Napa. He returned after his wedding and took a house in Oxford. It was in this year that a small collec-

tion of his poems was first published in book form; but Elodie, feeling that some of them were not up to the standard of which he was capable, persuaded him to buy back all copies of the book which were unsold. Later on, however, he included in *Sonnets and Verse* a selection of those contained in this early publication.

It is not difficult to trace the origin of a number of his poems to his experiences while at Oxford. His fierce derision of the dons, who, he felt, had cheated him of his rights; his enduring love of his Balliol friends; his exuberant republicanism—all these characteristics of the young Belloc overflow in his verse, and—which is more important—the individuality and vigour with which they are expressed are clues to the personality of the man himself. His unsparing, frontal attack upon all that he hated and despised could hardly be more ferociously marshalled than in his **"Lines to a Don"**; and in **"The Winged Horse"** we see the same attack transformed into the exhilaration of triumph as he passes in review the great heroes of chivalry and feels within himself an echo of their grandeur:

> I saw the Host of Heaven in rank and Michael with
> his spear,
> And Turpin out of Gascony and Charlemagne the
> Lord,
> And Roland of the marches with his hand upon his
> sword.
>
> For you that took the all-in-all the things you left
> were three,
> A loud voice for singing and keen eyes to see,
> And a spouting well of joy within that never yet
> was dried!
> And I ride.

Or again, in his poem **"To the Balliol Men still in Africa,"** the consuming love which he felt all through his life for his college and his undergraduate friends is brought into sharp contrast with his unbending sense of justice. He was torn between his strong opposition to the Boer War and his desire to be sharing with his friends the risks of battle:

> But angry, lonely, hating it still,
> I wished to be there in spite of the wrong.
> My heart was heavy for Cumnor Hill
> And the hammer of galloping all day long.

Then there is his **"Dedicatory Ode,"** which breathes the atmosphere of Oxford and his own enthusiasm for republicanism in that select club of four members—Phillimore, Eccles, Thornton, and himself—who

> kept the Rabelaisian plan
> And dignified the dainty cloisters
> With Natural Law, the Rights of Man,
> —Song, Stoicism, Wine and Oysters—

The hard fights of his life were yet to come. Oxford provided him with a training gymnasium and lusty sparring partners. But he was now married and he had failed to obtain the livelihood he had relied on. He set to work to earn money by coaching, by University Extension Lectures, and by the writing of books. *Lambkin's Remains* (another echo of Oxford) and **The Bad Child's Book of Beasts** were among the first. These were soon followed by *Danton and Robespierre,* the first of his studies of the French Revolution. But politics—his urge to see justice done—were soon occupying much of his time. Not only was he writing political articles for such papers as *The Speaker* and the *Daily News,* but he was travelling about the country making speeches in support of Liberal candidates for Parliament. In 1906 he became a candidate himself and entered Parliament as Liberal Member for South Salford, full of hope that he would be able to further the cause for which he had fought so vigorously. Once again he was to be disappointed. The House of Commons, which he had hoped would be the channel through which his strongly held ideas could issue in practical form, presented itself to him as a place full of hypocrisy and corruption; and so most of his time and energy, while there, was spent in exposing and attacking these evils. Disgusted with the party system as he found it—a sham fight conducted by place-hunters—at the next election he stood as an Independent. He was again elected, but at the end of that session he left Parliament for good and made up his mind to found a weekly review which would be a platform both for his own political views and for an attack upon those whom he regarded as enemies of truth and of the country of his adoption.

One has not far to look to find echoes of this period of his life. As well as innumerable articles in his paper *The Eye Witness* and its successors, there were his books. Some, such as *The Servile State* and *The Restoration of Property,* expressed his positive views, and others, *The Party System,* for example (written in conjunction with Cecil Chesterton), and his scathing political novels, drove home his attack upon the politicians. Among his poems, too, there are fierce thrusts at those whom he held to be betraying their country. They are scattered through his epigrams and concentrated in that terrible outburst **"The Rebel."**

But it was from the turn of the century, when he left his house in Oxford for one in Cheyne Walk, that a regular stream of books began to issue from his pen. On moving again, in 1906, to King's Land, a house in Sussex, near Horsham, where he finally made his home, the stream became a flood. With his roots in the county of his choice and in a home that he loved (though constantly away from both for weeks on end, travelling all over Europe to study *in situ* the historical events of which he was writing), he lived a full life after his own heart, entertaining his friends—Phillimore, Somers-Cocks, Baring, the brothers Chesterton, MacCarthy, Kershaw, and a host of others—interesting himself in the 50 acres of farmland that he had bought, attending debates in the House of Commons, and at the same time writing, writing, writing, in every conceivable vein—gay, satiric, profound, controversial.

Of the friends just mentioned, Gilbert Chesterton is the one most closely associated with Belloc by the general public. Because they held many views in common they are often represented as twin souls. Nothing could be further from the truth. Their friendship was deep, but their talents and characters were utterly different. Chesterton was a philosopher and a student with a wide knowledge of literature, whereas Belloc was primarily a man of action and, for one of his literary eminence, had read little. At their first meeting, as may be seen from his autobiography, Chesterton was attracted by Belloc's exuberance and mental vigour. Belloc, in his turn, soon found in Chesterton a man receptive to his own strong views on English politics and to the remedies he proposed, and because of this, always felt himself to be the teacher and Chesterton the pupil, for Belloc was a man who learnt little from other men. In addition, Belloc's outlook was essentially European and authoritative, Chesterton's English and persuasive; and it is perhaps significant that Belloc considered "Lepanto" (the most European poem Chesterton wrote) to be far and away his finest. Although they were always close friends, their temperaments and manner of approaching a subject had little in common.

The years between 1906 and 1914 may perhaps be said to be the peak period of his life. His powers as a writer and an orator had come to full fruition, and through the increasing sale of his books his financial circumstances, which had caused him so much anxiety in the Oxford and Chelsea days, were improving. His fame was beginning to spread. In 1907 he employed his first full-time secretary and did much of his dictating at King's Land. At the end of the day, when the secretary was wilting under the thousands of words he had poured out upon her, he would come in to dinner full of vigour, prepared to invent impromptu verses, sing French marching songs or a selection of his own, discuss historical problems or current events, while at the same time playing a complicated game of patience by the light of candles at the end of his dining table, and drinking his beloved wines of France. He appeared to be tireless both in mind and body.

Of the many books published during these years, *The Four Men* has proved to be one of the most popular. It is in the same class as that earlier masterpiece *The Path to Rome,* but whereas the latter is an account of an actual journey made on foot by the author from his old garrison town of Toul to Rome, in the former the walk across Sussex was never undertaken in the way described, and the four men who converse as they walk together are no more than mouthpieces of Belloc's own thoughts and moods. But both books give an insight into certain sides of him. A third, *The Cruise of the Nona,* published thirteen years later, is written in a similar, though more serious vein; but here the background against which his thoughts chase one another is the sea and the hazards of sailing.

In all this whirl of activity Elodie was his constant support and helper. Highly cultured and with an extensive knowledge of literature (Hilary considered her literary judgment to be superior to that of any of his contemporaries), she shared with him the reviewing of books sent him by the *Morning Post,* and often gave him valuable advice about his own writings. She devoted herself to her family of five children, managed the household with skill and loving care, was friend in need to all who lived round about, and was universally loved.

Belloc could write with the biting scorn of a prophet confronted by treachery and deceit, or with the humility of one who knows the fallibility of all human strivings; with the tenderness of a child, or with the ferocity of a soldier in battle.

—Reginald Jebb

With Elodie's premature death in 1914 (she was only forty-three) and the outbreak of the First World War, Belloc's life underwent great changes. Broken-hearted and thereafter always dressed in black, he tried to obtain an active service appointment. Disappointed in this, he began writing weekly explanatory articles on the progress of the war in *Land and Water,* and toured the country giving lectures on it. In his spare moments he took up sailing again, which he had largely discontinued during the previous eight years. His friends rallied round him in his sorrow and his fame continued to grow, but it was not till the end of the war that he seriously resumed the writing of books. From that time, right up to the moment of his illness in 1941, he plunged once again into every variety of literary output. It was in those years between the wars that his most sustained, and in the view of many critics his greatest, poem was completed, **"An Heroic Poem in Praise of Wine."** But these later years of his life, despite the activity he continued to display, are noteworthy more for the maturity of the work done in them than for new experiences leading to new fields of exploration. The formative days are over; the mind has reached its full stature.

In April 1941, following upon the death of his youngest son Peter on active service, he was taken ill, and at the beginning of the next year he had a stroke which brought him very near to death. His recovery was slow, and for some years his memory remained confused. However, thanks to his iron constitution, he got better, but his massive power of concentration had gone, and he never wrote again. His last years were passed peacefully at King's Land, his house in Sussex, and he enjoyed constant visits from his friends. Though no longer the brilliant talker he had been, he never failed to delight all who came to see him with his unquenchable humour, and was always ready to sing or to discuss the past. He died on 16th July 1953.

If this brief sketch of a few of the events and influences that surrounded Belloc as he grew to maturity helps to put into their setting some of the poems contained in this book it makes no pretension to be a full diary of his life—still less an assessment of the greatness of the man. All his immense output of writing, so diverse that it would be difficult to find any domain of life and thought that he had

not explored, all the compelling oratory with which he held audiences of every shade of opinion, the personality that endeared him to high and low alike, even to thousands who had never seen or spoken to him; above all, that high sense of honour that never deserted him—all this is outside the scope of this short introduction. He could write with the biting scorn of a prophet confronted by treachery and deceit, or with the humility of one who knows the fallibility of all human strivings; with the tenderness of a child, or with the ferocity of a soldier in battle. He could create beauty seen through the eyes of a lover. He could communicate the exhilaration of those who dare upon the high seas. The flamboyant braggadocio of a Cyrano was his to flaunt, as was the loveliness of the South Country his to enshrine. He could do all these things because each was a part of him.

But to give a picture, even in the merest outline, of the man himself (and one must repeat the man is greater than his work), two things must be emphasized beyond all others: his Catholic Faith and his marriage. There are poems in this book that directly avow his unswerving allegiance to the one and the ecstatic happiness that the other brought him. But direct avowal is no more than the overflow of those two guiding influences. It is they more than anything else, each strengthening the other, that give unity to all his work and to his crowded life.

The University of Leeds Review **(essay date 1970)**

SOURCE: "The Cosmic Pessimism of Hilaire Belloc," translated by Philip Thody, in *The University of Leeds Review,* Vol. 13, No. 1, May, 1970, pp. 73-88.

[*In the following essay, the anonymous critic analyzes Belloc's* Cautionary Verses *from a metaphysical perspective and compares it to other works of English literature.*]

The serious foreign reader of Hilaire Belloc's **Cautionary Verses** cannot fail to be impressed by the immense and tragic discrepancy between the misdeeds described and the punishments inflicted. A small boy called James runs a few steps from his nurse while on an innocent visit to the zoo, and is eaten alive by a lion. A little girl called Matilda indulges in the harmless practical joke of summoning a fire brigade when there is no conflagration to be extinguished, and is later consumed in the flames that devour her aunt's residence. And another little girl, Rebecca Offendort, is presented by the author as receiving nothing more than her just deserts when a marble bust of Abraham knocks her flat and kills her—all because she had 'slammed the door for fun'. The similarity with the tragic world described by Lukàcs, in a passage quoted by Lucien Goldmann in *The Hidden God,* is quite remarkable, for when we read that the God of this world 'sweeps from the ranks of men all those who have, by the slightest gesture, made in the most fleeting and forgotten moment of time, shown that they are strangers to the world of Essences' we seem to be precisely in the universe depicted by Belloc's poems, and in the same atmosphere of cosmic pessimism.

In contrast, those of Belloc's characters whose misdemeanors are serious escape virtually unscathed. While Henry King dies in agony for having eaten a few harmless little bits of string, Algernon the doctor's son is only reprimanded for attempting to assassinate his sister. George, whose failure to exercise proper care over a balloon is the direct cause of the death of seven adults and one other child, suffers merely 'a nasty bump behind the ear', while Hildebrand, whose cowardice is a blot on the record of a noble family, seems likely to receive several motor cars as a gift which he has done nothing to deserve. We are indeed, in a book which the English themselves affect to regard as amusing, in the tragic and meaningless universe so well described by the Preacher, Ecclesiastes, when he wrote that he 'returned under the sun' and saw 'that the race is not to the swift, nor the battle to the strong, neither yet bread to the wise, nor yet riches to men of understanding, nor yet favour to men of skill; but time and chance happeneth to them all.' It is the purpose of the [essay] to examine, by a rigorous analysis of the patterns of structure of Belloc's **Cautionary Verses,** and with reference to his other opinions where appropriate, just what conclusions can be drawn from his work; to discover what kind of metaphysic it implies, what sort of social vision it involves; and finally to suggest, by way of conclusion, what comparable approaches can and should be made to other great works in English literature such as the Jeeves Saga in the work of P. G. Wodehouse of the sadly neglected William books by Richmal Crompton.

II

It should of course be noted, as part of any Prolegomena to the study of Belloc's verse, that it would be totally wrong to regard him as being in any real way preoccupied with children. No more telling proof of this can be found than the fact that the absurdity and unpredictability of the social and metaphysical universe described in his work impinges just as much, and perhaps even more, upon adults. It is, as he himself remarks, by 'a curious fluke' that Lord Lucky becomes 'a most important duke', though it should naturally be remembered that this elevation is brought about by the death of five innocent people. Lord Finchley is struck dead merely because he tries to mend the electric light 'himself', while Lord Lundy falls from high office because of a virtue: an intense sensitivity to the sufferings of all mankind which moves him to tears at the merest hint of difficulties to be overcome. Neither is the world view presented in these poems any more reassuring when we move from the social to the natural world, for man's relationship with the animal kingdom, like his presence in Society, is one of consistent failure brought about by unpredictable and insuperable odds. Both the Gentleman who stays to fight the Bear and the Person who turns to run are equally devoured. Judges are bitten by cobras, men infallibly die when bitten a second time by a viper, and Boers cannot even pronounce the name of the animal whom they might need to kill for their very survival. This pontentially fatal aphasia clearly symbolizes the unreliability of language in a world that perpetually escapes human control, just as the sudden emergence of a crocodile from a missionary's breakfast egg offers a striking parallel

to Kafka's *Metamorphosis* or to the passage in Sartre's *La Nausée* where a child's tongue turns into a centipede.

Similarly, man's dilemma when faced with a bear has a marked resemblance to the realization which comes over Camus's Meursault, in *The Outsider,* of the insoluble problems with which man is confronted in an absurd universe. 'What she said was: "If one goes too slowly, there's the risk of a heat-stroke. But, if one goes too fast, one perspires, and the cold air in the church gives one a chill." I saw her point. Either way one was for it,' is only an alternative way of expressing Belloc's conclusion that

> Decisive action in the hour of need
> Denotes the Hero, but does not succeed,

and both texts offer the same cosmic implications. Man is caught in a situation where the most harmless activity can have the most catastrophic consequences, where the throwing of a stone may lose a fortune—

> John Vavassour de Quentin Jones
> Was very fond of throwing stones

—in which one child's extravagance can reduce its parents to penury—

> They had to sell the house and grounds
> For less than twenty thousand pounds

—where parents behave in a totally unpredictable manner towards their off-spring—

> Then tell your papa where the Yak can be got,
> And if he is awfully rich
> He will buy you the creature—
> Or else he will *not.*
> (I cannot be positive which)

—where power lies, as it does for William Shand, 'on the side of their oppressors' (*Ecclesiastes,* IV, I), where scorpions lurk in bed, seeking whom they may devour—

> He dearly loves to bite;
> He is a most unpleasant brute
> To find in bed at night

—and where 'an aunt in Yutacan' dies of snake-bite while the serpent itself, 'more subtle than any beast of the field' (*Genesis,* III, I) survives.

A conviction of the essential injustice of the universe lies, of course, at the heart of any tragic vision, whether it be that of Pascal, Sartre, Camus or Hemingway ('That was what you did. You died. You did not know what it was about. You never had time to learn. They threw you in and told you the rules and the first time they caught you off base they killed you', *A Farewell to Arms*), but Belloc adds to this conviction an acute awareness of the futility of human endeavour which carries particularly interesting associations. Occasionally, the adults in his work are prevented by purely private characteristics from rendering one another that mutual help and assistance so frequently presented by humanist thinkers as man's sole but valid reply to the problems of living in an absurd universe. The honest keeper, for example, trying to save Jim from the lion,

> . . . almost ran
> To help the little gentleman.

Alas, however, he was too fat, and arrived too late. Maria's parents do everything possible to save her from the ills she has brought upon herself by pulling faces, but such is the unconquerable selfishness of the human species that none of the potential suitors they have selected for her—

> . . . Grand Dukes, Commanders of the Fleece,
> Mysterious Millionaires from Greece,
> And exiled Kings in large amounts,
> Ambassadors and Papal Counts . . .

—can master the horror which they feel at her self-inflicted ugliness, and she is condemned to as unhappy a marriage as any to be found in Mauriac. Yet the deeper structure of the work—for Belloc's **Cautionary Verses,** like Baudelaire's *Fleurs du Mal,* must be read as an organic whole, not an accidental collection of *poems*—reveals a more significant reason for human impotence and disarray. Medicine, perhaps the greatest science known to man, and certainly the one most esteemed by humanists, is consistently and deliberately depicted as inefficacious. 'Physicians of the utmost fame,' when summoned to the bedside of the dying Henry King, can do no more than acknowledge that there is

> . . . no cure for this disease.
> Henry will very soon be dead.

and their remarks echo the verdict of perhaps the noblest figure described in nineteenth-century French literature, Doctor Larivière in Flaubert's *Madame Bovary.* Summoned to Emma's bedside when she has poisoned herself with arsenic, he looks at her only for a moment before telling her husband: 'Il n'y a plus rien à faire,' and he differs from Belloc's specialists only in showing some slight traces of human emotion to mitigate his professional impotence. The specialist consulted by Lord Roehampton is so incompetent that he diagnoses as laryngitis what turns out to be a fatal heart condition—

> Your Larynx is a thought relaxed
> And you are greatly over-taxed—

and Belloc's hostility towards all scientific endeavour reaches its climax in the poem **"The Microbe"**, a conscious satire of the whole basis on which the medical developments of his day were made.

III

It is, moreover, in this hostility to science that the key to Belloc's cosmic pessimism can be found, for it must be noted that the catastrophes which overtake his characters are not, as the first part of this article might have erroneously suggested, totally random. They almost always arise from the different versions of the *hubris,* or overweening pride, which so characterizes the scientific outlook. Whether it be Jim imagining that he can do without his nurse, Lord Finchley attempting to practice a trade for which he has not been trained, the Dinotherium leaving its natural habitat in order to 'Roost in branches like a bird'—

> If you were born to walk the ground,
> Remain there; do not fool around.

—or Godfrey Horne, perhaps the most significant example, who is justly punished for being 'Deathly Proud' by becoming

> . . . the Boy,
> Who blacks the Boots at the Savoy,

all Belloc's most memorable characters attempt to fly beyond the natural limits of the human condition—attempting, as Pascal would say, to become angels, and yet acting like animals. It would, moreover, be a mistake to imagine that Belloc is merely concerned with those who try to rise above their natural lot or pre-destined social station. As I shall later show, he would have thoroughly endorsed the sentiments expressed in that stanza from *All Things Bright and Beautiful* which is now so unfortunately omitted from modern hymn-books and was last given a public performance in the opening few minutes of the Boulting Brothers' film, *Heavens Above*:

> The rich man in his castle
> The poor man at his gate
> God made them high and lowly
> And ordered their estate,

and the whole social vision of the **Cautionary Verses** is profoundly consistent with the ideas he expressed elsewhere on the notion of the corporate state. But what is more important, when one considers the over-all metaphysical implications of his poems—taken, for a moment, in isolation from his other work and examined like Mallarmé's 'Calme bloc ici-bas chu d'un désastre obscur'—is that *all* those who act in an unusual way are punished, not solely those who do so through pride. Henry King realizes this—alas too late, for he is already on his death bed—when he offers the advice:

> O my Friends, be warned by me,
> That Breakfast, Dinner, Lunch and Tea,
> Are all the Human Frame requires . . . ,

for he has come to appreciate the folly of deviating from the dietary norm. It is significant to compare his fate with that of Franklin Hyde, who after being chastised for playing with

> . . . Disgusting Mud
> As though it were a Toy!

is reassured by his Uncle that

Children in *ordinary Dress* (my italics)
May always play with Sand,

and these two poems offer a microcosm of the ethic of social conformity that is so integral a part of Belloc's world vision.

Indeed, as one reads through these verses, one comes again and again across the same message, sometimes implicit in the events, sometimes made explicit by the author's own conclusions. The very first story in the book ends with the famous piece of advice, neglected by modern parents for financial excuses rather than on financial grounds,

Always keep a hold of Nurse
For fear of finding something worse,

while the volume itself is concluded with the comprehensive message:

The moral is (it is indeed!)
You mustn't monkey with the Creed.

Like Pascal's, Belloc's cosmic pessimism has a message, for the aim of the *Pensées* was undoubtedly to lead men to conform, not to 'monkey with the Creed', and Pascal makes this totally clear in the concluding passage of the wager argument. 'Or, quel mal vous arrivera-t-il en prenant ce parti?', he asks the unbeliever. 'Vous serez fidèle, honnête, humble, reconnaissant, bienfaisant, ami sincère, véritable', and his implied assurance of the social benefits to be gained from belief recalls the portrait which Belloc gives of the happy fate awaiting those who do conform. Sometimes, of course, the rewards are small, as when Franklin Hyde is merely allowed to play with sand because he is wearing ordinary dress, but at other times they are more substantial.

The nicest child I ever knew
Was Charles Augustus Fortescue,

begins one of Belloc's most celebrated poems, and it will be remembered that Charles Augustus, because he 'Always Did what was Right', accumulated an 'Immense Fortune', one so great that he was able to build a

. . . Splendid Mansion which
Is called *The Cedars, Muswell Hill,*
Where he resides in Affluence still,
To show what Everbody might
Become by SIMPLY DOING RIGHT.

While Pascal's unbeliever is not promised quite so definite recompense in the goods of this world, the suggestion in Lafuma 343 is that the delights stemming from the daily exercise of virtue cannot fail to lead to what Lady Bracknell [from Oscar wilde's play *The Importance of Being Earnest*] calls 'a recognized position in good society', and the parallel between the two thinkers becomes even closer if the rest of the Wager argument is compared to the success story of *The Statesman,* in *Ladies and Gentlemen.* When the unbeliever suggests to Pascal that he might have

difficulty in totally abandoning his enquiring intellect when he makes the leap into faith, Pascal's reply is clear: conform to established practice, take holy water, have masses said '. . . cela vous fera croire et *vous abêtira'* ('make you stupid' [my translation and my italics]). The Statesman, it will be remembered, was the man who

. . . use to say
Not once but twenty times a day,
That in the turmoil and the strife
(His very words) of Public Life
The thing of ultimate effect
Was Character—not Intellect,

and the course of action which decides to follow in pursuit of this principle has markedly Pascalian overtones:

He therefore was at strenuous pains
To *atrophy his puny brains* (my italics)
And registered success in this
Beyond the dreams of avarice.

Like Franklin Hyde and Charles Augustus Fortescue, and like Pascal's convert, The Statesman is rewarded for his conformity, and in this respect, at least, there is a profound relationship between Belloc's cosmic pessimism and his social vision. Salvation is possible for those who conform, whether they do so blindly as the child is recommended to do in the lines on the Pig in *A Moral Alphabet*—

Learn from the Pig to take whatever Fate
Or Elder Persons heap upon your plate

—or whether they adopt a more conscious conformity after the manner of The Statesman. But at all events, they will avoid anxious and indiscreet inquiries. 'Oh, que c'est un doux et mol oreiller que l'ignorance et l'incuriosité, à reposer une tête bien faite,' wrote the Montaigne who so influenced Pascal, and it is this attitude which is finally recommended both in *Sarah Byng* and in *The Example.* Sarah Byng, it will be remembered, did not know how to read, and was tossed into a thorny hedge by a Bull. After this experience, she resolves, not to remedy her ignorance, but simply to go

A long way round to keep away
From signs, whatever they may say

—a decision which is linked to what Belloc also describes as her

. . . instinctive guess
That literature breeds distress—

and which the portrait accompanying the poem seems thoroughly to endorse. Her youth enables her to avoid the dangers which later overtake 'John Henderson, an unbeliever' who

. . . lately lost his Joie de Vivre
By reading far too many books

and

    Went about with gloomy looks,

for she has had an instinctive knowledge of a truth from Ecclesiastes—which the unfortunate Henderson discovers only when it is too late—that 'of making many books there is no end; and much study is a weariness to the flesh' (XII, 12). She is a creature from before the Fall, antedating the descent of man into the hell of knowldege and inquiry, of differences and problems, and from which it is the aim of Belloc's *Cautionary Verses,* as it was that of Pascal's *Pensées,* to save him.

IV

A comprehensive analysis of the human condition such as we find in Belloc's *Cautionary Verses* is not something which arises by accident. Only the dialectical method, with the encouragement that it gives to the reader to go perpetually, as Lucien Goldmann says so often in *Le Dieu Caché,* from the Whole to the Parts and then from the Parts to the Whole again, enables the work to be understood in all its complexity, and only the refinements brought to dialectical materialism by thinkers such as Georg Lukàcs and Monsieur Goldmann himself can reveal the full relationship of the work to the complex of social conflicts which gave it birth. That the overall metaphysical world vision of Belloc's verses is totally coherent, in spite of the social contradictions which a Marxist cannot avoid seeing in it, is sufficiently indicated by the way in which even apparent irrelevances fit together, providing the same kind of satisfying sense of unity that we find in poems such as Baudelaire's *Fleurs du Mal,* with their 'secret architecture'.

Take, for example, the question of food. In two separate poems, *"A Reproof of Gluttony"* and *"On Food,"* Belloc returns to the bewildering variety of nourishment pursued by human beings, remarking in the first on how ungrateful Man is not to be

    Contented with his Prandial lot

commenting in the second on the 'various tastes in food' which 'Divide the human brotherhood' and lamenting how

    . . . all the world is torn and rent
    By various views on nourishment.

The parallel with Pascal's and Montaigne's concern over the immense variety and unpredictability of human behaviour in the moral sphere is too obvious to be missed. 'Plaisante justice qu'une rivière borne! Vérité au deçà des Pyrénées, erreur au delà' writes the former, in a remark clearly inspired by the passage in the latter's *Apologie de Raymond Sebond,* pointing out that 'Le meurtre des enfants, meurtre des pères, trafic des voleries, il n'est rien en somme si extrême qui ne se trouve reçu par l'usage de quelque nation', but what is more important than this similarity is the solution which Belloc presents to this problem.

    F for a Family taking a walk
    In Arcadia Terrace, no doubt.

begins one of the poems in the *Moral Alphabet,* and it is obvious from their complete conformity with established custom—

    The parents indulge in intelligent talk,
    While the children they gambol about

—that this family is being presented, like Charles Augustus Fortescue, as something of an ideal. Yet this ideal is something realized through synthesis, in the true dialectical method, something attained through effort, not merely given through Grace as is the ignorance of Sarah Byng.

    At a quarter-past six they return to their tea,
    Of a kind that would hardly be tempting to me,
      Though my appetite passes belief.
    There is Jam, Ginger Beer, Buttered Toast,
      Marmalade,
    With a Cold Leg of Mutton and Warm Lemonade,
    And a large Pigeon Pie very skilfully made
      To consist almost wholly of Beef.

Consciousness, as Sartre has so convincingly argued, always separates the admirer from the object admired. Belloc can only gaze in admiration at this family, which has achieved a synthesis that is quite beyond his powers, great though they are—'Though my appetite passes belief'— and his situation once again parallels that of Pascal. For many critics, the unthinking acceptance of faith, like the double-think required by the wager argument, in which the unbeliever both forgets his intellect and remembers to forget it, remained forever—and understandingly so—beyond Pascal's own capabilities. So Belloc looks on longingly at this salvation attained through choice and conscious effort, in which the bewildering variety of the world is subsumed under the

    large pigeon pie very skilfully made
    To consist almost wholly of beef,

and tries to forget his own condition of metaphysical and social exile.

It is indeed a social exile which forms the basis of Belloc's cosmic pessimism, just as it did that of Pascal. As Monsieur Goldmann has so exhaustively argued, Pascal and Racine both represented, whether they were conscious of it or not, the contradictory position of the legal nobility in the second third of the seventeenth century in France, torn between its desire to oppose the King who was trying to deprive it of its power and its realization that it had no-one else on whom to depend. A comparable analysis can be made of Belloc's situation, and one that is especially relevant both to the themes of his *Cautionary Verses* and to his declared political views. It is this analysis which will solve many of the critical problems presented by his verse, for this can take on its true significance—as distinct from its subjective meaning—only in the light of what Belloc thought about modern society and its trends.

Like his friend, G. K. Chesterton, Belloc was well-known as an enthusiastic defender of the corporate state. Equally opposed, at least in principle, both to *laissez-faire* capitalism and to socialism, both men argued in favour of a return to a modified version of the mediaeval concept of a society divided according to the part which men played in it, in which individualism was kept in check by a strong central authority, but in which the existence of a recognized and respected Church also prevented the temporal authorities from becoming tyrannical. Objectively, and from any Marxist standpoint, this was a reactionary philosophy aimed at recreating a static society already condemned by History, and it is not surprising that it should have given rise to the kind of pessimism described in the first part of this article. The ideal society conceived by the *noblesse de robe* in seventeenth-century France had similarly reactionary features, and the only real difference lies in the presence in Belloc of an anti-semitism found nowhere in the Jansenist movement. In the **Cautionary Verses**, this is noticeable in at least two places—

> A wealthy Banker's Little Daughter
> Who lived in Palace Green, Bayswater,

> This gentleman (A Mr Meyer
> Of Rabley Abbey, Rutlandshire)

—and shows how easily the concept of a static society from which all possibility of social change has been excluded can merge into Fascism. Belloc's ideal world is one where butlers

> . . . know their place and do not play
> The Old Retainer night and day
>
> **("Lord Lundy")**

in which a strict separation of social duties is enforced, as it would be in any corporate state which reproduced anything of the mediaeval guild system—

> Lord Finchley tried to mend the Electric Light
> Himself.
> It struck him dead: And serve him right!
> It is the business of the wealthy man
> To give employment to the artisan

—in which those who have the privilege to serve a Lady (*A Moral Alphabet*)

> . . . take it in turn to observe:
> 'What a Lady indeed! . . . what a presence to feel! . . .
> What a woman to worship and serve!' . . . ,

and where the Law provides constant protection to those injured by the progress of modern, individualistic, technological civilization (see the fate of Ned, Maria's younger brother, 'Who walking one way, chose to gaze the other').

Occasionally, it is true, Belloc seems to be critical of established society, and we ourselves have heard Englishmen actually laugh as they read the closing stanzas of **"Peter Goole,"** who

> even now, at twenty-five, still has to WORK
> To keep alive!

little realizing the true meaning of the poem. For what Belloc is obviously describing here is the failure of the landed aristocracy to survive in an age of ruthless commercial competition, and what might seem at first sight like irony is a genuine lament. Those critics who choose to ignore the advantages of the structural and dialectical method of analysing literary works, and prefer to concentrate on such imponderables as tone, style, or atmosphere, are bound to misunderstand the books they attempt to study with such imperfect tools. They are like those French scholars, rightly stigmatized by Monsieur Goldmann, who persist in maintaining that *Iphigénie* and not *Eriphile* is the true tragic heroine in Racine's *Iphigénie,* that Agrippine and Néron are the centres of attraction in *Britannicus,* or that *Andromaque* is one of Racine's tragedies, instead of merely being a 'drama'. Such people will never learn, and it is critics of their kind who attribute a satirical intention to the last lines in *The Garden Party*:

> They married and gave in marriage,
> They danced at the County Ball,
> And some of them kept a carriage,
> AND THE FLOOD DESTROYED THEM ALL.

In fact, this poem is a concrete dramatization—or a dramatic concretization—of the contradictory situation in which both Belloc and the audience for which he was consciously or unconsciously writing (and which consciously or unconsciously inspired him; it does not matter which, once the dialectical method is being used), found themselves in the first third of the twentieth century. The Rich, for whom Belloc is clearly *not* writing, are sure of their position and it is for this reason that they

> talk of their affairs
> In loud and strident voices.

The Poor, whom Belloc was too honest an observer, for all his ideas, not to recognize as the new Rising Class, are cheerful: they are arriving in Fords, symbols of the triumph of the new mass production technology. They

> laugh to see so many Lords
> And Ladies all assembled

because they know that they will soon be replacing them, if not as the new ruling class, then at least as the class which will benefit from the next phase into which industrial civilization is bound, through the irresistible pressures of History, to move. It is the 'People in Between' who look

> underdone and harassed,
> And out of place and mean,
> And horribly embarrassed

—the petty bourgeoisie slowly being crushed between the upper millstone of the triumphant *entrepreneurs* and the nether millstone of the Rising Working Class. It is they who are his true public, the breeding ground for the Fascism of which Belloc's theory of the Corporate State was but a disguise.

V

That there are contradictions in Belloc's vision of society is inevitable. He was a bourgeois writer, and all bourgeois writers inevitably express contradictions. They are, indeed, for a Marxist, nothing but contradictions, and it would be pointless to expect Belloc to explain why conformity is valuable as a means of rising in society when this society itself is so obviously doomed. One finds the same contradiction in Stendhal's *Le Rouge et le Noir,* where Julien Sorel is presented as the hero but where the society within whose framework he wishes to triumph is depicted as worthless and inauthentic. It is sufficient, for a critic espousing a synthesis between the structural method and the methods of dialectical materialism, to note at one and the same time the consistency of an author's cosmic pessimism and the inconsistency of his social remedies. Indeed, the main advantage of a study of this kind is that it highlights the immense advantages available, for the creative and imaginative critic, in a method which enables him to move so smoothly from one field of enquiry to another, unhampered by outdated concepts such as a positivist respect for the sum total of an author's work or by a purely aesthetic concern for style or verbal rhythm. Moreover, the great advantage of this method lies in its flexibility and adaptability.

Gertrude M. White (essay date 1978)

SOURCE: "Different Worlds in Verse," in *The Chesterton Review,* Vol. IV, No. 2, Spring-Summer, 1978, pp. 232-45.

[*In the following essay, White contrasts the poetry of G. K. Chesterton and Belloc.*]

It is almost a Chestertonian paradox that an eyewitness cannot see clearly. Only at a distance, across a gulf of years and the confusion of a turbulent century, is it possible to see that mythical beast, the Chesterbelloc, in true perspective. "What is remarkable," says Belloc's biographer Robert Speaight [in *Spode House Review,* December 1974-January 1975] "is that two men whose temperaments were so diverse should have thought alike on every conceivable question." But what is even more remarkable is that the likeness of thought has been emphasised, not the diversity of temperament.

It is easier, perhaps, to isolate and discuss ideas, the matter and substance of a man's work, than to attend to the less tangible elements of tone, mood, and style. Yet—for a writer, at least—the style is the man. This is true even in prose. In poetry it is the root of the matter. And it is as poets that I wish to discuss and compare G.K. Chesterton and Hilaire Belloc.

This will seem positively perverse to readers of *The Chesterton Review* or G.K.'s *Centenary Appraisal.* These pages offer a riches of reflection on fiction, journalism, Distributism, biography, theology, literary history, and bibliography, but there is no mention of poetry. Well, one can see why. The verse of neither Chesterton nor Belloc is much read today. Though Chesterton was once a popular poet, he has long ceased to be. Belloc, save for his inimitable children's verse, never was. Neither enlarged the boundaries of a tradition; neither influenced any considerable poet of the past fifty years: and in consequence neither has attracted much critical attention. Like so many other Georgians, they have been rolled over and very nearly obliterated by the hosts of War, Modernism, and Social Significance. But the Georgians are now enjoying a modest revival, and perhaps it is time for a backward look.

Today, the causes which so largely engrossed the energies of the Chesterbelloc have either perished or assumed new and awful shapes, to be dealt with in contemporary terms. What is the Boer War to us, who live in a century of wars? The Marconi scandal pales before Watergate. Distributism is a word unknown except in small enclaves. All around us the plutocracy Belloc loathed and the servile state he predicted create the climate in which we live. But when we turn from the Chesterbelloc's valiant rearguard action against historical falsehood, political corruption, and social injustice, and look at each man's verse, the fabulous twin-headed monster vanishes. Verse—even verse not of the first rank—has a charm against time, change, and all mortality. Chesterton and Belloc live in their verse as vividly as they did in their day. And whatever their common opinions, they were indeed very different men and lived in very different worlds. These differences—to me—are more interesting than their similarities.

The world of Chesterton's verse is as strange and surrealistic as that of Bosch or Dali. His landscape is like a huge amusement park, crowded with fantastic shapes, shot through with vivid lights, brilliant with improbable colours. Forests are purple, grass a crawling carpet of green hair, the sea a fallen sky in which fish like diabolic cherubs swim, a daisy the one eye of a Cyclops, the four winds the sails of a gigantic windmill, turning for a child whose dolls are crowned and winged saints and seraphim. In this world, unlike that of the Lotus Eaters, it is never afternoon but always dawn, sunset, or midnight. Earth and heaven alike are the scene of a cosmic drama, of merry wars of flowers and trees, of holy wars of stars and angels. It is a fairyland, a magic world, in which anything may happen: fishes may fly, forest walk, the sun turn black or the moon to blood. Flowers smell of passion, of pardon, of mirth; the smallest seed is filled with "God Almighty, and with Him / Cherubim and Seraphim," and "with the wan waste grasses on his spear," a wild knight rides forever, seeking after God.

Chesterton's verse, in short, combines the vivid visual imagination of an artist with the intuitions and convictions of an excited theologian. He sees the world as intensely real but strange, the whimsical and playful creation of a cosmic artist, and he defined the main problem of philosophers as "how we can contrive at once to be astonished at the world and yet at home in it." His early nightmare was solipsism: the dreadful possibility that he alone might be real, all Creation only a projection of himself. "The Mirror of Madmen" is perhaps the most explicit expression of this hideous vision, but his early poems are nearly all, in one way or another, dominated by it and by the overwhelming relief and gratitude with which he refuted and rejected it.

Belloc's verse, though occasionally it states his faith, reveals a man who, if the everlasting arms of the Church were to relax for a moment, would be swallowed up in an abyss.

—Gertrude M. White

Chesterton, it has been said often enough, was a Christian before he knew what Christianity was. Its doctrines, when he discovered them, confirmed his earliest intuitions and enabled him to reconcile them with his reason. Henceforward, he illustrated dogma by imagination: he really did look at Christianity as he looked at the world, with the eyes of a man who is seeing it for the first time. This innocence, this capacity for wonder, is Chesterton's greatest gift, a large part of that genius for parallelism which Belloc identified as one of his leading characteristics and which made him perhaps the outstanding religious apologist of his day. His concern, in prose or verse, is always for the problem of existence; the objects of his scorn throughout his life were the Pessimists, the Puritans, and the Manichees.

> Not for me be the vaunt of woe;
> Was not I from a boy
> Vowed with the helmet and spear and spur
> To the blood-red banner of joy?

All Chesterton's windows open outward on the world, the world he recognised—with what enormous relief and joy his verse proclaims—not he but God had made, the world he declared not merely good but a marvel. And whatever his particular concerns, religion was always at the core of his thought.

But the world of Chesterton's verse, Christian as it is, is not specifically a Catholic world. I say this nervously but with conviction. The persons and events of the Christian story, the great symbols, the Christian view of man's life in God's world, indeed engage his imagination, but he was what might be described as a temperamental rather than an institutional Catholic. He joined the Catholic Church relatively late in life, from a firm conviction of its historical truth and divine authority, but he had in a very real sense been born a Catholic. Eventually he recognised

the fact because, as he himself put it, "I perceive life to be logical and workable with these beliefs, and illogical and unworkable without them." But that was written in 1903, when he was not yet thirty, and nearly twenty years before he became a Catholic. The impact of his conversion is not perceptible by any change of thought or feeling recorded in his verse. It is the tone, perhaps, that changes a little. The hectic and feverish atmosphere of *The Wild Knight*—an atmosphere not wholly unlike that of the aesthetes and decadents against whom he rebelled—blew away in the fresh air of health and sanity, and though his poetic world is still vivid with colour and ringing with rhetoric, the nightmares have faded as wonder, joy, and laughter possessed him ever more securely.

If Chesterton was a born Catholic who found his way slowly to the Church, Belloc, born a Catholic, clung to the Church as a bulwark against despair. For Chesterton the Church embodied in historical and visible form his own personal vision of truth. For Belloc, it was the sword and shield with which he could fight his way through the wilderness of this world. We know from his many and varied prose works what his view of the Church was: founder and defender of civilisation and social order, creator of Europe, guardian of truth, the Church Militant warring against the heathen of every kind, the citadel outside of which, as he wrote, "are only the puerilities and the despairs." Belloc was dogmatic because to him, a sceptic by nature, the Church was a great rock in a weary land. But with few exceptions his most moving and convincing poems are not poems of Christian faith, still less of Christian joy. Where Chesterton seldom wrote about anything but religion, Belloc is only rarely a religious poet at all.

Now this is a paradox, for we know that Belloc took his verse very seriously indeed, almost as seriously as he took his religion. He wrote prose for money, verse for love. More than once he said he wished to be remembered primarily by his verse and would be proud if he had added something, however small, to the tradition of English lyric verse. He took scant pains with much of his prose; his verse he worked at rigorously and long. The **"Heroic Poem in Praise of Wine"** took him twenty years to write. "To excel in poetry," he said, "is, after holiness, the highest of human achievements."

Chesterton never felt nor said anything of the kind. His verse, it is not too much to say, is a triumph of the imagination, of emotion, of vision, over a diction and technique only just adequate. Owing largely to the "White Horse" and "Lepanto," he was and still is far more widely known than Belloc, but the latter is a far more serious poet. Belloc's remarks on the nature and practice of verse are widely scattered through his books and essays and he never set forth a systematic theory of poetics. Nevertheless, he has said enough to make his views clear. He regarded the poet, in the old, grand manner, as a man inspired, used by some divine power for its own purposes. But he laid even more emphasis on craftsmanship, the labour through which the poem becomes, in his own phrase, "something made." In his essay on Chesterton written after the latter's death, Belloc avoids judging his friend's verse because, he says, it is too soon and also—illuminating phrase!—"because I know myself to be fastidious in the matter." Despite this disclaimer, he goes on to say that Chesterton's verse suffers from being too voluminous and therefore loose, but that he "struck perpetually the inward note."

As a man judges, he may fairly be judged. Belloc's verse is anything but voluminous or loose. His metrics are always careful, strictly controlled, highly traditional: epigram and sonnet, quatrain and ballade, even the heroic couplet so seldom used since Dryden's time to carry any sustained emotion but anger or humour. A far more "literary" poet than the better-read Chesterton, he clearly owes much to his studies of the classics, to French poetry, to the Elizabethans and seventeenth-century lyrists. That his sonnets are indebted—too indebted, perhaps—to those of Shakespeare is obvious. Belloc tells us that though he had learned most of what he knew of English literature from Chesterton, "with English verse I can claim a better acquaintance." These influences, and his careful craftsmanship, have been often enough noted. The same terms recur in notices and reviews of his verse: *form, classic, clarity, pellucid, music, beauty.* But what of that "inward note" that he himself held to be at the heart of the matter?

When Chesterton's verse strikes the inward note, it is that of joy, of thanksgiving, of celebration. Never, apparently, was he moved to express grief or sadness in verse. But Belloc's inward note is most deeply sad; not Christian resignation, but the true pagan sadness which he shares with the author of *A Shropshire Lad.* Strange but true: of all Belloc's contemporaries, the lyric poet he most closely resembles is A.E. Housman. Like Housman, Belloc is a stranger and afraid in a world he never made. Like Housman, he defends himself with wit, irony, and satire. And in his serious verse, like Housman, he gives vent to an incurable nostalgia, to a wistfulness and a self-pity welling up from deeper levels than those expressed in the biting wit of his epigrams, the rollicking jollity of his drinking songs, or the playfulness of his *Cautionary Tales.*

It is this sadness that lends the best of Belloc's verse a piercing poignancy Chesterton seldom or never attains. Chesterton's is the verse of a happy man, centered and secure, possessed by a faith at once passionate and serene. Belloc's is that of a melancholy man, deeply sceptical at bottom, who tells us that:

> . . . they that held through Winter to the Spring
> Despair as I do, and, as I do, sing.

Where Chesterton's best serious verse is narrative and rhetorical, Belloc's is lyrical. Chesterton is a philosopher and, in the best sense, a propagandist; Belloc is a suffering human being and an artist for whom verse is partly the creation of beauty in words and rhythms and partly the balm of a hurt mind. If we had no other testimony, Chesterton's verse alone would both express and explain his faith. Belloc's verse, though occasionally it states his faith, reveals a man who, if the everlasting arms of the Church were to relax for a moment, would be swallowed up in an abyss.

Chesterton's gaudily coloured and oddly shaped world is one all men can share for it is addressed to all, and the voice that speaks in his verse is that of a man declaiming to others. But Belloc's is an intensely personal and private world; his mental doors swing inward to express a state of mind, and his voice is that of a man singing to himself or to a few much loved friends. It is yet another paradox that Belloc's verse is a record of love and friendship to a far greater extent than Chesterton's, and that beside Belloc the more genial Chesterton seems oddly detached from personal affection, save always for his wife.

It is strange, too, that Belloc, so self-absorbed in private experience and private emotion, loves the real world in a way Chesterton does not. Chesterton, entranced as he is by the beauty and the strangeness of the world, at bottom loves it because God made it and because in and through it he senses its Creator. The fantastic scenery and apparent violence and melodrama of his world barely conceal the visible presence of God:

> But I saw him there alone
> Standing stiller than a stone
>   Lest a moth should fall.

Now Belloc loves the world too, and he was much more of the world than Chesterton ever was. But he loves the world as it is and for itself: the seasons, which he celebrated in a sonnet sequence, its opportunities for physical action and sensuous pleasure: eating, drinking, singing, sailing, riding, walking, lovely women, luxury. The difference is that which Arcite draws between his love for Emily and that of Palamon:

> Thyn is affeccioun of hoolynesse,
> And myn, is love as to a creature.

Belloc loves the world as a creature, loves a woman as a woman. Chesterton loves both world and beloved woman because they reveal God's grace and power. Belloc thus writes of real places and real experiences in a way Chesterton never does. We know where we are: on the Downs, in France, in the Pyrenees, on a particularly stormy passage between two real ports, on Cummor Hill, or at Balliol, in Arundel or Kings Land, his home in Sussex. Belloc's verse is located in space and time as Chesterton's seldom or never is.

But the real world, lovely and solid as Belloc finds it, leaves him forever longing, forever homeless and homesick. It was Chesterton who said that "men are homesick in their homes / And strangers under the sun," but it was Belloc who, in reality, felt himself a stranger whether on land or sea, in Sussex or in Spain. Fear, sadness, nostalgia; a sense of violent, threatening, anarchic forces; these are the climate of Belloc's serious verse, the climate not of the outer but of the inner world. His true voice sounds most clearly not in the over-praised sonnets but in a few lyrics and epigrams. And it is a voice of lament, the voice of an exile mourning with inconsolable sadness the loss of youth, of beauty, of love, of life, the coming of old age and death. These are, of course, prominent themes and moods of the lyric in all ages and Belloc thus stands in a direct line of descent that reaches back to the Greek anthology.

The inward note speaks most poignantly in brief passages, the tone often changing suddenly in the midst of description or action. Haunting lines unexpectedly take us by the throat and remain in the memory. In the midst of a celebration of the South Country, all at once we hear:

> A lost thing could I never find,
> Nor a broken thing mend:
> And I fear I shall be all alone
> When I get towards the end.
> Who will there be to comfort me
> Or who will be my friend?

The sailor pauses in the midst of a southwesterly gale to address his boat:

> We shall not round the granite piers and paven
> To lie to wharves we know with canvas furled.
> My little Boat, we shall not make the haven—
> It is not of the world.
>
> Somewhere of English forelands grandly guarded
> It stands, but not for exiles, marked and clean;
> Oh! not for us. A mist has risen and married it;—
> My youth lies in between.

The prophet lost in the hills at evening cries out on God:

> It darkens; I have lost the ford.
> There is a change on all things made.
> The rocks have evil faces, Lord,
> And I am awfully afraid.

The poet remembering the friends of his youth prays:

> Absolve me, God, that in the land
> which I can nor regard nor know
> Nor think about nor understand
> The flower of my desire shall blow.

The fine verbal dance **"Tarantella"** ends with a change of scene and mood:

> Never more,
> Miranda,
> Never more.
>
> . . . . .
>
> No sound
> In the walls of the Halls where falls
> The tread
> Of the feet of the dead to the ground
> No sound:
> But the boom
> Of the far Waterfall like Doom.

The most eloquent of Belloc's several sundials speaks:

> Here in a lonely glade, forgotten, I
> Mark the tremendous process of the sky.
> So does your inmost soul, forgotten, mark
> The Dawn, the Noon, the coming of the Dark.

The lovely **"Ha'nacker Mill"** is a lament for past and future both, for England and for all things:

> Sally is gone that was so kindly
> Sally is gone from Ha'nacker Hill.
> And the Briar grows ever since then so blindly
> And ever since then the clapper is still,
> And the sweeps have fallen from Ha'nacker
> Mill.
>
> Ha'nacker Hill is in Desolation:
> Ruin a-top and a field unploughed.
> And Spirits that call on a fallen nation
> Spirits that loved her calling aloud:
> Spirits abroad in a windy cloud.
>
> Spirits that call and no one answers;
> Ha'nacker's down and England's done.
> Wind and Thistle for pipe and dancers
> And never a ploughman under the Sun.
> Never a ploughman. Never a one.

"Never" and "nevermore" hang on the lips of Belloc's Muse as they do on the beak of Poe's raven, and with the same effect.

It will be objected, with some truth, that I am picking and choosing; that Belloc had many moods; that there is as much humour, robust love of life, not to mention satire, swagger, bluster, and bounce as of lament in the small volume of his collected verse. And, of course, this is true. The man who could celebrate Christmas in this mood was not always broken-hearted:

> Noël! Noël! Noël! Noël!
> A Catholic tale have I to tell!
> And a Christian song have I to sing
> While all the bells in Arundel ring.
>
> . . . . .
>
> May all good fellows that here agree
> Drink Audit Ale in heaven with me,
> And may all my enemies go to hell!
> Noël! Noël! Noël! Noël!

But though not as obtrusive as his high spirits, the sadness seems to me Belloc's deepest and most essential mood. This "most various" of authors was no less varied a man. There is ample testimony to the contradictions and complications of his nature. Where Chesterton was centripetal, Belloc was centrifugal. "There was in him," remarked one of his friends, "something strange and frightening and unknowable." Another, who saw Chesterton as Porthos and D'Artagnan, compares Belloc to a mixture of Athos and Aramis. Soldier, sailor, horseman, far wanderer, devoted husband and father, bitter enemy and better friend:

the varied surface of Belloc's life barely veils but does not conceal the truth that this robust and rowdy man had a central, ineluctable core of brooding gloom. And the loveliest flowers in the "rightful garden" of his verse bear witness to this rather than to the faith he proclaimed so loudly and for which he fought throughout his life so unselfishly and so bravely. In testimony to that faith, as well as to his fundamental melancholy, let me finish with what is perhaps his noblest expression of both, the end of his **"Heroic Poem in Praise of Wine"**:

> When from the waste of such long labour done
> I too must leave the grape-ennobling sun
> And like the vineyard worker take my way
> Down the long shadows of declining day,
> Bend on the sombre plain my clouded sight
> And leave the mountain to the advancing night,
> Come to the term of all that was mine own
> With nothingness before me, and alone;
> Then to what hope of answer shall I turn?
> Comrade-Commander whom I dared not earn,
> What said You then to trembling friends and few?
> 'A moment, and I drink it with you new:
> But in my Father's Kingdom.' So, my Friend,
> Let not Your cup desert me in the end.
> But when the hour of mine adventure's near,
> Just and benignant let my youth appear
> Bearing a Chalice, open, golden, wide,
> With benediction graven on its side.
> So touch my dying lip: so bridge that deep:
> So pledge my waking from the gift of sleep,
> And, sacramental, raise me the Divine:
> Strong brother in God and last companion, Wine.

Michael H. Markel (essay date 1982)

SOURCE: "The Poetry," in *Hilaire Belloc,* Twayne Publishers, 1982, pp. 24-53.

[*In the following essay, Markel discusses the defining characteristics of Belloc's poetry.*]

During a writing career of more than forty-five years, Hilaire Belloc turned out almost one hundred and fifty prose works. With only a handful of exceptions, writing these books was an enormous chore for him, what one commentator calls his "sad campaign for a livelihood." Belloc's aggressive and domineering personality prevented him from long remaining anyone's employee, so he turned his antipathy for socialists, atheists, and Darwinians into a lifelong vocation.

But Belloc's real love remained his poetry. What he wished to be remembered for is collected in a slim volume called **Complete Verse.** Had circumstances been otherwise, he probably would have written ten volumes of poetry and very little else. Whereas the subject of his prose was the struggle of men in the world, their attempt to create a set of reasonable and just institutions that would allow them to lead civilized lives, the subject of his poetry was the

perennial theme of man's struggle against his mortality. Belloc put into prose what he wanted the world to hear; he saved for his poetry what he *had* to say.

In addition to his serious poetry, Belloc wrote several books of light verse, most of which is collected today under the title **Cautionary Verses.** His first book of light verse, **The Bad Child's Book of Beasts,** appeared the same year as his first collection of serious poems and, much to his delight, sold briskly. Then twenty-six years old, and with a family, a prestigious First Honours in History from Oxford, and no prospects for a job, Belloc decided the serious poems would have to wait, at least for a while.

The Light Verse

The nineteenth century in England was the great period of light verse, or what is sometimes called nonsense verse. Perhaps as a reaction to the seriousness and solemnity of Victorian advice-books for children, the writers of light verse portrayed a world in which children, unencumbered by the restrictions of "civilized" behavior, romped freely through a world bounded only by their own imaginations. The two most famous writers of light verse were Edward Lear (1812-1888) and Charles Lutwidge Dodgson (1832-1898), who is known today as Lewis Carroll.

Lear, a landscape painter by profession, popularized the short verse form known as the limerick:

> There was an Old Man with a beard,
> Who said, "It is just as I feared!—
> Two Owls and a Hen,
> Four Larks and a Wren,
> Have all built their nests in my beard!"

Lewis Carroll, a minor church official and mathematics professor at Oxford, wrote mathematics books under his real name and children's books under his pseudonym. Best remembered today as the author of *Alice's Adventures in Wonderland* (1865) and its sequel, *Through the Looking-Glass* (1871), Carroll is known for his creation of nonsense words in the poems contained within the two famous books. "Jabberwocky," in *Through The Looking-Glass,* is the prime example:

> 'Twas brillig, and the slithy toves
>   Did gyre and gimble in the wabe:
> All mimsy were the borogoves,
>   And the mome raths outgrabe.

Although Belloc is often linked with Lear and Carroll as the third master of nonsense verse, he seems to have been largely indifferent to both of them. The limerick form appears in several of Belloc's letters to friends—he could apparently toss them off effortlessly—but it doesn't appear in any of his published verse. And Belloc seems to have been even less impressed by Carroll's nonsense verse. In fact, he was almost alone among his countrymen in not thinking *Alice's Adventures in Wonderland* a masterpiece. He described it as full of "the humour which is founded upon folly" and thus worthwhile but inferior to "the wit that is founded upon wisdom." He went on to predict—wildly incorrectly, as it has turned out—that the fame of *Alice* would not outlive the insular and protected garden of the Victorian period.

> Whereas the subject of Belloc's prose was the struggle of men in the world, their attempt to create a set of reasonable and just institutions that would allow them to lead civilized lives, the subject of his poetry was the perennial theme of man's struggle against his mortality.
>
> —*Michael H. Markel*

Belloc remained unmoved by Lear and Carroll because he was not principally interested in writing for children. Even though the titles of his light verse collections—such as *The Bad Child's Book of Beasts* and *More Beasts (for Worse Children)*—appear at first glance to be intended for children, the adjectives "bad" and "worse" clearly suggest an adult perspective. Unlike Lear and Carroll, Belloc never tried to assume the viewpoint of the child, and there is very little childlike delight in any of the cautionary tales. Instead, Belloc wrote from the perspective of the stern parent lecturing children on the ghastly consequences of their improper behavior. Belloc achieved his humor by overstating the perils. Most of the bad children in his books die a horrible death: several are eaten by wild animals, one dies in an explosion caused in part by his own carelessness, and another succumbs because he ate too much string. Those lucky children who do not die suffer other unkind fates. Maria, for instance, constantly made funny faces. One day, "Her features took their final mould / In shapes that made your blood run cold . . ." Her sad story is suggested by the title of the poem: **"Maria Who Made Faces and a Deplorable Marriage."** Unlike Lear and Carroll, whose strategy was to bridge the gulf between adults and children, Belloc startled his readers by exaggerating that gulf. Belloc's view of children did not look backward to the Victorian nonsense poets, but forward to the films of W. C. Fields.

The Bad Child's Book of Beasts (1896) was the first appearance of Belloc's irascible narrator, who innocently announces his intentions in an introduction:

> I call you bad, my little child,
>   Upon the title page,
> Because a manner rude and wild
>   Is common at your age.

> The Moral of this priceless work
>   (If rightly understood)

Will make you—from a little Turk—
  Unnaturally good.

But the real personality of the narrator soon emerges. In **"The Lion"** he warns little children to beware:

> The Lion, the Lion, he dwells in the waste,
> He has a big head and a very small waist;
> But his shoulders are stark, and his jaws they are grim,
> And a good little child will not play with him.

The next poem is **"The Tiger"**:

> The Tiger on the other hand, is kittenish and mild,
> He makes a pretty playfellow for any little child;
> And mothers of large families (who claim to common sense)
> Will find a Tiger well repay the trouble and expense.

Enhancing Belloc's humor are the drawings by his friend Basil T. Blackwood that accompany the text. **"The Lion"** is printed around a sketch of a terrified child gazing at the ferocious animal rearing on its hind legs before him. **"The Tiger"** has two sketches: in the first, a hungry-looking tiger is approaching a smiling toddler. In the second, the tiger is walking away, licking its lips. This was one of Belloc's strategies in the book: the words express the seemingly innocent advice; the drawings portray the narrator's—and the reader's—real thoughts.

This kind of macabre humor obviously is not intended for the average child. The parents are the real audience, as several other verses in the collection make clear. **"The Marmozet"** and **"The Big Baboon"** gave Belloc a chance to have a little fun with the evolutionists, with whom he was constantly quarreling, while satirizing the poverty of the modern spirit. The drawing accompanying **"The Marmozet"** shows three figures: a statue of a burly caveman wearing an animal pelt and carrying a club, an anemic-looking young man perspiring as he pedals his bicycle, and a marmozet casting a scornful eye on the young man.

The four-line poem makes the point:

> The species Man and Marmozet
>   Are intimately linked;
> The Marmozet survives as yet,
>   But Men are all extinct.

"The Big Baboon" focuses Belloc's satire a little more:

> The Big Baboon is found upon
>   The plains of Cariboo:
> He goes about with nothing on
>   (A shocking thing to do).

> But if he dressed respectably
>   And let his whiskers grow,
> How like this Big Baboon would be
>   To Mister So-and-so!

The drawings that go with this poem show a happy baboon in the wild, a baboon gazing at a pretentiously dressed African, a baboon gazing into a mirror while his valet helps him on with his coat, and finally several baboons walking happily down a city street, outfitted with luxurious overcoats, fashionable hats, and canes.

Some of the verses in *The Bad Child's Book of Beasts* are funny without being violent or satirical, and many of the drawings are innocently clever, but for the most part Belloc was writing in the tradition of Jonathan Swift and Mark Twain, not Lear and Carroll. Belloc chose animals for his subject not because every child likes to read about them, but because they are strong, self-sufficient, and unaffected. Belloc accepted them as creatures that know what they are, never aspire to be anything else, and never are needlessly cruel. In this way they serve as a perfect contrast to the foolish and vain species called Man. Belloc's book of nonsense verse, reminiscent of Swift's parable of the Yahoos and the Houyhnhnms in Part IV of *Gulliver's Travels,* turns the hierarchy of nature upside down. Published in Oxford, *The Bad Child's Book of Beasts* sold out in four days. A second printing began immediately, and the author arranged for publication in the United States. The critics were very enthusiastic, but, as biographer Speaight remarks, they usually failed to see that the comic verse was not really nonsense.

The critics also applauded *More Beasts (for Worse Children)* (1897), which Belloc published quickly to capitalize on the success of the earlier book. Its plan is the same, but on the whole the humor is forced. Several of the verses are clever. **"The Microbe,"** for example, pokes fun at scientists who describe fantastic microscopic organisms they have never seen. "Oh! let us never, never doubt / What nobody is sure about!" intones the narrator solemnly. But the violence and cruelty of many of the verses is gratuitous: the woman who is devoured by a python in this book "died, because she never knew / Those simple little rules and few" about how to care for it. Her fate is neither humorous nor revealing.

Belloc found his mark again the next year with *The Modern Traveller* (1898), a satirical parable about imperialism. His criticism of the British role in the struggle with the Boers in South Africa was already taking shape; despite its clever verse and Blackwood's drawings, *The Modern Traveller* was obviously intended for adults, not children.

The poem describes how the narrator and two friends—Commander Sin and Captain Blood—travel to Africa to establish the Libyan Association "whose purpose is to combine 'Profit and Piety.'" Recently returned from Africa and looking over the page proofs of his memoirs, the narrator invites a reporter from the *Daily Menace* over for an exclusive article on his expedition. The explorer has plenty of pencils ready for the reporter, because the story is going to be a long one,

> Of how we struggled to the coast,
> And lost our ammunition;

How we retreated, side by side;
And how, like Englishmen, we died.

He begins by introducing Henry Sin:

> Untaught (for what our times require),
> Lazy, and something of a liar,
>   He had a foolish way
> Of always swearing (more or less);
>
>   And, lastly, let us say
> A little slovenly in dress,
> A trifle prone to drunkenness;
> A gambler also to excess,
>   And never known to pay.

In short, he was "A man Bohemian as could be— / But really vicious? Oh, no!" The other hero of the expedition, William Blood, while equally unsavory, was more at home in the modern world. He was:

> A sort of modern Buccaneer,
> Commercial and refined.
> Like all great men, his chief affairs
> Were buying stocks and selling shares.
> He occupied his mind
> In buying them by day from men
> Who needed ready cash, and then
> At evening selling them again
> To those with whom he dined.

When the narrator and his two partners arrive in Africa, they enlist an accomplice, the Lord Chief Justice of Liberia, who gives them "good advice / Concerning Labour and its Price":

> "In dealing wid de Native Scum,
> Yo' cannot pick an' choose;
> Yo' hab to promise um a sum
> Ob wages, paid in Cloth and Rum.
> But, Lordy! that's a ruse!
> Yo' get yo' well on de Adventure,
> And change de wages to Indenture."

A brief mutiny results—"We shot and hanged a few, and then / The rest became devoted men"—but soon the three adventurers find the land they wish to develop. The narrator describes Blood's triumphant pose:

> Beneath his feet there stank
> A swamp immeasurably wide,
> Wherein a kind of fœtid tide
> Rose rhythmical and sank,
> Brackish and pestilent with weeds
> And absolutely useless reeds . . .
>
>   . . . . .
>
> With arms that welcome and rejoice,
> We heard him gasping, in a voice
> By strong emotion rendered harsh:
> "That Marsh—that Admirable Marsh!"

The Tears of Avarice that rise
In purely visionary eyes
Were rolling down his nose.

The development of Eldorado, as Blood christens it, is thwarted. After a confrontation with an international commission against imperialism, which concludes that they are too mad to cause any harm, the three are finally captured by a native tribe. Captain Blood is chopped up and sold by the slice ("Well, every man has got his price") and Commander Sin finds himself floating in a large kettle ("My dear companion making soup"). The narrator endures so well under incredible torture that the tribesmen finally decide he must be a god and release him. His final words to the reporter are that Sin and Blood "Would swear to all that I have said, / Were they alive; / but they are dead!"

The Modern Traveller, like Belloc's two previous books of light verse, was very popular with the public, but it received some unenthusiastic reviews in newspapers, probably because of the satirical portrait of *The Daily Menace*. Sir Arthur Quiller-Couch explained the critical reaction by noting the link between the newspapers and imperialism: since the newspapers had been championing the cause of imperialism, they could not be expected to review fairly a book that criticizes it. The outbreak of the Boer War was in fact the most revealing comment on the book. Belloc in *The Modern Traveller* had shown that light verse could be the vehicle for serious satire without losing its popular appeal.

Belloc appreciated Quiller-Couch's praise, but his financial situation left him no leisure to savor it. Most of his time was being devoted to his first serious prose work, a full-length biography of the French Revolutionary figure Danton that could not hope to bring in much. So Belloc wrote *A Moral Alphabet* (1899). The alphabet format, in which each letter introduces a short verse, gave him a ready-made structure for verses on various subjects; unlike the *Beast* collections or *The Modern Traveller*, an alphabet book needs no unifying theme.

Signs of hasty composition are apparent in *A Moral Alphabet*, but the book is interesting in that it reveals Belloc's awareness of his audience and his growing self-confidence. Four of the twenty-six rhymes refer directly to this or one of his other books. "A," for instance, "stands for Archibald who told no lies, / And got this lovely volume for a prize." When he comes to the nemesis of all alphabet rhymsters, *X,* Belloc effortlessly turns the situation to his advantage:

No reasonable little Child expects
A Grown-up Man to make a rhyme on X.
        MORAL
These verses teach a clever child to find
Excuse for doing all that he's inclined

A Moral Alphabet marks the end of the first phase of Belloc's professional literary career. With the coming of the new century he turned to more substantial formats; he

had already proven himself a reigning master of comic verse in English. Between 1900 and 1905 he produced, among other works, a second biography, two prose satires, a book of literary criticism, a translation, a novel, and several travel books.

In 1907 Hilaire Belloc, member of Parliament, must have sensed that the public was ready for another book of light verse. *Cautionary Tales for Children* follows in the tradition of his first *Beast* book, but it shows a new direction in Belloc's thinking. Almost all of the children in this collection who pay so dearly for their misdeeds belong to the upper class. The title of one verse, **"Godolphin Horne, Who was cursed with the Sin of Pride, and Became a Boot-Black,"** is representative of Belloc's new interest in satirizing the rigid class system of England. His characteristic mask in this book is that of the defender of the class system, but occasionally the real author peeks out and winks at his readers. One example is **"Algernon, Who played with a Loaded Gun, and, on missing his Sister, was reprimanded by his Father."** The most subtle verse is the final one, **"Charles Augustus Fortescue, Who always Did what was Right, and so accumulated an Immense Fortune."** Here Belloc takes particular advantage of Blackwood's drawings by making one statement with words and another with pictures. The verse describes how this perfect child sailed through life successfully,

And long before his Fortieth Year
Had wedded Fifi, Only Child
Of Bunyan, First Lord Aberfylde.
He thus became immensely Rich,
And built the Splendid Mansion which
Is called *"The Cedars, Muswell Hill,"*
Where he resides in Affluence still,
To show what Everybody might
Become by SIMPLY DOING RIGHT.

The drawing accompanying this idyllic tale, however, shows the groom with a slightly pained expression on his face as he gazes at his decidedly unattractive bride, Fifi. Thus, Belloc's final suggestion for the best way to punish the indolent rich of England is simply to let them go about their own business unmolested. *Cautionary Tales for Children* was successful in part because a popular singer, Clara Butt, performed the verses in concert throughout England.

Belloc's unorthodox parliamentary career kept him in the public eye. Frequently squabbling with his own party, he became known as something of a national eccentric, with a reputation apart from his literary renown. Just as nobody was surprised when he decided not to stand for reelection in 1910, nobody was surprised when in 1911 he published *More Peers*, a collection of cautionary verses for adults. One verse describes the unfortunate plight of a physician whose patient, a Lord Roehampton, dies without leaving enough to pay the medical fee. The furious doctor storms away when he learns this tragic news, "And ever since, as I am told, / Gets it beforehand; and in gold." Another lord, Henry Chase, wins a libel suit against *The Daily*

Howl, "But, as the damages were small, / He gave them to a Hospital."

A Lord Finchley learns that excessive thrift has its penalties:

> Lord Finchley tried to mend the Electric Light
> Himself. It struck him dead: And serve him right!
> It is the business of the wealthy man
> To give employment to the artisan.

The highlight of *More Peers* is a story that never gets told:

> Lord Heygate had a troubled face,
> His furniture was commonplace—
> The sort of Peer who well might pass
> For someone of the middle class.
> I do not think you want to hear
> About this unimportant Peer,
> So let us leave him to discourse
> About Lord Epsom and his horse.

Nineteen years were to pass before Belloc got around to *New Cautionary Tales* (1930), published near the end of his long career. This collection is tired, partly because Belloc was then sixty years old, but mostly because he feared that the good fight against the forces of privilege had been lost. He could not escape the realization that fifty years of struggle and one hundred and fifty books had not changed the world. One verse tells the story of how young John loses his inheritance when he tosses a stone that hits his wealthy uncle William. The old man calls to his nurse, Miss Charming,

> "Go, get my Ink-pot and my Quill,
> My Blotter and my Famous Will."
> Miss Charming flew as though on wings
> To fetch these necessary things,
> And Uncle William ran his pen
> Through "well-beloved John," and then
> Proceeded, in the place of same,
> To substitute Miss Charming's name:
> Who now resides in Portman Square
> And is accepted everywhere.

Belloc's last book of comic verse, *Ladies and Gentlemen*, was published two years later, in 1932. It was quite obviously the work of a weary man who no longer felt that the foibles of society were a thoroughly suitable subject for humorous verse. **"The Garden Party,"** the opening verse, describes an affair attended by "the Rich," "the Poor," and "the People in Between":

> For the hoary social curse
> Gets hoarier and hoarier,
> And it stinks a trifle worse
> Than in the days of Queen Victoria . . .

The verse concludes with a reference to the fate of an earlier corrupt civilization: "And the flood destroyed them all." The final verse in the collection, **"The Example,"** is a parable of two modern types. The man is a miserable

agnostic whose only joy is to read the books written by the prophets of doom. The woman leads a life of mindless intemperance:

> The Christians, a declining band,
> Would point with monitory hand
> To Henderson his desperation,
> To Mary Lunn her dissipation,
> And often mutter, "Mark my words!
> Something will happen to those birds!"

Mary Lunn dies, "not before / Becoming an appalling bore," and Henderson is "suffering from paralysis." *"The moral is (it is indeed) / You mustn't monkey with the Creed."* Appropriately enough, Belloc's last book of comic verse concludes with a deadly serious joke.

The comic verse, except for *The Modern Traveller*, was collected under the title *Cautionary Verses* in 1940. The critical reception was highly enthusiastic. *The New Yorker,* for example, called *Cautionary Verses* "a grand omnibus." The collection remains Belloc's most popular single volume. An ironic reminder of the extent to which the satirical element in Belloc's comic verse has remained unrecognized is the fact that *Cautionary Verses* is generally catalogued among the children's books in the library. Taken together, the comic verse is a remarkable achievement. Belloc wrote too much of it, as he did of everything, but the best represents the extraordinary diversity of his imagination, which could combine pure nonsense of the highest quality and serious political and social satire. Perhaps the best insight into the origins of the comic verse is provided by Belloc himself in a poem he originally published in 1910 but which serves as an epigraph to *Cautionary Verses.* The poem, which begins "Child! do not throw this book about," ends with this stanza:

> And when your prayers complete the day,
>   Darling, your little tiny hands
> Were also made, I think, to pray
>   For men that lose their fairylands.

The comic verse is of course very funny, but behind the laughter is the sadness of an idealistic man in a real world.

The Serious Verse

In one of his comic verses Belloc wrote a couplet, "Upon the mansion's ample door, / To which he wades through heaps of Straw . . ." and added a footnote: "This is the first and only time / That I have used this sort of Rhyme." In his comic verse he was scrupulous about following the technical conventions, including such matters as the crispness of the end rhymes. He once wrote that comic verse "has nothing to sustain it save its own excellence of construction, . . . those who have attempted it [find] that no kind of verse needs more the careful and repeated attention of the artificer." This is surely overstatement, for the rate at which he produced his comic verse would have made such refinement and polishing impossible. However, the remark suggests the importance Belloc placed on "the excellence of construction" in all of his verse.

In his relatively few serious poems, in particular, he allowed himself the luxury of slow and careful construction, for in no other kind of writing would he speak so candidly. Almost everything else he wrote was intended to pay the bills. But in his serious poems he expressed his essence, the melancholy and even the despair that tested his Catholic faith. While the rest of Belloc's massive output contains the record of his many opinions, the serious poetry is his purest literary expression.

Belloc put into prose what he wanted the world to hear, he saved for his poetry what he *had* to say.

—*Michael H. Markel*

Belloc's poetic principles were classical. He deplored the contemporary trends in poetry whose origins he saw in the tenets of the Romantics of a century earlier. He insisted that "the greatest verse does not proceed immediately from the strongest feeling. The greatest verse calls up the strongest emotion in the reader, but in the writer it is a distillation, not a cry."

Thus, Belloc dispensed with Wordsworth's theory that poetry is born of "emotion recollected in tranquility" and with the rest of what he saw as "the romantic extravagance, the search for violent sensation, . . . the loss of measure . . ." The rest of the nineteenth century was for Belloc further decay. In a grouchy mood once he wrote to a friend expressing a desire to write a series called "Twelve Great Eunuchs of the Victorian Period." He reserved his most caustic comments, however, for the modern poets. One poet, "spared to middle age in spite of the wrath of God," Belloc called "famous for that he could neither scan nor rhyme—let alone think or feel." And modern English lyric poetry was mere "chopped up prose."

Fairly early in his life Belloc gave up trying to endure modern poetry. Except for the books written by his friends, he read little but the Latin and Greek classics in their original languages. His poetic principles are defined clearly in his book on Milton, whom he considered the last major classical poet in English:

> He felt to his marrow the creative force of restraint, proportion, unity—and that is the classic . . . Rule and its authority invigorated the powers of man as pruning will a tree, as levees a pouring river. Diversity without extravagance, movement which could be rhythmic because it knew boundaries and measure, permanence through order, these were, and may again be, the inestimable fruits of the classical spirit.

To the opinion that the classical style was tired, Belloc responded that "those whose energy is too abundant seek for themselves by an instinct the necessary confines without which such energy is wasted," and that "energy alone can dare to be classical."

Despite his many comments on the necessity of classical restraint, Belloc did not believe that great poetry was merely the result of regular rhythms and rhymes. Like the Romantics he scorned, he felt that a poet is more than a craftsman. Just as the Romantics spoke of the divine inspiration for which they served as a vehicle, Belloc wrote that "something divine is revealed in the poetic speech, not through the poet's will but through some superior will using the poet for its purpose. It is the afflatus of the God. . . . [t]he seed of Poetry floats in from elsewhere. It is not of this world." His definition of poetic inspiration is thus explicitly theistic—god-oriented—whereas the Romantics were more likely to think of poetry as a revelation of the god in Man. Basically, the difference is a matter of terminology and external beliefs, not of essentials. But Belloc was adamant in his views on poetic form, and so he went his own unpopular way during the years of poetic upheaval and innovation.

Belloc's respect for the classical conception of poetry is immediately apparent in his first volume of poetry, *Verses and Sonnets* (1896). Establishing a pattern that he was to follow in all of his books of poetry, Belloc arranged his work according to genre: sonnets, songs, epigrams, and satires. Like the ancients, he believed that poetry is a deliberate and self-conscious utterance and that an idea or emotion has to be expressed in an appropriate genre to achieve its meaning.

Belloc's concern for the plight of the poor, for example, is expressed in two poems, one a satire and one a sonnet. **"The Justice of the Peace,"** the satire, is a scathing dramatic monologue that begins with this stanza:

> Distinguish carefully between these two,
>   This thing is yours, that other thing is mine.
> You have a shirt, a brimless hat, a shoe
>   And half a coat. I am the Lord benign
> Of fifty hundred acres of fat land
> To which I have a right. You understand?

In his sonnet on the same subject, **"The Poor of London,"** Belloc ignores the conflict among the social classes and focuses instead on the plight of the poor:

> Almighty God, whose justice like a sun
> Shall coruscate along the floors of Heaven,
> Raising what's low, perfecting what's undone,
> Breaking the proud and making odd things even,
> The poor of Jesus Christ along the street
> In your rain sodden, in your snows unshod,
> They have nor hearth, nor sword, nor human meat,
> Nor even the bread of men: Almighty God.

The different perspectives on this situation are achieved through Belloc's careful use of the two genres. The satire is grimly cheerful, as befitting the confrontation between the rich man and the beggar. The sonnet, on the other hand, is almost a prayer to Christ to alleviate the suffering of the poor. The sonnet, the most popular genre of love poets, is perfectly appropriate for this different kind of love poem.

Social justice was one of Belloc's two major concerns at this time in his life. The other was Elodie, whom he married in 1896, soon after the publication of *Verses and Sonnets.* "The Harbour" dramatizes his frustration in waiting five years for her consent. Belloc uses a metaphor that was popular during the Renaissance in Europe:

> I was like one that keeps the deck by night
> Bearing the tiller up against his breast;
> I was like one whose soul is centred quite
> In holding course although so hardly prest,
> And veers with veering shock now left now right,
> And strains his foothold still and still makes play
> Of bending beams until the sacred light
> Shows him high lands and heralds up the day.

In "Love and Honour" he uses another favorite strategy of the Renaissance: the personification of abstract concepts. The impatient male is always Love, the reluctant female is Honour. In the traditional conflict Love tries unsuccessfully to conquer Honour, who retreats and thus conquers him by her virtue. After Belloc waits "a full five years' unrest," Honour appears to him one night:

> But when he saw her on the clear night shine
> Serene with more than mortal light upon her,
> The boy that careless was of things divine,
> Small Love, turned penitent to worship Honour.
>   So Love can conquer Honour: when that's past
>   Dead Honour risen outdoes Love at last.

Belloc loved Elodie, but he was also in love with English poetry.

Time, the enemy of all lovers, is the subject of many of the poems in Belloc's first collection. In "Her Music" he expresses the fear that the enchantment of his love will "stir strange hopes" of immortality, "And make me dreamer more than dreams are wise." The theme of mutability is explored in the highlight of the volume, *Sonnets of the Twelve Months,* which contain some of Belloc's best descriptive poetry. "January," for instance, contains this chilling portrait:

> Death, with his evil finger to his lip,
> Leers in at human windows, turning spy
> To learn the country where his rule shall lie
> When he assumes perpetual generalship.

The brisk March wind is described in a line that combines perfectly the sense and the sound: "Roaring he came above the white waves' tips!" The sonnets of the early summer months provide a gentle interlude before the declining half of the year. In several of the sonnets about the later months Belloc builds the poem around a famous European battle scene. In "July," for instance, he describes the Christian kings returning from the Crusades and states, "I wish to God that I had been with them . . .". In "August" Belloc's

historical imagination transports him to Charlemagne's great victory at Roncesvalles. In "September" he becomes a participant in the French Revolution: "But watching from that eastern casement, I / Saw the Republic splendid in the sky, / And round her terrible head the morning stars." The best of the twelve sonnets is "December," which ends with this sestet:

> For now December, full of agéd care,
> Comes in upon the year and weakly grieves;
> Mumbling his lost desires and his despair;
> And with mad trembling hand still interweaves
> The dank sear flower-stalks tangled in his hair,
> While round about him whirl the rotten leaves.

This passage, reminiscent of *King Lear,* is an appropriate conclusion to the sonnet sequence, for it unifies and transcends the individual battle scenes in a final portrait of human suffering. Belloc's love of European history, which was to become apparent in his numerous prose studies, is here given its shape by the poet's sensibility.

Mankind's suffering and despair are not meaningless, however. Belloc focuses on the proud and defiant warriors, such as Charlemagne with his "bramble beard flaked red with foam / Of bivouac wine-cups . . . ," because they represent man's attempt to confront and conquer the forces of disorder and anarchy. Similarly, Belloc the poet enters into their world in his attempt to give meaning to their stories through his sonnets. "The sonnet," he wrote, "demands high verse more essentially than does any other looser form. . . . [T]he sonnet is the prime test of a poet." In his first book he proudly announced his allegiance to the powers of poetry in its fight against the transience of man.

With his prose and then his parliamentary career occupying his time, Belloc did not publish his next volume of poetry until 1910. *Verses* includes many of the poems from *Verses and Sonnets.* Distinguishing the new verses from the old is not difficult, however, for the fourteen intervening years had changed Belloc dramatically. Whereas the first volume is marked by a youthful vitality and exuberance, *Verses* is permeated by a sense of spiritual fatigue and loss that characterized all of Belloc's work in the second half of his life. The death of his wife and then of his son Louis a few years later was to make this outlook permanent, but in 1910 Belloc was already beginning to characterize his life as a painful battle and to look backward to his youth as a carefree period of harmony with mankind and nature.

Yet the comic spirit is still alive in several poems. "Lines to a Don," for instance, is a comic diatribe against a "Remote and ineffectual Don / That dared attack my Chesterton." It is full of cascading insults such as these:

> Don puffed and empty, Don dyspeptic;
> Don middle-class, Don sycophantic,
> Don dull, Don brutish, Don pedantic . . .

A comic self-portrait, "The Happy Journalist," describes Belloc's pleasures:

I love to walk about at night
    By nasty lanes and corners foul,
All shielded from the unfriendly light
    And independent as the owl.

    . . . . .

Policemen speak to me, but I,
    Remembering my civic rights,
Neglect them and do not reply.
    I love to walk about at nights!

The comic verses, however, represent only a small part of the newer poetry. Belloc's alienation from society is portrayed most characteristically as violent combat. In **"The Rebel,"** for example, he pictures himself as a soldier fighting against the forces of "lies and bribes." After describing how he would, like Paul Revere, "summon a countryside," and kill the evil men, he vows to:

    . . . batter their carven names,
And slit the pictures in their frames,
And burn for scent their cedar door,
And melt the gold their women wore,
And hack their horses at the knees . . .

In **"The Prophet Lost in the Hills at Evening"** this violent struggle is transferred to the battlefield of Belloc's soul as he envisions himself as God's warrior:

I challenged and I kept the Faith,
    The bleeding path alone I trod;
It darkens. Stand about my wraith,
    And harbour me, almighty God.

Belloc at this point in his life was a curious mixture of public ferocity and private anxiety. In public he was a courageous and selfless fighter, unafraid to elicit the wrath of the English people because of his unpopular pro-Boer stand, unafraid to speak out against the political corruption in his own party, and unafraid to attack the socialists, the atheists, and the Darwinians. Considering that he was always short of funds and that he could easily have earned far more money writing comic verse and less provocative histories, his decision to engage in these constant battles shows a remarkable strength of character. Poems such as **"The Prophet,"** however, demonstrate the price he paid to maintain this public posture. Not only did he turn inward, he began to see himself as a divine messenger, a martyr who was being destroyed by the evil forces of the world.

The more successful poems in the 1910 collection are less self-consciously dramatic. **"The South Country"** pays homage to his native Sussex in simple and natural language:

If I ever become a rich man,
    Or if ever I grow to be old,
I will build a house with deep thatch
    To shelter me from the cold,
And there shall the Sussex songs be sung
    And the story of Sussex told.

I will hold my house in the high wood
    Within a walk of the sea,
And the men that were boys when I was a boy
    Shall sit and drink with me.

Sussex became for Belloc not so much a county as a fortress. He was fully aware that this final scene is a fantasy, as are his self-portraits as a warrior or a religious martyr. The power of **"The South Country"** is his point that even though his dream is apparently humble, it is as unattainable as any attempt to turn back the clock.

The best poem in the collection, **"Stanzas Written on Battersea Bridge During a South-Westerly Gale,"** dramatizes this thought rather than just stating it. Although Belloc never tired of criticizing Wordsworth, this poem shows that he learned the techniques of the meditative lyric from him. As his title suggests, the strategy of the poem is similar to Wordsworth's in "Lines Composed a Few Miles Above Tintern Abbey." Wordsworth begins his meditation by describing his impressions on revisiting the countryside that had meant so much to him when he was a boy. Belloc, on the other hand, pictures himself in London:

The woods and downs have caught the mid-
    December,
    The noisy woods and high sea-downs of home;
The wind has found me and I do remember
    The strong scent of the foam.

After describing his desperate wish to return to Sussex and his youth, he realizes that:

There is no Pilotry my soul relies on
    Whereby to catch beneath my bended hand,
Faint and beloved along the extreme horizon,
    That unforgotten land.

    . . . . .

Somewhere of English forelands grandly guarded
    It stands, but not for exiles, marked and clean;
Oh! not for us. A mist has risen and marred it:—
    My youth lies in between.

So in this snare that holds me and appals me,
    Where honour hardly lives nor loves remain,
The Sea compels me and my County calls me,
    But stronger things restrain.

    . . . . .

England, to me that never have malingered,
    Nor spoken falsely, nor your flattery used,
Nor even in my rightful garden lingered:—
    What have you not refused?

Unlike Wordsworth, whose realization of loss is tempered by a growth of understanding, Belloc sees no redemption in the passage of time. Like A. E. Housman, Belloc characterizes the journey from innocence to experience as a cruel joke. The last stanza is touched by an unreasonable self-pity, the indignation of a man who feels that his country has treated him unfairly—from the time of Oxford's refusal of the fellowship to his more recent struggles in the literary and political arenas. This treatment, Belloc is saying, is particularly unfair, considering the great energy he expended trying to do the right thing. Rather than remain in his "rightful garden"—the sheltered world of poetry—he confronted his enemies tirelessly.

But this self-pity is offset by the simple beauty of the last line. As W. H. Auden says in "In Memory of W. B. Yeats,"

> Time that is intolerant
>   Of the brave and innocent . . .
> Worships language and forgives
>   Everyone by whom it lives . . .

Belloc never did understand the ways in which he made his life more difficult than it might have been. **"Stanzas Written on Battersea Bridge"** is a complete failure as a logical argument, but it is a beautiful and moving evocation of his confusion.

The 1910 volume received little critical notice. *The Times Literary Supplement* [22 December 1910], however, called Belloc "specially successful with the music of a simple primitive rhythm."

Belloc's analyses of the war occupied his mind during this period of personal loss; he wrote little poetry. His third book of verse, *Sonnets and Verse,* was not published until 1923, thirteen years after his second book, twenty-seven years after his first. By this time he had had a chance to contemplate his disappointments and his grief. Despite his increasing activity as a Catholic apologist, he never was able to integrate his personal experience and his faith. Almost all of the new poems included in the 1923 volume record Belloc's struggle to understand his tragedies; in none of them does he offer a Christian explanation. Like the classical poets whose work he studied and emulated, he remained essentially a pagan. And like the pagans who stoically accepted death, he finally came to an uneasy peace with his fate.

Not all of the poems, of course, concern death. **"Tarantella"** is a song about a subject Belloc knew well—"the fleas that tease in the High Pyrenees"—and **"The Chanty of the 'Nona'"** is a sea song commemorating a sail he took in 1914 along the western and southern coasts of England. For these songs, and for many others he wrote, he composed melodies that he loved to sing aloud. *Sonnets and Verse* also contains a number of stinging epigrams, such as **"Epitaph on the Politician Himself"**:

> Here richly, with ridiculous display,
> The Politician's corpse was laid away.
> While all of his acquaintance sneered and slanged
> I wept: for I had longed to see him hanged.

"On his Books" is a clever statement of a professional writer's aspirations:

> When I am dead, I hope it may be said:
> "His sins were scarlet, but his books were read."

The mood of the volume, however, is most closely expressed by **"The False Heart"**:

> I said to Heart, "How goes it?" Heart replied:
> "Right as a Ribstone Pippin!" But it lied.

The bulk of *Sonnets and Verse* is love sonnets to Elodie. Several of them may in fact have been written before her death. The reader cannot tell because Belloc has stripped the poems down to an essential emotion—his love for her—which never changed in the sixty years following their first meeting. Any one of these sonnets demonstrates the timeless quality of his love:

> They that have taken wages of things done
> When sense abused has blocked the doors of sense,
> They that have lost their heritage of the sun,
> Their laughter and their holy innocence;
> They turn them now to this thing, now to t'other,
> For anchor hold against swift-eddying time,
> Some to that square of earth which was their
>   mother,
> And some to noisy fame, and some to rhyme:
>
> But I to that far morning where you stood
> In fullness of the body, with your hands
> Reposing on your walls, before your lands,
> And all, together, making one great good:
>   Then did I cry "For this my birth was meant.
>   These are my use, and this my sacrament!"

Belloc's definition of the sonnet form was very strict in one sense: he felt that the poet has to establish a clear break between the octave—the first eight lines—and the sestet—the other six. About the various rhyme schemes Belloc was silent, but he felt that the essence of the sonnet is the contrast between the unity of the octave and the response or elaboration of the sestet.

In this sonnet to Elodie the octave-sestet contrast embodies the meaning. The octave is the definition of how people attempt to deal with the passage of time. The first quatrain is Belloc's description of the ravages of time; the second quatrain is the description of how people react. Without identifying who these people are, he subtly distinguishes them from himself by using the distancing pronoun "they" in the first quatrain and the parallel grammatical structure in the second. Phrases such as "now to this thing, now to t'other" suggest the helplessness of these anonymous victims as they are buffeted uncontrollably by the seas of "swift-eddying time."

To the chaotic movement Belloc opposes his image of the stillness of Elodie. The contrast is introduced immediately by the transitional "But" and the first-person pronoun. His realization—the "cry" in the final couplet—is an exclamation of joy that contrasts with the "noisy fame" to which other people devote themselves. By creating this perfectly refined image of beauty, Belloc manages to cheat time.

The point made by this poem is that his image may have occurred in 1900 or 1923. Man can freeze time in a memory, and an artist can convey that memory in a timeless work of art.

If several of Belloc's sonnets demonstrate the poet's ability to capture an image and thereby stop time, others confront the issue of Elodie's death directly. One attitude characteristic of some of these sonnets is the consolation that Elodie enjoyed and contributed to all of the valuable aspects of mortal life. This attitude is expressed, for instance, in the sestet of **"When you to Acheron's ugly water come,"** in which Belloc describes the majesty and nobility with which Elodie died:

> Then go before them like a royal ghost
> And tread like Egypt or like Carthage crowned;
> Because in your Mortality the most
> Of all we may inherit has been found—
>   Children for memory: the Faith for pride;
>   Good land to leave: and young Love satisfied.

Unlike the "formless mourners" who stretch their hands longingly toward death, Elodie demonstrated in her death the grace she embodied in her life. Significantly, Belloc uses the pagan metaphor of crossing the river of death, despite his reference to the Catholic faith. His focus remains on the values of the living, not on the joys of the Christian afterlife. This poem was probably written some years after her death, when he was finally able to write about it with a more peaceful stoicism.

If Belloc could ultimately accept Elodie's death in some of his poetry, he was less successful in dealing with it in his real life. He wrote, as late as 1922, one year before the publication of **Sonnets and Verse,** that "my cancer of loss gets worse and worse with every year and I grow fixed in the void of my wife and my son . . ." Belloc never tried to forget his wife and son; on the contrary, he seems to have derived some solace from the rituals of grief. He wore only black from the day of Elodie's death, used funereal stationery, and traced the sign of the Cross upon her door before he went to bed every night at King's Land.

Belloc's inability to let go of Elodie is dramatized in several of the poems in **Sonnets and Verse.** One sonnet in particular shows this response:

> We will not whisper, we have found the place
> Of silence and the endless halls of sleep:
> And that which breathes alone throughout the deep,
> The end and the beginning: and the face
> Between the level brows of whose blind eyes
> Lie plenary contentment, full surcease
> Of violence, and the passionless long peace
> Wherein we lose our human lullabies.
>
> Look up and tell the immeasurable height
> Between the vault of the world and your dear head;
> That's death, my little sister, and the night
> Which was our Mother beckons us to bed,

> Where large oblivion in her house is laid
> For us tired children, now our games are played.

Here Belloc pictures the death of his wife and himself as a peaceful sleep, a respite from the shocks of the world. Death will be safe, for he and Elodie are only children who are obeying their mother's request that they go to bed. In an epigram, **"The Statue,"** he explores the same idea of his accompanying Elodie:

> When we are dead, some Hunting-boy will pass
> And find a stone half-hidden in tall grass
> And grey with age: but having seen that stone
> (Which was your image), ride more slowly on.

This beautiful and simple poem epitomizes **Sonnets and Verse.** The poet and his beloved are now gone, but life continues as always on earth, except that a passerby will be struck by her beauty as it is reflected by her gravestone. These love poems that Belloc wrought out of his grief were his memorial to Elodie. **Sonnets and Verse** thus represented for him a catharsis. By defining himself as Elodie's companion, he was able finally to stop the aching movement of time without his wife, just as in the earlier love poems he was able to create a fixed image of her.

The 1923 volume of poetry brought considerable critical reaction, largely because Belloc had become by that time one of the best-known English men of letters. An article in the *Saturday Review* [November 10, 1923], for example, was titled "Mr. Belloc—Poet" and speculated that one of the reasons he was not taken as seriously as a poet as he might have wished was that he wrote so much prose. The anonymous reviewer suggested that "he might, if he had confined himself to poetry, have been hailed as a master . . ." Along with several other commentators, the reviewer argued that "it is in rare gleams of an essential and peculiar loveliness, where the poet's strength and tenderness meet, that his bid for immortality is made." [In December 2, 1923] Filson Young, writing in the *New York Times,* also commented on the relative slimness of Belloc's poetic output: "He seldom will condescend to be merely an artist, but in this book of later poetry he returns, not without a shade of irony, to his old trade of using language as an instrument to evoke beauty." Belloc had become a respected and admired poet of the classical style.

The final volume of poetry, also called **Sonnets and Verse** (1938), is distinct from the 1923 volume in that it offers only a few brief lyrics to the memory of Elodie. In all other respects, however, Belloc remained unchanged. The generic classification system that the poet maintained emphasized this continuity. The "Epigrams" section of the 1923 volume, for instance, concludes with **"Partly from the Greek."** The 1938 collection, without skipping a beat, simply continues with the next epigram, **"From the Same."**

"The Fire," a melancholy description of how time has destroyed his hopes, is the best example of Belloc's later poetry. The self-assured pleasures of youth are described in the opening stanza, which gallops along carelessly in tetrameter lines.

We rode together all in pride,
They laughing in their riding gowns
We young men laughing at their side,
We charged at will across the downs.

The assault by time, however, cannot be resisted: "The golden faces charged with sense / Have broken to accept the years." The speaker, now alone and perplexed, demonstrates Belloc's ability to change the tone radically while maintaining the tetrameter lines:

Were they not here, the girls and boys?
I hear them. They are at my call.
The stairs are full of ghostly noise,
But there is no one in the hall.

Also characteristic of Belloc are the biting epigrams. One victim is a pacifist: "Pale Ebenezer thought it wrong to fight, / But Roaring Bill (who killed him) thought it right." Another victim, a Puritan, Belloc would classify a religious eccentric: "He served his God so faithfully and well / That now he sees him face to face, in hell And, as always, Belloc loved to define the political animal, as in **"On Two Ministers of State"**:

Lump says that Caliban's of gutter breed,
And Caliban says Lump's a fool indeed,
And Caliban and Lump and I are all agreed.

Belloc's poetic masterpiece, **"Heroic Poem in Praise of Wine,"** is also included in the 1938 *Sonnets and Verse.* Both poetically and philosophically, it is his most mature composition. The term "heroic poem" in the title refers to the poetic form: rhymed iambic pentameter couplets, sometimes called heroic couplets or heroic verse. By choosing this demanding poetic form for a work of over two hundred lines, he was distinguishing himself from the world of modern poetry and allying himself with the classical Greek and Roman writers and, in England, with Dryden and Pope.

Belloc chose the heroic couplet because it complemented the world and the spirit he wanted to celebrate:

To exalt, enthrone, establish and defend,
To welcome home mankind's mysterious friend:
Wine, true begetter of all arts that be;
Wine, privilege of the completely free;
Wine the recorder; wine the sagely strong;
Wine, bright avenger of sly-dealing wrong,
Awake, Ausonian Muse, and sing the vineyard song!

This classical invocation leads into a description of Bacchus, driving his chariot pulled by a team of panthers, swooping down over Europe and creating, everywhere, "The Vines, the conquering Vines!" (1. 35)

After this definition of the creation of the vineyards, Belloc begins his greatest passage of high comic verse:

But what are these that from the outer murk
Of dense mephitic vapours creeping lurk

To breathe foul airs from that corrupted well
Which oozes slime along the floor of Hell?
These are the stricken palsied brood of sin
In whose vile veins, poor, poisonous and thin,
Decoctions of embittered hatreds crawl:
These are the Water-Drinkers, cursed all!
On what gin-sodden Hags, what flaccid sires
Bred these White Slugs from what exhaust desires?

The conflict between the misguided water-drinkers and the godly wine-drinkers is not resolved; despite his comic treatment, Belloc is portraying nothing less than the struggle of Catholics "in these last unhappy days / When beauty sickens and a muddied robe / Of baseness fouls the universal globe."

The final movement of the poem begins on an elegiac note:

When from the waste of such long labour done
I too must leave the grape-ennobling sun
And like the vineyard worker take my way
Down the long shadows of declining day,
Bend on the sombre plain my clouded sight
And leave the mountain to the advancing night,
Come to the term of all that was mine own
With nothingness before me, and alone;
Then to what hope of answer shall I turn?

Raising his chalice of sacramental wine to the God he cannot see, he prepares to reenter "my Father's Kingdom." **"Heroic Poem in Praise of Wine"** combines a sustained technical virtuosity with Belloc's most sophisticated vision: a subtle mingling of the pagan earth and the Christian sky. He worked on the poem for some twenty years. More important, however, he lived most of his life before he could understand and articulate—just this once—the essential unity of comedy and tragedy on earth.

The critical essay that most insightfully defines how the 1938 volume illuminated Belloc appeared in *The Catholic World* [August, 1939]: ". . . the volume contains more than one indication that his faith, robust and virile as it is, has been wrested from the teeth of doubt." The other journals concentrated on Belloc's pursuit of the classical poetic virtues of craftsmanship, control, precision, and clarity of expression. The *Times Literary Supplement* [May 28, 1938] contrasted Belloc with the "new severe young men" who sacrificed form for intellectual content. Critic George Sampson wrote, in 1941, that:

Belloc's serious poems, slight in quantity, are exquisite in quality. His sonnets are the finest modern examples of that much tried form. His songs can laugh and laud and deride with the ribald vigour of the past and the effective point of the present. No one in recent times has touched sacred themes with such appealing delicacy. The poems of Belloc show triumphantly how a modern writer can follow an old tradition and remain master of himself.

Belloc was characteristically—and extravagantly—humble about his poetry. He once wrote that "I am one who by nature writes commonplace verse, which I then slowly tinker at and turn into less commonplace." He did not believe this for an instant, of course, but just as he refused to call his verse "poetry"—a term he considered too exalted for his efforts—he would not allow himself a public display of pride. But when the critics praised the poems he sculpted and polished, Belloc must have smiled inwardly.

A. N. Wilson (essay date 1984)

SOURCE: "Early Married Life: 1896-1899," in *Hilaire Belloc,* Atheneum, 1984, pp. 66-91.

[*In the following excerpt from his biography of Belloc, Wilson offers a mixed assessment of Belloc's poetry.*]

The first book which Belloc published was a small collection entitled *Verses and Sonnets* in 1896. 'I do not think that this book excited a ripple of attention at the time, and yet some of the poems in it have lived, and are now found in many anthologies, where as the verse which at this time was received with a clamour of applause is nearly all of it not only dead but buried and completely forgotten." That was Maurice Baring's judgment in 1922. Since that time, Belloc's reputation as a poet has declined to the point where his serious verse is only known or appreciated by a small band of enthusiasts. At the best of times, he is a very uneven poet. And the things he was good at have never been less admired by critics than now: lyric facility, metrical fluency, and the self-consciously 'beautiful' effects which have made 'Georgian' almost a term of abuse. At times, in this 1896 volume he approaches (though never here achieves) the technical virtuosity of A. E. Housman or Yeats, only to cascade into rhymes which seem too casy, or effects which seem mannered rather than meant.

> The Moon is dead. I saw her die.
> She in a drifting cloud was drest,
> She lay along the uncertain west,
> A dream to see.
> And very low she spake to me:
> 'I go where none may understand,
> I fade into the nameless land,
> And there must lie perpetually.'
> And therefore, loudly, loudly I
> And high
> And very piteously make cry:
> 'The Moon is dead. I saw her die'.

This could be any reasonably competent Nineties poet, steeped in the rhythms of Swinburne and the lethargic postures of *la Décadence*. Its 'spake' and 'drest' make it embarrassing now. Yet, in the same volume, there are poems which display three very distinctive qualities of Belloc's best verse: three qualities which were all part of his personality and which create the most authentically Bellocian *sound* when read aloud: bombast, lyricism and satire.

The first is bombast. It is a quality little esteemed in poets nowa-days, but which is not wholly to be despised. One sees it in some of his sonnets on the twelve months of the

year, mingled with an elegiac tone which is completely Belloc's; as in his '**November**' poem in which he likens the month to Napoleon.

> November is that historied Emperor
>   Conquered in age but foot to foot with fate
> Who from his refuge high has heard the roar
>   Of squadrons in pursuit, and now, too late,
> Stirrups the storm and calls the winds to war,
>   And arms the garrison of his last heirloom,
> And shakes the sky to its extremest shore
>   With battle against irrevocable doom.
>
> Till, driven and hurled from his strong citadels,
>   He flies in hurrying cloud and spurs him on,
> Empty of lingerings, empty of farewells
>   And final benedictions and is gone.
> But in my garden all the trees have shed
> Their legacies of light and all the flowers are dead.

The effect of the poignant last couplet, after all the swirling and bombastic storm of the previous lines, shows that Belloc had a wholly distinctive poetic voice, and that had he only 'polished up' his verse as Elodie urged him to do, he might have achieved great things.

Simple lyricism is the second quality which was apparent in Belloc's poetry from the beginning, lyrics as simple as the best medieval songs, lyrics which reflect his essential simplicity of form but which are so technically accomplished that in poems like '**Auvergnat**' or '**On a winter's night long time ago**' one could only take the perfect rhythms for artlessness. '**The Early Morning**' is another such poem, which has some of the smiling simplicity which was always a part of Belloc's nature:

> The moon on the one hand, the dawn on the other:
> The moon is my sister, the dawn is my brother.
> The moon on my left and the dawn on my right.
> My brother, good morning: my sister, good night.

But there is a third, and quite different category of poem in his *Verses and Sonnets* of 1896. Technically as accomplished as the other kinds of poem in the volume, it has the satirical edge which one thinks, perhaps wrongly, to be Belloc at his most distinctive.

On Torture, a Public Singer

> Torture will give a dozen pence or more
> To keep a drab from bawling at his door.
> The public taste is quite a different thing—
> Torture is positively paid to sing.

And, appropriately, it was his savage gifts as a comic poet which made his verses for children so abidingly successful. In much of his later prose, as in his conversation, Belloc's delight in strong speech won him many enemies. Some of the same qualities which made him such an impassioned controversialist, when channelled into magical nonsense, produced pages in which generations of children have revelled.

A Python I should not advise,
It needs a doctor for its eyes,
And has the measles yearly.
However, if you feel inclined
To get one (to improve your mind,
And not from fashion merely),
Allow no music near its cage;
And when it flies into a rage
Chastise it most severely.
I had an aunt in Yucatan
Who bought a Python from a man
  And kept it for a pet.
She died, because she never knew
These simple little rules and few;—
  The Snake is living yet.

In the forty-five years after the publication of *The Bad Child's Book of Beasts*, he wrote over a hundred and fifty prose works of history, of political and economic theory, and of religious apologetics. Almost none of these works is in print, and the general opinion even (or especially) among Catholics is that he spent his life talking and writing nonsense; violent, vitriolic, and, the general opinion would be, frequently dangerous nonsense. This huge output of books never sold very well, and it is now almost completely neglected. But his early doodlings, when he was deliberately writing violent nonsense, remain in print and are the possession of every literate, English-speaking child. The paradox is positively Chestertonian. Belloc had a keen desire to make his readers see Sense, about Economics, Politics, History and Religion. But, when he encapsulated all this Common Sense in lucid prose, it was dismissed for two or three generations as Nonsense. But Nonsense, so very undesirable in prose, was apparently an excellent thing in verse. Even today, when many of Belloc's political and social prophecies have been proved to be luminously common-sensical, the paradox remains. Parents who would shudder to read *The Servile State* or *The Jews* urge their children to recite the unhappy end of Rebecca Offendort, flattened by a marble bust of Abraham in her banker-father's Bayswater residence.

The Bad Child's Book of Beasts sold 4,000 copies within three months of publication, and has been in print ever since. *More Beasts for Worse Children* followed it in 1897 and was equally successful. In 1898, he published *The Modern Traveller*, illustrated, as were the previous two volumes, with ludicrously apposite drawings by Basil Blackwood. It tells the story of two explorers called Commander Sin and William Blood. As Arthur Quiller Couch noted in his review of the book, it specifically satirises the British Press and the Imperialist ideal: 'The exploration business, the "Anglo-Saxon" *entente*—can a journalist who has been watering these plants with emotion for months past be expected to welcome a book which hints that some recent and practical applications of his creed have been absurd and others more than a little base?' William Blood is

A sort of modern Buccaneer,
Commercial and refined.
Like all great men, his chief affairs
Were buying stocks and selling shares.

He occupied his mind
In buying them by day from men
Who needed ready cash, and then
At evening selling them again
To those with whom he dined.

But, although the 'satirical' elements in the tale reflects Belloc's perennial political preoccupations, the glory of it is in the inventiveness of its rhymes, the absurdity of its plot, and the wonderful arbitrariness of its general observations:

And yet I really must complain
About the Company's Champagne!
  This most expensive kind of wine
In England is a matter
Of pride or habit when we dine
  (Presumably the latter)
Beneath an equatorial sky
And stern indomitable men
Have told me, time and time again,
'The nuisance of the tropics is
The sheer necessity of fizz'.

The extraordinary magic of Belloc's light verse, as anyone who enjoyed it in childhood can testify—is that one can revel in this, and know it by heart before one has even seen a bottle of champagne. The parts of the poem which relate to 'grown-up' life are not distinguished, in the minds of the children who read it, from the combustiously absurd pace of those parts of the narrative which are not remotely 'satirical'.

On June the 7th after dark
A young and very hungry shark
  Came climbing up the side.
It ate the Chaplain and the Mate—
But why these incidents relate?
  The public must decide
That nothing in the voyage out
Was worth their bothering about,
Until we saw the coast, which looks
Exactly as it does in books.
Oh! Africa, mysterious land!
Surrounded by a lot of sand
  And full of grass and trees . . .

A man who was capable of writing those lines need not have striven to capture the attention of posterity.

But, of course, Belloc, at that date, if he had an eye on posterity at all, was pursuing fame of an altogether different kind; and his children's verses were only the most minimal interlude, as far as he was concerned, in a life dominated by his two over-riding concerns, of history and politics.

Michael H. Market (essay date 1986)

SOURCE: "The Manuscript Poetry of Hilaire Belloc," in *The Chesterton Review*, Vol. XII, No. 2, May, 1986, pp. 221-29.

[*In the following essay, Markel asserts that some of Belloc's unpublished verses are "equal in quality to his best published poetry."*]

On January 13, 1911, the Northern Newspaper Syndicate responded to Hilaire Belloc's offer to write an article for them:

> We are pleased that you are agreeable to write for us and as to title, we think if the article is called "What can be done with a Million" it would serve our purpose. As to terms, for the short article we require we do not see our way to pay more than £7.7s.

Could Belloc himself have written two sentences with more of a sting? He needed the £7.7s, so he wrote about how to spend a million, just as he wrote scores of other articles that he did not care about. His attitude toward his prose— including most of his one hundred and fifty books—was simple: "Write and write and write and then offer it for sale, just like butter."

But Belloc loved his poetry. With the sole exception of the novel, *Belinda,* the poetry was the only writing that he took seriously enough to revise. He concludes **"Stanzas Written on Battersea Bridge During a South-Westerly Gale"** by describing himself as one who "nor even in my rightful garden lingered." The manuscript poetry in the Boston College collection offers an unique glimpse inside the poet's garden. The collection shows that many of the classic poems that he published in his fifties were begun when he was barely out of his teens. A number of the poems in the collection exist in several versions, giving us that rare pleasure of watching a great craftsman struggle to create an "effortless" poem. Another bonanza is the new poetry: works that for one reason or another Belloc decided not to publish—or merely never got around to publishing. Some of this material is equal in quality to his best published poetry.

> The poetry in the Boston College collection covers the entire range of what he called his verse: several sonnets, a number of lyrics, a series of political epigrams, and some light verse. In addition, the collection contains several brief comic verse dramas, a lyric in French, and a large number of published but uncollected poems.

What condition are the manuscripts in? Ironically, the earlier material is the best preserved, for as a young man Belloc used notebooks. One small, leather notebook, which contains early versions of several of the great poems, is inscribed "Hilaire Belloc / San Francisco / March 31, 1891." Another is inscribed "Notes / on / Matters which I ignore, which I have ignored / or / Which I well may / Ignore / In the Future. / Together with / Those things which are too important. / to remain with a mere / Shadow / Of Doubtfulness / Hilaire Belloc / The 25th day of Veudemaire / In the year of liberty / 101" [25 September 1894]. Belloc appears to have abandoned the notebooks soon, however, as the bulk of the poetry is written on stationery, scraps of paper, backs of envelopes, and letters he had received. Much of this paper has begun to disin-

tegrate, in some cases destroying portions of the verse. The problems of legibility are compounded by several other factors, including Belloc's habit of scribbling notes on the same pages on which he was writing poetry. The phrase "Holy Saturday 1916 / Late at night / *Wine* tomorrow: Gallons of it!" for example, crowds out the poetry on one manuscript page.

Most troublesome, however, is Belloc's handwriting. His working method was to copy a poem over many times, revising each version. In the early drafts the handwriting is terrible, probably because he was writing quickly; in many cases the handwriting suggests that he was traveling by train or car. After a number of drafts of a poem, the handwriting becomes much neater. Several of the manuscripts, in fact, could be called fair copies. And the collection contains several typescripts, some of which are completed.

Belloc apparently did not keep careful records of the poetry that he published in newspapers and magazines. Although W.N. Roughead begins his preface to the **Complete Verse** with the comment that the volume contains "what I believe to be the whole of Belloc's poetry," the Boston College collection shows Roughead to be mistaken. Amassing the total body of Belloc's poetry will be an enormous task made more difficult by the fact that he at least occasionally used pseudonyms. In addition, the collection indicates that Belloc contributed to journals that the average scholar would never think to check, such as the *Gramophone,* a technical magazine.

Belloc wrote a series of "Epigramophones," four-line epigrams complemented by Nicolas Bentley's illustrations. The following example, employing the curmudgeon mask which Belloc used successfully in his later light verse, indicates one of the kinds of poetry that remains uncollected:

> Oppressed of years, the Human Organ grows Less pleasing—as the Prima Donna shows. The gramophone escapes our common curse. Bad to begin with, it becomes no worse.
>
> (*Gramophone,* December 1929)

Belloc's tone was considerably sharper in the manuscript versions of some of his familiar political epigrams. For instance, **"On Another Politican"** was published in this form in **Sonnets and Verse** (1938):

> The Politician, dead and turned to clay, Will make a clout to keep the wind away. I am not fond of draughts, and yet I doubt If I could get myself to touch that clout.

In the Boston College manuscripts, the first line reads, "Marconi Isaacs, dead and turned to clay, . . ." The reference is to the famous Marconi scandal, publicised by Belloc and Cecil Chesterton. The most infuriating aspect of this conflict-of-interest scandal for Belloc was that Parliament covered it up, even going as far as to defeat a motion censuring Lloyd George and other implicated members.

What difference does the substitution of "The Politician" for "Marconi Isaacs" make? The published version, like a Jonsonian epigram, requires only that the reader accept political corruption as highly possible, if not inevitable. Within that context, the poet directs the reader's attention to the poem's intellectual cleverness and prosodic perfection. The generic "politician" lets Belloc keep his hands clean while at the same time allowing his readers to make any plausible associations or even insert any name that fits in two-and-a-half iambic feet.

Did Belloc make the substitution because he feared legal repercussions or because he realized that it would improve the poem? The manuscript version is certainly more interesting as political journalism, for it reminds the modern Belloc student not only of the particulars of the Marconi scandal, but also of the writer's unsuccessful lifelong struggle against the forces of privilege in contemporary England. For those of us who see Belloc as fundamentally a poet who was diverted from his real work by the awful combination of his personal temperament and the climate of the times, the manuscript version is a chilling document: it is extraordinarily bitter because Belloc held Lloyd George accountable for a crime no less serious than attempting to destroy England. In the manuscript Belloc was not being clever; he was merely telling what he saw as the truth.

The Marconi version of the poem also exists in a holograph manuscript along with eight other political epigrams written on the same stationery, probably around the same time. A holograph title page, *"A Collection of Political Poems* / The Author H. B. / (May 9th 1924)," suggests that these nine epigrams were intended as the core of a volume that Belloc was contemplating.

The best of the nine is **"On Prime Ministers,"** which Belloc originally designated number five in the sequence but later changed to number one:

Of all Prime Ministers I ever saw
The least remarkable was Bonar Law:
Unless it were Macdonald, by the way,
—Or Baldwin, it's impossible to say.

This poem names names, but its tone is completely different from that of the Marconi version of **"On Another Politician."** For one thing, the accusation—that the three prime ministers are unremarkable—is less vitriolic than merely weary. Perhaps of more importance, however, is Belloc's skillful use of colloquial rhythms and diction in the second couplet. Without violating the heroic meter, the poet achieves a natural spontaneity and simplicity that reinforces the universality of the statement.

In addition to these epigrams, the Boston College collection contains some light verse characteristic of Belloc's earlier, gentler period. One of the most interesting is a five-stanza fragment, **"The European Gentleman,"** which Belloc introduces with a quotation from a (probably fictitious) book called *Modern Manners:*

The principal mark of good breeding is restraint, and the more perfect the manners of an individual, the less will he show by any outward sign the emotions of surprise, anger etc. Still less will he give way to expressions or gestures of annoyance on the occurrence of some untoward event. The European Gentleman is always at his ease.

The first extant stanza, which is labeled "III," is typical of the fragment's easy grace:

According to the author you will probably displease
If you shine about the elbows or are baggy at the
    knees;
But the words you should especially insist upon are
    these:
"A European Gentleman is always at his ease."

The last stanza of the fragment shows the careful deliberation of the craftsman at work:

    Well, the Gentlemen of Greenland, I am sorry
to repeat
    Are not above saluting total strangers in the
street
(1) They will argue with a Lady with unnecessary
heat,
or (2) They will hug a passing traveller with
violence & heat
(3) They will follow up a subject with
unnecessary heat
(4) They gesticulate with totally unnecessary heat
(5) They rub the nose fraternally with anyone
they meet
    Now here, to put it mildly, we should call it
indiscreet.

Belloc apparently was content to delay the moment of decision. What is surprising about this quatrain is the large number of variants the poet was willing to consider.

For more substantial poetry we would, of course, expect such care. A look at the evolution of the sonnet **"That which is one they shear and make it twain"** reveals something of Belloc's working methods. In the 1891 notebook, the sonnet appears in the following form:

That which is one, they split it up in twain
    Who do Love's light & dark discriminate:
His pleasure is one essence with his pain.
    Even his desire twin brother to his hate.
My mistress has all sweets in her sweet eyes
    In her sweet eyes the very smarts of hell:
Being all my life she's sweet, smart, laughter sighs
    Being all my heaven is day & night as well.

I am acquainted with misfortunes [*sic*] fortune.
Better than herself her dowry know
For she that is my fortune & misfortune
Making me hapless makes me happier so.

In which conceit as elder men may prove
Lies manifest the very core of Love.

The glaring weakness in this version, written some three decades before Belloc published the completed sonnet in the 1923 *Sonnets and Verse,* is the second quatrain of the octave. The first quatrain introduces the classical theme of love's complexity; the second quatrain merely repeats the theme without developing it. In addition, the quatrain is bad poetry, almost a parody of Belloc's favourite technique of repeating key words and phrases. Whereas in his best poems he uses the catalogue (see **"The Rebel"** or **"Lines to a Don"**) or selective redundancy ("beyond" in **"O my companions, O my sister Sleep"**) to establish a tone of poignancy or comic excess, here the three repetitions of the vapid adjective "sweet" suggests only that Belloc did not know where he was going. The quatrain rings false. For some readers, the damage might be more severe: it sounds like the utterance of a Restoration fop.

The 1894 notebook includes the poem in virtually the same form. The only real difference is that line 7 now reads, "She being all my life is laugh and sighs." The major change appears on a holograph manuscript in a green leather notebook inscribed "To Maurice from Hilary, Dec 30th 1924." This notebook, which has the title, **Verses and Sonnets,** embossed on its spine, begins with page proofs of six of the poems that first appeared in the 1923 collection and then includes holograph versions of **"That which is one . . ."** and several other poems. In this version, the second quatrain appears virtually in the published form:

> With him alarmed attempt is full achieving
> And being mastered, to be armed a Lord
> And doubting every chance is still believing;
> And losing all one's own is all reward.

In the published version, the first line of the quatrain has been changed to "With him the foiled attempt is half achieving." With this final revision, Belloc reduces the overstatement, meshing the quatrain seamlessly and transforming what had been an uneven exercise into a moving and evocative sonnet.

What does the manuscript's inclusion in the green notebook suggest about Belloc's working methods? Perhaps nothing conclusive. The poet might have been working on the poem steadily for more than thirty years. My guess, however, is that Belloc made the crucial revisions under the pressure of the 1923 volume's deadline, after having ignored the poem since his youth. In the intervening three decades, Belloc achieved the wisdom necessary to do full justice to his theme.

In 1933 an Italian journalist requested that Hilaire Belloc provide a brief description of his own poetry. Although he felt uncomfortable about the request ("I think it very difficult indeed for a man to write about himself!"), Belloc sent three paragraphs that include this sentence:

> His best work . . . in serious verse, is to be found in the few lyrics he has published, which have a special note of poignancy, though as sober as his more classical

verse, and careful to avoid extravagance of metaphor or neologism.

The Boston College collection includes several complete, unpublished lyrics that show the qualities which the poet ascribed to his published lyrics. One of the best of these manuscript poems is **"Her Garden"**:

> You have a garden up amongst the hills,
> Fenced in with rocks and close against the sky:
> This is the place a voice of far-sea fills,
> Here grass bends and great sea clouds go by.
>
> Love that no lover yet refused to pardon,
> Love that can take a young man by the hand,
> Love making wiser, Love that understands,
> Love loving lovers brought me to your garden.
>
> Where you your habitation have and where
> More blest than I might hope to dwell forever,
> I mortal and with memory quick will dare
> To pluck such blossoms as the immortals bear
> In misty gardens lapped of Lethe river.

"Her Garden" is remarkable in its avoidance of extravagant metaphors and neologisms; in fact, the poet is almost unnaturally restrained in metaphor and diction. Yet the poem conveys extraordinary poignancy, primarily because of Belloc's consummate metrical skill.

Almost every line is a lesson in how to vary the standard iambic pentameter to achieve a special effect. Line 4 is a typical example:

Here / grass bends // and great / sea clouds / go by. Certainly a great part of the effect here is achieved through the alliteration of the "g" and "s" sounds and the long vowel sounds. But, in addition, Belloc uses an unusual sequence of nine monosyllables, impeding the pace and thereby reinforcing the majestic scale suggested by the image. Of the nine monosyllables, only the conjunction *and* following the caesura is unaccented. To further strengthen the line, Belloc begins with the suspended iambic foot, "Here." The result is an iambic pentameter with only one true iambic foot.

Line 7 is even more impressive:

Love mak/ing wis/er, // Love / that un/derstands,

The spondaic initial foot immediately establishes the emotional urgency. After the rest provided by the iambic second foot, Belloc creates a striking effect by inserting the caesura in the middle of the third foot. Thus the unaccented second syllable of *wiser* functions as a feminine ending, sustaining the note that is pulled up short by the accented *Love* that follows. The last two feet I read as a pyrrhic and an iamb: with this rhythm Belloc accelerated the pace as he approaches the final accented syllable. Line 7, then, shows how a master technician can mix a pedestrian thought, uninspired diction, and unparallel modifiers (a participial phrase in one case, a noun clause in the other) into a line that communicates great emotion.

The final stanza begins with the poem's only regular iambic line, a rest after the emotional crescendo of the second stanza. But even this line functions actively in creating the intended effect: the caesura before the final foot enjambs the line, accelerating the pace of line 10 until it concludes with the mournful extra syllable in *forever*. The main clause that begins in line 11 starts with the emphatic spondee, followed by the pyrrhic. The spondee in the fourth foot reinforces the idea of quickness by reducing *memory* to two syllables. Line 11 is enjambed into line 12, which features an extra syllable in the fourth foot, an anapest. This line, too, is enjambed, which further sustains the pacing. The final line, which skillfully exploits the vowel sounds as does line 4, is a regular iambic line except for the extra syllable in the feminine *river*. The modulating effect of the iambic pattern effectively concludes the poem by sustaining the overall tone of yearning.

Scholars are always pleased to get a chance to study manuscripts, and the Boston College collection will provide many such opportunities. But the real treasures are the new poems, which, like **"Her Garden,"** bear comparison with the best of Hilaire Belloc's published lyrics. When the poetry is edited and published, it will be a substantial addition to the canon of a fine poet.

Michael H. Markel (essay date 1989)

SOURCE: "Hilaire Belloc's Uncollected Political Verse," in *English Literature in Transition 1880-1920,* Vol. 32, No. 2, 1989, pp. 143-56.

[*In the following essay, Markel surveys the style and themes of Belloc's unpublished political poetry, maintaining that he "succeeded in transforming contemporary political intrigue and corruption into sharp-edged satires."*]

W. N. Roughead begins his preface to the 1970 revised edition of Hilaire Belloc's **Complete Verse,** "This book contains what I believe to be the whole of Belloc's poetry." However, Belloc published some thirty additional poems, most of which are political satires, that he himself did not include in any of his verse collections and that Roughead apparently did not know existed. Most of the verses date from 1911-1913, when he was devoting the bulk of his energies to muckraking journalism. These political poems are, on the whole, technically sophisticated yet aesthetically flawed. Several, however, most notably those in which Belloc invokes himself as a comic character, are first-rate. The uncollected verse shows the considerable extent to which Belloc succeeded in transforming contemporary political intrigue and corruption into sharp-edged satires.

Several of the uncollected poems are nonpolitical lyrics and light verse that might have fit comfortably in one or another of Belloc's collections. **"Stop-Short,"** for instance, is a characteristic meditation on mortality:

> Ramonde, Alise, Inalfas, Amoreth
>   In mountain-guarded gardens vainly gay
> Wasted the irrevocable breath,
>   And sought to lose in play
> The fixed, majestic questioning eyes of Death,
>   By turning theirs away.

Belloc also wrote four "epigramophones" for the journal *Gramophone,* the following being one example:

> The owners of the Gramophone rejoice
> To hear it likened to the human voice.
> The owners of the Human Voice disown
> Its least resemblance to the Gramophone.

Then there is **"A Modernist Ballade,"** a clever parody of free verse, in which Belloc turns his own beliefs inside out: in justifying why he isn't using "ordinary rhythm [which] might have been neater," he explains that "thought loses freedom under the stress / Of rules, dogmas, and everything of that sort or race."

"A Modernist Ballade" provides a key to understanding Belloc's decision not to collect his political verse. He believed firmly in the rules and dogmas. He was as fastidious about the quality of his verse as he was casual about the quality of his prose. In a letter to Evan Charteris written on 24 October 1939, near the end of his long career, Belloc stated:

> I am writing verse again merely in order to cheat the Camard, which is French for the Snub Nose and is one of the names for Death. I am afraid I will leave a great deal unfinished and that is a pity because I publish so little, but I have before me the example of many poets good and bad who did a lot in their last year or two. Unfortunately I am always over-ashamed of my own work and it is only after years that I can decide whether it is worth publishing. . . .

Belloc never wavered from his thoroughly classical poetic principles. His models were the ancients (whom he read in the original languages) and the English and French Renaissance as well as neoclassical poets. His masterpiece, **"Heroic Poem in Praise of Wine,"** is high comedy in the style of Pope:

> . . . But what are these that from the outer murk
> Of dense mephitic vapours creeping lurk
> To breathe foul airs from that corrupted well
> Which oozes slime along the floor of Hell?
> These are the stricken palsied brood of sin
> In whose vile veins, poor, poisonous and thin
> Decoctions of embittered hatreds crawl:
> These are the Water-Drinkers, cursed all! . . .

In *Avril* (1904), his study of the French Renaissance poets, Belloc wrote that "those whose energy is too abundant seek for themselves by an instinct the necessary confines without which such energy is wasted," and that "energy alone can dare to be classical." Energy and classical restraint are indeed the main characteristics of Belloc's best verse. He used his vast prosodic talents to render his particular—and sometimes idiosyncratic—subjects impersonal and compelling.

In *Milton* (1935) he wrote that "the greatest verse does not proceed immediately from the strongest feeling. The greatest verse calls up the strongest emotion in the reader, but in the writer it is a distillation, not a cry." He considered Milton the last great classical poet in English:

> He felt to his marrow the creative force of restraint, proportion, unity—and that is the classic. . . . Rule and its authority invigorated the powers of man as pruning will a tree, as levees a pouring river. Diversity without extravagance, movement which could be rhythmic because it knew boundaries and measure, permanence through order, these were, and may again be, the inestimable fruits of the classical spirit.

Although Belloc's political verse is often technically accomplished, too often it does not meet this standard; it fails to achieve "permanence through order" because it fails to transcend its parochial subject matter and evoke in the reader the emotion that Belloc himself felt, or at least enable the reader to understand and feel the source of that emotion.

Many of the verses concern the Marconi scandal. The fact that today the Marconi scandal is of interest primarily to historians does not in itself explain the limitations of the verse. Yeats's "Easter 1916" is a triumph not because its subject matter is "important," but because it creates a context that renders the speaker's assertions credible. Belloc's political verse is limited because he chose to hit hard rather than to hit squarely. Instead of poetically evoking the situation that justifies his outrage, Belloc too often resorted to sarcasm and raillery. With a swagger Belloc asserted that leading political figures such as Lloyd-George, Herbert Samuel, and Rufus Isaacs (Lord Reading), were corrupt. Although modern scholarship has supported many of Belloc's assertions regarding the Marconi scandal, he of course knew that no mainstream publisher would have entertained the thought of publishing a sardonic parody of Longfellow's "Song of Hiawatha," full of unsubstantiated accusations, in which the Indian tribe consists of Herbert Samuel and his family, caught up in the embarrassing Indian silver scandal of 1913. Belloc and the Chestertons enjoyed publishing this sort of barb in their own journals, which had limited circulations. They relied on the idea that prosecuting them would be more trouble—and bad publicity—than it was worth. Except for one successful action against Cecil Chesterton, they were right.

Yet among the uncollected poems are a number of masterpieces in which the idea and the expression merge to create a witty indictment of the poverty of contemporary political life. At its best, the political verses are as intimate as his essays and as elegant as his light verse.

Belloc's first muckraking venture was *The North Street Gazette,* a collaboration with Maurice Baring that lasted only one issue, in 1908. The bulk of his uncollected political verse was published in the *Eye-Witness* and its later incarnation, the *New Witness.* The *Eye-Witness,* which first appeared in June 1911, was a weekly muckraking journal financed by Charles Granville and edited by Belloc. Its purpose was to follow the lead of Belloc and Cecil Chesterton's *The Party System* in exposing the corruption of the English political establishment. With contributors including Shaw, Wells, and Quiller-Couch, the *Eye-Witness* became for a time the second most popular weekly in England.

Weary of his editorial duties, Belloc resigned the position in June 1912. Cecil Chesterton edited the paper until its official demise in November of that year, at which time he revived it under the name of *New Witness,* largely due to the financial generosity of his father. During its year and a half of life, the *Eye-Witness* took up several causes, most notably the opposition to Lloyd-George's Insurance Bill on the grounds that because participation was mandatory for almost all workers it would strengthen the state's bureaucratic control of labor.

Writing in the *New Witness,* Belloc and Chesterton campaigned against political abuses such as the sale of honors (a practice Belloc had attacked as a member of Parliament), the enforced sterility clause of the Mental Deficiency Bill, and, most spectacularly, what came to be known as the Marconi scandal. Under the editorship of Cecil Chesterton, the paper became stridently anti-Semitic (especially in the columns of F. Hugh O'Donnell), a trend that worried Belloc.

The *New Witness* survived for eleven years, almost always on the edge of bankruptcy. Bernard Shaw, a frequent contributor, called the *New Witness* "a very remarkable paper" and expressed the hope that it would not fold. "I do not mind seeing Mr Samuel and Sir Rufus Isaacs and the rest treated as malignant dragons, giants, serpents."

A politician who frustrated all parties, but most especially his own, Belloc wrote and collected many poems on political subjects. These poems are as effective as any of his verse in demonstrating his skill in evoking a single, unadorned emotion. Usually that emotion was some combination of contempt and disgust. **"Epitaph on the Politician Himself,"** which was collected first in the 1923 **Sonnets and Verse**, is a typical example:

> Here richly, with ridiculous display,
> The Politician's corpse was laid away.
> While all of his acquaintances sneered and slanged
> I wept: for I had longed to see him hanged.

The wit here is considerable. "I wept" at the start of the last line sets up the reversal with its spondee. Following the colon we expect to see a eulogy. His acquaintances might sneer and slang; what else could be expected of those who were not close to the late politician, those who knew him only as a tough-minded public servant who occasionally had to make enemies in his quest for the greater good? But I, the speaker intones with the luxurious "longed," *I* wished for a more fitting farewell. When the reader reaches the punch line, the feminine rhyme "slanged/hanged" creates an extra resonance for Belloc's disgust. But this poem is, for all its vitriol, humorous, because the politician is generic; readers think of their own favorite targets and envy the poet's skill in telling a truth.

Contempt is also the emotion in **"On Two Ministers of State,"** but in this case the tone is icy rather than hot:

> Lump says that Caliban's of gutter breed,
> And Caliban says Lump's a fool indeed,
> And Caliban and Lump and I are all agreed.

Here too the generic names distance the readers from any real situation, so that they concentrate on the witty exposition of the speaker's amused disgust with both ministers.

An example of the difference in tone between Belloc's collected and uncollected verse is the curious case of **"The grocer Hudson Kearley, he,"** which appears in Roughead's collection with the tantalizingly uninformative note, "hitherto unprinted." Following is the version that appeared in the *Eye-Witness* in 1912:

II. The Noble Lord

> The Grocer Hudson Kearley, he
> When purchasing his barony,
> Was offered as we understand
> The title of Lord Sugar-Sand,
> Or might alternatively have been
> Lord Overweight of Margarine,
> But being of the grander sort
> Preferred the style of DEVONPORT,
> Which brazenry now stands and flames
> High to the front of English names,
> And where the Dockers starve and die
> Is worshipped to Idolatry.
> So may the noble House still,
> Their ancient Leadership fulfil,
> And knit with pity, sense and skill
> That commonwealth whose strengthening tie
> Is still her old nobility.

And here is the version Roughead published:

> The grocer Hudson Kearley, he
> When purchasing his barony,
> Considered, as we understand,
> The title of Lord Sugarsand,
> Or then again he could have been
> Lord Underweight of Margarine,
> But, being of the nobler sort,
> He took the name of Devonport.

Hudson Ewbanke Kearley, first Viscount Devonport (1856-1934), founded International Stores in 1880 and served as Liberal M.P. (1892-1910) and as the first food controller (1916-1917). (He also served as the model for the unscru-

pulous but inept Boss Mangan in Shaw's *Heartbreak House.*) In the eight lines that the two versions share, the only substantive difference is that Lord Overweight becomes Lord Underweight. This emendation surely does little damage to Belloc's reputation as a wit, although it probably makes a bad joke inexplicable.

In ending the poem at this point, however, Belloc effectively declaws it. In the editorial pages of the *Eye-Witness,* Belloc enthusiastically supported the dock strike of 1911. The uncollected poem derives its force from the contrast between the well-fed grocer, whom all his readers would know, and the anonymous, starving dockers. The reference to the docker's strike is skillfully introduced in a modifying clause. With the line "So may the noble houses still," Belloc borrows Keats's play on words from the Grecian urn ode: the English nobility remains inactive in the face of terrible social injustice. The poet repeats "still" in the last line—"Is still her old nobility"—to emphasize the upper class's lack of true nobility. The original version of the poem is strikingly effective: sarcastic, self-righteous, and whole. The collected version looks over its shoulder for the lawyers.

In his collected poems, especially the light verse, Belloc was extremely conscientious about his prosody. He believed that light verse "has nothing to sustain it save its own excellence of construction. . . . those who have attempted it [find] that no kind of verse needs more the careful and repeated attention of the artificer." In his 1911 collection **More Peers,** Belloc footnotes the couplet "Upon the mansion's ample door, / To which he wades through heaps of Straw." The note reads, "This is the first and only time / That I have used this sort of Rhyme."

The bulk of the topical political poems, however, were probably written at a single sitting. Desmond MacCarthy, reminiscing about the early days of the *Eye-Witness,* [in *G. K.'s: A Miscellany of the First 500 Issues of G. K.'s weekly,* 1934], wrote,

> If, late on the day of going to press, the paper was two or three articles short, Belloc or Cecil Chesterton supplied them. The men of the round table were great improvisors. If, when the sheets came in, there were blank spaces of different sizes, there was never a thought of altering the make up; something was written to length. Often it turned out as spirited as anything else in the paper, though it was necessary sometimes not to disguise that it was only a last-moment fill up.

The uncollected verse contains prosodic compromises that, common enough in most verse, are seen nowhere else in Belloc's poetry. An example is **"An Ode (Dedicated to the Under-Secretary for India in expectation of his immediate promotion to Cabinet rank through the Postmaster-General),"** one of Belloc's many attacks on the Samuel family, led by Herbert Samuel, the Postmaster-General implicated in the Marconi scandal. This poem is marred by instant iambs ("And oh!" "But oh!") and padded lines ("He's waiting on from day to day," "But who so happy, tell me, who").

Other poems are flatfooted in a more serious way; Belloc fails to evoke the emotion he wishes to communicate. He merely asserts it, without creating a character or a circumstance to justify it. The final stanza of **"The Voice of the People,"** concerning a three-way by-election in Crewe, begins with these lines:

> When all was over somebody had won.
> To be precise it was his father's son,
> His own son's father and his sister's brother;
> And, for the rest, some any-one-or-other,
> Fated by all the Gods before and after
> To fill his pockets and provide our laughter.

These lines leave the reader unmoved. When Belloc writes, later in the stanza, "The weary pressman notes / What idiots in what numbers cast what votes," the readers wonder why he is wasting his time writing about an election if he cannot even justify his disgust. He was apparently quite agitated about the election; unfortunately, he was not similarly intent on communicating his idea. The account of the election in the *Times* provides no clues about his thinking; Ernest Craig, a Unionist mining engineer, won the election because a Labour candidate and a Liberal split the remaining votes. "Interesting as this election has been to the observer from outside the constituency, it has aroused very little passion on the spot, and there is none of the delirious excitement which marked the closing stage of the Hanley contest," another recent three-way by-election.

Other poems begin promisingly, then falter. Following are the first stanza of **"A Ballade of Interesting News,"** then its final stanza and envoi:

> "Hullo!" said Mr. Creasy of Crouch End
> At breakfast as he read his *Daily Mail.*
> "I see the Marylebone Club intend
> To alter the position of the bail
> Upon the stumps; a thing that cannot fail
> To change the commonly accepted views
> With all that innovation must entail.
> It is extremely interesting news.

Belloc captures perfectly the orotund syntax of the vapid reader who finds a slight alteration in the cricket rules "extremely interesting." After another stanza describing some other items in the paper, Belloc concludes with this awkward, moralizing stanza:

> It is indeed! The Daily Papers lend
> A Something to our jaded lives and stale,
> Which energises them, and seems to send
> A thrill of life from Bow and Maida Vale:
> It also helps them to increase their sale
> (A motive it is easy to abuse),
> And now and then the writers go to gaol—
> It is extremely interesting news.

Belloc's prosodic gift often abandons him when his wit goes stale. In this case, the whole stanza is unnecessary, and the poem would be stronger without it. Line two's

"jaded lives and stale" is the sort of convoluted, anachronistic syntax he would parody in another poet. And line three's "and seems to send" shows that he is one foot short in the line. To compound his problems, Belloc adds this envoi:

> Prince, I suppose in sex you are a male,
> In politics a servant of the————(Help!)
> In your religion curiously pale——
> It is extremely interesting news.

The coy anti-Semitism is both objectionable in itself and in that it has nothing to do with the point the poem is making.

Perhaps even more frustrating than the obviously flawed poems are the verses that are technically skillful yet too obscure for the modern reader. I am not referring to every poem about the Marconi scandal; many of them are effective poetic statements that pose no problems for the reader who is supplied with the necessary background. A few footnotes on the subject make this sordid episode of political collusion and insider trading startlingly contemporary.

However, during 1912 and 1913 Belloc was so deeply involved with the scandal that he composed satirical verses for virtually every issue of the paper. As he and Cecil Chesterton described some minute aspect of the scandal in the news and commentary pages of the journal, Belloc would write another little poem on the subject. Some of these verses could be understandable only to the most serious students of the scandal. An example is **"The Samuel Pie,"** one of a series of parodies of nursery rhymes:

> Sing a song of Samuels,
>   Marconis firm and high,
> Five-and-Twenty fingers
>   Groping in the pie,
> When the pie was opened,
>   The Press began to sing.
> And wasn't that a sad surprise
>   For Alexander King?

Modern readers can admire the naturalness and directness, as well as the subtle exploitation of the "s" sound throughout. And a little research reveals that Sir Alexander King (1851-1942), Second Secretary of the Post Office, was called by the Select Committee to testify on the actions of Herbert Samuel, Postmaster-General, during the Marconi scandal. Yet that information doesn't make the poem work. Readers still cannot visualize the Second Secretary; the phrase "sad surprise" depends for its effectiveness on a certain familiarity with the person, the kind of familiarity one has with the manner of a reasonably prominent public figure. Belloc and perhaps a few dozen others in England shared that familiarity. By way of comparison, King was probably as well known to the contemporary reading public as is the current Assistant Secretary of State. The poem fails to justify itself from within.

Yet among Belloc's uncollected political verses are some excellent poems. Two strengths characterize these works.

First, they are self-sufficient in that they provide the evidence to justify their tones. And second, they are technically polished.

One early example of a fine topical poem is **"Done Into Verse,"** which appeared in the *Bookman*. This piece is fourteen stanzas of sharp but cheerful satire. Subtitled "A Suggestion for a Rhymed 'Who's Who,'" the poem operates on two levels. On the surface it is a portrait of a literary nonentity, similar to Belloc's indictments of worthless and inept aristocrats in **More Peers**. On a slightly deeper level it is a mock cry of frustration by Belloc; the fictional subject of the poem enjoys many of the advantages that Belloc envied. The poem begins with the fictional entry from a who's who:

> KEANES, HERBERT. B. 1846. The son of Lady Jane O'Hone and Henry Keanes, Esq., of 328, St. James's Square, and "The Nook," Albury. *Clubs:* Beagles, Blues, Pitt, Palmerston, the Walnut Box, the Two-and-Two's, etc. *Education:* Private tuition, Eton and Trinity College, Cambridge. Has sat for Putticombe, in Kent, 1885-1892. Nephew and heir of the Right Hon. the Earl of Ballycairn. *Occupation:* Literature, political work, management of estate, etc. Has written: "Problems of the Poor," "What, indeed, is Man?" "Flowers and Fruit" (a book of verse), "Is there a Clifford?" "The Future of Japan," "Musings by Killarney's Shore," "The Ethics of Jean-Paul," and "Nero." Is a strong Protectionist and a broad Churchman. *Recreations:* Social.

The satire, as well as the poet's envy of his subject, are announced as early as the first stanza:

> There is a literary man
>   Whose name is Herbert Keanes:
> His coat is trimmed with astrachan.
>   He lives on private means.

This is the sort of literary man who is best described by reference to his financial portfolio. Belloc often lamented his inability to be precisely the sort of wealthy man of letters he describes here. For three more stanzas Belloc describes Keanes's current wealth and lists the five considerable properties he will inherit when his uncle ("a lord") dies.

After a private education Keanes buys his way into Trinity College, Cambridge. About his collegiate career Belloc, significantly, has nothing to say; however, Keanes has an active social life:

> His clubs are these: the Beagles, Blues,
>   Pitt, Palmerston, Riviere,
> The Walnut Box, the Two-and-Two's,
>   Throgmorton's, Pot o' Beer.

Like Belloc, Keanes enjoys a brief Parliamentary career.

> Has sat for Putticombe, in Kent,
>   But lost the place he won
> By boldly saying what he meant,
>   Though meaning he had none.

Keanes shows the enthusiasm that only the ignorant can muster. Belloc, on the other hand, was barely reelected in 1910 because of his stubborn refusal to compromise on the Education Bill and because of his stirring tax-the-rich speeches. As a private man of means, Keanes fills his days profitably:

> OCCUPATION—
>   Composes verses and prose, and shoots
>   And talks to other men
>   On politics; takes off his boots,
>   And puts them on again.

The enjambed second line sets up Belloc's characteristic comic deflation in lines three and four. A partial list of Keanes's writings shows that he was even more versatile than Belloc:

> WORKS—
>   Has written "Problems of the Poor,"
>   "The Future of Japan,"
>   And "Musings by Killarney's Shore,"
>   And "What, indeed, is Man?"

The portrait of Keanes ends with these telling comments:

> RECREATIONS, ETC.—
>   A strong protectionist, believes
>   In Doctor Arnold's Heaven.
>   For recreation: dines, receives;
>   Unmarried, fifty-seven.

Of course Keanes believes in Dr. Arnold's Heaven; why shouldn't he? Belloc's comment self-consciously betrays his own envy of the liberal Protestant who served as professor of history at Oxford, a position for which he himself unsuccessfully applied on several occasions.

More indicative of what Belloc might have accomplished in political verse is **"Sonnet for the Seventh of August"**:

> As some grey fool, half blind with age and tears
> Lighting by chance upon a rusty toy,
> Murmurs: "My pop-gun, when I was a boy!
> Before the coming of the Brazen years!"
> Or as some wastrel from long exile come
> Sees his fifth love in a magenta hat
> And turns about most hastily thereat
> A-muttering in his last few teeth, "By Gum!"
>
> So I—with guns of Flanders on the gale—
> Read strangely how Lord Selborne and Lord Crewe,
> Lord Curzon—and I think Lord Charnwood too—
> Debated mine antiquities: the sale
> Of Peerages, the Party Funds, and all
> The Bag of Tricks. . . . Oh! God! Oh! Montreal!

Lords Selborne and Charnwood in 1914 had moved that honors not be awarded to persons solely because they had contributed to party funds. In 1917 they and the other two Lords succeeded in a resolution that the prime minister publicly justify his choices for honors and that he satisfy himself that the honor is not connected with any payment or expectation of payment to any party fund. Lloyd-George disregarded this resolution and created more and more peers as he increased his war chest, the Lloyd-George Fund.

The wit in this poem derives from Belloc's leavening his disgust with humor, including self-depreciating humor. The octet is vintage Belloc: the dismissive phrase, "some grey fool," and the precise adjectives that seem almost far-fetched, "fifth love" and "magenta hat." The sestet appears to be mere prose, but the phrases "mine antiquities" and "Oh! God! Oh! Montreal!" create a meaningful context.

The references are to Samuel Butler's "A Psalm of Montreal," first published in the 18 May 1878 *Spectator.* Butler's comic poem is a dialogue between the author and a custodian in the Montreal Museum of Natural History. Visiting the museum, Butler notices that two statues—of the Greeks Antinous and Discobolus—are obscured in a room with "all manner of skins, plants, snakes, insects, etc., and, in the middle of these, an old man stuffing an owl." The custodian responds to Butler's inquiry about why the statues are not displayed prominently:

> "The Discobolus is put here because he is vulgar—
> He has neither vest nor pants with which to cover
>   his limbs;
> I, Sir, am a person of most respectable
>   connections—
> My brother-in-law is haberdasher to Mr. Spurgeon."
> O God! O Montreal!

Belloc, who began campaigning against the sale of honors and the misuse of party funds while he was a member of Parliament and continued as editor of the *Eye-Witness,* portrays himself comically, not as a martyr but rather as a treasure that is considered a vulgar embarrassment. Belloc wisely resists the impulse to argue that the abuses of party funds and honors have created the war, although the case could be made that the weakening of the British government from within was to have serious consequences that cost many lives.

Taken as a group, Belloc's uncollected political poems fall somewhere between his collected light verse and his political prose. Although they are distinguished by a generally high-quality prosody and sharp wit, many of them are marred by the shortcomings of the political prose: hasty composition, lack of perspective, and a parochial assumption that the reader shares the author's particular knowledge and political assumptions. Had Belloc wished, he could have improved their overall quality by writing them from within, rather than from without, by animating his ideas within the scope of the poems themselves. Instead, he was too often content to preach to the converted, the readers of the *Eye-Witness* and the *New Witness.* In short, he did not envision these political poems as art.

Belloc's least successful political poems are solemn; Belloc has something to say—some wrong to right—and he

won't trivialize his subject by being merely witty or humorous. After all, politics is serious business, and the politicians' shameful behavior causes real human misery. In his best political poems, however, such as **"Done Into Verse"** and **"Sonnet for the Seventh of August,"** he exploits himself as a character rather than relying on his considerable gifts as a ideologue. In so doing he achieves perspective, a distancing that allows him the space in which to arrange the props for his brief drama.

Ironically, when he focuses on his subject to the exclusion of the context, the poems too often remain solipsistic exercises in invective when he involves himself, the poems transcend him and become effective political satires. Had he seen in the political world the material for art and not just propaganda, he might have allowed himself the luxury of lingering in what he called his "rightful garden." Belloc might have transformed the turbulent political events of his time into a more substantial body of first-rate satirical verse.

Jeffrey Hart (essay date 1989)

SOURCE: "The Poet of Europe," in *Acts of Recovery: Essays on Culture and Politics,* University Press of New England, 1989, pp. 83-92.

[In the following essay, Hart emphasizes the importance of history and politics in Belloc's work.]

> Have you seen the Pope's gentle remarks to the Modernists? They are indeed noble! I could not have done it better myself. He gently hints they can't think, which is true. The old Heretics had guts, notably Calvin, and could think like the Devil, who inspired them. But the Modernists are inspired by a little minor he-devil, with one Eye and a stammer, and the result is poor.
>
> *Belloc to Dorothy Hamilton*
> *October 8, 1907*

In England before the First World War it seems (in historical reverie) always to have been a summer afternoon. This may owe something to half-conscious effects lingering in the mind of scenes in Impressionist paintings, their joy in light and foliage and, above all, their virtually uninterrupted affirmation of gaiety and color and pleasure. It may owe something to late nineteenth-century poetry and its celebration of landscape. Certainly it owes much to the fact that, since the First World War, the emotions of the West have undergone a shattering confrontation with a barbarism far worse—colder and more malignant—than anything in previous Western experience.

In this historical reverie, pre-war England is a place of long, sunlit summer afternoons and bandstands, of little boys in sailor suits and weekends at spacious country houses with lawn parties and baccarat and billiards and riding to hounds, of lazy punting trips down the Thames from Oxford and picnics at the Rose and Crown. It is the world of Saki and Beerbohm and Rupert Brooke (a world which James, because of his greater depth, loved even more than they did), and of Compton Mackenzie's Oxford, with its dreaming spires, still the aristocratic Oxford of Arnold and Newman and Benjamin Jowett.

It is as a part of that England that Belloc first comes clearly into view, Belloc of Balliol and the Oxford Union. It was there, in that particular milieu, that he could flourish. For all his quarrels with it, the England of that time was his proper home. His central views were all formed before 1918. The very terms of his quarrels belonged to pre-war England. This is very far from saying that Belloc is a figure of "merely historical interest," as the saying goes. Indeed, it is because he was so firmly rooted in that pre-war world, and therefore connected in so many ways with a continuous European past, that he remains so important.

Hilaire Belloc was born in France, but he was raised in England; he attended Newman's Oratory School, then presided over by Newman himself—a sensitive, remote, fragile, august man in the full glory of his last phase. There is a symbolic quality to Belloc's presence at Newman's school. Both devoted their lives to bringing the truths of the past to bear on the present; both were gifted with deep historical consciousness; both were soldiers in a sense—Newman with the rapier of dialectic, Belloc with the "sound of the guns," a phrase that occurs often in his work, at Valmy, at Waterloo, at the Marne. Yet, though they were very different, one cannot quite say that they were opposite kinds of men, for both knew, as Manning remarked to Belloc, that "all human conflict is ultimately theological." Once, in Belloc's Latin class, Cardinal Newman burst into tears over some haunting passage in Virgil and had to leave the room. It is staggering to learn that the boys called him "Jack."

And after the Oratory came Oxford itself—Balliol and the Union. At the Oratory, Belloc had imbibed Catholicism and the classics. At Balliol, he read history, and the three things came together in his powerful mind. The classics, Catholicism, and history; Europe, the Church, and the West—kind of analogue of the Trinity itself; the three things were one.

When Belloc went up to Oxford in 1893, the Oxford Union was still in its great period. Today, a feeble-minded uplift and a low sincerity ruin all prospect of thought. But then the art of debate was assiduously cultivated and practiced for sheer intellectual pleasure. Such debate was only possible under conditions of disinterestedness: there was a whole range of ideas that could be entertained, and no one's life—more precisely, status—was at stake. The snarling, violent, moralistic mobs of the democratic campus had not yet made their appearance in history. The Union of 1893 was the Union of F. E. Smith and John Simon—and then, suddenly, of Hilaire Belloc. As Basil Matthews recalls:

> It was one of those rare nights in the Oxford Union when new ideas are discovered. Simon had denounced the Turk in Thessaly and Smith had held up the Oriental

to admiration. Men whispered to each other of the future Gladstone and Dizzy whom Oxford was to give to the nation. No one would be fool enough to speak after such brilliant rhetoric. . . . Suddenly a young man walked to the table. He was broad of shoulder and trod the floor confidently. A chin that was almost grim in its young strength was surmounted by a large squarely-built face. Over his forehead and absurdly experienced eyes, dark hair fell stiffly. As he rose, men started up and began to leave the house; at his first sentence they paused and looked at him—and sat down again. By the end of his first sentence, with a few waves of his powerful hands, and a touch of unconscious magnetism and conscious strength, the speeches of J. A. Simon and F. E. Smith were as though they had never been. For twenty minutes the new orator, Mr. Hilaire Belloc, who was soon to sit in the seat of Gladstone, Salisbury, Milner, Curzon, and Asquith as President of the Union, held his audience breathless.

Some of this was theater, of course, but for the most part it represented a genuine curiosity about what intelligence could do with a particular subject. The egalitarian and cloddish impulse to "commitment" about everything under the sun was absent.

Of course, politics in its way was a serious thing, and it attracted men of surpassing abilities. Simon and F. E. Smith went on to notable parliamentary careers. The Liberal ministry that came to power in 1906 was the most brilliant ever to assemble at Westminster: Asquith, Grey, Campbell-Bannerman, Haldane, Bryce, Winston Churchill. Yet it was the last time that most men agreed on most things.

Governments of both parties agreed, for example, that money should be allowed to "fructify in the pockets of the people." Because government had not extended itself into the very texture of existence, government was not awfully controversial. It was not yet in every hamlet, kitchen, and schoolroom. As the marvelous symbolic story has it, Simon and F. E. Smith, before going down from Oxford to London, tossed a coin to determine which would be Liberal, which Tory. There was no sense in entering the same party. One might block the other's path. If a crank called Marx had written some tracts in the British Museum, what of it?

Of course, men could be serious about serious things, and politics before the First World War has a flavor—no, not a flavor, a distinctive character—that separates it from later politics. This point is worth pausing over. It was very much a part of the pre-war atmosphere that candidates were not universally expected to caress the voters, much less lick their feet. Holding office was not *that* important. When Belloc ran for Parliament in 1906, he was told that the voters of South Salford might not vote for a Catholic. This is how he handled the problem, making his first campaign address to a packed house:

> Gentlemen, I am a Catholic. As far as possible I go to Mass every day. This [taking a rosary out of his pocket] is a rosary. As far as possible I kneel down and tell these beads every day. If you reject me on account of

my religion, I shall thank God that He has spared me the indignity of being your representative.

After a shocked pause. Belloc was cheered to the rafters and, later, elected. (A comparison with John F. Kennedy before the Houston ministers is instructive here.) This incident is usually held up as evidence of Belloc's unique courage and integrity. Yet, though the incident is extreme and special, it is also in many ways representative. When John Stuart Mill was standing for Parliament, he once spoke before a tough crowd of Victorian workmen. In the midst of his remarks, a billboard was brought forward bearing the deadly words from his *Thoughts on Parliamentary Reform: "The Lower Classes, though mostly habitual liars, are ashamed of lying."* The audience demanded to know whether Mill had written that. Said Mill clearly, "I did." The workmen cheered and stamped their feet, and their leader arose to say fervently that "the working classes had no desire not to be told of their faults; they wanted friends, not flatterers." Both episodes are very much in the vein of Burke's speech to the electors of Bristol. *Non serviam!*

Such an attitude is unthinkable today. Belloc and Mill and Burke would have disagreed on practically everything. Belloc had no time for Burke, and both would have looked on Mill as almost impossible. The essential point is that each believed that certain things were in fact true and that, beside the truth, any office was a bauble. The modern politician, in contrast, is other-directed. He finds out what is true by responding to his antennae. Mussolini's name now is mud, but largely because he was an ignominious failure; until 1940 his prestige in the West was very high indeed. His failure should not blind us to the fact that his technique of total reliance upon mass manipulation and mass appeal was not so different from modern politicians generally. In Ivonne Kirkpatrick's excellent biography of Mussolini, *Duce* (1964), we learn that he believed in almost nothing at all, at least not until his awful last month, and that at the height of his power he often made up his policy on the spot, even made momentous decisions, as he read the emotions of the crowd from the balcony of the Palazzo Venezia. Was Bobby Kennedy much different?

England before 1914 is usually called Liberal England by historians, after the name of the dominant party, but of course the word "liberal" had not yet reversed its meaning. Despite the overwhelming triumph of the Liberal Party in 1906, Liberal England was almost finished. Lloyd George was in the 1906 cabinet. In 1909 he would present his People's Budget with its sharp increase in taxes. Soon he would preside over the People's War of 1914-1918— the first war in history in which the use of mass civilian armies dictated a politics of mass manipulation at home. The future of mass taxation and mass government and mass emotion was suddenly radiant. At the center of the great empire, the end came almost unnoticed. In the spring of 1914 Belloc overheard the following conversation on a train going down to Horsham:

> "Terrible news from the Balkans."
> "Yes, but they're only barbarians."

During the weekend of June 29, he attended Mass at Salisbury. The congregation was asked to pray for the soul of the Archduke Franz Ferdinand, who had just been murdered at Sarajevo. Belloc had some sense but no immediately clear idea of the likely repercussions of the assassination on European peace. Then came the chilling moment. On July 20, cruising off Plymouth in the *Nona*, Belloc saw the British Grand Fleet, "like ghosts, like things made themselves out of mist", hastening eastward. He knew then there would be war—and the end of a world.

The crippling event in Belloc's own career was his failure to get a post at Oxford. He expected one, and with good reason, for his record had been excellent. He had really been one of the great undergraduates of all time, and he loved Oxford to the point of idolatry. His powers were recognized to be formidable, yet he was passed over for candidates no one ever heard of again. Belloc was a natural don, a don par excellence, with his thorniness and his total inability to work as a team member—he was a disaster as a party politician and a total failure in corporate journalism. But he had the potential of being a great historian. On the evidence of the history he did write, it is safe to say that, given the leisure of an academic environment, he would have produced work of classic quality. His moment as a historian had arrived. He wished to demolish the then-dominant Whig interpretation of history, according to which history was the happy-ending story of the advance of liberty under Whig and Protestant auspices, with heroes and villains suitably arrayed back through the ages. Such a view, Belloc believed, was no longer tenable, and it operated as a block to the understanding. But Belloc was condemned to a lifetime of journalism, one-night lectures, and hurried writing. He could not concentrate his resources upon writing a few great works, and we have had to wait until 1959 for Herbert Butterfield to accomplish Belloc's appointed task regarding Whig history.

Belloc was so much the natural don that he even had some of the weaknesses of the academic mind. As a historian and as a moral and religious thinker, he was admirably concrete, but when he wrote on current political and social matters, a don-like abstraction took over. He tirelessly attacked the English party system, arguing that because the governing class was linked by a web of family relations and because the parties always seemed to agree, they were therefore in conscious collusion and even agreed to alternate in office. The truth was more mundane. As a class and as members of a common culture, they did largely agree, but it is unlikely that any member agreed to lose an election out of collusion with his rival.

Similarly, in his book *The Jews,* he has many incisive things to say about the relations between Jews and non-Jews, but defining the Jews as a "dispersed nation"—which is, to a point, fair enough—he "reasons" to the absurd conclusion that English Jews ought actually to approximate a nation, have their own laws, courts, judges, be free from military service, taxes, and so on. This is a rationalist farrago. Belloc's plan might well accommodate the Jewishness of an individual, but it forgot all about his Englishness. In the real world, the Jews maintained their distinctive social and cultural institutions within the ordinary structure of law.

Again, he had shrewd things to say in *The Servile State.* The capitalist system does tend to lead to collectivism. It does concentrate property in the hands of a few. It engenders wide insecurity. Yet, from this, he again "deduced" a servile system in which the capitalists would rule over forced labor. It is only by stretching the definitions all out of shape that Belloc's predicition can be seen as having any relevance to the real world of power relations today.

Belloc always believed that his rejection at Oxford was due to his Catholicism, and he was bitter about it to the end of his days. The subject crops up again and again in his conversation, and he even cultivated a deliberate attitude of anti-academicism. Actually, he probably was not rejected because of his religion. The fact is, he tended to be a monologist, and dominating brilliance, after awhile, can become a bore. In addition, he was obsessive on some points. The Fellows of an Oxford college might well hesitate a long time before submitting themselves to a lifetime of disquisitions on distributism and the Jewish problem. Whatever the truth here, Belloc ended up at Fleet Street and missed his calling. But Oxford was his home, and he should have had that fellowship at All Souls.

In consequence, his achievement was fragmentary, though not on that account ephemeral. His grasp of essential things was a firm one, as is manifest wherever we look in his work. F. D. Wilhelmsen's subtitle for his study of Belloc, an absolutely first-rate piece of modern criticism, is an accurate one: *Hilaire Belloc: No Alienated Man* (1953). For though Belloc was, increasingly, at odds with the twentieth century, he was not alienated from the Western tradition or from the sources of anything positive that remains in Western culture. He held in balance the necessary coordinates of the fully human existence. He symbolized these in a little book called *Four Men,* which he published early in his career. The book is an allegory, recounting the journey of four men across Sussex in an autumnal setting: Myself, Grizzlebeard, the Poet, and the Sailor. As the journey and the conversations unfold, we see that Belloc means for each of the three men accompanying Myself to represent an essential quality of the fully human. The Poet represents spiritual aspiration, vision, and the sense of belonging to a world not present to the senses. He embodies a religious impulse that goes back to Plato and beyond. The Sailor belongs to this world, to its sudden landfalls and its hills against autumnal skies. His health saves man from mystical excess, solipsism, and decadence. Grizzlebeard is tradition incarnate: full of songs, lore, legends, and the wisdom of the past. Without Grizzlebeard's living connection with the past, man is isolated in time, a "stranger lost in a wilderness of pavements," as Wilhelmsen eloquently says. So thoroughly a part of the West was Belloc, so finely did he bring together these three essential elements that he found himself alienated from much around him. But the modern sensibility is alienated from itself; for it, as Wilhelmsen observes, nation, Church, and West, the past, roots, and origins are always wrong.

Looking at Belloc's work, we see that the three essential elements are always present, making each work an expression of the integral Western man behind it. He possessed the historical imagination as Eliot defines it: he wrote history with the past of Europe in his bones. History pervades his life at every point. Michelet was a friend of his father. A friend of his grandmother, a Mlle de Montgolfier, told him how as a girl she had been present at the storming of the Bastille. Belloc went over the roads and the battlefields of Europe foot by foot, and he attempted not only to record the past but to think his way back into it, to imagine it as it really was, when it was not past but present, and then to bring it forth re-created. He did not always succeed, and sometimes his imagination led him astray, but his method led to real discoveries. He knew, for example, that the eighteenth-century Whig oligarchy was not on the side of freedom. He knew that Cromwell had nothing further from his mind than religious liberty and that he would have been horrified by the thought of political liberty. He knew that James II had not been overthrown by any great wave of popular revulsion. Belloc's critical gaze liberated the past from the liberal dogmas of his present, and it did so at a moment when those dogmas, for sensitive minds, were in a state of dissolution. The main tendency of Belloc's historical polemic is now generally accepted by historians.

Belloc was a poet of Europe's past, and his prose, gaining resonance from his meditative involvement, moves us, often, as Burke's does. When Belloc wrote the following passage, he was entirely on the side of the Revolution, yet listen to his epitaph for the French monarchy:

> So perished the French monarchy. Its dim origins stretched out and lost themselves in Rome; it had already learnt to speak and recognized its own nature when the vaults of the Thermae echoed heavily to the slow footsteps of the Merovingian kings. Look up that vast valley of dead men crowned, and you may see the gigantic figure of Charlemagne, his brows level and his long white beard tangled like an undergrowth, having in his left hand the globe and in his right the hilt of an unconquerable sword. There also are the short, strong horsemen of the Robertian house, half hidden by their leather shields, and their sons before them growing in vestment and majesty, and taking on the pomp of the middle ages; Louis VII, all covered with iron; Philip the Conqueror; Louis IX, who alone is surrounded with light; they stand in a widening interminable procession this great crowd of kings; they lose their armour, they take their ermine on, they are accompanied by their captains and their marshalls; at last, in their attitude and their magnificence they sum up in themselves the pride and the achievement of the French nation. But time has dissipated what it could not tarnish, and the process of a thousand years has turned these mighty figures into unsubstantial things. You may see them in the grey end of darkness, like a pageant standing still. You look again, but with the growing light and with the wind that rises before morning they have disappeared.

Burke, Gibbon, Macaulay—and Belloc: in meditative evocation, he was their equal.

Yet although the past lived and was present to him, he possessed also his allegorical Sailor's intense communion with the world that is present to the senses. He knew the English landscapes, and he loved the English inns; he had walked through Normandy and Burgandy, and from Paris to Rome, and from Paris over the Pyrenees to Madrid. The physical world became a part of him, producing, as all intense experience of the senses does, both pleasure and melancholy. He did not see through things to something else—he saw the things themselves—and his attachment to them made him poignantly aware of transience. The elegiac note is not peculiar to the West, but it is integral to it, to its historicity and its sense of mortal limitation, to its knowledge that the world is immensely important, but that it is always dying.

> **Belloc always insisted upon the historical reality, and the Church was, historically, European and followed European expansion.**
>
> *—Jeffrey Hart*

His Catholic faith was, in its quality, also an extension of an older Europe. If he had been told that anyone could discuss the Resurrection as a "significant" thing without first inquiring whether it had actually occurred, he would have thought that he was hearing about a half-wit. Belloc had been born a Catholic and had attended the Oratory School. At Balliol his faith had been attenuated, but not lost. In his mature years it became crystalline. It was hard, irrefragable, based upon truth rather than on transitory relevance, on reason rather than on emotion. It had almost a military character. St. Dominic was his favorite saint. Belloc reasoned thus: Christ claimed to be divine. He was crucified, and three days later He rose from the dead. Such is the evidence, both written and traditional, and it goes back to eyewitnesses. Other views of the matter substitute theories, for which there is no evidence, for events for which there is much evidence. Faith does not rest on speculation or emotion—these may help or hinder it and are thoroughly marginal—but on evidence, available to everyone. Belloc's position is hard and sane and admirable.

As for the Catholic Church, here too he was a historian with the past of Europe in his bones. He knew that the Church, both in its liturgy and its creed, was traceable back to the origins, to those who had seen and talked with Christ, and that it was not a new thing but was continuous with those origins. He embraced the scandal of the concreteness of the Church in his famous formula, "Europe is the Faith and the Faith is Europe." Of course the proposition is phrased polemically: *contra* idealism. Belloc always insisted upon the historical reality, and the Church was, historically, European and followed European expansion. Theoretically, the Church is universal and might have

emerged in the Egyptian empire or in China. Theoretically, God might have been born in Brazil. In fact, Christ was a Jew, and the Church is European. The history of Europe cannot be understood without reference to the central role of the Church, and the Church cannot be understood apart from its actual history in Europe. Belloc's scandalous formulation is really a way of saying that grace perfects nature and that Providence would not have rooted the Church in Assyria rather than in Rome. This is a scandal to idealists and universalists everywhere, and Belloc meant it to be one.

A. N. Wilson (essay date 1991)

SOURCE: An introduction to *Complete Verse,* Pimlico, 1991, pp. iii-x.

[In the following essay, Wilson provides a brief and favorable overview of Belloc's poetry.]

When my biography of Hilaire Belloc appeared in 1983, it was discussed on a television programme. I watched with some trepidation, since the reviews of my book, which had been appearing in the English newspapers during the previous two weeks, had displayed a passionate hostility to Belloc—one critic stating that 'as a man, Belloc must have been about as congenial as nuclear waste', and another writing about Belloc's supposed 'malignity' in tones which would have required little modification if he had been describing Dr. Goebbels. Was all this hatred inspired solely by Belloc's anti-Semitism? If so, why was not similar odium heaped on the work of Dickens, or Thackeray, or T.S. Eliot, or G.K. Chesterton, or Virginia Woolf, or Proust, by the *bien-pensant* critics? They were all writers who had written anti-semitic things, quite as offensive as Belloc at his worst. Then I began to notice that some English writers do on occasion write with positively virulent hatred of Proust; a more likely explanation of the English critics' hatred of Belloc was that he was half French.

They disliked his uncompromisingness, his disparaging view of English political systems and (often the same thing) English humbug, as of English food and English religion. They were made uneasy by his combination of political radicalism (he was the only non-socialist journalist in London who supported the General Strike of 1926) and Catholicism, which was of a very French kind—at once off-hand and belligerent. They disliked his lapidary literary style and his elegance. And all these things are more characteristically French than they are English (as was the anti-Semitism).

When the television discussion of Belloc got under way it became clear that two of the three critics had never read a word that he had written. 'Why should we take Belloc seriously?' one of them complained. And a third replied, 'Because he was very nearly a poet.'

This was actually the most damning of all the damning remarks that had been made about Belloc during that fortnight. The sad thing is, one sees what this particular critic meant. Many of Belloc's best verses are spoilt by hamfistedness, and some of his most famous lyrics have about them a sort of boozy innocence which is not to the austere taste of the post-modernist generation. 'God be with you, Balliol men', or 'the grace of God is in courtesy', or

> And there shall the Sussex songs be sung
> And the story of Sussex told.

And yet Belloc the poet had a distinctive voice, without which literature would be poorer. No one else did what he did or wrote what he wrote. He is not merely a production-line Georgian.

Though he was a very funny writer, the core of Belloc's mood as a poet is despondent. He is a man on his own in the world, as is seen in his uneven series of sonnets beginning with the words, 'The world's a stage':

> The scenery is very much the best
> Of what the wretched drama has to show,
> Also the prompter happens to be dumb,
> We drink behind the scenes and pass a jest
> On all our folly; then, before we go,
> Loud cries for 'Author' . . . but he doesn't
> come

or

> The only part about it I enjoy
> Is what was called in English the Foyay.
> There will I stand apart awhile and toy
> With thought, and set my cigarette alight;
> And then—without returning to the play—
> On with my coat and out into the night.

These are possibly the best lines he ever wrote. In all his best poems he is alone, reminding me of his friend G.K. Chesteron's words, 'if we wish to depict what a man really is we must depict a man alone in a desert or on a dark sea sand. So long as he is a single figure he means all that humanity means; so long as he is solitary, he means human society . . . Add another figure and the picture is less human, not more so.'

Sometimes, in his poems, Belloc is lonely in love, and missing his wife Elodie:

> But when I slept I saw your eyes,
>   Hungry as death, and very far.
> I saw demand in your dim eyes
> Mysterious as the moons that rise
>   At midnight, in the Pines of Var.

(That is a poem which, for me, passes A.E. Housman's gooseflesh test in 'The Name and Nature of Poetry'.) Sometimes the solitary voice in Belloc's poetry is homesick for childhood and for the Sussex of boyhood. Sometimes he is exuberant in his solitude, as in his mysterious song of the Winged Horse (of which there exists an excellent gramophone record with Belloc singing his own

words). Sometimes, as in his epigram on 'The Telephone', he is simply lonely in town:

> Tonight in million-voicèd London I
> Was lonely as the million-pointed sky
> Until your single voice. Ah! So the sun
> Peoples all heaven, although he be but one.

It is not his most skilful epigram, but it is one of his most poignant, the more so when we remember how compulsively sociable he was. I imagine he wrote it one evening in London during his widowerhood, when he returned from a dinner to one of the rooms he rented from time to time from friends such as Charles Somers Cocks and 'Bear' Warre; and I imagine that the voice was that of Juliet Duff, with whom he was platonically in love.

He is at his best when this essentially melancholy view of life is expressed through comic means, as in his matchless **'Ballade of Hell and Mrs Roebeck'** (a poem, like Larkin's 'Vers de Société', which comes into my mind every time I attend a party) or as in his epigrams such as **'Fatigue'**:

> I'm tired of Love: I'm, still more tired of
>   Rhyme.
> But Money gives me pleasure all the time.

The Belloc who has perhaps travelled less well is the Georgian sentimentalist who wrote **'The Moon's Funeral'**, or **'Twelfth Night'** or **'Duncton Hill'**, one of his most famous anthology pieces, marred for the modern reader by such lines as

> He does not die, but still remains
> Substantiate with his darling plains.

Still, while seeing these limitations, I would rather have such poems on my shelves than not.

Belloc's earliest published work was poetry and it was a poet, primarily, that he wanted to be in his early years of literary struggle when, having married young, he was trying to make a living as a professional journalist and historian. To this early phase, too, belong those verses for which he will always be remembered, the *Cautionary Tales* and *The Modern Traveller*, followed by *Peers* and *More Peers* with their marvellous BTB [Basil T. Blackwood] illustrations. The 'serious' verse is of uneven quality but the comic stuff he polished continually and it has the hard-edged surprisingness which always accompanies true poetry. The world of Henry King, who perished through his 'chief defect' of chewing little bits of string, or of dishonest Matilda whose dreadful lies led to her death by burning, or of Goldolphin Horne, who 'held the human race in scorn' and ended as the boy 'who blacks the boots at the Savoy' has a surreal quality all Belloc's own. His sentimental lyrics invite comparison with Alfred Noyes or A.E. Housman. His cautionary verses are incomparable. Children of all generations have responded to them, quite regardless of whether they themselves are ever going to move in circles where they meet the likes of Lord Lundy who spoils his chances of being 'the next Prime Minister but three' by being 'far too freely moved to tears'.

In these poems Belloc revealed what he thought of England—its crazy institutions from the House of Lords to the Fire Brigade, its social divisions, its bogus moralism. It is a farcical place where grown-ups and children alike will get into scrapes. But it is guided by no true principles, either religious or political. This total pessimism about the land of his mother's birth informed much of Belloc's historical writing and his journalism, as well as his works of political and economic analysis, such as *The Servile State,* a prophetic book, whose wisdom is clearer now than ever before. He saw Capital and Capitalism as ruining everything, and he realised that most political systems calling themselves socialist would eventually succumb to the power of Capital, because both State Socialism and Capitalism pursue collectivist solutions to human problems, and place money before soul.

In his prose works, Belloc found only one acceptable collective, and that is the Catholic Church, which he believed to provide hearth and home for the human spirit. In his poems—though there are some pious lyrics—he writes less as a Catholic than as a solitary, whose world has been wrecked.

> Ha'nacker Hill is in Desolation:
>   Ruin a-top and a field unploughed.
> And Spirits that call on a fallen nation
>   Spirits that loved her calling aloud:
>   Spirits abroad in a windy cloud.
>
> Spirits that call and no one answers;
>   Ha'nacker's down and England's done.
> Wind and Thistle for pipe and dancers
>   And never a ploughman under the Sun.
>   Never a ploughman. Never a one.

Before I began work on my biography of the man, I had assumed that this mood of solitude and desolation came upon Belloc as a result of some personal crisis in his life, such as the death of his wife in middle age, or the collapse of his faith in the Liberal Party—in whose interest he sat in the 1906 to 1910 Parliament as MP for Salford. But I soon became aware that Belloc had been an elegist before he could talk and that his sense that 'Ha'nacker Hill is in Desolation' was inborn. The outward events of his life— the early death of his father, the defeat of France by the Prussians in 1870, Belloc's failure to secure a much-coveted Oxford Fellowship, the loss of his wife, the death of two grown-up sons, the Fall of France in 1940—all fitted into a pattern for which his imagination had been preparing him from the beginning—as did his pathetic final decade of existence.

> Life is a long discovery, isn't it?
> You only get your wisdom bit by bit.
> If you have luck you find in early youth
> How dangerous it is to tell the Truth;
> And next you learn how dignity and peace
> Are the ripe fruits of patient avarice.
> You find that middle life goes racing past.
> You find despair: and, at the very last,
> You find as you are giving up the ghost
> That those who loved you best despised you
>   most.

The man who wrote those lines cannot have been all bad. But, as I discovered when I tried to paint a sympathetic portrait of him, it is not surprising that the English did not find his presence very comforting during his lifetime; nor, thirty years after he was dead, did they much wish to be reminded of what he thought of them.

FURTHER READING

Biography

Speaight, Robert. *The Life of Hilaire Belloc.* London: Hollis & Carter, 1957, 552 p.
    Biographical and critical study of Belloc.

Criticism

Sherbo, Arthur. "Belated Justice to Hilaire Belloc, Versifier (1870-1953)." *Studies in Bibliography* 45 (1992): 251-64.
    Analyzes Belloc's revisions to his poetry.

White, Gertrude M. "True Words in Jest: The Light Verse of Chesterton and Belloc." *The Chesterton Review* VI, No. 1 (Fall-Winter 1979-1980): 1-26.
    Compares and contrasts the comic verse of the two poets.

Additional coverage of Belloc's life and career is contained in the following sources published by The Gale Group: *Contemporary Authors,* Vols. 106, 152; *Dictionary of Literary Biography,* Vols. 19, 100, 141, 174; *DISCovering Authors: Poets Module*; *Twentieth-Century Literary Criticism,* Vols. 7, 18; and *Yesterday's Authors of Books for Children,* Vol. 1.

Rupert Brooke
1887-1915

English poet, critic, dramatist, essayist, travel writer, and journalist.

INTRODUCTION

Considered England's foremost young poet at the time of his death in 1915, Brooke is best known today for his war poetry and for his personal mystique as the embodiment of idealized youth. Of the war sonnets in *1914, and Other Poems,* Brooke's "The Soldier," celebrating a life gladly given in England's service, is world-renowned—hailed for its noble sentiments by many, and scorned for its naiveté by others.

Biographical Information

One of three brothers, each of whom died before reaching age thirty, Brooke was born in Rugby, England, where his father served as a schoolmaster at Rugby School, which he attended. He composed two prize poems while at Rugby and entered King's College, Cambridge, in 1906. In 1911 he published *Poems,* which was regarded even by its detractors as a herald of a major talent. Brooke suffered an emotional breakdown in 1912, following a failed love affair. Brooke embarked on a trip to North America and the South Pacific in 1913. At the outbreak of World War I, he returned to England and received a commission in the Royal Navy. While preparing for the assault on Gallipoli, Turkey, Brooke died of blood poisoning aboard ship in the Aegean Sea. He was buried in an olive grove on the island of Scyros.

Major Works

Brooke is best remembered for his poems influenced by the onset of World War I. Commissioned an officer in the Royal Naval Division, he completed his famed *1914* sonnets during the early stages of the war, demonstrating in them a romantic, crusading vision typical of the English civilian spirit at that time. His travel poems also have attracted critical attention. Considered one of his best sonnets, "Tiare Tahiti" was inspired by his love for one of the natives he met while visiting the South-Sea island. Another well-regarded poem is his "The Old Vicarage, Grantchester," a whimsical, sentimental revelation of his homesickness while traveling.

Critical Reception

The idolatrous praise heaped upon Brooke following his death attracted a tremendous readership to his poetry. Often nostalgic and sentimental, his verse fueled the trag-

ic "young Apollo" image against which critics have struggled to assess his literary achievement. Shortly after World War I, Brooke's poetry was rejected by critics who viewed his work as little more than the idealistic musings of a pampered darling, objecting most emphatically to his war sonnets for their glorification of war and of the soldier's martyrdom. Present-day commentators, however, while acknowledging Brooke's excesses, have drawn favorable attention to his skill as a sonneteer, his gift for language, and the romantic intensity of his best verse, focusing on a renewed appreciation of Brooke's stylistic accomplishments. More importantly, however, Brooke has come to be viewed, in recognition of both the qualities and the defects of his poetry and character, as the embodiment of his age, closely reflecting the thoughts and sentiments of his pre-War generation. As such, he remains an important figure in the history of English literature.

PRINCIPAL WORKS

Poetry

Poems 1911
The Collected Poems of Rupert Brooke 1915

1914, and Other Poems 1915
The Poetical Works of Rupert Brooke 1946

Other Major Works

Lithuania (drama) 1915
John Webster and the Elizabethan Drama (essay) 1916
Letters from America (travel essays) 1916
The Prose of Rupert Brooke (essays and criticism) 1956

CRITICISM

G. Wilson Knight (essay date 1971)

SOURCE: "Rupert Brooke," in *Neglected Powers: Essays on Nineteenth and Twentieth Century Literature,* Barnes & Noble, 1971, pp. 293-308.

[*In the following essay, Knight discusses the defining characteristics of Brooke's verse.*]

Rupert Brooke belongs, not to a generation, and certainly not to posterity, but to a date: in so far as his name survives, it does so in inevitable connection with 1914. Although it was his generation—the generation of Pound and Eliot, of Joyce and Lawrence, of Epstein and Picasso and Stravinsky—that made the modern world of art, Brooke has no place among them, and consequently no living contact with the present moment. He is a poet of his time, but his time was those few first months of the First World War, when Englishmen still believed that it was sweet and proper to die for one's country, and when Brooke's war sonnets could be read without bitterness or irony.

We think of Brooke, then, as a War Poet. But quite inaccurately. In the first place, it would be more precise to call him an On-the-way-to-the-war Poet, for, with ironic appropriateness, he died of natural causes en route to the Dardanelles campaign, and the emotions that his war sonnets express are not those of a combatant, but of a recruit. The *real* War Poets—Owen and Sassoon and Graves and Blunden and Rosenberg—came along later, out of the trenches, and spoke with a different tone; indeed, one might say that their poems exist to contradict the ignorant nobilities of Brooke. Sassoon recalled [in *Siegfried's Journey,* 1945] that

> while learning to be a second-lieutenant I was unable to write anything at all, with the exception of a short poem called '**Absolution**', manifestly influenced by Rupert Brooke's famous sonnet-sequence. The significance of my too nobly worded lines was that they expressed the typical self-glorifying feelings of a young man about to go to the Front for the first time. The poem subsequently found favour with middle-aged reviewers; but the more I saw of the war the less noble-minded I felt about it.

Poor Brooke never got past the self glorifying stage, because he did not get to the war.

But Brooke was a would-be War Poet for only the length of those last five sonnets. Until then, through nearly a hundred poems, he had been a lyric poet of Youth, Love and Death, who developed from a Late Decadent to an Early Georgian. Most of these poems are hard going now, not because they are particularly bad, and certainly not because they are difficult, but because they are uniformly and conventionally dull; they are poems that might have been written by any of a number of mediocre pre-war poets, or by a committee of Georgians. They have no distinguishable individual voice, and this is no doubt one reason for Brooke's popularity among people who don't ordinarily read verse; his poetry sounds the way poetry *should* sound, because it sounds like so many poems that have already been written. Echoes of Marvell and Donne, of Shakespeare, Blake, Housman, Dowson and Yeats haunt the **Collected Poems**; the only ghost that is not there is Brooke's.

Almost any poem from **Poems 1911** (the only book that Brooke published during his lifetime) will confirm these strictures. Take, for example, this sonnet:

> Oh! Death will find me, long before I tire
>   Of watching you; and swing me suddenly
> Into the shade of loneliness and mire
>   Of the last land! There, waiting patiently,
> One day, I think, I'll feel a cool wind blowing,
>   See a slow light across the Stygian tide,
> And hear the Dead about me stir, unknowing,
>   And tremble. And *I* shall know that you have died.
>
> And watch you, a broad-browed and smiling dream,
>   Pass, light as ever, through the lightless host
> Quietly ponder, start, and sway, and gleam—
>   Most individual and bewildering ghost!—
> And turn, and toss your brown delightful head
> Amusedly, among the ancient Dead.

Not exactly a bad poem, and far from Brooke's worst, but a poem without any distinguishable merit—the diction abstract and conventional, the images the worn poetical coinage of the past, the theme Death, the most poetical subject that Brooke knew. Out of poems like this one a list of favourite words and gestures could be made that would constitute Brooke's sense of what was poetic, and that turn up again and again, rearranged, but essentially the same: dream and gleam, heart, tears, sorrow, grey, yearning, and weary cries and sighs, and of course, everywhere, Love and Death. In a rare moment of self-criticism Brooke composed a table of contents for an imaginary anthology, to which his own contribution was to be '**Oh, Dear! Oh, Dear! A Sonnet**'. This is very perceptive, for nearly half of his poems are conventional sonnets, and most of them, like '**Oh! Death will find me**', say little more than 'Oh Dear!'

This body of boring verse suggests not so much a man who wanted to write a poem as a man who wanted to be a poet; or perhaps in Brooke's case a man who took poeticalness as his destiny. For if the poems are in the most conventional sense *poetic,* so was Brooke. No one ever looked so much like a poet as he did—not a *poète maudit*, but an ideal English poet, a gentleman poet, a Rugby-and-Cambridge poet, a healthy, pink-cheeked, blond, games-playing poet. He was, as Henry Nevinson said, almost ludicrously beautiful, and with his long hair and his flowing ties he made his own beauty poetical. (Even Beatrice Webb, who was deaf to poetry and immune to a pretty face, called Brooke 'a poetic beauty', though she thought him otherwise a commonplace, conceited young man.) With such looks, great personal charm, and a modest talent, no wonder that he had such friends, that he dined with the Prime Minister and called Winston Churchill by his first name and never worked for a living. He was a Doomed Youth from the beginning, but his doom was his extravagant good fortune; as Henry James said, felicity dogged his steps.

More than any of his other admirers it was James who understood the expense of Brooke's beauty. 'Rupert expressed us all', James wrote after his death [in the preface to *Letters from America,* 1916] 'at the highest tide of our actuality, and was the creature of a freedom restricted only by that condition of his blinding youth, which we accept on the whole with gratitude and relief—given that I qualify the condition as dazzling even to himself'. The expressive self, the 'blinding youth' became a myth in his own time. Brooke was twenty-three and scarcely known when Frances Cornford published her epigram about him:

> A young Apollo, golden-haired,
> 　Stands dreaming on the verge of strife
> Magnificently unprepared
> 　For the long littleness of life.

And he remained mythical in his life and in his death. [In *Letters,* edited by Aldous Huxley, 1932] Even D. H. Lawrence—a man not given to classical allusion—wrote of Brooke's death that

> he was slain by bright Phoebus' shaft—it was in keeping with his general sunniness—it was the real climax of his pose. I first heard of him as a Greek god under a Japanese sunshade, reading poetry in his pyjamas, at Grantchester,—at Grantchester upon the lawns where the river goes. Bright Phoebus smote him down. It is all in the saga.

But as James perceived, the myth dazzled Brooke, too. He confessed to Ka Cox that he had 'always enjoyed that healthy, serene, Apollo-golden-haired, business' and in most of his poems he allowed himself to be absorbed in it, so that the personal role and the poetic role were the same, and there is no creative tension between them. If one asks who wrote **'The Funeral of Youth'** or **'The Great Lover'** or **'Tiare Tahiti',** the answer can only be, 'Apollo-Brooke did'.

A few poems suggest, however, that Brooke did recognize the danger of the myth to him as a poet, and that he was trying to destroy, or at least modify it by writing poems that were aggressively anti-Apollonian. His five so-called 'ugly poems' are all attempts to get beyond conventional poetic subject matter and language, to a more acrid reality. **'Channel Passage',** the most noticed of these, is about seasickness and lovesickness; **'Dead Men's Love'** is a vision of dead lovers kissing; **'Dawn'** describes snoring Germans on a train; **'Wagner'** shows a fat man at a concert; and **'Lust'** is an anti-erotic love poem. I don't think it is only the changes of modern taste that make these poems seem better and more realized than most of Brooke's other work; they do manage to suggest that they were written out of actual life, and not out of the postures of poetry.

The motive that Brooke offered for including **'Lust'** in his first book of poems is the motive for all of the ugly poems:

> My own feeling is that to remove it would be to overbalance the book still more in the direction of unimportant prettiness. There's plenty of that sort of wash in the other pages for the readers who like it. They needn't read the parts which are new and serious. About a lot of the book I occasionally feel like Ophelia, that I've turned 'Thought and affliction, passion, hell itself . . . to favour and to prettiness'.

The poems were Brooke's effort to shake off the felicity at his heels. But they were also 'new and serious'—that is, they were his principal attempts at 'modernism'. Brooke was a very up-to-date young Edwardian, who went to 'Hello Ragtime' and the Post-Impressionist Show, and read Pound and Bennett and Forster, but his 'ugly poems' are a demonstration of the fact that you can't be modern simply by knowing what *is* modern. The five poems are very traditionally imagined (three are sonnets), and none shows the slightest affinity with the work that was then being done by his most advanced contemporaries—by Pound, for example, and Hulme.

But even though the poems seem tame, they were opposed bitterly by Brooke's editors and friends. Edward Marsh complained that he preferred poems he could read at meals (which seems an odd place to read serious poetry), and particularly objected to one line in **'Lust':** 'And your remembered smell most agony'. 'There are some things', he wrote, 'too disgusting to write about, especially in one's own language'. The editor of the *Nation* wanted one of the poems (probably **'Channel Passage'**) changed before he would consider it, and Brooke's publishers, Sidgwick & Jackson, urged him to omit both **'Lust'** and **'Channel Passage'** from *Poems 1911,* on the grounds that reviewers would single them out for criticism. The poems were kept in the book, but only after the title of **'Lust'** had been changed to **'Libido';** and the reviewers did indeed attack these poems.

One may explain the opposition of editors and publishers as expression of a cautious Edwardian regard for propriety; but in the case of Brooke's friends I think the Apollo-myth enters, too; that is, poems like these tarnished the image of the 'blinding youth'. Would Apollo vomit? Would he feel Lust? Would he bend his gaze upon snoring Germans and fat music-lovers? Henry James, noting the inclination of all men to spoil Brooke, took the 'ugly poems' as 'a declaration of the idea that he might himself prevent the spoiling so far as possible'. But in fact it wasn't possible. None of these poems went into Marsh's *Georgian Poetry* anthologies, which spread Brooke's reputation with their enormous sales; none appears in any anthology that I have seen. The Brooke canon remains pretty much what Marsh chose, the poems of 'unimportant prettiness' that Brooke worried about, the songs of Apollo.

There is only one poem of Brooke's in which a self speaks in what one can believe are the accents of an actual man. In **'The Old Vicarage, Grantchester'**, Brooke looked at his own posturing and sentimentalizing with a mild ironic eye. Perhaps because he was writing about Englishness from a café in Berlin, perhaps because he used a verse form that encourages a pointed facility, Brooke managed in this poem to sustain a tension of attitudes that is missing from his other work. England is both loved and laughed at, and he himself, though he confesses his sentimental homesickness, is also an object of amusement, a half-romantic, half-comic bard-in-exile. He intended to make the irony unmistakable by calling the poem 'The Sentimental Exile', but Marsh chose the present title instead—no doubt because the other seemed self-denigrating. He also asked for revision, which happily Brooke declined to make; and so it remains what he called it, 'a long lanky laxlimbed set of verses' which is nevertheless his most sustained, most richly felt poem. It is also the least Apollonian, the least self-consciously posed: the self in the poem is 'sweating, sick, and hot', as well as sentimental, and this self, one must infer, comes close to the Brooke whom his friends so cherished.

One other poem by Brooke that shows something like the same attractive wit is not included among his **Collected Poems** (though Edward Marsh quotes it in his Memoir). It is his rendering of Shakespeare's first twenty sonnets in the 'short, simple, naive' style of his friend Frances Cornford:

"Triolet"

If you would only have a son,
  William, the day would be a glad one.
It *would* be nice for everyone,
  If you would only have a son.
And William, what would *you* have done
  If Lady Pembroke hadn't had one?
If you would only have a son,
  William, the day *would* be a glad one!

This little joke demonstrates a number of Brooke's more attractive qualities—his cleverness, his good ear, his technical skill, his geniality. It is perhaps still the work of a clever undergraduate, but it is very well done, nevertheless, and in a manner very far removed from the Apollo myth.

Wit is perhaps the first human quality to go when a war is declared, and it is not surprising that Brooke's war poems show no sign of his natural wittiness. It is at first glance surprising, though, that they also completely lack that ugliness that he had been at such pains to insert into

his 'ugly poems'. One might surely expect ugliness from a War Poet. But the point of poems like **'Channel Passage'**, Brooke had said, was that 'there are common and sordid things—situations or details—that may suddenly bring all tragedy, or at least the brutality of actual emotions, to you'. In his war poems there are no actual emotions, no situations, no details; there are only the clichés of imagined heroism, 'the typical self-glorifying feelings', as Sassoon put it, 'of a young man about to go to the Front for the first time'. For this reason Brooke's poems have no proper place among the genuine poems of the First World War, all of which are about real ugliness. Still, they have a value which one would not want to lose, for they tell us with a terrible accuracy of the delusions of nobility which Brooke's generation carried into the war. It seems impossible that any young man should feel that way again; but the delusions were nevertheless historically real, a part of that dreadful time, and it is well to have them set down in these, the last poems by a serious English poet that treat war as romantic. It is also worth recognizing how, in a poem like **'The Soldier'**, Brooke had to fill an empty rhetoric with too-easily weighted words—*England* four times and *English* twice in fourteen lines, *heart, dreams, heaven, eternal mind,* and the vaguely comforting *somewhere*—to falsify the truth of dying, and glorify death by calling it sacrifice. It is no wonder that Winston Churchill should have responded to Brooke's death with the same plaster rhetoric. 'During the last few months of his life', Churchill wrote in *The Times* [April 26, 1915],

> months of preparation in gallant comradeship and open air, the poet-soldier told with all the simple force of genius the sorrows of youth about to die; he was willing to die for the dear England whose beauty and majesty he knew; and he advanced towards the brink with perfect serenity, with absolute conviction of the rightness of his country's cause and a heart devoid of hate for fellow-men.

> The thoughts to which he gave expression in the very few incomparable war sonnets which he has left behind will be shared by many thousands of young men moving resolutely and blithely forward into this, the hardest, the cruellest, and the least-rewarded of all the wars that men have fought. They are a whole history and revelation of Rupert Brooke himself. Joyous, fearless, versatile, deeply instructed, with classic symmetry of mind and body, ruled by high undoubting purpose, he was all that one would wish England's noblest sons to be in days when no sacrifice but the most precious is acceptable, and the most precious is that which is most freely offered.

The eulogy is as false to reality as the poem, but both are true to the time; neither Brooke nor Churchill was exploiting false emotions, they were simply sharing them. As D. H. Lawrence said when he heard of Brooke's death, 'Even Rupert Brooke's sonnet, which I repudiate for myself, I know now it is true for him, for them'.

It is *that* truth, the true delusions of the ignorant young man on the way to war, that has survived, and has become Rupert Brooke. It is in a way only an extrapolation of the old Apollo myth, the beautiful young man in uniform, and when Churchill wrote his eulogy, three days after Brooke's death, that myth was already fixed. Brooke was the dream of English Youth, as an older generation might dream it, and his death became at once the symbol of England's sacrifice, the perfection of English manhood self-immolated on the altar of the war. Brooke-the-man, what there was of him beneath the fatal felicities, could scarcely survive such swift mythologizing.

The making of the myth continued after his death, at the hands of his mother and Edward Marsh, his executor. Friends did their part by withholding compromising records, and even now, nearly sixty years after his death, there are still letters—the correspondence between Brooke and his friend James Strachey—that are not to be made available for several years. Nevertheless, we do now know a good deal about Brooke's private life, thanks to the careful biography of Christopher Hassall, and he begins to emerge as a man who was both less and more than the Apollo myth—an attractive, troubled young man—immature (his favourite play was *Peter Pan*), provincial, puritanical, frightened by sex and harassed by a tyrannical mother who could end a typical letter, 'Why are you so unsatisfactory?'

That this young man wrote poems is interesting, but it is not of central importance: what is important is the way the story of his life and death becomes an obituary of a class and a generation that was destroyed in the war. The more we know about Brooke, and the more carefully we read his poems, the more he will be diminished as an important literary figure, and as a hero. And this is only proper: he has been Apollo too long. But myths are rarely killed by facts, and no doubt Brooke will remain the bard-like spirit to sentimental and immature minds like his own.

Poor Brooke: it is his destiny to live as a supremely poetical figure, shirt open and hair too long and profile perfect—a figure that appeals to that vast majority that doesn't read poetry, but knows what a poet should look like. But as a poet he is not immortal—he is only dead.

Samuel Hynes (essay date 1972)

SOURCE: "Rupert Brooke," in *Edwardian Occasions: Essays on English Writing in the Early Twentieth Century,* Oxford University Press, 1972, pp. 144-52.

[*In the following essay, Hynes offers a mixed assessment of Brooke's poetry.*]

On the mention of Brooke's name we think first either of his five war sonnets or of the famous bare-shouldered photograph by S. Schell, used for the 1915 collection of his *Poems* and the original of the plaque in Rugby Chapel by Havard Thomas, whose version is in the National Portrait Gallery, where copies are sold. I shall indicate a relation between Brooke's poetry and this portrait, called by Christopher Hassall in his biography *Rupert Brooke* 'A visual image that met the needs of a nation at a time of crisis'.

Brooke was not obviously fitted for the role of patriot. He had, it is true, certain social advantages. He struck a figure at Rugby and Cambridge, his poetic powers rapidly won attention, and he mixed with leading personalities in literature and politics. He had brilliance and wit. But the general tone of his conversation and writing was iconoclastic and unorthodox; he was a Socialist in politics and a pagan if not atheist in religion. His poetry was often of a kind to shock. He links the aestheticism of the nineties to the realism of postwar writing; he has affinities with both Wilde and Eliot.

Like Byron and Wilde, he had a strong personal impact. His appearance was striking; men such as Henry James, Walter de la Mare, and Sir Ian Hamilton were conquered by it. The many records are extraordinary: 'astounding apparition' with eyes 'like the sky', 'so beautiful that he's scarcely human'; 'a young man more beautiful than he I had never seen'; one who summed 'the youth of all the world'. But the accounts vary. Though he had the 'rosy' skin of a 'girl', of 'girlish' smoothness, his appearance was all male, 'there was nothing effeminate', and we hear also of a deeply tanned face and sturdy form, large feet and hands, and clumsy movements. It seems that he could appear variously male and female, clumsy and ethereal, according to mood. His complexion was rich, as though the blood 'was near the surface'. An inward power radiated out through the blood to the complexion, the eyes, and red-gold waves of hair, and it was some inner, spiritual, reality that gave him a 'shining impression' as of one 'from another planet', so that he entered a room 'like a prince'. According to Henry James, much of Brooke's importance as both poet and person could not be conveyed to posterity, since it depended on 'the simple act of presence and communication'.

He was an *embodiment* of poetry: 'There are only three good things', he once said, 'in the world. One is to read poetry, another is to write poetry, and the best of all is to *live* poetry'; it 'kept one young'. Siegfried Sassoon felt poetry in his presence, as of a 'being singled out for some transplendent performance, some enshrined achievement'. He had the baffling bisexuality of such persons. Though he could oppose bisexual doctrines, he also admitted that 'the soul of persons who write verse is said to be hermaphroditic'. He was aware of his endowments: 'I looked at myself, drying, in the glass, and I thought my body was very beautiful and strong, and that I was keeping it and making it splendid for you'. 'For you': but also, perhaps more, for himself, since there was in him an element of Whitmanesque narcissism. He was bodily conscious: 'While the Samoans', he once wrote, 'are not so foolish as to "think", their intelligence is incredibly lively and subtle'; even a European living among them 'soon learns to *be* his body (and so his true mind) instead of using it as a stupid convenience for his personality, a moment's umbrella against the world'.

He preserved a child's bodily self-interest and a child's integrity; as 'both man and boy' he was 'the child he must have grown from'; he was 'a symbol of youth for all time', doing up his shoes with 'the absorbed seriousness of a child'. Brooke remembered as a child often touching a 'higher level' of existence and recognizing that we are normally 'asleep', and the experience could be repeated in maturity, when he could say 'I more than exist'. In the South Seas he came near to a full recapture of this childhood magic.

He was obsessed with nakedness, usually in relation to bathing, at Grantchester, the South Seas, or by a Canadian lake, 'lying quite naked on a beach of golden sand'. In the South Seas he wrote of himself 'in a loin-cloth, brown and wild' by a 'sun-saturated sea', among 'naked people of incredible loveliness'. Here men were strong and beautiful in their unclothed bodies, and with finer sensibilities than Europeans, so that 'one's European literary soul begins to be haunted by strange doubts'. When war came, Brooke expected to 'find incredible beauty in the washing place, with rows of naked, superb men', either by sun or moon. If the many revulsions in his poetry point on to Eliot, his body obsession points to Lawrence. It is less likely that this obsession came from knowledge of his own beauty than that that beauty flowered from the inward obsession. He was, in fact, an integrated, or near-integrated, man.

His sex life was difficult. Living within the presexual or super-sexual, Nietzschean and lonely, integration at an age of physical maturity may be hard. His experience in the South Seas was not, he said, that of a love paradise; it was the opposite to alcohol according to the Porter's definition in *Macbeth,* 'for it promotes performance but takes away desire'. That is, presumably, sex functioned without a partner. Brooke had known intense love in England, but it had failed. He had had a severe breakdown. He had contemplated suicide, feared madness and was reluctant to have children. Hassall refers to 'some obscure emotional distemper', but leaves the 'root of his unsureness' undefined. Here is a late self-diagnosis:

> Oh, I've loved you a long time, child: but not in the complete way of love. I mean, there was something rooted out of my heart by things that went before. I thought I couldn't love wholly, again. I couldn't worship—I could see intellectually that some women were worshipful, perhaps. But I couldn't find the flame of worship in me. I was unhappy. Oh, God, I *knew* how glorious and noble your heart was. But I couldn't burn to it. I mean, I loved you with all there was of me. But I was a cripple, incomplete.

In some moods he was an antifeminist, rating friendship above love. But he does not appear to have experienced male romantic friendships; imagination was turned inward, narcissistically, on himself.

We pass now to the poetry. It strongly attacks romantic love. The two sonnets **'Menelaus and Helen'** show knightly romance giving place to blear-eyed impotence and nagging. **'The Beginning'**, **'Sonnet Reversed'**, **'Beauty and Beauty'** tell the same story. In **'Kindliness'** youth's infinite hunger has to make terms with a 'second-best'. In **'Mutability'** our 'melting flesh' aims at impossible absolutes. **'Jealousy'** contrasts young love with the slobbering age which follows, and in **'A Channel Passage'** there is

little difference between 'a sea-sick body or a you-sick soul'. In **'Dead Men's Love'** love is reduced to 'dust and a filthy smell'. There appears to be some achievement in **'Lust'**, but the only real gleams are, as we shall see, in some new dimension beyond earth.

Brooke's sense of physical perfection led to a corresponding reaction. Man's body could so easily be repellent: in **'Wagner'** and **'Dawn'** physical nausea is emphatic. Brooke questions the human form itself: in **'Heaven'** the fishes must see God as a great fish, and **'On the Death of Smet-Smet'** shows savages worshipping a hippopotamus goddess. Our human valuations are arbitrary. **'Thoughts on the Shape of the Human Body'** is a critique of sexual intercourse:

> . . . We love, and gape,
> Fantastic shape to mazed fantastic shape,
> Straggling, irregular, perplexed, embossed,
> Grotesquely twined, extravagantly lost
> By crescive paths and strange protuberant ways
> From sanity and from wholeness and from grace.

What is wanted is a more harmonious love 'disentangled from humanity', 'whole', a 'simplicity' like a 'perfect sphere', loving 'moon to moon'; the kind of love so often found in Platonic-homosexual engagements, though there seems to be nothing of primary importance recorded of Brooke. The moon's radiance is white, and whiteness is Brooke's colour, as it was Powys's, for beyond-earthly intimations.

Brooke was thrown back on himself. In **'Success'** his loved one's 'white godhead', 'holy and far', is entangled with 'foul you', 'shame' and a 'black word', leaving the poet 'alone'. In **'I said I splendidly loved you'** he admits the lie, conscious that he has been following 'phantoms' or 'his own face'. **'Waikiki'** shows him correspondingly 'perplexed'. In **'The Voice'** a love assignation horribly interrupts his lonely meditations in the night-darkened woods: 'By God! I wish—I wish that you were dead!' Elsewhere, in the dark woods of **'Flight'**, he has left daytime loves for the night's scents, weeping and stroking his own face. **'Paralysis'** shows him in his 'white neat bed' laughing in his 'great loneliness'. In **'Town and Country'** two lovers may be 'drunk with solitude' in the city, but in the woods by night love dissolves into a vaster, cosmic, loneliness. **'The Chilterns'** tells us that:

> . . . a better friend than love have they,
> For none to mar or mend,
> That have themselves to friend.

He will have freedom enjoying the roads and winds and hedgerows. He is with Wordsworth and John Cowper Powys, for whom the natural partner of the human soul is, not a sexual partner, but the objective universe. **'The Great Lover'** is a key poem, listing a fine assortment of loves ranging through all the senses from wet roofs, the smell of burning wood, 'the rough male kiss of blankets' and 'furs to touch', to the miracles of earth nature. This Powysian mystique is expanded in a remarkable letter to Ben Keeling, quoted in Hassall's biography.

Perfection is attainable in young beauty or in sense enjoyment of external objects. But what of the future? In **'The Great Lover'** he knows that life beyond death must be very different. He is ready to distinguish body from soul or spirit. In sleep the 'soul' leaves the body like a 'dress' laid by, and yet why then can the countenance appear troubled? Or smile? Surely, too, the sensuous is itself spirit-born, as in the mysterious sleep of **'Doubts'**:

> And if the spirit be not there,
> Why is fragrance in the hair?

This was Powys's concern. On its bodiless excursions the soul still, even at a great distance, uses the senses of the body it has left behind.

This thought-teasing paradox of soul and body is brilliantly handled in a poem from Fiji, on the old cannibal practice of letting the victim see parts of himself eaten. Will this be his own fate? In comic if almost unreadable couplets, composed as for a past lover, he traces the horrors:

> Of the two eyes that were your ruin,
> One now observes the other stewing.

The verses are simultaneously a critique of physical glamour and an assertion of the mind's, or soul's, independence. Perhaps nowhere else, apart from Byron, are crucial metaphysics so lightly handled.

Brooke was as strongly obsessed with the spiritual as with the physical. Though love fails on earth, there is hope for it beyond. **'The Goddess in the Wood'** sets, in mythological terms, a type. In 'The Call' lovers may be 'one' *above* the 'Night', and in 'Victory' 'beyond all love or hate', 'perfect from the ultimate height of living', they challenge 'supernal' hosts. Wounded on earth, love may win success at the 'eventual limit of our light', in **'The Wayfarers'**. **'Choriambics II'**, balances solitude in dark woods and some 'face of my dreams', gleaming down through the forest 'in vision white'. White is for Brooke, as for Powys, a mystical colour. In **'Blue Evening'**, after 'agony' and 'hatred' the poet's love is felt within the moon's 'white ways of glamour', blessing him with 'white brows'. **'Finding'** shows him after love's failure 'lone and frightened' in the 'white' moonlight's 'silver way', with around him trees 'mysteriously crying', 'dead voices' and 'dead soft fingers', and 'little gods' whispering, and he sees his love radiant beyond 'the tides of darkness', so that nothing was true

> But the white fire of moonlight
> And a white dream of you.

Such love is not sexually limited. **'Sleeping Out: Full Moon'** shows him alone under the lonely Moon-Queen, and he feels the whole world pressing toward 'the white one flame' of a 'heatless fire' and 'flameless ecstasy'; 'earth fades'; 'radiant bands' and 'friendly' presences help the stumbler to the 'infinite height' and *maternal* eyes. We remember Brooke's desire for a perfect, unentangled, love, loving 'moon to moon' in **'Thoughts on the Shape**

of the Human Body'. The visions are beyond sexuality in line with the contrast, in 'Success', of 'white godhead' with 'that foul you'—a contrast, in some vital way, of spirit with personality. We are all, already, part of some other, spiritual dimension. **'In Examination'** develops a vision of ordinary life transfigured, revealing the 'scribbling fools' as with flaming hair, God-like, 'white-robed' in the 'white undying Fire' among archangels and angels; as beings in a dimension of which our normal seeing refracts only a miserable simulacrum. **'Desertion'**, on the death of a loved friend, asks pathetically *why* he has gone? Had he known something that made him distrust earth's 'splendid dream'? Is perhaps earth's seeming splendour—and often to Brooke it seemed sordid enough—a mere nothing in comparison?

Such intuitions touch Spiritualism. Though **'The True Beatitude'** asserts 'an earthly garden hidden from any cleric' Brooke's poetry can be intensely spiritualistic, as when in 'Oh, Death will find me. . . . ' he imagines his love's arrival in Hades tossing her hair 'among the ancient Dead'. **'Dust'** vividly exploits the freedoms of an after-life. Though the 'white flame' of love's earthly visions has gone and we 'stiffen' in darkness, yet, in the manner of Byron's *Childe Harold* (III. 74):

> Not dead, not undesirous yet,
>   Still sentient, still unsatisfied,
> We'll ride the air, and shine, and flit,
>   Around the places where we died . . .

Beyond 'thinking' and 'out of view' (i.e. in an existence impossible to define):

> One mote of all the dust that's I
> Shall meet one atom that was you.

The old love reflames in the 'garden'; all senses are mixed— is it 'fire', 'dew', of 'earth' or the 'height', 'singing, or flame, or scent, or hue'? All that can be said is that it is 'light' passing on to 'light'.

Brooke had extrasensory experience. **'Home'** recounts how, returning by night to his room, he was aware of

> The form of one I did not know
>   Sitting in my chair.

Then it goes. All night he 'could not sleep'.

He wonders variously about the after-life. **'The Life Beyond'** imagines it as hideous. **'Mutability'** asks if indeed there is 'a high windless world and strange' beyond time? 'Our melting flesh' fixes Beauty there and 'imperishable Love', but all we actually know is earth experience, where kisses do not last. The poem **'Clouds'** ponders the belief that 'the Dead' remain close to those on earth, but suggests rather that they pass above like clouds, reflecting 'the white moon's beauty, and 'break and wave and flow' like a silent sea. But shall we remember the past? **'Hauntings'** imagines a 'poor ghost' 'haunted' by vague recollections of earth-life—as earth beings are 'haunted' by spirit-life—which are unintelligible:

And light on waving grass, he knows not when,
And feet that ran, but where, he cannot tell.

Official Spiritualism is given the **'Sonnet (Suggested by some of the Proceedings of the Society for Psychical Research)'.** After death we shall

Spend in pure converse our eternal day;
  Think each in each, immediately wise;
Learn all we lacked before; hear, know, and say
  What this tumultuous body now denies;
And feel, who have laid our groping hands away;
  And see, no longer blinded by our eyes.

The lines report what Spiritualism tells us: speech by telepathic immediacy, halls of learning and progress; the earth body as a limiting factor which narrows and constricts, so that we feel more keenly and see more clearly without it, as in Andrew Marvell's 'Dialogue between the Soul and the Body'. The next plane, where sound and colour are one, is richer, not poorer, in sense experience; depending not on a mentalized summation derived from separate sense-inlets, we shall respond directly to the totality of which these allow parts only to trickle through and which we can on earth only approach by attempts at some total dramatic art blending intellectual awareness with sound and colour.

Brooke came near such a total experience in the South Sea Islands. **'Tiare Tahiti',** rejecting the 'broken things' of earth, introduces us to a world of Platonic archetypes, to 'the Face, whose ghosts we are' and to 'Dance' without 'the limbs that move', all lovely things meeting in 'Loveliness'. All colours, white especially, but also coral, pearl, green, gold, red, are there; all earth beauty recaptured and eternalized. And yet—must 'feet' become 'Ambulation', and what of kisses? Meanwhile, let us enjoy the 'flowered way' and 'whiteness of the sand', 'well this side of Paradise'. We may be nearer the spirit reality at choice, sense-summing moments of earthly life than with *mental* accounts, however accurate, of that reality, which is all, and more, of what we experience on earth. Such is the truth flowering from this cleverly balanced poem.

Brooke lived and wrote on the border between earth and paradise, life and death. The transition, as with Powys, involves what may be called the 'elemental'. In nature Brooke loved night woods and the moon, and also his own, and others', nakedness, swimming and water. These are as transition mediums between modes of existence.

Herein lies the importance of the poem **'The Old Vicarage, Grantchester'.** It contrasts the regulated officialdom of Berlin, where the lines were composed, with the luxuriant freedoms and 'unofficial rose' of Grantchester; more widely, civilized constrictions with elemental freedom. At Grantchester one runs on 'bare feet' to the river 'deep as death':

In Grantchester their skins are white;
They bathe by day, they bathe by night. . . .

Spirits are here: 'His ghostly Lordship swims his pool', and among the trees flits 'the sly shade of a Rural Dean'. It is a place of 'lithe children lovelier than a dream' and 'youth', where suicide is preferable to 'feeling old'.

The phrase 'deep as death' is important. In the Hades of Byron's *Cain* and in Ibsen's *Lady from the Sea* and *Little Eyolf* water naturally blends with the dimension of death. Brooke once, in imaginative vein, described his Grantchester night bathing:

I stood naked at the edge of the black water in a perfect silence. I plunged. The water stunned me as it came upwards with its cold, life-giving embrace. . . .

Then a figure appeared, some 'local deity' or 'naiad of the stream', who urged him, as Powys often urged us, not to search beyond present existence. But with the elements, especially by night, we are already on the border-line, living life-and-death. Diving into blue-green waters at Fiji was perhaps better than poetry. Water is death and life. The dead of **'Clouds'** 'break and wave and flow' like a silent sea. The visionary figure of **'Blue Evening'** comes 'rippling' down the moon's 'glamour'. **'Day That I Have Loved'** imagines the day as a dead loved one, gone out to sea, and darkness. **'Finding'** tells of 'the words of night' and 'dead' spirit-voices and 'the dark, beyond the ocean'. Brooke's lines in **'Seaside'**:

In the deep heart of me
The sullen waters swell towards the moon,
And all my tides set seaward

correspond exactly to the conclusion to Powys's *Rodmoor*. In both Powys and Brooke we meet a mystique of water, darkness, and a great *white* peace. In **'The Jolly Company'** the stars are a 'white companionship' of 'lonely light'.

Sea life is as a new dimension. **'The Fish'** blends life and death:

The strange soft-handed depth subdues
Drowned colour there, but black to hues,
As death to living, decomposes—
Red darkness of the heart of roses,
Blue brilliant from dead starless skies,
And gold that lies behind the eyes,
The unknown unnameable sightless white
That is the essential flame of night. . . .

As elsewhere, *darkness* is one with the *white* vision. 'Behind the eyes' corresponds to Eliot's 'more distant than stars and nearer than the eye' in **'Marina'**. A fish's life contrasts with love's unrest; it is a lonely self-enjoyment of the blood rhythms. In Powysian vein, for these cool, atavistic depths are exactly Powysian, 'His bliss is older than the sun'

Brooke's progress through love-agony and love-failure to a lonely delight in his solitary, narcissistic, childlike, integrated self, body and soul, to a superb culmination of swimming naked among the glorious nakedness of the South Sea Islanders, was not all easy and innocent. It had its violent, non-moral aspect: 'I had to have a bath and dance many obscene dances, in lonely nakedness, up and down my room, to get sober'. In the early **'Song of the Beasts'** the 'sober' and 'dull' consciousness of 'common day' is contrasted with 'shameful night' when 'God is asleep':

> Have you not felt the quick fires that creep
> Through the hungry flesh, and the lust of delight,
> And hot secrets of dreams that day cannot say?

The night 'calls' and we leave the house, going

> Down the dim stairs, through the creaking door,
> Naked, crawling on hands and feet. . . .

We are 'Beast and God', serving 'blind desire', past 'evil faces' and 'mad whispers', out of the 'city', 'beyond lust', to level moonlit waters, and the 'calling sea'. An embarrassment, half-shame, half-pride, is written into **'Mary and Gabriel'**, wherein Mary feels both 'her limbs' sweet treachery' and her 'high estate', to be used for some high purpose. She feels 'alone', her 'womb'—or Brooke's own beauty—not exactly hers, and yet, we are told, it *will* be; some half-glimpsed purpose will be fulfilled and known.

Death is, and yet is not, the end. In the early (1908) **'Second Best'** the poet is 'alone with the enduring Earth, and Night'. Death, he thinks, is the end. If so:

> Proud, then, clear-eyed and laughing, go to greet
> Death as a friend!

The poem advances to a sense of death as containing all that was life:

> Exile of immortality, strongly wise,
> Strain through the dark with undesirous eyes
> To what may lie beyond it. Sets your star,
> O heart, for ever! Yet, behind the night,
> Waits for the great unborn, somewhere afar,
> Some white tremendous daybreak. And the light,
> Returning, shall give back the golden hours,
> Ocean a windless level, Earth a lawn
> Spacious and full of sunlit dancing-places,
> And laughter, and music, and, among the flowers,
> The gay child-hearts of men, and the child-faces,
> O heart, in the great dawn!

Brooke's earthly poetry is mostly a night-time poetry. Brightness, the sun, the white dawn—like that in the penultimate chapter of Powys's *Weymouth Sands*—all seem to lie, apart from his experiences in the South Seas, beyond. **'The Little Dog's Day'** (1907) is an early forecast of his death. After these supreme experiences in the South Seas, he had had his day: on his chosen line, there was little more. He had realized himself on the border where supreme self-enjoyment touches a new dimension, and he knew himself ripe for death. There was, he said, 'point in my not getting shot', but 'also there's point in my getting shot';

'life might be great fun' and 'death might be an admirable solution'. The famous war sonnets are less like patriotic trumpetings than paeans in praise of death. As in R. C. Sherriff's *Journey's End,* war is simply an elemental power, or death force: the sonnets could be applied, *mutatis mutandis,* to a young German.

The first, **'Peace'**, contrasts the inadequacies of poetry and love with 'swimmers into cleanness leaping' and a consequent 'release'. Only the body will be broken, and Death is both 'enemy' and 'friend'.

In the second, **'Safety'**, war, or death, 'knows no power'. One will be 'safe' whatever happens: 'And if these poor limbs die, safest of all'. 'Poor' registers both Brooke's emotional self-involvement and a recognition of the body's inadequacy.

'The Dead' celebrates 'honour', but remains typical in 'the rich Dead' who 'poured out the red sweet wine of youth'. Youth's sacrifice is more than patriotism. Called 'holiness', it is a thing in itself, youth's perfect hour.

The fourth, also called **'The Dead'**, remembers how they, as in **'The Great Lover'**, had known the varied sense-impressions of earth. 'All this is ended.' Instead, the glittering wavelets are now frosted to

> a white
> Unbroken glory, a gathered radiance,
> A width, a shining peace, under the night.

Moonlight is assumed, or stars.

In **'The Soldier'** Brooke concentrates on his body, made by England, after dying in a foreign land, where there shall be 'in that rich earth a richer dust concealed'. The 'heart' (i.e. mind or spirit) will preserve the sounds and scents of its earthly experience. The impressions are both physical and eternal.

These sonnets necessarily avoid extended statements on spirit-life. The problem of war sacrifice is one mainly of *body* sacrifice, as in Masefield's remarkable quatrain, printed in *The Times,* 16 September 1938, on the occasion of Neville Chamberlain's meeting with Hitler:

> As Priam to Achilles for his Son,
>   So you, into the night, divinely led,
>   To ask that young men's bodies, not yet dead,
> Be given from the battle not begun.

Those lines and Brooke's five sonnets preserve necessary limits.

We now return to the Schell portrait. The mockery it at first received at Cambridge as 'obscene' or as 'your favourite actress' signals the nature of its importance. It was used as a frontispiece to the 1915 collection of his poems and copied for the Rugby Chapel plaque. It became symbolic: 'bare-shouldered, long-haired, Greek god-like, mystic, wonderful', it was 'on the retina of the public eye, the soldier poet, the nation's sacrifice' (Richard Usborne, 'The Lost Heroes', *Sunday Times Magazine,* pictorial supplement, 29 January 1967).

Brooke was as strongly obsessed with the spiritual as with the physical. Though love fails on earth, there is hope for it beyond.

—G. Wilson Knight

What is its secret? The head rising from bare shoulders suggests a totality unconstricted by the mufflings of civilization. The profile of lips and nose, the waves of hair, the upward tilt of the head and eager eyes, are riveting. Its deliberated pose may have seemed 'a travesty' of one whose attractions were normally 'unconscious', lacking the 'candour' of glance his friends knew, but though critics thought the Rugby plaque 'sentimentalized', his mother saw it as the living image of the youth she had loved, and liked its appearance of 'pressing forward'.

The upward challenge of its meaning corresponds to Brooke's desire in the early **'Second Best'** to 'greet Death as a friend', 'clear-eyed and laughing', and to the use of 'lifts' in the 1913 poem **'The Night Journey',** wherein a rushing train symbolizes human destiny:

Hands and lit faces eddy to a line;
    The dazed last minutes click; the clamour dies.
Beyond the great-swung arc o' the roof, divine,
    Night, smoky-scarv'd, with thousand coloured
    eyes

Glares the imperious mystery of the way.
    Thirsty for dark, you feel the long-limbed train
Throb, stretch, thrill motion, slide, pull out and
    sway,
    Strain for the far, pause, draw to strength again. . . .

As a man, caught by some great hour, will rise,
    Slow-limbed, to meet the light or find his love;
And, breathing long, with staring sightless eyes,
    Hands out, head back, agape and silent, move

Sure as a flood, smooth as a vast wind blowing;
    And, gathering power and purpose as he goes,
Unstumbling, unreluctant, strong, unknowing,
    Borne by a will not his, that lifts, that grows,

Sweep out to darkness, triumphing in his goal,
    Out of the fire, out of the little room. . . .
- There is an end appointed, O my soul!
    Crimson and green the signals burn; the gloom

Is hung with steam's far-blowing livid streamers.
    Lost into God, as lights in light, we fly,
Grown one with will, end-drunken huddled

dreamers.
    The white lights roar. The sounds of the world
    die.

And lips and laughter are forgotten things.
    Speed sharpens; grows. Into the night, and on,
The strength and splendour of our purpose swings.
    The lamps fade; and the stars. We are alone.

Compulsion that 'lifts'; the darkness; the white lights roaring, sound and sight one in the new dimension; the intoxicating purpose and the conclusion on 'alone'—here is Brooke's total metaphysic, nobly stated.

The Schell portrait is, in its quiet way, a statement of this empowered message. It shows, necessarily, nothing of the blood radiance or red-gold hair which Brooke's friends knew. The definition is faint, a shadow kills the head's outline at the nape, and the far shoulder is lost in light (the definition is stronger in Havard Thomas's plaque). The dominating effect is of whiteness, as of a spirit body, its nakedness that of the 'naked seraph' of Shelley's additional lines to 'Epipsychidion' or the 'immortal nakedness' of the young Caponsacchi's ecstatic sacrifice in Browning's *The Ring and the Book* (VI. 971). Some lines of Brooke's 1908 **'Choriambics II'** were prophetic. They address a dream-figure who

Somewhere lay, as a child sleeping, a child
    suddenly reft from mirth,
White and wonderful yet, white in your youth,
    stretched upon foreign earth,
God, immortal and dead!

The child, or youth, may seem to sleep, but the seraph awakes, eager, as in the portrait. 'Immortal' yet 'dead': death in youth, and youth in death.

The bare-shouldered portrait was Brooke's own idea. Michael Hastings writes: 'When Brooke posed for Sherril Schell, the photographer claimed it was Brooke's idea to have, out of the twelve frames, a picture of himself naked from the waist up.' This was the basis of the famous portrait, of which Brooke wrote:

Nothing's happened: except that my American photographer has sent me a photograph of me—very shadowy and ethereal and poetic, of me in profile, and naked-shouldered. Eddie says it's very good. I think it's rather silly. But anyhow, I don't look like an amateur popular preacher—as in those others.

And no one will ever be able to put it into an interview, with the words 'We want great serious drama' underneath.

His self-exploitation might, he knew, incur mockery, but at least it distinguished him from conventional religion and the literary intelligentsia.

Brooke's death was in attunement with his life and thought. It came as an inevitable, half-willed, instinctive flowering.

This does not detract from the sacrifice but rather raises it to artistic and universal status. It was not by chance but rather, to quote *Coriolanus,* by a certain 'sovereignty of nature' that his dying became, like Byron's, symbolic. His memorial at Skyros was well devised by the sculptor Tombros as a nude statue not so much of Brooke himself as of 'a young man symbolizing Youth'.

Derek Stanford (essay date 1975)

SOURCE: "How Bad was Rupert Brooke?" in *Books & Bookmen,* Vol. 20, No. 235, April, 1975, pp. 64-6.

[*In the following essay, Stanford traces the decline of Brooke's literary reputation.*]

Even to have framed this question fifty years ago would have appeared a blasphemy. Rupert Brooke was still our national sacrificial object; our dear dead Anglo-Saxon Apollo. Only one year after his death, in her book *Studies of Contemporary Poets* (1916), Mary Sturgen identified him with England. 'In him . . . was manifested the poetic spirit of the race, warm with human passion and sane with laughter.' He had not died on 23 April—Shakespeare's birthday and St George's Day—for nothing. Inscribing his panegyric in *The Times* for 26 April, 1915, Winston Churchill assured the readers of Brooke's place in posterity: 'A voice had become audible, a note had been struck, more thrilling . . . than any other . . . the voice has been swiftly stilled. Only the echoes and the memory remain; but they will linger.' Churchill was Churchill but even voices less prone to sound the trumpet or the clarion attest to the premium put on Brooke at his decease. 'There was no one like him,' declared Harold Munro. 'No one has his frankness, no one his ingenuity, his incisiveness, or his humour.' By 1938, however, when Frank Swinnerton published his somewhat façile classic *The Georgian Literary Scene,* the climate of opinion had changed. 'Brooke,' he wrote, 'had all the talent of a happy and charming boy . . . but it was not a powerful talent, and it is not likely to survive in the memory of a later generation.' Mr Swinnerton is not an original critic, distinguished for independence of judgement, so one can take his verdict here as reflecting a switch in critical fashion.

Such a reversal of reputation is, of course, by no means unusual in poetry. One has but to think, say, of Stephen Phillips who before 1910 was being compared with Milton and the Elizabethans, only to be dismissed after the Great War as a creator of shallow bombast. But the case of Brooke is rather different; whereas no one read Phillips after 1918, Brooke's poems have gone into edition after edition. The *Collected Poems* containing Edward Marsh's Memoir appeared in July 1918 and by January 1920 had reached its seventh impression: and this was in addition to reprints of two smaller collections *Poems 1911-1914* and *1914 and Other Poems.* To these volumes, continually in print, was added Geoffrey Keynes's *The Poetical Works of Rupert Brooke* (1946) in which he included thirty-eight new pieces, itself becoming a paperback in 1960. This is hardly a matter of failing to survive 'in the memory of a later generation,' but that not unheard-of dichotomy between the assessment of fashionable professional critics and the response of the common reader.

Both his elevation to the heights and his later depreciation were originally the result of extra- or non-literary considerations. It was the patriotism rather than the poetry which first wafted Brooke to fame, just as it was the force of pacifism and internationalism which led to his demotion in the Thirties. It is a thousand pities, for his good name, that Brooke's long lecture on *Art and Democracy* (delivered to the Fabian Society in 1910 but not published till 1946) was not in print at that period, since it was political gestures of this order which caught the votes of the influential parlour Socialists busily engaged in separating the sheep of God from the goats of Mammon. Then, too, there came the fashion for a second phase of Great War verse: that written by the 'Trench War' poets (Wilfred Owen and Siegfried Sassoon) instead of the poetry of heroes and the cavalry charge (as represented by Brooke and Julian Grenfell). History, which at first had been on Brooke's side, now turned emphatically against him; but the verdicts of the history are not to be confused with the 'purer' judgements of criticism. Just how good or bad was Brooke in literary rather than in social terms?

Source of so many denigrative or reductive assessments, F. R. Leavis had written as far back as 1932: 'Brooke had considerable personal force and became himself an influence. He energised the Garden-Suburb ethos with a certain original talent and the vigour of a prolonged adolescence. His verse exhibits a genuine sensuousness rather like Keats's (though more energetic) and something that is rather like Keats's vulgarity with a Public School accent.' With a critical sneer that is never civil, he adds that 'Brooke's complexity amounts to little more than an inhibiting adolescent self-consciousness in an ironical disguise [which] in its extreme form is painfully embarrassing.' The tone of Dr Leavis is so irritating in its narrow 'superior' exclusiveness that one would be only too glad to dismiss, in turn, his dismissal. Can it be, though, that fair examination must lead us to endorse this belittlement? Before answering this question, I intend to pass quickly through Brooke's poems, commenting on the influence behind them, their style, their merits and de-merits. The following is a brief survey roughly in chronological order.

The first considerable and longest-lasting influence on Brooke was the poetry of Ernest Dowson. In a paper on *Modern Poetry* read to the sixth form at Rugby, he commended Dowson's verse to them. He told them that just as Hugo observed that Baudelaire had created 'a new shudder', so one might remark of Dowson that he had created 'a new sigh.' Imitate the sigh of a master, however, and you get something as consciously obtrusive as a stage-whisper:

> Where I can sleep, and rest me, and—forget.
> **("The Return," 1905)**

> Hast *thou* forgotten? . . . Dost thou remember?
> **("In January," 1905)**

This requiem swan-note persisted, with decreasing occurrence, until within two years of his death:

> "Not the tears that fill the years
> After—after—"
>
> ("**Beauty and Beauty**," 1912)

> "Heart from heart is all as far
> Fafäia, as star from star."
>
> ("**Fafäia**," 1913)

In his interesting book *Rupert Brooke: A Reappraisal and Selection* (1971) Timothy Rogers rightly regrets this strong Dowsonian influence although, one suspects, for the wrong reason. Dowson was bad for Brooke not because he was a bad poet (he was a far surer craftsman than Brooke and a better poet than him in all but a dozen of the latter's poems), but because he was a bad (inimitable) model. Dowson had husbanded his limited stock of imagination and brought it to a purified expression. There was no room for development along the Dowsonian track.

Another bad fairy at the christening of the poet was Algernon Charles—that 'outsider' of The Pines, Putney; and many of Brooke's early pieces are messy with the residue of a Swinburnian after-birth. Vast accretions of these intense but vaguely applied adjectives and adverbs—fiery, splendid, glorious, passionate, sweet, pallid, bitter, *etc*—clutter up poem after poem. It is true that Swinburne, with his great metrical inventiveness, provided a good training-ground for Brooke the eager apprentice. The technique of verse fascinated him; and notebooks dating from his Granchester days show his conscious deep concern with the elements of composition, one volume containing analyses and comments on the prosodic structure of the poems he had been reading *"Choriambics I & II"* (1908) clearly attest to this discipleship as do such twelve-syllabled line poems as "**Ante Aram**" (1907), "**Day that I have Loved**" (1908) or "**The Vision of the Archangels**" (1906), a sonnet in Alexandrines.

But Dowson and Swinburne were unfortunate influences for Brooke, imaginatively speaking. Both were emotionally retarded men who had never grown to maturity, and certainly did not help to wean Brooke from his own considerable immaturity. Rather they confirmed him in his protracted adolescence in the supposed belief that their moods were the concomitants of high poetry. Someone defined sentimentality as a response of feeling in excess of the stimulus, a gesture beyond that called for by the nature of the situation. Two notes often sounded in sentimental poetry are the melancholic and the hectic; the self-pitying and the pseudo-passionate. Dowson and Swinburne abound in both of these—a psychological weakness which they often carry off through their sheer virtuosity of technique. Brooke, who was not their equal here, is frequently left with the half-baked emotion clearly exposed for what it is. Sometimes, it is even Laurence Hope more than the two earlier poets of whom we are reminded.

> It does but double the heart-ache
> When I wake, when I wake
>
> ("**Sometimes Even Now**," c1912)

That he questioned these reactions and what he made of them is apparent from his own poems:

> Dearest, why should I mourn, whimper, and whine,
> I that have yet to live
>
> ("**Choriambics I**," 1908)

> They are unworthy, these sad whinning moods,
> Shall I not make of love some glorious thing?
>
> ("**My Song**," 1907)

But to question a response and to move beyond it may prove two quite different things; and although Brooke grew in imaginative terms, in emotional terms—above all, concerning the relationship between men and women—he remained undeveloped to the end of his life; and Dr Leavis is right to stigmatise 'his adolescent yearning for a maternal bosom'. "**Retrospect**" (1914), written only one year before his death, celebrates a poet's sexual partner in terms appropriate to a feather-pillow:

> O mother-quiet, breasts of peace
> Where love itself would faint and cease
> And a long watch you would keep;
> And I should sleep, and I should sleep!

Yeats once remarked of Brooke that if he could rid his poems of 'languid sensuousness', he would be a great poet. Be this as it may, Yeats's own influence—that of his Celtic Twilight period—was neither a bracing nor refining one for Brooke. *There's Wisdom in Women* (1913) shows him producing a poor copy of *The Sally Gardens. The Voice* (1909) also utilises Celtic Twilight atmospherics in a serio-comic poem which does not come off.

To Brooke's sentimentality and tendency to imitativeness (leading to inefficiently personalised pastiche) must be added a general patchiness or failure to achieve unity. This he was himself aware of, remarking on his over-addiction to what he called 'romantic devices'—'devices which aim at the beauty or power of some single line or part of the work rather than at the effect of the whole'. As with most young poets, such a cult of the line resulted in poems which were often like the curate's egg. "**In Freiburg Station**" (1912) is a sort of poetic sandwich where the top and bottom slice—

> In Freiburg's station, waiting for a train,
> I saw a Bishop in puce gloves go by

—is of good quality, but where the 'filling' has an artificial flavouring to it. Most of his poems tail off at the end, but "**Sonnet: in time of Revolt**" (1908) presents an example of a rather feebly facetious composition which concludes strongly:

> So shall I curb, so baffle, so suppress
> This too avuncular officiousness,
> Intolerable consanguinity.

What I have stated here has been the case for the prosecution. That there is also a case for the defence might be expected from the frequency with which new and old editions or selections of this poet appear or reappear upon the market. The latest and most esoteric of these is Geoffrey Keynes's *Rupert Brooke: Four Poems*, being 'drafts and fair copies in the author's hand' of four of the poet's most famous pieces (**"The Fish," "Grantchester," "The Dead," "The Soldier"**), together with a Foreword and Introduction by his most loyal and appreciative editor. Whatever his place as a poet, Brooke was a fascinating—though deeply disturbed—personality, and it is therefore right and fitting that those who subscribe to his cult should busy themselves with his remains. The publication in this album-sized folder with stiff bindings of drafts from the Library of King's College, Cambridge, together with a fair copy from the Fitz-William Museum will facilitate the evolution of these familiar pieces as well as proving of interest to those who take classes in practical criticism in schools and universities, since, as Sir Geoffrey observes, 'successive drafts of famous poems are not easy to come by in facsimiles of this quality'. There is much here which any defence counsel for Brooke might find convenient to employ.

Derek Stanford (essay date 1975)

SOURCE: "How Bad was Rupert Brooke? Part 2" in *Books & Bookmen,* Vol. 20, No. 8, May, 1975, pp. 50-1.

[*In the following essay, published as the second installment of Stanford's essay, he deems Brooke's poetry important during his time, but not in the realm of contemporary literature.*]

In *Rupert Brooke: Four Poems* Sir Geoffrey Keynes remarks on the poet's tendency to preserve any small scrap or draft of a poem. The two factors behind this retention were, he believes, laziness (making disposal too troublesome a business) or vanity (inducing thoughts of posthumous fame). Just how well, one might ask, were these conceits of immortality justified?

To measure the degree of success or failure towards which these little scraps of paper point, we have to take Brooke on his own terms and assess him on his merits in writing a quite conscious poetry of youth. This, of course, means not merely seeking to measure how far he incapsulated this personal youth-cult in words but how far he expressed it in words which remain memorable. To exclude from our minds, in the judging of Brooke, all other considerations is not as easy at it may seem. Ever since Matthew Arnold's time, we have, almost automatically, looked to poetry to provide a sort of religious surrogate ('More and more', wrote Arnold in 1880, 'mankind will discover that we have to turn to poetry to interpret life for us, to console us, to sustain us. Without poetry, our science will appear incomplete; and most of what now passes with us for religion and philosophy will be replaced by poetry'). Whether Arnold was right or wrong about this, his idea obtained the widest currency; and such a notion is specifically unsuitable in helping us assess Brooke's achievement. Of

the English poets of Romanticism, Arnold has said that 'they did not know enough', while Lytton Strachey, once a close friend of Brooke, commented contemptuously on his 'academic inadequacy'. In connection with this, it is interesting to see the answer Brooke gave Frances Cornford when she asked him for his 'View of Life'. 'Life', he replied, 'as it appears to me, is a chain of sensations and experiences (thoughts and colours, wind, food, and talk) . . . I care not greatly if they 'exist', or if the whole is only my dream or another's. All I know is these sensations and experiences, I cannot prove that I know them'. Such an impressionist's credo as this would not have impressed the followers of Arnold.

There are three phases in Brooke's poetry of youth: the decadent, the ironic, the patriotic. In the first, he plays the sedulous ape to Swinburne and Dowson, exercising his technique but producing little authentic poetry of his own (though one must certainly allot marks to **"Desertion"** for the virtuosity of its internal rhyming). In the second, he is doing two things: attacking a large body of verse written in the pseudo-sublime-and-spiritual manner, as well as protecting his own thin-skinned and self-conscious emotions. Of the verse of his friend Frances Cornford and her school, he wrote that 'they are known as the Heart-criers, because they believed poetry ought to be short, simple, naïve and a cry from the heart; the sort of thing an inspired only child might utter if it was in the habit of posing to its elders. They object to my poetry as unreal, affected, complex, "literary", and full of long words'. English poetry certainly stood in need of some such reversion from the 'soulful' ideal; and Brooke, whose intimacy with Donne was daily increasing, helped a little to establish a more 'disinfected' way of writing; though his own combination of the romantic and ironic was by no means always successful. At the same time, this cult of irony and the anti-romantic must be seen as an aspect of Brooke's own inhibited emotions. 'I think it's hard', wrote Lytton Strachey to him, 'that you should have erected the preposterous convention by which no one may ever be serious unless he's satirical, for fear of being considered "squashy" or "sentimental"'; but this convention was an armour Brooke could seldom dispense with till he came to write his *1914* sonnets. It is in this second phase of his work—ironic or semi-ironic—that nearly all of his best work is contained.

The third phase—all too brief—is, of course, the patriotic in which irony and emotional inhibition are completely transcended. Brooke, who found it difficult to be forthcoming and single-minded in the genuine expression of a *personal* relationship, found himself suddenly unshackled when it came to acting out on paper his feelings in a *national* context. These famous *1914* sonnets are also to be seen as a conscious extension of Brooke's cult of youth. In them, an element of world-weariness and certainly a touch of the death-wish ('Come and be killed. It will be fun', he wrote to a friend at the time) assume a chivalric dress. Brooke's third phase presents the poet as the young 'parfait knight', a sacrifice predominantly pure and unspotted. Whatever one may think of these last poems qua poems, their rhetorical utility-value to Britain at the off-set of war cannot be over-estimated. What Churchill's oratory achieved in 1940 was achieved by Brooke twenty-five years earlier. Their *poetic* quality I shall return to later.

Of Brooke's pseudo-decadent poems, the best by far is **"Wagner"**—the idea of which might well have been drawn from Aubrey Beardsley's drawing *The Wagnerites* (where one man, with almost 'hairless face' sits among 'women in a crowded place'—the only male in evidence). It is more to the point, however, to group **"Wagner"** with the ironic poems of the second phase, particularly those pieces which Brooke deliberately spoke of as his ' "unpleasant" poems', and of which the most obvious example is **"A Channel Passage"** ('I don't claim great credit for [it]: but the point of it was . . ."serious" '). Nor should the legerdemain of **"Dawn"** ('Opposite me two Germans snore and sweat') be forgotten. Lighter in kind but working along the same lines of romantic disintoxication is the piece of deliberated bathos **"Sonnet Reversed."** However irritating Lytton Strachey may have found Brooke's satirical pose, one can see that, even in fairly good poems, flaws appeared when he lowered his guard. Even such a late composition as *The Busy Heart* (1913) is weakened by the capital letter abstractions 'Love', 'Wisdom', 'Song'; and by such an old-fashioned apostrophe as 'O heart'. One year before his death, Brooke had still failed to break himself of this lazy sentimental shorthand. **"Retrospect"** (1914) shows him—in the first verse-paragraph—coming nearer to an understanding of aspects of feminine psychology. It shows him, too, advancing from irony to a sense of paradox:

> In your stupidity I found
> The sweet hush after a sweet sound

But even this poem is marred by sentimental abstractions:

> Wisdom slept within your hair,
> And Long-Suffering was there,
> And, in the flowering of your dress,
> Undiscerning Tenderness.

If Brooke declared himself the enemy of the sentimental, it was because he knew he was deeply infected.

Of the purely ironic poems belonging to Brooke's second phase **"Heaven,"** with its clever travesty of Christian Platonic thought, is the neatest. The problem of a realm of Pure Ideas, an aftermath of Permanent Forms is pondered over by the fish:

> And, sure the reverent eye must see
> A Purpose in Liquidity.
> We darkly know, by Faith we cry,
> The future is not Wholly Dry.
> Mud into mud!—Death eddies near—
> Not here the appointed End, not here!
> But somewhere, beyond Space and Time,
> Is wetter water, slimier slime.

A few months before his death, Brooke described himself as 'a cheerful atheist', and **"Heaven"** is one of the wittiest

parodies (though hardly a study in depth) of what to many must seem the unwarranted nature of religious thinking. **"Tiare Tahiti,"** written on the same theme one year later, seems to me less successful since it attempts a more lyrical and 'serious' treatment; its fluent descriptiveness on a higher level than the somewhat banal *carpe diem* hedonism of its thought.

Many of Brooke's pieces assay a blending of the romantic and ironic, but only one is perfectly successful: his finest poem **"The Old Vicarage, Granchester."** It is noteworthy that this was written in 1912, since of the thirty odd pieces contained in the collected poems written later only a small handful come near to it in achieved rightness throughout. This also is all the more puzzling in that Sir Geoffrey Keynes has shown in *Rupert Brooke: Four Poems* that the poet's habit of revision—as evident from manuscripts and drafts—points to a general and progressive improvement. One can only conclude that the felicities of **"Grantchester"** are those that may accompany a happy accident, a windfall of a situation presented to Brooke's imagination at just the very aptest moment. It is a poem of home-sickness which miraculously succeeds in re-creating all the most telling details of the absent scene; more than this, it evokes a 'little world' powerfully personal to the poet: an ethos as well as a topography, a way-of-living and a rural region.

Herbert Read once said that the only true politics were local politics; and perhaps one might go on to argue that the truest patriotism is the most local. Certainly there is much more of that *sense of one's country* in **"Grantchester"** than in those perfervid lines of **"The Soldier."** The whole countryside of the Granta—an image of the river and its environs—is potently present in the poem which Brooke was inspired to write in Berlin. The words 'England' and 'English' are used six times in **"The Soldier,"** but in each case could be replaced by 'Germany' or 'German' without any loss of meaning. Of the *specific* feeling of his own country, there is nothing in this poem. It is one of those universalized statements of patriotic feeling whose application is interchangeable.

"Grantchester" is unique, also, in the compound which results from its interaction of irony and romance: a species of light-hearted whimsical fantasy which is both, at times, elegant and nostalgic:

> Curates, long dust, will come and go
> On lissom, clerical, printless toe;
> And oft between the boughs is seen
> The sly shade of a Rural Dean . . .

There are passages, too, of what might be termed Symbolist Impressionism, more subtle and melodic than can elsewhere be found in Brooke's poems:

> A tunnel of green gloom, and sleep
> Deeply above; and green and deep
> The stream mysterious glides beneath,
> Green as a dream and deep as death.

Even such occasional cosy postcard touches as 'little room' or 'little kindly winds' are carried on the current of the poem, barely registering on the reader.

Next to **"Grantchester"** in general appeal—though far beneath it as a well-rounded poem—comes **"The Great Lover,"** a later composition. Little more than a *catalogue of partialities,* the poem has an opening of twenty-five lines ('I have been so great a lover . . .' down to 'Out of the wind of Time, shining and streaming') full of vague emotion and over-blown diction. Then, to the end—but particularly for the next nineteen lines—it becomes an anthology of finely-realised images; verbal simulacra assembled from epithets of the most effective order. A long way behind **"The Fish,"** with its Marvell-like fluency and elegance, **"The Great Lover"** has a firmer hold on the popular imagination, as indeed it deserves to. Few poems have incapsulated so vividly and briefly the texture, shape and scent of a host of homely things.

What was once regarded as the poet's crown—the five *1914* sonnets—are little to our taste today. There are lines and expressions of Elizabethan memorability within them; but what we might loosely call their metaphysic appears both inadequately argued and unsympathetic in its bearing. At the same time, we should remind ourselves of something which liberal-progressive critics have tried to obscure, namely that—as Christopher Hassall put it— 'Brooke never glorified war, but celebrated in exultation the discovery of a moral purpose'. Our fashionable bigots allow to John Cornford what they will not allow to Brooke.

Allen Walker Read (essay date 1982)

SOURCE: "Onomastic Devices in the Poetry of Rupert Brooke," in *Literary Onomastics Studies,* Vol. IX, 1982, pp. 183-208.

[*In the following essay, Read explores the diversity and use of place names in Brooke's poetry.*]

My interest in the subject of Rupert Brooke's use of place names has arisen from the great diversity of opinion concerning his famous sonnet entitled, **"The Soldier."** When I was coming into young manhood, in the early 1920s, in the aftermath of World War I (or "The Great War," as its usual name then was), Rupert Brooke's reputation was extremely high. Most people thrilled to his lines:

If I should die, think only this of me:
　That there's some corner of a foreign field
That is for ever England.

But in the next decade, the 1930s, when the pacifist outlook became ascendant, Brooke's reputation began to fade, and some of my friends poured scorn on his famous lines. It is a false sentimentality, they pointed out, to say that "some corner of a foreign field" should be called "England." They were not willing to accept what I am now calling an "onomastic device."

[In this essay] I wish to consider this and other onomastic devices in the whole context of Rupert Brooke's work, including his famous **"Grantchester"** poem, so filled with delectable English local names.

Though he is most famous for using English names, Rupert Brooke drew upon several other onomastic worlds. One of these worlds was the classical. It is sometimes forgotten, especially in America, how deeply steeped the English schoolboy was in the classics. At Rugby Brooke's principal reading for years was in Greek, and the fantasy life of his class and age was among the Greek gods. When Brooke used names from Greek myth, then, they were not decorative but represented an area where he was deeply at home.

Representative of this use of names are his sonnets on the Trojan war, entitled **"Menelaus and Helen,"** which begin:

Hot through Troy's ruin Menelaus broke
　To Priam's palace, sword in hand. . . .
High sat white Helen, lonely and serene.

At the end of the poem, showing the contrast with their old age, back in Greece, Brooke writes:

Menelaus bold . . .
. . . wonders why on earth he went
Troyward, or why poor Paris ever came.
Oft she weeps, gummy-eyed and impotent;
　Her dry shanks twitch at Paris' mumbled name,
So Menelaus nagged; and Helen cried;
And Paris slept on by Scamander side.

Rupert Brooke had a strange uncertainty about his **"Menelaus and Helen."** He wrote to a close friend (another poet, Frances Cornford) in a letter of July 8, 1910: "I wish I knew what you thought in the middle of the night about Menelaus & Helen. It is probably very important, and would entirely alter the whole of the poems I am just about to write." We do not have her reply, but Brooke's response to it was thoughtful. In a letter later in the same month, he said: "I'll ponder on Helen & Menelaus: pointing out (for what it's worth) . . . that the last line of the first sonnet, has a touch of a giggle behind it, perhaps, in some lights—though that probably makes the offence worse. Thanks for what you said about it."

During the last few weeks of his life, on a ship in the Aegean, Brooke returned to this theme and wrote:

They say Achilles in the darkness stirred,
And . . . Hector, his old enemy,
Moved the great shades that were his limbs.

　　Death and Sleep
Bear many a young Sarpedon home.

And Priam and his fifty sons
Wake all amazed, and hear the guns,
　And shake for Troy again.

From this ship, in a letter of March 12, 1915, he wrote presciently to the actress Cathleen Nesbitt: "And my eyes fell on the holy Land of Attica. So I can die."

The ancient world provided other exotic names, as in his poem **"On the Death of Smet-Smet, the Hippopotamus Goddess,"** described as "Song of a Tribe of the Ancient Egyptians." The name *Babylon* was relegated to a nursery rhyme that he sent to the "problem's page" of the *Westminster Gazette:*

"A Nursery Rhyme"

Up the road to Babylon.
   Down the road to Rome,
The King has gone a-riding gut
   All the way from home.

I have discounted the names that appear in his early poems, **"The Pyramids"** and **"The Bastille,"** because they were written on a set subject in order to win a prize as a schoolboy at Rugby. But his treatment of the Bastille did have a ringing climax, giving dramatic significance to the very name:

And all the resonant heavens clanged one name,
"To the Bastille!" and lo!— . . .
   a great cry goes crashing heavenward,
And the Bastille is won!

He read this on Speech Day in 1905, when he was eighteen years old, and reported in a letter shortly afterward that "half the audience were moved to laughter, the other half to tears."

Another onomastic area for Brooke's use of names was that of continental Europe, because from childhood on he went there on vacations with his family. The first poem he wrote reflecting actual personal experience was in 1907 on a train in Italy between Bologna and Milan, second class. The name *Milan* appears:

      There are . . .
Two hours to dawn and Milan; two hours yet.
   Opposite me two Germans sweat and snore.

And in another poem, *Verona:*

Helen's the hair shuts out from me
   Verona's livid skies.

Brooke seems to have been much attracted by names in Germany, where he spent part of 1912 in learning German and escaping certain English emotional problems. His poem **"In Freiburg Station"** notes:

In Freiburg station, waiting for a train,
I saw a Bishop in puce gloves go by.

Really delightful is his poem **"Travel,"** in which he refers to a set of German town names:

'Twas when I was in Neu Strelitz
I broke my heart in little bits.

So while I sat in the Müritz train
I glued the bits together again.

But when I got to Amerhold
I felt the glue would never hold.

And now that I'm home to Barton Hill,
I know once broken is broken still.

Even in his poem about a little dog, he called on Germanic names:

But this morning he swore, by Odin and Thor
And the Canine Valhalla—he'd stand it no more!

He noted the interchangeability of names in a poem on Easter, sent in a letter to a friend on March 27, 1910, from Rugby:

Easter! the season when One had rebirth Whom some
call Ishtar, some call Mother Earth, And others Jesus,
or Osiris.

I do not know how to classify his use of a star name, as in the following passage:

Could we but . . .
Love moon to moon unquestioning, and be
Like the star Lunisequa, steadfastly
Following the round clear orb of her delight.

When Brooke escaped to the South Seas for several months in 1913 and 1914, recovering from a near nervous breakdown, he met an entirely different onomastic world, and several of his best poems are studded with exotic names from there, especially in personal names. His poem **"Tiare Tahiti"** begins:

Mamua, there awaits a land
Hard for us to understand. . . .
You and Pupure are one,
And Taii, and the ungainly wise.

The name *Pupure* refers to himself, as he explained to his mother in a letter of February 4, 1914: "P. S. They call me *Pupure* here—it means 'fair' in Tahitian—because I have fair hair!"

The young women of Tahiti are further memorialized:

And all lovely things, they say,
Meet in Loveliness again;
Miri's laugh, Teipo's feet
And the hands of Matua, . . .
And Teüra's braided hair.

In Fiji a few weeks later another young woman is referred to:

Heart from heart is all as far,
Fafaia, as star from star.

His poem **"Waikiki"** has the memorable line: "Over the murmurous soft Hawaiian sea."

Rupert Brooke crossed North America twice, but apparently he was not attracted by American names. In a bit of doggerel in a letter of June 21, 1913, from Boston, he wrote:

All the way, from Americay,
My heart goes out to G. and J.

And he mentioned California once in some further doggerel written on shipboard as he was returning to England:

The world's great painter soul, whom we deplore,
Loved California much, but music more.

In mentioning the Pacific Ocean in a letter of October 12, 1913, to the actress Cathleen Nesbitt, on the ship taking him west from San Francisco, he made an onomastic pun. He wrote: "The Pacific has been very pacific. God be thanked!" The place name *Pacific Ocean* has been regarded as the very model of the "misnomer."

But we come now to the onomastic world of England, in which Rupert Brooke was truly at home, by birth, by nurture, and by emotional attachment.

One of his loveliest poems was entitled **"The Chilterns,"** concerning the aftermath of a failed love affair. Though his mood was bitter, he made good use of a number of Midland place names:

Thank God, that's done! and I'll take the road
    Quit of my youth and you,
The Roman road to Wendover
    By Tring and Lilley Hoo,
    As a free man may do.

His use of place names could be satirical, too. His reference to Balham, a suburb of London, calls attention to dull, middle class life. These are the lines:

Ah, the delirious weeks of honeymoon!
    Soon they returned, and, after strange adventures,
Settled at Balham by the end of June. . . .
                                    Still he went
Cityward daily.

A contest was held in the *Westminster Gazette* for parodies of A. E. Housman's "Shropshire Lad," on the occasion of that poet's appointment as Professor of Latin at Cambridge University. Brooke's entry made use of the names of Cambridge colleges, as follows:

Emmanuel, and Magdalene,
    And St. Catherine's, and St. John's,
Are the dreariest places,
    And full of dons.

It will be noted that he left out his own college, King's College, but that omission was remedied in a bit of doggerel that he sent back to a friend, written early in his visit to Canada:

My heart is sick for several things
Only to be found in King's—
I do recall those haunts with tears,
The Backs, the Chapel, and the Rears.

The letters of Rupert Brooke are replete with statements about his love for English place names. To Cathleen Nesbitt in October, 1913, he wrote: "I would like to make a litany of all the things that bind me to the memory of holiness—of peaks. It would run—'The Chilterns—Hampton Court . . . ' and a few more names." Then, in the next year, he wrote again to her from Washington, D. C.: "I sail from New York on May 29: and reach Plymouth (o blessed name o loveliness! Plymouth—was there ever so sweet and droll a sound? Drake's Plymouth! English, western Plymouth! . . . I will make a Litany—by Torquay . . . and by Paignton . . . past Ilsham . . . and Apoledore . . . by Dawlish . . . within sight of Widdecombe . . . by Drewsteignton. . . . And to Exeter. And to Ottery St. Mary . . .) on Friday June 5." As he came closer to his return to England, he burst forth to Edward Marsh, from New York City, concerning—"a day or two before we sight Scilly. Oh! these names!"

In telling about a motor trip from Rugby, in a letter of July, 1914, he dallied with various names: "Finally I chose Hampden-in-Arden. I remembered once passing through a station of that name. And I've always wanted to see the forest of Arden. Hampden-in-Arden. What a name to dream about!" At nearly the same time he wrote on a post card to a poet friend as follows: "It's made me start a poem for you—

The world may go from worse to worst
I shall recline at Chislehurst
And in a neuropathic attitude
Feed my subconsciousness with platitude."

The famous poem on Grantchester, with its rollicking lilt, did not spring forth without forerunners. In a letter of March 27, 1910, to a close friend, Brooke enclosed the following doggerel poem:

This year the ways of Fordingbridge won't see
So meaty and so swift a poet as me
Mouthing undying lines. Down Lyndhurst way
The woods will rub along without us.
                                    Say,
Do you remember . . .   Cranborne Town
By night? and the two inns? the men we met?

His biographer, Christopher Hassall, says of this poem [in *Rupert Brooke,* 1964]: "It was a crude exercise in a style he was to try once again, in very different circumstances, and with more success."

Earlier still, when Brooke was twenty years old, was a doggerel poem to Lulworth, a vacation spot on the south coast in Dorset. In a letter of July, 1907, to a schoolboy friend, he wrote: "Tomorrow I'm going to the most beautiful place in England to work. It is called West Lulworth. I have made seven poems on it, some very fine, and all resting on the fact that Lulworth Cove rhymes with love: a very notable discovery." In a later letter to Geoffrey Keynes, he gave some samples, such as the following:

> Oh give our love to Lulworth Cove,
>   And Lulworth Cliffs and Sea!
> Oh Lulworth Down! Oh Lulworth Town!
>   (The name appeals to me.)
> If we were with you today in Lulworth,
>   How happy we should be!

Rupert Brooke's association with Grantchester began in 1909, when he wanted more solitude than King's College afforded. In a letter of June, 1909, he wrote: "I am still uncertain, a little, whether I may not continue in King's and achieve complete solitude here. If not, I am going to try to get rooms in Grantchester, or further, even. I passionately long to shut myself wholly up, and read only and always." He moved to The Orchard that same month.

His letters thereafter show an increasing love for the place. He wrote in a letter of September 26, 1909, from The Orchard: *The orchard* is golden & melancholy and sleepy & enchanted. I sit neck-deep in dead red leaves." And in a letter of January 2, 1910: ". . . the place where I am happier than anywhere, (*no,* not Cambridge—Grantchester!)" And in a letter of January 20, 1910: "If you know how . . . solitarily happy I am in my hut at Grantchester—and with Spring coming on!"

I understand full well Rupert Brooke's feeling, because many of the happiest days in my own life have been spent in Grantchester. Back in the 1930s I frequently went to England to do research at the British Museum, but I took a day off now and then for an outing in Cambridge. I would punt on the river up to Grantchester, have tea at the Orchard, and then go on to Byron's Pool for a swim. In those old days the swimming was good below the wooden dam, before the recent cement dam was built. And I went again to Grantchester, this time sharing its loveliness with my wife, on the way back from the International Congress on Onomastics at Cracow, Poland.

When Brooke went to Germany in the spring of 1912, he was dogged by a certain homesickness. In a letter of April, 1912, he wrote on a train to the girl he was in love with: "I'm just passing through Potsdam. I've a fancy you may be just now, in Grantchester. I envy you, frightfully. That river and the chestnuts—come back to me a lot. Tea on the lawn. Just wire to me, and we'll spend the summer there."

In May, sitting in the Café des Westens of Berlin, behind its big window, he composed the first draft of the Grantchester poem in a pocket account book. He later told his girl friend that the germ of the poem was in the lines:

> Ah God! to see the branches stir
> Across the moon at Grantchester!

They may have been the first composed.

The title was originally "Home," but when it was first printed in the King's College magazine, *Basileon,* in June, 1912, it was changed to **"Fragments from a Poem to be entitled 'The Sentimental Exile'."** Then the final title, **"The Old Vicarage, Grantchester,"** was used when it was reprinted in book form for the first time in *Georgian Poetry* (London, 1912). The change of title was made at the suggestion of Edward Marsh. His biographer, Christopher Hassall, comments: "This was perhaps a pity, since the poem lost its clue to the key in which it was pitched." But was it, I would ask, really "sentimental"? I do not agree with Hassall, for the place names give it a "down to earth" quality that takes off the curse of being sentimental.

The first draft in the account book still survives, and when he copied it for publication he made very few changes. Written in the margin was a list of the villages in the vicinity of Cambridge that he intended to put in:

He originally wrote as a couplet:

> At Over they fling oaths at one,
> And worse than oaths at Comberton.

But he changed *Comberton* to *Trumpington,* and so *Comberton* was left out altogether. It is a happy circumstance that he used *Trumpington,* because of its echoes of Chaucer.

Some of his other changes are amusing. He omitted four lines that described the people of Grantchester:

> And so at General Elections
> They have the strength of their convictions.
> The atheists vote Liberal
> And many do not vote at all.

The famous concluding couplet:

> . . . yet
> Stands the Church clock at ten to three?
> And is there honey still for tea?

originally had the clock standing at "half past three," as the clock during most of 1911 had actually been stuck at that time. His biographer notes that "the poet took only forty minutes' worth of license!" After his death the suggestion was made that the church clock should be set permanently at "ten to three" as a memorial to him.

His own attitude toward the poem can be gathered from his letters to friends. Shortly after writing it, he reported to Frances Cornford, his fellow-poet: "I scrawled in a Café a very long poem about Grantchester, that seemed to me to have some pleasant silly passages. I sent it to the King's May week Magazine Basileon." And then on August 21, 1912, to a woman friend: ". . . did you see—a long lanky lax-limbed set of verses I wrote about Grantchester and published in a King's magazine?"

His writing about Grantchester actually made a difference in his plans. While on a train *en route* to the Hague to see an art exhibit, he wrote in a letter of June 24, 1912: "I've determined to come to England again. There's not much point in being anywhere—but writing about Grantchester gave me a bit of *Heimweh;* & your statement confirmed my dim remembrances that England held some nicish spots." The poem was appreciated in Grantchester itself. He noted in a letter of July 19, 1912, to Maynard Keynes: ". . . the youth of Grantchester quote my local patriotic poetry to me as I ride by on a bicycle." It was immediately much praised. While it was still called "The Sentimental Exile," his friend St. John Lucas wrote to him as follows: "Well, it's a lovely poem. I'm not sure the line I like best isn't 'From Haslingfield to Madingley.' You certainly have the art of using proper names."

Brooke was not afraid to parody his own work. In a letter on January 9, 1913, from Cornwall, to Geoffrey Keynes, he wrote, still showing his love for English place names:

I have written nothing for months, till I came here, except a fragment which I composed soon after I left you in September (August?): it's called **'Motoring'.**

The part of motoring I like
Is luncheon near the Devil's Dyke.
—The country's really very fair,
From beyond Ditchling Beacon there:
The view is very *sweet* and very *Pretty,* from there
   to Chanctonbury:
But still, the part of it *I* like
Is luncheon near the Devil's Dyke. . . .

It went on a long time: but I omitted to write it down: & have now forgotten it.

Even more of a parody was written on the ship taking him to America in May, 1913. Again writing to Keynes, he gave a sample: "I've already begun an interminable series of poems about England, entitled *Nostalgia.*

'In England oh the cauliflowers
They blow through all the English hours.
And all New York's clam chowder is
Less dear than Rugby strawberries.'

I can keep it up for days."

It remains now to deal with Rupert Brooke's most famous poem beginning, "If I should die." When he says, "there's some corner of a foreign field / That is for ever England," I am at a loss to find a good name to describe this onomastic device. In a way, it is a form of personification, raising "England" into an anthropomorphized being. Brooke's principal biographer holds that for Brooke "England" became a Platonic entity. Since I do not believe in the existence of Platonic entities, I attribute the effect of the word *England* to a linguistic abstraction that gained strong emotional associations by its usage in a habitual social setting. Brooke himself was wrestling with this problem when he wrote to the actress Cathleen Nesbitt, a few

months before he composed the sonnet, speaking of "some idea called England." As he said in the letter: "All those people at the front who are fighting—muddledly enough—for some idea called England—it's some faint shadowing of the things you can give that they have in their heart to die for."

The sonnet was begun on Wednesday, December 23, 1914, and finished early in January, while Brooke was on leave from the Hood Battalion. He had already experienced a disastrous expedition in Belgium and was looking forward to another foray in the eastern Mediterranean at Gallipoli. In his only excursion into autobiography, he contributed a prose essay to the *New Statesman* of August 29, 1914, under the title, "An Unusual Young Man." He described a "friend" (who was clearly himself), giving his feelings at the outbreak of war. This passage is especially significant: "Something was growing in his heart, and he couldn't tell what. But as he thought 'England and Germany' the word 'England' seemed to flash like a line of foam. . . . His astonishment grew as the full flood of 'England' swept over him on from thought to thought. He felt the triumphant helplessness of a lover." However cloudily, *England* is being treated as a linguistic abstraction.

Brooke's way of talking about "English thoughts" is also presaged in an earlier letter. I refer to his noble lines:

            . . . this heart . . .
   A pulse in the eternal mind, no less
   Gives somewhere back the thoughts by England
      given.

While at sea between Samoa and San Francisco, in a letter of April 5, 1914, he wrote the following rather enigmatic, but revealing, passage: "Lately, I have been having English thoughts—thoughts certainly of England—and even, faintly, yes, English thoughts—grey, quiet, misty, rather mad, slightly moral, shy & lovely thoughts. But very faintly so. England is too vague & hidden & fragmentary & forgotten a thing."

Out of the welter of English patriotic poetry, two sources have been noted that may have had an actual influence on Brooke. One of these is William E. Henley's poem "Pro Rege Nostro," written in January, 1892. It begins:

What have I done for you,
   England, my England?
What is there I would not do,
   England, my own? . . .

Ever the faith endures
   England, my England:—
'Take us and break us: we are yours,'
   England, my own!

There is considerable bombast here, and it is very different in spirit from Brooke's poem, but it at least shows the tug of the name *England.*

It can be shown that the Henley poem played some part in Brooke's life. In his last term as a schoolboy at Rugby, in 1906, he gave a paper before a local society on modern poetry, in which he discussed Henley, who stood, he felt, for what was best in imperialism. As Brooke wrote: "One may hate, as I do, the *way* in which he loved England, but one cannot deny the sincerity of his love and the power of his expression of it." Then he quoted the whole of the "England, my England" poem. His biographer says of this theme—"one of his own war sonnets would be a variation" of it.

Two years later, then an undergraduate at Cambridge, he wrote to a French friend, Jacques Raverat, in a letter of February, 1908: "And I am glad to hear, moreover, that you are coming (or have come?) to the only land in the world; as I increasingly affirm. 'England! my England!' in the superb words of the late W. E. Henley; the home of Freedom, of Blank Verse, of The Best People . . ." These last phrases have a strong satirical element, to take the curse off such naive patriotism. A further reference to Henley was given in a letter of April 15-20, 1909, to Geoffrey Fry: "I envy you your Italy. . . . Yet England ('my England' [Henley]), is to use an old-fashioned word, nice."

The second important forerunner of Brooke's poem was one by Hilaire Belloc, in his small volume of 1912, *The Four Men*. It concerned a character who was deeply rooted in his home piece of earth. Brooke revealed to a friend that he had committed it to memory. This stanza by Belloc is significant:

> He does not die that can bequeath
> Some influence to the land he knows,
> Or dares, persistent, interwreath
> Love permanent with the wild hedgerows;
> > He does not die, but still remains
> > Substantiate with his darling plains.

These lines, "He . . . still remains / Substantiate with his darling plains," carry the same message as Brooke's "corner of a foreign field / That is for ever England."

Another forerunner might appear to be in certain poems of Rudyard Kipling. However, Kipling was held in considerable disfavor by the social class in which Brooke moved, and it is unlikely that Brooke was susceptible to his influence.

Even in the final weeks before his tragic death on a ship in the Aegean, on April 23, 1915, at the age of 27 years and nine months, Brooke was engaged on an extensive **"Ode—Threnody on England."** A few days before his death he wrote to his friend Edward Marsh in a letter of April, 1915: "My long poem is to be about the existence—& non-locality—of England. And it contains the line—'In Avons of the heart her rivers run.' Lovely, isn't it?"

After his death, a fellow-soldier, W. Denis Browne, wrote concerning the "ode he was working on," saying: "But it must have been mostly in his head, for he spoke of it as being a great new thing he was doing. He quoted once to me the line—(In Avons of the heart her rivers run)—as being one he was delighted with: 'supreme' he said."

This line that pleased Brooke so much, "In Avons of the heart her rivers run," exemplifies some very complicated onomastic devices that are hard to analyze. A river name (in itself meaning "river" in Celtic) is generalized into a plural and then attributed to the human heart.

Only a few other fragments were returned, along with some personal effects, from the Aegean. The lines that survive have great nobility:

> And she for whom we die, she the undying
> Mother of men
> England! . . .

> She was in his eyes, but he could not see her,
> And he was England, but he knew her not.

Jon Stallworthy (essay date 1990)

SOURCE: "Who Was Rupert Brooke?" in *Critical Survey*, Vol. 2, No. 2, 1990, pp. 185-93.

[*In the following essay, Stallworthy challenges the prevailing impression of Brooke as a tormented poet.*]

This may seem an odd question to ask on a poet's hundredth birthday, but it was one asked by his oldest friend forty years after his death. Geoffrey Keynes, having selected and edited his letters, had just sent a set of proofs to each of his fellow literary trustees and to a few of Brooke's other friends. To his consternation, several responded with horror, saying in effect: 'The letters to me show the *real* Rupert, but his posturing in the others distorts the portrait out of all recognition.' In vain did Keynes point out that they each regarded the letters to him or to her (Frances Cornford was one of those most troubled) as expressing the *real* Rupert and shook their heads over the rest. In vain did he remind them of Brooke's undergraduate letter to *him* saying 'I attempt to be "all things to all men"; rather "cultured" among the cultured, faintly athletic among athletes, a little blasphemous among blasphemers, slightly insincere to myself . . .' So strong was the feeling among the poet's friends that Keynes's selection misrepresented him that the book was put on ice, and Christopher Hassall was commissioned to write a biography that would reveal the *real* Rupert Brooke.

What is interesting here is not that he adopted a different tone in writing to different people—we all do that—but that they cared so passionately that the world should know the *real* Rupert, *their* Rupert. It is worth remembering, too, who they were, these friends who valued him so highly; friends that included the Asquiths, the Cornfords, Hugh Dalton, E. M. Forster, David Garnett, Edmund Gosse, Henry James, Geoffrey and Maynard Keynes, Cathleen Nesbitt, Stanley Spencer, Edward Thomas, and Virginia Woolf.

Looking for an answer to the question 'who was Rupert Brooke?' I went back to the testimony of his friends and found a common denominator that had hitherto escaped my attention—and the attention of most who never met him. Geoffrey and Margaret Keynes used to say how funny he was, and in a letter of 1905 Rupert asks Geoffrey 'Have I not often made you laugh?' Frances Cornford wrote, in a poem entitled 'Rupert Brooke':

> Perhaps
> A thousand years ago some Greek boy died,
> So lovely-bodied, so adored, so young,
> Like us they grieved and treasured little things
> (And laughed with tears remembering his laughter)

[As quoted in Hassall's *Rupert Brooke: A Biography,* 1964] David Garnett remembered him as 'tall and well built, loosely put together, with a careless animal grace and a face made for smiling and sudden laughter': while A. C. Benson recalled him laughing 'rather huddled, in his chair'. [As quoted in John Lehmann's *Rupert Brooke: His Life and Legend,* 1980] Sybil Pye wrote: 'His gay unembarrassed laugh of pleasure still rings in one's head—one knew so well the sound of it.'

Brooke himself set great store by laughter, writing to Jacques Raverat from the South Seas:

> laughter is the very garland on the head of friendship.
> I will not love, and I will not be loved. But I will have
> friends round me continually, all the days of my life,
> and in whatever lands I may be. So we shall laugh and
> eat and sing and go great journeys . . .

Returning to England in 1914, he was introduced to Lascelles Abercrombie and reported to Ka Cox: 'He laughs very well'. There is much talk of laughter in Brooke's letters and much occasion for it. It is hard not to warm to the Rugby schoolboy who, suffering from pink-eye, explains that 'The disease comes of gazing too often upon Butterfield's architecture'; or to the dying man who, informed that Dean Inge had read his sonnet **'The Soldier'** aloud in St Pauls, praising it but saying 'it fell somewhat short of Isaiah's vision', responded that 'he was sorry Inge did not think him quite as good as Isaiah.' I suspect a fear that this Brooke—the laughing Brooke—would be overshadowed by the tormented lover may have been a factor in the adverse reaction to Keynes's original *Selected Letters.* The figure to emerge from Hassall's biography (1964) and Keynes's edition of *The Letters* (1968) was much more complicated, confused, and credible than the 'young Apollo' of Marsh's Memoir in the **Collected Poems** (1918). Most critical attention since has tended to concentrate on the tormented lover of 1911-13, losing sight of the happier man who, in the years before and after, wrote the poems by which he is today remembered.

The quality Brooke looked for in his friends he celebrated in a review of the 1912 edition of his favourite poet:

> as Donne saw everything through his intellect, it
> follows, in some degree, that he could see everything
> humorously. He could see it the other way, too. But
> humour was always at his command. It was part of his
> realism; especially in the bulk of his work, his poems

dealing with love. There is no true lover but has sometimes laughed at his mistress, and often at himself. But you would not guess that from the love-songs of many poets. Their poems run the risk of looking a little flat. They are unreal by the side of Donne. For while his passion enabled him to see the face of love, his humour allowed him to look at it from the other side. So we behold his affairs in the round.

But it must not appear that his humour, or his wit, and his passion, alternated. The other two are his passion's handmaids. It should not be forgotten that Donne was one of the first great English satirists, and the most typical and prominent figure of a satirical age. Satire comes with the Bible of truth in one hand and the sword of laughter in the other.

In an earlier essay, Brooke had quoted the remark of Hugo to Baudelaire, 'You have created a new shudder,' and went on to suggest that one might say of Ernest Dowson, 'He has created a new sigh.' Similarly, one might say of Brooke that he created a new laugh. Laughter is audible in no less than a third of the poems and fragments in Keynes's edition, a statistic doubly surprising given the nature of his central subject.

This emerges in one of his earliest extant poems, **'It Is Well'**, written when he was sixteen. It begins:

> Nay, love, I weep not, but laugh o'er my dead,
> My dreams long perished; though I forfeited
> To save thee sorrow, joy unutterable—
> I would not have it otherwise; 'twas well.

I suspect *that* laughter was meant to sound despairing, but it is possible to hear it also as self-mocking in wry acknowledgement of the nineties' archaic diction, the dreams and sorrow borrowed from Yeats and others. The laughter and death, life and death, juxtaposed in the first line re-emerge in the poem's last stanza:

> And when our Death dawns pale, and we must go,
> Though infinite space may part us, this I know;
> If, looking upward through the bars of Hell,
> I see that face in Heaven, it will be well.

We notice, however, that the vision is conditional: '*If,* looking upward . . .' The speaker may not—or may not be able to—look upward.

Two years later, flaunting the fashionable nihilism of the decadent poets of the nineties, Brooke addresses one of their favourite themes in his poem **'Man'**:

> Time drew towards its ending: everywhere
> Bent with their little sorrows and old pain,
> Men cried to God.

As Apocalypse approaches, the poet records that cry:

> Why are we vexed with yearning? Surely it is
> Enough for us to crouch about the fire

And laugh the irretrievable hours away,
Heedless of what may wait us in the gloom,
The muttering night beyond? Yet though we strive
So to live in the present and forget,
Ever the voice returning wakes again
The old insatiate yearning in our hearts,
Whispering words incomprehensible,
Infinity, Eternity, and—God.

Man's lament ends with a call to the incomprehensible Godhead for an incomprehensibly 'eternal End'. Brooke's letters of this time play with eschatological themes: 'With advancing years I find one's thoughts turn increasingly towards the Hereafter and the Serious Things of Life.' And again: 'I love to think of myself as seated on the greyness of Lethe's banks, and showering ghosts of epigrams and shadowy paradoxes upon the assembled wan-eyed dead.' A sonnet of this year, beginning **'When on my night of life the Dawn shall break,'** shows him playing once again with just such a fantasy. The beloved is more sharply imagined than in the earlier dawn of **'It Is Well.'**

She now has a 'brave smile', 'bright swift eyes', and a Yeatsian, Pre-Raphaelite, 'pale cloud of tossing hair', but the earlier conditional ('If looking upward . . . I see that face in Heaven') reappears reformulated:

Only—I fear me that I may not find
That brave smile . . .

The death of God is a recurrent theme of Brooke's early poems, but the Great Incomprehensible (and His Mother) return in a sonnet of 1907, **'My Song'**, to preside over another vision of the last dawn, another version of the beloved's entry into the Hereafter:

Yes, in the wonder of the last day-break,
God's Mother, on the threshold of His house,
   Shall welcome in your white and perfect soul,
Kissing your brown hair softly for my sake;
   And God's own hand will lay, as aureole,
My song, a flame of scarlet, on your brows.

We are not told whether the poet is to be present at the investiture, but he is certainly and centrally present in the final retake of this scene, a sonnet written in April 1909:

Oh! Death will find me, long before I tire
   Of watching you; and swing me suddenly
Into the shade and loneliness and mire
   Of the last land! There, waiting patiently,

One day, I think, I'll feel a cool wind blowing,
   See a slow light across the Stygian tide,
And hear the Dead about me stir, unknowing,
   And tremble. And *I* shall know that you have
   died,

And watch you, a broad-browed and smiling dream,
   Pass, light as ever, through the lightless host,
Quietly ponder, start, and sway, and gleam—
   Most individual and bewildering ghost!—

And turn, and toss your brown delightful head
Amusedly, among the ancient Dead.

This is a dramatic advance on anything Brooke had written before—a fact he recognised by putting it first in his first book of poems. The voice is a relaxed voice of 1909 rather than a literary voice of the 1890s. The speaker is now at the centre of the poem, and the solemnity of the occasion—a solemnity that had made the earlier poems portentous—is held in check by the good-humoured tone and the fact that the *ghost* is good-humoured, a 'smiling dream'. Seen first as 'a slow light' in the shade of the last land, she passes 'light as ever, through the lightless host', her light and lightness lightly re-emphasised when he sees her

. . . turn, and toss your brown delightful head
Amusedly, among the ancient Dead.

Amusedly—the key word—is quintessential Brooke, as is the ironic counterpoint on which the poem comes to rest. Alliteration links that adverb to 'the ancient Dead' (just as the new ghost is linked to the old), but the fact that she views them *amusedly* mocks and calls in question their ancient authority.

Brooke himself continually questioned, and increasingly denied, the ancient and modern authorities, positing the existence of an afterlife. His handling of this theme takes on the character of a debate. **'The Hill'**, a sonnet of 1910, rejects the comforting mythology of **'Oh! Death will find me'**. The setting is *this* world, which the poet endows with the splendour ascribed by others to the *next*:

                              'And when we die
   All's over that is ours; and life burns on
Through other lovers, other lips,' said I,
   'Heart of my heart, our heaven is now, is won!'

'We are Earth's best, that learnt her lesson here.
   Life is our cry. We have kept the faith!' we said;
   'We shall go down with unreluctant tread
Rose-crowned into the darkness!' . . . Proud we
   were,
And laughed, that had such brave true things to
   say.
—And then you suddenly cried, and turned away.

Brooke's rhetoric here gets the better of him, and the turn from laughter to tears is markedly less successful than the earlier sonnet's turn from solemnity to amusement.

It is generally agreed that his best period was his *wanderjahr* in the South Seas, and finishing there the poem **'Mutability'** begun in London, he puts both sides of the debate. The ancient Dead are quoted first:

They say there's a high windless world and
   strange,
   Out of the wash of days and temporal tide,
   Where Faith and Good, Wisdom and Truth abide,
Eterna corpora, subject to no change.

The counter-argument, however, carries the day and, as in so many of Brooke's other poems, *laugh* seems synonymous with *life*:

> Dear, we know only that we sigh, kiss, smile;
>   Each kiss lasts but the kissing; and grief goes
>   over;
>   Love has no habitation but the heart.
> Poor straws! on the dark flood we catch awhile,
>   Cling, and are borne into the night apart.
>   The laugh dies with the lips, 'Love' with the
>   lover.

The debate continues in two other sonnets of 1913. **'Suggested by some of the Proceedings of the Society for Psychical Research'** and **'Clouds'** both appear to reject the idea of a remote heaven but settle for an intermediate state not perhaps so very different. In the sestet of **'Clouds',** the ancient Dead and the speaker seem to agree:

> They say that the Dead die not, but remain
>   Near to the rich heirs of their grief and mirth.
>   I think they ride the calm mid-heaven, as these,
> In wise majestic melancholy train,
>   And watch the moon, and the still-raging seas,
>   And men, coming and going on the earth.

The authorities, the ancient Dead, are cited again in the poem **'Heaven'**, only now it is not '*They* say' but '*Fish* say':

> Oh! never fly conceals a hook,
> Fish say, in the Eternal Brook,
> But more than mundane weeds are there,
> And mud, celestially fair;
> Fat caterpillars drift around,
> And Paradisal grubs are found;
> Unfading moths, immortal flies,
> And the worm that never dies.
> And in that Heaven of all their wish,
> There shall be no more land, say fish.

This is a more cunning version of the debate than any hitherto, in that the authorities seem to have the floor to themselves, but of course their testimony is invalidated by the speaker's satiric voice. The targets of his satire are generally taken to be Platonism and Christianity, but there is I think another target: that signalled by 'the Eternal Brook', the poet so attracted to representations of an afterlife. This poem is not only a more cunning but also a more successful version of the Eternal Brooke's eternal debate, partly as a result of his switch to the shorter line. The slow march of the iambic pentameter encouraged his tendency to indulge in what, with characteristic self-mockery, he described as 'the purest Nineteenth Century grandiose thoughts, about the Destiny of Man, the Irresistibility of Fate, the Doom of Nations, the fact that Death awaits us All, and so forth. Wordsworth Redivivus. Oh dear! Oh dear!'

He continued to have such grandiose thoughts, but in his best poems he engages them with 'the sword of laughter'.

Both the tone and the rhetorical structure of **'Tiare Tahiti'** owe something to Marvell's 'To His Coy Mistress'. Brooke's mistress, the Mamua of his poem, was not coy so he does not have to persuade her to surrender to his advances, but he opens with another playful vision of a Platonic eternity:

> Mamua, when our laughter ends,
> And hearts and bodies, brown as white,
> Are dust about the doors of friends,
> Or scent a-blowing down the night,
> Then, oh! then, the wise agree,
> Comes our immortality.
> Mamua, there waits a land
> Hard for us to understand.
> Out of time, beyond the sun,
> All are one in Paradise,
> You and Pupure are one,
> And Tau, and the ungainly wise.
> There the Eternals are, and there
> The Good, the Lovely, and the True,
> And Types, whose earthly copies were
> The foolish broken things we knew;
> There is the Face, whose ghosts we are;
> The real, the never-setting Star;
> And the Flower, of which we love
> Faint and fading shadows here;
> Never a tear, but only Grief;
> Dance, but not the limbs that move;
> Songs in Song shall disappear;
> Instead of lovers, Love shall be;
> For hearts, Immutability;
> And there, on the Ideal Reef,
> Thunders the Everlasting Sea!

The first movement of the poem puts the arguments of 'the wise' but simultaneously undermines them. Its conclusion:

> And there's an end, I think, of kissing
> When our mouths are one with Mouth

is at once more light-hearted and more tender than the comparable conclusion of Marvell's first movement:

> The grave's a fine and private place,
> But none, I think, do there embrace.

The wise had celebrated

> Types, whose earthly copies were
> The foolish broken things we knew

but in the poem's second movement Brooke introduces a re-evaluation of their terms. Their wisdom is the 'foolishness' to be washed away 'in the water's soft caress', the Pacific tide that hears and answers 'the calling of the moon', unlike 'the Everlasting Sea' of the Platonic realm where 'moons are lost in endless Day'. The poem earns its conclusion—'There's little comfort in the wise'—and convinces us (I doubt if Mamua needed convincing) that there is more than comfort in those 'foolish things' that time will break.

'Tiare Tahiti' is dated February 1914. Brooke left Tahiti in April, writing to Cathleen Nesbitt:

> It was only yesterday, when I knew that the Southern Cross had left me, that I suddenly realised that I'd left behind those lovely places and lovely people, perhaps for ever. I reflected that there was surely nothing else like them in this world and very probably nothing in the next . . .

Four months later, the outbreak of war prompted a general resurgence of 'grandiose thoughts about the Destiny of Man, the Irresistibility of Fate, the Doom of Nations, the fact that Death awaits us All, and so forth'. In South Africa, Isaac Rosenberg, envisioning an exhausted civilisation rejuvenated by conflict, ended his poem 'On Receiving News of the War':

> O! ancient crimson curse!
> Corrode, consume.
> Give back this universe
> Its pristine bloom.

In France, Wilfred Owen used the same word at the same time to develop a similar natural image in the sestet of his sonnet **'1914'**:

> For after Spring had bloomed in early Greece,
> And Summer blazed her glory out with Rome,
> An Autumn softly fell, a harvest home,
> A slow grand age, and rich with all increase.
> But now, for us, wild Winter, and the need
> Of sowings for new Spring, and blood for seed.

In England, Brooke began work on the first of the 1914 sonnets that were to make his name. Paradoxically entitled **'Peace'**, it celebrates the discovery of a cause, a vision resembling Owen's and Rosenberg's: the regeneration of 'a world grown old and cold and weary'. The solemnity of the occasion prompted grandiose thoughts and, forsaking Marvellian tetrameters for Tennysonian pentameters, Brooke yielded to the temptations of a high style that in his better poems he had resisted. Despite the change of style, however, his subject remains the same: the place of life and laughter after death. His fourth sonnet, **'The Dead'**, comes to the same conclusion as **'Tiare Tahiti'**:

> These had seen movement, and heard music; known
>   Slumber and waking; loved; gone proudly friended;
> Felt the quick stir of wonder; sat alone;
>   Touched flowers and furs and cheeks. All this is ended.
>
> There are waters blown by changing winds to laughter
> And lit by the rich skies, all day. And after,
>   Frost, with a gesture, stays the waves that dance
> And wandering loveliness. He leaves a white
>   Unbroken glory, a gathered radiance,
> A width, a shining peace, under the night.

What is new in this is the closing metaphor's implication that human laughter has returned to its natural source, is now a part of nature. Although 'Frost, with a gesture, stays the waves that dance', sun and moon will in time release them and the changing winds blow them to laughter once again.

Brooke's fifth and most famous sonnet reverts, in its sestes, to the Platonic position he had so often mocked:

> And think, this heart, all evil shed away,
>   A pulse in the eternal mind, no less
>   Gives somewhere back the thoughts by England given

'The Soldier' would not have had the success it has had if it were not, in its way, a good poem, but I wonder whether some of the unease that over the years has crept into its readers' response may not be related to a lack of conviction on the part of its author as he tried to convince himself of the existence of an afterlife in which he did not believe. The irony is, of course, that whether or not Brooke *is* now 'A pulse in the eternal mind', he *does* give back, in the best of his poems:

> . . . the thoughts by England given;
> Her sights and sounds; dreams happy as her day;
> And laughter, learnt of friends; and gentleness,
>   In hearts at peace, under an English heaven.

Rupert Brooke is not a War Poet. He is a poet of peace, a celebrant of friendship, love, and laughter.

Paul Moeyes (essay date 1991)

SOURCE: "Georgian Poetry's False Dawn," in *Neophilologus,* Vol. LXXV, No. 3, July, 1991, pp. 456-69.

[*In the following essay, Moeyes discusses Brooke's place in literary history, asserting that he "is a transitional figure, entering a new age for which he was not prepared."*]

Rupert Brooke is regarded as one of the leading lights among the Georgian Poets, the group of poets Edward Marsh anthologised in his five volumes of *Georgian Poetry* (1911-1922). The Georgians have largely been ignored since the moment they went out of fashion in the mid-1920s, mainly because the Modernists labelled them reactionary, but more recent criticism has convincingly shown that they were in fact, like the Modernists, reacting against the late-Victorian Tory imperialist tradition, represented by such poets as Kipling, Newbolt, Henley, Watson, and Noyes. The Georgians resented their patriotism, rhetoric and pomposity, and instead wanted a poetry that dealt with even the humblest of subjects, written in a more natural language, though, unlike the Modernists, they still believed good poetry could be enjoyed by a large reading audience. The Georgians were, on the whole, Liberal, anti-

Victorian, and anti-imperialistic, and from the time the first *Georgian Poetry* anthology was published in 1912, the Georgians were considered an innovative movement, headed by Rupert Brooke.

Even before that time he had made a name for himself as the voice of a new generation: while at Cambridge, he had been the centre of a group of friends called the "Neopagans". Previous commentators, however, have already noted that Brooke's paganism "was a wilful, sometimes desperate attempt to escape from his engrained puritanism", and it is indeed noticeable that a religious undercurrent is a constant presence in his poetry. It is surprising, therefore, that Brooke's reputation as a rebel-innovator has never been seriously questioned, the more so since no commentator has been able to explain how an arch-rebel came to write a cycle of fervently patriotic *War Sonnets*. These are the questions, then, that this essay seeks to answer.

. . . . .

It was Brooke's mother, yet another example of that nineteenth century type of fiercely Evangelical, dominating women, who instilled in him the Victorian values that were to burden him for the rest of his life. In his adolescent years he discovered the poets of the Nineties, and their decadence inevitably clashed with his mother's religious upbringing. This is evident in his early poetry, for the most part consisting of decadent pastiches with strongly religious overtones. The earliest poem included in the *Poetical Works* is "God Give" (1903), and two years later he wrote a poem in which, despite the inflated language, he successfully sums up his own post-Victorian dilemma:

Why are we vexed with yearning? Surely it is
Enough for us to crouch about the fire
And laugh the irretrievable hours away,
Heedless of what may wait us in the gloom,
The muttering night beyond? Yet though we strive
So to live in the present and forget,
Ever the voice returning wakes again
The old insatiate yearning in our hearts,
Whispering words incomprehensible,
Infinity, Eternity, and—God.

("**Man**", ll. 11-20)

In retrospect, this is oddly enough one of his most honest poems, expressing as it does both a concern with fleeting youth and a latent religiosity. Despite its world-weary tone, Brooke was only 17 when he wrote it; what is perhaps most significant about this poem is that it shows what a talented poseur its author is.

The adolescent Brooke seems to have developed a strong need to be loved, and in the letters he wrote in this period he is quite honest about his dishonesty, frankly admitting to his friend Geoffrey Keynes that it is his intention to cultivate a public persona and to be "all things to all men". In combination with his desire to get away from his mother's Evangelical influence and the Classical education he received at Rugby, this accounts for his eagerness to take

up fashionable new ideas, thus at the same time reacting against his elders and gaining popularity among his contemporaries. By 1906 Brooke had sufficiently worked out his own creed, and he explained it in a letter to Geoffrey Keynes:

All art rests on the sexual emotions which are merely the instruments of the Life-force—of Nature—for the propagation of life. That is all we live for, to further Nature's purpose. Sentiment, poetry, romance, religion are but mists of our own fancies, too weak for the great nature-forces of individuality and sexual emotion.

For the moment, then, both the Christian religion and Platonic Love were apparently dead for him. He expressed this new stage in his thinking in two dramatic poems. In **"The Vision of the Archangels"** (December 1906), four archangels carry a small coffin ("where a child must lie") up a steep peak:

They then from the sheer summit cast, and watched it fall, Through unknown glooms, that frail black coffin—and therein God's little pitiful Body lying, worn and thin, And curled up like some crumpled, lonely flower-petal.

Two years later he returned to this theme in **"Failure"**. The speaker's rebellious mood in the opening lines of this sonnet is reminiscent of a similar defiant mood in the first lines of George Herbert's "The Collar", but in Brooke's poem the blaspheming speaker, incensed by thwarted Love, vows to go up the Golden Stair and curse God on his throne. But on entering the Iron Gate he finds the Kingdom of God deserted, "the glassy pavement" covered in moss, the council-halls dusty, and an "idle wind [blowing] round an empty throne".

. . . . .

When he wrote this poem, Brooke was already the centre of that group of friends Virginia Woolf later dubbed the "Neo-Pagans", a term that may require further explanation. Calling them a "group" is largely misleading, evoking, as it does, a picture similar to that of the Bloomsbury group. But the Neo-pagans were basically no more than some young people who were at Cambridge together, united by friendship and some shared pet-hates, and their ideas, if any, were fashionable rather than heartfelt or original. As Paul Delany puts it [in the *Neo-Pagans,* 1988]:

When the Neo-pagans came together . . . many ways for the new generation to escape from Victorianism were in the air, but they had no thought of any formal manifesto to found their group on. They were friends of Rupert, and friends of each other, who had a common style of youthful unconventionality, and overlapping links to Bedales, Fabianism, Cambridge and the Simple Life.

Also it is essential to interpret "pagan" as meaning "rustic" rather than "unbeliever" or "non-Christian". Brooke's theory about the "Life-force" might as well be ignored altogether, for in comparison with Bloomsbury's promiscuity the Neo-pagan summer camps had all the libertinism of a Sunday school outing.

Too many people seem to have been taken in by the Brooke persona. This strikingly handsome young man, who proclaimed his belief in the Life-force, Fabianism and the Simple Life was in fact a very insecure romantic with a yearning for a spiritual dimension. For how otherwise can it be explained that in his *Poetical Works* there is only one poem that could be said to be dealing with the "Life-force" (**"Lust"**), and only one about Fabianism (**"Second Best"**), whereas the God he buried in **"The Vision of the Archangels"** is resurrected in such poems as **"My Song,"** **"Song of the Children in Heaven"** and **"The Song of the Pilgrims"**.

The only real development that is noticeable in his Neo-pagan phase is regressive rather than progressive. Brooke's first poems (1903-06) were heavily influenced by his friendship with the local decadent poet St John Lucas, and as a result of that they are drenched in pessimism and Weltschmerz and filled with lost loves, fading petals and purple kisses. But in the first stage of his "Neo-pagan poetry" (1907-9), when love is still his main subject and he still lacks any first-hand experience of it, Brooke's inspirational sources lie further back in the nineteenth century: Wordsworth, Keats, Meredith and the pre-Raphaelites are now the new, dominating influences.

The nature-mysticism present in **"Seaside"** and **"Pine Trees and the Sky: Evening"** is purely Wordsworthian. In the love poems the beloved is now a distant, nymph-like ideal (reminding one of Keats as well as of the renewed interest in chivalry in Victorian art & literature); she is described as a "flower", "white" and "innocent", and with long flowing hair (thus evoking the picture of a pre-Raphaelite "stunner"). And the fact that she is distant and unattainable is essential, as is illustrated by two poems written within a month of each other, in April and May 1909. In **"The Voice"** the poet is alone "in the magic of my woods" about to reach "the hour of knowing". But then the silence is disturbed by the arrival, on her "ignorant feet", of his flesh-and-blood beloved: "The spell was broken, the key denied me / And at length your flat voice beside me / Mouthed cheerful clear flat platitudes". The exact opposite is described in **"Blue Evening,"** where, again in a sylvan setting, the lover/poet admires an idealised nymph: "A flower in moonlight, she was there / Was rippling down white ways of glamour / Quietly laid on wave and air". The important difference being that in this poem the woman is beyond the poet's reach, only to be admired from a distance.

Further evidence of a Victorian influence can be found in many other poems. In **"Day That I Have Loved,"** the day itself is personified, and the poet carries her "to the shrouded sands / Where lies your waiting boat, by wreaths of the sea's making". The imagery here is purely Tennysonian, either The Lady of Shalott or the Fair Elaine (both very popular subjects in Victorian painting). The setting of his sonnet **"Oh! Death will find me,"** on the other hand,

appears at first sight to have been derived from Dante: the poet pictures himself in the Underworld, waiting for his love to arrive from across "the Stygian tide". But it seems more likely that Brooke found this idea (including the "Oh!") in Bridges, the last stanza of whose "Elegy—on a lady whom grief for the death of her betrothed killed" (1890) describes the dead betrothed in a similar situation: "And thou, O lover, that art on the watch / Where, on the banks of the forgetful streams / The pale indifferent ghosts wander". What is obvious is that the world evoked in all these poems is very much like the dream world F.R. Leavis considered characteristic of the nineteenth century.

Brooke entered the second stage of his Neo-pagan phase towards the end of 1909, and it lasted until his nervous breakdown in 1912. It is characterized by a growing desire to escape from reality, culminating in a return to Platonism and, though perhaps less obviously, Christianity. There are two reasons for Brooke's increasing need to get away from reality. By 1909 he began to lose his centre stage position as the Neo-pagans broke up into several courting couples. At the same time Brooke himself felt unable to fall in love, which caused both sexual frustration and jealousy, and when he sought release from his sexual frustration in a homosexual encounter with a Rugby schoolfriend this only filled him with an intense self-disgust.

The intensity of his emotion can be felt in **"Jealousy"** (1909), in which the speaker addresses a girl who refused him in favour of somebody else. The poem expresses an enormous desire to hurt the girl and console the speaker's damaged pride, and this is achieved by picturing the couple in their decrepit old age:

> When all that's fine in man is at an end,
> And you, that loved young life and clean, must tend
> A foul, sick fumbling dribbling body and old,
> When his rare lips hang flabby and can't hold
> Slobber

The concern for fleeting youth expressed so vaguely and unconvincingly in the early poems is now juxtaposed with an evocative and horrible image of old age. But the poet is trapped by his own image when in the last line of the poem he realises that she, and by implication he, will be old and "dirty" too. This is what makes the second poem in which he deals with this idea of the flower of youth ending up in a mire of old age so extremely interesting.

In **"Menelaus and Helen"** (1909) he makes use of a classical setting: Homer ends his account of Menelaus and Helen with their return to Sparta after the fall of Troy; Brooke picks up their story at this point and paints the once perfect lovers as ageing, ugly and bored by each others' company ("her golden voice / Got shrill as he grew deafer"), but a new ingredient is the suggestion in the concluding lines of the poem that early death is infinitely more preferable: "So Menelaus nagged, and Helen cried / And Paris slept on by Scamander side". This denial of the possibility of ideal human love, convinced as he is that it will ultimately wane as Youth slips away and Old Age approaches, is also a denial of the Neo-pagan ideals, and the classical setting he chooses in expressing this rejection marks a return to his Rugby education, again suggestive of a reactionary rather than a progressive development.

From 1909-10 onwards, then, Brooke is gradually moving away from Neo-paganism. As a result of the courtships among his friends, his own failing in love and the disgust he felt after his homosexual affair the one-time leader of the Neo-pagans was thrown off his pedestal, and left in a state of emotional upset and insecurity. His major concern in the poetry written at this time is to find a new creed to hold on to and which will exonerate him from any personal failing. More and more this leads him back to his Platonic/ Puritan starting-point".

The new creed now gradually emerging in his poetry is a belief in friendship with distinct Platonic and Christian overtones. Brooke shies away from earthly love and its physical aspects, instead "love" changes into a purely spiritual "Love", a Platonic Ideal existing in an eternal realm separate from this world, and therefore unattainable for mortal man. In relation to this Love the poet becomes a worshipper, and Love his God. At the same time the poet celebrates friendship as the only ideal human relationship attainable on earth.

Brooke was desperately in search of peace of mind, and for the moment this creed seems to have helped him find a new equilibrium. It is in this period that he wrote two poems about friendship, **"Dining-Room Tea"** and **"Kindliness"**. The first poem reveals that Brooke experiences friendship, as he did with with "love" in the Neo-pagan phase, with a religious fervour. The speaker in the poem is among friends, and then suddenly experiences a vision of ideal friendship, a brief and yet timeless moment which for him has all the intensity of a religious revelation:

> Under a vast and starless sky
> I saw the immortal moment lie.
> One instant I, an instant, knew
> As God knows all.

In the second poem, **"Kindliness,"** Brooke returns to his earlier theme, the fallacy of perfect human love. But this time he is able to take a more detached view of the subject, which results in a convincing and at times even moving poem. He starts out by reiterating the point that, no matter how perfect love is, the fire of passion cannot last: "the best that either's known / Will change, and wither, and be less / At last, than comfort, or its own / Remembrance". So what to do at that stage, when love has changed to kindliness? The poet suggests suicide, or going separate ways, but then, with a serenity that is new in Brooke, he proposes friendship as another viable alternative, one that enables him to accept the inevitable with quiet resignation:

> Or shall we stay
> Since this is all we've known, content
> In the lean twilight of such day,
> And not remember, not lament?

It is this tone of submission that makes the poem stand out in Brooke's oeuvre. He himself thought it one of his best, possibly for this very reason. For the way love continued to be his main subject, and the passionate and often frantic quality of his writing in this period suggests that he was still emotionally upset.

. . . . .

In his 1968 review of Brooke's *Letters* [*Required Writings,* 1984], Philip Larkin noted that in the period 1909-1912 "Brooke almost obsessively overworked the adjectives 'clean' and 'dirty'." In his poetry this clean/dirty contrast is only one of the many puritanical good/evil, Heaven/Hell juxtapositions that serve as a framework for his writing. His particular obsession is physical love, which he considers both sinful and dirty, and this is juxtaposed with the Platonic "Love", which is like a state of grace, and where the ecstacy is purely spiritual.

Brooke's nature imagery also becomes part of this Heaven/Hell juxtaposition. In an earlier poem, **"Paralysis"** (1909), the poet is alone in his house in the town, his beloved nymph having left him to return to "the world beyond the town". Lying in his bed, he is tormented by the idea that she will forget him as soon as she is alone with her "hills and heaven". This somewhat literal symbol of a hill or mountain as the closest point to heaven recurs in several other poems. A sonnet describing two happy lovers is called **"The Hill,"** but more interesting is another sonnet, in which Brooke blames Katherine Cox for awakening sexual desires in him, which had been the cause of the emotional upset he was still suffering from. This sonnet is called **"The Descent,"** and in the opening lines the symbolic meaning is explicitly stated: "Because you called, I left the mountain height / Bleak nurse and neighbour to Infinity".

Religious references abound in these poems, varying from oblique references to the Eucharist in **"Mummia"** to the image of the disappointed lover as a Christ figure in **"Song"** ("'Oh! Love,' they said, 'is King of Kings'").

Too many people seem to have been taken in by the Brooke persona. This strikingly handsome young man, who proclaimed his belief in the Life-force, Fabianism and the Simple Life was in fact a very insecure romantic with a yearning for a spiritual dimension.

—Paul Moeyes

Brooke's complete collapse occurred towards the end of 1911. After the previous crisis he had sought solace in another creed, adopting friendship as his new ideal, but after his 1912 breakdown there was no attempt to comfort his feelings in new beliefs. The poems he wrote in the period between his breakdown and his departure for

America and the Pacific in May 1913 are all purely escapist: as when he wrote **"Dining-Room Tea,"** he needed to calm his nerves and therefore avoided any "disturbing" subjects. Instead he wrote pieces of pure escapism: mostly they are "Songs" (in his letters he had expressed his admiration for the Elizabethan lyricists), and there are only a few longer poems of some interest. The allegorical **"The Funeral of Youth: Threnody"** again displays Brooke's tendency towards self-dramatisation: among the friends who appear at his Youth's grave-side are Friendship ("not a minute older") and Contentment ("who had known Youth as a child"), with Love as the only absentee ("Love had died long ago"). A most remarkable poem is **"Mary and Gabriel"**. This poem marks the culmination of Brooke's puritanical obsession with sex, and in **"Mary and Gabriel"** he escapes from this physical dirtiness by writing a poem about the Immaculate Conception!

Brooke's belief in love was somewhat restored on Samoa, where he found both sex and solace with a native girl, but the influence this had on his poetry was not altogether a beneficial one. The poems he wrote in the Pacific still deal with a Platonic paradise, the important difference being that Brooke was obviously in much better spirits, and this affected the tone of the poems. [In Christopher Hassall's *Rupert Brooke: A Biography,* 1972] Harold Monro said that Brooke was "stimulated to write by the oddness rather than by the intensity of an idea", and the humorous tone already present in **"The Old Vicarage, Grantchester,"** now becomes more pronounced: poems like **"Heaven,"** the self-mocking **"The Great Lover,"** and **"Tiare Tahiti"** are basically clever jokes. In **"Tiare Tahiti"** Brooke even mocks his Neo-Platonic creed, saying that in his Platonic heaven there is no possibility for physical love: "And there's an end, I think, of kissing / When our mouths are one with Mouth . . .".

. . . . .

There is a enormous contrast between the witty poems Brooke wrote during his stay in the South Pacific and the highflown tone of the *War Sonnets* he wrote in November-December 1914. This contrast has never been satisfactorily explained and is in most cases simply ignored. As war poems, they are usually discussed in combination with some of the war poems of Siegfried Sassoon and Wilfred Owen, a comparison which then results in a dismissal of Brooke's poems as blindly patriotic and warlike. But it should never be forgotten that the early war poetry of both Sassoon and Owen is at least as patriotic and warlike.

Apologists, on the other hand, fare little better: Brooke's biographer Christopher Hassall is far from convincing in claiming that "Brooke never glorified war . . . but he celebrated in exultation the discovery of a moral purpose". This is an explanation for Brooke's enthusiasm for the war rather than a denial, and besides, "moral purpose" sounds a bit too elevated for what was basically an escape from trouble, confusion, and indecision. Similarly, C.K. Stead [in *The New Poetic,* 1964] offers no explanation at all; after stating that "Brooke prepared the ground for the work of better poets", he can only say that "when the war came

Brooke departed from the manner most characteristic of the Georgians", and in his Introduction to *Rupert Brooke: A Reappraisal and Selection,* Timothy Rogers fails to prove his claim that "Brooke was always capable of thinking for himself" in that he can only explain the contents of the *War Sonnets* by saying that Brooke "captured the thoughts and feelings of the moment, and gave eloquent expression to them".

After his return from the Pacific, Brooke still claimed that his main desire in life was to get married: the young actress Cathleen Nesbitt seemed a suitable candidate, and his sexual problems seem more or less to have been resolved on Samoa. But if this was indeed the case it seems strange that he was so enthusiastic about the war, and had no hesitations about leaving his beloved behind. The truth seems to have been, as Delany suggests, that he did not really love her enough; for one thing she was an actress and the puritan Brooke did not approve of that. But to me it seems that there also is a far more important reason. The many masks and poses obscure the fact that Brooke was in essence a follower rather than a leader. He was seldom an original thinker: it should not be forgotten that in all the phases in his life he started out by following and imitating the people around him, whether it was the poet St John Lucas in his decadent phase, or his friends from Bedales in his Neo-pagan phase. At the root of his problems is his desire to escape from his mother's Evangelicalism and his Rugby education. But though his desire to run away from this was all too genuine, he never realized that both qualities were ingrained in his personality. Rupert Brooke is an emblem of his age in the sense that in his eagerness to what was in effect an desire to escape from himself, he was always willing to open his mind to anything that was new and fashionable in the Edwardian Age, be it Decadence, Fabianism, Neo-paganism, or an interest in the Metaphysical Poets. But these attempts all failed, and their influence therefore remained essentially superficial, never affecting either the heart of his being, or of his poetry.

In September 1914 he confessed in a letter that "I am . . . carried along on the tides of my body, rather helplessly." His mother's religion had never suited him, because he was too active and passionate. But when he took up love as his new religion, his puritanism proved to be enough of an inhibition to prevent him from taking up free love or anything permissive. It is this that explains his desire to marry: he wanted to channel his passions in a socially acceptable way. But after the 1912 breakdown, the idea of having to drop his mask and give himself completely proved too great a stumbling-block, and besides, Brooke's fears of settling down, ending up in a rut and growing old were all too real.

All these points help to explain the appeal the war held for him, it was a temporary escape into the relative safety of camaraderie, a way out from all the choices that had to be taken and the adult responsibilities that had to be accepted. This is the interpretation John Press favours [in *A Map of Modern English Verse,* 1979]: "[Brooke's] war sonnets can no longer be read as a simple clarion call to arms: they are a desperate attempt by a tormented man to find emotional relief from a morbid self-disgust". But the problem with this view is that one does not get the impression that Brooke was particularly tormented when he wrote the sonnets: the poems written in the Pacific suggest that he had at least partly recovered from his breakdown, and neither the tone of his letters nor that of the sonnets is that of a man in great emotional distress.

A more likely explanation is that, some time before the outbreak of the war, Brooke had entered a new phase. And it was this new focus of attention that was to determine the course of the last part of his life. This new and decisive influence on the tone of Brooke's *War Sonnets* was the social circle he was now moving in.

Towards the end of 1912, Brooke had become a protégé of Edward Marsh, the future editor of the *Georgian Poetry* anthologies and at that time Private Secretary to Winston Churchill, the First Lord of the Admiralty. Marsh introduced Brooke to "Winston" (as Brooke called him in his letters), and at the outbreak of the war he arranged for Brooke to be commissioned in Winston's private army, the Royal Naval Division. But he also introduced Brooke to London's high-society, and by the summer of 1914 Brooke was a frequent guest at the Admiralty and 10 Downing Street. Among his close friends were Lady Eileen Wellesley, daughter of the Duke of Wellington, and Violet Asquith, eldest daughter of the Prime Minister. H. H. Asquith himself was also quite taken with Brooke: in a letter to his confidante Venetia Stanley, he wrote that "it would not be a bad thing if Violet & Rupert Brooke came together". Critics have never fully appreciated the fact that Brooke's chameleon-like qualities never deserted him. They have too often regarded him as the epitome of Neo-paganism, whereas in fact this phase, especially in his poetry, lasted only a relatively short time. It left him disgusted with love and sex, but he did value friendship, and by 1914 he had found a new circle of friends. Timothy Rogers may well be right in saying that Brooke was always capable of thinking for himself, but in his poetry his thinking was mainly prompted by his escapist desires.

The author of the *War Sonnets,* then, has nothing to do with the erstwhile Neo-pagan; rather he is a latter day Soul, a role for which he was ideally suited: handsome, charming, witty and intelligent, and eager to please rather than to probe. Many of his hosts had been leading members of the Souls: Violet's stepmother, Margot Asquith, had been at the centre of the group, in April 1913 Brooke was the guest of the Conservative MP and former Soul George Wyndham, in his day referred to as "the handsomest man of England", and when Enid Bagnold asked Lady Horner about another leading Soul Harry Cust, she was told that "he was the Rupert Brooke of our day".

This is the background against which the *War Sonnets* should be read. Brooke had found a new voice, a voice that went down well with his new friends. As a schoolboy at Rugby in 1905, Brooke had held a talk on modern poetry in which he said that he hated W. E. Henley's patriotism and that reading Kipling was like "reading life by flashes of superb vulgarity". Ten years later Edward Marsh had no problems converting Brooke into an admirer of Kipling's poetry, and the fact is that in the *War Sonnets* the tone is hardly distinguishable from that of the imperialist poets, Henley, Kipling and Sir Henry Newbolt. Brooke's rhetoric in these sonnets is that of an evangelist preaching a new gospel to the masses, though at the same time, as at the beginning of his Neo-pagan phase, he is trying to lose himself in a popular cause: as before the preaching of the public figure seems primarily intended to take his mind off and divert his own attention from the disturbing problems of the private individual.

This is not to say that the *War Sonnets* are mere propaganda pieces written to boost the numbers of Kitchener's Army. In the opening sonnet especially there are unmistakable references to his personal problems, but the point is that in adopting the Happy Warrior pose Brooke simply reflected the image that was prevalent in the society in which he now moved. Julian Grenfell, that other epitome of early war enthusiasm and himself the son of a leading Souls hostess, wrote his "Into Battle" from personal experience, whereas Brooke, as in his Neo-pagan phase, was fantasising about his new role rather than describing his deepest feelings and experiences.

The *War Sonnets* are hardly concerned with the war, and not at all with victory. They are about early death, and the desirability of early death, and it is this welcoming of an early death as an escape from growing old that links the *War Sonnets* with his 1909 poem **"Menelaeus and Helen"**. In this poem Brooke suggested that Paris's early death was a blessing in disguise, and this idea recurs in the first of the *War Sonnets*.

The opening poem of the cycle, **"Peace,"** is the most personal of the *War Sonnets* in that it is only in this poem that Brooke refers to what went before. The paradoxical title is particularly revealing, referring as it does to the inner peace Brooke thought he had refound in the year war broke out in Europe. Since it was no more than an escape and had done nothing to actually solve any of his problems, it also indicates an element of self-deception Brooke seems not to have been aware of.

"Peace" opens with a thanksgiving to the Christian God he had abjured in his Neo-pagan period: "Now God be thanked, Who has matched us with His hour / And caught our youth, and wakened us from sleeping". Brooke returns to his God as a repentant sinner, welcoming war as a baptism, a possibility to cut loose from the immediate past, including his love-worship, and redeem himself:

> To turn, as swimmers into cleanness leaping,
> Glad from a world old and cold and weary,
> Leave the sick hearts that honour could not move,
> And half-men, and their dirty songs and dreary,
> And all the little emptiness of love!

The "sick-hearts" and "half-men" could well be a reference to his hated enemy Lytton Strachey, like other "Bloomsberries" a conscientious objector, but the most revealing line is of course "the little emptiness of love", followed by the equally telling "Oh!, we, who have known shame, we have found release there". The last line of **"Peace"** introduces Death as a young man's "worst friend and enemy", and the desirability of a heroic Death is the subject of the following three sonnets. Whereas the rhetorical "we" in the first sonnet was but the faintest disguise for Brooke's own voice, the "we" in these poems does seem to refer to the young soldiers in general. But there is a sudden departure from this plural form in the last four lines of **"Safety,"** where after four separate references to "we" Brooke reverts to the first person singular to repeat his main theme: "And if these poor limbs die, safest of all".

The third sonnet continues the theme of the cleansing effect of wars, welcoming the return of such Platonic ideals as Honour, Nobleness and Holiness, and referring in passing to old age as "that unhoped for serene". This unlikely to be enjoyed serene old age is juxtaposed in the fourth sonnet with the desirability of early death, which is described as an "unbroken glory", since it preserves the soldiers' eternal youth.

The last and perhaps most famous sonnet of the sequence, **"The Soldier,"** introduces an imperialist note that puts Brooke on a par with Henley and Newbolt. The poem reads as the imperialist's answer to Thomas Hardy's bleak "Drummer Hodge", but on a more personal level it also seems an attempt by the poet to reconcile himself with death. In February 1915 Prime Minister Asquith reported to his friend that "Rupert Brooke is quite convinced that he will not return alive". In the event he did not return at all, and was buried on the isle of Skyros. It is impossible to say if he indeed thought he would die, or if this was all part of the new role of a romantic hero he had adopted.

. . . . .

There is no point in thinking about Brooke's personae in terms of Yeatsian masks. For Yeats the mask was a symbol of the creative process, for Brooke the poses he adopted were an attempt to compensate for a reality he could not accept. But the essential difference between Yeats and Brooke must be that Yeats lived for his poetry, whereas Brooke's approach remained essentially that of an amateur: he never used it as a means to analyse and investigate the truth, but to escape from and compensate for a reality he could not cope with.

Thinking of Brooke as the leader of the Neo-pagans is to misunderstand him completely: holding court at Grantchester was never a role that suited him, still adhering as he was to Christian morality as well as lacking in the necessary qualities of leadership. It was his last role, that of the poet laureate of the young English upper classes, that suited him best. In this capacity he created an imaginary portrait of an idealised self, the Happy Warrior of the *War Sonnets,* and found that it was a portrait that appealed to a whole generation. By that time he had completely distanced himself from his Cambridge past, both as a Neo-pagan and as a Cambridge Apostle and follower of G.E.

Moore's philosophy, which held that one had to base one's judgement "strictly on the exercise of reason, each man his own severest judge in his own case."

It is this basic insincerity and lack of depth that make his poetry ultimately disappointing. Even more so since his unmistakable craftsmanship and popularity would have enabled him to make a far more important and lasting contribution to that much maligned new school of Georgian Poetry.

Brooke is a transitional figure, entering a new age for which he was not prepared. It was the following generation, led in America by the young F. Scott Fitzgerald and the Flappers, and in England by Evelyn Waugh and the Bright Young Things, that succeeded where Brooke failed: cutting loose from the past, rejecting all responsibilities and flouting nineteenth century morality, they enjoyed life to the full and gathered as many rosebuds as they could.

Brooke never succeeded in breaking away from the nineteenth century, and that must have been a contributory factor in his failing to fulfil his promise as a talented and innovative young poet. It is a subject he avoids in his correspondence, but in one of his last letters, written to one of his closest friends, he gives up all pretence and frankly admits that "the realization of failure makes me *unpleasantly* melancholy."

It was a letter only to be opened in the event of his death.

William D. Laskowski (essay date 1994)

SOURCE: "Brooke's Poetry," in *Rupert Brooke,* Twayne Publishers, 1994, pp. 31-63.

[*In the following essay, Laskowski provides a thematic and stylistic analysis of Brooke's verse.*]

Readers of Geoffrey Keynes's edition of *The Poetical Works* of Brooke, initially published in 1946, will be immediately struck by Keynes's unusual arrangement of the poems in reverse chronological order, with the exception of some fragments Brooke wrote en route to the Dardanelles in 1915. In his edition Keynes has added 38 previously unpublished poems to the 82 originally included in *Poems* (1911) and *1914 and Other Poems,* some of them of little intrinsic merit or interest, perhaps with less justification than Anthony Thwaite's controversial additions to the *Collected Poems* of Philip Larkin. The effect of such an arrangement gives the appearance of protecting, or at least admitting the lesser value of, Brooke's earliest works. It tacitly—almost implicitly—gives credence to the theory that Brooke's main poetic appeal lies in his legend, which is inextricably linked to the later poems: the myth endorses the work. Keynes's strategy is reminiscent of what has now become a cliché in the organization of biographies, to begin with the death of one's subject, particularly since the first poem in *The Poetical Works* is **"Fragment"** (which is separated from Brooke's other final fragments, which are placed at the end of the volume). This poem ends with the proleptic phrase "soon to die / To other ghosts—this one, or that, or I," allowing no reader to forget that the writer of these lines did die soon after. Of course, a reader can begin at the end of the volume and work through to the beginning, but even that strategy does not remove the impression of a poetic life viewed through the wrong end of the telescope.

Prizewinner

Two of Brooke's longest sustained poetical works are **"The Pyramids"** and **"The Bastille,"** poems written to set historical themes for the poetry competition at Rugby. (The latter won first place, while the other received a *proxime accessit.*) Since Brooke is attempting in these works for the most part to reproduce an attitude that would win a prize, many of the themes and expressions in these poems are not only derivative, but uncharacteristically derivative. Some ideas Brooke explores here are worth noting, however, both those which are unique to these works and those which foreshadow certain directions Brooke's work would take.

Both poems are studded with themes and tropes connected to the decadent phase Brooke was exploring in his private poetry of the time, but most of these are underplayed, since the judges of a school contest would not look favorably on such a pose were it extravagantly expressed. Thus, the Sphinx in **"The Pyramids"** is more reminiscent of that at Giza than that of St. John Lucas (who wrote a novel called *The Marble Sphinx*). "The gloom that men call Death" awaits all in **"The Pyramids,"** and "Summer . . . Languid with roses" takes place unknown to those trapped in **"The Bastille"**: both images are from decadence, but conventional views more often prevail in these works. The climax of **"The Pyramids,"** for instance, invokes "The Eternal Music that God makes," obviously a concession by the unbelieving Brooke to the pieties of the judges. Despite such genuflections, however, one cannot assume, as does Ronald Pearsall [in *Rupert Brooke: The Man and Poet,* 1974], that other aspects of the poems, such as "The eternal day" in **"The Bastille,"** represent "a Christian eternity, something that would be acceptable to the judges of the contest." **"The Bastille"** concludes with the declaration "Men shall be Gods," an unmistakably non-Christian sentiment, an affirmation of the serpent's promise to Eve in Genesis. This vision of a utopian future is more revealing of the political themes Brooke explores in these poems, themes that, for all of Brooke's political involvement, he rarely explores or expresses elsewhere in his poetry.

The main thrust of **"The Pyramids,"** besides the standard meditations on the evanescence of human life, is the ultimate ephemerality of political empires: Egyptian, Greek, Roman, and, though never stated, that of the British Empire. Lives have been wasted "In the vain merciless mad race / For dreams of 'Empire' and 'Supremacy.'" Such a stance in 1904 was somewhat unusual for an English public school boy to adopt; although Brooke's beliefs on empire are never clearly stated elsewhere, he seems to have been a "little Englander," his patriotism, like Belloc's, not extending beyond the British isles. In **"The Bastille"** he confronts the political problem of revolution. His image for that upheaval is traditional: the darkness inside the Bastille will yield to "the slow inevitable day" of revolution; a political poster Brooke would have seen later, in Ben Keeling's room, for instance, was titled "Forward the Day Is Breaking." Much of the other imagery in the poem is traditional, but in its last section Brooke makes a prescient remark: the dreams of the French Revolution, as viewed from the perspective of 1905, have faded, "For we know / Not by one sudden blow / Are peace and freedom won." This declaration shows that Brooke was at least ready to accept the Fabian philosophy of gradual socialism. The poem's final vision of "The eternal day," far from being Christian, is the heaven on earth of socialism, "sin and bondage past," because the reasons for such evils—"Grey poverty" and "tyrannous Wealth"—will have been removed. While the radicalism of these poems is mild, they provided two of the few opportunities for Brooke to assert such ideas poetically. In later life he reportedly wanted to write a long poem on modern economic conditions that would climax in a depiction of revolution but gave up on it. As the weaknesses of these prize poems show, Brooke was essentially a miniaturist; most of the longer works he attempted gave him some difficulty, particularly in matters of tone.

Decadent

Many of the early poems Keynes added to *The Poetical Works* are eminently forgettable, evocative of no other writer; the decadent poems, while derivative, at least indicate some of the characteristic subjects Brooke would continue to write about. Since decadence is in part a reaction to Victorian sincerity, most of the emotions appearing in these poems are artificial, almost patently unauthentic, as are those emotions when they appear in the writings Brooke was imitating. One of the decadents' principal subjects is a morbid concern with death. As Pearsall points out, "The death note of Decadent writing caught thousands of hearts at the turn of the century. . . . But it seldom sticks as it stuck to Brooke." Much of Brooke's preoccupation with mortality arises out of an adolescent fixation on death as a means of escape, intimately bound up with the posture of being unable to forget painful memories. The death of the earth, for instance, is described in fin de siècle terms reminiscent of the last chapters of H. G. Wells's *The Time Machine*: "Quenching the light . . . And bringing back the terrible night that was", the soul of the dead must face "the darkness that is God." The possibility of old age becomes an object of intense fear in these poems, and youth the subject of worship.

Youthful beauty is often described in floral images, with homoerotic overtones: "flesh more fair than pale lilies." Lilies become the emblematic flower in these poems, betokening everything but their traditional association with resurrection. The title flowers in **"The Lost Lilies,"** the symbol of dimly evoked, forbidden passion, are contrasted with the other favorite flower in these poems, "the roses' purple kiss"; the speaker in the poem mourns for "The immortal pallor of my lost lilies." Paleness, languor, a stud-ied enervation—all the poses Brooke absorbed from Wilde and Ernest Dowson are here. Some of these affectless exercises, however, do spring into life at times when Brooke engages certain emotions and strategies. The poem **"In January"** is the first hint of what has been called Brooke's later realism: the speaker declares he has not forgotten "The dripping bough: the sad smell of the rotten / Leaves," but the poem ends more conventionally as the speaker also remembers "A glorious light." **"Song of the Beasts"** is an outgrowth of Brooke's antisensualism, covertly celebrating that which it condemns. As its epigraph states, *"Sung, on one night, in the cities, in the darkness,"* the song is a combination of Dr. Hyde and Dr. Moreau: "Have you not felt the quick fires that creep / Through the hungry flesh, and the lust of delight, / And hot secrets of dreams that day cannot say?" In another twisting of Genesis, the speaker declares, "Ye are men no longer, but less and more, Beast and God." The poem concludes as the speaker leads the rest of the beasts, lemming-like, out of the city "To the black unresting plains of the calling sea," an image derived from the ambiguous comfort the ocean provides in such poems as Matthew Arnold's "Dover Beach."

While decadence gave Brooke a tradition he could explore and build on, more important, it gave him a series of conventions he could rebel against, just as decadence itself was a revolt against Victorian sensibilities.

—William Laskowski

Perhaps the poem that best foreshadows Brooke's later concerns is **"The Beginning,"** in which the speaker prom-ises to look for his beloved one day, remembering the "Touch of your hands and smell of your hair." Yet when they do meet that day, the speaker will "curse the thing that once you were, / Because it is changed and pale and old." This represents an interesting contrast to Brooke's later, more famous attacks on old age in **"Menelaus and Helen,"** since here the speaker turns around and curses the beloved for having the potential to grow old. While the poem ends more conventionally, as the speaker admits the beloved will also grow "old and wise," it is important because it introduces Brooke's continuing war against time, which would culminate in his attempt to freeze it in moments encapsulated like those in **"Dining-Room Tea."**

While decadence gave Brooke a tradition he could explore and build on, more important, it gave him a series of conventions he could rebel against, just as decadence itself was a revolt against Victorian sensibilities. One can see the more mature Brooke emerge gradually during 1907, the year in which he later said the young poet he had been "died." **"The Call,"** according to Christopher Hassall, was written (February 1907) about the death of his older broth-er, Richard, but this biographical connection is difficult to perceive under all the conventional decadent language:

"I'll write upon the shrinking skies / The scarlet splendour of your name." Perhaps the first poem fully in Brooke's mature, independent voice is the **"Dawn,"** in which the matching first and last lines, "Opposite me two Germans snore and sweat," indicate the direction Brooke's search for unconventional subject matter, particularly for the sonnet form, would take him—a subject matter later la-beled "realistic," "ugly," or "unpleasant." Brooke's clear-est declaration of poetic independence is the appropriate-ly titled **"Sonnet: in time of Revolt"** (January 1908), writ-ten in defiance of his uncle Alan Brooke, dean of King's College, who had seemingly chided Brooke for using mild profanity. Brooke's seeming overreaction—"I am no boy! I AM / NO BOY!"—is more understandable in light of his search for a wider subject matter for his verse, and the poem's last declaration—"So shall I curb, so baffle, so suppress / This too avuncular officiousness, / Intolerable consanguinity"—dimly echoes Stephen Dedalus's vow of "silence, exile, and cunning" as he resolves to break the ties of blood that bind him and also throws off the dec-adent posturings of the villanelle he writes in *A Portrait of the Artist as a Young Man.* Although Brooke's exper-iments were never to approach Joyce's in depth, from now on Brooke's poetry would, on the whole, be an attempt to voice an original expression, not an echo.

Georgian

Brooke, even more than its editor, Edward Marsh, worked to puff and publicize the first volume of Marsh's anthol-ogy, *Georgian Poetry*; as he wrote to Marsh, "When I lie awake o'nights—as I sometimes do—I plan advertisements for 'Georgian Poets,'" and he was constantly on the look-out for the volume in his travels in America and Canada, and distributed copies where none were available. Brooke also realized, however, that the concept of "Georgianism" in literature was a somewhat artificial construct of Marsh's; as he humorously noted, "And it's generally agreed that Marsh has got Georgianism on the brain, & will shortly issue a series of Georgian poker-work: & establish a band of Georgian cooks." Kenneth Millard has recently (1991) argued that Brooke was actually an Edwardian and that there really were no Georgians; however, Robert Ross in *The Georgian Revolt* (1965) and Myron Simon in *The Geor-gian Poetic* (1975) have more persuasively proven that Georgianism was an organized movement with its own co-herent aesthetic, however much it appeared to spring full-blown out of one editor's taste, so to speak. Brooke himself argued that its very name betrayed it: it was "too staid for a volume designed as the herald of a revolutionary dawn."

Of course, the chief problem with Georgian poetry is not its existence but its worth in the minds of critics, partic-ularly after the World War I. Georgians in their time, as Ross and Simon show, were considered to be as icono-clastic and revolutionary as other, more identifiable pre-modernists; Georgians' works were marked, as Ross says, by "spiritual euphoria, a sense of vitality, anti-Victorianism, realism, and freedom of poetic diction. But most of these tendencies were not uniquely Georgian; they rather marked the Georgians, like the Imagists, Vorticists, and even Fu-turists, as scions of their age." Yet in 1918 T. S. Eliot was criticizing the Georgians for "pleasantness": "the Georgians caress everything they touch." Two events led to the general modern critical devaluation of the Georgians. The first was the attenuation of the poetic material Marsh published in anthologies after World War I. As Ross points out, "In 1912 and 1915 'Georgian' had implied vigor, revolt, and youth. After 1917 it was to imply retrenchment, escape, and enervation." The second was the sheer immense fact of the war itself. In *A War Imagined* Samuel Hynes has shown what an unbridgeable gulf the First World War meant to people in all walks of life, but particularly the arts. Poets became divided into those who served and those who did not: Robert Graves, Siegfried Sassoon, and Wilfred Owen, however much antiwar their verse became, all still thought of themselves as Georgians, not as modernists. As the critical perception of the Georgians as poetic "dew-dabblers" solidified, their own attempts at artistic breakthroughs and boundary-extending were forgotten. Perhaps the most striking "forgotten" feature of the Georgian poets was their realism, and Brooke became briefly notorious for the few poems in his first volume, **Poems**, which concerned hitherto "unpoetic" subjects, when the public preferred, as did Marsh, "poetry that I can read at meals."

The reasons behind Brooke's realistic approach are not entirely clear. There is a remnant of adolescent rebellion, and perhaps, as Ross speculates, it may have been part marketing ploy: "they attracted public attention." Others have postulated a more philosophical basis. Simon finds Brooke's realism rooted in the philosophical principles of Moore and Russell: "the Georgians acknowledged a real world, external to them, the existence of which was not contingent upon their perception of it. But that world was available for their inspection, and the first principle of their realism was that they must attend carefully to the concrete particulars of external experience." The truth is somewhere in between the two explanations. Brooke's underlying psychological reason for the "ugliness" of certain of his poems is to shock, whether it be his mother; his uncle, the Dean of King's; the secretary to the lord of the admiralty, Edward Marsh; or, later, his former Cambridge friends. He is at the same time working through in his poetry his reaction to the philosophy of G. E. Moore he encountered with the Apostles, but he is not merely adapting or conforming to it. Some biographers have declared that Moore's principles provided Brooke with little inner strength when his psychic world began to crumble around him at Lulworth. Yet Brooke never really expected them to help; he was constantly using and testing Moorist postulates for his own agenda.

For instance, one of the most striking early realistic poems is **"Wagner,"** a poem that has been grossly misread as being about the composer (Millard has mixed up Wagner's physical appearance with Rossini's). Written at Queen's Hall in 1908, **"Wagner"** describes "the state of mind"— to use the famous Moorist touchstone—of a man "with a fat wide hairless face" who comes to listen to Wagner because "He likes love-music that is cheap" and "Likes women in a crowded place." As he hears the music, he fantasizes, "thinks himself the lover," because "He likes to feel his heart's a-breaking." The last stanza describes him externally, and he has obviously not been transfigured by his experience: "His little lips are bright with slime. . . . His pendulous stomach hangs a-shaking." Brooke here questions the validity of such an artistic experience. Is a "state of mind" thus evoked by Wagner's music so as to induce dreams of romantic conquest and sorrow any less authentic, any less "good," than a more noble fantasy by a more prepossessing subject? If not, what of the state of mind of the poet who describes such an experience? In one of his most important letters, Brooke came close to answering these questions. Ben Keeling had written Brooke that he was becoming a pessimist, and Brooke attempted to dissuade him. Brooke called his solution either "mysticism or Life," and it consisted of viewing the world as it really was: "What happens is that I suddenly feel the extraordinary value and importance of everybody I meet, and almost everything I see. In *things* I am moved in this way especially by some things; but in people by almost all people. That is, when the mood is upon me. I roam about places . . . and sit in trains and see the essential glory and beauty of all the people I meet. I can watch a dirty middle-aged tradesman in a railway-carriage for hours, and love every dirty greasy sulky wrinkle in his weak chin and every button on his spotted unclean waistcoat. I know their states of mind are bad. But I'm so much occupied with their being there at all, that I don't have time to think of that." Of course, this was written in one of Brooke's own "optimistic" phases, in which he is close to the top of a manic mood swing. In these moments Brooke was acutely aware of what he called "the enchantment of being even for a moment alive in a world of real matter (not that imitation, gilt stuff, one gets in Heaven) and actual people:" quotidian matter and people are therefore appropriate subjects for his poems, and by treating them he refutes Moore and his "states of mind." **"Wagner"** is thus a kind of picture-within-a-picture; the fat man "ignobly" appreciates Wagner, and Brooke "ignobly" appreciates the fat man's appreciation.

Another aspect of Brooke's "realism" is its antiromanticism. Brooke proffered this reason as a justification to Marsh when defending his most notorious realistic poem, **"A Channel Passage."** In it a lover finds himself becoming seasick on a channel ferry and, as a preventive, tries to recall anything, but the only image that comes to mind is that of his lover: "You, you alone could hold my fancy forever!" Such remembrance, however, leaves the speaker with only the choice of "A sea-sick body, or a you-sick soul!" Instead of being a prophylactic, his lover's image acts as an emetic, as he is wracked with "The sobs and slobbers of a last year's woe" and vomits. Many critics have pointed out that the poem is in itself weak, yet one assumes Brooke realized the undercutting effect that the inverted word order of "up I throw" would have. Complaining that such a dose of realism, "the brutality of human emotions," was necessary "after I've beaten vain hands in the rosy mists of poets' experiences," Brooke invoked to Marsh the example of Shakespeare's sonnet 130, "My mistress' eyes are nothing like the sun." Brooke's main reason for writing **"Channel Passage"** seems to have been to stake out his own territory, independent of Marsh and of whatever other "dew-dabblers" were writing at the time. His most unpleasant unpublished poem, for example, concerns a lover celebrating his beloved's becoming the main course at a cannibal feast (preceding Evelyn Waugh's *Black Mischief* by about 20 years); it was written in a letter from the South Seas to the daughter of the prime minister of England, Violet Asquith. Not for nothing was one of his papers to the Apostles titled "Why Not Try the Other Leg?". . . .

Brooke's only serious poem on religious themes is **"Mary and Gabriel,"** a surprisingly lengthy (for Brooke) treatment of the Annunciation. Its uniqueness has prompted one critic to misread it: according to Pearsall [in *Rupert Brooke: The Man and Poet,* 1974], Brooke "had entered the hell period and was seeking for a religious identification as a means of getting out. This is a paranoid development as understood in psychiatry, and a desirable human development as understood in theology." Besides its muddling of religion and psychology, this analysis more crucially fails to take into account the most important omission in the poem: it is solely the account of the two title characters and never mentions God. In another of Brooke's frozen-moment poems, Gabriel is an androgynous messenger of the Ideal: "Not man's nor woman's was the immortal grace . . . lighting the proud eyes with changeless light." The moment of conception is described in phrases reminiscent, as Pearsall points out, of Yeats's "Leda and the Swan": "She felt a trembling stir / Within her body, a will too strong for her / That held and filled and mastered all." The only problem is that Yeats's poem was published some 11 years after Brooke's. In another example of Brooke's desire to offend any lingering Victorian proprieties, he also examines Mary's sexual sensations at the moment: "Under her breasts she had / Such multitudinous burnings, to and fro, / And throbs not understood." As she tries to understand what has happened to her, she looks at Gabriel, who is described in terms showing that to Brooke he is the representative of the disembodied love Brooke values so much (and carrying that *fleur du mal* that also marks him as a representative of Brooke's decadent past):

> He knelt unmoved, immortal; with his eyes
> Gazing beyond her, calm to the calm skies;
> Radiant, untroubled in his wisdom, kind.
> His sheaf of lilies stirred not in the wind.

This is not a Christian vision; rather it is Brooke's own personal dream-myth about his relationship with women and his working out of his failure to cross that last barrier between adolescence and maturity: becoming a father. Gabriel is a sexually ambiguous figure who bears close resemblance to descriptions of Brooke: "hair he had, or fire, / Bound back above his ears with golden wire, / Baring the eager marble of his face." As he flies away, "The whole air, singing, bore him up, and higher, / Unswerving, unreluctant. . . . She stood alone." Carnal love has been reduced to a moment of speech—"He told his word"—given by a messenger closer to Apollo than God. Significantly, Brooke carefully selected the same subject for the Eric Gill statues he bought as gifts for both Ka Cox

and Cathleen Nesbitt (they may even have been the same statue; a photograph of Nesbitt's is in her memoir): A Madonna and Child.

What may be called Brooke's two political poems are similarly ambivalent. **"Seaside"** is an early (1908) work; Hassall claims it is his first poem "which could only have been conceived by a natural poet." This sonnet was supposedly inspired by Brooke's decision to sign the Fabian Basis, but no reader without outside biographical knowledge could ascertain this from the poem itself. At a seaside resort (in Brooke's case, Torquay), the speaker finds himself pulled away from the favorably described sensory impressions of people, "the friendly lilt of the band, / The crowd's good laughter, the loved eyes of men," to that ambiguous boundary between nature and humanity, the beach. Out beyond is "The old unquiet ocean." The speaker is suspended, "Waiting for a sign," a phrase emphasized by its placement at the head of the sestet, which although enjambed, is spatially offset. This sign has something to do with the direction of the speaker's life, as he is drawn to the ocean: "And all my tides set seaward." Now the sounds of humanity are not so soothing, as the speaker hears "a gay fragment from some mocking tune." What— or whom does the tune mock? As the tune "dies between the seawall and the sea," the poem ends. Not only is the poem ambivalent about this experience; it is for Brooke uncharacteristically ambiguous. At this point in his life he may have already realized that, although Fabianism held a certain promise for his intellectual visions, it would not lead to any firm personal satisfaction or vocation.

"Second Best," from that same year, is, according to Hassall, Brooke's "only Socialist poem," yet that becomes apparent only from the imagery near the end of the poem. In it the speaker apostrophizes a heart, probably his own, which he calls "O faithful, O foolish lover." In one of Brooke's favorite settings, outdoors at night, the heart is pondering immortality, and the speaker tells it to "Throw down your dreams," because "night ends all things." Death is final for both joys and sorrows: "That gladness and those tears are over, over," so Death should be greeted "as a friend." Hardened by this realization, the heart is "Exile of immortality." After all this stoic preparation, introduced by the simple conjunction *yet,* comes the image of revolution that Brooke employed in **"The Bastille"**: "Yet, behind the night, / Waits for the great unborn, somewhere afar, / Some white tremendous daybreak." The paradise that will come after this dawn is reminiscent of another of Brooke's Edens, Never Land:

> Ocean a windless level, Earth a lawn
> Spacious and full of sunlit dancing-places,
> And laughter, and music, and, among the flowers,
> The gay child-hearts of men, and the child-faces,
> O heart, in the great dawn!

The lost boys have been found here. This vision also closely resembles the antiseptic, asexual paradise of the Eloi in Wells's *The Time Machine.* Brooke, like many other Edwardians, distrusted optimistic Victorian assumptions about progress; however, how humanity would arrive at this paradisiacal stage with only the help of a poetic image about the day breaking is unclear. One can readily see why Brooke's longer "epic" about socialism proved unworkable. . . .

Traveler

Brooke's trip to the South Seas and his stay there were a relatively productive period for him, even though in his letters home he deplored his indolence (he jocularly asked Marsh in his capacity as editor to write a couple of poems for him). The poems that he did write reveal a poet trying to come to some sort of psychic reconciliation with his past. In **"It's not going to Happen Again"** Brooke has obviously been influenced by the slang and colloquialism he had heard in America and Canada (over which he got into an argument with Marsh, who edited his letters from America before publication). The first stanza of the poem is as full of overblown rhetoric as anything Brooke wrote in his decadent phase: "Like a star I was hurled through the sweet of the world." The second part of the poem collapses this rhetoric with a skilled use of the vernacular in describing those lovers who elsewhere in Brooke's poetry were conventional symbols of passion: "What Paris was tellin' for good-bye to Helen / When he bundled her into the train." The last two lines of the poem, which repeat with studied emphasis the declaration of the title, are addressed not to the "my boy" of the first stanza, Brooke himself, but to an "old girl," probably Noel Olivier. The poem **"Love"** seems to refer to his relationship with Ka Cox, as its lovers are together yet separate, "but taking / Their own poor dreams within their arms, and lying / Each in his lonely night, each with a ghost." In **"Mutability"** (a favorite poetic subject from Spenser to Shelley), Brooke's Platonism emerges again: "Faith and Good, Wisdom and Truth"—what Brooke calls the *Aeterna Corpora,* eternal bodies, presumably opposed to the physical human bodies doomed to decay—are "subject to no change," unlike human love, in which "The laugh dies with the lips, 'Love' with the lover." One assumes Brooke was referring to this poem when he wrote Marsh from Vancouver, "I contemplate two short Sonnet Sequences (one including *Aeterna Corpora*)."

These sonnet sequences were, however, never completed; had Brooke lived long enough to learn to apply himself, the sonnet sequence might have been his best genre, as **"1914"** indicates. Yet poems with similar themes, and similar attempts at a detached viewpoint, did follow. Death in these poems does not, as it did before in Brooke's poetry, offer a chance to attain a love impossible for beings of flesh; rather, it represents, as it does in his earliest poetry, a rest and surcease from pain. The august but removed beneficence of the **"Clouds"** becomes a simile for the attitudes of the dead who "remain / Near to the rich heirs of their grief and mirth" and "ride the calm mid-heaven . . . And watch the moon, and the still-raging seas, / And men, coming and going on the earth." The ghostly lover in **"Hauntings"** is able to remember only "the ecstasy of your quietude," and mainly "Is haunted by strange doubts, evasive dreams, / Hints of a pre-Lethean life, of men, / Stars, rocks, and flesh things unintelligible." In a sense, these are the feelings

Brooke had about England and, more particularly, his new upper-class friends, when he was in the South Seas, for he quoted almost identical lines in a letter to Marsh from Tahiti about missing his new circle of friends.

Several poems from this period reveal the reconciliation Brooke was trying to achieve in his mind about the three main women in his life. **"Doubts,"** originally titled "To Cathleen," is another investigation of the mind-body split; the speaker wonders where his beloved's spirit goes while she sleeps, as she lies "still and fair, / Waiting empty, laid aside, / Like a dress upon a chair." Brooke's old process of idealizing his beloved is fully at work: her soul has "Wings where I may never go." Yet the speaker doubts that her soul really does wander, because her body frowns and smiles as she is asleep. The concluding couplet asks, "And if the spirit be not there, / Why is fragrance in the hair?", thus cleaning up the olfactory image from **"Lust"** that landed Brooke in a major disagreement with Marsh and Sidgwick—"your remembered smell most agony." This connection of self with smell seems to indicate a tentative coming to terms with the Platonic dualism that had beleaguered him before. And since this dualism had the force of a religion for him, **"Doubts"** is an appropriate title for the poem. The sense of smell, heretofore associated with sexual desire, is now associated, however tentatively, with the beloved's inner being, as well as her body.

> **Whether Brooke could have continued to turn his pity away from the self and toward others is the great unanswered question about the direction that Brooke's war poetry—indeed all of his poetry—would have taken had he lived.**
>
> **—*William Laskowski***

The subject of **"A Memory,"** written in Hawaii, is probably Noel Olivier, and again the speaker confronts his beloved as she sleeps. As the speaker kneels next to her bed, her hand reaches out and unconsciously holds his head, and he "had rest / Unhoped this side of Heaven, beneath your breast." The sestet of the sonnet conflates this moment (which Brooke claimed to Nesbitt actually happened one night) with their whole relationship: "It was great wrong you did me; and for gain / Of that poor moment's kindliness, and ease, / And sleepy mother-comfort!" That last phrase reveals a great deal about what substitutes Brooke was seeking in his relationships with women, a "lap" that he found so comforting and for which he had searched so long. Although admitting all this happens while his beloved sleeps, the speaker cannot help implying a sense of volition to his beloved's actions: the fingers that hold his head are "waking," even if she is not. The conclusion of the poem indicates that in this case the speaker has not yet been able to control his feelings about the past: "And love that's awakened so / Takes all too long to lay asleep again."

According to Hassall, Ka Cox is the subject of **"One Day,"** **"Waikiki,"** and **"Retrospect."** **"One Day,"** however, from what Hassall calls Brooke's "Modern Love" sequence, seems to be more about Noel Olivier. The speaker asserts that he has been happy all day, while he "held the memory of you." He has "sowed the sky with tiny clouds of love" and "crowned your head with fancies . . . Stray buds from that old dust of misery." Poems about Cox rarely admit the *speaker's* love, and the garland of "fancies" fits in more with Brooke's constant image of Noel Olivier as a dryad. The sester is more ominous; these memories become "a strange shining stone" that a child plays with, ignorant that for its sake "towns were fire of old, / And love has been betrayed, and murder done, / And great kings turned to a little bitter mould." Such a stone is not as "harmless" as Hassall says it is, particularly when the poem ends with such images. The transferral of such feelings into the past may be hoped for, but it is not yet complete. The child (another characteristic image) who holds the stone may be unaware of its history, yet the speaker is not. **"Waikiki"** is more definitely about Cox, and Hassall perceptively points out its similarity to the earlier **"Seaside."** Again the speaker is at the ocean's edge, but this time it is the music of "an *eukaleli*" that reaches his ears. Now he is not "waiting for a sign," as in the earlier poem, but trying to deal with his memories, and as in **"One Day,"** the memory is objectified and distanced into the dim past and the third person: "I recall, lose grasp, forget again, / And still remember" a story "Of two that loved—or did not love— and one / Whose perplexed heart did evil, foolishly, / A long while since, and by some other sea," words that echo Othello's last speech: "Of one that loved not wisely, but too well; / Of one not easily jealous, but, being wrought, / Perplexed in the extreme." In Othello's case, however, it is easy to discern that he is blaming himself; the speaker in **"Waikiki"** is indeterminate about who is to blame at the shore of that "other sea," which Hassall identifies as the Starnberger See, where Brooke and Cox once stayed. The use of the adjective *perplexed* would nevertheless seem to indicate that the speaker himself is tentatively ready to accept the blame for the "evil" that had occurred between the lovers.

By its title **"Retrospect"** reveals the stance Brooke is taking toward his relationship with Cox, although again much of the language in this poem could apply to Noel Olivier as well. Although Hassall bases his identification of the subject of the poem on the use of the phrase "mother-quiet," a similar phrase ("mother-comfort") was used in a poem about Olivier. Perhaps unconsciously Hassall noted the brutality of its line "In your stupidity I found / The sweet hush after a sweet sound," and felt that since Brooke used such phrases in letters about Cox, the poem must have been about her. Brooke, however, was not above calling Olivier stupid as well (Nesbitt seems to be the only woman who escaped such epithets). At any rate, the fact that it is difficult to determine the poem's biographical source indicates that Brooke was coming closer to reconciling and healing his memories for both of his earlier major loves. The speaker declares, in images reminiscent of the nature scenes in **"Grantchester,"** that his "thoughts of you . . . Were green leaves in a darkened

chamber, / Were dark clouds in a moonless sky." The speaker's previous use of the word *stupidity* is softened when he remembers his beloved's "vast unconsciousness," which is precisely why he seeks her. The poem, written in Tahiti, cannot help but echo Robert Louis Stevenson's language from "Requiem": "And home at length under the hill!" The beloved's "mother-quiet" will cause "love itself" to "faint and cease," another psychologically revealing line. And in a return to images Brooke employed in **"A Memory"** and **"One Day,"** the speaker's final wish is to return and lay his head "In your hands, ungarlanded," while he sleeps and she keeps watch over him. There is little doubt that such metaphors, while conciliatory and perhaps therapeutic, are regressive. The speaker returns in imagination to a lover whose motherhood is quiet and whose protection will cause the love in him not to grow but to end.

Many critics have pointed out how Brooke's best poem about his experiences in the South Seas, **"Tiare Tahiti,"** represents a step forward. At its start the poem treats characteristic themes, as the speaker tells his beloved that when they die they will become "dust about the doors of friends, / Or scent a-blowing down the night"; the bodies are no longer for Brooke the habitation of corruption. The paradise they shall enter is Platonic, where "the Eternals are": "The Good, the Lovely, and the True, / And Types," and "instead of lovers, Love shall be; / For hearts, Immutability." In a line that looks forward semiseriously to **"The Soldier,"** the speaker declares that "my laughter, and my pain, / Shall home to the Eternal Brain" so far **"Tiare Tahiti"** contains few surprises. But in the second long section, the speaker begins to describe how physical objects shall be subsumed into what he has called in the first section "the Eternals": a laugh, feet, hands, braided hair, a head—all connected with the Polynesian names of their owners. He catalogs the visual aspects of nature that will be there as well: the colors of coral, rainbows, birds, sunsets and sunrises. Most important is the figure who will be absent from this scene, the former speaker in Brooke's poetry, who was consumed with the dooms of chronological passion: "one who dreams . . . of crumbling stuff, / Eyes of illusion, mouth that seems, / All time-entangled human love." If all these things subsided into the ideal, the speaker asks, then how can the lovers worship each other? "How shall we wind these wreaths of ours, / Where there are neither heads nor flowers?" Significantly, the speaker here, unlike in **"Retrospect,"** allows his own head to be garlanded as well, because the passion is mutual.

Thus, the last section begins with the command to his beloved to "Crown the hair, and come away!" In a line reminiscent of W.H. Auden's acceptance of mortal frailty in "Lullaby" ("Human on my faithless arm"), the speaker tells Mamua to "Hasten, hand in human hand, / Down the dark, the flowered way." The image of a dark floral place, which before had been separated from the speaker by space (**"Grantchester"**) and time (**"Retrospect"**), is here accepted and experienced. As Delaney has pointed out, the image of water in **"Tiare Tahiti"**—its "soft caress"— represents a transformation from its formerly absolute function in Brooke's poetry (and letters). Its use also shows that the speaker has become one with the world of **"The Fish"**: "Pursuing down the soundless deep / Limbs that gleam and shadowy hair." No longer is there "the strife of limbs"; indeed, the lovers are able to bring the world of color and individuality into the formless depths. The last litany shows that the speaker has embraced what has formerly been mistrusted in Brooke's poetry: "lips that fade, and human laughter, / And faces individual, / Well this side of Paradise!" While this is a crucial progression in Brooke's development, it ultimately proved to be a dead end, for he compartmentalized his experience in the South Seas as rigidly as he did other areas of his life, and he did not live long enough to re-integrate them into his life when he returned to England.

One final poem from this period is significant, since it represents Brooke's response to a criticism that later was to be made often of his poetry: that its language and imagery were too abstract. Marsh wrote to him, "I hope you are writing something objective"; there were too many words like *dear* and *love* in Brooke's recent poems for Marsh's taste. In response Brooke wrote **"The Great Lover."** Its first section is full of the bombast he could produce so unerringly, full of sly echoes of Victorian poetic rhetoric, such as Tennyson's in "Ulysses":

> Shall I not crown them with immortal praise
> Whom I have loved, who have given me, dared with
>   me,
> High secrets, and in darkness knelt to see
> The inerrable godhead of delight?

One cannot parody a style well without being somewhat in sympathy with it, so the catalog of specific sensory images that follows sometimes lapses into a rhetoric of its own, closer to Georgian conventions: "feathery, faery dust . . . And flowers themselves, that sway through sunny hours, / Dreaming of moths that drink them under the moon." Other images in the list smack of Belloc's heartiness: "the strong crust / Of friendly bread; and many-tasting food." Some are familiar from other of Brooke's poems, particularly those images involving smell: "Hair's fragrance, and the musty reek that lingers / About dead leaves and last year's ferns." None of them are overtly sexual. When this litany is complete, the speaker declares, "And these shall pass," and even boasts about their transitoriness: "They'll play deserter, turn with the traitor breath." He claims that he shall awaken in some afterlife but will never be able to reclaim the earthly loves he has listed:

> But the best I've known
> Stays here, and changes, breaks, grows old, is
>   blown
> About the winds of the world, and fades from
>   brains
> Of living men, and dies.
> Nothing remains.

Brooke faintly echoes the verbs of Donne's holy sonnet "Batter My Heart" ("to breake, blowe, burn and make me

new"), but while Donne praises God for destroying his personality in order to anneal it, Brooke is now able to exult in ephemerality. The traditional use of the impermanence of the physical world in poetry has been to contrast it to the immortality of art, as in Shakespeare's sonnet 55, "Not marble nor the gilded monuments," and, within that tradition, to immortalize the poet's portrait of his beloved: "So, till the judgment that yourself arise, / You live in this, and dwell in lovers' eyes." In Brooke's terms this Shakespearean vow becomes "that after men / Shall know, and later lovers, far-removed, / Praise you, 'All these were lovely'; say, 'He loved.'" In the act of treasuring the most ephemeral objects, Brooke is able to come to terms with what had before most troubled him, the inevitability of changing, growing older, and dying. As he wrote to Keeling in his letter on optimism, "I don't know that 'Progress' is certain. All I know is that change is. . . . All this present overwhelming reality will be as dead and odd and fantastic as crinolines or 'a dish of tay.' Something will be in its place, inevitably. And what that something will be, depends on me." Unfortunately, Brooke was never able to hold on to such moods consistently.

Soldier

It is almost impossible to disentangle an analysis of Brooke's war poems from the history of their reception, which in many senses mirrors the history of the transformations of attitudes toward the World War I. The poems were immediately grasped at by a wide segment of the public; the issue of *New Numbers* in which they first appeared quickly sold out. Brooke's death ensured that few reading them would be able to separate the poems from the man, and even more so from the myth he had become. When the war became stalemated along the Western front and casualty lists exploded, some began to question the emotions portrayed in Brooke's war poems, while others held on to them for consolation. After the war the poems slowly grew notorious, until their reputation today, when only **"The Soldier"** is included in anthologies as the archetypal statement of the "old Lie" that Wilfred Owen excoriated later in the war in "Dulce et Decorum Est."

Yet Brooke's war sonnets are the direct outgrowth of the themes and subjects Brooke had been exploring for years. They were not made-to-order propaganda; Brooke had tried and failed to get a job that would make use of any abilities he had in that line. The reality is that the first line of **"Peace"** ("Now, God be thanked Who matched us with this hour") was true: Brooke's own personal sentiments had been precisely matched with the needs of his time. Nowhere can the transition between personal and public sentiment be more easily seen than in his sonnet **"The Treasure,"** written in August 1914, and meant to be read with the five sonnets of **"1914."** It is a reverse sonnet, with the sestet preceding the octave. The meaning of the first line, "When colour goes home into the eyes," of which Brooke was inordinately proud, is obscure, but taken with the other five lines it seems to imply the moment of death. Images of sight and sound—"lights that shine," "dancing girls and sweet birds' cries"—are all closed behind an area Brooke is becoming increasingly interested in: "the gateways of the brain." Two symbols of color, "the rainbow and the rose," are also shut by "that no-place that gave them birth." Brooke's refusal to believe in an afterlife has led him to transform utopia into its literal meaning: "no-place," the blankness that precedes and follows life. The mind, which Brooke had heretofore imagined as capable of journeying anywhere, has now shrunk to the limits of the "brain," and the images that "go home" are an amalgam of England (the rose) and the South Seas (dancing girls). When the consciousness dies, so do the perceptions that, the poem strongly suggests, the consciousness has created.

The concluding octave of the sonnet develops the metaphor of **"The Great Lover"** as a cherisher of images and experiences but in a curious way. The speaker hopes that, before death, time will let him "unpack" his "store" (the alternative title for the poem) in "some golden space," and the poem ends on an extended simile of the memory

> as a mother, who
> Has watched her children all the rich day through,
> Sits, quiet-handed, in the fading light,
> When children sleep, ere night.

Brooke has taken the image of the mother, which is usually applied to various types of beloved women in his poetry, and internalized it into a figure of guardianship and appreciation. It is almost impossible not to be tempted to link this metamorphosis with the feeling he expressed in his letters just before he returned to England ("I've such a warmth for the Ranee"), and while Brooke was always temperamentally driven to love more warmly that from which he was absent, he showed an even more intense fondness toward England on his return, an emotion that never abated.

While **"The Treasure"** might imply some sort of progression in Brooke's development, **"Peace,"** the first of the **"1914"** sonnets, displays many of the unpleasant characteristics of Brooke's post-Lulworth metamorphosis. The image of the diving swimmer returns in the notorious simile of the recruits (the poem's alternate title was "The Recruit") as "swimmers into cleanness leaping." They are washing away all the evils of modern life, "a world grown old and cold and weary," including what is generally taken to be a kick at Bloomsbury, the "half-men, and their dirty songs and dreary," and a fault that even those who admired and liked Brooke found hard to accept, what he called "all the little emptiness of love!" The war will provide the recruits, whose principal weakness is that they "have known shame," with an opportunity, quite simply, when the rhetoric is stripped away, to die; "the worst friend and enemy is but Death." Thus Brooke has come full circle in his poetry, and the figure of Death that hovers over so much of his early decadent poetry reappears. Most of this would be of interest only to the psychobiographer, did not (as will be shown) so many of Brooke's fellow citizens did share his sentiments that the war represented the chance to flush away all the slackness and foreignness they felt had heretofore sickened and weakened English culture.

"Safety" is addressed to the speaker's beloved and thus narrows the rhetorical focus of the sonnets from the broad "we" of **"Peace,"** specifically the recruits but potentially all of England, to the narrow "we" of two lovers. The "safety" of the poem is, of course, not physical safety but emotional if not spiritual protection. The lovers' safety will be with "all things undying," and in listing them Brooke succumbs to Georgian rhetoric and his own hollow heartiness: "The winds, and morning, tears of men and mirth, / The deep night, and birds singing, and clouds flying, / And sleep, and freedom, and the autumnal earth." There is not one fresh or striking image among them: this is Brooke's "fill-in-the-blanks" method of writing poetry at its most vapid. The sestet once again leads up to death as the ultimate consolation: "And if these poor limbs die, safest of all." It is difficult to believe in the consolatory power of such images, even in a nation in desperate need of them, and while Brooke does allude to death's analgesic effect ("a peace unshaken by pain for ever"), in his own case it provides a cessation not of physical but of mental and emotional pain.

Not surprisingly, sonnets 3 and 4 are both called **"The Dead."** In both of them the dead are addressed in the third person, with sonnet 3 apostrophizing the bugles that will sound over the dead, and sonnet 4 describing them. The third sonnet contains the notorious simile for the blood that would be spilled in war, "the red / Sweet wine of youth," which provided the title for the worst book written about Brooke. Uncharacteristically, old age is here called "that unhoped serene," but the speaker does define youth's greatest sacrifice: the giving up of the chance to have children, "their immortality," a thought that had been growing in Brooke's own mind as one of the reasons for an urgent wartime marriage. The dead also bring back a series of abstractions—"Holiness," "Love," "Pain," and "Honour," and "Nobleness"—with the ambiguous prepositional phrase "for our dearth," which can mean either that they have come because the English lacked them before the war or that they have come to make up their insufficiency. The last line of the sonnet, "we have come into our heritage" supports the first reading of the phrase, that the war has given the English a chance to fulfill themselves, and continues the theme introduced in **"Peace"** that the war is a cleansing, revivifying event.

Sonnet 4 returns to the themes of **"The Treasure."** Those who have died have possessed dawn and sunset "and the colours of the earth," and the rest of the images in the octave follow Brooke's characteristic sensory catalog: "Touched flowers and furs and cheeks." "All this is ended," the octave concludes: Brooke does not say the dead have died, but they have stopped feeling. The sestet is an extended metaphor in which the movements of the sea, a favorite place of contemplation for Brooke, are stilled by "Frost, with a gesture." The description of the frozen sea is by extension a description of the dead: "a white / Unbroken glory, a gathered radiance, / A width, a shining peace." This is the sign Brooke has been waiting for since **"The Seaside."** Once again a moment has been frozen, but unlike **"Dining-Room Tea,"** in which a moment from life is forever captured, here death itself is embalmed. Peace, a powerful word for those who have suffered the agonies of war, is equally powerful for Brooke, who was ironically searching for peace while waging its opposite.

The last poem, **"The Soldier,"** is Brooke's most famous, the poem inscribed by Eric Gill on his memorial in Rugby chapel, the poem by which Brooke can most easily be identified to people who do not otherwise know his name. Its most famous image, "some corner of a foreign field / That is for ever England," has been exhaustively analyzed and even called a symbol of economic imperialism. More insightfully, the image's origin has been traced to one of Brooke's favorite books, Belloc's *The Four Men,* whose last chapter contains a poem establishing this sentiment: "One with our random fields we grow. . . . He does not die that can bequeath / Some influence to the land he knows . . . He does not die, but still remains / Substantiate with his darling plains." Brooke may have repeated the sentiment, but he vastly improved the rhetoric of the utterance. In an uncanny irony for a poem written in 1911, Belloc's poem also contains an allusion to no-man's land. The use of this phrase by both Belloc and those who fought on the Western front reveals one reason why **"The Soldier"** became so popular: death had become so anonymous (this war originated the memorials to the unknown solider), and the struggle for a small piece of territory so seemingly meaningless, that any means that could personalize and localize sacrifice were seized on. The image of the afterlife in **"The Soldier"** that Dean Inge criticized in his sermon— "a pulse in the eternal mind"—is a continuation of the tentative substitutes for the afterlife that Brooke had been exploring in his recent poetry. Adorned with dreams, laughter, and gentleness, this afterlife is in a sense a regression to the safe and sterile Platonic paradises of Brooke's earlier work. The heaven for which Brooke had been searching so long, now called specifically English, has washed clean the sin and pain of **"Peace"** ("all evil shed away"), and the "hearts at peace" in the last line of the poem fulfill the promise of the title of the first poem. War, not the political revolution of **"The Bastille,"** will remove guilt and sin.

The fragments Brooke wrote en route to the Dardanelles are curiously ambiguous. While they present certain characteristic images and themes and are thus a continuation of "1914," in several instances they offer hints that Brooke was ready to strike into out what for him would have been new ground and can be viewed as fitting in with various aspects of later English poetry of the war. For instance, in the **"Fragment"** that Keynes selects to lead off his edition of *The Poetical Works,* the speaker, wandering on deck at night and watching unseen his friends performing various actions, sees all of them in a Platonic simile: "Like coloured shadows, thinner than filmy glass." Then he imagines all of them as dead, "Perishing things and strange ghosts—soon to die / To other ghosts—this one, or that, or I." None of this is unusual for Brooke, but the second stanza of the poem, with its images of masculine beauty and its admission of pity, is strongly reminiscent of the poetry of Wilfred Owen:

> I would have thought of them
> —Heedless, within a week of battle—in pity,

Pride in their strength and in the weight and firmness
And link'd beauty of bodies, and pity that
This gay machine of splendour'ld soon be broken,
Thought little of, pashed, scattered. . . .

Similarly, **"Lines for an Ode-Threnody on England,"** some of which appropriately was written at 10 Downing Street before Brooke embarked, explores the paradox implicit in **"The Treasure"**: that England, while an external object, is also capable of being completely internalized: "She is with all we have loved and found and known, / Closed in the little nowhere of the brain." Since the poem is in such rough shape, it cannot, of course, bear rigorous analysis; for instance, it has been criticized for the line, of which Brooke was very fond, "In Avons of the heart her rivers run." The objection is that the line amounts to nonsense, because rivers are running in a river. Yet Brooke is working through the double process by which a national entity is created internally by the mind and by which it is extended through sacrifice into "a corner of a foreign field," so perhaps the echolalic metaphor is somehow appropriate.

The other fragments offer few surprises. One recounts how a song from the troop decks reminds the speaker of a memory with his beloved on a hill when "youth was / in our hands." Another connects the present war with the Homeric world: "Death and sleep / Bear many a young Sarpedon home." The last fragment Keynes includes seems like a sequel to **"The Soldier,"** and its last lines are obviously meant by Keynes to be taken as Brooke's epitaph just as much as the earlier sonnet often is: "He is / The silence following great words of peace." Only one fragment indicates any new direction, in which Brooke combines realistic and Georgian diction: "'When Nobby tried . . . To stop a shrapnel with his belly' . . . But *he* went out, did Nobby Clark, / Upon the illimitable dark." This comes closer to the voice and focus of Robert Graves and Siegfried Sassoon. "The Poetry is in the pity," Owen wrote in the preface to his poems. Whether Brooke could have continued to turn his pity away from the self and toward others is the great unanswered question about the direction that Brooke's war poetry—indeed all of his poetry— would have taken had he lived.

Clive Bloom (essay date 1995)

SOURCE: "The Falling House that Never Falls: Rupert Brooke and Literary Taste," in *British Poetry, 1900-50: Aspects of Tradition,* edited by Gary Day and Brian Docherty, St. Martin's Press, 1995, pp. 37-47.

[*In the following essay, Bloom argues that Brooke should be perceived as a modernist poet and urges a reassessment of his work.*]

'Rupert Brooke's poetry remains a firm favourite with readers and listeners alike': such might be the opinion of the popular poetry radio programmes broadcast by BBC Radio 4 or, perhaps, the comments in the introduction to yet another anthology of the slim collected works (with a selection of letters added for good measure). Brooke's reputation, which is at stake here, has never rested on anything other than quicksand. The 'worth' or quality of his poetic ability becomes, as has rarely been the case with any but Dylan Thomas, subordinated to a quasi-biographical determinism in which the poetry itself plays little part. It is ironic yet it can be said that the value of Brooke's reputation is independent of the very work he did to secure that reputation.

As a 'firm favourite', Brooke is damned as a lower-grade Kiplingesque populist by the academic community whose fare consists of the modernists and those the modernists chose to applaud. Meanwhile Brooke is relegated to the outer corridors of fame, conversing posthumously with the likes of both Ella Wheeler Wilcox and Longfellow. In such a way, Brooke is left to those whose poetic taste is untrained except by personal predisposition and whose 'love' of poetry consists of enjoying a large chunk of meaning laced with a keen disregard for free verse. Brooke's Georgianism is damned both by those who dislike it (academics) and those who applaud it ('untrained' amateurs). To like Brooke is a form of eccentricity, peculiar to the English upper middle classes, akin to that dilettantism which would prefer an elderberry wine to a vintage claret.

Having safely relegated Brooke's poetry to the realm of amateur taste, professional opinion can comfortably exist on the acceptable fare of modernism and pre- or post-modernist tendencies. This, I contend, has little to do with the merit or otherwise of particular writers, it is much more to do with the history of academic predisposition.

What might a typical poetry course look like? Most poetry courses would include Yeats and Eliot in their survey, they could then chose other rankers: Auden, Spender, MacNeice, and then, perhaps Larkin, Hughes and Heaney. At this point a loss of nerve would set in. They might have some Hardy, as a token of changes in poetic taste, but Kipling could be added only for the sake of debunking. Owen would represent war (*all* war). Plath, whose poetic abilities are not as great as claimed, would be included for the sake of form, and because she also represents a type of obligatory tokenism in British poetry courses despite being an American. Finally, new writing, where it was possible to include it, would consist of 'fringe' writers, writers found outside the 'canon', in order to appease students who dislike upper-middle-class-white-male-Oxbridge-educated-types and who need a dose of proletarian consciousness. The lecturer might turn gratefully to the very anthologies that inevitably prove pretty conclusively that the best poetry written in Britain in the last hundred years came from the very poets whose gender and education are now so out of fashion.

Although the canon of the literary great among novelists has been radically challenged, such a challenge to the canon of acceptable poets has not. Recent tastes masquerade as valid professional judgements, and female poets who indulge in four-letter words are acceptable primarily because the establishment (from which they come, to which they belong, and against which they intend no harm) can provide the very *fake* radical oppositional voices that half-educated students think are relevant. This amounts to a case of the emperor's new clothes. Alternative traditions and attitudes are always acceptable but not ever at the expense of the *full* and complex *real* history of poetry in this country.

Georgianism is the expression of British poetry in the twentieth century and yet modernism, with its primarily American base (Amy Lowell, H. D., Eliot, Pound and company) has taken the Georgians' place and stepped across the shadow they throw in order to obscure them. Which is simply to say that before we look for alternative new voices we must *recuperate* what has been lost and re-evaluate its relevance. This is *not* a question of the quality of the poetry produced—such is not the point. What is at stake is the very idea of poetry as having a real lived material history which one must explore. The names on such a 'lost' list are Housman, Brooke, de la Mare, Masefield, Graves, Hughes, Thomas (Edward and Dylan) and many others. The influence extends through much of the poetry of the First World War and that of the Second World War as well as to Larkin and the so-called post-modernism attributed to those anthologised in the *Penguin Book of Contemporary Verse* edited by Blake Morrison and Andrew Motion in 1982.

Let me repeat, this is not a question of the quality of the works produced but a simple form of justice to poetic history and its grounding in material history. The work of feminist publishing houses has recuperated much of the 'lost' in women's writing and this we must do for poetry. Most of the poets I have listed have never been out of print, so the books are readily available; what is missing is the breaking out from methods of constructing poetic histories which circle around T. S. Eliot, however massive his influence. The other still voice in the poetic history of Britain in the modern age is the voice exemplified in Brooke. And this voice, as we shall see, has much more in common with the modernism of Eliot than is usually accepted by those only concerned with Brooke's association with the Georgian anthologies. The equation lacks its constituent parts, for the work of Ezra Pound and T. S. Eliot must be seen in conjunction, in Britain, with the work of Rupert Brooke and Edward Marsh. Such was the complex parallelism of influence that lead to the 'English' modernism of Virginia Woolf and the horticultural design interests of her friend Vita Sackville-West. Indeed, hostility to Georgianism did not come from the major modernists, however much they wished to carve out a path for themselves. What existed was rather, on the one hand a techno-futuristic modernism whose interests were urban and functional, and on the other a ruralist modernism whose interests were countrified and decorative. The two strands were *not* incompatible in modernism's heyday but have been pronounced incompatible only retrospectively. The latter type of Georgianism has become out of fashion, stranded in a Laura Ashley whimsicality, whereas the former has gained strength as the *only* form of modernism acceptable.

What must be said is that Brooke's poetry, more than much of that of his contemporaries, *is* modern in the terms of either of these two types of modernistic approach. Why then does Brooke exist only as a 'reputation' and as a marker and yet Eliot exist as a full-blown poet whose work is studied?

Before looking for an answer to the question just set, we must pause to answer a real problem in literary history. If we are to recuperate historical writers who are rarely read, at what point do we stop? The ideological inconsistency of the canon of fiction as the Leavises (husband and wife) constructed it was undermined by those whose egalitarianism mistook popular for better. If the canon was to be taught, then so were Agatha Christie, Dorothy L. Sayers, Baroness Orczy and Mills and Boon. This, all in the name of relevance. Relevance to what? If to an idea of quality, then the list just given hardly dents even the shadow of the Leavises' Desert Island selection. If relevant only to history, then the questions posed by art and the formal conditions governing aesthetics would of necessity collapse. What happened was that the barriers did collapse and everything became acceptable; for the discovery of Kate Chopin or Alice Walker we have paid with the study of such dross as feminist science fiction and lesbian detective tales.

And yet this was not a real emancipation of lost, forgotten or half-remembered relevant texts, but a partial recuperation of what is now actually only fashionable but which disguises that fashionableness with an appeal to an unwritten agenda that suggests some texts are higher than others on the 'worthiness' scale. Any real recuperation, however, must also include the *unacceptable,* that which is racist, sexist, imperialist, ageist, rightist and elitist, and this is a hard pill to swallow. We long ago learned to turn away from the anti-semitic, misogynistic and religious T. S. Eliot in order to understand both his contribution to culture's understanding of itself (alienation) and his contribution to literary form (style). In some ways we have stripped Eliot of content in order to salvage his achievement.

It is the very opposite with Brooke—if only he'd not written those war sonnets! Brooke's contribution to formal practice (style) is relegated to a secondary position whilst stripped from a content highlighted for its naivety and gross nationalist romance. In Eliot's case we recuperate his verse and in Brooke's damn it with a classic double standard.

Let me pull some arguments together after this long digression, before returning to the question of Brooke's position in literary history. First, 'academics' (except in a form of tokenism) have not found an alternative poetic tradition to the one usually offered in courses. However, within those courses a radical suppression has occurred that has distorted poetic history by an act of omission. In general literary courses the idea of the canon has only been undermined by an inclusiveness so wide as to be meaningless. Hence two things have been lost: the first is a sense of what art is and what it does. These are formal questions reserved for the realm of aesthetic analysis. The second is a sense of real history at work in the formal properties of the text and from which the text emerges as a type of *dialogue* with its culture. By widening choice in

courses, the Leavises are not answered on any of their points (however right or wrong), they are merely *overrun.* By avoiding the forces of real historical process, the questions proper to the study of art (its discipline) do not even get approached. Brooke is a particular victim.

One must acknowledge that the forces that allowed Brooke to become a brilliant and urbane stylist (his class background, education, expectations etc.) also made much of what he said difficult to swallow. What too many people do is chuck out the baby with the bathwater: we must have the poet as a totality if he is to be seen and understood as a poet *qua* poet and if his poetry is to have any independent value.

People rarely die on cue. Brooke's glory and his tragedy is that he died 'on cue' in 1915. Unlike Owen (a poet technically of a lesser stature but able to put into words the horror of the war), Brooke's 'final' words were patriotic and, apparently jingoistic. Owen's hatred of war quite correctly gained the limelight once the war had finished but, in doing so, distorted the importance of Brooke's artistic (formal) achievement, which was 'suppressed' in favour of works whose content spoke of suffering banality.

Once dead, Brooke as the golden boy became the mythic tool of those who need heroes and hero worship. Brooke stood for an attitude which canonised him, his generation and his era and at the same time delivered his poetry over to non-professional advocacy. Parellel with the canonisation of Brooke by imperialist conservatives such as Winston Churchill, was the suppression of Brooke by the rising oppositional forces within Cambridge academics.

It was now indeed that in Cambridge, modern English literature made its appearance as an object of study for those released from the rigours of war and disillusioned by establishment (classical?) values. I. A. Richards's *Principles of Literary Criticism* became the standard text for what one did when studying literature. Such study was required to be *seen to be* impersonal and scientific and rigorous: as a former psychologist, Richards saw literature as a branch of communication and the study of literature as a branch of communication study (a behavioural process originating in neurology). This whole pseudo-scientific procedure was needed to give the fledgeling study of modern literature a real base, but its origin lay not in the human sciences such as psychology or sociology but actually in T. S. Eliot's essay 'Tradition and the Individual Talent'. This aesthetic base was predicated on the idea of impersonality and of art as a cultural artefact. Richards's work is deeply indebted to Eliot's functionalist approach, which, whatever else it did, would, through the *pedagogy* of Richards, force all poetry to conform to modernist canons of taste. Richards's version of scientific enquiry was ultimately a procedure based on an aesthetic of modernist taste. In such a process the romantic personality cult of Brooke could only fare badly at the hands of the professionals.

At the same time, the '*Scrutiny* Group' around F. R. and Q. D. Leavis were in an embattled position not only against the establishment in Cambridge but also against the philistines of 'Golders Green' (see Eliot's 'A Cooking Egg'). Although they were not interested in Brooke *per se,* his reputation does badly under the attacks on the reading habits of Cambridge dons (an attack led by Queenie Leavis). Donnish taste, it seems, was in the same lamentable condition as that of the philistine public. Brooke, it turned out, was liked by both readerships. In Q. D. Leavis's 'The Case of Miss Dorothy Sayers' she trounces Sayers and those academics whose lack of judgement support the latter's way of writing. In the essay, Leavis identifies those shelves kept for show in a don's house and those where the books are actually read and enjoyed. On *these shelves* all that is second-rate and 'easy' is collected, including the work of Brooke.

> Run your eyes over enough academic bookshelves—not those housing shop but those where they keep what they really choose to read—and you get accustomed to a certain association of authors representing an average taste which is at best negative: Edward Lear and Ernest Bramah's *Kai Lung* (delicious humour), Charles Morgan and C. E. Montague (stylists), Rupert Brooke (or Humbert Wolfe or some equivalent), . . . we can all supplement.

While Leavis and his wife acted as the opposition to Richards, Richards actually saw himself as a force for radical change in the gentleman's club of Cambridge. Of course, *both* Richards and the Leavis group felt themselves to be outside the establishment of Cambridge. How implicated in the establishment appeared Brooke and how loved by uninformed opinion! For Richards, whose work relied on Eliot's aesthetics, Brooke was outside the pale, because he was apparently an unregenerated romantic whose work did not conform to the aesthetic paradigm (clinically exact) of T. S. Eliot. For F. R. Leavis and his wife, Brooke's work belonged to those who *think* they are educated but who fail the acid test of culture (as defined by them and based firmly in the aesthetic of Eliot's seminal essay).

In such a way, and devoid of professional advocacy, Brooke's work fell foul of the very academic prejudice needed to launch modern literary studies in the first place. A pre-eminent modern writer, Brooke became a nowhere figure stranded helplessly at ten to three one sunny afternoon in Grantchester in 1912. For generations of English students modernism *was* English literature and T. S. Eliot was English poetry. Indeed, somehow one couldn't even study Brooke 'objectively' for his very emotionalism got in the way of the intellectual force of the argument; T. S. Eliot had convinced academics to convince themselves that poetry was a branch of philosophy or politics or theology.

The attack on the establishment by Richards and Leavis was doubly compounded when the New Left alliance in the 1960s and 1970s attacked Richards and Leavis themselves for being the voice of conservatism. In this attack, Brooke, imperialism, conservatism, liberal-humanist consensus were all crudely lumped together.

Those who supported Leavis were branded 'Leavisites', and the discipline of English letters as it had existed from 1917 to the mid-seventies began to fall apart. In this, Brooke became a casualty yet again—this time through association with perceptions about Leavis's conservatism—that very conservatism that had attacked Brooke years before!

On the Left, another story emerged. For the Left, a proper Marxist aesthetic has always been a problem, and an answer that allows for art has never really been successful. While historical materialism very adequately answers questions of cultural production and reception, it has no proper answer to questions about 'quality', 'value' and 'importance'. In a very basic sense, for Marxism, because all literature reveals the contradictions in social forces, the very best literature simply papers over the contradictions with greater skill. To such a Marxist view, the one levelled at Brooke, the work of art is always *faulty,* its perfection a deceptive bourgeois device to hide the contradictory tensions latent in society. In this view all art is *failure.* To Leavisite humanism the Brookian poetic is a failure because it says nothing true about the eternality of human values, whereas to the Marxist it is a failure because it says too much. On one count Brooke fails the quality test, on the other the test of being too obviously historical: a product of an imperialist élitist establishment. Curiously, the Leavis approach is the 'properly' formal examination as the Marxist would have to invoke outside criteria and then apply a *moral* caveat.

Thus has Brooke's reputation fared in scholarly debate— our loss of nerve over the empire and over our role in the world contributed to a worried condemnation of Brooke as representative of all we wished *not* to remember in the last hundred or so years.

For poets this was otherwise. By the 1940s modernism had lost its hold in Britain, Eliot was discredited because of his return to the church, Auden had scurried off to the United States when war broke out, Pound was in Fascist Italy, Yeats was dead. British poets, under the pressure of the War (and later Suez, with the introspective period that followed), rediscovered the Georgianism 'lost' previously. Yet the Georgianism they discovered was not that of Brooke but rather an emotionalised romantic ruralist poetry that appealed to 'ordinary folk' and which avoided the harsh, cynical and urbane note struck by Brooke. Rather than Brooke, we get a version of the world by a latter-day Edward Thomas or W. H. Davies.

The 'parochiality' actively sought by Larkin or the later Liverpool poets is quite against the grain of a parochial/lyrical content in Brooke, which is always at a distance from the metropolitan—international voice he employs. Quite simply, Brooke has more in common with T. S. Eliot than with Larkin and has more the tone of e. e. cummings or Noel Coward than that of Dylan Thomas.

> It's the very first word that poor Juliet heard
>   From her Romeo over the Styx;
> And the Roman will tell Cleopatra in hell

When she starts her immortal old tricks;
What Paris was tellin' for good-bye to Helen
  When he bundled her into the train—
Oh, it's not going to happen again, old girl,
  It's not going to happen again.

           ('**It's not going to Happen Again'**)

Georgianism is not a movement, despite any argument to the contrary—rather it describes another current in the modern movement sometimes parallel to and sometimes intermixed with imagism, vorticism and futurism. Despite the fact that many see Georgian poetry as a tag-end Victorianism, it is (again, despite its adherence to rhyme, metre and traditional content) a full branch of *modern* poetry. Note here, indeed, how Eliot himself adheres to strict metres and traditional rhyme.

If the tag 'Georgian' is dropped for a moment, then Brooke emerges as a modern writer with the concerns, both aesthetic and historical, of those who are known as modernists. His work is at once dextrous, urbane, metropolitan, 'free', distanced and ironic; his subject matter, modern life and experience. As a modern, his work also reveals the prejudice and posturing of that group of people at that time, and this cannot be ignored.

I do not intend in this essay to explore the importance of Brooke to the British version of the modernist movement or to attempt to prove in detail the relationship between modernist theory and Brooke's techniques. It must suffice that Brooke needs to be read with the same critical apparatus as T. S. Eliot and judged accordingly. Here, I reiterate that the question of quality is a separate issue and that I am only concerned to show that if a certain procedure is followed then Eliot and Brooke emerge as stablemates.

As a modernist, Brooke's best work compares more than favourably with that of Ezra Pound, and his work with Edward Marsh is every bit as distinguished as Pound's achievement with *Poetry*. What Brooke adds is a dimension rarely present in the functionalist performances of the imagists. In **"Grantchester"** (whose influence in terms of 'tone' on *The Waste Land* is rarely acknowledged) Brooke proves himself both a highly serious modernist and a Hogarthian humourist. His wit is founded on an attitude both distanced and yet comfortable. Brooke is both alienated and dispossessed, yet the seriousness of the meditation is only possible via the satiric panorama he puts before us.

Humour is a rarity in the modernist movement yet it goes with the urbane and sophisticated tone we expect of some aspects of modernism: those of Noel Coward, P. G. Wodehouse, Irving Berlin or Cole Porter. '**Grantchester**' is, in this sense, a supremely cool and controlled poem, with its roots in Alexander Pope rather than Wordsworth and with its message drawn from money, continental travel and speed. At every point that '**Grantchester**' has a Browningesque nostalgia it is undercut by a satiric distaste for the object of that nostalgia. Parochial in its subject matter yet international in its style, '**Grantchester**' is the 'other' of *The Waste Land* and should be read by the discerning as a prefiguring and a commentary on Eliot's work. Brooke's

work is almost *the* epic of the English character, both comic and yet, because comic, also true.

Brooke's achievement in the war sonnets, '1914 Sonnets I-V', is to provide a language the totality of which transcends its literal meaning. His phrasing displays a control of language which does not allow the musicality of that phrasing to be reduced to the banal jingoism of passions which hardly can have been felt by Brooke! Eliot 'proved' that sincerity was an unnecessary criterion in poetic appreciation. Whilst Brooke's message appears 'hot' and sincere, his control is as cool as a modernist's martini. The clean lines of the functional swimmer predominate. If we are embarrassed by nationalism we need not be embarrassed by the skill of the maker.

This might be special pleading on behalf of Brooke, but the message of modernism is the message of internal coherence. Purpose (moral integrity) had been replaced by organisation (aesthetic integrity), and the sonnets measure up to this criterion. The *skill* of the artist must be seen as integral to the message and the message as integral to the aesthetic (poetic) strategy of the poet in his culture. In such a way, Brooke can be seen as working complex emotional issues through a control of literary technical skills against which the overt anti-war messages of Owen appear dull and repetitive.

Brooke's oeuvre is slight, his reputation problematic, his future doubtful, yet despite all this it is necessary that he take his place as an important writer, whose main contributions to the history of British poetry, though slim, are probably the equal of the best of Eliot or Yeats and whose work demands to be read through the criteria of modernism and not relegated to the trashcan marked 'Georgian'.

For its part, Georgianism, which Brooke did so much to aid, is to be seen as a type of modernism rather than an outworn, outmoded, Victorianism finally defeated by the harsh *reality* of war.

I have described how Brooke's reputation has been caught between the rock of professional enquiry and the hard place of amateur enthusiasm. It may be that, as I suspect, Brooke's world was irrecoverably lost and will always be irrecoverably lost somewhere in our own 'Edwardian' mental space, and the half-life he suffers will continue much as before. But in a world intent on recuperating the lost to challenge the accepted, it is time we revisited the half-forgotten not merely for the sake of the historical record but also because we must, in the end, care about the value of art. In both these areas, Brooke deserves more than a passing mention.

FURTHER READING

Biography

Delany, Paul. *The Neo-pagans: Rupert Brooke and the Ordeal of Youth.* New York: Free Press, 1987, 270 p.

Chronicles the story of Brooke and his friends, and examines Brooke's poetical philosophy.

Hassall, Christopher. *Rupert Brooke: A Biography.* Salem, N.H.: Faber & Faber, 1964, 556 p.
Definitive biography on the English poet.

Hastings, Michael. *Handsomest Young Man in England: Rupert Brooke.* London: Joseph, 1967, 240 p.
Provides a biographical account of the poet.

Criticism

Cunliffe, J. W. "Masefield and the New Georgian Poets." In *English Literature in the Twentieth Century,* pp. 292-329. New York: The Macmillan Co., 1935.

Praises *1914, and Other Poems* for its power to fire the patriotic spirit of its readers.

Drinkwater, John. "Rupert Brooke." In *The Muse in Council: Being Essays on Poets and Poetry,* Boston: Houghton Mifflin, 1925. pp. 273-88.
Lauds Brooke's poetic technique.

Lehmann, John. *Rupert Brooke: His Life and Legend.* London: Weidenfeld & Nicolson, 1980, 178 p.
Biographical and critical study of Brooke.

Pearsall, Robert Brainard. *Rupert Brooke: The Man and Poet.* Amsterdam: Rodopi N.V., 1974, 174 p.
Provides critical as well as biographical information on Brooke and his poetry.

Additional coverage of Brooke's life and career is contained in the following sources published by The Gale Group: *Twentieth Century Literay Criticism*, Vols. 2 & 7; *DISCovering Authors: British; DISCovering Authors: Canadian; DISCovering Authors: Most Studied Authors Module; DISCovering Authors: Poets Module; World Literature Criticism, 1500 to the Present; Contemporary Authors,* Vol. 104; *Contemporary Authors New Revision Series,* Vol. 61; *Concise Dictionary of British Literary Biography 1914-1945; Dictionary of Literary Biography,* Vol. 19 and; *Major 20th-Century Writers.*

Dennis Brutus
1924-

South African poet and activist.

INTRODUCTION

Brutus is regarded as one of the most distinguished contemporary South African poets. He employs traditional forms and rich language in his poetry to detail, without self-pity or bitterness, the physical and mental anguish he had suffered as a political prisoner and as an exile. Brutus is well known for his involvement in the anti-apartheid movement and has opposed apartheid in his works. In *Aspects of African Literature,* R. M. Egudu has deemed Brutus's poetry as "the reaction of one who is in mental agony whether he is at home or abroad," adding that this agony is "partly caused by harassments, arrests, and imprisonment, and mainly by Brutus's concern for other suffering people."

Biographical Information

Brutus was born in 1924 in Harara, Zimbabwe, which was then called Salisbury, South Rhodesia. His parents, teachers Francis Henry and Margaret Winifred Brutus, were South African "coloureds" who raised their son in Port Elizabeth. After receiving a bachelor's degree in English at Fort Hare University College in 1946, Brutus taught at several South African high schools. In the late 1950s, Brutus began to protest apartheid actively, concentrating on the conflict over race in sports. He was instrumental in the sanction to exclude South Africa's segregated sports teams from most international competitions, including the Olympics. In 1963, Brutus was arrested at a sports meeting for defying a ban which prohibited him from associating with any group. He fled the country after his release on bail but he was apprehended and returned to Johannesburg. Brutus again tried to escape but was shot in the stomach by police who pursuing. He was subsequently sentenced to 18 months of hard labor at Robben Island Prison—a notorious, escape-proof facility off the South African coast. During his imprisonment, his first volume of poetry, *Sirens, Knuckles, Boots* (1963) was published. In 1965, Brutus was released and allowed to leave South Africa on the condition that he never return. He emigrated to England in 1966 and then to the United States in 1970.

Major Works

Sirens, Knuckles, Boots includes love poems as well as poems protesting South Africa's racial policies. These poems, like many of Brutus's later pieces, are highly personal and meditative, interweaving references to his personal experiences while developing such themes as love, pain, and anger. Brutus's work was awarded an Mbari Prize from the University of Ibadan, Nigeria. Because Brutus was forbidden to write poetry in prison, he instead wrote letters. These formed the basis of his next collection, *Letters to Martha and Other Poems from a South African Prison* (1968), which was not published until after he left South Africa for England in 1966. In this volume, Brutus recounted his prison experiences through letters to his sister-in-law; the poems, which describe the deprivation and fear of prison life, were praised for their objectivity and lucidity. Critics have noted that these poems are different in style from those in Brutus's first collection; Brutus acknowledged that he altered his technique in favor of simpler idioms that make his verse more accessible to the average reader. Although his first two volumes remained officially banned in South Africa, Brutus's *Thoughts Abroad* (1970), published under the pseudonym John Bruin, were widely circulated in the country. A collection of his poems about exile and alienation, *Thoughts Abroad* was an immediate success in South Africa, and it was even taught in several colleges there, until the government discovered that Brutus was the author.

Brutus's first volume of poetry published after leaving England, *A Simple Lust* (1973), includes his earlier work concerning prison and exile, as well as new poems. Tanure Ojaide has described Brutus's characteristic persona, which becomes most prominent in *A Simple Lust,* as "a troubadour who fights for a loved one against injustice and infidelity in his society." In the new poems in this collection, Brutus wrote with passion of the homeland for which he yearned and of his compatriots who remained behind. His anxiety over their suffering is intensified by the contrast between his life as a free individual and their restricted lives. In *Stubborn Hope: New Poems and Selections from "China Poems" and "Strains"* (1978) Brutus again wrote about his prison experiences and the inhumanity of apartheid. Endurance and hope are dominant themes in this volume, as Brutus extended his concern with the oppressive conditions of his homeland to a universal scale and assumed the role of spokesperson for all suffering people. Brutus continued to write poetry while in America, publishing *Salutes and Censures* (1984) and *Airs and Tributes* (1989). In these volumes, he undertook to educating the American public about apartheid in South Africa.

Critical Reception

Critical evaluation of Brutus's poetry depends on the individual critic's conviction about the political purposes of poetry. Many have argued that his experience of political repression and his opposition to apartheid impart force and breadth to his poetry. In regard to the sustained opposition to the South African government and to repression in general, Colin Gardner has maintained that Brutus's poetry "has found forms and foundations which dramatize an important part of the agony of South Africa and contemporary humanity." Myrna Blumberg has contended that in parts of *Letters to Martha,* Brutus "has grace and penetration unmatched even by Alexander Solzhenitsyn—or perhaps Brutus is just less shockable and less verbose about the levels of degradation and joy, the nature of human nature, he has seen and felt."

Few critics question that Brutus, as Egudu writes, is ". . . a capable poet fully committed to his social responsibility." Some, however, argue that the political context of the anti-apartheid movement has limited the potential of his poetry. Frank M. Chipasula has deemed *Sirens, Knuckles, Boots* as the height of his poetic achievement and argues that the pressures of political activity led Brutus toward a poetic style that lacked "both power and craftsmanship." Others have accused Brutus of using his poetry for propagandistic purposes, although some have faulted him for being too restrained in condemning the South African government. Most however, would agree with Chikwenye Okonjo Ogunyemi, who has argued that Brutus succeeds in generalizing his experience of repression to symbolize "the existential human predicament that man finds himself in."

PRINCIPAL WORKS

Poetry

Sirens, Knuckles, Boots 1963
Letters to Martha and Other Poems from a Sout African Prison 1968
Poems from Algiers 1970
Thoughts Abroad [as John Bruin] 1970
A Simple Lust: Selected Poems Including "Sirens, Knuckles, Boots," "Leters to Martha," "Poems from Algiers," "Thoughts Abroad" 1973
Strains 1975; revised edition, 1982
China Poems 1975
Stubborn Hope: New Poems and Selections from "China Poems" and "Strains" 1978
Salutes and Censures 1984
Airs and Tributes 1989

CRITICISM

Cosmo Pieterse (essay date 1967)

SOURCE: An interview with Dennis Brutus, in *Cultural Events in Africa,* No. 26, January, 1967, pp. I-III.

[*In the following interview, Brutus discusses with Pieterse some of the themes and techniques of his poetry, as well as his principal influences.*]

[Pieterse]: *Dennis, one notices in poems of yours that fairly frequently there are opposites, for instance in the third line of the introductory poem from your collection;* **Sirens, Knuckles, and Boots:**

> *A troubadour, I traverse all my land*
> *exploring all her wide flung parts with zest*
> *probing in motion sweeter far than rest*
> *her secret thickets with an amorous hand:*
> *and I have laughed disdaining those who banned*
> *enquiry and movement, delighting in the test*
> *of wills when doomed by Saracened arrest,*
> *choosing, like unarmed thumb, simply to stand.*
> *Thus quixoting till a cast-off of my land,*
> *I sing and fare, person to loved one pressed*
> *braced for this pressure and the captor's hand*
> *—no mistress'-favour has adorned my breast*
> *only the shadow of an arrow-brand.*

'Motion' and its antithesis 'rest', is this a feature, an element of your poetry that you consciously strive after, or does this come out of, can one call it an inner philosophic meaning that is behind your life, behind your work; something perhaps unconscious?

[Brutus]: A very large question—I must start off by saying that I hadn't noticed that particular contrast. I think it is true to say that in my work there is a tension and this tension is partly a deliberate desire to catch tension, because I think tension is of the essence of good poetry. On the other hand, I think the circumstances in which I, and most South Africans live, is one which creates tensions, so I suppose the answer is partly that it is a deliberate choice and partly it's an expression of temperament.

Would there be a philosophy that you subscribe to, that deals in terms of tensions; some kind of dialectic perhaps that is expounded in your verse?

A question like that could have a number of answers each dealing with a different aspect of South African life. The image, for instance, of an unarmed thumb, is in fact deliberately drawn from the salute of the African Congress, which at one stage was a thumbs-up signal.

Could I just interrupt there and ask whether this could also be the troubadour who is hiking, who is hitching?

Yes indeed, although I think you are giving my work a depth it does not really deserve. But just in the previous line the reference to 'Saracen', which is to me related at once to the Middle Ages, the Crusades, and the conflict between Crusader and Saracen; and on the other hand the use of Saracens as armoured cars by the South African police—they were imported from Britain; we nicknamed them 'Skerpions' or 'Scorpions'.

I noticed for instance you have the word 'quixoting' which one would normally think of as a proper noun, doing duty as a verb. And very often composites like 'mistress'—favour'. Could you comment on these?

Yes, I don't know how far they will illustrate my work. Broadly, the poem is a special one, I think. But Don Quixote is to me a variation on the troubadour idea. The man who goes 'tilting with windmills' is not very much different from the troubadour, the minstrel, or el travatore—I think this is the same thing—the man who travelled across Europe fighting and loving and singing. It's the combination of conflict and music which interests me—the man who can be both fighter and poet, and this is a kind of contradiction which is also present in Don Quixote.

The Don Quixote who 'tilts with windmills' is to me a romantic, and to some extent blind fighter. To what extent do you feel this would be true about the fight that goes on in your poetry? The struggle that you wage, it seems to me so physically and strongly? I don't see much of Don Quixote in you.

I would say there are three answers here. There is a political struggle in South Africa; there is my personal conflict which eventually brought me to prison with the apartheid regime; and then there is, as you point out, the conflict of tension in the poetry itself. Now I think it is true, and at least one person writing in *Transition* has said this, that there is an element of laughter in my work; it may be that I am engaged in a fight but at the same time I find a certain delight in it. I enjoy the fight; I can laugh at myself and see myself as a little like Don Quixote, tilting at windmills, or if you like, fighting a losing battle.

I think you do yourself an injustice—not a losing battle, certainly that is not the tenor, the resonance of your verse. There is zest in it—a kind of strength, which I find again very often expressed in your linking the physical, the human body with the physical of nature. Soul and soil, as it were are very often transmuted, fused together. Is that correct?

I think you've summed up very aptly and neatly when you said soul and soil. I do think that although I haven't used those exact terms I have that in mind. When I speak of South Africa as a mistress it is both woman and country—there is no doubt about that. So it is in fact a physical body, a physical presence in the sense of the flesh. At the same time it is the land I traverse. I do not know whether we should confine ourselves to this particular poem, but when I say 'I pressed to the loved one in an intimate contact', this is the kind of image one would use of a sexual embrace. But I also deliberately used the same image as a contact with the earth. And then the reference you made earlier to Mistress' favour. What I am trying to say is that my loyalty has not been to any woman in the sense that the troubadours wore a particular woman's favour. For me the favour has been instead the knowledge which I predicted in the poem—that I would eventually end in prison; because the arrow brand at the end is the symbol of a convict in prison—the uniform with arrows on. My loyalty has been to the country with the shadow of an arrow constantly over me—this would be my mistress' favour!

From what you've said, although I know we've just been touching the surface, and from some of my readings of your poems, it seems that there are very many meanings locked into single words, into single lines, and certainly innumerable meanings in a whole poem. Are there any influences of which you are aware?

Well certainly during my years at University, and since then as well, one of the principle poets in terms of approach to poetry, the principle influence has been John Donne. And in fact all the metaphysicals have a strong appeal for me. I have, too, been influenced to some extent I think by my repeated readings of Eliot, of Yeats, and possibly because I read him at a very impressionable age, the writings of James Joyce—particularly *Ulysses*.

All these many meanings—do they not make the poetry too complex, too rich, do they not stand between reader and poem?

Well, I'm glad you asked that question because its one I've often asked myself and to which I have given an answer which seems very unpopular with my current readers. Ever since I came out of Robben Island I've been trying to work towards a very much greater simplicity in my work—I felt my work was too clotted, too thick, there were too many strands knotted together, I was trying to make the language do too many things at the same time.

And so I've turned to a very much simpler, very prosaic use of the language and almost everybody who's read my later poetry is convinced that it is far inferior to the early poetry!

Your earlier poetry, was it intended for a certain kind of audience—say a literary-conscious audience, or did you have the man in the street, the man at home or the students?

I would say that every poem in **Sirens, Knuckles, and Boots** was written for a particular person or to serve a particular function and that not one of these poems was written with an audience in mind. I was, in fact, writing letters to particular people in the form of a poem, or making a point that I had failed to make in conversation, but not one of them was written for publication or for an audience.

How did the publication of these poems come about?

Some of my work got into the hands of Ulli Beier, who at that time was preparing a Penguin Anthology, and he wrote to me expressing regret that the work had reached him too late to include in the Anthology; but he suggested that if I sent some more it could be turned into a book. So I scratched around for the stuff some of which is ten or fifteen years old, and whatever I could find—I suppose about 80% is lost—I sent him, and the book came out while I was in prison and I was in fact interrogated about it.

Your post-Robben Island poetry, did you have an audience in mind here? Why the simplification?

Well, most of it is addressed to an individual—my sister-in-law in fact. My brother is in prison and I wrote to her in the form of letters largely about prison conditions, but I had hoped that they would ultimately reach a wider audience and this may be one reason why I try to pare my thoughts down to a very simple basic sort of structure. I did a lot of re-thinking about technique and expression and that is one of the things that persuaded me to seek a simpler idiom. And then of course, if one is writing as I would be principally for the people of my own continent, and particularly those who are just becoming familiar with the English language but who one hopes will develop a great love for the language because it is a fine vehicle for poetry, I think one must avoid embroidery or anything that could be an interference or a barrier to the communication between a writer and a listener.

Dennis, you are a man with many interests, poetry apart. You are an educationist, deeply interested in sports administration and participation, you are a thinker, a politician, and yet one finds that the athlete for instance, never comes into your poetry?

Yes you are right. I am not sure of the reason but I agree with you completely that there are whole areas of my life which seem to be shut out of my poetry; it may be that they do not make good poetic material. Alternatively they may not be so integral to my emotional reactions that they

are thrown out as images when I am writing poetry. I don't know. I would say, however, that to me the troubadour is not so far from the sportsman—the kind of man who can conduct a fight but not lose his sense of humour or his sense of balance about it is not so far from the gymnast who is doing the pole vault. Basically I don't think they are so different in temperament or in character that I don't use the images of sport is to me even odd, but I can't explain it.

Pol Ndu (essay date 1971)

SOURCE: "Passion and Poetry in the Works of Dennis Brutus," in *Black Academy River,* Vol. 2, No. 1-2, Spring-Summer, 1971, pp. 41-54.

[*In the following excerpt, Ndu maintains that the presence of passion is critical for creating great poetry and he argues that Brutus's poetry is limited by what the author calls his "cautious" emotional involvement in the anti-apartheid movement.*]

Dennis Brutus sows the needs of great poetry when he discusses themes of special intimacy to himself. Such themes could have arisen from some loss, some desire, some feeling or even the pain of the confrontation of the abominable regime. But in each case, the poet does not generalize or pose as the mouthpiece of a doomed race. He speaks from the labyrinths of his fear, his anger, the wells of his thirst. This is only when the two strands of passion are consumated in him and he knows that if oppression takes

> Out the poetry and fire
> or watch it ember out of sight
> sanity reassembles its ash
> the moon relinquishes the night.
> But here and here remain the scalds
> a sudden turn or breath may ache,
> and I walk on cindered pasts
> for thought or hope (what else?) can break.[2]

The revulsion and terror of the poet as "police cars cockroach through the tunnel streets;

> from shanties creaking iron-sheets
> violence like a bug-infested rag is tossed
> and fear is immanent as sound in the windswung
>   bell

is self expletive. Or when

> The sounds begin again;
> the siren in the night
> the thunder at the door
> the shriek of nerves in pain.
> Then the keening crescendo
> of faces split by pain
> the wordless; endless wail
> only the unfree know.

———————
my sounds begin again

(*Sirens, Knuckles, Boots*)

one does not need to be told that a great mind is facing a great upheaval. The words are familiar enough, but they are so selected and worked to a decrescendo that when 'his' sounds begin again the reader has tasted the bitter dregs of the poet's ordeal, but with a fresh determination. Each dominant word is loaded with poetic responsibility and meaning and a great intensity is achieved. This is of course because as I have said, the poet is writing from instances of direct personal import. He does not write to postulate some moral, philosophical, political theory or slogan. He is merely expressing his terror in the language of poetry.

These are not images to cheer you
—except that you may see in these small acts
some evidence of my thought and caring:
but still I do not fear their power to wound
knowing your grief, your loss and anxious care,
rather I send you bits to fill
the mosaic of your calm and patient knowledge
—picking jagged bits embedded in my mind—
partly to wrench some ease for my own mind.
And partly that some world some time may know

(*Letters to Martha:* Postscripts 1)[3]

It is interesting to note that Brutus does pick jagged bits embedded in his mind "partly" to "wrench some ease" for his mind. I would substitute principally for "partly". But whichever way, the ease of mind is only wrenched when pains and passions are manfully indulged. In this indulgence, the poet should face up his punishment with a relish that must necessarily astound the uninitiated.

More terrible than any beast
that can be tamed or bribed
the iron monster of the world
ingests me in its grinding maw:

agile as ballet-dancer
fragile as butterfly
I egg-dance with numble wariness
—stave off my fated splintering.

(*Sirens, Knuckles, Boots*)

Man's life is brittle as the butterfly's, fragile as an egg and in the jaws of the grinding "iron monster" the poet realises that his destruction is gradual but systematic. It is pathetic and frightening. He must do something. But

Time—ordinary time—
exerts its own insistent
unobstrusive discipline.

The beauty of these lines will certainly be watered down by any attempts at explication. Time is certainly "ordinary" but only to the free. To the unfree, every minute seems an eternity, an eternity of waiting, longing and pining. In these very personal poems, Dennis Brutus leads every reader deep down into the turbulence of his imagination. The reader becomes both spectator and participant in the tragic drama taking place there. The passion of sorrow for being considered sub-human in a basically human world, and the passion of pleasure for sustaining life through the vicissitudes of the deadly hostilities are merged and fine poetry is the synthetic result. But as soon as the poet takes the propagandist rostrum, poetry flies and what follows might be moving but never profound. In **"Mirror Sermon I"**,

Our images cavort
in silent dissonance
Or graceless dance
slow sarabands of passionless lasciviousness
and lace through a cacophonous gavotte.
        Marionettes
devoid of graceful antecedents
we pirouette
in senseless choreography . . .

(*Sirens, Knuckles, Boots*)

obsolete and almost out of the way 'ballet-dance' terms are incongruously strung together to lament the helplessness of the South African "marionettes". 'Cavort', 'sarabands', 'cacaphonous gavotte', 'pirouettc', 'choreography' make indeed a

cold reflection

of our interlocking nudity

which seems to moralise

ascetically
on sensual intellection
or morality

and one begins to wonder whether the guilt of the "cold reflection" in "sensual intellection" and "sensual morality" is the poet's or still that of his white oppressors.

When the passions are not completely experienced in a poet, his poetry is jagged often sentimental and intruding. That unusual fuse which breaks a poem into the highest orbits of the imagination and the deepest layers of feeling is absent. In the several works of Dennis Brutus, these passions have not been fully reconciled. His lot is quite a pitiable and pitful one. Hunted from pillar to post by an abominable regime, thrown into jail as often as he is caught, banned from the exercise of the simplest and most elementary rights of man—to talk and to write—separated for a time from a cherished family, he is still something of a dilettante. His bitterness remains mostly unresolved. He argues in **"Their Behavior."** (*Letters to Martha*, p. 28)

Their guilt
    is not so very different from ours
    —who has not joyed in the arbitrary exercise
    of power
    or grasped for himself what might have been
    another's

and who has not used superior force in the
   moment when he could
(and who of us has not been tempted to these
   things?)—

Brutus here attempts to be profound but his argument
does not quite click. It sounds like an inconclusive yard-
stick of anti-Marxist: Apartheid could be tolerated because, given the same circumstances as the whites, the
blacks would practise apartheid. This is as untrue as it is
begging the question. And because of the posturing, Brutus only succeeds in making plain unpoetic statements.
He apparently wants to fight. But his fight must not be
bitter. It is not a fight of life and death—for him. It is the
mercenary soldier's fight: gradual, curious but most
cautious.

. . . Much as Brutus' anti-Marxist theory of universal
bent to greed might sound intellectual, the practical
realities of the South African situation needs a realistic
and grim facing up, a combat. The anti-apartheid fighter
could lose the battle in the short run, even lose his life,
but at the moment of death, he should realize a special
expiation and satisfaction, a traumatic canonization. It is
this final leap into sainthood which Brutus severally
refuses or fears

> After the sentence
> mingled feelings:
> sick relief,
>
>   . . . . .
>
> vague heroism
> mixed with self-pity
> and tempered by the knowledge of those
> who endure much more
> and endure. . . .

                   (*Letters to Martha* I)

This unsuccessful counterposing of the commonplace
"mixed feelings" and "vague heroism" is unfortunate. . . .
Even Brutus himself knows this, for he names the impure
item in his experience as 'self pity'. This impure "self pity"
blunts the edge of his language and emasculates his poetry.
He is cowed down by an "awareness of the proximity of
death", and having handed in "nails and screws and other
sizable bits of metals" he falls to his knees in the "childhood habit of nightly prayers" perhaps remembering the
great Christian precept of "Blessed are the meek . . ." Even
when this meek child cries for vengeance, it is the cry of
a toothless cur, there is no sharpness, there is no weapon;
the cry is within him and muffled there.

>   . . . . .
>
>   . . . . .
>
> but our concern
> is how they hasten or delay
> a special freedom—
> that of those the prisons hold

and who depend on change
to give them liberty

> And so one comes to a callousness,
> a savage ruthlessness—
> voices shouting in the heart
> "Destroy! Destroy!"
> "Let them die in thousands!"
> really it is impatience

                   (*Letters to Martha* II)

But they never die, not even in fives and tens, because
the voices shout only "in the heart" and if evil comes
upon some men the way others wish it, very few, if any
people will be alive the next minute. What 'Change' actually do those in the prisons depend on for liberty? A
change of mind of the South African whites? That would
be a miracle in the 20th century. A change of government
by a revolution or a coup d'etat? The only 'change' that
can effectively alter the human tragedy in South Africa is
that which gives the 'coloured' man his due place as
human. For Brutus, this change will be far in coming,

>   . . . . .
>
> So one grits to the burden
> and resolves to doggedly endure
> the outrages of prison

                   (*Letters to Martha* 13)

realising that

> we were simply prisoners
> of a system we had fought
> and still opposed

                   (*Letters to Martha* 14)

In an article **Protest Against Apartheid** Dennis Brutus
himself states that his 'case is not an extreme one' and he
catalogues the series of bans and restrictions that had
been placed on him. "In fact, my Banning Order (which has
Mr. Voster's autograph!) specifically forbids me to compose
slogans so that, in fact, even a string of words could have
been illegal". I wonder whose 'case' could be more extreme!
Then he continues "I think one may say in all seriousness
that to write at all once you are banned from writing—and
it doesn't matter whether you write badly—constitutes a
form of protest against apartheid in South Africa."[5] This
is true. But it is not all the truth. It matters very much how
well you write, and how much you protest because the
power of the written word is onerous and immense. And
if the devil can cite the scriptures to support devilry, it is
the ambiguous and equivocal sections that he could cite.
Thus Brutus decided to start his classification of protest-
ers with "Alan Paton who represents one extreme of protest literature in South Africa, and then work slowly over
to some one like Alex la Guma who represents the other
extreme. In between, you will find today people like Nadine
Gordimer, and in terms of drama, Athol Fugard"[6] Brutus
condemns Paton as a white sympathizer and Nadine Gordimer
as an insensitive, cold machine, without "warmth and feeling." But Athol Fugard's *The Blood Knot* he says "cleverly

approached it [apartheid] from both angles—it is both conflict and unity—for the white and the black are, as often they are in South Africa, blood brothers. One has turned out to be black, and the other one has turned out to be white."[7] This is the pampered philosophy of the weaker man's live and let live. For the South African tragedy does not deserve so much understanding. If the white and the black in South Africa are so much blood brothers, meant to cooperate peacefully perpetually, why do some noble non-whites eventually decide to quit the cherished compromise into exile? Brutus himself for instance. The salient point is that blood is blood. Pathologists have shown that all blood at best is the same. If therefore at any point or place some people want to show that their 'blood' is more blood than the blood of others, they have to be condemned, in unequivocal terms. . . . The basic plague of the white South African is his feeling that white is the colour of the gods. The normal human being will readily acknowledge the differences between himself and others in terms of intellect, status, education or achievement. But there is no apology for anyone who refuses to accept his intellectual or social equal or even superior on the basis of colour. This is why protest writers in Africa have to be re-classified and delineated into those who regard the South African tragedy as normal and acceptable and those who regard it as abnormal, inimical and unpardonable in society. This is what John Povey partly does in "Profile of an African Artist" where, I think, he also sees Brutus as an artist who considers apartheid evil but pardonable. "Throughout Brutus' poetry" he says "runs an infinite and continuous love for his sad yet beautiful country." In Povey's terms then, Brutus' pathetic love for his country is love to a fault because being human, his love should remain finite even if nostalgic. Infinity should be left to divinity. Povey poses the question "what can the place of innocence and intimacy of human love be here, in a situation that requires a different dedication and loyalty" and answers that "to love a woman seems personal to the point of self-indulgence, an abdication of principle; and yet to Brutus that real tenderness is always urgent."[8] If "that real tenderness" is ever urgent to Brutus and Professor Povey knows that its insistence is an abdication of principle, I also feel that Brutus' indulgence is narcissistic and could have far reaching unwelcome consequences for himself. It is however interesting that Professor Povey regards the rest of Brutus' poetry as contradicting his stated view that

> under jackboots our bones and spirits crunch.

It is equally contradictory for Professor Povey to hold that Brutus' optimism is not delusive despite the obvious implication of delusion in his poetry. Such optimism could in fact sustain Brutus' survival, but can never sustain equity or the hope for it in South Africa. Brutus and Company "had fought" the system and probably lost but the 'still' continuous opposition is what I have called the 'mercenary' soldier's battle: gradual, curious but most cautious—because, if Brutus lost his fight, he left no immortal marks whereby any passerby might pause and say "ah! a mortal combat took place here." If the battle was lost, it was lost too early. This probably means that Brutus has not fully utilized the weapons or the abilities at his disposal. Since

he still lives and opportunities still abound, one would expect to see him back in the fray with fresh vigour, greater resolve and very serious weapons.

> Quite early one reaches a stage
> where one resolves to embrace
> the status of prisoner
> with all it entails,
> savouring to the full its bitterness
> and seeking to escape nothing:
>
> . . . . .
> . . . . .
>
> Later one changes
> tries the dodges,
> seeks the easy outs
>
> But the acceptance
> once made
> deep down
> remains.
>
> (*Letters to Martha* 16)

The emasculating and pervading influence of self pity still holds down the protagonist. He must break through the shells of the deep-laid 'acceptance' and though refusing "to escape nothing"; refuse also to try the "dodges" and the "easy outs" but decisively "take up arms" against the sea of troubles and quell them by facing them. I do not mean here that Brutus should turn out the proverbial Don Quixote and catch the bull by the horns with bare hands. Instead, he should allow his true nature to take possession of his poetry of the whites' inhumanity to the blacks in South Africa; his nature which feels a sickly revulsion at the "bleak hostility", at the

> Coprophilism, necrophilism; fellatic;
> penis-amputation;
> . . . in this gibbering society . . .
> Suicide, self-damnation . . .
> not to be shaken off.
>
> (*Letters to Martha* 5)

Until this true nature takes possession, the passion for sorrow and the passion for joy will not be reconciled in Dennis Brutus' poetry and he shall not have received the bitter baptism of torture which such great poets receive.

In an article "Of Mr. Booker T. Washington and Others" W. E. B. DuBois talks of categories of the critics of Mr. Booker Washington's approach to the racial impasse in Southern United States. One group, notably of Bowen, Kelley Miller and the Grimkes "acknowledge Mr. Washington's invaluable service in counselling patience and courtesy in (his) demands . . . but they also know and the nation knows, that relentless colour prejudices is more often a cause than a result of the Negro's degradation, they seek the abatement of this relic of barbarism, and not its systematic encouragement and pampering by all agencies of social power from the Associated Press to the Church of Christ . . . they are absolutely certain that the way for a people to gain respect is not by continually belittling and ridiculing themselves, that, on the contrary, Negroes must insist continually, in season and out of season . . . that colour discrimination is barbarism and that black boys need education as well as white boys . . . In failing thus to state plainly and unequivocally the legitimate demands of their people, even at the cost of opposing an honoured leader, the thinking classes of American Negroes would shirk a heavy responsibility."[9] The responsibility of the Negro thinking classes cannot in this circumstance be more onerous than that of South African black or coloured thinkers and writers. The South African black or coloured man who has the opportunity should shriek, even turn militant and use all available machinations to undermine the invidious regime. In a barbarian society, only the laws of the jungle hold.

If **Letters To Martha** is unsuccessful it is because the poet has not fused the reality of his bitter experiences effectively with his poetry. Or, where the poet feels fulfilled, the feeling is insincere. So, he puts down quite often, "phrases and aphorisms" and commonplaces that are quite touching and pitiful but not exquisite. . . .

As Hopkins said of Tennyson, Brutus' "gift of utterance is truly golden but go further home and you come to thoughts [and images] commonplace and wanting in nobility, it is genius uninformed by character"[14] because the poet has not resolved his passions well enough to press out from his mills the relevant imagery and symbolism he needs to produce great poetry. In the few places he resolves these passions, Brutus definitely shows great promise.

Notes

[2] *Sirens, Knuckles, Boots* Mbari: Ibadan, 1963.

[3] *Letters to Martha and other poems from a South African Prison* Heinemann: London, 1969, p. 20.

[5] Dennis Brutus, "Protest Against Apartheid" in *Protest and Conflict in African Literature,* ed. Cosmo Pieterse and D. Munro, Heinemann: London 1969, pp. 93-100.

[6] *Protest and Conflict in African Literature,* p. 95.

[7] *Ibid.,* p. 98.

[8] John Povey, "Profile of An African Artist," *Journal of the New African Literature and The Arts,* Stanford, No. 3, Spring 1967, pp. 95-100.

[9] W. E. B. DuBois, "Of Mr. Booker T. Washington and Others" in *Souls of Black Folk,* Longmans: London 1965, pp. 35-36.

[14] W. A. M. Peters, *G. M. Hopkins,* Oxford, June 1948, p. 38.

Palaver interview (essay date 1972)

SOURCE: "Interview with Dennis Brutus," in *Palaver: Interviews with Five African Writers in Texas,* Bernth Lindfors, Ian Munro, Richard Priebe, Reinhard Sander (eds.), The University of Texas at Austin, 1972, pp. 25-36.

[*In the following excerpt, Brutus speaks to an African literature class about the personal experiences and literary influences that shape his poetry.*]

I'm glad to be here, and it seems to me the most useful thing I can do is to spend most of the time answering questions on the things that interest you. I ought to warn you that I don't know all the answers, and when it comes to poetry, even my own, I don't always give the same answer to the same question. This may sound odd, but I believe one tends to look at the same thing at different times in different ways. I think only dead people don't change, and even they putrify so that there is a form of change.

Another thing I should say is that I feel I know what I try to mean by my own poetry and I think I know how it ought to be read in terms of meaning. So it seems to me sensible to read some of my poems while I'm here, partly because they tell you something about Africa and African writing and about the African predicament today and partly because they tell you something about my own work.

The first one I'm going to read is called "The Sibyl." You know, of course, that a sibyl was an old woman who made prophecies. There were sibyls or oracles in Greece. Now I had a friend called Sybil; it's really as simple as that. And so I would write, not a poem for her (because this would be a little "corny,") but a poem for her at a second or third remove by finding a new image, somehow. But as a tribute to her I would stick her name in the title. I'm really talking in the poem, as you can guess, about the politics of South Africa and the inevitable bloody kind of destruction that must come there.

But I shouldn't be explaining everything. If it's a good poem, it will explain itself.

> Her seer's eyes saw nothing that the birds did not,
> her words were sharp and simple as their song;
> that mutant winds had honed their teeth on ice
> that sap ran viscous in the oaks and senile pines—
> these things were common cause except to those
> whose guilty fear had made them comatose;
> who could not guess that red coagulate stains
> would burst from summer's grossly swollen veins
> or spell out from the leaves of opulent decadence
> that autumn's austere nemesis would come to
>   cleanse?

I think it comes off, and I think it says quite a number of things.

But perhaps we should go on to another, the poem about the troubadour. I haven't read this one for a long time, but I did look at it last night because I have always felt a little sad about a typographical error in it. It seems to me one can read the first line and it can sound terrible unless you put the accent on the first syllable of *tráverse.* It should be tráverse. This is because in geography, when you are using sextants and other things to map a country, it's called a "tráverse"—the actual process of measuring a piece of land from the angles of the hills and valleys—and I am using the geographical term as a verb. Once you've accepted that, the rhythmic structure, I think, becomes much more convincing as a poem. One needs that accent.

> A troubadour, I tráverse all my land
> exploring all her wide-flung parts with zest
> probing in motion sweeter far than rest
> her secret thickets with an amorous hand:
>
> and I have laughed, disdaining those who banned
> inquiry and movement, delighting in the test
> of will when doomed by Saracened arrest,
> choosing, like unarmed thumb, simply to stand.
>
> Thus, quixoting till a cast-off of my land
> I sing and fare, person to loved-one pressed
> braced for this pressure and the captor's hand
> that snaps off service like a weathered strand:
> —no mistress-favour has adorned my breast
> only the shadow of an arrow-brand.

I know I don't read that one with much conviction, but this is just because I'm self-conscious about it. It's really a rather intricate poem, and if you will be patient, I'll spend a little time talking about it.

First the genesis. I was writing a lot of terribly loose, very bad free verse at the time, most or nearly all of which I threw away, and it seemed to me that I needed the discipline of a very tight poetic form. The tightest form I could think of was the sonnet, which is a very demanding form. And of all the sonnets—the Shakespearean variation, the Spenserian, Hopkins' variations and so on—it seemed to me that the Petrarchan was the most difficult. The Petrarchan rhymes abba/abba and cde/cde, and I decided I would make mine even more difficult; there would be only two rhyming sounds, an "a" sound and a "b" sound throughout the whole poem, not merely octet and sestet. So I made up my mind that the next poem I was going to write would be a hell of a tight one and would have this kind of structure. I didn't know what it was going to be about, but I resolved that I needed some discipline.

At that time I was forbidden to leave a particular district in South Africa. I had an order from the secret police restricting me to Johannesburg. So for the hell of it, I used to think up excuses for having to travel. I would persuade my wife to find a pretext (she was about 700 miles away from me); I would smuggle a note down to her and back would come a telegram, "Baby seriously ill," or something like that. I would have to go to court, and there would be a legal process by which the banning order, the confining order, would be set aside for twenty-four hours or forty-eight hours. So I was allowed to dash away and come back. This happened fairly often. I liked those trips because I was doing what they were telling me I couldn't do. I was defying their orders and actually conducting underground political activity at the same time.

So, travelling around and having this notion of myself travelling around, the ideas began to fall into place with this shape. Gradually they came together. I wanted to catch a certain medieval quality—I forget why—and that's why you have a troubadour, a Don Quixote, quixoting in the poem. But you also have a line from a very early Latin hymn written by Thomas Aquinas, a very beautiful hymn from which I borrowed the phrase, ". . . motion sweeter far than rest."

Furthermore, the resistance movement in South Africa has as its signal an upraised thumb. So you can see the thumb is in the poem as well. This is a code signal. And "Saracen" refers to the armored cars the police drive which have searchlights on them and may have guns.

So there are all kinds of things woven into the pattern, but above all, there was an awareness that I was going to prison sooner or later. You can't go on doing this and not get caught. And I expected to go to the prison on Robben Island, the worst prison in the country, which is off the beach of Cape Town. So when I talk of a weathered strand, it's functioning in two ways: it's a bit of cloth from a garment that's frayed, weathered, worn out, but it's also the strand where the waves break. It's an anticipation of a particular prison.

And whereas you went into battle, Don Quixote and everybody else, wearing your lady's scarf or handkerchief wrapped around your lance, I knew that this was not for me, that what I would wear could be imaged by a rather old fashioned prison garb with big arrows on it. The only kind of mistress's favour I would wear—my mistress being my country—would be a convict's clothes.

I hope this doesn't make it too complicated. I think it's still a successful poem, even if you forget about all these complexities. It still comes off, I think.

Of course, it is also a sexual poem. It's a poem for a particular woman—very much so in the first stanza where one recognizes her posture.

As for "cast-off my land," I was thinking back to the time of Defoe, and further back to Fernando Po, to the man who had been a cast-off, a castaway, as Robinson Crusoe was. A castaway is a man who goes to an island, and I expected to be a castaway; I would go to Robben Island.

But in another sense I am talking of fabrics, mistress's favours, weathered strands, meaning bits of worn cotton, worn wool, and they're cast off in stitches in knitting because you "cast on" and "cast off" when you're knitting. I don't know whether it's overambitious, but I was trying to do three things at the same time there. It's an anticipation of what would happen to me politically.

But I'm also trying to stick within the strict imagery of the poem which is of a mistress, a beloved, who sits sewing in a castle. I'm sure you know the image from "The Lady of Shalott" and things like that. So it's working in three ways.

Of course, all my poetry is not so complicated. But the troubadour image is important throughout my work. There was a phase when this was the dominant image in my poetry.

Could you explain why you have moved from this kind of complex poetry to a poetry of plainer statement in **Letters to Martha**?

Yes. As you know, I spent a period in prison for my opposition to apartheid and racism. But you may not know that much of it was in fact spent in solitary confinement. And this meant that you were in very great danger of going insane, and I came very close to it. To keep yourself busy you would have to organize your day in such a way that you could use up the whole day, because you saw no one, you spoke to no one, your food was just pushed under your door on the floor—a bowl of porridge three times a day. So you said to yourself, "Well, I'll spend an hour thinking about literature and another hour thinking about movies," and you stayed away from things like your family and so on—you didn't dare think of them.

And eventually, having exhausted most of the common themes, I got onto looking at my poetry. And the more I looked at it, the more horrified I became. It seemed such utter rubbish. I could have, in a sense, committed suicide at the mere thought of it. I had reached that point. And you went through this kind of dark night, and then, sensibly, you would say, "All right, if it was so terrible, what's better than that? What would you do instead if you could start again?" Either you didn't write at all, which seemed to me the sensible thing to do, or you would write differently. I had even sent my wife a message (I was allowed one letter every six months) saying, "I want all my poetry destroyed and nothing published."

The first thing I decided about my future poetry was that there must be no ornament, absolutely none. And the second thing I decided was you oughtn't to write for poets; you oughtn't even to write for people who read poetry, not even students. You ought to write for the ordinary person: for the man who drives a bus, or the man who carries the baggage at the airport, and the woman who cleans the ashtrays in the restaurant. If you can write poetry which makes sense to those people, then there is some justification for writing poetry. Otherwise you have no business writing.

And therefore, there should be no ornament because ornament gets in the way. It becomes too fancy-schmancy; it becomes overelaborate. It is, in a way, a kind of pride, a self-display, a glorying in the intellect for its own sake, which is contemptible.

I don't know whether I would hold the same position now. I am only trying to explain how I arrived at that position then.

So I said, "You will have to set the thing down. You will 'tell it like it is,' but you will let the word do its work in the mind of the reader. And you will write poetry that a man who drives a bus along the street can quote, if he feels like quoting." Very ambitious indeed.

But this is based on the idea that all people are poets. Some are just ashamed to let it be known, and some are shy to try, and some write but don't have the guts to show it to others. But we all are poets because we all have the same kind of response to beauty. We may define beauty differently, but we all do respond to it.

So this was the assumption: don't dress it up; you will just hand it over, and it will do its own work. And I think in fact I may have succeeded in one or two poems. I'm going to read one where this may have come off.

It doesn't really need an explanation, but I'll just tell you that I was kept in a prison in Johannesburg after I'd been shot in the stomach by the secret police, and then put in a truck with about sixty other prisoners. We were chained together, hands and ankles, and put in trucks and taken down to Robben Island. That's a distance of about a thousand miles.

First they would strip you, take all your clothes from you, and you'd line up naked. Then they would come along and issue everybody these short trousers—a kind of Bermuda shorts!—and a little vest:, and then they would chain you. You'd be barefooted, of course. And you would travel about four in the morning in trucks escorted by security police and cops on motorbikes and in armored cars. (I don't know whether we needed that kind of security.) And halfway on the journey, in a little town called Colesberg, we stopped for the night and were given porridge and then put back in the trucks and sent off again. This is a poem about it.

> Cold
>
> the clammy cement
> sucks our naked feet
> a rheumy yellow bulb
> lights a damp grey wall
>
> the stubbled grass
> wet with three o'clock dew
> is black with glittery edges;
>
> we sit on the concrete,
> stuff with our fingers
> the sugarless pap
> into our mouths
>
> then labour erect;
>
> form lines;
>
> steel ourselves into fortitude
> or accept an image of ourselves
> numb with resigned acceptance;
>
> the grizzled senior warder comments:
> "Things like these
> I have no time for;
>
> they are worse than rats;

you can only shoot them."

Overhead
the large frosty glitter of the stars
the Southern Cross flowering low;

the chains on our ankles
and wrists
that pair us together
jangle
glitter

We begin to move
    awkwardly.

                                        "Colesberg"

Well, that's it. I don't know whether I ought to throw that out, and you will have to decide for yourself whether it achieves what it sets out to achieve. It may be that in time I can persuade people that my intentions were valid. Or it may be that I will have to be unpersuaded—this may well happen, judging from what I wrote yesterday. I would say that I seem to be occupying a kind of middle ground at the moment. But this may simply be because I lack the guts to maintain the position which I believe to be right and which people are persuading me is not right. I don't know. I have an open mind on the matter.

This Colesberg poem is in fact a more artistic poem than it appears to be. I think the art is just concealed. I think, for instance, the use of the word *awkwardly* at the end has more than one function. I think the use of the Southern Cross with a kind of religious overtone, a certain spirituality, helps the suggestion that awkwardness is gracelessness, is being without grace, is being ungraceful. But to be without grace, which is something given to you *gratis* by God, is a spiritual concept. And if someone is without grace, if one is graceless, if one is awkward, couldn't one also be, if without grace, forsaken by God? "My God, why hast thou forsaken me?": this—the loss of grace—is the absolute depth of deprivation. To be totally deserted by God, to be forsaken, is desolation. And what I am trying to achieve is an absence of grace so total that one is desolate, and I have made the word *awkwardly,* the absence of grace, function for it. So it is really perhaps a more arty poem than it would appear at first.

How long after the experience was this poem written?

At least a year.

Is that typical of most of the prison poems?

No, the *Letters to Martha* themselves were written earlier, but as you know, the *Letters to Martha* tend not to capture immediately an experience. They talk about it, but this one is immediate. And as the experience moved further away from me or I moved further away from it in time and it became less intense, it became more manageable. I could at first only write about it from the outside, but later on I could live inside it, to some extent. So some of the

Letters to Martha were written within maybe six months or eight months of coming out. But the sharper ones were written further and further away.

Do you regard this kind of poetry as protest poetry?

No, I don't.

But would you say these poems contain protest?

Yes, I think they may have a protest function. I'd like to believe I don't go around in my poetry saying "What a terrible thing racism is," or "What a terrible thing apartheid is." I would like to believe I don't say that in my poetry, except by indirection, by implication. By reporting a simple experience I ask people to make up their own minds. But I don't try to persuade them as to how they ought to make up their minds. I don't think I myself would call this protest. I would say it functions as protest; it has the effect of protest. But I think it's poetry and not protest; it's not propaganda. The politics is not imported into it.

I may be a little old fashioned in this, but I have tried not to preach about racism or to make political speeches about racism in my poetry because I really believe that there is a thing called artistic integrity. I really believe that one ought not to turn art into propaganda. I think this is not only dishonest, I think it's a prostitution of the art.

I know people don't always agree with me. There are some who say, "So what, all art is propaganda," and I think this, in another way, is true. But I feel myself that it would be dishonest and discordant to introduce crude political statement, raw political dogmas, preachments against racism, in poetry. I don't believe one ought to do this. . . .

R. N. Egudu (essay date 1976)

SOURCE: "Pictures of Pain: The Poetry of Dennis Brutus," in *Aspects of African Literature,* Christopher Heywood (ed.), Heinemann, 1976, pp. 131-144.

[*In the following excerpt, Egudu describes Brutus's poetry as the expression of "mental agony" and praises his use of emotional tension.*]

The poetry of Dennis Brutus is the reaction of one who is in mental agony whether he is at home or abroad. This agony is partly caused by harassments, arrests, and imprisonment, and mainly by Brutus's concern for other suffering people. Thus Brutus feels psychically injured in some of his poems. When he traverses all his land as a 'troubadour',[10] finding wandering 'motion sweeter far than rest', he is feeling the pinch of restiveness resulting from dislodgement. All the factors that make life uncomfortable are assembled in the poem: banning of 'inquiry and movement', 'Saracened arrest', and 'the captor's hand', and against them Brutus takes to roaming in freedom, 'disdaining', 'quixoting' (i.e. pursuing an ideal honour and devotion), singing all the time. His fight is purely psychological, not physical, for he puts up an attitude which his oppressors would least expect and which would disconcert them.

The emotional tension is palpable: to find 'motion' sweeter than 'rest' is in fact to have no rest. The conceit is as effective here as that used by John Donne when he wrote 'Until I labour, I in labour lie', in the poem 'Elegie: Going to Bed'. Like W. B. Yeats, Brutus is pursuing his mask, his anti-self or that which is least like him. His expression of love emotions towards the land is a pathetic dramatization of his want of love. Thus instead of a 'mistress-favour' he has 'an arrow-brand' to adorn his breast. Brutus is therefore seeking for 'something that is dear to him, but something that is out of reach'.[11] Tejani, however, has missed this point for he argues that Brutus's reference to himself as a 'troubadour' is an 'archaic description of himself, more relevant in the sunny non-racial climate of the Mediterranean,' and that this description and the mood of the poem show that the poet listens to the outside voices with a decisiveness which is his weakness.[12] This is of course in consonance with Tejani's former view that Brutus lacks the strength to engage in a physical action against apartheid, not realizing that the kind of action Brutus is concerned with is more psychological than physical.

But Brutus shows no weakness in the poem. He is fighting the forces of oppression with that 'tenderness' which, though it is 'frustrated, does not wither' (*SL,* p. 4). As in the previous poem, the agents of pain here touch the mainstay of the mind. There are the 'investigating searchlights'; there is the 'monolithic decalogue / of fascist prohibition', and above all there are 'patrols' which, like snakes, 'uncoil along the asphalt dark / hissing their menace to our lives'. These forces have organized that 'terror' with which 'all our land is scarred' and which 'rendered [it] unlovely and unlovable'. The fact that Brutus emphasizes his use of 'tenderness' and not malice or even physical action as a fighting weapon does not mean that he is not appreciative of the ugliness of his situation. He clearly states in 'I am the exile' (*SL,* p. 137), that although he is 'gentle' and 'calm' and 'courteous to servility', yet

> . . . Wailings fill the chambers of my heart
> and in my head
> behind my quiet eyes
> I hear the cries and sirens.

And this goes to emphasize the point that his pain is mental rather than physical.

For this kind of pain, Brutus devises a mental weapon, as he indicates in **'Off The Campus: Wits'** (*SL,* p. 12):

> So here I crouch and nock my venomed arrows
> to pierce deaf eardrums waxed by fear . . .
>
> and from the corner of my eye
> catch glimpses of a glinting spear.

In warfare it is the nature of attack that determines the type of weapons to be employed by the attacked for

defence. In South Africa, it is not so much the physical destruction of the blacks and coloured by the whites, as the dehumanization of these people, the dementing process of dehumanization, that is painful to Brutus. Even the 'shouts' of 'Nordics at their play', 'pursuing us like intermittent surf' make the blacks 'cower in our green-black primitive retreat'. The use of 'cower' and later 'crouch' indicate the presence of terror, and both words naturally lead up to and link with that 'fear' which 'waxed' people's 'eardrums'. To fight this terror and fear Brutus uses, not a gun, but the 'venomed arrows' and 'glinting spear' of his poetry.

That fear is the 'enemy' to fight is an insistent motif in Brutus's poetry. **'A letter to Basil'** (*SL*, p. 74) is entirely on this. Fear is a deadly enemy; it 'seeks out the areas of our vulnerability / and savages us'. If we do not appreciate how fear can reduce one to a bestial level, we tend in reaction 'to resort to what revolts us and wallow in the foulest treachery'. But

> To understand the unmanning powers of
> fear and its corrosive action
> makes it easier to forgive.

Here the humanity of Brutus, that tenderness of his, is shown not to the perpetrators of fear, but to its victims. He is as ready to show tenderness to injure his oppressors as to forgive his compatriots who, under the influence of fear, are tempted to be treacherous.

When in prison, one of his most harassing problems is fear—fear that is generated by memory and forethought. In **'Letters to Martha'** Nos 1-13 (*SL,* pp. 54-63), Brutus delineates the unnerving impact of fear in a prison-situation. In **'After the Sentence'** we hear of 'the load of the approaching days' and 'the hints of brutality'; and we are told that the only tempering factor is 'the knowledge of those / who endure much more / and endure . . . No. 2 of **'Letters to Martha'** shows the effect of the prisoner's merely hearing 'that nails and screws and other sizeable bits of metal / must be handed in' which forms part of that 'mesh of possibilities' that give rise to 'notions' cobwebbing 'around your head' and 'tendrils' sprouting 'from your guts in a hundred directions' (**'Letters'**, No. 3). Or it may be 'whispers of horrors / that people the labyrinth of self' (**'Letters'**, No. 5), or such intimations as 'At daybreak for the "isle"', and 'Look your last on all things lovely'—it could be these that constitute 'this crushing blow' (**'Letters'**, No. 13). Fear thus destroys the 'man' in man before the arrival of the possible actual death.

In addition to this consciousness of fear, Brutus felt much the separation from ordinary physical nature while he was in prison, and the pain resulting from this is as mentally torturing as that caused by fear. In **'Letters'** No. 17 (*SL,* p. 65), clouds and birds become rare things and therefore 'assume importance' because they are cut off from view by the 'walls / of black hostility':

> The complex aeronautics
> of the birds

and their exuberant aerobatics
become matters for intrigued speculation
and wonderment;

also,

—the graceful unimpeded motion of the clouds
—a kind of music, poetry, dance—
sends delicate rhythms tremoring through the flesh.

The plight of the poet in prison, who lacks freedom and motion, is the direct opposite of the condition of the birds and clouds which are free and moving; and this is implicit in the poem. The fact that 'clichés about the freedom of the birds' now 'become meaningful' to the poet underscores his consciousness of his lack of this basic need—the need to be free. One therefore wonders why Tejani, referring to those lines quoted above about the free movements of the birds, should doubt that there is 'poetry' in those lines, and say that 'the sense of distance which we need when thinking of the cloud or the bird [is] not present in the poem'.[13] If the two beautiful and powerful images contained in the first and third of those five lines are not 'poetry', then one is at a loss to say what else is 'poetry'. . . .

Notes

[10] 'A troubadour, I traverse all my land', in: *A Simple Lust* (London, 1973), p. 2. Subsequent references to this collection will be embodied in the essay with the abbreviation '*SL*'.

[11] Theroux, op. cit., p. 111.

[12] Tejani, op. cit., p. 133.

[13] ibid., p. 137.

Chikwenye Okonjo Ogunyemi (essay date 1982)

SOURCE: "The Song of the Caged Bird: Contemporary African Prison Poetry," in *Ariel,* Vol. 13, No. 4, October, 1982, pp. 65-84.

[*In the following excerpt, Ogunyemi charts how Brutus transformed his prison experiences into a "humanistic" poetry that grapples with the problems of existence.*]

Writing in the nineteenth century, in his poem "Sympathy," Paul Laurence Dunbar equated the incarcerated nature of black life in America to the life of a caged bird. As a black man with only the foretaste of genuine freedom that the Reconstruction Period in American society could provide, he could fully sympathize with the plight of the bird, and records it dolefully:

I know why the caged bird sings, ah me,
  When his wing is bruised and his bosom sore,—
When he beats his bars and he would be free;
It is not a carol of joy or glee,
  But a prayer that he sends from his heart's deep core,
But a plea, that upward to Heaven he flings—[1]

Although Dunbar was writing specifically about a disillusioned Afro-American population ostensibly freed from the bonds of slavery, his words would apply specifically and at higher levels of intensity, as Ralph Ellison might say, to a majority of the black prison population, which from all reports was apathetic, cringing, and prayerful.

The burden of the song of Dunbar's caged bird has been radically changed in recent times through the efforts of a vociferous, insightful minority of black prisoners in America and Africa. The new themes are international. Considering themselves political prisoners regardless of the legal status of their incarceration, the Americans Malcolm X, George Jackson, Eldridge Cleaver, and Etheridge Knight, on the one hand, and the Africans Dennis Brutus, Okot p'Bitek, and Wole Soyinka, on the other, sing no prayers nor carols of joy or glee. Rather, they have collectively developed what is by now a black tradition of stridency, violence, scurrility, rebelliousness, and irony. They fight their political opponents in a battle of words that has at least left the opposition psychically as scarred as the new songbirds.[2] As African political prison poets laureate, Brutus, p'Bitek, and Soyinka have had to deal with the private anguish and the public roles of the political prisoner. Certain themes tend to recur. Most importantly are politics, sexual deprivation, loneliness, boredom, prison brutality, lack of freedom, no privacy, imperceptible inroads into the prisoners' mental health, the waste of human potential, and, more globally, the psychological bondage of the African masses to their rulers, who in their turn are controlled by the Western world. From South Africa to West Africa, the song of the political prisoner bears a similar message. It comes out shrill and loud as the poets lament their personal plight or urge their audience to some form of revolution to spring the populace from the many forms of prison life that it has been subjected to. Indeed, any black poet who writes to liberate the black race from total submission in Western ways of life, thought, and culture is in a sense concerned with the prison theme. . . .

II

In his collection, ***Letters to Martha,*** Dennis Brutus gives a hint of his attitude towards his prison material: "I cut away the public trappings to assert / certain private essentialities." It is the private angle of prison life with its humanistic emphasis which the public figure, Brutus, examines urbanely and objectively and with a remarkable ironical distancing. This apparently calm exterior, a recognizable black South African pose in racial politics, covers up an inner turmoil and seething. In one dramatic vignette, he presents himself as unprotected, but we perceive an inner resilience that only the spiritually strong can possess when opposing a contemptible but powerful enemy. He declares his stance thus:

and I have laughed, disdaining those who banned
inquiry and movement, delighting in the test
of will when doomed by Saracend arrest,
choosing, like unarmed thumb, simply to stand.[3]

His courage in the unequal struggle is the mark of his victory and heroism. He can therefore afford to be matter of fact in reporting the deplorable conditions under which he and the other prisoners find themselves on Robben Island:

> Cold
> the clammy cement
> sucks our naked feet
>
> . . . . .
>
> we sit on the concrete,
> stuff with our fingers
> the sugarless pap
> into our mouths.[4]

As if such indignities and deprivations are not enough, the prisoners, these descendants of a race of slaves, are psychologically demoralized by being chained together in pairs. Brutus' choice of aspects of prison life to emphasize demonstrates his acute awareness of the humiliating experience that is prison life, its emasculation of the black South African in a hideous system that remains apparently unchanging.

Brutus touches on the perennial conflict between the warder and the gaoled, a relationship that the reader readily extends to the apartheid rulers and the black populace:

> the grizzled senior warder comments:
> 'Things like these
> I have no time for;
> they are worse than rats;
> you can only shoot them.'
>
> (p. 53)

The punctuation marks here are important, as if Brutus is reporting an actual speech he heard. It is with such disarming simplicity and a hint of innocence that the poet manages adroitly to put his enemy in the wrong. The factual reporting allows the reader to make even extreme associations, between the situation reported and the brutality of the Nazis towards the Jews, for example. It is intended to arouse the moral awareness of the international community, to get us to view seriously the individual scenarios that take place in South African prisons, and by extension, in South Africa itself. Brutus' strategy is to engage in a quiet, unobtrusive, and insistent attack on his enemies, in an approach that is compatible with Martin Luther King's philosophy of political non-violence. Part of his attitude is a modesty and humility that will not jubilate over victory in any form. Instead, Brutus feels a certain selflessness in his

> vague heroism
> mixed with self pity
> and tempered by the knowledge of those
> who endure much more
> and endure. . . .
>
> (p. 54)

Yet he too has endured, and has the poetic ability to let us share his experience.

Brutus maintains a detached mood and achieves self-effacement with the use of imprecise pronouns like "one," "you," "your" instead of "I." His objectivity lends an air of truth and sincerity to his account as he explores the degeneration of the human mind in prison through observing various prisoners and their ways of coping with their terrible status. Deprived of basic necessities of life like sex and music and prevented from watching objects of nature like stars and the carefree bird, some prisoners take recourse in psychosomatic illnesses or fantasizing. Others move towards "Coprophilism; necrophilism; fellatio; / penis amputation;" (p. 57). Sodomy is rampant. Many find peace from their cares in the very private world of the insane. Yet through it all, with patience and without self-praise, Brutus not only survivers the numerous hardships, the lot of the prisoner, but, like Malcolm X, matures through contact with so much hideousness and suffering. Here he differs markedly from Soyinka, as we shall see, who delights in engaging in battle with the enemy. Rather, Brutus acknowledges the status of the political prisoner and from that premise continues to fight the opposition:

> we were simply prisoners
> of a system we had fought
> and still opposed.
>
> (p. 64)

With such a limited day-to-day experience, "clichés about the freedom of the birds . . . become meaningful" (p. 66) and a subtle metamorphosis takes place in the prisoner. Brutus suggests the poignancy of his plight in an incident when he switches off the light in an attempt to catch a glimpse of the stars but receives a "warning bark" in reply that arouses fear and destroys the meditative, romantic mood that the poet found himself in. Brutus knows the psychology of fear, as shown in **"A Letter to Basil,"** and his knowledge gives him spiritual strength amidst the vicissitudes of his life:

> To understand the unmanning powers of fear
> and its corrosive action
> makes it easier to forgive.
>
> (p. 74)

These lines express the length and the roughness of the road that Brutus had patiently trod. He has learnt to forgive and even pity the offensive prisoner who cannot help being perfidious to his kind out of fear of the authorities. Also, Brutus' South African whites, referred to as "O my people" in a poem, **"The Mob,"** brutal from fear and so unmanly, become, in a sense, Brutus' fellow prisoners. In an ironic but humanistic mood, he pities them and forgives them for their wrongdoings in a surprising spirit of maturity and brotherhood reminiscent of Christ's indomitable reaction to Peter's denial of him. When Brutus arrives at the tragic conclusion that the whole of South Africa is a prison, he has to work out a *modus vivendi* for himself. To remain sane,

one comes to welcome the closer contact
and understanding one achieves
with one's fellow-men.

                                                                    (p. 60)

His feeling of pity is similar to Baldwin's in the American situation as expressed in his letter to his nephew in *The Fire Next Time.* Brutus triumphs over the sadism of the South African government through his humanism, which pleads for imitation by the authorities. His rebellion against the dehumanization is the act of writing; the power of his cosmopolitan truth and urbane tones all the more condemns the apartheid regime, which emerges by contrast as primitive.

It is therefore surprising that "an African writer thinks that the poet's social involvement in Dennis Brutus's poems is a check on the artistic effect," although, as D. S. Izevbaye is quick to add, "most critics do not endorse this view, nor do they agree that as a rule poets should be less vociferous about social problems."[5] This raises a perennial issue about aesthetics and the social involvement of the writer, and here the issue must be resolved in the writer's favour. It is obvious from the ***Letters*** that the occasion and experience of prison life that political imprisonment affords have given poetic inspiration to Brutus, as it has to other writers in other parts of the world.[6] His turning his experience into a work of art is certainly as valid as a poet who turns to nature for inspiration. Brutus deals with the nature of man in power, the artist as prisoner, and these are powerful modes of knowing man and his ways. Brutus' writing is artistic rather than overtly propagandistic. He writes to connect his inner life with the outside world and those who love him so that his mind and theirs can be, relatively, at rest. He is conscious of this as he informs us that his poetry is

some evidence of my thought and caring:

. . . . .

partly to wrench some ease from my own mind.
And partly that some world sometime may know.
                                                                    (p. 68)

That need to connect with posterity, a reason for the enduring, is a genuine artistic feeling. By handling the subject of prison life, mulling over it, seeing its corrosive effect on both the gaoler and the gaoled, Brutus grapples through it with the existential human predicament that man finds himself in. His message, even if ultimately didactic, as most good literature is, is humanistically convincing and artistically enunciated.

Notes

[1] Paul Laurence Dunbar, "Sympathy," in *The Complete Poems of Paul Laurence Dunbar* (New York: Dodd, Mead & Co., 1913), p. 102.

[2] Dennis Brutus acknowledges his victory over the South African authorities in a poem, "Let Me Say It."

[3] Dennis Brutus, "A troubadour, I traverse all my land," in *A Simple Lust* (London: Heinemann, 1973), p. 52.

[4] Brutus, "Letters to Martha," in *A Simple Lust,* p. 52. All further references are to this edition and appear in the text.

[5] D. S. Izevbaye, "Criticism and Literature in Africa," in *Perspectives on African Literature,* ed. Christopher Heywood (London: Heinemann, 1971), p. 30.

[6] The output of respectable prison writing from Socrates to Kafka to Solzhenitsyn, for example, and popular works like *Papillon,* should by this time demonstrate that prison writing has come to stay as a distinctive, acceptable genre.

Amiri Baraka (review date 1989)

SOURCE: A review of *Airs and Tributes,* in *Black American Literature Forum,* Vol. 23, No. 3, Fall, 1989, pp. 621-26.

[*In the following review, Baraka faults the poetry in* Airs and Tributes *as being written to please academics and for failing to fully serve the international "revolutionary struggle."*]

This new volume of Dennis Brutus carries a multiple significance. Because Brutus is one of the best known of the South African poets in the U.S., we are interested not only in the poetry qua poetry and the life it carries and introduces us to, but because of the nature of the world itself, independent of poetry, Brutus's name carries another set of registrations, which expand the poetry's meaning and at the same time cause the poetry to be covered.

For instance, many readers will probably remember when Ronald Reagan tried to deport Mr. Brutus back to South Africa, even though the poet was teaching at Northwestern at the time and there was no question about his being able to put down the freedman's deposit instead of being sent back to the plantation on a vagrancy charge.

And this is not "Lucky" Brutus (quite the contrary, Mr. Brutus was once incarcerated at the notorious Robben Island where Nelson Mandela was kept so long; he was also shot in the back in an escape attempt, though I guess he is lucky that he survived) or "Mad Dog" Brutus, only a very soft-spoken poet and professor, who now chairs the Black Studies department at the University of Pittsburgh. Brutus has already published ten books of poetry.

But since art itself is an ideological reflection of life, no matter what formalist job holders maintain, it stands to reason that if that ideology, that way of looking at the world that a particular work of art contains is in opposition to the rulers of whatever state the artist lives in, then that artist is in for trouble. Minimally it will mean that he or she will have trouble getting published. This is the more sophisticated Western imperialist way of doing the Khomeini on its dissident artists, though one wonders how it is that mainstream Western artists can pull an attack wail re Salman Rushdie and never have raised much of a voice about those writers actually murdered by imperialism every day, such as Walter Rodney in Guyana, Mikey Smith in Jamaica, Pablo Neruda in Chile, and Henry Dumas in the U.S.

Because the Pan-African people generally lack self-determination, internationally, it means we must rely on "others" to publish, record, produce us. This is also trouble, though the art itself is a form of self-determination and self-consciousness. But since Reagan and company oppose black self-determination in any form, the idea that Dennis Brutus would be off somewhere doing something the Bruderbund forbade would get the Reag hopping to correct this. So he wanted to ship Brutus back to his primitive Boer relatives to be dealt with like a bad Kaffir should.

Brutus's *Airs,* on the other hand, is a slender volume and exposes a quiet, introspective voice. The very title of the book would seem "unpolitical," but all art is political whether overt or covert. It is propaganda (Mao said) for one point of view or another. Some focused consciousness, some overflowing perception, some experience reflecting itself or whatever makes the art. Some I or Eye. So what does the soft, reflective cadence of Brutus, the muted impressionism of his perception, the almost hesitant stillness of the rationale convey? The poetry is a use most modest for a life so full of extremes. But this is what is important here: Why such poetry from such a life, and how does the verse reflect at various levels degrees of feeling and comprehension?

Brutus is a South African of mixed blood, like most people in the world. But the justification of the spawn of the northern war gods for being in the world with the rest of us, and yet "in charge," is that they are "white" and "pure white" at that. They have been chosen (by themselves) and the womanless abstraction of their J-Christian trinity to maintain their "in chargeness"—that is, superiority and its concomitant purity and luxury—through war and blood. But for the tragic cost, such mindlessness would be laughable.

Brutus's undercrime is that he claims humanity when animal reign says only animals are human. The Euro-American bourgeois world view upholds this basic view for most of the peoples on the planet, though, in terms of intention and results, the state and states of modern imperialism reek with squalid human degradation, self-deception, ignorance, and normal terror.

Du Bois' observation that the problem of the twentieth century is the color line and the fact that people are willing to live in luxury knowing it's based on the exploitation and oppression of other people are basics of twentieth-century ideological demography for a world controlled by imperialism and white supremacy, but with neo-Colonialism native inposts rise where once there were foreign outposts.

Certainly the disappearance of most of the straight out colonial world means that even superficial discussion of an oppressive and exploitative society must begin with a class analysis. Blacks and whites in South Africa (and certainly the U.S.) have been distended into an exposure of their class essence more and more. Injured negroes attacked Tawana Brawley and welcomed Ronald Reagan, just as blacks in South Africa are shooting down other black people. It is the class information that defines ultimately, no matter the color and nationality. A member of the African National Congress, Brutus is active in the largest South African liberation organization—an urban organization with a broad gathering of classes, including urban workers and the urban middle classes, including black and white intellectuals and the South African Communist Party. There are other major liberation organizations in South Africa, the Pan African Congress and the Black Consciousness Movement, but there is as yet no broad united front movement among these three organizations, much less some of the smaller forces.

The ANC has always been marked by its well-projected and often attacked stance of "integration" or multinationality. Its members that we come in contact with are often from one sector or another of the South African middle class. And, as the Freedom Charter has stated, ANC's aim is to govern a multinational democratic South Africa.

What is literary about this is the *color* class uses as its tongue. All classes have their specific interests, hence their own world views and organizations. In national liberation movements, because of the united front character of such groups, made up of several different classes who are sometimes in conflict with each other almost as much as they are with their common enemy, it can complicate analysis.

Brutus's poetry, for instance, at its least interesting, is the flat lyrical subjectivism of the petty bourgeois—given to being thrown into fits of depression as much by the greyness of a morning as by a foiled get-rich-quick scheme.

One wonders, when reading Brutus, for instance, how it is that we "know" so much of what is happening in South Africa, as well as the registration of the connectedness imperialism has made of the world, here in the U.S., because this somehow escapes mention in these poems.

Brutus begins "the divinity within me / aspires to reunion, to divinity." This is not a theist abstraction of traditional African animism. Divinity and "itself" can never be separated, nor can any other thing or consciousness—except in the mind, we know from being manhandled by the subjectivism of oppressors.

Perhaps it is oppression that has caused this seeming division between being and the consciousness Brutus speaks of. And this comes at the very beginning of the book. In **"March 21, 1987,"** Brutus writes that "Summer droops in Autumn / the dyings continue / and resistance grows: there are still those / willing to give their lives." It is an obvious alienation one feels. Yet "Sharpeville, Langa / you are sacred names" again inhabits the spiritual, religious realm—that holding of texts with which to worship, to focus life. Yet the poem ends, "in the center of our brains / the flame of desire for freedom / fiercely burns." So we see that the "flame," the "spirit" is "in the center of our brains," that it is an *intellectual* reverence, and awe.

In **"For the Prisoners in South Africa,"** Brutus says thinking about them turns his "brain to stone" and writes of "the wound of knowledge / knowledge of my power-lessness." But why *powerlessness,* except as estrange-ment from what does have power? The single "I," the individual exists only as an expression of the whole. It is the *true* self-consciousness of the individual that is the valorization of the whole, and the identification as part of that whole consciousness.

The petty bourgeois is pessimistic because it (the class) conceives of the world as its own class reality, hung adrift, isolated from and in between oppressed and op-pressor. The radical petty bourgeoisie is sympathetic to the idea of liberation. Cabral said "class suicide" is the only method of self-conscious unity with the people.

What is disturbing is that when Brutus brings us closest to the war and agony of the South African freedom strug-gle, we get sentiments like "so finally they have come / must eliminate an irritant / I think, relieved and satisfied, / wait for the ripping thud of bullets." Relieved? To be killed by fascist monsters? What is the relief in that? Is this not a position of acquiescence and willing impotence?

We look for Odes and Tributes to the revolutionaries, to the spirit of human struggle and the valorization of the human spirit. But these are not forthcoming, except as fragments of life we feel somewhere just beyond the pages of the book.

Instead we get "fertile fields / hymned by Greek poets," or as a recollection, we presume, of his own incarceration memories like "Our hands meet / in the blue Athenian dusk / and the years roll away." The "other" of alluded oppres-sion and monstrousness, we are told, will be punished by "divine ordinance," because these whoevers have sought "delight too greedily."

We know that "a woman's voice / lovely and unneeded / called across the miles / desolate and desperate." Why? And for whom? That, like much in the volume, is left unlettered. Of a "South African exile killed by letter-bomb in Mozambique," Ruth First, we are left with "in a bomb-wrecked office in Maputo / your bloodied corpse rested." But what does it mean? Where are we in this? What is the struggle, and what the goal? Is our only act in the real world to be impotent subjectivism?

No direct answers. No directness of image or focus. Just fragments and tidbits of disappointment, pessimism and a curious yearning for metaphysical resolution to the real disasters of material life. It's as if exile is a purgatory of unfocused desires, with no commitment to struggle or objective understanding. Moods, quiet tones, and tin-kles—a deep and binding subjectivism. We cannot see the real life of either the subject or the human struggle he strains to make allusions to.

But how can the tortured say "all human aspirations are valid"? Does that include the aspirations of the Boers and Bushes and Shamirs? Is it true that the majority of the world, the victims of imperialism, and its pre-human de-sires, must accept their victimizers' aspirations to enslave them? And is what we really "yearn" for "the crimson glim-mer that holds splendor and wonder and hope?" I think not.

At times the book reads like a text for the tentative petty bourgeois, victimized by their socialization and "educa-tion" to worship what imperialism has created, its ideolo-gy, carriers and artifacts, and at times even their own rejection which they worship like intellectual mantras of self-pity and petty martyrdom. This is the only sense I could make out of the poem **"Scarab,"** which ends, "I pierce centuries / and break through barriers / my world and birth / imposed on me."

The poem **"Tribute"** strikes an aggressive note, perhaps because it is dedicated to Kwame Touré (Stokely Car-michael). But even here Brutus posits a martyr's justifica-tion more than the actual struggle to rid the world of martyrs and the evil that murders them into martyrhood. "He does not die / who lives in the consciousness / of his people." Yet here, too, the fragmented, pessimistic muddle mindedness returns. "The day dies into dusk / . . . disclos-es the continuity of days / the constant questions / un-answered, unanswerable . . ."—like the priests propose an unknowable world, answered only by our disappearance into their sectarian meal ticket.

Revolutionary struggle is the principal answer to the ques-tions being asked now by our torture and lack of self-determination. It is the answer to Apartheid in South Africa, Naziism in Gaza and the West Bank, and Fascism from the dunce-hat-wearing Fascists in Beijing.

Dennis Brutus has written stronger, more beautiful, hu-manistic, and inspiring poetry than this. *Airs & Tributes* is par for the petty bourgeois international university crowd; it is their sound and their song. What we need from Brutus, and what he needs from himself, is a poetry that is revolutionary in its politics and aesthetically powerful. We demand strength not weakness, nor the tinseled yearn-ing to be a peaceful, sensitive professor, like the rest of the dead flesh misleading our youth in these various schools who masquerade as artists and intellectuals, there-by forfeiting both poetry and revolution.

Frank M. Chipasula (essay date 1993)

SOURCE: "A Terrible Trajectory: The Impact of Apartheid, Prison and Exile on Dennis Brutus's Poetry," in *Essays on African Writing: A Re-evaluation,* edited by Abdulrazak Gurnah, Heinemann, 1993, pp. 38-55.

[*In the following essay, Chipasula argues that the strains and pressures of the apartheid state, rather than inspir-ing Brutus, actually limited the extent of his poetic achievement.*]

In contemporary African literature very few poets have attracted as much international attention for their extra-literary efforts as the exiled South African activist-poet, Dennis Brutus. Having been nurtured on a 'diet of eloquent delectable accolades',[1] he has grown into somewhat of a sacred bull one approaches with great trepidation. However, our reverence for Brutus has less to do with his poetic achievement than his stand against apartheid. Awestruck by the presence of this heroic 'fighter' who survived eighteen months of incarceration on Robben Island and has valiantly lived with the scar of a bullet wound, we have tended to place him constantly among the 'world's finest poets'.[2] A veteran of a life-and-death battle against injustice, Brutus has thus garnered rewards for an art that might not have attracted a stare had it been otherwise.

With eleven volumes currently to his credit, Brutus's poetic career appears impressive.[3] However, a reassessment based on three of his poetry collections, **Sirens, Knuckles, Boots** (1963), **Letters to Martha and Other Poems from a South African Prison** (1968) and **Stubborn Hope** (1978), reveals the terrible trajectory of his poetic performance, which can be attributed to apartheid's restrictive and reductive definition of human beings, and to imprisonment and exile. All the same, Dennis Brutus's career is remarkable, considering that he lived and functioned for many years under immense constraints, risking his very life when he challenged the apartheid system in sport (not in poetry, which came later). Although he has produced the bulk of his poetry in exile, in his work he has nevertheless focused on the South African landscape which he has always imagined as a lover's body.

Several factors encourage a reassessment of Dennis Brutus's poetic career and output. Firstly, the presence of younger poets in South Africa necessitates a revaluation not only of Brutus's poetic oeuvre but also his stature as a black South African poet. Unfortunately, a great deal of Brutus's poetry not only lacks the 'amazing suppleness and subtlety', and perhaps the ingenuity with which urban music confronts black people's experiences in the townships, but it also exhibits what Lewis Nkosi further describes as the 'cracks and tension of language working under severe strain'.[4] In terms of technical refinement, thematic development and poetic verve, Brutus's poems do not approximate the dexterity and linguistic innovativeness of the prematurely plucked Arthur Nortje, Brutus's own erstwhile student whom he himself has called not only the 'beautiful singer', but also 'the finest poet to come out of South Africa and probably out of Africa'.[5]

A recontextualisation of Brutus's poetry within the scheme of anti-apartheid poetry reveals the stunting impact of racial segregation, imprisonment and exile on his creativity. Yet unlike his disadvantaged compatriots within the country, Brutus, as poet and sports politician, has been nurtured and groomed by a group of dedicated and sympathetic critics willing to suspend negative observations on the shortcomings of his work, and he has thus found himself effortlessly in print abroad.[6] Apparently, as long as the poetry exhibited some elements of protest against apartheid and commitment to the cause for the restoration of justice in South Africa, it was worth publishing.

Should we expect or even demand more than protest and political commitment from a black South African poet? In the case of Dennis Brutus, we are justified in our expectation of aesthetic beauty in his poetry because of what his early verse had shown. Further, in a poetry such as Brutus's we expect something profound, what Pablo Neruda, in his essay 'The Poet Is Not a Rolling Stone' terms the 'essences' of his native country. According to Neruda, the 'first stage of a poet's life must be devoted to absorbing the essences of his native land: later, he must return them . . . His poetry and his actions must contribute to the maturity and growth of his people.'[7] However, unless such poetic maturity occurs in the poet, we cannot expect the contribution towards 'maturity and growth' of his people.

Apartheid's worst impact on Brutus's life was to create psychological barriers that apparently engendered a complex and deep-seated identity crisis during his early years, a consequence of his having been reductively classified as 'Coloured', that is, neither 'European' nor 'African', in a racially stratified society. Brutus's description of the racial divisions in Port Elizabeth during his childhood is illuminating, for it indicates the deep chasms the Group Areas Act created among the various 'races':

> Certainly we were not white, and *out there* were the white people who controlled our destiny . . . There were also the Africans, the 'natives' who lived even *further out on the edge of the city* and who passed through *our area,* or the outskirts of it, on the way to *their area,* each morning going to work and each evening coming from work.

> (*TriQ 69*, p. 366)

The implicit distance and lack of contact among the three groups, with the 'natives' occupying the marginal or peripheral spaces, indicate the degree of cultural isolation the young Brutus experienced.[8] The resultant psychic distortion and fragmentation are revealed in his subsequent doubts about his African identity when he expressed his 'misgivings' about his 'right to be called an "African Voice"; how far were my ideas and opinions and art peculiarly African?' (**Poems from Algiers,** p. 21).

Brutus's doubts and questions concerning his true identity are genuine, and they are a consequence of a breach between his individual imagination and the complex traditions within which it might have functioned had apartheid laws not closed off from him certain *essential* cultural experiences. This identity crisis is also apparent in the implicit discomfort and ambivalence with which Brutus recalls part of his family history:

> My mother talked of the days of slavery, of how her mother had in fact known slavery, may have been a slave herself. She was of African descent, but of mixed heritage: an English family called Webb, apparently.

> (*TriQ 69*, p. 366)

His grandmother's strong traditions of orature might have empowered Brutus to experiment with the many genres of poetry such as the Izibongo praise poetry, proverbs, riddles, tales, curses, initiation chants and dirges as well as war-songs, wedding and hunters' songs that are prevalent in southern Africa. Apartheid's fragmenting laws must be held responsible for Brutus's apparent lack of exposure to the region's rich oral traditions whose metaphors, symbols, images, and other poetic devices might have authenticated and anchored his work in genuine South *African* traditions.

Although he began writing poetry in the mid-1940s, Brutus's emergence in the early 1960s as the major Coloured South African poet coincides simultaneously with the intensification of the struggles for freedom in the region as well as the alliances among the colonial powers and the apartheid regime. Constantly persecuted by the South African political police, he was arrested, and in 1963 banned for his anti-apartheid activities in the field of international sport. In a bid to escape from the country, he was caught in Mozambique, detained and then handed back to the South African authorities. In another attempt to escape he was shot in the stomach, hospitalised and then tried for subversion. While incarcerated on the notorious Robben Island prison off Cape Town, his manuscript of poems, which had won the Mbari Poetry Prize in 1962 (although he returned the prize money because the award was racially based), was published as *Sirens, Knuckles, Boots* in 1963, in Nigeria.

Ironically, the Mbari Creative Society, in a gesture meant to encourage indigenous creativity, placed the rejected laurels on a poet who declared in a sonnet, **"A troubadour, I traverse all my land."** Within the coupled quatrains followed by the two tercets, Brutus's rhyming of 'land' with his probing 'hand', alternating 'zest' with 'rest', expressed his intense, urgent and passionate love for South Africa. This is all in order, except that Brutus, with all his love for the land, adopts an alien persona, a troubadour, perhaps to convince us of his knowledge of Mediterranean poetic traditions and aesthetics. Couldn't Brutus find, in African, or southern African traditions, an equivalent for this 'quixoting' troubadour? Did he really have to borrow an alien tongue to express his love for his native land? Perhaps we can condone this as merely apprentice poetry, and yet, even then couldn't he have apprenticed himself to such local poets as Vilakazi, Dhlomo and Mqayi and other Imbongi whose works must have crossed his eyes as he stealthily 'traversed' his land during his underground years?

This question becomes critical when one recalls Brutus's own assertion that he functions within the African poetic tradition,[9] which invites comparisons with such traditionalists as Okot p'Bitek, the late Acoli poet, and Mazisi Kunene who not only composes in the Zulu language and then renders his works into English, but also consciously operates within the Imbongi tradition of Zulu court poetry. Since African traditions are diverse and various it is perhaps not unjustified to ask: To which African tradition does Brutus's poetry belong?

A subtle process of self-definition and hence empowerment is implicit in his early poems that reflect a mind intensely at work, a burgeoning artist trying to wring meanings out of the complex, chaotic, and hostile yet beautiful landscape of his country. *Sirens, Knuckles, Boots* demonstrates a mind busily meditating on mastering anger by channelling it into forceful similes and metaphors. Brutus's economy of means creates a terse zestful line that attempts to link soul to soil, to fuse woman to land, and to project his double love of both, as in **"Nightsong: City"** (*A Simple Lust,* p. 18). Poems such as these, which express his love for land in startlingly erotic images of passionate and intimate sexual embrace, also cryptically reference his relationship with a white woman, in defiance of the Immorality Act.[10] A simple lust, for Brutus, metaphorically conjures a man's intimate contact with his beloved country. In the most powerful of these poems Brutus distils multiple meanings into single words, phrases and lines loaded with intense emotion, generating great tensions in the poems.

Nowhere in Brutus's exile poetry is the imagery as vivid and forceful as it is in these early poems. The volume's terse and richly imaged verse, endowed with lavish figurative language, perhaps more than the fact of Brutus's wounding and incarceration, may have impressed the jurors about the poet's now largely unrealised potential. Notice his vivid and harrowing description of the wastelands called the Transkei homeland in **"Erosion: Transkei"**:

> Under green drapes the scars scream,
> red wounds wail soundlessly,
> beg for assuaging, satiation;
> warm life dribbles seawards with streams.
> (A Simple Lust, p. 16)

Here is a forceful verbal portrait of a wounded, eroded land that becomes more poignant as the poet fuses implicitly the land's physical wounds with the people's psychic wounds. Yet there is always a possibility of 'warm life', new horizons, even as the streams that will be created by 'the quickening rains' carry the rich soil to the sea.

Curiously, the same poet who could deftly conjure up such an apt simile as 'violence like a bug-infested rug is tossed', or the metaphorical 'long day's anger pants from sand and rocks' (**"Nightsong: City"**, p. 18), could degenerate to such flatness as contained in:

> Bruised though we must be
> some easement we require
> unarguably, though we argue against desire

('This sun on this rubble after rain', p. 9)

The initial immediacy of **"This sun on this rubble"** is totally diminished from a poem that has such powerfully defeatist imagery as 'under jackboots our bones and spirits crunch/forced into sweat-tear-sodden slush'. Alternating pessimism with optimism, the poet may be excused for understating the possibility of regeneration, of something new being born out of this rubble and debris of humanity spiritually crushed under the brutal boots of apartheid.

This defeatist rhetoric takes on an intense preoccupation with the self, becomes almost solipsistic in **"Off the Campus: Wits"**, a poem which recalls and recreates an aspect of his student days at the University of Witwatersrand where he experienced segregation on the sports field. His bitterness attains the heights of irrationality when he describes white students, who are unjustly implicated in a policy of victimisation, as 'obscene albinos'.[11] What is strangely curious though is the sudden shift from the collective 'we look', 'we cower' to 'I crouch'—from 'us' to the solitary 'I', the oppressed community to the lone 'fighter' poet writing these venomed lines:

> to pierce deaf eardrums waxed by fear
> or spy, a Strandloper, these obscene albinos
> and from the corner of my eye
> catch a glimpse of a glinting spear.
>
> (*A Simple Lust,* p. 12)

There is a hint of the cult of the lone poet figure characteristic of the early Soyinka or Okigbo as well as intimations of an impending liberation struggle in the 'glinting spear' which the persona merely glimpses but does not wield. The cyclic nature of this oppression is quite clearly portrayed in the following twelve lines:

> The sounds begin again:
> the siren in the night
> the thunder at the door
> the shriek of nerves in pain.
>
> Then the keening crescendo
> of faces split by pain
> the wordless, endless wail
> only the unfree know.
>
> Importunate as rain
> the wraiths exhale their woe
> over the sirens, knuckles, boots;
> my sounds begin again.

"The sounds begin again", *A Simple Lust,* (p.19)

Three simple nouns—'siren', 'thunder' and 'shriek'—effectively conjure the violence that black South Africans had to endure nightly. However, the vicious cycle of these oppressive sounds implied in the rhyming of 'again' with 'pain' is mysteriously broken by the intruding natural force of rain. Thus one caught in the repetitive, odious cycle finds redemptive respite in the rain that presages a rebirth and regeneration.

'The sounds begin again' fairly succeeds with its terse, end-stopped lines, its intricate rhyme-scheme which weaves not only words but stanzas into a neat, coherent whole though again one wishes Brutus had heeded T. S. Eliot's advice to poets to find an 'objective correlative' to emo-

tions in a poem. John Pepper Clark asserts as much when he comments that Brutus is a 'man battering his head against the bars of a cage', yet it is difficult to hear the 'shouting' that Clark hears.[12] The tragedy in Brutus's poem does not become mere melodrama. The poem does vividly project the incessant nature of oppression in apartheid South Africa, and the acceptance in the last line, which is no mere variation on the opening line, might imply the speaker's stoical response to this reality.

Brutus's early volume remains his strongest to date and worth one more word if only to speculate on what manner of poet he might have become had apartheid's prison and exile not stunted his growth. His post-Robben Island poetry is marked by a simplicity and directness quite unlike the earlier poems. But his conscious decision to reach a much wider audience than before meant a great sacrifice in technical virtuosity. Upon his release from prison he was placed under house arrest for twelve hours of each day, and he was served with a new set of bans that made it a crime to draft or write anything, except letters, that might be published. As a result Brutus adopted the epistle form for his poems addressed to Martha, his sister-in-law, whose husband was himself a prisoner on Robben Island. Though not intended for publication, the poems were gathered together into *Letters to Martha and Other Poems from a South African Prison* (1968), a volume that remains the most tangible testament to the adverse effects of apartheid censorship restrictions and prison on this intrepid fighter for justice. The poems belong to the genre of prison poetry, all written under house arrest but exploring the meaning and implications of his prison experiences.

Although the poems lack in both power and craftsmanship, such an otherwise perceptive critic as Adrian Roscoe accredits the prison experience with having enabled Brutus to produce some of the most refined poems he had hitherto written, as he so articulately claims:

> Imprisonment not only pushed the poet to explore the deepest recesses of mind and soul, but also demanded, constantly and at their highest pitch, all those imaginative and spiritual resources necessary for his survival as a man of dignity and self-respect.[13]

Contrary to Roscoe's lavish praises, Brutus's own volume contains hardly any evidence to bolster such an eloquent and over-generous defence of the poet. More valid than these accolades are perhaps Es'kia (Ezekiel) Mphahlele and Lewis Nkosi's observations regarding Brutus's over-reliance on flat statement in that very volume.[14] As the poems lack any depth of feeling, they may serve to demonstrate just how thoroughly prison experience has stamped the 'art' out of these prosaic pieces. Strangely defeatist in tone, these poems rather intimate to us the shrinking and warping impact such extreme conditions can have on a fine artist.

The very first poem in *Letters to Martha* belies Roscoe's contention that this is some of the best verse ever written by Brutus.[15] In that poem, **"Longing"**, the speaker poses the following rhetorical question:

Can the heart compute desire's trajectory
Or logic obfusc with semantic ambiguities
This simple ache's expletive detonation?

(p. 46)

The response, of course, would have been positive had Brutus heeded Eliot's injunction to poets to seek an objective correlative for that 'simple ache' to resolve all the 'semantic ambiguities' which follow. I find it hard to empathise with the speaker whose 'heart knows now such devastation' because he makes no effort at projecting that devastation vividly through emotive language. The letters' major flaws are outright philosophising and over-use of polysyllabic diction which results in such flat and unevocative words as 'ease*ment*', 'lodge*ment*', 'intrigued speculation and wonder*ment*' (my emphases); or 'reformation / (which can procure promotion)', 'the impregnation of our air', or 'a pugnacious assertion of discontent / . . . the boundless opprobrium of life / a desperation: despair', or 'after the entertainment / Beethoven with his sonorous percussive exaltation' (p. 93); or when he is 'transcendentally watching the Irish jigsaw' (p. 95) as he flies from London to New York! And when the racists 'yearn unassuagedly', when the SANROC fighter blasts them 'unforgettably' and 'the diurnal reminders excoriate their souls' (p. 90), what emotions or images do these lines evoke in the reader's mind? It is the language, not the experience, that is at fault here.

Ploughing through the eighteen letters and postscripts (written, apparently, *in two days*),[16] another twenty-seven letters, and 'diary-entry-like' meditative verses, is rather taxing on the reader's patience, for the majority of the work here relies so heavily on prosaic and flat statement that one delights even in the rare sparks of vivid imagery. This is not to say that the movement (which the reader must reconstruct) from the trial, the charge, the journey to Robben Island with its stop-overs in various jails and the speaker's apprehensions about prison as well as the harrowing prison experiences is without value. Where is the depth of feeling one expects in a poem about incarceration? In the poem **"On the Island"**, we are meant to feel the deathly atmosphere of solitary confinement, but unfortunately the over-repeated compound modifier 'cement-grey' becomes irritatingly monotonous and redundant:

Cement-grey floors and walls
cement-grey days
cement-grey time . . .
(**"On the Island"**, *A Simple Lust,* p. 71)

Neither lyrical nor narrative, the poems depend too heavily on flat statements and rhetorical questions: 'who has not joyed in the arbitrary exercise of power'. Lacking emotive or figurative language, the **Letters** are level-headed meditations of a wronged man and a tired artist who is capable of such 'bad stumbling verse' (**Poems from Algiers,** p. 21) as the following:

the complex aeronautics
and the birds

and their exuberant acrobatics
become matters for intrigued speculation
and wonderment.

(**Letter 17,** *A Simple Lust,* p. 66)

This, of course, is mere posturing on dangerous verbal stilts not many prisoners can afford. Indeed, one is filled with a sense of 'wonderment' why Brutus couldn't simply lament, 'Oh had I a pair of wings!' Where is the precision and 'intensity of imagery', the 'apt image' that Daniel Abasiekong and Romanus Egudu applauded in Brutus's poetry?[17] Unlike Paul Theroux, I see more total misses from Brutus's wild swinging punches than we have hitherto been willing to acknowledge (Beier, p. 122).

Scribbled at lightning speed, under house arrest—itself a worse form of imprisonment since it alienates one from one's own home—these poems, whose purpose was 'partly to wrench ease' for himself, show the paralysing impact of both apartheid and prison on the poet. There is more moralising, didacticism and rationalisation of actions as well as unwitting revelations about Brutus's own fear that he may have been psychologically tainted by his prison experiences.

In the **Letters,** as in the previous collection, Brutus exposes the injustices the majority suffer in a police state which arbitrarily exercises and displays force through its various 'Special Branches'. Major themes here include the denial of freedom and dehumanisation of both the oppressors and the oppressed who nevertheless retain a measure of their humanity through endurance, tenderness and love. Imprisonment results in further fragmentation of lives and distortion of moral values, as the poems on prison sexuality indicate. The dominator-dominated dichotomy finds its parallel in the homosexual relations between the men and youths in prison. We notice, for instance, the changes and transformations that occur to 'Blue Champagne', a youthful male who plays the role of 'girl' in the sexual embrace, but when he grows older he becomes the dominant 'man' in the unions. Certainly, such 'random pebbles' as **Letters 3, 6, 7** and **8** could not console a wife whose husband might not only be driven to such 'desperate limits' as to seek relief from sexual tension in 'this' but also find it 'preferable, / even desirable' (**Letter 7,** p. 58). **Letters 9** and **10** do little to allay her fears, try as the persona may to reassure her.

What then is the real motive for composing these letters, and are the statements Brutus has made over the matter credible and conclusive? **Letter 13** reveals more about the letter-writing project itself than Brutus or his critics have acknowledged (*A Simple Lust,* p. 63). Deliberately misplaced in the sequence, the letter recalls the eve of his departure for Robben Island. What begins as a moment of personal illumination:

"So, for a beginning, I know
there is no beginning"

becomes suddenly generalised, as is Brutus's wont, to pre-empt any charges of a preoccupation with the self that borders on narcissism:

So *one* cushions the mind
    with phrases
    aphorisms and quotations
    to blunt the impact
    of this crushing blow.   [my emphasis]

The placement of the 'letter' here indicates its function. If these poems are about the human condition, they do less to enlighten us about that condition as it is modified by prison than they do about the poet himself. Brutus's apartheid prison is hardly unique to South Africa and might not particularly enrage sensitive audiences abroad. Rather, the *Letters* project, undertaken after Robben Island, is apparently a futile effort to 'cushion' his own mind and to conceal the psychic scars left by the 'outrages of prison' (p. 63).

Artistically, Brutus does not fare any better in exile, as his later work indicates. Just as chaotic as the other volumes, *Stubborn Hope* (1978) continues in the monotonous vein of his earlier verses, with flat statements, intriguing self-accusations, imagined questions or objections, without thematic linkages or apparent order, save for the sameness of voice.

Characteristically brief, yet more prosaic than before, these poems reveal an anguished heart, sometimes curiously 'remorseful', and a turbulent mind, understandably so considering that the poet is finally recognising the wounds garnered from incarceration in the notorious island prison and under house arrest, as he states in the verbose "**A Comparative Peace**":

One requires
more
an intellectual acceptance
assent
the erasure of sharp memories.
           (*Stubborn Hope*, p. 19)

an erasure which is next to impossible as the exile is continually haunted by the fact that other detainees still languish in the country's prisons. Hence:

One knows
only an unquiet ease
only a comparative peace.

           (p. 19)

The half-rhyme on 'ease' and 'peace' hints at the turmoil beneath, which is clearly discernible in the following poem, 'It is without the overtones': for despite the poet's efforts at concealment of his dis-ease, he cannot 'find (in the Abergavenny hills) some small easement' (p. 19).

Again, over-reliance on flat, sometimes even partially abstract, statement weakens Brutus's work here. And, although the poet is himself aware of this slackness in his verse, he is apparently unable to do anything about it. Brutus himself is his own best critic, as the following poems indicate, both from *Stubborn Hope*, his next substantial volume after *A Simple Lust*. Both poems are framed

as crucial questions an artist in Brutus's position might ask, caught in a circumstance where, although he is intensely aware of his artistic failures, his admirers think otherwise. The reference to that 'something beautiful' and the nostalgic tone of **"When Will I Return"** force one to re-examine the technical aspects of Brutus's earlier work to which these poems refer. The following claims need to be taken seriously because they are made by Brutus the reader of his own past performance, who simultaneously laments the loss of his artistic dexterity in sadly prosaic lines. 'When will my heart / ever sing again?' the poet prosaically laments in one poem, and in another he nostalgically asks, 'when will I return / to the tightly organised / completely structured / image and expression / rich in flying tangential associations'. (p. 13) Is this also perhaps a case of a poet's over-rating of his own past achievements? For beyond the few poems, such as **"The sounds begin again"**, which is compact yet in need of Eliot's 'objective correlative', not much in his accumulated work can support such a claim. Indeed, these large claims cannot be substantiated by many of his pre- and post-prison poetry. Besides, one would have to go to great pains to find that rich, complex, and resonant imagery in abundance among those issued during the earliest phase of his exile. The few exceptions are nevertheless marred by their own glaring flaws.

If these poems do not yield much in terms of issues, they nevertheless crack open the door into the poet's pained mind as he grapples with the reality of his continuing exile and the uncertainty of his country's future. They also offer us insights into the exile mind, the poignancy of his memories, as in **"At Odd Moments"** which reveals psychic ordeal and torment, as the pain surges without warning:

At odd moments
my bullet scars will twinge:
when I am resting,
or when fatigue
is a continuous shriek in my brain.
           (*Stubborn Hope*, p. 43)

What one encounters over and over in these very personal poems is an acutely lonely man estranged from both his family and perhaps friends, futilely concealing his guilt and bitterness in political (SANROC) work, as revealed in the poems: 'These are times (2)' (p. 17); 'How are the shoots of affection withered at the root?' (p. 17), and all those obviously futile attempts at self-justification for every little move the persona takes, even when he reminisces over prison experiences, as in **"Beyond Sharp Control"** (p. 21); **"I would not be thought less than a man"** (pp. 21-2) and **"I come and go"** (p. 25), for instance.

We encounter here a mind that is constantly groping for the meaning of exile, death of political prisoners, friends and the meaning of friendship, loneliness, the oppressor-oppressed dichotomy and the meaning of the life of a wandering man. Nostalgia, a significant aspect of the external exile, returns him again and again to the island prison as this sequence in which, after many lines of 'tired prose' (as his compatriot Mphahlele once described this verse), we are shown into the image-laden chamber that constitutes the memory of prison. Yet the imagery is often forced, as in 'the bright airy air / lightwoven, seawoven, spraywoven air' (p. 59); or his description of the water as 'rushing wave water / lightgreen or colourless, transparent with a hint of light' (p. 59).

The third, final, section is perhaps the most effective in its vivid portrayal of the tragicomic lot of prisoners lining up 'for hospital', only to receive castor oil (p. 60). However, a good portion of this section remains prosaic; **"Sharpeville"** (p. 89) consists of prose lines chopped up into verse. Also there are axioms and aphorisms masquerading as poetry, for instance: 'Perhaps / all / poems / are simply / drafts' (p. 55), or the one tucked towards the end of the South African sequence 'Exile / is the reproach / of beauty / in a landscape, / vaguely familiar / because it echoes / remembered beauty' (p. 94).

Further, the presence of such a prophetic poem as **"On the Coming Victory"** (p. 95) which presages the impending victory of the liberation forces and the dawn of a new day raises a very important issue. Strangely, the declaration he makes in 'I am a rebel and freedom is my cause' recalls Brutus's reticence regarding his relationship to the major liberation movements in South Africa. In this regard comparisons with two other central and southern African poets, Antonio Agostinho Neto, the late combat poet of Angola, and José Craveirinha, the Coloured poet of Mozambique who threw in his lot with the liberation movement in his own country, need to be highlighted. Curiously, finding himself in similar conditions, Brutus did not lend his harp entirely to the principal liberation movement in South Africa, though he claimed that he wrote 'a poetry which sings people to battle' (Alvarez-Pererye p. 137).

Brutus's claim that he wrote poetry that 'sings people to battle' must also be interrogated closely, for while Brutus was having a tryst with his lover-land, his contemporaries in Angola and Mozambique were injecting courage into their fighting arms with songs. While Brutus indulged in highly eroticised fantasies about the 'far flung flesh' of his land, Antonio Agostinho Neto, Antonio Jacinto, Marcelino dos Santos, Jorge Rebelo and José Craveirinha were not only vilifying the colonial masters while chiding and inciting the docile African peasants to revolt, but they were also reinterpreting African values through their poetry and offering a vision of democratic and racially integrated societies after the wars. They were actually engaged in an armed struggle to reclaim their lost lands and to reinstate their cultures. While Rebelo, for instance, saw 'bullets beginning to flower' in Mozambique Brutus was reflecting: 'somehow we survive'.

The most memorable word from this collection is 'stubborn', which is so over-used and worn thin that it ceases to have any impact on the reader. From stubborn hope to stubborn love, one plods through a myriad redundant phrases and words whose unintended effect is to create 'stubborn' verse, a great deal of which saps the reader's

energy. One feels drained, not emotionally but physically worn out by this poetry, as if the poet had been wrestling with the reader to try and wring some reaction from him or her.

If aesthetic value is not a strong element in this poetry, its social value cannot be underestimated or denied. Brutus's work, bearing witness to an epoch, a long dark season in South African political and social history, is indispensable. Characterised by the cacophony of violent sounds: thundering boots breaking down doors of Africans suspected of subversion, sirens wailing in the night as police cruisers cart transgressors of apartheid's irrational laws to prisons and concentration camps, the clang of handcuffs on wrists and prison doors slammed shut, vociferations of curses and insults as policemen search black people for passes; separate amenities; hard labour in prisons as innocent men engage in senseless drudgery of breaking stones in quarries; the murders and 'suicides' in prison, the whole image of a police state and its brutality are fairly successfully delineated in these verses. Present also is the tenderness, surprisingly, in victims of this system, moments of respite when even with torn, bleeding lips, blacks and whites caught in immorality acts, exchanged stolen and forbidden kisses before the final raid.

This exposure of an evil system that simultaneously harbours an implicit call for its destruction or total transformation defines the functional nature of this poetry. But it also suggests the beauty that is possible in a post-apartheid society. If, as critics, we have tended to turn a blind eye to Brutus's technical failures, our admiration has often focused on the fact that he has apparently heroically borne his physical and psychic wounds. However, a systematic reading of the work reveals the acute pain, loneliness, and mental anguish that dog him: that is, the work as a whole brings down our hero to a more human level where we are able to appreciate his suffering, whose origins are located in the evil apartheid state currently in the process of being dismantled.

Finally, Brutus has not realised his potential as a result of the disappointments and pain of exile; constant doubts seemed to plague him even when, as in *Poems from Algiers* and *China Poems,* he takes stock of his triumphs in his campaign against apartheid in international sport in cold, factual prosaic lines totally devoid of emotive language and vivid imagery. Anyone looking for memorable lines will not find them in *Airs and Tributes* either. The spectre of apartheid appears to have so paralysed the poets that they found it difficult to transmute the 'social facts' that they most often present to us in their verses into literary art.

Notes

[1] 'No Banyan, Only', *A Simple Lust,* London: Heinemann, 1973, p. 14.

[2] Lamont Steptoe, publisher's statement in Dennis Brutus, *Airs and Tributes,* Camden, NJ: Whirlwind Press, 1989, p. iv.

[3] Dennis Brutus has published the following collections of poems: *Sirens, Knuckles, Boots,* Ibadan: Mbari Publications/Evanston: Northwestern University Press, 1963;
Letters to Martha and Other Poems from a South African Prison, London: Heinemann, 1968;
Poem from Algiers, Austin: African and Afro-American Research Institute, University of Texas, 1970;
Thoughts Abroad, Del Valle, Texas: Troubador Press, 1970;
A Simple Lust, 1973 (which collects *Sirens, Knuckles, Boots; Letters to Martha; Poems from Algiers; Thoughts Abroads;* and the Brutus section of *Seven South African Poets,* London: Heinemann, 1971);
China Poems, Austin, Texas: African and Afro-American Research Institute, University of Texas, 1975;
The Ordeal, Austin, Texas: University of Texas Press, 1975;
Strains, Del Valle, Texas: Troubadour Press, 1975;
Stubborn Hope, Washington, DC: Three Continents Press, 1978;
Salutes and Censures, Lagos: Fourth Dimension, 1982.
Airs and Tributes, Austin, Texas: University of Texas Press, 1989.

[4] Lewis Nkosi, 'Fiction by Black South Africans', in Ulli Beier, ed., *Introduction to African Literature: An Anthology of Critical Writing,* London: Longman, 1979, p. 221.

[5] David Bunn and Jane Taylor, eds, *From South Africa: New Writing, Photographs and Art, TriQuarterly 69* (Spring/Summer 1987), Evanston, Illinois: Northwestern University, p. 366.

[6] During the 1974-5 academic year Brutus and Bernth Lindfors published three volumes of Brutus's poetry, as follows: *China Poems* (1975); *Strains* (1975) and *The Ordeal* (1975).

[7] Pablo Neruda, *Passions and Impressions,* New York: Farrar Straus Giroux, 1983, p. 331.
[8] See Brutus's 'Childhood Reminiscences' in Per Wastberg, ed., *The Writer in Modern Africa,* New York: Africana Publishing Co, 1968, p. 96.

[9] Introduction to a new edition of *Salutes and Censures,* published in Bunn and Taylor, eds, *From South Africa* (1987), p. 364.

[10] J. Alvarez-Pererye, *The Poetry of Commitment in South Africa,* London: Heinemann, 1984, pp. 133-4.

[11] Theroux and Pererye have discussed this issue at length. See Paul Theroux, 'Voices Out of the Skull: A Study of Six African Poets', in Ulli Beier (1979), p. 122; and J. Alvarez-Pererye (1984), p. 139.

[12] John Pepper Clark, *The Example of Shakespeare,* Evanston: Northwestern University Press, 1970, p. 50.

[13] Adrian Roscoe, *Uhuru's Fire: African Literature from East to South,* Cambridge: Cambridge University Press, 1977, p. 163.

[14] Ezekiel Mphahlele, *Voices in the Whirlwind and Other Essays,* New York: Hill and Wang, 1972, p. 92; Lewis Nkosi, *Tasks and Masks: Themes and Styles in African Literature,* Harlow: Longmans, 1981, pp. 166-7.

[15] Page references will be to *A Simple Lust* where *Letters to Martha* has been collected and slightly rearranged.

[16] See *Letters to Martha:* Letters 1-11 are dated 11 November 1965; he may also have written 'Letter to Basil', 'Presumably' and 'For Bernice' on the same day. On 16 December 1965 he wrote four poems: 'Blood River Day', 'The Impregnation of the Air', 'Their Behaviour' and 'For X. B.'. Letters 12-18 are dated 20 December 1965; although the six postscripts are undated, they may have been composed on the same day as well.

[17] Romanus Egudu, *Modern African Poetry and the African Predicament,* London: The Macmillan Press, 1978, p. 64; Daniel Abasiekong, 'Poetry Pure and Applied: Rabearivelo and Brutus', *Transition,* Vol. 23 (1965), p. 46.

Ronald Ayling (essay date 1995)

SOURCE: "Statements and Poetry: *Salutes and Censures* Re-Examined," in *Critical Perspectives on Dennis Brutus,* edited by Craig W. McLuckie and Patrick J. Colbert, Three Continents Press, 1995, pp. 135-141.

[*In the following excerpt, Ayling offers an assessment of the poems in* Salutes and Censures *and criticizes Brutus for writing poetry without tension.*]

Dennis Brutus was already a well known poet and activist by the time in the early 1980s that he came to collect together the occasional writings that eventually appeared as **Salutes and Censures.** Of the eight previous collections of his poems, three were of major proportions in quality as well as length: **Letters to Martha, A Simple Lust** and **Stubborn Hope,** for all their unevenness, have yet a scope and humane compass that make their author a poet whose contribution to South African letters must be taken into account in any future critical assessment and revaluation of that burgeoning literature. It is highly unlikely, however, that the mixed batch of blasts and benedictions that comprise his **Salutes and Censures** will ever need to be consulted in reaching any final verdict on Brutus' poetic career. Most of these writings were still born, long before they appeared in print. They neither illuminate his thought and art nor add anything of consequence to his stature as poet or even (as he would seem to claim implicitly in this volume) as social conscience for the Third World.

Salutes and Censures gathers together thirty poems on a wide assortment of topics, though with certain significant themes concerning oppression and resistance predominating. A majority of the poems were written in the late 1970s (mostly, from 1977 to 1980) but **"After the stubbornly cheerful day"** was composed in 1967 and **"You may not see the Nazis"** was dated 1966-1967. It is strange to find these early works published here; they do not deserve resurrection.

There is in **Salutes and Censures** abnegation of the self (a conspicuous absence of the first person singular which had been pervasive throughout his earlier prison writings in the 1960s, for instance, and new emphasis on "we" and "us") and virtual elimination of the individual consciousness and of bodily experience, that "unarticulated simple lust" of a people and, necessarily, of himself that Brutus had sought to realize in his early work. The emphasis on "protest, picket, pamphlet" that he had celebrated in his notable Luthuli poems is, however, even more strongly pronounced here. Among tributes or memorial elegies to resisters to apartheid in South Africa and oppression elsewhere, there are poems to Steve Biko (then little known outside his native land when Brutus wrote his tribute), the heroic children of Soweto, a notable executed freedom fighter (Solomon Mahlangu), the newly victorious Sandinista rebellion in Nicaragua, Karen Silkwood and Beatrix Allende, among others. The censures are widely distributed to the masters (and monsters) in power in the poet's native land, and in the United States (where Brutus has lived for many years), Britain and France.

Brutus' very first collection of poems, which appeared twenty years earlier was aptly entitled *Sirens, Knuckles, Boots.* The same subject matter—encompassing arbitrary arrests, brutal confinement and routine state oppression of a defenceless populace—is encountered in *Salutes and Censures,* but a comparison of the two is salutary. The earlier volume, as the pithy title suggests, is more sharply focused on particular images, and it is, above all, concrete and specific. *Salutes and Censures,* on the other hand, is diffuse, abstract (as title and verse), and slackly generalizing; it is more ambitious in its range of reference (the abuses of human rights now embrace North and South America as well as South Africa) but those evils are less vividly realized and the all-pervasive horrors less memorably apprehended. *Salutes and Censures* as a title honestly suggests the volume's scope and limitations. It acknowledges the public nature to both sides of the experience that are embodied here and, at the same time, reveals the lack of a personal dimension and of what one can only describe as poetic intensity; almost imperceptibly, the tension at the heart of his work has somehow slackened. The imagination is not as actively engaged, as it is in a good deal of his prison writings. The salutes are just that—public gestures rather than strongly felt elegies or passionate commemorative tributes. And the censures, similarly, never rise to the level of true satire; obdurately, they remain little more than downright denunciations, censorious criticism of a mostly abstract and portentous nature. In such a context, the writing, while it appears more wideranging than in the early work, is deceptive even in this regard. It is not, paradoxically, as universal.

Often, the universal in art is achieved by means of the specific, the local, the regional—witness Faulkner, Hardy, Achebe, poets of a particular region, whose major concerns and preoccupations, once deeply explored and actualized in appropriate native speech and imagery, can be seen to have all-encompassing implications and relevance. In *Salutes and Censures,* Brutus as a public figure reaches for a larger significance in the world as global village; attempting oracular utterance, he succeeds in speaking more as a politician than a poet; certainly, he is more the activist-critic than a true voice of the people—a distinction, that could not as often be made, I think, in *Letters to Martha* and some of the other earlier verses. The best of that work, though admittedly uneven, combined the private and the public, the confessional and the committed, the sentient as well as the sententious in characteristically individual and arresting ways. The susceptible man and the apprehensive man was discernible in addition to the social critic and reformer; and not only did the two sides of his poetic sensibility not clash, they actively set off and complemented each other. The criticism and social commitment is intensified and reified by the depth of personal involvement and vulnerability exposed in both the pre-Robben Island and the Robben Island periods in Brutus' poetry. The same claim cannot as surely be made for *Salutes and Censures* and other post-Robben Island verse by him.

Obviously, Brutus has deliberately simplified his later poetic style—usually to emphasize unambiguous straightforward

statements, uttered without ornamentation or any kind of poetic diction and with no discernible traces of literary artifice, influence or reverberations. By means of plain unvarnished invocation and reiteration, the poet clearly aims to speak to the oppressed peoples of the world. It is evident that the exile feels compelled to speak, to give utterance to his concerns and fears, to express his solidarity with the oppressed—and, above all, to let them know that. Understandably, direct simple statement seems called for, and it is interesting that Brutus' playwriting compatriot, Athol Fugard, went through a period in the 1970s where he, likewise, placed a good deal of emphasis on similarly didactic expression. A volume of three of his most obviously antiapartheid plays was published under the general title of *Statements* at this time and the longest of the three appeared as *Statements After an Arrest Under the Immorality Act.* Yet Fugard never abstracts the language and characterization to serve his message and, in the use of mime and humorous effects, in *The Island,* he humanizes and individualizes prison life and the horrors of apartheid for the blacks in South Africa.

Brutus, in seeking to serve what he sees as the need to communicate more widely with a largely non-literary public in the Third World, has sacrificed linguistic complexity and individual expressiveness, putting his thoughts and feelings into common speech patterns that, more often used by journalists and politicians, fall into hackneyed images and predictable pronouncements even in a poet's deployment. I am not complaining of the parallelism and repetition, functional elements in much black South African poetry designed for oral delivery (in the work of Serote, Madingoane, Mafika Gwala, for instance), where the poets need to repeat things in a large hall crowded with kids running around and mothers with babies on their backs. It is the pervasive abstraction and lack of particularity that is troubling. From very early in *Salutes and Censures* we find both: in the first poem, **"Salute to Our Allies,"** we never learn who are "our allies" and who are "our friends," so the salute becomes something of a private message, which surely defeats the poet's apparent intention to reach out to a large audience, world-wide and Africa-wide. Cliches and pedestrian phrases abound throughout. The illuminations of London's West End are "garish pyrotechnics"; England's parliament is

> that place of shame
> spawner of slavery's systems,
> hoarse-throated still with lust
> for Africa's rape
> they plot fresh perfidy
> emerge smiling
> dripping their fetter of festering lies
>
>   (Brutus, 7).

Certain benedictory elegies are hackneyed throughout, moreover, as in these lines **"For the Kent State Martyrs,"** which would assuredly have been excised from earlier collections by Brutus:

> We will remember them
> as long as we live

we will remember them
at the rising of the sun
and its going down
we will remember
the martyrs of Kent State
who died in May 1970

For justice they died
for justice here in this place
and for justice in a far-off place
thousands of miles away
they died by the guns of oppressors

And we will remember them
we swear we will remember them
and keep their memory alive

(Brutus, 24).

Occasional poems in this collection do rise above the generally pervasive banality though none, to my mind, entirely surmount it. One of the better examples, written in 1980, is **"Robben Island,"** the last poem to be gathered here. Perhaps, in recollecting a nightmare experience from his prison days almost twenty years earlier and using it for memorial purposes, the verse regains some earlier vivacity:

In a long shot down the rectangular enclosure
stone-walled, with barred windows I find myself
anonymous
among the other faceless prisoners

I see myself again bent on my stone block
crouched over my rockpile
and marvel

I see the men beside me
Peake and Alexander
Mandela and Sisulu
and marvel

All the grim years.
And all the marvellous men
who endure beyond the grim years.
The will to freedom steadily grows
The force, the power, the strength
Steadily grows

(Brutus, 38).

Despite some slackness toward the end of the poem, there is a certain stark objective grandeur about this lyric, like a commemorative statue in granite. Something of an exception among the abstract aridity of this collection, even this achievement is put into its properly minor perspective by comparison with the more moving personal idiom of his early prison poems. *Letters to Martha*, at their best, can be indelibly commemorative and transcend the individual while yet being firmly rooted in the private and the personal for (as he wrote in letter 5) his verse there sought to "people the labyrinth of self" in a manner stoutly resisted in most of his subsequent work. In *Salutes and Censures*, while eschewing (largely) the personal and private, there is also a commensurate ignor-

ing of the physical—that which, earlier, was vibrantly celebrated as the "body's expression of need" and its vulnerability too—as well as banishing the occasional romantic and lyrical outbursts to be found effectively harnessed as counterpoint to brutal daily indignities in the early verse. One would wish Brutus to return to first principles such as these—perhaps tempered by occasional flashes of humour that existed there too—that, collectively, enlivened the best of his earlier writings. Does the poet not remember his own wise words—acute in self-criticism as well as in understanding the strengths in his work—in the fine interview he gave to Cosmo Pieterse in 1966? There, he said: "I think tension is of the essence of good poetry," and went on to acknowledge that "there is an element of laughter in my work; it may be that I am engaged in a fight but at the same time I find a certain delight in it. I enjoy the fight; and this is where the laughter and the music, the gaiety and the humour come in" (Duerden, 54-5). Tension, laughter, music and gaiety are largely absent from Brutus's later writings though not from his life and personality.

Brutus should himself be saluted for trying to reach out to a large (and largely unlettered) audience, but need one throw out the poetry in the attempt? Of course, greater poets in our period have pursued a somewhat similar path: T.S. Eliot, for instance, in trying to find a place for poetry in the modern theatre became less and less intricate in thought and speech to the extent, finally, that his later plays are hardly poetic drama at all. The sophisticated West End audience that Eliot had in mind is far removed from Brutus's intended readership, but both writers have traversed the same arid terrain. It is questionable whether either man has succeeded in breaking through to a new public for poetry. A strong case can be made out for trying to do so, however, and, in the case of Dennis Brutus's protracted experiment, a final judgement has to be suspended for the time being. The same cannot be said, unfortunately, for the particularly shallow instances gathered together as *Salutes and Censures.*

Works Cited

Brutus, Dennis. *Salutes and Censures.* Enugu, Nigeria: Fourth Dimension Publ. Co. Ltd., 1984.

Duerden, Dennis and Cosmo Pieterse, eds. *African Writers Talking.* London: Heinemann, 1972.

John Lent (essay date 1995)

SOURCE:"'Turning Stones to Trees:' The Transformation Of Political Experience in Dennis Brutus' *Strains*," in *Critical Perspectives on Dennis Brutus,* edited by Craig W. McLuckie and Patrick J. Colbert, Three Continents Press, 1995, pp. 99-112.

[*In the following excerpt, Lent examines how the concrete landscape imagery in* Strains *embodies the abstract emotions of suffering and exile.*]

At the end of **Strains**, Dennis Brutus suggests this paradox regarding artistic expression and silence: "Music, at its highest / strains towards silence." (**Strains**, 44) In a curious way, it identifies an artistic issue that lies beneath the composition of the poems in this volume: how can a writer take the rather extreme human experiences represented in some of the poems—The Sharpeville massacre, the death of friends such as Teruggi and Nortje, memories of the poet's own imprisonment—and say anything worthwhile about them without the art being either too direct, or too rhetorical, or too flat in its expression? In other words, is it possible to address such experiences in art when silence is so much more powerful in some ways? The answer, of course, is that yes, it *is* possible, and not only possible but imperative that the silence be broken. It is not easy, however, and Dennis Brutus knows this (see Lindfors *et alia,* 24). Though in an abstract sense all poetry is political, there are poets like Brutus who use the technical conventions of the lyrical poem to focus on political experiences more directly than most poets do. As a poet myself, writing in a North American context, I worry that direct political poetry, written about political experiences on this continent, always seems to run the risk of being overwhelmed by either arbitrary points of view or a rhetoric that can be predictable. As a result, the poets I know who are fascinated by politics—a Canadian poet like Tom Wayman, for example—will use the authority of individual experience and the technique of working meticulously conceived image complexes to achieve political poetry that is not overwhelmed by arbitrariness or rhetoric. In my own poetry over the years, I have focused rather directly on lower-middle-class experiences in the Canadian West, but I always place those experiences in detailed physical contexts that grow out of individual experience. If I didn't do this, if I tried to speak more abstractly and politically, I would fear that my voice would become hollow, stagey, even obvious. For me, then, there must be a carefully orchestrated balance between abstract and concrete elements in the lyrical poem. An imbalance either way can overwhelm the poem and inhibit its potential power. An imbalance of directly stated ideas or emotions, for example, seems especially dangerous, for it moves the lyric in the direction of philosophy or rhetoric that can denude the poem of its emotional power, its humanness, and turn it into something else. However admirable that something else might be, it won't have the power of poetry. When I turn to the poetry of Dennis Brutus, then, I bring this wariness about political poetry to his work. I worry in advance that his poetry might simply move on the surface of abstract political events and be overwhelmed by a singular point of view and a rhetoric that accompanies that view. Having said these things, however, I have to say that I am moved when I read Brutus' poems in **Strains**.

Here is a contemporary writer who cannot afford to work huge political experiences from a purely individual point of view. His political context is far more clear and harrowing than mine. The life and death of people, including the poet himself, are always hanging in the balance. His material is not the seizing of experiences growing up in a mid-Western city in Canada, however simple or complex that material

might be. Instead, his is the political context of South Africa: the racism of its apartheid policies, the systematic murder of the poet's friends and people. In order to express this reality, Brutus uses the lyrical poem, and especially elemental / landscape imagery, to transform sweeping political events into condensed seizures of those events. To a great degree, the transformation is executed through understatement and a careful building of image complexes. Typically, Brutus maneuvers sharp, specific landscape images to suggest political events and to suggest, too, the awful distance those political events have carried human beings away from that landscape. I admire this work, even the weaker poems, for I am aware as a writer of the artistic risks Brutus has taken to speak at all, artistically or politically. Here is a voice that will be criticised either way. He will be too political; he will not be political enough. The trap is inescapable and Brutus knows this, too. And yet the voice still chooses to speak, to break the silence. . . .

In *Criticism and Social Change,* Frank Lentricchia discusses the power of rhetoric in literature and points to the fundamental choice a writer like Brutus must make concerning the use of this power:

> Burke insists that art conceived as rhetoric opens up radically divergent social functions for the writer. He may work, as in the writer's classical vocation, on behalf of a dominant hegemony by reinforcing habits of thought and feeling that help to sustain ruling power . . . Or he may work counter-hegemonically as a violator, in an effort to dominate and to reeducate (*in*form), to pin us to the wall, in order to assist in the birth of a critical mind by peeling off, one by one, and thus revealing to us for what they are, all bourgeois encrustations of consciousness. In the widest sense of the word, he would encourage cultural revolution.
>
> (Lentricchia, 147-8)

It is clear that Dennis Brutus is writing against a dominant hegemony and that his work encourages both cultural and political revolutions. Here is a writer who has made a commitment to his people, and who has paid some of the prices involved, too, both on a human and on an artistic level sometimes. In an essay that focuses on Brutus eventually, Chidi Amuta discusses the kind of choice and commitment Lentricchia has spoken of. Following a rather arbitrary political view, however, Amuta essentially dismisses most attempts to express political experience in poetry:

> Even if the bourgeois poet strives, through technical innovations such as the adoption of simple ideas and the rhythm of popular speech, to reach a popular audience, his efforts will not nullify his essential alienation, for the original creative force of poetry belongs to that spontaneity of relationship between the poet and his live audience which was the norm in the oral tradition of all societies.
>
> (Amuta, 176)

Amuta goes on to discuss bourgeois poets including Brutus and praises Brutus for his political action and his technical attempts to speak to a wider audience: "Brutus' career as a poet, which is an accompaniment to his other involvements, is conditioned by the same socio-political pressures as his political action. In essence, the struggle for freedom consitutes the overriding concern in Brutus' poetry" (179). For me, however, the more Amuta pushes a 'Marxist' line in his analysis of Brutus' work, the more clear it is to me that he is drawn to the weakest of Brutus' poems. He declares that he likes the fact that sometimes Brutus abandons conventional poetics and moves towards a "more direct, declamatory and structurally uncomplicated verse" (180) which, he says, suffers "no significant loss in artistic effect" (180). As examples of such a shift to simplicity in Brutus' poems from **Stubborn Hope**, Amuta includes the following:

> I have been bedded
> in London and Paris
> in Munich and Frankfurt,
> Warsaw and Rome—
> and still my heart cries out for home!
>
> (Quoted in Amuta, 181)

> I am a rebel and freedom is my cause:
> Many of you have fought similar struggles
> therefore you must join my cause:
> My cause is a dream, of freedom
> and you must help me make my dream reality:
> For why should I not dream and hope?
> I not revolution making reality of hopes?
>
> (Quoted in Amuta, 182)

Amuta admires these poems because, he says, they advance a "political message." I find them weak because they are too abstract, too direct, and have lost their power as poems. They may be emotional declarations that I can agree with or admire, but they are not good poems. In **Strains**, too, there are a few poems that, like the examples above, suffer the same weakness of abstraction and rhetoric. Here is **"10 April 67"**:

> When I think what I have done
> I have stridden across the world
> I have come and gone like a comet
> crossing continents and oceans
> scattered sparks and ashes in the bushes:
> I have lighted fire in men's minds
> and I will do it again.
>
> (**Strains**, 6)

This poem has little of the power of some of the other poems in **Strains** because it never moves out of the abstract; it never acquires the muscle of imagery and as a result seems flat and self-promotional. Here is a less political poem in **Strains** that suffers a similar weakness:

> All I ask
> nervously,
> now:
> you might,
> once again,
> unexpectedly,

> revive,
> gratefully,
> a dead heart.
>
> (**Strains**, 25)

This 'simplicity' takes away from the power that is in most of the poems in **Strains** and likely has a source in what Amuta observes as Brutus' attempt to reach a wider audience. They do not undermine the considerable achievement of **Strains**, however. It remains a powerful commitment and it succeeds in transforming almost unspeakable experiences into voice. I simply worry that the more abstract, direct, or 'simple' poems end up, ironically, patronizing the very audience they intend to uplift. In their obvious attempts to manipulate an audience, they do exactly that, and end up insulting the intelligence of that audience, no matter how literate or privileged.

What fascinates me about most of the poems in **Strains** is how they transform the abstract nature of human experiences—of violence, exile, and suffering—into concrete expressions by implementing elemental landscape images. This transformation provides unity and consistency in the volume. Images of earth, air, fire and water, vivid scenes of African and American landscapes, the flights of birds, all suggest the complex worlds of the exile, the writer, the lover. Brutus' technique seems to be to transmute human emotions through physical images. It is a strong procedure that seems to suit his voice and strengths.

Early in the volume, bird images suggest complex ideas about Brutus as exile and about his homeland, too. **"In the friendly dark,"** (4) develops the image of responsibility and love by sticking to one image complex of the bird, and exhausting it:

> In the friendly dark, I wheel
> as a bird checks in flight
> to glide down streams
> and planes of slanting air.
>
> so I turn, worn by work
> and the dull teeth of care
> to find your face, your throat
> and the soft dark of your hair;
>
> flesh lies snugged in sheets
> the brain, wrapped close in folds
> of the still-blanketing night,
> awaits the easy balm of dreams,
>
> but my heart soars and wheels
> hurtling through the friendly dark
> to find your mouth and your heart
> and nest quietly there.
>
> (Brutus, **Strains**, 4)

The hesitant, buffeted flight of the bird into the surcease of dreams and love, is wonderfully complete and carefully executed. In the description of its 'wheeling' flight Brutus makes this image complex suggest the realms of public and private responsibilities and the struggle to breach them. In

"**Tehran: 3 May 68**" Brutus develops the elemental images of water and trees to play strengths in the concrete landscape against the abstract fragility of humans trapped behind 'barbed wire':

> At night
> on the smooth grey concrete of my cell
> I heard the enormous roar of the surf
> and saw in my mind's eye
> the great white wall of spray rising,
> like a sheet of shattering glass
> where the surge broke
> on the shore and rocks and barbed wire
>
> and going to the shed
> in hope of a visitor
> I greeted the great cypresses
> green and black
> dreaming in their poised serenity
> in the limpid stillness of the brilliant afternoon
> gracious as an Umbrian Raphael landscape
> but more brilliant and more sharp.
>
> (7)

Even when Brutus is considering the American landscape of his exile, in "**To Indianapolis: 17 Nov 71**," he works emotions of love against the elemental imagery of winter:

> A mauve haze
> the serried winter branches make
> at the end of the avenue:
> I grow dizzy with lust
> and yearning
> soon age will add
> another patina
> to insulate me
> against delight
>
> and around me the tight-buttocked girls
> romp, ogle and frolic
> and still one burrows
> makes a place of impact,
> in some crevice of the globe.
>
> (15)

By the end of the poem, the winter landscape, the narrator, the girls he sees and the crevices he imagines filling, all become fused in a delicate interweaving of phenomenal and psychological landscapes. It is this interweaving that distinguishes Brutus' work. In "**18 Nov 71**," referred to earlier, for example, Brutus takes the theme of "our allies are exiles," and like the Czech catalogue poems, lists the names of those exiles who have, like him, been involved in political struggles, sometimes killed by them. The difference, however, between the Czech list and Brutus' is that he expands the power of the list by placing it within the carefully conceived image complex of a forest clearing and, on the rim of the clearing, animals in the dark waiting to enter it, to join together: "they prowl and howl / like gaunt wolves / at the edge of the besieged clearing" and "now a penumbra, / a spectral flame / burning like an ideal / on the horizon of our awareness / great victim / of the world's racist plague" (17). Brutus works the image of the clearing in the forest until it yields a complex, political reality. The "dark flames beating / on the rim of a dark world" become "an ideal /on the horizon of our awareness" so that something is always being redeemed because of the exiles on the periphery of "besieged clearings." In "**Ibadan, Lagos, Kano, London: 5 Jan 72**," Brutus is direct about the relationship between the elemental landscape and his emotional reality:

> Africa's jacaranda dusk
> descends on Ibadan;
> the trees poise
> against the grey sky
> while the red earth glows:
> this is my sustenance
> the spirit is refreshed
> the flesh renewed
> while the sun smoulders
> and the trees tower.
>
> (23)

In "**Brazzaville: 22 Feb 72**," Brutus draws the reader into the African landscape, and emphasises the connection between that landscape and his heart:

> but suddenly one was home:
> the spirit stretched at ease
> and the music of rain on leaves
> of birdsong in the clear dawn
> sang the soundless music
> that was in my heart.
>
> (26)

By manipulating us into psychological realities through such vivid images of landscape in this way, I believe Brutus succeeds in forcing the love and horror in his homeland out into the relief of our own consciousness, and this, more than simplicity or rhetoric, is the real political achievement in this volume of poetry.

Even in the poems that concentrate on Brutus' frustrations in exile and in love, he utilizes this procedure that interweaves emotional and physical landscapes. In "**Seattle: 7 May 72**," he realises that even in love he cannot escape history or politics: "we cannot shut out time and persons / from our circled intimacies," (28) and in "**Evanston: 4 June 72**," Brutus perceives the landscape of a woman's body he is making love to as the landscape of Vietnam. Here again, love, responsibility, commitment, history and landscape all become fused in a human and complex vision in which nothing can be separated from anything else. By fusing psychological and phenomenal landscapes in this way, Brutus succeeds in emphasising their inseparability which is, in itself, a political theme in these poems. I feel compelled to add that I don't believe this fusion of internal and external landscapes is simply a theoretical procedure, but comes from something fundamental in the poet: a vision of the connectedness of human beings and the landscape they are born to. There is an impulse deeply rooted here, I suspect, and intensified by exile, that contributes to the power of such a fusion.

In *Strains* Dennis Brutus hauls the reader into a 'friendly dark' made up of two landscapes, a series of physical landscapes which, when evoked, release psychological landscapes. The latter are full of frustration, sorrow, rage, struggle and, ultimately, a fierce kind of joy. In "Easter, 1916," W. B. Yeats writes of his politically committed friends, "Too much sacrifice / can make a stone of the heart." He is worried, of course, about the emotional prices paid by humans overwhelmed by political struggle. But the "terrible beauty" Yeats sees in this poem would not be born without that struggle and the prices paid by it. The amazing thing about Dennis Brutus' work is that while it is so engaged in the struggle, it has not turned his heart to stone. On the other hand, his mission is to "turn stone to trees," (**"New Orleans: 30 Oct 71"**), and he even echoes Yeats' "terrible beauty" in this regard in **"5 Jan 72"** when he writes:

> how time and circumstance have changed
> in ways not to be imagined
> and where so much may be done—
> time and the world transformed.
>
> (22)

As Creina Alcock suggested, the world 'transcends defeat' through love, and is transformed if only one voice connects through the silence: "Neruda is dead; / No matter" (41).

Works Cited

Amuta, Chidi. *The Theory Of African Literature*. New Jersey: Zed Books Ltd., 1989.

Brutus, Dennis. *Strains*. Austin: Troubadour Press, 1981.

Kogawa, Joy. *Obasan*. Markham: Penguin Books Ltd., 1981.

Lentricchia, Frank. *Criticism And Social Change*. Chicago: University of Chicago Press, 1983.

Lindfors, Munro, Priebe, Sander, eds. *Palaver*. Austin: African and Afro-American Research Institute, The University of Texas at Austin, 1972.

Malan, Rian. *My Traitor's Heart, A South African Exile Returns To Face His Country, His Tribe, & His Conscience*. New York: Vintage International, 1991.

Ondaatje, Michael. *Rat Jelly*. Toronto: The Coach House Press, 1973.

FURTHER READING

Biography

Alvarez-Pereyre, Jacques. "The First Generation of Committed Black Poets." In *The Poetry of Commitment in South Africa*, Clive Wake (trans.), pp. 130-145. Heinemann Educational Books, 1984.

Provides an overview of Brutus's political activity and his commitment to the anti-apartheid movement.

Legum, Colin, and Legum, Margaret, "Dennis Brutus: Poet and Sportsman." In *Choice: Eight South Africans' Resistance to Tyranny*, pp. 1149-166. Cleveland: The World Publishing Company, 1968.

Surveys Brutus's early involvement with poetry, sports, and politics in South Africa.

Criticism

Beier, Ulli. "Three Mbari Poets." *Black Orpheus* No. 12 (1963): 46-50.

Praises the themes and passions of Brutus's poetry, as well as his precise use of language.

Elimimian, Isaac I. "Form and Meaning in the Poetry of Dennis Brutus." *The Literary Half-Yearly* XXVIII, No. 1 (January 1987): 70-78.

Explores the themes of love and hate in Brutus's poetry and emphasizes his ultimately peaceful relationship with apartheid.

Gardner, Colin. "Brutus and Shakespeare." *Research in African Literatures* 15, No. 3 (Fall 1984): 354-64.

Explores some of the traditional influences on Brutus's poetry.

Lindfors, Bernth. "Dennis Brutus' Mousey Tongue." *World Literature Written in English* 15, No. 1 (April 1976): 7-16.

Examines *China Poems* and how Brutus transformed Chinese poetic conventions to suit his own political and aesthetic goals.

——. "Dialectical Development in the Poetry of Dennis Brutus." In *The Commonwealth Writer Overseas: Themes of Exile and Expatriation*, Alastair Niven (ed.), pp. 419-429. Bruxelles: M. Didier, 1976.

Traces the evolution of Brutus's poetic development through *China Poems* and identifies four stages: complexity, simplicity, balance, and economy.

Nkondo, Gessler Moses. "Dennis Brutus: The Domestication of a Tradition." *World Literature Today* 55, No. 1 (Winter 1981): 32-40.

Explores Brutus's relationship with the English poetic tradition—particularly John Donne and William Butler Yeats.

Ojaide, Tanure. "Troubadour: The Poet's Persona in the Poetry of Dennis Brutus." *Ariel* 17, No. 1 (January 1986): 55-69.

Shows how Brutus modeled his poetic persona on the troubadour from medieval European love poetry.

Onuekwusi, Jasper A. "Pain and Anguish of an African Poet: Dennis Brutus and South African Reality." *Literary Criterion* 23, Nos. 1-2 (1988): 59-68

Responds to critics who fault Brutus for being excessively passionate and emphasizes the political purposes that his poetry serves.

Povey, John F. "I Am the Voice—Three South African Poets: Dennis Brutus, Keorapetse Kgositsile, and Oswald

Mbuyiseni Mtshali." *World Literature Written in English* 16, No. 2 (November 1977): 263-280.

> Examines how South African poetry meets the challenge of furthering social and political goals while satisfying aesthetic criteria.

Rawick, Alain J. A review of *Letters to Martha and Other Poems from a South African Prison* and *Poems from Algiers*. *African Report* 16, No. 2 (February 1971): 36-37.

> Finds that Brutus's poetry expresses a range of human experience and achieves a cultural identity that "has become Africa's humanistic voice."

Roscoe, Adrian. "Writers in South Africa." *Listener* 100, No. 2583 (October 26, 1978): 533-34.

> Argues that South African literature is realistic, valuing "camera-like exactitude," while still rising above the terrible events it reports.

Salt, M. J. "On the Business of Literary Criticism: With Special Reference to Bahadur Tejani's Article: 'Can the Prisoner Make a Poet?'" *African Literature Today* No. 7 (1975): 128-41

> Disputes Tejani's criticism of Brutus, arguing that a more careful and fair-minded reading of his poetry shows it to be worthy of praise.

Sweetman, David. "Children of the Lion." *New Statesman* 99, No. 2561 (April 18, 1980): 592-93.

> Criticizes Brutus for using too many words to express simple insights and argues that his best poetry is a "straight presentation of experience."

Tejani, Bahadur. "The Prison Poems of Dennis Brutus." *Standpoints on African Literature,* Chris Wanjala (ed.), pp. 323-43. Nairobi: East African Literature Bureau, 1973.

> Criticizes both the aesthetic and th. political foundations of Brutus's poetry.

Theroux, Paul. "Voices Out of the Skull." *Black Orpheus* No. 20 (August 1966): 41-58.

> Explores Brutus's role as an artist under a repressive regime.

Additional coverage of Brutus's life and career is contained in the following sources published by The Gale Group: *Contemporary Literary Criticism*, **Vol. 43,** *Black Literature Criticism*; *Discovering Authors*: *Multicultural Authors Module*; *Discovering Authors*: *Poets Module*; *Black Writers*, **Vol. 2;** *Contemporary Authors*, **Vol. 49-52;** *Contemporary Authors Autobiography Series*, **Vol. 14;** *Contemporary Authors New Revision Series*, **Vols. 2,27,42; and** *Dictionary of Literary Biography*, **Vol. 117.**

James Weldon Johnson
1871-1938

American novelist, poet, autobiographer, historian, and critic.

INTRODUCTION

Johnson is regarded as an influential black American author whose novel *The Autobiography of an Ex-Colored Man* (1912) impacted the work of later writers concerned with the nature of racial identity. Seen as an accurate sociological depiction of the lives of black Americans by his contemporaries, Johnson's novel is today viewed as a complex work providing an ambiguous psychological study of its anonymous title character. Although literature for Johnson was only one aspect of an active and varied professional life, he produced accomplished works in several literary genres, including the novel, conventional and experimental poetry, popular songs, literary and social criticism, and autobiography. As a poet, Johnson is best known for *God's Trombones* (1927), a collection of seven poems which capture the rhythmic and spiritual essence of traditional black sermons. He is furthermore recognized for his groundbreaking editorship of *The Book of American Negro Poetry* (1922).

Biographical Information

Johnson was born in Jacksonville, Florida, where his father worked as headwaiter at a luxury resort hotel and his mother taught grammar school. At Jacksonville's Straton Grammar School he showed early virtuosity in both music and literature, but because secondary education was not available to black students, he was sent to a preparatory school at Atlanta University in Georgia. Johnson graduated in 1894 and was recommended for, and received, a scholarship to Harvard University medical school; however, he turned down this offer in order to return to Straton Grammar School as its principal. Although he continued at Straton for several years, Johnson simultaneously pursued other careers: as a lawyer with a private practice; as founder of the *Daily American,* believed to have been the first black daily newspaper in the country; and as a lyricist for Cole and Johnson Brothers, writing successful songs with his younger brother Rosamond and his song-and-dance partner Bob Cole. In 1906 Johnson abandoned his show business activities to accept a position in the U. S. Consular Service. He began his work at a small post in Venezuela, and it was at this time that he wrote most of *The Autobiography of an Ex-Colored Man.* Later he was advanced to a position in Nicaragua, where he completed the novel.

In 1913 Johnson resigned from the service and in January of that year his poem "Fifty Years," commemorating the

Emancipation Proclamation, appeared in the *New York Times.* Johnson's literary reputation soared and the work's popularity prompted publishers of the *New York Age* to hire him as an editorial writer in 1914. His popular column in this newspaper offered a conciliatory view toward the opposing black political factions aligned with either Booker T. Washington or the militant W. E. B. Du Bois. In 1916 Johnson joined the National Association for the Advancement of Colored People and served as the organization's executive secretary from 1920 to 1930. His active association with the NAACP also marks the years Johnson published the poetry collections *Fifty Years, and Other Poems* (1917) and *God's Trombones,* as well as wrote the historical study *Black Manhattan* (1930) and edited the works of lesser-known black poets in an anthology titled *The Book of American Negro Poetry.* In 1931 he returned to education as a professor of creative literature at Fisk University in Nashville, Tennessee. Johnson died in 1938 in an automobile accident.

Major Works

The nature of Johnson's early poetic works is demonstrated in the collection *Fifty Years, and Other Poems*—comprised of traditional verse and dialect poetry, in the manner of Johnson's contemporary Paul Laurence Dunbar, which seeks to approximate the language of southern blacks of the period. The sixteen poems in the latter mode are grouped together in the section entitled "Jingles and Croons." These pieces generally touch upon transitory or humorous subjects, though they occasionally confront more significant themes, such as lost love in "Sense You Went Away." The remaining, conventional pieces of the collection primarily document serious, racial topics—slavery, lynching, black rights, interracial relationships—and include the protest poems "To America" and "Brothers." Johnson's second volume of poetry, *God's Trombones,* represents a significant departure from his earlier verse. Containing seven poetic sermons in free verse, the work evokes what critics perceive as a powerful and natural black voice in the idiom of the traditional southern Negro preacher. As such, the themes of *God's Trombones* are throughout religious and spiritual, drawing significantly from Biblical narrative in such works as "The Creation," "The Prodigal Son," "Noah Built the Ark," and "The Crucifixion." Johnson's final poetry collection, *St. Peter Relates an Incident: Selected Poems* (1935), features very little new material aside from the long, satirical *Saint Peter Relates an Incident of the Resurrection Day.* The poem's narrative offers a parable of racial prejudice recounted by St. Peter. In it, a collection of whites watch as the body of the Unknown Soldier is exhumed on the day of resurrection. To their dismay, they learn that the soldier is black and watch him as he proceeds into heaven while singing a Negro spiritual.

Critical Reception

Johnson's early *Fifty Years, and Other Poems* attracted only slight interest at the time of its publication, and has since been largely dismissed by critics who see the collection as a very modest composition in standard poetic forms and of verse characterized by the minstrel dialect often used by poets of the time. Additionally, the poem *Saint Peter Relates an Incident of the Resurrection Day* has been viewed as a disappointing satire marred by stylistic and structural flaws. In contrast, critics have regarded *God's Trombones* as an impressive poetic achievement and have lauded its superb translation of the rhythms and metaphors of black preachers into literary form. It is for this work that scholars have generally acknowledged Johnson as a poet of considerable influence and vision, equaling that of his accomplishments in fiction as the author of *The Autobiography of an Ex-Colored Man.*

PRINCIPAL WORKS

Poetry

Fifty Years, and Other Poems 1917
The Book of Negro American Poetry [editor] 1922
God's Trombones 1927
St. Peter Relates an Incident: Selected Poems 1935

Other Major Works

The Autobiography of an Ex-Colored Man (novel) 1912
Black Manhattan (history) 1930
Along This Way: The Autobiography of James Weldon Johnson (autobiography) 1933

CRITICISM

Benjamin Brawley (review date 1918)

SOURCE: A Review of *Fifty Years and Other Poems,* in *The Journal of Negro History,* Vol. III, No. 2, April, 1918, pp. 202-203.

[*In the following review, Brawley lauds "the simple, direct, and sometimes sensuous expression" of several poems in Johnson's* Fifty Years, and Other Poems.]

From time to time for the last fifteen years Mr. James Weldon Johnson has been remarked as one of the literary men of the race. He has now brought together his verses in a little volume, **Fifty Years and Other Poems,** an introduction to which has been written by Professor Brander Matthews, of Columbia University. The task was eminently worth while.

The book falls into two parts. The first is made up of poems in the commonly accepted forms, though there are one or two examples of *vers libre;* and the second is entitled *Jingles and Croons.* This second division consists of dialect verses, especially the songs that have been set to music, most frequently by the poet's brother, Mr. J. Rosamond Johnson. Outstanding are the very first lines, "Sence you went away." It is well that these pieces have been brought together. For artistic achievement, however, attention will naturally be fixed upon the first division. **"Fifty Years"** was written in honor of the fiftieth anniversary of the emancipation of the race. Professor Matthews speaks of it as "one of the noblest commemorative poems yet written by any American—a poem sonorous in its diction, vigorous in its workmanship, elevated in its imagination, and sincere in its emotion." This is high praise, and yet it may reasonably be asked if there are not in the book at least four pieces of finer poetic quality. These are, first of all, the two poems that originally appeared in the *Century [Magazine],* **"Mother Night"** and **"O Black and Unknown Bards,"** and **"The White Witch"** and **"The Young Warrior."** The first of these four poems is a sonnet well rounded out. The second gains merit by reason of its strong first and last two stanzas. **"The White Witch"** chooses a delicate and difficult theme, but contains some very strong stanzas. **"The Young Warrior"** is a poem of rugged strength and one that deserves all the popularity it has achieved with Mr. Burleigh's musical setting. Mr. Johnson is strongest in the simple, direct, and sometimes sensuous expression that characterizes these latter poems, and it is to be hoped that he may have the time and the inclination to write many more like them.

Harriet Monroe (review date 1927)

SOURCE: A Review of *God's Trombones,* in *Poetry* (Chicago), Vol. XXX, No. V, August, 1927, pp. 291-93.

[*In the following review, Monroe praises Johnson's* God's Trombones *as "his own highest achievement as a poet."*]

For some time Mr. Johnson has been known as a leader among the American Negro poets, and as by all odds their best editor. His *Book of American Negro Poetry,* and his two books of *Spirituals,* with their prefaces, are monuments of patient and sympathetic scholarship and of devotion to his race in its highest achievements.

The present volume [*God's Trombones*] is his own highest achievement as a poet. The author says modestly in his excellent preface:

> I claim no more for these poems than that I have written them after the manner of the primitive sermons.

But it is something of an achievement to suggest, as he does, the spirit and rhythm of those sermons, and to do it without the help of dialect or of antiphonal repetitions. There may be two opinions about the tradition of dialect; at least Mr. Johnson makes a very good argument against it in his preface, and gets on very well without it.

With the old-time Negro, religion was a grand adventure. It exalted him into rapture, and his imagination lavished gymnastic figures upon it. Here, for example, are two stanzas from **"The Creation"**:

> Then God himself stepped down—
> And the sun was on his right hand,
> And the moon was on his left;
> The stars were clustered about his head,
> And the earth was under his feet.
> And God walked, and where he trod
> His footsteps hollowed the valleys out
> And bulged the mountains up.
>
> Then he stopped and looked and saw
> That the earth was hot and barren.
> So God stepped over to the edge of the world
> And he spat out the seven seas;
> He batted his eyes, and the lightning flashed;
> He clapped his hands, and the thunders rolled,
> And the waters above the earth came down,
> The cooling waters came down.

We have space for only a hint of the book's quality. Mr. Johnson does not claim to have originated the sermons; like Joel Chandler Harris he has set down what he heard—the essence of it; and he is entitled to credit of the same kind. Hardly to the same degree, however, as the authenticity is less complete, the art less perfect. I wish he could have let himself go a little more rashly; for the creation myth, as I heard Lucine Finch repeat her old mammy's version, was more powerfully poetic than Mr. Johnson's.

However, we should be grateful for this book. As the author says:

> The old-time Negro preacher is rapidly passing, and I have here tried sincerely to fix something of him.

The Canadian Forum (review date 1927)

SOURCE: A Review of *God's Trombones,* in *The Canadian Forum,* Vol. VII, No. 84, September, 1927, pp. 380, 382.

[*In the following review, the critic calls* God's Trombones *"a striking achievement of . . . reverence."*]

[*God's Trombones*] contains what the author calls 'seven negro sermons in verse' Readers of *The Century Magazine* and of *The American Mercury* will have seen two of the poems, since **'The Judgment Day'** appeared in the former, and **'Go Down, Death'**, in the latter periodical. Mr. Johnson will add to an already enviable reputation by this latest experiment, for such it must be called. He has taken seven of the stock themes of the old-time preachers of his race, **'The Prodigal Son'**, **'Noah Built the Ark'**, **'The Crucifixion'**, **'Let My People Go'**, **'The Judgment Day'**, and the two already mentioned. These he has put into verse form, with a striking achievement of impressiveness and reverence, striking only, to be sure, when one recalls that for many years now the negro sermon of the old type has been used chiefly as a subject for very hackneyed parody at rural garden parties and other ready-made entertainments.

The chief means whereby Mr. Johnson has avoided the possibility of giggling, a possibility which no amount of sympathy with the negro preacher or his point of view can deny, is the non-employment of dialect, as he explains in his exceedingly interesting introduction. I have heard two of these stock sermons, preached by semi-literate negroes, with a dignity and an exaltation that have left a lasting impression, and find it difficult to account for the retention of the intimate simplicity and peculiar power of the old sermon when the dialect has been discarded. All the vividness and directness have been retained, all the quick alternation of solemn far-away objectivity and apocalyptic imagery with sudden, familiar evangelistic appeal, with the stress naturally shifted to the former.

Not the least arresting feature of the book is the fine series of eight drawings by the negro artist, Aaron Douglas. The whole makes an important contribution to the study of the negro folk-culture, by two men who possess the gift, rare indeed among their people, it seems to me, of being able to stand off and analyze their old culture without losing genuine feeling for it.

Countee Cullen (review date 1927)

SOURCE: "And the Walls Came Tumblin' Down," in *The Bookman* (New York), Vol. LXVI, No. 2, October, 1927, pp. 221-22.

[*In the following review, Cullen favorably assesses the poems of Johnson's* God's Trombones.]

And seven priests shall bear before the ark seven trumpets of rams' horns; and the seventh day ye shall compass the city seven times, and the priests shall blow with the trumpets.

And it shall come to pass, that when they make a long blast with the ram's horn, and when ye hear the sound of the trumpet, all the people shall shout with a great shout; and the wall of the city shall fall down flat. . . .

James Weldon Johnson has blown the true spirit and the pentecostal trumpeting of the dark Joshuas of the race in *God's Trombones,* composed of seven sermon-poems and a prayer. The seven sermons are like the seven blasts blown by Joshua at Jericho. **"The Creation"**, **"The Prodigal Son"**, **"Go Down Death—A Funeral Sermon"**, **"Noah Built the Ark"**, **"The Crucifixion"**, **"Let My People Go"**, and **"The Judgment Day"**, they are all great evangelical texts. And the magnificent manner in which they are done increases our regret that Mr. Johnson was not intrigued into preaching "The Dry Bones In the Valley", the *pièce de résistance* in the repertoire of every revivalist to whom a good shout is a recommendation of salvation well received.

An experiment and an intention lie behind these poems. It will be remembered that in *The Book of American Negro Poetry* Mr. Johnson spoke of the limitations of dialect, which he compared to an organ having but two stops, one of humor and one of pathos. He felt that the Negro poet needed to discover some medium of expression with a latitude capable of embracing the Negro experience. These poems were written with that purpose in view, as well as to guarantee a measure of permanence in man's most forgetful mind to that highly romantic and fast disappearing character, the old time Negro preacher.

The poet here has admirably risen to his intentions and his needs; entombed in this bright mausoleum the Negro preacher of an older day can never pass entirely deathward. Dialect could never have been synthesized into the rich mortar necessary for these sturdy unrhymed exhortations. Mr. Johnson has captured that peculiar flavor of speech by which the black sons of Zebedee, lacking academic education, but grounded through their religious intensity in the purest marshalling of the English language (the King James' version of the Bible) must have astounded men more obviously letter-trained. This verse is simple and awful at once, the grand diapason of a musician playing on an organ with far more than two keys.

There is a universality of appeal and appreciation in these poems that raises them, despite the fact that they are labeled "Seven Negro Sermons in Verse", and despite the persistent racial emphasis of Mr. Douglas' beautiful illustrations, far above a relegation to any particular group or people. Long ago the recital of the agonies and persecutions of the Hebrew children under Pharaoh ceased to chronicle the tribulations of one people alone. So in **"Let My People Go"** there is a world-wide cry from the oppressed against the oppressor, from the frail and puny against the arrogant in strength who hold them against their will. From Beersheba to Dan the trusting wretch,

rich in nothing but his hope and faith, holds this an axiomatic solace:

Listen!—Listen!
All you sons of Pharaoh,
Who do you think can hold God's people
When the Lord himself has said,
Let my people go?

In considering these poems one must pay unlimited respect to the voice Mr. Johnson has recorded, and to the pliable and agony-racked audience to whom those great black trombones blared their apocalyptic revelations, and their terrible condemnation of the world, the flesh, and the devil. Theirs was a poetic idiom saved, by sincerity and the heritage of a colorful imagination, from triteness. If in "Listen, Lord", they addressed the Alpha and Omega of things in a manner less reverent than the frigidity of the Christian's universal prayer, it is not to be doubted that their familiarity was bred not of contempt, but of the heart-felt liberty of servitors on easy speaking terms with their Master. What people not so privileged could apostrophize Christ so simply and so humanly as merely "Mary's Baby"?

In like manner certain technical crudities and dissonances can be explained away. The interpolation here and there of a definitely rhymed couplet among the lines of this vigorous free and easy poetry will not jar, when one reflects that if poetry is the language of inspiration, then these black trumpeters, manna-fed and thirst-assuaged by living water from the ever flowing rock, could well be expected to fly now and then beyond their own language barriers into the realms of poetic refinements of which they knew nothing, save by intuitive inspiration. And if on occasion the preacher ascended from *you* and *your* to *thee* and *thou,* this too is in keeping with his character.

To me **"The Creation"** and **"Go Down Death"** are unqualifiedly great poems. The latter is a magnificent expatiation and interpretation of the beatitudes; it justifies Job's "I know in Whom I have believed" to all the weary, sorrowbroken vessels of earth. It is a revelation of to what extent just men shall be made perfect. The repetitions in **"The Crucifixion"** are like hammer-strokes of agony.

It is a tribute to Mr. Johnson's genius that when a friend of mine recently read **"Go Down Death"** to an audience in Mr. Johnson's own natal town, an old wizened black woman, the relic of a day of simpler faith and more unashamed emotions than ours, wept and shouted. Perhaps many a modern pastor, logically trained and multi-degreed, might retrieve a scattering flock, hungry for the bread of the soul, by reading one of these poems as a Sunday service.

Harold Rosenberg (review date 1936)

SOURCE: "Truth and the Academic Style," in *Poetry* (Chicago), Vol. XLIX, No. I, October, 1936, pp. 49-51.

[*In the following review of* St. Peter Relates an Incident, *Rosenberg observes that Johnson's conservative poetic temperament undercuts the harsh political realities of his subject matter.*]

The title poem [of *Saint Peter Relates an Incident, Selected Poems*] is the author's expression in satirical terms, of the indignation he felt on reading in the newspaper of a morning in 1930 that the U. S. government was sending a group of gold-star mothers to France to visit the graves of their sons slain in the World War, and that the Negro gold-star mothers would not be allowed to travel with the white, but would be sent over later on a second-class ship. The incident, related in Eternity by Saint Peter, deals with the discovery on Resurrection Day that the Unknown Soldier, buried in Washington, happens to be a Negro.

It is grievous to report that the outrageous act of public discrimination against his race which inspired Mr. Johnson to write his poem strikes very little fire in the poem itself. Naturally, the blurb on the book tries to capitalize on the genius of the Negro people by claiming for the poem "something of the simple charm of Negro lore." As a matter of fact, however, the Saint Peter poem, as well as the rest of the volume, is less typical of the poetry produced out of the labor, anguish, courage, and awakening consciousness of the Negro race in America, than of the literary products of the conservative upper-class nationalist of any race or nation. Mr. Johnson is a Negro poet only in the sense that he applies his academic art to the situation of the American Negro. So far as literary qualities are concerned, a conservative Chinese nationalist, a conservative Zionist, a conservative Hindu nationalist, a conservative celebrator of American accomplishment, all resemble Mr. Johnson in their comfortable idealization of nature-sentiments, their reliant appeals to abstract Justice, their self-solacing trust in an after-death rectification of what their people have suffered. Amid the most brutal assaults upon the lives and liberties of their beloved people, these patriots manage to remain aloft and dignified, the official mourners, the official voices of hope in the future. With respect to nationality, they exist as Chinese, Jews, Hindus, Americans; with respect to poetry, they are all one thing—academicians: an internationalism of mediocrity forever seeking to disguise itself under racial and geographic borderlines.

Whatever part it may play in the social and political progress of the people it aims to represent, the official gesture is irreconcilable with good poetry. The chemistry of interaction between experience, imagination, and language is completely unknown to the stencil-designer of monumental shadows of good will. When Mr. Johnson, in the poem called **"Brothers—American Drama,"** gives an account of the burning alive of a member of his race, he does not say that the victim was lynched because he was a Negro—that would be too horrible; he is lynched because he is not a Negro at all but

> The monstrous offspring of the monster, Sin,

a criminal, whom Mr. Johnson is careful to dissociate from

> That docile, child-like, tender-hearted race
> Which we have known three centuries.

And the only admonition he can give to the righteous mob which has "avenged" some "fiendish crime" are the dying man's last words,

> Brothers in spirit, brothers in deed are we—

in short, an absurd application (Why "brothers in deed"?—did the victim lynch himself?—or did he lynch the mob?) of the apostolic slogan to be found in all idealistic versions of crime and punishment. Is this the speech of a Negro poet? Of any Negro in concrete imaginative contact with the ultimate dread and horror of the black man's history? Such a falsely conceived, slave-mongering piece of high-society propaganda, overlooking its lynch-condoning implications in order to raise the "problem" of mass-servitude to a metaphysical height, could only be constructed in the most wooden language imaginable. With its calculated juggling of old figures, it has the poetic and intellectual value of a false financial report.

Such being the condition of Mr. Johnson's talents, it is possible to respond favorably to his verses on two occasions only: when the great folk-song tradition of his people flows over his poetry, as in some of the dialect poems; and when it happens to fall within his philosophy to make a clear statement of fact:

> This land is ours by right of birth,
>   This land is ours by right of toil;
> We helped to turn its virgin earth,
>   Our sweat is in its fruitful soil.

Stephen H. Bronz (essay date 1964)

SOURCE: "James Weldon Johnson," in *Roots of Negro Racial Consciousness, The 1920's: Three Harlem Renaissance Authors,* Libra Publishers, 1964, pp. 18-46.

[*In the following excerpt, Bronz examines the social importance of Johnson's early poetry in* Fifty Years, and Other Poems *and comments on his later work as a precursor to the Harlem Renaissance.*]

His First Poems: History, Polemics, and Croons

[Johnson's] first poem to reach a large audience, **"Lift Every Voice,"** has become known as the Negro National Anthem.[14] Johnson wrote the anthem together with [his brother John] Rosamond in 1900, to be sung by Jacksonville school children on Lincoln's Birthday. The following snippets give a fair summary:

> Lift every voice and sing
> Till earth and heaven ring,
> Ring with the harmonies of liberty;
>
> . . . . .
>
> We have come, treading our path through the blood
>   of the slaughtered, . . .

Till we stand at last where the white gleam of
   our star is cast . . .
God of our silent tears,

. . . . .

Keep us forever in the path, we pray

. . . . .

Lest, our hearts drunk with the wine of the world,
   we forget Thee;
Shadowed beneath Thy hand,
May we forever stand.
True to our God,
True to our native land.

These are curious lines to have come from Johnson. First, he was an admitted agnostic.[15] Second, the anthem's sentiments stress only the Negro's duties instead of also the white man's and God's obligations to the Negro. Even more curious is Johnson's own comment many years later that "nothing I have done has paid me back as fully in satisfaction. . . . I am also carried back . . . to . . . the exquisite emotions I felt at the birth of the song." In 1935, he wrote that he and Rosamond had all but forgotten the anthem after moving from Jacksonville. Only after the song had spread across Negro America, and was proclaimed the Negro National Anthem by the NAACP in 1920, did Johnson apparently recall such "exquisite emotions." Even though Johnson doubtless would have written a very different Negro anthem in 1935, he probably saw no point in disavowing what had become a mainstay of Negro school pageants.[16]

In the same spirit, Johnson wrote **"Fifty Years,"** a rousing if not quite heroic commemorative published in the New York *Times* on January 1, 1913, the fiftieth anniversary of the Emancipation Proclamation. It begins with a summary view:

O brothers mine, to-day we stand
Where half a century sweeps our ken,
Since God, through Lincoln's ready hand,
Struck off our bonds and made us men.

We have made great strides, it continues, since we were "a naked, shivering score, / . . . wild-eyed on Virginia's shore." We thank God for our progress, and pray that "we may grow more worthy of this country and this land of ours." Though we came from Africa, we are no longer Africans, or mainly Negroes, but Americans:

This land is ours by right of birth,
This land is ours by right of toil;
We helped to turn its virgin earth,
Our sweat is in its fruitful soil.

In the poem's conclusion, Johnson views the sacrifices whites have made for Negroes, as part of God's plan:

Think you that John Brown's spirit stops?
That Lovejoy was but idly slain?

Or do you think those precious drops
From Lincoln's heart were shed in vain?

That for which millions prayed and sighed,
That for which tens of thousands fought,
For which so many freely died,
God cannot let it come to naught.

Despite the apparent passivity of its message, **"Fifty Years"** poses an implicit challenge. To make America as much the Negro's land as the white man's and to ensure continued progress would involve more change than most whites were ready to accept in 1913. Possibly with a sense of relief at the poem's apparent mildness, the *Times* ran an editorial the next day praising **"Fifty Years"** as a "great subject . . . greatly treated."[17]

In 1917, **"Fifty Years"** was published in a volume by that title with other poems Johnson had written since about 1900.[18] (**"Lift Every Voice"** was not published in a volume until 1935.) Some of the poems in *Fifty Years* discuss race and the Negro, some are dialect poems, and the remainder are the sorts of third-rate expression of sentiment and moralism one finds tucked away near the drug store ads of small town newspapers. Besides **"Fifty Years,"** Johnson's most powerful poem about race is **"To America"** which reads:

How would you have us, as we are?
Or sinking 'neath the load we bear?
Our eyes fixed forward on a star?
Or gazing empty at despair?

Rising or falling? Man or things?
With dragging pace or footsteps fleet?
Strong, willing sinews in your wings?
Or tightening chains about your feet?

This appeal to whites' self-interest as well as to simple justice, though reminiscent of Booker T. Washington's Atlanta Exposition speech, implies that prejudice oppresses the white man as well as the Negro.

In **"Brothers,"** Johnson depicts a Negro, accused of rape, telling his white captors, in elevated language, who he really is, and how he came to be that way. "Are not you," the lynchers ask him, "who seem more like brute than man" sprung from "that more than faithful race which through three wars / Fed our dear wives and nursed our helpless babes / Without one single breach of trust?" "I am, and am not," the Negro replies,

The bitter fruit I am of planted seed;
The resultant, the inevitable end
Of evil forces and the powers of wrong

. . . . .

Lessons in degradation, taught and learned,
The memories of cruel sights and deeds,
The pent-up bitterness, the unspent hate

Filtered through fifteen generations have
Sprung up and found in me sporadic life.

. . . . .

Brothers in spirit, brothers in deed are we.

Notwithstanding their captive's eloquence, the whites proceed to lynch him brutally, and to divide his charred bones among themselves as mementos. One vagrant thought, however, still troubles them: "What did he mean by those last muttered words, 'Brothers in spirit, brothers in deed are we?'" The irony of the poem's ending—a man brutally lynched by those who made a brute out of him in the first place—may seem heavy-handed, but the sociology stated in the poem's first section is more sophisticated. Johnson seems to be making three main points: that racial hatred as well as slums and broken homes can produce criminals, that American Negroes potentially can become violent revolutionaries, and that a lynching is as degrading to the lynchers as rape to the lynched, if, indeed, rape was committed.

The dialect poems, together entitled "Jingles and Croons," ring authentic as folk poetry. Their imagery is vivid and the equal of the best efforts of Dunbar, the popular dialect poet, whom, in fact, Johnson was emulating.[19] The most famous, the folk blues **"Sence You Went Away,"** has been recorded by Paul Robeson and provided with a violin obligato by Fritz Kreisler.[20] The first and last stanzas read:

Seems lak to me de stars don't shine so bright,
Seems lak to me de sun done loss his light,
Seems lak to me der's nothin' goin' right,
    Sence you went away . . .
Seems lak to me I jes can't he'p but sigh,
Seems lak to me ma th'oat keeps gittin' dry,
Seems lak to me a tear stays in ma eye,
    Sence you went away.

Johnson's dialect poems and their later counterpart, *God's Trombones,* form an integral part of his work. They show that he was not only an earnest race leader, but a man able to love and enjoy the folk life of the very people he was trying to uplift. . . .

As Harlem Renaissance Leader: Critic and Author

Throughout the 'twenties, Johnson helped to lead the Harlem Renaissance, both as poet and elder statesman. Observations he made on the meaning and problems of the movement were penetrating and sophisticated. As early as 1918, he had foreseen that "it may be . . . that what many are looking for, perhaps unconsciously, from the Negro poet is something not necessarily good, but something different, something strange . . . something new."[48] It was indeed by writing something different, strange, and new that many of the Negro authors of the 'twenties achieved their popularity. Good poetry and fiction often was received no more enthusiastically than the very poor.

Ten years later, with the Renaissance in full swing, Johnson spoke to the same problems, with a somewhat different emphasis. The dilemma of the Negro author, he wrote, is the "problem of the double audience." While most Negro authors try to reach both Negro and white readers, many fall in between and reach neither. The problem arises, he said, because Negro and white readers each read Negro authors with certain preconceptions in mind. Whites, nurtured on Uncle Remus and romantic Southern novels, expect Negro characters to behave like Sambos or low-living hedonists. Negro readers, equally obsessed with the same stereotypes, demand that Negro authors present to white readers only Negroes who belie the stereotypes, heroes with middle-class virtues. Though Johnson did exaggerate—some whites were more knowledgeable and some Negroes, including Johnson himself, were less obsessed with presenting a pleasing image to Whites—the dilemma was a real one, and exerted strong influence on such a writer as Countee Cullen. As Johnson commented: "I judge that there is not a single Negro writer who is not, at least secondarily, impelled by the desire to make his work have some effect on the white world for the good of his race."[49]

In another critical essay, his introduction to an anthology of Negro poetry, Johnson commented on Negro poets' choices of style and subject. Dunbar, America's first well-known Negro poet, represented the only real tradition Negro authors writing as Negroes possessed. Dunbar, however, writing almost exclusively in dialect, stood for a tradition to rebel from, rather than to emulate. Johnson himself carefully thought out his own reasons for breaking with dialect in his own poetry. Traditional Negro dialect, he said, is inextricably associated with the Sambo image of the Negro, "and by that very exactness it is an instrument with but two full stops, humor and pathos." Hence, he pointed out, dialect is inadequate for dealing with new social conditions, especially urban life. But language was not a crucial problem in the Negro Renaissance. A handful of poets used traditional dialect, but most wrote in the King's English or in a newer, idiomatic, urban slang. Subject matter, on the other hand, was a crucial issue. Because an author writes most convincingly about material closest to him, Johnson said, Negroes' poems on race problems have far greater "power and artistic finality" than poems dealing with less specifically Negro themes.[50]

Johnson's final important series of poems, and probably his best, closely followed these precepts. Published in 1927, and printed for the fifteenth time in 1955, *God's Trombones,* a free verse rendition of a Negro folk-sermon, is steeped in folk imagery yet written in straight English.[51] It is distinctly Negro, yet it carries scarcely any explicit propaganda. And it is aimed at Negro audiences rightly proud of their own heritage, and at white audiences who, if they had trouble accepting a Negro as a lawyer, still could appreciate the more familiar figure of the Negro preacher. White readers in the 'twenties, one imagines, expected Johnson's preacher to be a comic figure, but instead were surprised and even awed by the noble, sonorous rhythms of the sermons. Johnson quotes a definition of trombone that not only explains the poem's title, but prepares one for its special kind of music:

trombone: A powerful brass instrument of the trumpet family, the only wind instrument possessing a complete chromatic scale enharmonically true, like the human voice or the violin, and hence very valuble in the orchestra.

The second section of the sermon, **"The Creation,"** begins:

> And God stepped out on space,
> And he looked around and said:
> Im lonely—
> I'll make me a world.
>
> And far as the eye of God could see
> Darkness covered everything,
> Blacker than a hundred midnights
> Down in a cypress swamp.
>
> Then God smiled,
> And the light broke,
> And the darkness rolled up on one side,
> And the light stood shining on the other,
> And God said: That's good!

And the beginning of the third section, **"The Prodigal Son"**:

> Young man—
> Young man—
> Your arm's too short to box with God.

After the majesty of **"The Creation"** and the evangelic fervor of **"The Prodigal Son,"** Johnson turns to engrossing drama in relating the serpent's temptation of Eve, and to shivering poignancy in describing the Crucifixion. Only once does a clear, racially-oriented note of protest manifest itself. It is in the spirited ending of the section on Exodus, made the climax of a dramatization of *God's Trombones* which opened off-Broadway in December, 1963.

> And the waves rushed back together,
> And Pharaoh and all his army got lost,
> And all his host got drownded.
> And Moses sang and Miriam danced,
> And the people shouted for joy,
> And God led the Hebrew Children on
> Till they reached the promised land.
>
> Listen!—Listen!
> All you sons of Pharaoh.
> Who do you think can hold God's people
> When he himself has said,
> Let my people go?

It is quite possible that *God's Trombones* was as much compilation from sermons Johnson had heard as original creation, but that question need not bother us, as it doubtless did not bother Johnson. The Negro poet, he wrote,

> needs to do . . . something like what Synge did for the Irish; he needs to find a form that will express the racial spirit by symbols from within rather than by symbols from without—such as the mere mutilation of English spelling and pronunciation. He needs a form that is freer and larger than dialect, but which will still hold the racial flavor; a form . . . which will . . . be capable of voicing the deepest and highest emotions and aspirations . . . [52]

Johnson was a modest man, and did not mean to imply that *God's Trombones* made him the Negro's Synge. But he did, it seems clear, mean to guide younger Negro poets towards expressing their own heritage. If the results are not only good poetry, but strengthened pride in being a Negro, so much the better.

For all his urbanity, Johnson could react furiously to injustices that especially piqued him. His capacities for both restraint and anger even seemed to be reflected in his appearance. Johnson was always quietly and carefully dressed, and his face, in later years, was dominated by deep-set, narrow, cat-like eyes which peered out from under bushy eyebrows and a balding head, and over jowled cheeks and a sloping, trim, grey mustache. One infuriating injustice inspired his last major poem, **"St. Peter Relates an Incident of the Resurrection Day,"** written in 1930, and published in 1935. In the summer of 1930, Johnson writes in the poem's introduction, he read in a newspaper that the U. S. Government was sending contingents of gold-star mothers to visit the graves of their soldier sons in France. The Negro gold-star mothers, notwithstanding the bond in war and death of the Negro and white soldiers, were to be sent on a separate ship, and second class. The incident, which St. Peter relates in the poem to a group of spell-bound angels, describes the resurrection of the Unknown Soldier. The word went forth that the Unknown Soldier was to be resurrected, and his identity thus revealed. All veteran and patriotic organizations, including the G.A.R., the D.A.R., and the Confederate Veterans, marched to the banks of the Potomac. Led by the Ku Klux Klan, they picked away with shovels at the Unknown Soldier's grave. Finally,

> He, underneath the debris, heaved and hove
> Up toward the opening which they cleaved and
>   clove,
> Through it, at last, his towering form loomed big
>   and bigger—
> "Great God Almighty! Look!" they cried, "he is a
>   nigger."

The Klansmen and associates were mortified, but the black Unknown Soldier rose to heaven, singing, "Deep river, my home is over Jordan, / Deep river, I want to cross over into camp-ground." Johnson tells us in his foreward that he wrote **"St. Peter"** in a single sitting, and there is little reason to question his honesty. The poem is not one of his better efforts; it is far too long, and its irony, because of the unimaginative reaction attributed to the Klansmen, is blunted. Still, it demonstrates that even as late as 1930, Johnson could feel quite bitter towards the adversaries with whom he was trying to deal as calmly as possible.

Notes

[14] Reprinted in Johnson, *St. Peter Relates an Incident* (New York, 1935), pp. 101-102.

[15] Johnson, *Along This Way,* pp. 30-31, 154.

[16] Johnson, *St. Peter Relates an Incident,* p. 99; *Along This Way,* p. 156. See also Ernest Lyon, *A Protest against the Title of James Welden* [sic] *Johnson's Anomalous Poem as a 'Negro National Anthem' as Subversive of Patriotism* (1926), and advertisement quoting "Lift Every Voice and Sing" for Mutual Life Insurance Company of Chicago in Johnson Folder, Schomburg Collection.

[17] "A Negro Speaks for his Race," New York *Times,* 2 Jan. 1913.

[18] Johnson, *Fifty Years and Other Poems* (Boston, 1917).

[19] Johnson, *Along This Way,* p. 158.

[20] *Ibid.,* pp. 153-154.

[48] Johnson's reply to Floyd Dell's review of *Fifty Years and Other Poems, The Liberator,* v. 1 (April 1918), p. 43.

[49] Johnson, "The Dilemma of the Negro Author," *American Mercury,* v. 15, no. 60 (Dec. 1928), pp. 477-481.

[50] Johnson's "Preface to the Revised Edition" of Johnson, ed., *The Book of American Negro Poetry* (New York, 1931), pp. 3, 4, 7.

[51] Johnson, *God's Trombones* (New York, 1927). On the poem's origins see Johnson, *Along This Way,* pp. 335-336.

[52] Johnson, *St. Peter Relates an Incident,* pp. ix, 13-22.

Lynn Adelman (essay date 1967)

SOURCE: "A Study of James Weldon Johnson," in *The Journal of Negro History,* Vol. LII, No. 2, April, 1967, pp. 128-45.

[*In the following essay, Adelman reflects on Johnson's life, writing, and contributions to African-American culture between the 1890s and 1930s.*]

The period running roughly from the 1890's to the 1930's was a particularly harsh one for the American Negro. It was characterized in many ways by a deterioration in the Negro's status both in the South and the North. And although the Negro made some important gains, especially in the latter part of this period, the South's capitulation to racism and to the Jim Crow code of discrimination, which began in the 1890's, ran unabated until well into the depression years.[1] These conditions placed heavy demands on Negro leadership, which was itself torn, at least until 1915, by the bitter split between Booker T. Washington and W. E. DuBois and their followers.

The adult life of James Weldon Johnson spanned approximately these years. Johnson lived from 1871 until 1938. Study of his career yields substantial insight into the period and into the way in which it affected an individual Negro. Johnson's problems and responses were, to be sure, not altogether typical, for he was an unusually gifted and versatile person. But in some ways both his personal career and the nature of the leadership which he provided demonstrate the difficulties the Negro faced and the harsh limitations on the possible approaches to those difficulties.

I.

Johnson had the benefit of an unusual childhood.[2] He was born in Jacksonville, Florida, where his family provided a comfortable and culturally stimulating home. His father was a native of New York and held the position of head-waiter at the St. James Hotel. The St. James was a haven for wealthy tourists[3] and the Johnson family became familiar, at least as spectators, with an aristocratic way of life. Johnson's mother was the daughter of Stephen Dillet, who was the Postmaster of the city of Nassau and one of the best known Negroes in the Bahamas. She was proud, sensitive, and musically talented; her unique background of Nassau and New York had given her no conception of her "station." From this proud and cosmopolitan home, Johnson gained a deep sense of dignity.

Other factors worked to his advantage. His childhood years were spent in that hazy period in the history of Southern race relations before the violent settlement of the Negro's position had been reached. Systematized discrimination and segregation did not come until later. And in this period—when attitudes had not yet hardened into laws—Jacksonville was considered a particularly good town for Negroes. Thus, Johnson was able to grow up free of the effects of the ghetto or the slum. He never learned to view his Negritude as a burden. When he finally did encounter the problem of race he was able to meet it on a more or less rational level and with an already keen intelligence.

At the age of sixteen Johnson entered Atlanta University. Because of the lack of a Negro high school in Jacksonville, his parents sent him to Atlanta for both his high school and college educations. Thus, he was at Atlanta for practically all of his early manhood and the impact of the school upon him was profound. Atlanta was Johnson's introduction to the problem of race. Awareness of race was pervasive and the subject was constantly discussed. The school sought to foster a sense of mission in its students. It had been founded twenty years before by a white philanthropist whose hope was to develop individual Negro talent, provide inspiration and leadership for Negro communities, and train teachers.[4] Johnson began to write poetry with racial themes and he began to think of his purpose in life as one peculiar to a Negro.

So, too, did the school's philosophy of education influence him. Atlanta stressed the classical liberal education. This became central in Johnson's thinking. He would consistently argue that education was the most potent weapon in the Negro's struggle;[5] that the liberal education, in particular, could improve and uplift the Negro. Concerning Booker Washington's emphasis on vocational training, Johnson once pointed out that Washington himself had been liberally educated.[6] In stressing academic education, Johnson—who was proud of his own intellectual accomplishments—generalized, in part, from his own experience. This experience may, in some ways, have limited his perspective on the race problem. He seemed sometimes to underestimate the many barriers impeding Negroes from gaining an education. His exhortations, while certainly sensible, occasionally seemed naive as, for example, when he urged Harlem Negroes to spend more time in the library.[7]

II.

Johnson graduated from Atlanta in 1894. Having by this time become well thought of by the Negroes in Jacksonville, he was offered and accepted the job as principal of Stanton School, which was the elementary school that he had attended and the largest Negro school in Florida. At Stanton he was both a teacher and an administrator and he made a distinguished record. By adding one grade each year, he made Stanton a high school as well as a grade school. His ability was widely recognized, leading, in 1900, to his election as President of the Negro State Teachers Association.

Teaching and school administration, however, were not entirely fulfilling either his ambition or the sense of responsibility to his race which had been developed at Atlanta. These feelings were strong ones and in 1895 they impelled him to start a newspaper. *The Daily American,* as the paper was called, was aimed primarily at the Negro and was to provide an instrument for the expression of the Negro's feelings. According to one of Johnson's first editorials, the *American* would champion the rights of the Negro but would criticize him when he deserved it. It would be Republican in politics, objective in its news coverage, and adamant in its fight against wrongdoing, both in personal conduct and in government.[8]

With the *American,* for the first time Johnson assumed the role of spokesman for his people and exhorter to them. Alternately he urged the Negro to demonstrate his proven ability[9] and to strive to improve himself. Present but less conspicuous in his editorials was the bitter indictment of discrimination and prejudice which would characterize his work for the *New York Age* twenty years later. The difference in tone was part of the difference in the situations. At the time of the *American* he was a young man trying to gain support for a new paper, in a time and place where there was virtually no tradition of strong Negro protest.

Johnson was seeking most to increase respect for the Negro in the eyes of both Negroes and whites. The *American* itself was a symbol of this purpose. Its prosaic style, its puritanical emphasis on clean living and clean government, its explicit attempts at objectivity all were part of his attempt to improve the image of the Negro. Each copy was to be proof that Negroes were not illiterate and irresponsible.

The paper made a good start, but failed after eight months of publication because of insufficient financial support. Johnson himself was not sure whether the failure was because the Negroes of Jacksonville were not yet ready

for such a paper, or because of his own failings.[10] It was clear that in seeking to provide a voice for the Southern Negro and to encourage pride and self respect Johnson was waging a lonely and uphill struggle. Virtually everything in the Southern system tended to beat against the black man's pride. As Paul Buck has written: "Early in life the Negro child learned the hazards of the color line. It was the lot of every Negro to accept, as most of his race did, the badge of inferiority or to carry within his inner soul an important yet agonizing spark of rebellion against the fateful injustice of his position."[11]

With the failure of the *American,* another side of Johnson came to the fore. He decided to take up the study of law and arranged to "read law" in the office of Thomas Ledwith, a young white lawyer whose father had been a prominent Republican. Here was the more conventional aspect of his ambition asserting itself. While he wanted to serve his race, he also wanted to succeed in a way more or less unrelated to race. The tension between these two sides of him would be a consistent theme for many years of his life.

He studied law for eighteen months and then, at the urging of Ledwith, decided to take the Florida bar examination. At that time there were several Negro lawyers in Jacksonville but none had been admitted through open examination in a state court. Johnson's examination was an ordeal, with one of the examiners calling him a "nigger" and walking out, but his answers were right and he managed to pass.

Law, however, was not the career for him. He opened an office, but practiced only for a short time. Although he was not unsuccessful in getting business, he may have seen that opportunities for Negro lawyers in the South were limited. Few were able to devote themselves to practice and fewer appeared in court. For a Negro client, white counsel often was more helpful than the best Negro representation.[12]

Besides this, he had found a new interest. His brother Rosamond, who was a musician, wanted him to help compose a comic opera. Rosamond was to write the lyrics and James, the words, the ultimate plan being to sell it in New York. Johnson was receptive to the idea. He had been writing verse since college and he was fascinated by the world of theatre and music, which his brother, who had spent seven years studying and working in the North, inhabited.

Together they produced "Toloso," a comic opera satirizing United States imperialism, and in the summer of 1899, set out for New York. Although the opera itself was never produced, the trip was an important one in their lives. "Toloso" served as a passport to the inner circles of the Negro show business world. Johnson was exposed to Negro artists and he saw for the first time the great potentialities of Negro art. His love of New York, which he had visited as a child, was revived. Although he returned to Jacksonville in the fall, it as only a few years later that Johnson left Jacksonville for good. Between 1899 and 1902, he spent his winters at the Stanton School and his summers in New York, writing songs and musical comedies. In the summer of 1900, he and Rosamond formed a combination songwriting-vaudeville team with Bob Cole. And in the summer of 1902, as they became increasingly successful, Johnson resigned from Stanton.

Show business was his fourth new venture in the five years since Atlanta. This darting from one project to another was a commentary on the conditions in which he found himself. A particular kind of identity crisis was involved. There were no clear paths for Johnson to follow. He was a talented and ambitious Negro living in a society which had little place for such types. As the plight of the Negro laborer at this time was poor, so too was that of the Negro aristocrat. As John Hope Franklin has put it: ". . . the American melting pot, so far as Negroes were concerned, was not boiling; it was hardly simmering."[13] Johnson's desire to be a racial spokesman had been dampened by the failure of the *American*. Being a lawyer in Florida offered an uncertain future and a high school principalship was not enough for a life's work. One of the few areas of opportunity was the world of show business. It lacked the dignity and the seriousness which were so much a part of him, but it offered glamor and excitement.

III.

In the years between 1900-1906, the team of Cole and the Johnson Brothers flourished. They were among the top composers of American popular music and were signed to a lucrative contract by Klaw and Erlanger, a major theatrical firm. Johnson lived at the Marshall Hotel and was a leading figure in New York's Black Bohemia. He and his partners toured the United States and played the Palace Theater in London. They lived the gay life—in a three-month stay in Europe they spent some ten thousand dollars and had to borrow money to tip the ship's steward on the return trip.[14]

Artistically, Johnson's work was less successful. Before becoming a professional songwriter, he had written essentially two kinds of poetry: more or less conventional verse, sometimes with racial themes, and dialect poems. The dialect, at that time, posed a particular problem for an aspiring Negro poet. Dialect, which had first been popularized by white local colorists after the Civil War, consisted mainly of rhymed and metrical misspellings. It was widely accepted as the verse best fitted to describe Negro life, and Negro poets generally wrote in dialect. The subject matter of dialect, however, rarely rose above the stereotype of the harmless plantation Negro.[15] It rendered an inaccurate and often insulting picture of the Negro.

Johnson had mixed feelings about the dialect. He liked it because of its particularly Negro quality but he saw its limitations, or as he later wrote, its "artificiality . . . exaggerated geniality, childish optimism, forced comicality, and mawkish sentiment . . ."[16] Further, he had had some success with conventional form in expressing racial themes. In 1900 he wrote **"Lift Every Voice and Sing,"**[17] a powerful poem which, when set to music, later came to be adopted by Negroes as a Negro National Anthem.

During his tenure in show business, however, he was unable to break away from the dialect. Such a course was made more difficult by the demands of his new profession. As show business represented something of a compromise for him, so his writing saw the same compromise. Negro entertainers were bound largely by the white man's stereotypes and prejudices; the time had not yet come for the Negro rebel, in politics or in art. Johnson, as yet, was no exception.

Even while he continued to write dialect, however, Johnson was able to express more than surface emotions. In **"A Banjo Song,"**[18] for example, he wrote of a plantation bacchanal held not for innocent fun but to forget very real troubles.[19] And he strove consciously to avoid portraying the stereotype of the happy, gluttonous Negro.[20]

Johnson was never entirely satisfied by show business and these feelings persisted. In 1903 he wrote to the Atlanta University newspaper, reassuring it that he had not given up life's serious pursuits. He also found time to study literature at Columbia, and to head a Colored Republican Club in New York. When he returned from Europe the sense that show business was neither dignified enough nor important enough continued to weigh heavily upon him. He began to consider the suggestion of Charles Anderson, a politician, that he try for a position in the United States Consular Service. Two of his qualifications were fluent Spanish and past service for the Republican Party. He passed the examination, and in 1906 he took the next step in his already staccato career when he received the appointment as United States Consul in Puerto Caballo, Venezuela at a starting salary of $2,000.

IV.

Johnson was, of course, not the first Negro in government service. McKinley alone appointed twice as many Negroes to federal positions as had any previous President.[21] As a consul his primary duties were to overlook international commercial affairs and to assist American citizens. He found the work enjoyable and sometimes exciting—as when he became at least peripherally involved in the turbulence of Latin American politics—and after a time he began to consider making it his life's work. In 1909 he received a promotion to consul at Corinto, Nicaragua, with a thousand dollar increase in pay. His years in Latin America were productive in other ways. In February of 1910, on one of his trips to New York, he married Grace Nail, who came from a wealthy long-established Negro family in Brooklyn.

Residence in Latin America also had a good effect on his development as an artist. Musical comedy had been a hindrance in many ways. He had been hemmed in by the demands of his audience, and the gay life which he led was not conducive to the expression of deep feeling. In Latin America there was no immediate audience and few distractions. Removed from the American racial scene, he could observe with greater clarity.

Nearly all his poems now were racial in theme. He was able to discard competely the dialect, and the feelings which he expressed were no longer the dialect's "pathos and humor." Particularly noteworthy were such poems as **"O Black and Unknown Bards"** and **"Mother Night."** Some of his poems were protests, a note not often heard in Negro poetry since before the Civil War. An example is **"O Southland"**[22] which begins,

> O Southland, fair Southland
> Then why do you still cling
> To an idle page
> To a dead and useless thing?

He also found time to write a novel, *The Autobiography of an Ex-Coloured Man,*[23] the story of a Negro who is able to "pass." The hero of the story wanders through the American South, to New York, and to Europe, having adventures and making various observations on the race question. He ultimately marries a white girl and decides to pass permanently. The book was revolutionary in several respects. Its treatment of the miscegenation theme was new in that both parties were aristocrats.[24] Further, Johnson portrayed a dimension of Negro life rarely present in stories about Negroes. Consider this description of his hero's life in Black Bohemia:

> . . . my regular time for going to bed was somewhere between four and six o'clock in the morning. I got up late in the afternoon, walked about a little, then went to the gambling house or the club.[25]

The novel was, in its own way, a statement of racial pride. Johnson's hero leads a life that would make anyone envious and, in the end, he has the last laugh on the white man by intermarrying. The novel was, in fact, frightening to its author. Johnson was worried about its potential shock effect and had no desire, with a possible government career ahead of him, to become controversial. Also, he had hopes that the story would be taken as true. He, thus, chose to publish it anonymously. The book, published in 1912, turned out to be a financial success and received no particular denunciation;[26] in 1927 it was republished by Knopf above its author's name.

Johnson's hopes of a career in the foreign service were not to be fulfilled. In 1913, when Woodrow Wilson took office, he was expecting his second promotion and, in fact, had been nominated by President Taft to be Consul to the Azores. When no action was taken on the matter Johnson went to Washington to talk to Secretary of State Bryan. The Wilson Administration's attitude toward the Negro was equivocal, if not hostile; its policy regarding the foreign service was generally to substitute neophyte Democrats for experienced men.[27] Bryan was not encouraging and Johnson left feeling victimized by race and politics. Shortly afterward he resigned from the Consulate.[28]

His frustration was, of course, nothing new. Now forty-two, he had come some way since Atlanta University—publisher, educator, lawyer, composer, artist, and diplomat—yet in a way he was back where he began. In none of his pursuits—except the *American*—had he failed, but

each had brought frustration. He had started as a Negro in the South, trying to make his own way and to improve the lot of his race, but his efforts had been blocked by Negro indifference and white prejudice. He had gone North and found that there, too, opportunities were limited. He was a successful songwriter but had to write juvenile and sometimes demeaning verse. The latest roadblock had come in government service. In some ways, he had been a Negro doing white men's work. Not since his short-lived publishing attempt was his work directly related to the Negro struggle. His poems indicated his feelings, but his time had been spent living the good life in Negro Bohemia or being a functionary in Latin America, far away from the turbulence of racial conflict.

After 1913, Johnson turned back to the central issues and identified himself totally with the cause of the Negro. While this course was, in part, forced upon him by the circumstances in which he found himself, he did not choose it reluctantly. His ambition to be a leader and a spokesman had only been in abeyance. None of this was clear to him in 1913. First he went to Jacksonville to gather his thoughts. But Jim Crow signs were more common and Grace Nail Johnson was unhappy. In 1914 they headed for New York and when, several weeks later, he was offered the job as head of the editorial staff of the *New York Age,* New York's oldest Negro newspaper, Johnson quickly accepted.

v.

Johnson's editorship of the *Age* thrust him to the forefront of American Negro spokesmen. For the first time he had to face squarely and state his position on the many issues of the day. The outlines of his thought had already been made clear in *The Autobiography of an Ex-Coloured Man.* Underlying all his ideas was the belief that the race problem was, at root, a question of attitude. The Negro, through years of subjugation, had become apathetic and resigned.[29] The problem of white attitudes lay mainly in their misconceptions about the Negro. Johnson realized that the myth of inferiority was often a cover-up for complex emotional forces, but he believed that the first step towards equality was to prove that inferiority was nonsense. Thus, he advocated a two-pronged approach of seeking to awaken the Negro and to enlighten the white.[30]

Johnson turned with alacrity to his new role as agitator. He wrote a daily column called "Views and Reviews," which contained the strongest race protests he had yet uttered. No longer was he inhibited by worries about a career as a diplomat; his only responsibility now was to the Negro. Johnson passionately defended the Negro and the Negro's ability. No important Negro activity missed his attention. He praised Negro artists and performers and defended the Negro soldier.[31] He also berated the Negro for not helping himself in such columns as "Cut Out the Comedy."[32]

Nor did he hesitate to attack prejudice. Particularly biting were such pieces as "Tom Watson, Apostle of Prejudice"[33] and "Staying in the Ditch"[34] which opened as follows:

We doubt that Mississippi has ever produced a man who has contributed to the progress of the world.

He could see the debilitating effect of racism on both its protagonists—"The solving of the race problem," he said, "involves in large measure the salvation of the black man's body and the white man's soul."[35]

The freedom and power evident in his editorials could also be seen in the poetry he was now writing. Besides his own maturity, the spirit of the times was more conducive to militance. People were using the term "New Negro," whose spirit was, perhaps, best represented by DuBois. This new feeling had not yet reached Negro art but Johnson was to lead the way. The Harlem Renaissance was imminent.

The best example of this spirit in Johnson's work is his poem **"Brothers—American Drama,"**[36] written in 1916, about the burning of a Negro by a white mob. It was a thoroughly realistic social justice poem[37] and the most vigorous poem yet heard from any Negro poet.[38] The horror of the burning is vividly described:

> Now let it blaze again. See there!
> He squirms! He groans!
> His eyes bulge wildly out.

But Johnson's calm wisdom is also present. The act is

> The bitter fruit . . . of planted seed;
> The resultant, the inevitable end
> Of evil forces and the powers of wrong.

Thus, after 1913, Johnson seemed to find himself as a spokesman and a poet. In both media he spoke with increasing strength. His efforts did not go unnoticed. In 1916 Joel Springarn, president of the recently formed NAACP, invited him to attend a conference on questions relating to the Negro at Amenia, New York. The Amenia Conference was an important event both for the Negro and for Johnson. It marked the first time that Negro leadership was more or less united, a unity caused partly by the death of Washington and partly, said DuBois, "by the concentration of effort . . . which rising race segregation, discrimination, and mob murder were compelling us to follow."[39]

Johnson according to Arthur Spingarn, "hit it off perfectly with everybody."[40] After the Conference the NAACP's Board of Directors, headed by the Spingarns and DuBois, decided they wanted Johnson in the Association. The only problem, both for the Association and for Johnson, involved Johnson's ideological position.[41] During the long conflict between Washington and DuBois, Johnson had never really taken sides. His thinking was much closer to that of DuBois, which his editorials, emphasizing full equality and denouncing race prejudice, clearly showed. But Johnson had long been close to Washington and owed him a debt of gratitude; for it was only through Washington's efforts that Johnson had received his appointment in the Consulate.[42] And even had he wanted to criticize Washington he would have been prevented by the policy of the *Age,* which at one time had been partially owned by Washington, of never criticizing Washington in print.[43] The Association, not sure of his position but hoping to bring him into their camp, offered him a position. Johnson accepted and, in 1916, assumed the newly created position of Field Secretary, beginning what was to be his major work for the next fifteen years.

VI.

Johnson's principal duties as Field Secretary were organization and expansion. His first major contribution was to convince the Board of the importance of organizing a Southern section. In January 1917, he began an organizing tour of the South addressing conferences in every major city. Johnson was encouraged by the response of Negroes at the mass meetings. Walter White, then in his early twenties, described the meeting in Atlanta and Johnson's approach as follows:

> The . . . meeting . . . was so packed with eager faced Negroes and even a few whites that we had difficulty wedging the platform party through the crowd to enter the auditorium. Mr. Johnson, calm, slender, and immaculate, stood hazardously between the footlights and a painted backdrop . . . There was none of the sonorous flamboyant oratory of that era in the meeting . . . only the quiet irrefutable presentation of the facts and the need to wipe out race prejudice before the hate . . . destroyed both the victims and the perpetrators.[44]

The sum of Johnson's efforts was an organizational success for the Association. By 1919, there were 155 Southern branches, over half of its total number.[45]

The general outlook for the Negro at this time, however, was bleak. The War and the migration of Negroes from South to North and from country to city were bringing new racial tensions, tensions which erupted in Coatesville, in East St. Louis, and elsewhere. The Association was also having its problems. It was threatened by the black nationalism of Marcus Garvey, and it was divided internally, mainly by DuBois, who insisted on running the *Crisis* independently of the Association and who had already caused the resignation of Oswald Garrison Villard. Its leadership was faltering as Executive Secretary, John Shillady, had been frightened since being beaten by a mob in Austin, Texas. Besides this, it had already been branded by many as radical and irresponsible.[46]

In 1920, these problems were thrown squarely into Johnson's lap. The Board of Directors appointed him to succeed Shillady as Executive Secretary. He was to be the first Negro to hold this position. His first act was characteristic. He accepted; but only on the condition that his salary at least equal Shillady's.[47]

Johnson was not as sure of himself as his demand to the Board might have indicated. The problems he faced were grave and often he had no answers to them. One of these problems was the Negro laborer, who was just beginning to be heard from. Jobs for unskilled laborers were rare and the Negro was, as the saying went, "the last to be hired, the first to be fired." High wartime wages had only whetted his appetite.

Johnson recognized the problem and was deeply concerned. He saw the grim struggle for existence that was the real, behind-the-scenes story of Harlem.[48] He could make, however, no effective response. He advocated a pragmatic, more or less opportunistic policy, stressing organization, if possible, in white unions, otherwise in Negro associations. He also suggested boycotts and an effort to convince whites of the abilities of Negro laborers.

Johnson rarely took any action particularly aimed at helping the Negro laborer. Probably there was little he could have done; but it was also true that he was hard pressed to personally involve himself in the laborers' struggle. He had little in common with the laborer. DuBois pointed out that Johnson, except for isolated incidents, never had any personal contact with the urban laborer.[49] Johnson abhorred a working class philosophy. So middle class was his orientation that in a later book on the alternatives facing the Negro, he had to be urged even to mention Communism.[50] As an artist and an intellectual, a psychological approach to prejudice appealed to him more than did an economic one.

Another evidence of the difficulties of Johnson's and the NAACP's pragmatic and necessarily long-range approach was the rise of Garveyism in the 1920's. Garvey's effect on the unlettered and inexperienced Negro urban element was magnetic; by 1923 Garvey could legitimately claim at least a half million supporters.[51] Johnson could not help but admire Garvey, who had awakened Negroes in a way that he himself could never do. But he had no sympathy for "Back to Africa." Garveyism was to him the "Apotheosis of the Ridiculous."[52] He felt no great bond with Africa. Although he felt some cultural unity with the African people,[53] he took little interest in plans that included Negroes of the world, such as DuBois's Pan-African Congress.

More than that, he loved America. He felt little of the despair or the bitterness of a DuBois. He tended to generalize from his own life. Wasn't he himself an example of the distance a Negro could go? Whatever his frustrations had been, he was very much at home in a white culture. DuBois even criticized him for too often asking advice from whites.[54] He was not only an American Negro, who, as C. Vann Woodward has pointed out, is possessed of a realism bred into his bones and marrow,[55] but he was an American Negro for whom that realism was not an unpleasant one.

Johnson was somewhat more successful in other areas. One of the Association's major efforts in the years 1921-24 was to pass the Dyer Anti-Lynching Bill. Johnson spent much of those years lobbying in the halls of Congress. The bill passed the House in 1922, but succumbed to the Senate in 1924. Although an anti-lynching bill was not passed until 1937, the effort had aroused substantial enthusiasm among American Negroes. Johnson also made an investigation of the brutality of the U. S. Marines and of U. S. imperialism on the island of Haiti. He wrote an

expose[56] and told the story personally to Warren Harding who later made the problem a campaign issue although he did nothing once elected.

But by far Johhnson's most important contribution as Executive Secretary was in building the NAACP. Here, the qualities which left him helpless in the face of Garveyism served him well. When he began, in 1920, the organization had few funds, faltering leadership, and an insecure reputation. Under his leadership all this changed. He was a masterful fund raiser. From a state of near bankruptcy in 1920 the NAACP was by 1930 a financially stable organization. Johnson's distinguished style and personality were, according to Arthur Spingarn, the Association's greatest selling point.[57]

Johnson also brought to the NAACP courageous leadership; during his tenure the leadership moved from the Board of Directors to the Executive Secretary.[58] The ideology of the Association did not change under him. The objectives remained full political, economic, and social equality. The methods remained lobbying, propaganda, and legal reform. Johnson's contribution was to maintain and implement these principles in a period when the Association could have been destroyed by timidity.

Furthermore, Johnson was the crucial force in maintaining the harmony and integrity of the Association. His mere presence was a cohesive force. Mary White Ovington ascribed to Johnson the quality of "sweet reasonableness." "Given authority," she said, "he knew when and when not to use it."[59] Johnson and DuBois, for example, worked well together. "They got along," said Carl Van Vechten, "because Johnson got along with DuBois."[60] No other act demonstrated his "sweet reasonableness" more than did his resignation. In 1930 he took a year's leave of absence because of ill health. During his absence he delegated most of his responsibility to Walter White. When Johnson returned he found that White had become accustomed to the job and would be unhappy to give it up. The job was still Johnson's, but he had no desire for a power struggle within the Association.[61] Johnson, the reasonable man, stepped down.

VII.

Johnson lived seven more years in which he taught and continued to write. The poetry he had written during his years with the NAACP was the finest he had ever done and among the best Negro poetry that had been written. He had found a new form, the idiom, which could express themes and emotions peculiar to the Negro but which, unlike the dialect, was pure and truthful and did not smack of the minstrel stage.[62] He had arrived at this form by studying the traditional Negro folk sermons, and in it he wrote such poems as **"The Creation," "Go Down Death"** and **"Let My People Go."**[63] There were also several books including an autobiography. In 1938 he was killed in an automobile accident in Great Barrington, Massachusetts.

Johnson had started out to build a life of his own and be an asset to his race. Circumstances limited the life of his own; all had to go to the race. As a race leader there were also limitations. DuBois called Negro leadership in the 1920's both a great success and a colossal failure. But whatever ideological or tactical criticisms one might make of Johnson and others, the most imposing fact about the period is that a foundation was created for the road ahead.

Notes

[1] C. Vann Woodward, *The Strange Career of Jim Crow* (New York, 1955), p. 102.

[2] For some of the biographical information about Johnson's early years this paper relies on his autobiography, *Along This Way* (New York, 1933).

[3] Thomas Davis, *History of Jacksonville, Florida and Vicinity* (Jacksonville, 1925), p. 488.

[4] Willard Range, *The Rise and Progress of Negro Colleges in Georgia, 1865-1949* (Athens, Ga., 1951), p. 21. 90% of Atlanta graduates became teachers. See. *Atlanta University Catalogue,* 1877-78 (Atlanta), p. 7.

[5] See, e.g., Johnson's class oration at Atlanta in 1892 (James Weldon Johnson Collection, Yale University, New Haven, Conn.).

[6] Johnson to Florida *Times Union,* December 21, 1897 (James Weldon Johnson Collection).

[7] See Johnson's editorial, "The Harlem Public Library," *New York Age,* Nov. 5, 1914 (James Weldon Johnson Collection).

[8] *Daily American,* probably May, 1895 (James Weldon Johnson Collection). There are no known extant copies of the *American* and all references are to clippings in the Johnson Collection.

[9] Johnson tried, for example, to persuade the Negroes of Jacksonville to enter a display in the Jacksonville Exposition of 1895. *Daily American,* probably June, 1895 (James Weldon Johnson Collection).

[10] Johnson, *Along This Way,* pp. 139-40.

[11] Paul Buck, *The Road to Reunion 1865-1900* (New York, 1959), pp. 300-01.

[12] See Gunnar Mydal, *An American Dilemma* (New York, 1944), p. 326.

[13] John Hope Franklin, *From Slavery to Freedom* (New York, 1947), p. 405.

[14] Oswald G. Villard, "Issues and Men," *The Nation,* OXLVII (July, 9, 1938), p. 44.

[15] Eugenia Collier, "James Weldon Johnson: Mirror of Change," *Phylon,* XXI (Winter, 1960), 351.

[16] Johnson, *Along This Way,* pp. 158-59.

[17] In Robert Eleazer, *Singers in the Dawn* (Atlanta, 1934), p. 22.

[18] In James Weldon Johnson, *Saint Peter Relates an Incident: Selected Poems* (New York, 1935), p. 73.

[19] Collier, "James Weldon Johnson: Mirror of Change," *loc. cit.,* pp. 352-53.

[20] Sterling Brown, *Negro Poetry and Drama* (Washington, D. C., 1937). Johnson's pop music is also of relatively high quality; see, e.g., "Mandy," "The Maiden with the Dreamy Eyes," "The Congo Love Song" (James Weldon Johnson Collection).

[21] Franklin, *From Slavery to Freedom,* p. 427.

[22] The poems mentioned in this paragraph and others are collected in James Weldon Johnson, *Fifty Years and Other Poems* (Boston, 1917).

[23] New York, 1912.

[24] Sterling Brown, *The Negro in American Fiction* (Washington, D. C., 1937), p. 105.

[25] Johnson, *The Autobiography of an Ex-Coloured Man,* p. 113.

[26] Interview with Carl Van Vechten, Feb. 11, 1960.

[27] Paul Haworth, *The United States in Our Own Times 1865-1920* (New York, 1920), p. 23.

[28] Johnson, *Along This Way,* pp. 291-93.

[29] Of the lower class Negroes, he wrote, in *The Autobiography of an Ex-Coloured Man,* of their "unkempt appearance, the shambling, slouching gait and loud talk and laughter," p. 56.

[30] The fullest exposition of Johnson's views on Negro strategy is his *Negro Americans, What Now?* (New York, 1934).

[31] See Bolton Smith, "The Negro in Wartime," with a rejoinder by James Weldon Johnson, 1918 (James Weldon Johnson Collection).

[32] *New York Age,* March 3, 1917 (James Weldon Johnson Collection).

[33] *Ibid.,* Sept. 2, 1915 (James Weldon Johnson Collection).

[34] *Ibid.,* Feb. 6, 1918 (James Weldon Johnson Collection).

[35] Johnson quoted by Walter White, *A Man Called White* (New York, 1948), p. 34.

[36] In Johnson, *Saint Peter Relates An Incident: Selected Poems,* p. 27.

[37] Margaret Just Butcher, *The Negro in American Culture* (New York, 1956), p. 122.

[38] Brown, *Negro Poetry and Drama,* p. 51.

[39] W.E.B. DuBois, *Dusk of Dawn* (New York, 1940), p. 243.

[40] Interview with Arthur Spingarn, March 4, 1961.

[41] *Ibid.*

[42] *Ibid.*

[43] See Emma Thornbrough, "More Light on Booker T. Washington and the *New York Age,*" *Journal of Negro History,* XLIII (Jan., 1958), p. 34-49.

[44] White, *A Man Called White,* p. 34.

[45] NAACP, *Annual Report,* 1919, p. 9.

[46] Franklin, *From Slavery to Freedom,* p. 439.

[47] Interview with Arthur Spingarn.

[48] James Weldon Johnson, *Black Manhattan* (New York, 1930), p. 161.

[49] Interview with W.E.B. DuBois, March 1, 1961.

[50] Interview with Arthur Spingarn.

[51] Franklin, *From Slavery to Freedom,* p. 482.

[52] *New York Age,* Aug. 19, 1922 (James Weldon Johnson Collection).

53 See James Weldon Johnson, *Native African Races and Cultures* (Charlottesville, 1927).

54 Interview with W.E.B. DuBois.

55 C. Vann Woodward, "Comment," *Studies on the Left*, VI (Nov.-Dec., 1966), 42.

56 James Weldon Johnson, "Self Determining Haiti," *The Nation*, CXI (Sept. 4-Sept. 25, 1920), 2878.

57 Interview with Arthur Spingarn.

58 *Ibid.*

59 Mary White Ovington, *The Walls Came Tumbling Down* (New York, 1947), p. 177.

60 Interview with Carl Van Vechten.

61 Interview with W.E.B. DuBois.

62 Brown, *Negro Poetry and Drama*, p. 68.

63 These poems and others are collected in James Weldon Johnson, *Gods Trombones* (New York, 1927).

Richard A. Long (essay date 1971)

SOURCE: "A Weapon of My Song: The Poetry of James Weldon Johnson," in *Phylon*, Vol. 32, No. 4, Winter, 1971, pp. 374-82.

[*In the following essay, Long surveys Johnson's poetic works, assessing his evolving notion of "the function of the poet."*]

The verse output of James Weldon Johnson falls into four groups: lyrics in standard English, poems in the dialect tradition, folk-inspired free verse, and a long satirical poem. The first two groups are contemporary and were published in the volume *Fifty Years and Other Poems* (Boston, 1917). The prayer and seven Negro sermons of the third group constitute *God's Trombones* (New York, 1927). The last group is represented by the poem "**St. Peter Relates An Incident of the Resurrection Day**," privately printed in 1930, and republished with a selection of earlier poems in 1935.

The early poetry of Johnson belongs to the late nineteenth century tradition of sentimental poetry in so far as its techniques and verse forms are concerned, seldom rising above the mediocrity characteristic of American poetry in the period 1890-1910, during which it was written for the most part. In purpose, however, Johnson's early verse was a species of propaganda, designed sometimes overtly, sometimes obliquely, to advance to a reading public the merits and the grievances of blacks. In this sense the poetry of Johnson is an integral part of a coherent strain in the poetry of Afro-Americans beginning with Phillis Wheatley:

> Remember, Christians, Negroes, black as Cain,
> May be refined, and join th' angelic train.

> (Phillis Wheatley, "On Being Brought from Africa
>   to America")

More particularly, we may note the relationship of Johnson's early poetry to that of Paul Lawrence Dunbar, his much admired friend and contemporary. Though they were about the same age, Dunbar was by far the more precocious, and his virtuosity had an obvious impact on Johnson, though little of Dunbar's verse bears any obvious burden of racial protest, in spite of the real personal suffering Dunbar underwent because of misunderstanding and neglect that he ascribed to his color.

Another factor of importance in the early verse of Johnson is his composition of verses to be set to music by his brother J. Rosamond Johnson; the search for euphony and piquancy and the use of devices such as internal rhyme betrays the hand of the librettist.

The division of Johnson's poetry into standard lyrics and dialect verse, as in the case of Dunbar's poetry, reflects a self-conscious distinction made by the author himself. Johnson's first collection of his poetry, which appeared eleven years after Dunbar's death, presents forty-eight standard poems, followed by a segregated group of sixteen "Jingles and Croons." The dialect poems reflect of course a literary tradition of their own since in point of fact the themes and forms of such dialect poetry as was written by Dunbar and Johnson and many others reflect no tradition of the folk who used "dialect." In point of fact, it is useful to remember that the dialect poets learned mainly from their predecessors and employ for the most part uniform grammatical and orthographic conventions which suggest that they did not consciously seek to represent any individual or regional dialect. Johnson himself gives a brief account of the dialect literary tradition in his introductions to Dunbar and other dialect poets in *The Book of American Negro Poetry* (New York, 1931).

One of Johnson's dialect poems, because of its popular musical setting, is widely known and thought by many to be a genuine folk-product. The low-key sentimentality of "**Sence You Went Away**" is nevertheless that of the stage and not of real life. The last stanza will illustrate the point:

> Seems lak to me I jes can't he'p but sigh,
> Seems lak to me ma th'oat keeps gittin' dry,
> Seems lak to me a tear stays in ma eye,
>   Sence you went away.

The other dialect poems in Johnson's first collection which should be classified among the "croons" are "**My Lady's Lips Are Like De Honey**," "**Nobody's Lookin' But de Owl and de Moon**," "**You's Sweet to Yo' Mammy Jes de Same**," "**A Banjo Song**." The titles are sufficiently indicative of their range and content. The "jingles" are frequently in the form of dramatic monologue, and while they (partly because of their later publication), have never become platform rivals to Dunbar's monologues, "**Tunk (A Lecture on Modern Education)**" and "**The Rivals**" can challenge comparison. The first is an exhortation to a truant schoolboy in which the light duties of white folks in offices are contrasted with the labors of black folks in the fields. The second is an old man's reminiscences of a crucial episode in the courtship of his wife. Both poems are written in long line rhyming couplets, Johnson's preferred verse form for his dialect verse, though a variety of stanza forms and rhyme schemes is employed, some with great versatility as the refrain from **"Brer Rabbit, You's de Cutes' of 'Em All"** illustrates:

> "Brer Wolf am mighty cunnin',
> Brer Fox am mighty sly,
> Brer Terrapin an" Possum—kinder small;
> Brer Lion's mighty vicious,
> Brer B'ar he's sorter 'spi'cious,
> Brer Rabbit, you's de cutes' of 'em all.'

Of the standard poems of Johnson collected in *Fifty Years*, at least ten are more and less overtly on the race problem and among these are several of Johnson's most important poems. In contrast, the more generalized poems have hardly more than a passing interest except for a group of six poems "Down by the Carib Sea" in which Johnson treats images from his Latin-American experience as a U.S. consul in Venezuela and Nicaragua. Unfortunately, even here, conventionality of diction vitiates what might have been a poetic expression of enduring interest and value.

The group of ten race poems includes three of the "appeal" genre in which the black poet addresses his white compatriots and invites an improvement in their attitudes toward the blacks. This genre of Afro-American poetry runs from Phillis Wheatley to Gwendolyn Brooks, and may be said to have been already conventional when Johnson essayed it, though the sincerity with which he takes up the form cannot be doubted. In the short poem **"To America"** he asks:

> How would you have us, as we are?
> Or sinking 'neath the load we bear?
>
> . . . . .
>
> Strong willing sinews in your wings?
> Or tightening chains about your feet?

"O Southland" makes the poet implore

> O Southland, fair Southland!
> Then why do you cling
> To an idle age and a musty page,
> To a dead and useless thing.

And in **"Fragment"** he declares

> See! In your very midst there dwell
> Ten thousand blacks, a wedge
> Forged in the furnaces of hell. . . .

The somewhat stern Calvinistic fervor of this poem suggests that the system is foredoomed to divine malediction.

Another genre in the race poems is that of pointing out the virtuous black and inviting sympathy and understanding. **"The Black Mammy"** and **"The Color Sergeant"** illustrate this genre. The theme of the Black Mammy who has nursed with tenderness the white child who may some day strike down her own black child has its own kind of immortality, combining as it does the mawkishness of mother love with America's quaint racial customs. **"The Color Sergeant"** is based on a real incident in the Spanish-American War and may be said to prefigure the Dorie Miller and similar poems of succeeding wars.

A lynching poem is called **"Brothers"** and is a stilted dramatic exchange between a lynch victim and the mob who burn him alive. The division of objects from the ashes is intended perhaps to recall the casting of lots for Christ's clothes:

> "You take that bone, and you this tooth, the chain—
> Let us divide its links; this skull, of course
> In fair division, to the leader comes."

Still another poem which I classify as a race poem because of its obvious symbolism and because Johnson places it at the end of that group in the arrangement of the poems in *Fifty Years* could be read simply as a poem of ghostly circumstance. **"The White Witch"** describes a beauteous apparition who lures young men to their death. The poem's progenitors are the Romantic literary ballads. It is possible that Johnson had heard of the Jamaican ghost legend of the White Witch of Rose Hall, but there is no obvious patterning of his scenario on the legend.

In two of the race poems Johnson addresses black people specifically. One of these is the famous ode to the dead creators of the spirituals, **"O Black and Unknown Bards."** The harmony and dignity of the poem are fully deserving of the praise it has received. The poet marvels continually:

> There is a wide, wide wonder in it all,
> That from degraded rest and service toil
> The fiery spirit of the seer should call
> These simple children of the sun and soil.

But his conclusion seems timid and apologetic,

> You sang far better than you knew; the songs
> That for your listeners' hungry hearts sufficed
> Still live,—but more than this to you belongs:
> You sang a race from wood and stone to Christ.

The bulk of the poems written by Johnson which fall into the two categories just discussed were written before 1910. The poem which serves as the title poem to his first collection is itself a commemorative poem written in 1912 to mark the fiftieth anniversary of the Emancipation Proclamation. The poem begins with an apostrophe to his fellow blacks:

> O brothers mine, today we stand
> Where half a century sweeps our ken. . . .

He then invokes the scene of the first blacks arriving in Jamestown in 1619. And from these few (aided, as the poet does not note, by the energetic exploitation of the slave trade) have come a race "ten million strong / An upward, onward marching host." He goes on to declare

> This land is ours by right of birth,
> This land is ours by right of toil;
> We helped to turn its virgin earth,
> Our sweat is in its fruitful soil.

He cites the labors of blacks and their frequent defense of the flag. He observes that despite these things blacks are maltreated and persecuted, but he urges

> Courage! Look out, beyond, and see
> The far horizon's beckoning span!
> Faith in your God-known destiny!
> We are a part of some great plan.

And the poem closes with expression of faith in God's intentions for the best. The poem is in twenty-six octosyllabic quatrains, rhyming a ba a b, in *Fifty Years and Other Poems*. Johnson abridged it to twenty stanzas for its appearance in *The Book of American Negro Poetry*. In the 1935 collection it appears as a poem of twenty-four stanzas, with a prefatory note.

One poem, related in tone and character to "Fifty Years," written in 1900, was not included in *Fifty Years and Other Poems*, but was included in the 1935 collection. This is the famous song lyric "Lift Every Voice and Sing," known far and wide as the "Negro National Anthem." Its heroic language, fully sustained by the harmonies of J. Rosamond Johnson, have played a role in the life of black America that no patriotic song could have fulfilled.

> We have come over a way that with tears has been
>   watered,
> We have come, treading our path through the blood
>   of the slaughtered,
> Out from the gloomy past,
> Till now we stand at last
> Where the white gleam of our bright star is cast.

The second decade of the twentieth century was a period of innovation and change in American poetry. The establishment of *Poetry Magazine,* the Imagist manifesto, the appearance of Frost, Masters, Sandburg, Lindsay and Pound all bespeak the new spirit. The annual anthologies of Magazine verse edited by William Stanley Braithwaite beginning in 1913 which were one of the chief forums of the new spirit despite Braithwaite's own conservatism were surely well-perused by his friend James Weldon Johnson. Accordingly, it is not surprising to find a sudden modification in Johnson's poetic practice develop during this decade, for his poem "The Creation" precedes by almost a decade its publication with companion pieces in *God's Trombones* in 1927. He recounts his immediate inspiration for "The Creation" in the Preface to *God's Trombones*:

> . . . He [a rural black preacher] strode the pulpit up
> and down in what was actually a very rhythmic dance,
> and he brought into play the full gamut of his wonderful

voice. . . . He intoned, he moaned, he pleaded—he blared, he crashed, he thundered. I sat fascinated; and more, I was, perhaps against my will, deeply moved; the emotional effect upon me was irresistible. Before he had finished I took a slip of paper and somewhat surreptitiously jotted down some ideas for the first poem, "The Creation."

"The Creation" was conceived, as it were, in the heat of the moment. Only gradually did Johnson develop the series of poems which constitute the seven sermons and the opening prayer of *God's Trombones*. The principles he employed in writing these poems, based closely on the practice of the folk preacher, are explained in the Preface. He explains why he did not write them in dialect (in the sense of an attempted indication of folk speech):

> First, although the dialect is the exact instrument for
> voicing certain traditional phases of Negro life, it is,
> and perhaps by that very exactness, a quite limited
> instrument. Indeed, it is an instrument with but two
> complete stops, pathos and humor. This limitation is
> not due to any defect of the dialect as dialect, but to
> the mould of convention in which Negro dialect in the
> United States has been set, to the fixing effects of its
> long association with the Negro only as a happy-go-
> lucky or a forlorn figure. . . .

> The second part of my reason for not writing these
> poems in dialect is the weightier. The old-time Negro
> preachers, though they actually used dialect in their
> ordinary intercourse, stepped out from its narrow
> confines when they preached. They were all saturated
> with the sublime phraseology of the Hebrew prophets
> and steeped in the idioms of King James English, so
> when they preached and warmed to their work they
> spoke another language, a language far removed from
> traditional Negro dialect. It was really a fusion of
> Negro idioms with Bible English; and in this there may
> have been, after all, some kinship with the innate
> grandiloquence of their old African tongues. To place
> in the mouths of the talented old-time Negro preachers
> a language that is a literary imitation of Mississippi
> cotton-field dialect is sheer burlesque.

Johnson says in the Preface that "the old-time Negro preacher is rapidly passing." Nothing could have been further from the truth. "Old-time" Negro preaching is not only fully present in 1971 in large churches as well as in store-front meeting rooms, but its eloquence has dominated political forums and civil rights meetings, sometimes to the exclusion of action. This eloquence underlies much of the prose of Ellison and Baldwin as well as that of many writers of the sixties.

The medium Johnson chose for the sermon poems is a cadenced free verse which very effectively reflects the rhythmical speech of the folk preacher. Johnson uses the dash to indicate "a certain sort of pause that is marked by a quick intaking and an audible expulsion of the breath. . . ." The arrangement of prayer and sermons in *God's Trombones* is

> Listen, Lord—A Prayer
> The Creation

The Prodigal Son
Go Down Death—A Funeral Sermon
Noah Built the Ark
The Crucifixion
Let My People Go
The Judgment Day.

"Listen, Lord," "The Creation," "Go Down Death," and "The Crucifixion" are generally of a more exalted interest than the other pieces, but all of them capture effectively the imagery, the intensity, the sly humor, and the hypnotic grandeur of the black sermon tradition. In "Listen, Lord" the blessing of God is invoked on the preacher in these terms

Put his eye to the telescope of eternity,
And let him look upon the paper walls of time.
Lord, turpentine his imagination,
Put perpetual motion in his arms,
Fill him full of the dynamite of thy power,
Anoint him all over with the oil of thy salvation,
And set his tongue on fire.

The actual events of awful moments are iterated in "The Crucifixion":

Jesus, my lamb-like Jesus,
Shivering as the nails go through his feet.
Jesus, my darling Jesus,
Groaning as the Roman spear plunged in his side;
Jesus, my darling Jesus,
Groaning as the blood came spurting from his
 wound.
Oh, look how they done my Jesus.

In "Noah Built the Ark" Satan is depicted with familiarity:

Then pretty soon along came Satan.
Old Satan came like a snake in the grass
To try out his tricks on the woman.
I imagine I can see Old Satan now
A-sidling up to the woman.
I imagine the first word Satan said was:
Eve, you're surely good looking.

After the story of the exodus is told in "Let My People Go" the preacher concludes with a magnificent coda:

Listen!—Listen!
All you sons of Pharaoh.
Who do you think can hold God's people
When the Lord God himself has said,
Let my people go?

The general technique developed by Johnson for *God's Trombones* constitutes a giant leap from his archaizing early poetry. Unfortunately the many pressures of his life as a public man and as a cultural mentor prevented him from utilizing his new freedom in a substantial body of work, though the continuing popularity of *God's Trombones* since its initial publication and its appeal to a broad stratum of readers have given this slim volume an impor-

tance in American poetry enjoyed by few other works of comparable scope.

A special irony of Johnson's creations is that they have often themselves reentered the folk stream they were intended to fix and commemorate, and have in turn sustained through countless recitations the continuation of a living tradition.

While Johnson expressed no overt ideological objectives concerning his verse sermons, it is significant that they were not offered either in the spirit of his early standard verse or of his "jingles and croons." The sermons are an assertion of black pride and black dignity with no reference to perspectives and standards of others.

A further direction in his poetic practice was revealed by Johnson in the long satirical poem "St. Peter Relates an Incident of the Resurrection Day." Johnson describes the genesis of the poem in the third person in his 1935 foreword:

. . . The title poem of this volume was originally printed in 1930, in an edition of 200 copies for private distribution. In the summer of that year the author was busy on the manuscript of a book. He read one morning in the newspaper that the United States government was sending a contingent of gold-star mothers to France to visit the graves of their soldier sons buried there; and that the Negro gold-star mothers would not be allowed to sail on the same ship with the white gold-star mothers, but would be sent over on a second and second-class vessel. He threw aside the manuscript on which he was working and did not take it up again until he had finished the poem, "Saint Peter Relates an Incident of the Resurrection Day."

The poem, arranged in six sections of varying length, presents St. Peter, long after Resurrection Day, recounting to some of the heavenly host the unburying of the Unknown Soldier. The discovery that the man who had been honored by generations of Americans in his magnificent tomb was black is the O'Henryesque reversal in the poem. The limpidity of Johnson's handling of the theme in quatrains of rhyming couplets, a favorite meter for narration and monologue with him in his earlier verse, is illustrated by his description of the reaction to the Klan's suggestion that the soldier be reburied:

The scheme involved within the Klan's suggestion
Gave rise to a rather nice metaphysical question: Could he be forced again through death's dark portal, Since now his body and soul were both immortal?

The publication of "St. Peter Relates an Incident of the Resurrection Day" in 1935 provided the occasion for Johnson to issue a new selection of his poems. Thirty-seven poems, including eight in dialect, from *Fifty Years and Other Poems* were reprinted, as well as "Lift Every Voice and Sing." Four additional poems were a sonnet "My City," a celebration of Manhattan, and "If I were Paris," a lyric of twelve lines, both in his earlier manner; a free-verse poem "A Poet to His Baby Son" written in a later colloquial manner; and a translation from the Cuban poet Placido, **"Mother, Farewell!"** a sonnet which Johnson had published in the 1922 edition of *The Book of American Negro Poetry* and again in the 1931 revised edition. *Fifty Years and Other Poems* had included the translation of another poem of Placido.

An untitled envoy, the last poem in *Fifty Years and Other Poems,* contains the following lines, central to its thought:

> . . . if injustice, brutishness and wrong
> Should make a blasting trumpet of my song;
> O God, give beauty and strength—truth to my
>   words. . . .

Eighteen years later a revised and now titled **"Envoy"** closes the second and final selection of Johnson poems:

> . . . if injustice, brutishness, and wrong
> Stir me to make a weapon of my song;
> O God, give beauty, truth, strength to my words.

In this revision two important points are presented in capsule. Johnson continued to revise and modify his poems, a fact which should be taken account of in any future study devoted primarily to the texts. The second point is that Johnson's conception of the function of the poet, the black poet particularly, had evolved from the apologetic tradition, in which racial justice is implored and in which an attempt to show the worthiness of blacks is made by showing their conformism, to a militant posture, in which the poet uses his talent as a weapon with concern only for beauty, truth and strength. In both phases, Johnson was a poet who recognized the propriety of propaganda. His earlier concern was with influencing opinion ("a blasting trumpet"); his later concern was asserting the verities, with a willingness "to make a weapon of my song."

Jean Wagner (essay date 1973)

SOURCE: "James Weldon Johnson," in *Black Poets of the United States: From Paul Laurence Dunbar to Langston Hughes,* University of Illinois Press, 1973, pp. 351-84.

[*In the following excerpt, Wagner explores the conventionality of Johnson's early verse and describes the poet's ambivalence toward agnosticism and dialect poetry.*]

Religious and Patriotic Conformism

Since the avowal made in his autobiography five years before his death, we know that all Johnson's religious poetry came from the pen of an unbeliever.[29]

Under the influence of his maternal grandmother, who would have liked to see him become a minister, from the age of nine he had been forced into religious observances, inappropriate for a child, in the Methodist church which she attended. When she wanted him to be accepted as a full-fledged member, an argument broke out between her and her son-in-law; this aroused anxiety in the child. With it was blended his dislike for certain external religious practices common in the popular Negro churches:

> These combined factors at length produced reluctance, doubt, rebellion. I began to ask myself questions that frightened me. I groped within the narrow boundaries of my own knowledge and experience and between the covers of the Bible for answers, because I did not know to whom I could turn . . . I was alone with my questionings and doubts. . . . At fourteen I was skeptical. By the time I reached my Freshman year at Atlanta University I had avowed myself an agnostic.[30]

His openly proclaimed agnosticism led to some friction in Atlanta University, "a missionary-founded school, in which playing a game of cards and smoking a cigarette were grave offenses."[31] This experience, in which his frankness was poorly rewarded, may have given rise to the reserve with which he would henceforth surround his metaphysical convictions. Not only did he reveal nothing of his agnosticism in his poetry; quite the contrary, he strewed left and right declarations of trust in God the Creator and in Providence, as though he were speaking on his own account.

One sole feeble echo of his doubts regarding life after death can be heard in the last two lines of the sonnet **"Sleep"**:

> Man, why should thought of death cause thee to
>   weep,
> Since death be but an endless, dreamless sleep?[32]

But this is slight, compared to the numerous passages that could convince one of his religious orthodoxy.

Since he did not believe in God, why did he turn to him in prayer? Thus the envoi at the end of the 1917 collection begs the Almighty for inspiration and persuasive force:

> O God, give beauty and strength—truth to my
>   words,[33]

and if that other personal request, **"Prayer at Sunrise,"** does not expressly invoke the Deity, there can be no doubt that Johnson is thinking of him when he addresses the "greater Maker of this Thy great sun."[34] How could anyone guess he was an agnostic, hearing him proclaim:

> . . . God's above, and God is love[35]

or again, when he offers this assurance to Horace Bumstead, president of Atlanta University:

> . . . sure as God on His eternal throne
> Sits, mindful of the sinful deeds of men,
> —The awful Sword of Justice in His hand,—
> You shall not, no, you shall not, fight alone.[36]

While maintaining that the universe had no purpose, in **"Fifty Years"** he nevertheless twice utters the conviction that the Negro's destiny is a part of God's great design:

A part of His unknown design,
We've lived within a mighty age;[37]

. . . . .

Faith in your God-known destiny!
We are a part of some great plan.[38]

And in the celebrated poem **"O Black and Unknown Bards,"** the principal merit he discerns in these bards who composed the spirituals is to have converted a race of idolators to Christ:

> . . . the songs
> That for your listeners' hungry hearts sufficed
> Still live,—but more than this to you belongs:
> You sang a race from wood and stone to Christ.[39]

Faced with such categorical declarations, one might feel tempted to conjecture that Johnson's agnosticism sometimes grew faint along the path, and that there were periods in his life when traditional religiosity gained the upper hand. But nothing authorizes such a supposition,[40] and if we may trust his belated avowal in *Along This Way* (1933), his agnosticism remained unwavering to the very end.

> I have not felt the need of religion in the commonplace sense of the term. I have derived spiritual values in life from other sources than worship or prayer. . . .

> As far as I am able to peer into the inscrutable, I do not see that there is any evidence to refute those scientists and philosophers who hold that the universe is purposeless; that man, instead of being the special care of a Divine Providence, is a dependent upon fortuity and his own wits for survival in the midst of blind and insensate forces.[41]

Thus Johnson's religious poetry does not express his personal feelings; it merely conforms—in a way whose precise meaning is, in our view, most clearly apparent in certain commemorative poems that are semi-official in nature. The first of these, written in 1900, is **"Lift Every Voice and Sing,"** which Black America spontaneously adopted as a Negro national anthem, and which ends with a fervent prayer to a providential God:

> God of our weary years,
> God of our silent tears,
> Thou who hast brought us thus far on the way;
> Thou who hast by Thy might
> Led us into the light,
> Keep us forever in the path, we pray,
> Lest our feet stray from the places, our God,
>   where we met Thee,
> Lest, our hearts drunk with the wine of the world,
>   we forget Thee;
> Shadowed beneath Thy hand,
> May we forever stand
> True to our God,
> True to our native land.[42]

The last two lines sum up the twin conformity of religion and patriotism that sounds the dominant note in *Fifty Years and Other Poems*. It is as though Johnson realized that, in a country where the inalienable rights of all men are officially derived from a gift made by their Creator,[43] the Negro could hardly expect to be heard until he had at least formally professed his faith in the existence of this Creator and his loyalty to his country.

God and country are no less closely associated in **"Fifty Years,"** the commemorative poem written for the fiftieth anniversary of Emancipation and published by the *New York Times* on that very date: January 1, 1913. In it the liberation of the slaves is presented as God's handiwork, with Lincoln acting as the instrument of the Divine will:

> . . . God, through Lincoln's ready hand,
> Struck off our bonds and made us men.[44]

On the soil of America, Negroes have undergone a multiple transformation;

> Far, far the way that we have trod,
> From heathen kraals and jungle dens,
> To freedmen, freemen, sons of God,
> Americans and Citizens.[45]

One may note, incidentally, the unflattering expressions used by Johnson in his references to Africa. Negroes had been living there in "heathen kraals" or even in dens like animals, from which God chose to remove them out of sheer mercy:

> Then let us here erect a stone,
> To mark the place, to mark the time;
> A witness to God's *mercies* shown,
> A pledge to hold this day sublime.[46]

The word "mercies" was bound to serve as an unpleasant reminder of that line of Phillis Wheatley's:

> 'Twas mercy brought me from my pagan land[47]

—as Johnson probably realized, for in the 1935 edition he put in its place the word "purpose," and also dropped from the poem the two following stanzas whose humility and submissiveness, both to God and to White America, was absolutely not the right thing, after the swath cut in its stormy passage by the nationalism of the Negro Renaissance:

> And let that stone an altar be,
> Whereon thanksgivings we may lay,
> Where we, in deep humility,
> For faith and strength renewed may pray.

> With open hearts ask from above
> New zeal, new courage and new pow'rs,
> That we may grow more worthy of
> This country and this land of ours.[48]

As was true of Dunbar, nothing in Johnson evokes rebellion or rebels. The heroes of whom he sings are all loyal, faithful national heroes, and not racial heroes. Most of them, too, are whites: the abolitionists Garrison, Phillips, and Lovejoy; John Brown, of course, and Lincoln the Emancipator.[49] He praises only two blacks: Crispus Attucks,[50] the first to fall in the struggle for the country's independence, and the humble standard-bearer who, though despised by all, loyally gave his life for his country at the battle of San Juan Hill:

> Black though his skin, yet his heart as true
> As the steel of his blood-stained saber.
>
> . . . . .
>
> Despised of men for his humble race,
> Yet true, in death, to his duty.[51]

His attitude toward the South is almost more submissive and sentimental than [Paul Laurence] Dunbar's. **"O Southland!"**[52] is the humble appeal of a weakling who asks for charity, and one would seek in vain for even the most muted protest against the abominations to which, as Johnson well knew, Negroes were being subjected in his own country.

Must we then brand Johnson a hypocrite?[53] His parade of religious orthodoxy is a paradoxical phenomenon, it must be confessed. Even Dunbar, though he seems to have been less grievously afflicted by doubt than Johnson, had bravely confided to his verses moving accounts of his problems with religious belief. But Johnson does not reveal himself, and speaks rather in the name of the racial or national community without allowing his own emotions to pour out. As for the avowal of his agnosticism, that will be judged opportune only in his declining years.

His behavior might appear to be dictated, in the first place, by a certain discretion, by the desire not to shock majority opinion and to respect its convictions. In any event, the following passage from his autobiography, in which he speaks of his lack of religion, would tend to convey that impression: "But I make no boast of it; understanding, as I do, how essential religion is to many, many people."[54]

Nevertheless, without making any display of his unbelief, he might have avoided affirming the antithesis of his real convictions and maintained a discreet neutrality. The miming of strong religious feeling was not called for.

Thus the thought arises that he conformed, to a very large degree, for reasons of diplomacy. Like humor in the dialect poems, the facade of religious orthodoxy fulfills the function of dissimulation and self-defense. In either case, the individual hides his real feelings behind ramparts constructed *ad hoc,* and the outer world, whose hostility must be appeased, is allowed to see only a mask which, in every respect, corresponds to the mythical portrait that prejudice has put together. Since, in the eyes of the majority, the Negro is deemed especially religious, it is better to acquiesce and to put on the externals of religion, if necessary, rather than offend the majority by showing oneself

as one is. This is a kind of moral camouflage, or mimicry. As we have already stated, it is in order to strengthen the Negro's claim to equal treatment that Johnson presents him as absolutely identical with the national ideal, which treats as indivisible belief in God and loyalty to one's country.

But Johnson's conformist behavior looks not only to the opinions of the white majority. In the tradition of his own race, too, the themes of religious orthodoxy have always been so closely intertwined with those of race that to separate them is almost unthinkable. Thus the religious themes survive and assert their authority, even after genuine religious feeling has practically evaporated. Involved here is a transfer of values, causing the religious theme to lose its sacral substance and to stand only for one racial theme among many others. The transfer seems to have occurred all the more easily because sacred and profane had been almost indistinguishable in the overall concept of Negro religion. This was true for both the ambivalent language of the spirituals and for the ambivalent figure of the Negro pastor, who was a racial as well as a spiritual leader.

Thus the poet, through the totality of signs constituted by the religious context of his poetry, no longer proclaims his adhesion to a metaphysical notion he had set aside long before. He announces his decision to remain one with a community that is at the same time national and racial.[55] How this finds expression is determined, ultimately, by social constraints no less powerful than those Dunbar had known. As a consequence, the bulk of Johnson's 1917 volume of poems, constructed around a conventional outlook, appears to us sadly lacking in that "spontaneous overflow of powerful feelings" which, according to Wordsworth,[56] is the distinctive mark of all good poetry.

Johnson and the New Spirit

If Johnson's lack of lyric upsurge and spontaneity leaves most of the poems in *Fifty Years and Other Poems* lagging behind Dunbar's work, an exception must nevertheless be made for a few poems which are characterized by a more mature racial consciousness, a less rudimentary critical sense, and a firmer tone with respect to White America. It is permissible, on the strength of these poems, to see in Johnson an immediate forerunner of the Renaissance.

Yet one must not follow John Hope Franklin[57] and base this assertion on **"Fifty Years,"** in which the poet comes nowhere near the spirit that would imbue the New Negro. It contains fleeting references to Africa that are hardly laudatory, the estimate of the race's progress since reaching American shores seems excessively optimistic, and declarations of humility and loyalty far outweigh protest. This attitude was deliberate, for the poet thought it more appropriate to the celebration of Emancipation's fifty years than were the despairing stanzas that originally had concluded the manuscript poem, and which Johnson suppressed prior to publication.[58] Yet his dignity and moderation do not hinder his roundly denouncing injustice and servitude, with no attempt to minimize them, nor his restating forcefully the black race's right to an equitable share in the national heritage:

> For never let the thought arise
> That we are here on sufferance bare;
> Outcasts, asylumed 'neath these skies,
> And aliens without part or share.
>
> This land is ours by right of birth,
> This land is ours by right of toil;
> We helped to turn its virgin earth,
> Our sweat is in its fruitful soil.[59]

Johnson was not the man to throw down the gauntlet to America. He preferred to appeal to its reason and to persuade it that, since blacks and whites are irrevocably destined to live in association, the welfare of one group can only be maintained through assuring the welfare of the other. **"To America"** tries to convince America that it has the choice of making the black minority an element of strength for the nation or, on the contrary, a brake on its progress:

> How would you have us, as we are?
> Or sinking 'neath the load we bear?
>
> . . . . .
>
> Strong, willing sinews in your wings?
> Or tightening chains about your feet?[60]

But the question arises whether, in the poet's mind, the hour of this choice has not already passed. That, at least, is the conclusion one might derive from **"Fragment,"** which offers a vision of the future hopelessly bogged down in past mistakes. While the country persisted in its prejudices and injustice, Johnson argues, its black population had unnoticeably been transformed for it into a divisive factor, a wedge inserted ever more deeply until the day came when, the split completed, the two halves of the nation rose against each other in bloody conflict:

> See! In your very midst there dwell
> Ten thousand thousand blacks, a wedge
> Forged in the furnaces of hell,
> And sharpened to a cruel edge
> By wrong and by injustice fell,
> And driven by hatred as a sledge.
>
> A wedge so slender at the start—
> Just twenty slaves in shackles bound—
> And yet, which split the land apart
> With shrieks of war and battle sound,
> Which pierced the nation's very heart,
> And still lies cankering in the wound.[61]

The wound in the nation's heart has not been cured thereby, the valor of the combatants has been expended in vain, and Johnson predicts that America's sin against its black minority will continue to weigh upon the future generations until it is at last expiated. . . .

Folklore and Race: Their Rehabilitation

No less paradoxical than the religious feeling he displays in his poetry is the strange attraction felt by Johnson the agnostic for the religious folklore of his race. One of the most remarkable poems in *Fifty Years* already expressed his admiration for the unknown authors of the spirituals, and his amazement that such noble songs could have sprung from the heart of a race so obscure and so despised:

> O black and unknown bards of long ago,
> How came your lips to touch the sacred fire?
> How, in your darkness, did you come to know
> The power and beauty of the minstrel's lyre?
> Who first from midst his bonds lifted his eyes?
> Who first from out the still watch, lone and long,
> Feeling the ancient faith of prophets rise
> Within his dark-kept soul, burst into song?
>
> . . . . .
>
> Not that great German master in his dream
> Of harmonies that thundered amongst the stars
> At the creation, ever heard a theme
> Nobler than "Go down, Moses." Mark its bars,
> How like a mighty trumpet-call they stir
> The blood. Such are the notes that men have sung
> Going to valorous deeds; such tones there were
> That helped make history when Time was young.
>
> There is a wide, wide wonder in it all,
> That from degraded rest and servile toil
> The fiery spirit of the seer should call
> These simple children of the sun and soil.
> O black slave singers, gone, forgot, unfamed,
> You—you alone, of all the long, long line
> Of those who've sung untaught, unknown,
>   unnamed,
> Have stretched out upward, seeking the divine.[78]

Of course, the poet did not share the faith whose expression he admires in the spirituals, and if with evident sincerity he praises their authors for having raised their souls to God, despite their debased condition, this merely proves that he was not narrowly sectarian. But, basically, the religious content of these songs did not interest Johnson except to the extent that it might move the nation's white majority. If he undertook to make the beauty of Negro folklore better known and appreciated, and with this purpose in mind brought out his two collections of spirituals, it was because he expected that the artistic and religious emotions thus awakened in the public would create a favorable climate likely to shake the foundations of the nation's prejudices. Significant in this connection is one passage in the preface to *The Second Book of Negro Spirituals* (1926) where Johnson, speaking of the spirituals, states:

> For more than a half century they have touched and
> stirred the hearts of people and effected a softening
> down of some of the hard edges of prejudice against

the Negro. Measured by lengths of years, they have wrought more in sociology than in art. Indeed, within the past decade and especially within the past two or three years they have been, perhaps, the main force in breaking down the immemorial stereotype that the Negro in America is nothing more than a beggar at the gate of the nation, waiting to be thrown the crumbs of civilization; that he is here only to receive; to be shaped into something new and unquestionably better.

This awakening to the truth that the Negro is an active and important force in American life; that he is a creator as well as a creature; that he has given as well as received . . . is, I think, due more to the present realization of the beauty and value of the Spirituals than to any other one cause.[79]

He had said the same thing about Negro poetry four years earlier, in the preface to his anthology *The Book of American Negro Poetry:*

The final measure of the greatness of all peoples is the amount and standard of the literature and art they have produced. The world does not know that a people is great until that people produces great literature and art. No people that has produced great literature and art has ever been looked upon by the world as distinctly inferior.

The status of the Negro in the United States is more a question of national mental attitude toward the race than of actual conditions. And nothing will do more to change that mental attitude and raise his status than a demonstration of intellectual parity by the Negro through the production of literature and art.[80]

These remarks hold true not only for the spirituals and for written poetry, but also for the sermons in *God's Trombones.*

Just as his two volumes of *Negro Spirituals* were intended primarily to make these songs better known, so it was the main object of *God's Trombones* to reveal the existence of the Negro folk sermon to the wider public. "A good deal has been written on the folk creations of the American Negro: his music, sacred and secular; his plantation tales, and his dances; but that there are folk sermons, as well, is a fact that has passed unnoticed."[81]

This is not the whole truth, however, for even before the earliest collections of slave songs, spirituals, and Negro sermons began to appear in the years following the Civil War, the general public had known of spirituals and Negro sermons, though in strange fashion, through the caricatures and parodies provided by the minstrels on the stage.[82] We have also seen the Negro sermon find its way into popular poetry with Irwin Russell, his example followed by Dunbar and some of his contemporaries. But, like the minstrels, all these poets treated the sermon as funny, with the ill-intentioned stock jokes further underlined by the use of a degraded form of speech baptized "Negro dialect" for the occasion. Thus the Negro sermons in verse of *God's Trombones* cannot properly be classified

as a revelation, but rather as a rehabilitation—in the first place, of the Negro preacher, who here for the first time is no longer presented as a comic figure, and whose historic role in the service of the black people is thus emphasized:

The old-time Negro preacher has not yet been given the niche in which he properly belongs. He has been portrayed only as a semi-comic figure. He had, it is true, his comic aspects, but on the whole he was an important figure, and at bottom a vital factor. It was through him that the people of diverse languages and customs who were brought here from diverse parts of Africa and thrown into slavery were given their first sense of unity and solidarity. He was the first shepherd of this bewildered flock.[83]

But from the rehabilitation of the Negro preacher it was Johnson's intention to proceed to that of the whole race. With that in mind, he at once forbade himself the use of Negro dialect, so that the reader would not be induced to adopt any of the unkind mental attitudes that dialect traditionally served to convey. For this reason it is possible, to some extent, to look on the sermons in *God's Trombones* as pieces of evidence in the indictment that Johnson, after 1917, took it into his head to pursue against Negro dialect. This consideration had such an influence on the composition of *God's Trombones* that we must linger over it for a moment before dealing with the work itself.

The Condemnation of Dialect

Shortly after Johnson had published *Fifty Years and Other Poems* (1917)—a third of which, let it not be forgotten, was made up of poems in Negro dialect similar to Dunbar's—he became this idiom's principal detractor.[84] His new stand seems to have been decided on by 1918, since **"The Creation,"** which dates from this year and which he placed as the first sermon in *God's Trombones*, is not written in dialect. But not until 1922, in the preface to his anthology *The Book of American Negro Poetry*, did he first formulate his reasons for having come to condemn the dialect. He blamed it especially for being "an instrument with but two full stops, humor and pathos,"[85] and asserted "that there are phases of Negro life in the United States which cannot be treated in the dialect either adequately or artistically."[86] In these terms, the problem is obviously very poorly stated, and Johnson, as if aware of this, took it up again on the following page, specifying: "This is no indictment against the dialect as dialect, but against the mold of convention in which Negro dialect in the United States has been set."[87] But if the dialect was to be pronounced innocent the moment it had been accused, why was it brought into the case at all?

The real story behind this about-face may perhaps be found elsewhere. Much had changed since the days when Johnson reveled in his easily won successes on Tin Pan Alley, for now he was on the staff of a New York paper and was secretary general of the N.A.A.C.P, had an "in" with Congress and even the White House, and rubbed shoulders in New York and Washington, not with thespians any longer, but with people in society's loftiest circles. In a word he had become, as McKay put it, "the aristocrat of Negro Americans."[88] By repudiating dialect, Johnson at the same time turned his back on a whole segment of his own past and voiced his desire for a respectability whose usefulness, in his new situation, became more apparent every day.

Yet the dialect was too ready an alibi. If he had sought to be entirely sincere with himself, would he not have had to tell himself that he felt far less guilty for having written in dialect than for having presented his fellow blacks as idlers and thieves?[89] What, other than his own ambition, his eagerness to see his name displayed at the entrance of Broadway's music halls, had locked him into this "conventional mold"? If Dunbar had let himself be pulled in this direction, at least he had the excuse of financial need. But Johnson had never known hunger. He had a college degree, he had become a school principal and a lawyer at the Jacksonville bar, and he had abandoned all that for the vainglory and the royalties offered by the world of song and show business.

These are some personal aspects that must be borne in mind when evaluating Johnson's attitude toward dialect. He himself unintentionally revealed how inauthentic his attitude was, in the preface to the second edition of *The Book of American Negro Poetry,* in a passage that discusses the dialect poetry of Langston Hughes and Sterling Brown: "Several of the poets of the younger group, notably Langston Hughes and Sterling A. Brown, *do* use a dialect; but it is not the dialect of the comic minstrel tradition or of the sentimental plantation tradition; it is the common, racy, living, authentic speech of the Negro in certain phases of real life."[90] The distinction is valid, of course, but why not say outright that what has changed is not so much the dialect as the writers' basic outlook, and that in this lies the whole difference between the minstrel tradition of former days and the Negro poetry of the rising generation? The important thing is not any changes that Langston Hughes or Sterling Brown may have made in spelling the dialect, but the fact that they no longer portray other blacks as ignoramuses, lazybones, and thieves; they no longer present them exclusively as clowns who pass their lives laughing and strumming the banjo, but as human beings confronted by life's many problems—who laugh, of course, but who also weep, struggle, suffer, and die, crushed beneath the weight of injustice and their color. This is what makes good the sin of omission of which the minstrel and plantation traditions were guilty, and which such poets as Dunbar and Johnson, often too lightheartedly, chose to assume. The dialect itself was not evil; instead, it too often was but the innocent vehicle for evil.

Thus Johnson's thesis can scarely be defended. As it turned out, it won him no disciples, and a poet like Sterling Brown briefly but energetically expressed his refusal to participate in any condemnation of dialect.[91]

Notes

[29] The definition of his agnostic attitude will be found in *Along This Way,* pp. 413-14. On his religious experience at home, see *ibid.,* pp. 21-31.

[30] *Ibid.,* p. 30.

[31] *Ibid.*

[32] *Fifty Years,* p. 50.

[33] *Ibid.,* p. 93. In the 1917 edition this poem does not bear the title "Envoy," which is to be found only in *Saint Peter Relates an Incident—Selected Poems by James Weldon Johnson* (1935), p. 103.

[34] "Prayer at Sunrise," *Fifty Years,* p. 51.

[35] "O Southland!" stanza 3, line 7, *ibid.,* p. 9. This passage may be compared with the last line of "Fragment," *ibid.,* p. 18: "God is not love, no, God is law."

[36] "To Horace Bumstead," *ibid.,* p. 10.

[37] "Fifty Years," stanza 5, lines 1-2, *ibid.,* p. 1.

[38] *Ibid.,* stanza 23, lines 3-4, p. 4.

[39] "O Black and Unknown Bards," *ibid.,* p. 8.

[40] Except, perhaps, for this detail: during the summer of 1888, when there was an epidemic of yellow fever in Jacksonville, Johnson was in the employ of a local medical man, Dr. Summers. In the doctor's library he read *Some Mistakes of Moses* and *The Gods and Other Lectures,* but also *The Age of Reason* by Thomas Paine. This recollection, together with that of Ingersoll, may have helped to lend a slight tinge of deism to his agnosticism. But this influence, if indeed it ever existed, must have been minimal. See *Along This Way,* pp. 94ff.

[41] *Ibid.,* p. 413. To round out Johnson's confessions as contained in his autobiography, let us point out the existence of an essay on the foundations of morals, "The Origin of Sin," to the best of our knowledge never published, consisting of a six-sheet typescript preserved in the James Weldon Johnson file of the Negro Collection in Atlanta University. After making the arbitrary declaration that the origin of sin remains one of theology's mysteries, Johnson in this essay reaches the conclusion that the notion of sin was invented by man to enhance the natural pleasure he took in certain acts by adding that of the forbidden fruit. In the course of his argument he deplores the existence of a moral sense which, by bringing man into conflict with himself, is in large part responsible for making him unhappy. In a certain way, too, his moral sense makes man inferior to the animals. Johnson illustrates this point by citing Walt Whitman ("Song of Myself" 32, lines 1-5); but the way in which the problems are tackled awakens the impression that another influence was that of Mark Twain's *The Mysterious Stranger.*

[42] "Lift Every Voice and Sing," *Saint Peter Relates an Incident,* p. 102. Though this poem was written as early as 1900, it is not included in the 1917 collection.

[43] Declaration of Independence, par. 2.

[44] "Fifty Years," stanza 1, lines 2-3, *Fifty Years,* p. 1.

[45] *Ibid.,* stanza 4. In the 1935 edition, the second line has been changed to read: "From slave and pagan denizens." Stanzas 4 and 7 have also changed places.

[46] *Ibid.,* stanza 7 (italics added).

[47] See above, Ch. 1.

[48] "Fifty Years," stanzas 8 and 9, *Fifty Years,* p. 2.

[49] *Ibid.,* stanzas 24 and 25, p. 5.

[50] *Ibid.,* stanza 14, p. 3.

[51] "The Color Sergeant," *ibid.,* p. 11.

[52] *Ibid.*, pp. 8-9.

[53] Johnson's own view was that the prayer meetings held at Atlanta University encouraged students in a hypocritical, conformist attitude: "I doubt not that there were students who enjoyed their prayer meetings and were spiritually benefited, but I believe the main effect was to put a premium on hypocrisy or, almost as bad, to substitute for religion a lazy and stupid conformity" (*Along This Way*, p. 81). For a similar remark on prayer, see *ibid.*, p. 44.

[54] *Ibid.*, p. 413.

[55] An analogous intention should probably be seen behind Johnson's gesture of agreeing, not long before he left for Fisk University, to become a deacon of Saint James Presbyterian Church in Harlem. On other occasions Johnson was a severe critic of the Black Church, which he charged with pretentiousness, corruption, inefficacy in practical matters, and a purely formal morality. On this, see *Negro Americans, What Now?* pp. 20-26.

[56] William Wordsworth, preface to *Lyrical Ballads* (1800 ed.).

[57] John Hope Franklin, *From Slavery to Freedom*, p. 493.

[58] On the writing of this poem, see *Along This Way*, pp. 289-91, where Johnson speaks of fifteen discarded stanzas. In *Fifty Years and Other Poems*, the poem has been cut down from 41 stanzas to 26 stanzas, and in the 1935 edition only 24 will remain.

[59] "Fifty Years," stanzas 10 and 11, *Fifty Years*, p. 2.

[60] "To America," *ibid.*, p. 5.

[61] "Fragment," stanzas 2 and 3, *ibid.*, pp. 17-18.

[78] "O Black and Unknown Bards," stanzas 1, 4, 5, *Fifty Years*, pp. 6-7. The "great German master" of the text is probably Joseph Haydn.

[79] Pp. 18-19.

[80] P. 9 in the 1931 ed.

[81] *God's Trombones*, p. 1.

[82] *The Book of American Negro Spirituals*, pp. 13-14.

[83] *God's Trombones*, p. 2.

[84] For Johnson's attitude to dialect, see *The Book of American Negro Poetry*, pp. 3-5, 40-42; *The Book of American Negro Spirituals*, pp. 42-46; *God's Trombones*, pp. 7-9; *Along This Way*, pp. 159, 336; *Saint Peter Relates an Incident*, pp. 69-70.

[85] *The Book of American Negro Poetry*, p. 41.

[86] *Ibid.*

[87] *Ibid.*, p. 42.

[88] See note 1 above.

[89] See Sec. 2 above, "Dunbar's Disciple: Poetry in Dialect."

[90] *The Book of American Negro Poetry*, p. 4.

[91] Brown, *Negro Poetry and Drama*, p. 77.

Blyden Jackson and Louis D. Rubin, Jr. (essay date 1974)

SOURCE: "The Search for a Language, 1746-1923," in *Black Poetry in America: Two Essays in Historical Interpretation*, Louisiana State University Press, 1974, pp. 1-36.

[*In the following excerpt, Jackson and Rubin recount Johnson's influential creation of a true black voice in American poetry.*]

When James Weldon Johnson, putting together his first book of verse in 1917, entitled the final section "Croons and Jingles," he was making an ironic comment not only upon his own early work but upon the situation of the American poet who was black. For by croons and jingles, Johnson was referring to the modes of poetry in which the black poet was expected to write. He could produce sentimental songs like Johnson's own **"Sence You Went Away"**:

Seems lak to me dat ev'ything is wrong,
Seems lak to me dat day's jes twice es long,
Seems lak to me de bird's forgot his song,
Sence you went away.

Or he could write quaintly comic lyrics like Paul Laurence Dunbar's lines in "When De Co'n Pone's Hot":

Why, de'lectric light o'Heaven
    Seems to settle on de spot,
When yo'mammy says de blessin'
    An'de co'n pone's hot.

He could, in other words, write what in the case of the black writer was indeed a loaded term: local color literature. . . .

As Dunbar's friend James Weldon Johnson reported, "Often he said to me: 'I've got to write dialect poetry; it's the only way I can get them to listen to me.'" In so saying, Dunbar spoke for all his fellow black writers. Anyone who would seek to understand the poetry and prose of black Americans must keep in mind one central truth: that almost every line they wrote, until comparatively recently, was written to be read by an audience not of other blacks, but of white people. . . .

What was . . . to be achieved, . . . was the discovery of a language whereby the black poet could render the particular subtleties and urgencies of black American life. James Weldon Johnson, who was almost two years older than Dunbar, . . . composed his earlier poetry very much in the two modes that Dunbar used: dialect and literary English. Like Dunbar, Johnson felt the inadequacy of stereotyped dialect very keenly, but he also recognized, without yet knowing what to do about it, the limitations of the ornate literary language of genteel poetry as well. A native of Jacksonville, Florida, Johnson was, unlike Dunbar, a highly educated and widely read man. After teaching high school and qualifying for the Florida bar, he collaborated with his brother Rosamond, a talented musician, in writing popular songs and musical comedy lyrics. Johnson's words to such songs as **"Under the Bamboo Tree," "Oh, Didn't He Ramble,"** and **"The Congo Love Song"** are still popular.

Dissatisfied with his poetry, Johnson knew that something was lacking, not only in his poems but in Dunbar's and those of all other black poets as well. (Apparently Johnson did not see the potentialities in the several free verse poems that W. E. B. DuBois was publishing at this time.) Johnson became intrigued with Walt Whitman's *Leaves of Grass:* "I was engulfed and submerged by the book, and set floundering again," he recollected many years later in his brilliant autobiography, *Along This Way.* When Dunbar came to visit Johnson in Jacksonville, he showed him poems he had written after the manner of Whitman. Dunbar "read them through and, looking at me with a queer smile, said, 'I don't like them, and I don't see what you are driving at.'" Taken aback, Johnson got out his copy of *Leaves of Grass* and read him some of the poems he most admired: "There was, at least," he wrote, "some personal consolation in the fact that his verdict was the same on Whitman himself."

Apparently Johnson acquiesced in Dunbar's verdict, for as late as 1917, when he published his own first book of verse, **Fifty Years and Other Poems,** he included in it no work that seems especially akin to the poetry of Walt Whitman. That volume did contain his memorable **"O Black and Unknown Bards,"** however, in which, writing in the formal literary English of the day, he achieved an almost classic precision and simplicity of utterance. There was also skillful dialect poetry. But Johnson was still dissatisfied. As he wrote in his introduction to *The Book of American Negro Poetry,* "Negro dialect poetry had its origin in the minstrel traditions, and a persisting pattern was set. When the individual writer attempted to get away from that pattern, the fixed conventions allowed him only to slip over into a slough of sentimentality. These conventions were not broken for the simple reason that the individual writers wrote chiefly to entertain an outside audience, and in concord with its stereotyped ideas about the Negro."

What was needed was what Johnson discovered while in Kansas City in 1918, when he was engaged in field work for the National Association for the Advancement of Colored People. On a Sunday evening, after having already given four talks to Negro church groups, he heard a famed black evangelist give a sermon:

> He was a dark brown man, handsome in his gigantic proportions. I think the presence of a 'distinguished visitor' on the platform disconcerted him a bit, for he started in to preach a formal sermon from a formal text. He was flat. The audience sat apathetic and dozing. He must have realized that he was neither impressing the 'distinguished visitor' nor giving the congregation what it expected; for, suddenly and without any warning for the transition, he slammed the Bible shut, stepped out from behind the pulpit, and began intoning the rambling Negro sermon that begins with the creation of the world, touches various high spots in the trials and tribulations of the Hebrew children, and ends with the Judgment Day. There was an instantaneous change in the preacher and in the congregation. He was free, at ease, and the complete master of himself and his hearers. The congregation responded to him as a willow to the winds. He strode the pulpit up and down, and brought into play the full gamut of a voice that excited my envy. He intoned, he moaned, he pleaded—he blared, he crashed, he thundered. A woman sprang to her feet, uttered a piercing scream, threw her handbag to the pulpit, striking the preacher full in the chest, whirled round several times, and fainted. The congregation reached a state of ecstasy. I was fascinated by this exhibition; moreover, something primordial in me was stirred. Before the preacher finished, I took a slip of paper from my pocket and somewhat surreptitiously jotted down some ideas for my . . . poem.

Johnson saw now that he had been looking in the wrong place for his idiom. The place to find the diction and pattern of imagery and idiom for a poetry that could embody the experience of black Americans was not in the convention of dialect poetry, for that was not black experience, but a caricature of it written to fulfill the expectations of a white audience. Neither was the literary English of the poetry of idealism a suitable vehicle; its demands, expectations, and vocabulary were alien to the racial idiom. The model must instead be the folk tradition of black America itself, with its own cadences and metaphors. As he declared a few years afterward in his introduction to *The Book of American Negro Poetry:* "What the colored poet in the United States needs to do is something like what Synge did for the Irish; he needs to find a form that will express the racial spirit by symbols from within rather than by symbols from without, such as the mere mutilation of English spelling and pronunciation. He needs a form that is freer and larger than dialect, but which will still hold the racial flavor; a form expressing the imagery, the idioms, the peculiar turns of thought, and the distinctive humor and pathos, too, of the Negro, but which will also be capable of voicing the deepest and highest emotions and aspirations, and allow of the widest range of subjects and the widest scope of treatment."

The poem that Johnson produced as the result of what he discovered that evening in Kansas City was **"The Creation,"** published in *The Freeman* for December 1, 1920, and later the basis for his book of seven black sermons, **God's Trombones** (1927). The first three stanzas authoritatively set the mood and tone:

> And God stepped out on space
> And he looked around and said:
> I'm lonely—
> I'll make me a world.
>
> As far as the eye of God could see
> Darkness covered everything.
> Blacker than a hundred midnights
> Down in a cypress swamp.
>
> Then God smiled,
> And the light broke,
> And the darkness rolled up on one side,
> And the light stood shining on the other,
> And God said: That's good!

In place of the singsong rhymings and the contrived semi-literacy of cotton-field dialect, here was the flowing, pulsating rise and fall of living speech, making its own emphases and intensifications naturally, in terms of the meaning, not as prescribed by an artificial, pre-established pattern of singsong metrics and rhyme. Here indeed was the influence of Walt Whitman, not woodenly imitated but used creatively and freely. Instead of abstract rhetorical platitudes couched in ornate literary English, there was colloquial speech—"I'll make me a world." Colloquial in the true sense, however, because drawn from the actual language of men and women, not the self-conscious cutenesses of dialect. Nor was there any self-imposed limitation on emotion: "Blacker than a hundred midnights / Down in a cypress swamp" was language and metaphor that was at once expansive and natural. The diction, the cadence, the range of feeling permitted a freedom of metaphor and a flexibility of language and imagery that allowed him to express his meaning in a voice that could move from formal intensity to colloquial informality and then back again, without confusion or incongruity:

> And there the great God Almighty
> Who lit the sun and fixed it in the sky,
> Who flung the stars to the most far corner of the
>   night,
> Who rounded the earth in the middle of his hand;
> This Great God,
> Like a mammy bending over her baby,
> Kneeled down in the dust
> Toiling over a lump of clay
> Till he shaped it in his own image . . .

To realize the potentialities and possibilities of the new form that Johnson discovered with **"The Creation,"** one need only compare such a stanza with lines from several of the poems in *Fifty Years and Other Poems.* Here are the opening lines of **"Prayer at Sunrise"**:

> O mighty, powerful, dark-dispelling sun,
> Now thou art risen, and thy day begun.
> How shrink the shrouding mists before thy face.
> As up thou spring'st to thy diurnal race!

The contrived stiffness of diction of this poem, with its ornate literary idiom, its forced imagery and sententious attitudinizing, seems artificial and lifeless by comparison with the far greater force and natural intensity of **"The Creation."** Contrast "Now thou art risen, and thy day begun" with "Who lit the sun and fixed it in the sky"; not only is the metaphor of God lighting the sun as if it were a lantern far more striking than anything in the other line, but the desired sense of power and vastness comes across far more convincingly.

Now compare the lines from **"The Creation"** to these lines of an early dialect poem by Johnson entitled **"A Plantation Bacchanal"**:

> W'en ole Mister Sun gits tiah'd a-hangin'
> High up in de sky;
> W'en der ain't no thunder and light'nin' a-bangin'
> An'de crops done all laid by . . .

The need to make the idea picturesque and quaint by referring to "ole Mister Sun" who "gets tiah'd" robs it of almost all potentiality for dramatic intensity and wonder. The fact that the speaker must express himself in folksy images designed to exhibit his unlettered, primitive status thoroughly dissipates any chance for serious commentary. The best that can be managed with such a speaker is homely philosophizing. By contrast, the language of **"The Creation"** can permit simple and authentic colloquial diction—"the most far corner of the night," "Like a mammy bending over her baby"—while also allowing for great intensity—"Who flung the stars," "Toiling over a lump of clay."

With **"The Creation,"** Johnson had indeed achieved a momentous breakthrough in the search of the black American poet for his proper language. Here at last was a way to deal with the unique particularities of black experience, while at the same time achieving the dignity and intensity of imaginative literary utterance. In his own way, Johnson had pointed the way toward a discovery for the black poet fully as useful as that which the Chicago poets and, more importantly, T. S. Eliot and Ezra Pound were making for American poetry in general: he had found the idiom for writing important poetry about the circumstances of twentieth-century American life.

Though Johnson went on, in the middle and late 1920s, to add six more sermons to **"The Creation"** and complete the book he entitled *God's Trombones,* it cannot be said that he himself chose to follow up and develop the implications of what he had been first to discover. Johnson was never a full-time poet; he wrote verse only intermittently, and by far the greater part of his energies was devoted to his work with the National Association for the Advancement of Colored People. Feeling as he clearly did that his formidable intellect and irrepressible energies could best be utilized in leading the legal and moral fight to ameliorate conditions under which the vast majority of black Americans were forced to live as second-class citizens in a nation in which Jim Crow laws still went almost unchallenged, Johnson had little time for the writing of verse. Save for the six-part poem he entitled **"St. Peter Relates an Incident,"** and a few other shorter poems, he produced no additional poetry. It would be left to other and younger men and women to create the poetry of twentieth-century black America. But it was Johnson, more than any other man, who opened the path, and the achievement that followed was in an important sense possible because of what he first demonstrated. The leading poets who came afterward—Toomer, Hughes, Tolson, Hayden, Brooks, LeRoi Jones—can truly be said to have followed along James Weldon Johnson's way.

Saunders Redding (essay date 1975)

SOURCE: "James Weldon Johnson and the Pastoral Tradition," in *The Mississippi Quarterly,* Vol. XXVIII, No. 4, Fall, 1975, pp. 417-21.

[*In the following essay, Redding investigates Johnson's use of dialect and the "Southern Negro idiom" in his poetry.*]

In a book entitled *Some Versions Of Pastoral,* published in 1935,[1] the English critic and poet William Empson set forth a definition of the pastoral that differed from both the ancient classical and the later Elizabethan concept, both of which comprehended poetry only. Empson's definition more or less ignored the elements of form, of meter, and of subject matter in order to emphasize technique and intent. He conceived of the pastoral as a "device for literary inversion," a method for "putting the complex into the simple," and of expressing, in whatever literary genre, "complex ideas through simple personages" and dramatizing these ideas through the imitation of actuality and the representation of the concrete and the real: "Any work in any genre which sets forth the simple against the complicated, especially to the advantage of the simple, is a pastoral."

If one accepts this definition—and in view of the topic of our discussion one must accept it—it is scarcely to be argued that much if not all of the fiction and a good deal of the poetry of the South is pastoral. Applied to the one novel and practically all of the verses of James Weldon Johnson, this critical proposition should not need to be documented. But unfortunately it does, and for the reason that Johnson's use of Negro dialect has struck some critics as the only defining characteristic of his verse, while other, kindlier critics, hoping to redeem Johnson from the pejorative designation "dialect poet" which so embittered one of his well-known contemporaries, have ignored Johnson's work in dialect and focused upon such pieces as **"Lift Every Voice and Sing," "My City," "Fifty Years," "The Glory of the Day Was On Her Face,"** and the seven Negro sermons in verse in ***God's Trombones.***

In the beginning Johnson did not seem to want to be redeemed. He deliberately set out to write dialect verse, with, as he tells us in his autobiography, "an eye on Broadway." If he judged these pieces to be somewhat trite and trivial, he nevertheless declared himself "fully satisfied" with the recognition they brought him. And he wrote many "coon songs" and pastoral lyrics in dialect, some of which his brother Rosamond set to music for the stage, and some of which he included in a section entitled "Croons and Jingles" in his first volume of poetry, ***Fifty Years and Other Poems,*** published in 1915. In his own estimation the best of these was **"Since You Went Away":**

> Seems lak to me de stars don't shine so bright,
> Seems lak to me de sun done loss his light,
> Seems lak to me der's nothin' goin' right,
>   Sence you went away.

> Seems lak to me de sky ain't half so blue,
> Seems lak to me dat ev'ything wants you,
> Seems lak to me I don't know what to do,
>   Sence you went away.

> Seems lak to me dat ev'ything is wrong,
> Seems lak to me de day's jes twice as long,
> Seems lak to me de bird's forgot his song,
>   Sence you went away.

> Seems lak to me I jes can't he'p but sigh,

> Seems lak to me ma th'oat keeps gittin' dry,
> Seems lak to me a tear stays in my eye,
>   Sence you went away.

But by 1915 he had come to the realization of a vexing problem, and that was the problem of trying to depict Negro life and the Negro character in a language taken to be distinctly expressive of the Negro, but which at the same time communicated the wide range of human experiences and values. Dialect was limited and, as Dunbar had discovered, could not do this. Dialect was expressive of the pastoral component in Southern Negro life, but it had also been employed to reflect the cultural abasement of Negro life in the city; and wherever Negro life was lived, the acceptable mythology represented it as basically simple, irresponsible, mimetic, and, even in moments of pathos, amusing. The mythology was not created by the Negroes themselves. It was created largely, but, considering Washington Irving and J. F. Cooper, not exclusively, by Southern whites, among them J. P. Kennedy, Edgar Allan Poe, William Gilmore Simms, and Thomas Nelson Page; and it had been kept current by a host of lesser writers who, like those already named, used the mythology to justify an amused contempt for the Negro people. In short, the myths projected a life and life styles that encouraged the concept of the Negro as a lower species of the human animal. And this posed a problem for certain black writers which Johnson called "the author's dilemma," and which he defined in terms of the duty of the black writer to appeal to and to promote the receptive disposition of two audiences, one white and the other black. Dialect had been used primarily to appeal to the white audience, and it was not altogether a failure in appealing to the black, which had the heaven-sent capacity for recognizing and finding amusing the limitations dialect suggested. This audience's amusement derived from its knowledge that whites were incapable of perceiving the essence and the spirit which underlay the dialect. It was in-house amusement, coterie humor, nurtured by an ironic perception. But Johnson, who by this time—circa 1910—had passed the point of apprehending literature merely as entertainment, wanted to get at the white audience with the deeper truths of Negro life while avoiding giving direct offense to that audience's preconceptions.

But how was this to be done? His friend and early contemporary, Paul Dunbar, had tried to do it with dialect and to a degree had succeeded, but his approach was on the level of sentimentality, of humor and pathos, and when, pitching his appeal to higher levels of emotional and intellectual perception, he employed standard English to this end, he was rebuffed.

> He sang of life, serenely sweet,
>   With, now and then, a deeper note.
>   From some high peak, nigh yet remote,
> He voiced the world's absorbing beat.

> He sang of love when earth was young,
>   And love, itself, was in his lays.
>   But ah, the world, it turned to praise
> A jingle in a broken tongue.

Johnson, too, had tried as a novelist in *The Autobiography of an Ex-Coloured Man,* his only work of fiction, and he smashed into a stone wall of white indifference and even resistance to the recognition of the Negro as a complicated human being, all of whose problems could not be solved by the emotional and moral equivalent of a stick of peppermint candy. The *Autobiography* was the story of the development of a Negro youth from pastoral simplicity to complex sophistication through his experiences in some of the great cities of the world. Published in 1912, it sold fewer than 500 copies. And when his volume of poetry, *Fifty Years and Other Poems,* was published seven years later, the few white critics who commented on it fixed their attention on the "Croons and Jingles" section and virtually ignored all the rest. Johnson wrote:

> What the colored poet in the United States needs to do is something like what Synge did for the Irish; he needs to find a form that will express the racial spirit by symbols from within rather than by symbols from without, such as the mere mutilation of English spelling and pronunciation. He needs a form that is freer and larger than dialect . . . and which will . . . be capable of voicing the deepest and highest emotions and aspirations [of the Negro] and allow of the widest range of subjects and the widest scope of treatment. Negro dialect is at present a medium that is not capable of giving expression to the varied conditions of Negro life in America, and much less is it capable of giving the fullest interpretation of Negro character and psychology. This is no indictment against the dialect as dialect, but against the mold of convention in which Negro dialect in the United States has been set.[2]

By 1926 Johnson thought he had found what he sought— a form or language that held the racial flavor but which was also capable of "voicing the deepest and highest emotions and aspirations" and allowing for the treatment of Negro life and experience in all of its great variety. He thought he had found it in the Southern Negro idiom, with its syntactical and metaphorical peculiarities. He was laboring under this illusory discovery when he wrote "The Seven Negro Sermons in Verse" already referred to, which do indeed voice deep emotions and high aspirations, but which do not define the character of nor encompass the experience of Negroness in America. In this regard the Negro idiom is nearly as limited as Negro dialect. And the irony is that Johnson the poet's use of the idiom was a contradiction of all that Johnson the social and political being believed and fought to establish practically all of his life: the validity of the concept of the Negro as man, motivated by the same forces and responding to life's circumstances and experiences like any other man. The Negro is not different from other Americans except in the color of his skin, Johnson declared in his book, *Negro Americans, What Now?,* and in another place, "the sooner they write American poetry, the better."

Finally, Johnson both as poet and sociopolitical man would have been appalled by what is happening now in Negro writing and in the mind of the Negro community. The concept and the current use of so-called Black English would have dismayed him, although he was the unwitting godfather of the concept, and although it in great part succeeds in doing what he failed to make dialect and idiom do: it holds the racial spirit by symbols from within; and it is more flexible, versatile and truer than both dialect and idiom. Johnson would have decried it, and the more especially because it is the instrument of communication between Negro and Negro; because it is employed as a kind of thieves' jargon to express the delusory differences of perception and response between Negro and white, and because it is a reflection of the contemporary Negro masses' conscious wish to keep the white man at arm's length and to reject so-called white values.

Johnson was all for promoting the receptive disposition of whites, for promoting understanding between the races; in short, he was for integration. And the present crop of Negro writers and poets—Imamu Baraka, Don Lee, Nikki Giovanni, etc.—are cultural and national separatists. They want no part of Whitey and they say so in a language that Whitey is scornfully challenged to understand. Johnson would have prayed for the day he prayed for all his life, the day when black Americans would write "American" poetry and make their contribution to the whole corpus of American literature.

Notes

[1] (Norfolk, Conn.: New Directions Books).

[2] "Preface," *The Book of American Negro Poetry* (New York: Harcourt, Brace, 1922).

Susan J. Koprince (essay date 1985)

SOURCE: "Femininity and the Harlem Experience: A Note on James Weldon Johnson," in *CLA Journal,* Vol. XXIX, No. 1, September, 1985, pp. 52-56.

[In the following essay, Koprince relates Johnson's presentation of women as temptresses or as saintly mothers in the poems of God's Trombones *to his impression of Harlem in the 1920s.]*

God's Trombones (1927), James Weldon Johnson's collection of folk sermons in verse, has long been celebrated for its innovative language[1]—in particular, for its rhythmic, free-verse lines, which recreate the art of the "old-time Negro preacher."[2] But these poetic sermons can also be examined profitably in terms of the literary characters which occur in them. A study of the women in Johnson's sermons, for example, not only reveals the poet's attitude toward the female sex, but, in a broader sense, helps to explain his enchantment with Harlem during the 1920s— the same Harlem which Johnson evokes so vividly in his cultural treatise *Black Manhattan* (1930).

Several poetic sermons in *God's Trombones* make clear Johnson's view of women as powerful temptresses. The poem **"Noah Built the Ark"** introduces the figure of Eve, the archetypal temptress "With nothing to do the whole day long / But play all around in the garden" (p.32) with her consort, Adam. Although Eve disobeys God out of vanity ("You're surely goodlooking," Satan tells her, offering her a mirror), Adam does so out of uxoriousness and a fatal desire for this beautiful, sensuous woman. "Back there, six thousand years ago," says Johnson, "Man first fell by woman— / Lord, and he's doing the same today" (p. 33).

Johnson describes the temptress even more explicitly in his sermon **"The Prodigal Son."** Here the prodigal son journeys to the great city of Babylon, where he associates with "hot-mouthed" and "sweet-sinning" women (pp. 24-25). Dressed colorfully in yellow, purple, and scarlet, and adorned with bright jewelry, the women are "Perfumed and sweet-smelling like a jasmine flower," and their lips are "like a honeycomb dripping with honey" (p. 24). Much in the manner of Eve, these temptresses usher a man into a world of sin and profligate living, confounding his powers of reason with their sexual allure and bending him completely to their will.

But Johnson also presents a different image of women in *God's Trombones:* that of the saintly mother, the sympathetic and loving comforter. In his sermon **"The Crucifixion,"** for instance, Johnson pictures the Virgin Mary at the scene of her son's death, weeping as she watches "her sweet, baby Jesus on the cruel cross" (p. 42). In **"Go Down Death,"** the poet celebrates the simple human dignity of Sister Caroline, a wife and mother who has "borne the burden and heat of the day" and "labored long in [God's] vineyard" (p. 28). When at last it is Sister Caroline's turn to be comforted, Death takes her in his arms like a baby and then places her "On the loving breast of Jesus" (p. 30). This last image, it should be noted, transfers the maternal role from Sister Caroline to Christ; and the Savior Himself becomes her eternal comforter:

> And Jesus took his own hand and wiped away her
>   tears,
> And he smoothed the furrows from her face,
> And the angels sang a little song,
> And Jesus rocked her in his arms,
> And kept a-saying: Take your rest,
> Take your rest, take your rest.
>
>   (p. 30)

The deification of maternal love is likewise evident in Johnson's well-known poem **"The Creation,"** where the act of divine creation is compared to a scene of maternal devotion, and where God Himself is portrayed as the tender-hearted mother of mankind:

> This Great God,
> Like a mammy bending over her baby,
> Kneeled down in the dust
> Toiling over a lump of clay
> Till he shaped it in his own image;
>
> Then into it he blew the breath of life,
> And man became a living soul.
>
>   (p. 20)

In the poet's view, motherhood is sacred, partly because the earthly mother shelters and nurtures her offspring, but also because, like the Divine Maker Himself, she has the power to create new life.

So important for Johnson is this dichotomy between the sensual and the spiritual, between the whorish and the maternal, that he employs it not only to describe the women of *God's Trombones,* but to depict Harlem of the twenties in his cultural study *Black Manhattan.* Just as Johnson tends to divide women into two extreme types— the sexual temptress and the saintly mother—so does he picture Harlem as a city containing the extremes of sensuality and spirituality. For Johnson, Harlem is at once a voluptuous temptress and a spiritual mother—a force which inspires both amorous passion and creative genius—a city which is seductive and vibrant.

Thus, like the "sweet-sinning" women of Johnson's poems, Harlem is "farthest known as being exotic, colorful, and sensuous."[3] The city is noted not only for its flashy night life, with music, dancing, and laughter, but for its underworld "of pimps and prostitutes, of gamblers and thieves, of illicit love and illicit liquor, of red sins and dark crimes" (p. 169). Just as the prodigal son in Johnson's poem is tempted to "[waste] his substance in riotous living" (p. 24), so may the visitor to Harlem "nose down into lower strata of life" (p. 160). He may become initiated, explains the author, "in all the wisdom of worldliness" (p. 169). This black metropolis entices "the pleasure-seeker, the curious, the adventurous, the enterprising, the ambitious, and the talented of the entire Negro world"; indeed, *"the lure of it,"* says Johnson, "has reached down to every island of the Carib Sea and penetrated even into Africa" (p. 3; italics added).

Yet Harlem of the twenties is also a life-giving force, a kind of spiritual and artistic mother. The city can boast, for example, of an abundance of churches, which serve as a crucial stabilizing force in the community. Like mothers, these churches provide their members with a sense of identity and belonging, offering not only spiritual inspiration, but the feeling of being part of an extended family.[4] Harlem's ability to bring about the "*birth* of new ideas" (p. 231) and "opportunities for the *nurture and development* of talent" (p. 226; italics added) is also a maternal characteristic. As the center of the Negro Renaissance and the repository of a new black culture, Harlem possesses a truly regenerative force. The spiritual (or maternal) side of Harlem comprises more, in other words, than mere religiosity. According to Johnson, Harlem encourages black people to believe in their own potential and to discover for themselves their unique powers and abilities. Like a mother, this black city ultimately builds self-confidence; it gives a new hope and vitality to the individual creative artist.[5]

Although Johnson's image of women in *God's Trombones* can indeed be compared with his image of Harlem in *Black Manhattan,* one distinction should be kept in mind; whereas Johnson divides women into two different roles—temptress and mother—he unites these two roles in the city of Harlem itself. Harlem thus resembles not an individual woman, but womankind, for it expresses all aspects of femininity, from gaiety and sensuous charm to spiritual emotion and creative vigor. Like a temptress, Harlem lures the black man, exhilarates him, and overwhelms him; but like a mother, it also shelters him, inspires him, and gives him his identity. For James Weldon Johnson, Harlem of the twenties was much more, therefore, than a place to which to "jazz through existence" (p. 161); it was the scene of the black people's cultural rebirth—the home of their racial awakening.

Notes

¹ See, for example, Jean Wagner, *Black Poets of the United States,* trans. Kenneth Douglas (Urbana: Univ. of Illinois Press, 1973), pp. 377-84; and Richard A. Long, "A Weapon of My Song: The Poetry of James Weldon Johnson," *Phylon,* 32 (Winter 1971), 374-82.

² James Weldon Johnson, Pref., *God's Trombones: Seven Negro Sermons in Verse* (New York: Viking, 1927), p. 2. Future references are to this edition.

³ James Weldon Johnson, *Black Manhattan* (1930; rpt. New York: Atheneum, 1968), p. 160. Future references are to this edition.

⁴ According to Johnson, a Harlem church is really much more than a place of worship: "It is a social centre, it is a club, it is an arena for the exercise of one's capabilities and powers, a world in which one may achieve self-realization and preferment" (p. 165).

⁵ In his preface to *Black Manhattan* (New York: Atheneum, 1968), Allan H. Spear emphasizes that "Johnson's vision of Harlem was more a dream than a reality." By 1930 the city was already largely transformed from a "community of great promise" to a saddened ghetto.

Robert E. Fleming (essay date 1987)

SOURCE: "The Composition of James Weldon Johnson's 'Fifty Years,'" in *American Poetry,* Vol. 4, No. 2, Winter, 1987, pp. 51-56.

[In the following essay, Fleming suggests that Johnson significantly revised his poem 'Fifty Years' prior to its publication in order to make it more acceptable to white audiences.]

James Weldon Johnson (1871-1938) has frequently been recognized as the sort of black writer and leader who achieved a great deal by working within the American legal and political system. Educated at Atlanta University, Johnson taught in an all-black rural elementary school and in a black high school and college, practiced law in Florida, wrote for black newspapers and magazines, and worked for his race as secretary of the National Association for the Advancement of Colored People. Always a political realist, he campaigned among black voters for the election of Theodore Roosevelt, and after Roosevelt's election he gladly accepted diplomatic appointments as U.S. consul in Venezuela and later in Nicaragua. Through all these careers, Johnson also found time to write prose, poetry, and song lyrics. His first major poem to find a large audience was the occasional poem "Fifty Years," a work that still represents Johnson in many anthologies of Afro-American literature.

"Fifty Years" serves as an example of the side of Johnson to which many modern readers object. Written to commemorate the fiftieth anniversary of the Emancipation Proclamation, "Fifty Years" traces the history of the black race from slavery to freedom, noting its accomplishments in clearing and settling the new nation and in defending its principles from the Revolutionary War on. Implicit in the poem is the idea that the black population should be content to be assimilated into American culture and to wait patiently for full citizenship to be granted. In only three of the twenty-six stanzas of the poem does Johnson suggest that black Americans are still held down by law and custom:

> And yet, my brothers, well I know
>   The tethered feet, the pinioned wings,
> The spirit bowed beneath the blow,
>   The heart grown faint from wounds and stings;
>
> The staggering force of brutish might,
>   That strikes and leaves us stunned and dazed;
> The long, vain waiting through the night
>   To hear some voice for justice raised.
>
> Full well I know the hour when hope
>   Sinks dead, and 'round us everywhere
> Hangs stifling darkness, and we grope
>   With hands uplifted in despair.
>
>   (11, 77-88)¹

More typical of the tone of the poem are lines that stress the gradual nature of the process of assimilation and the necessity for black people to grow into the new roles to which they aspire:

> Far, far the way that we have trod,
>   From heathen kraals and jungle dens,
> To freedmen, freemen, sons of God,
>   Americans and Citizens.
>
>   (11, 13-16)
>
> With open hearts ask from above
>   New zeal, new courage and new pow'rs,
> That we may grow more worthy of
>   This country and this land of ours.
>
>   (11, 33-36)

Especially during the years of the "black is beautiful" movement, such sentiments, like those expressed in Phillis Wheatley's "On Being Brought from Africa to America," seemed to accept a second-class citizenship for the black race and thus alienated the black reader.

Reading the poem as it was published, first in the *New York Times* of 1 January, 1913, and later in Johnson's first collection of poetry, **Fifty Years and Other Poems** (1917), it is hard to disagree with Johnson's biographer Eugene Levy, who says that the poem is "much closer in spirit to *Up from Slavery* than to *The Souls of Black Folk*."² Yet Johnson had to overcome deep feelings of bitterness before he was able to produce a poem full of so much sweet reasonableness. A study of the manuscript drafts of **"Fif-**

ty Years" in the Beinecke Rare Book Room and Manuscript Library, Yale University, shows that Johnson's first efforts to write the poem resulted in a diatribe against racial bigotry and would probably have shocked his white readers and created a mood of despair among his black readers. Four drafts and a number of fragments exist in the collection of autograph manuscripts of "Fifty Years," but the entire first draft of nine stanzas was scrapped by Johnson and never found its way into the published poem because, as Johnson reflected some twenty years later, the omitted portion would have "nullified the theme, purpose, and effect of the poem as a whole."[3]

Nevertheless, an examination of Johnson's first draft helps to clarify not only Johnson's mental attitude, but the state of black morale in the first years of the twentieth century. Johnson wrote "Fifty Years" in the American consulate in Nicaragua, where he was enjoying his reward for his political efforts on behalf of the Republican Party. If he was tempted to despair while assessing the racial progress since the Emancipation, what must have been the attitude of black people who were less fortunate than he?

Draft one begins not at the beginning of the poem as published, but at the end. The first lines that came to Johnson were the stanzas with which he would close the poem, to bring "into view the other side of the shield, and [end] on a note of bitterness and despair."[4] Having planned to recount the history of the fifty years just past, Johnson asks if the strides that have been made will truly lead to the goal the race has been striving for:

But, Oh, my brothers, if the tears
You've shed, the fight that you have fought,
The grueling struggle of the years,—
If none of these should count for ought,

If what you've built in faith and hope,
To make you worthy of this Land,
Is sneered at by the misanthrope,
And struck down by the bigot's hand

. . . . .

If on the ladder you would climb,
They force you downward rung by rung,
Into the quagmire and the slime,
Back down into the dirt and dung,

Then loose your hold, your grip let free,
No longer strain, no longer try,
Slip back where they would have you be
And wallow where you're forced to lie.

(11, 1-8, 13-20)[5]

These lines refer not only to the losses suffered by former slaves following their first successes after the Civil War, but to some particularly disturbing developments shortly before Johnson wrote the poem: Thomas Dixon's *The Leopard's Spots: A Romance of the White Man's Burden, 1865-1900* had appeared in 1902, and was soon followed by Dixon's *The Clansman* (1905). Both books enjoyed

widespread popularity. Johnson saw in the attitudes which Dixon's books epitomized an American tendency to turn away from the former slaves, or as he put it, to "refuse your need of help and love, / And balk each effort made to rise" (11, 11-12).

In an apparent allusion to Paul Laurence Dunbar's famous poem "We Wear the Mask" (1896), Johnson ironically urges his black readers to

Drop off the shamming mask of man,
Go backward, downward, grovelling,
Till you are more than they would plan,
A vile, polluted, dying thing.

(11, 25-28)

At the end of the century, the prevailing strategy of Booker T. Washington, like that of Johnson's alma mater, Atlanta University, was to put on the best possible face for the white race, a strategy which Johnson had personally adopted in making his way through careers in education, law, musical comedy, and politics. Here, however, he found himself suggesting, though rhetorically, that black people deliberately display to whites the negative side of human nature, to show to what depths humanity can fall if it is forced to respond always to the most adverse conditions.

The final lines of Johnson's first draft reveal how this degradation of the black race will affect the rest of the nation.

Then one more struggle—Leap the length
Of one last goal before your eyes,
And with your all remaining strength
Up to your trembling feet arise.

Stretch out your hands, leprous and lean,
One curse, one last despairing cry!
Touch them, and leaving them unclean,
Sink back, and die!

(11, 29-36)

Far from ending in a positive, conciliatory way, "Fifty Years" would have anticipated Claude McKay's lines in "If We Must Die":

What though before us lies the open grave?
Like men we'll face the murderous, cowardly pack,
Pressed to the wall, dying, but fighting back!

(11, 12-14)[6]

But Johnson, even though he needed to purge these bitter feelings from his system, was not ready to abandon his moderate approach. As he later stated in his autobiography, *Along This Way*, "I saw that I had written two poems in one," and his "artistic taste and best judgement" caused him to cut the bitter stanzas from the poem.[7] He set aside the section of the poem that he had excised, intending to use it as the basis for another poem someday, but he never wrote a poem using those exact lines. Their main idea, however, appears in the poem directly following "Fifty Years" in Johnson's first collection. In "To America," first published in *The Crisis* in 1917, Johnson rhetorically asks his country:

> How would you have us, as we are?
> Or sinking 'neath the load we bear?
> Our eyes fixed forward on a star?
> Or gazing empty at despair?
>
> Rising or falling? Men or things?
> With dragging pace or footsteps fleet?
> Strong, willing sinews in your wings?
> Or tightening chains about your feet?[8]

It is a sign of the times in which Johnson lived that even this cool literary spokesman of black America should have been haunted by racism to the extent that he was. Like his contemporary, Paul Laurence Dunbar, Johnson learned to stifle his anger so that he might produce art acceptable to a broad audience and affirm the positive side of life in America. But the lost stanzas of **"Fifty Years"** show that Johnson's placid exterior concealed a raging awareness of the wrongs committed against his race.

Notes

[1] James Weldon Johnson, "Fifty Years," in *Fifty Years and Other Poems* (Boston: Cornhill Publishers, 1917), p. 4. All subsequent references to "Fifty Years" refer to this edition and appear in parentheses.

[2] Eugene Levy, *James Weldon Johnson: Black Leader, Black Voice* (Chicago: University of Chicago Press, 1973), p. 144.

[3] James Weldon Johnson, *Along This Way: The Autobiography of James Weldon Johnson* (New York: Viking Press, 1933), p. 290.

[4] James Weldon Johnson, *St. Peter Relates an Incident* (New York: Viking Press, 1935), p. 91.

[5] Draft I of "Fifty Years" is in the Collection of American Literature, the Beinecke Rare Book Room and Manuscript Library, Yale University, item + 206. It is a pencil draft on 81/2 x 14 unlined paper.

[6] Claude McKay, *Selected Poems of Claude McKay* (New York: Harcourt, Brace & Would, 1953), p. 36.

[7] *Along This Way*, p. 290.

[8] *The Crisis* 15 (1917): 13.

Robert E. Fleming (essay date 1987)

SOURCE: *James Weldon Johnson*, Twayne Publishers, 1987, 123 p.

[*In the following excerpt, Fleming traces Johnson's development from a writer of conventional poetry to one of experimental free verse in* God's Trombones.]

During his Atlanta years Johnson began to write poetry. From the 1890s through his publication of *Fifty Years and Other Poems* (1917) the form and subject matter of his poems are characteristic of the period in which he wrote; that is, they are written in conventional stanzaic forms, in rhymed verse, and they address subjects that are either the conventional subject matter of the poet or the specialized subject matter of the Afro-American poet, as handed down from early protest writers such as George Moses Horton and Frances Watkins Harper. During the 1920s, however, Johnson began to experiment with more modern forms, eventually producing in *God's Trombones* (1927) a free verse form calculated to recall the style and rhythm of the southern black minister. These later poems are the ones most likely to appear in literary histories, despite the popularity of some early poems such as **"Lift Every Voice and Sing."**

FINDING A VOICE

Characteristic of Johnson's early poetry is a Petrarchan sonnet, **"Mother Night,"** that he wrote while serving as consul in Venezuela. The night is personified as "a brooding mother" out of which the universe evolved and to which it will return. In the sestet Johnson applies the lesson of the universe to the life of the individual:

> So when my feeble sun of life burns out,
>   And sounded is the hour for my long sleep,
>   I shall, full weary of the feverish light,
>   Welcome the darkness without fear or doubt,
>   And heavy-lidded, I shall softly creep
>   Into the quiet bosom of the Night.[1]

Another poem of the same type is the English sonnet called **"Sleep"** in *Fifty Years* and **"Blessed Sleep"** in *St. Peter Relates an Incident*. Reminiscent of Sir Philip Sidney's Sonnet 39 from *Astrophel and Stella*, **"Sleep"** praises the value of sleep, its ability to "soothe the torn and sorrow-laden breast." But near the end the poem diverges from Sidney's theme, reflecting on the fact that pain "lives again so soon as thou art fled." The final couplet moves on to another form of sleep: "Man, why should thought of death cause thee to weep; / Since death be but an endless, dreamless sleep?" (*FY*, 50). While he wrote several of these conventional poems, which display the sort of competence and deftness with rhyme and meter that made him a successful songwriter, Johnson would probably never have merited a place in literary history for any of this class of poetry. Even in his early period, however, he did write a number of poems whose racial themes gained them a place in Afro-American literary history. Certain of his occasional or commemorative poems are widely anthologized, while some protest poems produced between 1893 and 1917 deserve to be better known than they are.

The fiftieth anniversary of the Emancipation Proclamation was the occasion for **"Fifty Years,"** the well-known title poem of his first volume of verse. Johnson begins his long poem by recalling how far the race has come, not only in the fifty years since Emancipation, but since its introduction to America three centuries earlier:

> A few black bondmen strewn along
>   The borders of our eastern coast,
> Now grown a race, ten million strong,
>   An upward, onward marching host.
>
>   (*FY*, 2)

He asserts the rights of America's black citizens to equal partnership with white citizens because "this land is ours by right of toil," and he details the contributions of black men and women to clearing the land and making it productive. Johnson also points out that from the martyrdom of Crispus Attucks to his own day black Americans had rallied to the flag in times of war; he forcefully concludes this section, "We've bought a rightful sonship here, / And we have more than paid the price" (*FY*, 4). The black American, then, has no need to take a position inferior to that of the newly arrived European immigrant who, black leaders such as Booker T. Washington feared, might replace black workers in the desirable jobs in the industrialized North. On the other hand, **"Fifty Years"** acknowledges that black people are still persecuted and that many have grown discouraged. Johnson ends the poem, therefore, with an exhortation to the black reader to maintain his courage, to look beyond the present:

> That for which millions prayed and sighed,
>   That for which tens of thousands fought,
> For which so many freely died,
>   God cannot let it come to naught.
>
> (FY, 5)

"Fifty Years" appeared in the *New York Times* on 1 January 1913[2] and has been frequently anthologized since, but it is more noteworthy for the sentiments it expresses than for the excellence of the poetry itself. While at times genuine emotion breaks through its formality, the modern reader may be inclined to read it more as a social document than as a great poem.

Similar to **"Fifty Years"** is **"Father, Father Abraham,"** written on the anniversary of Abraham Lincoln's birth and first published in the *Crisis* in February 1913. Johnson pays tribute to the Great Emancipator, a traditional hero of the race, in a prayerlike poem of sixteen lines. As the biblical Abraham gave birth to the Jewish people, Lincoln is viewed as the spiritual progenitor of the black race. Furthermore, Lincoln's death is seen as an act of martyrdom to "ransom" the black race. The poem not only offers a tribute to the statesman, but also contains an inspirational note:

> To-day we consecrate ourselves
>   Anew in hand and heart and brain,
> To send this judgment down the years:
>   The ransom was not paid in vain.
>
> (FY, 13)

Also in this category is **"Lift Every Voice and Sing,"** a poem which Johnson's brother Rosamond set to music. Designed to be sung by a large chorus of school children. **"Lift Every Voice"** was first performed at a celebration of Lincoln's birthday in Jacksonville in 1900. In later years it was adopted by the NAACP and became known as the "Negro National Hymn" or the "Negro National Anthem." Like **"Fifty Years,"** **"Lift Every Voice"** looks back to the hardships faced by the race in the past—"stony the road we trod, bitter the chastening rod"—and also looks forward to "the rising sun of our new day begun."[3] While he

details some of the pains of slavery, Johnson's emphasis is on the moderate course: the race should learn from the "dark past," should persevere in its faith in God and the nation, and should never cease to press toward its eventual victory.

Less artificial and more moving than the public poems discussed above is Johnson's **"O Black and Unknown Bards,"** a commemoration of the anonymous composers of the spirituals. In this justly popular poem Johnson allows his honest emotion to break through the conventional diction of turn-of-the-century popular verse and pays a beautiful tribute to the folk poets who produced the spirituals. He opens the poem by posing an unanswerable question:

> O black and unknown bards of long ago,
> How came your lips to touch the sacred fire?
> How, in your darkness, did you come to know
> The power and beauty of the minstrel's lyre?
>
> (FY, 6)

Throughout the poem he weaves lines from the actual spirituals—"Steal Away to Jesus," "Swing Low, Sweet Chariot," "Go Down, Moses," and others—marveling at the ingenuity of the composers, who produced their works without any training and under the worst possible conditions. And it is not merely as artistic successes that Johnson views the songs, but as signs of the spiritual depths of their creators. Himself an agnostic, Johnson nevertheless empathizes with the "hungry hearts" of the listeners for whom the songs were composed. Implicit in the poem is a recognition of the importance of religion in helping an enslaved people to survive with their spirits intact.

Like many black poets, Johnson frequently turned to the writing of protest poetry. At times the protest is mild, as in **"O Southland,"** where his love for the South is mingled with his desire to see it progress toward racial harmony to the benefit of both races. More typically, however, his protest poems display a bitterness and a militancy that are surprising in the poetry of a man who normally took moderate stands on civil rights issues. The earliest published poem of this type, **"A Brand,"** appeared in 1893 during Johnson's junior year at Atlanta University. The poet describes a despised wanderer:

> Upon his brow he wore a brand,
>   And on his back,
> A thousand stripes for it he bore:
>   His skin was black.[4]

Yet, at the end of a miserable life, the wanderer faces his God and is admitted to heaven because of his pure heart. Johnson progressed from the mild protest of **"A Brand"** to a warning in **"To America"** that the fate of the nation itself is tied to the fate of its black population. Hardly militant, **"To America"** states that if black people are kept "sinking 'neath the load we bear," the race will throw chains about the feet of their country instead of helping the nation to prosper (*FY*, 5).

Protest poems such as **"Brothers"** and **"The White Witch"** go a step further by addressing the twin southern problems of lynching and miscegenation. **"Brothers"** begins with words spoken by a member of the lynch mob, observing a victim "more like brute than man" and asking if this creature is from the same "docile, child-like, tender-hearted race" that has served southern whites for three centuries. The victim replies that he is "the bitter fruit . . . of planted seed" and details the "lessons in degradation, taught and learned," that have been the lot of the race through fifteen generations of slavery and oppression: the slaves separated from their families, the murders and the rapes he has seen. The poem then shifts from dramatic dialogue to detailed description of the lynching itself as the mob refuses to hear more accusations. The fire is built carefully so that it will not burn too fast and deprive the watchers of the joy of watching their victim die slowly. When it begins to burn too vigorously, they throw water on it. At last the black man dies, and the crowd comes forward for grisly souvenirs of the burning: "You take that bone, and you this tooth; the chain— / Let us divide its links; this skull, of course, / In fair division, to the leader comes." Finally, their brutal actions over, the members of the mob have time to ponder the last words of the dying man, but they fail to unlock the riddle. His words, in the last line of the poem, are "Brothers in spirit, brothers in deed are we" (*FY*, 14-17). Although much of the dialogue of this poem is artificially formal, given the heated context, the poem on the whole makes a powerful statement about violence and brutality begetting more brutality.

"The White Witch" is more subtle, though it is unlikely that any black reader would mistake its message.[5] **"The White Witch"** appears to be a fanciful supernatural ballad, in which a vampirelike witch threatens to lure away young men and kill them. Beneath the surface, however, it is clear that Johnson is treating black-white sexual relations, the complex of psychological ills that accompany the thought of miscegenation, and the very real physical danger to the black man who succumbs to the lures of white women. The white witch is described by one who speaks, perhaps from the grave, about his own temptation and fall. He warns his younger brothers not to test their strength against the witch or even to look at her, "For in her glance there is a snare, / And in her smile there is a blight" (*FY*, 19). The witch is not like the witches the boys have heard of in children's stories; this is no "ancient hag" with "snaggled tooth," but a beautiful woman "in all the glowing charms of youth." The third and fourth stanzas create a portrait of her as the archetypal white woman: "her face [is] like new-born lilies fair," her eyes are blue, and her hair is golden. Although she appears young, "unnumbered centuries are hers" (*FY*, 19); her origins go back to the beginning of the universe.

The speaker then tells his brothers how he has been trapped by the witch. At first he enjoyed the kisses from her unnaturally red lips and the bondage of her white arms and the golden hair that entangled him. But then a transformation took place, and the red lips began to "burn and sear / My body like a living coal" (*FY*, 20). The temptress has led her victim to the stake, and the glow of her beauty

becomes the glow of the lynch mob's fire. What motivates the white witch? In anticipation of much later works such as Calvin C. Hernton's *Sex and Racism in America* (1965) or Eldridge Cleaver's *Soul on Ice* (1968) her victim answers:

> She feels the old Antaean strength
> In you, the great dynamic beat
> Of primal passions, and she sees
> In you the last besieged retreat
> Of love relentless, lusty, fierce,
> Love pain-ecstatic, cruel-sweet.
>
> (*FY*, 21)

The poem ends with the repeated warning to the younger brothers not to be enticed by the witch. Johnson operates with considerable subtlety in this poem. Nowhere is it stated that the speaker and his brothers are black, but given the imagery of the white enticer and the nature of the speaker's fate, it is apparent that the poem is a social fable on one level even though it may be read on another.

Although Johnson's later experiments with free verse in *God's Trombones* were extremely successful, he never completely abandoned traditional verse. Just three years after the publication of *God's Trombones*, a news story that caught Johnson's eye provided the occasion for another poem. As he tells the story in his foreword to *St. Peter Relates an Incident*, he read about a contingent of gold-star mothers being sent to France to visit their sons' graves. White mothers were to travel on one ship and black mothers on another, the latter being a "second-class vessel" (*SP*, ix). Johnson laid aside the manuscript that he had been working on and began to compose the long satirical title poem of his last collection of poetry.

In the 161 lines and six sections of **"Saint Peter Relates an Incident of the Resurrection Day"** Johnson uses various stanza forms, rhyme schemes, and meters, but most of the work is in quatrains made up of rhyming couplets. The first two sections set up the framework for the tale itself: to enliven the cloying sameness of heaven, St. Peter tells the assembled angels and saints a story. On the day of the resurrection all of the living and dead members of the various patriotic groups of the United States, including the Ku Klux Klan and Confederate veterans, gathered in Washington to honor the Unknown Soldier and escort him to heaven. Since the tomb of the Unknown Soldier is so massive, he could not emerge immediately, and the assembled masses had to dig him out. For his part, the Unknown Soldier worked from inside, until at last

> He, underneath the débris, heaved and hove
> Up toward the opening which they cleaved and
>   clove;
> Through it, at last, his towering form loomed big
>   and bigger—
> "Great God Almighty! Look!" they cried, "he is a
>   nigger!"
>
> (*SP*, 18)

The crowd debated the best way to handle the situation. The Klan suggested reburying the soldier, but skeptics argued that divine will would not be foiled by mere concrete. While they were discussing him, the Unknown Soldier climbed to heaven, singing "Deep River." St. Peter recalls:

> I rushed to the gate and flung it wide,
> Singing, he entered with a loose, long stride;
> Singing and swinging up the golden street,
> The music married to the tramping of his feet.
>
> > (*SP*, 20)

The poem ends with the heavenly perspective on the incident as the assembled host disperses while making a noise "that quivered / 'twixt tears and laughter" (*SP*, 22). Characters and incident, meter and rhymes—all contribute to the humorous effect of the poem.

In addition to the title poem, Johnson's last collection of poetry contains four other poems not included in *Fifty Years*, all but one of which revert to conventional verse forms. In his formal traditional poetry he breaks no new ground, but his poetry is competent, and, because of the unique racial perspective from which it approaches life, it is worth reading. One further contribution that Johnson made to black poetry of his period is a body of dialect verse.

THE DIALECT POEMS

When Johnson began his poetic career in the 1890s, dialect poetry was in fashion. One well-known black poet of the period, Paul Laurence Dunbar, had been encouraged to create dialect verse by the influential novelist and critic, William Dean Howells. When Johnson moved to New York, the conventions demanded dialect in the songs and shows that he wrote for the stage. It is not surprising, then, that of the poems in *Fifty Years and Other Poems*, the last sixteen are grouped under the heading "Jingles & Croons," meaning dialect poems. As he read and edited poetry during the early twentieth century, however, Johnson began to have reservations about dialect in poetry; by the time he published his last collection of poetry, he had already experimented with an alternative to the stylized dialect he and Dunbar had earlier used, and he no longer believed that dialect was a proper part of the black poet's repertoire. Accordingly, *St. Peter Relates an Incident: Selected Poems* reprinted only eight of the sixteen dialect poems that had appeared in *Fifty Years*. Furthermore, Johnson prefaced these poems with a two-page statement of his later position on dialect poetry.

By the middle of the 1930s, Johnson says, dialect poetry as it was known in the latter half of the nineteenth century and the early years of the twentieth was a dead form, never used by black writers. If black poets of the thirties used dialect at all, it was "the racy, living speech of the Negro in certain phases of contemporary life." Modern black poets, including Johnson, had left behind the "smooth-worn stereotype" of "contented, childlike, happy-go-lucky, humorous, or forlorn 'darkies' with their banjos, their singing and dancing, their watermelons and possums . . ." (*SP*, 69). He regrets the tainted origins of conventional black dialect, which came to the black poet

via the white minstrel show and the plantation tradition, for that dialect could be used powerfully, as when it was used by folk poets who were composing unselfconsciously, "solely to express and please themselves" (*SP*, 69). Had black poets "been the first to use and develop the dialect as a written form, . . . to work it in its virgin state, they would, without doubt, have created a medium of great flexibility and range, a medium comparable to what Burns made of the Scottish dialect" (*SP*, 70). But the form came to the black poet too heavily freighted with old associations and conventions, and he was never able to break it free from its past. The future, Johnson predicts, would have to see a new idiom evolve to capture the spontaneity and "racial flavor" that dialect poets attempted to convey.

Johnson had been hesitant about including any of his own dialect poems in his last collection, but he reflects that some great poems had been written in dialect: "To take Dunbar's dialect poetry out of American literature would cause both a racial and a national loss" (*SP*, 70). The same might be said of some of Johnson's dialect poems, such as **"Sence You Went Away,"** which has often passed for a genuine folk poem, and even **"Brer Rabbit, You's de Cutes' of 'Em All,"** which is indebted to the plantation tradition.

"Sence You Went Away" laments a lost love. The speaker finds all of nature wanting now that his loved one has left him:

> Seems lak to me de stars don't shine so bright,
> Seems lak to me de sun done loss his light,
> Seems lak to me der's nothin' goin' right,
> > Sence you went away.
>
> > (*FY*, 63)

Although Johnson employs the sort of conventional dialect Dunbar used, **"Sence You Went Away"** is restrained in its tone and contains none of the malaprops that cause some dialect poems to belittle the speaker. The persona created by the speaking voice is dignified in his grief, and, dialect aside, the poem speaks to and for anyone who has lost a lover.

Another sort of tenderness is captured in **"De Little Pickaninny's Gone to Sleep,"** which Johnson published in *Fifty Years* but omitted in the final volume of his poetry. The speaker is a worried father who fears that something is wrong with his child:

> Cuddle down, ma honey, in yo' bed,
> Go to sleep an' res' yo' little head,
> Been a-kind o' ailin' all de day?
> Didn't have no sperit fu' to play?
> Never min'; to-morrer, w'en you wek,
> Daddy's gwine to ride you on his bek,
> 'Roun' an' roun' de cabin flo' so fas'—
> Der! He's closed his little eyes at las'.
>
> > (*FY*, 83)

But the father's relief gives way to uneasiness as the child sighs and groans in his sleep, and when the father goes to the trundle bed to reassure himself, he finds that the child has died. Johnson may have omitted the poem from his final book believing that it was too sentimental, but the sorrow expressed by the poem is understated:

> W'at's dat far-off light dat's in his eyes?
> Dat's a light dey's borrow'd f'om de skies;
> Fol' his little han's across his breas',
> Let de little pickaninny res'.
>
> (*FY*, 83)

The rest that the father had wished for his child has become the eternal rest.

More typical of dialect poetry from the turn of the century is **"Tunk,"** a dramatic monologue based on Johnson's conception of one of his students in the rural Georgia school. The speaker is an angry mother who has tried to do the best thing for her son Tunk, only to have him refuse to cooperate in his education:

> Heah I'm tryin' hard to raise you as a credit to dis
>   race,
> An' you tryin' heap much harder fu' to come up
>   in disgrace.
>
> Dese de days w'en men don't git up to de top by
>   hooks an' crooks;
> Tell you now, dey's got to git der standin' on a
>   pile o' books.
>
> (*FY*, 66-67)

Tunk's mother warns him that a "darkey" has to work hard from first light in the morning to sundown, never earning more than he needs to stay alive, and never owning more than his clothes. On the other hand, she naively sees the lives of white workers as ideal. Not only do they work a much shorter day, but their work seems easy:

> Dey jes does a little writin'; does dat by some
>   easy means;
> Gals jes set an' play piannah on dem printin' press
>   machines.
> Chile, dem men knows how to figgah, how to use
>   dat little pen,
> An' dey knows dat blue-back spellah f'om
>   beginnin' to de en'.
>
> (*FY*, 67-68)

While the moral of the poem, that black youth needs education to be upwardly mobile, is unassailable, the portrait of the mother that emerges from her speech is unflattering. She attempts to motivate Tunk for the wrong reasons, seeing education as a license to practice a life of idleness. Her naiveté about the lives of white people and her acceptance of the term "darkey" for her race suggest a condescension on the poet's part that was far from Johnson's true attitude. Yet, as Dunbar's rise proves, such an image of the southern Negro fit white America's stereotypes, as conditioned by the plantation school, and Johnson was not immune to the effects of the stereotypes and conventions that he found established in dialect poetry when he began to write it.

No such social questions arise to spoil the enjoyment of another class of Johnson dialect poems—works like **"Possum Song"** and **"Brer Rabbit, You's De Cutes' of 'Em All."** The first of these is a comic warning to "Brudder Possum" that fall is coming and with it hunting season. The second, a more complex poem, praises not only the physical "cuteness" of the traditional black trickster figure, but also the acute instinct for survival that made Brer Rabbit a folk hero since the days of slavery. The creatures of the wilderness have a meeting to determine "Who is de bigges' man?" An owl is appointed judge and renders his decision in an oracular formula:

> "Brer Wolf am mighty cunnin',
> Brer Fox am mighty sly,
> Brer Terrapin an' 'Possum—kinder small;
> Brer Lion's mighty vicious,
> Brer B'ar he's sorter 'spicious,
> Brer Rabbit, you's de cutes' of 'em all."
>
> (*FY*, 81)

When each of these animals except Brer Rabbit claims to have won the competition, the wily rabbit "jes' stood aside an' urged 'em on to fight" until all of the other animals were exhausted, then "he jes' grabbed de prize an' flew" (*FY*, 82), proving that he was the "cutest" in more than one sense.

While Johnson's achievements in traditional rhymed verse and in dialect poetry are not remarkable, he was among the foremost black poets of his day. If his work seems dated, so does much of the work of his famous contemporary Dunbar. But Johnson lived longer than Dunbar, lived to observe the experimentation in poetry that occurred during his lifetime and to modify his own writing accordingly.

God's Trombones

Johnson's greatest contribution to Afro-American poetry was nearly ten years in the making. In 1918, while lecturing in Kansas City, he was invited to speak at a black church, where he was to follow a visiting minister who had a considerable reputation as a preacher. It was late in the evening, and the prepared sermon began prosaically, but when he sensed that the attention of the congregation was wandering, the visiting preacher

> stepped out from behind the pulpit and began to preach. He started intoning the old folk-sermon that begins with the creation of the world and ends with Judgment Day. He was at once a changed man, free, at ease and masterful. The change in the congregation was instantaneous. . . . It was in a moment alive and quivering; and all the while the preacher held it in the palm of his hand. . . . He strode the pulpit up and down in what was actually a very rhythmic dance, and he brought into play the full gamut of his wonderful voice, a voice—what shall I say?—not of an organ or a trumpet, but rather of a trombone, the instrument possessing above all others the power to express the wide and varied range of emotions encompassed by the human voice. . . . Before he had finished I took a slip of paper and somewhat surreptitiously jotted down

some ideas for the first poem [of *God's Trombones*], **"The Creation."**[6]

Published in the *Freeman* in 1920, that first poem elicited favorable responses and was reprinted in several anthologies. However, the press of his work with the NAACP was so great that, in spite of some false starts on new free-verse poems, it was seven years before Johnson completed a second poem for *God's Trombones,* **"Go Down Death."**[7]

The book published in 1927 consists of seven free-verse sermons introduced by a preface in which Johnson explained the origin of the poems and the language in which they were written; he added a prayer, also in free verse, such as might have been offered in a real congregation before the sermon. He considered and discarded the notion of writing *God's Trombones* in dialect, he says in his preface, first because dialect verse is "a quite limited instrument. . . . with but two complete stops, pathos and humor" (*GT,* 7). Second, when they were preaching, the black preachers the poems attempt to capture did not really use black dialect but an elevated form of language, "a fusion of Negro idioms with Bible English" (*GT,* 9), and it is this language that Johnson set down in his verse sermons. In *Along this Way* he explained his use of free verse by saying that he chose "a loose rhythmic instead of a strict metric form, because it . . . could accommodate itself to the movement, the abandon, the changes of tempo, and the characteristic syncopations of his material" (*A,* 336).

"Listen, Lord," the opening prayer, gives a sort of preview of what is to come in the sermons. The inspiration that is called down upon the minister is couched in earthy, figurative language:

> Hang him up and drain him dry of sin.
> Pin his ear to the wisdom-post,
> And make his words sledge hammers of truth—
> Beating on the iron heart of sin.
>
> . . . . .
>
> Put his eye to the telescope of eternity,
> And let him look upon the paper walls of time.
> Lord, turpentine his imagination.
> Put perpetual motion in his arms,. . . .
>
> (*GT,* 14)

Because of the unexpected nature of some of these images, they strike the reader with a force that recalls Edward Taylor's use of metaphysical conceits—such as "Who in this bowling alley bowled the sun?"—to approach religious subjects. Such language does not cause the reader to find an intellectually inferior speaker ridiculous but makes him admire the daring and strength of the basic metaphors.

This technique continues into **"The Creation,"** although the diction of the first sermon is elevated appropriately above that of **"Listen, Lord."** God's motivation for the creation is human, basic, and understandable: "I'm lonely— / I'll make me a world" (*GT,* 17). The actual mechanics

of creation are treated in detail chosen to form a mental picture of real activity in the mind of the listener:

> Then God reached out and took the light in his
>   hands,
> And God rolled the light around in his hands
> Until he made the sun;
> And he set that sun a-blazing in the heavens.
> And the light that was left from making the sun
> God gathered it up in a shining ball
> And flung it against the darkness,
> Spangling the night with the moon and stars.
>
> (*GT,* 17-18)

One can easily imagine a preacher miming such actions. In the creation of Man a specifically black image is created.

> This Great God,
> Like a mammy bending over her baby,
> Kneeled down in the dust
> Toiling over a lump of clay
> Till he shaped it in his own image;
>
> Then into it he blew the breath of life,
> And man became a living soul.
>
> (*GT,* 20)

The anthropomorphic God who appears in these lines is maintained consistently throughout the poem. He is not the remote, formal, all-knowing God of the Scriptures so much as an approachable, questioning, evolving Being with whom the listener could identify. Creation is an act of problem-solving, as God seeks to remedy the loneliness that has plagued Him; thus He is not only an understanding but an understandable Being. The use of long and short lines suggests the changing tempo of the preacher's speech, and the occasional dashes indicate "a certain sort of pause that is marked by a quick intaking and an audible expulsion of the breath . . ." (*GT,* 10-11). On the whole, **"The Creation"** is a dignified poem whose tone and diction are appropriate to its solemn subject.

In later sermons, where the object is to sway the emotions of the congregation and to foster repentance, Johnson's preacher becomes more earthy and his idiom more colloquial, as in the second, fourth, and seventh sermons: **"The Prodigal Son," "Noah Built the Ark,"** and **"The Judgment Day."** In **"The Prodigal Son,"** after the famous opening of "Your arm's too short to box with God," the preacher immediately makes clear the central analogy of the parable:

> A certain man had two sons.
> Jesus didn't give this man a name,
> But his name is God Almighty.
> And Jesus didn't call these sons by name,
> But ev'ry young man,
> Ev'rywhere,
> Is one of these two sons.
>
> (*GT,* 21)

The preacher paints a rather specific picture of the prodigal son's debauchery, detailing the charms of

. . . the women of Babylon!
Dressed in yellow and purple and scarlet,
Loaded with rings and earrings and bracelets,
Their lips like a honeycomb dripping with honey,
Perfumed and sweet-smelling like a jasmine flower. . . .

(*GT,* 24)

But he reminds his congregation that, like the prodigal son, each man must someday face the end of riotous living. "But some o' these days, some o' these days, / You'll have a hand-to-hand struggle with bony Death, / And Death is bound to win" (*GT,* 25). This grim metaphor leads him to the obvious conclusion: like the prodigal son, his listeners will do well to mend their ways and return to their Father before it is too late.

"Noah Built the Ark" and **"The Judgment Day"** are similar warnings. The former sermon traces the origins of sin back to the Garden of Eden and then on to Noah's time, lightening the sermon with an occasional touch of humor: when Noah warns of the deluge to come, "Some smart young fellow said: This old man's / Got water on the brain" (*GT,* 35). The preacher leaves the moral of his tale to God, who "hung out his rainbow cross the sky" and warned that the next time He will "rain down fire" on mankind (*GT,* 37). This same image of fire raining down is the beginning of the final sermon of the book, **"Judgment Day."** Here no humor relieves the solemn descriptions: the graves yielding up their dead to the sound of "the clicking together of the dry bones" (*GT,* 54), the division of the sheep from the goats, and the casting of the damned into hell. The poem, as well as the volume, ends on this somber note: "Sinner, oh, sinner, / Where will you stand / In that great day when God's a-going to rain down fire?" (*GT,* 56). Thus, in nearly half of the verse sermons Johnson emphasizes the fire-and-brimstone messages delivered by the old-time preachers.

But the sermons in *God's Trombones* can comfort the flock as well as threaten it with reminders of God's wrath. **"Go Down Death—A Funeral Sermon"** offers consolation to the "heart-broken husband," the "grief-stricken son," and the "left-lonesome daughter" of a woman who has died. The preacher dramatizes God's reaction when, looking down into the world, He sees "Sister Caroline, / Tossing on her bed of pain" (*GT,* 27) and orders Death to report to Him. Death is described in terms that are not so much fearful as majestic: his horse's hooves strike sparks from the golden streets of Paradise as he rides to the throne of God, and he leaves a trail like that of a comet in the sky as he embarks on his mission. Though the arms that he puts around Sister Caroline are cold, they soothe the pain she has felt, and Death looks "like a welcome friend" (*GT,* 29). Receiving the dead woman into heaven, Jesus

. . . smoothed the furrows from her face,
And the angels sang a little song,
And Jesus rocked her in his arms,
And kept a-saying: Take your rest. . . .

(*GT,* 30)

If Death is not the mother of beauty, at least it is a welcome sleep after a lifetime of pain, a concept with

which black congregations of the 1920s and even Johnson's more sophisticated black readers could empathize.

Although **"The Crucifixion"** also ultimately treats the salvation of mankind in its last lines, most of the poem deals in heartrending detail with the passion and death of Christ. At first there is no attempt to relate the sufferings of the Savior to those of the black people of the United States—sufferings of which Johnson was all too aware after his years of service with the NAACP—but a black congregation hearing such a sermon, like the black reader, would not need to be reminded of the parallel. However, after the preacher has taken his listeners through the mental anguish of Gethsemane and on through the trial, he incorporates the black folk belief about the race of Simon of Cyrene as Jesus carries the cross up to Golgotha:

I see my drooping Jesus sink.
And then they laid hold on Simon,
Black Simon, yes, black Simon;
They put the cross on Simon,
And Simon bore the cross.

(*GT,* 41)

Now the connection has become explicit, and, along with Jesus, the black listener could shudder at the sound of the hammer and feel the pain being inflicted.

The preacher reaches his high point in the poem as he dwells on the agony of Christ during the crucifixion; the repetition of key words and the alternate pattern of the lines relates this section of the poem to traditional litanies.

Jesus, my lamb-like Jesus,
Shivering as the nails go through his hands;
Jesus, my lamb-like Jesus,
Shivering as the nails go through his feet.
Jesus, my darling Jesus,
Groaning as the Roman spear plunged in his side;
Jesus, my darling Jesus,
Groaning as the blood came spurting from his wound.
Oh, look how they done my Jesus.

(*GT,* 42)

The end of the poem again separates the identities of listener or reader from that of the martyred Jesus as the preacher reminds his congregation, echoing the words of a familiar spiritual, how awesome was the sacrifice that redeemed them:

It causes me to tremble, tremble,
When I think how Jesus died;
Died on the steeps of Calvary,
How Jesus died for sinners,
Sinners like you and me.

(*GT,* 43)

Yet Jesus the scapegoat is also "King Jesus" in the poem, and **"The Crucifixion"** implicitly reminds its audiences—the fictional listener and the real reader—that the downtrodden do not remain down forever. A transfiguration awaits Jesus and may await His most humble follower.

"Let My People Go" also appeals to the black audience through identification of black people with the enslaved children of Israel in Exodus. Here Johnson draws on a traditional association between the two peoples of which, as a collector of spirituals, he was well aware. But the sermon "Let My People Go" depends little on the song of the same name, merely sharing a few lines with it. The preacher begins his account of Moses with the prophet's first encounter with God in the burning bush. The preacher's God soon shows Himself to be a Being of plain speech:

> And God said to Moses:
> I've seen the awful suffering
> Of my people down in Egypt.
> I've watched their hard oppressors,
> Their overseers and drivers;
> The groans of my people have filled my ears
> And I can't stand it no longer;
> So I'm come down to deliver them. . . .
>
> (*GT,* 46)

The terminology is that of slavery—overseers and drivers as opposed to the term "taskmasters" in the King James Bible—and God's double negative marks Him as having proletarian sympathies. He then delivers his order to Moses in nearly the same words as in the spiritual: "tell Old Pharoah / To let my people go" (*GT,* 46). The preacher relates the plagues and the death of the Egyptian firstborn that led to the release of the children of Israel, but he reserves his greatest power for the end of his sermon. In great detail he tells of the mighty army called up by Pharoah to pursue the fleeing slaves, picturing for his congregation the multitude of chariots raising dust "that darked the day" (*GT,* 51), and emphasizing the earthly power assembled against God's chosen people.

But all this power is useless when Pharoah and his hordes attempt to cross the Red Sea:

> Old Pharoah got about half way cross,
> And God unlashed the waters,
> And the waves rushed back together,
> And Pharoah and all his army got lost,
> And all his host got drownded.
>
> (*GT,* 52)

The broader implications of the biblical story are clear when the preacher warns metaphorical "sons of Pharaoh" that they can never hold the people of God, a meaningful message to black people of the 1920s, who had been subjected to mistreatment ranging from discrimination to lynching, and who had seen the widely publicized Dyer antilynching bill killed by the 67th Congress early in the decade. "Let My People Go" is in many ways the most powerful work in *God's Trombones*; treating as it does the theme of God's rescue of the enslaved and the downtrodden, the poem strikes an old and responsive note in black literature.

RESPONSES TO JOHNSON'S POETRY

Johnson's first book of poetry was largely ignored by the literary establishment, perhaps understandably. When *Fifty Years* appeared under the imprint of the Cornhill Company of Boston, Johnson was relatively unknown, having produced, in addition to his anonymously published novel, only a little more than a dozen poems, some of which appeared in periodicals of very limited circulation. Nevertheless, William Stanley Braithwaite, the black critic and poet who reviewed *Fifty Years* for the *Boston Evening Transcript,* stated that Johnson had proved himself to be the heir to Dunbar's position as "the most important poet of the race,"[8] and even suggested that Johnson was superior to Dunbar intellectually. Brander Matthews, Johnson's teacher at Columbia, praised the poet in the introduction he wrote for the volume, singling out the title poem as an example of superior diction, imagination, and craftsmanship. Benjamin Brawley, reviewing the volume for the *Journal of Negro History,* especially liked "Mother Night," "O Black and Unknown Bards," "The White Witch," and "The Young Warrior."[9] While some half-dozen other periodicals noted the publication of *Fifty Years and Other Poems* from 1917 through 1919, these favorable opinions did not prevail in the marketplace—the book sold slowly—or in the critical opinions of others, for the book was ignored by most reviewers. This is not to say that Johnson had no reputation as a poet. The popularity of some of his works, especially the song "Lift Every Voice and Sing," gave him a sort of underground reputation among black people that is impossible to quantify. Maya Angelou tells, for example, of the pride she felt in 1940 when she and her classmates replied to the segregationist speech of a white politician by singing the "Negro National Anthem" as an assertion of their dignity and their determination to endure.[10]

God's Trombones, on the other hand, was very well received by the literary press. Unlike *Fifty Years*, it was published by a major firm, Viking Press, and its author was by 1927 perhaps the most visible black American alive. In literature he had made a name for himself as a critic of poetry with his anthology, *The Book of American Negro Poetry* (1922), and as an expert on spirituals with his two collections published in 1925 and 1926. His novel *The Autobiography of an Ex-Colored Man* was republished under Johnson's name in the same year that *God's Trombones* came out.

However, the reception of *God's Trombones* was not just a response to the reputation of its author, but a recognition of the excellence and originality of the poetry itself. Harriet Monroe, reviewing *God's Trombones* for her journal *Poetry,* had some reservations about the success of individual poems but felt that, on the whole, readers "should be grateful for this book,"[11] while the anonymous critic for *Saturday Review of Literature* felt that no student of black literature could afford to miss the book. The *New York Times Book Review* praised *God's Trombones* for its "sensitivity, artistic judgment, and a sustained emotional beauty."[12] Thomas Munroe, in the *New York Herald Tribune Books,* found "The Creation" to be "almost Miltonic" although he felt that some of the other poems might have been helped by the inclusion of dialect.[13]

Among black critics, Johnson fared even better than in the mainstream publications. *Opportunity* not only published a favorable review by Joseph Auslander but also awarded Johnson its first prize in literature for 1928.[14] Poet Countee Cullen, writing for the *Bookman,* felt that the attempt to replace dialect was successful and called **"The Creation"** and **"Go Down Death"** magnificent.[15] W. E. B. DuBois agreed with Cullen about the success of Johnson's attempt to convey the black idiom through means other than conventional dialect and identified Johnson as a trailblazer in black poetry, while Alain Locke termed Johnson a major poet.[16] Of the black critics reviewing *God's Trombones,* the faintest praise came from satirist Wallace Thurman, who lumped Johnson with Dunbar in the category of important minor poets. Yet even Thurman had to acknowledge that the free-verse sermons were among the best poems written by black poets.[17]

Half a century after its publication *God's Trombones* is recognized as Johnson's best poetry, and its influence on later black poets has been widely noted. Eugene B. Redmond, in *Drumvoices,* calls *God's Trombones* "one of the most precious [volumes] in the annals of Afro-American writing" and sees Johnson as an influence on Margaret Walker, Langston Hughes, and Sterling Brown.[18] Arthur P. Davis recognizes Johnson as "a pioneer influence" and suggests that "because of its folk undergirding, *God's Trombones,* in all probability, will outlast the rest of Johnson's poetry."[19] Blyden Jackson and Louis D. Rubin, Jr., conclude that "it was Johnson, more than any other man, who opened the path [to the creation of a new black poetry], and the achievement that followed was in an important sense possible because of what he first demonstrated. The leading poets who came afterward—Toomer, Hughes, Tolson, Hayden, Brooks, LeRoi Jones—can truly be said to have followed along James Weldon Johnson's way."[20]

So Johnson, who had abandoned early poetic ambitions in order to work in the fields of politics, journalism, and race relations, returned to poetry at various times during his life, and with considerable success. While only a few of his early poems merit inclusion in a list of significant works of Afro-American literature, *God's Trombones* is clearly his crowning achievement as a poet and will be remembered for its influence on later poets as well as enjoyed for the freshness and beauty of its imagery and language.

Notes

1 *Fifty Years and Other Poems* (Boston: Cornhill Co., 1917), 22; hereafter cited in parentheses in the text as *FY* with page number.
2 *New York Times,* 1 January 1913, p. 16, columns 5-6.

3 *St. Peter Relates an Incident: Selected Poems* (New York: Viking Press, 1935), 101; hereafter cited in parentheses in the text as *SP* with page number.

4 *Bulletin of Atlanta University,* no. 44 (March 1893):1.

5 However, Richard Long, in "A Weapon of My Song: The Poetry of James Weldon Johnson," *Phylon* 32 (Winter 1971):377, feels it necessary to defend the inclusion of "The White Witch" in the category of "race" poems.

6 *God's Trombones: Seven Negro Sermons in Verse* (New York: Viking Press, 1927), 6-7; hereafter cited in parentheses in the text as *GT* with page number.

7 *Along This Way,* 336-37. See also Levy, *Johnson,* 306.

8 William Stanley Braithwaite, "The Poems of James Weldon Johnson," *Boston Evening Transcript,* 12 December 1917, part 2, p. 9.

9 Benjamin Brawley, review of *Fifty Years and Other Poems, Journal of Negro History* 3 (April 1918):202-3.

10 Maya Angelou, *I Know Why the Caged Bird Sings* (New York: Random House, 1969), 178-79.

11 Harriet Monroe, "Negro Sermons," *Poetry: A Magazine of Verse* 30 (August 1927):29.

12 "Poetry and Eloquence of the Negro Preacher," *New York Times Book Review,* 19 June 1927, p. 11.

13 Thomas Munroe, "The Grand Manner in Negro Poetry: *God's Trombone {sic},*" *New York Herald Tribune Books,* 5 June 1927, p. 3.

14 Joseph Auslander, "Sermon Sagas," *Opportunity* 5 (September 1927):274-75.

15 Countee Cullen, "And the Walls Came Tumblin' Down," *Bookman* 66 (October 1927):221-22.

16 W. E. B. DuBois, "The Browsing Reader," *Crisis* 34 (July 1927):159; Alain Locke, "The Negro Poet and His Tradition," *Survey* 58 (1 August 1927):473-74.

17 Wallace Thurman, "Negro Poets and Their Poetry," *Bookman* 67 (July 1928):555-61.

18 Eugene B. Redmond, *Drumvoices: A Critical History* (Garden City, N.Y.: Doubleday, 1976), 187, 189.

19 Arthur P. Davis, *From the Dark Tower: Afro-American Writers, 1900 to 1960* (Washington, D.C.: Howard University Press, 1974), 29.

20 Blyden Jackson and Louis D. Rubin, Jr., *Black Poetry in America: Two Essays in Historical Interpretation* (Baton Rouge, La.: Louisiana State University Press, 1974), 26.

Robert E. Fleming (essay date 1992)

SOURCE: "James Weldon Johnson's *God's Trombones* as a Source for Faulkner's Rev'un Shegog," in *CLA Journal,* Vol. XXXVI, No. 1, September, 1992, pp. 24-30.

[*In the following essay, Fleming suggests the influence of Johnson's* God's Trombones *on William Faulkner's southern black preacher in* The Sound and the Fury.]

Studies of Faulkner's relationship to the black race have usually treated his depiction of black characters, his position on civil rights questions, the place of African Americans in Faulkner's South, or Faulkner's influence—positive and negative—on later black writers from Ralph Ellison to William Melvin Kelley.[1] It has generally been assumed that Faulkner, as a Southerner, needed no sources for his successful black characters. He grew up among black people and had ample opportunity to observe their speech and mannerisms. However, comparing the Easter service at Dilsey's church with James Weldon Johnson's book of African-American sermons in verse, *God's Trombones* (1927), suggests that Faulkner knew the book and used it in his depiction of Reverend Shegog, the visiting preacher from St. Louis.

God's Trombones was the culmination of nearly a decade of experimentation in which Johnson attempted to capture the idiom of the black Southern preacher without resorting to the usual dialect spellings associated with the comic "darkies" of the white minstrel show. In 1920 he published **"The Creation"** in *The Freeman,* and over the next seven years worked sporadically, as his duties with the NAACP permitted, on the remaining six poems that would make up *God's Trombones.* Faulkner, in touch with Sherwood Anderson's New Orleans literary set, could hardly have been unaware of a book that was reviewed in the *Saturday Review,* the *New York Times Book Review, Bookman, The Nation,* and *Poetry.* Also, Faulkner was corresponding with black poet and critic William Stanley Braithwaite in 1927.[2] Braithwaite, a friend of Johnson's, might easily have called *God's Trombones* to Faulkner's attention.

Looking for a metaphor for what he termed the "full gamut of [the] wonderful voice" of the Negro preacher, Johnson finally decided that it most resembled not the sound of "an organ or a trumpet, but rather of a trombone, the instrument possessing above all others the power to express the wide and varied range of emotions encompassed by the human voice—and with greater amplitude. He intoned, he moaned, he pleaded—he blared, he crashed, he thundered."[3] Johnson, who knew his music, notes that the trombone possesses a complete chromatic scale, "enharmonically true, like the human voice or the violin" (7). While Faulkner does not mention the trombone, he too uses the image of the wind instrument. Rev. Shegog's voice, once he gets warmed up, is "as different as day and dark from his former tone, with a sad, timbrous quality like an alto horn, sinking into their hearts and speaking there again when it had ceased in fading and cumulate echoes."[4] Again as Shegog grows more engrossed in his preaching, Faulkner refers to his voice ringing "with the horns" (295) as his scholarly air is stripped away.[5]

The whole presentation of Shegog echoes the tone of Johnson's introduction to *God's Trombones,* which insists that, although the black preacher may be personally ridiculous, his rhetoric allows him to transcend his personal limitations. Johnson tells the story of how a black preacher read a cryptic biblical passage and then announced: "Brothers and sisters, this morning—I intend to explain the unexplainable—find out the undefinable—ponder over the imponderable—and unscrew the inscrutable." (4-5) Faulkner's Rev. Shegog does not make himself ridiculous by anything that he says, but his appearance is all against him as Frony notes when she says, "En dey brung dat all de way fum Saint Looey" (293). Beside the congregation's regular preacher, who is a large, light-colored man of "magisterial and profound" bearing, the visitor appears disappointing:

> The visitor was undersized, in a shabby alpaca coat. . . . And all the while that the choir sang again and

while the six children rose and sang in thin, frightened, tuneless whispers, they watched the insignificant looking man sitting dwarfed and countrified by the minister's imposing bulk, with something like consternation. They were still looking at him with consternation and unbelief when the minister rose and introduced him in rich, rolling tones whose very unction served to increase the visitor's insignificance. (293)

What happens when Rev. Shegog begins to preach is almost exactly what Johnson reports having witnessed in Kansas City while he was a guest at a black church. Johnson recalled that he had arrived at a church where he was to speak for the NAACP following the service. The congregation had been lulled nearly to sleep by an "exhorter" who had concluded a dull sermon just as Johnson arrived. After two more short sermons, the visiting minister rose to speak.

> He appeared to be a bit self-conscious, perhaps impressed by the presence of the "distinguished visitor" [Johnson himself] on the platform, and started in to preach a formal sermon from a formal text. The congregation sat apathetic and dozing. He sensed that he was losing his audience and his opportunity. Suddenly he closed the Bible, stepped out from behind the pulpit and began to preach. He started intoning the old folk-sermon that begins with the creation of the world and ends with Judgment Day. He was at once a changed man, free, at ease and masterful. The change in the congregation was instantaneous. . . . (6)

Faulkner's treatment of the parallel scene in *The Sound and the Fury* is strikingly similar to Johnson's account of the transformation of the visiting preacher in Kansas City. When Rev'un Shegog begins to speak, his performance seems as disappointing as his appearance, and although his manner is impressive in a scholarly sense, it does not appeal to his audience:

> When the visitor rose to speak he sounded like a white man. His voice was level and cold. It sounded too big to have come from him and they listened at first through curiosity, as they would have to a monkey talking. . . . They even forgot his insignificant appearance in the virtuosity with which he ran and poised and swooped upon the cold inflectionless wire of his voice, so that at last, when with a sort of swooping glide he came to rest again beside the reading desk with one arm resting upon it at shoulder height and his monkey body as reft of all motion as a mummy or an emptied vessel, the congregation sighed as if it waked from a collective dream and moved a little in its seats. (293-94)

The performance seems to be over, and Frony's low expectations seem to be fulfilled. But the visitor is not done. Like Johnson's preacher, he recaptures his audience with his "Brethren and sisteren. . . . I got the recollection and the blood of the Lamb!" (294). He becomes more mobile, walking "back and forth before the desk, his hands clasped behind him. . . ." The congregation has sat quietly during his scholarly delivery of the formal, prepared sermon, but now, he is answered by "a woman's single soprano: 'Yes, Jesus!'" As the preacher further departs from his Northern persona, his speech becomes more earthy:

"Breddren en sistuhn!" His voice rang again. . . ."I got de ricklickshun en de blood of de Lamb!" They did not mark just when his intonation, his pronunciation, became negroid [sic], they just sat swaying a little in their seats as the voice took them into itself. (295)

He goes on to preach a sermon that, while devoid of any continuity or organization, enthralls the congregation and leaves it emotionally drained when he is finished.

The power of the preacher is attested to by several members of the congregation as they leave the church:

"He sho a preacher, mon! He didn't look like much at first, but hush!"

"He seed de power en de glory."

"Yes, suh. He seed hit. Face to face he seed hit." (297)

There are few direct word-by-word parallels between what Johnson's preachers and Faulkner's say, but both share the theme of the coming of Judgment Day: Johnson's first six sermons on such topics as the Prodigal Son, the death of the individual, and the Flood pave the way for a treatment of the last judgment in the seventh; likewise, Faulkner has been building toward the notion of a day of reckoning throughout *The Sound and the Fury*. Thus, a recurring theme in each work is, "There comes a time, / There comes a time" (*God's Trombones* 22), or "dey'll come a time" (*Sound and Fury* 295) when the individual will be judged. Both preachers call for salvation by the faithful washing "their robes in the blood of the Lamb" so that they are "clothed in spotless white" (*God's Trombones* 55) or urge "de ricklickshun en de blood of de Lamb!" (*Sound and Fury* 295). And Dilsey's final pronouncement, "I've seed de first en de last" (297) mirrors the structure of *God's Trombones*, which begins with the Creation and ends with Judgment Day.

What is more striking than verbal echoes is the outline of Rev'un Shegog's sermon. The seven-verse sermons of *God's Trombones* are:

"The Creation"
"The Prodigal Son"
"Go Down Death—A Funeral Sermon"
"Noah Built the Ark"
"The Crucifixion"
"Let My People Go"
"The Judgment Day."

Faulkner employs allusions to five of the seven within Rev'un Shegog's sermon of less than 500 words. **"Go Down Death"** is echoed by Shegog's reminder that "dey'll come a time. Po sinner saying Let me lay down wid de Lawd, lemme lay down my load" (295). The Flood is referred to by Shegog when he says, "I sees de whelmin flood roll between; I sees de darkness en de death everlastin upon de generations" (296). The crucifixion is treated in a paragraph which calls up "Calvary wid de sacred trees . . . de thief en de murderer . . . [and] de wailin of

women en de evening lamentations" (296). Shegog reminds the congregation of those who "passed away in Egypt . . . de generations passed away" (925) just as Johnson's preacher has done in **"Let My People Go."** And as previously mentioned, Shegog's sermon begins and ends with reminders of the subject of Johnson's last poem: Judgment Day.

Although one recent critic sees a resemblance between Shegog and Johnson's portrait of the black preacher but sees more contrasts than similarities and pronounces Faulkner's sermon "not completely successful,"[6] a comparison of the two preachers and their sermons justifies a more positive conclusion. The success of both sermons depends heavily on the dramatic shift in style by each preacher, a shift that elicits a corresponding change in the reaction of the congregation—and of the reader. In spite of the obvious stylistic difference caused by the facts that Johnson elected not to use dialect and Faulkner did use it, the sermons are remarkably similar in both style and substance, and Faulkner's description of the reaction to Rev'un Shegog closely echoes Johnson's account of the reaction of the Kansas City congregation in his preface to *God's Trombones*.

James Weldon Johnson's *God's Trombones* appears to have exerted a significant influence on Faulkner as he completed one of his most important novels. Admittedly, Rev'un Shegog is a minor character in *The Sound and the Fury*, and Johnson's influence extends to no more than some five pages. However, that influence is important in that Rev'un Shegog's sermon has been called "an extraordinarily memorable event in American fiction that, with a readily acknowledged power and poignancy, brings to a climax the agony and the ecstasy of *The Sound and the Fury*. . . ."[7]

While the success of Shegog's sermon has been questioned by some critics, the fact that Faulkner was influenced by James Weldon Johnson in the creation of a significant black character and a scene characteristic of black life is both noteworthy and suggestive. Faulkner, whose commitment to the black race has sometimes been suspect among black readers and critics, showed a willingness and ability to achieve insights denied to white observers by consulting the work of a respected black author of his day and in doing so strengthened the final section of one of his best works.

Notes

[1] See, for example, Charles H. Nilon, *Faulkner and the Negro* (New York: Citadel, 1965); Lee Jenkins, *Faulkner and Black-White Relations: A Psychoanalytic Approach* (New York: Columbia UP, 1981); Thadious M. Davis, *Faulkner's "Negro": Art and the Southern Context* (Baton Rouge: Louisiana State UP, 1983); and Richard Beards, "Parody as Tribute: William Melvin Kelley's *A Different Drummer* and Faulkner," *Studies in Black Literature*, 5 (Winter 1974), 25-28.

[2] Joseph Blotner, *Selected Letters of William Faulkner* (London: Scholar Press, 1977) pp. 35-36.

3 James Weldon Johnson, *God's Trombones: Seven Negro Sermons in Verse* (New York: Viking, 1927), pp. 6-7. Future references are to this edition and appear parenthetically in the text.

4 William Faulkner, *The Sound and the Fury*, New, Corrected Edition (New York: Random, 1984), p. 294. Future references are to this edition and appear parenthetically in the text.

5 Shegog's effective use of the black oral tradition and Faulkner's skill at conveying that tradition have been treated by Bruce A. Rosenburg, "The Oral Quality of Reverend Shegog's Sermon in William Faulkner's *The Sound and the Fury*," *Literatur in Wissenschaft und Unterricht*, 2 (1969), 73-88, and Andre Bleikasten, *The Most Splendid Failure: Fulkner's The Sound and the Fury* (Bloomington: Indiana UP, 1976), p. 200.
6 Davis, p. 122.

7 Arthur F. Kinney, introd., *Critical Essays on William Faulkner: The Compson Family* (Boston: G. K. Hall, 1982), p. 2. See also Irving Howe, *William Faulkner: A Critical Study* (New York: Random, 1962), p. 48; Arthur Geffen, "Profane Time, Sacred Time, and Confederate Time in *The Sound and the Fury*," *Studies in American Fiction*, 2 (1974), 175-97; Joseph R. Urgo, "A Note on Reverend Shegog's Sermon in Faulkner's *The Sound and the Fury*," *NMAL*, 7, No. 1 (1984), item 4; and Bleikasten, p. 197.

Holly Eley (review date 1993)

SOURCE: "Committed to the Conduit," in *Times Literary Supplement*, No. 4721, September 24, 1993, p. 27.

[*In the following review of* St. Peter Relates an Incident, *Eley summarizes Johnson's career and the significance of his poetry.*]

James Weldon Johnson's reputation no longer rests—if it ever truly did—on his poems. Although his work includes the gospel hymn, **"Steal Away to Jesus,"** he arguably deserves most respect as an exemplary member of W.E.B. Du Bois's "talented tenth": black Americans who, having managed to surmount the difficulties encountered by the descendants of slaves and having joined the middle class, neither abandon their brothers nor burn out.

Johnson was born in 1871, in Florida, the son of a waiter and a schoolmistress, and church was an influential part of his upbringing. Extraordinarily energetic and highly disciplined, by the age of twenty-three he had become principal of a segregated school and, a year later, the founding editor of the *Daily American*, the first national US newspaper for blacks. He then qualified as a lawyer (the first black to be admitted to the Florida Bar since Reconstruction), and wrote memorable songs for Broadway such as **"Under the Bamboo Tree"** and **"O Didn't He Ramble,"** while avoiding involvement in the racially exploitative minstrel shows of the time.

In 1906, on the advice of Booker T. Washington, who had just delivered the black vote to the Democrats, Theodore Roosevelt appointed Johnson to the US Consulate in Venezuela. Soon afterwards, he was made consul in Nicaragua. He served with distinction in both postings, but found time to write his only novel, *The Autobiography of an Ex-Colored Man*. His truer autobiography, *Along This Way*, was written in the 1930s; it emphasizes his achievements and makes light of the near-impossibility of reconciling loyalties to his race and to the political and cultural policies of his country. Johnson was active in the NAACP, and in the aftermath of the First World War, made sure that black commitment to the American cause was at least minimally rewarded with jobs in industry.

But literature had always seemed to him likely to be the main conduit through which black culture would reach the wider world. When, as an adolescent, he first addressed himself to it, he wrote dialect verse, a form he was soon to discard and too much of which has been included in this new selection. His political crusades are better reflected in protest poems such as the 1916 **"Brothers,"** a dialogue between a lynch mob and its victim, and the sardonic poem from which the selection takes its title, **"St Peter Relates an Incident of the Resurrection Day,"** in which the Unknown Soldier, symbol of America's heroic war dead, turns out, having been given a Washington state funeral attended by the Daughters of the American Revolution and other diagnitaries, to have been a nigger.

As a writer, Johnson is best remembered for his religious poetry. *God's Trombones: Seven negro sermons in verse* (in which he captures the rhythm, sentence structure and repetitions of the illiterate folk-preacher without the distortions and limitations of dialect) was published in 1927, during the Harlem Renaissance. He was not as much appreciated by the niggerati and their white avant-garde supporters as he should have been; his free verse sermon poems (only one is included in this volume) precede the acclaimed innovations of folkloric poets such as Sterling Brown. Apart from **"Steal Away to Jesus,"** his most successful poem, also included here, is **"Lift Every Voice and Sing."** Written in 1900, and set to music by his brother, J. Rosamond Johnson, it is known today as the African-American national anthem.

FURTHER READING

Bibliography

Mason, Julian. "James Weldon Johnson." In *Fifty Southern Writers After 1900: A Bio-Bibliographical Sourcebook*, edited by Joseph M. Flora and Robert Bain, pp. 280-89. New York: Greenwood Press, 1987.

> Bibliography of primary and secondary sources preceded by an introduction to Johnson's life and the major themes of his work.

Biography

Brawley, Benjamin. "Protest and Vindication-James Weldon Johnson." In *The Negro Genius: A New Appraisal of the Achievement of the American Negro in Literature and the Fine Arts*, pp. 206-214. New York: Dodd, Mead & Company, 1937.

Provides a sketch of Johnson's life which includes a brief survey of his works of poetry.

Broun, Heywood Hale. "James Weldon Johnson." In *Collected Edition of Heywood Broun,* pp. 452-54. New York: Harcourt, Brace and Company, 1941.

Gives a short biographical assessment of Johnson.

Desjardins, Lucile. "James Weldon Johnson." In *Rising Above Color,* edited by Philip Henry Lotz, pp. 98-104. New York: Association Press, 1943.

Offers a biographical study of Johnson that concentrates on his poetic achievements and work with the National Association for the Advancement of Colored People (NAACP).

Levy, Eugene. *James Weldon Johnson: Black Leader, Black Voice.* Chicago: University of Chicago Press, 1973, 380 p.

Provides an exemplary, full-length biography of Johnson.

Criticism

Collier, Eugenia W. "James Weldon Johnson: Mirror of Change." *Phylon* 21, No. 4 (1960): 351-59.

Evaluates the pivotal 1920s emergence of Johnson's verse in the southern black idiom, which elevated the genre of stilted and traditional African-American dialect poetry.

Whalum, Wendell Phillips. "James Weldon Johnson's Theories and Performance Practices of Afro-American Folksong." *Phylon* 32, No. 4 (Winter 1971): 383-95.

Examines Johnson's writings as they pertain to the style and performance of black American spirituals.

Additional coverage of Johnson's life and career is contained in the following sources published by The Gale Group: *Twentieth-Century Literary Criticism,* **Vols. 3, 19;** *Black Literary Criticism,* **Vol. 2;** *DISCovering Authors: Multicultural Authors Module; DISCovering Authors: Poets Module; Black Writers,* **Vol. 1;** *Contemporary Authors,* **Vols. 104, 125;** *Concise Dictionary of American Literary Biography 1917-1929; Children's Literature Review,* **Vol. 32;** *Dictionary of Literary Biography,* **Vol. 51;** *Major 20th-Century Writers;* **and** *Something About the Author,* **Vol. 31.**

Juana Inés de la Cruz
1651-1695

(Born Juana Ramírez de Asbaje) Mexican poet, playwright, and autobiographer.

INTRODUCTION

Juana is recognized as one of the most important female writers of her time. Her most acclaimed poem *El sueño,* is praised for its personal, lyric qualities as well as its incorporation of images from history, mythology, science, physiology, and philosophy. Her passionate defense of female intellectual rights has led many critics to cite her as a significant feminist poet and scholar.

Biographical Information

Juana was born on November 12, 1651, on a small farm southeast of Mexico City. Her parents were not married, and the fact that she was born illegitimate was a stigma that followed her the rest of her life. She was a precocious reader, and her obsessive interest in scholarly topics was considered very unusual for young girls at that time. At the age of eight, she had already composed poetry and a prologue to a play. She was sent to Mexico City to live with relatives, and it was at that time she came to the attention of the viceroy, the marquis of Mancera, and his wife. Her wit and sharp intelligence made her a favorite in their court, and she was recognized as a formidable intellectual presence. It was at court that she was asked to write verse commemorating special social or political events of the day. She entered the Carmelite convent on August 14, 1667, but a year later left to join the convent of St. Jerome. The religious life allowed her a limited degree of social independence and intellectual pursuit, and she continued to study philosophy, history, and literature. Near the end of her life, she was pressured to concentrate on only serious poetry and theological essays; her response, *Respueta a Sor Filotea de la Cruz,* is considered a strong self-defense of her intellectual development and has become a recognized hallmark of feminist literature. Disillusioned at the publicity this document generated, Juana withdrew from public life. She died of an unidentified plague on April 16, 1695.

Major Works

A prolific writer, Juana composed personal lyrics, poetic portraits, religious verse, and *villancicos.* Primarily sonnets, her lyrics are characterized by conventional structure, an intellectually rational approach, and autobiographical subject matter. Her verse expresses the themes of love, jealousy, duty, and absence and incorporates elements of mythology, theology, science, literature, and

history. In her twelve sequences of *villancicos*—poems sung by a choir on major feast days—Juana presents an innovative, often humorous celebration of Mexican life.

Critical Reception

Juana is almost universally lauded for her concise, spirited poems that reflect the public, religious, and social life of Mexico in the seventeenth-century. Critics note how she fused traditional poetic forms with fresh use of language to create vibrant, innovative verse. *El sueño,* her best-known poem, has been studied for its deft treatment of philosophical and autobiographical issues. Juana has been praised for her incorporation of images and subject matter from a diverse group of intellectual interests, such as literature, mythology, science, theology, physiology, and history. The influence of many major and minor Spanish poets have been found in her poetry, from Lope de Vega, Gongora, Quevedo, and Agustin de Salazar y Torres. Many commentators have analyzed the feminist ideology in both her prose and her poetry and consider her a strong feminist icon and a courageous, talented writer.

PRINCIPAL WORKS

Poetry

Poemas 1690
Fama y obras pósthumas 1700
Obras poéticas 1715
El sueño [*The Dream*] 1951
Obras completas. 4 vols. (poems, essays, and plays) 1951-1957

Other Major Works

Auto sacramental del divino Narciso (play) 1690
Respuesta a Sor Filotea de la Cruz [*A Woman of Genius: The Intellectual Autobiography of Sor Juana Inés de la Cruz*] (autobiography) 1691

CRITICISM

Robert Graves (essay date 1955)

SOURCE: "Juana de Asabaje," in *The Crowning Privilege: The Clark Lectures 1954-1955,* Cassell & Co., 1955, pp. 166-84.

[*In the following essay from 1955, Graves categorizes Cruz as a woman of poetic genius and compares her to other great female poets.*]

Every few centuries a woman of poetic genius appears, who may be distinguished by three clear secondary signs: learning, beauty, and loneliness. Though the burden of poetry is difficult enough for a man to bear, he can always humble himself before an incarnate Muse and seek instruction from her. At the worst this Muse, whom he loves in a more than human sense, may reject and deceive him; and even then he can vent his disillusion in a memorable poem—as Catullus did when he parted from Clodia—and survive to fix his devotion on another. The case of a woman poet is a thousand times worse: since she is herself the Muse, a Goddess without an external power to guide or comfort her, and if she strays even a finger's breadth from the path of divine instinct, must take violent self-vengeance. For awhile a sense of humour, good health, and discretion may keep her on an even keel, but the task of living to, for, and with herself alone, will sooner or later prove an impossible one. Sappho of Lesbos, Liadan of Corkaguiney, and Juana de Asbaje belonged to this desperate sisterhood: incarnations of the Muse-goddess, cut off from any simple gossiping relation with their fellow-women, who either adored them blindly or hated them blindly, and from any spiritual communion with men on equal terms. Though a woman so fated cannot help feeling physical desire for a man, she is forbidden by her identity with the Goddess from worshipping or giving herself wholly to him, even if he desires to worship and give himself wholly to her. It is possible that Clodia was another of these unfortunates, so that the harder Catullus tried to please her, the more despairingly she fought him off: playing the society harlot rather than consent to burn with him in a mutual flame.

About Clodia little is known, and about Catullus no more than his poems reveal. Even the story of Sappho survives only in fragmentary form. We learn that she was early married on Lesbos to one Cercolas, a man of no distinction, and bore him a daughter; that her learning and inventive faculties were memorable; that she tutored girls of literary promise; that she rejected the advances of Alcaeus, the leading poet of his day; that she fled to Sicily from some unnamed trouble and, after an unhappy affair with one Phaon, a common sailor, 'took the Leucadian leap': which implies some spectacular act of self-destruction. The inter-relation of these bare facts remains obscure; yet it seems that a possessed woman poet will rather subject herself to a dull husband or ignorant lover, who mistrusts her genius and may even ill-treat her physically, than encourage the love of a Catullus or Alcaeus, which demands more than it is hers to give.

The story of Liadan is also fragmentary. She was a brilliant young Irish *ollamh* (or master-poet) of the seventh century A.D., privileged to make semi-royal progresses from one great mansion to another, preceded by a peal of golden bells, and followed by a train of lesser bards and pupils. On one of these she went to Connaught, where the *ollamh* Curithir welcomed her to an ale feast. After the long exchange of riddling poetic lore in Old Goidelic, customary on such occasions, he burst out suddenly: 'Why should we not marry, Liadan? A son born to us would be famous.' She was startled into answering: 'Wait until my progress is done; then visit me at Corkaguiney and I will come with you.' He did so, only to find that Liadan, regretting her lapse, had meanwhile taken a religious vow of chastity. In despair and anger, Curithir took a similar vow, and when they went away together, as agreed, it was to the monastery of Clonfert, where Liadan insisted on placing herself under the spiritual direction of St Cummin, a hard and severe abbot. Curithir followed suit. Cummin found them two separate cells, offering Curithir the choice of either seeing Liadan without addressing her, or addressing her without seeing her. He chose the second alternative; and Liadan consented to this arrangement. They were then each in turn allowed to wander around the other's wattled cell; until Liadan persuaded Cummin to grant Curithir greater freedom, of which she must have known that he would try to take advantage. As a result, he was banished from Clonfert, and sailed away to the Holy Land; but Liadan let herself die of remorse, because she had foolishly involved him in her ruin.

Unlike Sappho and Liadan, Juana de Asbaje was born into a society where she must have seemed as portentous as a talking dove, or a dog which does long division. Neither in Lesbos nor ancient Ireland had limits been set to a woman's learning. Sappho was no freak, but merely the truest of several famous women poets. Liadan, to win her peal of golden bells, had passed the *ollamh's* twelve-year course in literature, law, history, languages, music, magic, mathematics, and astronomy—one of incredible stiffness—and that a woman should so distinguish herself was not considered abnormal. In seventeenth-century Mexico, however, the Church had gained such a stranglehold on learning and literature that women, doctrinally debarred from the priesthood, and despised as the intellectual and moral inferiors of their fathers and brothers, could nurse no aspirations beyond a good husband, many children, and a Christian death. Only at the Viceregal Court might a lady read poems or romances, and thus equip herself for the games of chivalry in which etiquette required her to assist the courtiers; but even so, a confessor always stood by to check all signs of vanity or immodesty.

Juana, born on November 12, 1651, was the daughter of Don Pedro Manuel de Asbaje, an immigrant Vizcayan, and Dona Isabel Ramirez, whose father, the head of a family long established in Mexico, owned a substantial estate near Chimalhuacán, and seems to have been a man of some cultivation. Juana's mother, however, could neither read nor write and, when she died some thirty years later, it transpired that Juana and her two sisters had all been born out of wedlock: presumably because the father had left behind a wife in Spain. Though he seems to have legitimized the three of them before they grew up, it has been suggested that the shame of having been born a bastard encouraged Juana to excel as a poet, while it soured her against marriage; but this is mere speculation.

One morning, when she was three years old, her sister said: 'Mother cannot have you about the house today. Come with me to school and sit quietly in a corner.' Juana went . . .

> . . . and seeing that they gave my sister lessons, I so burned with a desire to know how to read that, deceiving the teacher, as I thought, I told her that my mother had ordered her to give me lessons. She did not believe this, as it was incredible, but to humour me, she acquiesced. I continued to attend and she to teach me, not in mockery now, because experience had undeceived her; and I learned to read in such short time that when my mother (from whom the teacher had hidden the matter in order to give her the pleasure and receive the reward all at once) found out, I was already proficient. I, too, had concealed it, thinking that they would whip me for acting without orders. She who taught me still lives, God preserve her, and can testify to the truth. . . . I recall that in those days I had the appetite for sweets and delicacies that is common at such an age, but that I abstained from eating cheese because I had heard it said that taking this made one dull-witted; for my desire to learn was stronger than the wish to eat, which ordinarily is so powerful in children.

At the age of six or seven, she pleaded to be enrolled at Mexico City University and, since the statutes barred women from taking the course, to have her hair cut and be dressed as a boy. When her mother laughingly refused, Juana took possession of her grandfather's library, which no punishment could deter her from reading; and when she found that the most desirable books were in Latin, mastered the elements in fewer than twenty les-

sons and, before she was eight, could read and enjoy Plato, Aristophanes, and Erasmus. Juana now made life so difficult for her mother that she was sent to her uncle's house in Mexico City, where she taught herself literature, science, mathematics, philosophy, theology, and languages. At the age of thirteen she was presented at Court by the uncle; there her exceptional talents, vivacity, and beauty—wide-set chestnut-coloured eyes, broad brow, quick smile, straight nose, determined chin, delicate fingers—qualified her to be the darling and first lady-in-waiting of the Vicereine. For three years Juana took part in all the gallant diversions of the Viceregal Court, the cultural centre of the New World, and became its principal ornament, next to the regal pair themselves: studying every book that came to hand, and writing a profusion of court verse in Castilian, Latin, and Aztec—besides theatrical sketches, satires, verses of commendation and occasional trifles, some of them 'highly seasoned'; and finding time for poetry of a truer and more personal kind. A great many well-born young men asked her hand in marriage, but she behaved with admirable discretion and refused their offers, though the Viceroy and Vicereine would doubtless have provided a dowry.

When she reached the age of sixteen, the Viceroy heard her decried as having only a smattering of knowledge, and therefore summoned forty learned men—University professors, theologians, poets, mathematicians, and historians—to examine her in their various subjects. He afterwards recorded with satisfaction:

> Like a royal galleon beating off the attacks of a few enemy sloops, so did Juana fight clear of the questions, arguments and objections that so many specialists, each in his own department, propounded. . . .

Father Calleja, of the Society of Jesus, her first biographer, asked Juana what impression this triumph, capable of puffing up even the humblest soul to self-importance, had made upon her. She replied: 'It left me with no greater satisfaction than if I had performed a small task of hemstitching more neatly than my embroidery-teacher.' About this time she first expressed a total aversion to marriage. Her motives have ever since been hotly debated. Father Calleja suggests that she recognized the glitter of Court life as empty delusion; never fell in love with a man; and soon realized that only service to God could give her lasting happiness. This is still the view of the Church, despite her plainly autobiographical love-poems, written at the age of sixteen: *Este amoroso tormento que en mi corazón se ve,* and: *Si otros ojos hé visto, matenme, Fabio, tus airados ojos*; and the poems of disillusion which followed, especially the famous:

> *Hombres necios que acusáis*
> *a la mujer sin razón;*

and the two scorching farewell sonnets to Silvio, whom she hates herself for having loved so well.

Juana presently decided to become a nun, although, as she wrote later: 'I knew that the estate implied obligations (I am referring to the incidentals, not the fundamentals) most repugnant to my temperament.' In this course she was encouraged by her confessor, Father Antonio Nuñez de Miranda, to whom 'she broached all her doubts, fears, and misgivings'. Her first attempt failed: after three months as a novice among the Barefoot Carmelites, her health broke down, and she withdrew on doctor's orders. Fourteen months later, however, she was well enough to enter a Jeronymite convent and in February 1669, having completed a short novitiate, took the veil as Sor Juana Inéz de la Cruz, the name by which she is now generally known.

Father Antonio did not insist that she should abandon her studies and, since the Jeronymites were the most liberal of the Orders in seventeenth-century Mexico, her cell soon became an academy, lined with books and filled with the instruments of music and mathematics. Juana learned to play several instruments, wrote a treatise on musical harmony, made a name as a miniaturist, became proficient in moral and dogmatic theology, medicine, canon law, astronomy, and advanced mathematics. Her library swelled to four thousand books, the largest in the New World, and it is recorded:

> . . . the *locutorio* of the Jeronimas was frequented by many of the highest in Mexico, thanks to the renown of Sor Juana. She had loved solitude but [her presence] brought her many distinguished visitors. Not a Viceroy of that epoch but desired to know her and, from the highest to the lowest, they all consulted Juana on weighty affairs. A natural affability and graciousness made her lend herself with good will to these fatiguing visits.

Juana continued to write verses, though none for publication: mostly birthday and name-day greetings addressed to her friends at Court, dedications, epitaphs, commemorations, rhymed letters of thanks for books or musical instruments—all smooth, eloquent, and highly rhetorical. To these she added sacred sonnets, dirges, roundelays, carols, panegyrics of saints, lively allegories, and religious plays. She was also a famous cook and for ever sending her friends gifts of confectionery: almond rings, nuns' sighs (to use the politer phrase), cakes, and puff pastry of every kind. Accompanying these went humorous verses, such as this:

> *To Her Excellency again, with a shoe embroidered in Mexican style, and a parcel of chocolate:*
>
> > A cast glove is challenge:
> > *Contrariwise,*
> > A cast shoe, my Lady,
> > *Surrender signifies.*

Frequent balls, concerts, and ballad-recitals were given in the Convent and patronized by the Viceregal pair who never failed to attend vespers there as an excuse for amusing and instructive conversation with the 'Mexican Phœnix'. It was an easy life, since no limit was put on the number of Indian serfs owned by the sisters; one convent of a hundred nuns had five hundred such serving-women working for them. Juana was unlucky, at first, to be under a jealous and narrow-minded prioress, at whom she once shouted in exasperation: 'Hold your tongue, you ignorant fool!' The prioress complained to the then Archbishop of Mexico who, as an admirer of Juana, endorsed the prioress's complaint with: 'If the Mother Superior can prove that this charge is false, justice will be done.'

Unlike Sappho and Liadan, Juana de Asbaje was born into a society where she must have seemed as portentous as a talking dove, or a dog which does long division.

—Robert Graves

Juana performed all the religious tasks laid on her, though not greedy of ecclesiastical advancement and, when on one occasion unanimously elected prioress, declined the honour. The gay times at the Convent seem to have ended with the Viceroy's term of office; but her 'passion to know' remained as strong as ever, and this, she wrote, subjected her to more criticism and resentment than the massive learning she had already acquired. On one occasion a 'very holy and candid prelate' ordered her to cease from her studies. She obeyed in so far as she read no more books . . .

> . . . but since it was not within my power to cease absolutely, I observed all things that God created, the universal machine serving me in place of books.

During the three months of the prelate's continuance in office, she studied the mechanics of the spinning top, and the chemical reactions of convent cookery, making important scientific discoveries. Later, when she fell seriously ill, the doctors also forbade her to read, but . . .

> . . . seeing that, when deprived of books, her cogitations were so vehement that they consumed more spirit in a quarter of an hour than did four days' reading,

they were forced to withdraw their prohibition.

Juana's confessor, still the same Father Antonio, now tried to dissuade her from seeing and writing to so many friends and learned laymen, on the ground that this was irreconcilable with her profession; and when she would not listen to him, resigned his charge. Next, she was ordered by an unnamed superior to refute an admittedly unorthodox sermon preached by a famous theologian, the Portuguese Jesuit Father Antonio Vieira; which Juana did in a letter of such masterly argument, that when it was published (without her knowledge or permission) the most learned doctors of Spain and Portugal were highly diverted to find that this Mexican nun had completely demolished Vieira's thesis; and sent her profuse congratulations. But one old friend, the Bishop of Puebla, qualified his praises with the suggestion that the letter proved how sadly she had wasted her talents in writing shallow verses and studying irrelevant and profane subjects; instead, she should have devoted herself to the unmasking of doctrinal error, now so rife in Christendom. Juana, deeply offended, replied that she made no claim to academic distinction, had written the letter only because ordered to do so and, when she saw it in print, had burst into tears, 'which never come easily to me'. Then, rather than become a theologian, to the exclusion of all her other studies, she grimly sold her entire library for the benefit of the poor, together with all her musical and mathematical instruments; and submitted to the severest conventual discipline, which Father Antonio, returning in joy, unsuccessfully begged her to moderate. This spectacular event created such a stir that the new Archbishop of Mexico similarly sold all his books, jewels, valuables, and even his bed.

In 1695, some of the sisters fell ill of the plague, and Juana, though weakened by nearly two years of rigorous penance, set herself to nurse them; but presently caught the infection and succumbed. The Jeronymite records contain this sentence, scratched with Juana's fingernail dipped in her own blood—because she had renounced the use of pen and ink:

> Immediately above will be noted the day, month and year of my death. For the love of God and of His Purest Mother, I pray that my beloved sisters, both those now living and those who have gone before, will recommend me to Him—though I have been the worst woman in the world.
>
> Signed: I, Juana Inés de la Cruz.

Juana de Asbaje wrote true poetry before she was seventeen; but what of her heiress and successor, Sor Juana Inés de la Cruz? We can applaud the dazzling fantasy of Sor Juana's religious verse, its perfect sense of rhythm and sure balance of phrases, its essential clarity, which shames the interlaced extravagances of contemporary Gongorists, and the universality of knowledge displayed by the incidental references. Yet the appeal is almost wholly to the intellect. Juana never became mystically involved with Christ. She accepted Him as a theological axiom, rather than as the divine bridegroom whom St Teresa knew, and of whom the medieval Irish nun wrote:

> Jesukin, my Jesukin
> My small cell doth dwell within!
> With prelates have I nought to do:
> All's untrue but Jesukin.

She was no longer the Muse of every Mexican gallant, though flatterers continued to call her 'The Tenth Muse'; and as an intelligence she now functioned in a field which the ecclesiastics, to whom she had promised obedience, were always seeking to reduce; being forced to play a religious part in which she could not wholly believe, because it was repugnant to her temperament, yet at last playing it so successfully as at once to shame them and defeat her own ends. When she had sold her books and

cut herself off from the world, the only solace left was the fellowship of her ignorant sisters, and even this seems hardly to have been an unmixed blessing:

> It happened that among other favours, I owe to God an easy and affable nature and the nuns loved me for it (without taking notice, like the good people they were, of my faults) and greatly enjoyed my company; knowing this and moved by the great love I had for them—since they loved me, I loved them more—there were times when they intruded somewhat, coming to me to console themselves and to give me the recreation of their company.

It was in no spirit of mock-humility that she described herself as the worst of women; writing the confession in her own blood. She meant that when she first took the Leucadian Leap by becoming a nun, it had not been into the sea of pure religion. Still keeping her intellectual pride, her thirst for scientific knowledge and her pleasure in profane authors, lay visitors and the minor pleasures of the flesh, she could remember what it had been to love and to write poetry; and her ancient powers still occasionally reasserted themselves, for instance in some of the songs, based on the *Canticles,* which enliven her religious play *The Divine Narcissus.* Juana called herself the worst of women, it seems, because she had lacked sufficient resolution either to stick it out as a Muse, or make a complete renegation in the style of Liadan.

Now, though both Liadan and Juana were young and famous women poets who took vows of celibacy and submitted to ecclesiastical discipline, it was Juana's Irishness, rather, that first led me to compare them. Juana not only combined Christian ethics with pagan emotion, and profound learning with easy lyricism, like the *ollamhs,* but had inherited their technique by way of the early medieval Latin hymns and the anti-monastic ballads of the Goliards. She too loved the short rhymed quatrain, and the internal rhymes of her *Carol to St Peter*:

> Y con plumas y voces veloces
> Y con voces y plumas las sumas
> Cantad . . .

were in the purest Bardic tradition, like St Bernard of Cluny's *Rhythm,* which begins:

> Hora novissima, tempora pessima
> Sunt; vigilemus
> Ecce minaciter imminet arbiter
> Ille supremus . . .

Moreover, she excelled in satire of the scorching Irish sort that would raise blotches on the victim's face: her **"Lines to Sour-Faced Gila"** might have been written by the arch-*ollamh* Seanchan Torpest himself, notorious for having rhymed rats to death. Perhaps Juana's Vizcayan blood was at work; an ancient tie of kinship and religion bound the Western Irish with the Northern Spanish—both peoples had worshipped the same pre-Christian Muse-goddess and the doomed hero Lugos, or Lugh, her gifted son.

Gerard Flynn (essay date 1971)

SOURCE: "The Poetry of Sor Juana," in *Sor Juana Inés de la Cruz*, Twayne, 1971, pp. 82-98.

[*In the following essay, Flynn provides a stylistic and thematic overview of Cruz's poetry.*]

Sor Juana was in effect a poet laureate who had to write many poems for the important occasions of Church and State. For the Church she wrote a series of *villancicos* celebrating certain feast days of the year. Most of them were to be combined with the prayers of matins, and a few were to be sung at the Epistle, the Offertory, and the *Ite missa est* of the Mass.

Those *villancicos* that were written as "complete sets for matins" were broken up into three nocturnes matching the three parts of matins. The first nocturne had the task of introducing the mystery of the feast day or the history of the saint whose memory was being celebrated. The second nocturne was generally less grave and drew images from the arts and sciences: medicine, music, fencing, astronomy, philosophy, teaching, painting, physics, and history. In most cases the second nocturne also had the *jácara*, a lively piece that provided relief for the congregation. In the *villancicos* for the Immaculate Conception, 1689, Sor Juana describes the purpose of the *jácara*; the chorus has sung very well and now: "one singer alone wanted / in a jacarandina / to soothe with levity / the gravity of the tones."

The third nocturne had the remaining two poems of the set and usually repeated a previous theme. One of these poems was the *ensalada*, a mixture of verses that were for the most part frivolous. Nevertheless, it is the *ensalada* that has the one durable part of all these *villancicos*, the poetry of the Negro.

The Negroes appear in the following verses of the *villancicos*: Assumption 1676, VIII; Immaculate Conception 1676, VIII; St. Peter Nolasco 1677, VIII; Assumption 1679, VIII; Assumption 1685, VIII; St. Joseph 1690, VIII. The purpose of the Negro verses was to amuse a congregation that was tired after a long time at prayer, but in effect they capture the religious spirit of the occasion better than the other verses.

The Church preaches the gospel of the uncircumcision, which is not confined to any nation because of its purity of blood, superior law, politics, economics, or philosophy. The gospel is meant for all, the meanest slave and the greatest king. And so the Negroes can sing to their mother Mary, who is also the mother of God.

The Feast of the Assumption 1676

The Spanish of the Negroes	The same verses in ordinary Spanish.	An English translation.
1. *Cantemo, Pilico,* *que se va las Reina*	1. *Cantemos, Perico,* *que se va la Reina*	1. Petey, let's sing, the Queen is going away
y dalemu turo *una noche buena.*	*y démosle todos* *una noche buena.*	let us all bid her good night.
2. *Iguale yolale* *Flacico, de pena,* *que nos deja ascula*	2. *Igual es llorar* *Blasico, de pena,* *que nos deja oscuros*	2. Better to cry Blaisey, from sorrow since she leaves us dark (in darkness)
a turo las negla.	*a todos los negros.*	all us Negroes.
1. *Si las Cielo va*	1. *Si al Cielo va*	1. If she's going to Heaven
y Dioso la lleva	*y Dios se la lleva*	and God takes her away
¿pala qué yolá *si Eya sa cuntenta?*	*¿para qué llorar* *si Ella está contenta?*	why should we cry if She is happy?
Sará muy galana *vitita ri tela* *milando la Sole* *pisando la Streya.*	*Estará muy galana* *vestida de tela* *mirando el Sol* *pisando las Estrellas.*	She must be beautiful dressed up in silk seeing the Sun walking the Stars.
2. *Déjame yolá* *Flacico por Eya* *que se va, y nosotlo* *la Oblaje nos deja.*	2. *Déjame llorar* *Blasico por Ella* *que se va y nosotros* *el Obraje nos deja.*	2. Let me cry Blaisey for her for she's going and she leaves us the workhouse.
1. *Caya, que sa* *siempre* *milando la Iglesia;*	1. *Calla, que está* *siempre* *mirando la Iglesia;*	1. Quiet, she will always be watching the Church;
mila las Pañola	*mira a la Española*	look at the Spanish lady
que se quela plieta.	*que se queda prieta* *(or apretada).*	how somber she is.
2. *Bien dici, Flacico*	2. *Bien dices, Blasico*	2. You are right, Blaisey
tura sa suspensa; *si tú quiele, demo* *unas cantaleta.*	*toda está suspensa;* *si tú quieres, demos* *una cantaleta.*	she is all amazed; if you want, let us sing in jest.
1. *Nomble de mi* *Dioso*	1. *Nombre de mi* *Dios*	1. By God's name
que sa cosa buena!	*que es cosa buena!*	that's a good idea!
Aola, Pilico	*Ahora, Perico*	Now, Petey
que nos mila atenta.	*que nos mira atenta.*	since she's looking at us.
Estribillo	*Estribillo*	Refrain
¡Ah, ah, ah, *que la Reina se nos va!*	*¡Ah, ah, ah,* *que la Reina se nos va!*	Ah, ah, ah, the Queen has gone and left us!
¡Uh, uh, uh, *que non blanca como tú,*	*¡Uh, uh, uh,* *que no es blanca como tú*	Hu, hu, hu, She is not white like you,
nin Pañó que no sa buena;	*ni Española que no es buena*	nor Spanish, which is not good,
que Eya dici: So molena	*que Ella dice: soy morena*	cause she says I am dark
con las Sole que milá!	*con el Sol que me miró!*	from the Sun that looked on me!
¡Ah, ah, ah, *que la Reina se nos va!*	*¡Ah, ah, ah,* *que la Reina se nos va!*	Ah, ah, ah, the Queen has gone and left us!

Here is the sentiment of the poor and downtrodden. The Queen has gone to heaven where she's looking after all her friends, not just the people from high society. She is a dark queen (la Virgen Morena) who has a special love for Petey and Blaisey. Even for the poor, life is a comedy.

In the last *villancico* of the Immaculate Conception 1676 series, a Negro sings his praises of the Virgin. He is happy and he is singing because he knows how to praise his queen as well as the next man:

> Acá tamo tolo
> Zambio, lela, lela,
> que tambié sabemos
> cantaye las Leina.

> All we mixed bloods (*zambos*)
> Are here, lela, lela,
> cause we too know how
> to sing to the Queen.

He is told to go away on this feast of purity and light, for anything black doesn't fit in with the celebration. But he answers:

> Aunque neglo, blanco
> somo, lela, lela,
> que el alma rivota
> blanca sa, no prieta.

> Although black, we are
> white, lela, lela,
> cause the good soul
> is white, not black.

There is no stopping this fellow. The rest of the verses are his. The devil grew bold and tried to harm the Virgin, but she gave that scoundrel (dirty dog) just what he deserved.

The *villancicos* of St. Peter Nolasco 1677 also show the feeling of the Negroes towards the whites. The black man is the poor man who works hard for little pay. He has heard that St. Peter Nolasco redeems the slaves but he cannot believe he did anything for the blacks because he knows from experience the whites get all the good things and live up there in that palace. In a primitive way his thought is very cynical and uncharitable, and the Negro repents for having had it:

> La otra noche con mi conga
> turo sin durmi pensaba
> que no quiele gente plieta
> como eya so gente branca.
> Sola saca la Pañola;
> ¡pues, Dioso, mila la trampa
> que aunque neglo gente somo

> aunque nos dici cabaya!
> Mas ¿qué digo, Dioso mío?
> ¡Los demono, que me engañu,
> pala que esé mulmulando
> a esa Redentola Santa!
> El Santo me lo perrone,
> que só una malo hablala,

> que aunque padesca la cuepo
> en ese libla las alma.

> The other night with my wife
> I couldn't sleep and thought
> he doesn't like black people
> as well as his own white.
> He only helps the Spaniard;
> well, God, see the hitch
> cause we are people,
>   though we're black
> though they call us *burro!*
> But what am I saying, God?
> the devil he deceives me,
> to make me gossip
> about that redeeming Saint.
> I hope the Saint will pardon me,
> and all my evil chatter
> for though the body suffers
> that's what frees the soul.

In the Assumption 1679 series of *villancicos* there are two princesses from Guinea with bundles, who are on their way to market. These salesladies put down their bundles and start to sing:

> 2. *Dejemoso la cocina*
> *y vamoso a turo trote,*
> *sin que vindamos gamote*
> *nin garbanzo a la vizina:*
> *qui arto gamote, Cristina,*
> *hoy a la fieta vendrá.*

> Let us leave the food
> and go as fast as we can
> without selling sweets (potatoes)
> or chickpeas to the women:
> for many sweets, Christina,
> will come to the fiesta today.

The Lady Mary ("Ledy Melly") was a good slave and that's why they freed her and sent her up to heaven:

> Milala como cohete
> que va subiendo lo sumo.

> See her like a skyrocket
> climbing in the sky.

For the theologian the Assumption is a mystery of Faith that demands careful study, but for these two princesses with their graphic minds the Assumption is like the path of a skyrocket.

In the Assumption 1685 series the *camotero* (vendor of sweet potatoes) is a man on very personal terms with his heavenly mother. He would never think of calling himself "one of the faithful," but only "your black Tony" (tu negro Antón), and he asks Mary to wait before ascending until he can bring his gifts to her:

> Espela, aun no suba,
> que to negro Antón

te guarra cuajala
branca como Sol.

Wait, don't go yet
for your black Tony
has curds for you
white as the Sun.

God must delay His plan in History until Antón can deliver
his salted chickpeas, fine sweets, and curds to his mother,
Mary. Like the two princesses of Guinea, Antón has a graphic
way of saying things. Who but he would think to say:

¡Oh Santa María
que a Dioso parió
sin haber comadre
ni tené doló!

Oh Holy Mary,
who delivered God
without a midwife
or labor pains!

The Negro verses appear in the last *villancico* of each
set. Of all the verses they alone have preserved for us the
religious meaning of the occasion.

A good many poems that Sor Juana composed for State
occasions (the birthday of the king, the birthday of the
victory, and so forth) will not stand the test of literary
criticism; the same may be said of the *villancicos,* which
she wrote for Church occasions. Sor Juana led a liturgical life, of which the feasts of the *villancicos* were a
part, and so they have a certain sincerity and genuineness
not to be found in many of her secular pieces; nevertheless, they are not poetry.

The *villancicos* rely too much on paradoxes and other trick
devices. If the reader will picture for a moment the Cathedral of Mexico or Puebla in the early hours of the morning
with the choir and religious singing the prayers of matins,
he can see the problem of the nun. In between antiphon,
psalm, and lesson, she had to supply *villancicos* that were
also to be sung, and she could not appeal to the eyes of
those present but only to their ears, since the *villancicos*
do not provide the spectacle of theater. Sor Juana had to
create means of attracting and holding attention.

Thus she puts a paradox in one of her poems: did the
Blessed Mother descend or ascend when she was assumed
into heaven? She ascended with joy into the arms of her
Son; "the rest was a descent."

Another paradox is the bet between St. Joseph and God,
and the idea that Joseph wakes up when he sleeps, because an angel reveals to him in a dream that his virgin
wife is to bear the Son of God.

Another trick device is an enigma or riddle:

—I shall propose a riddle.
—And I shall answer it.

One singer argues that the Feast of the Assumption is
August 15, and another argues that it is March 25 (the
Incarnation) because the real assumption or rising of the
Mother of God was her union with Christ. Perhaps no
theologian will object to this argument but the literary
critic will have to agree with Menéndez Pelayo, who called
these verses mental gymnastics and disapproved of them.

In some of the *villancicos* Sor Juana mixed Spanish and
Nahuatl, or Spanish and Latin:

Yo al Santo lo tengo
mucha devoción,
y de Sempual Xuchil
un Xuchil le doy.
  (Feast of St. Peter Nolasco 1677, *Villancico* VIII)

Tristes te invocamus:
concede, gloriosa,
gratias quae te illustrant,
dotes quae te adornant.
  (Feast of the Assumption 1679, *Villancico* II).

The *villancicos* are important documents for the biographer of Sor Juana and for the historian of the seventeenth
century. One of the *villancicos* is written with the simplicity of a catechism; another shows that Sor Juana knew
the doctrines of latria and hyperdulia; another shows she
knew the procedure of a Scholastic debate; in another she
applies the idea of hylomorphism to the Assumption. There
are scores of ideas and expressions such as those just
mentioned in the two-hundred-odd pages of the *villancicos.* As for the historian, he will find many social and
cultural references in these verses: a Negro vendor of
sweet potatoes; a Biscayan; two sacristans; an idea from
physics; an image from the science of the day; the translation of the Bible by the Seventy-Two, comparisons from
music, rhetoric, teaching, philosophy, and fencing; some
Portuguese; even a reference to the *mal francés!*

. . . . .

The lyrical poetry of Sor Juana consists of metrical combinations known as *romances, endechas, redondillas,*
décimas, glosas, sonetos, liras, ovillejos, and *silvas.* A
careful reading of this lyrical poetry will show that it can
be divided into three parts: (A) the courtly poems, that is,
poems Sor Juana wrote for the viceroy's court, for dig-
nitaries, or for the king; (B) the love poems; and (C)
thirteen sonnets.

A. *The Courtly Poems*

The courtly poems, which comprise about three-fourths
of Sor Juana's lyrical poetry, are not distinguished verses. Some of these poems are for an archbishop, a
marchesa, the viceroy, the king, a young doctor; others
are based on an anagram; others are written in Latin or
translate a Latin poem; others praise contemporaries of
Sor Juana and ask them for verses. Other courtly poems
accompany a gift Sor Juana is sending to a friend; they
answer the poem of another writer; they are entries in a

poetic contest; or they play with the language of Scholastic philosophy. Most of these poems are little more than clever exercises.

Occasionally the reader comes upon some good verses in the courtly poems; for example, the following lines from the *romance* **"Si daros los buenos años,"** which was presented to the viceroy on his birthday:

> Grey hairs must be sought
> before they are painted by time:
> whoever would have them finds joy,
> affliction whoever awaits them.
> The fool who finally walks
> the premise of old age,
> combs shame rather than locks,
> repeats outrages rather than years.
> The wise young man in short
> leaves an eternal frame
> for his Life, and with his fame
> marks eternity.

B. *The Love Poems*

The second group consists of some fifty love poems, about a fifth of Sor Juana's lyrical poetry. Most of these are as undistinguished as the courtly poems, but a dozen of them are worthwhile and two are excellent. The better love poems seem to come from Sor Juana's own experience rather than from an occasion of Church or State, or from a literary fashion of the day, such as an anagram or a polite poetical debate.

The *romances* are the least inspired of Sor Juana's love poems and do not impart any personal warmth. They deal with themes that border on the philosophical; for example, the poem **"Supuesto, discurso mío"** argues the problem of love and disdain. The poetess loves Fabio, who does not return her love, and she is loved by Silvio, for whom she has no feeling. What is she to do? Is she obligated to Silvio?

> It is not harsh, not tyranny
> the passions being the same,
> his lack of self-restraint
> and his desire that I myself restrain?
>
> To love him because he loves me
> is not rightly called love,
> for he loves not, who supposes
> that to love he must be loved.
> Love is not correspondence;
>
> . . . . .
>
> And indeed, though so much truth
> were wanting on my behalf,
> my will belongs to Fabio,
> Silvio and the world please pardon.

In the *romance* **"Ya que para despedirme"** the theme is the absence of the lover. This absence and the jealousy

accompanying it are the most common themes in the *romances,* and they carry over into the sonnets and *endechas.* For example, in the *endecha* **"Prolija memoria,"** the reader comes upon the lines:

> Why do you air
> the idle question,
> whether inconstancy
> be the child of absence?
> I well know the frailty
> of nature
> whose one constancy
> is to be not so.

The *endechas* are rather better than the *romances,* but they do not measure up to Sor Juana's sonnets and *liras.* For example, in the poem **"Si acaso, Fabio mío"** the reader finds these lines:

> hear, in this sad dirge
> the tender harmony
> that soothes, a funeral rite,
> the dying swan.
> And ere eternal Night
> with deadly opaque key
> the dim light snuffs
> of my fainthearted eyes,
> give me the last embrace,
> whose tender ties
> unify bodies,
> thus identify souls.
> Let night hear thy sweet voice
> and let it not smother
> in troubled cadence,
> thy words entire.
> From thy countenance on mine
> make in love an image
> and bathe these frigid cheeks
> with ardent tears.

Although these verses show more warmth than the *romances,* they retain a certain intellectual aloofness. In the lines "unify bodies / thus identify souls" ("siendo unión de los cuerpos / identifican almas") the thought would have made a splendid verse if it had not been expressed so prosaically. Once again Sor Juana is abusing the language of philosophy.

The two best sonnets are **"Esta tarde, mi bien, cuando te hablaba,"** and the **"Detente, sombra de mi bien esquivo"**:

> This eve, my love, when I spoke with thee
> I saw by thy gesture and face
> How with words I could not move thee
> And I wanted thee to see my heart.
> And Love, who helped my design
> Conquered what seemed scant of gain
> For amongst the tears that sorrow poured
> My heart fell in drops undone.
> No more rigor, my love, no more;
> Jealous tyrants need torment thee no more,

Nor vile suspicion test thy quietude
With foolish shades, with empty clue,
Since in liquid humor thou hast seen and touched
My heart between thy hands undone.

Hold on, shade of my evasive love,
Image of the spell I most adore,
Fair illusion for which happily I die,
Sweet fiction for which painfully I live.
If for the lodestone of thy grace
My breast serves, obedient steel,
Why must thou please and enamor,
If fleeting thou willst to fool me?
But thou may not boast self-satisfied
That thy tyranny vanquished me,
For though thou leavest the close tie deceived,
Which thy fantastic form has wound,
It little matters thou foolest arms and breast
If my phantasy has captured thee in chains.

In many of the other sonnets Sor Juana unfortunately returns to the clever manner of the *romances,* for example:

He who ungrateful leaves me, lovingly I seek;
He who lovingly seeks me, ungratefully I leave;
Constant I adore him who disdains my love;
I disdain him who constantly seeks my love.

For the present writer, the best of Sor Juana's love poems is the one called **"Amado dueño mío,"** which is written in *liras.* This poem expresses the feelings that come from the absence of the loved one. Here are some selections:

My beloved lord,
Hear a while my tired lament
which I to the wind confide
that quickly it might reach thine ear
if the dolorous plaint does not vanish
like my hope, in air.
 (vv. 1-6)

If thou seest the loquacious stream
woo the meadow's flowers,
a pleasing lover that charms
and tells them of his care,
my grief will have thee know
how his current laughs fed by mine own woe.
 (vv. 19-24)

If thou seest the wounded stag
down the mountain, hurried,
seeking anguished
ease in a frozen stream,
and thirsty plunge the waters,
in anguish not ease he follows me.
 (vv. 37-42)

If thou seest clear the sky
such is the candor of my soul;
and if, avaricious of light

the day is veiled with gloom,
it is in inclement obscurity
the image of thine absence and my life.
 (vv. 49-54)

When will thy sonorous voice
wound these ears;
and when will the soul that loves thee,
drowned in joy's delights,
abandon these eyes to laughter
as it hastens from them to greet thee.
 (vv. 67-72)

When shall I behold the gracious line
of thy quiet countenance
and that unspoken joy,
beyond the pale of human pen,
for all is ill defined
that does not fit experience.
 (vv. 79-85)

C. *The Philosophical and Historical Sonnets*

The rest of Sor Juana's lyrical poetry consists of thirteen sonnets with philosophical or historical themes. The eight philosophical sonnets repeat the theme of man's return to dust; one of them combines the *return to dust* with the theme of *carpe diem (seize the day).* Here are three of these sonnets: [This sonnet concerns a portrait of Sor Juana.]

This hued deceit thou seest,
which boasting art's comeliness
with colors' false syllogism
is a delusive betrayal of sense;
yes this, where flattery has thought
to reprieve the horrors of years,
and by subduing time's arrogance
to triumph over age and oblivion,
is esteem's vain dissimulation
is a fragile flower to the wind
is a useless refuge against fate
is foolish errant diligence
is decrepit care, and understood,
is corpse, is dust, is shade, is nought.

[This sonnet is a stricture for a rose, and for those like a rose.]

Rose divine in tender bloom,
thou art in thy fragrant grace
beauty's teacher, born to the purple,
a white snow tenet of comeliness.
Model of the human form
example of charm's emptiness
in whose being nature has joined
the happy cradle and wan sepulchre.
How haughty is thy pomp, how presumptuous,
how proud, thou scornest the threat of death
and later, faint and withdrawn,
of thy withered self givest the despondent sign,
for in foolish life and wise demise
thou teachest dying and living showest deceit.

[This sonnet says that Death is better than exposure to the outrages of old age.]

> Celia watched a meadow rose
> happily boasting empty splendor,
> while with carmine salve and scarlet
> it bathed its soft made countenance;
> and she said—Enjoy with no fear of Fate
> thy buoyant years' quick course
> for tomorrow's death cannot quit
> what today thou hast possessed;
> and though death will come now soon
> and thy scented life will away,
> thou shalt not mind thy dying, so beautiful, so gay:
> see how experience teaches thee
> thou art fortunate dying in bloom
> not knowing old age's vehemence.

There are five historic-mythological sonnets, which concern women from antiquity. Two of them praise the gallant Lucretia, a favorite of Sor Juana, who fought so bravely to preserve her purity against the lecherous Tarquino. The best of these sonnets is about Pyramus and Thisbe.

Pyramus and Thisbe appear in the *Metamorphoses* of Ovid. They were legendary lovers of Babylon who spoke to each other through an opening in a wall between their houses. One night they planned to meet by a white mulberry tree. Thisbe arrived first at the tree but fled when she saw a lioness. She left a blood-smeared garment, which Pyramus found. Thinking her dead, he took his own life with a sword, and she, on returning, did the same by plunging the weapon into her breast. Pyramus blood caused the white mulberries to turn red, and Thisbe's, mixed with his, caused them to turn purple.

Here is Sor Juana's sonnet on their tragic love:

> Of a mournful mulberry the black shade,
> of a thousand horrors and confusions full,
> in whose hollow trunk today there still resounds
> the echo that sorrowfully invokes the name of
>   Thisbe;
> this shade covered the green-hued carpet
> where Pyramus in love opened the vein
> of his heart, and This be in her pain
> made the mark that still astounds the world.
> But seeing Love in so great affliction,
> Death took pity on them
> and joined their breast in one tight bond.
> Alas, poor and unhappy is she
> who offers not her breast to her own Pyramus
> not even for a sword's hard blade.

. . . . .

A writer's attitude towards nature is important since it throws light on the ultimate meaning of his literature. The writings of Sor Juana Inés reveal that her basic attitude towards nature comes from Scholasticism, the doctrine of the medieval school and Golden Age Spain. Sor Juana may have exalted nature in *The Dream* and in some of her other verses, for example the passage in which Echo tempts Narcissus with her possessions, but it is Scholasticism that permeates everything she wrote.

Nature in Scholastic philosophy has a strict order of inanimate matter, vegetable life, sensitive life, and rational life. These various levels of being come under the Aristotelian doctrine of hylomorphism, according to which all bodies consist of two essential principles, matter and form. In her *loa* to Friar Diego Velázquez, Sor Juana has a figure called Nature say: "since I am Nature/ in common, to whose wise/ always operative idea/ the sweet union/ of matter and form is due. . . . In short I am she/ who makes the vegetal grow/ the rational discourse/ the sensitive to feel."

The language of hylomorphism appears in *The Divine Narcissus.* Here is an example: In the era before Christ's coming, Gentilism (the pagan world) has an argument with Synagogue (the world that knows divine revelation). Gentilism has many beautiful myths and stories to tell, but Synagogue has the truth. It would be nice if they could come to some sort of an agreement. Gentilism says that she will provide the *matter* for a sacramental play if Synagogue will supply the *form* or meaning. She concludes her speech to Synagogue: "I do not understand you well, but since you propose that I give you the matter so that you may inform it with another soul, another meaning my eyes do not recognize, I shall give you from my literature the poetic beauty of the story of Narcissus." ("So that you may inform it with another soul": according to hylomorphism, the form of a living being is its soul.)

According to Scholasticism there is a strict order within every part of nature. All material beings are composed of matter and form, that is, informed matter. Forms, however, differ in dignity and the resultant beings fall into a hierarchy:

Man—rational form (spiritual soul)

Animals—sensitive form (material soul)

Plants—vegetable form (material soul)

Minerals—a non-vital form.

[Sor Juana] brings up this doctrine in **The Dream.** Furthermore, Sor Juana frequently uses the word "order" to describe nature. In the third *loa* for the birthday of the king she writes: "For he [the king] who from the common order / is exempt, / does not need years / to be wise." Sor Juana is saying here that owing to the order of nature all men must have sense perception and experience if they are to acquire knowledge; that is, they must grow old in years to become wise. The glorious king, however, does not need to grow in years to acquire knowledge and wisdom since he is above nature. Sor Juana is exercising a poetic license in order to praise the king. She does not mean to be taken literally.

Sor Juana's attitude towards nature has an effect on her attitude towards the social order. Society has a strict hierarchy. This explains Sor Juana's, profound respect for the monarchy in all the *loas.*

Scholastic theology also sees an order in nature, but it allows for God's taking exception to that order. In the first *loa,* to Charles II, the figure called Love says that the various figures in the poem must speak according to their grade and must keep "the natural order the powerful Hand of God put on us when He took us out of Chaos." Love is talking here about Fire, Air, Water, and Earth, the four elements who must praise King Charles in their natural order. This order in nature is extremely important to Sor Juana.

Nature is the creation of God and its main purpose is to reflect the Beauty of the Creator, to follow Him. He is nature's polestar:

> If you can in Narcissus [he has not yet become
> Christ in the play]
> so much perfection suppose,
> for you say his beauty is
> of hearts the lodestone
> and that nymphs and shepherds follow him
> and not these alone
> but birds and beasts
> mountains, dales
> streams and fountains
> meadows, trees and flowers;
> with how much greater truth
> is this high perfection
> seen in God
> for whose Beauty the Spheres
> in mirrors' guise
> behold themselves unworthy;
> and for Whom all creatures
> (though there were not cause
> of so many gifts
> and marvellous favors)
> for His Beauty alone
> would owe Him adoration
> and Whom Nature
> (that's my name) raptly
> seeks as its Center,
> follows as its Star?

Nature glorifies God and gives Beauty back.

The order of nature does not stand by itself but has a relation to grace that has changed several times in the past. In the beginning nature and grace were wedded so that nature was benign, but the devil trapped man into offending God and many special graces were removed.

This separation of grace and nature caused man to be unhappy, reduced him to misery, and caused nature to cease being benign. There was, for example, the Deluge. God is not a passive witness to nature and its relation with grace. He can if He will arrest the operations of nature or go beyond them, as He did when He brought about the virgin birth. God also refused to admit the separation of grace and nature in the instance of the Immac-

ulate Conception, which is alluded to when Narcissus looks into the fountain (Mary) and marvels at the untarnished beauty there. God also takes exception to nature when he allows miracles. In the sacramental play *Joseph's Scepter* there is a miracle above nature when the boy Joseph foretells the future fat and lean years of Egypt. No natural knowledge can account for this prophecy, which is made possible only by special grace.

Sor Juana may have exalted nature in **The Dream** and a few other passages of her works, but her verses constantly show that for her nature comes from the Hand of God and imposes order. This is the nature of the Scholastics.

Arthur Terry   (essay date 1973)

SOURCE: "Human and Divine Love in the Poetry of Sor Juana Inés de la Cruz," in *Studies in Spanish Literature of the Golden Age,* Tamesis Books, 1973, pp. 297-313.

[*In the following essay, Terry analyzes Juana Inés de la Cruz's treatment of divine and romantic love in her verse.*]

The "sincerity" or otherwise of Sor Juana's love poems no longer seems a crucial question; in the words of Octavio Paz [in *Las peras del olmo,* 1957]: "Poco importa que esos amores hayan sido ajenos o propios, vividos o soñados: ella los hizo suyos por gracia de la poesía". This should make it easier to see her work in relation to earlier seventeenth-century love poetry, and perhaps especially to that of writers like Polo de Medina and Bocángel who make a point of reproducing the kind of theoretical discussion which seems to have been common in the Academies of the time. It also enables one to do justice to her strong dramatic talent (by no means confined to her plays), by suggesting a type of experience in which imagination and intellect are continually brought to focus on the materials of real life. Nevertheless, certain problems remain: one of them is to know how seriously to take such poems—not in biographical terms, but as a way of expressing certain themes and attitudes; another, which follows from this, is to find a way of defining their relationship to other aspects of Sor Juana's writings.

Some years ago [in his *Baroque Times in Old Mexico,* 1959], Professor Irving A. Leonard attempted to solve the second problem by suggesting that certain of the love poems might be read allegorically. The ones he had in mind were the three consecutive sonnets on the theme of "encontradas correspondencias": **"Que no me quiera Fabio, al verse amado . . .", "Feliciano me adora y le aborrezco . . ." and "Al que ingrato me deja, busco amante. . . ".** Each of these poems turns on the same situation: the speaker loves A, who does not love her; at the same time, she is loved by B, whom she rejects. The treatment is extremely schematic: taken as a group, the poems seem to represent what Professor Elias Rivers [in *Antología,* 1965] has called "una 'cuestión de amor' trovadoresca", in which the poet's own feelings are perhaps not very deeply engaged. On Leonard's reading, however, they form a code which, once deciphered, can be seen to relate to a quite different situation which, for obvious reasons, could not be described directly. So A (Fabio-Feliciano) stands for the spirit of intellectual enquiry which runs counter to the demands of Sor Juana's religious vocation and B (Silvio-Lisardo) for the love of the Church which she is unable to accept unconditionally. Unfortunately, there is no real evidence to justify such a theory; as Dario Puccini has pointed out [in *Sor Juana Inés de la Cruz,* 1967], there is nothing to suggest that Sor Juana's desire for knowledge affected the basic orthodoxy of her ideas, or that her moments of self-criticism ever induced her to see her difficulties in such clear-cut terms. Here, once again, one is forced to dismiss the possibility of biographical interpretation; if the poems have a deeper meaning, it is hardly likely to be of this kind, and it seems better to confine one's speculations to the kind of tradition with which Sor Juana herself was familiar.

At the same time, if one attempts to read her love poems at their face value, they may appear disconcerting, especially if one tries to see them as a whole. Several of the finest, like **"Si acaso, Fabio mío . . ."** and **"Detente, sombra de mi bien esquivo . . ."** are moving and accomplished poems by any standard, and lose none of their effect when read in isolation. Others—the majority—contain a good deal of theorizing, which is not always applied to a particular situation. It is here that one might expect to find an explanation of the attitudes which are embodied in the more directly emotional poems, though, in fact, this is not always so.

This can best be illustrated by comparing two poems on the same theme, **"Supuesto, discurso mío . . ."** and **"Al amor, cualquier curioso . . ."**. Like the three sonnets already mentioned, both these poems hinge on the idea of "correspondencia", that is to say, on the possibility of a mutual relationship between a pair of lovers. In the first, the problem is stated succinctly, though with a certain ambiguity:

> Manda la razón de estado
> que, atendiendo a obligaciones,
> las partes de Fabio olvide,
> las prendas de Silvio adore; . . .

The argumentative part of the poem begins at line 81:

> ¿Qué hace en adorarme Silvio?
> Cuando más fino blasone,
> ¿ quererme es más que seguir
> de su inclinación el norte?

All that we are told of Silvio and Fabio is that the former possesses "méritos" which, it is implied, are inferior to the latter's "perfecciones"; nor is there any suggestion that Fabio returns, or even recognizes, the speaker's love. The argument itself, though it occupies the remaining sixty lines of the poem, is clear enough. Silvio's fault is to have *chosen* to love the speaker: his kind of love costs him no sacrifice, and to return another person's love sim-

ply because one is loved would be a form of self-indulgence, a worshipping of one's own mirror image. In contrast to this, true love is *fated,* and may run contrary to mere "inclination":

> No es amor correspondencia;
> causas tiene superiores:
> que los concilian los Astros
> o lo engendran perfecciones.

The lines which begin "Ser potencia y ser objeto, / a toda razón se opone; . . ." support this view by an appeal to traditional logic: "To be a potentiality and at the same time the object of that potentiality would be contrary to reason, since it would be to exercise one's own operations on oneself. The object which it (i.e. the potentiality) knows is distinguished by its separateness—that is to say, by its status as an object; therefore the potentiality aims at that which is worthy to be loved, not at that which loves." And in the concluding lines, "correspondencia" is once more dismissed as alien to love's purpose:

> Amor no busca la paga
> de voluntades conformes,
> que tan bajo interés fuera
> indigna usura en los dioses.
> No hay cualidad que en él pueda
> imprimir alteraciones,
> del hielo de los desdenes,
> del fuego de los favores.

A great deal of the effect of such a poem comes from the careful balancing of terms like "inclinación" and "destino", and from the ease with which logical commonplaces are torn from their normal context and worked into the natural flow of the verse. The same is true of 104, though here the intention is entirely theoretical, and there is no attempt to refer the argument to a specific situation. The opening statement of the theme immediately recalls the previous poem:

> Al amor, cualquier curioso
> hallará una distinción:
> que uno nace de elección
> y otro de influjo imperioso.

Yet already there is a difference: where the first poem recognized only a single form of love, the distinction is now between two kinds, neither of which is necessarily false. This distinction between irresistible love and "amor de elección" is amplified, more or less schematically, in the rest of the poem. The first is described as "amor afectivo"—passionate love. It is "más afectuoso", "más natural" and "más sensible"; it demands from the lover worship ("veneración") and "rendimiento de precisa obligación"; above all, it paralyses the will and is hostile to reason and the understanding. "Amor de elección", on the other hand, is rational and may extend to friendship and other natural bonds; in whatever form, it is based on the understanding, whence its superiority to the other kind: "digo que es más noble esencia / la del (amor) de conocimiento." As the title of the poem emphasizes, it is this second type of love which deserves to be reciprocated: ". . . amar por elección del arbitrio, es sólo digno de racional correspondencia".

Two qualifications need to be made if we are to grasp the full sense of the poem. In the first place, passionate love is described for the most part as a force which acts against the will of the lover, even though he may despise the object of his love. (The possibility that the lover may be helpless and at the same time consenting to his love does not arise.) In the last stanza, this is slightly modified:

> A la hermosura no obliga
> amor que forzado venga,
> ni admite pasión que tenga
> la razón por enemiga;
> ni habrá quien le contradiga
> el propósito e intento
> de no admitir pensamiento
> que, *por mucho que la quiera,*
> no le dará el alma entera,
> pues va sin entendimiento.

>   (my italics)

This last-minute concession, however, scarcely weighs against the general tenor of the poem. The crucial thing is the rôle of the understanding, without which no love can be complete. In the second place, there is the tone which is used in judging the claims of irrational love, the dismissive wit which appears whenever the two kinds of love are contrasted:

> Mas en mi ánimo altivo,
> querer que estime el cuidado
> de un corazón violentado,
> es solicitar con veras
> que agradezcan las galeras
> la asistencia del forzado.

The ingenious play on the lover-galley slave metaphor could hardly be more pointed; an apparently casual stroke of humour is aimed at a whole tradition of amorous complaint with an economy quite beyond the possibilities of plain statement.

Each of these poems, then, speaks for an opposing view. They are, in fact, the two extremes of a whole series of poems which deal with the subject of "correspondencia", and which between them make up a fairly comprehensive range of possible attitudes. Comprehensive, but not, of course, coherent; this is the real point, and for some readers, one imagines, the stumbling-block. The question is, quite simply, how are we to take such poems? Are they merely examples of Sor Juana's skill in arguing both sides of a case, or is she arguing with herself in a more responsible sense, as part of a constantly shifting dialectic? Reading them as a whole, they may strike us rather as the poems for an unwritten pastoral novel; that is to say, in spite of their inconsistencies, they revolve around a limited number of central ideas which they debate from different, though related, points of view. Or, thinking of the artistic process behind the poems, one might put it

another way: although their author is not necessarily committed permanently to a particular attitude, she has had at different times to imagine the circumstances in which any given one might be true. Sor Juana, of course, is not alone in this: the whole tradition of love poetry from the *cancioneros* onward shows similar inconsistencies which need only trouble us if we insist on relating them to direct personal experience, rather than to a developing literary convention. What Sor Juana's poems have in common is a rational framework of thought which rests on certain traditional polarities: reason-passion, as in the poems just discussed, and elsewhere soul-body and intuition-logic. These polarities are more often than not combined with more specific features of earlier love poetry, with concepts taken from Neoplatonism or the theory of courtly love, though here again it would be wrong to look for a complete exposition of any one set of ideas.

This brings us back to the original question. One need hardly insist on the dangers of devising simple equations between poems and "contemporary ideas". Where seventeenth-century poetry is concerned, this error can only be made worse by attempting to see a particular body of poems in terms of some basic unity of idea, so that any apparent exception has to be explained as a conscious retraction. As Professor Frank Kermode has said of Andrew Marvell [in *The Selected Poetry of Andrew Marvell*, 1967]: "(such poems) ask of the critic a respect for their relationship to traditions not invented by the poet, and not to be resolved in some generalization about his thought; his penetration and judgement must respect, in this sense, his singularity." In the case of Sor Juana, one could argue, the real unity of the poems comes from the sense of a strong personality which binds together a large number of heterogeneous elements—something in which the tone of the voice which speaks through the verse is at least as important as the biographical facts. This is hard to demonstrate in detail, though some such explanation is needed to account for the contrast between the almost line-by-line derivativeness of many of her poems and the extraordinary freshness of the whole. This is not to deny her lapses: many passages, and occasionally whole poems, strike one as overingenious or at times merely arid; her best verse succeeds, however, precisely because her imagination is able to find new patterns in traditional clusters of thought without accepting them schematically.

Allowing, then, for conflicting points of view, how comprehensive is the range of attitudes which Sor Juana presents? This is not the irrelevant question it might seem at first sight. The traditions on which she draws, though varied, are not unlimited, and it is quite possible to detect a preference for certain types of situation rather than others. It is noticeable, for example, that even in the poems which emphasize the idea of mutual love, there is little idea of what mutual love might be like. Here, one feels the pressure of that part of the courtly love tradition which equates love with suffering and postponement, or, occasionally, a suggestion of "platonic love" in the conventional meaning of the phrase. What one never finds is the sense of a relationship which, for better or for worse, involves the whole process of living. Significantly, the only social criterion which affects Sor Juana's poetry is "decorum": this is the principle which gives way in the face of passion, or, alternatively, to which one appeals as a means of evasion.

Nor is there much evidence of the characteristic Neoplatonic progression from sensual to spiritual love. Though the love of beauty is described in a number of poems, notably in those addressed to the Marquesa de la Laguna, there is no suggestion that this may lead to the contemplation of God, just as, at the other end of the scale, there is no indication that the woman's reflected beauty may be legitimately possessed. If this is so, the idea of a "scale" scarcely applies: what we have instead is a static situation which moves neither up nor down. Consider, for example, the poem which begins **"Si el desamor o el enojo . . .".** Here, the immediate occasion is annoyance ("enojo") at what appears to have been a sensual lapse. The speaker admits that her love is irresistible ("aunque no quise, te quise"), and for once this love is reciprocated. This balance, however, is threatened:

> No hagas que un amor dichoso
> se vuelva en efecto triste,
> ni que las aras de Anteros
> a Cupido se dediquen.

Anteros, traditionally, is the less harmful brother of Cupid; Méndez Plancarte equates him with "el amor puro o dichoso en el sacrificio". The following stanza pursues this distinction between sensual passion and spiritual love:

> Deja que nuestras dos almas,
> pues un mismo amor las rige,
> teniendo la unión en poco,
> amantes se identifiquen.

Later, the two souls are imagined passing into eternity as an "unidad indivisible"; in this last part of the poem there is an obvious play on "unión" and "unidad": sexual union, as against the more permanent unity of souls. Yet this unity, however much it may transcend mere sexual attraction, remains a self-sufficient ideal: the "siempre amantes formas" are finally to achieve an openly pagan kind of immortality in which their happiness will be envied by the great lovers of antiquity.

Clearly, there is little in such a poem which could not be related, in one way or another, to earlier traditions. The condemnation of Cupid, for example, figures largely in Bembo and, by extension, in Gil Polo, whom Sor Juana had almost certainly read, and this is one of the things which set them apart from the more medieval notions of a León Hebreo. Yet in Bembo, this forms part of an attack on the whole idea of "fatal love" on which Sor Juana's poem is based. This is what one means when one speaks of "finding new patterns in traditional clusters of thought": as here, certain older, and originally inconsistent, ideas are fused into a new kind of unity, partly through the sheer conviction of the voice which presides over the poem. Moreover, as I have already argued, it is difficult not to see a consistency in the type of situation described. If the terms of this particular poem—the emphasis on love as a thing of the soul—lead it quickly away from the sphere of the senses, there are others which hardly rise to a spiritual level at all. These, on the whole, are the poems which speak of a love based on the acceptance of jealousy and suffering, the kind of love one associates with the older *cancionero* lyric. The title of one of these, **"En que describe racionalmente los efectos irracionales del amor,"** introduces a long series of paradoxes which the reason is powerless to resolve. For the most part, these hinge on the contrast between irresistible desire and the fear of disillusionment. Yet one stanza seems to go beyond this:

> Ya sufrida, ya irritada,
> con contrarias penas lucho:
> que por él sufriré mucho,
> y con él sufriré nada.

"El" refers to the man with whom the speaker is in love: the lines express, with unusual directness, a shying-away from the intimacy of mutual feeling, a rejection of the final commitment which here, at least, has no justification in a superior form of love.

Such qualifications are not meant as a criticism of Sor Juana, but are simply an attempt to indicate the area in which her love poetry moves and, if possible, the kind of central situations on which it is based. One of these, as we have seen, is the notion of "correspondencia"; another, surely, is the tendency to think in terms of a spiritual love which does not appear to lead on to the love of God. This love is an "amor del entendimiento" which resides in the soul and which scorns the senses. Moreover, as is apparent from one of the poems already discussed, it can transcend differences of sex in a way which one is inclined to think characteristic of Sor Juana. As she says to the Marquesa de la Laguna:

> Ser mujer, ni estar ausente,
> no es de amarte impedimento;
> pues sabes tú, que las almas
> distancia ignoran y sexo.

Such statements are common in the poems addressed to friends, where there is no reason to suppose that she is acting a rôle. In poem 39 (**"Señor Diego Valverde . . ."**), she writes to a male acquaintance whose attractions are purely intellectual:

> Y también sabéis, que como
> es mi amor de entendimiento,
> no ha menester de la vista
> materiales alimentos,
>   pues radicado en el alma,
> independiente y exento,
> desprecia de los sentidos
> el inútil ministerio.

The difference between this and the language of certain love poems is very slight: if there *is* a "scale" in Sor Juana's love poems, it is not a "spiritual ladder" in the

Neoplatonic sense, but one which runs through the varieties of "amor por elección", from spiritual love between the sexes to the natural demands of kinship. And at the back of all these possibilities is the idea of sexual neutrality which she expresses so strikingly in poem 48: (**"Señor, para responderos . . ."**):

> Con que a mí no es bien mirado
> que como a mujer me miren,
> pues no soy mujer que a alguno
> de mujer pueda servirle;
>   y sólo sé que mi cuerpo,
> sin que a uno u otro se incline,
> es neutro, o abstracto, cuanto
> sólo el alma deposite.

Here, certainly, it is safe to assume that Sor Juana is speaking from the standpoint of her religious vocation, though the attitude she is expressing seems almost a logical consequence of the conduct she envisages in several of the love poems. It would be tempting to draw the connection tighter, were it not for the existence of other poems which present emotional situations of some intensity. Significantly, the most serious of these relate either to absence or death, or, in the one notable exception, to the failure of the loved one to return the speaker's love. In poem 78 (**"Agora que conmigo . . ."**), the woman is lamenting the death of her "esposo": though she calls on love to overcome her reason, there is no attempt to convey the quality of the relationship on which it was based. Poem 76 (**"Si acaso, Fabio mío . . ."**) is a different matter: in many ways this is the finest, and certainly the most moving, of Sor Juana's love poems, not merely because of the situation itself. This is exceptional enough (the woman who speaks is dying in the arms of her lover), yet the most striking thing is the complete absence of rhetoric and the effect of tenderness which this creates. This is not merely a question of restraint or the avoidance of sentimentality: the boldness of a metaphor like "De tu rostro en el mío / haz, amoroso, estampa" and a phrase like "Unidas de las manos / las bien tejidas palmas" are more physical than anything else in Sor Juana's poems. But what controls these details is the same voice which can contemplate death as an "eternal night" and, a moment later, can move wittily through a series of legal metaphors which issue with sudden appropriateness in the image of a pagan underworld:

> Dame por prendas firmes
> de tu fe no violada,
> en tu pecho escrituras,
> seguros en tu cara,
>   para que cuando baje
> a las Estigias aguas,
> tuyo el óbolo sea
> para fletar la barca.

It would be difficult to deny the sense of intimacy; yet one suspects that such a mood has been achieved precisely because of the imminence of death. At one point in the poem, the speaker says:

> . . . dame el postrer abrazo

> cuyas tiernas lazadas,
> siendo unión de los cuerpos,
> identifican almas.

This may recall one of the poems discussed earlier, in which the unity of souls was directly opposed to the idea of physical union. Here, there is no such opposition, but rather a telescoping of the two states, so that one is indistinguishable from the other. It would be wrong, of course, to expect complete consistency between the two poems; at the same time, the terms in which Sor Juana speaks of the love of the soul scarcely vary. In this particular poem, there is a sense in which the physical union, such as it is, achieves a dignity which it is not allowed elsewhere simply because of the unrepeatable nature of the situation, as if the urgency of the request guaranteed the merging of body and soul.

Many passages, and occasionally whole poems, strike one as over-ingenious or at times merely arid; her best verse succeeds, however, precisely because her imagination is able to find new patterns in traditional clusters of thought without accepting them schematically.

—Arthur Terry

These invented situations lead one to reflect on the part played by the imagination in Sor Juana's work. This is not merely a question of invention, but also, in certain poems, a possible means of dominating the experiences which she presents. One cannot fail to notice, for instance, how many of her love poems are concerned with absence. A relatively trivial example of this occurs in the poem which begins **"Aunque cegué de mirarte . . ."** where the male speaker claims that the woman he loves, though physically absent, is present—and more powerfully so—to the "eyes of the soul". Though in this particular poem the idea is hardly more than a conventional hyperbole, it is the emphasis itself which strikes one: the notion that "gustos imaginados" are actually superior to those which are literally experienced. One sees the significance of this when one turns to a much finer poem, the sonnet which begins **"Detente, sombra de mi bien esquivo . . ."**. As Carlos Blanco Aguinaga explains in his excellent analysis of this poem [in *MLN*, 1962], its whole strategy consists in deceiving the expectations aroused in the opening quatrains. Just at the moment when it seems likely that the shadow of the elusive lover will finally escape her, the speaker quietly announces her victory:

> que aunque dejas burlado el lazo estrecho
>   que tu forma fantástica ceñía,
> poco importa burlar brazos y pecho
>   si te labra prisión mi fantasía.

Absence here has become crucial: it is no longer a temporary condition, as in the previous poem, though neither is it the total absence of death. Quite simply, it is a state which, because of the power of the imagination, has ceased to be a deprivation at all; the only state, moreover, in which the imagination is at liberty to exercise its powers to the full. It seems doubtful whether the attitude of this poem is as unique as Blanco Aguinaga suggests; there is, in fact a whole group of poems which tend in the same direction, though none of them achieves such a complete expression as this one. At this level, certainly, it hardly seems to matter whether the situation is invented or not: without exception, the men and women of Sor Juana's love poems are "shadows" evolved by the imagination. As Ramón Xirau has observed [in *Genio y figura de Sor Juana Inés de la Cruz,* 1967]: "sucede como si Sor Juana quisiera alejar el objeto amoroso para mejor amasarlo; como si quisiera guardarlo en el recuerdo para mejor poseerlo en las imágenes de la memoria." Hence the importance, not only of absence, but of all the other devices and arguments by which her poems elude the tensions of a living relationship. In all the situations she presents, there are two ways of dominating experience, one intellectual, the other emotional, though the second is never entirely divorced from the first. As many critics have pointed out, her mind habitually works in terms of traditional dualities. Her intellect is such that it can argue for opposing points of view; it is emotionally, through her imagination, that she comes closest to achieving a synthesis of contraries, a precarious undertaking which can only succeed in the face of rational impossibility and which, when it fails, plunges straight into disillusionment.

One might end there, were it not that the subject of human love also occurs in Sor Juana's religious poems. In divine love, predictably, all contraries are resolved: "Que amor que se tiene en Dios / es calidad sin opuestos". In Sor Juana's presentation of divine love, therefore, there are none of the contradictory attitudes one finds in her poems on secular love. What problems there are come from a different source: roughly speaking, there are tensions involved in achieving divine love, and these come from the weaknesses of human nature, and particularly from the tendency of the attitudes of human love to intervene. Hardly surprisingly, therefore, several of the religious poems contain contrasts, open or implied, with human love, and these are all the sharper for being expressed in a common terminology.

Once again, the key concept is "correspondencia", which not only appears in several of Sor Juana's religious poems, but is also vital to the argument of the *Carta atenagórica,* her famous reply to the Portuguese Jesuit, Padre Antonio Vieira. The latter, in his *Sermão do Mandato* of 1650, had argued that the greatest sign of Christ's love for humanity was neither the Eucharist nor his death on the Cross, but his willingness to absent himself from man while at the same time loving him more than his own life. Moreover, he went on to say, Christ had not wished his love to be returned for his own sake, but for that of man, and that consequently his greatest act of favour ("fineza") was to love without "correspondence". Sor Juana

attacks both arguments: her own view, basically, is that the full extent of Christ's love for man is shown by his actual death, and that, in dying, "quiso mucha correspondencia, y no la renunció, sino que la solicitó". We do not need to follow the rest of her reasoning; in the present context, what is interesting is the confrontation between two kinds of relationship. As she says at one point: "el no querer correspondencia fuera fineza en un amor humano, porque fuera desinterés; pero en el de Cristo no lo fuera, porque no tiene interés ninguno en nuestra correspondencia . . . El amor humano halla en ser correspondido, algo que le faltara si no lo fuera, como el deleite, la utilidad, el aplauso, etc. Pero al de Cristo nada le falta aunque no le correspondamos . . . (Mi proposición) es que Cristo quiso la correspondencia para sí, pero la utilidad que resulta de esa correspondencia la quiso para los hombres": At this distance in time, the actual theological point may seem overingenious; remembering her poems, however, it is surely revealing that, where human love is concerned, Sor Juana allows for two opposing views and then goes on to argue that the love of Christ is unlike either.

In poem 56 (**"Traigo conmigo un cuidado . . ."**), she speaks of the difficulties of achieving disinterestedness in a divine context. On the face of it, she has rejected all kinds of human love—"amor bastardo, . . . de contrarios compuesto"—in favour of the one legitimate love, that of God. The problem arises when her spiritual desires become overlaid with human expectations; her suffering comes about because she wishes God to return her love, though she regards this as a human weakness. In one sense, of course, it is not: there is nothing in the least unorthodox about wishing to receive divine grace. However, as Méndez Plancarte points out, the kind of disinterestedness Sor Juana has in mind belongs to the tradition of "No me mueve, mi Dios, para quererte . . .", though her own poem, by comparison, is lacking in conviction. Instead, there is division:

> Tan precisa es la apetencia
> que a ser amados tenemos,
> que, aun sabiendo que no sirve,
> nunca dejarla sabemos.
> Que corresponda a mi amor,
> nada añade; mas no puedo,
> por más que lo solicito,
> dejar yo de apetecerlo.

Méndez Plancarte slightly misinterprets these lines: the speaker's "dolor de amor" is not "el anhelo de la absoluta seguridad de su correspondencia", but her grief at not being able to rise above the desire for "correspondence". It would be a mistake to suppose that she were denying the existence of God's love for man: in view of the earlier lines in which human love is rejected, it seems that what she really fears is that the purity of her love for God will be harmed by an excessively human idea of "correspondence".

Despite the possible echoes of Santa Teresa, there is nothing especially "mystical" about this poem or the two which follow. In **"Mientras la Gracia me excita . . . "**, the suffering lies more vaguely in the conflict between reason and "la costumbre", though the final paradox—

>   Padezca, pues Dios lo manda;
> mas de tal manera sea,
> que si son penas las culpas,
> que no sean culpas las penas.

—suggests that the suffering caused by guilt may not itself be guilty; that it may, in fact, be a source of good. Here, as in all Sor Juana's writings, divine love is equated with reason and virtue, never with less rational qualities; unreason, on the other hand, is part of the normal fabric of human life, just as it belongs to a certain kind of secular love. And in **"Amante dulce del alma . . . "**, the last of the group, the distance between the human and the divine is once more asserted through a variation on a familiar strategem.

Several of Sor Juana's poems on human love describe the effects of jealousy. In one of them, **"Si es amor causa productiva . . . "**, it is taken to be the one infallible sign of love: "Sólo los celos ignoran / fábricas de fingimientos. . . ". Conversely, Christ's love for man is disinterested, though in order to bring this home in her poem, she momentarily entertains the idea that it might be no more than jealousy. The speaker has just taken Communion: Christ has now "entered her heart", and she asks:

>   . . . ¿ Es amor o celos
> tan cuidadoso escrutinio?
> que quien lo registra todo,
> da de sospechar indicios.

For a moment we are made to think of the human world, in which a man may examine a woman's appearance or conduct for signs of infidelity. But immediately she pulls herself up with a sense of shock: nothing, after all, is hidden from Christ—"¡ . . . como si el estorbo humano / obstara al Lince Divino!"—implying, perhaps, that jealousy exists precisely because human beings do not have the power of seeing into one another's souls. So she moves to her conclusion: since the circumstances for jealousy are lacking, Christ's presence in her heart must be a sign of love:

>   Luego no necesitabais
> para ver el pecho mío,
> si lo estáis mirando sabio,
> entrar a mirarlo fino.

The poem not only confirms the unique nature of divine love by deliberately inviting human comparisons; it also presents the relationship between Christ and the believer in a way which seems characteristic of its author. At such moments, as Ramón Xirau has observed, "más que ver, Sor Juana siente que es vista". The contemplation of God, in the strict sense of the term, seldom enters her work, even as an ideal. What one finds instead, of course, is the constant humility of someone for whom divine favours are granted without regard to merit and for whom any thought of a more direct relationship with God would seem arrogant. And this may lead us to reflect once again on the

love poems: if this is Sor Juana's view of her relations with God, is it surprising that her poems should avoid the idea that, through human love, one may rise to the contemplation of divinity?

One might be tempted to argue that there are inconsistencies in her religious poems as well. However, this would be to ignore the two traditional ways of approach to God, the negative and the affirmative, which are complementary, rather than mutually exclusive. God, in Sor Juana's poems, may be present or absent, yet his absence is never final. As she says in the *Carta atenagórica,* "No ver lo que da gusto es dolor; pero mayor dolor es ver lo que da disgusto", a remark which has its implications for both human and divine love. In both cases, absence is a time for reflection as well as suffering and, where God is concerned, deprivation is only another stimulus to love.

In all Sor Juana's religious writing, there is one major theme: divine love is rational, consequently there can be no direct, intuitive knowledge of God. This is why, in her sacred poems, the idea of divine love is continually approached through comparisons with human love, which is partly known, though limited by various kinds of convention. In the end, the contradictions of the love poems seem to indicate—how consciously, one cannot say—that such partial knowledge is the most one can hope to achieve. What matters for Sor Juana is not so much knowledge as the search for knowledge, though this can best be seen in the one major poem which lies outside this study. As Octavio Paz has said: "*Primero sueño* no es el poema del conocimiento, sino del acto de conocer." Explicitly or implicitly, Sor Juana's treatment of love confirms this with a richness of attitudes that is often tested by the intellect, but which has little to do with intellectual certainties.

Octavio Paz (essay date 1976)

SOURCE: "Sor Juana Inés de la Cruz," in *The Siren & the Seashell, and Other Essays on Poets and Poetry,* translated by Lysander Kemp and Margaret Sayers Peden, University of Texas Press, 1976, pp. 3-15.

[*In the following essay, Paz explores the autobiographical aspects of Juana Inés de la Cruz's work and places her within the context of historical and political events of seventeenth-century Mexico.*]

In 1690, Manuel Fernández de Santa Cruz, bishop of Puebla, published Sor Juana Inés's criticism of the Jesuit Antonio de Vieyra's famous sermon, "Christ's Proofs of Love for Man." This *Carta atenagórica* [Letter worthy of Athena] is Sor Juana's only theological composition, or at least the only one that has survived.

Taken up at a friend's behest and written "with more repugnance than any other feeling, as much because it treats sacred things, for which I have reverent terror, as because it seems to wish to impugn, for which I have a natural aversion," the *Carta* had immediate repercussions. It was most unusual that a Mexican nun should dare to criticize, with as much rigor as intellectual boldness, the celebrated confessor of Christina of Sweden. But, if her criticism of Vieyra produced astonishment, her singular opinion on divine favors must have perturbed even those who admired her. Sor Juana maintained that the greatest beneficences of God are negative: "To reward is beneficence, to punish is beneficence, and to suspend beneficence is the greatest beneficence and not to perform good acts the greatest goodness." In a nun who loved poetry and science and was more preoccupied with learning than with her own salvation, this idea ran the risk of being judged as something more than theological subtlety: if the greatest divine favor were indifference, did this not too greatly enlarge the sphere of free will?

The bishop of Puebla, the nun's publisher and friend, did not conceal his disagreement. Under the pseudonym of Sor Filotea de la Cruz, he declared, in the missive that preceded the *Carta atenagórica*: "Although your discretion calls them blessings [the negative beneficences], I hold them to be punishments." Indeed, for the Christian there is no life outside of grace, and even liberty is a reflection of that grace. Moreover, the prelate did not content himself with demonstrating his lack of conformity with Sor Juana's theology but manifested a still more decided and cutting reprobation of her intellectual and literary affinities: "I do not intend that you change your nature by renouncing books, but that you better it by reading that of Jesus Christ . . . it is a pity that so great an understanding lower itself in such a way by unworthy notice of the Earth that it have not desire to penetrate what transpires in Heaven; and, since it be already lowered to the ground, that it not descend further, to consider what transpires in Hell." The bishop's letter brought Sor Juana face to face with the problem of her vocation and, more fundamentally, with her entire life. The theological discussion passed to a second plane.

Respuesta a Sor Filotea de la Cruz [Reply to Sister Filotea de la Cruz] was the last thing Sor Juana wrote. A critical autobiography, a defense of her right to learn, and a confession of the limits of all human learning, this text announced her final submission. Two years later she sold her books and abandoned herself to the powers of silence. Ripe for death, she did not escape the epidemic of 1695.

I fear that it may not be possible to understand what her work and her life tell us unless first we understand the meaning of this renunciation of the word. To hear what the cessation of her voice says to us is more than a baroque formula for comprehension. For, if silence is "a negative thing," not speaking is not: the characteristic function of silence is not at all the same thing as having nothing to say. Silence is inexpressible, the sonorous expression of nothingness; not speaking is significant: even in regard to "those things one cannot say, it is needful to say at least that they cannot be said, so that it may be understood that not speaking is not ignorance of what to say, but rather is being unable to express the

many things that are to be said." What is it that the last years of Sor Juana keep silent from us? And does what they keep silent belong to the realm of silence, that is, of the inexpressible, or to that of not speaking, which speaks through allusions and signs?

Sor Juana's crisis coincided with the upheaval and the public calamities that darkened the end of the seventeenth century in Mexico. It does not seem reasonable to believe that the first was an effect of the second. This kind of linear explanation necessitates another. The chain of cause and effect is endless. Furthermore, one cannot use history to explain culture as if it were a matter of different orders: one the world of facts, the other that of works. Facts are inseparable from works. Man moves in a world of works. Culture is history. And one may add that what is peculiar to history is culture and that there is no history except that of culture: the history of men's works and the history of men in their works. Thus, Sor Juana's silence and the tumultuous events of 1692 are closely related facts and are unintelligible except within the history of colonial culture. Both are consequences of a historical crisis little studied until now.

In the temporal sphere New Spain had been founded as the harmonious and hierarchical coexistence of many races and nations under the shadow of the Austrian monarchy; in the spiritual sphere, upon the universality of the Christian revelation. The superiority of the Spanish monarchy to the Aztec state was somewhat similar to that of the new religion: both constituted an open order capable of including all men and all races. The temporal order was just, moreover, because it was based upon the Christian revelation, upon the divine and rational word. Renouncing the rational word—keeping silent—and burning the Court of Justice, a symbol of the state, were acts of similar significance. In these acts New Spain expressed itself as negation. But this negation was not made against an external power: through these acts the colony negated itself and renounced its own existence, but no affirmation was born out of this negation. The poet fell silent, the intellectual abdicated, the people rebelled. The crisis led to silence. All doors were closed and colonial history was revealed as an adventure without an exit.

The meaning of the colonial crisis may be misunderstood if one yields to the temptation of considering it as a prophecy of independence. This would be true if independence were solely the extreme consequence of the dissolution of the Spanish Empire. But it was something more and also something substantially different: it was a revolution, that is, the exchange of the colonial order for another. Or say it was a complete beginning again of America's history. In spite of what many think, the colonial world did not give birth to an independent Mexico: there was a rupture and, following that, an order founded on principles and institutions radically different from the old ones. That is why the nineteenth century has seemed remote from its colonial past. No one recognized himself as being in the tradition of New Spain because, in fact, the liberals who brought about independence were of a different tradition. For more than a century, Mexico has lived without a past.

If the crisis that closed the period of the Austrian monarchy did not prophesy independence, then what was its meaning? Compared to the plurality of nations and tongues that comprised the pre-Hispanic world, New Spain presented a unitarian structure: all peoples and all men had a place in that universal order. In Sor Juana's *villancicos* ("Christmas carols") a heterogeneous multitude confesses a single faith and a single loyalty, in Nahuatl, Latin, and Spanish. Colonial Catholicism was as universal as the monarchy, and all the old gods and ancient mythologies, scarcely disguised, could be accommodated in its heavens. Abandoned by their divinities, the Indians, through baptism, renewed their ties with the divine and once again found their place in this world and in the other. The uprooting effect of the Conquest was resolved into the discovery of an ultraterrestrial home. But Catholicism arrived in Mexico as a religion already formed and on the defensive. Few have pointed out that the apogee of the Catholic religion in America coincided with its European twilight: sunset there was dawn among us. The new religion was a centuries-old religion with a subtle and complex philosophy that left no door open to the ardors of investigation or the doubts of speculation. This difference in historical rhythm—the root of the crisis—is also perceivable in other orbits, from the economic to the literary. In all orders the situation was similar: there was nothing to invent, nothing to add, nothing to propose. Scarcely born, New Spain was an opulent flower condemned to a premature and static maturity. Sor Juana embodies this maturity. Her poetry is an excellent showcase of sixteenth- and seventeenth-century styles. Assuredly, at times—as in her imitation of Jacinto Polo de Medina—she is superior to her model, but she discovered no new worlds. The same is true of her theater, and the greatest praise one can offer of *El divino Narciso* [The divine Narcissus] is that it is not unworthy of the Calderonian sacramental plays. (Only in *Primero sueño* [First dream], for reasons that will be examined later, does she surpass her masters.) In short, Sor Juana never transcended the style of her epoch. It was not possible for her to break those forms that imprisoned her so subtly and within which she moved with such elegance: to destroy them would have been to repudiate her own being. The conflict was insoluble because her only escape would have demanded the destruction of the very foundations of the colonial world.

As it was not possible to deny the principles on which that society rested without repudiating oneself, it was also impossible to propose others. Neither the tradition nor the history of New Spain could propose alternative solutions. It is true that two centuries later other principles were adopted, but one must remember that they came from outside, from France and the United States, and would form a different society. At the end of the seventeenth century the colonial world lost any possibility of renewing itself: the same principles that had engendered it were now choking it.

Denying this world and affirming another were acts that could not have the same significance for Sor Juana that they had for the great spirits of the Counter Reformation or the evangelists of New Spain. For Saints Theresa and Ignatius, renunciation of this world did not signify resignation or silence, but a change of destiny: history, and human action with it, opened to the other world and thus acquired new fecundity. The mystic life did not consist so much of quitting this world as of introducing personal life into sacred history. Militant Catholicism, evangelical or reformist, impregnated history with meaning, and the negation of the world was translated finally into an affirmation of historical action. In contrast, the truly personal portion of Sor Juana's work does not touch upon either action or contemplation, but upon knowledge—a knowledge that questions this world but does not judge it. This new kind of knowledge was impossible within the tenets of her historical universe. For more than twenty years Sor Juana adhered to her purpose. And she did not yield until all doors were definitely closed. Within herself the conflict was radical: knowledge is dream. When history awakened her from her dream, at the end of her life, she ceased to speak. Her awakening closed the golden dream of the viceroyship. If we do not understand her silence, we cannot comprehend what **Primero sueño** and *Respuesta a Sor Filotea de la Cruz* really mean: knowledge is impossible, and all utterance flows into silence. In understanding her silence one

> deciphers glories
> amid characters of devastation.

Ambiguous glories. Everything in her—vocation, soul, body—was ambivalent. While she was still a child her family sent her to live in Mexico City with relatives. At sixteen she was lady-in-waiting to the Marquesa de Mancera, vicereine of New Spain. Through the biography by Father P. Diego Calleja we are able to hear the echoes of the celebrations and competitions in which the young prodigy Juana shone. Beautiful and alone, she was not without suitors. But she chose not to be the "white wall upon which all would throw mud." She took the habit, because, "considering my totally negative attitude toward matrimony, it seemed the most fitting and most decent thing I could choose." We know now that she was an illegitimate child. Had she been legitimate, would she have chosen married life? This possibility is dubious. When Sor Juana speaks of her intellectual vocation she seems sincere: neither the absence of worldly love nor the urgency of divine love led her to the cloister. The convent was an expedient, a reasonable solution, offering refuge and solitude. The cell was an asylum, not a hermit's cave. Laboratory, library, salon, there she received visitors and conversed with them; poems were read, discussions held, and good music heard. She participated from the convent in both intellectual and courtly life. She was constantly writing poetry. She wrote plays, Christmas carols, prologues, treatises on music, and reflections on morality. Between the viceregal palace and the convent flowed a constant exchange of rhymes and civilities, compliments, satirical poems, and petitions. Indulged child, the tenth Muse.

"The tender phrases of the Mexican language" appear in her *villancicos* along with black Congolese and the unpolished speech of the Basque. With complete awareness, and even a certain coquetry, Sor Juana employs all those rare spices:

> What magic infusions
> known to the Indian herbsmen
> of my country spread their enchantment
> among my writings?

We would be in error if we confused the baroque aesthetic—which opened doors to the exoticism of the New World—with a preoccupation with nationalism. Actually one might say precisely the opposite. This predilection for languages and native dialects—in imitation of Luis de Góngora—does not so much reveal a hypothetical divination of future nationalism as a lively consciousness of the universality of the empire: Indians, Creoles, mulattoes, and Spaniards form one whole. Her preoccupation with pre-Columbian religions—apparent in the prologue to *El divino Narciso*—has similar meaning. The functions of the church were no different from those of the empire: to conciliate antagonisms and to embrace all differences in one superior truth.

Sor Juana transmutes her historical and personal ill fortunes, makes victory of her defeat, song of her silence. Once again poetry is nourished by history and biography. Once again it transcends them.

—Octavio Paz

Love is one of the constant themes in her poetry. Scholars say that she loved and was loved. She herself tells us this in various lyrics and sonnets—although in *Respuesta a Sor Filotea de la Cruz* she warns us that everything she wrote, except for **Primero sueño**, was commissioned. It is of little importance whether these were her loves or another's, whether they were experienced or imagined: by the grace of her poetry she made them her own. Her eroticism is intellectual; by that I do not mean that it is lacking in either profundity or authenticity. Like all great lovers, Sor Juana delights in the dialectic of passion; also, for she is sensual, in its rhetoric, which is not the same as the rhetorical passions of some female poets. The men and women in her poems are images, shadows "fashioned by fantasy." Her Platonism is not exempt from ardor. She feels her body is like a sexless flame:

> And I know that my body—
> never inclining to one or the other—
> is neuter, or abstract, everything
> the soul alone safekeeps.

The question is a burning one. Thus she leaves it "so that others may air it," since one should not attempt subtleties about things that are best ignored. No less ambiguous is her attitude toward the two sexes. The men of her

sonnets and lyrics are fleeting shadows exemplifying absence and disdain. However, her portraits of women are splendid, especially those of the vicereines who protected her, the Marquesa de Mancera and the Condesa de Paredes. Sor Juana's poem that "paints the beautiful proportions of the Lady Paredes" is one of the memorable works of Gongoristic poetry. This passion should not scandalize:

> To be a woman and to be absent
> is no impediment to loving you,
> for souls, as you know,
> ignore distance and gender.

The same rationale appears in almost all her amorous poetry—and also in the poems that treat the friendship she professes for Phyllis or Lysis: "Pure love, without desire for indecencies, can feel what profanest love feels." It would be excessive to speak of homosexuality; it is not excessive to observe that she herself does not hide the ambiguity of her feelings. In one of her most profound sonnets she repeats:

> Though you may thwart the tight bond
> that enclasped your fantastic form,
> it is little use to evade arms and breast
> if my fantasy builds you a prison.

Her loves, real or imagined, were without doubt chaste. She loved the body with her soul, but who can trace the boundaries between one and the other? For us, body and soul are one, or almost so: our idea of the body is colored by the spirit, and vice versa. Sor Juana lived in a world based on dualism, and for her the problem was easier to resolve, as much in the sphere of ideas as in that of conduct. When the Marquesa de Mancera died, she asked:

> Beauteous compound, in Laura divided,
> immortal soul, glorious spirit,
> why leave a body so beautiful,
> and why bid farewell to such a soul?

Sor Juana moved among shadows: those of untouchable bodies and fleeting souls. For her, only divine love was both concrete and ideal. But Sor Juana is not a mystic poet, and in her religious poems divinity is an abstraction. God is Idea and Concept, and even where she visibly follows the mystics she resists mixing the earthly and the heavenly. Divine love is rational love.

These were not her great love. From the time of her childhood she was inclined toward learning. As an adolescent she conceived the project of dressing as a man and attending the university. Resigned to being self-taught, she complained: "How hard it is to study those soulless marks on the page, lacking the living voice of the master." And she added that all these labors "were suffered for the love of learning; oh, had it only been for the love of God—which were proper—how worth-while it would have been!" This lament is a confession: the knowledge she seeks is not in sacred books. If theology is the "queen of the sciences," she lingers on her outer skirts: physics and logic, rhetoric and law. But her curiosity is not that of the specialist; she aspires to the integration of individual truths and insists upon the unity of learning. Variety does not harm general understanding; rather, it exacts it; all sciences are related: "It is the chain the ancients imagined issuing from the mouth of Jupiter, from which all things were suspended, linked one with another."

Her interest in science is impressive. In the lines of *Primero sueño* she describes, with a pedantry that makes us smile, the alimentary functions, the phenomenon of sleep and fantasy, the curative value of certain poisons, the Egyptian pyramids, and the magic lantern that

> *reproduces, feigned*
> *on the white wall, various figures,*
> *helped no less by the shadows*
> *than by light in tremulous reflections . . .*

Everything blends together: theology, science, baroque rhetoric, and true astonishment before the universe. Her attitude is rare in the Hispanic tradition. For the great Spaniards learning resolved into either heroic action or negation of the world (positive negation, to state it differently). For Sor Juana the world is a problem. For her, everything stimulates questions; her whole being is one excited question. The universe is a vast labyrinth within which the soul can find no unraveling thread, "shifting sands making it impossible for those attempting to follow a course." Nothing is further removed from this rational puzzle than the image of the world left us by the Spanish classics. There, science and action are blended. To learn is to act, and all action, like all learning, is related to the world beyond. Within this tradition disinterested learning is blasphemy or madness.

The church did not judge Sor Juana mad or blasphemous, but it did lament her deviation. In *Respuesta a Sor Filotea de la Cruz* she tells us that "they mortified and tormented me by saying, These studies are not in conformance with saintly ignorance, she will be lost, she will faint away at such heights in her own perspicacity and acuity." Double solitude: that of the conscience and that of being a woman. A superior—"very saintly and very candid, who believed that study was a matter for the Inquisition"—ordered her not to study. Her confessor tightened the ring and for two years denied her spiritual assistance. It was difficult to resist so much opposing pressure, as before it had been difficult not to be disoriented by the adulation of the court. Sor Juana persisted. Using the texts of the church fathers as support, she defended her right— and that of all women—to knowledge. And not only to learning, but also to teaching: "What is unseemly in an elderly woman's having as her charge the education of young ladies?"

Versatile, attracted by a thousand things at once, she defended herself by studying, and, studying, she retreated. If her superiors took away her books, she still had her mind, that consumed more matter in a quarter of an hour than books in four years. Not even in sleep was she liberated "from this continuous movement of my imagination; rather it is wont to work more freely, less encumbered, in my sleep . . . arguing and making verses that would fill a very large catalogue." This is one of her most beautiful confessions and one that gives us the key to her major poem: dreaming is a longer and more lucid wakefulness. Dreaming is knowing. In addition to diurnal learning arises another, necessarily rebellious form of learning, beyond the law and subject to a punishment that stimulates the spirit more than it terrorizes it. I need not emphasize here how the concept that governs *Primero sueño* coincides with some of modern poetry's preoccupations.

We owe the best and clearest description of the subject matter of *Primero sueño* to Father Calleja's biography: "It being nighttime, I slept. I dreamed that once and for all I desired to understand all the things that comprise the universe: I could not, not even as they are divided into categories, not even an individual one. The dawn came and, disillusioned, I awoke." Sor Juana declared that she wrote the poem as a deliberate imitation of *Soledades* [Solitudes]. But *Primero sueño* is a poem about nocturnal astonishment, while Góngora's poem is about daytime. There is nothing behind the images of the Cordovan poet because his world is pure image, a splendor of appearances. Sor Juana's universe—barren of color, abounding in shadows, abysses, and sudden clearings—is a labyrinth of symbols, a rational delirium. *Primero sueño* is a poem about knowledge. This distinguishes it from Gongoristic poetry and, more finally, from all baroque poetry. This very quality binds it, unexpectedly, to German Romantic poetry and through that to the poetry of our own time.

In some passages the baroque verse resists the unusual exercise of transcribing concepts and abstract formulas into images. The language becomes abrupt and pedantic. In other lines, the best and most intense, expression becomes dizzying in its lucidity. Sor Juana creates an abstract and hallucinatory landscape formed of cones, obelisks, pyramids, geometric precipices, and aggressive peaks. Her world partakes of mechanics and of myth. The sphere and the triangle rule its empty sky. Poetry of science, but also of nocturnal terror. The poem begins when night reigns over the world. Everything sleeps, overcome by dreams. The king and the thief sleep, the lovers and the solitary. The body lies delivered unto itself. Diminished life of the body, disproportionate life of the spirit, freed from its corporeal weight. Nourishment, transformed into heat, engenders sensations that fantasy converts into images. On the heights of her mental pyramid—formed by all the powers of the spirit, memory and imagination, judgment and fantasy—the soul contemplates the phantasms of the world and, especially, those figures of the mind, "the clear intellectual stars" of her interior sky. In them the soul re-creates itself in itself. Later, the soul dissociates itself from this contemplation and spreads its gaze over all creation; the world's diversity dazzles it and finally blinds it. An intellectual eagle, the soul hurls itself from the precipice "into the neutrality of a sea of astonishment." The fall does not annihilate it. Incapable of flight, it climbs.

Painfully, step by step, it ascends the pyramid. Since method must repair the "defect of being unable to know all of creation in an intuitive act," it divides the world into categories, grades of knowledge. *Primero sueño* describes the progress of thought, a spiral that ascends from the inanimate toward man and his symbol, the triangle, a figure in which animal and divine converge. Man is the site of creation's rendezvous, life's highest point of tension, always between two abysses: "lofty lowliness . . . at the mercy of amorous union." But method does not remedy the limitations of the spirit. Understanding cannot discern the ties that unite the inanimate to the animate, vegetable to animal, animal to man. Nor is it even feasible to penetrate the most simple phenomenon: the individual is as irreducible as the species. Darkly it realizes that the immense variety of creation is resolved in one law but that that law is ineffable. The soul vacillates. Perhaps it would be better to retreat. Examples of other defeats rise up as a warning to the imprudent. The warning becomes a challenge; the spirit becomes inflamed as it sees that others did not hesitate to "make their names eternal in their ruin." The poem is peopled with Promethean images; the act of knowing, not knowledge itself, is the battle prize. The fallen soul affirms itself and, making cajolery of its terror, hastens to elect new courses. In that instant the fasting body reclaims its own dominion. The sun bursts forth. Images dissolve. Knowledge is a dream. But the sun's victory is partial and cyclical. It triumphs in half the world; in the other half it is vanquished. Rebellious night, "recovered by reason of its fall," erects its empire in the territories the sun forsakes. There, other souls dream Sor Juana's dream. The universe the poem reveals to us is ambivalent: wakefulness is dream; the night's defeat, its victory. The dream of knowledge also means: knowledge is dream. Each affirmation carries within it its own negation.

Sor Juana's night is not the carnal night of lovers. Neither is it the night of the mystics. It is an intellectual night, lofty and fixed like an immense eye, a night firmly constructed above the void, rigorous geometry, taciturn obelisk, all of it fixed tension directed toward the heavens. This vertical impulse is the only thing that recalls other nights of Spanish mysticism. But the mystics seem to be attracted to heaven by lines of celestial forces, as one sees in certain of El Greco's paintings. In *Primero sueño* the heavens are closed; the heights are hostile to flight. Silence confronting man: the desire for knowledge is illicit and the soul that dreams of knowledge is rebellious. Nocturnal solitude of the consciousness. Drought, vertigo, palpitation. But, nevertheless, all is not adversity. In his solitude and his fall from the heights man affirms himself in himself: to know is to dream, but that dream is everything we know of ourselves, and in that dream resides our greatness. It is a game of mirrors in which the soul loses each time it wins and wins each time it loses, and the poem's emotion springs from the awareness of this ambiguity. Sor Juana's cyclical and vertiginous night suddenly reveals its fixed center: *Primero sueño* is a poem not of knowledge but of the *act of knowing*. And thus Sor Juana transmutes her historical and personal ill fortunes, makes victory of her defeat, song of her silence. Once again poetry is nourished by history and biography. Once again it transcends them.

Frederick Luciani (essay date 1986)

SOURCE: "The Burlesque Sonnets of Sor Juana Inés de la Cruz," in *Hispanic Journal,* Vol. 8, No. 1, Fall, 1986, pp. 85-95.

[*In the following essay, Luciani places Juans In*és *de la Cruz's burlesque sonnets within the context of the courtly love tradition.*]

In his controversial psychoanalytic study of Sor Juana Inés de la Cruz, Ludwig Pfandl offers her five burlesque sonnets as proof that the Mexican nun suffered from a chronic mental disorder, because of which she sometimes slipped into an abnormal and indecent deficiency of sensibility and taste. Says Pfandl [in *Sor Juana Inés de la Cruz, la décima musa de México: Su vida, Su poesia, Su psique,* translated by Juan Autonio Ortega y Medina, 1963]:

> Por último podemos también aqui mencionar esos cinco malos sonetos que los biógrafos de nuestra monja no saben precisamente cómo justificar y declarar inofensivos y tampoco saben cómo ponerlos en consonancia con el elevado estado intelectual de la Décima Musa. . . . Nosotros . . . consideramos que los cinco malcriados incubos son productos de la Juana ya madura y monacal, pues sabemos cómo renovaba y resbalaba reiteradamente hacia un anormal estado de sensibilidad.

Pfandl's observations neatly summarize the general critical posture with regard to the burlesque sonnets: they have long been both a source of perplexity for critics and an object of direct or indirect censure. Their rather frivolous, discordant rhymes have not been to everyone's taste, and their presentation of a picaresque sort of love (unrefined, even bawdy), along with the occasional indelicate word or reference, have struck a number of modern critics as incongruous and inappropriate, especially considering Sor Juana's sex and religious calling.

A quick description of the form and content of the burlesque sonnets will help to explain why, as Pfandl correctly noted, critics have been hard-pressed to explain their presence within Sor Juana's oeuvre. All five are written in forced consonantal rhyme, and use farcical, sometimes coarse, language to describe aspects of love among the lower classes. The characteristic rhymed consonant of the first sonnet, "Inés, cuando te riñen por bellaca . . . ," is /c/; the person addressed, perhaps by her suitor, is Inés, who is scolded for her loquacity in terms which do not exclude the scatologic. The second sonnet, "Aunque eres, Teresilla, tan *muchacha* . . . ," has a characteristic *ch* in its rhyme scheme, and deals with the deceitful Teresilla and her cuckolded husband Camacho. The only peculiarities in rhyme of the third sonnet, "Inés, y con tu amor me refocilo . . . ," are the use of the prefix *re* in the rhymed words of the first quatrain and the first tercet, and the final *o* of all the lines. In this poem, an

Inés is again addressed, this time by a suitor who describes his reactions to her fickle, and sometimes violent, moods. The consonant *f* is characteristic of the rhyme scheme in the fourth sonnet, "Vaya con Dios, Beatriz, el ser *estafa* . . . ," in which a Beatriz receives the complaints of her *rufo,* who accuses her of being deceitful and unfaithful. In the last sonnet, "Aunque presumes, Nise, que soy *tosco* . . . ," the characteristic rhyme is *-sco.* In this poem, a Nise is assured by the man in her life that he is not deceived by the traps she sets for him.

Where critics have gone wrong is to divorce these sonnets from the literary context which makes them intelligible: the courtly love tradition, in both its serious and burlesque forms. When examining this tradition, a convenient place to start is with Guillaume IX of Aquitaine, generally acknowledged as the first troubadour, at least the first whose works are extant. Guillaume's lyric manifests many of the refined notions of courtly love whose echoes are heard in the Baroque age of Sor Juana, yet in his songs on *con,* for example, Guillaume treats the most earthy aspects of physical love in a broad and bawdy fashion. But the presence of the exalted and the base is not schizophrenic in Guillaume, any more than it is in Rabelais or Quevedo, or for that matter, Sor Juana. Rather, high and low treatments of love coexist as parallel and connecting modes, in constant dialogue with each other. Refined courtly love depends upon its burlesque counterpart; its elegant attitudes need to be somehow grounded in baser reality so as not to become empty posturing. Similarly, burlesque views of love depend on their refined counterpart for their humor and surprise; only as thematic and linguistic deformations of an ideal are they ingenious, and therefore amusing.

This element of dialogue, a dialogue of texts, of voices and attitudes, to which the attentive reader is sensitive, is important in Sor Juana as well. Her burlesque sonnets do indeed stand in contrast to her sublime amorous lyric, a contrast whose intention is to surprise and delight. Pfandl is of course correct when he suggests that these poems cannot be put "in consonance" with Sor Juana's more elevated moments; his mistake is to view the dissonance of the burlesque sonnets in ethical and psychological terms rather than in terms of an evolving tradition.

The third sonnet is a good example of how burlesque love poems can best be appreciated as a deformation of the ideal courtly love lyric. It reads:

Inés, yo con tu amor me *refocilo*
y viéndome querer me *regodeo*;
en mirar tu hermosura me *recreo,*
y cuando estás celosa me *reguilo.*

Si a otro miras, de celos me *aniquilo*
y tiemblo de tu gracia y tu *meneo*;
porque sé, Inés, que tú con un *voleo*
no dejarás humor ni aun para *quilo.*

Cuando estás enojada no *resuello,*
cuando me das picones me *refino,*
cuando sales de casa no *reposo*;

y espero, Inés, que entre esto y entre *aquello,*
tu amor, acompañado de mi *vino,*
dé conmigo en la cama o en el *coso.*

The sonnet is essentially a lover's lament, but this lover is not a courtier, and the object of his affections is no lady. As in serious courtly love poetry, the beloved enjoys a superior position relative to her suitor, who rejoices in any sign of affection or attention on her part. And as in courtly love connection, the beauty of the lady, which the lover contemplates with delight, is the source of love. The beginning of the poem, then, presents a perfectly traditional situation: the lover rejoices in his lady's beauty and attentions. But the serious tone of this beginning is undermined by the discordant forced consonants of the quatrain; the last word of each line, the key verb which expresses the lover's emotions, begins with the prefix *re-,* a prefix which suggests repetition and intensification. Each of these verbs is also reflexive, preceded by the pronoun *me.* The repetition of these verbs ("me refocilo," "me regodeo," "me recreo") vulgarizes the essential message, suggesting emotions that are more self-indulgent than courteous.

The lover goes on to treat the theme of jealousy; he is devastated when his beloved looks at another, and trembles when she herself is jealous. The lover's trembling recalls that of the ideal courtly lover, who manifests symptoms of love illness (*hereos*). However, this lover trembles, not because of his extreme humility, not because his worship of the lady leads him to fear her slightest sign of displeasure, but rather, as it turns out, because of her habit of walloping her man when provoked. The ideal courtier's *heroes,* caused by the alteration of humors in his lady's presence, is thus parodied by the lower-class lover, the *rufián,* whose nervous trembling is a result of the fear of physical violence: "tú con un voleo / no dejarás humor ni aun para *quilo.*"

The first tercet of the sonnet returns to the use of words beginning with *re-,* and each line recalls a traditional courtly love theme. In the first line, the lover notes how he does not dare to breathe when Inés is angry. This corresponds to both a symptom of *hereos* (the "impedido aliento" found elsewhere in Sor Juana's verse) and the theme of the silent adorer, the *fenhedor* of courtly love lyric. But here Sor Juana's lexical choice, the verb *resollar,* colors the concept with a more vulgar shade of meaning: it recalls the noisy respiration of animals as well as the familiar meaning of "breathing a word," speaking up. The next line echoes the courtly theme of the refining effect of love; the lover's courteous service is a source of virtue, a process of self-improvement through the exercise of humility, devotion, and self-discipline. But this lover's service is of a more prosaic nature; it is Inés' henpecking that keeps him in line. The last line recalls the courtly theme of the wakeful lover, Petrarch for example, whose lonely bed is his *duro campo di battaglia.* But in Sor Juana's sonnet, the lover's sleeplessness is not a result of unrequited passion; it is a more practical kind of vigilance, directed towards Inés' activities outside the house.

The sonnet ends with an expression of hope or expectation; this corresponds to the courtly lover's role of *precador,* or beseecher. But the *guerdón* that this lover anticipates is ambiguous: He expects that Inés' love will land him in bed or out on the street. If bed is his fate, he will either have won the object of his heart's desire, or else he will be convalescing. If the street is his fate, he will either have been dismissed by his disdainful lady, or else he will have joined her in some mutually profitable enterprise.

The fifth burlesque sonnet by Sor Juana also constitutes a humorous deformation of courtly love commonplaces. It reads:

> Aunque presumes, Nise, que soy *tosco*
> y que, cual palomilla, me *chamusco,*
> yo te aseguro que tu luz no *busco*
> porque ya tus engaños *reconozco.*
>
> Y así, aunque en tus enredos más me *embosco,*
> muy poco viene a ser lo que me *ofusco,*
> porque si en el color soy algo *fusco,*
> soy en la condición mucho más *hosco.*
>
> Lo que es de tus picones, no me rasco,
> antes estoy con ellos ya tan *fresco*
> que te puedo servir de helar un frasco:
>
> que a darte nieve sólo me enternezco,
> y.asi, Nise, no pienses darme *chasco,*
> porque yo sé muy bien lo que me *pesco.*

As with so many poems in the courtly love mode, this sonnet hinges upon the antithetical contrast of images and metaphors of heat and cold, light and darkness. But the lover who speaks in this poem uses these antitheses to systematically deny similarity between himself and the traditional courtier.

The first quatrain constitutes a reworking of one of the oldest and most common metaphors of courtly love verse: the lover as a moth attracted to the flame. The standard metaphor is well suited to the commonplaces of courtly love sentiment: just as the moth flits about the flame, unable to approach and unable to depart, so is the courtly lover trapped in a perpetual state of longing, of frustrated desire, of "have-and-have-not"; the moth's attraction is ultimately fatal, just as the lover's passion is self-destructive. Poets traditionally noted the madness of the moth in its attraction to flame (in the words of the troubadour Floquet de Marseille, "parpaillos qu'a tant folla natura"), as well as its artless, ingenuous nature (Petrarch's "semplicetta far alla," Herrera's "simple mariposa"), and its literal and figurative blindness (in Góngora's words, "Mariposa, no sólo no cobarde, mas temeraria, fatalmente ciega").

In Sor Juana's sonnet, all of these commonplaces are alluded to, but with a difference: the lover who speaks denies the relevance of the traditional metaphor; his is not the classic situation. He is not stupid ("tosco") despite what Nise may think. He is not blinded with passion, but rather, exceedingly clear of eye: he sees Nise for what she is without seeking her "light": "tu luz no busco," "tus engaños reconozco." In short, he is no butterfly, and no dreamy courtly lover; his love is lucid and self-interested, and he is not be its victim.

The second quatrain continues to contrast images of light and darkness. The lover, however deeply involved he may be with Nise, and even entangled in her deceitful plots, denies being confused ("ofuscado"); his skin color may be dark ("fusco") but his disposition is even darker ("más hosco"). These lines recall many of Petrarch's which contrast the lover's dark and depressed state with Laura's bright and serene nature: "Che'l nostro stato è inquieto a fosco, / Si come'l suo pacifico e sereno." But such sentiments are corrupted in Sor Juana's sonnet; the lover who speaks is not only dark of disposition, but also of skin color. He is probably a mulatto or mestizo, that is to say, of the lower classes. Thus, a kind of racial joke is used to parody the traditional courtly lover's spiritual darkness and despair.

> **Even allowing for differences in taste and humor between Sor Juana's century and our own, one cannot help but sense a certain ponderous quality in these sonnets; without judging them ethically or censuring them aesthetically, one can still recognize that they are something of a vulgar stunt.**
>
> **—Frederick Luciani**

In the tercets, the contrast of light and darkness gives way to the contrast of heat and cold, in antithetical image that recall qenerations of European love lyric. But here again, the classic situation is reversed: the lover is cool and collected, not burning with passion. He is the one whose heart is cold, who offers his snowy disdain to the lady. The poem ends on a defiant note: the lover knows what he is about, and is not to be trifled with.

This affirmation of control over the amorous relationship on the part of the suitor is a direct negation of courtly lover sentiment, and of the traditional roles of courtly lovers. Nise is warned not to play the cruel mistress, for her man is not the courtier of love lyric, and has no intention of being dominated. He is clever, self-possessed, keen of visions; even his skin color is a denial of resemblance to the poetic ideal. This denial of resemblance is carried out in the poem on the rhetorical level: standard comparisons are employed, but vulgarized or trivialized so as to stand the conventions of love lyric on their ear. The difference is obvious if one juxtaposes Petrarch's "stato fusco" with the "color fusco" of the lover in Sor Juana's sonnet, or if on one compares the standard expression of amorous disorientation, the "camino errado" of so many courtly love poets, with this lover's colorful and impudent expression of self-assurance: "yo sé muy bien lo que me pesco."

As the preceding analysis has suggested, it is the final word of each line which gives the five burlesque sonnets their farcical tone. Aside from the peculiar consonantal rhymes which they possess, these words are unique in their general semantic, morphological, and acoustic properties. Among them one finds examples of onomatopoeia (*triquitraque, chasco*), of *germanía* and colloquialisms (*mequetrefe, cuca,* and so on), of popular variants of words (*ducho,* rather than *docto*), and of *poliptoton (ofusco, fusco, hosco*). In addition, the first sonnet includes one common scatological word (*caca*), and the fourth sonnet concludes with a line that mimics the laughter of which the *rufián* will be the object ("afa, ufo, afe, ofe . . .") and ends by naming the characteristic consonant of the sonnet, *efe*. In short, these final words are deliberately and self-consciously anti-poetic, if by "poetic" we mean mellifluous, idealized, euphemistic, and erudite. They are the direct antithesis of "poetic" language, just as the plebeian lovers who are referred to are, in their actions and emotions, the antithesis of the prototypical lovers of courtly tradition.

Antipoetic too, by traditional standards, is the consonantal rhyme of these sonnets, the insistent repetition of sound which is percussive but not musical. The result is a kind of vertical alliteration, read or heard downward from line to line, not the linear, mimetic alliteration of traditional verse. This alliteration is used in a playful, nonfunctional way; the forced consonants are, to borrow Severo Sarduy's words [in *América Latina en su literatura,* edited by César Fernández Moreno, 1972], a "divertimiento fonético," an intratextual operation which invites an unorthodox, nonlinear reading, and which, like the anagram and so many other "curiosities of Baroque verse," is ultimately self-referential. If there is a correspondence, a harmony of sound and sense in these poems, then it is a cacophonous harmony; the acoustic discord of the final words reminds the reader of the general nature of the sonnets: their deliberate corruption of courtly love ideology, their lexical deviation from conventional poetic language, in short, their carefully contrived dissonance with regard to traditional amorous lyric.

The burlesque sonnets, then, can be regarded as poems of contrived dissonance. The reader can attune his ear to the acoustic and intertextual dissonances of the poems, but what about the elements of contrivance? How can one explain the sonnets' systematic rhetorical and thematic upending of the courtly love tradition? They are obviously meant as humorous pieces; one must assume that their buffoonish humor was more engaging in the seventeenth century than in our own. And certainly the ingeniousness of the metrical tricks performed must have appealed to the Baroque Age's love of wit. Yet even allowing for differences in taste and humor between Sor Juana's century and our own, one cannot help but sense a certain ponderous quality in these sonnets; without judging them ethically or censuring them aesthetically, one can still recognize that they are something of a vulgar stunt. When read within a literary tradition, and especially when juxtaposed with serious treatments of courtly love, they are more then comical and clever: they are somewhat aggressive, even subversive. The triviality of the situations presented does not change the fact that these sonnets turn back on the tradition in a critical way; this is cumbersome parody, but with a pointed tip.

Sor Juana's burlesque sonnets refer constantly to a poetic tradition, and ultimately, to themselves. This circular referentiality makes determining the fundamental sense and purpose of these poems a difficult task. But the task can be made practicable by stepping briefly outside the circle, by looking to another writer and another text as points of comparison. The humorously parodic nature of the burlesque sonnets, their metaliterary consciousness, their constant reference to an established literary genre, are all reminiscent of similar tendencies in the *Quixote*. Cervantes and Sor Juana share, among other things, a keen awareness of the permutations that can be realized by the writer who works with topoi that are over-familiar, time-worn. The *Quixote* offers a wealth of comparative possibilities, but one episode in particular, that of Don Quixote's penitence in the Sierra Morena, can serve as a virtual simulacrum for the feats performed by Sor Juana in the burlesque sonnets.

As the reader of the *Quixote* will remember, in part I of the novel the hero sends his squire on a mission: Sancho must ride to Dulcinea and communicate his master's love to her. During Sancho's absence, Don Quixote proposes to imitate the mad fury of Orlando and Amadis, two of his principal models in knight-errantry. The purpose of Don Quixote's imitation will be to prove his love for Dulcinea, to give, in his words, "testimonio y señal de la pena que mi asendereado corazón padece." To this end, it is necessary that Sancho be his medium; he must observe some of Don Quixote's actions before leaving and report them to Dulcinea: "'Por lo menos, quiero, Sancho . . . que me veas en cueros, y hacer una o dos docenas de locuras, . . . porque habiéndolas tú visto por tus propios ojos, puedas jurar a tu salvo en las demás que quisieres añadir . . .".'

Sancho immediately begins to suspect what Don Quixote never does, namely that such actions will not make sense out of their conventional context. He notes that, while the chivalric heroes had sufficient cause to lose their sanity, Don Quixote's "madness" will be unprovoked. His master's answer is too pragmatic, too well reasoned, and is a reminder of the totally contrived nature of his enterprise: "'Ahi está el punto . . . , y ésa es la fineza de mi negocio; que volverse loco un caballero andante con causa, ni grado ni gracias: el toque está en desatinar sin ocasión y dar a entender a mi dama que si en seco hago esto, ¿qué hiciera en mojado?'" Don Quixote's purpose is too obviously rhetorical; he hopes to physically enact the figures and topoi of amorous convention in order to *convince* Dulcinea that he indeed is in love. As most often is the case in the novel, Don Quixote's real madness lies in his inability to recognize what Cervantes makes refreshingly clear to the reader: that literary conventions make sense only on a literary plane, that they cannot be translated into action without becoming absurd.

Sancho, again, realizes that his *amo* is embarked upon an enterprise doomed to failure. When Don Quixote mentions that he proposes to smash his head against the rocks as part of his amorous derangement, Sancho advises: "Por amor de Dios . . . , que mire vuestra merced cómo se da esas calabazadas: que a tal peña podrá llegar, y en tal punto, que con la primera se acabase la máquina desta penitencia. Y seria yo de parecer que . . . se contentase . . . con dárselas en el agua, o en alguna cosa blanda, como algodón." Sancho's premonitions turn out to be valid ones: Don Quixote's mad fury is never quite realized in action. His descriptions to Sancho of his proposed derangement are most of what constitutes his imitatio. Beyond that, all he does is to half undress, and, just as Sancho embarks upon his mission, stand upon his head, "descubriendo cosas, que, por no verlas otra vez, volvió Sancho la reinda a Rocinante, y se dió por contento y satisfecho de que podia jurar que su amo quedaba loco." Once Sancho is gone, Don Quixote decides, in a wave of pragmatism, to imitate the gentle penitence of Amadis rather than the violent variety of Orlando. Mostly he wanders and prays the rosary, and occasionally carves a love poem on a tree or traces one in the sand, since without a witness, a reader of his actions, and without the powers of linguistic figuration, his crazed actions are meaningless, merely absurd.

Within the story of Don Quixote's adventures, his penitence in the Sierra Morena is a dismal failure. His attempts to physically enact the figures of literary convention are impossible; the message he endeavors to send to Dulcinea never arrives, and even his medium, Sancho, does not understand the spirit in which his penitence is intended, even if he understands its concrete implications only too well. But the episode of Don Quixote's penitence is remarkably successful novelistically. The artificiality of Don Quixote's stunts effectively turns the convention upside down, and reveals the ridiculousness of the original literary theme. Don Quixote's imitation of his literary heroes' penitence may be a disaster for Don Quixote, but it is something of a novelistic coup for Cervantes; the episode is utterly successful as a parody of hyperbolic declarations of love.

Somewhat the same thing can be said for Sor Juana's burlesque sonnets. As love poetry, they are a deliberately garish failure, a grotesque inversion both of courtly love sentiment and of love poetry's euphonic metrics. A parallel can be drawn between Don Quixote's contrived poses and Sor Juana's contrived verses; in both cases, the trick is pre-announced. The consonants in the burlesque sonnets are indeed "forced" upon the reader; each line seems to be contrived so as to produce the prearranged word, which strikes the ear with its gratuitous discord. As with Don Quixote's physical displays of madness, the metrical trick performed comes across as too pre-meditated, too heavy-handed.

But as parody the sonnets are very effective. By presenting a farcical lower-class version of the idealized love of courtly tradition, the sonnets, like Don Quixote's penitence, demonstrate how the themes and tropes of a given literary mode are untranslatable from their conventional context; the parodic deformation of the convention, in turn, reveals the latter's artificial and arbitrary nature. If the trick performed is absurd, so are the original literary commonplaces which it apes. On this plane, the intrusive metrical design of the sonnets serve to complement their parodic mission: the percussive noise heard at the end of each line, in the repetition of the forced consonants, is really the sound of literary clichés being exploded, clichés which, too, have long been forced upon the reader.

It is this rather violent final image of the burlesque sonnets that perhaps best captures their essense and importance. These poems struggle to deal with a decadent and stifling courtly love mode, a mode which, in the seventeenth century, could be reworked or debunked but never sidestepped or merely ignored. But Sor Juana's struggle was carried forth without the eminently convenient persona of Don Quixote, who, living in a twilight world between literature and physical reality, could slip back and forth between the two, and thereby act out the fancies of Cervantes' sophisticated metaliterary consciousness. Without this mediating figure, Sor Juana's gymnastics are confined to the rhetorical plane, but as Pfandl and others have sensed without understanding, the trick performed in the burlesque sonnets is not just a brief, frivolous, somewhat scandalous cartwheel; it is also an aggressive and revealing one. As the sonnets turn literary convention upside down, they uncover a defiant and irreverent attitude with regard to tradition, an assertion of authorial will, a celebration of the generative power of the artist.

Frederick Luciani (essay date 1987)

SOURCE: "Emblems of Praise in a *Romance* by Sor Juana Inés de la Cruz," in *Romance Quarterly,* Vol. 34, No. 2, May, 1987, pp. 213-21.

[*In the following essay, Luciani discusses stylistic elements of Cruz's panegyric poem to Condesa de Galve.*]

The panegyric verse of Sor Juana Inés de la Cruz is, for most modern readers, of rather limited appeal. The intricate court hierarchies and systems of protection and patronage which gave rise to this kind of poetry now seem remote and obscure; the kind of flattery in which this poetry indulges now often seems vacuous, at times fulsome. What is more, Sor Juana's panegyric verse seems to have little to recommend it alongside the formal excellence and ideological profundity of some of her major works, such as the **Sueño,** the *Respuesta,* or the *autos.*

But when this poetry is considered within the context of both the viceregal society in which Sor Juana held a prominent place, and the European tradition of courtly verse of which it was a part, it begins to reveal both ideological coherence and artistic felicities. This is precisely the context that Octavio Paz has outlined in his recent book, *Sor Juana Inés de la Cruz o las trampas de la fe.* His succinct definition of Sor Juana's panegyric compositions can be regarded as a kind of maxim: "Son emblemas verbales de una relación política sobrentendida. Aunque esta relación asume muchas formas, puede reducirse a la más simple: el vínculo que une al señor y sus vasallos." Verbal *emblems,* with an attendant and fairly consistent code, a system of representation—this is what Paz postulates and what I hope to take as my point of departure, with the goal of delineating the *emblem,* in perhaps a more literal sense than that intended by Paz, in a particular poem by Sor Juana.

This poem, a *romance* written in praise of the Condesa de Galve, one of the several vicereines of Mexico to be honored by Sor Juana's pen, can be placed in an important subcategory of Sor Juana's panegyric verse: the poetic portrait. This subcategory includes some of Sor Juana's most unusual and least-studied works and embraces everything from the lengthy *ovillejo* which describes Lisarda and is a kind of subversive anti-poem, to elegant and highly stylized portraits which employ the standard Petrarchan conceits in ingenious ways. What all of these poems have in common is an ideological stratum subjacent to the sociopolitical one laid open by Octavio Paz. The essence of these poems is metaphor: the lady is like or unlike something else. But here metaphor is more than a device used to convey a message; it is a topic as well as a trope. The nature of resemblance is what these poems are fundamentally "about," the resemblance of a person to a thing, of a word to its referent, of art to the world. It is this *artistic* ideology which remains to be elucidated in Sor Juana's poetic portraits.

The particular portrait of interest to this study has an epistolary, even conversational tone. It begins, as letters often do, with a reference to its own redaction:

> Sobre si es atrevimiento
> bella Elvira, responderte,
> y sobre si también era
> cobardia el no atreverme,
> he pasado pensativa,
> sobre un libro y un bufete
> (porque vayan otros *sobres*)
> sobre el amor que me debes,
> no sé yo qué tantos días;

This self-reflective quality is developed as the *romance* goes on. The poetess presents herself in the act of planning a reply to the Vicereine, a reply in the form of a poetic portrait. The *romance* is thus, ostensibly, the *petite histoire* of the writing of a poem, or rather, as shall be seen, the failure to write one. The poetess continues:

> y si no lo has por enojo,
> después que estaba el caletre
> cansado asaz de pensar
> y de revolver papeles,
> resuelta a escribirte ya,
> en todos los aranceles
> de Jardines y de Luces,
> de Estrellas y de Claveles,
> no hallé en luces ni colores
> comparación conveniente,

> que con más de quince palmos
> a tu hermosura viniese . . .

The standard objects of comparison—stars and flowers—are unsuited to the task, as is the precedent offered by other poets:

> Pues a los Poetas, ¡cuánto
> les revolví los afeites
> con que hacen que una hermosura
> dure aunque al tiempo le pese!

There follows a long list of the great poets and painters of history (Timantes and Apeles, Petrarch the painter of Laura, Homer the painter of Helen, Virgil of Dido) and also the great beauties of literary history (Proserpine, Lucrecia, Florinda la Cava, and others). None of these precedents are equal to the task of describing the Condesa de Galve, although Ovid's *Metamorphoses* offers a veritable treasure trove of possibilities:

> En Ovidio, como es
> Poeta de las Mujeres,
> hallé que al fin los pintares
> eran como los quereres;
> y hallé a escoger, como en peras,
> unas bellezas de a veinte . . .

There follows a list of Ovidian beauties from Galatea to Circe, Dephne and Atlanta, but none is a worthy predecessor of the Condesa, and Sor Juana concludes:

> y en fin, la Casa del Mundo,
> que tantas pinturas tiene
> de bellezas vividoras,
> que están sin envejecerse,

> . . . . .

> revolví, como ya digo,
> sin que entre todas pudiese
> hallar una que siquiera
> en el vestido os semeje.

The only solution to the problem will be to abandon the descriptive task altogether, to reject comparison, that is, metaphor:

> Con que, de comparaciones
> desesperada mi mente,
> al ¿viste? y al *así como*
> hizo ahorcar en dos cordeles,
> ya sin tratar de pintarte,
> sino sólo de quererte . . .

The concluding stanzas of the *romance* express Sor Juana's love, obeisance, and humility in conventional terms, slyly inserting the kind of solar metaphor that the poetess had earlier rejected:

> Y en fin, no hallo qué decirte,
> sino sólo qué ofrecerte,

adorando tus favores,
las gracias de tus mercedes.
   De ellos me conozco indigna;
mas eres Sol, y amaneces
por beneficio común
para todos igualmente.
   Por ellos, Señora mía,
postrada beso mil veces
la tierra que pisas y
los pies, que no sé si tienes.

The panegyric message in this *romance* is not difficult to discern. It is hyperbolic in the most extreme degree: it is descriptive praise that presents its subject as beyond description. The beauty and charms of the Condesa are simply ineffable. This ineffability topos is, of course, an integral part of laudatory rhetoric, and it is well represented in the courtly love lyric. In Sor Juana's verse, it appears frequently, usually as a rather transparent screen for a rhetorical trick. The trick, in this case, is to make the Vicereine the winner of the literary beauty pageant by default; the other contestants simply cannot compete. The real compliment, of course, with the hyperbole discounted, is to even include the Condesa in such an impressive list. And, not incidentally, the compliment accrues nicely to Sor Juana herself: by implication, the author of the poem as well as its subject is to be admitted to a literary pantheon inhabited by the likes of Homer and Petrarch, Helen of Troy and Laura.

Sor Juana's poetic portraits—and non-portraits, like this *romance*—are almost always framed in terms of literal *painted* portraits, with the appropriate nomenclature, rules of composition, and thematic corpus. They therefore must be considered within the pictorial tradition of seventeenth-century poetry, that is, the close partnership of the "sister arts" of poetry and painting in the Baroque Age. The importance of this partnership, especially as evidenced in the emblem books of Alciato, Ripa, and others, books that were immensely popular in seventeenth-century Europe, has been studied with respect to Sor Juana's *Neptuno alegórico* by Karl-Ludwig Selig, Octavio Paz, and Georgina Sabat de Rivers.

To summarize Baroque literary pictorialism would require many pages, indeed, volumes: witness the magnificent studies by Mario Praz, Jean Hagstrum, and in particular regard to seventeenth-century Spain, Julián Gallego. For the purposes of this paper, the examination of one specific representation of *ut pictura poesis*, "as a painting, so a poem," will suffice. This representation is itself an emblem, a symbolic picture accompanied by a verbal description and explanation: I refer to the emblem for "Ars Pictoria" in the 1758-60 edition of Cesare Ripa's *Iconologia*. The pertinent elements of this complex emblem are the following: Painting is personified by a woman with a cloth bound over her mouth, a standard reference to the notion that painting is mute poetry. She rests one arm on a canvas upon which is drawn the allegory of Poetry: another reference to the sister arts. At the foot of the emblem is the inscription "Imitatio." And behind the personification of Painting is

hanging a self-portrait of Gottfried Eichler, the illustrator of this edition of the *Iconologia*. In this self-portrait the artist points back over his shoulder to one of his works. These are the elements to keep in mind: painting as mute poetry, poetry in turn as a speaking picture, the painting within a painting, the self insertion of the artist and his *oeuvre,* the all embracing idea of mimesis.

Although all of the literary allusions in Sor Juana's *oeuvre* are relevant to the pictorial tradition it is Ovid's *Metamorphosis* that offers the most striking possibilities. First, it must be kept in mind that *illustrated* versions of this work were immensely popular in seventeenth-century Europe. An important example is the Spanish translation of Sánchez de Viana, *Las transformaciones de Ovidio,* published in Valladolid in 1589. A persual of the lists of book shipments to the New World provided by Irving A. Leonard shows that this version of Ovid crossed the Atlantic. It very possibly was part of Sor Juana's library. Thus, when the poetess says that she found in Ovid "unas bellezas de a veinte," she very likely refers to both poetic descriptions and actual illustrations of Ovid's mythological ladies.

But the *Metamorphoses* was connected with pictorial art in more important ways. It provided abundant material for visual spectacle: the paintings of a Rubens or a Velázquez, the court masques of Ben Jonson and Inigo Jones. The artists who illustrated the *Metamorphoses* also sometimes illustrated emblem books: Virgil Solis (1514-1562) of Germany is an example. And emblem books themselves often used mythological figures from the *Metamorphoses* to represent a vice or a virtue: thus, in Alciato's *Emblemata,* Phaeton is used to represent temerity, Narcissus to represent self-love, and so on.

The reasons for this seventeenth-century and, indeed, perennial link between Ovid and pictorial art are not difficult to fathom. Ovid himself owed much to a poetic tradition that, since the foggy prehistory of Hellenic culture, had been linked closely with a tradition of mythological painting and sculpture. His tales have an obvious pictorial quality: color, form, movement, and above all, metamorphosis—people are transformed into creatures or things to which they then stand in some sort of metaphorical relationship. If to this is added the fact that Ovid's tales are easily read as moral allegories, their metaphorical essence becomes apparent. It may be noted in passing that the Viana translation of the *Metamorphoses* was augmented, as its title indicates, "con el comento y explicación de las Fábulas: reduziéndolas a Philosophía natural y moral y Astrología e Historia. . . ." This tendency to read the *Metamorphoses* as allegory is well documented in Baltasar Gracián's *Agudeza y arte de ingenio*: Gracián seems to regard the metamorphosis as a kind of trope, not unlike a simile or metaphor. Of the metamorphosis he says: "Consiste su artificio en la semejanza con lo moral, explicada por transformación o conversión fingida del sujeto en el término asimilado; de donde es, que cualquiera símil se pudiera convertir en metamorfosis, lo mismo del jeroglífico, que se funda en la semejanza."

But if, as Gracián suggests, the essence of metamorphosis is similitude, resemblance, it should also be remembered that the idea of artistic similitude took a peculiar twist in the Baroque Age. Art can reflect life or nature, but it also can reflect art, can reflect itself. The seventeenth was the century that discovered the amusing possibilities of mirrors: they can reverse an image, distort it, displace it. They can be set up face to face so that something placed between them reflects away into nothingness in an abysmal infinite regression. This is the technique used by Velázquez in *Las hilanderas,* a series of paintings within a painting whose figures seem to float somewhere between represented spaces and whose subject matter is the story of Minerva and Arachne, the weavers of tapestries, a story taken, of course, from Ovid.

But let us return to Sor Juana's *romance.* Its allusions to the *Metamorphoses* may be regarded as a cue to examine more carefully the question of artistic resemblance in the poem. As has been seen, the *romance* pretends to reject metaphor, since the Condesa is incomparable; this is the panegyric message. But if the Condesa is absent except in terms of what she is not, no such anti-mimetic presentation is professed for the poetess herself. The poem is framed, as it were, by vivid images of Sor Juana: in the opening stanzas, she is at her writing table, anxiously poring over her books; in the closing lines, she is prostrate at the feet of her beloved patroness. These two images—really stylized poses—in effect turn the *romance* into a self-portrait and they merit individual attention.

The image of Sor Juana at her writing table, surrounded by her books, is self-representation that, given the circumstances of the nun's life, borders on self-exaltation. As an international literary celebrity and darling of the court, Sor Juana could attribute her fame to her books and her pen, that is, to her astonishing scholarly bent, her prodigious literary talent. She was, put simply, a phenomenon: a woman who moved easily in a world of cultural signs to which few men and far fewer women had access. Thus, Sor Juana's listing of literary greats is also a survey of her own physical and mental library, her cultural lexicon. It is equivalent to the self-portrait in which the painter points over his shoulder to his own past work. It is also equivalent to the painting of the artist's studio: when Sor Juana refers to the "casa del mundo" in which she searches for something with which to compare the Condesa, she refers not only to the world at large, but also to her own cloistered world, literally a *casa,* a *celda.* As Octavio Paz explains, Sor Juana's cell, with its collections of books, instruments, and curious objects, was indeed a universe in miniature, a universe of signs. Finally, the *petite histoire* of the poetess composing her poem can be compared to the painting of the artist at work—*Las meninas,* for example. But as with Velázquez, the *petite histoire* becomes, in fact, the big story, one in which the self-glorification of the artist has no small part.

The *romance*'s final image of the poetess, prostrate at the feet of the Condesa, is one which can be found in a number of Sor Juana's panegyric poems. It has the quality of a rather formulaic epistolary closing. But in the *ro-*

mance it also has a particularly graphic quality; it nicely summarizes the various attitudes struck by Sor Juana throughout the poem: her despair before a subject matter beyond the talents of her pen, her humility before the Condesa's beauty and majesty, her love for her patroness and gratitude for her favors. If this image of the poetess were conceived as a kind of emblem, it might look something like the illuminated miniatures of the Renaissance that showed an author presenting his book to his patron. The pose is the same: the author kneels humbly, the patron acknowledges the gift with benevolence and dignity. Renaissance books sometimes contained such a miniature as a frontispiece, the *petite histoire* of the writing of the book thus preceding the book itself and, incidentally, implying a kind of infinite regression: a picture within a book within a picture within a book.

But Sor Juana's *romance* is, ostensibly, not a finished work of art. It is a poem which professes to be a non-poem, the story of why the poem, the portrait, never came to be. The Condesa is, among all the world's beauties, only like herself. Therefore, the poetess must abandon metaphor, poetic or pictorial—the "falsos silogismos de colores" of the famous sonnet—and simply love her patroness, that is, reflect back some of the splendor which the Condesa radiates like the sun. The final emblematic image of the *romance* can thus be modified: ultimately, it most resembles another stock theme of Renaissance painting, that of Venus admiring herself in a mirror held by a kneeling, fascinated Cupid.

The mirror that Sor Juana humbly holds up to the Condesa's incomparable face is both art's faithful mirror held up to nature—for the poem deftly communicates its panegyric message as well as depicts the essence of the patron-client relationship—and also the maddeningly tautological mirror of the Baroque: seen only in reflection, reflexively, the Condesa's countenance seems to elude our perception. Like other artists of her time, Sor Juana seems to have both held to the idea that art is like a mirror and recognized that this idea is itself a simile, a simulacrum. Undeterred by the dizzying incongruities of mimetic theory, Sor Juana bends them to her own purpose: she devises a work of art which both exalts its subject and pushes it out of the picture, one in which the self-abasement of the poetess covers itself with glory.

Octavio Paz (essay date 1988)

SOURCE: "Music Box," in *Sor Juana or, the Traps of Faith,* translated by Margaret Sayers Peden, Belknap Press, 1988, pp. 307-25.

[*In the following essay, Paz traces the development of the villancico and surveys Cruz's poems in this genre.*]

Poetic forms are like plants: some are native to the soil they grow in and others are the result of grafting and transplanting. The sonnet and terza rima are Spanish by naturalization, the *romance* and *villancico* by birth. The last of these, according to a noted specialist in metrics, Tomás, Navarro Tomás, comes from Galician-Portuguese *cantigas de estribillo,* which derived from the Mozarabic *zéjel.* From the medieval period to the twentieth century, the poetic fortune of the *villancico* has been extraordinary.

In the fifteenth century the *villancico* split away from the *cantigas de estribillo* to acquire its own form. Despite changes over the centuries, the form has survived to our day. The basic model is the following: a poem in short lines, almost always eight or six syllables, composed of a two- or four-line *estribillo* (refrain) that sets the theme; a variation or *mudanza* (change), ordinarily a quatrain; and a *vuelta* (envoi) that repeats the *estribillo* in whole or in part. In its beginnings the word *villancico* did not designate a specific poetic form but, rather, referred in broader terms to compositions in the manner of the songs sung by peasants and villagers. They were both amatory and devout in theme. In the sixteenth century, and now under that name, "the *villancico* became the most prevalent form of the lyric song." The themes continued to be those of secular love or, as in the case of St. Teresa, divine love. *Villancicos* also appear as insertions in plays and pastoral novels. The seventeenth century is the high noon of the form, and some of the *villancicos* of Lope, Góngora, and Valdivielso are among the purest lyric poems in the Spanish tongue.

Complexity and simplicity, refinement and spontaneity: the charm of the *villancico* resides perhaps in this mixture of conflicting tonalities. There is an incessant swinging back and forth, especially during the Baroque period, between the secular amatory and the religious, the popular and the erudite: a bullfight is transformed into theological allegory; with the panache of a lady of Madrid, the Virgin treads on the head of the serpent; and St. Peter wanders the alleyways of Rome cutting a swath like a swordsman. During the second half of the seventeenth century in Spain, there are no figures comparable to Góngora, Lope, or even Valdivielso. In contrast, during those same years in New Spain the *villancico* was reaching a second but no less resplendent high noon in the works of Sor Juana. Hers was not merely a continuation, it was a rebirth.

The *villancico* came early to these shores, along with other poetic forms. The Franciscans presented in Spanish and in Indian tongues *autos, coloquios,* and other theatrical works on religious themes. The first recorded *villancico* is one sung during an *auto* illustrating the fall of Adam and Eve, performed in Tlaxcala in 1538:

> Why did she eat,
> the first wedded woman,
> why did she eat
> fruit that was forbidden?

In the second half of the sixteenth century a poet of real merit appeared, Hernán González de Eslava; *villancicos* and religious songs make up the best of his work. Following him, the *villancico* became enormously popular in New Spain.

Almost all the poets who wrote in Sor Juana's time composed *villancicos,* but the truth is that none of the others could compare with her; they were not peers or rivals, only a chorus. But it was a chorus of melodic voices and well-trained throats: those poets were heirs to a century and a half of great poetry, from Garcilaso to Calderón. As skillful versifiers, masters of a repertory of images, figures, metaphors, and mythological allusions and a vocabulary of great richness, it was not difficult for them, even with moderate ability, to achieve a poetic level that Spanish neoclassical and romantic writers never reached. In fact, Mexico and the entire Hispanic world was not again to see writing of such purity and elegance until the Spanish-American *modernista* poets at the turn of this century. In this sense, even if not in philosophy or science, the literary atmosphere surrounding Sor Juana was beneficial and stimulating.

For the Spanish American poets of that generation Góngora's aesthetic revolution was still taking place, a revolution also indebted to his rivals and enemies, Lope de Vega and Quevedo. This is another of the notable differences between Spain and America. Espinosa Medrano, known as El Lunarejo, had written in Lima, "We criollos arrive late." But that tardiness was at the same time a sign of vitality: the criollos were younger. For that reason this was in Mexico a period of great experimentation, especially in the field of metrics. Sor Juana surpassed her contemporaries in this area, as she surpassed almost all the poets of the seventeenth century. In preparing a summary of the metrics and changes in Spanish verse during the Golden Age, Navarro Tomás lists the great innovators. Significantly, he omits Quevedo and Calderón, reducing the names to four: Cervantes (primarily as a humorist in verse), Góngora, Lope de Vega, and Sor Juana Inés de la Cruz.

Until early in the seventeenth century, as now, the word *villancico* referred to the Christmas carols of the shepherds of Bethlehem. This was the mode in which Góngora and Lope de Vega excelled. But around 1630, says Méndez Plancarte, [in Cruz's **Obras completas**], the term was restricted to the compositions sung at matins on religious holidays, "leaving the simple generic name 'lyrics' for all other forms." Matins are divided into three nocturnes, each consisting of three psalms. *villancicos* adopted the same division: three nocturnes of three lyrics each, although often the last lyric was replaced by the Te Deum. Thus, each of these *villancicos* was a set or series of eight or nine lyrics. In Mexico the custom of singing *villancicos* of three nocturnes to celebrate matins on liturgical holidays goes back to the second half of the seventeenth century. The cathedrals of Mexico City, Puebla, Oaxaca, and Valladolid (Morelia), among others, celebrated all important annual holy days with these songs. The frequency of the celebrations, the accompanying pomp, and the number of faithful who attended meant there had to be a permanent organization in charge of them. The *villancicos* were a spectacle—and spectacles, besides authors, actors, and audience, require stage directors, administrators, and managers: a bureaucracy.

The institutional aspect of the *villancicos* has not been studied by historians of New Spain, regrettably. Such ceremonies fulfilled a religious function but also had so-cial and, in the strict sense of the word, political uses. Religious, patriotic, or revolutionary holidays are ceremo-nies in which a society, by means of symbol or image, is made one with itself. They are a joining together of the elements that compose the society into a whole that is also a *unit*: I mean, a united whole. But they are also the society's reunion with its past—with its dead, its heroes, its saints, its founders—and with its future: its tomorrow in history and in the immeasurable time of the beyond. In New Spain, essentially a heterogeneous society, as much for its class differences as for its diversity of pasts, be-liefs, and races—Spanish, criollo, Indian, mestizo, black—religious holidays were ceremonies of celebration and participation. Celebration of the principles that supposed-ly gave the society its being, and of the figures in whom those principles were embodied; participation of each group and of each element in a totality that encompassed all differences and annulled all hierarchies. And also a cele-bration of the Other, the divine, and participation in the *other* reality, the supraterrestrial. In the darkness of the church, a darkness dimly lit by flickering candles and the dawn breaking in the east, a multitude communed with a reality both marvelous and familiar: warrior angels, danc-ing virgins, sainted theologians, Indians and blacks, Basques and Moors, devils and lawyers. Pedantry, chant-ing, and soaring flight.

The existence of a permanent administration responsible for organizing such ceremonies required sufficient funds to maintain it and to pay all those who carried out their assigned tasks: poets, musicians, singers, printers of texts (booklets were illustrated with vignettes and other engrav-ings), those responsible for decorating the altars with flowers and for the lighting, those who hung the tapestries and raised the standards, doorkeepers and ushers. None of this has been researched. We do not know how much poets were paid, or musicians, or whether some of them were permanently attached to any of the churches or cathedrals. But some basic information is available. The September 1730 issue of the *Gazeta de México* contains some interesting facts about the matins foundations of the Mexico City cathedral. The *Gazeta* lists the wealthy do-nors, mentions the sums they contributed to their foun-dations, and names the holiday to which each sum was designated: matins for the Nativity of Our Lady, six thou-sand pesos and three hundred in revenues donated by Don García de Legaspi y Velasco; matins for the Concep-tion, five thousand pesos and two hundred fifty in reve-nues donated by someone already familiar to us, Don Juan de Chavarría, the man who provided Sor Juana with a sum of gold on the day of her profession as a nun; matins for Our Lady of Guadalupe, eight thousand pesos and four hundred in revenues donated by Don Bartolomé de Que-sada; the list continues, to include all the liturgical hol-idays celebrated in the cathedral. The *Gazeta* mentions eleven foundations—two sponsored by Chavarría—each receiving from four to eight thousand pesos, plus reve-nues, except for one endowed with twenty thousand pe-sos and another with twelve thousand. Property and hous-es that produced rental income were given as well as cash.

Seventeenth-century foundations were not very different from our modern ones. Without them, the continuity of the *villancicos* would have been impossible: they were sung in the churches of New Spain from 1650 through the first third of the eighteenth century. These poems and tunes were, yes, the expression of poets' and musicians' fervor, but they were equally the result of generous financial patronage. Between 1676 and 1691 Sor Juana wrote twelve complete sets of *villancicos*, each composed of eight, nine, or more lyrics. She also composed thirty-two lyrics for the dedication of the church of the nuns of San Ber-nardo, three for the holy day of Our Lady, four for the Incarnation, two for the Nativity, and four for a nun's profession. In addition to all these there are another ten sets of *villancicos* that can be attributed to her and in all likelihood are hers. She wrote two hundred thirty-two of these poems. To this truly impressive quantity must be added frequency: there was scarcely a year, following 1676, when she did not write at least one set of *villancicos* and sometimes two or even three. Finally, there is geo-graphical range: she did not limit herself to writing for the Mexico City cathedral and other churches of that city; she wrote nine series for the cathedral in Puebla and one for the Oaxaca cathedral. When we add the courtly poems—*romances*, *décimas*, sonnets, *bailes*, *loas*—we see that more than two-thirds of all that she wrote was commis-sioned. It is paradoxical that this literature addressed to the general public was an often enigmatic literature filled with recondite mythological allusions and embellished with displays of erudition.

Sor Juana's poetic activity was not unrewarded: the court paid her for her *loas*, *bailes*, and spectacles, and the Church compensated her for the *villancicos* and sacred lyrics. The income she collected from this writing helps to explain how over the years her financial condition passed from poverty and insecurity to comfort. But financial ad-vantages, great as they were, were not the only or the most important rewards: writing for the Church provided prestige and power. What I have said about her influence at court and her use of this influence to benefit her con-vent and her own situation can be applied, with some reservations, to her relationship with the Church. Less centralized than that of the state, the power of the Church was distributed among the major prelates and the religious orders. This division of power and influence protected Sor Juana from the hostility of Aguiar y Seijas, at least until 1692. A nun devoted to secular literature and enmeshed in an active literary and worldly life had constantly to con-front her superiors, those outside as well as within the convent. This is why she sought always to win the pro-tection of Princes of the Church. . . . For now, I want to emphasize simply the material and political aspects of her collaboration with the cathedral of Mexico City and other churches, especially the cathedral in Puebla, whose Bish-op, Manuel Fernández de Santa Cruz, was her friend and protector. The ambition of so many ideologues and rev-olutionary leaders—social poetry, art at the service of the people, and so on—was actually realized by the poets of New Spain, except that social poetry did not represent criticism and opposition but rather poetry celebrating the social order and its ideology. Official poetry was the result, then as now, of a system of rewards and punishments: on the one hand, the protection of the palace and the Church; on the other, censure and the Inquisition. The idea of the "organic intellectual" propounded by modern revolutionaries was a reality in the seventeenth century. In reaction to that reality there arose, in the eighteenth century, the idea of the critical intellectual, without a Church and without a lord.

When Sor Juana began to compose *villancicos,* the genre was already established and it was not possible to change either the structure imposed by Church ritual or its literary and musical conventions. But even though she was not free to modify the form, with her imagination she gave it new life and with her grace gave it flight. Creative joy animates many of these poems—the almost physical pleasure born of doing things well. We sense that she enjoyed composing those singing, dancing verses. It is remarkable that using well-worn materials she was able to build such light and airy constructs. Frequently the first *villancico* of the first nocturne announces the theme and summons the audience, like a street vendor attracting the attention of people in the plazas and fairs. The tone is imperative and promises marvels, as we can see in these examples from several poets of New Spain: "Gather round, see this burning bush / that blazes, that glows, but is not consumed"; "Hurry, hurry, hurry"; "Make way, make way!"; "Pause a while, lend an ear, don't miss this, hey, there!" Sor Juana manages, while respecting the formula, to instill new freshness in the lines, as in this unusual combination of meters (poem lxvii) with an echo of Góngora's *Polifemo*:

> To sing the glory of divine Pedro,
> come one, come all,
> those that come to a whistle
> or live in a sheepfold!

Or in these *seguidillas* in which a blessed event, more glimpsed than seen, rises like an exhalation from the depths of time:

> Listen, hear me a moment,
> for I want to sing,
> about the blessed Moment that
> was outside of time!

The basic characteristic of the *villancico* is the blending of disparate elements. This blending at times produces the marvelous and at others the grotesque. Valdivielso's shepherdesses flirt with the Holy Spirit as they would with a lover:

> My beloved Husband,
> how beautiful your body.
> I adore its elegance.

But fifty years later a mischievous girl, Marizápalos, appears in a León Marchante *villancico* and meets the recently incarnated Jesus. She can think of no words to utter except, as she is dressed in green, this culinary joke: "if this is the night in which the Flesh triumphs, / it is not out of line that I bring the parsley." A *de*scending

metaphor, Basho and Breton would say in unison. Sor Juana almost always avoids such risks: when she is on the verge of falling into the puddle, she spins away and continues along the edge of a reflection. The Virgin Mary, to whom she dedicated several sets of *villancicos,* appears in one of them as a superior student of theology: she studied all subjects, even, Sor Juana adds with wit, some she studied in herself, such as *de Incarnatione.* Mary appears later in varying guises: as the mistress of the Supreme Choir of the universe, directing the choirs "through the signs of the stars"; as a "female knight-errant"—"Bradamante in bravery, / Angelica in beauty"—torn from a page of *Orlando furioso,* "golden locks" floating on the air, surrounded by as many abject Rolands as hairs on her head; as a "great astronomer," and herself a star that "sheds beneficent influences over the Earth," outwitting even the sun and the moon; finally, in an unforgettable fantasy, as the "holy herb": the *Sánalo-todo* (Heal-all Herb), *Celidonia* (Greater Celadine) that "clears the sight"; *Mejor-Ana* (marjoram, and Ana, for the mother of Mary), and *Siempre-Viva* (Eternal Flower):

> No one need, from this day on, fear deadly poison,
> for with this antidote, none can be fatal.

If the Virgin is a specialist in theology, St. Peter is a student of Latin prosody and metrics, expert in syllabic quantities, in verse feet and caesuras, although, remembering that he thrice denied Christ, Sor Juana comments with irony:

> he started in *heroic verse,*
> thrice did falter,
> then, limpingly, did imitate
> pentameter.

An obligatory reference is the malicious allusion to poor Simon Magus, customary since the Acts of the Apostles—"With an ungainly air he flies through the air"—as well as the rejoicing in his fall, which is compared to a "line of *pie quebrado*" (broken [poetic] foot). What is most surprising is to see St. Peter as a fencing master who outfences the famous Spanish masters, Carranza and Pacheco. Naturally, Sor Juana takes advantage of the occasion to recall the "act" of the apostle who struck off the ear of Malchus, servant to the high priest.

But there are serious moments, as when she refers in poem 302 to the passage in Matthew in which an angel appears to Joseph in a dream, bidding him not to abandon a pregnant Mary, "for that which is conceived in Her is of the Holy Ghost":

> Jealousy with dream,
> dream with jealousy,
> in Joseph alone
> are not contradictory.

Sometimes the lyrics have genre subtitles: *jácara, ensalada, canario, cardador,* and others. The *jácara* is a *romance* written in the language of the *jaques,* that is, braggarts and rogues; the *canario* and *cardador* were dances, and the *ensalada* (salad) was a mixture of meters and, especially, of modes of speech of blacks, Moors, Basques, Galicians, and Portuguese. In New Spain the Indians, and Indian language, took the place occupied by the Moors in Spain. A *tocotín* contained lyrics written in Nahuatl, or was colored with Aztec phrases. The tradition of the *tocotín*—probably an Indian dance—originated in the earliest evangelizing theatrical works of the missionaries. There is a *tocotín* in the first set of *villancicos* written by Sor Juana on the theme of the Assumption, in 1676. The poem is written entirely in Nahuatl, but in the Castilian style of six-syllable lines of assonant rhyme.

> *Tla ya timohuica,*
> *totlazo Zuapilli,*
> *maca ammo, Tonantzín,*
> *titechmoilcahuíliz.*

Ángel M. Garibay made a literal translation: "If you go now / our beloved Lady, / do not, our Mother / forget us." The poem, says Garibay, is written "with notable grace and fluidity." Probably Sor Juana called on the help of someone who knew Nahuatl well. Here is still further indication that the composition of *villancicos* was not a solitary task but the work of a group; occasional collaborators were involved in addition to poets, musicians, and singers. The same was true of the courtly *bailes, sainetes,* and *loas.* Sor Juana's life was not strictly that of an anchorite.

Góngora had wrought marvels with the speech of Moors and blacks; the wonderful onomatopoeia of his *villancicos* foreshadows, and at times surpasses, the "black poetry" of modern writers such as Palés Matos, Ballagas, and Nicolás Guillén. Sor Juana's ear, and her oral gifts, rival those of Góngora, as is seen in these lively, inventive, and curiously modern resonances:

> *Ha, ha, ha!*
> *Monan vuchilá!*
> *He, he, he,*
> *cambulé!*
> *Gila coro,*
> *Gulungú, gulungú,*
> *hu, hu, hu!*
> *Menguiquilá,*
> *ha, ha, ha!*

How must these syllables have sounded sung beneath the vaulted ceiling of the criello cathedral? . . .

> Tumba, la-lá-la; tumba, la-lé-le;
> when dey be Pete, dey won' be no slave-girl!
> Tumba, tumba, la-lé-le; tumba, la-lá-la,
> when dey be Pete, no slave-girl dey'll be!

The Latin of the *ensaladas* is an ecclesiastical Latin with Spanish prosody and metrics; it is also a hybrid Latin studded with Spanish words, the macaronic Latin of students and sacristans. Similarly, Sor Juana's Portuguese verses are actually written in Spanish with a Portuguese accent: "Timoneyro, que governas / la nave do el Evange-

lio . . ." (Helmsman, you who steer / the ship of the Gospel . . .). She always prided herself on her Basque heritage, so that when in an *ensalada* a Basque sings in a harsh voice we are warned that no one is to whisper, "for that is the [tangled] tongue / of my grandfathers."

Sor Juana had the ear of a dramatic poet, and may have been the first to reproduce the speech of Mexican *rancheros,* as we see in this *copla* in which two country men enter with "jingling footsteps," singing "without the *estribillo*" (the refrain) because "up to now their feet / have disdained *estribillos*" (a pun on *estribos,* stirrups):

> God bless you, my little beauty,
> off on your way to see God!
> I think you're just as pretty
> as a picture from Michoacán.
> You rise up tall like the palm tree,
> just like the plane tree you tower,
> Those Uruápans could never catch you
> if they chased you for an hour.

The real *ensalada* is tossed not from meters or dialects but with fresh lettuce from Toluca, oil, vinegar, salt, and lime. Yet we should not take too much pride in the products of our land, as Sor Juana says in poem 311:

> Because I am so spicy,
> I like to bring salt,
> five hundred varieties
> my voice will exalt.
> You may have a fine voice, but
> don't be conceited,
> for the salt of Mexico
> is *tequesquite* [saltpeter].

Villancico 312, from a series about St. Catherine, the martyr of Alexandria, is as melodic and meandering as the river itself:

> Be calm, O sinuous Nile,
> soothe your musical waters,
> slowly, slowly,
> pause, and rejoice in seeing
> the beauty you make fertile:
> of the earth and the heavens, the Rose and Star.
> For her, the Rose, sacred Nile,
> bid your sounding waters go
> singing, singing,
> in concerted harmony
> your swift-moving waves will be
> syllables, language, numbers, and voices.

Villancico xxxiv contains lines in *ecos,* a form also found in the *loas:*

> The waxing Moon, how beautiful,
> with grace that none can disavow,
> goes, to the rhythm of the day,
> gliding,
>   gilding,
>   golden hours.

There is a little of everything in the *villancicos*. The eleven-syllable *romance* typical of the time appears alongside traditional *romances* of eight- and six-syllable lines. One of these deserves separate commentary. It is the *villancico* that begins the second nocturne of the set of eleven lyrics dedicated to St. Catherine, sung in the cathedral of Oaxaca in 1691. . . . 315 is, however, noteworthy for a different reason. It begins by alluding to the translation of the Bible made at the order of Ptolemy Philadelphus by seventy wise men in Alexandria in the third century before Christ. Sor Juana comments that if a pagan king had instructed that the Holy Book be translated, he did it through divine inspiration, thus unknowingly preparing for Catherine's defense of Scripture centuries later. In this passage, faithful to her "Egyptian" hermeticism, Sor Juana underlies the special place ancient Egypt held in the divine plan:

> And who could doubt the plan, it was the cross
> Judea and the Roman Empire scorned,
> that Egypt, among all its hieroglyphs,
> upon the breast of Serapis adored.

Sor Juana is alluding, elliptically, to the cross (or crosses; the number varies according to the author) found among the hieroglyphs of the Serapeum, the sanctuary of Serapis in Alexandria, which was a wonder of the ancient world. The cult of Serapis, a Hellenized form of Osiris and Apis, was founded by Ptolemy Soter in the fourth century B.C. The Serapeum was destroyed in 391, a barbaric act of the monk and Archbishop Theophilus during the cruel reign of the Christian Emperor Theodosius. Actually, that cross is nothing more than the ancient hieroglyph *ankh*, a cross shaped like a T with a small loop or circle at the top: the *crux ansata* or ansate cross. It was later used by Coptic Christians, and also by St. Anthony, the anchorite of the *Thebaid*. Sor Juana writes that the Egyptian cross was engraved on the chest of Serapis. She thus accepts a very ancient tradition, but one whose ramifications should have disturbed a Christian conscience. In fact, among the ancient Egyptians the *crux ansata* was a phallic sign signifying eternal life and was an attribute of certain divinities, as seen in representations of Isis, Osiris, and other deities. Although Sor Juana could not have been unaware of those associations of the *crux ansata,* motivated by her desire to exhibit her knowledge and, at the same time, obeying a deeper impulse in a poem of fervent feminism and during a time of bitter dispute, she evokes the ancient Egyptian symbol. Was she, to use current jargon, obeying an unconscious urge? Or was it conscious defiance?

According to Marsilio Ficino, the influence of the heavens is greater when its light descends in rays perpendicular to the cardinal points, thus forming a cross. That is why, he adds, the Egyptians used the sign of the cross that was for them the bearer of long life, and that was also why they engraved it on the breast of the god Serapis. For Ficino the *crux ansata* was a powerful astral talisman. But, he adds immediately, the Egyptians unknowingly adored the sign because it was a prophecy of the coming of Christ. Giordano Bruno took this idea but radically, and perilously, transformed it. Some of the documents of

Bruno's trial reveal that he believed that the Christians had surreptitiously appropriated an ancient and powerful Egyptian talisman. A fellow prisoner informed the inquisitors that he had heard Bruno say that "the sign [of the cross] was sculptured on the breast of the goddess Isis, and . . . was stolen by the Christians from the Egyptians." During his interrogation, Bruno said: "I think I have read in Marsilio Ficino that the virtue and holiness of this character [the cross] is much more ancient than the time of the Incarnation of Our Lord, and that it was known in the time in which the religion of the Egyptians flourished, about the time of Moses, and that this sign was affixed to the breast of Serapis, and that the planets and their influences have more efficacy . . . when they are at the beginning of the cardinal signs." Bruno believed that the *crux ansata* was the "true cross" and that it had magical powers, a belief that sealed his doom.

> **Even though Sor Juana was not free to modify the form of the *villancico*, with her imagination she gave it new live and with her grace gave it flight.**
>
> —*Octavio Paz*

Kircher records in his *Oedipus Aegyptiacus* (1652) the story of the Egyptian cross graven on the breast of Serapis. He states that Hermes Trismegistus himself invented this form of the cross, which he calls the *crux hermetica*. He also cites the passage from *De vita coelitus comparanda* in which Ficino speaks of its astral and talismanic powers: the *crux hermetica* is a sign that, as it reproduces the form in which the solar rays intersect the cardinal points, creates a powerful talisman. In the second volume of *Oedipus Aegyptiacus* there is an engraving representing a *crux ansata*: each bar terminates in one of the signs of the four elements, the cross rests on a serpent, and the Ptolemaic universe is suspended within the ring, which is transfixed by a horn, the emblem of Isis. Of course, Kircher does not allude in any way to the episode of Bruno; he, too, and with greater reason than Sor Juana, "wished no quarrel with the Holy Office." He consistently strove to stay within the bounds of orthodoxy, which is why he never accepted the new astronomy and why from time to time he denounced in his writings the "impious doctrines of Hermes Trismegistus." In his attempt to present Egypt as the origin of all civilizations, Kircher finds the *crux ansata* even in the *lingam,* the phallic symbol of the Hindu god Shiva, whom he calls Insuren (Osiris). In this "infamous and monstrous disguise," the divine sign is adored in India. Sor Juana alludes to all this in the following quatrain from her *villancico* to St. Catherine (315):

> And Catherine inherited with her blood
> (though in a perverted cult) a burning zeal
> for Law and Cross, and God in her
> transformed what was perverse to the ideal.

Later, in another quatrain, and by means of an extraordinary figure, she transforms the martyrdom of Catherine into a demonstration of geometry that in turn outlines a virtuous paradigm:

> Her martyrdom was like a Cross; the wheel,
> with its opposed diameters, creates
> the holy and supreme shape of the Cross,
> which into four right angles separates.

This is the image that impressed Ficino, Bruno, and Kircher: the mysterious relationship between the cross and the circle. As the arms of the cross rotate, they engender the circle; for its part, the circle contains a cross. More than two centuries later, Alfred Jarry—in one of his most complex and still little explicated works, *César-Antéchrist*—uses the same demonstration to present a blasphemous allegory. In this enigmatic text a heraldic band appears as a character: it is also a horizontal staff, and thus symbolizes, dually, the phallus and the minus sign. As the staff-phallus rotates, exactly as in Sor Juana's quatrain, it turns upward and forms a cross that is also the plus sign, represented by a Templar who is prepared for combat against the adverse sign. There is no battle; the Templar lays aside his weapon, and the figure drawn by the two hostile signs is the sign that can only be defined negatively: zero. In its circle the two adversary principles are reconciled and annulled: phallus and cross, minus and plus, yes and no, life and death. Identity of opposites: zero is the belly of Ubu, and without contradiction, the circle that ceaselessly begins again at the exact point where it ends. The circle is Christ and it is Caesar. It is also the torture wheel to whose revolutions Catherine is bound and on which, transfigured, she escapes death:

> Catherine was bound upon the ring,
> symbol of God, the infinite hieroglyph,
> but did not die on it, and there, instead
> of circling to her death, encountered life.

Like Iphigenia, snatched by Artemis from the sacrificial altar, Catherine ascends to Heaven on the revolutions of the wheel, the emblem of the infinite God. The image of God as a circle of which the center is everywhere—a proposition both irrefutable and undemonstrable—comes from Nicholas of Cusa, although Sor Juana, as she herself says in the *Response,* took it from Kircher. In his *De docta ignorantia* Nicholas of Cusa had written that "the world has no circumference; for if it had a center and a circumference there would be some space and some thing beyond the world . . . [For this reason] it is not in our power to understand the world whose center and circumference are God." The paradox posed by Nicholas of Cusa follows in the tradition of the negative theology of Dionysius Areopagiticus. As Arthur O. Lovejoy has said [in *The Great Chain of Being,* 1936] Cusanus was concerned not so much with questions of astronomy as with a species of mystical theology. But Giordano Bruno uses these speculations to defend his concept of an infinite universe, and again and again repeats

the metaphor of God as a circle whose center is everywhere. This image, with different shadings, reappears in two of Sor Juana's essential texts, in the central passage of *First Dream* and in the *Response*: "All things issue from God, who is at once the center and circumference from which and in which all lines begin and end." It is revealing that even in a *villancico,* a popular and devout genre, Sor Juana did not abandon her philosophical and hermetic preoccupations.

The merit of Sor Juana's *villancicos* is not only, or predominantly, historical, social, philosophical; metrical, or literary, but, in the strictest sense of the word, poetic. These works seduce us at times with their fluid grace, at times with their iridescent transparency, and, always, with the inexplicable attraction poetry holds for us:

> See how Love stands shivering
> in the icy blast,
> how the frost and snow
> are holding him fast.
> Who comes to his aid?
>   Earth?
>   Water?
>   Air?
> No, none comes but Fire!

More deeply felt than *villancico* 283, just quoted, is 287, especially the *estribillo,* sung in two voices. Here is simple beauty, piercing beauty:

> "Since my Lord was born for pain,
> let him stay awake."
>   "Since he is awake for me,
> let him lie asleep."
>   "Let him stay awake;
> for one who loves, there is no pain
> as great as lack of pain"
>   "Let him lie asleep,
> for he who sleeps is, in his dream,
> practicing for death."

Not limpid, but sumptuous and crisscrossed with cruel sensuality, are the verses of *villancico* 314 in which the poet sings to two heroic "gypsies" (Egyptians)—Cleopatra, who committed suicide for human love, and Catherine, a martyr for divine love:

> Lovingly to snowy breast
> Cleopatra pressed the asp,
> But how redundant is the asp
> when one has lain within love's grasp!
> Ay, what tragedy, dear God!
> Ay, what hapless fate!
>
> And thus heroic Catherine
> yields up a throat of ivory
> to the cruel blade, that hell shall never
> triumph over constancy;
> and, in dying, she defeats
> those who her death decreed.

We marvel at the perfect harmony and the contrasting movements and oscillations of *villancico* xxxvii. It is the dawn of the Assumption, and

> Stars fall to the earth,
> dawns rise in the skies.
> Bright sunrays shine,
> sweet perfumes rise,
> quadrilles of jasmine,
> carnations and broom,
> that run,
>   that fly,
> that strew,
>   that festoon,
> with blossoms,
>   with gleams,
> with roses,
>   with flames.

The *estribillo* of *villancico* 242 is memorable for its combination of different meters and for the play of adjectives, which make us hear writing and see voices:

> O winged seraphim and celestial finches,
> muffle your feathers and ruffle your voices,
> ruffled voice, and feather,
> muffled feather and voice,
> warble and write of Peter's exploits.

One of the most enjoyable *villancicos* is a diaphanous paraphrase of the Song of Songs. It was one of the first Sor Juana wrote and was sung in 1676 in the cathedral of Mexico City, at the feast of the Assumption. The *coplas,* in verses of six syllables, are simplicity itself; in contrast, the *estribillo* mixes lines of various lengths. In the *estribillo* we see Mary as a miraculous skyrocket that ascends until it is lost in the clouds. No commentary can substitute for the slender poem, the whirlwind of airy words rising from the page.

> That Shepherdess
> with the serene gaze,
> enchantment in the grove
> envy of the skies,
> captured with one hair,
> wounded with one eye,
> the Sublime Shepherd
> who dwells on high;
> to her, her Beloved
> was a bundle of myrrh,
> her lily-white breasts
> gave him shelter;
> she wears rich garments
> and, for cleanliness,
> has a bowery bed
> and a cedar-filled house . . .
> to enjoy the arms
> of her Master and love,
> she exchanged humble valley
> for the Mountain above . . .

> To the Mountain, to the Mountain on High,
> Shepherdesses, run, run, fly,

María is leaving, rising through the skies!
Hurry, hurry, run, quickly, quickly fly,
for she is stealing away our souls and lives,
bearing off in her Person all that we prize,
leaving our Earth barren, of all treasures deprived!

Edward H. Friedman (essay date 1990)

SOURCE: "Signs of Nature and the Nature of Signs in the Sonnets of Sor Juana Inés de la Cruz," in *RLA: Romance Languages Annual 1989,* Vol. I, edited by Ben Lawton & Anthony Julian Tamburri, Purdue Research Foundation, 1990, pp. 435-39.

[*In the following essay, Friedman offers a semiotic reading of three sonnets composed by Cruz.*]

Recent literary theory and criticism perhaps most differ from their precedents by reducing the role of interpretation and expanding the role of self-analysis. One might call this phenomenon a crisis of the critical conscience or an urge for accountability in the analytical process. The prefix *meta*—as in metacommentary, metacriticism, metatheater, metafiction, metapoetry, metadiegetic narrative, and so forth—is a watchword of contemporary critical sensibility, an identifying sign of the self-conscious approach to literary texts. Deconstruction and the new rhetoric, inspired by structuralism even as they deviate from it, point to the structures and strategies which underlie texts and which often run counter to apparent or surface structures. A tenet of the "new historicism," currently in fashion in Elizabethan studies, is that, through distance, one may determine the ideological forces behind a given text, forces "invisible to the culture in which the text was produced and accessible only from the privileged perspective of remoteness" [Catherine Belscy, *Critical Practice*]. There is, thus, a radical distinction between the North American New Criticism of the 30s, 40s, and 50s—which viewed poetic texts in isolation from their creators and consumers, and, in a sense, from the historical record—and the "newer," self-reflective, and often more skeptical views espoused since the early 60s. Semiotics, the science of sign systems, provides a type of mediation between the divergent critical currents of the present. Semiotics treats all objects as signs, and the various semiotic models work to place signs, including the language of literature, in context, to study its forms and signifying functions. Whatever one's critical orientation might be, it would be difficult to discuss the poetry of Sor Juana Inés de la Cruz without reference to the "self and circumstance" of the author or to the contexts implicit in or generated by her poetic creation.

There is an obvious paradox in the life and works of Sor Juana, a paradox captured in the subtitle of Octavio Paz's important study, *Sor Juana Inés de la Cruz o las trampas de la fe.* Sor Juana the poet and intellectual vies with Sor Juana the nun. Sor Juana the woman contends with a social hierarchy and with a literary canon invented and sustained by men. The interplay of social, spiritual, and creative impulses marks the historical Sor Juana, as well as the Sor Juana reconstructed through readings of her texts. In his essay on Fray Luis de León and San Juan de la Cruz in *Reality and the Poet in Spanish Poetry,* Pedro Salinas calls attention to what he terms the "peculiarity of our mystics, their realistic sense, their exact and selfless performance of the daily duties of their calling, and at the same time their prodigious capacity for detachment from the temporal, for living in the absolute." The principal motif of this poetry—escape—becomes paradoxical when the poet uses symbols of "profound material reality" to describe pure spirituality. The message here is that the poet intent upon seeking the higher spiritual realm must take recourse to the signs of this world. (This is a dilemma not unlike the double bind of deconstruction, which refutes the linguistic, or logocentric, premises of Western culture by means of the discursive conventions being refuted.) The conflict widens when the poetic goals are more profane than sacred, when the person who has taken holy vows wishes to practice "art for art's sake," to explore secular feelings and language. And the gap becomes especially notable when the poet is a woman.

In a chapter entitled "The Word Made Flesh: Magic and Mysticism in Erasmian Spain" in his study *The Birth and Death of Language: Spanish Literature and Linguistics, 1300-1700,* Malcolm K. Read notes that Erasmus "gave birth to a religious movement characterized by a profound suspicion of language." Recognizing the corrupting potential of language, the Erasmians favored "a kind of language that had been stripped of all its refinement. The humanistic delight in the aesthetic value of language has gone: the word serves merely to 'sprimir los concetos de vuestros ánimos,'" as Juan de Valdés puts it in the *Diálogo de la lengua.* In addition, in Renaissance Spain there lingers a dichotomy based on gender, in which deeds connote the masculine and words the feminine. And according to Read, "Being a sexual activity, speech is more suspect in some groups than in others, particularly when it is affected and ornate. Feminine indulgence in language is condemned by Alfonso de Valdés [Juan's twin brother, in the *Diálogo de Mercurio y Carón*]: ' . . . porque el callar en las mugeres, especialmente donzellas, es tan conveniente y honesto como malo y deshonesto el demasiado hablar.'" Baroque discourse is the antithesis of direct speech and of directed silence. The language of Golden Age Spanish poetry contains its own theoretical presuppositions, which would certainly include an interest in words both as conveyers of ideas and as things of beauty. By appropriating the poetic conventions of Baroque Spain—by breaking the silence, as it were—Sor Juana strays from accepted protocol for a member of a religious order and for a woman. As a poet, she seeks a voice of her own and a place in earthly and celestial domains.

Sor Juana's most ambitious work, the *Primero sueño,* is truly impressive in its synthesis of Baroque form with theological and philosophical subtleties lacking, for example, in the *Soledades* and in the *Polifemo* of Góngora. The *Sueño* possesses what may be termed Baroque decorum, a self-consciously difficult language at the service of an equally difficult conceptual scheme. The most strik-

ing feature of the sixty-five sonnets of Sor Juana may be their range—not of subjects, which are fairly traditional—but of treatments, or poetic modes. The sonnets alternately respect and violate decorum to produce an internal movement or dialectic. Sor Juana not only rewrites the intertext, as do all poets, but she rewrites her own work. [This essay] will consider this process in three of Sor Juana's sonnets, those numbered 147, 148, and 158. I would like to suggest that this sonnet sequence exemplifies, or reifies, the crisis facing the artist whose authority is always in question. The first sonnet offers a variation on a common theme, the second a refashioning of the conventional message, and the third a deconstruction of sorts of the initial premise. Gerard Flynn notes in Sor Juana's attitude toward nature the influence of Scholasticism, which adheres to a strict order within every part of nature and which allows only God to take exception to that order. This explains, for Flynn, what he calls the poet's "profound respect" for the social order. What I will attempt to show is, to a degree, an opposing perspective: that in her poetry Sor Juana perhaps may find a means to circumvent the rigid hierarchies that dominate her existence. The enterprise more likely stems from psychological than from political stimuli, so that in the case of Sor Juana poetic expression is not an act of rebellion, but a form of release. It is also, I would submit, a commentary on the nature of signs.

The three sonnets by Sor Juana bear a relation to a process described by Julia Kristeva in an essay entitled "From Symbol to Sign" [found in *The Kristeva Reader,* 1986] although Kristeva refers specifically to narrative. The essay focuses on a lessening of faith in the power of the word, a shift from absolute and predetermined meanings to more capricious or contextually determined meanings. Kristeva argues that "from the thirteenth to the fifteenth century, the symbol was challenged and weakened. This did not make it altogether disappear but it did assure its passage (assimilation) into the sign. The transcendental unity supporting the symbol—its other-worldly wrapping, its transmitting focus—was called into question." The *symbol* has its own history; in the words of C. S. Peirce, it "operates above all by virtue of an institutionalised and learnt contiguity between signifier and signified" (quoted in Kristeva). The *sign,* on the other hand, depends on conditional rather than prescribed meanings. According to Kristeva, once the sign "is free from its dependence on the 'universal' (the concept, the idea in itself), it becomes a potential mutation, a constant transformation which despite being tied to one signified, is capable of many regenerations. The ideologeme [or semantic thrust] of the sign can therefore suggest what is not, but *will be,* or rather *can be.* And this *future tense* is accepted by the sign not as something caused by extrinsic factors, but as a transformation produced by the possible combinations within its own structure." The essay concludes with a list of the basic characteristics of the sign, stressing its difference from the symbol:

—It does not refer to a single unique reality, but *evokes* a collection of associated images and ideas. While remaining expressive, it nonetheless tends to distance itself from its supporting transcendental basis. (It may be called arbitrary.)

—It is part of a specific structure of meaning and in that sense it is *correlative*: its meaning is the result of an interaction with other signs.

—It harbours a principle of *transformation*: within its field, new structures are forever generated and transformed.

Within this framework, the "reading" of symbols is an acquired knowledge, a learned activity, a positing of universals, while "reading" of signs is a more open venture, in which such factors as function and context affect meanings. The fact that signs may be devalued or reconstituted symbols not only gives the signs a multiple temporal base, but frequently also leads to an ironic juxtaposition of signifiers. Kristeva contrasts the immediacy of the sign with the permanence of the symbol. Equally significant is the symbolic "residue" of the sign, that is, the deferred significance of the symbol as it becomes a sign. The present (or future) status of the sign depends upon its lost—or, more properly, recast—symbolism. In sonnets 147, 148, and 158, Sor Juana takes the rose "from symbol to sign." The stability of the symbol in the first poem moves toward a glorification of the instability of the sign in the third poem, which is, in effect, a metacritical response to the conventions that inform it.

The rose is, arguably, the ideal poetic symbol. From classical antiquity onward, it has represented beauty and the impermanence of youth, of beauty, and of earthly existence. It has been the source of numerous images and a model for themes such as *carpe diem*. Sor Juana's three sonnets are apostrophes to the rose and, it would seem, apostrophes—respectively—to poetic tradition, semantic variation, and literary ingenuity. There is a feeling of past, present, and future, as well as an increasing subjectivity, in the poems. If in the first sonnet Sor Juana confronts the work of previous poets, in the second and third she makes herself the subject—or the target—of the composition. She challenges the symbol around which she constructs the first poem and, in a manner of speaking, frees it from the binds of tradition. The rose is, of course, the most obvious common denominator of the sonnets, but the rhetorical structure of each poem also has points of contact with the others. The refurbishing on the formal level has a conceptual counterpart in the modified messages and changing "voices" of the sonnets. Sor Juana experiments with poetic expression and with the rules of decorum that govern her life as a woman, as a nun, and as a writer. Her personal history is relevant if one is to appreciate the daring nature of her work and the reciprocity (one might be inclined to say conversion) of medium and message. The emergence of the authorial persona—the poetic, subjective "I"—stands in opposition to the woman isolated from the world and part of a community which shuns the egocentric and the defiant. The very act of creating poetry is a symbolic gesture, and the sonnets directed to the rose may add to the intellectual autobiography of the poet.

In sonnet 147, Sor Juana captures the rose in all its glory: in full bloom, fragrant, vividly colored, basking in its beauty, and oblivious to its fate. There is an irony in the adjective *divina* in line one. The poet begins with a deceptive description as a correlative of the theme of mortality. The lesson of the poem is that the rose is not divine and that we must learn from its example, that we must recognize the brevity of this life. "Magisterior purpúreo en la belleza" in line 3 and "enseñanza nevada a la hermosura" in line 4 operate on two planes: the rose is a model of beauty—a teacher, a guide—which also demonstrates the destruction of this beauty. The two metaphors are themselves guides to the motif of learning by example. The hidden conceits of verses 3 and 4 are "activated" by the following lines, "Amago de la humana arquitectura, / ejemplo de la vana gentileza." The metaphor (or periphrasis) within the metaphor of line 5 addresses the true object of the apostrophe: humankind. The movement from positive example to negative example is reflected in the semantic shift from "gentil cultura" in line one to "vana gentileza" in line 6. Nature unites life and death—the joyful cradle and the somber grave—in the rose and in the "human form," and the poet makes this fundamental point by joining antithesis, chiasmus, prosopopoeia, and metonymy.

The tercets add an exclamatory flourish to the message of exemplarity. The haughty rose scorns the threat of death, but as it withers it gives off "signs" of death and proof of life's vanities. In the final verses, the poet sustains the antithesis and the lesson: ". . . con docta muerte y necia vida / viviendo engañas y muriendo enseñas." The rose is a guide, not to beauty but to mortality. Its "learned death" is the consequence of its "foolish life," a life in which it did not heed signs of imminent destruction. Through these signs ("en señas"), the rose may teach ("enseñas") men and women to guard against the illusions of immortality. The disillusionment—*desengaño*—follows a careful reading of the signs. By inverting the force of the early metaphors, the poet gives readers a similar task by asking them to analyze these signs in another context. The sonnet teaches us about beauty by rejecting the aesthetic vision of the first quatrain in favor of an analogy between the dying rose and human beings facing death. The rose as a symbol of beauty and of the brevity of life is ultimately a teacher, whose short-lived splendor is a reminder of the human condition.

Sonnet 148, well grounded in tradition, is noteworthy for its reversal of expectations. The first quatrain would seem to introduce a lesson on time and beauty reminiscent of the preceding poem, and perhaps an admonition to "seize the day." The poetic lexicon draws from Sonnet 147, as in the case of "la vana gentileza" and "cuán altiva en tu pompa," which become "ostentaba feliz la pompa vana." The poetic speaker Celia (not Juana) has a message for the rose. In the *carpe diem* paradigm, a man generally gives advice to a young woman. Here, the woman apostrophizes to a rose. Despite the familiar admonition ". . . Goza . . . / el curso breve de tu edad lozana" of lines 5 and 6, the particular execution and the rationale to follow affect the direction and significance of the statement. If sonnet 147 warns against youthful presumption, sonnet 148 delights in the moment of glory. Celia directs herself to the rose—and, one may assume, "a sus semejantes"—not in cautionary terms, not with her mind on spiritual matters, but to foreground the present. She indeed wants the rose to relish its brief luxuriance, and, indeed, the rose will die on the morrow, but what precisely is the message here? It is, simply, that the beauty enjoyed today cannot be destroyed by death and that it is preferable to die young ("siendo hermosa," line 13) so as to avoid the ravages of age ("y no ver el ultraje de ser vieja," the final verse). In order to remove the message from a specifically Christian context, the poet refers to "hado" (line 5) and "fortuna" (line 13). To a degree, the sonnet inverts the hierarchy of heaven and earth. Through its beauty, the rose attains a type of immortality, something akin to fame, which will remain even after death. Death, as represented in the second tercet, is desirable, not by virtue of Christian dogma and the superiority of eternal life over the mundane, but because death may "freeze" youth and beauty in their highest state. And one may accept this option without fear of fate ("sin temor del hado"), without the burden of theology.

In Sonnet 148, Sor Juana distances herself from the speaker and gives the message a secular edge. The poem lauds beauty for its own sake and sees death as a means of preserving the glow of youth. It is as if Sor Juana's "deceptive" portrait, to which she addresses her most famous sonnet (145), were no longer a "false syllogism of colors" or a "delicate flower in the wind," but something more permanent and more powerful than its subject. Old age is no longer a logical transition to eternal life, but a final affront to vanity. And for Celia, whose thoughts are on this life, experience teaches—"la experiencia te aconseja," line 12—that the lucky die young. Sonnet 147 censures the rose (and the young and beautiful) for their pride. It points to the end of the road and to the lesson to be learned from the rose's brief moment in the sun. Sonnet 148 exalts—seeks to immortalize—that moment. In the first poem, the "divine" rose is shown to be ephemeral. In the second, what is called the "empty splendor" of the rose becomes a sign of everlasting beauty. Sonnet 158 does not employ this kind of internal shift; its course and its deviation from the traditional course are clear from the beginning. In the third sonnet, Sor Juana once again addresses the rose, but without the moral-theological underpinnings of the first or the earthly alternatives of the second. Sonnet 158 is a metapoem, a poem whose subject is poetry itself. It is a work about tradition, about signification, about the author as poet, and about the sonnets that precede it.

The opening apostrophe to **"Señora doña Rosa"** sets a jocular tone. The rose is no longer "amago de la humana arquitectura" but "hermoso amago de cuantas flores miran sol y luna." The double metaphor and the lesson of sonnet 148 are now rendered in tautological or anticlimactic terms: the rose is like all other flowers. Verses 3 and 4 further question the nobility of the rose by challenging the description of sonnet 148 and the intertext in general. How can the rose be a lady if she is still in the metonymical "cradle" of youth, and how can she be subject to the ravages of human time if she is "divine"? The author of the *Primero sueño* here examines the validity—the logic—of figurative language. The second quatrain continues to pursue the issue of logic, ironically through a rhetorical question and with recourse to hyperbaton, prosopopoeia, and periphrasis. The quatrain essentially asks how the rose—tied to this world, and defenseless against the whims of nature—can presume to contemplate what lies beyond? And yet the poet, through her use of the apostrophe, implies that this meditative rose is capable of understanding her figurative discourse and offers the image of a rose "begging" for nourishment, for water, the "turbio humor de un cenagoso lago" of line 8. The rose's fall from divinity is thus punctuated by linguistic mudslinging.

The tercets of sonnet 158 recall Lope de Vega's "Soneto de repente" ("Un soneto me manda hacer Violante"), the second verse of which is "que en vida me he visto en tanto aprieto." After a conventional show of authorial modesty—"mi mal limada *prosa* (!)," line 10—Sor Juana supplies a concluding statement, or warning: "y advierta vuesarced, señora Rosa, / que le escribo, no más, este soneto / porque todo poeta aquí se roza." This ending completes the trivialization—demystification, deconstruction—of the earlier poem and of its literary roots. The rose loses its symbolic vigor as an ideal of beauty and as an admonition to those who would overvalue this beauty. It becomes, instead, the sign of a poetic rite of passage. One must get one's feet wet—as conveyed through the pun, *se roza*—by composing a poem about a rose. In the sonnet to her portrait, Sor Juana curses the illusions of art and reduces the subject (ironically, herself) to nothingness. In sonnet 158, the rose becomes a marker, not of existential but of expository concerns, a shadow of its former self. In lines 9 and 10, Sor Juana speaks of losing respect, when, in fact, it is her poem which treats the rose with disrespect. In the sonnet sequence, she would seem to place her allegiance on the side of creativity, of individual authority, and of changing signs. She is not betraying the rose but bestowing her trust on poets who may create it anew in their verses. In this implied *ars poetica,* she anticipates Vicente Huidobro, who invokes his colleagues thus [in *Obras completas de Vicente Huidobro,* 1976]: "Por qué cantáis la rosa, ¡oh Poetas! / Hacedla florecer en el poema." When Sor Juana sings of the rose, she makes and remakes her object. And her voice is, if nothing else, polyphonic.

Sor Juana's examination of the rose reflects her affinity to letters and her need for self-expression. In the *Respuesta a Sor Filotea,* she comments: ". . . desde que me rayó la primera luz de la razón, fue tan vehemente y poderosa la inclinación a las letras, que ni ajenas represiones—que he tenido muchas—ni propias reflejas—que he hecho no pocas—han bastado a que deje de seguir este natural impulso que Dios puso en mi." This was a woman with more than one calling, who believed that both serving God and pursuing one's God-given talents were possible. For her, God was the source, not the adversary, of reason and intelligence. And it is precisely "this natural impulse" that led her to consider the validity, and the stability, of signs. Sor Juana's poetry, like her life, is informed by the security of her faith, a faith unintimidated by reason. The writings show "the anxiety of influence" in the most comprehensive sense, for the poet must justify her endeavor and her role. The literary object is not just a manifestion of the self, but an extension of the sheltered and inspired persona.

Jacqueline C. Nanfito   (essay date 1991)

SOURCE: "*El sueño:* The Baroque Imagination and the Dreamscape," in *MLN,* Vol. 106, No. 2, March, 1991, pp. 423-31.

[*In the following essay, Nanfito explores the function of spatial forms and their interrelationships in Cruz's* El sueño, *asserting that the poem is "a dream of height which enables the reader to transport himself to the domain of the imaginary, to the cosmic realm of the infinite, where one is free to experience the dynamics and depth, the intensity and immediacy of the immanent and the intimate, both features of the fantastic landscape."*]

The maximization of the spatial dimension figures among the fundamental organizational principles in Sor Juana's poem, *El sueño.* Her masterful blending of language and aerial imagery has produced a poetic text which transcends the boundaries of time and space through the establishment of relationships—horizontal and vertical—among distinct spatio-temporal realities, and surmounts the temporal barrier of sequence inherent in the literary act through the techniques of juxtaposition and simultaneity. More than a geometry of universal experience, this composition of the Latin American Baroque is a lyric, oneiric topology of psychic expanses and privileged moments, a fantastic landscape which reveals the dynamic quality of Sor Juana's time consciousness, and where time and space become the vehicles of freedom and flight.

The principal coordinates of Sor Juana's art are spatial forms and their interrelationships. Yet there is in the poetic text of Sor Juana a new conception and treatment of the poematic space that is distinct from that of her predecessors. Whereas the baroque poet seeks to exalt and transform reality, often replacing it with an elaborate ideality, Sor Juana's objective in *El Sueño* is to transgress the material world, etherealize it, internalize it, thereby rendering the fantastic landscape apprehensible only by the enlightened eyes of the intellect. Her principal concern is not with the glorification of external realities, but rather with an inner essence, that, like herself, is in a process of development. While the baroque poet responds to novelty and variety, associating colors and forms, and moving in the direction of more superficial transformation, the imagining forces of Sor Juana's spirit are guided by the search for that which is essential and eternal. The landscape that is evoked and painted in *El sueño* is of a highly geometric, stylized nature, a fundamentally mental construct; the description that prevails throughout the verses is that of a natural world that is not sensuous by nature, but rather abstract, conceptual. Sor Juana strives for the creation of an imaginative poetry that, freed from the yoke of description, renounces immediate reality and converts it into a fully and authentically human space of lyrical, subjective intimacy. She acts directly and dynamically upon material reality in order to successfully translate it into an intelligible surreality, at once particularly human and universal.

In an attempt to surpass the limits inherent in the human condition, and transcend the unknown dimension of the intellect and the threshold of illimitable reaches of interior space and time, physical reality is defiantly challenged as this seventeenth century Mexican writer strives to attain a truly authentic creative style that is capable of encompassing the totality of a reality which is increasingly more mutable and polymorphic. Among the dialectics of physical space exploited in this quintessential baroque composition are such qualities as depth, in the colonization of interior, subjective states and places, and the philosophical profundity of the poetic thought; polarity, in the dualistic opposition of imagistic forms and thematic principles, and in the dialectic unity and coexistence of contraries; height, in the identification of the soul with those images of elevation—particularly winged beings—which are associated with the celestial sphere, thereby conferring upon the poematic space a moral dimension; expansion, in the exuberant amplification of significant motifs, and in the establishment of distance—physical and psychic, spatial and temporal—between the images, and between the distinct planes or spheres of the poetic reality; and centrality, in the inferences and references to the mystic Center:

> y a la Causa Primera siempre aspira
> —céntrico punto donde recta tira
> la línea, si ya no circunferencia,
> que contiene, infinita, toda esencia

It is, however, the dialectics of verticality/horizontality and ascent/descent, visible in the numerous images of forward and upward movement, which perhaps most singularizes this poetic text and elevates it to the apex of the poetic canon of the Latin American Baroque.

El sueño is fundamentally a poem of the aerial, an "invitation au voyage" as Gaston Bachelard (1943) would designate it. While the poem may spring from concrete material reality and objective physiological events or occurrences, it nonetheless is superior to these and transcends the limits of time and space inherent in these, transporting them to another, more fantastic sphere where their contingencies are displaced and their semantic function becomes multivalent.

The violation of spatial and temporal boundaries inherent in the poem serves to liberate the poetic expression of the most intimate dimension of the ontological process manifested in the oneiric odyssey of the soul. In the course of just one night, which constitutes the actual literary time of the text, the reader traverses multiple coextensive spaces, accompanying the soul to such remote corners of the universe as the island of Pharos, in the reference to the legendary lighthouse; the ancient capital of Egypt, Cairo, with reference to the two pyramids; and the island of Crete, in the suggested presence of the labyrinth from which Icarus escaped on wings of wax. With the soul acting as visionary and guide, the reader passes symbolically from the subterranean depths of Hades, or the nether world, ruled by Pluto to beyond the celebrated heights of Olympus, higher than the symbolic flight of the eagle, and far above the Egyptian pyramids and the Tower of Babel ("aquella blasfema altiva Torre"), two architectural marvels of antiquity that testify to man's innate desire to scale the heights and to construct an edifice that affords communication with the celestial sphere of Eternal Truth.

The significance of this poem is it rigorous exploration of both time and space as a means of examining subjective experiences, with its emphasis not on the verifiable chronology of events, rather upon the vertical structure of reverie and unrestricted imaginings. Here space and psychic time not only function as organizational principles, in the decisive contrast between "inner" and "outer" time, but also contribute to the overall aesthetic effect of time as an image of space. Through the system of interreferences by which allusions are made simultaneously to past, present and future, through the coincident presentation of mythological, physiological and fantastic phenomena, through the harmonious and poetic fusion of diachronic and synchronic aspects of time operative on all levels of reality, Sor Juana succeeds in transcending time and in creating one of the most solemn and affecting images landscape has ever offered.

The artistic value of Sor Juana's perceptions of the nature of time lies in the poetic energy that these generate, and much of this energy is produced by a pervasive and relentless conflict between the mind's thirst for eternal knowledge and immutability, and its perceptions of an organic changing universe. The opposition of successive temporal phases that comprises a substantial portion of the text of *El sueño* is essentially symbolic of a moral duality in which the forces of darkness struggle to wrest power from the positive forces of the celestial sphere, the latter of which ultimately triumph. The poetic recreation of the two entities of Darkness and Light by means of the temporal notions of Day and Night serves to advance the notion of the dichotomies existence/essence, rational/irrational, masculine/feminine. These immensities are evoked not merely as particular spaces within the Cosmos, but more importantly, for the sake of their unities. For night and day are but singular, circumstantial moments of darkness and brightness, death and rebirth. And the union of these opposing cosmic forces by means of the poetic word signifies the momentary, motionless crystallization of the particular and the universal. There is within the individual being, just as there exists on all levels of the cosmos, this dialectical and symbolic tension between the light and the darkness: the successive triumph and defeat of reason and passion, intellect and imagination, manifested in the alternation in each of us between the diurnal man, governed by reason, and the nocturnal self, characterized by free and unrestricted flights of imaginative fancy.

El sueño has a timeless, cosmic perspective, the action occurs in the interval that is night but extends into the vast realms of all our yesterdays and tomorrows. The landscape in the poem, with its visionary texture and symbolic topography, has a penumbral aspect. The central image of the initial verses, as well as that of the final stanzas of the text, for example, is that of the night as a bellicose geometric configuration that engages in battle with the diurnal forces of light and reason. It never completely triumphs, as the presence of the qualifying adjective "vanos" suggests—a foreshadowing literally and figuratively of the futile attempt by the soul to scale the summit of intellectual supremacy. Rather, Night, the shadowy conical projection of the Earth ("piramidal . . . de la tierra nacida sombra"), is limited in its capacity as a ruling force and must exercise its powers within the confines of the sphere of air, which is, coincidentally, the sphere of sound. The dominion of the night over the air is manifested in the very silence which no living creature nor any one of the elements can disturb.

The poet's sensitivity to light is revealed in her treatment of certain themes in a dramatic gray register, thereby transfiguring the fantastic landscape into the atmosphere of the dream. The chiaroscuro interplay between the twilight tonality of the netherworld evoked in the initial verses and the blinding light of Paradise at the end of the poem is but one illustration of the artist's intensification and manipulation of light, which not only contributes to the creation of a centrifugal force that heightens the sense of dynamism and movement in the overall design of the poematic space, but more importantly, modifies space and transvalues local and geometrically exact space into a tonality, a psychic topography. Sor Juana's vision of landscape is like a dream, for her poetic imagination catches the pulsation of oneiric light that works a metamorphosis of space and actual places, establishing a dramatic, pictorial illusion. The fantastic landscape offered in the poem allows interchanges of precision and imprecision, vague distances and vanishings into worlds not realized but only suggested. Such interchanges in space imply interchanges in time, the alternation between outer, chronometric time—episodic, isolating acts in sequence—and inner, psychic time, or the experience of interpenetrating moments felt by the human spirit in a continuum that expresses a condition or dimension of selfhood.

The world of outer time is not defeated by inner time, it is simply left behind, as the soul disengages itself from the temporal chains of the body and embarks upon an inward, intellectual flight to the heights of knowledge. Time in *El sueño* is best conceived as a progressive image, a process of transfiguration and of mythical evolution, from negative to positive, from darkness to light, from ignorance to enlightenment, all of which can be traced in the gradated presentation of ascendent images, at once particular and timeless. The poetic imagination at work within the poem is based upon the concept of time not as a social construct of horizontality, but rather, as a fundamentally human, interior time whose vertical axis provides a means of evasion from the realm of material reality into the diaphanous sphere of poetic thought and form.

Psychic time for Sor Juana is a reflex of the psychic landscape that one would call poetic or fantastic with its shifting planes of reality, its enchanted atmosphere. Such poetic space is the vehicle of flight and freedom.

Throughout the poem time is segmented and structured into nonsequential relationships and surprising juxtapositions so as to give the impression of pictorial simultaneity in space, and to repeatedly distract the reader from the progressive temporal linearity inherent in the literary text. The processes of simultaneity and self-reflexiveness at work within the composition engender a series of interrelated correspondences totally independent of any temporal/causal sequence, as can be observed, for example, in the fusion of distinct spatiotemporal realities—the mountain Olympus, the magnificent Egyptian pyramids, the Tower of Babel, etc.—in the lengthy passage devoted to the pyramids and in the verses that depict the soul's ignorance concerning natural processes, such as the flow of the river and the attributes of the rose. By having to continually apprehend the poem's images and symbols by means of a single, instantaneous effort, the reader is forced to mentally map out the entire system of references and internal relations suggested in the poem in order to fully comprehend the ultimate significance of *El sueño.* And consequently, the successful apprehension of the poem's images and symbols is achieved only by means of this reflexive act in a particular instant in time.

While the poem transpires in the course of one night, a night that is at the same time every night and all nights, in actuality the principal diegetic, or poetically narrated, event—the ascendent flight of the soul—is outside the exclusively causal/temporal sequence. In order to amplify and optimize the poematic space to allow for the unfettered flight of the poetic idea, Sor Juana fuses distinct temporal spheres in a dramatic amalgamation of past and present times, superimposing, for example, the imaginative world of mythology upon other spheres—physical, physiological, oneiric—activated during the course of the narrative act. The creation of a mythical dimension of time symbolically reflects the repeated, universal effort of the individual to transcend physically spatial and temporal realities in order to enter into the realm of total knowledge.

As the reader can observe from a perusal of the poem's several hundred verses, Sor Juana employs a combination of present and past tenses to describe the events of the soul's oneiric odyssey, thereby imparting a sense of impreciseness and vagueness to this internally spatial and temporal action. After the presentation of night and of sleep as cosmic images, Sor Juana turns away from the exterior world in order to focus on the activities—physiological, psychic, oneiric—of internal space and time, thereby initiating the narration of the soul's lyrical adventures through the open skies of a spatially and temporally boundless imagination:

> El alma, pues, suspensa
> del exterior gobierno—en que ocupada
> en material empleo,
> o bien o mal da el día por gastado—,

> solamente dispensa
> remota, si del todo separada
> no, a los de muerte temporal opresos
> lánguidos miembros, sosegados huesos,
> los gajes del calor vegetativo,
> el cuerpo siendo, en sosegada calma,
> un cadáver con alma,
> muerto a la vida y a la muerte vivo,
> de lo segundo dando señas
> el del reloj humano
> vital volante que, si no con mano,
> con arterial concierto, unas pequeñas
> muestras, pulsando, manifiesta lento
> de su bien regulado movimiento.

The emphasis here is decidedly upon the actions of retardation ("lánguido", "muestras, pulsando, manifiesta lento") and suspension ("suspensa", "sosegada calma"), in terms of both physical and temporal realities ("muerte temporal"), and with regard to the narrative sequence. The alternation of the present tense with the past tenses, particularly in the section of the poem which treats the lyrical events of the philosophical dream, serves not only as a conscious literary device for securing greater vividness, but more importantly, for interrupting the continuity of progression of the narration and alluding to the supreme significance of the internal logic of emotional, psychological states over the causal logic of discourse.

The notion of suspension throughout this passage also alludes to a reality beyond the parameters of the narrated events of the text. The reader, like the protagonistic soul, is left suspended temporarily in the poematic space while the poetess turns away from the linear discourse which constitutes the narration of the epic flight of the soul in order to digress at length upon the regulatory functions of the body which know neither the spatialized time of the clock, nor the human time of the psyche, but follow, rather, the natural and constant, patterned rhythms of biological time. It is primarily through the rhetorical device "digressio" that Sor Juana succeeds in departing from and thereby detaining the central theme of the discourse and enlarging the poetic universe with her knowledge of physiological, psychological, and mythological phenomena.

The idea of separation—"remota, si del todo separada / no . . ."—denotes the release, or physical detachment of the Intellect, or the soul, from the corporal chains that bind it to the diurnal task of perceptive awareness. The periodic repose and suspension of the physical being during the state of nocturnal slumber does not necessarily imply a parallel quiescence within the realm of mental and psychological activity; rather it opens the doors and windows onto the limitless horizons of oneiric activity. The emphasis on suspension in these verses is an echo of the platonic conception of the relationship between the soul and the body developed throughout the poem. No longer bound by the tethers of sense perception that restrict it to the material realm, the Intellect embarks upon unrestrained pursuits in the limitless spheres of knowledge and imaginative endeavors. Accompanied by the reader, who as an active participant in the recreation of the poetic universe must allow himself to be suspended in the literary act, the soul proceeds along an axis of verticality on its intellectual ascent, through an oneiric time that belongs essentially to the world of poetic forms and images, traversing the fantastic regions of the dreamscape mapped out by the creative imagination of the poetess.

Essential to the comprehension of the poem is the recognition of the insistence of the human spirit on transcendence, on the overcoming of obstacles, both external and internal, in spite of defeat and failure. The recurrent use of certain symbols and images—particularly those of a dynamic aerial and ascensional nature—serves to heighten and confirm the syncretic fusion of multiple spatial and temporal spheres: the physical, the physiological, the psychological and the mythical. Essentially, the reader is confronted with what could best be called a Bergsonian conception of time (Bergson, *Oeuvres,* 1970): real time or human time ("durée", the constant creative flow of Becoming, suffused with *élan vital,* or the force that drives it) fuses with time in the narrow sense, spatialized or clock time, in order to create a temporal reality within the poem which is based primarily upon the principle of synchrony rather than diachrony.

The extremely private, human time of the creative imagination, not heedful of the ordinary logical relations of ordered, sequential discourse of the literary text, contracts and expands at will, arbitrarily sequencing and juxtaposing imagistic fragments pertaining to distinct temporal realities, thereby contributing to the amplification of the poematic space, and enhancing the reader's apprehension of *El sueño*'s inherently spatial form. The coalescence, by means of the poetic word, of the dynamic, vertical time of interior, human subjectivity and the horizontal time of causality, further enables Sor Juana to construct a reality that is at once particular and universal, a fantastic dreamscape that transpires beyond the limits of successive time, unfolding within the spatialized moment of the poetic act.

The opening of the world by the poetic word is simultaneously the creation of the world, the postulation of other realities, the perpetual suggestion of coextensive spaces and times. In *El sueño,* the primary function of the poetic word is amplified, so as not to limit it to merely the creation of an object that corresponds mimetically to a contemplated reality, but rather to transfigure and transform that poetic function, and consequently endow the poetic word with a more plastic, flexible creative capacity. The poetic imagination that reveals itself in Sor Juana's poem is at once the essence and the very experience of becoming. Accordingly, the reader encounters an infinity of threshold images, images which allude to the point of entering or beginning, the place from which the ontological process departs, symbolized in the fantastic flight of the soul.

With its labyrinthine plan of reciprocal relations and reflexive references, it associations, suspensions, interruptions, and imprecisions, *El sueño* gives poetry the velocity of the dream where temporal relations are lived as a rhythm of intensities and measures that evade strict chronological sequence and spatial logic. Unfolding within the immobilized instant of spatialized time, *El sueño* is a dream of height which enables the reader to transport himself to the domain of the imaginary, to the cosmic realm of the infinite, where one is free to experience the dynamics and depth, the intensity and immediacy of the immanent and the intimate, both features of the fantastic landscape.

Elaine Granger Carrasco   (essay date 1991)

SOURCE: "Sor Juana's Gaze in *Romance 48*," in *Mester,* Vol. XX, No. 2, Fall, 1991, pp. 1926.

[*In the following essay, Carrasco discusses Juana Ines de la Cruz's treatment of sexuality in* Romance 48.]

The essence of Sor Juana's ***Romance 48*** is situational: it is a response, the other half of a conversation. It invokes a dialogue and brings into focus the Peruvian who apparently inspired it. In the *advertencia* that precedes the poem, we are advised that Sor Juana is "respondiendo a un caballero del Perú, que le envió unos barros diciéndole que se volviese hombre." Even without the clarification, the text itself represents an existential reality in relation to an Other as well as in relation to another's text.

The *advertencia* allows us to imagine that Sor Juana receives word that a gentleman has come to see her or has left her something. She accepts what probably were indigenous artifacts from Chile, the *"barros"* mentioned above, and an accompanying note or poem in which this stranger, who has undoubtedly heard of Sor Juana and knows of her poetic inspiration as well as of her worldly fame as a writer, tells her she should turn herself into a man. Perhaps his poem was not openly insulting. Yet the *romance* strongly suggests that the gentleman made reference to Sor Juana's physical attraction and that she was deeply offended that his gaze should be on her "womanhood" and not on her "writerhood," if you will. He seems to have associated her success as a writer with masculinity, hence his request that she negate her sex. Her taking offense at his posture becomes apparent in the constant presence of the Peruvian in her own poem where Sor Juana's regard is directed at him and his poem, while, at the same time, her gaze is directly focused on the meaning of his request that she change herself into a man. Sor Juana frames his request in the ontological woman/artist problem.

Sor Juana begins the poem with a salutation, like a letter:

Señor: para responderos
todas las Musas se eximen,
sin que haya, ni aun de limosna,
una que ahora me dicte;

The pivotal word seems to be *eximir.* The muses, all feminine, are not only exalted by the Peruvian's lines, they are completely used up, *gastadas,* and none are left to inspire Sor Juana's poem. We can cautiously begin by pointing out an exaggerated false modesty on Sor Juana's part which serves to put down the Peruvian's poetic inspiration—she is master of a dramatic irony that says one thing in such a way as to deny it at the same time. We can also see here Sor Juana's general exaltation of women which Georgina Sabat de Rivers has discovered functioning in many of her other texts. Elevating the status of the Virgin Mary to a level with God himself, her overwhelming use of feminine nouns in **The Dream,** her frequent enumerations of female biblical and historical figures and, of course, her *villancicos* dedicated to Santa Catarina show an unmistakable desire to praise females.

Indeed, as Sor Juana continues to refer to the muses, she calls them sisters and mothers:

> y siendo las nueve Hermanas
> madres del donaire y chiste,
> no hay, oyendo vuestros versos,
> una que chiste ni miste.

"Madres del donaire y chiste" associates the creative process with the female biological function through a metaphor that serves to reinforce the power of female figures in the creative process. Also the opposition of the phrase, *ni-una, no-hay-una,* from the first stanza is repeated and points to one muse among many, possibly a suggestion of the poet herself.

The next mythological figure is male and the entire stanza creates a burlesque image of both the Peruvian gentleman/ poet and the Roman God:

> Apolo absorto se queda
> tan elevado de oírle,
> que para aguijar el Carro,
> es menester que le griten.

Ironically, I am reminded of Lord Byron's *Don Juan* whose quartets begin in praise of woman and whose last two lines satirically expose her. Likewise, Sor Juana begins the stanza with a traditionally Gongorine hyperbaton but ends with the image of the population shouting at Apollo (dumbfounded by the Peruvian's poem), lest he drop the sun. This unexpected carnavalesque twist places the masculine figure in an inferior intellectual position amidst the already exalted female ones.

> Para escucharlo, el Pegaso
> todo el aliento reprime,
> sin que mientras lo recitan
> tema nadie que relinche.

As we have just seen in the above stanza, spectators are called in as witnesses, as it were, of a spectacle, and this presence points to the community of New Spain. Here as earlier, the poet publicly satirizes the unfortunate man, definitely no match for Sor Juana's wit. The image is of Pegasus, a horse present at the recital of the Peruvian's poem, holding back his neighing, in order to give full respect to the speaker. The praise is so hyperbolic as to make the irony unmistakable:

> porque sus murmurios viendo,
> todas las Musas coligen
> que, de vuestros versos, no
> merecen ser aprendices.

Left without any possible poetic inspiration from the muses, Sor Juana then says she can only be inspired by the Peruvian himself and she asks him to be her Apollo:

> Sed mi Apolo, y veréis que
> (como vuestra luz me anime)
> mi lira sonante escuchan
> los dos opuestos confines.
>
> Mas ¡oh cuánto poderosa
> es la invocación humilde,
> pues ya, en nuevo aliento, el pecho
> nuevo espíritu concibe!

A new spirit has been conceived in her by the Peruvian. But not the fruit of sexual union, it is the fruit of the artistic process, of a dialogue which entails the feminine as well as the masculine: "Nuevas sendas al discurso / hace . . ." "New paths to discourse" that are inspired by *dos opuestos confines,* two opposite confines, two ends of the earth, perhaps, Peru and Mexico, but two sexual poles as well— her poem and his inspiration for it are these two opposing forces. Apollo and the unspoken name of the poetic voice, Muse. There is a clear male/female dichotomy that begins to work here which softens her satire and, albeit not abandoning the irony, prepares the way for a more serious look at art itself and a kindlier tone in reference to the Other.

"Pensaréis que estoy burlando," "You probably think I'm joking," Sor Juana says, and then reasons that since she cannot find poetic inspiration in the poet she will give up this display of dramatic irony and move her regard from the poet to his gifts: the artifacts he has brought to her from Chile. These Chilean vases or bowls of clay, in their humble representation of beauty, whet her appetite for Art, she says. She refers to the sharpness of the instrument that must have carved designs on them, *filis,* and concludes that it must have been the Peruvian himself that carved them. The Greek word *Filis* suggests lover, as well as file, which needs no semiotic nor Freudian analysis. Her next line refers to his attack on her sexuality connecting the idea of sharp and cutting to his request that she turn herself into a man. "I am going to muster up all the strength that I can," says Sor Juana, "but you cannot really fertilize strength, that is, make a man's essence grow artificially," and she gives a further reason:

> porque acá Sálmacis falta,
> en cuyos cristales dicen
> que hay no sé qué virtud de
> dar alientos varoniles.

Is she serious now when she says that there's no Salmacis around to give her the "who knows what virtue of male breaths"? We shall see in a moment that Salmacis is a highly charged sexual metaphor that embodies an androgynous symbol of knowledge and that by giving herself the pretended character or *persona* of a simple and naïve "dama boba" she pretends that she thinks that an androgyne's breath is only male. She negates the female half of the symbol just as the Peruvian forgot to include the female element and Sor Juana's sexuality in her creative writing process. The intentionality of Sor Juana's gaze here is no longer only to elevate the position of the female for its own sake. Her regard, her look is on the mistake the Peruvian made in not being able to accept her biological sex and possibly even her gender in relation to her work as a poet and playwright.

"I do not understand such things," Sor Juana continues, referring to the much critiqued stanza just quoted, "because, if I am a woman, no one will ever verify it." And she continues in this vein:

> Y también sé que, en latín,
> sólo a las casadas dicen
> úxor, o mujer, y que
> es común de dos lo Virgen.

In other words, she does not know anything about the virtues of men, males' breaths (or expressions?). All she knows is Latin, intellectual language of mostly only men at that time, a language that allowed her to participate in the male world. In her stance of innocence/ignorance, all she knows is that both sexes experience the virgin state, associating once again those *opuestos confines* of the male and female poets.

The word *confines* is certainly appropriate considering the historical context of Sor Juana and her Peruvian, which demanded strict adherence to hegemonic ideas that molded sexual roles. She even refers to this social force in her next stanza pointing to the fact that his drawing attention to her sexuality is very definitely inappropriate. But not only because the eyes of the hegemony see it that way, rather because sexuality is determined by the Other, by the subject-in-situation, and she will not ever be thus available for definition. The only thing she knows about her body is that since it does not incline one way or the other in relation to him, it is or should be respected as neutral, abstract,

> (. . .) cuanto
> sólo el Alma deposite.
> Y dejando esta cuestión
> para que otros la ventilen,
> porque en lo que es bien que ignore
> no es razón que sutilice.

The tone of the poem changes again here and Sor Juana, still clever, but more open with him now, refers once more to his file, his *lima,* to his attack on her being, and as she does in many other places, refers to the deadly circumstance of being special in an envious world. She suggests that he leave his *lima,* his sharp edge, in Lima and come to Mexico where he may be accepted more openly than he has been able to accept her.

Sabat de Rivers, pointing to the presence of the Other in Sor Juana's **Dream,** the intellectual Other as well as the social Other, associates this masculine presence with a desire on Sor Juana's part to negate sexuality, as if the presence of both sides would render the soul asexual:

> Cuando sor Juana lanza al Alma hacia las alturas—alma que es, al mismo tiempo, la suya propia y la del 'otro'—la hace asexual para que cada ser humano pueda identificarse con ella (el Alma) y darle así dimensiones universales.

It is possible that such a desire on Sor Juana's part to identify with the soul reveals not so much an asexual and neutral image of mankind, but rather a union of the sexes, the creation of a space where man and woman can live on a plane, bound in love and not opposed by their attraction to each other.

Critics have said that Sor Juana defines her sexuality in this poem. For Octavio Paz, for example, the **Romance 48** is another expression of her sought-after asexuality, her creation of an asexual self-image, and supports his suggestion of unconscious sublimation of her lesbianism. But Paz may be guilty of the same mistake the Peruvian made: the removal of the woman from her own literary production. It was not, then, so much a question of what the Peruvian gentleman said, but more, what he did not say and what he implied. Sor Juana seems to have filled in this gap for him, if you will, and Paz seems to have missed it.

Suggesting that Sor Juana expressed a repressed lesbianism through neoplatonic thought and imagery, Octavio Paz points to this poem in Chapter 15 of his book, *Sor Juana Inés de la Cruz or, the Traps of Faith.* When Sor Juana says that she cannot change herself into a man because there is no Salmacis around, Paz assumes that the hermaphroditic image inherent in the metaphor of Ovid's Salmacis, is sexual for Sor Juana. But he agrees with Méndez Plancarte in that the use of the Ovidian reference was a careless mistake on the part of Sor Juana because this fountain did not transform maidens into youths, it changed Hermaphroditus into an androgyne. Méndez Plancarte says that what Sor Juana meant to say was Iphis, who was a real female figure whom Isis changed into a man. The mythological figure of Iphis belongs to a separate story in the *Metamorphosis.* Paz bases further conjecture on this assumption although admitting that what he interprets as a sort of Freudian slip provides tempting territory for a professional psychologist:

> But maybe we do not need psychoanalysis to be able to explain this small error. To begin with, it is difficult to believe that Juana Inés, considering everything we know about her, would refer to the episode about Iphis: it was too similar to her own situation. Iphis . . . asks Isis to turn her into a man.

Iphis most likely represents what Sor Juana would really wish: a male body so she could be with her beloved, the Marquesa de la Laguna, Sor Juana's good friend and protector. Both critics, readily willing to admit that the poet has made an essential error in the use of an Ovidian image of the *Metamorphosis,* totally forget or consider irrelevant two very important facts in Ovid's myth of Salmacis: 1) Hermaphroditus, a male love-child of Aphrodite and Hermes, is also converted into the androgyne along with Salmacis, and 2) the name of a sensuous fountain, is also a sexually aggressive heterosexual female (Ovid, Book IV). Ironically, Paz briefly outlines the Salmacis myth and mentions Sor Juana's reference to hermaphroditism, but leaves that reference unexplained. Here is the story of Salmacis, a story that two of Sor Juana's most well-known critics cannot accept as part of the textual message of the *Romance 48*:

It begins when Hermaphroditus, who wanders by the shores of undiscovered rivers and unimagined places because he delights in the unknown, finds Salmacis, a Naïde, the only nymph unknown to Diana, who resides by a fountain: symbol of the unknown which is the object of Hermaphroditus' desire. Salmacis falls madly in love with Hermaphroditus when she sees him; but he repulses her and, so, she tells him that she will leave him alone. But she hides instead. After a time of thinking himself alone and lingering by the shore of the fountain, Hermaphroditus is seduced by the pool of water itself—its clear warm-cool liquid, soothing and irresistible, acts on him and he disrobes and enters the water to the absolute delight of Salmacis hiding in the bushes. She flings off her clothes and dashes into the water too, attacking him, clinging, embracing, kissing him while breathlessly panting. But she still remains chaste. Ovid compares her to a serpent, symbol of knowledge, and also to ivy, and he compares Hermaphroditus to figures that correspond to the serpent and the ivy: an eagle, and an oak tree. The metamorphosis that Salmacis and Hermaphroditus undergo is to become an eagle with a snake entwined about its legs. The image of a flying eagle with a snake wrapped around his legs, as seen in William Blake's *The Marriage of Heaven and Hell,* for example, also recalls Quetzalcoatl, who, curiously, is represented as a plumed snake in Aztec renderings of him. In the metamorphic myth, the bodies of Hermaphroditus and Salmacis become one, the Hermaphrodite figure, and anyone who enters the fountain of Salmacis after that must leave its waters half man and half woman.

It is clear to me that Sor Juana made no mistake in choosing her images in this poem and it is also clear that her voice, at least here, is heterosexual. She approached the Peruvian as a woman and as an artist and tried to enlighten him to the fact that the artistic process, not her own body, is androgynous. Not only the use of the Salmacis metaphor, but her invocation of the Peruvian, "Be my Apollo," points to an ironic coquetry, not a flirtation, a tease. In commenting on Sor Juana's phrase, "If true that I am a female," Paz says that she "diminishes and almost places in doubt her female condition." I argue that she is cleverly rebuking the *caballero* from Peru, implying that "none of you gentlemen will ever know for sure." She seems to be asserting her sexuality and artistic dignity at the same time. The jauntily erotic basis seems an intentional background for a discourse of art and knowledge

which she roots in the androgyne/hermaphrodite archetype. The discourse moves from sex to gender, female *persona* to androgynous symbol, particular to universal. By employing such a metaphor as Salmacis, Sor Juana brings an image of heterosexual aggression to bear on her poem, an inversion of the dominant ideology and an indication that she was aware that "Female-authored work cannot escape varieties of sexual malaise; identification with dominance has colonized most imaginations" [Adrienne Munch, *Making a Difference. Feminist Literary Criticism,* 1985]. Even more compelling than her awareness that her identity is defined in relation to the world in which she lives, is her ability to demonstrate such awareness through the construction of situations—relation in situation. Thus even the static world of Colonial, Creole Mexico filters through her gaze to reflect a mutable space that can at once be intimate and public, saintly and erotic, reproachful and attractive: an image that may not yet be harmonious with the confines of our own gaze resting on the achievement of a Catholic nun in the New World.

Georgina Sabat de Rivers (essay date 1991)

SOURCE: "A Feminist Rereading of Sor Juana's *Dream,*" in *Feminist Perspectives on Sor Juana Inés de la Cruz,* edited by Stephanie Merrim, Wayne State University Press, 1991, pp. 142-58.

[*In the following essay, Sabat de Rivers asserts that* El sueño *was written from a female perspective and discusses its feminine characteristics.*]

Undoubtedly there were many more women writing works of literature in colonial Spanish America than those whose names appear in our records from Hispaniola (the present-day Dominican Republic), from Peru, and from New Spain (Mexico). And it is no accident that the names preserved derive precisely from those geographical areas where, in different periods, the major cultural centers were located. It was especially in these centers that women insisted on their right to be heard and read, along with the men who did most of the writing. If our records are fragmentary and sometimes names have been lost, this is due to a strong tradition that held literature to be a realm in which women were not supposed to be active, a tradition that was reluctant to accept those women who dared to cross cultural boundaries in their desire to make themselves known literarily. In Spanish America people generally followed the customs of Spain, where "Maidens and decent ladies were expected to live in the custody of severe domestic guardians—husbands, fathers, or brothers—who, in order to keep their own manly honor above suspicion, were obliged to keep their charges under lock and key, in the tradition of Arabs and Turks, or to have them always accompanied by squires or duennas." Nonetheless, we need only recall that Sor Juana Inés de la Cruz, our supreme example of the Hispanic woman's effort to participate in a literary world where she could measure herself intellectually with men, is neither a unique case nor a miracle; her case is "a peak, not in a plain, but in a mountain range." For reasons that may have something to do with the shift from Renaissance to Baroque thought, the fate of Sor Juana Inés de la Cruz was fortunately not the same as that of the earlier Clarinda and Amarilis, literary names that are the only way we have of identifying two excellent Peruvian poetesses. Sor Juana, even though her literary reputation has suffered from the critical ups and downs of *culteranismo,* never had to conceal her own name and has always been fully recognized as a major figure in Mexican and Hispanic letters.

Sor Juana, as we know, openly and deliberately refused to be involved in the activities usually assigned to her sex when, as a nun, she insisted on devoting herself fully to the life of the mind. She . . . claimed her neuter status as a virgin, free from the domination of any man, and thus established her fundamental liberty:

> Yo no entiendo de esas cosas;
> sólo sé que aquí me vine
> porque, si es que soy mujer,
> ninguno lo verifique.
> Y también sé que, en latín,
> sólo a las casadas dicen
> *uxor,* o mujer, y que
> es común de dos lo virgen.
> Con que a mí no es bien mirado
> que como a mujer me miren,
> pues no soy mujer que a alguno
> de mujer pueda servirle:
> y sólo sé que mi cuerpo,
> sin que a uno u otro se incline,
> es neutro o abstracto, cuanto
> sólo el Alma deposite.

> (I don't understand these matters; all I know is that I came here so that, if in fact I am a woman, no one could find it out. I also know that, in Latin, only married women are called *uxor* or feminine, and that *virgin* is of common gender, neither masculine nor feminine. So

> I do not consider it proper to be considered a woman, for I am not a woman to serve as wife to any man; and I only know that my body without inclining to one sex or another, is neuter or abstract, solely the dwelling of my soul.)

The final stanza reminds us of what Calderón himself had said: "So let them fight and study, for to be brave and learned is a matter of the soul, and the soul is neither male nor female." María de Zayas took advantage of this in her struggle for women in her day, as did Sor Juana later on in a poem she addressed to the Countess de Paredes (no. 403):

> Ser mujer, ni estar ausente,
> no es de amarte impedimento;
> pues sabes tú que las almas
> distancia ignoran y sexo.

> (Neither being a woman nor being far away keeps me from loving you, for, as you know, souls are ignorant of distance and of gender.)

To give the title of the "Tenth Muse" to María de Zayas and to Sor Juana (and to Anne Bradstreet, too, in colonial New England), favored in those days as a way of recognizing distinction in women who had made their mark in literature, was a somewhat ambiguous act. It combined the ideas of being abnormal and of being a woman or mother, reinforced in the case of Sor Juana by her status as a nun. We may wonder whether the glory accorded to this woman in her own day, in a post-Renaissance period, was due to her genius itself or to those Baroque ideas of being unusual, extraordinary, and amazing in a topsy-turvy world. She herself seems to have suspected this when, after several lines of false modesty, she writes the following (no. 506):

> Si no es que el sexo ha podido
> o ha querido hacer, por raro,
> que el lugar de lo perfecto
> obtenga lo extraordinario.

> (Unless it be that my sex, so peculiar, could or would be the cause for the extraordinary to be accepted as perfection.)

Many different examples can be found in Sor Juana's writings of her active concern for women's status, of her identification with her sex. In fact, I think that we may say that the whole of her literary production is permeated by her feminine consciousness of her society's patriarchal character and of her exceptional status as a female writer and intellectual. I therefore cannot accept what has sometimes been asserted: that she wished to be identified with the masculine sex. Born a woman and an intellectual, what she did do was to assert herself and demand the same rights that were conceded to enlightened men. She did not resign herself to being a female poet with no rights or opinions of her own within the paternalistic system; she was a woman who offered, who continues to offer, "a series of suggested alternatives to the male-dominated membership and attitudes of the accepted canon." The conviction that she had of her own capacity and her consequent desire for recognition as a woman intellectually comparable to men led her to rectify, by her own practice, the prejudice against women and to demonstrate by example what a woman writer was capable of achieving within the level of Golden Age literature. She did all this in a way that still moves us, by not accepting her "natural" condition of being what a woman was supposed to be but by showing what a woman could become culturally. She did not write specifically for women "sewing by parlor lamp-light," but instead managed to place her books on the library shelves of her period's intellectual men. In her poetry and prose she uses the stylistic and syntactic devices found in her feminine predecessors in the New World, her "native land": false modesty, catalogues of illustrious women, contradictions, indirect ways of insinuating facts, sisterhood. But our Mexican nun, taking up the battle begun by women before her, did not limit herself to the more or less subtle characteristics of feminine writing; she went much further.

On only a few occasions did Sor Juana speak out directly against men. The most famous examples of this are her quatrains beginning **Hombres necios** (Foolish Men), and even this poem can be seen as part of the pastoral tradition, in combination with her feminist concerns. What really mattered to her was to give to the feminine sex a literary and intellectual status equal to that of men, as can be seen explicitly or implicitly throughout her works.

In the light of all this, and especially of recent feminist criticism focusing on the modes of expression used by the writer as woman, it is revealing to reread Sor Juana's beloved "papelillo" or "scrap of paper," her *Sueño* or *Dream.* It is true that, in this, her most important poem, she presents intellectual concerns that are not limited to woman but belong to the human race in general, concerns always considered essential to man's thought, such as how to establish knowledge of a universal sort. In so doing, she converts her protagonist, the Soul, into pure intellect engaged in reflections of a universal sort. But at the same time we can detect—and not only in the definitive last line of the poem, "el mundo iluminado, y yo despierta" (the world bathed in light, and the feminine I awake)—other emphases and characteristics that give evidence of the woman behind the pen that did the writing: "Feminine values penetrate and undermine the masculine systems that contain them." Rosa Perelmuter Pérez, arguing against the impersonal character of the poem, has found in the *Sueño* many deictics that indicate the more or less veiled presence of the writer as she intervenes in the poem's discourse.

The first thing to attract my attention in this rereading of the *Sueño* was the preponderance and importance of feminine characters and of feminine nouns. Naturally, in the latter case it is a matter of Spanish grammar: all of us have to use nouns of both genders. And yet it is not easy to explain the fact that this poet, perhaps unconsciously, preferred feminine nouns in a proportion far exceeding that of masculine nouns. As for the feminine characters, what is most interesting is the significance she attributes to them, their relevance within their context, and their importance. If multiplicity and variety, besides being Baroque, can be considered characteristics of women's writing, there is no doubt that Sor Juana was doubly at home as she wrote this poem.

Immediately after the opening lines, with two feminine nouns—"Piramidal, funesta, de la tierra / nacida sombra . . ." (the funereal, pyramidal shadow born of the earth, that tries in vain to scale the stars [also feminine])—the moon makes her appearance, but the shadow cannot reach her either (lines 9-13):

> que su atezado ceño
> al superior convexo aun no llegaba
> del orbe de la diosa
> que tres veces hermosa
> con tres hermosos rostros ser ostenta . . .

> (whose dark frown could not even reach the upper curve of the orb of that goddess who shows herself to be thrice beautiful with three beautiful faces . . .)

The moon is presented in her triple mythological role of the goddess of three faces: as Hecate in the sky; as Diana on Earth; and as Proserpina in the underworld. Thus, Sor Juana establishes, from the beginning of the poem, a universe where woman rules as a cosmic force. (And she will return to Proserpina later on, as we shall see.)

In this prologue, which we have entitled "Night and the cosmos go to sleep," the birds of night are the next to appear. Unlike other such passages in Golden Age poetry, these birds are all associated with mythological figures, and all of them except Ascalaphus are female. Although all of these figures, the sinister companions of Night, are presented with negative connotations, we can perceive a tone of sympathy for the feminine characters. It is probably no accident that Sor Juana, an illegitimate daughter who hardly knew her father, lists among the birds of night a certain Nyctimene, punished by being turned into an owl for her crime of incest with her father (lines 27-28):

> la avergonzada Nictimene acecha
> de las sagradas puertas los resquicios . . .

> (shameful Nyctimene lurks about the cracks in the sacred doors . . .)

Our nun-poet seems to present a somewhat ambivalent image of this character. On the one hand, she tries to attenuate her crime, perhaps in a gesture of feminine solidarity, by using the adjective "avergonzala" which evokes our sympathy insofar as it suggests *arrepentida* (repentant or remorseful), which, according to the *Diccionario de autoridades,* was one of the word's meanings in the Golden Age. But, on the other hand, in the lines that follow she also calls Nyctimene "sacrilegious" as she relates her to the chaste, intellectual figure of Minerva, where olive oil (the olive tree is referred to periphrastically as "el árbol la Minerva", Minerva's tree). Nyctimene drinks from the temple's lamps.

Let us now read closely four lines from this passage which refer to the daughters of Minyas, who worked so hard that they ignored the festivities due to the deity of Bacchus and were punished by being transformed into bats (lines 47-50):

> aquellas tres oficïosas, digo,
> atrevidas hermanas,
> que el tremendo castigo
> de desnudas les dio pardas membranas . . .

> (I mean those three industrious, daring sisters who received the awful punishment of dark, naked membranes . . .)

According to the above-mentioned dictionary, *oficïoso* meant both officious and industrious. This is the ambiguity underlying Sor Juana's treatment of the three sisters: she recognizes the hardworking virtue of their overzealous vice, which cost them so dearly. The word "tremendo" (awful) seems to imply that the punishment was disproportionate to the crime. This ambiguity or doubt in the mind of the poet is emphasized by her presence in the word "digo," a rhetorical *figura correctionis* that makes us aware of the writer's self-consciousness.

As for the figure of Ascalaphus, "el parlero ministro de Plutón" (Pluto's garrulous minister), who betrayed Proserpina and hence was transformed into an owl by her, I will only note at this point that the poet has chosen a masculine character who was punished for what has been considered to be one of the vices most characteristic of women: being too talkative.

As she follows the coming of night, which slowly covers the whole world, preparing it for sleep, Sor Juana next speaks to us of the sea (lines 86-94):

El mar, no ya alterado

. . . . .

y los dormidos, siempre mudos, peces,
en los lechos lamosos
de sus obscuros senos cavernosos,
mudos eran dos veces;
y entre ellos, la engañosa encantadora
Almone . . .

(The sea, no longer disturbed . . . and the sleeping fish, always mute, in the slimy beds of their dark and cavernous recesses were twice mute; and among them, the deceptive enchantress Almone . . .)

The latter is the only fish to which the poet attributes a name, a name that places her within a mythological tradition according to which she was known as deceptive. At the same time, in contrast to this negative attribute, the poet asserts the ambiguous charm of the enchantress.

As we enter the section of the poem that deals with man's intellectual sleep or dream (for in Spanish the word *sueño* is related etymologically and semantically to both Latin words *somnus* and *somnium*), the poet devotes a series of beautiful lines to the evocation of sleep's, and death's, leveling power, which ranges from the grammatically feminine symbol of power (line 184: "la soberana tiara," the sovereign tiara) to the grammatically feminine symbol of humility (line 185: "la pajiza choza," the straw hut). Immediately afterward there comes to center stage "el Alma" (the Soul), also grammatically feminine, although it theoretically represents the neuter intellect which joins both sexes and genders, as for example in line 293: "su inmaterial ser y esencia bella" (her immaterial being and beautiful essence; the first noun masculine and the second feminine). But, as a matter of fact, the Soul, "de lo sublunar reina soberana" (line 439: sovereign queen of everything under the moon), which will be the protagonist of this Baroque attempt to grasp the whole cosmos in a philosophical or scientific way, is a constantly feminine character that, like Sor Juana herself, combines intelligence and beauty in "sus intelectuales bellos ojos" (line 441: her intellectual, beautiful eyes).

In the lines that follow, which deal with the lighthouse of Alexandria, feminine nouns are emphasized even more: "la terse superficie" (the smooth surface) of "la azogada luna" (the quicksilvered plateglass) upon which Fantasy does her industrious labor (lines 280-91):

así ella, sosegada, iba copiando
las imágenes todas de las cosas,
y el pincel invisible iba formando
de mentales, sin luz, siempre vistosas
colores, las figuras
no sólo ya de todas las criaturas
sublunares, mas aun también de aquellas
que intelectuales claras son estrellas,
y en el modo posible
que concebirse puede lo invisible,
en sí, mañosa, las representaba
y al Alma las mostraba.

(Thus she calmly proceeded to copy the images of all the things, and her invisible brush began to sketch, with mental, lightless color s always showy, the outlines not only of all sublunary creatures, but also of those which are bright intellectual stars, and insofar as the invisi-

ble can possibly be conceived of, within herself she skillfully represented them and showed them to the Soul.)

This whole passage is highly significant as an example of how the nun's baroque language, centered around a feminine protagonist, becomes scientifically analytical and precise.

Another feminine noun worthy of note is the pair of pyramids that, as the poet explains (line 403), "especies son del alma intencionales" (are the intentional faculties of the soul) aspiring to reach the "Primera Causa" (line 408: First Cause), a feminine noun here used to refer to a traditionally masculine God as creative power. A similarly feminine circumlocution for God the Creator is "Sabia Poderosa Mano" (line 670: the Wise and Powerful Hand). And close to God we find Thetis, a mythological sea goddess and mother figure, performing an essentially female function as she offers "sus fértiles pechos maternales" (lines 627-28: her fertile maternal breasts) to vegetation, the first level of Creation, extracting "los dulces . . . manantiales de humor terrestre" (lines 630-31: sweet springs of earthly water) as nourishing irrigation. And before finally mentioning the human being as the culmination of Creation, she refers to him or her by means of these feminine abstractions: "Naturaleza pura" (line 661: the essence of Nature), "bisagra engarzadora" (line 659: the linking hinge, that is, the mediator between God and subhuman creatures), and "fábrica portentosa" (line 677: the prodigious structure), a series of three feminine nouns displacing the usually masculine *man*. Similar feminine circumlocutions are found in "espantosa máquina inmensa" (lines 770-71: immense and fearful machine) for the cosmos, and "cerúlea plana" (line 949: blue sheet of paper) for the sky, replacing Góngora's similar but masculine metaphor (*Soledad I,* line 592: "papel diáfano del cielo").

Let us now review a few lines appearing in the section we have entitled "Intellectual Sobriety," a section particularly rich in feminine characteristics. Sor Juana, who was probably at this point following the Florentine Platonic tradition that asserted knowledge to be impossible unless revealed to the soul, has by now in her poem described two different methods of seeking truth—Plato's intuitive method and Aristotle's discursive or analytical method—both of them failures. She goes on to say (lines 704-11):

> Estos, pues, grados discurrir quería
> unas veces, pero otras disentía,
> excesivo juzgando atrevimiento
> el discurrirlo todo
> quien aun la más pequeña,
> aun la más fácil parte no entendía
> de los más manüales
> efectos naturales . . .

(These levels, then, [the Soul] would try sometimes to analyze, but other times she dissented, judging it to be excessively daring for one to analyze everything who could not understand even the smallest, accessible aspects of the most tangible natural phenomena . . .)

She goes on to offer us two examples of those simple aspects of nature that the human mind is incapable of comprehending: the underground course of a spring, personified mythologically as Arethusa, and the feminine flower.

Arethusa, a Nereid or nymph who was transformed into a spring so that she could flee the persecution of the river Alpheus, had asked Diana, the chaste goddess, to help her escape in this way, to go underground and there to proceed (lines 715-22):

> deteniendo en ambages su camino
> —los horrorosos senos
> de Plutón, las cavernas pavorosas
> del abismo tremendo,
> las campañas hermosas,
> los Elíseos amenos,
> tálamo ya de su triforme esposa,
> clara pesquisidora registrando . . .

(as she slowed down and began to wander about—examining as a bright investigator the dark chambers of Pluto, the frightful caverns of the awful abyss, the beautiful Elysian fields so pleasant, now the wedding bed of his threefold bride . . .)

This bride is, of course, Proserpina, the daughter of Ceres, goddess of agriculture and abundance. Proserpina (Persephone in Greek) was abducted by Pluto, the god of the underworld, while she was playing on a meadow with her sisters, and was taken away to "the awful abyss." Arethusa, turned into an underground spring as she passed through "the dark chambers of Pluto," saw her down there, and when she came to the surface in Sicily she told Ceres where her daughter was. Ceres, wishing to save her favorite daughter, begged permission from Jupiter, Proserpina's father, to go down into the underworld to rescue her,

but he set one condition: that Proserpina must not have eaten anything in Pluto's realm (a harsh condition discriminating against woman, strangely reminiscent of the fruit forbidden to Eve). When Ceres reaches the underworld, Proserpina was beginning to eat a pomegranate and had in fact already swallowed a few grains. The person who told Jupiter about this was Ascalaphus, later changed into an owl by Proserpina as punishment. After all that had transpired, the only thing Ceres could settle for was to have her daughter stay with her for half of each year, spending the rest of the year at the side of the man who, by rape, had made her his bride.

It is impossible, it seems to me, to attribute to mere chance the fact that Sor Juana chose precisely such mythological characters as these to illustrate the intellectual argument of her great poem. Their relevant characteristics are the motherly love identified with Ceres, the bond of sisterhood between her and Arethusa, Proserpina's filial loyalty to her mother, and also the abundance represented by the mother figure; and these feminine figures suffer at the hands of the masculine figures who intervene in their lives. Let us read closely the following passage, in which "the bright investigator" of the underworld reports to Ceres the whereabouts of her daughter (lines 723-29):

> útil curiosidad, aunque prolija,
> que de su no cobrada bella hija
> noticia cierta dio a la Rubia Diosa,
> cuando montes y selvas trastornando,
> cuando prados y bosques inquiriendo,
> su vida iba buscando
> y del dolor su vida iba perdiendo.

(a useful curiosity, though prolix, which yielded positive news of her beautiful unfound daughter to the Blond Goddess when, searching high and low through woods and forests, inquiring of meadows and groves, she was seeking for her beloved and was losing her life in grief.)

In addition to Sor Juana's usual emphasis on the positive characteristics of her feminine figures, here we have a striking example of her capacity to bring together in a single complex reflection two different aspects of her own personality: her concern about being a woman and her concern about being an intellectual. Let us recall what she tells us in her *Reply* to the bishop about the scientific discoveries she made while she was in the kitchen or on the playground watching girls spin a top, discoveries leading her to consider the advantages of being a woman and having access to fields of observation closed to men, to a fuller perspective on the world: "If Aristotle had been a cook, he would have written a great deal more." In this case, too, Sor Juana's ultimate purpose is to give us an example to illustrate a philosophic point about the limitations of human knowledge, an example based on observing underground water coming up from a spring. For this she chooses a feminine character, Arethusa, and brings her into a personal relationship involving intimate maternal feelings of suffering for a lost daughter.

The other example she uses to illustrate the same episte-mological concerns is that of the "breve flor," or short-lived flower, a variation on a similar feminine theme: when she mentions "her fragile beauty," we cannot help think-ing of the traits traditionally attributed to woman as a "weak and lovely being." It is easy for us to imagine, behind the following lines of Baroque poetry, a seven-teenth-century nun bent over a flowerpot on the window-sill of her convent cell, concentrating her attention on the most beautiful carnation, and trying in vain to compre-hend it (lines 733-41):

> . . . mixtos, por qué, colores
> —confundiendo la grana en los albores—
> fragante le son gala;
> ámbares por qué exhala,
> y el leve, si más bello,
> ropaje al viento explica,
> que en una y otra fresca multiplica
> hija, formando pompa escarolada
> de dorados perfiles cairelada . . .

(not knowing why mixed colors—combining crimson with white light—adorn it with fragrance; why it exhales perfumes and unfold in the wind its loveliest thin garment, multiplying itself in one new daughter after another, forming a frilly fringe fluted with bold streaks . . .)

She notes, incidentally, the flower's reproductive func-tion, multiplying itself in daughters, and then immediately decides to follow the Renaissance poetic tradition of com-paring the carnation's combination of red and white to women's cosmetics, using the flower as an exemplum in a sermon against the dangers of deception (lines 751-56):

> preceptor quizá vano
> —si no ejemplo profano—
> de industria femenil que el más activo
> veneno hace dos veces ser nocivo
> en el velo aparente
> de la que finge tez resplandeciente.

(a reproof perhaps in vain—if not a bad example—of feminine wiles that make the deadliest poison doubly noxious in the deceptive veil of a fictiously glowing complexion.)

These are the incidental thoughts that occur to Sor Juana as she comments on how problematic it is for human science, which cannot understand a single, simple object, to try to comprehend the entire universe. From the topos of the rose, traditionally compared with woman because of her fleeting, fragile beauty and her cosmetics, the poet moves in a sophisticated leap to epistemological ques-tions of philosophy. This gives us insight into how an extraordinary nun in New Spain invents a new feminine rhetoric to theatricalize everyday aspects of women's lives, making them significantly relevant to the adven-tures of scientific thought.

Let us turn now to the final section of the poem, the dra-matic battle between night and day. Before the appearance of the "father of burning light" in line 887, Sor Juana has three feminine characters precede the sun: Venus, the plan-et goddess representing intelligence, love, and female beau-ty; Aurora, the goddess of the dawn; and Night, also, like Aurora, presented as an Amazon (lines 895-906):

> Pero de Venus, antes, el hermoso
> apacible lucero
> rompió el albor primero,
> y del viejo Titón la bella esposa
> —amazona de luces mil vestida,
> contra la Noche armada,
> hermosa si atrevida,
> valiente aunque llorosa—
> su frente mostró hermosa
> de matutinas luces coronada,
> aunque tierno preludio, ya animoso,
> del planeta fogoso . . .

(But first the lovely peaceful star of Venus broke the dawn, and the fair bride of aged Tithonus—an Amazon clad in many rays, armed against the Night, lovely while daring, brave though tearful—showed her beautiful forehead crowned with morning light, a vigorous though tender prelude to the fiery star . . .)

Venus leads the way and helps Aurora show her ray-crowned head in an attack on Night. Aurora sheds tears of dew, in a traditional way, but Sor Juana is innovative in having her armed and brave, vigorous in her onslaught as she leads the fight against Night—also an Amazon, but dark (lines 914-16):

> y con nocturno cetro pavoroso
> las sombras gobernaba,
> de quien aun ella misma se espantaba.

(and with her fearsome nocturnal scepter she ruled the shadows, which frightened even her.)

Upon the attack of "la bella precursora signífera del sol . . . tocando al arma todos los süaves / si bélicos clarines de las aves" (lines 917-20: the fair forerunner and stan-dard-bearer of the sun . . . sounding in alarm all the sweet yet warlike clarions of the birds), the Night "ronca tocó bocina / a recoger los negros escuadrones / para poder en orden retirarse" (lines 936-38: sounded her hoarse horn for the black squadrons to gather and be ready to retire in order). But they were unable to do so since the Sun's arrival was already imminent (955-58):

> y llegar al ocaso pretendía
> con el (sin orden ya) desbaratado
> ejército de sombras, acosado
> de la luz que el alcance le seguía.

(and so she tried to reach the west with her now shattered and disorderly army of shadows, attacked by the light that was pursuing them.)

But Night—and this is most significant—was only tem-porarily defeated (lines 959-66):

Consiguió, al fin, la vista del ocaso
el fugitivo paso,
y—en su mismo despeño recobrada,
esforzando el aliento en la rüina—
en la mitad del globo que ha dejado
el sol desamparada,
segunda vez rebelde determina
mirarse coronada . . .

(Her fleeing step at last brought her in sight of the west
and—recovering even as she fell, taking courage in
defeat—in the half of the globe that the sun has left
unoccupied she decides, again rebellious, to have herself
crowned as queen.)

The dramatic quality of this final scene depends primarily on the two feminine characters, Aurora and Night. The intervention of the sun (and Sor Juana could not have avoided considering Apollo a supremely masculine figure), though narrated in beautiful verse, is relatively passive (lines 943-49):

Llegó, en efecto, el sol cerrando el giro
que esculpió de oro sobre azul zafiro:
de mil multiplicados
mil veces puntos, flujos mil dorados
—líneas, digo, de luz clara—salían
de su circunferencia luminosa,
pautando al cielo la cerúlea plana . . .

(The sun arrived in fact, closing the circle that he drew
in gold on sapphire blue: from a thousand points multiplied
a thousand times, a thousand golden rays—lines I mean
of bright light—shone from hisluminous circumference,
drawing straight edges on the sky's blue sheet . . .)

What is emphasized in these lines is the light projected by the sun. However, the poet avoids presenting the sun as a personal individual or specific mythological character, as Phoebus or Apollo, while this is precisely what she does with Venus, and especially with Aurora and the Night. Since woman has been credited with an ability to endure and adapt in a flexible way, characteristics also attributed to Baroque culture, I should like to point out something that has not, I believe, been commented on before, and that is the Night's attitude toward defeat: she undertakes the battle knowing that she is going to lose but also knowing, at the same time, as Sor Juana had remarked before apropos of Phaeton (lines 785-826), that she can repeat her efforts interminably, like Sisyphus, "segunda vez rebelde." If the sun is a masculine character, the Night is feminine; if daytime belongs to the sun, the Night takes courage from defeat and succeeds the sun in endless rotation. This poem is a dream that will be repeated night after night, the obverse of daily activities under patriarchal vigilance. Sor Juana was fully aware of the literary tradition of the dream as reality, of the close relationship between what we do during the day and what we dream of doing at night. The daylight classical brilliance of the Renaissance had given way to twilight zones of light and darkness in the Baroque period. The nun's dream is not the ethical *Bildungstraum* of Calderón's *La vida es sueño*

(Life Is a Dream); it is an epistemological dream that reveals the impossibility, for human beings, of comprehending the universe and at the same time urges persistence in the face of defeat as a sufficient compensation for that impossibility.

Night as a character is given emphasis by being placed at the end of the poem; in this way the poet reinforces what she had said apropos of Phaeton. Both of these figures represent an urge to succeed and to rebel, even though in vain, to strive to comprehend the universe, which was Sor Juana's own major aim in life. This is the aspiration incarnated in these two figures. Like Phaeton and like Night, the nun decides to repeat in her poem what she indefatigably tries to do with every new day that begins, even though she accepts in advance the inevitability of defeat: during long and patient hours she studies, affirming in this way her right to existence as effort, and she does this centuries before Camus and his existentialist theories. As Octavio Paz says [in *Sor Juana Inés de la Cruz, o Las trampas de la fe,* 1982], *El Sueño* is a poem that represents "the last example of one genre and the first of another." In a world that made no space available to woman as a thinking being, it was a woman, a nun, who, by making use of every recourse available to women, offered new solutions to the old problems of man, inscribing herself fully within a universal human problematic. With Sor Juana, Woman (with a capital W) enters the literary history of the Spanish-speaking world; after her, no one could exclude the female intellectual from Spanish American letters. If it is true that the writings of women have always been heroic, it has never been truer than in the case of this extraordinary nun who concludes her long philosophical poem, unique in Hispanic literature, by asserting her faith in womankind with her single explicit reference to her feminine self, a reference made by means of the first-person singular pronoun modified by a feminine past participle, the last word of *El Sueño*:

. . . quedando a luz más cierta
el mundo iluminado y yo *despierta.*

(leaving the world illuminated by a more certain light,
and me *awake;* [author's] emphasis)

Jacqueline C. Nanfito   (essay date 1992)

SOURCE: "Time and Space in Sor Juana's *El sueño,*" in *Hispanic Journal,* Vol. 13, No. 2, Fall, 1992, pp. 345-52.

[*In the following essay, Nanfito examines Cruz's treatment of time and space in her most famous poem.*]

If Renaissance poetry tended toward simplicity in its use of tense and time reference, the baroque poem exhibits an explicit, accentuated awareness of the passage and multivalent nature of time, and an unparalleled inclination toward the manipulation of time and the exploitation of its paradoxes. The existing union between life and death in the essence of all living creatures, along with the notion of time as an inexorable agent, constitute some of the central themes or motives recurring throughout the Hispanic Baroque, particularly in the "metaphysical poetry" characteristic of this period, distinguished by its emphatic and impassioned inclination toward ingenuity and obscurity.

The question of time recurs in the literary texts of the Latin American Baroque, and in particular, in the poetic compositions of Sor Juana Inés de la Cruz. Her poems reveal a preoccupation with such philosophical problems as the meaning of time, transience and death; the question of eternity and immortality; and the significance of the relationship between mind and matter, body and soul. The subject of ephemerality is manifest in a number of texts, such as **"En vano tu canto suena,"** one of the "Glosas en décimas," and in nearly all of the sonnets of a philosophical-moral nature: **"Este que ves, engaño colorido," "Rosa divina que en gentil cultura," "Miró Celia una rosa que en el prado," "Si los riesgos del mar considerara,"** and **"Diuturna enfermedad de la Esperanza."** Yet nowhere is the topic of time more rigorously addressed and investigated than in her most celebrated poetic text, *El sueño.*

As an intellectual and metaphysical poem, *El sueño* confers upon time an active role as a structuring force in the realization of Sor Juana's poetic idea. What is so distinctive about this poem is that it exemplifies an inherently temporal work that is at times arrested by a fundamentally spatial conception of art. The tendency to spatialize in this baroque poem is not restricted to the form and content. It also pervades the temporal aspect of the composition, thereby contributing to the creation of an illimitable poematic space whose temporal ambiguity suggests at once the concurrence of distinct spatiotemporal realities, and their harmonious fusion into the concept of a universal time and space.

For just as the soul aspires to possess knowledge of the cosmos in its complexity and entirety, the author of *El sueño* ambitiously endeavors to encompass within her composition the totality and the multidimensionality of these two abstract categories, time and space. Critical to our comprehension of the spatialization of time in this composition is a careful scrutiny of Sor Juana's characteristic methods of indicating time and its passing, as these methods will reveal the manner in which she perceived time and hence the manner in which she wished her readers to perceive it.

More often and more effectively, Sor Juana uses the natural situation to identify a moment or measure duration. In *El sueño* the notion of a regulated universal time is repeatedly conveyed. As in her ordering of sense experience Sor Juana retains the spatial structure of phenomenological reality, so in her treatment of subjective experience she retains always the sense of an objective measurable time to which it can be related. These are invaluable sources of the clarity and rigor with which she attempts to order her experiences, microcosmic echoes of a more vast, universal system of continuity and consistency.

Yet the notion of time that informs and conditions the verses of *El sueño,* and serves to support the entire poetic mechanism is the intimate, imperceptible clock of human subjectivity. As the predominant temporal rhythm at work within the poem, this inner, interior time is the means by which the poet leaves behind the realm of strict, linear chronology of human events, and journeys into the shadowy terrain of psychic experiences and ontological reveries. It is here, in the space of unrestricted flights of imaginative fancy, that Sor Juana succeeds in transcending time and utilizing it as a means of scrutinizing subjective experience.

For Sor Juana the time-space arrangement includes the mind and its many moods. Human time is the quintessence of time, and the only time that ultimately bears any consequence upon being. Not only is it important that the reader acknowledges that human consciousness is an integral component of space-time, but also that this matter be transposed from a philosophical matter to a poetic act. It is not merely that human observation is at times modified or distorted by nervous and emotional sensibility; the human mind has a tendency to remember and count.

There is no real counterpoint of cyclic and progressive patterns in *El sueño.* Sor Juana's journey is only the semblance of a journey, for her course is fundamentally circular, a poetic expression of the myth of the *eterno retorno.* The poem suggests an essential optimism with regard to the continuity of life, for example, in the ultimate triumph of Day over Night in the final verses of the poem, and presents the notion of time as a fundamentally synchronic, spatial phenomenon. This poetry forms a natural bridge between the human and the cosmic travelers. There is no progression. Sor Juana takes refuge in the planetary motion, conjuring up a spurious sense of invulnerability in the repeated alteration of seasons and star systems. The human mind, however, remembers and counts and does not confuse similarity with sameness; and although this day may be exactly like a certain day many years ago, it is not the same day. The soul's flight to the heights may be reminiscent of other attempts to scale the heavens, yet it is a singularly and unequivocably unique experience.

The opposition of successive temporal phases that comprises a substantial portion of the text of *El sueño* is essentially symbolic of a moral duality in which the forces of evil struggle to wrest power and control from the positive forces of the celestial sphere, the latter of which ultimately triumph. The sun is the time reference, fixing the poematic moment not as an entry in a diary or a date in a biography, rather as a means to fully represent the anagnorisis and self-knowing of which that moment is an essential element. Night, on the other hand, is the mythological daughter of chaos, and thereby symbolizes the realm of disorder and disruption that temporarily displaces the reality of regular, linear time. As a result of her traditional association with the material realm, she is symbolic of original sin whose consequences impede the evolution and ultimate perfection of the human individual. In Sor Juana's poem, Night assumes the form of a shadowy emanation of the black vapors ("negros vapores") that are given off by the processes of corruption and decay that characterize the state of entropy reigning in the terrestrial sphere.

Day, on the other hand, and by extension light, is the dualistic opposite of Night, and as such is symbolic of the creative force, and of cosmic energy, because of its emanation from the sun. In the dualism of light/darkness, it is the manifestation of morality and order, of virtue and of the intellect. Light is characteristically equated with the spirit, and its magnificence and superiority are immediately recognizable by its luminous intensity. Symbolically, illumination is associated with the East and Dawn, or the hour of the rising sun. Psychologically speaking, as well as in mystic terms, to become "illuminated" or "enlightened" is to become aware of a source of a Higher Light, and consequently, of a superior spiritual strength.

There is within the individual being, just as there exists on all levels of the cosmos, this dialectical and symbolic tension between the light and the darkness: the successive triumph and defeat of reason and passion, intellect and imagination, manifested in the alternation in each of us between the diurnal man, governed by reason, and the nocturnal self, characterized by free and unrestricted flights of imaginative fancy.

The poetic recreation in *El sueño* of the two entities of Darkness and Light not only serves to advance the notion of such dichotomies as existence/essence, irrational/rational, feminine/ masculine, but also to amplify the composition's essentially spatial form, as they necessarily implicate spatial vision on the part of the reader who contemplates Sor Juana's poematic universe. These immensities are evoked not merely as particular spaces within the Cosmos, but more importantly, for the sake of their unities. For night and day are but singular, circumstantial moments of darkness and brightness, death and rebirth. The union of these opposing cosmic forces, by means of the poetic word signifies the momentary, motionless crystallization of both the particular and the universal.

Time in *El sueño* is best conceived as a progressive image, a process of transfiguration and of mythical evolution, from negative to positive, from darkness to light, from ignorance to enlightenment, all of which can be traced in the gradated presentation of ascendent images, at once particular and timeless. The winged creatures that appear in the initial verses of the poem—the bats, or daughters of Minyas, and the owls in the mythological figures of Nyctimene and Ascalaphus—all contribute to the creation of a song of silence which is properly Night's dirge:

> solos la no cañora
> componían capilla pavorosa,
> máximas, negras, longas entonando,
> y pausas más que voces, esperando
> a la torpe mensura perezosa

de mayor proporción tal vez, que el viento
con flemático echaba movimiento,
de tan tardo compás, tan detenido,
que en medio se quedó tal vez dormido.
Este, pues, triste són intercadente
de la asombrada turba temerosa,
menos a la atención solicitaba
que al sueño persuadía;
antes sí, lentamente,
su obtusa consonancia espaciosa.

In the language of hermeticism, night, and therefore darkness, has traditionally been associated with the mystic state of Nothingness or Selflessness, and as such signifies a path leading back to the profound mystery of the Origin. San Juan de la Cruz's mystic poetry, for example, is perhaps best symbolized by the night, with its suspension of temporal and material reality which enables the soul to gaze upon and enter into communion with the Divine. Such symbolism seems to set the tone for *El sueño* as Sor Juana's protagonistic soul, freed temporarily from the corporal chains—temporal, spatial—which characteristically bind it, embarks upon an ascent to the highest of intellectual heights in the middle of a night that is, in essence, many nights, in a world in which mobility is made simultaneously immobile. For Sor Juana's view of time in relation to poetry is very similar to that of Gaston Bachelard: "It is in the vertical time of an immobilized moment that poetry finds its specific dynamism." For the poetic imagination at work within *El sueño* is based upon the concept of time not as a social construct of horizontality, but rather, as a fundamentally human, interior time whose vertical axis provides a means of evasion from the realm of material reality into the diaphanous sphere of poetic thought and form.

True to the principle of spatiality as delineated and elucidated by Joseph Frank, time assumes a subservient role in the conception and artistic elaboration of the literary compositions that are fundamentally spatial in form, in that there is a consequential diminution of the temporal aspect inherently characteristic of the literary work. In *El sueño,* although time never fully loses its fundamentally diachronic character, it does acquire a resonant mythical dimension, most evident on the formal level in the structuring of the work upon natural processes or physical/physiological states that are successive and thus cyclic: night and day, sleeping and waking. The recurrence of those images of natural and material phenomena that are cyclical in nature similarly heightens the notion of a repetitive time that transcends the finite temporality of the poetic discourse: the successive phases of the moon (". . . la Diosa / que tres veces hermosa / con tres hermosos rostros ser ostenta," vv. 13-15); the heart as a human clock ("reloj humano . . . de su bien regulado movimiento," vv. 205, 209); the action of breathing in and out sustained by the body even during sleep:

> —pulmón, que imán del viento es atractivo,
> que en movimientos nunca desiguales
> o comprimiendo ya, o ya dilatando
> el musculoso, claro arcaduz blando,

hace que en él resuelle
el que lo circunscribe fresco ambiente
que impele ya caliente,
y él venga su expulsión haciendo activo
pequeños robos al calor nativo,
algún tiempo llorados,
nunca recuperados,
si ahora no sentidos de su dueño,
que repetido, no hay robo pequeño—;
éstos, pues, de mayor, como ya digo,
excepción, uno y otro fiel testigo,
la vida aseguraban,

The symbolic crown, whose circular shape is first evoked
to suggest the never-ending responsibilities and duties of
a prudent and diligent monarch

. . . misteriosa,
circular, denotando, la corona,
en círculo dorado,
que el afán es no menos continuado.

is suggested by the description, in the closing verses, of
the full circle of the sun's apparent movement, a movement traced "in gold on sapphire blue":

Llegó, en efecto, el sol cerrando el giro
que esculpió de oro sobre azul zafiro:

The cyclical nature of all life processes is further intimated in the allusion to the myth of Persephone. As
Montross indicates,

> The myth of Persephone (the daughter of Jupiter, goddess
> of agriculture and queen of the underworld and therefore,
> "triforme") provides an explanation for the seasons, the
> cycle of life and death of the plants, that, in turn, suggests
> the cycle of life, death, and rebirth of man [Constance
> M. Montross, *Virtue or Vice? Sor Juana's Use of
> Thomistic Thought,* 1981].

Throughout the poem time is segmented and structured
into non-sequential relationships and surprising juxtapositions so as to give the impression of pictorial simultaneity in space, and to repeatedly distract the reader from
the progressive temporal linearity inherent in the literary
text. The processes of simultaneity and self-reflexiveness
at work within this intrinsically mobile apparatus engender a series of interrelated correspondences totally independent of any temporal/causal sequence, as can be
observed, for example, in the fusion of distinct spatiotemporal realities—the mountain Olympus, the magnificent
Egyptian pyramids, the Tower of Babel, etc.—in the
lengthy passage devoted to the pyramids and in the
verses that depict the soul's ignorance concerning natural processes, such as the flow of the river and the
attributes of the rose. By having to continually apprehend the poem's images and symbols by means of single, instanteous effort, the reader is forced to mentally
and visually map out the entire system of references and
internal relations suggested in the poem in order to fully
comprehend the ultimate significance of *El sueño.* Con-

sequently, the successful apprehension of the poem's
images and symbols is achieved only by means of this
reflexive act in a particular instant in time.

As a literary art form, poetry by its very nature implies
progressive movement and development in time and across
the page of a composition. However, the linear temporal
development of the poetic act in *El Sueño* is subordinated
to a predominantly spatial form with which Sor Juana
constructs this work with its emphasis on the visual aspect. The coordinates of her art are principally physical,
geometric, spatial forms and their interrelationships. Here
space and psychic time function not only as organizational principles, but also contribute to the overall aesthetic
effect of time as an image of space. Through the system
of interreferences by which allusions are made simultaneously to past, present and future, through the coincident presentation of mythological, physiological and fantastic phenomena, through the harmonious and poetic
fusion of diachronic and synchronic aspects of time operative on all levels of reality, Sor Juana succeeds in
transcending time. We, the reader, like the protagonistic
soul, are suspended temporarily in a moment in time due
to the spatialization of form, content and time in the poetic
construct.

Lisa Rabin   (essay date 1995)

SOURCE: "The *Blasón* of Sor Juana Inés de la Cruz:
Politics and Petrarchism in Colonial Mexico," in *Bulletin of Hispanic Studies,* Vol. LXXII, No. 1, January, 1995,
pp. 28-39.

[*In the following essay, Rabin discusses the literary and
political implications of Cruz's use of the* blasón *in her
poetry.*]

The frontispiece of the *Fama y obras pósthumas* (1700),
one of Sor Juana Inés de la Cruz's first published collections of verse, proclaims her Petrarchan poetry as the
vehicle of eloquence in a foreign land. The official pillars
of empire, the *plus ultra* of Castile and Aragon, have
been converted into a knight of 'Europa' and an Indian of
'América' to embrace the primitive regions of Mexico. And
written on the cornices of the *plus ultra* is a revealing
invitation to Sor Juana's readers: *Mulierem forte(m) q(u)is
inveniet / Procul et de ultimis finib(us)?* Or, 'Who will
discover a courageous woman / at the farthest extremes
of the earth?' According to her Spanish editors, Sor Juana is heroic to be writing poetry (and promoting civilization) in the far-flung reaches of the Empire.

Yet it is Sor Juana's Petrarchan poetry that makes her
truly noble. First, the poet's image is surrounded by laurel, the quintessential symbol of Petrarchan fame. And
below the poet's picture, the mountains of her native
village Nepantla (the volcano Popocatépetl and the snow-
capped mountain Ixtaccíhuatl) are inscribed with the epigraphs 'unde lix ardet' and 'unde nix lucet'—which are
reminiscent of Petrarch's 'icy fire', the paradox of unre-

quited love. Clearly, Sor Juana's Petrarchan poetry is the means through which a remote, uncivilized Mexico can receive European traditions—and become, in other words, a true extension of the Empire.

The frontispiece of the *Fama* is an example of what Stephen Greenblatt has called 'linguistic colonialism'—or the promulgation of eloquence and poetry as a form of cultural imperialism. The *Fama* editors' focus on Petrarchism as a valuable instrument of the Empire reflects its importance in the development of a Spanish imperial identity in the Renaissance. The rejuvenation of poetic forms in Peninsular poetry, and the ushering in of Petrarchism in Spain, accompanied the political expansion of the Spanish crown in America. The Renaissance Spanish *courtier* often had two roles—that of a soldier, politician or cleric, and that of a Petrarchan poet. Military officers like Garcilaso de la Vega (and even Hernán Cortés) were also poets. Members of court society or the Church, like Quevedo and Sor Juana, were well known for their lyric verse.

On the frontispiece of the *Fama,* although Sor Juana wears a nun's habit and Mexico is her obvious home, she is most strongly identified as a European Petrarchan poet. This is a representation that presents her creole identity as a mere appendage of Spanish culture, and overlooks her roles as a woman poet and nun in the colonial milieu. The *Fama* editors are impartial on one account—Sor Juana did write a large amount of Petrarchan poetry. Yet this poetry suggests an extraordinary problem: how can a colonial woman poet and nun unambiguously adopt a European, male and secular form of lyric verse?

The facile translation of European metaphor into an American setting on the frontispiece is a much more complex endeavour in Sor Juana's poetry itself. One of Petrarch's major contributions to the western lyric was to stylize an individual voice in vernacular poetry through the musicality of his verse and a classical register of tropes. Throughout his famous lyric collection the *Rime sparse* (1372), Petrarch cultivates a myth of Rome—from his political poems that yearn for Italy's epic past to his use of Ovid's *Metamorphoses* to represent the transformations of the poet in love. Sor Juana's poetry abounds with Petrarchan convention. Yet instead of reflecting the classical world, many are reflective of her own perspective: the laurel is exchanged for a walnut tree in *romance* 23; the beloved's form is described like a banana plant in *romance* 61. These metaphors are a puzzle, because they are at once both European and American. Seventeenth-century Mexico was very far from ancient Rome, both temporally and geographically. How, then, should we interpret Sor Juana's Petrarchan tropes? By emulating Petrarch, does Sor Juana—like the *Fama* editors—see Mexico as the extension of Rome and imperial Spain? Or is Mexico indeed a 'new Rome', as Balbuena intimated, a new empire of flora, fauna and exotic metaphors?

The question of Sor Juana's Petrarchism becomes even more compelling when we consider Sor Juana's unique relationship to her female beloved. Petrarch wrote poetry to a silent beloved, who was largely a figment of his imagination. Sor Juana's lyric, however, is often directed towards her patrons the Mexican vicereines—Laura, or the Marquesa de Mancera, Lísida, or the Condesa de Paredes, and Elvira, or the Condesa de Galve. Sor Juana's relationship with her female patrons in the court was friendly and political: the vicereine supported her intellectual skills and served as a protector of the poet's autonomy in the convent. Sor Juana's posture towards her patron is thus clearly very different from Petrarch's towards Laura, even though both poets employ the same literary devices to express praise. Sor Juana's beloved is the object not of the poet's desire but of her identification and self-promotion. In Sor Juana, Petrarchan strategies of desire become political strategies.

This adds an interesting slant to the question of Sor Juana's infusion of classical rhetoric with American tropes. On the one hand, since the vicereine is a surrogate of the Empire, Sor Juana's praise of her can be seen as legitimizing its system. But since Petrarchan love characterizes the self as well as the beloved, Sor Juana's praise of the Mexican vicereine is also a way of legitimizing her American situation. Thus, just as Sor Juana's Petrarchan poetry affirms her devotion to the colonial infrastructure, so it also expresses the poet's own conception of Mexico. When Sor Juana describes Lísida's stature as a banana plant, then, we are presented with the vicereine's embodiment of a creole sensibility.

The description of the vicereine's form as a banana plant is perhaps an odd metaphor, yet the poem itself belongs to a popular Renaissance convention—that is, the Petrarchan *blasón,* or the metaphorical description of the woman as a series of parts. The *blasón,* which was derived from medieval heraldry, was first used in the Renaissance epic, and became codified in the lyric with Petrarch's *Rime sparse.* Although we never get a complete picture of Petrarch's Laura, we recognize her teeth as pearls, her hair as gold knots, and her lips as red as coral. Because Petrarch's desire for his lady is never fulfilled, her whole body is never described.

In Golden-Age Spanish texts, the desire for an unattainable beloved is often coupled with aspirations of empire. Columbus, for example, describes the western hemisphere as a woman's breast; in Quevedo, the lady's eyes and hair are rubies and gold to be won in the Indies. In light of these texts, Sor Juana's *blasón* of her patron Lísida seems a parody of the Petrarchan eroticization of America: a banana plant could not be either a more phallic or utilitarian metaphor. In another *blasón* in poem 80, Sor Juana constructs the body of her patron Elvira as a series of triumphalist heroes, depicting the Mexican vicereine as an authority more powerful in her totality than each of her European parts. Sor Juana's *blasones* of her patrons are political 'bodies' of New Spain, where America is not the silent object of European fantasies, but the creole author of its own eclectic image.

Before I undertake a close analysis of Sor Juana's poems, it is important to examine further the *blasones* of her precursors in Spain. Columbus and Quevedo's projection of male fantasies of the New World in the body of the woman is a frequent convention in texts of the discovery and conquest. As Margarita Zamora points out [in her *Reading Columbus,* 1993], Jan van der Straet's 1575 drawing of an encounter between 'America', or a naked Indian woman, and 'Europe', or a clothed, white male, characterizes a long-standing discourse: America is already gendered when the first conqueror arrives. Yet the Golden-Age *blasón* is an even more complex version of this phenomenon. To understand this, we must look to its origins in heraldry and Petrarch.

The French *blason* and English *blazon* first meant the depiction of coats of arms upon shields. By 1250 *blazon* meant a verbal description of arms. By the sixteenth century, the word *blasón* in various European languages meant 'a description' in general, and the *blason* in French came to be known as a poem of praise or blame through description. The literary device of the *blasón,* then, represents the achievement, or authority, of the poet in the Petrarchan tradition. In Columbus and Quevedo, the *blasón* marks both literary authority and historical achievement, as the beautiful parts of the lady symbolize resources of the Spanish Empire in the New World. These authors create a verbal *blazon* or shield of Spain in the image of the woman's body, substituting the conventional terms of the heraldic emblem for poetic commonplaces.

The shift from poetic to imperial authority in the Golden-Age *blasón* is not only facilitated by the device's heraldic origins. A rhetoric of quest and domination is embedded within the language of the *blasón* itself. Let us first look to a famous poem of Petrarch's, poem 90 from the *Rime*:

> Erano i capei d'oro a l'aura sparsi
> che 'n mille dolci nodi gli avolgea,
> e 'l vago lume oltra misura ardea
> di quei begli occhi, ch' or ne son sì scarsi;
>
> e 'l viso di pietosi color farsi
> (non se vero o falso) mi parea:
> i' che l'esca amorosa al petto avea,
> qual meraviglia se di subito arsi?

Here, the spark of the lady's features causes the poet's desire to catch fire. This desire is both sexual and creative: Laura so arouses Petrarch that her body parts become poetic language. Indeed, his beloved must always remain a *blasón*—or permanently unattainable—for Petrarch to write beautiful poetry.

Yet the perpetual deferral of Petrarch's *blasón* is not only creative, it is also destructive. The lady's fiery gaze is a threat to Petrarch, invoking the sexual taboo: his own desire for her may consume him. In order not to be destroyed, he destroys her first, fragmenting her into innocuous parts. Echoing its origins in heraldry, the *blasón* thus becomes an emblem of Petrarch's authority over Laura, an instrument of gender domination in his text. In the same way, the Spanish *blasón* of the New World

represents the attempt to possess what is unknown by reducing it into a series of manageable parts.

Let us look now to several Golden-Age *blasones.* In his third voyage, Columbus compares the Western hemisphere to a woman's breast:

> . . . falle que (el mundo) no era redondo en la forma que escriben, salvo que es de la forma de una pera que sea toda muy redonda, salvo allí donde tiene el pezón, que allí tiene más alto, o como quien tiene una pelota muy redonda y en un lugar de ella fuese como una teta de mujer allí puesta, y que esta parte de este pezón sea la más alta e más propinca al cielo. . . . Yo no tomo que el Paraíso Terrenal sea en forma de montaña áspera como el escribir de ellos nos amuestra, salvo que él sea en el colmo allí donde dije la figura del pezón de la pera . . .

In this passage, Columbus' 'discovery' of Paradise is imagined in the highly eroticized fragment of the woman's body. In Columbus, the Petrarchan lady's sensuality is the site of utopian ideals.

Columbus' use of the *blasón* in a utopian fantasy is also found in a poem by Góngora. Here, the lady's eyes are given power over Spain and its overseas empire: 'Divinos ojos, que en su dulce Oriente / dan luz al mundo quitan luz al cielo / y espera idolatrallos Occidente'. In Góngora's poem, the lady's eyes are suns that rise and set in the East, or in Europe; while in the West, or America, the gentiles will worship them. The *blasón*'s image of the woman's influence across the seas again refers to a new, utopian world.

To return to Columbus, the 'pera' is a metaphor not only of sexual conquest and utopia, but also of material gain. The allure and sensuality of the Petrarchan beloved is thus an allegory for a New World rich with exotic substances. This continues in Quevedo, whose *blasón* describes the woman's attributes as material treasures in the Indies:

> En breve cárcel traigo aprisionado,
> Con toda su familia de oro ardiente,
> El cerco de la luz resplandiente,
> Y grande imperio del Amor cerrado.
> [. . .]
> Traigo todas las Indias en mi mano,
> Perlas que en un diamante por rubíes
> Pronuncian con desdén sonoro hielo, . . .

In Quevedo's depiction of a ring that carries the woman's portrait, the lady's physical attributes have been displaced by the material wealth of the Indies. Quevedo's poem cleverly uses the 'grande imperio del Amor'—or the Petrarchan *blasón*—to imagine a lucrative 'imperio' in America.

In Petrarch, the lady's body is the poet's projection of his own identity. Columbus, Góngora, and Quevedo similarly use the *blasón* to construct the New World as a projection of the Old: The New World is the Paradise of a woman's breast, the gentiles of America will begin to worship Christ as the beloved's eyes are so worshipped, the Spaniards will be rich in treasures as they are rich in poetic devices to describe the woman. For these European poets, the mystery of America is simplified in an erotic fantasy. Here, like Petrarch's Laura, the New World is the silent receptor of identity.

Yet in the *blasón* of Sor Juana Inés de la Cruz, the New World is a speaking creole subject, continually questioning of its Spanish design. Sor Juana's *blasón* of her political patron, the Mexican vicereine, is the colonial poet's representation of the political body of New Spain. This strategy highlights Mexico's authority not merely as an appendage of the Empire, but as a new manifestation of the Empire itself.

In *romance* 61, for example, Sor Juana writes a *blasón* of Lísida, or the Condesa de Paredes. In the second stanza, the poet says,

> Cárceles tu madeja fabrica:
> Dédalo que sutilmente forma
> vínculos de dorados Ofires,
> Tíbares de prisiones gustosas.

In this poem, Lísida is the incarnation of Mexico's treasures. First, her hair is a labyrinth of golden knots, creating 'prisiones gustosas' of gold stones ('Ofires' and 'Tibares'). This gold (especially as it is described in exotic metaphors) reminds us of the wealth desired by the crown in the conquest of the New World. Yet while Quevedo uses the *blasón* to represent the Spanish desire for New World riches, Sor Juana's *blasón* imagines such riches as the Mexican vicereine's political authority— and, correspondingly, as Mexico's own legitimacy. If Lísida is gold, then by extension, Mexico has political and economic prestige.

In other stanzas, Sor Juana's poetic corpus of Lísida includes thoroughly New World parts. As I have related, the vicereine's figure is described as a banana plant:

> Plátano tu gentil estatura,
> flámula es, que a los aires tremola:
> ágiles movimientos, que esparcen
> bálsamo de fragrantes aromas.

Here, because Lísida's 'estatura' is her eminence as well as her form, Sor Juana's image of the vicereine as a banana plant implies that she literally 'shades' or influences Mexico with her stature. Although the plantain was a fruit imported to Mexico, by Sor Juana's time it had become thoroughly Americanized. The banana tree is thus a profound metaphor for Lísida, who herself, according to Sor Juana, has also become Americanized. Thus, while in Golden-Age texts America is imagined as the conventional attributes of the Petrarchan lady, in Sor Juana this lady's body—or European poetry—has been obliged to adapt to an American paradigm.

In another stanza in poem 61, Sor Juana describes the vicereine's physique as so unique, she can only be de-

scribed as modelled after herself ('tu talle / . . . / émula su labor de sí propia'). Her shape, indeed, far surpasses traditional doric columns and ionic pillars ('dóricas esculturas asombra: / jónicos lineamientos desprecia'). These structures are metonymic figures for the lady's form in conventional Petrarchan poetry. Furthermore, they are also reminiscent of the *plus ultra,* the famous symbol of the Castilian and Aragonese Empire. Thus, just as Sor Juana's patron transcends the Petrarchan lady, so does colonial Mexico—a model only for itself—surpass the imperial Spanish paradigm.

Another fine example of Sor Juana's political *blasón* occurs in *seguidilla* 80, which praises the Condesa de Galve. Here, Elvira's body is a series of triumphalist heroes:

> Con los Héroes Elvira
> mi amor retrata,
> para que la pintura
> valiente salga.
>
> Ulises es su pelo,
> con Alejandro:
> porque es sutil el uno,
> y el otro largo.
>
> Un Colón es su frente
> por dilatada,
> porque es quien su Imperio
> más adelanta.
>
> A Cortés y Pizarro
> tiene en las cejas,
> porque son sus divisas
> medias Esferas.

Sor Juana's ingeniousness in this *blasón* centres on the question of Elvira's 'Imperio'. Is the Condesa de Galve's Empire (or her body) an allegory for Spain's New World possessions? This would make Sor Juana's poem the consummate Golden-Age fantasy, the literal fulfilment of epic deeds in a Petrarchan lady.

Yet Elvira is explicitly not an erotic body in this poem. Right from the beginning, Sor Juana states that she desires her portrait of Elvira to appear 'valiente'. The poet thus wants to reflect her patron's epic stature, as opposed to making the Condesa de Galve the object of sexual fantasies. Indeed, Sor Juana makes clear that she will not describe the vicereine's sensual parts: the poet cannot find an appropriate hero for the lady's mouth ('no encuentro / con alguno que tenga / tan buen aliento'), and she cannot describe her feet ('nunca a un Valiente / [los pies] le sirven'). In this poem, Sor Juana cleverly keeps herself from describing the mouth and feet, or fetishistic images of the woman, because they would identify Elvira's sexuality—which is incompatible with her epic stature.

Elvira, like Lísida in poem 61, is a political, not an erotic body. The vicereine is the culmination of a triumphalist history—the latest in a long line of epic figures, a protagonist as equally viable as classical and Spanish heroes. Elvira is Sor Juana's image of colonial Mexico, taking its place among the great empires of the past. Sor Juana imagines Mexico as a series of influences: classical, in Ulysses and Alexander here, and in Caesar, Hannibal, and Hercules elsewhere in the poem; and Spanish, in Columbus, Cortés and Pizarro. Yet as the assembly of great imperial heroes, Elvira is more powerful than each that has preceded her, just as Mexico, according to Sor Juana, has surpassed the empires before it.

. . . . .

The *blasones* of Elvira and Lísida, the Mexican vicereines, are a challenge to Spanish imperial models of the New World. In Sor Juana, Mexico is no mere 'extremity' of Spain, as the **Fama** editors describe it. Instead, Sor Juana's images of her patrons praise Mexico as an empire unto itself, a creole domain that capitalizes on European and native triumphalist histories and merges European metaphors for the state with new and indigenous Mexican ones.

At the most basic level, moreover, Sor Juana's *blasones* are startlingly different from conventional Petrarchan representations of the beloved. Lísida and Elvira (who after all, are real women) appear as sound and intact bodies, organic realms that seem to consolidate the scattered parts of the Petrarchan lady. As such, Sor Juana's *blasones* are a meaningful reinterpretation of Petrarchism. Sor Juana, a colonial poet so very far from classical Rome, cannot satisfactorily depend on the ruins of a European past to define an American present. In Sor Juana, Mexico is not the scattered fragments of European metaphor and history, but the unification of these elements and indigenous ones in the image of a creole state. Sor Juana's gathering of metaphors in Lísida and Elvira is Utopia reconstructed as a political body, a cue to the creole world to imagine its own fantasies of the future.

Georgina Sabat de Rivers   (essay date 1995)

SOURCE: "Love in Some of Sor Juana's Sonnets," in *Colonial Latin American Review,* Vol. 4, No. 2, 1995, pp. 101-23.

[*In the following essay, Sabat de Rivers explores the defining characteristics of Cruz's love sonnets.*]

The love sonnets of Sor Juana Inés de la Cruz belong to the long and varied tradition of love poetry in the Western World, which goes back at least to Greek literature, when the militant, masculine poetry of Homer gave way to the feminine sensibility of Sappho. As the first great love poet of Greece, she developed a voice that was totally different from that of Homer, a voice that was personal and introspective, focused on intimate emotions, whether pleasant or unpleasant, even at times anguished and associated with pathological symptoms. In her poetry woman occupies the center of the stage and cultivates the typically West-

ern individual personality, subtly analyzing a great variety of affective states. Anacreon, another archetypal but masculine love poet in Greece, was entirely different, singing the pleasures of wine, sex, and music.

Catullus, the first great love poet to write in Latin, renewed the Sapphic tradition, synthesizing emotional conflicts in his epigrams, such as this one, for example: "Odi et amo . . . ," "I hate and I love. Perhaps you ask me why: / I don't know, but I feel it, and it keeps me in agony". This typical epigram, anticipating some of Sor Juana's sonnets, consists of a single elegiac distich, that is, of a metrically asymmetric pair of lines, the first being an hexameter and the second a pentameter. The elegy, or lament, written in a series of such distichs, was the best-known genre of love poetry in Latin; besides Catullus, love elegies were written by Propertius, Tibullus, Ovid, Ausonius, and other poets. In elegiac distichs Ovid wrote a whole series of poems that were well-known during the Middle Ages and the Renaissance; among them are the *Heroides*—the laments of women betrayed by their lovers—, the *Ars amatoria* or art of love, and the *Remedia amoris* or remedies for love.

With the rebirth of vernacular poetry in the Christian Middle Ages, especially in twelfth-century France, there developed another historic dichotomy between epic poetry, or *chansons de geste,* recited orally by men and for men, especially warriors, and the songs of the troubadours, which we now call courtly love poetry, written and sung by men for great ladies and lords in the Provençal courts. This poetry, although still influenced by the Ovidian tradition, marks the foundation of a new concept and code of aristocratic love; according to this code, which was highly conventional and stylized, the masculine lover, generally imagined as an unmarried youth without great power of his own, was supposed to exalt and adore an unnamed married lady, the Provençal *dons,* who during the absences of her husband was the all-powerful mistress of court and castle, and was endowed by the poet with supreme physical beauty and insuperable moral virtues. This self-abasing and passionate literary devotion imposed upon the poet-lover a feudal discipline that supposedly ennobled him; he learned to delight in the suffering caused by the unbridgeable distance between himself and his lady. According to the code, it was the frustration of desire that lay at the root of the poet's song. In addition to Ovidian and feudal influences, there are obvious religious parallels between courtly love and the glorification of the crucified Christ's humble suffering (*gloria crucis et passionis*), as well as the Gothic cult of the Virgin Mary, the source of all beauty and divine grace. From the south of France, the troubadours traveled from court to court, taking with them to Germany, England, Portugal, Catalonia, Italy and even Sicily their songs of courtly love; in this way, the vernaculars of each region gradually adopted this poetic code and formed local schools of love poetry.

It was in the Sicilian school that a court notary, Giacomo da Lentino, invented in the thirteenth century a new "little song", or "sonetto", fourteen lines long, divided into an octet and a sestet with different rhymes: this was the birth of the love sonnet, an invention that soon achieved success in northern Italy with Dante's youthful sonnets addressed to Beatrice. Then, in the fourteenth century, Petrarch spent part of his long life creating and perfecting his own *canzoniere* devoted to Laura. This collection of songs and sonnets is an artistic combination of poems in which the poet expresses and analyzes minutely each state of mind and each stage in the story of his passionate spiritual development. Petrarch's *canzoniere* became the most influential body of love poetry during the vernacular Renaissance; Petrarchism became in the sixteenth century an important literary movement, not only in Italy but also in Spain and the other countries of Europe.

The first Spanish sonnets, which are probably the first sonnets written outside of Italy, belong to the fifteenth century, when at long last there had developed in Castile a school of courtly love; the Marquis of Santillana (1398-1458) translated and imitated in Spanish some of the more spiritual love sonnets by Dante and Petrarch. But Santillana's sonnets were not widely circulated. The history of the Spanish sonnet begins in effect with the publication, in 1543, of the poetry written by Juan de Boscán and by Garcilaso de la Vega; the triumph of the Spanish hendecasyllabic line, which is the iambic pentameter, brought with it the sonnet, which immediately achieved a prestige that it has maintained until the present throughout the Hispanic world.

The Spanish love sonnet began as a close imitation of its Italian and Petrarchan models in rhyme-schemes and structure, syntactic, semantic, and thematic; for two centuries the Spanish and the Italian sonnet developed side by side, influencing one another mutually. The basic argument of the love sonnet combines the conventions of courtly love with Classical and mythological motifs, but the themes vary widely, from those of religious spiritualism and of refined human love to the grossest pornographic parodies. In his commentaries on Garcilaso's sonnets Fernando de Herrera established the relation between the witty concision of the sonnet and that of the Latin epigram. Baroque poets, with their characteristic wit, further complicated the paradoxical, antithetical, and contradictory aspects of previous Spanish poetry; Sor Juana participates fully in this tendency.

Petrarch's *Canzoniere* or *Rime sparse*, consisting principally of sonnets and *canzoni*, is arranged to form a poetic chronology based on a love for a real woman (Laura), which was a more or less imaginary experience; it is divided into two sections, "in vita" and "in morte", before and after Laura's death. Boscán's *cancionero*, made up of ten *canciones* and 92 sonnets, clearly imitates Petrarch's collection in its binary chronological structure, but the division is quite original: there is an abrupt transition from a traditional courtly love affair, filled with sinful erotic anguish, to a chaste love within matrimonial bliss. Garcilaso's approximately thirty love sonnets, on the other hand, are not integrated with his five *canciones*, nor do they form a coherent whole; they are individual sonnets, more or less Petrarchan in tone, and frequently mythologically pictorial. Toward the end of the sixteenth century Fernando de Herrera constructed a *cancionero* following closely the Petrarchan model, but Garcilaso's loose sequence of individual sonnets was the model that predominated in Spain and her colonies.

Sor Juana, in the history of Hispanic poetry, was clearly the last great poet in the tradition that had begun in Spanish with Boscán and Garcilaso and that came to an end with her death on this side of the Atlantic Ocean, in New Spain, as Mexico was then known. Although she was well acquainted with the Petrarchan tradition, reflected in her poetry, her love sonnets do not form a *canzoniere*. We may group her sonnets by the persons to whom they are addressed, but when we consider her sonnets as a whole, we find that they are addressed to many different persons, and although they do not constitute a love story, they do reflect her social and personal relations with a number of other people.

Sor Juana was thoroughly familiar with the sonnets written by the great poets of Europe, and by minor poets both in Spain and in the colonies. Her poetry echoes the traditions of New Spain; in her literary world she was the poet who commanded the widest range of previous poetry. She was of course conversant with the Renaissance practice of *imitatio*, which in her case was never servile. She adapted to her own purposes a wide range of models from different sources, addressing a public that ranged from the clerical writer, the aristocratic courtier, and the learned scientist to the more modest world of musicians and poets involved with cathedral carol sequences and street recitations. Her world of poetry was international, according to Eugenio de Salazar's *Epístola a Herrera*, ranging from the "mil riquezas" of Spain and "las lindezas" of Italy to the poetry of Provence and of Greece. In New Spain there had lived sonneteers from Seville, such as Gutierre de Cetina and Juan de la Cueva, local poets such as Francisco de Terrazas, Francisco Bramón, Miguel de Guevara, as well as others from Spain who had become fully adapted to the *criollo* world: Bernardo de Balbuena, Fernán González de Eslava, and the bishop of Puebla and viceroy Juan de Palafox y Mendoza. Later there were other Mexican-born sonneteers such as Catalina de Eslava (the author of a sole surviving sonnet on the death of her uncle), María de Estrada, and Sor Juana's contemporary Diego de Ribera. Such poets as Luis de Sandoval Zapata, for example, had written sonnets shortly before Sor Juana did. Thus we see that her local poetic environment, which directly influenced her sonnets, was a rich one. The diversity of themes, motifs, and voices which she appropriates as a poet give evidence of this whole literary world as transformed by a learned Mexican-born writer, conscious of her unique role as an intellectual woman. She tells us in her *Respuesta* that she could not help being a writer; she wrote many different sorts of sonnet, seeking recognition, within her convent and outside, of her right to be a writer.

Before beginning to analyze Sor Juana's sonnets, we should emphasize one of their most unusual aspects: the fact that the poetic self who speaks is in her case not masculine but feminine. The courtly love tradition, including Petrarch, had always been based on the premise of a poet-lover who was male and adored his lady. But Sor Juana inverts or varies this established norm, speaking in different voices: the poetic self is sometimes feminine and addresses a male beloved; it is sometimes masculine and tells his lady of his suffering; it is sometimes ambiguous, of unidentifiable gender; and occasionally, whether male or female, it simply reflects upon a love situation.

Turning now to the study of Sor Juana's love sonnets, we may note that she normally follows the tradition of posing a problem in the octet and, after the usual pause or transition, of resolving the problem in the sestet. But sometimes the posing of the problem continues into the tercets, as is frequent in Baroque sonnets, and the resolution or reversal comes only in the final lines. Taking into account the whole category of Sor Juana's love sonnets, a category that is not always easily defined, with their different semantic postures, we may divide them into two large groups: in the first (A) we find the traditional, orthodox concepts of courtly or Petrarchan love organized from the personal point of view of the poet-lover; in the second (B) heterodox group, we find a parodical or burlesque point of view, which is perhaps more characteristic of Sor Juana's Baroque art.

Group A. Orthodox Concepts of Love.

Within this group, two sonnets belong to a sub-group that we may call (1) "Mutual undying love" (numbers 169 and 183 in, **Obras completas** edited by Méndez Plancarte, 1951). Fabio, the vocative addressed by the poet's voice in number 169, is the poet's favorite masculine name, always applied to the ideal beloved. In sonnet 169 we find a process of logical reasoning that is typical of Sor Juana:

Enseña cómo un solo empleo en amar es razón y
   conveniencia.

> Fabio: en el ser de todos adoradas,
> son todas las beldades ambiciosas,
> porque tienen las aras por ociosas
> si no las ven de víctimas colmadas.
>
>   Y así, si de uno solo son amadas,
> viven de la Fortuna querellosas,
> porque piensan que más que ser hermosas
> constituye deidad el ser rogadas.
>
>   Mas yo soy en aquesto tan medida,
> que en viendo a muchos, mi atención zozobra,
> y sólo quiero ser correspondida
>
>   de aquél que de mi amor réditos cobra;
> porque es la sal del gusto el ser querida,
> que daña lo que falta y lo que sobra.

In this sonnet, the voice of a woman, as the feminine grammatical agreement indicates, addresses a man with the classical pronoun "tú." The poet in the octet describes what normally occurs: beautiful women want to be adored by many men, for to be a "deity" does not depend on a

woman's beauty in itself but on the number of her worshippers, of the sacrificial victims heaped on her altar. But in the sestet the poet declares that she is much more moderate ("medida") in her pretensions, because her attention cannot be focused on so many different objects, and she only wants to be loved by the one that "collects a return (*réditos*) from his investment," in other words, a man that she can repay with love. In the epigrammatic *sententia* of the last two lines, the poet sums up her attitude: love is like salt, the lack or the excess of which ruins the taste of a dish. The images of the octet belong to the exalted level of religious worship; those of the sestet bring us down to earth with the language of commerce and kitchen recipes.

Sonnet 183 is addressed to Celia, and the voice of the poet is presumably masculine, although in this case it is not confirmed by any grammatical agreement. This difficult sonnet is based on an elaborate simile, or allegory, involving scholastic modes of thought concerning the superiority of form to matter.

> Para explicar la causa a la rebeldía, ya sea firmeza de
> un cuidado, se vale de opinión que atribuye a la
> perfección de su forma lo incorruptible en la materia de
> los cielos; usa cuidadosamente términos de Escuelas.

> Probable opinión es que conservarse
> la forma celestial en su fijeza
> no es porque en la materia hay más firmeza
> sino por la manera de informarse,
>
>   porque aquel apetito de mudarse
> lo sacia de la forma la nobleza,
> con que, cesando el apetito, cesa
> la ocasión que tuvieran de apartarse.
>
>   Así tu amor, con vínculo terrible,
> el alma que te adora, Celia, informa;
> con que su corrupción es imposible,
>
>   ni educir otra con quien no conforma,
> no por ser la materia incorruptible
> mas por lo inamisible de la forma.

The octet provides a scholastic explanation for the incorruptibility of heavenly bodies; in the sestet the persistence of love, a "vínculo terrible" which cannot be broken, is presented in comparable terms, incorruptible not because of the appetite of matter, or the body, but because of the permanence of the form, or the soul. By implication, then, love is immortal, like the stars.

This sonnet by Sor Juana presents, in an oblique way, a defense of woman's intellectual rights. In other poems she overtly uses a masculine voice; but in this sonnet her voice does not declare explicitly whether it belongs to a male or to a female. She knew that scholastic philosophy in her world was the intellectual property of men, not women, and perhaps she did not want to challenge this openly; but her own feminine authorship of the sonnet was, of course, no secret.

Let us now read a sonnet (number 182) from another sub-group that we have called (2) "Rational love"; it was written by Sor Juana in reply to a sonnet by an admirer, and in it she uses the same rhymes that he had used. We can see from this exchange not only the high cultural level of social communication surrounding the famous poet-nun in the City of Mexico but also this society's delight in literary games, pure poetic fantasy and fiction. Sor Juana wrote other sonnets with predetermined rhymes; this sonnet is related to number 181, beginning **"Dices que no te acuerdas, Clori, y mientes."** It is obvious that the person who sent her his sonnet was a reader of her sonnets and that she knew him; this indicates that Sor Juana's poetic manuscripts circulated within a network of her readers, that they commented to one another on her poems, and that they even dared to intervene directly by sending her poems and requests, as in this case. Her responding sonnet that we shall now see is, of all her sonnets with predetermined rhymes, the only one that we can consider as belonging to our group of "orthodox" sonnets:

> Que respondió la Madre Juana en los mismos
>   consonantes.
>
>   No es sólo por antojo el haber *dado*
> en quererte, mi bien, pues no *pudiera*
> alguno que tus prendas *conociera*
> negarte que mereces ser *amado*.
>   Y si mi entendimiento *desdichado*
> tan incapaz de conocerte *fuera*,
> de tan grosero error aun no *pudiera*
> hallar disculpa en todo lo *ignorado*.
>   Aquella que te hubiere *conocido*,
> o te ha de amar o confesar los *males*
> que padece su ingenio en lo *entendido*,
>   juntando dos extremos *desiguales*;
> con que ha de confesar que eres *querido*,
> para no dar improporciones *tales*.

The reasoning of this sonnet—spoken by a feminine voice and addressed to a "tú", and belonging to the poet's own category of "rational love"—is based on the merits or graces observed in a person; that is, this is not a case of capricious love, the love "por antojo" of line 1. The reasoning is based on the words "conocer", "ingenio", and "entendimiento": the understanding must be capable of recognizing the good qualities of the person in order to love him; otherwise it would be a case of "improporciones" that would make us realize the lover's lack of reason. This is an example of Sor Juana's emphasis on the importance of one's mental capacities. As usual, there is a rational transition from octet to sestet, leading to the poet's conclusion.

In her *décimas* that begin **"Al amor, cualquier curioso"** (number 104), Sor Juana explains what she means by "rational love", which she contrasts with a love based on "amor imperioso," or pure emotions, deriving from the influence of a star or destiny. She tells us that the love that she calls rational is based on free choice and has different names, depending on the relationship between the persons:

> Y así, aunque no mude efectos,
> que muda nombres es llano:

al de objeto soberano
llaman amor racional,
y al de deudos, natural,
y si es amistad, urbano.

She goes on to say, in the same poem, that only a love based on choice deserves gratitude because it is based on understanding, that is a recognition of the virtues and graces of the beloved, which is quite different from the "imperious" love that forces itself upon us and does violence to our heart in an irrational way. Sor Juana concludes in the last two lines of these *décimas* that one can give one's whole heart only in rational love, a love based on the understanding, which reinforces its faith with logic and reason. We should recall that in Sor Juana's play *Los empeños de una casa,* Leonor's love is based on Carlos's merits, and that he is faithful despite appearances that might make him doubt Leonor's love: he is courteous, kind, and well-balanced, and their love is mutual.

We find similar ideas in poem number 99, beginning **"Dime, vencedor rapaz",** in which the understanding and the will struggle against "inclinación" and refuse to give in; or if the will does give in, reason resists. In poem number 5, **"Si el desamor o el enojo",** we also find the topic of love based on merits: "Si de tus méritos nace / esta pasión que me aflige, / ¿cómo el efecto podrá / cesar, si la causa existe?" (vv. 45-48); in number 100 (**"Cogióme sin prevención"**) these ideas are compared to the fall of Troy. Our sonnet apparently is opposed to the topic that we may call "to see is to love", or love at first sight, found in her poems dealing with courtly love.

Sub-group 3. The Power of Fantasy.

The sonnet that we will now read is one of Sor Juana's most famous (number 165), and justly so:

> Que contiene una fantasía contenta con amor
>   decente.
>
>   Detente, sombra de mi bien esquivo,
> imagen del hechizo que más quiero,
> bella ilusión por quien alegre muero,
> dulce ficción por quien penosa vivo.
>   Si al imán de tus gracias atractivo
> sirve mi pecho de obediente acero,
> ¿para qué me enamoras lisonjero
> si has de burlarme luego fugitivo?
>   Mas blasonar no puedes, satisfecho,
> de que triunfa de mí tu tiranía:
> que aunque dejas burlado el lazo estrecho
>   que tu forma fantástica ceñía,
> poco importa burlar brazos y pecho
> si te labra prisión mi fantasía.

In this sonnet the poet overtly adopts the feminine voice (with the usual pronouns "yo / tú"). The key words used in the first quatrain ("sombra", "imagen", "ilusión", "ficción") have Latin roots and are based on Aristotelian concepts dealing with the mind, which the poet uses at the same time to address her beloved. In the second quatrain the virtues of the beloved become a magnet that attract her breast, enclosing her heart, which responds as a piece of steel, conveying the idea of armor against the attacks of love, quite different from the soft wax ("cera") used by Garcilaso de la Vega in one of his sonnets. The idea of his virtues as a magnet that attracts her is related to what we have seen in her "rational love": he has sufficient merits to be loved, but he does not love her in return. We discover the reason for the opening imperative "detente" when we reach the reproachful question of the final two lines of the second quatrain: why do you make me fall in love with you if you then run away from me? His flight explains why she has had recourse to complex mental concepts. The feminine voice of the poet, aware of her beloved's deceitful game, decides in the sestet to teach him a lesson: your tyrannical treatment, she says, cannot triumph over me, for, although you attempt to flee me, my "fantasía" can hold you fast, in spite of yourself. She is triumphant because of her mental possession of the beloved's image. Note that the "forma fantástica" that runs away from her arms is already a product of her imagination; being fantastic, his form can be captured by her mind. My inner self, she tells him, imprisons you, and this establishes a close relationship between the sentiments of love and the faculties of the mind.

In Cruz's more unorthodox phases, we hear the same voices—masculine, feminine, or ambiguous—insisting now on love as subject to time and to change, as subject to practical decisions based on the human understanding.

—Georgina Sabat de Rivers

This sonnet, highly intellectual and at the same time highly lyrical, can be compared, in the attitude that it expresses, with the *Carta Atenagórica* and the "Carta de Monterrey"; it is one more expression of Sor Juana's intellectual self-confidence, of her faith in the triumph of mind over matter. The mind is so powerful that it can destroy prisons as well as create them; as she says in poem 42, which seems to anticipate this sonnet:

> Para el alma no hay encierro
> ni prisiones que la impidan,
> porque sólo la aprisionan
> las que se forma ella misma.

Among the many excellent examples of related topics in previous authors that Méndez Plancarte cites in his notes, the following seem particularly appropriate: Martín de la Plaza's "Amante sombra de mi bien esquivo" (already noted by Abreu); Quevedo's "A fugitivas sombras doy abrazos / . . . / Búrlame y de burlarme corre ufana"; Calderón's "Adorando estoy tu sombra, / y, a mis ojos aparente, / por burlar mi fantasía / abracé al aire mil veces" and his "Detente, espera, / sombra, ilusión . . ."

These concepts, drawn from Aristotelian psychology, were a common patrimony; Sor Juana uses them in a splendid sonnet, adding as a personal note the great power of the mind; her originality lies in the fact that she centers the action within her self, a woman in love, and not in the beloved who flees and who, in the final analysis, cannot escape her mind.

There are two other poems by Sor Juana, a group of *décimas* (number 101) and a *glosa* (number 142), in which she deals with similar ideas in connection with the theme of absence. The lover, by means of thought, never leaves the beloved, no matter how far away he may be; she says that she will have "siempre el pensamiento en ti, / siempre a ti en el pensamiento". She converts the philosophical ideas of our sonnet into an almost religious love, when she says "Acá en el alma veré / el centro de mis cuidados / con los ojos de mi fe: / que gustos imaginados, / también un ciego los ve". But our sonnet is poetically superior to these two poems.

We should not forget that Sor Juana's *Sueño* contains some of the same topics that we find in the sonnet, including the word "imán", in connection with the lungs that attract air; more important, there is a passage in which the Pharos of Alexandria is compared with the faculty of Phantasia. The stomach, says the poet,

> al cerebro envïaba
> húmedos, mas tan claros, los vapores
> de los atemperados cuatro humores,
> que con ellos no sólo no empañaba
> los simulacros que la estimativa
> dio a la imaginativa
> y aquésta, por custodia más segura,
> en forma ya más pura
> entregó a la memoria que, oficiosa,
> grabó tenaz y guarda cuidadosa,
> sino que daban a la Fantasía
> lugar de que formase
> imágenes diversas . . .

In both the sonnet and the *Sueño,* Phantasia—capitalized as a personified character—mediates between thought and the sensations received by the five physical senses, as the "common sense" that combines them. In the sonnet, Phantasia forms the image of the beloved and has it retained by Memory. This faculty of the human mind plays a leading role in our sonnet; once again Sor Juana converts scientific terms into love poetry.

Group B. Heterodox Ideas about Love.

What we have called Sor Juana's heterodox sonnets can also be divided into several sub-groups. In all of them Sor Juana deviates from the orthodoxy of courtly and Petrarchan love; she gives us a love that adapts to circumstances and even ignores the beloved if that seems best.

Sub-group 1. Love and hate.

Two sonnets fall within this category. The first is Méndez Plancarte's number 176:

Que da medio [= manera, modo] para amar sin
   mucha pena.

    Yo no puedo tenerte ni dejarte,
ni sé por qué, al dejarte o al tenerte,
se encuentra un no sé qué para quererte
y muchos sí sé qué para olvidarte.
    Pues ni quieres dejarme ni enmendarte,
yo templaré mi corazón de suerte
que la mitad se incline a aborrecerte
aunque la otra mitad se incline a amarte.
    Si ello es fuerza querernos, haya modo,
que es morir el estar siempre riñendo;
no se hable más en celo y en sospecha,
    y quien da la mitad no quiera el todo;
y cuando me la estás allá haciendo,
sabe que estoy haciendo la deshecha.

The topic is a familiar one, dating from Martial, Catullus, and Ovid, which might be called "an in-between love": one can live neither with nor without the beloved. Castillejo summed it up in the sixteenth century: "Ni contigo ni sin ti / mis penas tienen remedio, / contigo porque me matas / y sin ti, porque me muero"; the fourth line, found in the courtly love tradition, is familiar to us from the religious version of Santa Teresa. In this sonnet the gender of the speaker and of the addressee cannot be identified; s/he speaks of the special pain of this guarded sort of love, which seeks a way to relieve its suspicions and jealousy by getting even, but which cannot expect to receive more than it gives. This sonnet, while elaborately witty, has some of the charm of spontaneously colloquial language. As is normal, the question is posed in the octet and resolved in the sestet: the final line seems to mark the finale of the love affair.

The "no sé qué" of line 3, implying ineffability, derives from Petrarch; there are examples of the use of this phrase in Boscán and in St. John of the Cross, among others. Our poet, however, gives it a lighter turn by converting it into a "sí sé que" in the following line, implying that there is a real cause to believe in the beloved's infidelity; this would justify forgetting the beloved, hardening the lover's heart. The word "fuerza" implies that this love is predestined by the stars, the sort of love that Sor Juana elsewhere rejects as irrational; true love, according to her, would be based on reason and mutual appreciation. The poet, who as a woman believes in equal obligation on both sides, concludes on a note of recrimination and perhaps final separation. It is as though, throughout the sonnet, the speaker had been thinking over the whole situation and considering different options, while at the same time talking to the addressee; the poem seems to present us with thought being overheard.

The second sonnet in this sub-group reads as follows:

Un celoso refiere el común pesar que todos padecen, y advierte a la causa [the "causa" is the person who causes the problem] el fin que puede tener la lucha de afectos encontrados.

    Yo no dudo, Lisarda, que te quiero,

aunque sé que me tienes agraviado;
 mas estoy tan amante y tan airado,
que afectos que distingo no prefiero.
    De ver que odio y amor te tengo, infiero
que ninguno estar puede en sumo grado,
pues no le puede el odio haber ganado
sin haberle perdido amor primero.
    Y si piensas que el alma que te quiso
ha de estar siempre a tu afición ligada,
de tu satisfacción vana te aviso,
    pues si el amor al odio ha dado entrada,
el que bajó de sumo a ser remiso,
de lo remiso pasará a ser nada.

This is once more the same love problem that we saw in the previous sonnet, but with no apparent ambiguity; the theme dates back at least to the distich ("Odi et amo . . .") by Ovid that we saw earlier in this essay. The conflict of opposing emotions takes place within a single person, the "speaker" of the sonnet, who plays the role of a man addressing a woman: he begins by asserting his love, but gradually he moves from doubt to doubt. At first he does not know whether to prefer, or put in first place, love or hate, since neither one reigns supreme. In the sestet he moves toward undeceiving the lady: his love may well descend to the nadir of non-love, making room for hate to take over.

Sub-group 2: Love's Temporality

We have already seen that love may change, but the two sonnets belonging to this sub-group focus directly upon time itself. The first one that we will analyze is Méndez Plancarte's number 174:

Aunque en vano, quiere reducir a método racional el pesar de un celoso.

    ¿Qué es esto, Alcino? ¿Cómo tu cordura
se deja así vencer de un mal celoso,
haciendo con extremos de furioso
demostraciones más que de locura?
    ¿En qué te ofendió Celia, si se apura?
¿O por qué al Amor culpas de engañoso,
si no aseguró nunca poderoso
la eterna posesión de su hermosura?
    La posesión de cosas temporales,
temporal es, Alcino, y es abuso
el querer conservarlas siempre iguales.
    Con que tu error o tu ignorancia acuso,
pues Fortuna y Amor, de cosas tales
la propiedad no han dado, sino el uso.

The voice of the poet in this case is that of a disinterested adviser; it addresses Alcino (a conventional pastoral name) and tries to reason with him about his love for and jealousy of Celia. In the first quatrain it tells Alcino that his yielding to jealousy is a failure of right-thinking and causes him to act with mad fury; in the second the voice of the poet tries to reason with him, and to cause him to reason, by using rhetorical questions. The second question clearly means that Love does not have the power to guarantee anyone the eternal possession of the beloved. In the sestet the problem is resolved: human beings are subject to time, and so are all their affairs, including love; to wish it were otherwise is to ignore the nature of things. Not to understand this is not to realize that Love, like the wheel of Fortune, can only confer temporary usufruct, not permanent property rights. This use of legal concepts and a mercantile process of sensible reasoning urge Alcino in effect to be practical, not idealistic, about love.

Jealousy is not a Petrarchan theme, and Sor Juana treats it negatively, even though in one poem she admits it may be considered a sign of love. Love's temporality, or mortality, is not a Petrarchan theme either: for the orthodox Petrarchan, love is eternal and not subject to the laws of human life. The motifs or topoi that were most used in Golden Age poetry to exemplify or emblematize temporality and the wasting away of feminine beauty were the images of ancient ruins and of the rose; Sor Juana does not use the image of ruins but she does devote three sonnets to the rose, the passing of time and feminine beauty. These three poems, however, are not specifically love sonnets.

As a final example of love's temporality, let us look at the second sonnet belonging to this sub-group:

Que consuela a un celoso, epilogando la serie de los amores.

> Amor empieza por desasosiego,
> solicitud, ardores y desvelos;
> crece con riesgos, lances y recelos,
> susténtase de llantos y de ruego.
>   Doctrínanle tibiezas y despego,
> conserva el ser entre engañosos velos,
> hasta que con agravios o con celos
> apaga con sus lágrimas su fuego.
>   Su principio, su medio y fin es éste;
> pues ¿por qué, Alcino, sientes el desvío
> de Celia que otro tiempo bien te quiso?
>   ¿Qué razón hay de que dolor te cueste,
> pues no te engañó Amor, Alcino mío,
> sino que llegó el término preciso?

We see at once that this sonnet is closely related to the previous one: the human characters have the same names and play the same roles, and the poet continues to be an arbiter, calling upon Alcino to reflect realistically on his situation. In addition, this sonnet's quatrains belong to a tradition of poetic definitions of love; the definition in this case consists of a process that moves from uneasiness ("desasosiego") and concern ("solicitud") to the grievances and jealousy that extinguish, with their tears, the flames of love. Following the break that comes after the generalizing octet, the sestet is applied to the special case of Celia and Alcino. The first line of the sestet sums up the process of love: like everything else in life, it has a beginning, a middle, and an end. Then the poet asks Alcino why he should resent Celia's decision to leave him, for all she has done is to bring the process to its natural end: women, like men, have the right to stop loving.

. . . . .

The masochistic suffering of courtly love took different forms in different poets and periods, from the theological spiritualization of Dante to the humanistic introspection of Petrarch to the burlesque indecency of unprintable sonnets. The love sonnet, with its medieval roots, was the most widely known poetic genre, and one of the most prestigious, during the sixteenth and seventeenth centuries. In studying Sor Juana's love sonnets we should always keep in mind that Renaissance and Baroque poetry has little to do with the cult of sincerity and autobiographical directness that became popular during the Romantic period, which cultivated a sensibility much closer to our own. From the simple objective idealism of the neo-Platonic Renaissance we move to the complex, disillusioned subjectivism—dynamic and Protean—of the Counter-Reformational Baroque period. Reality can no longer be trusted; Sor Juana's many voices do not give us accounts of personal experiences, which come to the surface only as remembered fantasies. In our case, these fantasies take concrete form as sonnets, with strict formal rules; they are often poetic games invented to amaze and astound. Baroque poetry, to which we attribute such complex and interrelated tendencies as both "conceptismo" and "culteranismo", reflects a perplexed and tortured world-view, according to Maravall, and a need to exercise and cultivate the mind during a difficult cultural crisis; Gracián urges the intellectual to be highly attentive and on guard, so as to be able to decipher the traumatic events that take place, events that cause one to doubt the evidence of one's own senses. Baroque wit thrives on contradictions.

In this study we have separated Sor Juana's love sonnets into two major groups. We have called the first group orthodox or idealistic; it evokes a pure, disinterested, and permanent love, or a rational love based on the merits of the beloved. The second group is heterodox in the sense that love is seen as problematic and relativistic, mixed with hate, aware of its own impermanence.

The most noteworthy fact is that Sor Juana is a woman who reinvents love poetry from a feminine perspective; she knows the established tradition, but she finds herself immersed in the disquieting Baroque world that we have described. She sometimes assumes the traditional male voice of the courtly love tradition; sometimes she applies to love her knowledge of scholastic science to characterize it as incorruptible and based on reason. In her more unorthodox phases, we hear the same voices—masculine, feminine, or ambiguous—insisting now on love as subject to time and to change, as subject to practical decisions based on the human understanding. Her language, though complex, reflects at times lovers' contact with the everyday world.

In her sonnets we can see that, from within her cloister, Sor Juana took a leading role in the cultural life of New Spain; she exchanged with the outside world not only sonnets but other manuscripts and probably books. Her poetry reflects this cultural world and shows pride in her personal knowledge of intellectual trends, both scholastic and more recent. But it also allows us to see her social role as a female arbiter and adviser in a real world of courtly gossip and family intrigue, of flirtation and changing relations among aristocrats born in Spain or in the New World; she taught lessons to others on how to react in the face of amorous deception, how to break off a sentimental engagement, why one should reject an unworthy beloved and recognize love's time-bound nature. As is shown in the case of the *Enigmas* that Sor Juana wrote for a group of Portuguese nuns who knew they could find in her poetry the answers to her riddles, she was widely known for her mental agility and respected for her writings, which had a strong influence on people even before they were printed.

As for the unique poem that stands out amidst all of her sonnets, **"Detente, sombra de mi bien esquivo",** which has been called "the masterkey to her love poetry," it is a compendium of the poet's own literary and personal characteristics, among which we will point out again the following two. First, she emphasizes the inner life of the mind, analyzed here in terms of Aristotelian psychology: she reviews the process by which memory stores the "sombras", illusions and fictions that have been caught by the senses and converted into the "imagen del hechizo que más quiero", becoming in this way imprisoned by fantasy in her mind, from which there is no escape. And, second, she emphasizes the feminine perspective: in this sonnet she ignores the will of the male beloved and acts with a profoundly and daringly "feminist" determination. This sonnet reflects not only her pride as an intellectual woman capable of analyzing the mind with an erudition acquired by her own independent studies, but also her ability as a plain and simple woman to find a way to escape the "tyranny" of a fleeing lover and win the upper hand over him.

Sor Juana's intellectual and literary creativity takes advantage of a long, rich tradition to rise to new poetic heights as she analyzes with great sophistication the sentimental relationships between people belonging to her world of New Spain; she knew this world well, she was thoroughly familiar with the literary tradition dealing with questions of love, and she had a powerful human intuition that took poetry to levels that cannot be excelled.

FURTHER READING

Biography

Paz, Octavio. *Sor Juana or, the Traps of Faith,* translated by Margaret Sayers Peden. Cambridge, MA: Belknap Press, 1988, 547 p.

> Definitive biographical and critical study.

Criticism

Barnstone, Willis. "Sor Juana Inés de la Cruz." In *Six*

Masters of the Spanish Sonnet, pp. 59-85. Carbondale: Southern Illinois University Press, 1993.

> Provides a biographical and critical study of Cruz and her work.

Dixon, Paul B. "Balances, Pyramids, Crowns, and the Geometry of Sor Juana Ines de la Cruz." *Hispania* 67, No. 4 (December 1984): 560-66.

> Analyzes the role of geometry in Cruz's poetry, asserting "that some of the central themes with which her poetry is concerned are based upon a geometric model."

Feder, Elena. "Sor Juana Inés de la Cruz; or, The Snares of (Con)(tra)di(c)tion." In *Amerindian Images and the Legacy of Columbus,* edited by René Jara and Nicholas Spadaccini, pp. 473-529. Minneapolis: University of Minnesota Press, 1992.

> Offers a gender-historical focus on Cruz's major works.

Flynn, Gerard Cox. "The Alleged Mysticism of Sor Juana Inés de la Cruz." *Hispanic Review* XXVIII (1960): 233-44.

> Discusses the role of mysticism in Cruz's work.

Johnson, Julie Greer. "A Comical Lesson in Creativity from Sor Juana." *Hispania* 71, No. 2 (May 1988): 442-44.

> Traces the way in which Cruz adapts and employs conventional images of women and womanhood in her satirical poetry.

Lowe, Elizabeth. "The Gongorist Model in *El Primero Sueño.*" *Revista de Estudios Hispanicos* X, No. 3 (October 1976): 409-27.

> Presents a very detailed stylistic and thematic analysis of Cruz's poem.

Luciani, Frederick. "Anamorphosis in a Sonnet by Sor Juana Inés de la Cruz." *Discurso Literario* 5, No. 2 (Spring 1988): 423-32.

> Explores the role of visual perception in "Este, que ves, engaño colorido."

Pallister, Janis L. "A Note on Sor Juana de la Cruz." *Women & Literature* 7, No. 2 (Spring 1979): 42-6.

> Promotes a critical rediscovery of Cruz's work.

Reyes, Alfonso. "The Tenth Muse of America." In *The Position of America and Other Essays,* edited and translated by Harriet de Onís, pp. 117-27. New York: Alfred A. Knopf, 1950.

> Provides a general overview of Cruz's life and work.

Schwartz, Kessel. "*Primero Sueño*—A Reinterpretation." *Kentucky Romance Quarterly* XXII, No. 4 (1975): 473-90.

> Offers a psychoanalytic reading of Cruz's poem, asserting that "the reader must seek the truth behind Sor Juana's feelings and slight suggestions in his own way, but it seems fairly clear that Sor Juana elucidates unconscious motives, activated by sleep, to achieve gratification through dream content."

Additional coverage of Juana Ines de la Cruz's life and career is contained in the following sources published by The Gale Group: *Literature Criticism,* **Vol. 5.**

Li-Young Lee

1957-

American poet and autobiographer.

INTRODUCTION

Lee is the author of two acclaimed collections of poetry, *Rose* (1986), which won New York University's Delmore Schwartz Memorial Poetry Award, and *The City in Which I Love You,* which was the 1990 Lamont Poetry Selection of the Academy of American Poets. Deeply personal, Lee's poetry explores identity, particularly his sense of being part of a vast, global Chinese diaspora.

Biographical Information

Lee was born in Jakarta, Indonesia, to parents who had been exiled from China. His maternal grandfather had been the first president of the Republic of China, and his father had been a personal physician to Mao Zedong in China before leaving for Indonesia. In Jakarta Lee's father helped found Gamaliel University, where he taught English and philosophy. In 1959 the family fled from anti-Chinese persecution in Indonesia, embarking on a five-year trek through Hong Kong, Macau, and Japan, arriving finally in the United States in 1964. After studying theology in Pittsburgh, Lee's father became a Presbyterian minister in a small town in Pennsylvania where Lee attended high school. Lee continued his studies at the University of Pittsburgh, the University of Arizona, and State University of New York. He has taught at Northwestern and the University of Iowa.

Major Works

Lee's background and upbringing are reflected in several issues that recur in his poetry, which explores the question of individual identity in a world where people have been uprooted from traditional cultures, but have not found complete acceptance in their adopted lands. His desire to understand and accept his father, whom he both loves and fears, is the central motif of *Rose,* while the nature of his own identity dominates his second collection, *The City in Which I Love You.* Lee records his experiences with great detail, often connecting seemingly disparate and occasionally abstract thoughts with a single image, such as a rose, persimmon, or cleaver.

Critical Reception

Lee's poetry, particularly those poems in his second collection, has been lauded for its emotional depth and skilled use of language. Many critics have sought out Lee's poetic influences, noting Walt Whitman in particular, although the majority agree that his finest poems, such as "The Cleaving," depart from American poetic tradition. Several scholars have focused on the significance of Lee's Chinese heritage, which has sparked some critical debate. Zhou Xiaojing has responded by claiming that such readings "are not only misleading, but also reductive of the rich cross-cultural sources of influence on Lee's work and the creative experiment in his poetry." Zhou added, "Li-Young Lee's poems enact and embody the process of poetic innovation and identity invention beyond the boundaries of any single cultural heritage or ethnic identity."

PRINCIPAL WORKS

Poetry

Rose 1986
The City in Which I Love You 1990

Other Major Work

The Winged Seed: A Remembrance (autobiography) 1995

CRITICISM

Roger Mitchell (essay date 1989)

SOURCE: A review of *Rose,* in *Prairie Schooner,* Vol. 63, No 3, Fall 1989, pp. 135-37.

[*Mitchell names "tenderness" as the most salient quality of Lee's poetry and judges this a shortcoming in* Rose.]

Rose, Li-Young Lee's first book, begins the career of a promising poet. Lee is one of a rising number of Asian-American writers, though in *Rose* that background is not an issue. One line refers to someone "exiled from one republic and daily defeated in another." Two other lines recall someone "who was driven from the foreign school-yards / by fists and yelling, who trembled in anger in each retelling." There is a poem, too, about relatives singing and remembering China. But Lee does not dwell on grievances. He recreates, instead, "immedicable woes" (Frost's term) about his love for his father. I don't think Lee set out to write a book about the loss of his father, . . . but the dead father enters almost all of these poems like a half-bidden ghost. So close is the father that Lee asks at the end of **"Ash, Snow or Moonlight,"** "Is this my father's life or mine?"

Lee has committed himself to tenderness the way other poets commit themselves to reality, the imagination, nature, or some other enveloping generalization.

—Roger Mitchell

In a book that records many gifts, small and large, intended and unintended, **"The Gift"** describes the son's principal debt to his father. In taking a metal splinter from his son's hand years before, his father recited a story in a low voice. Years later the son performs a similar service for his wife.

> I can't remember the tale,
> but hear his voice still, a well
> of dark water, a prayer.
> And I recall his hands,
> two measures of tenderness
> he laid against my face.

The point is not just that his father taught him something about love, but that in teaching him that, he also kept him from having to hate. "I did not hold that shard / between my fingers and think,"

> *Metal that will bury me,*
> christen it Little Assassin . . .
> And I did not lift up my wound and cry,
> *Death visited here!*

Thus the boy is prevented from an inward and egotistical hatred of the world. He can go out to the world and love it, as he does in loving his wife. **"The Gift"** may be a little self-congratulatory, but it deflects much of that by attributing the wisdom to his father.

The book is named for a flower, and Lee writes well about them, particularly in **"My Indigo"** and **"Irises."** The title poem, unfortunately, does not discover the flower but uses it, ready-made, for a host of metaphoric ends which, while ambitious, strains credulity. The indigo, on the other hand, "blossoms / like a saint dying upside down."

> I've come to find the moody one, the shy one,
> downcast, grave, and isolated . . .
> my secret, vaginal and sweet,
> you furl yourself shamelessly
> toward the ground.

The irises are praised for "beauty and indifference." Beauty, sweetness, love, joy, wisdom, tenderness, these are the qualities Lee has extracted from experience so far. They

come to him either as gifts from his father or accidentally, indifferent as the iris.

If I had to isolate the most evident quality in Lee's poems, I would use the word tenderness. Lee has committed himself to tenderness the way other poets commit themselves to reality, the imagination, nature, or some other enveloping generalization. Tenderness is certainly a virtue, and it is scarce. But I have to ask, at the risk of sounding like a curmudgeon, is tenderness enough? Would tenderness have given us the poetry of—to pick names at random—Donne, Wordsworth, Blake, Browning, Dickinson, Pound, Eliot, Frost, Rich, etc.? There is tenderness in the work of all these poets, but there is much more than tenderness. Tenderness is not enough for someone trying to realize an understanding of life or reach a truce with it. The "infinitely gentle, infinitely suffering thing" is not—and I will risk saying, cannot be—the poet. For one thing, tenderness is not an aesthetic matter. The poet determined to be tender will come to care less how a thing is said than that tenderness be displayed. For another, tenderness does not always mix well with the truth. While I hope for tenderness, I would prefer no compromises from poetry. Let things be called by their real names. Where it is awful, let it be called awful; and where sublime, sublime. That is what Eliot meant, I think, when he called for tough reasonableness. We need more of it today.

Judith Kitchen (essay date 1991)

SOURCE: "Auditory Imaginations: The Sense of Sound," in *The Georgia Review,* Vol. XLV, No. 1, Spring, 1991, pp. 154-69.

[*In the following review of* The City in Which I Love You, *Kitchen extols Lee's "verbal and visionary imagination."*]

Li-Young Lee's second book, ***The City in Which I Love You,*** is the 1990 Lamont Poetry Selection of The Academy of American Poets. This is a work of remarkable scope—musically as well as thematically—offering a sweeping perspective of history from the viewpoint of the émigré. He speaks for the disenfranchised, but from the particular voice of a late-twentieth-century Chinese-American trying to make sense of both his heritage and his inheritance. Positioning himself as father and son, Chinese and American, exile and citizen, Lee finds himself on the cusp of history; his duty, as he sees it, is to "tell my human / tale, tell it against / the current of that vaster, that / inhuman telling."

The City in Which I Love You picks up where Lee's first book, ***Rose,*** left off. The opening poem, **"Furious Versions,"** is a long, seven-part account of his family's exile. Fueled with the sense that he is the only one who has lived to tell it, Lee recounts his father's fractured life and the loss of his brother. The effect is more than personal; it is admonitory—as if to warn us that we cannot face the "next nervous one hundred human years" without a knowledge of what his past represents. But whereas the central figure in *Rose* is the father, here the "furious versions" belong to the son—because his "memory's flaw / isn't in retention but organization." This long poem seems to fill in some gaps left by the previous book, but its language is angrier, less elegiac:

> It was a tropical night.
> It was half a year of sweat and fatal memory.
> It was one year of fire
> out of the world's diary of fires,
> flesh-laced, mid-century fire,
> teeth and hair infested,
> napalm-dressed and skull-hung fire,
> and imminent fire, an elected
> fire come to rob me
> of my own death, my damp bed
> in the noisy earth,
> my rocking toward a hymn-like night.

Although the story is personal and unique, the poems are declamatory, public even in their intimacy. They have as two of their sources Whitman and the Bible, and they have as their intention a passionate need to synthesize and instruct. They challenge us with their heightened rhetoric, exhibiting the dangers (as well as the glories) of eloquence. Lee's very strengths are his potential weaknesses. The echo of Whitman may need to be muted; even Lee's own tremendous verbal resources may demand modulation in order to achieve their finest realization. One more adjective, one more item in a list, and the poem could tip over into excess.

The ambitious title poem, 166 lines in the middle of the book, marks a turning point where the experience of exile is no longer the speaker's alone. **"The City in Which I Love You"** is a collage of twentieth-century horror rendered in an onrush of fragments, some evoking the nightly news, others surrealistic nightmare. In a devastated cityscape, the "I" of the poem searches for a "you"—an other. The other is more than a beloved (the epigraph is from the *Song of Songs*); rather, it seems to signify some impossible fulfillment, a connection to humanity through which love might still be possible, and suffering redemptive. Informing the poem is a dense language, thick with urgent rhythms and relentless desire—as though language itself were the other, the body of the beloved.

In the face of the larger history, Lee must discover the meaning of his individual life: "He was not me," "They are not me," "None of them is me." This discovery is central to the book, for the next several poems are rooted in a quiet family life—love poems to a woman who tastes like iron and milk, a child who wants a story, a father whom death has made giant. **"Goodnight"** is a lullaby, in slant-rhyme couplets, sung to his son. It moves, ultimately, toward full rhyme:

> Where did you, so young, learn
>
> such sacrifice? Now
> I no longer hear the apples fall. But how

they go! Incessantly, though
with no noise, no

> blunt announcements of their gravity.
> See!
>
> There is no bottom to the night, no end
> to our descent.
>
> We suffer each other to have each other a while.

The book ends with another long poem, **"The Cleaving."** Here Lee looks to the present; the immigrant figure is no longer his father, the story no longer only autobiographical. It has become a text. A young man with his own identity and history enters a butcher shop. The butcher is familiar—he could be grandfather, father, brother, nomad, Gobi, Northern, Southern. He is American, a man at work:

> He lops the head off, chops
> the neck of the duck
> into six, slits
> the body
> open, groin
> to breast, and drains
> the scalding juices,
> then quarters the carcass
> with two fast hacks of the cleaver,
> old blade that has worn
> into the surface of the round
> foot-thick chop-block
> a scoop that cradles precisely the curved steel.

The language is packed, sound clicking against sound, consonants hacking their own blades, reminiscent of Lowell. The sounds are American—harsh, hurried, energetic—and they carry the reader toward meaning as Lee, self-conscious that this is as much the making of poetry as the telling of tale, comes to terms with the violent wrenchings of his immigrant experience. He savors the taste of meat—a hunger at last satisfied, because it is a hunger that *can* be satisfied. He accepts his varied, though finite, human ties. He finds, in the body of a fish, a shape that complements the shape of his mind: "I take it as text and evidence / of the world's love for me, / and I feel urged to utterance, / urged to read the body of the world, urged / to say it / in human terms, / my reading a kind of eating, / my eating / a kind of reading, / my saying a diminishment, / my noise / a love-in-answer."

"The Cleaving," is the intellectual flip side of the title poem. In it, Lee accepts his body and its appetites, accepts his inevitable death, eschews the need for transcendence. With its exploration into every nuance of the title, its love of detail, and its journey into the abstract, **"The Cleaving"** has the feel of a major American poem. It throws aside some of the American traditions he has previously followed: "I would eat these features, eat / the last three or four thousand years, every hair. / And I would eat Emerson, his transparent soul, his / soporific transcendence." Above all, **"The Cleaving"** predicts change—a change that is necessary if Lee is to grow into other books.

It is the birth of the self out of personal and global history, a self that is not the sum of its stories but of its experience—assimilated, whole, and wholly alive in a chamber of sound:

No easy thing, violence.
One of its names? Change. Change
resides in the embrace
of the effaced and the effacer,
in the covenant of the opened and the opener;
the axe accomplishes it on the soul's axis.
What then may I do
but cleave to what cleaves me.
I kiss the blade and eat my meat.
I thank the wielder and receive,
while terror spirits
my change, sorrow also.
The terror the butcher
scripts in the unhealed
air, the sorrow of his Shang
dynasty face,
African face with slit eyes. He is
my sister, this
beautiful Bedouin, this Shulamite,
keeper of sabbaths, diviner
of holy texts, this dark
dancer, this Jew, this Asian, this one
with the Cambodian face, Vietnamese face, this
    Chinese
I daily face,
this immigrant,
this man with my own face.

With its mixture of verbal and visionary imagination, *The City in Which I Love You* is reminiscent of Kinnell's *Book of Nightmares,* maybe even of Eliot's *Waste Land.* The personal nightmare becomes general. Lee's poetry makes us look hard at the world and the place our own "furious versions," at once interconnected and isolated, have in it.

Jessica Greenbaum (essay date 1991)

SOURCE: "Memory's Citizen," in *The Nation,* October 7, 1991, pp. 416-18.

[*In the following essay, Greenbaum offers a favorable evaluation of both* Rose *and* The City in Which I Love You.]

Sometimes poets seem like the orators at Speakers' Corner—I can see them now, stacking their well-built stanzas like orange crates, stepping to the top with a deep breath and saying what they have to say. Readers, meanwhile, mill about the edges of the literary park, hoping to be caught by a poet's music or gossip, by the telescopic insinuation of worlds or by the expansive description of them. Sometimes a poet's voice distinguishes itself by carrying authority and by addressing a singular authority. That has been my experience reading Li-Young Lee's poems.

Lee's first book, *Rose* (1986), opens with **"Epistle,"** his letter to the world, as Dickinson called her poems. It ends:

Before it all gets wiped away, let me say,
there is wisdom in the slender hour
which arrives between two shadows.

It is not heavenly and it is not sweet.
It is accompanied by steady human weeping,
and twin furrows between the brows,
but it is what I know,
and so am able to tell.

Some of the biographical background for this solemn introduction is well known by now. Both Lee's books carry biographical notes (a whole page in *The City in Which I Love You*) and his interview in Bill Moyers's WNET series *The Power of the Word* supplied more. Lee was born in 1957, to Chinese parents then living in Jakarta, Indonesia. His father had been Mao's personal physician and then professor of English and philosophy at Gamaliel University in Jakarta. The senior Lee ended up a political prisoner under Indonesia President Sukarno and spent two years in prison before escaping and fleeing the country. A nearly five-year trek through Hong Kong, Macao and Japan led the family to the United States, where Lee's father, "the critical 'myth'" of Lee's work, became a "Presbyterian minister in a tiny western Pennsylvanian town, full of rage and mystery and pity, blind and silent at the end." Lee's father died in 1980.

The above quotations are from Gerald Stern's introduction to *Rose.* In the late 1970s, Stern was Lee's mentor at the University of Pittsburgh, and Stern's preface to *Rose*—his introduction of Lee to the literary world—still stands as the most valuable prose about Lee's work. The plain-spokenness of Lee's poems is coupled with a fearlessness of direction which Stern calls "a willingness to let the sublime enter his field of concentration." This "willingness," paired with Lee's unorthodox imagery, makes a powerful team. In *Rose* we hear this brave combo in the last stanza of **"Dreaming of Hair":**

Sometimes my love is melancholy
and I hold her head in my hands.
Sometimes I recall our hair grows after death.
Then, I must grab handfuls
of her hair, and, I tell you, there
are apples, walnuts, ships sailing, ships docking,
    and men
taking off their boots, their hearts breaking,
not knowing
what they love more, the water, or
their women's hair, sprouting from the head,
    rushing toward the feet.

Lee's task seems sometimes to remember the life of his father *for* him, to plot the moving figure, the migrant political prisoner whose character kept evolving when the mad dash was over. We often get the sense that Lee feels only one step ahead of the oblivion of inarticulateness (and always a few steps behind his father). Unlike the picture one gets of other poets—Ashbery, for instance, who comes to mind (regardless of his incalculable labors) as being in repose or absently surveying a garden—Lee comes across as a man bent over a drafting table, erasing, rewriting, sweating more than he wishes. In *Rose*'s poem **"Mnemonic"** he says:

> A serious man who devised complex systems of
>   numbers and rhymes
> to aid him in remembering, a man who forgot
>   nothing, my father
> would be ashamed of me.
> Not because I'm forgetful,
> but because there is no order
> to my memory, a heap
> of details, uncatalogued, illogical.

Rose announces Lee's obsessions but also bears the innate triumph of ordering language. In the poem **"Persimmons"** Lee takes revenge on the teacher who humiliated him for confusing the fruit's name with the word "precision." And who is more precise than the poet, writing about persimmons that a blind father painted from precise memory? In the poem, the father, when handed his own scroll-painting of persimmons, says:

> Oh the feel of the wolftail on the silk,
> the strength, the tense
> precision in the wrist.
> I painted them hundreds of times
> eyes closed. These I painted blind.
> Some things never leave a person:
> scent of the hair of the one you love,
> the texture of persimmons
> in your palm, the ripe weight.

Rose won the Delmore Schwartz Memorial Poetry Award from New York University and, like its title, offers the reader a complicated, beautiful, burdened, opening blossom. *The City in Which I Love You,* published four years later, was the Lamont Poetry Selection for 1990. In *The City,* dreaminess and the urgency of ordering memory still seem braided; dream, or the travel between the dead and the living, between truth and the imagination, and between refugee status and citizenship, seems, in fact, to be the vehicle for ordering memory. Blind feeling, or feeling memorized onto the soul, as with the father's painting of persimmons, is still the way to the truthful depiction of life's experiences.

The long opening poem of the volume, **"Furious Versions,"** gives the impression of the poet floating, like a Chagall figure, through the lives of his family, scouting for their stories through a kind of relaxed levitation in liquid time. The poet observes the world's images metamorphosing, like a lava lamp, and tries to metamorphose with them. Aside from the first line's awkward verb— "These days I waken in the used light"—the poem generally feels effortless and effervescent.

> Or I might have one more
> hour of sleep before my father

> comes to take me
> to his snowbound church
> where I dust the pews and he sets candles
> out the color of teeth.

>   · · · · ·

> And I wonder
> if I imagined those wintry mornings
> in a dim nave, since
> I'm the only one
> who's lived to tell it,
> and I confuse
> the details; was it my father's skin
> which shone like teeth?
> Was it his heart that lay snowbound?
> But if I waken to a Jailer

>   · · · · ·

> what name do I answer to?

There's a fabulous passage in part 5 of the poem, an image that another, more opportunistic poet might have used to wrest an entire poem:

> Once, while I walked
> with my father, a man
> reached out, touched his arm, said, *Kuo Yuan?*
> The way he stared and spoke my father's name
> I thought he meant to ask, *Are you a dream?*
> Here was the sadness of ten thousand miles,
> of an abandoned house in Nan Jing,
> where my father helped a blind man
> wash his wife's newly dead body,
> then bury it, while bombs
> fell, and trees raised
> charred arms and burned.
> Here was a man who remembered
> the sound of another's footfalls
> so well as to call to him
> after twenty years
> on a sidewalk in America.

Once the imagination is receptive, Lee might be saying, you can find anyone.

Perhaps one of his "simpler" poems, but one whose concept and execution I still find wonderful, **"This Room and Everything in It,"** describes another "mnemonic," another formula for memory, as taught by the speaker's father:

> I am letting this room
> and everything in it
> stand for my ideas about love
> and its difficulties.

> I'll let your love-cries,
> those spacious notes
> of a moment ago,
> stand for distance. . . .

. . . . .

and so on, each thing
standing for a separate idea,
and those ideas forming the constellation
of my greater idea.
And one day, when I need
to tell myself something intelligent
about love,

I'll close my eyes
and recall this room and everything in it.

The room is one architecture for memory, the stanza another.

Lee has been compared to Whitman; in fact, Judith Kitchen, writing in *The Georgia Review,* has said Lee may sound *too* much like him. The father-of-us-all does stride through the book's last and most challenging poem, **"The Cleaving"** (which, for all the hoopla, including a Pushcart Prize, doesn't swoop me up). The poem's speaker finds himself—while ordering roast duck at the Chinese grocery—in an epiphanic moment. His relationship to the butcher, to food, to the machinery of the body, and the interrelationship of all these elements, swirl about him and illuminate his relationship to his own soul and the soul of others. A string of images about lovemaking begins, "The noise the body makes / when the body meets / the soul over the soul's ocean and penumbra," and ends, "an engine crossing, / re-crossing salt water, hauling / immigrants and the junk / of the poor." And so the poet gives us something else to remember.

Zhou Xiaojing (essay date 1996)

SOURCE: "Inheritance and Invention in Li-Young Lee's Poetry," in *MELUS,* Vol. 21, No. 1, Spring, 1996, pp. 113-32.

[*In the essay below, Zhou contends that "Li-Young Lee's poems enact and embody the processes of poetic innovation and identity invention beyond the boundaries of any single cultural heritage or ethnic identity."*]

Li-Young Lee's two prize-winning books of poetry, *Rose* (1986) and *The City in Which I Love You* (1990), contain processes of self-exploration and self-invention through memories of life in exile and experiences of disconnection, dispossession, and alienation. While providing him with a frame of reference to explore the self, autobiographical materials in his poems also serve as a point of departure for Lee to re-define and re-create the self as an immigrant in America and as a poet. At the same time, the process of Lee's construction and invention of identity is accompanied by his development of a set of poetic strategies through which the acquired knowledge and identity are forcefully articulated and expressed.

However, both Lee's identity re-creation and his poetic innovation are overlooked by critics who attempt to explain his poetry by emphasizing his Chinese ethnicity. In his complimentary foreword to *Rose,* Gerald Stern writes that what "characterizes Lee's poetry," among other things, is "a pursuit of certain Chinese ideas, or Chinese memories. . . ." For Stern, Lee's father and his Chinese cultural heritage are fundamental components to his poetry: "Maybe Lee—as a poet—is lucky to have had the father he had and the culture he had. Maybe they combine in such a way as to make his own poetry possible. Even unique." Stern's attribution of the making of Lee's poetry and its characteristics to his Chinese heritage is reiterated by L. Ling-chi Wang and Henry Yiheng Zhao, editors of *Chinese American Poetry: An Anthology* (1991), who claim that the unique "quality" of Lee's poetry "boils down to 'a pursuit of certain Chinese ideas, or Chinese memories.'" To illustrate what they mean by the Chineseness in Lee's poetry, Wang and Zhao cite Lee's poem **"My Indigo"** as an example. Lee's method of expressing his feelings and state of mind by describing a phenomenon in nature in this poem may be borrowed from Chinese classical poetry. But rather than showing any particular "Chinese ideas," the directness of erotic feelings and the celebration of sexual love in **"My Indigo"** bear some affinity to "The Song of Songs" which is one of Lee's favorite books of poetry. And the speaker's comment on the indigo flower's condition of isolation and living "a while in two worlds / at once," expresses Lee's own feelings resulting from his experience of life in exile, wandering from country to country within a short period of time, rather than illustrating any ideas or memories which can be defined as typically Chinese.

Ethnocentric readings of Lee's poems by Stern, Wang, and Zhao are not only misleading, but also reductive of the rich cross-cultural sources of influence on Lee's work and of the creative experiment in his poetry. Their readings presuppose a misconception that a pure and fixed Chinese culture has been inherited and maintained by Chinese immigrants and their descendants in America. As Sau-ling Cynthia Wong has pointed out, "Asian American writers, however rooted on this land they or their families may have been, tend to be regarded as direct transplants from Asia or as custodians of an esoteric subculture." This tendency in reading Asian American writers risks relegating their works to a marginalized niche. As a corrective to ethnocentric misreading of Asian American poetry, Shirley Lim proposes "an ethnocentered reading" based on "an ethnopoetics" which will function on three levels— stylistic, linguistic, and contextual. In my view, the contextual level is more important than the other two, for the context of the creative subject and act, to a large extent, determines the stylistic and linguistic aspects of the work. Ethnocentric readings of Asian American writers such as Li-Young Lee result from a narrow focus on the poet's heritage of Chinese culture which, by implication, is enclosed. Without contextualizing the heritage of Lee's poetry beyond his ethnicity, interpretations of his style or use of diction exclusively in terms of his ethnicity still cannot escape an ethnocentric misreading, as shown in Wang and Zhao's comments on Lee's **"My Indigo."**

By contextualizing the heritage of Lee's poetry, I mean examining Lee's poems within their "horizon" in the sense of Hans-Georg Gadamer's hermeneutics. For Gadamer, the concept of "horizon" suggests "possibility of expansion," of "opening up of new horizons." The limits of horizon are never fixed; "the closed horizon that is supposed to enclose a culture," Gadamer contends, "is an abstraction." He argues that

> The historical movement of human life consists in the fact that it is never absolutely bound to any one standpoint, and hence can never have a truly closed horizon. The horizon is, rather, something into which we move and that moves with us. Horizons change for a person who is moving.

This concept of horizon is shaped by history, by the particular situations of people's lived lives, and by their consciousness. Gadamer notes that "Our own past and that other past toward which our historical consciousness is directed help to shape this moving horizon out of which human life always lives and which determines it as heritage and tradition." In other words, one's heritage is not possessed once for all, nor is it necessarily inherited through ethnic lineage. Rather, it is changed and renewed with the changing conditions of human life and human consciousness.

In this sense, Li-Young Lee's poems cannot be fully understood or appreciated by tracing his heritage, which is mistakenly categorized as exclusively Chinese. Lee learned to love poetry from his exposure to Chinese classical poems and the Psalms. As a child, Lee learned to recite classical Chinese poems from his father, who had a classical Chinese education and used to recite poems from the Tang Dynasty to his children. His father also used to read to his family constantly from the King James Bible, which became one of Lee's favorite books. Lee's poems and poetics are largely shaped by his experience as a refugee and immigrant and by his readings in English, being educated from grade school through college in the United States. He was born in 1957 in Indonesia of Chinese parents. His mother is the granddaughter of China's provisional president, Yuan Shikai, elected in 1912 during the country's transition from monarchy to republic. Lee's paternal grandfather was a gangster and an entrepreneur. Thus his parents' marriage in communist China was much frowned upon, and his parents eventually fled to Indonesia, where Lee's father taught medicine and philosophy at Gamliel University in Jakarta. In 1958, Lee's father was incarcerated by Sukarno because of his interest in Western culture and ideas; he loved Shakespeare, opera, Kierkegaard, and the Bible. After nineteen months imprisonment, he escaped, and the family fled Indonesia with him. For several years, they traveled throughout Indochina and Southeast Asia before finally settling down, first in Hong Kong and then in the United States. In the U.S., his father studied theology at a seminary in Pittsburgh and later became a Presbyterian minister in a small town in Pennsylvania.

Because of this background, Lee finds that "the wandering of the children of Israel" in the Book of Exodus "has profound resonance for [him]" (Moyers). And his consequent feelings of loss, disconnection and dislocation are often reflected in his poems. One of his early poems, **"I Ask My Mother to Sing,"** deals with the emotional reality of his family as refugees and immigrants:

> She begins, and my grandmother joins her.
> Mother and daughter sing like young girls.
> If my father were alive, he would play
> his accordion and sway like a boat.
>
> I've never been in Peking, or the Summer Palace,
> nor stood on the great Stone Boat to watch
> the rain begin on Kuen Ming Lake, the picnickers
> running away in the grass.
>
> But I love to hear it sung;
> how the waterlilies fill with rain until
> they overturn, spilling water into water,
> then rock back, and fill with more.
>
> Both women have begun to cry.
> But neither stops her song.

This poem marks several losses: the death of the father, a vanished world within the Forbidden City in Peking and its way of life in the royal palace, and the speaker's inability to connect himself to that world and its culture of his Chinese heritage. As Lee observes in an interview, seeing his father's name in Chinese characters on his tomb stone with all these American flags on the other graves makes him feel strange rather than nostalgic. "I don't know what to feel nostalgic *for*," says Lee. "It's simply a feeling of disconnection and dislocation" (Moyers). Here in the poem, the speaker does not share his mother's and grandmother's memories, nor their nostalgia. But that lost world and its culture, in whatever fragmentary fashion, has been passed on to the speaker through the song.

The difference between the speaker's feeling of disconnectedness and his mother's and grandmother's feeling of dislocation and nostalgia shows a generational disparity which is characteristic of immigrants' experiences. This difference indicates discontinuity and fragmentation in the speaker's inherited Chinese history, culture, and identity, which at the same time are opened to "new horizons," to use Gadamer's words again. The speaker's, or rather Lee's, position of straddling different cultures and histories leads to an expansion of his conceptual and perceptual horizon. This position, according to Mikhail Bakhtin, can be creatively productive. Bakhtin emphasizes that "the most intense and productive life of culture takes place on the boundaries of its individual areas and not in places where these areas have become enclosed in their own specificity" (*Speech Genres*). This productiveness, Bakhtin indicates, is the result of interactions of different points of view:

> In the realm of culture, outsidedness is a most powerful factor in understanding. It is only in the eyes of *another* culture that foreign culture reveals itself fully and profoundly. . . . A meaning only reveals its depths once it has encountered and come into contact with another, foreign meaning: they engage in a kind of dialogue, which surmounts the closedness and one-

sidedness of these particular meanings, these cultures. We raise new questions for a foreign culture, ones that it did not raise itself; we seek answers to our own questions in it; and the foreign culture responds to us by revealing to us its new aspects and new semantic depths.

Li-Young Lee's bi-cultural heritage enables him to escape "closedness and one-sidedness" in his perception and views. His cross-cultural experience helps generate and enrich his poems.

Part of Lee's creative impulse is motivated by his urge to inscribe the presence and experience of his father, his family, himself, and other immigrants in poems as a measure of conquering mortality.

—Zhou Xiaojing

To deal with his cross-cultural experience and to show culturally conditioned ways of perception in his poetry, Lee employs and develops a major technique which relies on a central image as the organizing principle for both the subject matter and structure of the poem. This method gives him much freedom in exploring various perspectives in relation to the central image. At the same time, Lee incorporates the method of using narrative as the material for meditation, the concrete frame of reference for abstraction and the shifting point of departure for transition or development within the poem.

In one of his early poems, **"Persimmons,"** Lee's method of organizing the narrative, description, and meditation around a central image enables him to present several different periods of his life, including his cross-cultural experience in grade school. The poem begins with narrative of an incident in the classroom:

> In sixth grade Mrs. Walker
> slapped the back of my head
> and made me stand in the corner
> for now knowing the difference
> between *persimmon* and *precision*.
> How to choose
>
> persimmons. This is precision.
> Ripe ones are soft and brown-spotted.
> Sniff the bottoms. The sweet one
> will be fragrant. How to eat:
> put the knife away, lay down newspaper.
>
> Peel the skin tenderly, not to tear the meat.
> Chew the skin, suck it,
> and swallow. Now, eat
> the meat of the fruit,
> so sweet,
> all of it, to the heart.

Lee's precise descriptions with respect to persimmons here illustrate his knowledge of both persimmons and precision, which undermines the reason Mrs. Walker punished him. His empirical knowledge of persimmons also provides a contrast to how his teacher and classmates have their first taste of a persimmon in another class described later in the poem.

In association with persimmons, Lee introduces fragments of memories into the poem. The poem thus progresses with Lee's shifts of topics and narratives all related to the central image of persimmons. The memory of his punishment for confusing "persimmon" with "precision" reminds him of teaching "Donna" how to say certain Chinese words, and then leads to further memory of "Other words / that got me into trouble." One of these words, "yarn," evokes Lee's memory of his mother. Then in connection to persimmons, another classroom scene is described:

> Mrs. Walker brought a persimmon to class
> and cut it up
> so everyone could taste
> a *Chinese apple*. Knowing
> it wasn't ripe or sweet, I didn't eat
> but watched the other faces.

In juxtaposition to Mrs. Walker's teaching of "persimmon" and the classmates limited and obviously unpleasant experience of this *"Chinese apple,"* Lee describes his parents' feelings about and ways of looking at persimmons.

> My mother said every persimmon has a sun
> inside, something golden, glowing,
> warm as my face.
>
>   . . . . .
>
> Finally understanding
> he was going blind,
> my father sat up all one night
> waiting for a song, a ghost.
> I gave him the persimmons,
> swelled, heavy as sadness,
> and sweet as love.
> This year, in the muddy lighting
> of my parents' cellar, I rummage, looking
> for something I lost.
> My father sits on the tired, wooden stairs,
>
>   . . . . .
>
> He's so happy that I've come home.
> I ask how his eyes are, a stupid question.
> *All gone,* he answers.

After the father had lost his eyesight, he could still paint persimmons with precision. The two in one of his paintings look "so full they want to drop from the cloth." At the end of the poem, persimmons have taken on different significations and have become one of the things which stay in the reader's memory. As the father says:

Some things never leave a person:
scent of the hair of one you love,
the texture of persimmons,
in your palm, the ripe weight.

The central image, persimmons, while allowing Lee a wide range of associative narratives, meditations, and descriptions, always pulls these associations back to its center, thus giving coherence to the disconnected incidents described in the poem and to the poem itself. At the same time, this composition method renders the development and transitions of the poem spontaneous and smooth, like the movements of musical variations on the same theme.

Similar techniques of composition by associations with a central image are also employed in a number of other poems, such as **"Always a Rose," "Water," "Dreaming of Hair,"** and **"Braiding."** Again, the central image in these poems gives a great deal of elasticity to various associations. **"Always a Rose,"** for instance, consists of ten parts, each dealing with a segment of Lee's life, memory, and thought in association with the rose. With its elastic and binding function, the image of a rose also allows Lee to confront the painful loss of his father, to recall his father's difficult struggle in life and the different facets of his personality; it also enables him to express his love and respect for his father and eventually to meditate on his own mortality. Throughout the poem, there is a pervasive sense of the transitory temporality of all living things. This sense is accompanied by the father's death, which haunts the living in the poem. In Part 1 and Part 2, the dead father is presented as part of the speaker's life and memory. That death is part of living is hinted at in the beginning of the poem and in its imagery:

Dead daisies, shriveled lilies, withered bodies
of dry chrysanthemums. Among these, and waste
    leaves
of yellow and brown fronds of palm and fern,
I came, and found
a rose
left for dead, heaped with the hopeless dead,
its petals still supple.

. . . . .

my sister would rival its beauty,
my mother bow before it, then bear it
to my father's grave, where
he would grant it seven days,
then return and claim it forever.
I took it,
put it in water,
and set it on my windowsill.

2.
In the procession of summers and the arrivals of days
the roses marched by in a blur: the roses burning
in the coffin between my father's stiff hands.

By associating roses with the father's death, the speaker begins to reflect upon his own mortality through the rose.

He speaks to the rose, which he has put in water and set on his windowsill, about their drying:

When with arrows, night pierces you, rose,
I see most clearly
your true nature.
Small, auroral, your death is large.
You live, you die with me, in spite
of me, like my sleeping wife.
Lying here, with her at my right and you at my left,
the dying lies between the dying.

Lee's keen awareness of mortality shapes his presentation of images and gives weight and meaning to his description of the physical parts of the self: "Each finger is a brother or sister, / in each thumb is smudged the deaths I'm losing count of," says the speaker. The rose also evokes the speaker's memory of his birth, at which his father dreaded that the birthmark on his body was ominous, that he was born "half girl." So he was given the rose to eat whole as a "remedy."

With this autobiographical incident in connection to the rose, another major idea emerges in the poem—eating, or rather swallowing, something bitter is a way of learning to understand and master the unknown.

Odorous and tender flower-
body, I eat you
to recall my first misfortunate.
Little, bitter
body, I eat you
to understand my grave father.
Excellent body of layers tightly
wound around nothing,
I eat you to put my faith in grief,
Singed at the edges, dying
from the flame you live by, I
eat you to sink into
my own body. Secret body
of deep liquor,
I eat you
down to your secret.

This idea of confronting and getting down to the bottom of "good, grave" bitterness in life is to be further developed in Lee's later poems with the idea of changing and strengthening the self by learning to know and master the unknown as an immigrant and poet.

Lee's use of the rose as the binding agent for a succession of lyrical and narrative moments makes it possible for him to deal with several thematic concerns within the same poem. Through association with how the rose is "fed by what dies" and revitalized by last year's "leaves, mown grass, rotten apples, dead roses," the speaker meditates on the possibilities of overcoming death through poetry.

If with my mouth,
if with my clumsy tongue, my teeth,
if with my voice, my voice
of little girl, of man, of blood, and if

with blood, if with marrow, if with groin, lungs,
if with breath bristling with animal and vegetable, if
with all
the beast in me, all the beauty,
I form one word,
then another, one
word
for every moment
which passes, and if I do so until
all words are spoken, then ·
begin again,
if I adore you, Rose,
with adoration become nonsense become
praise, could I stop our dying?
Could we sit together in new bodies. . . .

The inevitability of physical decline and death is indicated by Lee's descriptions of the rose in response to his question. Here the rose is described in such a way as to evoke the human body and human mortality:

You sag,
turn your face
from me, body
made of other bodies, each doomed.

The bodily image as indication of inevitable decay and death suggested here is later developed into an image which has the possibility of transformation and renewal in the concluding poem of Lee's second book.

Poems in Lee's second book are marked by a shift from the memories of his father to an emphasis on Lee's own life and identity. In **"Furious Versions,"** the opening poem of this second collection, the identity of the speaker as an immigrant who came to America "on my father's back, in borrowed clothes" is merged with his identity as a poet who is in the process of creation:

I wait
in a blue hour
and faraway noise of hammering,
and on a page of poem begun, something
about to be dispersed,
something about to come into being.

. . . . .

I'll tell my human
tale, tell it against
the current of that vaster, that
inhuman telling.

This process of poetic creation involves "the ceaseless invention, incessant / constructions and deconstructions" of the past and the given.

The past and the given consist of memories, experiences, received knowledge, established notions, and culturally and historically constructed ethnic identity, which are re-constructed, questioned, challenged, and re-created in Lee's poems. Through this multidimensional process of

creative act, Lee articulates and affirms his identity as a Chinese-American and a poet in the concluding poem, **"The Cleaving."** In this richly textured long poem, Lee's major thematic concerns and technical strategies converge and render his assertions effective and forceful. In **"The Cleaving,"** the implications of eating and detailed descriptions of the speaker's own physical features explored in Lee's early poems such as **"Always A Rose"** are integrated with the specific social and racial contexts of America. Lee's special attention to physical features in **"The Cleaving"** is related to the racialized and politicized body in America, where images of Asians have been misrepresented and stereotyped. Bakhtin has pointed out that social values and other people's opinions are constituent of our own conceptions, feelings, and evaluations of our looks. He argues:

[O]ur own relationship to our exterior does not, after all, have an immediately aesthetic character; it pertains only to its possible effect on others. . . . That is, we evaluate our exterior not for ourselves, but *for* others *through* others.

(*Art*)

In this sense, the act of self-presentation is an act of finding an axiological position in relation to others. How each individual's body, the particular features of a race, and the appearance of an ethnic group are regarded by themselves and others is not purely a matter of aesthetics but of values. In the Japanese-American poet David Mura's poem "The Colors of Desire," the color of the body becomes the racial dividing line between us and them as he describes his teenage father's bewilderment when he

stepped on a bus to find white riders
motioning, "Sit here, son," and, in the rows beyond,
a half dozen black faces, waving him back,
"Us colored folks got to stick together."
How did he know where to sit? . . .

Decades later, Mura, as a teenager himself, also suffers from identity crisis, seeing no presentation of any body of his skin color among the black and white bodies which embody Americans. "[W]here am I, the missing third?" asks Mura in the poem.

For Asian American poets, presentation and celebration of Asian physical features are an act of resistance to racial stereotypes. As Cathy Song asserts in her poem "Out of Our Hands": "The poem about being Chinese, / skin the glorious color of chicken fat" is "a subversive act." In a poem which records "a conquering barbarian" whispering "the racist song" in his Chinese girl's ear: "*bye-bye chinky butterfly*," Marilyn Chin insists on celebrating the color of Asian skin:

If ecstasy had a color, it would be
yellow and pink, yellow and pink
Mongolian skin rubbed raw.

The affirmation of their own ethnicity in these poems is part of the creative and dialogic processes in which Asian

American writers engaged for the purpose of self-definition and self-invention.

Similarly, Li-Young Lee's treatment of looks of particular racial and ethnic groups in **"The Cleaving"** is at once a position and a strategy for articulating particular values and beliefs in response to racial misrepresentations. The poem begins with the speaker's observation of and identification with a Chinese butcher in Chinatown.

> He gossips like my grandmother, this man
> with my face, and I could stand
> amused all afternoon
> in the Hon Kee Grocery,
> amid hanging meats he
> chops: roast pork cut
> from a hog hung
> by nose and shoulders,
>
> . . . . .
>
> Such a sorrowful Chinese face,
> nomad, Gobi, Northern
> in its boniness
> clear from the high
> warlike forehead
> to the sheer edge of the jaw.
> He could be my brother, but finer,
>
> . . . . .
>
> In his light-handed calligraphy
> on receipts and in his
> moodiness, he is
> a Southerner from a river-province;
> suited for scholarship, his face poised
> above an open book, he'd mumble
> his favorite passages.
> He could be my grandfather;
> come to America to get a Western education
> in 1917, but too homesick to study,
> he sits in the park all day, reading poems
> and writing letters to his mother.

Complex meanings are condensed in the detailed description of this Chinese butcher, whom Lee presents with appreciation as an individual, unique in his own ways, yet possessing familiar aspects others can identify with. Both the emotional and physical hardships immigrants endure are captured in "Such a sorrowful Chinese face" and the butcher's "engorged" and "sinewy" left forearm. Lee's description of the butcher's face as being "suited for scholarship" and his absorption in reading among hanging carcasses of meats reflect immigrants' displacement in a new country, where they are stuck with a job for survival, unable to pursue their own interests or develop their talents. Association of the butcher's reading in the grocery store with the persona's grandfather, who read poems but was "too homesick to study," partly suggests their feelings of exile and alienation in a strange land and partly shows the importance of their cultural heritage, which nourishes them and sustains and defines their identity. In addition, refer-

ences to different types of features and to the butcher's manner of calligraphy, which is supposed to reflect personality, reveal the ethnic variety and individual diversity of Chinese people, thus undermining their imposed homogeneity.

Li-Young Lee's poems, like the poems of Marilyn Chin and others, illustrate that Chinese-Americans can remake themselves in images of their own invention.

—Zhou Xiaojing

As the poem develops, the speaker's sympathy and love are extended beyond Chinese immigrants to people of different races and ethnicities. His appreciation of and identification with immigrants and oppressed racial groups assert Lee's position, which embraces others who are different from and yet bound to him by their common humanity and social status.

> An engine crossing,
> re-crossing salt water, hauling
> immigrants and the junk
> of the poor. These
> are the faces I love, the bodies
> and scents of bodies
> for which I long
> in various ways, at various times,
>
> . . . . .
>
> In a world of shapes
> of my desires, each one here
> is a shape of one of my desires, and each
> is known to me and dear by virtue
> of each one's unique corruption
> of those texts, the face, the body:
> that jut jaw
> to gnash tendon;
> that wide nose to meet the blows
> a face like that invites;
> those long eyes closing on the seen;
> those thick lips
> to suck the meat of animals
> or recite 300 poems of the T'ang;
> these teeth to bite my monosyllables;
> these cheekbones to make
> those syllables sing the soul.
> Puffed or sunken
> according to the life,
> dark or light according
> to the birth, straight
> or humped, whole, manqué, quasi, each pleases,
> verging

on utter grotesquery.
All are beautiful by variety.

Lee's celebration of physical heterogeneity and diversity in all people resists and counters notions of "racial hierarchy."

His celebration and descriptions of all sorts of physical features, including those which verge "on utter grotesquery," can be understood as a subversive strategy like what Bakhtin calls the function of "the carnival-grotesque" image. Bakhtin defines this function as:

> to consecrate inventive freedom, to permit the combination of a variety of different elements and their rapprochement, to liberate from the prevailing point of view of the world, from conventions and established truths. . . .
>
> (*Rabelais*)

This subversive function of Lee's embrace of heterogeneous racial and ethnic physical features anticipates his challenge of Emerson's remarks later in the poem. Lee's enthusiasm in honoring diversity is accompanied by his urge to devour all:

What is it in me would
devour the word to utter it?
What is it in me will not let
the world be, would eat
not just this fish,
but the one who killed it,
the butcher who cleaned it.
I would eat the way he
squats, the way he
reaches into the plastic tubs
and pulls out a fish, clubs it,

. . . . .

The deaths at the sinks, those bodies prepared
for eating, I would eat,
and the standing deaths
at the counters, in the aisles,
the walking deaths in the streets,
the death-far-from-home, the death-
in-a-strange-land, these Chinatown
deaths, these American deaths.
I would devour this race to sing it,
this race that according to Emerson
managed to preserve to a hair
for three or four thousand years
the ugliest features in the world.
I would eat these features, eat
the last three or four thousand years, every hair.
And I would eat Emerson, his transparent soul, his
soporific transcendence.

Eating for Lee is "a kind of reading" and a kind of mastering the familiar and the unknown. Eventually, his eating will enable him to give voice to all: "I would eat it all / to utter it."

Lee's response to Emerson's words brings his narrowly conceived generalization to dialogue with multiple and heterogeneous specificity presented in the poem. The validity of the assumed universal truth in Emerson's remarks, acquired through transcendental consciousness, is challenged within a wider cultural horizon and from a different point of view. In the context of racial violence suggested earlier in the poem ("that wide nose to meet the blows / a face like that invites"), Emerson's transcendental generalization about a whole people becomes dangerously limited. Slavery, genocide, and colonialism are justified by biased generalizations of certain races as categories of inferior Other. Like his Whitmanesque statement, "All are beautiful by variety," Lee's recognition of individual uniqueness and insistence on the equality of skin color, "dark or light," and of various appearances, including those "verging / on utter grotesquery," not only enrich his artistic creation with visual heterogeneity; they are also a moral gesture that refuses to regard people in terms of general categories in a multiracial and multicultural society with a history of slavery and racial discrimination.

Lee's embrace of different others is informed by an awareness of the necessity of change and of the pain and violence it involves. The complex meanings of violence suggested in the motifs of eating, devouring, chopping and cutting are further supplemented by a deepened understanding of the self in relation to others with a widened social, ideological, and cultural view in the last part of the poem, which returns to the butcher's cleaving and his sorrowful face.

No easy thing, violence.
One of its names? Change. Change
resides in the embrace
of the effaced and the effacer,
in the covenant of the opened and the opener;
the axe accomplishes it on the soul's axis.
What then may I do
but cleave to what cleaves me.
I kiss the blade and eat my meat.

. . . . .

The terror in the butcher
scripts in the unhealed
air, the sorrow of his Shang
dynasty face,
African face with slit eyes. He is
my sisters, this
beautiful Bedouin, this Shulamite,
keeper of sabbaths, diviner
of holy texts, this dark
dancer, this Jew, this Asian, this one
with the Cambodian face, Vietnamese face, this
    Chinese
I daily face,
this immigrant,
this man with my own face.

Like the physical violence in the butcher's cleaving, emotional and spiritual violence are an inevitable part of change. Transformation entails action that reaches out to what hurts, frightens, and enriches. Throughout the poem, the metaphorical expressions of the speaker's desire to devour the world, to swallow the way the butcher chops, to eat deaths, and to eat Emerson, including his notions and beliefs, is to understand and master "the effaced and the effacer." At the same time, eating suggests a voluntary eagerness to open oneself to new things, a courage to encounter the unknown, and a capacity to absorb all with ease or pain. This understanding of the necessity of being open to others leads to a bond among people of different cultures, religions, and ethnicities. Lee's description of the Chinese butcher's face as a "Shang dynasty face" alludes again to Emerson's remarks about Chinese features, by going back "three or four thousand years" to the Shang dynasty of 1765-1112 B.C. This face, which at the beginning of the poem is only related to different types of Chinese features, is now identified with African, Arabic, Jewish, Cambodian, and Vietnamese faces, as well as the face of the speaker himself.

These violent and physical images in **"The Cleaving"** and Lee's other poems can be better understood through Bakhtin's discussion of the principles and implications of grotesque images. Bakhtin contends: "The grotesque image reflects a phenomenon in transformation, an as yet unfinished metamorphosis, of death and birth, growing and becoming" (*Rabelais*). Moreover, "the grotesque body" is inseparably bound to "the rest of the world." Bakhtin argues:

> It [the grotesque body] is not a closed, completed unit; it is unfinished, outgrows itself, transgresses its own limits. The stress is laid on those parts of the body that are open to the outside world, that is, the parts through which the world enters the body or emerges from it, or through which the body itself goes out to meet the world.

For Lee, his devouring all is a way of outgrowing his own limits, a way of meeting the world and letting the world enter him and then emerge from him in his poems.

Furthermore, Lee's eating, described in great detail, is motivated by an impulse to resist death and its void:

> I would eat this head,
> glazed in papper-specked sauce,
> the cooked eyes opaque in the their sockets.
> I bring it to my mouth and—
> the way I was taught, the way I've watched
> others before me do—
> with a stiff tongue lick out
> the cheek-meat and the meat
> over the armoured jaw, my eating,
> its sensual, salient nowness,
> punctuating the void
> from which such hunger springs and to which it
>   proceeds.

The last three lines here are reminiscent of the speaker's questions in an earlier poem, **"Always a Rose"**:

> If with my mouth,
> if with my clumsy tongue, my teeth,
>
>   . . . . .
>
> I form one word,
> then another, one
> word
> for every moment
> which passes, and if I do so until
> all words are spoken, then
> begin again,
>
>   . . . . .
>
> could I stop our dying?

The creative impulse to capture every living moment in a form with words against dying, implied in these lines, underlies many of Lee's poems. His keen sense of human mortality is intricately related to his deeply felt sense of loss in his parents' lives, particularly his father's life as a refugee and immigrant, which to Lee was a "waste" for a man with tremendous talent and the ability to speak seven languages.

Part of Lee's creative impulse is motivated by his urge to inscribe the presence and experience of his father, his family, himself, and other immigrants in poems as a measure of conquering mortality. As the speaker of **"Furious Versions"** asserts:

> But I own a human story,
> whose very telling
> remarks loss.
> The characters survive through the telling,
> the teller survives
> by his telling. . . .
>
>   The past
> doesn't fall away, the past
> joins the greater
> telling, and is.

Through this telling, death becomes just "a phrase"; "nothing is ever / lost, and lives / are fulfilled by subsequence."

Eventually, Lee's "telling" of the Chinese-American immigrants' experiences in his poems involves the processes of self-exploration and self-invention. His presentation and invention of the Chinese-American experience and identity not only dismantle racial stereotypes, but also replace the single image of Chinese-American, which Marilyn Chin laments in her poem "A Chinaman's Chance":

> The railroad killed your great-grandfather.
> His arms here, his legs there . . .
> *How can we remake ourselves in his image?*

Li-Young Lee's poems, like the poems of Marilyn Chin and others, illustrate that Chinese-Americans can remake themselves in images of their own invention. However, rather than rejecting the broken image of the "great-grand-father" who helped build America's railroads, the invention of new Chinese-American images in Lee's poems is rooted in the reality of Chinese-Americans' lives. As Lee articulates passionately in **"The Cleaving,"** his singing of the world and his people must be proceeded by embracing and understanding both. His singing is made possible by transformations of the self and experience; the renewal of the self is accompanied by a renewal of the traditional poetic form and language.

As a poet, Lee must wrestle with the limits of poetic form, and search for new possibilities of language, in order to tell his "human tale." Lee wrote in a letter, "I can't tell if my being Chinese is an advantage or not, but I can't imagine anything else except writing as an outsider." He added: "It's bracing to be reminded [that] we're *all* guests in the language, any language." In another letter, Lee expressed his hope that the reader of **"The Cleaving"** will note the "richness" and "earthiness" of its language. Li-Young Lee's poems enact and embody the processes of poetic innovation and identity invention beyond the boundaries of any single cultural heritage or ethnic identity.

Works Cited

Bakhtin, Mikhail. *Art and Answerability: Early Philosophical Essays.* Ed. Michael Holquist and Vadim Liapunov. Trans. and notes by Vadim Liapunov. Austin: U of Texas P, 1990.

———. *Speech Genres and Other Late Essays.* Trans. Vern W. McGee. Ed. Caryl Emerson and Michael Holquist. Austin: U of Texas P, 1990.

———. *Rabelais and His World.* Trans. Hélène Iswolsky. Bloomington: Indiana UP, 1984.

Chin, Marilyn. "A Portrait of The Self as Nation, 1990-1991." *The Phoenix Gone, The Terrace Empty.* Minneapolis: Milkweed, 1994. 92-97.

———. "A Chinaman's Chance." *Dwarf Bamboo.* New York: The Greenfield Review Press, 1987. 29-30.

Gadamer, Hans-Georg. *Truth and Method.* Trans. Joel Weinsheimer and Donald G. Marshall. New York: Crossroad, 1992.

Lee, Li-Young. *Rose.* New York: BOA, 1986.

———. *The City in Which I Love You.* New York: BOA, 1990.

———. *The Winged Seed: A Remembrance.* New York: Simon, 1995.

Lim, Shirley. "Reconstructing Asian-American Poetry: A Case for Ethnopoetics." *MELUS* 14.2 (Summer 1987): 51-63.

Moyers, Bill. Interview with Li-Young Lee. *The Language of Life: A Festival of Poets.* New York: Doubleday, 1995. 257-69.

Morrison, Toni. *Playing in the Dark: Whiteness and the Literary Imagination.* New York: Vintage, 1990.

Mura, David. "The Colors of Desire." *The Colors of Desire.* New York: Anchor, 1995. 4-9.

Song, Cathy. "Out of Our Hands." *School Figures.* Pittsburgh: U of Pittsburgh P, 1994. 31-32.

Stern, Gerald. Foreword. *Rose.* By Li-Young Lee. 8-10.

Uba, George. Rev. of *Chinese American Poetry: An Anthology.* Ed. Li Ling-chi Wang and Henry Yiheng Zhao. *MELUS* 18.3 (Fall 1993): 103-105.

Wang, L. Ling-chi and Henry Yiheng Zhao. Introduction. *Chinese American Poetry: An Anthology.* Santa Barbara: Asian American Voices. Distributed by U of Washington P, 1991. xv-xxix.

Wong, Sau-Ling Cynthia. *Reading Asian American Literature: From Necessity to Extravagance.* Princeton: Princeton UP, 1993.

FURTHER READING

Baker, David. "Culture, Inclusion, Craft." *Poetry* CLVIII, No. 3 (June 1991): 158-75.

    Includes commentary on *The City in Which I Love You.* Baker states: "I have to admit that I admire the desires this book expresses more often than I am able to admire the writing."

McDowell, Robert. "Li-Young Lee." In *Contemporary Poets,* Sixth Edition, ed. Thomas Riggs. Detroit: St. James Press, 1996.

    Biographical and critical survey of the poet.

Miller, Matt. "Darkness Visible." *Far Eastern Economic Review* 159, No. 22 (May 30, 1996): 34-6.

    Biographical portrait that stresses the influence of Lee's family history on his poetry.

Moyers, Bill. "Li-Young Lee." In *The Language of Life: A Festival of Poets,* 256-69. New York: Doubleday, 1995.

    Interview in which Lee discusses his family history and the impact of religion on his poetry.

Neff, David. "Remembering the Man Who Forgot Nothing." *Christianity Today* 32, No. 12 (September 2, 1988): 63.

    Emphasizes Lee's interest in the Bible and detects Scriptural influences in his poetry.

Stern, Gerald. "Foreword." In *Rose,* by Li-Young Lee, pp. 8-10. Brockport, N. Y.: Boa Editions, 1986.

    Asserts that what characterizes Lee's poetry is "a certain humility, a kind of cunning, a love of plain speech, a search for wisdom and understanding."

Waniek, Marilyn Nelson. Review of *The City in Which I Love You. The Kenyon Review* n.s. XIII, No. 4 (Fall 1991): 223-25.

    Maintains that Lee's second collection "is more than interesting. One or two of its poems are, in my opinion, necessary. Elegant, delicate, and reticent, they achieve in graceful form the fulfillment of Lee's remarkable childhood history."

Additional coverage of Lee's life and career is contained in the following sources published by The Gale Group: *Contemporary Authors,* Vol. 153; and *Dictionary of Literary Biography,* Vol. 165.

Howard Nemerov
1920-1991

American poet, critic, novelist, short story writer, nonfiction writer, essayist, editor, and playwright.

INTRODUCTION

Nemerov is known for a diverse body of poetry that has been praised for its technical excellence, intelligence, and wit. Writing verse in a variety of forms and styles—including lyrical, narrative, and meditative—Nemerov examined religious, philosophical, scientific, and existential concerns. Although Nemerov frequently has been labeled an academic poet because of his detached stance, his firm grounding in formal verse, and the moralistic tone of some of his work, he often incorporated irony, satire, and colloquial language into his works. In addition to winning numerous prizes for his verse, including the Pulitzer Prize and the National Book Award for *The Collected Poems of Howard Nemerov* (1977), Nemerov was appointed poet laureate of the United States in 1988.

Biographical Information

Nemerov was born in New York City, where his father was president and chairman of the board of an exclusive clothing store. After graduating in 1937 from the elite Fieldston School in New York, Nemerov earned his bachelor's degree from Harvard University in 1941. Nemerov served in the Royal Canadian Air Force from 1941 to 1944 and in the U.S. Army Air Force from 1944 to 1945. He later incorporated his war experiences into such poetry collections as *Guide to the Ruins* (1950) and *War Stories* (1987). After World War II, Nemerov returned to New York and published his first poetry collection, *The Image and the Law,* in 1947. He worked as assistant editor of the irreverent magazine *Furioso* from 1946 to 1951 and was appointed consultant of poetry to the Library of Congress in 1963. During his academic career, Nemerov taught at such colleges as Brandeis University, Washington University, and Bennington College. At Bennington, he met such notable literary figures as Kenneth Burke, Bernard Malamud, and Stanley Edgar Hyman. Nemerov died in 1991 in St. Louis, Missouri, of cancer of the esophagus.

Major Works

In *The Image and the Law* Nemerov utilized a variety of poetic forms and introduced themes that would recur in his subsequent collections, including war, urban blight, art, death, and religion. The poems in this volume, the title of which reflects Nemerov's examination of the dichotomy between what he called "the poetry of the eye"

and "the poetry of the mind," are often pessimistic in outlook. "The Situation Does Not Change," for example, contains a description of New York City: "Only the dead have an enduring city, / Whose stone saints look coldly on a cold world." In the war poem "For W——, Who Commanded Well," which centers on a military officer who served in World War II, Nemerov wrote: "Money is being made, and the wheels go round, / And death is paying for itself." *Guide to the Ruins,* which also contains a variety of poetic forms, including sonnets, epigrams, and ballads, addresses similar concerns, particularly World War II and "the ruins" of post-war life. For example, in "Redeployment," Nemerov proclaimed: "They say the war is over. But water still / Comes bloody from the taps."

The Salt Garden (1955) marks a shift in the tone, style, and themes of Nemerov's poetry. Although his earlier poems were often abstract, esoteric, formal, and derivative of the works of such poets as T. S. Eliot, W. H. Auden, and Wallace Stevens, the poems in this volume are less rigid, impersonal, and bitter; they explore such subjects as perception, nature, and the duality of man. With this volume, Nemerov reached what many critics consider his poetic maturity; *The Salt Garden* was also the first verse collection to bring Nemerov widespread critical and popular attention. *Mirrors and Windows* (1958), which won the Blumenthal Prize from *Poetry* magazine, reveals Nemerov's increasing confidence as a poet. In addition to addressing the limits of perception and the boundaries between the inner and outer worlds, many of the poems in this volume examine the nature of poetry writing, including the difficulty of capturing reality in verse. In "A Day on the Big Branch," for example, Nemerov provided an ironic look at himself and his literary and academic contemporaries. In *The Next Room of the Dream* (1962), which contains two verse plays devoted to biblical themes, Nemerov simplified his poetic approach, emphasizing description, observation, and direct language over abstract philosophical concerns. *The Blue Swallows* (1967) is considered another turning point in Nemerov's career. In this volume, which won the Theodore Roethke Memorial Prize, Nemerov was less pessimistic than in earlier collections and used more short-lined poems in keeping with his trend toward simplicity. *The Blue Swallows* also evinces Nemerov's continuing concern with nature and his increasing interest in science and technology. In *The Western Approaches* (1975) Nemerov returned to the more formal metaphors and conceits of his earlier works. The poems in this collection, most of which are short lyrics, are divided into three sections: "The Way" contains ironic poems about modern life, "The Mind" includes verse about art and culture, and "The Ground" focuses on nature. *War Stories* draws on Nemerov's war experiences and addresses illusions and misconceptions about war and military life. In the poem "The War in the Air," for example, Nemerov declared, "That was the good war, the war we won / As if there were no death, for goodness' sake."

Critical Reception

Critical reaction to Nemerov's verse has been as diverse as his poetic oeuvre. Scholars have consistently praised his technical mastery of various verse forms and the diversity of his subject matter; James Billington, at the time of Nemerov's appointment to U.S. poet laureate, stated that Nemerov's subject matter ranges from "the profound to the poignant to the comic." Joyce Carol Oates has also emphasized the diversity of Nemerov's works, writing that as "romantic, realist, comedian, satirist, relentless and indefatigable brooder upon the most ancient mysteries—Nemerov is not to be classified." Critics have also lauded his emphasis of philosophical themes, particularly his examination of individual consciousness and how it is affected by the external world. However, Nemerov has also been decried as an academic poet because of the difficulty of his verse. Similarly, his works have been called self-indulgent, cocky, obscure, and overly pessimistic. Nemerov's use of humor has also been called into question, with some stating that it sometimes descends into mere wittiness or sarcasm. Others, however, have observed that Nemerov's humor provides a counterbalance to the urbanity and intellectual weight of his poems. Despite mixed reaction to his poetry and a lack of what some consider serious scholarly study of his work, many critics have applauded Nemerov's ability to address contempo-

rary concerns, including the dichotomy between inner and outer life, the isolation of the individual, and the limits of language, in a way that is relevant, compassionate, and thought provoking. Ross Labrie has observed: "No modern writer has more eloquently traced the subtle emanations of consciousness and its shadowy journeying through the fine membrane of language out into the strangeness of the external world."

PRINCIPAL WORKS

Poetry

The Image and the Law 1947
Guide to the Ruins 1950
The Salt Garden 1955
Mirrors and Windows 1958
New and Selected Poems 1960
The Next Room of the Dream: Poems and Two Plays 1962
The Blue Swallows 1967
The Painter Dreaming in the Scholar's House 1968
The Winter Lightning: Selected Poems 1968
Gnomes and Occasions 1973
The Western Approaches: Poems, 1973-1975 1975
The Collected Poems of Howard Nemerov 1977
By Al Lebowitz's Pool 1979
Sentences 1980
Inside the Onion 1984
War Stories: Poems about Long Ago and Now 1987
Trying Conclusions: New and Selected Poems, 1961-1991 1991

Other Major Works

The Melodramatists (novel) 1949
Federigo: Or the Power of Love (novel) 1954
The Homecoming Game (novel) 1957
A Commodity of Dreams and Other Stories (short stories) 1959
Endor: Drama in One Act (drama) 1961
Poetry and Fiction: Essays (nonfiction) 1963
Journal of the Fictive Life (autobiography) 1965
Stories, Fables, and Other Diversions (short stories) 1971
Reflexions on Poetry and Poetics (essays) 1972
Figures of Thought: Speculations on the Meaning of Poetry and Other Essays (nonfiction) 1978
New and Selected Essays (nonfiction) 1985
The Oak in the Acorn: On Remembrance of Things Past and Teaching Proust, Who Will Never Learn (nonfiction) 1987
A Howard Nemerov Reader (collected works) 1991

CRITICISM

F. C. Golffing (review date 1947)

SOURCE: "Question of Strategy," in *Poetry* (Chicago), Vol. LXXI, No. 11, November, 1947, pp. 94-7.

[*In the following mixed review of* The Image and the Law, *Golffing questions the dichotomy between images and ideas in the volume.*]

Mr. Nemerov tells us—on the dust-jacket [of *The Image and the Law*], of all places—that he dichotomizes the "poetry of the eye" and the "poetry of the mind," and that he attempts to exhibit in his verse the "ever-present dispute between two ways of looking at the world." Though usually skeptical of programmatic statements, I find this particular one quite serviceable as a clue—a "way in"— to the plexus of Nemerov's poetry.

The dichotomy itself is fashionable, and it is peculiar. It has almost assumed the status of doctrine in the work of Wallace Stevens, who disassociates mind and eye while paying homage to both, and in the work of W. C. Williams, who, while exploiting sensory perception, makes short work of the mind. There are other poets—none of them of comparable rank—who would, on the basis of the same antinomy, dismiss sense-perception for the sake of pure intellection.

What matters here is not the individual emphasis of the poet but the fact that the underlying assumption is unsound. Eye and mind are not two contrary ways of looking at the world but two interdependent modes of prehension, the perceptual mode subserving the conceptual and normative. The poet who tears the two modes asunder and presents them as inimical commits a meaningless act of violence, which is likely to vitiate the intellectual framework of his poetry.

The fact that both Stevens and Williams have written a great deal of excellent verse cannot be regarded as proof of the soundness of their methods: verse as good as theirs or better has been written on principles that are now generally recognized as either flimsy or perverse (*vide* Shelley, Swinburne, Whitman, Hart Crane). While there is evidently no simple correlation between a writer's doctrine and his poetic practice, it is equally plain that a half-baked or wrong-headed philosophy will tend to have an ill effect on his manner of composition. I am convinced that most of the failures in the work of both Stevens and Williams must be traced to a defect, not in sensibility or formal mastery, but in envisagement or, as Kenneth Burke might say, poetic strategy.

Being largely under the sway of Wallace Stevens, Mr. Nemerov has appropriated not only the basic dichotomy of that poet but also his special tactics of treating ideas and perceptions severally and oppositionally. About half of his pieces deal with "images," while the other half are concerned with the "law," i.e., the normative function of the mind. I can discern no methodological connection between the two sets, not even the dialectical one of active contrasts moving toward some kind of synthesis. Not a few of the "images"—that is, the strictly descriptive or anecdotal pieces—are quite good in their whimsical way; though rarely witty they have to their credit a certain mordancy, acumen, and lightness of touch. Stylistically they hover between Stevens and K. Rexroth, with occa-sional sallies—no spoils resulting—into Empson's domain. When Mr. Nemerov deals with ideas he is as a rule less satisfactory; partly through simple lack of style—his identification with Rexroth becomes intolerable at times, especially in his most ambitious attempt, **"The Frozen City,"** which despite several impressive lines is a towering monument to bathos, cf. "Moving, I saw / The murderer staring at his knife, / Unable to understand, and a banker / Regarding a dollar bill with fixed / Incomprehension," etc.—partly through conceptual confusion, as in **"The Place of Value,"** where a plea for relevance is made in the most irrelevant terms: the neurotic individual versus the healthy statistician, fortuitous versus expiatory death, etc. Yet, oddly enough, it is in this category that we must look for Nemerov's best poems: **"Warning: Children at Play," "An Old Photograph"** and, particularly, **"Lot's Wife"**—poems which suggest that ideation may after all be this poet's forte and that, by turning division of mind and eye into collaboration, he may yet achieve a fine body of poetry. **"Lot's Wife"** deserves to be quoted in full; though ostensibly an animadversion on religious and other revivals, the piece rises far above the level of controversy and assumes the grave beauty characterizing all consummate symbolic statements:

> I have become a gate
> To the ruined city, dry,
> Indestructible by fire.
> A pillar of salt, a white
> Salt boundary stone
> On the edge of destruction.
>
> A hard lesson to learn,
> A swift punishment; and many
> Now seek to escape
> But look back, or to escape
> By looking back: and they
> Too become monuments.
>
> Remember me, Lot's wife,
> Standing at the furthest
> Commark of lust's county.
> Unwilling to enjoy,
> Unable to escape, I make
> Salt the rain of the world.

Arvid Shulenberger (review date 1950)

SOURCE: A review of *Guide to the Ruins,* in *Poetry* (Chicago), Vol. LXXVI, No. VI, September, 1950, pp. 365-70.

[*In the excerpt below, Shulenberger provides a mixed review of* Guide to the Ruins, *commenting on Nemerov's poetic style and the influence of Ezra Pound and William Shakespeare on his works.*]

Among the forty poems in Mr. Nemerov's second book [*Guide to the Ruins*] there are several kinds: epigram, song, sonnet, fragment, and brief essay. They are written in formal or near-formal verse, and are concerned chiefly with the contemporary scene, "the ruins" of a post-war world. In the absence of many positive qualities, their striking characteristic is chiefly their conventionality. They employ conventions of tone, meter, and attitude. The most widely conventional tone of modern serious verse since at least the early work of E. A. Robinson has been that of irony, and many of these poems are heavily ironic. In "Song" the author writes of a dead friend:

> And write him letters now and then
> Be sure to put them in the post
> Sound cheerful as you can
> Care of the holy ghost.

(It is incidental to the matter of irony that the grammar here seems determined by the rhyme scheme.)

The chief metrical convention in modern poems has been that of variation from the traditional line, and of "prose rhythms" in verse lines. It is a delicate question, at what point of variation a given meter ceases to be interestingly new or experimental, and becomes merely bad. We can cite an extreme example, however, and observe that Mr. Nemerov does not often write this badly:

> The art of writing an honest prose
> Is no very difficult one, and may
> Be mastered in little time by persons
> Willing to obey such simple rules
> As are to be found in almost any
> Comprehensive handbook of the subject.

Such lines are not honest verse or prose; they have in fact only the weight of a recent and unstable tradition of accentual verse to recommend them to the reader at all.

The attitude informing a majority of the poems in **Guide to the Ruins** is humanitarian, and the defect of humanitarian feeling in literature is simply that it tends to become emotionally pretentious. It too often deals in entities which exist for the reader only as newspaper abstractions. And it is an attitude which has its own clichés; the tragedy of the recent war for example cannot be forcibly suggested by means of the figure of a totally disabled soldier, a "basket case," brought home and exhibited at a "world's fair." Even a shocking figure can become banal. It should be added, however, of these poems in general that their concern for the real political world and its people is one of their admirable qualities.

Mr. Nemerov writes of other modes of poetry than his own:

> Whole traditions existed
> For which the strict imitation of the predecessors
> And not originality, was the matter of pride.

He seems largely unaware of the tradition within which he works. Yet most of the conventions of twentieth century poetry have existed now for nearly forty years, and can be considered a minor tradition in their own right. It is a

tradition of elliptical, highly connotative verse, in meters that are generally accentual variations from older norms. Its virtues have been the beauty of sound and richness of suggestion displayed in the poetry of its few masters.

Mr. Nemerov's poems are highly diverse in form and style; he has plainly read both Shakespeare and Pound. There is hardly a "typical" poem in the book, or one which seems to show a strong quality which is the writer's own. The verses are in fact exercises in several modes, and many of them are modestly interesting when read as such exercises. The unresolved, suggestive epigram which Pound developed out of imagist verse is represented, and also the literary-archaic language of Pound's early adaptations, as in "Madrigal":

> To such a year no springtime riseth,
> Nor is no excellence in May,
> But darkness in the sky abideth
> Where the world wanders astray.

Not many writers can show an actual Shakespearean influence in a "Shakespearean" sonnet, and Mr. Nemerov's "Four Sonnets" have virtues of hardness and clarity not evident in his poems in the newer conventions.

> Your beauty once the profit of your scorn
> Blinded almost the burning eye of time,
> Which from the head of heaven being torn
> Had left the world lit by your lonely prime;
> But having burned your days to brilliant light,
> Feeding expression on your own cold blood,
> The waste of this is reckoned up to night
> And that you cannot keep which kept you proud.
> So to the blackness of an unloved day
> Your mortal flare condemns the world and you,
> Which locked in mutual contempt display
> The scars of married rage, bound to be true
>   With neither love nor pride nor beauty won
>   From your proud pacing of the lonely sun.

Carolyn Kizer (review date 1958)

SOURCE: "Nemerov: The Middle of the Journey," in *Poetry* (Chicago), Vol. XCIII, No. 3, December, 1958, pp. 178-81.

[*In the generally positive review of* Mirrors and Windows *below, Kizer praises the intelligence, daring, and maturity of Nemerov's poetry, but states that some of the poems in the volume are too long.*]

With this book [**Mirrors and Windows: Poems**], his fourth, Howard Nemerov now belongs to that group of poets who are most difficult to review. To express joy in the accomplished poems, yet receive them ungraciously! For, alas, the homage a serious reviewer pays to a serious poet is a vigorous appraisal. Still, the poems must be handled with care, care in many of its meanings: *mental effort, a sense of responsibility, solicitude, affection,* and *concern*. Nemerov's own criticism has been distinguished by these qualities, so there is the added obligation of trying to serve him as well as he has served other poets.

Howard Nemerov is brave, intelligent, resourceful, crafty, accomplished and grown-up. He not only takes chances with poems and ideas, he is unflinching: The poem, **"A Day on the Big Branch,"** provides us with, among other things, a long, frank and tenderly ironic look at himself and his contemporaries: the generation that was abruptly certified as adult in 1941, and that felt like surplus property from about 1945 on. How many of us marked or saved this poem when it appeared in *Poetry* because through it we saw our own unpoetic lives glowing with poetry? Hu Shih once said that to arouse sentiment, the speaker must not be sentimental about himself, or must have the art to conceal his feelings.

Though Nemerov uses technique and style to conceal his feelings, occasionally he uses them to conceal the absence of feeling, when the motive seems to be a poem-for-poem's sake. Then his equipment stands, polished but empty, like armor in the hall: the mechanical writing of **"A Primer of the Daily Round"** (the kind of thing that most of the younger English writers can toss off before tea); the long poem, **"Orphic Scenario,"** where no amount of forcing can mobilize the dead-tired ideas; the rather limp self-consciousness of most of the Orient-influenced poems, as if they were written on borrowed energy from an imperfectly assimilated world. The long, discursive poem, **"To Lu Chi,"** has a grave and thoughtful central theme, muffled by too many unnecessary lines. Certain phrases and tags are embarrassing: "this somehow seems oddly Chinese . . ." "your words have not failed / to move me with their justice and their strength . . ." "so now / Goodbye, Lu Chi, and thank you for your poem." Though Nemerov may clog the poem with these bits of debris from time to time, there are lovely intervals when the flow is quite pellucid:

> And then you bring, by precept and example,
> Assurance that a reach of mastery,
> Some still, reed-hidden and reflective stream
> Where the heron fishes in his own image,
> Always exists. I have a sight of you,
> Your robes tucked in your belt, standing
> Fishing that stream, where it is always dawn
> With a mist beginning to be burned away
> By the lonely sun . . .

The hard fact remains that many of the long poems are too long. The shorter pieces show that he has a firm sense of dramatic structure, but in poems like **"The Loon's Cry"** or **"Ahasuerus"** the thrust of the poem is hampered by a good deal of off-side activity: whole stanzas of near-irrelevancy wander in, the focus shifts, the intensity diminishes. Sometimes because he does not trouble to whip a line, he sends a stanza to do a line's work. Sometimes when he is preoccupied with exposition, or with over-explicit ironies, the poetry flattens out into prose. Nemerov has what one might call an untrammeled intellect; he is capable of convincing himself that a sensibility or a

concept is sufficiently poetic in itself: the poem becomes a vehicle to carry these responses or ideas. But when he subordinates his intellect to the verbal and linear demands of the poem, the result is a magnificently sustained, fulfilled poem like **"Brainstorm"**:

> The house was talking, not to him he thought,
> But to the crows; the crows were talking back
> In their black voices. The secret might be out:
> Houses are only trees stretched on the rack.
> And once the crows knew, all nature would know.
> Fur, leaf and feather would invade the form,
> Nail rust with rain and shingle warp with snow,
> Vine tear the wall, till any straw-borne storm
> Could rip both roof and rooftree off and show
> Naked to nature what they had kept warm . . .

That passage, with its felicitious echo of Hardy, is ripped from the center of a poem of thirty-nine lines. Most of Nemerov's long poems would be greatly strengthened if they were pared to more nearly this length.

Although Nemerov's ear is not always listening as hard as it should, his eye is, in Dr. Williams' phrase, infinitely penetrant:

> People are putting up storm windows now,
> Or were, this morning, until the heavy rain
> Drove them indoors. So, coming home at noon,
> I saw storm windows lying on the ground,
> Frame-full of rain; through the water and glass
> I saw the crushed grass, how it seemed to stream
> Away in lines like seaweed on the tide . . .

Or these lines, from **"The Town Dump"**:

>   . . . From cardboard tenements,
> Windowed with cellophane, or simply tenting
> In paper bags, the angry mackerel eyes
> Glare at you out of stove-in, sunken heads
> Far from the sea; the lobster, also, lifts
> An empty claw in his most minatory
> Of gestures; oyster, crab and mussel shells
> Lie here in heaps, savage as money hurled
> Away at the gate of hell. If you want results,
> These are results . . .

That magnificant line about money! But, oh, the flatness of those "results". This trick of word repetition in Nemerov is nearly always a signal that his mind is playing fast and loose with his poem: ". . . you may say / There should be ratios. You may sum up / The results, if you want results. But I will add . . ." This passage of "fill" occurs later in the poem, perhaps appropriately in a poem about a dump. But, leafing through his book, one finds: "modern American rocks, and hard as rocks . . ." "never batter that battered copy of *Walden* again . . ." "a venomous tense past tense", "Shadows emerge and merge . . ." "Miraculous result would have resulted . . ." "Could happen only as they let it happen, / Refused to let it happen . . ." and so on. Nemerov, now that he is mature, should renounce the verbal playground. However, the kind of mind which puns easily, can, under pressure, produce the well-wrought irony and the stern paradox which turns the whole world upside down:

> On Saturday, the power-mowers' whine
> Begins the morning. Over this neighborhood
> Rises the keening, petulant voice, begin
> Green oily teeth to chatter and munch the cud.
>
> Monsters, crawling the carpets of the world,
> Still send from underground against your blades
> The roots of things battalions green and curled
> And tender, that will match your blades with blades
> Till the revolted throats shall strangle on
> The tickle of their dead, till straws shall break
> Crankshafts like camels, and the sun go down
> On dinosaurs in swamps. A night attack
> Follows, and by the time the Sabbath dawns
> All armored beasts are eaten by their lawns.

This is the kind of writing that separates the men from the boys: unusual syntax firmly manipulated, artful punctuation, a texture clarified but never thin, an almost arrogant virtuosity. The poet, engaged in the sunlit nightmare of the contemporary world, both hotly observes it and coolly notes it down. Certain poems of Wallace Stevens, Stanley Kunitz, Richard Wilbur, come to mind. . . . That marvelous quality, opulent yet rigorous, of twentieth-century pentameter at its best.

Thom Gunn (review date 1961)

SOURCE: "Outside Faction," in *The Yale Review,* Vol. 1, No. 4, June, 1961, pp. 585-96.

[*In the following excerpt, Gunn offers a laudatory review of* New and Selected Poems *and discusses Nemerov's place in contemporary American poetry.*]

Poetic theory in America is at present in an extremely curious state, resembling that of England during the Barons' Wars rather than that of a healthy democracy or well-run autocracy. It is not even a decent civil war, traditionalist against modernist. At one extreme, it is true, there are the academic-suburban poets who aim so low that it is difficult to see why they bother to aim at all; at the other there are the remnants of the neo-Bohemians, who aim everywhere and thus nowhere. Between these comparative majorities of those who are timid or eccentric on principle exist the Barons, each commanding a troop of ill-equipped and determined fighters, and each against all the rest: Baron Bly, recommending a slightly surrealist imagery that looks a little old-fashioned nowadays; Baron Rexroth, exdirector of the Beat advertising campaign; Baron Fitts, who has just announced that the one distinguishing characteristic of true poetry is Strangeness, and a host of others who are convinced that they, and they alone, have discovered *the* criterion for good poetry. What is interesting, or rather, distressing, is that none of the Barons' retainers are good poets. Or if they are ever good, it is only when they can

forget the precepts of their masters. Just as Herbert is good in so far as he is unlike the rest of the School of Donne, so James Wright, for example, is at his best only when he is not trying to write like Robert Bly.

The Barons certainly get the ear of the public; for one thing, they are mostly good journalists, and for another, they are so original. The result is that a Ginsberg, a Starbuck, an O'Gorman receives unlimited publicity for a brief season, while Howard Nemerov, Louis Simpson, Edgar Bowers, and a few others scarcely inferior are acknowledged only here and there, and often grudgingly. But it is these last, I suspect, who will still be read in fifty years' time. Part of their virtue lies in the very fact that they have not been seduced into literary politics: they have learned from the whole of literature, not merely from writers of a special kind; and they do not view the writing of poetry as a group activity, but as a lonely and difficult task for which the rules are so extraordinarily difficult to define that each poet must reformulate them for himself.

If one associates Nemerov with other poets, it would be only with the contributors to the defunct *Furioso,* who made up a group so loose that it hardly counted as such, including men as different as Coxe and Kees. He has always been, very individually, one of the best poets of his generation, but with the emergence of his *New and Selected Poems* it becomes necessary to class him outside the category of a mere generation; for the book makes it clear that he is one of the best poets writing in English.

Nemerov's early poems were like marvelous tricks, brilliant in themselves, but each in a sense isolated from the rest. In some of them it almost looked as if he were setting himself difficult problems in style and tone for their own sake. **"History of a Literary Movement"** and **"Carol,"** for example, though they are excellent light verse, bear little relation to each other (in the way all of Robert Lowell's early poems bear a closely definable relation to each other) except in so far as they show an unusually efficient use of two different styles, parody and folksong. But the value of the apprenticeship served in the early poems becomes apparent in his succeeding work: for rhetoric is now an instrument with which he can pry open what he pleases.

He is at equal ease in the modes of epigram, comic poem, meditation, and narrative, yet his work in each is now clearly related to his work in all the rest. His style has great range. He can write the abstract statement of the following passage from **"The Murder of William Remington,"** statement which is careful and qualified, and derives much of its strength from Renaissance writing.

> There is the terror too of each man's thought,
> That knows not, but must quietly suspect
> His neighbor, friend, or self of being taught
> To take an attitude merely correct;
> Being frightened of his own cold image in
> The glass of government, and his own sin,
>
> Frightened lest senate house and prison wall
> Be quarried of one stone, lest righteous and high

Look faintly smiling down and seem to call
A crime the welcome chance of liberty,
And any man an outlaw who aggrieves
The patriotism of a pair of thieves.

He can also, however, elaborate images in the much more casual, seemingly random manner of the beginning of **"Writing"**:

The cursive crawl, the squared-off characters,
these by themselves delight, even without
a meaning, in a foreign language, in
Chinese, for instance, or when skaters curve
all day across the lake, scoring their white
records in ice.

What the two passages have in common, perhaps, is an easy authority of tone, by means of which particular observation is generally placed and generalization is seen in relation to a particular context.

The latest poems, occupying more than the first quarter of the book, are the most exciting. For from traditional materials he has fashioned a kind of blank verse which I believe to be, in Pound's sense, an invention. Its most striking characteristic is the almost continuous use of runovers. It is normally difficult to run-over many consecutive lines and still write good poetry, since the metrical norm tends to get lost, as we can see for example in the more breathless passages of **"Endymion,"** by which Keats was protesting—a bit inadequately—against the tightness of eighteenth-century verse. The effect in Nemerov's poems, in say **"Mrs. Mandrill"** or **"Death and the Maiden"**—two of the best—is of an unceasing flow, an unchecked movement *without* looseness or breathlessness: the unit of the line is never destroyed or forgotten (though it is true, as often in blank verse, it has become less important than the unit of the paragraph), and the constant use of runovers, instead of causing the distintegration of form, has created a new form. I find this a technical invention of great importance, and have little doubt that Nemerov will have his imitators within a few years. What is more, the speed at which the verse moves enables the writer to introduce a great many juxtapositions of detail which would seem forced in a slower-moving verse. Seemingly discrepant images are caught up and absorbed by the swift movement to bring about a continuous enrichment and qualification of meaning.

On the night that Mrs. Mandrill entered Nature,
squirrels and mice and crickets everywhere
were squeaking, while the dark spilled up the sky
and the marble moon rolled out over the hills. . . .

"God?" Mrs. Mandrill said, "I have no God,
and not afraid or ashamed to tell Him so
either, if it should come to that. I am
fatigued, and would find no fault with these
　　arrangements,
did they not cause me pain."
　　　　　　　　　But while she said,
her skinny feet troubled the waters, rattled

the leaves, and picked at the nervous vines where
　　crossed
every last telephone in the weird world,
with all the crickety conversations of them
describing how the moon rolled out like a marble
and how the dark spilled up instead of down . . .

Nemerov gets a wide range of material and tone into these passages, yet there is a unity of effect. There is in fact a concentration of experience without the loss of richness and variety that concentration can involve.

Most of the poems in this selection possess a similar authority, and are composed—to apply to him one of his own phrases—with "a singular lucidity and sweetness." It is a distinguished and important book.

Nemerov on poetic vision:

The poet hopes to articulate a vision concerning human life; he hopes to articulate it truly. He may not be much of a poet, he may not be much of a human being, the vision is not so special either; but it is what he hopes to do.

This "vision" need not be thought of in religious terms, as a dramatic one-shot on the road to Damascus; its articulation may be slow indeed, and spread over many works; the early and late parts of it may elucidate one another, or encipher one another still more deeply.

For the substance of this vision the poet listens, he watches, and when he speaks in his character of poet it is his conviction, possibly his illusion, that something other speaks in him.

Howard Nemerov in "The Muse's Interest,"
Poetry and Fiction: Essays, *Rutgers University Press, 1963.*

Hayden Carruth   (review date 1963)

SOURCE: "Interim Report," in *Poetry* (Chicago), Vol. CII, No. 6, September, 1963, pp. 389-90.

[*Below, Carruth calls most of the poems in* The Next Room of the Dream *"wisecracks" and discusses what he considers Nemerov's "technical failures."*]

Half of this book [*The Next Room of the Dream*] is taken up by two verse plays on Biblical themes, and since I'm not qualified to discuss them, I'll pass them over; remarking only that the language seems to me nearly successful, but not quite; it lacks the vivacity or tone which we want from dramatic verse, even when the plays are, like these, reflective in intent. But the other considerations of struc_ ture, pace, theatrical expediency, etc., I must leave to critics of the stage, though I earnestly recommend these two plays as excellent texts for their attention.

The rest of the book consists of short poems, most of which are wisecracks. For my purpose here, I define the wisecrack as a poem of wit in which the two parts fail to cohere. A proper conceit, as we know, consists of a joke and a moral; they must resist each other fiercely yet remain locked together—a sort of terrified embrace; and when they fall apart the joke becomes merely a joke, the moral becomes merely a platitude. Which is what happens in too many of Nemerov's poems. Why? When I reviewed his last book, I said flatly it was a defect of meter and let it go at that, and my friends chided me, quite justly, for being so short with a fine poet. Nemerov has a good ear for all verbal effects, as we know from his best earlier work; for example, that much-anthologized piece about the lady and the whale. There meter does what it should; it fixes the tone of voice, emphasis, and ultimately the meaning of the poem. Meter is, after all, what makes any artifice of language come alive, and I hope it's clear I'm not talking about metronomic or syllable-counting techniques. Nemerov's verse is far from these; his meter is varied and flexible; but I still think that in his recent work his metrical effects have become rather mechanical, rather predictable and repetitious. We recognize Nemerov all right, but a Nemerov who is copying his own manner by rote, turning the stuff out too easily and slickly. The general tone betrays fatigue; and the result is a meter which fails to do its work, fails to sustain and consolidate the feeling, in Nemerov's case the feeling—verve, élan—of wit in a forcing moral action. It isn't always a failure; there's a poem in this book, **"At a Country Hotel,"** which is close to the whale poem in excellence, perhaps good enough to become a new anthology piece. But one poem will not support a book. The reviewer does not inquire, of course, into the deeper cause of a technical failure, especially in the case of a poet as gifted as Nemerov. One can only wish him, as I and I'm sure all readers do, the best of luck, and assure him we will wait for his next book with every anticipation of renewed enjoyment.

Peter Meinke (essay date 1968)

SOURCE: "Twenty Years of Accomplishment," in *The Critical Reception of Howard Nemerov: A Selection of Essays and a Bibliography,* edited by Bowie Duncan, The Scarecrow Press, 1971, pp. 29-39.

[*In the following essay, which was originally written on the occasion of the publication of* The Blue Swallows *and published in* Florida Quarterly *in October 1968, Meinke examines the first twenty years of Nemerov's poetic career, stating "more than any other contemporary poet, Nemerov speaks to the existential, science-oriented . . . liberal mind of the 20th century."*]

It's a bad word, perhaps, but Howard Nemerov is really a philosopher. And judging from the scant space allotted him in the latest books on modern poetry, he is still one of our most underrated poets, despite a steadily widening audience (his *New & Selected Poems,* for example, is in its fourth printing). His latest book confirms what really has been evident since 1955 and *The Salt Garden*: more than any other contemporary poet, Nemerov speaks to the existential, science-oriented (or -displaced), liberal mind of the 20th century.

The Blue Swallows, published exactly 20 years after his first book, is Nemerov's seventh book of poetry, and the 67 new poems it contains represent not so much a culmination of his efforts as another step along a clearly defined technical evolution, and another elucidation (another series of examples) of what might be called a philosophy of minimal affirmation. Like his gulls and swallows, Nemerov circles around and around the things of this world, finding them insubstantial, frightening, illusory, beautiful, and strange. Nowhere is his basically pessimistic view of man as both hopeless and indomitable better expressed than in the conclusion of his new poem, **"Beyond the Pleasure Principle"**:

> There, toward the end, when the left-handed wish
> Is satisfied as it is given up, when the hero
> Endures his cancer and more obstinately than ever
> Grins at the consolations of religion as at a child's
> Frightened pretensions, and when his great courage
> Becomes a wish to die, there appears, so obscurely,
> Pathetically, out of the wounded torment and the
>   play,
> A something primitive and appealing, and still
>   dangerous,
> That crawls on bleeding hands and knees over the
>   floor
> Toward him, and whispers as if to confess:
> *again, again.*

In Nemerov's first two books, *The Image and the Law* (1947) and *Guide to the Ruins* (1950), the same pessimism is evident, but without the technical control, the assimilation of influences. In these early books Nemerov, an ex-RAF pilot, is "writing the war out of his system," as they say; he is also, more importantly, writing A) Eliot, B) Yeats, and C) Stevens out of his system:

> A) Descending and moving closer
>   I saw the sad patience of
>   The people awaiting death
>   (They crossed their bony legs,
>   Their eyes stared, hostile and
>   Bright as broken glass).
>
> B) But I, except in bed,
>   Wore hair-cloth next the skin,
>   And nursed more than my child
>   That grudge against my side.
>   Now, spirit and flesh assoil'd,
>   I lace my pride in,
>   Crying out odd and even
>   Alas! that ever I did sin,
>   It is fully merry in heaven.

C) What, Amicus, constitutes mastery?
   The perdurable fire of a style?

The early poems in general have an abstract, literary quality, an esoteric vocabulary, many allusions. One marked tendency in Nemerov's technical development has been a growing simplicity and directness, not toward the "country" simplicity of Robert Frost, but the simplicity of a highly educated man trying to convey the substance of his meditations clearly.

Critics often note in his earlier work the influence of Auden. While one can find it in an occasional flatness of tone, Nemerov's wit is his own. (In the same way his novels have been compared to Evelyn Waugh's, but both of these similarities are only real insofar as wit is similar to wit.) Wit is certainly a constant element in Nemerov's work: puns, irony, satire, epigrams, jokes; these are not extrusive from his main body of poetry, but integral to it. Nemerov has said, "The serious and the funny are one." This is even more true of *The Blue Swallows* than of his earlier books.

The other main element besides wit that is carried over from his early poetry is a concern with theological questions, reflected often in Biblical subject matter (e.g., his two verse plays, **"Cain"** and **"Endor"**), but more often in a running dialogue with Christianity. Nemerov's own religious position seems to be that of a non-practicing Jew who is constantly wrestling with the problem of faith. An early sonnet ends: "The question is of science not to doubt / The point of faith is that you sweat it out." This is still an important theme in his latest book (e.g., **"Creation of Anguish," "Cybernetics"**).

It was in his third book, *The Salt Garden,* that Nemerov first pulled together his talent and intelligence; originally a "city" poet, Nemerov moved to Bennington, Vermont, in 1948; and nature has been a unifying element in his work since *The Salt Garden* (in 1967 he was given the $1000 St. Botolph Club Arts Award for "a poet of accomplishment and promise, native to, or primarily associated with, New England). **"The Goose Fish," "The Pond," "I Only Am Escaped Alone to Tell Thee," "The Salt Garden,"** are just a few of the poems from *The Salt Garden* which have become familiar to readers of contemporary poetry.

Also in *The Salt Garden* the two main influences on Nemerov emerge. His subjects and the flexible rhythms of his meditative blank verse reflect a close study of Wordsworth and Frost: he is one of the few poets to really learn from these masters:

Line, leaf, and light; darkness invades our day;
No meaning in it, but indifference
Which does not flatter with profundity.
Nor is it drama. Even the giant oak,
Stricken a hundred years ago or yesterday,
Has not found room to fall as heroes should . . .

The typical adjective used to describe nature is "brutal," and the link between brutal nature and "decent" bumbling man is found in the liquids, ocean and blood, which fuse into man's "salt dream," the submerged and subconscious call of the wild. And while Nemerov's lyrical intelligent voice brooding over nature and man dominates this book, there is also great variety of tone and subject: e.g., the telescoped images of **"I Only Have Escaped Alone to Tell Thee,"** the surreal dream sequence **"The Scales of the Eyes."**

The trend toward nature begun in *The Salt Garden* continues in *Mirrors & Windows* (1958), the difference being that in the latter book Nemerov is consciously aware that he is a *poet* looking at nature, trying to capture it in his poems: "Study this rhythm, not this thing. / The brush's tip streams from the wrist / of a living man, a dying man. / The running water is the wrist."

"A Day on the Big Branch" is a good example of Nemerov's attitude, which might be called realistic romanticism. That is, the poems seem to be composed by a romantic sensibility which is at the same time too analytical and honest to see things other than as they are. Nemerov's rocks are "hard as rocks" and when the half-drunk card players climb into the wilderness nothing very glorious happens—except that as they talk of the war and of life, the majestic beauty of nature forces them into "poetry and truth":

so that at last one said, "I shall play cards
until the day I die," and another said,
"in bourbon whiskey are all the vitamins
and minerals needed to sustain man's life,"
and still another, "I shall live on smoke
until my spirit has been cured of flesh."

Another outstanding poem of minimal affirmation is **"The Town Dump,"** a savage metaphor for civilization (in Nemerov's novels the pessimism is redeemed by the humor; generally speaking, in Nemerov's poetry the pessimism is redeemed by beauty, often symbolized by birds):

. . . . You may sum up
The results, if you want results. But I will add
That wild birds, drawn to the carrion and flies,
Assemble in some numbers here, their wings
Shining with light, their flight enviably free,
Their music marvelous, though sad, and strange.

Mirrors & Windows often reminds one of Hart Crane's lines which Nemerov used as an epigraph for his novel, *Federigo*: "As silent as a mirror is believed / Realities plunge in silence by . . ." The object of poetry is to catch as in a mirror the beauty and terror of life, not to make life prettier, not to make it easier for us, not even to help us understand it. "Some shapes cannot be seen in a glass, / those are the ones the heart breaks at." The poems in this book are life-reflecting mirrors, and windows through which we see with the poet's "infinitely penetrant" eye. Nemerov's poetry has become considerably more visual:

It was as promised, a wonder, with granite walls
enclosing ledges, long and flat, of limestone,

or, rolling, of lava; within the ledges
the water, fast and still, pouring its yellow light,
and green, over the tilted slabs of the floor,
blackened at shady corners, falling in a foam
of crystal to a calm where the waterlight
dappled the ledges as they leaned
against the sun; big blue dragonflies hovered
and darted and dipped a wing, hovered again
against the low wind moving over the stream,
and shook the flakes of light from their clear wings.

New & Selected Poems (1960) contains only fifteen new poems; the new note is an overriding concern with his "deare times waste." Time and the loss of innocence, of friends, of hope, are the themes: "I cried because life is hopeless and beautiful," he writes, and the beauty teaches him to "endure and grow." The central poem—Nemerov's longest—is **"Runes,"** symmetrically consisting of fifteen-line stanzas (a stanza form very suitable to his talent, e.g., **"The Beekeeper Speaks"** in *The Blue Swallows*). Like **"The Scales of the Eyes," "Runes"** is a sort of dream sequence, but more tightly organized, the fifteen stanzas being meditations clustered around the images of water and seed, "Where time to come has tensed / Itself." The smooth run-on blank verse lines match rhythm and content:

> Consider how the seed lost by a bird
> Will harbor in its branches most remote
> Descendants of the bird; while everywhere
> And unobserved, the soft green stalks and tubes
> Of water are hardening into wood, whose hide,
> Gnarled, knotted, flowing, and its hidden grain,
> Remember how the water is streaming still.
> Now does the seed asleep, as in a dream
> Where time is compacted under pressures of
> Another order, crack open like stone
> From whose division pours a stream, between
> The raindrop and the sea, running in one
> Direction, down, and gathering in its course
> That bitter salt which spices us the food
> We sweat for, and the blood and tears we shed.

The water streaming in the seed streams through our world, our bodies, holding everything together in its always-changing permanence. The subtle rhythms support the imagery in a fusion of form and content; run-ons, alliteration, repetition, all playing important roles in the structure. The "s" sound in "soft green stalks and tubes," the "d" sound in "hardening into wood, whose hide, / Gnarled, knotted" reinforce the meaning; the rhythm, stopped by "whose hide, / Gnarled, knotted," flows forward again with "Flowing, and its hidden grain." The end of the first sentence holds the paradox of permanent impermanence in the ambiguous "streaming still." The onomatopoeic "crack" splits the second sentence, whose alliteration and longer phrases ("gathering in its course / That bigger salt which spices us the food / We sweat for") underline the stanza's conclusion.

Nemerov's sixth book of poems, *The Next Room of the Dream* (1962), continues his trend toward a more simple and clear verse, emphasizing natural description: "Now I can see certain simplicities / In the darkening rust and tarnish of the time, / And say over the certain simplicities, / The running water and the standing stone . . ." And yet, as he writes in another poem, **"Nothing will yield"**: art smashes on the rocks of reality. Often attacked for being too "cold" or "cerebral," Nemerov's poetry is actually quite the opposite: a passion disciplined, but passionate and humanitarian nevertheless, with cries of anguish constantly breaking through: "—Nothing can stand it!" Poems like **"Lion & Honeycomb"** and **"Vermeer"** express his *ars poetica,* his striving for rhythms "Perfected and casual as to a child's eye / Soap bubbles are, and skipping stones"; poems like **"The Iron Characters"** and **"Somewhere"** express his humanitarianism; poems like **"To Clio, Muse of History"** and **"The Dial Tone"** are metaphysical expressions of his belief in the unreality of reality, the reality of the void.

The Blue Swallows is a worthy successor to these books. Divided into four sections, it has the variety, wit, and technical skill we have come to expect; it is also full of wisdom and gentleness:

> . . . even the water
> Flowing away beneath those birds
> Will fail to reflect their flying forms,
> And the eyes that see become as stones
> Whence never tears shall fall again.
>
> O swallows, swallows, poems are not
> The point. Finding again the world,
> That is the point, where loveliness
> Adorns intelligible things
> Because the mind's eye lit the sun.

While the themes and images are often specifically contemporary (Auschwitz, burning monks, a Negro cemetery, cybernetics), Nemerov is mainly concerned with finding timeless metaphors for the human condition, "relation's spindrift web." In poem after poem we are likened (without his saying so explicitly) to cherries picked off trees, snowflakes falling in black water, lobsters waiting in a tank, days falling into darkness, planted rows dwindling to wilderness, fields becoming shadow. These poems are used more or less contrapuntally with tremendously effective satire on The Great Society (**"Money," "On the Platform," "To the Governor & Legislature of Massachusetts"**). A typical example (not best, but chosen for brevity) is **"Keeping Informed in D.C.":**

> Each morning when I break my buttered toast
> Across the columns of the *Morning Post,*
> I am astounded by the ways in which
> Mankind has managed once again to bitch
> Things up to a degree that yesterday
> Had looked impossible. Not far away
> From dreams of mind, I read this dream of theirs,
> And think: It's true, we *are* the bankrupt heirs
> Of all the ages, history *is* the bunk.
> If you do not believe in all this junk,
> If you're not glad things are not as they are,
>   You can wipe your arse on the *Evening Star.*

Nature, still treated unromantically, permeates these poems; in **"The Companions,"** which is a sort of modern "Immortality Ode," Nemerov describes the pull towards nature that, for example, Frost writes about in "Directive." But Nemerov refuses to see "messages" there: "That's but interpretation, the deep folly of man / To think that things can squeak at him more than things can." A fascination with light, "Firelight in sunlight, silver pale," also plays over these pages, and indeed these poems can be thought of as the "small flames" which conclude the book's final poem:

> So warm, so clear at the line of corded velvet
> The marvelous flesh, its faster rise and fall,
> Sigh in the throat, the mouth fallen open,
> The knees fallen open, the heavy flag of the skirt
> Urgently gathered together, quick, so quick,
> Black lacquer, bronze, blue velvet, gleam
> Of pewter in a tarnishing light, the book
> Of the body lying open at the last leaf,
> Where the spirit and the bride say, Come,
> As from deep mirrors on the hinted wall
> Beyond these shadows, a small flame sprouts.

One reason that Nemerov speaks to this age is that his poetry attempts to come to terms with science: not just psychology (in which Nemerov is well versed, *vide* his *Journal of the Fictive Life*), but "hard" science. Light years and nebulae, the speed of light, electrodes, a heterodyne hum, physicists and particles, are typical subjects for him. His general position seems to be that science is "true," but never quite accounts for our lives (though it tries): science lacks "blood" and "mystery;" it misses the essential:

> For "nothing in the universe can travel at the speed
> Of light," they say, forgetful of the shadow's speed.

While Nemerov's typical form is the loose blank verse line, in *The Blue Swallows* he uses more short-lined poems, trimeter and dimeter, than in his earlier work, keeping with his trend toward simplicity. In this form, too, his rhythms are varied and subtle, as in the first stanza of **"Celestial Globe"**:

> This is the world
> Without the world.
> I hold it in my hand
> A hollow sphere
> Of childlike blue
> With magnitudes of stars.
> There in its utter dark
> The singing planets go,
> And the sun, great source,
> Is blazing forth his fires
> Over the many-oceaned
> And river-shining earth
> Whereon I stand
> Balancing the ball
> Upon my hand.

To sum up. *The Blue Swallows* is the work of a poet who is a master of his craft; rhythm, image, sound fuse in poem after poem. And the poetry speaks to us, as poems should. There is no certainty, much agony, our minds bow down "Among the shadows / Of shadowy things, / Itself a shadow / Less sure than they." Nemerov's general intelligence and craftsmanship perhaps seem old-fashioned today, when blood-and-guts, a confessional softness, and a sort of sloppiness are thought to be more "honest" or "spontaneous"; he is perhaps closer in spirit to, say, Pope, who is also out of favor (nevertheless the 18th century is called the Age of Pope). And underneath the darkness Nemerov continally strikes the existential spark, as in the conclusion of his poem describing an oil slick polluting a stream:

> The curve and glitter of it as it goes
> The maze of its pursuit, reflect the water
> In agony under the alien, brilliant skin
> It struggles to throw off and finally does
> Throw off, on its frivolous purgatorial fall
> Down to the sea and away, dancing and singing
> Perpetual intercession for this filth—
> Leaping and dancing and singing, forgiving
>   everything.

Douglas H. Olsen (essay date 1971)

SOURCE: "Such Stuff as Dreams: The Poetry of Howard Nemerov," in *Imagination and the Spirit: Essays in Literature and the Christian Faith Presented to Clyde S. Kilby,* edited by Charles A. Huttar, William B. Eerdmans Publishing Company, 1971, pp. 365-85.

[*In the following essay, Olsen provides a stylistic and thematic overview of Nemerov's poetry, focusing on the unifying elements in his works.*]

> The serious and the funny are one. The purpose of Poetry is to persuade, fool, or compel God into speaking.
>   —Howard Nemerov, in a letter to Robert D. Harvey.

The poetry of Howard Nemerov is conventional and conversational; it has been called "academic" and even prosaic. His best poetry, however, is among the best American poetry written since World War II, partly because it is poetry that comes so close to being prose. Much postwar poetry, in reaction to the Eliot-Pound influence, attempts to communicate outside the classroom by using colloquial idioms and even slang, a conversational and even flippant tone, and contemporary subjects, such as Old Dutch Cleanser, television, Merritt Parkway, and J. Edgar Hoover. The danger in such poetry, of course, is that it may communicate to our time and our time only. It may be only Instant Poetry or Disposable Poetry (reflecting perhaps a fear that there will be no centuries to communicate to after ours). Howard Nemerov's best poetry, however, succeeds in being both contemporaneous and universal; it succeeds often in being both prosaic and poetic—prosaic on the surface for our prosaic times, yet intensely poetic beneath. Hayden Carruth in a review (*The Nation,* January 21, 1961) said that he was not tempted to reread Nemerov's poems because they had "strayed into prose." Though the statement may be true of some of the poems, such a wholesale dismissal is unwarranted; it is almost as unfair as dismissing Eliot's poetry because it strays into nonsense.

Some of Nemerov's verse appears to be less than poetry because of a seeming lightheartedness, a tendency toward wit and satire.

—Douglas H. Olsen

Nemerov, it is true, is quite at home with prose. He has published three novels (*Melodramatists, Federigo, The Homecoming Game*), a collection of delightful short stories (*A Commodity of Dreams*), an autobiographical journal-novel (*A Journal of the Fictive Life*), and a collection of essays and literary criticism (*Poetry and Fiction*). But he is at his best in his six volumes of poetry (of which the last two are best): *The Image and the Law* (1947), *Guide to the Ruins* (1950), *The Salt Garden* (1955), *Mirrors and Windows* (1958), *New and Selected Poems* (1960), and *The Next Room of the Dream* (1962). The last volume includes two biblical plays (modernized) in verse.

His poems comment on a great range of subjects—dandelions, autumn, snowmen, TV cartoon shows, a dial tone, modern religious attitudes, war, a town dump, lovers, the fairy tale "Sleeping Beauty"—with the calm, sometimes gently ironic voice of a leisurely observer out for a stroll. This quiet style, which is sometimes mistaken for prose, is achieved with much art. Consider, for example, one of Nemerov's best poems, **"Storm Windows."**

> People are putting up storm windows now,
> Or were, this morning, until the heavy rain
> Drove them indoors. So, coming home at noon,
> I saw storm windows lying on the ground,
> Frame-full of rain; through the water and glass
> I saw the crushed grass, how it seemed to stream
> Away in lines like seaweed on the tide
> Or blades of wheat leaning under the wind.
> The ripple and splash of rain on the blurred glass
> Seemed that it briefly said, as I walked by,
> Something I should have liked to say to you,
> Something . . . the dry grass bent under the pane
> Brimful of bouncing water . . . something of
> A swaying clarity which blindly echoes
> This lonely afternoon of memories
> And missed desires, while the wintry rain
> (Unspeakable, the distance in the mind!)
> Runs on the standing windows and away.

Despite the iambic pentameter—most of Nemerov's poetry is in blank verse—the entire poem has a looseness of sentence structure and rhythm associated more often with prose than with poetry. The first four lines especially seem like prose: there is no paradox, no metaphor, no original phrasing, no vivid imagery, no compression of thought. So far it is what you might notice about Frost's

> Whose woods these are I think I know.
> His house is in the village though;
> He will not see me stopping here
> To watch his woods fill up with snow.

But Frost's lines have rhyme and a more definite meter, instantly identifying it as verse. In Nemerov's lines even the iambic pentameter does not distinguish it as verse, since iambic pentameter is so close to natural speech rhythm. There is, however, slant rhyme in these lines—*now, rain, noon, ground*—an arrangement that would not occur in prose. These slant rhymes further chime with other words—*windows, indoors, windows.* Also the sound *or* is in each of the lines—*storm, morning, indoors, storm*—and there are repetitions of *m* and long *o*. If it is prose, it is a pleasantly skillful prose.

In addition to these subtle rhythmic effects, there are two subtle tensions of thought in the four lines. The first is the qualification, "Or were, this morning, until the heavy rain / Drove them indoors." This qualification may cause the reader to suspect Nemerov of wordiness, for these four lines can easily be condensed to three:

> People were putting up storm windows when
> The heavy rain drove them indoors. At noon
> I saw storm windows lying on the ground, . . .

Apparently the meaning has not been changed, but does the revision improve the lines? If it does, obviously the poem is flawed, and we can call Nemerov's original lines prose. In this case, however, one thing that the revision changes is the style. Nemerov's style is a relaxed style; the revised lines, on the other hand, seem to rush too fast—they are not as graceful, as natural, as the original. Also, something quite important to the meaning has been left out: the qualification has been removed. Still it might seem that the qualification was pointless in the first place, since it seems to contradict and even negate the idea of the first line, that "people are putting up storm windows *now*." The *now* is essential to the whole poem, however: the people are still in the process of putting up storm windows; when the rain stops, they will come out and finish the job. The qualification, therefore, only qualifies; it does not negate. The situation, therefore, as in many poems, is a frozen moment, an eternal now. Another of Nemerov's poems, **"Moment,"** illuminates this idea.

> Now, starflake frozen on the windowpane
> All of a winter night, the open hearth
> Blazing beyond Andromeda, the sea-
> Anemone and the downwind seed, O moment
> Hastening, halting in a clockwise dust,
> The time in all the hospitals is now,
> Under the arc-lights where the sentry walks
> His lonely wall it never moves from now,

The crying in the cell is also now,
And now is quiet in the tomb as now
Explodes inside the sun, and it is now
In the saddle of space, where argosies of dust
Sail outward blazing, and the mind of God,
The flash across the gap of being, thinks
In the instant absence of forever: now.

The people are putting up storm windows *now,* the poet is
writing the poem *now,* we are reading the poem *now*—art
blends the time differences into a single *now.* Furthermore, putting up storm windows is as seasonal as the fall
of leaves; in a sense, therefore, people are always putting
up storm windows, as there always is an autumn.

The second tension of thought in the first four lines of
"Storm Windows" is the irony that the people, while
trying to protect their houses from storms, were driven
indoors by a storm. Man's constant struggle against Nature and the ultimate futility of that struggle are thus symbolized at the poem's outset.

"Frame-full of rain" in line 5 is the first slightly unusual,
more "poetic" (because compressed) phrasing in the poem.
It comes as a mild surprise after the relaxed lines preceding it; moreover, the image is set at the beginning of the
line and followed by a caesura. It is the central image of
the poem, and Nemerov makes us see it. Then the image
is described in four lines as though the frame contained a
painting. The poet, however, paints the picture with similes. The observed fact of crushed grass is transformed
into an underlying reality—the natural kinship of grass
with wheat and seaweed. Likewise, the storm and glass
become tide and wind as the imagination of the poet takes
us from the original scene to the sea and country, and
even into elemental Nature.

The similes make sharp pictures, but they are, nevertheless, only similes. The grass "*seemed* to stream." The grass
is "crushed," the glass is "blurred," the clarity sways and
"blindly echoes." In Nemerov's poetry windows and mirrors are used frequently as metaphors or symbols for the
way we perceive the world: in a mirror reversed or distorted (as through a glass darkly) or through a window in
which the glass is a tangible, though invisible, barrier
between the observer and reality. So in this poem the image
seen through the glass is not seen clearly, it seems in
imagination to be what it is not in fact (though the imagination may be closer to Reality than the fact is). In the next
six lines the image of rain on glass *seems* to be even more.
It seems to say something very important, some truth
perhaps. But what it says is not nearly so clear as the
seaweed and wheat. It is only *something.* It is an intuition,
a memory, a longing, a note of beauty or nostalgia perhaps, but unformed. How can one describe a sunset or
love or rain on storm windows? "If only we had words,"
we often think. The poet is one whose job it is to have
words, but here he can only record the fact itself and say
it said "something." The situation, therefore, comes to stand
for abstract truth itself. We sense a greater reality behind
observable fact, but cannot ultimately define it, cannot
know it forever into words. But it is there; it is *something.*

"Unspeakable the distance in the mind!" Within itself the
mind can travel infinitely far from the storm window starting place; but when it returns, it is like the man who saw
heaven and was unable to tell about it. For Nemerov this
"secret of life," which can be known intuitively but not
empirically verified, is often symbolized by water, itself a
mysterious source of life. For example, Section xv of
"Runes":

> To watch water, to watch running water
> Is to know a secret, seeing the twisted rope
> Of runnels on the hillside, the small freshets
> Leaping and limping down the tilted field
> In April's light, the green, grave and opaque
> Swirl in the millpond where the current slides
> To be combed and carded silver at the fall;
> It is a secret, but to have it in your keeping,
> A locked box, Bluebeard's room, the deathless thing
> Which it is death to open. Knowing the secret,
> Keeping the secret—herringbones of light
> Ebbing on beaches, the huge artillery
> Of tides—it is not knowing, it is not keeping,
> But being the secret hidden from yourself.

Here this intuitive knowledge is transformed into *being,*
which paradoxically is unknowable (it can only be *experienced*).

In **"Storm Windows"** the key phrase is "swaying clarity."
That is, after all, what the rain on the glass seemed to say
something of. The phrase is similar to "swaying form" in
Nemerov's essay "The Swaying Form," which discusses
the relationship of art and religion. The term, *une forme
maistresse,* comes from a passage by Montaigne, as translated by Florio; Nemerov applies it to poetry and explains,

> The form . . . is simultaneously ruling and very variable,
> or fickle; shifting and protean as the form of water in
> a stream, where it is difficult or impossible to divide
> what remains from what runs away.

The "swaying clarity," therefore, is first of all that which
the combination of grass, window, and rain evokes in the
observer—the memories, desires, feelings, mood—and,
second, a term appropriate for the poem itself. The poem
as an objective correlative creates the same clear yet vague
feelings in the reader: the situation, the imagery, the sense
of loneliness are clear; yet any message of truth, any
"moral," runs away like seaweed on the tide or water on
windows. According to Nemerov, this is often the nature
of poetry. It is art working against itself to reveal and yet
not reveal. The reason for this is that the "truth" in poetry
is not a theology, not a systematic philosophy, not an
outline of any doctrine, but a re-creation of a situation.

> The poet's business . . . is to name as accurately as
> possible a situation, but a situation which he himself
> is in. The name he gives ought to be so close a fit with
> the actuality it summons into being that there remains
> no room between inside and outside; the thought must
> be "like a beast moving in its skin." (Dante)

[Poetry and Fiction]

The situation named in **"Storm Windows"** is "This lonely afternoon of memories / And missed desires." More specifically, the situation may be one of unrequited love or a broken love affair with the "you" of line 11. "The dry grass bent under the pane / Brimful of bouncing water" reflects the mood of the speaker, a protected (though bent) condition, a numbness perhaps—"After great pain a formal feeling comes," to quote Emily Dickinson. The temptation toward an outpouring of emotion bounces off and away. That the windows in the last line are not the ones lying on the ground, but are standing, suggests a resoluteness of the speaker, a squaring of the shoulders and walking on (undoubtedly under an umbrella). Even our deepest emotions affect us with a "swaying clarity." Grief is often mixed with relief.

Further "meaning" is suggested by the seasonal setting, the tide, the water running off the windows, the poet's passing by the scene. The "message" of the poem is that life goes on, thank goodness, whether we like it or not. This is the message of many great poems. By itself it is a rather banal message; in the great poems it is profound truth. That is why naming a situation is so important: the new name is fresh, and the situation is more than an abstract generalization—it becomes life itself. The poem attempts to give us life itself so clearly that if there is any meaning to life we can read that meaning from the poem. Actually, therefore, the entire poem is the named situation; the meanings of its words should evoke a response similar to that observed by the poet from the real situation. Poems ideally should mean no more than trees do, but

> Poems or people are rarely so lovely,
> And even when they have great qualities
> They tend to tell you rather than exemplify
> What they believe themselves to be about,
> While from the moving silence of trees,
> Whether in storm or calm, in leaf and naked,
> Night or day, we draw conclusions of our own,
> Sustaining and unnoticed as our breath,
> And perilous also—though there has never been
> A critical tree—about the nature of things.

This didactic excerpt from **"Trees"** (*New and Selected Poems*), is—like MacLeish's "A poem should not mean / But be"—unfaithful to its own advice. **"Storm Windows"** more effectively names a situation.

It may still seem to some, however, that **"Storm Windows"** does not name the situation accurately, that the diction and sentence structure are still too prose-like. So many of the great poets of this century—Eliot, Cummings, Thomas, Roethke, Stevens, Hart Crane, Robert Lowell—pack so many implications into each word and line that a readily readable poet like Nemerov, especially in a period dominated by the New Criticism, seems to have the same fault of wordiness as some of the popular nineteenth-century poets, such as Bryant and Longfellow. Or his diction may seem too colloquial and commonplace for poetry. In some of his poems the diction does fail, but that is not a fault of the diction. "To be, or not to be: that is the question" is not intrinsically less poetic than "The slings and arrows

of outrageous fortune," despite the former's plain language. Since Wordsworth, at least, there has been a line of poets—such as Whitman, Frost, and even Eliot—who have sought to write in a common language. Nemerov is in this tradition; he uses ordinary words, avoiding both poetically contrived phrasing and, as a general rule, colloquialisms and slang. He uses a communicative and enduring language. His method is summed up in **"Vermeer"** (in *The Next Room of the Dream*):

> Taking what is, and seeing it as it is,
> Pretending to no heroic stances or gestures . . .
>
> If I could say to you, and make it stick,
> A girl in a red hat, a woman in blue
> Reading a letter, a lady weighing gold . . .
> If I could say this to you so you saw,
> And knew, and agreed that this was how it was
> In a lost city across the sea of years,
> I think we should be for one moment happy.

That is exactly what **"Storm Windows"** does, and in reading it we are, despite the loneliness in the poem, "for one moment happy." It is an aesthetic happiness that comes from our being able to agree that that was exactly how it was; Nemerov has succeeded in naming the situation accurately.

Some of Nemerov's verse appears to be less than poetry because of a seeming lightheartedness, a tendency toward wit and satire. For example, **"Absent-Minded Professor"**:

> This lonely figure of not much fun
> Strayed out of folklore fifteen years ago
> Forever. Now on an autumn afternoon,
> While the leaves drift past the office window,
> His bright replacement, present-minded, stays
> At the desk correcting papers, nor ever grieves
> For the silly scholar of the bad old days,
> Who'd burn the papers and correct the leaves.

Some of his poems satirize materialistic religious attitudes. **"Boom!"** is based on an actual statement by President Eisenhower's pastor that we are in a time of "unprecedented religious activity." After describing some of this activity, Nemerov sums it up:

> Never before, O Lord, have the prayers and praises
> from belfry and phonebooth, from ballpark and
>   barbecue
> the sacrifices, so endlessly ascended.

Then he comments,

> It was not thus when Job in Palestine
> sat in the dust and cried, cried bitterly;
> when Damien kissed the lepers on their wounds
> it was not thus; it was not thus
> when Francis worked a fourteen-hour day
> strictly for the birds; when Dante took
> a week's vacation without pay and it rained
> part of the time, O Lord, it was not thus.

The long satiric prayers ends with a promise to

> give to Thee,
> if Thee will keep us going, our annual
> Miss Universe, for Thy Name's Sake, Amen.

Another poem, **"Santa Claus,"** attacks in a fresh way the commercialization of Christmas.

> Somewhere on his travels the strange Child
> Picked up with this overstuffed confidence man,
> Affection's inverted thief, who climbs at night
> Down chimneys, into dreams, with this world's
> goods.
>
> . . . . .
>
> . . . His name itself
> Is corrupted, and even Saint Nicholas, in his turn,
> Gives off a faint and reminiscent stench,
> The merest soupcon, of brimstone and the pit.
>
> . . . . .
>
> Played at the better stores by bums, for money,
> This annual savor of the economy
> Speaks in the parables of the dollar sign:
> Suffer the little children to come to Him.
>
> At Easter, he's anonymous again,
> Just one of the crowd lunching on Calvary.

A few of Nemerov's poems gently poke at literary attitudes. For example, **"On the Threshold of His Greatness, the Poet Comes Down with a Sore Throat"** has, in parody of "The Waste Land," sixteen footnotes and a "Note on the Notes":

> These notes have not the intention of offering a complete elucidation of the poem. Naturally, interpretations will differ from one reader to another, and even, perhaps, from one minute to the next. But because Modern Poetry is generally agreed to be a matter of the Intellect, and not the Feelings; because it is meant to be studied, and not merely read; and because it is valued, in the classroom, to the precise degree of its difficulty, poet and critic have agreed that these Notes will not merely adorn the Poem, but possibly supersede it altogether.

Carruth calls such poems "wisecracks," which he defines as poems of wit in which the two parts—a joke and a moral—"fail to cohere" (*Poetry,* September 1963). This very criticism shows a serious intention behind such poems, and Nemerov has stated, "In general, to succeed at joking or at poetry, you have to be serious." A poem in which the humorous and serious combine for effect is **"Make Big Money at Home! Write Poems in Spare Time!"**

> Oliver wanted to write about reality.
> He sat before a wooden table,
> He poised his wooden pencil

> Above his pad of wooden paper,
> And attempted to think about agony
> And history, and the meaning of history,
> And all stuff like that there.
>
> Suddenly this wooden thought got in his head:
> A Tree. That's all, no more than that,
> Just one tree, not even a note
> As to whether it was deciduous
> Or evergreen, or even where it stood.
> Still, because it came unbidden,
> It was inspiration, and had to be dealt with.
>
> Oliver hoped that this particular tree
> Would turn out to be fashionable,
> The axle of the universe, maybe,
> Or some other mythologically
> Respectable tree-contraption
> With dryads, or having to do
> With the knowledge of Good and Evil, and the Fall.
>
> "A Tree," he wrote down with his wooden pencil
> Upon his pad of wooden paper
> Supported by the wooden table.
> And while he sat there waiting
> For what would come next to come next,
> The whole wooden house began to become
> Silent, particularly silent, sinisterly so.

The title immediately gives away the humorous intent, and the colloquial phrase "all stuff like that there" establishes the speaker's mocking attitude toward Oliver. The poem appears to be light verse satirizing many would-be creative writers who find they have nothing to say. But it is not light verse; by the time the last line is reached, the tone has changed. As **"Storm Windows"** begins casually and ends profoundly, this poem begins lightly and ends chillingly. The mocking tone is aimed not only at Oliver, but at his high moral intentions in the third stanza (contrast Nemerov's attitude in the passage from **"Trees"** quoted above). Oliver, therefore, represents at the end any poet who tries to make meaning from the silent universe. It may be that there is nothing to say. Compare Ferlinghetti's "poet like an acrobat" who is "constantly risking absurdity / and death" in his attempt to catch Beauty.

> And he
> 　　a little charleychaplin man
> 　　　　　who may or may not catch
> 　　her fair eternal form
> 　　　　　spreadeagled in the empty air
> 　of existence.

This is the modern existentialist attitude: because God is dead, the artist creates in a vacuum of meaning, "the empty air of existence." This note occurs in other Nemerov poems; for example, his four-line **"The Poet at Forty."**

> A light, a winged, & a holy thing,
> Who if his God's not in him cannot sing.
> Ah, Socrates, behold him here at last
> Wingless and heavy, still enthusiast.

A recent poem, **"Projection"** (*The Atlantic,* May 1967), also pictures the existentialist attitude of making the best of the world despite the loss of God.

> They were so amply beautiful, the maps,
> With their blue rivers winding to the sea,
> So calmly beautiful, who could have blamed
> Us for believing, bowed to our drawing boards,
> In a large and ultimate equivalence,
> One map that challenged and replaced the world?
>
> Our punishment? To stand here, on these ladders,
> Dizzy with fear, not daring to look down,
> Glue on our fingers, in our hair and eyes,
> Piecing together the crackling, sticky sheets
> We hope may paper yet the walls of space
> With pictures any child can understand.

Note the underlying humor, the slight tongue-in-cheek tone that is in tension with the seriousness. The suggestion is that the effort to wallpaper space is futile, but the effort itself is called a punishment. Is Nemerov claiming universal absurdity and Divine Injustice—that the punishment is really not deserved? ("Who could have blamed / Us," he asks.) Is the punishment for having once believed in the maps, or is it for now rejecting them? In any case, the actions of "Us"—modern mankind—are ludicrous, absurd. They are only a new (and apparently inferior) version of the old attempts to find meaning. It is like Oliver's trying to make his imagined tree into the axle of the universe: it is going about things the wrong way. What Oliver failed to observe was the relationship between the wooden pencil, the wooden paper, the wooden table, and the wooden house—the essential "woodenness" of these things. Section xi of **"Runes"** illuminates this.

> A holy man said to me, "Split the stick
> And there is Jesus." When I split the stick
> To the dark marrow and the splintery grain
> I saw nothing that was not wood, nothing
> That was not God, and I began to dream
> How from the tree that stood between the rivers
> Came Aaron's rod that crawled in front of Pharaoh,
> And came the rod of Jesse flowering
> In all the generations of the Kings,
> And came the timbers of the second tree,
> The sticks and yardarms of the holy three-
> masted vessel whereon the Son of Man
> Hung between thieves, and came the crown of
>   thorns,
> The lance and ladder, when was shed that blood
> Streamed in the grain of Adam's tainted seed.

Nemerov's existentialism, therefore, seems to be mixed with a form of transcendentalism. God may be silent in that He does not speak to us personally, but He is not dead. God is the very process of life, the Life Force we might call Him. The clearest embodiment of this idea is perhaps **"Mrs. Mandrill"** (*New and Selected Poems*). The lady, busy with activities, believed not in God, until she died and became part of Nature. The poem ends,

> ". . . .
> It hasn't been easy," Mrs. Mandrill cried
> to the crickets and other creatures who now silenced
> their conversations at her heart, "for though
> I knew the lead behind my looking-glass
> better than some, I was the more deceived
> by the way things looked. But for the love of God
> all's one, I see that now, since I shall be
> converted even against my will, and my will
> converted with me, hearing this creature cry
> before her wet heart spills and goes to seed."

In being converted to seed (the source of life) she is converted to belief in God. Rather, all that remains of her is that which is God. Her personality is lost, and it is not life after death as we usually dream of it. In fact, it seems ultimately to be a joke, for such a "meaning" is virtually a lack of meaning: such a "God" may as well not exist as far as any individual human soul's awareness is concerned. Such a God may be impersonal, but at least he is not the burned-out star that many of the existentialists seem to make him. And such paradoxical faith in God is not a giving up to absurdity, despair, negation; it is a positive commitment to life.

One of Nemerov's most frequent metaphors for life, however, is that of the dream. Life is a dream, or *like* a dream; God is the Great Dreamer; our little lives are rounded by a sleep. But men are also dreamers; we dream by imagining things and by wishing for things, but also by trying to interpret the Dream with science, philosophy, history. But "As with a dream interpreted by one still sleeping, / The interpretation is only the next room of the dream."

Poetry also is "the next room of the dream." In "Bottom's Dream: The Likeness of Poems and Jokes," an amusing essay, Nemerov quotes as a definition of poetry Bottom's line: "It shall be called Bottom's Dream, because it hath no bottom." The definition suggests the resonances of meaning a good poem can sound in interpreting the complexities of life.

Nemerov's poems are not dreamlike themselves in the sense that those of Poe, Edwin Muir, or Walter de la Mare are. That is, except for a few—such as **"Fables of the Moscow Subway," "The Stare of the Man from the Provinces,"** and **"Brainstorm"**—they do not use fantastic and surrealistic imagery. If real life itself is considered a dream, if the stuff of life is dreamlike, then even a poem using realistic images can be considered dreamlike. As an example read Nemerov's **"Death and the Maiden."**

> Once I saw a grown man fall from a tree
> and die. That's years ago, I was a girl.
> My father's house is sold into a home
> for the feeble-minded gentlefolk who can't
> any longer stand the world, but in those days
> there was money to maintain the mile or so
> of discipline that kept the hungry grass
> parading to the lake, and once a year
> bring men to prune the files of giant trees
> whose order satisfied and stood for some

euclidean ancestor's dream about the truth:
elms, most of them, already dying of
their yellow blight, and blackened with witches'
  broom
in the highest branches—but they could die for
  years,
decades, so tall their silence, and tell you nothing.
Those men came in October every year,
and among the last leaves, the driven leaves,
would set their ladders for assault and swarm
like pirates into the shrouds, thrusting with hook
and long-handled bill against the withered members
of those great corporations, amputating
death away from the center. They were called
tree surgeons, on the ground they were surly-
polite and touched their caps, but in the air
they dared. I would watch one straddle a branch
on a day of rainy wind, his red shirt patched
on the elm's great fan of sky, his pruning-claw
breaking the finger-bones from the high hand
which held him, and I'd dream of voyages.
My father said: "It looks more dangerous
than really it is." But if your hand offend,
I thought, cut off the hand, and if your eye
offend, pluck out the eye. I looked at him
out of my window all one afternoon,
and I think he looked back once, a young man
proud and probably lecherous, while I—
was a maiden at a window. Only he died
that day. "Unlucky boy," my father said,
who then was dying himself without a word
to anyone, the crab's claw tightening
inside the bowel that year to the next
in a dead silence. I do not know if things
that happen can be said to come to pass,
or only happen, but when I remember
my father's house, I imagine sometimes
a dry, ruined spinster at my rainy window
trying to tally on dumb fingers a world's
incredible damage—nothing can stand it!—and
watching the red shirt patched against the sky,
so far and small in the webbed hand of the elm.

In one sense the whole poem is a dream in that it is a product of the imagination. In a kind of daydream the poet plays the role of a spinster. The man falling from the tree may or may not have been actually witnessed once by Nemerov; within the poem, however, the incident itself is "real," while the poem is imagined, or "dreamt." That it was dreamt differently from "Kubla Khan" makes it no less a dream.

The first reference to a dream—"euclidean ancestor's dream about the truth"—is apropos. The ordering of the trees is analogous to the poet's ordering of words; a poem is also a "dream about the truth." And does not the line imply that Euclid's theories were likewise dreams—intangible, impermanent products of imagination?

The other reference to a dream—"I'd dream of voyages"—is interesting because it comes immediately after the image of the red-shirted man in the tree. The tree has already reminded the speaker of a ship; now she dreams of voyages. Again we see the unspeakable distance in the mind. In the same moment she is safely in her house, up in the tree with the man, and far away from both. How like a dream! How like a poet to transform by means of metaphors one thing into another, trees into ships, tree surgeons into pirates, himself into a spinster.

Her dreaming of voyages, of course, has another meaning: she wishes to escape the reality of the man's death. But she cannot, for as her mind voyages, her body goes nowhere. This is significant because the poem is very much about the limitations of the human body. The trees, for example, are likened to the body collectively in "the withered members of those great corporations," and the one tree is likened to a hand. The disease of the trees is paralleled by the cancer killing the father. The metaphor for the cancer—"crab's claw"—connects it with the tree surgeon's "pruning claw / breaking the finger bones from the high hand which held him." The hand-claw similarity suggests that blight is universal throughout Nature, affecting trees, crabs, human beings. The trees, the tree surgeon, the father, and the spinster "trying to tally on dumb fingers a world's incredible damage" are all caught in this slow grip of death. The allusion to the words of Christ suggests the wrath and judgment of God, especially since the tree surgeon's eye is "probably lecherous." Christ's original words were a warning against adultery.

> You have heard that it was said, "You shall not commit adultery." But I say to you that every one who looks at a woman lustfully has already committed adultery with her in his heart. If your right eye causes you to sin, pluck it out and throw it away; it is better that you lose one of your members than that your whole body be thrown into hell. And if your right hand causes you to sin, cut it off and throw it away; it is better that you lose one of your members than that your whole body go into hell.

This reference to lust in the poem fits in with the rest of the references to the body; however, Nemerov's point here is not a traditional condemnation of the sinner to hell. The point is that everything dies, perhaps because of original sin, perhaps regardless of sin—the emphasis is on death, not sin. The allusion to Christ's words is, therefore, ironic. The disease cannot be cut out, the lecherous eye will not be plucked out for its lechery. The trees and the father will die anyway; the tree surgeon will die, not because he is "probably lecherous" (and only probably) but, if anything, because he is an "Unlucky boy." Chance is suggested, not Divine Purpose; and it is only *suggested*. It remains an open question, for the speaker says, "I do not know if things / that happen can be said to come to pass / or only happen." Interpretations, after all, are only "the next room of the dream."

What comes to pass or only happens is clear, however; in the poem everything disintegrates. "Among the last leaves" the geometric order of the estate has been given over to feeblemindedness, disease, and death. The speaker has gone from maiden to "dry, ruined spinster," an indication of the fruitlessness of things. As geometry and surgery could not save the trees or her father, she is left to imagine herself trying to tally up the damage—the Euclidean theorems are reduced to counting on the fingers, the surgeon's skill is reduced to "dumb fingers."

Life appears to us as prosaic, yet Nemerov reveals it full of poetry—of correspondences, metaphors, essential order; life appears to us as tragic, yet for Nemerov the tragedy is ultimately not so terribly serious—death is the inevitable and necessary order of things; life appears to us as fixed and tangible reality, yet Nemerov sees it as kaleidoscopic and evanescent as dreams— the only reality is flux, Being, Aliveness.

—*Douglas H. Olsen*

Notice that she only *imagines*—dreams. And again the observing is separated from reality by a window. It is a picture of human noninvolvement in tragedy; yet it is *involved* noninvolvement. She is like the poet who can record and try to make some order from a situation he is in but cannot completely comprehend, even if that order he creates is only a "swaying clarity." Or if she cannot make order from it, she can at least feel it—"nothing can stand it!" she thinks. Still, like the poet, she is only an observer, a recorder. It is interesting that "if your eye / offend, pluck out the eye" is followed immediately by "I looked at him." The implications are, (1) her eye offends her by the tragedy it sees; (2) she too, not only the proud and lecherous tree surgeon, will die (have her eye plucked out); (3) her eye offends because it can only see and not understand.

That which she sees at the end of the poem is the image that ties the poem together; it is, therefore, important to understand it. Nemerov may have meant to evoke Stephen Crane's "The red sun was pasted on the sky like a wafer" and the death of Jim Conklin that precedes it. In any case, the synecdoche "red shirt" disembodies the man, making him an effigy or merely a remembered image. "Patched" implies an attempt to repair the sky, as the daring tree surgeon by pruning trees was in effect trying to correct nature. The "webbed hand" may suggest an insect in a spider web, but it is more likely to mean an amphibious hand (like a claw of a crab). At this point in the poem we are in a rainy world, as we were in **"Storm Windows."** Whether the world is wet or dry (notice the spinster is called "dry"), this hand of blight and death is acclimated to it.

Another poem, **"The View from an Attic Window,"** helps us interpret two of the symbols involved—the tree and the rain.

But what I thought today, that made me cry,
Is this, that we live in two kinds of thing:
The powerful trees, thrusting into the sky
Their black patience, are one, and that branching
Relation teaches how we endure and grow;
    The other is the snow,

Falling in a white chaos from the sky,
As many as the sands of all the seas,
As all the men who died or who will die,
As stars in heaven, as leaves of all the trees;
As Abraham was promised of his seed;
    Generations bleed,

Till I, high in the tower of my time
Among familiar ruins, began to cry
For accident, sickness, justice, war and crime,
Because all died, because I had to die.
The snow fell, the trees stood, the promise kept,
    And a child I slept.

The rain in **"Death and the Maiden"** has associations similar to the snow and the seeds in the lines just quoted. Nemerov further clarifies the imagery in *Poets on Poetry* (edited by Nemerov, the book contains contemporary poets' answers to a questionnaire); he says that water images represent for him "an emblem for human life and the life of the imagination" as opposed to stone images, which he associates with monuments and statues "as representing the rigid domination of past over present." Rain, running streams, and snow are also all representative of the natural flux of life—they suggest the seasons, erosion, growth. The life of the imagination must partake of this natural flux; it cannot be rigid, conservative, tradition-bound. The life of the imagination must adapt to change, even to tragedy and death.

Trees, on the other hand, are immovable like stone; yet they are alive and growing. They seem to represent human endurance, which resists for a time the natural flux but finally succumbs to it. In **"Learning By Doing"** (*The Kenyon Review,* Vol. XXVI, Spring 1964) Nemerov describes the cutting down of a supposedly diseased tree, which when sectioned turns out to be healthy. The poem concludes:

There's some mean-spirited moral point in that
As well: you learn to bury your mistakes,
Though for a while at dusk the darkening air
Will be with many shadows interleaved,
And pierced with a bewilderment of birds.

It is a "mean-spirited moral" because the moral is, in effect, that we can do nothing about the seeming injustices of life except endure them; they are a natural and inevitable part of life. In the many interleaved shadows of life man is bewildered as the birds. He can try to tally the injustice on his fingers, he can put up storm windows, he can cry, he can write poems, but he cannot stop the flux of life. He will be driven indoors, he will die trying.

M. L. Rosenthal, in *The Modern Poets: A Critical Introduction* (New York, 1960), comments concerning **"Storm**

Windows" that "the rain falling on the windows and grass crushed beneath them are seen in a momentary frame that gives the whole thing the illusion of having a point—though what is really being seen in the frame is essential chaos." This is true, but what must be emphasized is that the chaos for Nemerov is *essential.* Man may be caught in the web of death, and his attempts to prune out the death may be as futile as trying to patch the sky with red cloth; the "world's incredible damage" may seem like chaos as we perceive it through our windows; yet this chaos is not necessarily evil, is not even necessarily chaos. For Nemerov this chaos is the ongoing process of life; it is the working of God himself. Man is "far and small" compared to it, but like the daring tree surgeon in the elm he is caught up in it. He is himself caught and yet a vital part of the process. He might be considered—in a sense similar to that meant by Emerson, Thoreau, and Whitman—"divine." That is, man as a part of Nature is a part of God. Nemerov is not so optimistic as the transcendentalists—there is no indication that the process is constantly improving itself—yet neither is he so pessimistic as the naturalists and the existentialists.

The poet in this scheme of things could perhaps be thought of as a priest serving the God who is Being Itself (as the transcendentalists tended to think of the poet).

> Poetry and institutionalized religion are in a sense the flowing and the static forms of the same substance, liquid and solid states of the same elemental energy. . . .

> So the work of art is religious in nature, not because it beautifies an ugly world or pretends that a naughty world is a nice one—for these things especially art does not do—but because it shows of its own nature that things drawn within the sacred circle of its forms are transfigured, illuminated by an inward radiance which amounts to goodness because it amounts to being itself.

The poet is, in a sense, a spokesman for God; his vocation is to capture, not in stone but in a living form, life itself.

Therefore, it is appropriate that Nemerov's poetry is so like prose, so like jokes, so like dreams. Distinctions between prose and poetry, comic and tragic, dream and reality, pass away. Life appears to us as prosaic, yet Nemerov reveals it full of poetry—of correspondences, metaphors, essential order; life appears to us as tragic, yet for Nemerov the tragedy is ultimately not so terribly serious—death is the inevitable and necessary order of things; life appears to us as fixed and tangible reality, yet Nemerov sees it as kaleidoscopic and evanescent as dreams—the only reality is flux, Being, Aliveness.

All this may perhaps seem to be making too much of the philosophy behind Nemerov's poems. It is, of course, not a systematic philosophy but rather a viewpoint, an attitude toward life; besides, Nemerov again and again shows the futility of drawing any final philosophic conclusions—that almost becomes his philosophy, in fact. Nevertheless, Nemerov's viewpoint unifies his poems; almost all of them show in different lights his way of looking at the world as

though it were God. Furthermore, in each individual poem this "philosophy" is virtually another of his poetic devices: like metaphors, iambic pentameter, alliteration, it helps hold the poem together and give it form. It is not a moral tag applied at the end of each poem, but an integral part of the art of each poem. To misunderstand his outlook is to misread the poems. Many of them at first glance may appear to be saying the opposite—that is, have the opposite attitude toward the situation—from what they actually say. They seem to show universal loneliness, meaninglessness, alienation. But Nemerov treats these contemporary attitudes with a tone of irony and paradox and transcends them. The spinster's attitude in **"Death and the Maiden"**—her attitude of helpless hand-wringing anguish at the world's injustices—is not wholeheartedly Nemerov's. (That she is not really wringing her hands, but counting on them, is a clue to her insincere sincerity.) If anything, he is on the side of the tree surgeon daring death (and probably on the side of the absent-minded professor who would correct the leaves—does not the poet "correct" nature, too?). He may regret, he may dream, he may wish it were otherwise, but he does not cry about it; he does not sit in sackcloth and ashes like so many modern Jobs who have not heard the Voice from the Whirlwind. Nemerov has apparently heard the Voice and seeks to comfort (or perhaps discomfort) our modern Jobs. As **"The View from an Attic Window"** (quoted above) suggests, it is even better to sleep than to cry. Or as the narrator of one of his short stories, "A Commodity of Dreams," says concerning the collection of dreams, over three thousand of them filed and cross-referenced in a museum, of Capt. Frank Lastwyn,

> They would at the British Museum look at it all twice, and imperturbably file it away under Dreams . . . which was probably where everything, after all, belonged. We were all, I thought sleepily, going down in history, whether as Tamerlane or Genghis Khan, Beethoven, St. Francis or Nesselrode who invented the pudding. Or as Capt. Frank Lastwyn, R. A. (ret.), or as anonymous nobodies, such as myself. And ho-hum to it all.

But that, too, needs to be taken with a grain of irony. Nemerov's attitude is usually not so flippant.

Wallace Stevens' "Men Made Out of Words" comes very close to summing up Nemerov's poetry.

> Life consists
> Of propositions about life. The human
>
> Revery is a solitude in which
> We compass these propositions, torn by dreams,
>
> By the terrible incantations of defeats
> And by the fear that defeats and dreams are one.
>
> The whole race is a poet that writes down
> The eccentricities of its fate.

But for Nemerov defeats and dreams *are* one; he has thus overcome the fear. His propositions will seem eccentric to those of us whose center is different from his, yet within his poems the eccentricity—the apparent conflict between good and evil, dream and defeat—is at the center. There good and evil, dream and defeat, are paradoxically *One*.

Nemerov on difficult poetry:

If poetry reaches the point which chess has reached, where the decisive, profound, and elegant combinations lie within the scope only of masters, and are appreciable only to competent and trained players, that will seem to many people a sorry state of affairs, and to some people a consequence simply of the sinfulness of poets; but it will not in the least mean that poetry is, as they say, *dead*; rather the reverse. It is when poetry becomes altogether too easy, too accessible, runs down to a few derivative formulae and caters to low tastes and lazy minds—it is then that the life of the art is in danger.

Howard Nemerov in his Reflexions on Poetry and Poetics, *Rutgers University Press, 1972.*

Howard Nemerov with Robert Boyers (interview date 1975)

SOURCE: An interview with Howard Nemerov, in *Salmagundi,* Nos. 31-32, Fall, 1975/Winter, 1976, pp. 109-19.

[*In the following interview, which was conducted in March 1975, Nemerov discusses such topics as his composition process, the relationship between poetry and meaning, politics, and the influence of other writers on his works.*]

[Robert Boyers]: *In the past year or so, Howard, you've written a great many poems, by any standards more than most poets expect to write in several years. Is there any way you can explain to yourself, or anyone else, how this came to be?*

[Howard Nemerov]: Well, I'd settled down thinking to myself, listen, you're 54 years old; who the hell goes on in this business, year after year, waiting for something to happen? You're supposed to grow up, you might as well cease to expect. And I said to my old lady, the minute classes stop I am facing the inner emptiness. After settling down, though, or trying to, I began saying things to myself, and appreciating again that when I think to myself, it's usually in blank verse, sometimes in rhyme. I'm very old-fashioned in this respect, you know, wrote all my free verse when I was 26, so I didn't have to do any after that. But how the new poems came so fast I can't say. All I know is every night I would go to bed and think, well, that's the end: look, you had another poem today, it could never happen again—all the while holding onto the sneaky notion that maybe it might happen again. What I love about poetry is, you don't know what you're going to do until you do it. You don't have to plan everything the way

you do when you write novels—it's terrifying to wake up every morning knowing what you have to do.

The new poems that I've had a chance to look at are as various as we'd expect from your previous work. Do you find yourself writing in verse forms that are new to you? Do you think about such things at all as you're going about the business of writing new poems?

Well, a new poem seems to start for me with a line, not an idea: if I get an idea I'm pretty sure I can't write it. I thought once, what a wonderful thing, write a poem about a deep-sea diver: get out a few books about deep-sea diving, and everything will turn out to be a metaphor for deep-sea diving, you know, heaven, hell, the rest of it— I was full of ideas, but no poem. A poem, or a part of a poem, just speaks itself in me when I'm composing. It's really kind of uncanny, though mind you I'm not claiming heaven-sent inspiration, because you would feel just as wonderful if you were writing the worst poem in the world, as long as it was coming that way. In fact, I've met people who do feel that way even though what is produced isn't much. But it feels like some kind of privileged condition. Nearest analogy: coming over on a little commuter-flight airplane from Binghamton this morning, I got this strong religious sense of being in the hand of something. You know, I used to fly in the war, and here I was, sitting up front, looking at the instruments, and I said to myself, I could fly this damned airplane, though I wouldn't know how to handle communications incessantly pouring in from the great beyond. Anyhow, we are intrepidly trudging on through clouds so thick you can't see an inch beyond the nose of the airplane, and this little guy doesn't even wear a smart cap. I had to think—one of those great fantasies— if the guy had a stroke and little Howard the hero has to guide us in, how the hell would I do it? My impulse would be suddenly to dive the hell out of the clouds so I could see what I was doing, and wind us up against the mountain, somewhere, whereas he just stays there, serenely flying, all the other passengers commuting like this full time, not terrified like me. You know, usually it's the unknown that's terrifying, but here it was the unknown that sustained, with people talking the blind aircraft in; they say, do this, steer that, descend 5000, descend 4000, and finally when they say—you're still in the clouds, can't see a damned thing—'O.K. 5-5-0, you're on your own, keep descending, you'll see the runway, in front of you,' and you do, it's just, well, miraculous, though maybe a pretty humble miracle compared with some. But imagine the industry, the ingenuity, the skill, the countless people which go into such an operation, performed all the time, guiding one tiny little airplane safely to its destination. And, above all, I was thinking, imagine the utter obedience and trust that goes with all this: you don't do what you think is right, you do what the guy tells you to, and practically all the time it works, that's remarkable. Well, it's an analogy, maybe there are better ones, and I don't want to make this all religious-sounding, but writing poetry does feel, when you're in the midst, as if something knows what you're doing, much better than you do. Of course, this is not to deny that you're supposed to have a little skill at carpentering the stuff together, so you find the rhyme at the right time, the rhyme that maybe gives you an idea you wouldn't have had if you didn't have to find a rhyme. But you can't deny that wonderful, wonderful things happen some mornings.

I agree, and the analogy does work, I think, though for me there's a problem in trying to identify what the obedience you describe would correspond to in composing verse. Clearly it's related to the more familiar idea of discipline, and would seem to involve attention to the processes of a poem's unfolding, the character of its dynamics. Do you want to say anything further about obedience in this sense?

Claude Levi-Strauss has a clue, I think, when he speaks of Bach as a composer of the code, so that everybody who's played Bach a little feels as if he just lets the language do it, you know, in the organ works, page after page, you feel you know every note and exactly where the next line will go. I like the idea of the composer of the code, of somebody who is not rebellious, who is just using the language because it says that is the way it is to be used. No doubt this is an illusion, like many others, except we've got to remember: the idea that we do things all by ourselves is equally unprovable and equally likely to be an illusion. The idea fixed in the human brain since, ah, somebody says William of Ockham, somebody says Roger Bacon, and so forth, since the 17th century maybe, that it's all done in the head and has nothing to do with out there seems to me to be very funny, tragic too, because some of its results are frightening. Is that really as clear as mud?

Clearer.

I've written satiric poems about it, of course. Sometimes I believe the business about codes, sometimes I'm not so sure. Now one of the writers who has expounded these ideas most clearly is your friend Erich Heller, who wrote, as from teacher to pupils, "be careful how you interpret the world—it is like that." That's nice, huh?

It's instructive, though in some ways hard to grasp. Your notion of the code seems to me very important if Heller's idea is to yield what it should. If the world "is like that," a fact we ignore only at great peril, then we can honor its actual presence only by having the proper words, the inevitable code-words, if you will. But doesn't this conflict with the rather more familiar contemporary notion of the poet as one who makes the language over, more or less in the image of his desire?

There is a conflict, I suppose, though when you come right down to it the real poets are doing pretty much the same thing with the language. I'm always surprised to discover, when I try to teach students to write poetry, that they rarely notice how omnipresent language is in our dealings with the world. I've often thought that poets don't have to know much about the outside world—they just have to know what things are called, the names even of strange things. It's alright to make up new ones, but that's rarer than has been supposed, I think. Karl Shapiro was being pretty silly when he proclaimed, rather arrogantly I

thought, that words in a poem have nothing to do with their dictionary meanings. I felt like shaking him. You know, the words are there when you come into the world, like other institutions—they're waiting for you; you're not a lonely individual cast out on a barren shore. And if the words didn't have their dictionary definitions, nobody could use them. Of course, people didn't have to wait for dictionaries, but words must always have had a consensual, lexical human meaning, even granting that there are idioms in which no word has its dictionary meaning. And this isn't something we should be sorry about.

I'm very strongly in favor of literal meanings. I try to stress the difference between what the poem says and what it means, which may be mysterious beyond belief and doesn't need to mean one thing.

—Howard Nemerov

You've written lately on the relation between poetry and meaning. In what sense does the poem's commitment to the poet's private meaning betray the code?

Well, I'm very strongly in favor of literal meanings. I try to stress the difference between what the poem says, which should be as clear as you can make it, and what it means, which may be mysterious beyond belief, because the universe is mysterious and vast, and doesn't need to mean one thing. But the reader should get a more or less literal vision of what's being talked about. What I passionately respect in reading Dante lately—he's been such a revelation to me this time around—what I passionately respect about his writing is his painstaking endeavour to make it clear. You never question that he is talking about what he's seeing. I don't know how he saw it, but it's absolutely marvelous. He's always talking about seeing—the act itself of seeing—and sees almost everything he writes about: he never tries to show you in the grand Miltonic manner. Me and Milton don't get along so well—I respect the old bastard, but I'm never going to love him.

Are there other writers you especially value, from whom you take regular instruction or inspiration? Writers, say, at once committed to 'the code' and to the mystery of things?

I really value the writers that I think of as friends, because they are ever so full of grandeur that they don't tell you. I have four in special: Socrates, Shakespeare, Montaigne, and Freud. Freud especially, because he tells you always the process of his thought and how he's getting there—says, oh, that won't do, we'll have to go back and try this other way. And Montaigne, because he is so generous about the world and so kindly in leading you throught it.

And he makes no vast claim—he says, in that last great essay "On Experience," "I have no subject but ignorance and profess nothing but myself."

What I love about poetry is, you don't know what you're going to do until you do it. You don't have to plan everything the way you do when you write novels— it's terrifying to wake up every morning knowing what you have to do.

—Howard Nemerov

The element of the mysterious, the unaccountable, which you've alluded to only intermittently in all this, seems to me of central importance when one distinguishes among the different kinds of verse you've written. Thinking about this recently, I was brought to think of something that Saul Bellow said at Skidmore a year ago in accounting for the differences among his various novels. He talked about the different kinds of inspiration involved in the composition of different books. When he wrote Henderson The Rain King, *he claimed, he had no feeling of polemical urgency in him, no axe to grind; he had no specific ideas that he wished to communicate, felt entirely at one with himself and with the world he was making. Thus he preferred* Henderson *to all his other books, feeling that somehow there was a relation between the success of a book and the feeling of the author at the time of its composition. Now my conviction is that the poems collected in parts 3 and 4 of* **The Blue Swallows** *are, in concentration at least, the most consummately beautiful poems that you've written. Could it be that there were special circumstances, spiritual or otherwise, which might account for the special merits of those poems?*

Well, applying a comparison even more exalted than Saul, notice in Shakespeare each of the great tragedies has its own absolutely unmistakable atmosphere and tonality. You know it's Shakespeare with every line, but you also know which play it is; in fact, there's one exception that proves the rule, a place where Hamlet talks just like Macbeth, very melo-dramatic and ranting, so that I think, my god, he must have had this left over from Macbeth, tucked away. But there's never a question about the authenticity of the passage. As to the parts of *The Blue Swallows* you speak of, they were written over a period of maybe four years. Each poem has its own peculiar history. I remember that the **"Bee-Keeper"** poem came, I'm ashamed to say, from a newspaper article about a beekeeper who said, not in the words of my poem, a good many of the things that get said there. **"The Mud Turtle"** was written while I was writing the *Journal Of The Fictive Life* one summer, and poems like **"Celestial Globe"** in part three were practically all written one summer in '66 when I was trying something special and rather different for me—you note

they're all little trimeter lines instead of blank verse, or rhymed iambics.

We mentioned the name of Auden in talking together earlier, and I would like to ask you about him—not only because he's died recently, but also because what most of us think about Auden is likely to say a great deal about the way we think about contemporary poetry in general. Lots of poets have become increasingly dissatisfied with Auden's verse, especially his late verse, and I suppose this feeling about Auden was most vividly expressed by Randall Jarrell many years ago, when he described much of the verse as "an invalid's diet, like milquetoast." Arguing that the dominant emotion in most of these poems was pity, he said that they tended to express an encompassing passivity. Do you feel this way about Auden? I know that at one time at least he meant a great deal to you.

Well, I guess I always admired Auden's poetry very much. Still, when asked to review his last book, or 1/2 book, collected and published by his friends, I got kind of stymied, and thought of a one-sentence review: "Dear reader, whatever you thought of Mr. Auden before this, you will continue thinking, and you won't change your mind on this account." I thought of his as a rather triumphal career in a way: here he had gone from a kind of boyish pseudo-fascism, through leftist pseudo-fascism, writing all kinds of nonsense, some of it terribly obscure, but learning at last to speak in a decent middle-range voice. He became a grown-up who could tell you lots of things, who had done more than any other poet to absorb the technological scientific sophistication of the time and make it go in his verses. At the same time, of course, as a declared devout Christian, he is also among the saved, and must be a happy man. If there is a great good place I hope he is in it, and I hope the cooking is good. All the same, this sort of thing makes me nervous, and I think—if that is all there is to being happy, I'm doomed, and maybe poetry as I know it is doomed too. And Auden doesn't improve the prospect much when he says, giving himself every freedom, that the poet *qua* poet is always a polytheist. Isn't that wonderful? When you're saved you can have it any way you like . . . Did you see the little remembrance by his friend Hannah Arendt in *The New Yorker* a few weeks back? The shocking revelation of loneliness and despair and not caring? I can conclude only that we human beings are a mass of contradictions, and anybody that tries to make sense of us must be a human being himself. In all, I wouldn't go quite as far as Randall Jarrell, but it is true that the later poems are mild-mannered, avuncular, full of crummy wisdom: if the word was still usable you could say that they were the poems of a godfather. He addressed one volume of them to his godson, you know, benign, witty, charming advice on how to get on through the world and how to put up with its contradictions and miseries. But I keep thinking, is that all? Maybe a great voice from on high wants to say, "yes, bub, that's all," to which I can reply only, "I have no rational argument, sir, to put up against that; if it's that way, so O.K." So Auden in his poetry and career raises some very poignant problems for anybody who is serious about writing. Whatever you feel about Auden, though, or about other writers, one thing at least can be said in favor of poetry: it doesn't kill you for not believing in it. Fair enough?

You bet. Still, it bothers me that work by writers a lot less famous than Auden, though very accomplished, is regularly overlooked, badly neglected, usually on behalf of another kind of verse which in our time has come to be known as naked poetry. I wonder whether we might talk a little bit about the obvious neglect of poetry decidedly more exacting, more reflective, than most of the poetry that my students tend to read. I'm thinking of poets like Ben Belitt and John Peck, whose work we both admire.

It's hard to talk about the situation in poetry; like all those large general things, as soon as you assert something about it you can instantly think of 3, 4, 8, a million exceptions. Still, what you suggest seems true enough. I like poets like Ben Belitt, very much as you do, and I like John Peck, who's much younger, and has only one volume to his credit so far—a very distinguished volume, I might add. But they are both extremely refined, elaborate, fastidious, and curious artists, whose effects you have to get familiar with for rather a long time. I don't think they yield themselves instantly at all, and of course, for I guess maybe two decades or so, people have been very much in favor of the immediate in poetry, what can be picked up like Kleenex—you use it and throw it away, the poem of strong opinion frequently. Naked poetry, the title of some silly anthology of several years ago, did suggest at least that if you want to go around naked you'd better be in a warm climate, and that it's best to be beautiful. When I looked at the book I had to say I'd rather write closed couplets. Again, old-fashioned.

There was a time when you wrote novels, but you seem to have given that up. Were there things that you felt you could express better in the poetry than in the medium of prose fiction?

Well, maybe I just gave in to natural laziness. Writing a novel is terrible hard labor, whereas in my new book [**The Western Approaches**] I have 4 or 5 poems about what a novelist thinks when he's writing a novel; you know, that's much easier, because you can do it in 14 lines. Maybe the decisive turning point came when I taught at Bennington over the way some years ago, and dear Stanley Edgar Hyman, now the late Stanley, was holding one of his typical benevolent despot department meetings. We were going to hire somebody, and Stanley said, we have to hire a novelist, and a voice from the back of the room, not mine, said, but Howard's a novelist, and Stanley said, Howard's a poet. So we hired Bernard Malamud instead. You know, it's trivial little things like that that mark where you have to go. I said to myself, now you know something your best friends wouldn't tell you; in fact, they've told you.

We're covering all of your various literary enterprises here, as you can see. You've written a great deal of criticism, published several volumes of it, in fact. Does writing criticism play any special function for you? Does it bear, say, a specific relation to the ups and downs of your verse writing? Do you make elaborate calculations to decide which medium you'll write in?

Hmm, I can remember when I began to think of all this in economic terms. When I was starting out, benign grey-haired publishers would explain to me how very proud they were that I was a poet, because that would be good training for when I went on to write the novels they wanted me to write. And, before I got out of commercial publishing and settled down with University presses, and other such unprofitable endeavours, the only way I could get my poems published in the main was by hooking a novel onto them. And you know, once I came through with a novel I could say, I will not sign a contract for this unless you promise to publish me a book of poetry. So that worked, twice I guess, or three times. Then a poet named Elder Olson at the University of Chicago said they were going to start publishing poetry and could they start with me? I said, oh dear, yes you could, and we've been friends ever since. It's a very gentlemanly relation, nobody makes any money or expects to, but they put out a handsome looking book, they keep it in print, it sells its respectable seven copies a year, and we seem to be reasonably happy that way. And so the same thing happened with Rutgers University Press and my essays: they published two books of those and sort of a novelist's creature called *Journal of the Fictive Life*. For me publishing seems to be largely a matter of going on record—I did this, see, here it is—and it doesn't much matter whether it's criticism or verse or fiction. It never occurred to me to write criticism as a conscious decision. When I was growing up criticism was a very serious industry, big time for such a little thing as literature. At 18 I thought the *Kenyon Review* was, well, eternity, and that John Crowe Ransom, who edited it, must have been there years and years and years. Only 20 years later, when John asked me if I wanted to succeed him as editor, I went back and looked at the files and found *Kenyon Review* had started only the year before I went to college, and had that imposing appearance of permanence and the imposing tone of authority, shared by the *Partisan Review* and the *Sewanee Review,* and one or two others in those days. Then one wrote because one felt that there was a literary community, life seemed to be a little smaller and more compact. I know I am talking like an elder, but I feel like an elder. About 1955 when Allen Ginsberg emerged from somebody's head, the whole thing exploded and it all got redefined, and among many of the effects of that period was that I generally stopped reading those magazines and even writing for them. Anyhow, you write criticism you make as many enemies as you need quite early in life, and I didn't think I needed to write any more: I had already done for myself. But I never gave up criticism, and have always alternated between poetry and prose, lately deciding to do only what can be accomplished in brief spans of time. Unlike our friend Ben Belitt I write very fast and concentratedly, and suffer with years of silence inbetween. People like Ben or Bernard Malamud seem to go to the desk every day; they know what they're working at and they steadily do a little something to bring it toward completion, whereas I have to do it all in a single day—if not a whole novel, then an entire episode or chapter at any rate.

You've written often about the public world in your verse, though your most memorable work seems to me meditative and personal, frequently even mystical, rather than ocasional. Would you say something about the poet and politics. It's a subject you've addressed once or twice in your essays, for example, "Poetry And The National Conscience."

I remember vividly the assassination of President Kennedy. It was, you know, a very terrible moment, and like a great many other poets I went right home and spent all day writing a poem of which I think it was *The New Leader* published only a part. When things had calmed down I recognized sadly that it was a terribly bad poem, and so I never reprinted it. When we poets believe that we are thinkers, moralists, or preachers, that we're going to give you the word—now this is wisdom, kid—we reveal more terribly than others how stupid we are. And so I mostly have stayed, I think, out of the preaching business. It's very hard to be sure because someone may think you're preaching when you didn't know you intended to at all. I like to think I've succeeded in writing poems that try to say what the world is, instead of what it ought to be, though I'm sure as I age I make my moralizing sententiae as nobly and with as grand a gesture as anybody else. But I don't think I've lately committed the sin on the scale I achieved in the Kennedy poem—that was awful slop. You can, of course, be moved by a political event and set out to write about your response, only to find that your poem isn't about the subject you were moved by at all. That's hard to tell without getting down to cases, and I just don't have any examples at hand to help me there. I do think I wrote a very good political poem, about the murder of William Remington, who nobody perhaps remembers now. In that great Alger Hiss-Whittaker Chambers scandal he was one of the not-innocent victims who went to prison, where he was beaten up by two thugs. He died there and I don't remember that I was terribly moved when I heard it, but I wrote a damned good poem, and managed not to moralize. At least there's no overt sermonizing about how the American people should behave better, or stuff like that.

You once wrote, I think it was years ago in Journal of the Fictive Life, *that you hate intelligence and have nothing else. I've been curious about that.*

That's one of those petulant things you say once in a while if you're writing a more or less confessional book. It doesn't mean that that is your settled habit of mind; after all, I wrote that book just at the beginning of those terrible middle years. Since then I've cheered up considerably. I now teach with a ruthless geniality, handing my misinformation out with the greatest good cheer.

That's good to hear, and something I'll try to remember when I reach my own terrible middle years. Speaking of terrors, though, I thought we might talk a little about the subject of anxiety (you've got to admire this transition).

I think I know where you're headed.

There's been much debate lately about what Harold Bloom calls The Anxiety of Influence. *In your recent review of Bloom's book for* Sewanee *you sound some skeptical notes on the theory. Without addressing the book itself, perhaps you'd care to say something further about the relation between influence and style.*

Well, Mr. Bloom may be correct, and there may well be an anxiety of influence for most people. If so, I guess I was just too stupid to be anxious, though I was influenced by everybody. I remember T.S. Eliot's first poetry recording, reading "Gerontion" on one side and "The Hollow Men" on the other—I got so I could imitate it even down to the scratch of the needle at the start of the record. My first girl-friend at college told me to cut out the parsonlike tone of voice, that it didn't have to sound that way. I went on from there to make up my own talent school of virtuosity exercises—Tate, Auden, Stevens, Pound. 20 years later somebody gave the exercises back to me and I swear there is a Stevens imitation there that could go in his *Collected Poems* and even he wouldn't know he hadn't done it. It always seemed to me a lot of cant to talk about finding your own voice—I never went looking for it. My way of saying this in the review of Bloom's book was that, when you're 20 you write "the grass is green" and they say "ah, Wallace Stevens." 20 years later you write "the grass is green" and they say "ah, sounds just like you." It's a very mysterious business. Seems to me that to learn to write poetry includes learning maybe to sound like Yeats at his most arrogant, putting on an attitude you couldn't afford in your personal life because people would kick your teeth in. What's always marvelous is at the end how the poem can sound like all the others and still be itself. Style is the making visible of the soul, about which Proust had a good thing to say, when he wrote that the universe is the same for all of us and different for each. I like that.

William Mills (essay date 1975)

SOURCE: "The Urban Landscape," in *The Stillness in Moving Things: The World of Howard Nemerov,* Memphis State University Press, 1975, pp. 119-42.

[*In the following essay, Mills states that Nemerov's poetry of the urban landscape "concentrates on the most powerful institutions of society" and "is particularly concerned with the tyranny of the past over the present."*]

Nemerov's poetry divides itself between contemplative poetry, which most often springs from his encounter with nature, and satiric poetry that finds its nourishment in disparities and paradoxes that reveal themselves in the urban scene. To say that the poetry is divided in subject matter and concern is not, however, to say that the poet is divided. These disparities and paradoxes are revealed by a vision that knows the difference in authentic and inauthentic existence, and knows the call of conscience. This vision knows that for someone to say there is a boom in religion because of increased affluence is to hear what Heidegger calls "idle talk."

And because this discoursing has lost its primary relationship-of-Being towards the entity talked about, or else has never achieved such a relationship, it does not communicate in such a way as to let this entity be appropriated in a primordial manner, but communicates rather by following the route of *gossiping* and *passing the word along*. What is said-in-the-talk as such, spreads in wider circles and takes on an authoritative character. Things are so because one says so. . . .

[Martin Heidegger, *Being and Time,* 1962]

Language of idle talk, since it does not mirror a primary relationship to what is being talked about, mirrors nothing. It only seems to mirror something, and so "takes on an authoritative character." As this kind of talk becomes public and authoritative, the inauthentic self seems released from the task of genuine understanding. "Because of this, idle talk discourages any new inquiry and any disputation, and in a peculiar way suppresses them and holds them back," continues Heidegger, in *Being and Time*. This kind of talk corresponds to what Nemerov calls "verbal effigies," of which we will hear more shortly.

The disparities and paradoxes that Nemerov reveals through his authentic vision often take the form of jokes—so say some of the critics, disparagingly, and so says Nemerov, but with an explanation.

It sometimes seems to me as though our relations with the Devil have reached that place, so near the end, where paradox appears immediately in all phenomena, so that, for example, the increase of life is the fated increase of mortal suffering, the multiplication of the means of communication is the multiplication of meaninglessness, and so on. At the obsequies for the late President of the United States the "eternal flame" was extinguished by holy water in the hands of children; in the material world that may have been an unfortunate accident, but in the poetic world, where one is compelled to listen to symbolic things, it appears as possibly a final warning, a witty and indeed diabolical underlining of the dire assassination itself.

So if paradox and accenting the hidden side of the paradoxical has always played such a part in my poetry, perhaps the seriousness of that view of life, its necessity even, may now begin to appear. The charge typically raised against my work by literary critics has been that my poems are jokes, even bad jokes. I incline to agree, insisting however that they are bad jokes, and even terrible jokes, emerging from the nature of things as well as from my propensity for coming at things a touch subversively and from the blind side, or the dark side, the side everyone concerned with "values" would just as soon forget.

[*Reflexions on Poetry and Poetics*]

Even though there appears to be a division in the body of the poet's work, he at least sees a unity.

Principally . . . I would like to take note of Nemerov's urban landscape: the parts that make him laugh, even if it means a subsequent kick in the stomach, and the parts that make him quietly rage. Often, as I have noted, the obser-

vations take the form of some kind of joke, though certainly this is not always so.

A number of the poems that embody jokes are grouped in a section of *The Blue Swallows* called "The Great Society." The second poem of the group illustrates a persistent ironic quality of this part of Nemerov's work.

"Sunday"

He rested on the seventh day, and so
The chauffeur had the morning off, the maid
Slept late, and the cook went out to morning mass.
So by and large there was nothing to do
Among the ashtrays in the living room
But breathe the greyish air left over from
Last night, and go down on your knees to read
The horrible funnies flattened on the floor.

It's still a day to conjure with, if not
Against, the blessed seventh, when we get
A chance to feel whatever He must feel,
Looking us over, seeing that we are good.
The odds are six to one He's gone away;
It's why there's so much praying on this day.

The setting is familiar in modern poetry, a Sunday on which the character or characters are not taking part in the ritual of the culture. Eliot's "Mr. Eliot's Sunday Morning Service" and Wallace Stevens' "Sunday Morning" are of course the most famous of such poems and much more elaborate than Nemerov's. In addition, Stevens' goes on to a kind of affirmation that is not evident in Nemerov's. In this one "the odds are six to one He's gone away." Perhaps, the speaker muses, we feel similar to God, since both of us are resting on the seventh day, but he suspects God is not in God's house as he is in his.

There are several senses in which this poet can be described as "religious," although not in a conventional way. If a deep concern for the world and even for metaphysics is religious, then truly Nemerov is. But it is also true that he persistently takes his shots at organized religion. For instance, consider **"Debate with the Rabbi"**:

You've lost your religion, the Rabbi said.
  It wasn't much to keep, said I.
You should affirm the spirit, said he,
And the communal solidarity.
  I don't feel so solid, I said.
We are the people of the Book, the Rabbi said.
  Not of the phone book, said I.
Ours is a great tradition, said he,
And a wonderful history.
  But history's over, I said.

We Jews are creative people, the Rabbi said.
  Make something, then, said I.
In science and in art, said he,
Violinists and physicists have we.
  Fiddle and physic indeed, I said.
Stubborn and stiff-necked man! the Rabbi cried.

The pain you give me, said I.
Instead of bowing down, said he,
You go on in your obstinacy.
    We Jews are that way, I replied.

Although the idea behind the poem is a serious one, this may well be described as "light verse." If such verse were the sole achievement of the poet, it would not be enough to create the reputation that he has. With this said, it can be observed that such verse complements his lyric voice and makes a different kind of statement. The rabbi's opponent will not be persuaded by categorical imperatives that he does not feel. He cannot affirm a "communal solidarity" because he does not "feel so solid." This play on words offers a kind of revelation that Nemerov is quick to point out shares a commonality with the lyric. His essay "Bottom's Dream: The Likeness of Poems and Jokes" explores this commonality.

> . . . one mechanism of economy in joking is the pun, either in the use of one word in two senses . . . or in the use of two words of similar sound which mean different things but still somehow establish a resemblance beyond that of the sound.

Concerning jokes he says:

> A joke expresses tension, which it releases in laughter; it is a sort of permissible rebellion against things as they are—permissible, perhaps, because this rebellion is at the same time stoically resigned, it acknowledges that things are as they are, and that they will, after the moment of laughter, continue to be that way. That is why jokes concentrate on the most sensitive areas of human concern: sex, death, religion, and the most powerful institutions of society; and poems do the same.

Accordingly, the rabbi's opponent says he does not feel solid, either in his belief or in his hunch about himself and the world; thus, he is unable to affirm "communal solidarity." The rabbi attempts to entice by an appeal to tradition, but his opponent insists that history is over, which it obviously is; but less obviously, the opponent thinks, the past should not tyrannize the present, an omnipresent theme of Nemerov.

As Nemerov searches the modern terrain he insists that "bad jokes, even terrible jokes" emerge from the nature of things and the nature of the "Great Society." In a vein that sustains this criticism of the contemporary church, he has written a poem called **"Boom!"** which was inspired by the daily newspaper. The passage in the Associated Press release that struck Nemerov was the following.

> Atlantic City, June 23, 1957 (*AP*).—President Eisenhower's pastor said tonight that Americans are living in a period of "unprecedented religious activity" caused partially by paid vacations, the eight-hour day and modern conveniences.

> "These fruits of material progress," said the Rev. Edward

L. R. Elson of the National Presbyterian Church, Washington, "have provided the leisure, the energy, and the means for a level of human and spiritual values never before reached."

The idea of opulence leading to spiritual values—values that had their origin in austerity, pain, and suffering—jars the poet's sensibilities. The poem begins:

> Here at the Vespasian-Carlton, it's just one
> religious activity after another; the sky
> is constantly being crossed by cruciform
> airplanes, in which nobody disbelieves
> for a second, and the tide, the tide
> of spiritual progress and prosperity
> miraculously keeps rising, to a level
> never before attained. The churches are full,
> the beaches are full, and the filling-stations
> are full, God's great ocean is full
> of paid vacationers praying an eight-hour day
> to the human and spiritual values, the fruits,
> the leisure, the energy, and the means, Lord,
> the means for the level, the unprecedented level,
> and the modern conveniences, which also are full.

The effect of asserting that the "churches are full" is rapidly neutralized by noting that everything else is full. Besides beaches and filling-stations, all the modern conveniences are full, with the suggestion that a particular convenience that we fill daily is now running over—with much the same substance as the minister's observations. The poem, of some forty-five lines, continues to build up details of the affluent society, but midway through the poet notes tersely: "It was not thus when Job in Palestine / sat in the dust and cried, cried bitterly." Nemerov would insist that if there are "jokes" in his poems, surely there is a horrible joke in the reality of the daily newspaper article.

Observations like those of the minister—repetitiously presented in the mass media—become increasingly dangerous, because their very repetition transforms them into dogma. This is the language of "idle talk," mirroring nothing but seeming to, and as such, taking on authoritative character. In addition, it keeps us from further inquiry. Nemerov explores this danger:

> The thought of statues as representing a false, historical immortality seems clearly related to the scriptural prohibition against the making of graven images; and the category in which the statues finally come, which I generalized out as "effigies," may include also photographs, mythological figures such as Santa Claus, even mannequins in shop windows, or anything that tends to confirm the mind in a habitual way of regarding the world, which habitual way is, to be short with it, idolatry. There are many examples in my work, and I have chosen one which represents newspapers, by a slight extension of the thought, as a sort of verbal effigy, idolatrously confirming human beings day after day in the habit of a mean delusion and compelling them to regard this mean delusion as their sole reality. I say this halfway as a joke with the name of a newspaper, *The Daily Globe*.

The poem **"The Daily Globe"** elaborates his criticism:

Each day another installment of the old
Romance of Order brings to the breakfast table
The paper flowers of catastrophe.
One has this recurrent dream about the world.

Headlines declare the ambiguous oracles,
The comfortable old prophets mutter doom.
Man's greatest intellectual pleasure is
To repeat himself, yet somehow the daily globe

Rolls on, while the characters in comic strips
Prolong their slow, interminable lives
Beyond the segregated photographs
Of the girls that marry and the men that die.

Nemerov says that for the benefit of foreign audiences he would point out that obituary pages in this country are almost exclusively of men and the matrimonial pages exclusively of women. Nemerov thinks that such habitual ways of regarding the world, described in the poem, are on the increase. One of the functions of the poet then is to help man see the world freshly. One way that poets have always done this is by holding up a mirror so that man may see himself, his own nature and the nature that is outside him. Nemerov notes that "if my poetry does envision the appearance of a new human nature, it does so chiefly in sarcastic outrage, for that new human nature appears in the poetry merely as a totalitarian fixing of the old human nature, whose principal products have been anguish, war, and history." Nemerov's satiric mirror helps man to see himself as he is, and the mirror held up to nature puts him in touch with the currents of being.

Nemerov has noted that makers of jokes and smart remarks resemble poets in another way in that they would also be "excluded from Plato's Republic; for it is of the nature of Utopia and the Crystal Palace, as Dostoevsky said, that you can't stick your tongue out at it." Turning from the church to politics, I might select three or four short instances where the poet's tongue is showing.

No bars are set too close, no mesh too fine
To keep me from the eagle and the lion,
Whom keepers feed that I may freely dine.
This goes to show that if you have the wit
To be small, common, cute, and live on shit,
Though the cage fret kings, you may make free with it.

So much for the lower end of the political scene, with its hangers-on and opportunists.

Another poem, **"The Iron Characters,"** in one way takes up the other end of the political spectrum, but part of its theme is a kind of commonality that is shared by the great and small.

The iron characters, keepers of the public
  confidence,
The sponsors, fund raisers, and members of
  the board,

Who naturally assume their seats among the
  governors,
Who place their names behind the issue of
  bonds
And are consulted in the formation of
  cabinets,
The catastrophes of war, depression, and
  natural disaster:
They represent us in responsibilities many and
  great.
It is no wonder, then, if in a moment of crisis,
Before the microphones, under the lights, on
  a great occasion,
One of them will break down in hysterical
  weeping
Or fall in an epileptic seizure, or if one day
We read in the papers of one's having been
  found
Naked and drunk in a basement with three
  high school boys,
Or one who jumped from the window of his
  hospital room.
For are they not as ourselves in these things
  also?
Let the orphan, the pauper, the thief, the
  derelict drunk
And all those of no fixed address, shed tears
  of rejoicing
For the broken minds of the strong, the torn
  flesh of the just.

There is a tension of sentiment in the poem that insists on our reflection here. The "iron characters" do represent us in responsibilities and because this is so, they are the "keepers of the public confidence." When Nemerov selects certain very pathetic and awful moments when the keepers of the confidence break, it is not with malice. In only one instance might the newspaper reader feel occasioned to laugh: at the figure found naked and drunk with high school boys, because our nervous attitude about sexual mystery quickly finds its outlet in some kind of laughter—sometimes. It may be the case of Profumo in England or of Senator Kennedy in the United States. But these are "horrible jokes" that are no jokes. Thus, there is an obvious sympathy in the selection of examples. On the other hand, there is an ironic pleasure or affirmation for "all those of no fixed address" when they discover that the mighty are made of flesh also. Surely it is ironic that the orphan and the pauper should shed "tears of rejoicing / For the broken minds of the strong, the torn flesh of the just." The "tears of rejoicing" are shed simply because of a commonality or brotherhood that becomes apparent when the characters cease being "iron" and appear as all too human.

"To the Governor & Legislature of Massachusetts" is turned out with a livelier hand than the preceding poem, and incidentally reflects a part of recent Americana—that following the McCarthy era and the great Communist scare. University professors, among many others, found themselves being forced to sign "security oaths" and to promise that they would not overthrow the government. Apparently this happened to Nemerov:

When I took a job teaching in Massachusetts
I didn't know and no one told me that I'd
    have to sign
An oath of loyalty to the Commonwealth of
    Massachusetts.
Now that I'm hooked, though, with a house
And a mortgage on the house, the road ahead
Is clear: I sign. But I want you gentlemen to
    know
That till today it never once occurred to me
To overthrow the Commonwealth of
    Massachusetts
By violence or subversion, or by preaching
    either.
But now I'm not so sure. It makes a fellow
    think,
Can such things be? Can such things be in the
    very crib
Of our liberties, and East of the Hudson, at
    that?

So if the day come that I should shove the
    Berkshire Hills
Over the border and annex them to Vermont,
Or snap Cape Cod off at the elbow and scatter
Hyannis to Provincetown beyond the twelve-
    mile limit,
Proclaiming apocalypsopetls to my pupils
And with state troopers dripping from my
    fingertips
Squeaking "You promised, you broke your
    promise!"
You gentlemen just sit there with my
    signature
And keep on lawyer-talking like nothing had
    happened,
Lest I root out that wagon tongue on Bunker
    Hill
And fungo your Golden Dome right into
    Fenway Park
Like any red-celled American boy ought to
    done
Long ago in the first place, just to keep in
    practice.

Perhaps incidental to the poem, there is here an example of Nemerov as liberal, which he certainly is. Though he handles the theme with wild hyperbole, there is a reasonable degree of serious anger. This is another occasion of the bad jokes that he insists constantly emerge from the contemporary ruins.

In the early 1950s when the United States was much troubled by the fear of Communist infiltrators, an economist for the U.S. Commerce Department, William Remington, was sentenced to three years for perjury, for denying he had given secret data to a Russian spy ring. Scheduled for release in August 1955 he was beaten to death by two fellow inmates in late November 1954. There was speculation that he had been beaten because of anti-Communist sentiment within the inmate population of the Lewisburg, Pennsylvania, prison. Nemerov reacts to the brutality of

the killing (the murderers used a brick inside a sock) in **"The Murder of William Remington,"** reflecting about the function of law and punishment, and that much punishment may be a grim joke the majority play on the few.

There is the terror too of each man's thought,
That knows not, but must quietly suspect
His neighbor, friend, or self of being taught
To take an attitude merely correct;
Being frightened of his own cold image in
The glass of government, and his own sin,

Frightened lest senate house and prison wall
Be quarried of one stone, lest righteous and high
Look faintly smiling down and seem to call
A crime the welcome chance of liberty,
And any man an outlaw who aggrieves
The patriotism of a pair of thieves.

"The Great Society, Mark X" picks up the phrase that was coined during the Johnson years, years that signaled to Americans that there may be rents in the fabric of their society. The affluence following World War II seemed to create as many problems as it solved, or it may have simply given Americans the leisure to reflect on them. Ralph Nader came along during the years of "The Great Society" with his expose of General Motors. It may also be that since the assembly line, with its association of Ford's Model T, helped to usher in the era of mass production that gives a foundation to the present affluent society, it is appropriate that Nemerov chooses an automobile which is falling apart to embody the erosion of the society.

The engine and transmission and the wheels
Are made of greed, fear, and invidiousness
Fueled by super-pep high octane money
And lubricated with hypocrisy,
Interior upholstery is all handsewn
Of the skins of children of the very poor,
Justice and mercy, charity and peace,
Are optional items at slight extra cost,
The steering gear is newspring powered by
Expediency but not connected with
The wheels, and finally there are no brakes.

However, the rear-view mirror and the horn
Are covered by our lifetime guarantee.

The criticism of the society in this poem has been heard with much greater frequency in the intervening years, as, some feel, the wealth continues to accumulate in the hands of the powerful few. This is the articulated voice of a liberal. "Interior upholstery is all handsewn / Of the skins of children of the very poor," is a bit melodramatic, but the last three lines are, I think, the most haunting. A contemporary American despair derives from the fear that there is no way of stopping the juggernaut, that "there are no brakes." It is yet to be seen whether the "automobile" can be steered by anything but expediency, or whether the machine will have to be destroyed and a new one built. Two things are guaranteed: there is a rear-view mirror through which we can see the wreckage-strewn past and see where we have been, and a frightening horn that can only blow, hoping everyone will get out of the way. All in all, this is a terrible, mad-cap machine.

The poet continues to examine the nature of greed, invidiousness, and injustice in **"Money."** The figure he examines is the "buffalo" nickel that is now out of circulation. As Nemerov recalls for us, there was a standing buffalo on one side and the face of an Indian on the other. As for the buffalo, "one side shows a hunchbacked bison / Bending his head and curling his tail to accommodate / The circular nature of money." The main effect of this is to accentuate the overpowering influence of money but it is another reminder of the way greed and unawareness "influenced" the buffalo almost right out of existence. By extension, modern industrial society has temporarily made the natural world "accommodate" itself to a very demanding will. Temporarily, because as we are now aware, it was with a price that we may not be able to pay back.

As to the figure of the Indian:

> And on the other side of our nickel
> There is the profile of a man with long hair
> And a couple of feathers in the hair; we know
> Somehow that he is an American Indian, and
> He wears the number nineteen-thirty-six.
> Right in front of his eyes the word *LIBERTY*, bent
> To conform with the curve of the rim, appears
> To be falling out of the sky Y first; the Indian
> Keeps his eyes downcast and does not notice this;

Wearing the number nineteen-thirty-six has the association of a prisoner, which of course the Indian was and to some extent continues to be; at the same time there is the association of "his days are numbered" or at least his numbers are scarce. Right before the Indian's eyes, the nature of money "bends" or perverts any real notion of liberty. In just one or two lines the poet reminds us of much of our American past that we are not proud of; and he helps to clarify what many have known about one kind of *laissez faire*—that it often means "Devil-take-the-hindmost."

This poem is also an example of the danger any poet runs, and that is over-writing, or once something has been said, to then take up the expansive process of prose and continue to explain. The passage I have just excerpted was quite enough, I think. But Nemerov goes on to explain,

> The representative American Indian was destroyed
> A hundred years or so ago, and his descendants'
> Relations with liberty are maintained with
>   reservations,
> Or primitive concentration camps.

While not commenting specifically on this poem, Miller Williams has noted in a review of **Blue Swallows** ["Transactions with the Muse," in *The Critical Reception of Howard Nemerov*], from which **"Money"** is taken, that "While the beginnings and resolutions of almost all Nemerov's poems are as tight as good craftsmanship can make them, a number have a curious way of going loose in

rhythm and almost rambling in the middle, so that the reader has the feeling of crossing a suspension bridge. These are faults, if I read fairly; but they are moved over without serious stumbling, and sometimes are no more than the peculiar mark of the man." The passage from **"Money"** supports this contention.

Nemerov is particularly concerned with the tyranny of the past over the present—a tyranny which is manifest in the way it compels habitual action and habitual ways of looking at the world

—William Mills

My own hunch is that this sort of thing occurs more frequently in the satiric poetry about the contemporary urban scene than it does with the more meditative poetry. This may be because abstract ideologies (political or otherwise) are more difficult to turn into poetic images than the insights that Nature may provide.

In addition to areas of the church, the state, and war (which are amply treated in the early volumes), there are several poems that reflect his attitudes about race. The first, an example of the terrible jokes that present themselves to the poet and which he continues to joke about, in a serious way, is entitled **"A Negro Cemetery Next to a White One."**

> I wouldn't much object, if I were black,
> To being turned away at the iron gate
> By the dark blonde angel holding up a plaque
> That said White Only; who would mind the wait
>
> For those facilities? And still it's odd,
> Though a natural god-given civil right,
> For men to throw it in the face of God
> Some ghosts are black and some darknesses white.
>
> But since they failed to integrate the earth,
> It's white of them to give what tantamounts
> To it, making us all, for what that's worth,
> Separate but equal where it counts.

After musing on the anomaly of a Christian turning another human being away because of color, the poet turns the situation further on its head and with irony by inversion observes that the earth is integrated surely in the end as the elements mix themselves and where no one's elements are separate, though truly they are equal.

The poem **"A Picture"** engages the racial problem in another way and the revelation of this poem is I think of a profounder order. The scene, from a photo in a newspaper, is the image of a group of people running down a city street after something; the first part of the poem isolates several of the people with comment, one a man in a "fat white shirt" who is "dutifully / Running along with all the others," and then:

> The running faces did not record
> Hatred or anger or great enthusiasm
> For what they were doing (hunting down
> A Negro, according to the caption),
> But seemed rather solemn, intent,
> With the serious patience of animals
> Driven through a gate by some
> Urgency out of the camera's range,
> On an occasion too serious
> For private feeling. The breathless faces
> Expressed a religion of running,
> A form of ritual exaltation
> Devoted to obedience, and
> Obedient, it might be, to the Negro,
> Who was not caught by the camera
> When it took the people in the street
> Among the cars, toward some object,
> Seriously running.

So much of the powerful inherited legacy of Man the animal, Man the descendant of *australopithecus africanus,* is rendered in this very haunting scene. The ritual of running is acted out as a matter of great solemnity, in the way a pack of hounds follows its prey with single-mindedness, a community effort. In the way that hounds are "driven," although they seem to drive, the people are "Devoted to obedience, and / Obedient, it might be, to the Negro, / Who was not caught by the camera." The poet's intelligence roves the contemporary landscape, in this instance an urban one, discovering strange rents in the fabric of civilization, rents that often appear to resemble bad jokes.

Another poem concerning race (of course all these poems embody more than a racial theme) but which does not fall into the category of jokes is **"The Sweeper of Ways."** The poet himself has written about the poem in his last collection of essays. The occasion for the poem was one of his habitual meetings with a Negro man who swept the sidewalk of leaves at a school where they both worked. Part of the poem reflects a middle-class, liberal embarrassment that anyone has to work at menial jobs because of his background and not because of his potential. The speaker reflects:

> Masters, we carry our white faces by
> In silent prayer, Don't hate me, on a wave-
> length which his broom's antennae perfectly
> Pick up, we know ourselves so many thoughts
> Considered by a careful, kindly mind
> Which can do nothing, and is doing that.

Nemerov has commented [in *Reflexions on Poetry and Poetics*] that "This kindly old man exemplifies a wrong in society. I didn't do it, but I have to feel responsible. And I detest about society this constant enforcing upon its members feelings of responsibility which are also deeply hopeless and despairing, so that one guilt evokes another, without remedy or end. For even if you could correct the future, what about the past? Many thousands gone." And

the poet is mightily impressed with the patience and apparent lack of bitterness.

Three other poems gradually pull back from specific areas of man's experience until the perspective is quite wide. The first of these, **"Cybernetics,"** is directed to someone who is ready to build a human brain, but in substance the poem is much more about the nature of man and his history. There is only profound, respectful admiration for man's complexity and his capabilities. The poet notes that for a cyberneticist to make a human brain, he would have to start with an area as big as Central Park and it would cost a little more than the Nineteen Fifty-Nine Gross National Product. He continues to enumerate many other problems the cyberneticist will have as he goes about his project. He observes, not resisting the pun, that the brain "must, of course, be absolutely free, / That's been determined." In the midst of its freedom, it is threatened with "yesterday's disasters" and must at the same time "assure itself, by masterful / Administration of the unforeseen, / That everything works according to plan." Out of the tension may be achieved that which permits man to endure: "something between / The flood of power and the drouth of fear: / A mediocrity, or golden mean, / Maybe at best the stoic *apatheia*." Further, if one intends to build a brain, he must install a "limiting tradition, / Which may be simple and parochial / (A memory of Main Street in the sunlight)" and the tradition should be as unequivocal as "'God will punish me if I suck my thumb.'"

If the brain-maker wants something rather elaborate, he can have it, but he must understand that this could be expensive.

> It runs you into much more money for
> Circuits of paradox and contradiction.
> Your vessels of antinomian wrath alone
> Run into millions; and you can't stop there,
> You've got to add at every junction point
> Auxiliary systems that will handle doubt,
> Switches of agony that are On and Off
> At the same time, and limited-access
> Blind alleys full of inefficient gods
> And marvelous devils.

And in the closing section of the poem, the speaker addresses the budding cyberneticist with irony that may be appropriate to someone who is now taking on the powers of Creator.

> O helmsman! in your hands how equal now
> Weigh opportunity and obligation.
> A chance to mate those monsters of the Book,
> The lion and serpent hidden from our sight
> Through centuries of shadowed speculation.
> What if the Will's a baffled, mangy lion,
> Or Thought's no adder but a strong constrictor?
> It is their offspring that we care about,
> That marvelous mirror where our modest wit
> Shall show gigantic. Will he uproot cities,
> Or sit indoors on a rainy day and mope?
> Will he decide against us, or want love?

How shall we see him, or endure his stride
Into our future bellowing Nil Mirari
While all his circuits click, propounding new
Solutions to the riddle of the Sphinx?

Some reviewers have commented on Nemerov's negativism, or in Meinke's words his "minimal affirmation." But over and over again Nemerov emphatically affirms man, and to use his own words [in *Poetry and Fiction: Essays*], he is a poet who has "got so far as to believe in the existence of the world." This is not the same thing as saying that he sentimentalizes the goodness of man and neglects man the beast. But who would believe a poet, or take him seriously, if he did offer such a sweeping, uncritical "affirmation"? **"Cybernetics"** is just such a poem that admits man's fantastic complexity and yet tacitly admires the courage he does show in the face of what he must confront. The poet chides the budding scientist for not being aware of just what he may be embarking on, and in so doing Nemerov affirms man. Nemerov affirms man in all his possibilities, authentic and inauthentic. It is man, and only man, who has the possibility of a relationship to being, who in his freedom can care, who can hear the call of conscience (Heidegger's *Dasein*). Just in what way the full ramifications of all of this can be labeled "minimal affirmation" is difficult to see.

"A Primer of the Daily Round" does not require any explication, it makes its statement clearly enough, but it is a delightful short poem and ends, to use a word that one has to use often with Nemerov, hauntingly.

A peels an apple, while B kneels to God,
C telephones to D, who has a hand
On E's knee, F coughs, G turns up the sod
for H's grave, I do not understand
But J is bringing one clay pigeon down
While K brings down a nightstick on L's head,
and M takes mustard, N drives into town,
O goes to bed with P, and Q drops dead,
R lies to S, but happens to be heard
by T, who tells U not to fire V
For having to give W the word
That X is now deceiving Y with Z,
  Who happens just now to remember A
  Peeling an apple somewhere far away.

The last two lines reinforce Miller Williams' comment that the "resolutions of almost all Nemerov's poems are as tight as good craftsmanship can make them" This poem, along with the next, is often selected for public readings; both lend themselves to a first hearing.

"Life Cycle of Common Man" is specifically about the "average consumer of the middle class." Nemerov estimates some of the consumables, ("Just under half a million cigarettes, / Four thousand fifths of gin and about / A quarter as much vermouth"), and the cost of putting him through life, his parents' investment and "how many beasts / Died to provide him with meat, belt and shoes / Cannot be certainly said." He pictures the man leaving a long trail of waste behind him. What did he do?

The usual things, of course,
The eating, dreaming, drinking and begetting,
And he worked for the money which was to pay
For the eating, et cetera, which were necessary
If he were to go on working for the money, et
  cetera,
But chiefly he talked. As the bottles and bones
Accumulated behind him the words proceeded
Steadily from the front of his face as he
Advanced into the silence and made it verbal.

There were countless greetings and good-byes, gratitudes, and "statements beginning 'It seems to me' or 'As I always say.'" The poem closes with a lonely figure, strangely modern.

Consider the courage in all that, and behold the man
Walking into deep silence, with the ectoplastic
Cartoon's balloon of speech proceeding
Steadily out of the front of his face, the words
Borne along on the breath which is his spirit
Telling the numberless tale of his untold Word
Which makes the world his apple, and forces him
  to eat.

This is the kind of affirmation that Nemerov makes, affirming the kind of courage that modern man must have in order to face a world that "forces him to eat."

One final poem, a very delicate and poignant poem, evokes the poet's stance and describes the kind of courage that a sensitive mind must possess to face the often dark, terrifying world.

"To D_____, Dead by Her Own Hand"

My dear, I wonder if before the end
You ever thought about a children's game—
I'm sure you must have played it too—in which
You ran along a narrow garden wall
Pretending it to be a mountain ledge
So steep a snowy darkness fell away
On either side to deeps invisible;
And when you felt your balance being lost
You jumped because you feared to fall, and thought
For only an instant: That was when I died.

That was a life ago. And now you've gone,
Who would no longer play the grown-ups' game
Where, balanced on the ledge above the dark,
You go on running and you don't look down,
Nor ever jump because you fear to fall.

The courage is perhaps an act of faith, or else a result of having nothing else to do or lose. One walks along the edge of what separates the known (or what we think we know) and what we know we do not know, the edge of order and chaos, of hope and despair. But, "you go on running."

In this survey of the poems about man and his city-socities there emerges a liberal mind, in this case a particularly civilized and witty mind, which responds to what it sees.

What Nemerov chooses to single out for comment and what is manifestly part of his uniqueness, comes from his talent for recognizing the paradoxes and bad jokes inherent in the most sensitive areas of human concern. The poetry that reflects the urban landscape concentrates on the most powerful institutions of society. Nemerov is particularly concerned with the tyranny of the past over the present—a tyranny which is manifest in the way it compels habitual action and habitual ways of looking at the world, whether it is the equation of greater numbers in church with a spiritual awakening, the customary selection of males for the obituary page and females for the matrimonial page, or the ritual force of our racial prejudices. As is true of all satire, there is affirmation, some assertion of value, and this is certainly true of Nemerov's. The poet helps us see the world freshly and, in so doing, reminds, us of our manly qualities and our strengths.

Julia Randall (review date 1976)

SOURCE: "Saying the Life of Things," in *American Poetry Review,* Vol. 5, No. 1, January/February, 1976, pp. 46-7.

[*In the positive review of* The Western Approaches *below, Randall compares Nemerov to English poet William Wordsworth.*]

> If you really want to see something, look at something else. If you want to say what something is, inspect something that it isn't. It might go further, and worse, than that: if you want to see the invisible world, look at the visible one.
>
> —[Howard Nemerov], "On Metaphor," *Reflexions on Poetry & Poetics*

If you really want to see Howard Nemerov, look at practically anybody else writing today. But I pick a non-controversial foil, Wordsworth, because the comparison is fun and, for me, illuminating. It clarifies both what Nemerov's poetry is, and what it is not.

Wordsworth and Nemerov share the plain style and the same grand epistemological theme. Both write many disarmingly simple poems that help the reader grasp the occasional intricate star. Both avoid the marketplace, lead quiet lives, and would like to see Elysium a simple produce of the common day. Wordsworth tries to convince us that he succeeds. Nemerov, who takes a more realistic view of human nature and does not go in for the Egotistical Sublime, assumes that the attempt is useless. As he wittily quotes a student boner: "Man is descended from the maneating ape." Wordsworth is witless. He is given to trance, whereas Nemerov always keeps both eyes open, even, we feel, in his dreams. Wordsworth came to Nature early, Nemerov late. Wordsworth is a moon and mountain man, Nemerov a sun and seed man. For both poets, the central problem is how the individual Mind is fitted to the external World. For Wordsworth the fitting is exquisite. Nemerov is fond of quoting Blake: "You shall not bring

me down to believe such fitting and fitted. I know better, and please your Lordship." Both the druidical Anglican and the sceptical Jew are mental travellers on the same track, and I like to see them there together, for they have precious little company today.

Nemerov's ninth volume of verse, *The Western Approaches,* is a substantial achievement—71 entries including two splendid translations (Rilke's "Kindheit" and a canzone from Dante's "Convivo") and two prose pieces, "The Measure of Poetry," and "The Thought of Trees." It divides into three sections: The Way, poems, largely ironic, about our gadgets and current preoccupations, e.g. **"Watching Football on TV"**; The Ground, poems mostly about Nature; The Mind, poems mostly about art and thought. It is quieter, more relaxed, more colloquial than its predecessor, *Gnomes and Occasions* (1973). It seems to me *slacker*—but to cast even mild aspersions on Nemerov's work makes me feel a bit like Francis Jeffrey, The *Edinburgh Review*'s prize ass, who could write in 1814 "The case of Mr. Wordsworth, we perceive, is now manifestly hopeless, and we give him up as altogether incurable and beyond the power of criticism." Jeffrey writ better than he wot, for WW was indeed incurable and beyond any criticism the *ER* could offer.

Nemerov can do what he likes with language, from the pun to the villanelle, and it is to his credit that he has (I imagine) curbed his aural gift, as Thomas and Auden, for instance, in their very different ways, did not always do. I like best his rough blank verse, for example Rune X from *New and Selected Poems* (1960).

> White water, white water, feather of a form
> Between the stones, is the race run to stay
> Or pass away? Your utterance is riddled,
> Rainbowed and clear and cold, tasting of stone,
> Its brilliance blinds me. But still I have seen,
> White water, at the breaking of the ice,
> When the high places render up the new
> Children of water and their tumbling light
> Laughter runs down the hills, and the small fist
> Of the seed unclenches in the day's dazzle,
> How happiness is helpless before your fall,
> White water, and history is no more than
> The shadows thrown by clouds on mountainsides,
> A distant chill, when all is brought to pass
> By rain and birth and rising of the dead.

Here the verse flows as naturally as the water that is its subject. It is our dialect, but purified. Not so these lines from **"The Metaphysical Automobile"** in the current volume:

> The idea of a car either has a dent
> In its left front fender or it downright don't.

This is both metaphysically and linguistically cute. I do not see the necessity of splitting off the apostrophe in these lines about a football that wants to wobble:

> and to make it spiral true
> 's a triumph in itself.

At the opposite extreme I object to the wordiness of

> And all the reborn sceptics smiled
> Over such fancies as could have beguiled
> No one who was not but a simple child,

which seems to mean "could not have beguiled a simple child." And then, Miltonics:

> Spreading in secret through the fabric vast
> Of heaven and earth.

Some lines are reminiscent of earlier and stronger ones, e.g. "as in the brilliant stillness of the sun" compared to "in the great room of the sun." Thematically, too, some of the poems in *The Western Approaches* seem to be overflows from poems in *Gnomes and Occasions.* Thus **"Learning the Trees"** (*Approaches*) is a paler version of **"Beginner's Guide"** (*Gnomes*), and **"Conversing with Paradise"** (*Approaches*) a footnote to the very fine **"Painter Dreaming in the Poet's House"** (*Gnomes*).

Despite such qualifications, *The Western Approaches* helps us to delimit Nemerov's world, and we are grateful that he has a world and an intellectual life instead of a platform and an autobiography. His Archimedean point is where seeing and saying meet. At least that is the point that moves the human world and produces our quadrivium—the arts, the humanities, the natural and the social sciences—through the creative agency of language. Neither Nemerov nor Susanne Langer, lacking the confidence of St. John, knows where language began. Both know that language made thought, and that thought made time, space, and human history.

> Great pain was in the world before we came.
> The shriek had learned to answer to the claw
> Before we came; the gasp, the sigh, the groan,
> Did not need our invention. But all these
> Immediacies refused to signify
> Till in the morning of the mental sun
> One moment shuddered under stress and broke
> Irreparably into before and after,
> Inventing patience, panic, doubt, despair,
> And with a single thrust producing thought
> Beyond the possible, building the vaults
> Of debt and the high citadels of guilt,
> The segregating walls of obligation,
> All that imposing masonry of time
> Secretly rooted at the earth's cracked hearth,
> In the Vishnu schist and the Bright Angel shale,
> But up aspiring past the visible sky.

> —from **"The Creation of Anguish"** (*The Blue Swallows*)

The great western question—Plato's, Kant's, Wordsworth's, Cézanne's, Stevens'—is a question about the premises of perception: can Mind see/say anything that is not defined and limited by its own powers? It may well aspire past the visible sky, but can it get anywhere on rods and cones, consonants and vowels?

Nemerov excludes the materialist's and the mystic's answers, but he is of several minds about the remaining possibilities. Language (hence thought, hence history) may after all be an insignificant game, as in the significantly titled **"Playing the Inventions"** (Bach's):

> And only being uninformative
> Will be the highest reach of wisdom known
> In the perfect courtesy of music, where
> The question answers only to itself
> And the completed round excludes the world.

Personal destiny, too, may be a weary plot (author anon.); freedom and creativity jokes or illusions. A life

> grows ghostly toward the close
> As any man dissolves in Everyman
> Of whom the story, as it always did, begins
> In a far country, once upon a time,
> There lived a certain man and he had three sons . . .
> —**"The Western Approaches"**

I may bring in here as evidence what I suppose to be a common experience of poets (and if poets aren't freely creative, who is?). You can sweat for hours or days getting a certain line perfect; you know it's out there and you've got everything but the words. Finally you get them—good job. Until some months later the editor points out that line 12 is by Yeats. Or the opposite case: I've read lines in other people's poems that are by me, when I know perfectly well that the author has never heard of me. Nemerov at times likens the world to a Great Writing in which we merely "play" the lines invented for us. The new volume contains several poems about novelists and their characters, "people who are not and whose non-being / Always depends on the next syllable."

Nemerov's first book was called *The Image and the Law,* and when he's not backing the Laws of thermo- and psycho-dynamics, he backs the Prophets. That is, he can imagine a future of which the human voice is shaper as well as sufferer. I think he would go at least as far as Wordsworth, and be still

> A lover of the meadows and the woods,
> And mountains; and of all that we behold
> From this green earth; of all the mighty world
> Of eye, and ear,—both what they half create
> And what perceive; well pleased to recognise
> In nature and the language of the sense
> The anchor of my purest thoughts, the nurse,
> The guide, the guardian of my heart, and soul
> Of all my moral being.
> —"Tintern Abbey"

Poetry in the hands of the great masters, writes Nemerov, makes statements

> about invisible mysteries by means of things visible;
> and poems, far from resting in nature as their end, use
> nature as a point from which they extrapolate darkly
> the nature of all things not visible or mediately

knowable by the reason—the soul, society, the gods or god, the mind—to which visible nature is equivocally the reflexion and the mask. Such poetry is magical, then, because it treats the world as signature, in which all things intimate to us by their sensible properties what and in what way we are.

> —"On Metaphor," *Reflexions on Poetry & Poetics*

In *The Approaches* he quotes Blake: "Poetry, Painting, & Music, the three Powers in Man of conversing with Paradise, which the flood did not Sweep away." But if we can converse with Paradise we have—to make a bad pun—made it. And lo! it *is* a produce of the common day, of that great room of the sun where thought and thing mate fruitfully to bring forth the knowledge that lies sleeping in them as long as they lie alone. The act of imagination, a repetition in the finite mind of the eternal act of creation—exactly so. Even if the finite mind requires Nature (or whatever is not-mind) as a partner, it is no mere stenographer. How much still lies sleeping in the world the true scientist knows as surely as the true artist, and both are ever ready for the protean encounter.

These are pretty high-flown words—HN's where they are not WW's or STC's—and I will deflate them by a simple example. In the course of writing this review I have found the poems come alive, shift shape, and start generating in me perceptions which were not there before and may not be in the poems either.

> How arbitrary it must be, the sound
> That breaks the silence; yet its valency,
> Though hidden still, is great for other sounds
> Drawn after it into the little dance
> Prefigured in its possibilities.
>> —**"Playing the Inventions"**

Poetry talks back. That is why it is our best model of the mind. History records finished mental acts; poetry retrieves them because it catches them *in verb,* because we have to *engage* with it, being and becoming all at once.

> My belief about poetry says that you write a poem not to say what you think, nor even to find out what you think—though that is closer-but to find out what *it* thinks.
>> —"The Sweeper of Ways," *Reflexions on Poetry & Poetics*

Doubtless some thoughts lie forever too deep for words. Meanwhile it would be well for us if more poets listened to what poems think.

Richard Howard   (review date 1976)

SOURCE: A review of *The Western Approaches. Poems 1973-75,* in *The Yale Review,* March, 1976, pp. 425-42.

[*In the excerpt below, Howard praises* The Western Approaches, *calling it Nemerov's "wisest" book.*]

Three years ago, when [Nemerov] published *Gnomes and Occasions,* even the vivid and lovable poems in that book were spiked and spooked by so many sour epigrams and put-downs of Others that it seemed Howard Nemerov must have forgotten Marianne Moore's hard truth: there never was a war that was not inward. Were all the enemies *out there,* one wondered, could none of the problems be played closer to the chest, even the medicine chest, than so much snarling seemed to suggest? Of course there were, as I say, vivid and lovable poems in the book—Nemerov is the master of his generation (he is fifty-seven), and since Auden's death he is the only poet of that generation in America who has found it possible to continue serving wisdom without forsaking intelligence or even knowledge; as long ago as 1961, James Dickey in a beautiful review of Nemerov's *New and Selected Poems* said the necessary things about this poet, the things necessary to make you go on reading him from beginning to

> the definite announcement of an end
> where one thing ceases and another starts.

But by 1973, one gasped at what Nemerov must endure at his own hands, from his own mirror, if he could speak so easily (it seemed), so icily about the rest of us and our defections from sanity and grace. This new book [*The Western Approaches*] is the assuaging answer to my fiction: the poet "unbelieving looked behind the glass / on razor, styptic, mouthwash and Band-aid" and came up, or out, with one of his enhancing formulations:

> . . . it has been my life's ambition since
> To elucidate the mirror by its medicines.

That is the program for this new and I may say sudden book, a much more generous and engaging affair than the last, a book of helpless pains and privileged affections where "on every front at once we reach the edge." It is organized into three parts—"the way," the way we live now, twenty-eight poems as mordant and skeptical as ever but including the poet in the bite, the doubt; "the ground," fifteen poems about the rhythms and figures of earth; and "the mind," twenty-six poems about the correspondences between those rhythms and figures and a language (poetry, painting, music) which "competes with / experience while cooperating with / experience." Thus the mirror is disciplined, and by a dose of its own medicines; and Nemerov (who else so much suggests Lucretius as this poet for whom "the motion of the many made the one / shape constant and kept it so"? Only Ammons) is enabled, is obliged by his most compassionate talents, to write his finest book among many very fine, and I am convinced his wisest.

The wisdom convinces me because it is intricate only after it is obvious; because it is subtle only once it appears simple. Nemerov is not, now, the kind of poet who makes you exclaim: I never would or could have thought of that! He is the kind of poet who makes you—or me, ever and again—exclaim: Of course I thought of that, but I never understood what my thinking meant, what it could make me feel! Poems about "First Snow," about "A Cabinet of

Seeds Displayed," about "Flower Arrangements" are not so much *about* these subjects as they are within them: such poems make the subjects happen in the mind, and so they become events, dramas, even tragedies. It is the elements, and elemental things (weather, darkness, decay; growth, change, form), which the wise poet broods on, and they speak to him, and he to us, in a chastised language whereby nothing solemn gets through without its test of observation and the wit which observation yields. *Privileged* is the new word in Nemerov's lexicon—over and over he acknowledges his debts to his condition ("you feel / upon your heart a signal to attend / the definite announcement") and declares himself privileged so to suffer, so to observe:

> . . . how privileged
> One feels to find the same necessity
> Ciphered in forms diverse and otherwise
> Without kinship—that is the beautiful
> In Nature as in art, not obvious,
> Not inaccessible, but just between.
>
> It may diminish some our dry delight
> To wonder if everything we are and do
> Lies subject to some little law like that;
> Hidden in nature, but not deeply so.

This language of Nemerov's which I call chastised (compared to Auden's, say, when both poets deal with such mortal ventures as taking a walk in the fall) is not thereby in a condition of privation, as the analyst says who may not touch his patient. Rather it is rich with its own constraints—as Nemerov says of the seeds displayed, "kept from act for reverence's sake"; the direct stanzas and the diligent iambics are *in keeping,* they hold onto the movement of the mind, and by such government the poems become "eternal return of the excluded middle," that kind of devotion to truth I have called wisdom because it leaves information and even knowledge behind in the privilege, just so, of wonder, of mystery, of myth:

> These correspondences are what remain
> Of the great age . . .

Such poems as **"Boy with Book of Knowledge"** and **"The Backward Look," "Playing the Inventions,"** and **"The Weather of the World"** are only instances of what is here so rifely extant, poems which do elucidate the mirror—by reflecting the world.

Robert Richman (review date 1988)

SOURCE: "Death and the Poet," in *The New Criterion,* Vol. 6, No. 5, January, 1988, pp. 72-7.

[*In the following review of* War Stories, *Richman discusses existential themes in Nemerov's poetry as a whole.*]

"They say the war is over," writes Howard Nemerov in **"Redeployment,"** one of his most memorable early po-

ems. "But water still / Comes bloody from the taps." Today, thirty-seven years after writing these lines, Nemerov's whole outlook on life is still haunted by the memory of war. This is the impression one has from Nemerov's new book, *War Stories: Poems about Long Ago and Now.* Nearly a third of the poems in this volume have their source in the poet's experiences, between 1942 and 1944, as a flying officer in the Royal Canadian Air Force, and as a first lieutenant, during the final two years of the conflict, in the U.S. Army Air Force. In the RAF, Nemerov's missions included the bombing of German shipping boats on the North Sea. A few poems are based directly on this experience, and others treat of the more banal aspects of war, such as Nemerov's dealings with his colleagues in the air force and his training as a flyer.

> **Nemerov has been called an existential poet, and for good reason. He believes that modern man must attempt an absurd task: to contrive meaning in a meaningless world.**
>
> **—*Robert Richman***

Nemerov's poetic response to war is not unusual. The dispassionate, ironic voice of the poems in *War Stories* has also been employed to good effect in the war poems of Randall Jarrell and Karl Shapiro. All the same, it is a fitting response to the particular absurdity Nemerov witnessed—what he calls the bloodless "clean war, the war in the air." Here is a poem entitled **"The Faith"**:

> "There are those for whom is a
> vocation. . . . They are mystic soldiers,
> devout—and killing is their calling.
> What of them?"—*Kenneth Burke*
>
> I knew a couple of these dedicates,
> The ones that loved the life and volunteered
> For more of it after they'd got home free
> And honorably discharged with all the
>   gongs . . .
>
> One aimed his aircraft at a battle cruiser
> (it turned out one of ours) and was blown
>   away;
> The other signalled from behind the Frisians
> That he and his crew were hit and going down,
>
> His voice as neutral as the evening news
> That we would hear on our return to base
> That night: "From these and other operations
> Seven of our aircraft failed to return." . . .

And here is **"Night Operations, Coastal Command RAF"**:

Remembering that war, I'd near believe
We didn't need the enemy, with whom
Our dark encounters were confused and few
And quickly done, so many of our lot
Did for themselves in folly and misfortune.

Some hit our own barrage balloons, and some
Tripped over power lines, coming in low;
Some swung on takeoff, others overshot,
And two or three forgot to lower the wheels.

There were those that flew the bearing for the
     course
And flew away forever; and the happy few
That homed on Venus sinking beyond the sea
In fading certitude. For all the skill,
For all the time of training, you might take
The hundred steps in darkness, not the next.

The truth is, another kind of war has always been in the forefront of Nemerov's consciousness. This is the war between man and the world that Nemerov considers to be the essential fact of the human condition. Indeed, the term "war stories" could be applied not just to Nemerov's many poems that deal with the Second World War but to most of the poems he has written. One has the sense that the poet turns so often to "real" war as a subject in his verse because he regards war as the most extreme example of the struggle between man and the spiritual void he occupies.

Shifting clouds and misty mountains are rare in the Nemerovian oeuvre because imagery, in Nemerov's estimation, dilutes the dramatic contest at the heart of the poem.

—Robert Richman

Nemerov has been called an existential poet, and for good reason. He believes that modern man must attempt an absurd task: to contrive meaning in a meaningless world. A poem that vividly reflects this existential stance is **"Quaerendo Invenietis"** (from *Gnomes and Occasions,* published in 1973). In this poem, Nemerov declares that "[w]ithout my meaning nothing, nothing means." An early war poem entitled **"September Shooting"** (from Nemerov's first book, *The Image and the Law,* published in 1947) also betrays something of existential philosophy. In it, the poet describes how an "anonymous bullet flies out of / An irrelevant necessity, and knows no evil."

Nemerov is commonly grouped with the other formalist poets of his generation—Richard Wilbur, Anthony Hecht, Donald Hall, and Peter Davison. Yet despite possessing a sense of language and form equal to any of these poets, he has often been viewed as the black sheep of the group. No

doubt this has to do with Nemerov's unalloyed pessimism. It is true, though, that where his contemporaries will focus on, say, a beautiful woman emerging from a town-house door, Nemerov fastens his eye on a hapless soul who was tossed into a river, his feet cemented into a bucket. Where his contemporaries are on the lookout for spiritual presences in the world—presences that may enrich their lives—Nemerov insists that we must "sweat it [i.e., life] out." Nemerov bridles at the idea of transcendence: "darkness invades our day," he says in **"Deep Woods,"** from *The Salt Garden* (1955); "[n]o meaning in it, but indifference." And he wonders sardonically, in **"Lines & Circularities"** (from *Gnomes & Occasions*), "How many silly miracles there are / That will not save us." When Nemerov does happen on a rainbow, he sees it in a polluted stream:

Oil is spilling down the little stream
Below the bridge. Heavy and slow as
     blood,
Or with an idiot's driveling contempt:
The spectral film unfolding, spreading
     forth
Prismatically in a breaking of rainbows. . . .

(**"The Breaking of the Rainbows"**)

The eclipse—like the rainbow, admired by many poets as an example of the miraculousness of nature—is also unmasked as a fraud by Nemerov. In **"During a Solar Eclipse,"** from the 1980 volume *Sentences* (the title itself is a diminishment of the book's contents), the poet concedes the eclipse's power to transform the day, but it cannot alter the speaker:

The darkening disk of the moon before
     the sun
All morning moves, turning our common day
A deep and iris blue, daylight of dream
In which we stand bemused and looking on
Backward at shadow and reflected light,

While the two great wanderers among the
     worlds
Enter their transit with our third, a thing
So rare that in his time upon the earth
A man may see, as I have done, but four,
In childhood two, a third in youth, and this

In likelihood my last. We stand bemused
While grass and rock darken, and stillness
     grows,
Until the sun and moon slide out of phase
And light returns us to the common life
That is so long to do and so soon done.

The speaker is "bemused"—the word is used twice in three stanzas—preoccupied, dreamy, abstracted; but not in the least bit transfigured by the experience.

Inevitably, death is—with war—one of Nemerov's favorite subjects. Everything reminds Nemerov of death because everything leads to it. As he writes in **"In the Glass of Fashion,"** from *The Image and the Law*:

> I am asked why I do not
> Stop writing about death
> And do something worth while.
> To write about what would be
> Not to write about death?

And in **"The Goose Fish,"** from *The Salt Garden,* the "moony grin" of the dead fish's head mocks the lovers:

> On the long shore, lit by the moon
> To show them properly alone,
> Two lovers suddenly embraced
> So that their shadows were as one.
> The ordinary light was graced
> For them by the swift tide of blood
> That silently they took at flood,
> And for a little time they prized
>   Themselves emparadised.
>
> Then, as if shaken by stage-fright
> Beneath the hard moon's bony light,
> They stood together on the sand
> Embarrassed in each other's sight
> But still conspiring hand in hand,
> Until they saw, there underfoot,
> As though the world had found them out,
> The goose fish turning up, though dead,
>   His hugely grinning head.

While in **"De Anima"**—from *The Next Room of the Dream* (1962)—Nemerov argues that "what lovers bring / Into the world is death."

Nemerov's poetry is not completely devoid of any acknowledgement of beauty. But on the rare occasion when he does refer to the beautiful, what is usually honored is the poet's ability to generate that beauty. What is "affirmed" in these poems is the inherent worthlessness of nature. In the title poem of *The Blue Swallows* (1967), Nemerov writes:

> O swallows, swallows, poems are not
> The point. Finding again the world,
> That is the point, where loveliness
> Adorns intelligible things
> Because the mind's eye lit the sun.

An analogous message is voiced in **"The Makers"** (from *Sentences*). Here, the "idiot world" is sung not only into beauty but into being by the poet:

> Who can remember back to the first poets,
> The greatest ones, greater even than Orpheus?
> No one has remembered that far back
> Or now considers, among the artifacts
> And bones and cantilevered inference
> The past is made of, those first and greatest poets,
> So lofty and disdainful of renown
> They left us not a name to know them by.

> They were the ones that in whatever tongue
> Worded the world, that were the first to say
> Star, water, stone, that said the visible
> And made it bring invisibles to view
> In wind and time and change, and in the mind
> Itself that minded the hitherto idiot world
> Spoke the speechless world and sang the
>   towers
> Of the city into the astonished sky.

> They were the first great listeners, attuned
> To interval, relationship, and scale,
> The first to say above, beneath, beyond,
> Conjurors with love, death, sleep, with bread
>   and wine,
> Who having uttered vanished from the world
> Leaving no memory but the marvelous
> Magical elements, the breathing shapes
> And stops of breath we build our Babels of.

This is Nemerov in his most confident mood. Even here, though, the poet's despair comes through. In his wish to get to "the truth of the matter" (the title of one of his earliest poems), Nemerov disdains certain poetical tools he judges will obscure the lucid expression of the "war" between man and universe. One such device is the sensuous image. Shifting clouds and misty mountains are rare in the Nemerovian oeuvre because imagery, in Nemerov's estimation, dilutes the dramatic contest at the heart of the poem. So does ornate language. Nemerov writes in bare, unadorned language because in his view it dispatches the "truth of the matter" best. The conclusion of **"The Biographer's Mandate,"** from *War Stories,* is iambic pentameter at its most demotic—and, alas, most mediocre: "For we don't give a shit about his work. / These are the things we give a shit about."

In *War Stories,* Nemerov's wish to unearth "the truth of the matter" continues unabated. In **"Economic Man,"** the poet contends that it is futile to look to nature for something to "profit by." Similarly, in **"A Christmas Card of Halley's Comet,"** the poet remarks sarcastically how "[w]ords fail us" when faced with the enormity of the comet's meaninglessness. And in **"On the Occasion of National Mourning"**—written in the wake of the Challenger disaster—Nemerov comments that "the silvery platitudes / Were waiting in their silos for just such / An emergent occasion. . . ."

In the book's war poems, Nemerov seeks to rid us of our illusions about military life. Since none of us any longer harbors illusions about military life, however, a few of the poems fall flat. In **"IFF,"** for example, the poet confesses that while in the air force he spared Hitler "hardly a thought," but loathed instead "Corporal Irmin," "Wing Commander Briggs," "station C.O. Group Captain Ormery," and "my navigator Bert," who "shyly explained to me that the Jews / Were ruining England." (A similar sentiment is expressed in Edward Thomas's 1915 poem, "This is no case of petty right or wrong.") In **"Double Negative,"** meanwhile, what is "exposed" is the "wisdom" of a senior pilot Nemerov had received instruction from. The old pilot assured Nemerov that it was a cinch to stop firing when—"as it's almost bound to happen"—"one of your chaps / Crosses his aircraft over in front of yours. . . ."

Though these poems may not be the last word in originality, they are harmless enough. But what are we to make of Nemerov's truth-seeking and plain speaking in the second half of the poem entitled **"Crotchets"**?

> At Breakfast this Morning
>
> She tells me out of the paper about this guy
> He's got leukemia and into the bargain AIDS,
> They give him maybe two more weeks to live
> When the oxygen tank outside the room
>   explodes
> And he winds up in emergency and then
> Intensive care all over third-degree burns.
> But they saved his life, they brought him back.
>
> So don't try to, she says, tell me there is no God.

Nemerov is attracted to disaster like a moth to light, and it was perhaps inevitable that he would write a poem on AIDS. But why use it as the occasion for mirth? **"Crotchets"** may be too much, even for Nemerov's most sympathetic readers.

Actually, Nemerov has always had a penchant for jokes in his poetry. The poem alluded to above, for example, **"The Truth of the Matter,"** revolves around a rather dark joke. In this poem, Nemerov writes of the "divine justice" of the death by diabetes of the head of a "great sugar refinery." The first two lines of **"Ultima Ratio Reagan,"** from *War Stories,* constitute another, considerably lighter, attempt at humor: "The reason we do not learn from history is / Because we are not the people who learned last time."

Many commentators have criticized Nemerov for his taste for the sarcastic quip. In his 1966 essay "Attentiveness and Obedience," the poet tried to respond to these charges. He wrote, in part: "The charge typically raised . . . has been that my poems are jokes, even bad jokes. I incline to agree, insisting however that they are bad jokes, and even terrible jokes. . . ."

One way to view these jokes is as a purely defensive reaction—the reaction of a mind so overwhelmed by the world's despair that it has no other response available to it *but* humor and sarcasm. In this view, gags are the response of a mind at the end of its tether. If one perceives Nemerov's jokes this way, it is easy to construe them as positive signs that the mind is still functioning in the face of the onrushing void.

But this is not a very satisfactory explanation of the impulse behind *all* of Nemerov's jokes, particularly the offensive ones, as in **"Crotchets."** For a possible clue to the impulse behind this dark humor, one must turn to Nemerov's 1965 prose volume *Journal of the Fictive Life.* In this book, Nemerov made a revealing statement. He wrote, "I hate intelligence, and it is all I have."

The joke at the end of **"Crotchets,"** and the joke about the sugar man's death, are jokes at their most vulgar and unappealing. Could these attempts at humor actually be the poet's desire to punish his intelligence for denying him a bigger poetic response to the world, by showing that intelligence in the worst possible light? Could it be that Nemerov wishes to exact revenge on his hated intelligence for forcing him to write verse devoid of standard poetic effects and limited in subject matter to "war stories"? A strange thought, but not implausible.

Fortunately, this punitive aspect of Nemerov's sensibility rears its ugly head fairly infrequently. In Nemerov's oeuvre there are many poems which not only remain free of this self-destructive joking, but, remarkably, transcend the poet's general aesthetic strictures as well. **"Redeployment,"** **"The Goose Fish,"** and **"The Makers"** are just a few examples.

"Models," from *War Stories,* is another. In this poem, the juxtaposition of the model airplane-building boy and the soldier the boy becomes underscores marvelously the gulf between the reality of war and the young boy's romantic dream of a dogfight:

> The boy of twelve, shaping a fuselage
> Of balsa wood so easy to be sliced
> Along the grain but likely to get crushed
> Under the razor when it was cut across;
>
> Sanding the parts, glueing and lacquering
> And pasting on the crosses and the rings
> The brave identities of Fokker and Spad
> That fought, only a little before his birth,
>
> That primitive, original war in the air
> He made in miniature and flew by hand
> In clumsy combat, simulated buzz:
> A decade away from being there himself. . . .

"The War in the Air," also from *War Stories,* succeeds despite Nemerov's poetic restrictions. Here, the poet shows how the mourning of the war dead need not be done with false eulogies, but through the unlikely combination of dispassion and stoicism:

> For a saving grace, we didn't see our dead,
> Who rarely bothered coming home to die
> But simply stayed away out there
> In the clean war, the war in the air.
>
> Seldom the ghosts came back bearing their
>   tales
> Of hitting the earth, the incompressible sea,
> But stayed up there in the relative wind,
> Shades fading in the mind,
>
> Who had no graves but only epitaphs
> Where never so many spoke for never so
>   few:
> *Per ardua,* say the partisans of Mars,
> *Per aspera,* to the stars.

That was the good war, the war we won
As if there were no death, for goodness' sake,
With the help of the losers we left out there
In the air, the empty air.

Poems like these are not all that rare in the poet's body of work. It is on the basis of them that Howard Nemerov should be regarded as one of our finest poets.

Louis D. Rubin Jr. on Nemerov's poetic achievements:

Whether Nemerov was a "major" or a "minor" poet I shall not dispute; what I am certain of is that at his best (which was often) he was a *great* poet. His poetry is unique in its magnificent fusion of idea and emotion in language. He was not afraid of thinking in his poems—yet neither was he cerebral. He wrote two kinds of poems. One kind was witty, acerbic, satirical; it was well done, but I did and do not care for it nearly as much as his lyric, philosophical, meditative poetry, so often about external nature—poems such as **"The Blue Swallows," "Runes," "Summer's Elegy," "Two Girls," "Again."** My favorite of all—though there are so many to choose from that I like—is his sestina, **"Sarajevo,"** which inexplicably was omitted from the *Howard Nemerov Reader.* Perhaps I like it so much because it *is* historical, as few of his poems are. It is hauntingly beautiful; the complexity of the verse form is played against the matter and manner of saying.

Louis D. Rubin Jr. in Sewanee Review, *Vol. 99, October 1991.*

Ejner J. Jensen (essay date 1988)

SOURCE: "Howard Nemerov and the Tyranny of Shakespeare," in *Centennial Review,* Vol. XXXII, No. 2, Spring, 1988, pp. 130-49.

[*In the essay below, Jensen examines the influence of William Shakespeare on Nemerov's verse, stating that Shakespeare is "the guide and genius of [Nemerov's] poetic achievement."*]

John Lehmann, writing in his autobiography, claimed for Shakespeare the greatest intellectual and creative sovereignty over the minds and feelings of both the writers who followed him and all those whose literary inheritance derives from the English tradition. Shakespeare, he declared,

was the key to the whole of English literature, the mastermind that determined its course and depth and vitality so fundamentally that we can scarcely conceive what our imaginative life—perhaps even our moral values—would be like without him.

His assertion, in its nature more of a celebratory declaration than a critical argument, was picked up and expanded upon by T. J. B. Spencer in his British Academy Lecture, "The Tyranny of Shakespeare." Spencer argued that "The history of Shakespeare criticism . . . . has connexions with the production of poetry; and it is likely to be an unreal thing if we attempt to write it abstracted from the moulding influence of Shakespeare's writings upon subsequent literature." In this, Spencer was not merely agreeing with Lehmann but with a host of nineteenth-century writers including, notably, Ruskin, who claimed that "the intellectual measure of every man since born, in the domains of creative thought, may be assigned to him, according to the degree in which he has been taught by Shakespeare."

But the tyranny of Shakespeare, at once so widespread and so various in its manifestations, is difficult to measure. In Spencer's words, "Influences that become too pervasive lose their bright particularity, and defy the ordinary methods of describing literary causation." Harold Bloom's more recent theoretical formulation of the problem Spencer described focuses less on the details of textual influence than on questions of the psychology of creation growing out of one author's awareness of another's presence in his literary-intellectual background and in his works. The consciousness, as Bloom puts it, of a strong poet, makes the tyranny of Shakespeare something that the modern author must confront directly, recognizing his indebtedness and coping in some fashion with the "anxiety of influence."

Among contemporary poets, Howard Nemerov offers a striking instance of a writer whose indebtedness to Shakespeare is both considerable and self-conscious. Nemerov is so aware of Shakespeare's presence in his work, so given to clinching his critical arguments with quotations from Shakespeare, so supple and inventive in his employment of Shakespearean allusions in his poetry that he may be said to have transformed the tyranny of Shakespeare into a benevolent timocracy in which he can claim a legitimate share.

One measure of Nemerov's debt to Shakespeare appears quite simply in the titles of several poems. **"In the Glass of Fashion," "The Second-Best Bed," "A Lean and Hungry Look," "Holding the Mirror up to Nature"** all depend for their understanding at least in part on a reader's sense of the allusion and the context that it summons up. Other poems, such as **"In the Market-Place"** or **"The Town Dump,"** use Shakespearean quotations as epigraphs. In the former instance, an exchange between Polonius and Hamlet—

Do you know me, my lord?
Excellent well; you are a fishmonger.—

introduces a poem packed with contradictions whose theme suggests the deep potential for evil in all of life. In this market-place "The armored salmon jewel the ice with blood"; and though it is noon and "soft August" still the speaker feels the power of the day to stir "a chill cloud" and raise "a silver flood To savage in the marrow of my weir." In the second case, Nemerov takes an epigraph from *King Lear*—

The art of our necessities is strange,
That can make vile things precious—

and quotes from the passage once more in the final section of the poem:

Among the flies, the purefying [sic] fires,
The hunters by night, acquainted with the art
Of our necessities, and the new deposits
That each day wastes with treasure, you may say
There should be ratios.

"Necessities" in the design of the poem become not required things but rather perceptions imposed upon individuals by certain habits of thought. Thus "dealers in antiques / . . . prowl this place by night" in the hope of some discovery,

on
The off-chance of somebody's having left
Derelict chairs which will turn out to be
By Hepplewhite, a perfect set of six
Going to show, I guess, that in any sty
Someone's heaven may open and shower down
Riches responsive to the right dream.

Thus too those who need to find ratios, says the speaker, "may sum up / The results, if you want results." But over against that summing up,

I will add
That wild birds, drawn to the carrion and flies,
Assemble in some numbers here, their wings
Shining with light, their flight enviably free,
Their music marvelous, though sad, and strange.

In place of "necessities" of thought, we have an alternative possibility. The mathematical "results" are not allowed to stand as a final solution; instead, the poet "will add" to them, and what he adds brings to the poem a final ambiguity reminiscent of that summoned by the pigeons at the close of Stevens' "Sunday Morning" sinking "downward to darkness, on extended wings."

Rosalie Colie once wrote of the shaping power of paradox in *King Lear,* remarking how the play turns so insistently to parodoxical figures as a means of arriving at its final truth. It is this aspect of *King Lear* that Nemerov seizes on in **"The Town Dump"**: this final depository where "nothing finishes," a sty that may become "Someone's heaven," "Being" which "ends up / Becoming some more" and—on another level, where paradox approaches oxymoron—"dreamy midden." All of these figures, along with more fully developed images—"the lobster," who "lifts / An empty claw in his most minatory / Of gestures"; "banana peels / No one will skid on, apple cores that caused / Neither the fall of man nor a theory / Of gravitation"—bring **"The Town Dump"** into a rewarding series of thematic connections with *King Lear.* Like the play, Nemerov's poem develops around a few related central themes that unite questions of perception and judgment, appearance and value, dissolution and redemption from loss. If the poem finally provides no clear answers, it does—like tragedy generally and like *Lear* in particular—force us to look at the most troubling questions. And like *Lear,* like all great tragedies, it invites us to contemplate the mystery of beauty sprung from waste, of wisdom not wholly accessible but undeniably present even in the midst of suffering and defeat. Thus Nemerov uses *Lear* not merely as a point of reference, not merely allusively, but as a means of enlarging his own poem's range of meaning and bringing its themes more strikingly into our field of awareness.

Critics have commented extensively on Nemerov's recurrent attention to the relationship between perception and reality, his continuing exploration of the question of "how thought ever emerged (if it ever did) out of a world of things." Julia Bartholomay has demonstrated how productive these concerns have been of images and symbols that abound in Nemerov's poetry; and Nemerov himself has written of a whole class of figures he describes as effigies, "including by analogy with the form and function of statues such metaphorical extensions as photographs, Santa Claus, mannequins in shop windows, snowmen, famous and influential people, and even the unsuccessful heroes turned to stone by the Gorgon's head."

Another figure of nearly comparable importance is that of the stage as a place of created or feigned reality. Often Nemerov will simply echo Jacques' famous speech as a shorthand means of bringing this figure into play. In an early poem, **"Portrait of Three Conspirators,"** one of the three figures of the title is a man "who no longer believes the world a stage." The line returns three more times during the course of the poem. In the fifth stanza,

It is night, and it is the season of winter.
It is time, and time passes, and
The world is not a stage.

In the seventh stanza, the speaker reports a kind of dialogue he has with his imperturable "assassins,":

I say to them, I must die, because the world
Is not a stage.

But they remain unmoved:

Nothing can change them. They sit there as if
Immortal, and mutter, like actors on a stage,
Of art and wisdom, and a change of life.

This final comment on the inefficacy of poetic creation suggests (even requires) a contrast with Yeats's golden bird, who sings "of what is past, or passing, or to come." Where the Irish poet speaks of escaping the limitations imposed by "any natural thing," Nemerov denies the power of art, whose "words . . . break against / Implacable existence."

In **"The Loon's Cry,"** from *Mirrors and Windows* (1958), Nemerov turns to the same problem, though here he provides it with a historical context. Set in a landscape that symbolizes the intrusion of modern life into the world of nature—"down where the railroad bridge / Divides the river from the estuary"—the poem presents a speaker "fallen from the symboled world" who envies "those past ages . . . / When . . . the energy in things / Shone through their shapes." That past, he believes, was far more readable than the present. Orderly and well-balanced, it was characterized by a satisfying economy of design and function:

> Each life played a part,
> And every part consumed a life, nor dreams
> After remained to mock accomplishment.

That past was, above all, purposive; "The world a stage," its inhabitants were actors in a drama of divine shaping, "maskers all / In actions largely framed to imitate / God and his Lucifer's long debate."

But the energy and meaning of art hold more promise here than in **"The Three Conspirators."** Midway through the poem the bird's "savage cry" causes the speaker to imagine himself as "Adam . . . / Hearing the first loon cry in paradise." Its final stanza brings the poem's two chief symbols together:

> The loon again? Or else a whistling train,
> Whose far thunders began to shake the bridge.
> And it came on, a loud bulk under smoke,
> Changing the signals on the bridge, the bright
> Rubies and emeralds, rubies and emeralds
> Signing the cold night as I turned for home,
> Hearing the train cry once more, like a loon.

Thus **"The Loon's Cry"** goes farther than most of Nemerov's poems in uniting the world of created reality (the world shaped and ordered by mankind) and the world of nature. The world is *not* a stage, but neither does it stand exclusively as a mockery of the artist's effort to understand its meaning.

The relation of the poet's vision to the world—specifically the world of nature—is again Nemerov's subject in **"Elegy for a Nature Poet."** Here too the poem turns in part on an allusion to *As You Like It*. Of the dead poet, the poet asserts that there was

> Nothing too great, nothing too trivial
> For him; from mountain range or humble vermin
> He could extract the humble parable—
> If need be, crack the stone to get the sermon.

Duke Senior's praise of rustic life and "the uses of adversity" celebrates an existence that

> Finds tongue in trees, books in the running brooks,
> Sermons in stones, and good in everything

As is often the case with Nemerov, the poetic working-out of an intellectual or philosophical problem offers as well a field for play. **"Elegy for a Nature Poet"** illustrates this habit in a variety of ways: in its sly joking with the terms of its basic oppositions, in its surprising shifts of tone, and in its deft management of the conventions of its genre.

The death of the nature poet comes, ironically, from too intimate a contact with nature. On his last walk, he ventured unprotected into her domain:

> The covered bridge,
> Most natural of all the works of reason,
> Received him, let him go.

Through the witty playfulness of the poem, Nemerov sets the poet's fictions over against nature's truth. The dead poet was, above all else, pleased with his role.

> His gift was daily his delight, he peeled
> The landscape back to show it was a story;
> Any old bird or burning bush revealed
> At his hands just another allegory.

But the final judgment on him (and on his work) is the ironic sentence that nature always imposes on those foolish enough to try shaping her to their desires.

> And now, poor man, he's gone. Without his name
> The field reverts to wilderness again,
> The rocks are silent, woods don't seem the same;
> Demoralized small birds will fly insane.
>
> Rude nature, whom he loved to idealize
> And would have wed, pretends she never heard
> His voice at all, as, taken by surprise
> At last, he goes to her without a word.

The small birds are "demoralized" as they fulfill conventional elegiac expectations; but more importantly they are "de-moralized" as they are free from the impositions of one who would see a pattern in their randomness.

Thus Nemerov challenges Duke Senior's sentimental pastoralism, bringing nature itself to witness against and rebuke those who would read in its mysteries easy truths. *As You Like It* does not come fully into view in the brief compass of **"Elegy for a Nature Poet,"** but one does see there a complex of attitudes arising from the major pastoral-romantic themes of the play. Nemerov confronts those attitudes with a skepticism that operates by means of comic deflation. The questions are the familiar and serious ones of reality and perception, of art as reflection or source of meaning. As in **"Small Moment"** one discovers death; whatever is invented cannot last: "Without his name / The field reverts to wilderness again."

The "Seven Ages of Man" speech of Jacques in *As You Like It,* apart from providing a set piece for generations of high school elocution students, serves in the play as a counter-poise to its romantic and pastoral idealism. Nemerov, writing on **"The Four Ages"** turns to another of Shakespeare's plays to aid his analysis, which proceeds in terms drawn from the art of music. It is, he says, "*de rigueur* for myths to have four ages," though "Nobody quite knows why." In any event,

> The first age of the world was counterpoint,
> Music immediate to the senses

Not yet exclusive in their separate realms,
Wordlessly weaving the tapestried cosmos
Reflected mosaic in the wakening mind.

Though he offers no explanation for the change, Nemerov reports the end and the broken remnants of that first stretch of time:

That world was lost, though echoes of it stray
On every breeze and breath, fragmented and
Heard but in snatches, henceforth understood
Only by listeners like Pythagoras,
Who held the music of the spheres was silence
Because we had been hearing it from birth,
And Shakespeare, who made his Caliban recite
Its praises in the temporary isle.

In *The Tempest,* Caliban attempts to comfort Stephano and Trinculo, who have been frightened by Ariel's music.

Be not afeard. The isle is full of noises,
Sounds and sweet airs that give delight and hurt not.
Sometimes a thousand twanging instruments
Will hum about my ears; and sometimes voices
That, if I then had wak'd after long sleep,
Will make me sleep again; and then, in dreaming,
The clouds methought would open and show riches
Ready to drop upon me, that, when I wak'd,
I cried to dream again.

In **"The Four Ages"** the poet's myth traces a breakdown. Moving from "Music immediate to the senses," in the second age "words / Entered the dancing-space and made it song." The third age left only words and poetry,

A thinner music, but
Both subtle and sublime in its lament
For all that was lost to all but memory.

Finally, the fourth age completes a movement from magical apprehension of pure sound to rational explanation. "Illusion at last is over" and one is left with "common prose," which is "Delighted to explain, but not to praise." It may be, though the poem's speaker seems not to think it a major issue, that myths require four ages so that they may match

Four seasons and four elements and four
Voices of music and four gospels and four
Cardinal points on the compass rose and four
Whatever elses happen to come in four.

What matters most is that

These correspondences are what remain
Of the great age when all was counterpoint
And no one minded that nothing mattered or meant.

Nemerov is careful in the poem to attribute to Shakespeare (not his creature Caliban) the power to detect echoes of the first age of the world. As argument, then, his

poem exempts Shakespeare from the conflict that opposes the world's reality to the artist's perception. Instead, he is viewed as one who has access to the wondrous immediacy of the first age—"the tapestried cosmos / Reflected mosaic in the wakening mind."

This is the ground of Nemerov's wish, expressed with such telling poignancy in *Journal of a Fictive Life*:

The predicaments of my most characteristic and intimate imagery strangely belong to Shakespeare too, who resolved them by magical poetry in his Last Plays. May it happen to me also one day that the statue shall move and speak, and the drowned child be found, and the unearthly music sing to me.

The resolution of such "predicaments" is most likely to take place in poems that work at some remove from the actual details of Shakespearean language and plot detail. Again and again, Nemerov's "characteristic and intimate imagery" illuminates his dilemma as poet and thinker. Ross Labrie describes that dilemma most economically: "The insatiable hunger for meaning co-exists with the awareness that the meaning sought by the mind will invariably turn out to be the meaning imposed by the mind." For the most part, the poems which come closest to the magical resolution Shakespeare achieved in his last plays are less analytical and self-reflexive than the poems *about* Shakespeare. Yet the poems that develop out of an allusion to Shakespeare or take some Shakespearean character or play as their subject exemplify a central aspect of Nemerov's thinking about poetry. They do so, moreover, by making full use of a public awareness of Shakespeare; the poet can count, to an extraordinary degree, on his audience's adding something of their own commitment to Shakespeare to the field of interest created by the poem. This seems especially true of two poems that grow out of the materials of *Hamlet*, **"Polonius Passing Through a Stage"** and **"Orphic Scenario,"** with its subtitle, "for a movie of *Hamlet*."

The first of these, **"Polonius Passing Through a Stage,"** belongs to a long tradition of poems that isolate single characters from the plays, subjecting them to analysis or allowing them to speak for (and try to explain or justify), themselves and their actions. Walter De La Mare wrote a series of such poems, including one on Polonius in which he imagines the fictional character recognizing Sir Frances Bacon as his court fellow in corruption. The Czech poet Miroslav Holub describes a Polonius whose wily usefulness is an available commodity—"a pound of jellied / flunkey."

Nemerov's Polonius is a genuinely puzzled figure laboring to explain himself and his fate. In his attempt, he seems both pitiable and vaguely comic; in some ways, his efforts at self-justification recall the Herod of Auden's "For the Time Being." But where Auden's character degenerates into rant and banality ("I've tried to be good. I brush my teeth every night. I haven't had sex for a month. I object. I'm a liberal. I want everyone to be happy. I wish I had never been born."), Nemerov's becomes more complex, seeing himself as both an individual and as a dramatic figure, a mere counter in the theatrical patterns arranged by the playwright Shakespeare. Thus too the "stage" of the poem's title is both a stage in the speaker's development and the stage on which he acts out his appointed Shakespearean role.

In both cases, as he reviews his life now with the wisdom of retrospection, he believes he followed that injunction received as a child and delivered years later to his son: "Try to be yourself." Yet he can only judge that in the effort to do so he has failed; and his defense is the familiar, helpless one of all whose failure perplexes and defeats them: "I tried." The poem, in three six-line stanzas rhyming ababcc, treats past, present, and more recent past. The first stage tells of the speaker's childhood and early maturity, the third of his age, while the second seems to be a perpetual present in which the plays of Shakespeare are forever being performed. Surprisingly, they are presented by "The company in *my* Globe theater," apparently the mind or imagination of Polonius rather than Shakespeare's Globe.

Both in life and art, Polonius' efforts to be himself meet with frustration. "The blue annuities of silence some called / Wisdom," stored up over his youthful years, cannot shut out the reality of "sunstorms and exploding stars, / The legions screaming in the German wood." For most men, "Ten heavenly don'ts / Botch up a selfhood,"—i.e. a life defined by the commandments, though it be ruined, is nevertheless given some sort of shape. But Shakespeare as creator provides even less than the negative guidance of the decalogue: "where there's a Will / He's away." The result for Polonius as a Shakespearean character is that he finds himself, in language drawn from the play's chief line of imagery, "Rotting at ease, a ghostly doll"; he is troubled and perplexed by his own sense of unease: "What is that scratching on my heart's wall?" Finally, he reaches a condition like that of Lear in his madness, a connection borne out by an allusion to *King Lear*: "The silence grew / Till I could hear the tiniest Mongol horde / Scuffle the Gobi, a pony's felted shoe." Lear, in his wild ranting, imagines that

> It were a delicate strategem to shoe
> A troop of horse with felt. I'll put't in proof,
> And when I have stol'n upon these son-in-laws,
> Then kill, kill, kill, kill, kill, kill!

Here is the issue of those "blue annuities of silence": a more profound and inescapable sense of evil, and finally death at the hand of Hamlet. It seems hard to say precisely what meanings are comprehended in "from the fiery pit that self-born bird / Arose"; but the immediate context suggests that the reference is primarily to Hamlet and that the phoenix, though certainly a plausible intention, fits less well. Hamlet is "self-born" as the images of "Among School Children" are ("both nuns and mothers worship images"), and he emerges from unearthly contact with his dead father to claim revenge on those responsible for the late king's death. The poem's closing lines once again merge the speaker of the poem and the Shakespearean character: "A rat! The unseen good old—/ That sort of

thing always brings the house down." Hamlet's exclamation and Gertrude's report make up the first line, while the second is the character's resigned evaluation of his theatrical fate. Even here, though, Polonius' double role is captured in a kind of pun. His death is invariable a *coup de theatre,* but it also marks the imminent destruction of his family line.

"Polonius Passing Through a Stage" is not, like many of the poems about Shakespeare's plays or the characters who inhabit them, particularly self-reflexive in its operation. It does not turn us back to the play with any sense that we have access to the heart of its mystery. Rather, it moves out of the play to make a more generalized point about how one shapes identity and about the essentially solitary nature of that task. Yet if one sees the poem as an answer to the question, "How would Polonius explain himself?" it does provide an interpretation of his character and grounds for understanding his behavior throughout the play. What "they told the child" remains for the aging court counsellor a first principle of behavior. He wants to please, and his eagerness to do so emerges as mindless obsequiousness joined to self-celebrating garrulity. In this poem, Nemerov strikes an effective balance between source and invention, using as givens the character of Polonius and some elements of Shakespeare's own language but supplying from his own poetic resources the central thematic concern and the intellectual playfulness that create the work's striking tone and undeniable power.

What Nemerov achieves with **"Polonius Passing Through a Stage"** he attempts on a much larger scale in **"Orphic Scenario,"** a poem from a section in *Mirrors and Windows* (1958) that includes **"The Loon's Cry," "Lightning Storm on Fuji (Hokusai)," "Home for the Holidays," "Sunderland," "Moses,"** and **"Ahasuerus."** While this seems not to be a rigorous grouping, there are sufficient likenesses among the poems to suggest possible reasons for their placement. **"The Loon's Cry,"** discussed earlier, treats the issue of art's relation to the world it proposes to imitate. This theme also shapes the poem on Hokusai's painting. **"Moses"** and **"Home for the Holidays"** explore the familiar Nemerov theme of contrasting (even opposed) perspectives. **"Sunderland,"**—which includes an allusion to *Romeo and Juliet*—and **"Ahasuerus"** are both self-consciously literary. In **"Orphic Scenario"** one sees the "predicaments of [Nemerov's] most characteristic and intimate imagery" expressed in a difficult and complex poem. The work's range—of allusion, of feeling—is enormous; in addition, it displays the poet's almost habitual disregard of consistency of tone. Thus a poem which takes up the grandest and most important of themes (time, the self, ways of knowing, orders of existence) contains as well gratuitous and ineffective puns (the egghead's Rorschach in the Holy Wood, "Meatier and more meet"). Perhaps it was her impatience with such unreconciled diversity that prompted Carolyn Kizer to say that in this poem "no amount of forcing can mobilize the dead-tired ideas."

The notion of "forcing," though, which implies a pattern or design into which the poet tries to fit pieces of his argument, seems foreign to the strategy of this poem, which works rather through the "predicaments" of imagery. Birth and death, egg and bleeding bull, constitute the encompassing extremities of this imagery. Light—as reflection, as stage device, as source of a version of reality (Plato's myth of the cave)—makes up its center. On this field of imagery, Nemerov develops his poem. **"Orphic Scenario,"** with its descriptive subtitle, "for a movie of *Hamlet,*" is circular in design. It moves from a description of the close of the play—

> Bear Hamlet, like a soldier to the stage
> (The world's a stage). And bid the soldiers shoot.
> Loud music, drums and guns, the lights go up.

to

> Goodnight.
>   The Soldiers shoot.
> That's what life is, you may be moved to say,
> Reality. And sometimes, in reality.
> You may remember how the honey and blood
> Fell from the huge lips of those murdered gods.

and from "Cheap? Yes, of course it's cheap." to "Cheaper, and yet more golden than before." Within this movement, the central theme of the poem is the relation of art and reality, the "tricks" of the stage or the camera set over against "the things we think we see and know."

The concerns of **"Orphic Scenario"** appear repeatedly in the other poems of *Mirrors and Windows* and in "The Swaying Form: A Problem in Poetry," first published in 1959. The knottiness of the poem—its circularity and reflexivity, the ambiguity of its reference—demonstrates the need to read it with certain words and ideas in mind, words and ideas that seem to dominate Nemerov's thought and writing during the period of the 'fifties and early 'sixties. These would include such words as "mirror," "window," "light," "lens," "screen," and objects or phenomena associated with them, such as reflection, illumination, shadowing, and many others. Thus it is true and not merely fashionable to say that **"Orphic Scenario"** is a poem about the creative process, about the writing of poetry; for the poem's design, or its struggle to achieve a design, illustrates perfectly Nemerov's definition of the writer's job of work:

> Writing means trying to find out what the nature of things has to say about what you think you have to say. And the process is reflective or cyclical, a matter of feedback between oneself and "it," an "it" which can gain its identity only in the course of being brought into being, come into being only in the course of finding its identity.

Thus the question of theatrical tricks—Is the close of *Hamlet* cheap?—grows into other questions which have the effect of joining this theatrical illusion to illusions of other sorts. The stage image alters into that of a camera and perhaps also of a card game, even an unfair one— "This dark malodorous box of taken tricks"—but with the

purpose of asserting that "reality's much the same"; and the speaker of the poem, anticipating a charge of begging the question, simplifies his responses:

> Reality's where the hurled light beams and breaks,
> Against the solemn wall, a spattered egg,
> The seed and food of being.

Julia Bartholomay, arguing that Nemerov's key theme is "reflexivity of thought," identifies its expression in "Runes," where it also appears through the imagery of seed and egg. In "Runes," she says, "The secret of the seed, extracted by knowledge, is death (IV), though it is also life (XVI)."

Paradox, a multiplicity of illusions, difficulty even in locating a starting point—these are the experiences of a reader of **"Orphic Scenario"** just as they are the subjects of the poem itself. Here one may see in Nemerov's own work an example of a major problem he identifies in modern poetry citing *Troilus and Cressida* to illustrate his point:

> This development [poetry that treats of the act of composition], where the mind curves back upon itself, may always be a limit, not only for poetry but for every kind of thought, for that "speculation" which Shakespeare says "Turns not to itself / Till it hath travell'd and is mirror'd there / Where it may see itself" adding that, "This is not strange at all."

But if such a limit imposes itself, one's only recourse is to accept it and, in that acceptance, work toward the best possible understanding. Reality, then, as "hurled light" or "spattered egg" is at least a beginning; and from that point, Nemerov goes on to posit other developments, all of them offered tentatively and in the subjunctive mood—"if," "should." Once the illusion is projected, "splayed as a blaze / On the blank of limit," it becomes a potential source of knowledge, able to "entrance / The vacant stare, fix it with visions of, / However dripping and impure, an order." And if this can be achieved, "That is enough, or the abstract of enough." But the speaker of the poem, never content to accept a single vision of reality, pressing always for still another logical possibility in this investigation of the limits of knowledge, goes one step further:

> And should the seed and food of order also
> Resemble the things we see and know,
> Lips, noses, eyes, the grimaces thereof
> Compounded, playing in the fetal night,
> That too is enough, if not too much.

"Human kind," says Eliot, "cannot bear very much reality"; and the reality of "lips, noses, eyes," recalling the torment of Othello, provides an instance of that truth even as it reminds us that the Moor's madness grows out of an illusion created by Iago.

The continuing movement in search of a ground for observation—which is both the poem's method and its meaning—culminates finally in a defense of art which may be described as Sidneyan:

sometimes, in reality,
You may remember how the honey and blood
Fell from the huge lips of those murdered gods.

This is an assertion, though admittedly an oblique and understated one. Any paraphrase of such a subtle argument runs the risk of Polonian specificity; but it is clear, I think, that Nemerov bases his defense of art on its moving power, on its ability to use a golden world—here a world of grand figures and actions with mythic resonance—to enhance and transform our vision of the world we experience. The instruments of that transformation are "effigies," of the sort described by Julia Bartholomay—in this poem primarily the cinema and images drawn from film technique and personalities but also the rich and violent world of mythology. In **"Orphic Scenario,"** however, the effigies do not confirm a mistaken notion of reality; instead, they force an observer to question the grounds of his belief about reality and to become aware of the terrifying mysteries that great art is capable of communicating. This, finally, is the poem's testimony to the power of Shakespeare's drama. The death of Hamlet shows us

How all the buildings rise in a golden sky
Cheaper, and yet more golden, than before,
More high and solemn, borne on a great stage
In a failing light.

For Nemerov, then *Hamlet* offers a paradigm of the function of great art. In its majesty (and even in its theatrical "cheapness") it confronts us with the need to test our vision of reality. Its very grandeur is a source of its moving power, and though that grandness be at times specious, a publicist's excess—"The new Veronica, the stiffened face / Light of the world, cast on a hanging cloth"—it is capable nevertheless of driving us to other and deeper awarenesses.

Nemerov's response to the tyranny of Shakespeare appears finally in a variety of strategies, all of them based on the modern poet's recognition that Shakespeare is a vital presence both for himself and for his contemporary audience. In his poetry, Nemerov introduces and uses Shakespeare in a wide variety of ways ranging from casual, apparently flippant allusions to instances in which the original Shakespearean materials are deployed extensively to create whole poems. This habitual returning has its basis in two beliefs that Nemerov has set out in a quite explicit fashion—the first related to his understanding of poetry, the second to his sense of Shakespeare's thought. The struggle to come to terms with what is, the poet's continuing effort to define the relation between mind and things, observer and observed world, is the key to his description of poetry:

Poetry, I would say, is, in its highest ranges, no mere playing with the counters of meaning, but a perpetual rederiving of the possibility of meaning from matter, of the intelligible world from the brute recalcitrance of things.

It was Shakespeare's glory, "a sublime and terrible treasure which afterwards was lost," to have created his match-

less dramas on the assumption that "there exist several distinct realms of being, which for all their apparent distinctness respond immediately and decisively to one another." In his continuing struggle as a poet, Nemerov has kept the example of Shakespeare before him, seizing upon occasional stray echoes of "The first age of the world" but recognizing his own less favored place in history. In **"The Four Ages"** the last age is described in a metaphor that recalls the poet's frequent denial that "All the world's a stage." Here the stage itself is dissolving and the show has come to an end:

The sentences break ranks, the orchestra
Has left the pit, the curtain has come down
Upon the smiling actors, and the crowd
Is moving toward the exits through the aisles.
Illusion at last is over.

This is a world Shakespeare never knew, a world of prose fit to explain but not to celebrate. In such an age, the tyranny of Shakespeare might seem especially inescapable and potent. But for Nemerov it becomes instead a spur to greater effort in the craft of writing, in the attempt "to find out what the nature of things has to say about what you think you have to say." In "the nature of things" Nemerov discovers that Hopkins knew: "there lives the dearest freshness." Shakespeare, as unattainable model, forces him to this discovery; and thus the tyrant Shakespeare becomes the guide and genius of his poetic achievement.

Miriam Marty Clark (review date 1990)

SOURCE: "'Between the Wave and the Particle': Figuring Science in Howard Nemerov's Poems," in *Mosaic,* Vol. 23, No. 4, Fall, 1990, pp. 37-50.

[In the review below, Clark examines Nemerov's incorporation of science and technology into his works.]

As reader, namer, knower, skeptic, Howard Nemerov has had a long and productive engagement with the material world and with the sciences which explore its laws, its oddities. His work alludes often to scientific and semi-scientific writing from Euclid to Einstein; his many, diverse sources include Goethe, Gödel, Eddington, Sherrington, Freud, Whitehead, Russell; Herbert Muller, Scott Buchanan, Owen Barfield and Lewis Thomas.

Such engagement, though generally acknowledged, has curiously been given little detailed attention by critics of Nemerov's work. Peter Meinke, for example, notes broadly [in his *Howard Nemerov,* 1968] that Nemerov has become a "spokesman for the existential, science-oriented (or science-displaced), liberal mind of the twentieth century," and Julia Bartholomay argues simply that the poet is one of the few to "incorporate science into his work" [in her *The Shield of Perseus: The Vision and Imagination of Howard Nemerov,* 1972]. Undoubtedly, partly responsible for failure to pursue the issue further is the way Nemerov himself has seemed not to encourage it. Thus early in his career, in *Journal of the Fictive Life* (1965), he observed: "Like many poets, I read a good deal of science, and like most of the poets who do, I do not read it for the sake of science but rather for the sake of metaphor." Later, in a 1979 interview with Ross Labrie [in *Southern Review,* Vol. 15, 1979], he added, "I've sort of despaired of ever knowing anything. . . . I can hunt around snapping up unconsidered metaphors where I can. But that oughtn't to be confused with the knowledge of physics and biology."

Disclaimers like these are not especially troublesome, however, for it can easily be demonstrated that, "unconsidered" as they may seem, Nemerov's metaphors are not divorced from their scientific contexts and are related in vital ways, not merely passing ones, to the questions the poet asks, the puzzles and paradoxes of the world he describes. More problematic, and therefore probably the real deterrent to a discussion of the centrality of science in Nemerov's poetry, is the question—alluded to by Meinke—of whether his interest should be viewed as "orientation" or "displacement." A poet of shifting moods, Nemerov swings, often within a single volume, between deep engagement and ironic detachment, between an empowering romanticization of science and a lingering distrust of it.

Furthermore, Nemerov's attitude toward science and technology, which he often treats—tellingly—as a single venture, has evolved over the years. Some of his early poems (**"The Bacterial War," "Fragment from Correspondence"**) and essays (**"A Dream of Reason"**) address science as an alien enterprise and one threatening both to poetry and to civilization. In this he is like many other poets of his generation, responding to World War II and to the rise of New Criticism (Nemerov's first volume of poems was published in 1947, the same year as Cleanth Brooks's *The Well Wrought Urn*), which Gerald Graff has described [in *The American Scholar,* Vol. 49, 1980] as "a socially committed movement, dedicated to the romantic project of saving the world from the demoralization inflicted by science."

Increasingly, however, Nemerov has come to see science as a discourse among discourses, in many ways adjacent to poetry and open, if not to genealogy in a poststructuralist sense (his guide in the matter being Whitehead, not Foucault), then to critique and to exploration. Ultimately, Nemerov is concerned not only with the figurative *possibilities* of science—its usefulness as a source of metaphors—but also with its figurative *nature* and its mythic properties.

This concern arises first and most enduringly, I believe, from a sense of the adjacency of scientific and literary discourses and an understanding of the aims and the limitations they share. In an important essay on his friend and teacher Kenneth Burke [in *Reflexions on Poetry and Poetics*], Nemerov points out that while Burke is often at odds with scientistic philosophies and with science itself, he is "adventured on somewhat the same quest as that of physics: he would bring the world of human action, as it

would the world of physical motion, under the dominion of few, simple and elegant laws."

Like Burke, Nemerov has a strong impulse to find in and bring to the world those "few, simple, and elegant laws." At the same time, however, he also has a powerful sense of the world as chaotic, in flux, fundamentally unruly. The problem of reconciling abstraction with particularity, form with chaos, is originally expressed in philosophical and poetic terms. Explaining the title of his first book, *The Image and the Law,* Nemerov observed to Labrie: "On one side the imagist sort of thing, the sharp, individualized perception which related to nothing but itself. And on the other side, the side of Platonism and the sort of scholastic philosophers before people like Abelard, Scotus and Ockham came along, the side which emphasized the governing similarity to other experiences and abstractions, the law." In his early volumes, Nemerov tries various strategies and tropes—aphorism, dialectic, metaphor—to reconcile the image and the law. Most prove inadequate even to the metaphysical complications the poems themselves set forth and certainly to the rich, diverse world Nemerov knows. Finally language itself fails to order and reveal the world fully.

Throughout the *Collected Poems* there is considerable tension between the belief that language is powerful to comprehend and order and the conviction that there are limits to its power. "It is as though the world / were a great writing," he says in one poem, but adds: "Having said so much, let us allow there is more to the world / than writing: continental faults are not / bare convoluted fissures in the brain." Here the metaphor—the world as writing—both does and does not succeed. Language *does* describe and circumscribe the world, but imperfectly. This realization leads to more sustained speculation, in poems and essays alike, on the power and the limits of language. In the course of that speculation, Nemerov turns again to science.

If nature, in its flux and particularity, resists the philosopher and the poet it also resists the scientist, and never more profoundly than in our own time. Physicist Stephen Hawking, describing the inconsistencies and uncertainties which have occupied his colleagues for most of our century [in his *A Brief History of Time,* 1988], notes simply that "It turns out to be very difficult to devise a theory to describe the universe all in one go." He goes on to elaborate the fundamental incompatibility between the "two basic partial theories" by which contemporary scientists describe the world—the general theory of relativity, which reckons with the large-scale structure of the universe, and quantum mechanics, which "deals with phenomena on extremely small scales."

For a variety of reasons, and in ways I will deal with more fully later, it is the terms of quantum mechanics which prove most tempting to Nemerov. Rather than resolve the old dilemma of the image and the law, they extend it radically and offer a whole new set of metaphors: waves, particles, uncertainties becoming principles. In **"This, That, and the Other,"** a verse dialogue, the poet seizes on those scientific terms playfully, if unscientifically, having his character "That" advance a theory of his own:

> The physicists are vexed between the wave
> And particle—would it not somehow save
> The appearances to think about snow
> As particles becoming waves below,
> Exchanging not their natures but their shapes?

Though the ease of such appearance-saving is deceptive (and though "That" later admits, sheepishly, "This isn't physics, but theology"), the lines are important ones, both exploiting the figurative possibilities of scientific discourse and suggesting again the figurative nature of it.

By the middle volumes of *The Collected Poems,* those published between 1955 and 1973, the problem of principle and diversity, of the image and the law, becomes the focus of virtually all of Nemerov's thinking about science and much of his thinking about the world. These middle poems are characterized by their keen attentiveness to the objects and arrangements of the physical world. While many take up the accoutrements of modern life—the telephone, the television, sun glasses, storm windows—others consider the natural world. In them Nemerov's point of view, language and metaphors are often broadly scientific. He writes about the taxonomy of trees and birds, the chemistry of the mysterious gingko, the geometric patterns of shells and leaves. He attends to singularities and variations in nature as well as to governing shapes and similarities. Sometimes he discovers truth in the relations between things; at other times he dismisses metaphysics and notions about truth.

Influenced by mathematician Scott Buchanan's books *Poetry and Mathematics* and *The Doctrine of Signatures,* Nemerov sometimes turns in these volumes to arithmetic as metaphor and as a way of reckoning the relations between things. In his poem **"Vermeer,"** it is "a holy mathematic" which can relate those daily things—moments, colors, gestures—for which the Dutch Master cares so unassumingly, so unspeculatively, to each other and to the larger forces of history, time and truth. A decade later, in **"Figures of Thought,"** truth is similarly reckoned in mathematical terms:

> To lay the logarithmic spiral on
> Sea-shell and leaf alike, and see it fit,
> To watch the same idea work itself out
> In the fighter pilot's steepening, tightening turn
>
> Onto his target, setting up the kill,
> And in the flight of certain wall-eyed bugs.

The repeated pattern, the shell-shaped spiral, becomes principle enciphered. "How secret that is," he continues, "and how privileged / One feels to find the same necessity / Ciphered in forms diverse and otherwise / Without kinship." In the end, Nemerov treats these hieroglyphs and the truth they encode less seriously than he does in **"Vermeer."** "It may diminish some our dry delight," he concludes, "To wonder if everything we are and do / Lies

subject to some little law like that; / Hidden in nature but not deeply so."

His attitude here, like his topic, echoes a much earlier poem, **"Shells."** There the form of the shell along the shore is "only cryptically / Instructive, if at all"; quite unlike the shell of Holmes's chambered nautilus, it is subject to a variety of readings. "It is a stairway going nowhere," Nemerov proposes, "Our precious emblem of the steep ascent." But then he suspends belief: "Perhaps, beginning at a point / And opening to infinity, / Or the other way, if you want it the other way." Eventually the shell's spirals are erased "with dust, then with water." The spiral continues to be a governing shape for Nemerov, however, and in other poems other figures serve as ciphers and emblems for relation. Maxwell Goldberg, for example, has identified the reticulum or network as an important configuration in some of Nemerov's poems; equally he employs alphabets, hieroglyphs and ideograms to encode the world.

Wry as his talk about relation and interpretation may be, Nemerov treats them elsewhere, as in **"Vermeer,"** seriously and with deep, even religious, feeling. In such moments his debts to Buchanan and to English writer and historian of consciousness Owen Barfield are evident. Already in his poem **"The Loon's Cry,"** published in the late 1950s, he considers in yearning ways the failure and recovery of the mind's power to construct relations between object and truth or meaning. What begins as a walk on a cool, late-summer evening soon becomes a meditation on the disappearance of meaning from the physical world. "This is a natural beauty," he writes of the setting sun, the rising moon, "it is not / Theology,"

> For I had fallen from
> The symboled world, where I in earlier days
> Found mysteries of meaning, form and fate
> Signed on the sky, and now stood but between
> A swamp of fire and a reflecting rock.

The dissociation is a double one—of the natural world from meaning and mystery, and of phenomena (sun and moon, river and sea) from each other. The poet's use of metaphor in the final line of the stanza is both ironic and hopeful, because such a figure depends on, even as it testifies to, the relations between image and meaning, image and image.

"I envied those past ages of the world," he writes, envisioning an ideal relation between the physical world and universal truth,

> When, as I thought, the energy in things
> Shone through their shapes, when sun and moon no less
> Than tree or stone or star or human face
> Were seen but as fantastic Japanese
> Lanterns are seen, sullen or gay colors
> And lines revealing the light that they conceal.

Allowing that his argument simplifies the history of consciousness, he then describes the present. "We'd traded all those mysteries in for things," he observes, "For essences in things, not understood—/ Reality in things! and now we saw / Reality exhausted all their truth." If what Nemerov is describing in these lines sounds like imagism, it also sounds like the scientific materialism he rejects resoundingly in his poems and essays. Hyatt Waggoner's characterization of imagism as a "defensive-imitative poetic response" to the mechanism and materialism of early twentieth-century· scientific philosophy [in his *American Poets from the Puritans to the Present,* 1984] is revealing here. Like positivism, Waggoner says, imagism revered the concrete, the verifiable, the economical; like positivism it saw experience and sensation rather than "truth" as the proper domain of poetry. Such a view, Nemerov argues in poems like **"The Loon's Cry,"** renders poetry and the things of the world meaningless.

In that poem, the speaker's sense of meaninglessness culminates in a moment of desolation and emptiness which serves also as a turning point. He becomes Adam, hearing the first loon's cry in paradise, and understands "what that cry meant":

> That its contempt was for the forms of things,
> Their doctrines, which decayed—the nouns of stone
> And adjectives of glass—not for the verb
> Which surged in power properly eternal
>
> Against the seawall of the solid world
> Battering and undermining what it built.

Elsewhere Nemerov puns on his own name—making himself a "namer-of"—but here he sees himself not as a noun-speaker but as a verb-utterer. To say the verb is to replenish nature and language; it is "the poet's act, only and always, in whatever time." Such an act becomes possible in the rediscovery of meaning. Thus, alluding both to Scott Buchanan and Jacob Boehme, he writes: "For signatures / In all things are, which leave us not alone / Even in the thought of death, and may by arts / Contemplative be found and named again." In noun and adjective, stone and glass, moon and stars, the contemplative mind finds the constant, the thing which abides through decay and dissociation, the force which informs and makes meaningful the phenomena of the physical world and which holds those disparate phenomena together.

Almost a decade later, in **"The Blue Swallows,"** Nemerov returns (though not for the first time) to the themes of the image and the law, relation and consciousness. Grammar and geometry again figure significantly. The shapes—seven blue swallows above the millstream—are "invisible and evanescent, / Kaleidoscopic." Watching them from the bridge, the speaker strives in vain to connect, to "Weave up relation's spindrift web." The mood of the poem, until its final stanza, is one of despair. Metaphor fails—swallows tails are not "nibs / Dipped in invisible ink." Neither mind, nor memory, nor abstraction ("history is where tensions were," "Form is the diagram of forces") nor theology holds sway over the fleeting and changing shapes below the bridge. In the world since William of Ockham, relation is unreal, a dream, a false grammar the mind imposes. Fully realized, such nominalism denies one of the most basic kinds of relation—reflection. "Even the water / Flowing away beneath those birds," Nemerov laments, "Will fail to reflect their flying forms."

Like **"The Loon's Cry," "The Blue Swallows"** asserts in the end the redemptive power of the mind. The relation which is discovered and named by "arts contemplative" in the earlier poem is here created and illuminated by the imagination. "O swallows, swallows, poems are not / The point," the speaker says,

> Finding again the world,
> That is the point, where loveliness
> Adorns intelligible things
> Because the mind's eye lit the sun.

Such a conception of mind is Romantic, much like (though more benign than) the view Nemerov attributes to Blake; it is also much like Goethe's and, more recently, like Owen Barfield's. Nemerov's affinity for the Romantics is evident both in his essays (particularly in "Two Ways of the Imagination") and in his poems. At the end of his introduction to Barfield's *Poetic Diction,* explaining the importance of poetic diction to the Romantic poets, he writes,

> Out of their efforts to reform this highly specialized diction and reach back instead to "nature" arose the deeper question of the extent of the imagination's role as creator of the visible and sensible world. For Blake that extent was total: Imagination is the Savior. For Wordsworth the relation was a more tentative and balancing one. . . . For both, and for their great contemporaries, the primacy of imagination was a point of considerable anxiety, too, because the view opposed, the view of a universe of independently and fatally moving *things,* the view named by Alfred North Whitehead as "scientific materialism," was so evidently triumphant in imposing its claims upon the general mind of Europe and America.

In Goethe, in Barfield, in others, Romanticism makes its own scientific claims and establishes its own approaches to scientific problems.

For Nemerov, the relevance of the Romantic vision to a discussion of science is twofold. On one hand, in poems like **"The Blue Swallows"** and the profoundly Romantic poem **"The Painter Dreaming in the Scholar's House,"** it is a luminous resolution of the old scientific and philosophical problem of the image and the law. For Nemerov, as for Stevens, imagination becomes both the source of and the informing, governing truth for the image, novelty, diversity. Meaning dwells in the mind; the verb surges from within, not from beyond the mind and nature.

On the other hand, such a view provides him with a significant point of connection to modern physics. In his essay "Goethe's Science in the Twentieth Century," Frederick Amrine suggests that the work of Werner Heisenberg and his colleagues has made an important place in modern science for Goethe's subjective, Romantic conception of the world. "A realm is uncovered," Amrine contends, "in which the contribution of the subject cannot be excised from *any* act of cognition. Quantum mechanics reveals that the observer influences the events that he observes; Heisenberg writes that 'the object of research is no longer nature itself but man's investigation of nature.'" Elsewhere [*Physics and Philosophy,* 1958] Heisenberg himself puts it this way: "The term 'happens' is restricted to the observation. Now this is a very strange result, since it seems to indicate that observation plays a decisive role in the event and that the reality varies, depending on whether we observe it or not. We have to remember that what we observe is not nature in itself but nature exposed to our questioning." And Herbert Muller, whose *Science and Criticism* is a book that Nemerov praises, describes the dawning period in science as one in which "knowledge is a transaction between the observer and the observed."

These principles and descriptions apply, as scientists are quick to point out, chiefly to the fundamental particles of the universe. "The equations describe the behavior of very small objects," physicist John Gribbin cautions [in *In search of Schrödinger's Cat,* 1984], "generally speaking, the size of atoms or smaller—and they provide the *only* understanding of the world of the very small." Yet like relativity, quantum physics finds its way, often in a very generalized or modified form, into poetry. For Nemerov, quantum physics, broadly interpreted, provides for his Romantic conception of mind and nature an appealing set of metaphors and paradigms. From physics he also derives a set of more tolerant or expansive principles to hold up to diverse and chaotic reality. The terms and hypotheses of quantum physics appear occasionally in the early and middle volumes but become increasingly important in the last two volumes of *The Collected Poems.*

In the middle volumes and on into the later ones, however, Nemerov's attitude toward science and scientists continues to be mixed and often sardonic. In **"Cosmic Comics,"** for example, he ponders the Freudian aspects of the "apocalyptic dream" of the black hole, "Through which, say our astronomers, / The whole damn thing, the universe, / Must one day fall," and concludes: "Where Moses saw the seat of God / Science has seen what's just as odd, / The asshole of the universe." About technology he is often even more wry. In **"Cybernetics,"** for example, he imagines a brain-building kit, complete with instructions. A more elaborate brain than the simple one in the package is "perfectly possible," these directions admit, but,

> It runs you into much more money for
> Circuits of paradox and contradiction.
> Your vessels of antinomian wrath alone
> Run into millions; and you can't stop there,
> You've got to add at every junction point
> Auxiliary systems that will handle doubt,
> Switches of agony that are On and Off
> At the same time, and limited-access
> Blind alleys full of inefficient gods
> And marvelous devils.

On much the same grounds he rejects computer-made poetry in a couple of essays written in the same period as

"Cybernetics." "The computer can never do more than imitate from the outside certain imitable characteristics of art," he argues. "Poetry tells us stories deep and rich with experience, with thought, with language. The technological—I would not say the scientific—pretension is that all this is artificially imitable; and technologically that might one day turn out to be true. And then?"

His opinion of technology is seldom much more favorable than this. In **"The Backward Look"** he compares Dante in heaven to the "sterile satellite" in its bored orbit through the "heaven of technology." In another poem, **"Druidic Rimes,"** he describes with regret astronomy's venture—via satellite—beyond the visible. He writes first of the mind going forth "with naked eye / To take a turn about the sky" and then of the deeply Romantic experience of seeing the sky through a telescope. "When the telescope was trained / Where only darkness reigned," he writes,

> Or seemed to, lights broke into being
> As if to marry the eye's seeing
> In the flowering of a cosmic spring
> That grew like anything.

Telescopes, however, give way to electronic methods of scanning the heavens; the Romantic experience gives way to scientific certainty. "Now mind went forth without the eye," he says ruefully,

> On waves beyond the visible sky:
> Impulses from what scarce was matter
> Bounced off a shallow platter
>
> Into the realm of number pure,
> The only measure made so sure
> That mind was guaranteed to mind it
> And always stand behind it.

As much as he rejects the satellite and the disembodied information it collects, then, so much does he embrace the telescope as a bit of technology which makes possible a wonderful engagement of mind and world. In **"Lines & Circularities"** it is the record player he praises:

> I watch the circling stillness of the disc,
> The tracking inward of the tone-arm, enact
> A mystery wherein the music shares:
> How time, that comes and goes and vanishes
> Never to come again, can come again.

Most recently, in **"Playing the Machine,"** he writes with grumpy satisfaction of opposing a computer at chess. "You can always, turn it off," he notes, "Declare a victory and leave it there, / Somewhat the way you leave a telling dream, / Taking its faithless memory away." It would seem, therefore, that it is to tools like the telescope and the phonograph that Nemerov refers in his essay "On Metaphor" when he argues that the physical sciences "have a relation to magic with respect to the material world, so that men can on their account do many things that before could only be thought or dreamed."

Such miracles of telescope and tone arm, however, do little to mitigate Nemerov's disapproval of technology in its higher varieties, for the science-assisted imagination is also the science-afflicted, even the science-endangered imagination. Accordingly, in the end, the threat posed by technology converges with the threat posed by scientific materialism. In an essay called "Poetry, Prophecy, Prediction," Nemerov recalls with feeling Blake's vision of the future. Blake's is a Newtonian universe, of course, but the world which he imagines is one that even a twentieth-century poet engaged by the terms and equations of quantum physics finds chilling. Thus to Nemerov, "The invention of machines in its turn produces the image of a giant machine as a metaphor for the universe, but also, inevitably, as a metaphor for the mind, whose servile ambition henceforth will be the progressively perfected imitation of relentless and mechanic order without other purpose than the maintenance of its sterile circularities, from which soul, spirit, mind itself at last, will be progressively excluded."

Yet, even as Nemerov's remarks address the frightening specter of science and technology, they make the case that metaphor is powerful and that language is what finally gives shape to consciousness. At the end of the same essay he calls scientific language "the language in which we tell each other myths about the motions and the purposes of mind disguised as world, as time, as truth." Later, in his poem **"Einstein, Freud & Jack,"** he makes a similar assertion when he depicts Einstein writing to Freud to ask what he thinks science might do for world peace. "Not much," Freud responds, adding that "science too begins and ends in myth." To call the language of science mythic is, in one sense, to devalue it in a world where fact and myth are antonyms. Nemerov adds to this effect by concluding slyly, "It scarce needs saying, that myth believed is never called a myth." In Nemerov's own lexicon, however, as in Blake's and in Freud's, myth is a way of telling the truth about the world and the mind.

For Nemerov, particularly in his four or five most recent volumes, the language, the laws, the metaphors of science do become deeply appealing ways of comprehending and revealing the world. Some of his metaphors are biological. In one poem, for example, he describes novelists talking, "In allegories of themselves that go down on paper like dividing cells." And in **"The Weather of the World"** a TV map is described as "a great sensorium, / The vast enfolding cortex of the globe, / Containing contradictions, tempers, moods."

More often both the metaphors and the principles come from physics. In particular, he works and reworks the second law of thermodynamics (which holds that the disorder or entropy of a closed system always increases), trying to find a way of resolving the old paradox of the image and the law. In **"Two Pair"** he compares the Old Law and the New of the Bible to the first and second laws of thermodynamics. "The first pair tells us we may be redeemed," he writes, "But in a world, the other says, that's doomed." "What boots it to be told both sets are true," he inquires a few lines later, "Or that disorder in the universe is perfectly legal, and always getting worse?" In

"Drawing Lessons" he considers some exceptions to the entropy principle. "Water," he notes,

> has the wondrous property
> And power of assembling itself again
> When shattered, but the shore cannot do that.
> The Second Law seems to reverse itself
> For water, but not for land.

Allowing the usefulness of the second law in predicting things like the gradual going to dust of the drawing student's pencil and of the body, he nevertheless looks on it as "The invention of a parsimonious people / Accustomed to view creation on a budget / Cut to economy more than to delight." To this assessment he adds smugly, "The sea's a little more mysterious than that." In the way of mind, not body, water defies the laws which would govern the novel, unruly world.

In his 1973 essay, [in *Salmaguadi*] James M. Kiehl notes—with respect to Nemerov's concern with the inadequacies of scientific thinking—"One response by the sciences to such limitations is to come back upon themselves, to devote attention to their own modes of expression and perception. They are at least noticing that their own modes are analogic and metaphoric and consequently they are learning the same sort of diffidence poets acquire as 'negative capability.'" Kiehl acknowledges that this turn toward the reflexive, particularly on the part of physicists, is important to Nemerov's thinking about science and his use of scientific images. Such thinking is most clearly worked out in the late poems where Nemerov turns to ways of seeing, of reckoning subatomic truths in daily life. "There," for example, describes the workings of the Romantic imagination in terms of physics. "Sacred is secret," he writes,

> at the confluence
> Where the unclean, the holy, the forbidden,
> Mingle their currents, there where mind and sense,
> An inch behind the eyes, perform their hidden
>
> And common ministry, turning a storm
> Of photons into this world of trees and rocks
> And stars and faces.

In **"Seeing Things"** he writes about metaphor-making: nature making metaphors for quantum physics, physics making them for sight and thought. "Close as I ever came to seeing things / The way physicists say things really are," he begins,

> Was out on Sudbury Marsh one summer eve
> When a silhouetted tree against the sun
> Seemed at my sudden glance to be afire:
> A black and boiling smoke made all its shape.
> Binoculars resolved the enciphered sight
> To make it clear the smoke was a cloud of gnats,
> Their millions doing such a steady dance
> As by the motion of the many made the one
> Shape constant and kept it so in both the forms
> I'd thought to see, the fire and the tree.

This scene in the marsh calls to mind first and most compellingly the Big Bang and those original particles which, as Gribbin puts it, "first jostled in close proximity in the cosmic fireball." It also recalls the "logarithmic spiral" which governs in **"Figures of Thought."** Yet this strange sight and the physics it alludes to provide something the spiral does not—a way of reconciling principle and chaos. The gnats make up and sustain the constant; and they summon, like the photons of "There," the powers of imagination to give them shape and meaning.

For Nemerov, particularly in his four or five most recent volumes, the language, the laws, the metaphors of science . . . become deeply appealing ways of comprehending and revealing the world.

—*Miriam Marty Clark*

In the long poems of *The Western Approaches* (1975), Nemerov uses the metaphors of wave and particle to describe the world (suggesting again that the models of science are themselves metaphoric). In **"Drawing Lessons"** particles and waves are the shapes that define the world. "Today we shall explore the mystery," he writes, "Of points and lines moving over the void— / We call it paper—to imitate the world." Breaking on the shore, wave becomes particles; later, particles and waves become consonants and vowels, matter and anti-matter. "Nature," he notes, "plays / Far ranging variations on the kinds, / Doodling inventions endlessly, as the pencil does." Though not so glib as the appearance-saving argument advanced in **"This, That & the Other,"** Nemerov's way of thinking about waves and particles here has something in common with That's logic. In both, a single nature or Nature is manifested in a variety of forms. In **"Drawing Lessons,"** however, the forms—themselves metaphors—generate other, fuller metaphors. Out of such generation, the world arises.

In **"The Measure of Poetry"** the wave (chiefly, this time, the sea wave) is the form in which the image and the law are reconciled. "The idea one gets from these waves," Nemerov writes, envisioning a shoreline, "whether the sea is / rough or calm, is the idea of a great consistency coupled with / A great freakishness, absolute law consisting with absolute rage." Like the wave, the measures of poetry begin "far from the particular / conformation of the poem, far out in the sea of tradition and the mind / even in the physiological deeps," and like the wave they are met by the hard particularity of the shoreline: "the objects which are to appear in the poem" or (in a different analogy which makes vowels the tidal impulse) the consonants which "are rock and reed and sand, and the steep or / shallow slope." Most like the wave, however, this measure is governed by laws, "simple and large, so that in the

/ scope of their generality room may remain for moments of / freedom, moments of chaos."

Implicit in this metaphoric working out of the image and the law is an equally metaphoric working out of wave-particle duality, the concept in quantum mechanics which holds, as Hawking puts it, "that there is no distinction between waves and particles; particles may sometimes behave like waves, and waves like particles." Treated as metaphors, wave and particle need not be mutually exclusive but can be enlarged and elaborated into ways of understanding the forms and forces of the world, of language. As ways of being and, more important, as ways of seeing, particle and wave are central to **"The Measure of Poetry"** and **"Drawing Lessons."** As paradox they are evident at every point in Nemerov's long career.

In the end, Nemerov seems to argue, metaphor is more powerful than law in any of its varieties—scientific, poetic, moral—to tell the truth about nature, the imagination, the universe. Science, understood as metaphor, becomes a potent way of imagining and ordering the world. At the same time, however, even in Nemerov's late volumes, set against this powerful romanticization of science is a keen distrust. In his essay "To Speak or Else to Sing," Paul Ramsey ventures an explanation of Nemerov's rejection of scientific positivism. "The fear of the damages scientific physicalism does to the poetic enterprise is real," he argues, "the fear of existential absurdity, unintelligibility, is real; the regret for the loss of the ontology of plainsong is very real."

It may be so; certainly the fear is there, with a measure of regret, in the early volumes. Yet elsewhere and later, Nemerov's inquiries, doubts, and even outright rejections of science seem based on a premise like Whitehead's in *Science and the Modern World,* a book he cites often. "If science is not to degenerate into a medley of *ad hoc* hypotheses," Whitehead writes, "it must become philosophical and must enter upon a thorough criticism of its own foundation." At the heart of Nemerov's interest in science—its aims, its data, its metaphors—is just such a philosophical examination of its presuppositions; beneath the irony and the inquiry of the science poems, there is just such a critique of its foundation, whereby—its metaphoric nature revealed, its paradoxes and mysteries acknowledged—science does not "degenerate" but becomes richly generative.

FURTHER READING

Bibliographies

Potts, Donna L. "Howard Nemerov: An Annotated Bibliography of Secondary Sources." *Bulletin of Bibliography* 50, No. 4 (December 1993): 263-67.
    Comprehensive bibliography about Nemerov's works.

Wyllie, Diane E. *Elizabeth Bishop and Howard Nemerov: A Reference Guide.* Boston: Hall, 1983, 196 p.

Contains an annotated list of works by and about Nemerov.

Biography

Labrie, Ross. *Howard Nemerov.* Boston: Twayne Publishers, 1980, 159 p.

Biographical and critical study of Nemerov that includes chapters on his poetry, novels, and criticism.

Criticism

Boyers, Robert. "Howard Nemerov's True Voice of Feeling." In *Excursions: Selected Literary Essays,* pp. 217-41. Port Washington, N.Y.: Kennikat Press, 1977.

States that "contrary to what so many have said of Nemerov, his characteristic idiom is not the language of unruffled calm or serenity. Always he has written with a sharp sense of troubled waters threatening beneath placid surfaces."

Burke, Kenneth. "Comments on Eighteen Poems by Howard Nemerov." *The Sewanee Review* LX, No. 1 (Winter 1952): 117-31.

Stylistic and thematic analysis of eighteen poems by Nemerov, including "Around the City Where I Live," "In the Last Hour of the Dream," and "When Black Water Breaks the Ice." Burke's comments were meant to be published with the poems.

Carruth, Hayden. "In Their Former Modes." *New York Times Book Review* (April 28, 1968): 7.

Negative review of *The Blue Swallows* in which Carruth comments on Nemerov's "tired" poetic irony and his predictable rhymes and metaphors.

Clark, Miriam Marty. "The Evolution of Consciousness in Howard Nemerov's 'The Painter Dreaming in the Scholar's House.'" *University of Dayton Review* 21, No. 1 (Spring 1991): 161-67.

Discusses Nemerov's struggles with post-modernist concerns and the influence of English philosopher and philologist Owen Barfield on the poet's works.

Costello, Bonnie. "Sympathy and Wit." *Parnassus: Poetry in Review* 9, No. 2 (Fall/Winter 1981): 169-83.

Compartive review of Nemerov's *Sentences* and William Meredith's *The Cheer.* Costello concludes that Meredith's work is sympathetic, emotional, and optimistic and Nemerov's is witty, "hard-edged and piercing."

Goldstein, Laurence. "The Wings of War." *Michigan Quarterly Review* 29, No. 3 (Summer 1990): 472.

Mixed review of *War Stories* in which Goldstein discusses Nemerov's irreverent tone and demythology of war.

Johnson, Tom. "Ideas and Order." *The Sewanee Review* LXXXVI, No. 3 (Summer 1978): 445-53.

Refutes two common misconceptions about Nemerov: that he was primarily an academic poet and that he focused mainly on middle-class concerns.

Kiehl, James M. "The Poems of Howard Nemerov: Where Loveliness Adorns Intelligible Things." *Salmagundi,* Nos. 22-23 (Spring/Summer 1973): 234-57.

Provides a thematic and stylistic overview of Nemerov's works, focusing on how his poems challenge the reader's perception of reality.

Kinzie, Mary. "The Judge Is Rue." *Poetry* CXXXVIII, No. 6 (September 1981): 344-50.

Mixed review of *Sentences* in which Kinzie concludes "*Sentences* is a disappointing and self-indulgent volume on the whole, but has some landmark poems."

————. "The Signatures of Things: On Howard Nemerov." *Parnassus: Poetry in Review* 6, No. 1 (Fall/Winter 1977): 1-57.

Overview of Nemerov's poetry and nonfiction. Kinzie comments on Nemerov's place in and influence on contemporary poetry.

Pritchard, William H. Review of *Gnomes and Occasions,* by Howard Nemerov. *The Hudson Review* XXVI, No. 3 (Autumn 1973): 579-97.

Positive assessment of *Gnomes and Occasions.*

Prunty, Wyatt. "Howard Nemerov: Mimicry and Other Tropes." In *"Fallen from the Symboled World": Precedents for the New Formalism,* pp. 143-92. New York: Oxford University Press, 1990.

Examination of Nemerov's use of figurative language in which Prunty argues that Nemerov rebelled against modernism to pursue "a more independent course."

Randall, Julia. "Genius of the Shore: The Poetry of Howard Nemerov." In *The Sounder Few: Essays from the Hollins Critic,* edited by R. H. W. Dillard, George Garrett, and John Rees Moore, pp. 345-57. Athens: University of Georgia Press, 1971.

Examines metaphysical aspects of Nemerov's poetry.

Senn, Werner. "Speaking the Silence: Contemporary Poems on Paintings." *Word & Image* 5, No. 2 (April-June 1989): 181-97.

Discusses Nemerov's poems on paintings, including "Nature Morte," "The World as Brueghel Imagined It," and "Vermeer."

Shaw, Robert B. "Making Some Mind of What Was Only Sense." *The Nation* 226, No. 7 (February 25, 1978): 213-15.

Mixed review of *Collected Poems* in which Shaw calls the volume repetitive and predictable but praises Nemerov's humor and intelligence.

Spiegelman, Willard. "Alphabeting the Void: Poetic Diction and Poetic Classicism." *Salmagundi* 42 (1978): 132-45.

Compartive review of the verse of Nemerov, A. R. Ammons, and Allen Tate.

Young, Gloria L. "Finding Again the Word." *Concerning Poetry* 20 (1987): 75-85.

States that Nemerov's poems often deal with "the philosophical problem of how—or if?—poetry unites mind and world (self and Other)."

————. "'The Fountainhead of All Forms': Poetry and the Unconscious in Emerson and Howard Nemerov." In *Artful Thunder: Versions of the Romantic Tradition in American Literature in Honor of Howard P. Vincent,* edited by Robert J. DeMott and Sanford E. Marovitz, pp. 241-67. Kent, Ohio: Kent State University Press, 1975.

> Discusses how American writer Ralph Waldo Emerson's ideas of the unconscious anticipate the psychological, linguistic, and aesthetic theories of Nemerov and psychologist Carl Jung.

Interview

Bowers, Neal, and Charles L. P. Silet. "An Interview with Howard Nemerov." *The Massachusetts Review* XXII, No. 1 (Spring 1981): 43-57.

> Interview in which Nemerov discusses such subjects as his writing technique, the relationship between his fiction and poetry, the pessimistic tone of his verse, and the influence of critics on his work.

Additional coverage of Nemerov's life and career is contained in the following sources published by The Gale Group: *Contemporary Authors,* Vols. 1-4 (rev. ed.), 134; *Contemporary Authors Bibliographical Series,* Vol. 2; *Contemporary Authors New Revision Series,* Vols. 1, 27, 53; *Contemporary Literary Criticism,* Vols. 2, 6, 9, 36; *Dictionary of Literary Biography,* Vols. 5, 6; *Dictionary of Literary Biography Yearbook, 1983; DISCovering Authors: Poets Module;* and *Major 20th-Century Writers.*

Algernon Charles Swinburne
1837-1909

(Also wrote under the pseudonym Mrs. Horace Manners)
English poet, dramatist, critic, essayist, and novelist.

INTRODUCTION

Swinburne is renowned as one of the most accomplished lyric poets of the Victorian era and as a preeminent symbol of rebellion against the conservative values of his time. The explicit and often pathological sexual themes of his most important collection of poetry, *Poems and Ballads,* delighted some, shocked many, and became the dominant feature of Swinburne's image as both an artist and an individual. Nevertheless, critics have found that to focus exclusively on the sensational aspects of Swinburne's work is to miss the assertion, implicit in his poetry and explicit in his critical writings, that his primary preoccupation was the nature and creation of poetic beauty.

Biographical Information

Born into a wealthy family, Swinburne was educated at Eton and at Balliol College, Oxford, but did not complete a degree. While at Oxford, he met the brothers William Michael and Dante Gabriel Rossetti, as well as other members of the Pre-Raphaelite circle, a group of artists and writers whose work emphasized medieval subjects, elaborate religious symbolism, and a sensual pictorialism, and who cultivated an aura of mystery and melancholy in their lives as well as in their works. He achieved his first literary success in 1865 with *Atalanta in Calydon,* which was written in the form of classical Greek tragedy. The following year the appearance of *Poems and Ballads* brought Swinburne instant notoriety. He became identified with the "indecent" themes and the precept of art for art's sake that characterized many of the poems of the volume. He subsequently wrote poetry of many different kinds, including the militantly republican *Song of Italy* and *Songs before Sunrise* in support of the *Risorgimento,* the movement for Italian political unity, as well as nature poetry. Although individual volumes of Swinburne's poetry were occasionally well received, in general his popularity and critical reception declined following the initial sensation of *Poems and Ballads.*

Throughout the 1860s and 1870s Swinburne drank excessively and was prone to accidents that often left him bruised, bloody, or unconscious. Until his forties he suffered intermittent physical collapses. In 1879, Swinburne's friend and literary agent, Theodore Watts-Dunton, intervened during a time when Swinburne was dangerously ill. Watts-Dunton isolated Swinburne at a suburban home in Putney and gradually weaned him from alcohol—and from

many former companions and habits as well. Swinburne lived another thirty years with Watts-Dunton, whose role remains controversial. He denied Swinburne's friends access to him, controlled the poet's money, and restricted his activities. However, commentators agree that Swinburne's erratic conduct could have resulted in his death, and Watts-Dunton is generally credited with saving his life and encouraging him to continue writing into his old age. Swinburne died in 1909 at the age of seventy-two.

Major Works

The most important and conspicuous quality of Swinburne's work is an intense lyricism. Even early critics, who often took exception to his subject matter, commended his intricately extended and evocative imagery, metrical virtuosity, rich use of assonance and alliteration, and bold, complex rhythms. At the same time, the strong rhythms of his poems and his characteristic use of alliteration were sometimes carried to extremes and rendered his work highly susceptible to parody. Critics note that his usually effective imagery is at times vague and imprecise, and his rhymes are sometimes facile and uninspired. After establishing residence in Putney, Swinburne largely abandoned the themes of pathological sexuality that had characterized much of his earlier poetry. Nature and landscape poetry began to predominate, as well as poems about children. Many commentators maintain that the poetry written during the years at Putney is inferior to Swinburne's earlier work, but others have identified individual poems of exceptional merit among his later works, citing in particular "By the North Sea," "Evening on the Broads," "A Nympholept," "The Lake of Gaube," and "Neap-Tide."

Critical Reception

During Swinburne's lifetime, critics considered *Poems and Ballads* his finest as well as his most characteristic poetic achievement; subsequent poetry and work in other genres was often disregarded. Since the mid-twentieth century, however, commentators have been offering new assessments of Swinburne's entire career. Forgoing earlier dismissals of his voluminous later writings and reexamining individual poems strictly on their own merit, critics have identified works of great power and beauty from all periods of his career.

PRINCIPAL WORKS

Poetry

Poems and Ballads 1866
A Song of Italy 1867
Songs before Sunrise 1871
Songs of Two Nations 1875
Poems and Ballads: Second Series 1878
Tristram of Lyonesse, and Other Poems 1882
Poems and Ballads: Third Series 1889
The Tale of Balen 1896
A Channel Passage, and Other Poems 1904

Other Major Works

The Queen-Mother and Rosamond (dramas) 1860
Atalanta in Calydon (drama) 1865
Chasteland (drama) 1865
Notes on Poems and Reviews (criticism) 1866
William Blake (criticism) 1868
Under the Microscope (criticism) 1872
Bothwell (drama) 1874
Essays and Studies (criticism) 1875
George Chapman (criticism) 1875
Erechtheus (drama) 1876
A Study of Shakespeare (criticism) 1880
Mary Stuart (drama) 1881
A Study of Victor Hugo (criticism) 1886
Locrine (drama) 1887
A Study of Ben Jonson (criticism) 1889
Studies in Prose and Poetry (criticism) 1894
Rosamund, Queen of the Lombards (drama) 1899
Love's Cross-Currents (novel) 1901
Shakespeare (criticism) 1909
Contemporaries of Shakespeare (criticism) 1919

The Complete Works of Algernon Charles Swinburne. 20 vols. (poetry, dramas, novel, essays, criticism, and letters) 1925-27
Lesbia Brandon (unfinished novel) 1952
The Swinburne Letters. 6 vols. (letters) 1959-62

CRITICISM

Antony H. Harrison (essay date 1978)

SOURCE: "The Aesthetics of Androgyny in Swinburne's Early Poetry," in *Tennessee Studies in Literature,* Vol. 23, 1978, pp. 87-99.

[*In the following essay, Harrison explores Swinburne's treatment of androgynous aspects of human sexuality.*]

Death and the achievement of organic continuity with the universe represent the end and culmination of sexual passion for the major figures in most of Swinburne's early poems. Yet it is the enduring *condition* of passion that provides the poet himself with his richest materials,

> For love awake or love asleep
> > Ends in a laugh, a dream, a kiss,
> > A song like this.

During his most productive years Swinburne undertook to characterize all conditions of passion and its concomitant suffering in men and women of all conceivable states of sexuality—from the noble masculinity of Tristram and Mary Stuart's courtier Chastelard, to Sappho's lesbian strivings for domination and penetration, to the perverse and "feminine" gentleness of the persona in **"The Leper."** Love is Swinburne's constant subject from his undergraduate lyrics of 1857 to his epic *tour de force,* **Tristram of Lyonesse,** published twenty-five years later. The diversity of his poems of passion and the complexity of the philosophical precepts which support and dominate them must be recognized in any evaluation of Swinburne's achievement. However, critics have not treated Swinburne's metaphysic of love with the seriousness it demands, and they have only begun to investigate the relationship between the philosophical and aesthetic principles central to his most important poems. Crucial to that relationship is Swinburne's recurrent exploration of androgynous aspects of human sexuality.

Frequently Swinburne's males possess what are normally considered feminine traits, and his women have male characteristics. But sexual ambiguities in his works, though apparent most often in sadistic females with masochistic male counterparts, extend beyond the mere reversal of roles. Mario Praz observes Swinburne's preoccupation with equivocal sexuality in noting the kinship between Moreau's painting *Necessity of Riches* and Swinburne's unfinished novel, *Lesbia Brandon:*

> Moreau's figures are ambiguous; it is hardly possible
> to distinguish at the first glance which of two lovers

is the man, which the woman; all his characters are linked by subtle bonds of relationship, as in Swinburne's *Lesbia Brandon*; lovers look as though they were related, brothers as though they were lovers, men have the faces of virgins, virgins the faces of youths; the symbols of Good and Evil are entwined and equivocally confused. There is no contrast between ages, sexes, or types: the underlying meaning of this painting is incest, its most exalted figure the Androgyne, its final word is sterility.

Similarly, Richard Mathews [in *Victorian Poetry,* 1971] notes Swinburne's fascination with the hermaphroditic iconography of his friend Simion Solomon's paintings, which were "greatly occupied with this ideal of male-female conjunction. . . . Swinburne was intrigued by this aspect of Solomon's art: 'In almost all of these [paintings] there is the same profound suggestion of . . . the identity of contraries.' The union of male and female is paralleled by the possibility of the marriage of all opposites—fire and water, good and evil, Heaven and Hell, high and low."

One should add to this list the marriage of body and spirit. Indeed, the key to understanding Swinburne's apparent equivocation between the mystical spiritualism of what he considered his most important philosophical lyric, **"Hertha,"** and his continual emphasis on the need for purely physical gratifications of passion, resides in his acceptance of a crucial Blakean doctrine. In his essay on Blake Swinburne explains,

> Those who argue against the reality of the meaner forms of "spiritualism" in disembodied life, on the ground apparently that whatever is not of the patent tangible flesh must be of high imperishable importance, are merely acting on the old ascetic assumption that the body is of its nature base and the soul of its nature noble, and that between the two there is a great gulf fixed, neither to be bridged over nor filled up. Blake, as a mystic of the higher and subtler kind, would have denied this superior separate vitality of the spirit; but far from inferring thence that the soul must expire with the body, would have maintained that the essence of the body must survive with the essence of the soul.

Swinburne more clearly defines the nature of man's sublime "essence" in **"Hertha,"** which characterizes the unitary, informing principle of all creation: "before God was, I am," Hertha asserts (II, 72). In this poem Swinburne attempts a reconciliation of all dualities, including sexual duality, which is the fundamental concern underlying his poems about passion: "Out of me man and woman," Hertha declares (II, 72).

These poems suggest that Swinburne imagined a primordial sexlessness in man which precluded the strife of passions men now suffer. This ideal of the "perfect spiritual hermaphrodite" can be seen, like Yeats's Byzantine spirits, as a mystical vision of the prelapsarian harmony of soul which characterized man before incarnation, or as the asexual organicism to which he returns after death. The androgynous ideal for Swinburne reflects the pure, eternal, "Herthian" potential of the soul beyond its temporary

embodiment in the mired complexities of blood. As Swinburne remarks of Blake's conception of the eternal androgyne, that being is "male and female, who from of old was neither female nor male, but perfect man without division of flesh, until the setting of sex against sex by the malignity of animal creation." Ironically, the sexual yearning for total physical integration with the beloved object, characteristic of Swinburne's personae, can be seen as an attempt both to escape the torture of insatiable passion and to regain this sexless ideal.

Swinburne was hardly alone in his hermaphroditic quest. As A. J. L. Busst has demonstrated [in *Romantic Mythologies,* edited by Ian Fletcher, 1967], the figure of the androgyne permeates nineteenth-century literature. In addition, Busst notes that C. G. Jung has powerfully reinforced a major intuition of those writers of the period now considered decadent: "that the androgyne is an archetype of the collective unconscious, that the human psyche is itself androgynous." When dealing with androgynous figures, Swinburne was aware that he was working in a tradition, one that retained unlimited potential for artistic development. Indeed, he seems to have perceived both the optimistic and pessimistic extremes intrinsic to the concept of androgyny that Busst has outlined. On the one hand, androgynous propensities in such figures as the speaker of **"The Triumph of Time,"** Chastelard, Sappho in **"Anactoria,"** and Meleager in *Atalanta in Calydon* reflect an ultimately positive yearning for completion and the sort of continuity with the world which necessitates dissolution of consciousness and quintessential union with the sexless and mystical source of all generation. Although the character of their suffering is largely the subject of the poems they appear in, these figures demonstrate a strength in the resignation to their destiny which borders on optimism and certainly mitigates the pathos we feel for them. This is especially true of Chastelard, for instance, who feels "a kindling beyond death / Of some new joys," and of Sappho at the end of her monologue when she at last perceives how her kinship with nature will immortalize her. On the other hand, androgyny, when conceived of in *purely physical* terms, results in the unbearable intensification of insatiable sexual passions that "shall not be assuaged till death be dead." This pessimistic view of androgyny is developed in **"Hermaphroditus,"** although it also complicates the depiction of figures like Phaedra, Sappho, and Mary Stuart, the heroine of Swinburne's remarkable trilogy of closet dramas. All three are sadistic women whose masculine attributes thrust them into a limbo of vain desires. Most often the optimistic and pessimistic possibilities of androgyny merge for Swinburne when a figure—like Rosamond, Sappho, or Tannhäuser in **"Laus Veneris"**—does not immediately perceive death as the destined and only complete gratification of his or her passions, as Meleager and Chastelard, for instance, unequivocably do.

The relationship of Swinburne's cast of usually sadomasochistic figures to the symbol of the androgyne is often further complicated by the issue of morality. Questions of good and evil dominate poems like **"Laus Veneris," "Dolores,"** and *Atalanta in Calydon,* while they are important motifs in *Rosamond, Chastelard, Lesbia Brandon, Love's*

Cross-Currents, and ***Tristram of Lyonesse.*** The questions of morality that result from insatiable desires and perverse indulgences arise primarily because passion is dramatized by Swinburne in a rigid pagan or Christian, rather than visionary Blakean, context. Both the constricting hostility of religious or social forces and the physical limitations of sexual indulgence are responsible for the intense frustration that Swinburne's characters suffer. At the same time, the relationship of sadism and masochism to a concept of androgyny is a logical one. As Busst observes, in nineteenth-century literature the figure of the hermaphrodite commonly symbolized sadism and masochism. Although there is nothing androgynous about a *male* sadist or a *female* masochist,

> a sadistic woman, in as far as she dominates her male victim, may be considered virile, since she exhibits strength, a male characteristic; and her ability to indulge in her vice depends to a large extent on the male's abdication of his own virility, his masochistic willingness to be ruled—even tormented—by the female[,] showing a weakness of character generally associated with effeminacy. His refusal to assert himself often indicates awareness of the vanity of all action, which must accompany loss of convictions in a world without values, where good is often indistinguishable from evil. It is therefore not surprising that male masochism and its necessary counterpart, female sadism, should be associated so frequently with the attitude of despair and disillusionment reflected in the pessimistic symbol of the androgyne.

While, for instance, Tannhäuser accepts external standards of good and evil and his own consequent damnation, the speaker in **"Dolores"** rejects the world's standards. Both, however, are deeply affected by accepted morality, whether its effect be manifested in martyred resignation or satanic challenge. Both also quiver under the lash of a burning passion, whose object is represented as a sadistic *femme fatale.* In this light Swinburne's frequent coupling of masochistic males with sadistic women can be seen not at all as perverse indulgence for its own sake, but as a reflection of his intuition that the most deep-seated human sexual yearnings are for a kind of androgynous existence that escapes physical desire, as well as the categories of good and evil, and that returns human energy and essence to its original sexless condition. The artistic result of this intuition is, naturally, either despair or hostility to the world's presiding forces on the part of Swinburne's personae because this ideal cannot be attained by them in life.

Among Swinburne's works, *Atalanta in Calydon* and **"Hermaphroditus"** most coherently exemplify his respectively positive and negative expressions of the androgynous ideal. *Atalanta,* which made Swinburne an overnight celebrity, has been widely discussed in formal terms as a Greek tragedy; it has been examined as a psychological document; it has been analyzed as a work of consummate poetic skill. I shall explore it, however, as an embodiment of Swinburne's positive vision of androgyny. I shall then discuss the neglected but magnificent brief sonnet sequence **"Hermaphroditus,"** contained in his 1866 volume of ***Poems***

and Ballads, which very nearly overturned his newly acquired reputation because of its sexual extravagances. This poem is Swinburne's most forceful and poignant representation of the androgyne as a pessimistic symbol.

The titular heroine of *Atalanta in Calydon* is an embodiment of the androgynous ideal, and, significantly, she is nearly bereft of human passions. Atalanta changes "the words of women and the works / For spears and strange men's faces." Although the play's chorus expresses hostility toward her, Meleager perceives Atalanta immediately *as* an ideal and strives to identify with her rather than to copulate with her. Indeed, in *Atalanta* Swinburne's representation of the nature and ends of human passion takes its least physical, most metaphysical form. Early in the poem the chorus perceives love as man's curse and articulates the mythology of Aphrodite's birth and man's concomitant fall into suffering. Beyond this, throughout the play the chorus expands upon Althaea's pessimistic view of the effects of passion:

> But from the light and fiery dreams of love
> Spring heavy sorrows and a sleepless life,
> Visions not dreams, whose lids no charm shall close
> Nor song assuage them waking; and swift death
> Crushes with sterile feet the unripening ear,
> Treads out the timeless vintage.
>
> (IV, 266-67)

Such pessimism culminates in the fourth chorus, which constitutes a hymn of vitriolic defiance to the source of all suffering—including that caused by vain passion—"the supreme evil, God." Yet neither the chorus nor Althaea is able to perceive the spiritual, worshipful quality of Meleager's love for Atalanta:

> Seeing many a wonder and fearful things to men
> I saw not one thing like this one seen here,
> Most fair and fearful, feminine, a god,
> Faultless; whom I that love not, being unlike,
> Fear, and give honour, and choose from all the gods.
>
> (IV, 269)

Meleager is entirely conscious that Atalanta is more divine than human, more ideal than real. Moreover, as Althaea and her brothers are at frequent pains to remind Meleager, Atalanta is by no means conventionally feminine. It makes sense, then, that the yearning for Atalanta that he feels results primarily from a respect for her martial accomplishments and his own aspiration toward the pure and self-contained spirit that he associates with her and with nature:

> My delight, my desire,
>   Is more chaste than the rain,
> More pure than the dewfall, more holy than stars are
>   that live without stain.
>
> (IV, 325)

Atalanta, devotee of Artemis, is continually associated with nature imagery and recognizes her own "forest holiness":

me the snows
That face the first o' the morning, and cold hills
Full of the land-wind and sea-travelling storms
And many a wandering wing of noisy nights
That know the thunder and hear the thickening
    wolves—
Me the utmost pine and footless frost of woods
That talk with many winds and gods, the hours
Re-risen, and white divisions of the dawn,
Springs thousand-tongued with the intermitting reed
And streams that murmur of the mother snow—
Me these allure, and know me.

(IV, 282)

By reputation and self-description, Atalanta, as a huntress and symbol of chastity, becomes almost an extension of the androgynous spirit of nature. Ironically, the figures in *Atalanta* who consider themselves most normal prove to be the least natural. Indeed, in killing the boar, only Atalanta and Meleager show themselves to possess the kinship with natural forces requisite to exert control over them.

Significantly, Meleager is not the first to wound the boar. The best he can do is follow and emulate his ideal. Although he can only approach identification with that ideal in this life, he *can* conceive of a posthumous coalescence with the natural world which Atalanta has come to symbolize. Meleager sees his fate after death as one of reunification, of achieved continuity with the world, analogous to the absorption of vital liquids by organic nature. In lieu of life, the gods will grant him:

the grace that remains,
    The fair beauty that cleaves
To the life of the rains in the grasses, the life of the
    dews on the leaves.

(IV, 328)

Thus, although seen by all except Meleager as an unnatural woman, "Virgin, not like the natural flower of things / That grows and bears and brings forth fruit and dies," Atalanta appears to Meleager as perfection, "a god," and "faultless." Despite the fact that his love for her is fatal and fulfills the prophecies of both Althaea and the chorus, his death is ultimately the result of his devotion to an ideal of androgyny. In Meleager's last speech, concerned that the manner of his death will effeminize his reputation, he asks Atalanta to "stretch thyself upon me and touch hands / With hands and lips with lips" (IV, 333). Significantly, he requests only symbolic intercourse. Such an identification with his ideal is all that he aspired to in the tragedy, and, insofar as he achieves this sort of union with her, his respectful passion and his fate become not so much pathetic as noble. His anticipated destiny of a continuity like Sappho's in **"Anactoria"** with the sexless organic world is the best that can be hoped for in this universe of suffering and strife.

Atalanta may be the only self-sufficient androgyne in this work, but, as Mathews notes, most of the major figures possess both masculine and feminine traits: "Atalanta is armed like a man; Meleager weak-voiced like a woman. Althaea possesses the spirit of a man; Oeneus knows the submission of a woman." Meleager's "effeminate" love for a masculine woman and Althaea's masculine strong will are responsible for all suffering in the play, along with Oeneus' negligence in worshiping Artemis, the androgynous goddess. That Meleager dies for worshiping Artemis' mortal counterpart is the final irony of the tragedy. Here, as in Swinburne's sadomasochistic lyrics, the corruption of clear divisions between the sexes and the pursuit in carnal reality of an androgynous ideal is the cause of suffering, whether through attempts to merge with the beloved, as in "Phaedra" and *Chastelard,* or to adopt traits properly belonging to the opposite sex. This is not to say that Swinburne rejected the androgynous ideal. On the contrary, Swinburne perceived the inevitably futile compulsion to attain that ideal as the most forceful aspect of human sexuality, at once the source of all passion and the cause of passion's pain. The ideal itself must, however, remain always purely ethereal, intellectual. The androgynous condition represents sexual completion and integrity; it therefore signifies an end to all striving motivated by passion and to all suffering caused by it. The perfected androgyne must be emotionally sterile, dead for the purposes of art. It provides a literary subject only as a counter for characters who are sexually "incomplete" and who exist in a state of perpetual passionate yearning. Atalanta, who is passionless and in every respect sterile, provides such a counter in Swinburne's play. The characters who surround her, however, represent the most sublime material for tragic art, because they strive and suffer tumultuously as a result of their sexual divisions.

Swinburne perceived, as did Gautier, that "it is precisely because [the hermaphrodite] does not truly exist in reality that [it] . . . is so beautiful. 'Rêve de poète et d'artiste,' it is the product of pure art, the 'effort suprême de l'art.'" Swinburne believed that the *idea* of the hermaphrodite "incarnate, literal, or symbolic, is merely beautiful," and that man's yearning toward the ideal, or a vision of the ideal achieved, constitutes the supreme subject for verse because it combines the ultimate state of passion with the ultimate pathos of suffering. However, the actual physical attainment of the ideal could, paradoxically, produce a monstrous exacerbation of the sufferings induced by human passion. The artistic paradigm for the whole mythology of androgyny thus becomes Swinburne's poem **"Hermaphroditus."** In *Notes on Poems and Reviews* he acknowledges both the perfection of the hermaphroditic ideal *and* the necessary sterility of any physical achievement of that ideal: "The sad and subtle moral of this myth, which I have desired to indicate in verse, is that perfection once attained on all sides is a thing thenceforward barren of use or fruit; whereas the divided beauty of separate woman and man—a thing inferior and imperfect—can serve all turns of life." Yet, *insofar as* an androgyne can be made to represent the absolute extreme of vain sexual desires, as it does in **"Hermaphroditus,"** it can serve all turns of art; it is "ideal beauty."

Apparently to Swinburne the most forceful aspect of a *purely physical* embodiment of the hermaphroditic ideal was its unnaturalness. Hermaphroditus, as depicted by the famous statue in the Louvre, possesses the physical characteristics of both sexes but is not sexually neutralized. On the contrary, his sexual desires and suffering are infinitely intensified by his inability in any way to satisfy the passions of either sex. In the myth, Hermaphroditus' refusal to gratify the nymph of Salmacis represents an unnatural act, and he is requited with an equally unnatural fate, one that equivocally incorporates both the nymph's passion and Hermaphroditus' fearful rejection of it. The poet asks, "Is it love or sleep or shadow or light / That lies between thine eyelids and thine eyes?" And he answers, "Yea, love, I see; it is not love but fear. / Nay, sweet, it is not fear but love" (I, 80). In fact, it is both fear and love, as well as a passion so intense that Hermaphroditus' fire of yearning can be quenched only with an inconceivable extinction:

> Where between sleep and life some brief space is,
>   With love like gold bound round about the head,
>   Sex to sweet sex with lips and limbs is wed,
> Turning the fruitful feud of hers and his
> To the waste wedlock of a sterile kiss;
>   Yet from them something like as fire is shed
>   That shall not be assuaged till death be dead.
>
> (I, 79)

Hermaphroditus is suspended physically "between sleep and life," the literal physical embodiment of the immobility dictated by the mythical Hermaphroditus' sexual duality. He exists only to be contemplated. By extension, conceived of as a real being, the hermaphrodite is not merely sexually impotent, but impotent for action in the world. A still birth, he is suspended in a perpetual state of yearning.

In Swinburne's poem the statue becomes the artistic vehicle for expressing the ultimate extreme of passions felt universally and intensely, by generating in the reader an identification with the hermaphroditic condition of insatiable passion. That identification, however, is mitigated by the self-conscious and highly crafted form of the poem, and it yields after the first sonnet to a mood of intense pathos that is primarily purgative.

In the first sonnet of **"Hermaphroditus,"** Swinburne is able to induce in the reader a state of yearning approaching that which the statue projects, but in order to do so, he must, in the last lines of the sonnet, dissolve the possibility for precise meaning to be derived from the language he uses. Ironically, the poet addresses this tragic embodiment of androgyny as a lover would:

> Ah sweet, albeit no love be sweet enough,
>   Choose of two loves and cleave unto the best;
>   Two loves at either blossom of thy breast
> Strive until one be under and one above.
> Their breath is fire upon the amorous air,
>   Fire in thine eyes and where thy lips suspire:
> And whosoever hath seen thee, being so fair,
>   Two things turn all his life and blood to fire;
> A strong desire begot on great despair,
> A great despair cast out by strong desire.
>
> (I, 79)

The last two verses force the viewer (and the reader) to identify with the statue. The rhetorical structure and effect of these lines is that of a paradox. Because of the simple syntactical inversion of the subject and object of the first line in the second, we are left in a momentary state of intellectual suspension parallel to Hermaphroditus' suspension in a purgatory of sexual desires which "shall not be assuaged till death be dead." Here Swinburne manages to dissolve precise meaning and to approach the perfect expression of an ineffably intense state of "desire" which results from the combination of both male and female sexual passions.

"Hermaphroditus" as a poetic creation imitates an art object which in turn imitates an idea—much as does Keats's "Ode on a Grecian Urn," but the significant difference between the two lyrics is that Swinburne's offers no clear resolution to the "problem" of the poem:

>   Or wherefore should thy body's blossom blow
> So sweetly, or thine eyelids leave so clear
> Thy gracious eyes that never made a tear—
>   . . . . .
> Yea, sweet, I know; I saw in what swift wise
>   Beneath the woman's and the water's kiss
>   Thy moist limbs melted into Salmacis,
> And the large light turned tender in thine eyes,
> And all thy boy's breath softened into sighs;
>   But Love being blind, how should he know of
>   this?
>
> (I, 80-81)

In the poem's last lines, by referring to the myth out of which the pessimistic concept of the androgyne originated and by projecting himself as a kind of aesthetic Tiresias who witnessed the origin of that concept, the lyric voice reaffirms the purely artistic force of the hermaphroditic ideal, its value in the realm of myth and literature. This realm is admittedly removed from life—a thing of barren hours—but nonetheless serves as a gloss on life. In life the passion for complete physical integration with the beloved, as we see it represented in **"Anactoria,"** "Phaedra," *Chastelard,* and ***Tristram of Lyonesse,*** and as it appears in most of Swinburne's poems of passion, can be consummated only in death and a return to original continuity with the world. But, according to Swinburne, in art it must never be consummated. For the passions which reflect our quintessential yearning for sexual integration provide the richest material for art, both because they are perennial and recognizably potent forces in all of us, and because art remains the only vehicle for adequately expressing and vicariously mitigating those passions by presenting them as objects of contemplation.

For Swinburne passions in art, no matter how earthy, must be ideal passions, "moral passions." He speaks of Shelley's poetry, "where description melts into passion and contemplation takes fire from delight." Ultimately, for Swinburne sensual experience is always secondary and inferior to intellectual experience. In both its pessimistic and optimistic formulations, the ideal of the androgyne for him, as well as for Gautier, Péladan, and the decadents, represents a "withdrawal from practical life." Swinburne's confidence in the value of such an ideal, the supreme value of art, and the necessity for such a withdrawal is reflected in both his art and his life.

David G. Riede (essay date 1978)

SOURCE: "The Putney Period: Solipsism without Fear," in *Swinburne: A Study of Romantic Mythmaking,* University Press of Virginia, 1978, pp. 187-214.

[*In the following essay, Riede urges a reassessment of Swinburne's later verse.*]

The enormous bulk of the poetry written in the last thirty years of Swinburne's life has been greeted with almost unmitigated disdain by the few readers who have gone to the trouble of looking at it. Swinburne, it is routinely said, devoted more than half of his creative life to the production of fatuous effusions of baby worship, political poems savoring of the rankest kind of imperialism, and nature poetry of the travel-book variety. The charges have been made so persistently that they must be met head-on, and, indeed, there is a certain amount of truth in them. The nature poetry, which makes up the bulk of the late verse and is of a far higher order than has been acknowledged, will be discussed separately and at some length, but the poems of baby worship and imperialism may be dismissed without extended comment—and without disdain. They are far fewer than Swinburne's detractors would have us believe, and those in praise of babies are inoffensive at worst and even, for the most part, lovely. The baby poems may, in a very limited way, be attributable to Swinburne's general tendency to celebrate regeneration in all things—sunrises, spring, flowering, and so on—but must be mainly attributed to a not unattractive foible, an aging and lonely man's love for children. Continuing to misread Blake, moreover, he probably felt that the precedent of *Songs of Innocence* sanctioned his adoption of the subject, and he must also have been encouraged by the example of Christina Rossetti's children's poems, which he loved. Though these poems do not attain to the level of high art, they hardly deserve the uninformed contempt they have received.

The imperialist poetry, unfortunately, is a different matter, and has fully earned its share of scorn. Nevertheless, though this rant cannot be excused, it can be briefly explained in terms of Swinburne's development and the development of his myth. His mythmaking had always extended from ancient myth to actual history, particularly English history—Mary Stuart, in the *Chastelard, Bothwell, Mary Stuart* trilogy, is a giantess à la Dolores and Faustine—and ultimately he created his own myth of British history. [In his *The Swinburne Letters,* 1959] Cecil Lang has observed that

> it was Swinburne's insularity, his very *Englishness,* that came to dominate his thinking. The most cosmopolitan of English poets was transformed into the most parochial and chauvinistic of British jingoes. The republican-turned-"English Republican" became English

first and last, and remained republican only by a semantic sophistry that would be as much at home in *1984* as in *Through the Looking Glass.* "People nowadays seem to forget . . . ," he wrote to his mother in 1886, "that the first principle of a Republican is and must be Unity (without which liberty can only mean license—or pure anarchy—or pretentious hypocrisy) and that Republican right is common consistency and honesty to the first to protest against a party of anarchists and intriguers whose policy is to break up the state."

This is, to be sure, sophistry, but it is perfectly consistent with the political philosophy of "Hertha," only brought out of the realm of abstraction into the realm of practice. All of Swinburne's mythmaking is aimed at unifying the human race under the aegis of love and art—the Apollonian song, after all, was the song of the *whole* of mankind. The organic metaphor of the tree in "Hertha" implies that there can be only one seed which will grow into the world-soul. For Swinburne, in effect, the tradition was all, and tradition, civilization, was more highly developed in England than elsewhere. As Oswald Spengler aphoristically put it [in *The Decline of the West,* translated by Charles Francis Atkinson, 1926] "Imperialism is Civilization unadulterated," and unadulterated civilization is precisely what Swinburne had always sought. The switch from republicanism to imperialism was not so radical a transformation as it appears, if only because the theory behind the former had always actually been more conducive to the latter. The jingoism of the late years, to use the metaphor of "Hertha," grew inevitably from the seeds of cultural monism apparent even in *Songs before Sunrise.* However deplorable we find poems like "The Commonweal," "The Armada," and "England: An Ode," they are consistent with Swinburne's political growth. Despite the praise that has been lavished on *Songs before Sunrise,* politics had never been Swinburne's strong point.

His strong point had, in fact, always been the poetry of the life of man confronting the life of nature, and it is to the late nature poetry that we must turn to find the unadulterated strength of the aging Swinburne. The critical contempt for this poetry, written under the auspices of Watts-Dunton at the Pines in Putney, has been so universal that one would think, with Samuel Chew [in *Swinburne,* 1929] that the critic's job should be simply to "call attention to the comparatively few pieces that have some lasting interest, attractiveness and individuality." The judgment of Chew and his contemporaries has echoed down the decades, like the Apollonian song, finding its most recent expression in Kerry McSweeney's article on "Thalassius" [in the *Humanities Association Bulletin,* 1971]: "From 1880 to his death in 1909 Swinburne wrote a great amount of nature poetry, the vast majority of the merely decorative or travel-book variety. Only infrequently do we find poems describing the naked encounter of poet and natural world. When we do find this, as in 'A Nympholept' (1894) and 'The Lake of Gaube' (1904), the results are two of Swinburne's greatest poems." Yet the problem of dealing with the huge bulk of Swinburne's poetry in these last thirty years is not, in fact, a paucity of good poems but a plethora; the problem is not to sort the grain from the chaff but to choose examples from an embarrassment of riches. And despite McSweeney's implication that little of the late poetry can be truly mythopoeic, a substantial portion of the nature lyrics is just that—the life of man confronting the life in nature. While it is true that such poems as **"A Nympholept"** and **"The Lake of Gaube"** stand out as supreme achievements in Swinburne's canon, many other exquisite poems should not be slighted, lyrics like **"To a Seamew," "Neap-tide," "Off Shore," "Evening on the Broads," "Adieux à Marie Stuart," "A Midsummer Holiday," "A Ballad of Sark," "Dedication: To William Morris,"** many poems of the lovely *Century of Roundels,* **"Astrophel," "On the South Coast," "A Swimmer's Dream," "Loch Torridon," "The Palace of Pan," "A Channel Passage," "The Promise of the Hawthorn," "Hawthorn Tide," "The Passing of the Hawthorn,"** and a long list of others. All of these poems, beautiful by any standards, exhibit Swinburne's powers of mythmaking and body forth the tenets of the achieved myth.

The most notable exception to what has been called the "rule of mediocrity" in the late verse is not a lyric at all, but the magnificent narrative *Tristram of Lyonesse* (1882), by far the best modern rendering of the Tristram legend. Both the **"Prelude,"** written as early as 1869, and the rest of the enormous narrative, not produced until the 1880s, reflect all of the achievements—technical and thematic— of his best mythopoeic poetry. [In *Swinburne: An Experiment in Criticism,* 1972] Jerome McGann has compared the rhetorical structures of *Tristram* to those of **"On the Cliffs,"** and the extraordinary inclusiveness of the syntax may even surpass that of **"On the Cliffs."** The overall structure, moreover, is antiphonal in the same sense as that of **"By the North Sea."** In addition to the awesome antiphonal response of the first forty-four lines of the **"Prelude"** in the first forty-four of the final book, **"The Sailing of the Swan,"** the poem continually picks up and metamorphoses image clusters and ideas. Allusions to Merlin's imprisonment by Nimue, for example, run throughout the poem, subtly shifting meaning in different contexts. Swinburne said he was "stimulated" by the music of Wagner when writing *Tristram of Lyonesse,* and his statement is not surprising, for even more than in **"Hesperia,"** *Erechtheus,* or **"On the Cliffs,"** the verse reverberates with the continually present, continually metamorphosing leitmotives of Wagnerian opera. Further, the metaphoric identification of man's attributes with the natural world, which reflects his experiential perception of a "Thou" in nature, could not be clearer. [In *Swinburne: Selected Poetry and Prose*] John D. Rosenberg notes the "erotic interpenetration of nature and man"; indeed, all of nature is alive with man's life, as almost any passage in the poem would serve to illustrate. Tristram, moreover, is, like Swinburne, a singer—and, like Swinburne's, his resurrection in song corresponds with nature's resurrection in spring. He and external nature merge in the great cosmic song:

> And the spring loved him surely, being from birth
> One made out of the better part of earth,
> A man born as at sunrise; one that saw
> Not without reverence and sweet sense of awe
> But wholly without fear or fitful breath

> The face of life watched by the face of death;
> And living took his fill of rest and strife,
> Of love and change, and fruit and seed of life,
> And when his time to live in light was done
> With unbent head would pass out of the sun:
> A spirit as morning, fair and clear and strong,
> Whose thought and work were as one harp and song
> Heard through the world as in a strange king's hall
> Some great guest's voice that sings of festival.
> So seemed all things to love him, and his heart
> In all their joy of life to take such part,
> That with the live earth and the living sea
> He was as one that communed mutually
> With naked heart to heart of friend to friend.

That the narrative is, in some sense, a myth of the creative poet should be clear from this passage—in which Tristram strikingly resembles the Swinburne of **"On the Cliffs"**— but it becomes unambiguously clear later in the poem, when the birth of the poet in **"Thalassius"** is recapitulated in terms of Tristram:

> And like the sun his heart rejoiced in him,
> And brightened with a broadening flame of mirth:
> And hardly seemed its life a part of earth,
> But the life kindled of a fiery birth
> And passion of a new-begotten son
> Between the live sea and the living sun.

His heart, like the spiritual life of the poet of **"Thalassius"**—or of **"By the North Sea"**—is born of the union of sea and sun.

The significance of the myth in *Tristram of Lyonesse* becomes even clearer when we recall that the sea consistently represents the world of process and the sun symbolizes thought and poetry for Swinburne. Tristram's development in the poem is primarily a growth toward acceptance of cyclical change, and the poem itself modulates from a celebration of love in the **"Prelude"** to a remarkable prolonged antiphonal celebration of fate in **"The Sailing of the Swan."** *Fate,* moreover, is merely another word for *change*:

> Fate, that was born ere spirit and flesh were made,
> The fire that fills man's life with light and shade;
> The power beyond all godhead which puts on
> All forms of multitudinous unison,
> A raiment of eternal change inwrought
> With shapes and hues more subtly spun than
>   thought,
> Where all things old bear fruit of all things new
> And one deep chord throbs all the music through,
> The chord of change unchanging. . . .

Fate and change, as changeably unchangeable as the sea, must be acknowledged before love or art can be made, for "Fate that was born ere spirit and flesh were made" is the one thing which must preexist "Love, that is first and last of all things made." For those who accept and merge with change and process, for those who participate in the cosmic song of universal change, life is "no discord in the tune with death"; immortality may be gained in song. The burden of the **"Prelude,"** as well as of **"The Sailing of the Swan,"** is that passionate lovers, become one with the cycles of nature, are resurrected by generations of singers just as organic growth is resurrected in spring or the day in the dawn—"short-lived things, long dead, live long / . . . in changeless change of seasons" because singers revive them. The one absolute necessity is that man recognize change as law and consequently recognize that life and death are one:

> If life were haply death, and death be life;
> If love with yet some lovelier laugh revive,
> And song relume the light it bore alive . . .
>
>   . . . . .
>
> Might he that sees the shade thereof not say
> This dream were trustier than the truth of day.

It must be noted at some point that Swinburne's myth of cyclical return in song makes him the most prolific user of the prefix *re* the language has ever known—just as Hardy, tormented by his agnosticism, was the most prolific user of *un,* and Wordsworth, pioneering the subconscious, the most persistent user of *under.* The importance of this passage, however, is its emphatic statement of the truth and life of the imagination—made possible by a clear recognition of mortality.

According to Kerry McSweeney, **"A Nympholept"** and **"The Lake of Gaube"** rise above **"Thalassius"** and "the mediocrity of so much of the poetry that was to come" because they "emphasize the difficulty and danger of direct confrontation with nature, the terror it inspires, and the difficult struggle to put aside those things that keep the poet from fully surrendering himself to the natural world." This is, as we have seen, true also of **"On the Cliffs," "By the North Sea,"** and *Tristram of Lyonesse,* but McSweeney is right in noting that the element of fear and terror is more pronounced, more central, in the later poems. **"A Nympholept,"** perhaps Swinburne's most perfect mythopoeic poem, is overtly concerned with the problem of overcoming fear of natural law, of change. The poem's ostensible deity, Pan, simply represents all of the natural world; like all of Swinburne's gods, he is man-made, created only by the soul's "strength to conceive and perceive [him] . . . / With sense more subtle than senses that hear and see." Pan's wife, the natural complement of nature, is *change,* and the fear of the poet springs from a recognition of the inseparability of the two:

> No service of bended knee or of humbled head
> May soothe or subdue the God who has change to
>   wife:
> And life with death is as morning with evening
>   wed.

The central question, which immediately follows this perception, is whether hope, inspired by the beauty of the sunlit scene, is stronger than fear: "And yet, if the hope that hath said it absorb not fear, / What helps it man that the stars and the waters gleam?" The vision, the actual seizure (*-lepsy*) by the nymph, immediately ensues, and though this is never made explicit, the nymph seems to be none other than Pan's

wife, change itself, for she is described as a strange oscillation between shadow and light (death and life)—as change is frequently described in Swinburne. Recognition of the nymph transforms fear to delight:

> I sleep not: never in sleep has a man beholden
>   This. From the shadow that trembles and
>   yearns with light
> Suppressed and elate and reluctant—obscure and
>   golden
>   As water kindled with presage of dawn or
>   night—
>   A form, a face, a wonder to sense and sight,
> Grows great as the moon through the month, and
>   her eyes embolden
>   Fear, till it change to desire, and desire to delight.

Fear is conquered by a euphoric acceptance of natural process—the poet achieves a mergence with the All, which he had thought could come only with death:

> I lean my face to the heather, and drink the sun
>   Whose flame-lit odour satiates the flowers:
>   mine eyes
> Close, and the goal of delight and of life is one:
>   No more I crave of earth or her kindred skies.

The sleepless, unsatisfied urge of romanticism, the recognition that "Our lives and our longings are twain," which had preoccupied Swinburne since the first series of *Poems and Ballads,* is finally brought to an end in the ecstatic embrace of **"A Nympholept."**

As in **"By the North Sea,"** acceptance of mortal limits paradoxically leads to immortality, for the oblivious union with nature, a sort of death into the life of process, suddenly makes the poet realize his own power to create meaning. After the embrace, he asks, significantly: "My spirit or thine is it, breath of thy life or of mine, / Which fills my sense with a rapture that casts out fear?" And in the closing lines he realizes that the nymph is of earth, the ecstasy caused by his imagination, and that the power of the mind brings heaven to earth:

> Heaven is as earth, and as heaven to me
> Earth: for the shadows that sundered them here
>   take flight;
> And nought is all, as am I, but a dream of thee.

Even more clearly than in *Tristram of Lyonesse,* the final resolution is an affirmation of solipsistic creation from the void. Recognizing that he makes his own God, his own hope, his own passionate embrace and his own heaven, the poet celebrates the power of his imagination. The presiding deity of this poem is not Pan at all, but Apollo, the sun god and the singing god, whose rays pervade the noon landscape and unify poet, nature, and nymph in their splendor. The opening stanza sets the scene beautifully:

> Summer, and noon, and a splendour of silence, felt,
>   Seen, and heard of the spirit within the sense.
> Soft through the frondage the shades of the

sunbeams melt,
  Sharp through the foliage the shafts of them,
    keen and dense,
  Cleave, as discharged from the string of the
    God's bow, tense
As a war-steed's girth, and bright as a warrior's belt.
  Ah, why should an hour that is heaven for an`
    hour pass hence?

The concluding question indicates that the poet is not content merely to accept that his life and desires are twain, but the solution to his problem is implicit in the six preceding lines. The shafts from the God's, Apollo's, bow cleave—the word is used in the same sense as in **"On the Cliffs"**—all things into glorified unity. In an earlier poem, **"Pan and Thalassius"** (1889), Swinburne had used the myth of the singing contest of Pan and Apollo to suggest that the worshipers of nature, like Midas, are sadly mistaken. Thalassius, "seed of Apollo," given the final response in the lyrical dialogue, expresses the reasons for the superiority of Apollo. Pan has asserted that he is "All," but Thalassius answers:

     God,
  God Pan, from the glad wood's portal
    The breaths of thy song blow sweet:
  But woods may be walked in of mortal
    Man's thought, where never thy feet
     Trod.

     Thine
  All secrets of growth and of birth are,
    All glories of flower and of tree,
  Wheresoever the wonders of earth are;
    The words of the spell of the sea
     Mine.

Apollo occupies the "spirit within the sense"—an oft-reiterated phrase in late Swinburne—exalting man above nature by incorporating "mortal / Man's thought" in his song. At a more sophisticated level **"A Nympholept"** also recreates the contest between Pan and Apollo. The Wordsworthian joy in the unity of nature at the beginning of the poem results from a perception of a bond between heaven and earth, Apollo and Pan. The sun's rays, as in **"By the North Sea"** and many other poems, draw all things into harmony. The vision, however, does not reinforce this idea of unity; it shatters it, for the vision is of a shadow that separates the sun's rays from the earth, Apollo from Pan:

What light, what shadow, diviner than dawn or
  night,
  Draws near, makes pause, and again—or I
    dream—draws near?

Only when the divorce of sun and earth is complete, at the end of the poem, does the poet advance beyond Wordsworthian joy to a new conception of man in nature:

    Heaven is as earth, and as heaven to me
Earth: for the shadows that sundered them here

take flight;
  And nought is all, as am I, but a dream of thee.

The poem ends where it began, with a blissful, sun-soaked nature, but on a new level, for the poet has seen that the mind of man is necessarily separated from nature by the shadow of mortality and that the perceiving mind *creates* the harmony of man and earth. He comes, by virtue of his vision of the sundering shadow, to realize that the Apollonian mind is not only separated from nature but creates nature. In the beginning, the poet, Midas-like, celebrates "the one God, Pan," and it is only through immersion in process and recognition of change that he comes to the element missing from the All—the power of man's thought.

The recognition in **"A Nympholept,"** **"Pan and Thalassius,"** and a host of other late poems of the superiority of Apollo over Pan clearly establishes Swinburne's main line of divergence from Wordsworthian romanticism. Nature to him is not a great healer, but is, as it was to Tennyson and the other Victorians, "red in tooth and claw." His success in salvaging the visionary nature poetry of romanticism from the Victorian pragmatism that had ruined it for his contemporaries makes Swinburne unique in his period. Arnold, Mill, and others could praise Wordsworth and his fellow romantics even while knowing, sadly, that harmonious union with nature was no longer possible. Swinburne alone both saw the impossibilities of pantheism and was able to continue to see nature as imaginatively—mythopoeically—as his predecessors. Swinburne alone was able to fuse the truths of romanticism and Victorianism, the earlier generation's belief in the life of nature and his own generation's knowledge of nature's brute, impersonal carnality. In Nietzschean terms, Swinburne has recognized the need to incorporate Dionysian fear and ecstasy into a complete mythic view.

Swinburne was typical of his age in his preoccupation with the subject of personal immortality, but as **"A Nympholept"** and, even more emphatically, **"The Lake of Gaube"** illustrate, he was uniquely successful in dealing with the agnostic's traditional fear of death. More explicitly in **"The Lake of Gaube"** than anywhere else in his poetry, Swinburne is concerned with the fear of mortality that destroys the Wordsworthian joy of childlike immersion in nature. The salamanders that live near the lake, "living things of light like flames in flower," represent this total communion with sunsoaked nature—the communion finally achieved in **"A Nympholept"**—but

Fear held the bright thing hateful, even as fear,
  Whose name is one with hate and horror, saith
That heaven, the dark deep heaven of water near,
  Is deadly deep as hell and dark as death.

As in **"A Nympholept"** again, the fear is overcome by an ecstatic embrace of the terror—here, more explicitly death than change. The poet plunges into the waters of death:

Death-dark and delicious as death in the dream of a
  lover and dreamer maybe,
  It clasps and encompasses body and soul with

delight to be living and free:
Free utterly now though the freedom endure but the
    space of a perilous breath,
And living, though girdled about with the darkness
    and coldness and strangeness of death:
Each limb and each pulse of the body rejoicing,
    each nerve of the spirit at rest,
All sense of the soul's life rapture, a passionate
    peace in its blindness blest.

Complete surrender to the deathlike state, an experience in life of the oblivious mergence sought in so many of the early poems, makes him realize that death is not a negation of life but a fulfillment and that acceptance of death eliminates the fear of process which inhibits freedom. Comparing **"The Lake of Gaube"** with the **"Hymn to Proserpine,"** Kerry McSweeney has succinctly summarized Swinburne's maturation to this point of acceptance: "Death is no more a longed-for oblivion, a release from meaningless imprisonment in mutability. It is rather something intimately a part of man's relation to nature; a culmination, not an escape."

The comparison with the **"Hymn to Proserpine"** is instructive in other ways. We recall that in the earlier poems the depths of the sea represented the changeless void of death, the surface the perpetually shifting semblance of mortal life. In 1867 Swinburne had found consolation for mortality in contemplating the eternality of the void, the end of strife, but had found no instruction as to how he might best live out his days in the sun. In **"The Lake of Gaube"** he does not contemplate the void, he experiences it; his consolation is not philosophical but experiential, emotional, mythopoeic. After the experience he can return from the void to the ever shifting surface and live without fear; after the plunge into the depths he can return to swim on the surface, in the full light of the sun, and participate in the "sense of unison" of all living nature. The salamander is significant because, being amphibious, it can live both on land and in water and because, according to legend, it can live through fire. In other words, the salamander lives in harmony with all the elements, with nothing to fear from any of them. The swimmer, half in the water and half out, with the sun above him and the depths below, is in a precisely analogous state, a state of total surrender to the forces of the external world. The result, even more emphatically than in **"A Nympholept,"** is that life and death are as one:

As the silent speed of a dream too living to live
    for a thought's space more
Is the flight of his limbs through the still strong
    chill of the darkness from shore to shore.
Might life be as this is and death be as life that
    casts off time as a robe,
The likeness of infinite heaven were a symbol
    revealed of the lake of Gaube.

The diver is completely at one with the cosmic song of nature. At a precisely analogous moment in *Tristram of Lyonesse* after Tristram has plunged into the sea, the metaphor of the cosmic song is explicitly evoked:

each glad limb became
A note of rapture in the tune of life,
Live music mild and keen as sleep and strife.

Like Tristram and like the salamanders, which are described earlier in the poem in terms of song, the diver becomes a chord in the universal harmony.

The lesson of **"The Lake of Gaube,"** the cure Swinburne sets forth for the agnostic agony of the nineteenth century, is that surrender to the flux of experience, nurture of the whole self in the whole of nature, makes philosophical doubt irrelevant. The final section of the poem, after the description of the exhilarating plunge into elemental nature, begins with an agnostic litany:

Whose thought has fathomed and measured
    The darkness of life and death,
The secret within them treasured,
    The spirit that is not breath?
Whose vision has yet beholden
    The splendour of death and of life?

Wordsworthian romanticism does not ask such questions. Swinburne's contribution to the poetic succession is his incorporation of philosophical doubt into his myth and his triumphant affirmation of man's ability to make meaning. The answer vouchsafed for his question is, paradoxically, silence:

Deep silence answers: the glory
    We dream of may be but a dream,
And the sun of the soul wax hoary
    As ashes that show not a gleam.
But well shall it be with us ever
    Who drive through the darkness here,
If the soul that we live by never,
    For aught that a lie saith, fear.

All of this recapitulates, with heightened awareness, the implicit lessons of **"Hesperia,"** **"By the North Sea,"** and **"A Nympholept,"** that acceptance of our mortal part is the basis of creativity and that in creation from the void lies our salvation. Swinburne believed he had much in common with Blake, and so he had, but on the crucial question of the self in relation to nature, they disagreed entirely. Blake based his myth of the imaginative self entirely on a rejection of the natural, generative self, rhetorically asking of his mortal part in "To Tirzah," "Then what have I to do with thee?" Swinburne's answer, had he understood the poem aright (he did not) would have been *everything*: his own myth of imagination is based on the reality of experience—experience which tells him that freedom and peace are found in surrender of the self to cyclical change.

The uniqueness of Swinburne's myth in the late nineteenth century can best be appreciated by comparing it with the faith of the wholly antithetical but eminently Victorian Browning. Swinburne's final consolation lay in his belief—confirmed, he felt, by experience—that death would liberate him from the strife of time, Browning's in the Christian belief in personal immortality. Browning's last thoughts on the subject of death are set forth in the last stanza of the "Epilogue" to *Asolando,* published, ironically, on December 12, 1889, the day of his death. With the bravado of the true believer—both in Christianity and the Protestant work ethic—he exhorts us to

> Greet the unseen with a cheer!
> Bid him forward, breast and back as either should be,
> "Strive and thrive!" cry "Speed,—fight on, fare ever
>   There as here!"

For Browning, as for most Victorians—from Carlyle to the Evangelical Protestants to the Utilitarian industrialists—the lot of man was ever to work and to strive; but reaching the goal was unthinkable, for in fulfillment the purpose, the strife of humanity, would be ended. Even after death, Browning insists, man must "fight on" as he fought in life. . . . [The] early Swinburne had felt the same way, rejecting sterile completion in such poems as **"Hermaphroditus"** and asserting the need for perpetual striving until death. It is a mark of his development that in the late poetry he was able to find complete fulfillment in life, to find the joy Wordsworth had thought could only be known by the child.

No poet ever set himself a harder task, no poet ever worked so long and faithfully at achieving his ends, and no poet ever succeeded so fully at creating his own consolation in a bleak and cheerless world.

—David G. Riede

For Swinburne, unlike Browning, life was not to be a continual kicking against the pricks in order to prove the integrity of the individual; rather it was to be a complete surrender to and immersion in the flux of nature. The Wordsworthian child knows the freedom of wild animals, bounds over the mountains like a roe; Swinburne at the end of his life, knew the same joy: "As a sea-mew's love of the sea-wind breasted and ridden for rapture's sake / Is the love of his body and soul for the darkling delight of the soundless lake." The mythopoeic impulse in Wordsworth and Coleridge had died out when the moments of childlike rapture in nature had ceased to come, and their legacy to the Victorians had been the meager comfort that years bring the philosophic mind. Swinburne's distinction, as the finest of the heirs of romanticism, was to begin with the shattered vision of Wordsworth, the division of soul and sense, the philosophic mind, and work his way back to harmonious interpenetration of the self in nature. He utterly reversed the romantic process of growth from vision to philosophy, completing the cycle from fall to redemption by incorporating and subsuming the philosophical mind in his final vision. McSweeney, characterizing **"A Nympholept,"** accurately describes the balance of philosophy and experiential joy in both that poem and **"The Lake of Gaube"**: "None of the awareness of human

limitations and of nature's separateness from man . . . is forgotten or negated here. It is for the moment transformed, because of the speaker's acceptance of it, into something positive and joyous." Swinburne remained, contemplatively, agnostic while becoming, experientially, religious and mythopoeic. The fear he overcame in **"A Nympholept"** and **"The Lake of Gaube"** was the fear fostered on romanticism by rationalism.

The complete fusion of the self in nature is the first requirement of mythopoeic art, and **"The Lake of Gaube"** is as much a parable of the artist as a description of the loss of selfhood in the elements. In another late poem, **"By Twilight,"** Swinburne clearly stated the absolute irreducible base of his myth:

>   the supreme
> Pure presence of death shall assure us, and prove us
>   If we dream.

In **"The Lake of Gaube"** the supreme presence of death verifies the dream of man's significance and makes possible the perpetuation of dreams, of myths. The description of the diver's return to the surface suggests, in the light of Swinburne's Apollonian myth, a return to creativity: "And swiftly and sweetly, when strength and breath fall short, and the dive is done, / Shoots up as a shaft from the dark depth shot, sped straight into sight of the sun." He becomes as a shaft from the bow of Apollo returning to the quiver, revivified by acceptance of death. The lines recall the description of the unifying shafts of Apollo in the first stanza of **"A Nympholept"** and analogous descriptions in **"On the Cliffs"** and **"By the North Sea."** The salamander, whom the swimmer comes to resemble in his ability to live in joy in all elements, has been described by Meredith B. Raymond [in *Victorian Poetry,* 1971] as "the manifestation of art" because he is a "living synthesis of two worlds, the universal, eternal world and the particular world of man." This is true, but, even more significantly, the description of the salamander as a "flamelike tongue" suggests the Pentecostal image of the Holy Spirit, as a tongue of flame, coming to strengthen the apostles at a moment of doubt and fear. Swinburne, always rivaling the Christian myth, is creating a natural Pentecost, a trial by fire, in which doubt and fear are ousted and the soul is strengthened. Bolstered by a return to the elements, he is ready to sing again.

Just as **"A Nympholept"** and **"The Lake of Gaube"** are, in a sense, poems about art without ever mentioning art, so are dozens of the other late nature poems that have been dismissed as mere scene painting because readers have never realized that the myth of poetry and Apollo, arduously developed in other poems, unostentatiously pervades them. It would be impracticable—and redundant—to examine all of these lyrics, but it is worth while to glance at a few stanzas taken from Swinburne's last volume of lyrics, *A Channel Passage and Other Poems* (1904). Immediately following **"The Lake of Gaube"** in this volume is an exquisite trilogy of poems that has been all but ignored by critics. **"The Promise of the Hawthorn," "Hawthorn Tide,"** and **"The Passing of the Hawthorn"** do not merely describe the budding, blooming, and drooping of a flower but the joy of man and nature in the changeless change of the eternal song:

> A new life answers and thrills to the kiss of the
> young strong year,
> And the glory we see is as music we hear not, and
> dream that we hear.
> From blossom to blossom the live tune kindles,
> from tree to tree,
> And we know not indeed if we hear not the song
> of the life we see.

The experiential verification of the dream of the song once again overrides the rational doubts. All of nature is alive and singing, and the perceiving poet is singing in complete harmony:

> ever the sight that salutes them [flowers] again
> and adores them awhile is blest,
> And the heart is a hymn, and the sense is a soul,
> and the soul is a song.

Part of the reason for neglect of these poems, no doubt, is that the myth of poetry is evoked, at times, in words difficult of comprehension to one not already well versed in it:

> Music made of the morning that smites from the
> chords of the mute world song
> Trembles and quickens and lightens, unfelt,
> unbeholden unheard,
> From blossom on blossom that climbs and
> exults in the strength of the sun grown strong,
> And answers the word of the wind of the
> spring with the sun's own word.

Such verse has been condemned as facile word-music—"a tale of little meaning tho' the words are strong"—but for one who has read Swinburne carefully, they are highly charged with significance. Finally, in neglected lyrics of as late a date as **"Hawthorn Tide,"** Swinburne was still capable of such verbal tours de force as the description of a bank of flowering hawthorn as "One visible marvel of music inaudible." As in **"Hesperia,"** written some thirty years earlier, the dazzling harmony of synesthetic imagery still asserts a harmony of the senses that is purely a creation of the poet. Swinburne's language, as much as ever, if not more, is charged with metaphor to bring about a fusion of the soul and sense of man and the soul and sense of nature.

Two other poems included in *A Channel Passage and Other Poems* indicate the extent to which Swinburne drew comfort from his myth. He wrote **"The High Oaks: Barking Hall, July 19th, 1896"** at his mother's birthplace in celebration of her eighty-seventh birthday; Lady Jane Henrietta Swinburne died in November 1896, and he added an elegiac companion piece, **"Barking Hall: A Year After."** The first of the poems, a lovely evocation of the landscape, is filled with the images and ideas we have come to associate with the mature myth. The consolation

for mortality is so prominent that even this poem sounds like an elegy:

> Here we have our earth
> Yet, with all the mirth
> Of all the summers since the world began,
> All strengths of rest and strife
> And love-lit love of life
> Where death has birth to wife,
> And where the sun speaks, and is heard of man:
> Yea, half the sun's bright speech is heard,
> And like the sea the soul of man gives back his word.

Nature is alive with the love and speech of man; the sun and the sea, life and death, are in unison and all is alive and at peace. According to Edmund Gosse [in *The Life of Algernon Charles Swinburne,* 1917] the death of Swinburne's mother was a devastating blow: "The grief of her son was overwhelming, and it may be said that this formed the last crisis of his own life." It is of the greatest significance that Swinburne turned for comfort to the landscape, fulfilled of love and of song—including his own song of a year before. His lament for his mother begins as a celebration of wind, sun, and change:

> Still the sovereign trees
> Make the sundawn's breeze
> More bright, more sweet, more heavenly than
> it rose,
> As wind and sun fulfil
> Their living rapture: still
> Noon, dawn, and evening thrill
> With radiant change the immeasurable repose
> Wherewith the woodland wilds lie blest
> And feel how storms and centuries rock them still
> to rest.

The "sundawn's breeze"—a potent image in view of the myth—is different, "more heavenly," because the fulfilling force of "wind and sun" have added his love and his song to the scene. Change, which carried off his mother, is accepted and seen as a mere part, an ornament, of changelessness, "the immeasurable repose." All is in harmony with the light of the sun; change itself is "radiant." As in **"A Nympholept"** and **"The Lake of Gaube,"** however, the affirmation at the beginning must be earned in the course of the poem, must describe the pain of grief, the pain of knowing that the dead live only in our dreams. The last stanza returns to the consolation of the first, with greater impact because it has absorbed all of the pain of the intervening stanzas:

> Night and sleep and dawn
> Pass with dreams withdrawn:
> But higher above them far then noon may climb
> Love lives and turns to light
> The deadly noon of night.
> His fiery spirit of sight
> Endures no curb of change or darkling time.
> Even earth and transient things of earth
> Even here to him bear witness not of death but
> birth.

Love, born of the "transient things of earth," lives on in the eternal. The borderline between life and death is wholly eradicated and all change, leading to rest, is to be celebrated.

That much of Swinburne's late poetry is elegiac should not be surprising. His personal myth, evolved in response to his own fears of mortality, is perfectly adapted to the genre of consolation. He arrived slowly and arduously at a myth of "Art that mocks death, and Song that never dies" (**"A Death on Easter Day"**), and it was fitting that he should use it to mock death. Because a large part of the myth was concerned with the ability of the poet to fulfill the world with meaning by joining the cosmic Apollonian song of all generations of singers, it was fitting also that most of Swinburne's elegies should be about fellow poets. *Poems and Ballads* (Second Series), the volume in which the myth of poets and poetry is first fully set forth, consists largely of celebrations of dead singers, as do all the subsequent collections of lyrics. In mourning poets dead and gone, Swinburne not only paid tribute to them but expressed his own faith. The poignant **"In Time of Mourning,"** written after the death of Hugo in May 1885, is short enough to be quoted in full, and will serve as a perfect example of Swinburne's use of the elegiac mode:

> "Return," we dare not as we fain
>   Would cry from hearts that yearn:
> Love dares not bid our dead again
>   Return.
>
>   O hearts that strain and burn
> As fires fast fettered burn and strain!
>   Bow down, lie still and learn.
> The heart that healed all hearts of pain
>   No funeral rites inurn:
> Its echoes, while the stars remain,
>   Return.

The lesson is simple—the singer's heart never dies because the echoes of his song ring down the ages. The poem ties in perfectly with the idea of the eternal Apollonian song, the everlasting succession of poets and the immortal life of man, both aggregate man and the individual man, Victor Hugo.

The form of this simple little tribute exactly corresponds to its content. It is a roundel, a form enormously congenial to Swinburne, in which a word or phrase from the first line is caught up and used as a refrain. In this case the echoing of the word "return" rings in the perpetual returns of Victor Hugo, his heart redeemed in each succeeding poet who takes up his song. The song and the heart are metamorphosed in each return, of course, because the note of the new singer is added and the context of the song is changed. Hugo becomes Swinburnian Hugo. The roundel perfectly reflects this process of metamorphosis, this *repetitio ad differens,* because the refrain, like the poet's song, is transformed in the changing context. In **"The Roundel"** Swinburne beautifully characterizes the effects of the form,

> As a bird's quick song runs round, and the hearts
>   in us hear

> Pause answer to pause, and again the same strain
>   caught,
> So moves the device whence, round as a pearl or tear,
>   A roundel is wrought.

The answer of song to song is the basis of Swinburne's myth and the answer of image to image, thought to thought, and line to line the basis of much of his best art. The echo system of *Erechtheus,* the calling of image to image in **"On the Cliffs,"** and the recurring leitmotives of *Tristram of Lyonesse* all reflect, on a larger scale, the poetic concerns that led Swinburne to the roundel.

The principle of modulating echoes appears to form the basis of most of Swinburne's beliefs about lyric form. Relatively early in his career he had been able to accept and praise the free verse of Whitman, but as his myth of poetry developed and his own attitudes about poetic form hardened, he came to insist on the need for rigid structures in lyrical verse. He emphatically insisted on the need for rhyme, for example, and was adamant on the importance of a fixed, repeating stanza form. Irregular odes, such as Wordsworth's "Intimations Ode," suffer from the "lawless discord of Cowley's 'immetrical' irregularity" and a "lack of ordered rhythm and lyric law." Even Coleridge and Shelley, in Swinburne's opinion the greatest English lyricists, "could not do their very best when working without a limit and singing without a law." Stanzaic regularity in his own verse, which made possible the sort of dazzling antiphonal variation of **"By the North Sea,"** reflects a general tendency of Swinburne's lyrics to continually repeat sounds and thoughts, subtly shifting the implications. Most of his best lyrics, in fact, follow a circular pattern, returning in the end to the thoughts expressed at the beginning, but with a more profound understanding. As we have seen, **"On the Cliffs," "A Nympholept," "The Lake of Gaube,"** and **"Barking Hall"** all return in their closing lines to qualify and reaffirm the initial vision. The pattern is particularly significant in Swinburne both because it formally exhibits his belief in a continual expansion of the soul in the constant accumulation of song and because the final, qualified vision of his closing stanzas is almost always an assertion of man's solipsistic creation rather than of unqualified faith in external verities. The very form of these lyrics, a continuing modulation of song, is a microcosm of history as Swinburne perceived it. Man begins with unquestioning faith, falls into a period of doubts and speculation, and emerges triumphant in his own power to create. Significantly, the form is based on the Christian paradigm of fall and redemption only to refute Christian faith with the assertion, best expressed in the last stanza of **"A Nympholept,"** that earth and heaven are one and the same, that it is all a matter of perception. The two poems written in tribute to his mother, **"The High Oaks"** and **"Barking Hall,"** provide an informative example of the value of poetic form to Swinburne. The complex nine-line stanza, apparently invented for the first poem, is repeated in the second so that the elegy reverberates both the form and the content of the birthday tribute. Swinburne's recurrent use of standard forms throughout his career, in fact, is designed to echo the songs of earlier poets in the same way as **"Bark-**

ing Hall" is to echo "The High Oaks." A poem, Swinburne felt, could become a part of an earlier poem by being an antiphonal response to it. In a letter to D. G. Rossetti he wrote that "of all things I like (not repetition but) antiphony—if there be such a word—in poems—two notes struck in the same key—two companions mutually responsive and reinforcing." Swinburne is here discussing two poems by one author—like his own "Hymn to Proserpine" and "The Last Oracle"—but the principle would apply as well to two poems by different authors. "On the Cliffs," for example, is an antiphonal response to Whitman's "Out of the Cradle Endlessly Rocking." Formally, from his earliest experiments in pastiche to his resurrection of Greek and Elizabethan tragedy to his late use of highly formalized structures like the roundel and sonnet, he is self-consciously harmonizing with the eternal voices of the Apollonian song. Even his meters, as in "Sapphics" and "Hendecasyllabics"—or more subtly, in "On the Cliffs," where he adopts the rhythms of "Lycidas"—are often chosen to strike in the same key with a certain past singer or song.

Swinburne's astonishing gift for parody—"a kind of miracle of 'negative capability,'" Cecil Lang has called it—is, in a more profound way than one might expect, indicative of the nature of his genius. His parodies exhibit not only his "unsurpassed *maestria*," but also his uncanny ability to enter into the creative process of another poet. They are, in their own way, antiphonal responses to Swinburne's victims, pitched in precisely the same key. That the parodies are perfect echoes of form and ghastly distortions of content reflects yet another of Swinburne's aesthetic beliefs—the importance of a harmonious fusion of form and content. It was because he so clearly saw the need for such fusion that he so clearly saw the absurdity of separating the two, and it was on the basis of such a separation in the poems of his victims that he chose them. The division of soul and sense, for example, in the bodiless philosophizing of Tennyson's "The Higher Pantheism"—

> And the ear of man cannot hear, and the eye of
>   man cannot see;
> But if we could see and hear, this Vision—were it
>   not He?

—is only slightly exaggerated in Swinburne's antiphon, "The Higher Pantheism in a Nutshell":

> Body and spirit are twins: God only knows which
>   is which:
> The soul squats down in the flesh, like a tinker
>   drunk in a ditch.

The parodies, like everything else Swinburne wrote, from his mythopoeic poetry to his translations—also miracles of negative capability—reflect his two central aesthetic beliefs: all poems are conditioned by and responsive to other poems, and form and content in poetry are, ideally, inseparable.

It is altogether fitting that this discussion of Swinburne's poetry, which began with an analysis of his concept of form, should in the end, like a Swinburnian roundel, return to its beginning in an altered context. Swinburne's paradoxical insistence on the all-importance of form, his unabashed aestheticism, and his equally emphatic insistence on the importance of thought can now be resolved. Thought, in Swinburne, rarely means contemplative or philosophic meditation but rather designates the emotional and artistic truths of creative poetry, part of the collective soul of man, and has a set form, a defined body, that cannot be neglected. Further, though it may seem that mythopoeia should be a spontaneous reaction, uninhibited by arbitrary rules, to the whole life in nature, it must be remembered that, for Swinburne, the life in nature is the soul of man, the soul of man is poetry, and poetry is form. His mythopoeic creation and his myth are based not on perceptions of a chaotic nature but on perceptions of a nature vivified and "fulfilled" by the highly structured Apollonian song.

Finally, for Swinburne, form *is* thought. His vision is extraordinarily solipsistic, for he believes only in what he perceives, knowing all the while that "nought may be all," and the formal structures he employs are those that are best adapted to fill space, as it were, and cover the abyss of meaninglessness. The roundel, which typifies Swinburne's ideals of form, demonstrates more clearly than any form I know—except perhaps the triolet—that even words have no genuine, verifiable meaning outside the context which the individual, solipsistic intellect provides. The word "return," used three times in the elegiac roundel for Victor Hugo, has three distinct meanings. Swinburne believed in poetry more than he believed in anything else, but even poems, he knew, had different meanings at different times to different people. "On the Cliffs" shows that Sappho's song is immortal, but also shows that it has no single meaning to all men—that it, like Christianity, cannot be used as a universal verity on which to base a faith. Thus it is the form, the beauty, of Sappho's song that is carried on the wind, not its message or moral, and because it is the beauty of the song which uplifts and inspires Swinburne, it is the form which is, for him, the meaning.

Perhaps the most outstanding of Swinburne's many unusual qualities was his ability, perhaps unique, to make a virtue of solipsism. He was a born rebel who could not simply accept another man's creed, and his belief that no creed was externally verifiable, except by individual experience, not only encouraged but compelled him to create his own myth. Yet he was, nevertheless, following in the footsteps of Shelley. A final example of his poetic revisionism, his revision of Shelley's "Adonais," will serve to show both his essential romanticism and his atypically cheerful but typically Victorian solipsism. Like so many of Swinburne's late poems, "Adonais" is an elegy for a poet, and, like so many of Swinburne's early poems, it rejects all received myths of consolation to arrive at a longing for oblivion, a return to the All. In the most famous stanza of "Adonais" Shelley wrote:

> The One remains, the many change and pass;
> Heaven's light forever shines, Earth's shadows fly;
> Life, like a dome of many-coloured glass,
> Stains the white radiance of Eternity,

Until Death tramples it to fragments—Die,
If thou wouldst be with that which thou dost seek!
Follow where all is fled!

As in Swinburne's early elegy **"Ave atque Vale,"** the main consolation appears to be escape from the insignificance and suffering of mortality. In the final stanza of "Adonais," however, Shelley moves in the direction of a Swinburnian myth of poetry. The breath of Urania, which had vivified Keats's song, now descends on him and unites him in spirit with Adonais:

> The breath whose might I have invoked in song
> Descends on me. . . .
>
> . . . . .
>
> I am borne darkly, fearfully, afar;
> Whilst, burning through the inmost veil of Heaven,
> The soul of Adonais, like a star,
> Beacons from the abode where the Eternal are.

Shelley's poem, like many of Swinburne's, rejects received mythologies, acknowledges and accepts death, and then seeks consolation in a mythopoeic conception of an eternal song of man—the breath of Urania for Shelley, the Apollonian song for Swinburne. Yet though Shelley accepts death in "Adonais," he is not able to overcome the fear of it; and though he acknowledges mortal limits, he does not give thanks for them.

Swinburne's poetic revision of "Adonais," found in the final book of **Tristram of Lyonesse,** definitively establishes his point of departure from Shelleyan romanticism. After claiming that song will "relume the light {love} bore alive," Swinburne continues with a summation of his agnostic creed:

> If aught indeed at all of all this be,
> Though none might say nor any man might see,
> Might he that sees the shade thereof not say
> This dream were trustier than the truth of day.
> Nor haply may not hope, with heart more clear,
> Burn deathward, and the doubtful soul take cheer,
> Seeing through the channelled darkness yearn a star
> Whose eyebeams are not as the morning's are,
> Transient, and subjugate of lordlier light,
> But all unconquerable by noon or night,
> Being kindled only of life's own inmost fire,
> Truth, stablished and made sure by strong desire,
> Fountain of all things living, source and seed,
> Force that perforce transfigures dream to deed,
> God that begets on time, the body of death,
> Eternity: *nor may man's darkening breath,*
> *Albeit it stain, disfigure or destroy*
> *The glass wherein the soul sees life and joy*
> Only, with strength renewed and spirit of youth,
> And brighter than the sun's the body of Truth
> Eternal, unimaginable of man,
> Whose very face not Thought's own eyes may scan,
> But see far off his radiant feet at least
> Trampling the head of Fear. . . .

[emphasis mine]

Swinburne, far more than Shelley, emphasizes the impossibility of knowing absolute truth but affirms that the truth which thought cannot find may be created by emotional, experiential conviction, may be "stablished and made sure by strong desire." Though the lovers of **Tristram of Lyonesse** are irrevocably destined for death, the intensity of their passion, "life's own inmost fire," is sufficient to cast out fear, which, significantly, Swinburne goes on to equate with the received myth of Christianity. Shelley had discarded received myth to embrace his own agnostic mythmaking, but he never achieved enough conviction to cast out fear or to apprehend that the lack of external verities made man's life more, not less, meaningful. For Shelley the negative connotations remain in the statement that life "Stains the white radiance of Eternity." Swinburne's fundamental divergence from his romantic predecessors is apparent in his conscientious elimination of negative connotations from this simile. The white light of eternity is, as we have repeatedly seen, only a euphemism for the void of eternity, and for Swinburne the breath that stains the glass does not disfigure it but only makes life and joy visible to the soul. Man's breath, in Swinburne a symbol of both life and song, is all that has meaning because it is all man can know. Thus Swinburne's final poetic creed, though hopeful, is no facile optimism but a call for unblinking acceptance of death and pain and continual strife to live intensely and create continually. His insistence on agnostic mythmaking both as an aesthetic and ethical necessity was, in practice, no less than a challenge to himself to overcome solipsistic fears through incessant creation of myths, to fulfill the empty universe with meaning. No poet ever set himself a harder task, no poet ever worked so long and faithfully at achieving his ends, and no poet ever succeeded so fully at creating his own consolation in a bleak and cheerless world.

Rikky Rooksby (essay date 1985)

SOURCE: "Swinburne in Miniature: A Century of Roundels," in *Victorian Poetry,* Vol. 23, No. 3, Autumn, 1985, pp. 249-65.

[*In the following essay, Rooksby offers a close reading of Swinburne's roundel poems, and discusses the major themes of these works.*]

Swinburne, said T. S. Eliot in 1920, was among that group of poets whose work ought to be read in selection, not whole. That judgment seems to remain a sound one, despite the recent work of critics like David G. Riede [in *Swinburne: A Study of Romantic Mythmaking,* 1978] who has referred to the "embarrassment of riches" to be found in the thirty years of Swinburne's writing in Putney; one cannot accept, though, Eliot's view that a selection would be based pretty much on *Atalanta in Calydon* and *Poems and Ballads* (1866). There *are* poems written after 1878, the great watershed year of Swinburne's publishing, which it would be an error to omit. Criticism has hardly begun as yet to sift, analyze and evaluate the huge quantity of verse produced by Swinburne between 1879 and his death in 1909, a quantity which represents about half of his total output. The problem that faces student and teacher alike is the question of where to enter this dark continent of largely unexplored writing. The choice is an important one, because there are certain areas of land (to pursue the metaphor)—areas such as some of the very lengthy eulogistic odes, the poems in praise of babies and Bertie Mason in particular, and those expressing fervent nationalistic sentiments—whose general climatic conditions and terrain will strain the patience of the most hardened and enthusiastic Swinburnian to the point of wondering whether the old verdict that Swinburne was finished as a poet by 1878 was not correct after all. And yet to stumble from the oppressive jungle of these things into the power and beauty of poems like **"A Nympholept," "The Lake of Gaube," "Evening on the Broads,"** or, on a smaller scale, **"In a Rosary,"** is to have one's faith utterly restored. The disparity between the best and the worst of Swinburne's later poetry remains a puzzle, all the more so because from a technical point of view both classes of poems seem to be doing the same sorts of things with the same methods.

Apart from this question of selecting which poems to read from the later years, there is also the problem of the length of Swinburne's best poems. The length of a poem like **"Anactoria," "The Triumph of Time,"** or **"Evening on the Broads"** is one way in which Swinburne creates the beautiful panoramic effects of his land and seascapes, the peculiar emptiness that is bound within them, and the disturbed, charged and spiraling contemplations of his varied personae. But Swinburne could also achieve these things on a smaller scale. This is ably demonstrated by the poems published in 1883 as *A Century of Roundels,* a volume which in miniature features the vices and the virtues of the later poetry, and whose best individual pieces show how Swinburne, often considered crown prince of prolixity, could focus the Swinburnian "void" into a mere eleven lines.

A Century of Roundels was a departure from the formal concerns and content of the first collections of poetry published after his move to Putney. *Songs of the Springtides* and *Studies in Song* (both 1880) featured a small number of long poems and were succeeded by the nine-canto *Tristram of Lyonesse* (1882). Swinburne's parodies in *The Heptalogia* (1880) did represent a moment of light relief, though the lampoons were also lengthy. The impulse to write the roundels was explained by Sir Edmund Gosse [in *Algernon Charles Swinburne,* 1917] as a determination on Swinburne's part "for the sake of self-discipline, to abandon for a time his broad and sweeping measures, and to curb his Pegasus with a rigidly-determined fixed form." It seems Swinburne wrote them in a matter of two months or so; he began in mid-January and "by the 6th of February he had finished twenty, four more by the 9th, and three more on the following day." The *Century* was complete by the end of March. Gosse described the original work-drafts as bearing "very little mark of correction, and may be considered as almost improvisations." Though a certain lightness of touch and air of spontaneity is evident throughout the book, this

does not mean they necessarily failed in their original disciplinary function. Swinburne was given to referring to them in a cooing fashion as "a little book of songs" and "a tiny new book of songs or songlets" and disingenuously describing their composition by saying that he had taken "a fancy to the form and went on scribbling in it" until he had one hundred.

Needless to say, there has been very little critical writing on the roundels. They have tended to be either ignored in book-length studies or dismissed as "a charming series of rather slight pieces." [In his *Algernon Charles Swinburne: A Critical Study,* 1912] Edward Thomas described some of them as "the prettiest, saddest things alive" and Harold Nicolson [in *Swinburne,* 1926] found them interesting "only as a reflection of his early moods at Putney," though he praised the more remorseful roundels. [In *Swinburne,* 1929] Samuel C. Chew wrote that "to read the collection through is an exhausting experience; the studies of babyhood are particularly trying." Although "several of the poems have something of a quiet charm," they failed "to check the fatal fluency." Modern critics, such as Riede (cited above) and Jerome J. McGann [in *Swinburne: An Experiment in Criticism,* 1972], have supplied the best examples of discussion of the roundels; it is also refreshing to see a number of the roundels included in L. M. Findlay's *Selected Poems* of Swinburne (1982). A closer examination of some of these roundels will support the view that words such as "charm" really fail to do justice to the best things in the *Century.*

Swinburne's roundel is a variant upon the French rondeau, which has thirteen lines and three stanzas rhyming aabba, aab, aabba, with only two rhymes being used. Furthermore, the first word or phrase is employed as a refrain and is repeated in the eighth and last lines. The word "roundel" was used by Chaucer and others as a synonym for the roundeau and therefore has a long literary history. The poem entitled **"The Roundel"** will admirably serve as a description and illustration of Swinburne's variant form:

> A roundel is wrought as a ring or a starbright sphere,
> With craft of delight and with cunning of sound unsought,
> That the heart of the hearer may smile if to pleasure his ear
>   A roundel is wrought.
>
> Its jewel of music is carven of all or of aught—
> Love, laughter, or mourning—remembrance of rapture or fear—
> That fancy may fashion to hang in the ear of thought.
>
> As a bird's quick song runs round, and the hearts in us hear
> Pause answer to pause, and again the same strain caught,
> So moves the device whence, round as a pearl or tear,
>   A roundel is wrought.

Swinburne's change from the rondeau was to trim one line from each of the five-line stanzas to produce a structure eleven lines long and to move the refrain from line eight to line four. The chiming quality, created by the use of two rhymes only and the thrice-stated refrain—in this instance "A roundel is wrought"—gives the roundel its immediately apparent major formal distinction: its circularity. By contrast, it is helpful to think of the steady forward progression of a Shakespearean sonnet to its concluding couplet, where the structure is linear and does not formally turn back upon itself. Each break between quatrains is like a bridge we only cross once. The poem invites comparison, in particular, with Rossetti's sonnet on the sonnet ("A sonnet is a moment's monument"). The roundel, however, is more like the spiral of a seashell, the opening stanza making one circle and the remainder a second, ending where the poem began, with the refrain. But at the conclusion, this is read with increased perception. It is a kind of formal aesthetic embodiment of Eliot's famous lines:

> And the end of all our exploring
> Will be to arrive where we started
> And know the place for the first time.
> ("Little Gidding,")

The two rhymes set up a series of echoes with each recurrence recalling earlier lines; the echoes bridge the gaps between the tercet and quatrains and draw the poem into a resonant whole. This combination of words occurring once but their sound being picked up repeatedly makes the form of the roundel reflect more abstract paradoxes such as those of time and timelessness and changeless change, which are often evoked in the poetry by Swinburne's use of the forces of nature, especially the sea. Thus the roundel is peculiarly appropriate as a form for a poet whose concern is often with eternal flux, with permanence and impermanence, and the mixed joy and grief that arises from these facts when their effect on human life is considered.

The roundel is a spiraling circle, a single chord that begins with the tonic and ends on the octave; like the serpent of myth, it swallows its own tail. And these qualities are indicated by the images Swinburne uses in the poem as analogies for it. The roundel is likened unto a "starbright sphere," a jewel "round as a pearl or tear," and requires a careful diligence from the poet. This is referred to as "craft," and the poem must be "carven," fashioned, "wrought." The beauty of the roundel must be like that of a gem, its facets breaking the light a thousandfold, a jewel of music—a typically Swinburnian conjunction. Musicality is another quality of Swinburne's form, generated by the rhyme scheme and reinforced by his use of alliteration; **"The Roundel"** is a good example of the delicacy of the phrasing and music suggested by the simile of "a bird's quick song," as well as the modulation of vowel sounds in line three and the impish humor of the conceit of the roundel as a jewel to be hung in the "ear of thought." The craft of the images lies in the way we are able to move from ideas of music and birdsong to images of jewels without difficulty, until they blend into the whole summed up in the phrase "jewel of music." The poem defines the roundel form by what it structurally is, by what it says, and by the images which coalesce.

"The Roundel" exhibits several distinctive features of Swinburne's verse style. One can hardly fail to notice the metrical pulse produced by the five anapestic feet in most of the lines, though here they seem altogether defter than the driving force they impart to a poem like **"Hesperia."** It was Swinburne's use of anapestic and dactylic feet which overwhelmed his first readers, and after eighty years of relative metrical austerity, Swinburne's rhythms can be approached with a fresh sense of their energetic beauty. Secondly, there is ample evidence in the poem of his fondness for alliterative pairings like "love" / "laughter," "fancy" / "fashion," and "remembrance" / "rapture," and the antithetical pairs such as "rapture or fear." Swinburne habitually wrote and constructed poems on the principle of antithesis; as Cecil Lang pointed out to me, this is shown by a pair of roundels on love and fate entitled **"Two Preludes,"** and in contrasting sections of a longer work like *Tristram of Lyonesse.*

The best of the roundels show that Swinburne was able to write with his own kind of precision in a potentially restrictive form and to achieve miniature many of the effects he produces on the larger canvases of the longer poems.

—*Rikky Rooksby*

Having examined one roundel in detail to make clear exactly what Swinburne's blueprint was, one can note the structural variations he plays on this form through the *Century* as a whole. The line length varies from a dimeter, the sparse line of **"Babyhood"** (IV), to anapestic heptameter in the stormy **"The Death of Richard Wagner"**: "From the depths of the sea, from the wellsprings of earth, from the wastes of the midmost night." The refrain can either be a phrase such as "From the depths of the sea" or a single word for special emphasis, like "gone" or "friend." The exact tone of the three appearances of the refrain is also altered, so that it can become a question, answer, or proposition, tentative or bold. On a slightly larger scale Swinburne creates antiphonal effects by arranging some of the roundels as dialogues. **"Time and Life"** comprises two roundels, the first beginning "Time, thy name is sorrow, says the stricken / Heart of life," and the second being Time's answer, "Nay, but rest is born of me for healing." The three roundels entitled **"A Dialogue"** form a question, counter-question, and reply between humankind and death. In the first, the speaker says:

> Death, if thou wilt, fain would I plead with thee:
> Canst thou not spare, of all our hopes have built,
> One shelter where our spirits fain would be,
> Death, if thou wilt?

Death retorts, "Man, what art thou to speak and plead with me?" in the second roundel, and declares its lordship over all things. The pessimism thus suggested is modified by the stoic defiance of the third roundel, where the human speaker asserts, "Thy might is made out of our fear of thee." The three roundels form the three parts of a single roundel-like structure, representing the three stages of fear, despair, and hope.

A Century of Roundels also contains a number of separate poems which are antithetical pairs in their subject matter. **"Death and Birth"** is complemented by **"Birth and Death," "Discord"** pairs with **"Concord," "Plus Intra"** with **"Plus Ultra,"** and so on. The most telling two-part roundel is entitled **"On an Old Roundel."** Its first part carries the epigraph "Translated by D. G. Rossetti from the French of Villon." Swinburne had in mind Rossetti's "To Death, of his Lady," a poem in which Villon addresses death and laments the loss of his beloved. The subject of the first roundel is the emotional rapport and artistic influence between Rossetti and Villon's work that culminated in the former's translation:

> Death, from thy rigour a voice appealed,
> And men still hear what the sweet cry saith,
> Crying aloud in thine ears fast sealed,
>   Death.

Though Villon's lament could not change the reality of his loss, his lyric utterance retains its power even after his death and inspires an artist in a distant age, thus transcending death and time; the singer lives on in the song as long as the poem is remembered. The argument is the familiar one of the poem as echoing tomb, and the next three lines provide a vivid image for this:

> As a voice in a vision that vanisheth,
> Through the grave's gate barred and the portal
>   steeled
> The sound of the wail of it travelleth.

The image of the portal "steeled" is fittingly medieval, as the French poet's "wail" sounds out of the realms of death across the centuries; the effect of this is described in the concluding lines:

> Wailing aloud from a heart unhealed,
> It woke response of melodious breath
> From lips now too by thy kiss congealed,
>   Death.

Perhaps seeing in Villon's poem a reflection of his own grief at the loss of Elizabeth Siddal, Rossetti was sufficiently moved by it to respond to Villon's "wailing" with "melodious breath" and write the translation, an aesthetic resurrection of the dead through lyric song. But the sudden revelation of Rossetti's own death in the penultimate line is a potent shock and a distinctive Swinburne effect. The phrase "It woke response of melodious breath / From lips" implies the present actuality of Rossetti's translation, and since Villon is of the distant past, the reader expects Rossetti to represent the contrast of a living present. In fact, this living present turns out to be Swinburne's own song, since Rossetti's death is abruptly announced by the rest of line ten, "now too by thy. kiss congealed." The contrast between distant past and present celebration of Villon's art is destroyed almost before we have a chance to take it in. This kind of sudden snatching away of present into past is something Swinburne often does, usually with great success; other examples of the technique occur in **"A Forsaken Garden"** and **"In a Rosary,"** as well as elsewhere in the *Century.*

The first roundel of the pair clearly accords with Swinburne's vivid sense of a tradition of lyric poets stretching back to Catullus and Sappho, who sing almost with one voice. He makes specific reference to these kinds of artistic "conversations" across the ages in a passage from his essay on William Collins:

> There is yet another memorable bond of communion which connects the fame of Collins with that of Milton in the past and with that of Shelley in the future. Between the elegy on Edward King and the elegy on John Keats came the humbler and softer note by which Collins set the seal of a gentle consecration on the grave of the "Druid" Thomson; a note to be as gently echoed by Wordsworth in commemoration of his own sweeter song and sadder end.

The four elegies alluded to—"Lycidas," "Ode on the Death of Mr Thomson," "Remembrance of Collins," and "Adonais"—are explicitly linked, and the imagery of consecration and the term "echoed" give a strong sense of the art of these poets linking up across the ages, as Rossetti's and Villon's have in the first roundel. As Swinburne wrote elsewhere, "Art knows nothing of time; for her there is but one tense, and all ages in her sight are alike present."

This is apparent, too, in the second roundel, which is an "ave atque vale" for both poets:

> Ages ago, from the lips of a sad glad poet
> Whose soul was a wild dove lost in the whirling
>   snow,
> The soft keen plaint of his pain took voice to
>   show it
>   Ages ago.

The phrase "sad glad poet" recalls a line from Swinburne's earlier poem **"A Ballad of François Villon,"** "Villon, our sad bad glad mad brother's name"; the poem was published in *Poems and Ballads* (1878), which also contained Swinburne's own translations of the French poet. The second line is striking in its force and beauty; complex associations of purity and spirituality struggling with, and eventually overcome by, hostile conditions and the context of a poem that looks back down the centuries to a single individual turn the image into a symbol whose meanings are hardly to be pinned down. The effect of the line is exactly what Swinburne attributes to Villon's poetry itself when he writes of its "soft keen plaint." Further description comes in the remainder of the roundel:

So clear, so deep, the divine drear accents flow,
No soul that listens may choose but thrill to know it,
Pierced and wrung by the passionate music's throe.

For us there murmurs a nearer voice below it,
Known once of ears that never again shall know,
Now mute as the mouth which felt death's wave
          o'erflow it
          Ages ago.

The "nearer voice" is that of Rossetti, whose poetic "breath" now mingles with that of Villon's in death; its location "below" that of the French poet is perhaps a delicate value judgment on the comparative merit of Swinburne's contemporary and friend, though there is no slight on Rossetti being demoted in this way, since Villon was, in Swinburne's eyes, a truly colossal figure. Swinburne described him as

> a singer also of the future; he was the first modern and the last mediæval poet. He is of us, in a sense in which it cannot be said that either Chaucer or Dante is of us, or even could have been; a man of a changing and self-transforming time, not utterly held fast, though still sorely struggling, in the jaws of hell and the ages of faith.

The generality of the refrain, "Ages ago," successfully evokes the vast stretch of time that separates us from Villon, with just a hint of what that implies in historical and cultural terms. It is a typically Swinburnian effect. His best poetry is remarkable in its evocations of huge expanses of time or space. What is astonishing is that he manages to achieve the same effects of emptiness which are produced in the longer poems in the tiny span of the roundel. In this sense words like "pretty" do not reflect the focused power of some of these eleven-line poems. To complain that the final stanza of this second roundel is diffuse and vague, and that therefore the exercise in curbing a fatal facility was a failure is to be looking for the wrong things. Their brevity could not do anything but prevent prolixity. But the diffusion, which has sometimes been used to describe this quintessential Swinburnian emptiness, is there only in a positive sense, and its presence is a striking indication of poetic success. It can be felt all the way through **"On an Old Roundel,"** which ends with Swinburne's ultimate symbol of death and deathless flux, the sea. A wave passes over both Villon and Rossetti's mouths, bringing oblivion but perhaps a suggestion of life in a greater whole, quite apart from the relative immortality of their poetry, celebrated in the form of this roundel of Swinburne's. They live on in his song, and therefore the poem is both elegiac and lyric celebration.

The sea figures in the series of descriptive roundels called **"In Guernsey"** which close the *Century*; in them can be found echoes of that rapture which characterizes longer poems like **"A Swimmer's Dream."** Take, for example, the second roundel in the group:

My mother sea, my fostress, what new strand,
What new delight of waters, may this be,

The fairest found since time's first breezes fanned
          My mother sea?

Here is an example of the refrain being altered into a question on its second appearance, as the poem evinces Swinburne's close bond with the sea by referring to it as a "mother" (as in **"The Triumph of Time"**). The rapture is evident in the dizzy alliteration and bunched stresses of line three. The alliteration may contribute toward the impression one gets that there are extra unstressed syllables in the pentameter line, though in fact it is fairly regular. The tone becomes less demonstrative and more intensely personal in the tercet:

Once more I give me body and soul to thee,
Who hast my soul for ever: cliff and sand
Recede, and heart to heart once more are we.

The mode of expression is appropriated from love poetry, though the phrase "heart to heart" is hardly straining the sentiment, in that Swinburne's passion for the sea was probably the single enduring passion of his life from beginning to end. Considering the intensity of the lines, it is surprising to find this intensity has been achieved by very few and simple words. The beauty of Swinburne's verse takes two quite different forms, the rhythmic urgency of the choruses of *Atalanta* and the richness and Pre-Raphaelite color of a passage such as this from **"Anactoria"**:

Blossom of branches, and on each high hill
Clear air and wind, and under in clamorous vales
Fierce noises of the fiery nightingales,
Buds burning in the sudden spring like fire,
The wan washed sand and the waves' vain desire.
Sails seen like blown white flowers at sea, and words
That bring tears swiftest, and long notes of birds
Violently singing till the whole world sings.

But there is also the kind of writing that makes Swinburne, in the phrase of John D. Rosenberg [in *Victorian Studies,* 1967] the "supreme master in English of the bleak beauty of little words." This second type is characterized by rhythmic restraint, by a speaking rather than singing tone, and by its simple diction; it is evident in the lines of the tercet of the second **"In Guernsey"** roundel and throughout the book. Some of the most moving moments in his poetry are produced by an abrupt thinning out of the poetic texture, a shift from colorful, flaming images and plentiful use of adjectives to the curt monosyllabic phrase.

As cliff and sand recede into the distance we are led to suppose that the speaker is recollecting being in the sea, but this is really a tease, as the conclusion of the poem makes clear:

My heart springs first and plunges, ere my hand
Strike out from shore: more close it brings to me,
More near and dear than seems my fatherland,
          My mother sea.

The tercet turns out to be only anticipation of a pleasure not yet realized. Despite the very evident delight, there is a hint of deeper spiritual frustration in the phrase "more close it brings to me," since a total uniting with and dissolution in the sea is not possible. A certain longing remains as an unresolved tension in what otherwise seems a perfectly straightforward poem. Here the *Century* has revealed another characteristic of Swinburne's work, for his poetry is predominantly steeped in unslaked passion and unrealizable desires. Rarely do the speakers in his poems achieve peace, and when they do, it is usually after their individualities have been subsumed into a greater whole, as in "**Anactoria**," where Sappho leaps into the sea. In this sense, the conclusion of "**A Nympholept**" is unusual. Peace is not to be had by the living, but by the dead, as in the reconciliation of the roundel called "**Concord**":

> Both bright names, clothed round with man's
> thanksgiving,
> Shine, twin stars above the storm-drifts piled,
> Dead and deathless, whom we saw not living
> Reconciled.

The experience of the living is rapture and doubt, joy and sorrow, rage and fear—the kinds of unresolved dichotomies of human perception that occur throughout Swinburne's work. If any resolution or peace is possible it comes in a blend of mystery at the nature of things and moments of such intense joy that the fretful self is transported beyond itself and its conflicts, as in the third "**Guernsey**" roundel:

> Across and along, as the bay's breadth opens, and
> o'er us
> Wild autumn exults in the wind, swift rapture and
> strong
> Impels us, and broader the wide waves brighten
> before us
> Across and along.

Here Swinburne's own brand of sprung rhythm immediately establishes the breathless joy of the swimmer. The sea becomes metaphorical with the line, "Are we not as waves of the water, as notes of the song?"—a briny Swinburnian complement to the Heraclitean fire, a symbol of inexhaustible flux and energy. In context, the question becomes not an expression of doubt but a thoroughly rhetorical affirmation of unity, the unity of humankind with the ecological and biological forces of the planet. Here Swinburne, whose vision of nature is quite free of his century's mechanistic nuts-and-bolts view of the physical universe, is relevant to our egocentric and arrogant time. If the reader puts aside his idiosyncratic pain-pleasure bias in describing those forces, the poetry evinces an intense, imaginative, and what one can only describe as loving awareness of the sea, sky, and land which we have lost and desperately need to recover. The affirmation of such lines as those that end this roundel can fairly be called holistic:

> Like children unworn of the passions and toils that
> wore us,
> We breast for a season the breadth of the seas that
> throng,
> Rejoicing as they, to be borne as of old they bore us
> Across and along.

The specific incident of swimming becomes one with the metaphorical meaning that life is itself a sea, and nothing may be lost from it. The simile that compares humanity to children and the feeling of trust and support that comes from the phrase "as of old they bore us" may indicate for the modern reader something more than what might be dismissed as a touch of sentimental obsession in a man of forty-six. Perhaps it is time to go beyond the rather facile view of Swinburne's "mother" sea as a sign of a psycho-pathology and ask the question if this recurring figure/force in his poetry may not be read a different way? Perhaps Swinburne's life-and-death-giving "mother" sea is the entity Kit Pedler [in *The Quest for Gaia,* 1979] calls "Gaia": "the earth spirit, she is life, the ground, the air, the water and the interaction between all their inhabitants."

Convoluted syntax and a blurring of tenses in these last lines promote the sense of one moment merging with all moments, as the swimmer's delight is mirrored, via the pathetic fallacy, by the waves' "rejoicing." This is an example of the distinctive use Swinburne makes of this fallacy: he will often attribute ecstatic feelings to nature. The result is often a sense of plenitude and life that easily outweighs the loss of faith in any orthodox concept of a God behind or present in the Creation, so that one hesitates to say Swinburne's vision of nature is secular.

The broadening out of the roundel into wider meanings is done in a way that leaves a sense of mystery; Swinburne's methods are mythopoeic, not allegorical, and though his love of the sea and all wild places is intense, it never falls into sentimentality. The roundels frequently present, in miniature, a perception of the desolate and destructive aspects of nature, even as they rejoice in the power of the elements. This is especially true of the elegiac and more reflective roundels. Sometimes a landscape in itself will give pause for reflection, as in the opening stanza of "'**Insularum Ocelle**'":

> Sark, fairer than aught in the world that the lit
> skies cover,
> Laughs inly behind her cliffs, and the seafarers mark
> As a shrine where the sunlight serves, though the
> blown clouds hover,
> Sark.

Even when Swinburne is celebrating natural forces the poetry can become unsettling in its implicit relegation of humanity to simply a part of life, rather than the God- or self-appointed master of it. The illusion of our dominance of nature is gradually exposed in poems which subtly shift their perspective from a homocentric view to a view of nature as a greater entity.

A new apprehension of human vulnerability, with a touch of the "vanity, all is vanity" vision of Ecclesiastes, is felt in "The Way of the Wind." This roundel is an excellent example of how Swinburne manages to hollow out the form and create a sense of emptiness and desolation familiar in his longer poems. Unanswerable questions, images that become symbols of mysterious forces, a feeling of timelessness, and a monochromatic vocabulary all combine to produce a voidness reminiscent of that which surrounds the particularity of a haiku:

> The wind's way in the deep sky's hollow
> None may measure, as none can say
> How the heart in her shows the swallow
>   The wind's way.
>
> Hope nor fear can avail to stay
> Waves that whiten on wrecks that wallow,
> Times and seasons that wane and slay.
>
> Life and love, till the strong night swallow
> Thought and hope and the red last ray,
> Swim the waters of years that follow
>   The wind's way.

The refrain accumulates meaning with each repetition; in line one, no sooner do we get the reference to the wind than an aura of mystery is created by "None may measure," as the limits of human knowledge are alluded to. Being a force beyond our reckoning, the wind starts to take on a symbolic quality, as inscrutably motivated as the flight of the swallow. The bird enjoys here an affinity of being that makes it closer to the forces of nature than humanity; it moves in harmony with the elements, in contrast to the grisly prospect afforded in the tercet. The middle lines provide the most typical example of Swinburne's rhythmic patterning of all the roundels discussed so far: the linking of antithetical abstract nouns "hope" and "fear," the way "Times and seasons" is balanced by two verbs in the second half of the line, and the alliteration of "Waves that whiten on wrecks that wallow." The image of a shipwreck is a favorite of Swinburne's for showing the precarious vulnerability of some human enterprises (crossing seas) and the power of the elements to make toys out of grand artifacts. The import of these lines is clear: nature is indifferent to the desires of individuals, and her destructive side cannot be checked by wishful thinking. The phrase "Hope nor fear can avail to stay" seems to tilt at the consolations of Victorian religion.

The last stanza becomes even more general. The "strong night" of death claims all things, and until then all life is immersed in time and inextricably one with the forces of nature, just as the swallow in its flight. The metaphor of swimming is used again, with its delicate implication of life being a fusion of the concepts of individual form and yet immersion in a single element, oneness. (A careful moment's thought with this image, as with "my mother sea," takes us beyond the limits of a traditional psychological reading based on the incontestable fact that Swinburne was an enthusiastic swimmer.) The feeling of mystery heightens at the conclusion and the last use of the refrain, "the wind's way," leaving the reader with an expression of doubt and a symbol whose meanings shade off into a peculiar impression of emptiness and the absolute indifference of nature. But this indifference does not mean that there is no link between nature and humanity, no interdependance. The poem generalizes all into a holistic unity, a void of invisible and inscrutable energies. It is important to notice that this effect is largely produced by the words that should be attached to humans—"love," "thought," "hope," and so on—occurring as unattached entities. The generality this causes is exactly right in terms of rendering Swinburne's perception of nature. In his poems objects are replaced or melt into processes; nothing is static, everything moves, dances, or crumbles into decay according to the mood of the poem. The waves in the tercet are not white, they "whiten"; the wrecks "wallow." Adjectives become verbs as possessed qualities become something that happens. Something is not a color, but coloring moment by moment. Commonsense reality, the limited perception we need to get by with when engaged in activities other than contemplation or creation, indicates the world consists of objects that occasionally take part in processes, then cease and go back to being objects. But a truer picture is one that shows everything as process, as an ancient metaphysical system like Buddhism has long known and modern sub-atomic physicists have now discovered. In **"The Wind's Way,"** as in so many of Swinburne's poems, human life becomes not the actions of separate entities over and against the backdrop of nature, but processes and activities that are part of and dependent upon the overall energies of the planet. Very often in his land and seascape poems, humanity either appears as tiny figures in the vast surround or not at all. Just as the swallow is a mere speck in the "deep sky's hollow" and Villon was "a wild dove lost in the whirling snow," so we have become insignificant in the poetic vision, despite the compactness of the roundel. Swinburne's poetry repeatedly achieves this extraordinary panoramic effect and the complementary diminution of human concerns, whether it be in the eleven lines of **"The Wind's Way,"** the sonnet **"A Solitude,"** or much longer pieces like **"By the North Sea."** As Rosenberg pointed out in what remains one of the most thoughtful essays on Swinburne, his scale is macrocosmic, and the brevity of the roundel seems to intensify this, as though we were to receive an insight into the cosmos through the contemplation of a single star.

Perhaps the best example of these techniques at work in the *Century,* and certainly one of the finest poems in the volume, is **"Past Days,"** three elegiac roundels written for George Powell, the Welsh squire and minor man of letters whom Swinburne knew as a young man:

> Dead and gone, the days we had together,
> Shadow-stricken all the lights that shone
> Round them, flown as flies the blown foam's
>   feather,
>   Dead and gone.

The refrain makes its point with a painful finality, and the emphatic tone is backed up by the pulse of the five trochaic feet in each line. The fact of Powell's death now casts a shadow over memories of the past, times described as being insubstantial as seafoam. The important thing to notice is how the third line suggests a different way of experiencing time, where human life becomes a momentary flicker: a perspective more akin to the notion of geological time. There is an even stronger example of this later in the poem.

The tercet shows Swinburne's bleaker style of curt statement in monosyllabic words:

> Where we went, we twain, in time foregone,
> Forth by land and sea, and cared not whether,
> If I go again, I go alone.

The placing of "we twain" as an after-emphasis suggests the rhythms of speech, since we often add clauses when speaking regardless of the overall syntax of our statements. Just as Swinburne's diction can be sumptuous or barren, so his rhythms are not always racing anapests. The fact of Powell's death is evoked with emotional force by the slightly indirect "If I go again, I go alone," a line which owes much to its austerity. The final stanza contrasts their condition of spirit in the present:

> Bound am I with time as with a tether;
> Thee perchance death leads enfranchised on,
> Far from deathlike life and changeful weather,
>   Dead and gone.

The poet is "bound" in two ways: he is haunted by the past and still subject to the vagaries of time in the present, whereas Powell is now free, although the poem is careful to retain its doubt with regard to the kind of existence, if any, the deceased now has. Swinburne can only write "perchance," though what is certain is that Powell is free of the "deathlike life" in which the poet is still trapped. The phrase is one of those moments which occur from time to time in the later poetry where one catches hints of deep dissatisfaction and frustration on the part of Swinburne, perhaps at life at "The Pines" with Watts-Dunton (as in **"To a Seamew"**). But the element of hope in "perchance" is modified by the weight of the final refrain.

The second roundel contrasts with the first in providing a fuller treatment of the past and the memories to which he has already alluded. Trochaic rhythm gives way to the smoother effect of iambs:

> Above the sea and sea-washed town we dwelt,
> We twain together, two brief summers, free
> From heed of hours as light as clouds that melt
>   Above the sea.
>
> Free from all heed of aught at all were we,
> Save chance of change that clouds or sunbeams dealt
> And gleam of heaven to windward or to lee.
>
> The Norman downs with bright grey waves for belt
> Were more for us than inland ways might be;
> A clearer sense of nearer heaven was felt
>   Above the sea.

The first stanza shows how Swinburne can modulate from the plain expression of the second line, a line that causes a hiatus in the rhythm for a second, to the comparative richness of the third, where the iambs take over once more. What Swinburne gives the reader is neither specific events or photographic description, but rather the elements which he and Powell experienced, and which were

so clearly, for Swinburne at least, a large part of the pleasure of that time. The sea is present throughout as a tacit reminder of flux and impermanence that inexorably leads Powell to his death and Swinburne to the role of writing this elegy.

Impermanence and natural energies figure prominently in the third roundel which returns us to the present, though the span of attention has considerably widened:

> Cliffs and downs and headlands which the forward-
>   hasting
> Flight of dawn and eve empurples and embrowns,
> Wings of wild sea-winds and stormy seasons wasting
>   Cliffs and downs,
>
> These, or ever man was, were: the same sky frowns,
> Laughs, and lightens, as before his soul, forecasting
> Times to be, conceived such hopes as time
>   discrowns.

Clearly, Swinburne has now shifted into a more intense key than in the previous two roundels. This is evidenced by the change to trochaic hexameter which imparts a new urgency to the verse, alliteration, enjambment between the first and second stanza, the use of a single sentence for the first seven lines, the breathless repetition of "and"— six times in the first quatrain—and the unstinting occurrence of plurals. This last technique Swinburne used all the way through his poetry to build up a feeling of plenitude, of teeming life and vast natural landscapes. The overall impression is like watching a speeded-up film of clouds moving across the sky. The very seasons themselves seem to chase each other over the earth through the words "empurples and embrowns," which function as verbs and adjectives. Our time perspective has been altered as it was in the line "flown as flies the blown foam's feather" earlier. Years are passing as if they were mere seconds, with all that implies for us. The cliffs and downs of the refrain were there long, long before Swinburne and Powell enjoyed those "two brief summers." The roundel has altered our time sense from the conventional three-score-and-ten of the elegy to the millenia of the geological clock. Powell's life is actually crammed into lines six to seven, "his soul" introducing the subject of the elegy only for him to be "discrowned" by death and time a line later. This effect is similar to that seen in **"On an Old Roundel"** where Rossetti is introduced and snatched away in the same way.

The last quatrain completes the process of establishing an expanded time sense by shifting our attention to include humanity at large, not just Powell:

> These we loved of old: but now for me the blasting
> Breath of death makes dull the bright small seaward
>   towns,
> Clothes with human change these all but everlasting
>   Cliffs and downs.

Here the point is made that though nature is, from a human angle, virtually "everlasting" (though trust Swinburne to say "all but"), our losses color our perception of it and make nature sometimes seem expressive of a sorrow which is humanity's. The grief felt by the poet causes him to see the "bright small seaward towns" as "dull"; for a moment we are aligned with the elements, the cliffs and downs, the millennia, and look back to the world of men and women, their loves and ambitions, with a striking awareness of the fragility and fleeting quality of life. How small Swinburne makes those "seaward towns" seem! Rosenberg quotes disapprovingly these lines from **"A Midsummer's Holiday"** (II) where a similar image is being employed:

> Friend, the lonely land is bright for you and me
> All its wild ways through: but this methinks is best,
> Here to watch how kindly time and change agree
> Where the small town smiles, a warm still sea-side
>   nest.
>
>   (Rosenberg)

He cites these lines as an example of the decline in Swinburne's poetic powers, in contrast to successful larger-scale poems like **"By the North Sea"** or **"Evening on the Broads."** But we need to beware when we stumble across what may appear a cosy reference to pleasant days on the beach or promenade at one of the favorite Victorian bathing resorts on the south coast of England. The example Rosenberg gives may well represent a moment of insipid writing—though the very idea of a nest suggests a vulnerability. Elsewhere, we can find poems where the failure is quite evident, as in **"On the South Coast,"** whose hyperbolic treatment of its subject must bring a smile to the face of any English reader:

> Winds are glancing from sunbright Lancing to
> Shoreham, crowned with the grace of years;
> Shoreham, clad with the sunset, glad and grave with
>   glory that death reveres.

The connotations of the place name do not quite live up to such language. But there are also instances where Swinburne's use of the town image is quite devastating, such as the line in the last roundel of **"Past Days"**: "makes dull the bright small seaward towns." Another comes, infuriatingly enough in terms of the sporadic, fitful sparking into life of the later poetry, in the same sequence which yielded Rosenberg's "sea-side nest":

> Seaward goes the sun, and homeward by the down
> We, before the night upon his grave be sealed.
> Low behind us lies the bright steep murmuring town,
> High before us heaves the steep rough silent field.

"Murmuring" is an effective way of reducing humanity's bustle to something akin to the noise of insects. The passage goes on to contemplate the spectacle of collapsing cliffs in the late afternoon light, and the contrast with the town is a salutary reminder of mutability in the physical world. This confrontation with geological time and broader cycles of growth and decay causes both Powell's death and Swinburne's elegiac song to seem fleeting moments in a vast arena of time and change; thus the conclu-

sion of **"Past Days"** creates the same impression of space and emptiness that hangs about **"The Way of the Wind."**

The best of the roundels show that Swinburne was able to write with his own kind of precision in a potentially restrictive form and to achieve in miniature many of the effects he produces on the larger canvases of the longer poems. Poems like **"On an Old Roundel," "The Way of the Wind," "Past Days,"** and, to cite others not discussed here, **"The Death of Richard Wagner," "Recollections,"** and **"Three Faces,"** are hardly failures in discipline, even though their language and technique is neither metaphysically or imagistically precise in the mode of Donne or Pound. Many of the themes of the longer poems, such as impermanence, human grief, the consolations of the environment, and religious doubt, are there in the roundels. The most remarkable aspect of a poem like **"Past Days"** is that it does manage to achieve this unmistakably Swinburnian shift of the point of view, so that we find ourselves part of the elements and their time scales. Admittedly, the contrast between the "seaward towns" and the "cliffs and downs" of **"Past Days"** cannot be as marked as it is in a poem like **"Evening on the Broads."** In that poem, we have a lengthy and very elaborate evocation of sunset, sea and sand, and the inland waters, until after a hundred lines Swinburne springs a terrifyingly casual reference to standing "Here, far off in the farther extreme of the shore as it lengthens / Northward, lonely for miles, ere ever a village begin. Taken out of context, the power of these lines is a little muted, but one has a sudden apprehension of the discrepancy between the vast landscape and the tiny village. No other poet is able to get this unnerving effect and evoke a truly panoramic view of nature—nature vast, full of energy, without an informing God, bleakly beautiful. In "East Coker," Eliot laments "O dark dark dark. They all go into the dark" and proceeds with a list of different types of people. As he describes them, we watch them from inside looking out—that is, out of the familiar dwelling, the window of our narrow concerns, to the unknown. Swinburne's poetry can sometimes take us so far out into that darkness that we see the same window as nothing but a tiny speck of light in the surrounding black.

Melissa Zeiger (essay date 1986)

SOURCE: "'A Muse Funeral': The Critique of Elegy in Swinburne's 'Ave atque Vale'," in *Victorian Poetry,* Vol. 24, No. 2, Summer, 1986, pp. 173-88.

[*In the following essay, Zeiger explores Swinburne's innovative treatment of the elegaic form.*]

Elegy has traditionally been a search: until the last century, a search with a foregone conclusion. The elegist directed the elegy toward an ending in consolation, and the poem took its shape from that direction. But what does elegy seek when there can be no consolation? Where does it move, if not toward the self-ordained closure of a "Lycidas" or an "Adonais"? Different possibilities have emerged, and A. C. Swinburne offered one that would set the tone for modern elegies:

> Yet with some fancy, yet with some desire,
> Dreams pursue death as winds a flying fire,
> Our dreams pursue our dead and do not find.

The pursuit becomes primary, the *not* finding. **"Ave atque Vale"** evokes openness, mystery, enigma; it luxuriates in the baffling relation between its hypnotic surfaces and the unanswered question it poses. For modern poets, "Lycidas," with its consolation and strong closure, is the type of the old elegy, and **"Ave atque Vale"** confronts in direct dialogue both "Lycidas" itself and the burden of tradition which it represents.

The traditional elegy arrives at its resolution by a particularly linear and highly shaped narrative. The speaker begins by lamenting a death; he goes on to consider the ramifications of the individual death and of death in general, often in relation to his own life; he continues to lament until some avenue of consolation suggests itself; and he ends by rejoicing in that consolation. Elegiac consolation does not necessarily equal poetic closure, but the two overlap, and to reject the one, as Swinburne does, makes the achievement of the other problematic.

For triumphant answers, then, Swinburne substitutes echoing questions: he suggests at every turn the possibility of emptiness, of hollowness, the disturbing notion that there may be nothing beyond the surfaces which we would like to take as a promise of meaning. Religion, poetic convention, traditions of language are all just such empty promises. Thus he hollows out words, leaving us with sound and movement; he hollows out conventions, leaving tropes and patterns which, emptied of their original motive, work ironically; he places in every line of vision some image of emptiness, often of hollows within hollows, till we seem to be looking endlessly outward and downward. What perspective can we find, at that vertiginous height, from which to understand death?

"Ave atque Vale" has a purpose other than its explicit one: it serves as a critique of traditional elegy. Swinburne sets himself against not only the distant but also the recent past, in which loomed Tennyson's great elegy. *In Memoriam* must have seemed a formidable monument, epic and authoritative. But it presents a cul-de-sac for the elegist: Tennyson, unlike Milton, approaches the problems of closure in a revisionary spirit—only to turn back from them, finally, to a consolation, like Milton's, in religious faith. *In Memoriam,* moreover, comes to its consolation only after condemning elegy itself, casting that form aside for a more responsible, public utterance: something more befitting the sonorous voice of a Victorian sage. Swinburne reinstates the elegy but discards the consolation.

Swinburne's critique marks, and takes part in, the shift in poetics which will become modernism; elegy, as a form breaking with tradition in the late nineteenth century, finds ready to hand the metaphor of burying the dead past. Swinburne remakes the elegy, examining and evaluating the conventions of trope and form. These conventional elements, removed from their traditional basis in religion, emerge as the highly problematic raw material for the new elegy. We will find for the most part, in this and in most modern elegies, those conventions which further the lamentation—the procession of mourners, the shorn lock of hair, the invocation to the muses—rather than those which tend to introduce a consolation—images of returning spring, or of the beauty of the heavens (and hence the afterlife), or the transformation of the dead. The more equivocal kind appears in new roles.

Since Swinburne explicitly disallows any religious resolution, the drama for him comes not in a narrative of lament, crisis and consolation, but in a new poetic approach. His elegies do not tell a story, as classical and Christian elegies tend to do. He emphasizes the uncertainty and questioning which form the body of older elegies, but which in them is transformed by the closure of consolation. His stanzas stop, begin again, follow out a new idea, melt into trance or vision. They create for the elegy a new, unlinear shape, of relentless repetition, of unachieved closure.

When Swinburne's elegy does end, it does so only because it has proved that perception and language can pursue the subject no further, and it must move into the trance and silence which are his unorthodox version of poetic climax. Only the exploration consoles the mournful poet in **"Ave atque Vale"**: the poetic search itself provides pleasure. True consolation has been made impossible by the collapse of belief; but more importantly, **"Ave atque Vale"** presents a poetic world in which the more coherent story is no longer imaginable. In this regard, Swinburne begins the modern elegy.

The modern elegist faces a quandary. If the healing power of convention can no longer provide consolation, what is the poet to do? How can the elegiac task ever be finished? Poetic closure has been the central problem of elegy, a problem both of decorum and of structure. How may one give a shape to something as terrible and unwieldy as lamentation for a death? Are shaping and grief compatible? When may one move, without an appearance of callousness, from the lamentation? The turning toward consolation has been a moment of high drama between poet and reader, and like any good dramatic effect, it exists not only in itself, but in everything that comes before and after. What is the effect on the whole when there can be no consolation? And behind the poetic closure is a greater, but intimately related, problem of closure: the closure that is death. Elegiac closure struggles with its subject: inspired by death, it must begin as a protest against death, and yet it must leave its subject in order that the poet may go on living; therefore the elegist must finally assent to the death in question by giving up the lamentation, but still make it seem reasonable, even necessary and right, to be alive. On the one hand, the whole of such an elegy prepares for the consolation; on the other, the consolation seems to deny what has gone before. Behind this struggle is another paradoxical relation caused by the place of elegy in the literary tradition.

Harold Bloom situates elegy in the final chapter of his *Anxiety of Influence,* as the ultimate statement of the subject of his book—the rivalry of poets with their predecessors and the strategies which that rivalry takes. He describes the elegy as the poetic wish-reversal of *apophrades,* the fearful return of the dead. It is perhaps the most densely allusive of lyric forms, and whether any specific elegy situates itself in continuity with or in opposition to its antecedents, it criticizes them by implication. Sometimes it criticizes them explicitly. To complicate matters further, it often commemorates a specific antecedent—and with what strange mixture of admiration and vengefulness, one must look at the individual poems to say. Out of this welter emerges the modern elegy, with its own hesitancies and paradoxes to magnify those inherent in the form.

Swinburne modestly offers his elegy as a humble fourth to the three most famous English elegies: "Lycidas," "Adonais," and "Thyrsis." As his remark suggests, the poem is an acknowledgement of poetic influences as well as the commemoration of an individual. **"Ave atque Vale"** is most obviously in dialogue with "Lycidas," but it takes on the entire tradition. Swinburne knew his literary forbears thoroughly—Greek and Latin as well as English and French—and he shows that the conventions of elegy (presided over, in the tenth stanza, by the "Muse funereal") are still his raw materials, to be discriminated among at will.

In **"Ave atque Vale,"** Swinburne undoes the traditional structure of elegy, which closes in consolation, and creates a new, subtle kind of closure that exists almost as a parody of—certainly as an ironic counterpart to—elegy itself. He thus confronts the problem of literary tradition—and, by extension, of literary influence. He progresses on two parallel and indeed overlapping courses: he sets up the elegy as a poem that will rest in loss, rather than in regeneration; and he undoes the typical conventions of the elegy. In fact, he turns those conventions, especially those which would ordinarily herald returning joy, to the service of loss. And to supply the poetic climax thus removed, he introduces his own nonce convention: the trance state, a feature which appears throughout Swinburne's work but which, in the context of **"Ave atque Vale,"** crystallizes those issues of elegy that most occupy him.

[In *Swinburne: An Experiment in Criticism* 1972] Jerome McGann sees trance as a way of encountering the world:

> This state of trance, below or beyond ordinary consciousness, represents Swinburne's ideal of full human awareness. In such a state the light of sense goes out whereby the world is held as an aggregate of fixed things and relations. The world comes not as something to be possessed, mastered, or used but as a vitality one is to be possessed by. . . . To be mastered by that life, rapt into it, is to discover oneself to the world as a present incarnation of such life.

The trance state is Swinburne's revenge against Time, the all-destructive "secular sway / And terrene revolution of the sun" (*Atalanta in Calydon*). The trance states are a

relief from chronology: personal, literary, and historical. They also operate on the temporal quality of verse: they disrupt expectations of narrative and linguistic linearity. For a form such as the elegy, which has traditionally enacted an extremely linear and cumulative drama, the effect of such a disruption is radical.

In **"Ave atque Vale,"** trance takes the place of the closural effects which would ordinarily surround the consolation, and which suggest the implacable movement of time (within and without the poem) and the ultimate ending in death. The trances are closural, since they create a bridge or turning point from the lamentation. But since they are antilinear, an escape from time, they also work against closure. Perception fades out twice in the course of **"Ave atque Vale,"** once during the inquiry into the afterlife, and again at the end of the poem.

The epigraph to **"Ave atque Vale,"** lines from Baudelaire's own "La Servante au Grand Coeur," suggests immediately the problematic relations of the living to the dead, foreshadowing the similarly problematic relation of the living poet in particular to the dead one:

> We must nevertheless bring some flowers to her [or him]. The dead, the poor dead, have great sadnesses. And when October, the pruner of old trees, blows its melancholy wind in the vicinity of their marble tombs, then indeed they must find the living highly ungrateful.

Ironically banal, this stanza acts as a kind of miniature elegy, or mock elegy. With deadpan wit, Baudelaire points to some of the kinds of wishful fantasies elegy embodies: that we can know what death is like, that the dead are conscious, that we can communicate with them, that they are easily propitiated. He even sets the scene within the elegiac conventions of the strewing of the grave with flowers and of the death of the old year.

The epigraph, then, makes a suitable introduction to a poem which, an elegy itself, will also comment on the nature of elegy. But it creates a curious effect. Elegies often have epigraphs even though their conventional narrative pretext is (for all the artifice of the form) a spontaneous bursting forth of lamentation; artifice within artifice, the elegy conceals while displaying its literariness. Thus **"Ave atque Vale"** announces its status as poem, as made thing, before it begins. But Swinburne's choice of an epigraph from Baudelaire allows the dead Baudelaire a voice, and includes him as a ghostly presence within the body of the poem. So Swinburne's elegy is a made thing with two makers; Baudelaire's idiom will be heard throughout the poem, in Swinburne's elegant incorporation of Baudelairean metaphor and images from *Les Fleurs du Mal.* Swinburne thus acknowledges his recognition that any poem has ultimately more than one author, and that elegy must confront a particularly emphatic form of the anxiety of influence. Swinburne's epigraph would seem an unbelievably direct acknowledgment of—almost a slavish bow to—influence, if it were not for one more consideration—the power of a new context to make an extracted passage ironic. Baudelaire's detachment toward his speaker in the epigraph pales, placed as it is at the head of Swinburne's elegy, and what gains a new prominence is the condescension of the living toward the dead. We can feel and behave toward the dead as we like; and the image of Baudelaire as a discontented, petulant corpse who finds the living "bien ingrats" goes far to domesticate him. He has a good reason, too, to find Swinburne an ungrateful follower.

The black humor in Bloom's theory seems to govern the strange history of **"Ave atque Vale,"** an elegy truly brought forth by "false surmise." Swinburne wrote the poem in April of 1867 on hearing—falsely!—that Baudelaire was dead: "He had no sooner written it than he suffered the most embarrassing setback which could befall any writer of elegy. Baudelaire was still alive." The French poet really died in August 1868, and Swinburne brought out the poem in January of the following year.

The first lines treat the conventional bringing of flowers and address to the dead Baudelaire a melancholy question:

> Shall I strew on thee rose or rue or laurel,
> Brother, on this that was the veil of thee?

The lines recall the opening of "Lycidas":

> Yet once more, O ye Laurels, and once more,
> Ye myrtles brown, with Ivy never sere,
> I come to pluck your Berries harsh and crude.

Milton's speaker already knows what kind of shrub and what kind of poem he wants to offer to the mourned person. He gives less of a sense of having to make his way among the conventions. They bend to him, not vice versa. Later, he will return to the subject in an extended catalogue of flowers, a convention borrowed from classical elegy. But the flower catalogue, traditionally a bridge between grief and consolation and occurring late in the poem, dominates the whole of **"Ave atque Vale."** There, it comments on the progress of the poem. The flower catalogue in "Lycidas" announces itself as a metaphor for poetry too; in that poem, however, it has served as a distraction "to interpose a little ease."

Swinburne now must ponder the appropriate way to mourn Baudelaire. He summons the powers which have always motivated elegy—rose (love and the life-force); rue (grief and memory); and laurel (poetry and the desire for fame). He considers also the French poet's own mode of "Half-faded fiery blossoms" in the *Fleurs du Mal* (passionate and vital, but already partaking of death), and the traditional pastoral of "meadow-sweet or sorrel, / Such as the summer-sleepy Dryads weave," and his personal trope for poetry of "quiet sea-flower moulded by the sea." He will carry this conceit through the poem, pondering, with increasing pessimism, the possibility of poetic growth for the belated poet. Unlike Milton, Swinburne seems to hesitate, to be unable to choose.

In appearing to ponder explicitly the conventional choices, however, Swinburne has already chosen a convention, a formal one, by beginning with a rhetorical question. In doing so, he follows the traditional pattern of elegy, rather than differs from it. These questions abound in elegy because they record the mourner's frustration with his distance from his subject and, more generally, with the enigmatic nature of death and of a universe predicated upon death. That angry uncertainty takes the form of an anxiety about the continuance of the art:

> Who, ah, who will ever make music on thy pipe, O
> thrice-desired Bion, and who will put his mouth
> to the reeds of thine instrument? who is so bold?
> (Moschus, "The Lament for Bion")

or of a reproach to the guardian powers:

> Where were ye Nymphs when the remorseless
> deep
> Clos'd o'er the head of your lov'd *Lycidas?*
> ("Lycidas," ll. 50-51)

or else it expresses its ontological nature outright:

> Whence are we, and why are we? of what scene
> The actors or spectators?
> (Shelley, "Adonais," ll. 184-185)

Swinburne's questions resonate with other questions native to elegy: How may one honor the dead man? And what significance does the act of homage hold? How does the living poet find his relation to the dead one? By extension, how is that death related to one's own death? And most importantly, what does one do now? Swinburne's elegy will continue to question and to worry its own questions.

Swinburne proceeds to treat such questions by denying the answers suggested by traditional elegy. Immediately, he undermines the associations which might have led to a consolation. He invokes Sappho, "the supreme head of song," a great predecessor to Baudelaire. Her fame, or poetic legacy, or ascension to heaven might conceivably be made to redeem her death. But Swinburne never moves beyond the site of her death, the Ionian Sea whose waves bear her "Hither and thither, and vex and work her wrong, / Blind gods that cannot spare." The second line reiterates the sense of enforced distance from the subject which the first line has set up: the bedecking with flowers concerns not Baudelaire himself but "this that was the veil" of him. The living body as well as the corpse is an empty sign, and Swinburne is removed from Baudelaire not only by death and physical distance, but also by the essential unknowableness of the other. If the soul of another is hidden during life, how can one hope to know its fate after death?

Like Wordsworth's Lucy, Sappho is "rolled round" in the elements, undergoing an unbenign metamorphosis inflicted by indifferent, will-less forces. Here is no sympathetic mourning of nature, and Sappho's drowning will not be redeemed, like that of Lycidas, by an apotheosis. Older elegies call up the ugliness and horror of the decaying corpse, but in order finally to overcome it. Images such as the corpse which "welter[s] to the parching wind"

("Lycidas"), "Invisible Corruption" waiting "at the door" ("Adonais,"), and even bones "wrapt about" by the roots of the yew (*In Memoriam*), give over to images of extreme beauty: the Genius of the shore, the star "burning through the inmost veil of Heaven," the "diffusive power" felt in the universe. Swinburne and an increasing number of elegists after him retain the horror, come back insistently to the fact of the dead body: the "effaced unprofitable eyes" of the dead; Baudelaire's "dust" and "unmelodious mouth" which undergo no transformation into beauty and meaning. The emptiness of the corpse as sign in Swinburne's poem suggests that the transcendent afterlife to which death traditionally points in the elegy is also hollow. Certainly "Ave atque Vale" is especially concerned with an inquiry into the nature of that afterlife, but in terms which mock the search and the elegiac conventions surrounding that search.

Elegy partakes of the general futility:

> not all our songs, O friend,
> Will make death clear or make life durable.
>
> (XVI)

The poet perseveres in song nonetheless:

> with wild notes about this dust of thine
> At least I fill the place where white dreams dwell
> And wreathe an unseen shrine.
>
> (XVI)

The place of the white dreams must certainly indicate, as is generally held, that traditional province of the elegy, "the abode of the ghosts of the dead." But Swinburne gives it a new dimension as well; he makes it the realm, ambiguous and shifting (like so many of Swinburne's symbolic places), of fantasy—that fantasy which includes, indeed, our imaginings of the "faint fields" of afterlife but also that fantasy which is poetic production. An empty page looks very much like a place where white dreams dwell. The image calls attention to the fact of our reading, our contact with the words on the page. But it denies their status as words too; it makes them into inarticulately expressive "wild notes." The urge to fill up paper with poems is related to the urge to know what happens after one is dead; both are fantastic leaps into the unknown, working in language but aiming beyond it. Fantasy is the link; poems can go where people cannot, can "wreathe an unseen shrine." The uncertainty of what is next drives the poet on.

Swinburne celebrates in Baudelaire's poetry a refusal, similar to his own, to fall in with convention. He sees in *Fleurs du Mal* a realm of poetic imagination beyond language, beyond human experience, essentially solitary:

> Secrets and sorrows unbeheld of us:
> Fierce loves, and lovely leaf-buds poisonous,
> Bare to thy subtler eye, but for none other
> Blowing by night in some unbreathed-in clime.
>
> (III)

The poetry of trance, in short. This stanza envisions Baudelaire as operating, like Swinburne himself, within a newly conceived structure of meaning. Their conventions are, defiantly, nonce conventions. But the fact remains that the trance poem is tied both to time and to meaning, its very antagonists, and so its failure is inextricably tied to its success. The transience of the pleasure in self-abandon qualifies it, to be sure, but deepens it as well. Any investigation of death is just such a doomed venture, and successful failure is crucial to "Ave atque Vale."

Swinburne emphasizes the uncertainty and questioning which form the body of older elegies, but which in them is transformed by the closure of consolation. . . . They create for the elegy a new, unlinear shape, of relentless repetition, of unachieved closure.

—Melissa Zeiger

Swinburne's subject, then, remains not the movement toward consolation but the persistence of loss. The fourth stanza, with its pattern of negations, of "no"s and "-less"es, suggests at once the pain of generating such poetry (the pain which makes the poet long for trance or for death) and the pain of remaining behind in bereavement and ignorance:

> O sleepless heart and sombre soul unsleeping,
>   That were athirst for sleep and no more life
>   . . . . .
>   Is it well now where love can do no wrong,
> Where stingless pleasure has no foam or fang?

That fourth stanza initiates the inquiry into the nature of the afterlife with which the rest of the poem will be concerned. An ironic exploration, as Kerry McSweeney notes [in *Tennyson and Swinburne as Romantic Naturalists* 1981], because,

> as the . . . faintly mocking tone suggests . . . these questions are rhetorical. The answer they presuppose is: No, death is not at all like life and if it were (so the tone insinuates), it would be distastefully stale and insipid. Swinburne's point is George Santayana's: 'When . . . it is clearly seen that another life, to supplement this one, must closely resemble it, does not the magic of immortality altogether vanish'?

The quest assumes its own failure.

The first hallucinatory image of that afterlife comes from Baudelaire's own poem, "La Geante," with one of the female figures of grief who further the poem's concentration on loss:

> Hast thou found place at the great knees and feet
> Of some pale Titan-woman like a lover,
>   Such as thy vision here solicited,
>   Under the shadow of her fair vast head,

The deep division of prodigious breasts,
    The solemn slope of mighty limbs asleep,
    The weight of awful tresses that still keep
The savour and shade of old-world pine-forests
    Where the wet hill-winds weep?

                          (VI)

The giantess resembles the other women who have appeared and will appear in this elegy—Sappho, Proserpine, Venus, and Niobe—in being a traditional figure of grief. But all except Niobe are also periodically comforted figures of joy or abundance as well. Swinburne fixes them in their role as symbols of mourning: Venus—"That obscure Venus of the hollow hill"—"stains with tears her changing bosom chill"; Sappho's kisses are "salt and sterile" and she is lost in the sea; Proserpine is veiled, in "The low light" of Hades and surrounded by "unregarded tears"; the earth is like Niobe, empty-wombed, "chill," and "in the hollow of her breasts a tomb." All are larger than life, silent, deeply associated with a wintry land—or seascape— the "old-world pine-forests," Venus' Nordic Horsel, Proserpine's yearly stay underground corresponding to Ceres' winter vigil above. All are emblems of emptiness. And all suggest unmotherly mothers: women bereft of their children, or sterile, or huge and ominously distant.

McGann notes the near identity in **"Laus Veneris"** of Venus and Proserpine, arguing that "the Proserpine/Venus of **"Ave atque Vale"**

> becomes in the elegy a positive source of power and sympathy, an ideal figure to be solicited as a source not only of sleep, rest, and death, but also of eternal life, power, and light. The difference between the fallen Venuses of **"Laus Veneris"** and **"Ave atque Vale"** is simply this: in the former poem she is not associated with Proserpine whereas in the latter she is. Tannhäuser cannot die, being an unnatural, that is, a Christian, believer, but Baudelaire, the believer in the Proserpine/Venus, can and does. Tannhäuser is cut off from the motions and continuities of natural cycle; Baudelaire is not.

While McGann is right to acknowledge Baudelaire's affinity with Proserpine, he misinterprets the quality of the natural cycles of **"Ave atque Vale."** Like the hero of classical pastoral elegy, Baudelaire represents here a dying spirit of nature. The trouble is that he is not going to be brought back; the natural cycle in Swinburne's elegy is in fact no longer cyclic. Northrop Frye locates the movement of elegy in the repetitive aspects of nature—death is associated with sunset, winter, and sea; rebirth with sunrise, spring, and land. Logically, then, hope returns with spring in the flower catalogue. But for Swinburne nature is not reborn; final death, rather, threatens to replace cyclic regeneration. Venus appears in both **"Ave atque Vale"** and **"Laus Veneris"** as a moribund life-force. And **"Ave atque Vale"** ends with Frye's death images: the "chill" earth, Baudelaire "whose days are done," the stillness or sunset over the sea where "all winds are quiet as the sun, / All waters as the shore."

Swinburne's version of repetition does not move outward toward completion in a product, but inward toward self-

enclosure. This unending repetition threatens in previous elegy; according to C. Alphonso Smith, a contemporary of Swinburne,

> The elegiac mood, in which the thought turns back so often upon itself, is best voiced by some form of repetition. It is seen in David's cry: "Oh my son Absalom! my son, my son Absalom! would God I had died for thee, O Absalom, my son, my son!"

Usually, the repetition ends in the turn toward consolation; not so in **"Ave atque Vale,"** where repetition predominates but without moving toward any end. [In *Swinburne,* 1929] Samuel C. Chew says of the rhyme scheme of **"Ave atque Vale"**—ABBA, then a couplet, twice—that "the effect of this intermediate couplet is to bring the music to a pause, after which it mournfully renews itself." The short final line of each stanza intensifies the compulsive quality of this movement, as though the speaker paused in weariness and then urged himself on. And T. Earle Welby, Swinburne's first biographer, had earlier noted (Swinburnianly!) that **"Ave atque Vale"** afforded

> a supremely good example of flow and check, repetition and variation, of pure and stately diction, of phrasing that tightens on the substance without constricting it, of metrical movement precisely adjusted to the impulses and pauses and sad returns on itself of the thought!

           [*A Study of Swinburne,* 1926]

Swinburne's poetic narrative is not linear, not chronological: it moves outside of time. It wants to escape from time, and instead of tending toward the "poised repose" of the elegy that achieves consolation, it remains suspended in a kind of marine flux—like the unfortunate Sappho.

So even the cyclic fecundity of poetry is in question:

Hast thou found any likeness for thy vision?
    O gardener of strange flowers, what bud, what
        bloom,
    Hast thou found sown, what gathered in the
        gloom?

                          (VII)

Poetic flowers, whether *Fleurs du Mal* or some other sort, may well not transplant to the world below, and the silence of that world strikes a pessimistic note for poetry:

Does the dim ground grow any seed of ours,
    The faint fields quicken any terrene root,
    In low lands where the sun and moon are mute
And all the stars keep silence?

                          (VII)

This silence threatens, in several respects, to be catching: because the poet may be baffled by the enormity of his incomprehension; because his sense of himself as a belated poet may deprive him of inspiration; most obviously, because he too will die. The project of elegy becomes an urgent struggle: he writes so that he may keep on writing.

The only world of vitality, nonetheless, is this highly provisional world shared by poets. Stanza VIII treats—with utmost delicacy—the painfully charged relation between living and dead poet:

> Alas, but though my flying song flies after,
>   O sweet strange elder singer, thy more fleet
>   Singing, and footprints of thy fleeter feet,
> Some dim derision of mysterious laughter
>   From the blind tongueless warders of the dead,
>   . . . . .
> Some little sound of unregarded tears
>   Wept by effaced unprofitable eyes,
>   And from pale mouths some cadence of dead
>   sighs—
> These only, these the hearkening spirit hears,
>   Sees only such things rise.

The opening of this stanza, in its reference to Baudelaire's "more fleet / Singing," suggests more than the conventional complimentary disclaimer of worthiness to commemorate the noble dead. It relays also the post-Romantic obsession with having missed the appropriate era for writing poetry. This obsession will, in various guises, dominate the mood of the rest of the poem. For the moment, however, Swinburne displaces it.

In this instance, the anxiety of influence tries to hide by fading imperceptibly into a comment on elegy. Inquiry into the afterlife meets only with the frustration of meeting more veils, more unspeaking mouths: "Proserpine's veiled head," "the blind tongueless warders of the dead." The echo in this last of the "blind mouths" of "Lycidas" suggests the spiritual decline that has taken place; the gods themselves, not merely their earthly representatives, are now degenerate. Even the wicked, ravening energy of the priests' self-regard has abated: they figure now as the emblem of inaccessibility and mutilation.

Swinburne reiterates the impossibility of closure here in a tonal shift downwards. Darkness and silence begin to dominate this section, as they continue to do in the whole poem. This stubborn silence, more intense even than elsewhere in Swinburne, contrasts with the earlier elegy, loud in its lamentation—

> Begin then, Sisters of the sacred well,
>   . . . . .
> Begin, and somewhat loudly sweep the string

("Lycidas," ll. 15-17)

—and loud in its triumphant consolation:

> There entertain him all the Saints above,
> In solemn troops, and sweet Societies
> That sing, and singing in their glory move.

("Lycidas," ll. 178-180)

Adonais, initially wept by Urania, "Most musical of mourners," (l. 28) is finally

> made one with Nature; there is heard
> His voice in all her music, from the moan
> Of thunder, to the song of night's sweet bird.

(ll. 370-372)

Swinburne's maneuver of displacement has moved him away from one possible impasse, but face to face with another. Perhaps the question he is asking about the afterlife is so unanswerable, so rhetorical, that speech is simply futile. Perhaps it is impossible to ask the question in any meaningful way and that is why everything seems so silent.

> Thou art far too far for wings of words to follow,
>   Far too far off for thought or any prayer.
>   What ails us with thee, who art wind and air?
> What ails us gazing where all seen is hollow?

(IX)

What ails us is partly that speech itself is suspect, even if not being asked to move beyond the limits of human knowledge. We are calling across a void in any attempt to achieve meaning. The void of death to which Swinburne refers simply particularizes the problem.

In fact, that very emptiness becomes a motivation for poetry. In the first stanza, Baudelaire's dead body appears as an emptiness, as an imagined sight so unreadable that it stops thought. But now Swinburne finds a way to make that enigma motivate rather than repel inquiry. The hollowness becomes energy:

> Yet with some fancy, yet with some desire,
>   Dreams pursue death as winds a flying fire,
> Our dreams pursue our dead and do not find.

(IX)

The vacuum creates a force, pulling dreams—and thought, words, and poems, which for Swinburne are of the same stuff as dreams—after it. Swinburne finds in vacuum the impulse of poetry, and especially the impulse of elegy. This surging impulse gives him a sense of communion with Baudelaire, a communion mingled nonetheless with loss:

> Not thee, O never thee, in all time's changes,
>   Not thee, but this the sound of thy sad soul,
>   The shadow of thy swift spirit, this shut
>   scroll
> I lay my hand on, and not death estranges
>   My spirit from communion of thy song.

This tenth stanza is the one upon which arguments for a consolation in **"Ave atque Vale"** generally rest.

And if the elegy ended here, these lines would perhaps resolve the poem, leave the reader with consolation—although in the most muted way possible. The stanza does, in fact, form a turning point in the tone and content of the poem. But the shift is downward, into a quieter, deeper tone of despairing resignation. Swinburne sees himself as the last of the line of poets: "The youngest . . . singer / That England bore" (**"In Memory of Walter Savage Landor"**).

The tenth stanza is a lonely moment of glory, the loneliness of which is heightened rather than mitigated by the presence of the literary relic. The lines are ambiguous: is "shut scroll" the subject of "estranges"—suggesting the darker side of poetic influence—or does "not death estranges" mean "death can never estrange," suggesting some indissoluble bond? In either event, Baudelaire is at a greater distance than ever: "this that was the veil of thee" has become "this shut scroll." And, "As though a hand were in my hand to hold" recalls the loneliness of *In Memoriam*: "my heart was used to beat / So quickly, waiting for a hand, / A hand that can be clasped no more."

Poetry possesses a limited power. It cannot restore life or ward off death, but perhaps it can create something like a moment of contact—between Swinburne as reader and Baudelaire as poet, between Swinburne as poet and Baudelaire as subject. In looking at these complicated interrelations, Swinburne locates the point of intersection in poems about death: both poets have written them, prompted by the muse of elegy, the "Muse funereal":

> These memories and these melodies that throng
> Veiled porches of a Muse funereal—
>   These I salute, these touch, these clasp and fold
>   As though a hand were in my hand to hold,
> Or through mine ears a mourning musical
>   Of many mourners rolled.
>
> (X)

So the mourning continues, and Swinburne offers his tribute of poetry to Baudelaire, a poetry which partakes of its time and place:

> what of honey and spice my seedlands bear,
> And what I may of fruits in this chilled air.
>
> (XI)

The chilled air is, of course, that of England, in contrast to the tropical "bitter summer" evoked in the first stanza, its fruits recalling also the unknown seed, "faint fields," and fruit of the underworld in stanza VII. Even more importantly, it suggests the decline of poetry which he is about to mourn. The following two stanzas describe a wasting Apollo:

> For, sparing of his sacred strength, not often
>   Among us darkling here the lord of light
>   Makes manifest his music and his might.
>
> (XIII)

> he too now at thy soul's sunsetting,
>   God of all suns and songs, he too bends down
>   To mix his laurel with thy cypress crown,
> And save thy dust from blame and from forgetting.
>
> (XIV)

Significantly enough, Apollo appears not, as he does in "Lycidas," to comfort the mourner, but instead to add to the lamentation. Moreover, he comes with no gift of poetic power or promise of fame—he must conserve what little "of his sacred strength" he still has. Apollo, like Venus in the

next stanza, is "A ghost, a bitter and luxurious god"; and so his gesture of homage to Baudelaire is an ambiguous one. When he mixes "his laurel with [Baudelaire's] cypress crown," does he bestow fame or partake of mortality?

Swinburne associates poetry with warmth and fire and light,

> In hearts that open and in lips that soften
>   With the soft flame and heat of songs that
>   shine.
>
> (XIII)

But Baudelaire has reached the sunset of his soul; he is dust, his eyes are sunless. Is Swinburne suggesting that the kind of poetry Baudelaire wrote hastened his end, attuned him to mortality? His "Half-faded fiery blossoms," his "sick flowers of secrecy and shade," suggest a being which forsees and is even intertwined with its own end. To Baudelaire, "past the end," Swinburne says that "the end and the beginning / Are one thing"; perhaps they have always been for Baudelaire. This is the despondent key in which the elegy ends. In "Lycidas," foreknowledge of everlasting life helps to minimize the fear of death; in the modern elegy, the knowledge that death will come helps to undermine the meaning of life. And yet it is this break with conventional consolation which allows the poem to continue. Swinburne, ever contradictory, commemorates the death of poetry in verse. [In the *Georgia Review,* 1977] Leslie Brisman finds the source of Swinburne's power in just such paradox; in Swinburne's "difficult grammar," "in the newly asserted freedom from the conventions of speech and the conventions of morality—freedoms, either way, from referentiality to preexistent objects and codes—man finds his potentiality and his humanness." In an ultimate paradox, therefore, the shift from consolation—the central convention of elegy—supplies a new kind of consolation.

The sixteenth stanza confirms this tonal shift downward: "And now no sacred staff shall break in blossom." Tannhäuser's reprieve is not to be looked for. Nor shall he be greeted, Lycidas-like, with "choral saluation." Elegy itself does no good:

> not all our songs, O friend,
> Will make death clear or make life durable.
>   Howbeit with rose and ivy and wild vine
>   And with wild notes about this dust of thine
> At least I fill the place where white dreams dwell
>   And wreathe an unseen shrine.
>
> (XVI)

He has finally chosen his flowers: the rose, flower of passion, and ivy and wild vine, associated in his verse with Bacchanalian scenes. They mark the intensity and persistence of his task, but finally they only decorate. Their vitality, too, is on the wane, and with their energy dies that of the last stanza:

> For thee, O now a silent soul, my brother,
>   Take at my hands this garland, and farewell.
>   Thin is the leaf, and chill the wintry smell,

And chill the solemn earth, a fatal mother,
　　With sadder than the Niobean womb,
　　And in the hollow of her breasts a tomb.
Content thee, howsoe'er, whose days are done;
　　There lies not any troublous thing before,
　　Nor sight nor sound to war against thee more,
For whom all winds are quiet as the sun,
　　All waters as the shore.

Instead of anticipating, with the weary but vital swain, a move onward—"Tomorrow to fresh woods, and pastures new"—we are left with the dead Baudelaire, "For whom all winds are quiet as the sun, / All waters as the shore." We leave the economical concreteness of pasture and wood, the vigor suggested by the adjectival chiasmus (fresh woods, and pastures new), by the strong closure of the single ottava rima, by the half-open final vowel, by the confident iambic. Instead we get the sense of almost imageless vast space, of a drifting off, in the short last line, on the sighing open "o" of "shore."

Harold Bloom says that the consolation for Swinburne in this elegy is that he has consigned Baudelaire to eternal oblivion. That is certainly an incidental pleasure, but the greater one has to do with his genre, with the exploration he has set in motion. He has reexamined the basic premises of elegy, not merely dismissed them, by reopening possibilities for the form. In its most radical aspect, then, **"Ave atque Vale"** accomplishes the most conventional goal of elegy: a regeneration.

James Richardson (essay date 1988)

SOURCE: "Purity and Pain," in *Vanishing Lives: Style and Self in Tennyson, D. G. Rossetti, Swinburne, and Yeats,* University Press of Virginia, 1988, pp. 116-36.

[*In the following essay, Richardson provides a thematic and stylistic analysis of Swinburne's verse.*]

We had stood as the sure stars stand, and moved
　　As the moon moves, loving the world; and
　　　　seen
Grief collapse as a thing disproved,
　　Death consume as a thing unclean.
　　　　　　　　　　"The Triumph of Time"

Less a personality than, as he might have put it, a shoreline, Swinburne is visible only as the hypnotically shifting border of land and sea, solidity and fluidity, cold strength and smothering passion. Because he lacks the patience and—though it may seem strange to say this of a man so eccentric and explosive—the self-indulgence of his mentor Rossetti, Swinburne can dwell only briefly in the Rossettian closeness

　　Covered with love as a covering tree,
　　　　　. . . . .
　　Filled from the heart to the lips with love,
　　Held fast in his hands, clothed warm with his wings.

Though such swarming passions continuously inform his poetry, they are qualified, sometimes by enthusiastic wit, sometimes by poisonous guilt, and most often by that most remarkable aspect of Swinburne—his drive toward cold clarity, impossible innocence, superhuman strength, inhuman purity.

"The Leper" is an instructive example. The story of an apparent rapist and necrophiliac who imagines that intercourse with an at first unwilling and later dead leper is love "well seen of me and her" should be nearly unreadable. But **"The Leper"** is hardly even shocking. It is almost a critical venture in that it so consciously, almost self-consciously, exploits the voyeurism of Victorian poetry—its fondness for maidens dead, swooning, sleeping, or merely unaware—to discover its limits. But like Browning's "Porphyria's Lover" (from which, along with Morris's "The Wind," it clearly derives, and whose conclusion it echoes), **"The Leper"** transforms violence less with critical distance than with terrifying *innocence*:

It may be all my love went wrong—
　　A scribe's work writ awry and blurred,
Scrawled after the blind evensong—
　　Spoilt music with no perfect word.

But surely I would fain have done
　　All things the best I could. Perchance
Because I failed, came short of one,
　　She kept at heart that other man's.

I am grown blind with all these things:
　　It may be now she hath in sight
Some better knowledge; still there clings
　　The old question. Will not God do right?

On its own terms—those of the clear confusions of a dream, "A scribe's work writ awry and blurred"—**"The Leper"** is not revolting but strangely poignant. In order to be repelled by the corruption and closeness seemingly inherent in the situation, one must step outside the speaker's hallucinatory detachment and deliberately—and with some difficulty—reliteralize the narrative. The residue of the poem as it demands to be read is not diseased flesh but delicacy, naiveté, chill purity:

Nothing is better, I well know,
　　Than love; no amber in cold sea
Or gathered berries under snow:
　　That is well seen of her and me.

The Swinburnean poles of closeness and clean power exhibited by **"The Leper"** appear alternately and more typically in **"Laus Veneris,"** Swinburne's version of the Tannhäuser legend:

Inside the Horsel here the air is hot;
Right little peace one hath for it, God wot;
　　The scented dusty daylight burns the air,
And my heart chokes me till I hear it not.

Behold, my Venus, my soul's body, lies
With my love laid upon her garment-wise,

> Feeling my love in all her limbs and hair
> And shed between her eyelids through her eyes.
> . . . . .
> Ah yet would God this flesh of mine might be
> Where air might wash and long leaves cover me,
> Where tides of grass break into foam of flowers,
> Or where the wind's feet shine along the sea.

Virtually swamped with love, the second of these stanzas would have made a worthy (and almost undetectable) addition to *The House of Life.* But there may be a shade of almost boyish comedy in the emphatic alliteration of *Horsel-here-hot* and the rhyme *God wot,* and this distance predicts the more convincing "would God." Smothered in this humid interior, the knight yearns for the purity and high windy light of the seacoast, Swinburne's truest element. Swinburne is more convincing than Tennyson or Rossetti at both luridness and heroic freshness, though he can hardly hold them apart, as here in **"The Triumph of Time"**:

> Sea, that art clothed with the sun and the rain,
> Thy sweet hard kisses are strong like wine,
> Thy large embraces are keen like pain.
> Save me and hide me with all thy waves,
> Find me one grave of thy thousand graves,
> Those pure cold populous graves of thine
> Wrought without hand in a world without stain.
>
> I shall sleep, and move with the moving ships,
> Change as the winds change, veer in the tide;
> My lips will feast on the foam of thy lips,
> I shall rise with thy rising, with thee subside.

What is remarkable here is the near simultaneity of Swinburne's three intensest loves. One—the faintest—is guiltily painful, poisonous, insidiously damaging. The second, exhilarating, is vast, cold, impersonal, heroic—as clean as those "pure cold populous graves." The third, in the troughs of the waves, is rest, oblivion. All three are imaged in the sea, as they might, in another moment, all be imaged in a woman, for there are few fixed symbols in Swinburne. There are instead perceptions. The meaning of objects in his poetic landscape is determined by the hardness or softness of the love felt in them at any given moment—their balance of cruelty, tenderness, coldness, shame, purity, pain, passion.

The Hades of rest is an inevitable subdivision of Victorian consciousness, and it is especially important in Swinburne who, more strongly than any of his contemporaries, feels the Keatsian inseparability of pleasure and pain. As the most intense of the Victorian poets, he also exhibits the most intense longing to sleep and be done. In his various and without exception touching renderings, Hades is the image of the elegiac consciousness, an existence, in Browning's words for Andrea del Sarto, "all toned down":

> I wish we were dead together to-day,
> Lost sight of, hidden away out of sight,
> Clasped and clothed in the cloven clay,

> Out of the world's way, out of the light,
> Out of the ages of worldly weather,
> Forgotten of all men altogether,
> As the world's first dead, taken wholly away,
> Made one with death, filled full of the night.
> How we should slumber, how we should sleep,
> Far in the dark with the dreams and the dews!
> And dreaming, grow to each other, and weep,
> Laugh low, live softly, murmur and muse.

"As the world's first dead"—the image is at once stunning and almost touchingly possessive, both faded and fresh. Hades, where "subtler natures taste in air less dense / A life less thick and palpable than ours," is the dimness of life, the only refuge from Swinburne's round of furious and painful loves. Elsewhere, pain is inextricable from intensity, inextricable also from clarity, purity, strength. This bears directly on the well-known but often only half-read **"Hymn to Proserpine."** It is not merely that its pagan speaker resists Christian immortality in his desire for the oblivion of sleep, for he laments not only Proserpine, queen of Hades, but Apollo, "a bitter God to follow, a beautiful God to behold." The new regime denies not only the possibility of eternal sleep, but, within life, denies intensity by separating pain and pleasure. When he exclaims "Thou hast conquered, O pale Galilean; the world has grown grey from thy breath," he regrets not only the new deathlessness but the accompanying new lifelessness.

Hardly anyone has failed to notice Swinburne's idiosyncratic rhythmic textures but the reports of readers are strangely contradictory. "Swinburne's most novel rhythms are those which are extremely speedy and those which are extremely languorous," says E. K. Brown [in *Victorian Literature: Modern Essays in Criticism,* edited by Austin Wright, 1961], and Lionel Stevenson notes his "two distinctive"—and seemingly opposite—"effects, speed and emphasis" [*The Pre-Raphaelite Poets,* 1974]. [In *Swinburne: The Critical Heritage,* edited by Clyde K. Hyder, 1970] Saintsbury cites Swinburne's "impulse to quicken, to quick time," but his absolutely accurate statement that "the intricate and massive stanza of **'The Triumph of Time'** swells and swings like a wave" seems to describe quite other qualities than speed. The implied confusion about the velocity of Swinburne's verse should be reminiscent of the discussion of Tennysonian flow above, and leads to similar conclusions about Swinburne's desynchronized apprehension of time— that speed and languor are simultaneous, without contradiction, and without strain. Take the stanza of **"A Forsaken Garden"**:

> In a coign of the cliff between lowland and highland,
> At the sea-down's edge between windward
> and lee,
> Walled round with rocks as an inland island,
> The ghost of a garden fronts the sea.
> A girdle of brushwood and thorn encloses
> The steep square slope of the blossomless bed
> Where the weeds that grew green from the graves
> of its roses
> Now lie dead.

Brown uses this stanza as an example of Swinburne at his most languorous and dirgelike, and one certainly knows what he means. But no matter how slowly the stanza is read, a complementary impression of speed will not disappear. This is partly a matter of the uneven pacing of lines composed of blends of duple and triple feet. The unstressed syllables of an anapest (of the cliff) are read quickly to make it equivalent in time to the disyllabic feet. Accordingly, slowness is felt not in isolation but as the restraint of a swiftness somehow inherent in the lines, a wavelike swell and fall.

Swinburne's mixture of double and triple feet results in a rhythmic undulation at once more exaggerated and more effortless than Rossetti's. The texture of the lines is unlike Rossetti's "arduous fulness," and even farther from Browning. Swinburne's counter-motions meet, like Tennyson's, without standard tension. We are conscious of changes in gravity, of acceleration and deceleration, moving up and down to go forward. Change is rapid, progress slow—the lines become their own restraint. This dovetails with the brooding, obsessive quality of Swinburne's emotions, and is supported by myriad habits of sound.

The alternation of masculine and feminine rhymes, sets up a second wavelike motion. The weakly rhymed lines seem to end only tentatively and are somehow not complete until the strong rhyme of the following line. Consequently, the motions of the lines cross as if—to push Saintsbury's wave metaphor—they were inrushing and subsiding waves. (What is in question here, of course, is not an accurate "depiction" of the ocean, but the Swinburnean swell and fall of emotion that led him to feel his strange and exhilarating kinship with the sea in the first place). Then, too, in "the weeds that grew green from the graves of its roses," each element—*weeds-grew-green-graves-roses*—repeats a previous sound, drops one, adds another, in a kind of relay that provides an illusion of momentum. In the end, the line returns figuratively to earth, but momentum, surviving the qualifications of meaning, surges on into the suddenly short line "Now lie dead." Too small to quite disperse the motion, the line is perceived in terms of *reticence,* which is, after all, the transfer of motion from reluctant words to willing reader. The reticence Hardy and Browning achieve with metrical roughness, understatement, or irony, Swinburne here produces with an almost imperceptible blend of motions. The effect is exaggerated and perhaps even more moving when the words in the short line are in themselves general and inconclusive:

> So long have the grey bare walks lain guestless,
> > Through branches and briars if a man make
> > > way,
> He shall find no life but the sea-wind's, restless
> > > Night and day.

The motion that swells through this ambiguous closure, that of endless ending, is inescapably Swinburnean.

But lest the Swinburnean tone seem inherent in the bare outline of a rhythmic pattern rather than in his special adaptations, it should be pointed out, on one hand, that

Hardy, a vastly different poet, uses similar blends of double and triple feet—arranged, syllabified, and paused differently—and, on the other, that this logaoedic rhythm has in general been used for comic verse. In his superlative study of poetic rhythm, Derek Attridge [in *The Rhythms of English Poetry,* 1982] summarizes the difficulties of triple rhythms:

> Duple rhythms are much commoner than triple in the English literary tradition, and it is worth asking why this should be so. . . . One feature of English speech [is] the tendency towards an alternation of stronger and weaker stresses; verse in duple metre embodies this tendency as its basic rhythmic principle, and is therefore able to draw on the full resources of the spoken language, accommodating polysyllables and stretches of monosyllables with relative ease. Triple metres, on the other hand, have to work against this tendency in order to create an alternative rhythmic pattern, which can tolerate certain words only by suppressing their natural stress contours. Moreover, duple verse matches the two rhythmic principles of English, the stress-timed rhythm and the syllabic rhythm, by providing one syllable for a rhythmic peak and one for a trough; triple verse, on the other hand, favours stress-timing, both in its implied equivalence of one strong to two weak syllables, and in its overriding of the alternations of the language. This alliance with the stronger, and probably more fundamental, rhythmic principle produces a prominent rhythm that tends to simplify the contours of speech. A strong triple rhythm will often force a bad poet (or even tempt a good one) to subordinate semantic and syntactic choices to metrical choices, producing verse which is more gesture than expression.

"Gesture" has its obvious dangers, but is alien neither to Swinburne's aspirations to the condition of music, nor to his virtually symphonic mode of thinking, nor to his preference for emotion that has not yet quite specified itself in words. And his meter, for all its limitations, turns out to have other advantages. In triple or mixed meters, the stress pattern, as Attridge notes, must be strongly marked. The differential—difference in value between stressed and unstressed syllables—of such lines is high. And it is relatively rigidly enforced—we are less likely to hear several degrees of stress among the stressed syllables. This evenness of emphasis counteracts some of the dipody native to the tetrameter but potential even in the pentameter, as in the Tennyson line "The woods decaý, the woods decaý and fall." Swinburne's stresses, in contrast, tend to retain one high value throughout the line—"I have pút my daýs and dreams out of mind"—and the effect, though potentially wearying, is more often that of an enforced monotone, a strong restraint. This is true especially when the line is heavily monosyllabic. And despite one's aftermemory of a certain ornateness in Swinburne's poems (this is the residuum of the heavy patterning of sound and rhythm, and the blurring of individual words, not the actual quality of the diction) he is in fact among the most monosyllabic poets in the language. Rosenberg justly praises him as the master of "the bleak beauty of little words" [Introduction to *Swinburne: Selected Poetry and Prose,* 1968].

Swinburne, indeed, learned to put this fierce monotone, with its suggestion of awful stoicism, even into the strictly duple blank verse of *Atalanta*;

> Night, a black hound, follows the white fawn day,
> Swifter than dreams the white flown feet of sleep;
> Will ye pray back the night with any prayers?
> And though the spring put back a little while
> Winter, and snows that plague all men for sin,
> And the iron time of cursing, yet I know
> Spring shall be ruined with the rain, and storm
> Eat up like fire the ashen autumn days.

The verse, in its severe deliberation, is almost reversed. It favors initial trochees after breaks which, despite their steepness, carry forward little momentum, and its most conspicuous caesuras are early—they devour momentum. With its monosyllabic drag, its tendency to bridge over the normal positions for the medial caesural sag, and its evenness of stressing, the passage hints at the ferocious restraint, the terrible dismissal of love by Althaea, that will make *Atalanta in Calydon* the greatest of the Victorian verse dramas.

In stichic verse, moreover, unconfined by the stanza or by Rossettian agoraphobia, Swinburne can push his paradoxical method—microscopic restraint of macroscopic abundance—to its extreme:

>   yea, she felt
> Through her own soul the sovereign morning melt
> And all the sacred passion of the sun;
> And as the young clouds flamed and were undone
> About him coming, touched and burnt away
> In rosy ruin and yellow spoil of day,
> The sweet veil of her body and corporal sense
> Felt the dawn also cleave it, and incense
> With light from inward and with effluent heat
> The kindling soul through fleshly hands and feet.
> And as the august great blossom of the dawn
> Burst, and the full sun scarce from sea withdrawn
> Seemed on the fiery water a flower afloat,
> So as a fire the mighty morning smote
> Throughout her, and incensed with the influent hour
> Her whole soul's one great mystical red flower
> Burst, and the bud of her sweet spirit broke
> Rose-fashion, and the strong spring at a stroke
> Thrilled, and was cloven, and from the full sheath
>   came
> The whole rose of the woman red as flame:
> And all her Mayday blood as from a swoon
> Flushed, and May rose up in her and was June.

This is two sentences, but it is almost one line—at least one hardly pauses to notice the couplet rhymes. End-stopped couplets will arrange themselves along a medial axis, almost slowing down to avoid their rhymes, but Swinburne's never pause. Each phrase seems to leap out from the farthest exhausted reach of the last. Something like escape velocity is quickly reached. Freed from the gravity of syntax, words begin to bleed into what Rosenberg—characterizing Swinburne generally, but with partic-

ular relevance for the pictorial qualities of this passage—calls "a single Turnerian chord of color." We are, as Rossetti might well have said but as Swinburne actually did, "enmeshed in multitudinous unity."

Swinburne is a poet of macroscopic abundance and microscopic restraint, a poet of vast passion in search of heroic silence.

—James Richardson

In this passage, as generally in Swinburne and Rossetti, it is difficult to distinguish actor from object. It is nearly impossible to know which of the myriad lights, heats, and colors radiate from the sun and which from the awakened soul of Iseult. There is a remarkable fusion of self and world, flesh and light—the whole has the intense, vague color of strong sun driving through closed eyelids. The syntax supports these ambiguities. Like Rossetti, Swinburne snatches away the solidity of long-sought grammatical objects by making them subjects, and the distinction is further blurred by his fondness for linking both active and passive verbs to a single subject as in "Thrilled, and was cloven" or "flamed and were undone." The setting of metaphor within metaphor similarly confuses the tenor-vehicle distinction so that all of the sensuous qualities of both belong to the moment described, and we forget that some are imported from outside through the agency of a half-dozen similes. Mind and reality are reduced to that line of turbulence which is their meeting. This kind of dissolution of the border between self and world is a constant in Swinburne's poetry, and has been described in different ways by his best readers. Rosenberg, for example, sees Swinburne as the poet "not of natural objects but of natural energies, less of things seen than of forces felt." McGann says that "like Shelley and Mallarmé" Swinburne "strives to render not the thing but the effect it produces." [In *The Sacred Wood,* 1920] T. S. Eliot remarks that though a "bad poet dwells partly in a world of objects and partly in a world of words, only a genius could dwell so completely and consistently among words as Swinburne." These assessments differ mainly in degree, and could be ordered according to the extent that they interiorize poetic reality—from "forces felt," the most external, to "effects," to "words," the most internal. Along these same lines, Browning intolerantly but predictably found Swinburne's style "a fuzz of words." He called it "florid impotence," echoing Pope's description of Sporus in "Epistle to Dr. Arbuthnot," and he tried his hand at it: "the *minimum* of thought and idea in the *maximum* of words and phraseology. Nothing is said and done with, left to stand alone and trust for its effect in its own worth. What a way of writing is that wherein, wanting to say that 'a man is sad,' you express it as, 'he looketh like to one, as one might say, who hath a sadness and is sad indeed, so that beholders think "How sad is he!" ' " Though this hardly approaches Swinburne's parody of Browning's "James Lee's Wife" in deadliness, Browning, despite his exasperation, hits on some truths: first, Swinburne's elegiac tone; second, his habit of looking at words in various contexts; finally his related habit of looking at minds, objects, and feelings from so many angles that they dissolve into the atmosphere of the poem. To a poet of otherness who dwindled into a poet of paraphrase, Swinburne's poetry of "prolonged mildly mixed metaphor" would have seemed obfuscatory and threatening in either half of his career, for it is precisely Swinburne's purpose to let "nothing stand on its own." [In *Swinburne: An Experiment in Criticism,* 1972] McGann calls the stylistic features discussed above Swinburne's "techniques for suggesting the unity of existence," for their end is not clarity but the richness of the Rossettian oxymoronic vision. A Swinburne poem takes all ways at once:

> Heart handfast in heart as they stood, "Look
> thither,"
>   Did he whisper? "look forth from the flowers
>   to the sea;
> For the foam-flowers endure when the rose-
> blossoms wither,
>   And men that love lightly may die—but we?"
> And the same wind sang and the same waves
> whitened,
>   And or ever the garden's last petals were shed,
> In the lips that had whispered, the eyes that had
> lightened
>   Love was dead.
>
> Or they loved their life through, and then went
> whither?
>   And were one to the end—but what end who
>   knows?
> Love deep as the sea as a rose must wither,
>   As the rose-red seaweed that mocks the rose.
> Shall the dead take thought for the dead to love
> them?
>   What love was ever as deep as a grave?
> They are loveless now as the grass above them
>   Or the wave.

The passage is full of equations, large and small. There is hardly a line that does not contain some leveling repetition of a word or phrase—"rose" occurs four times, forms of "love" seven. "The *same* wind sang and the *same* waves whitened." "Whither" is "wither." Lovers, by the grace of simile, are the same as the grass above them, and rose-red seaweed "mocks" the rose. Things are fused by their relation to a third term—foam and roses are equal because both bloom. Swinburne's double simile, "Love deep as the sea as a rose must wither" is covert synesthesia—as its tenor-vehicle relations blurs, qualities float free. For the duration of "deep as the sea as a rose," a flower has vast depths; for the time of "sea as a rose must wither," the odorous sea dies, and for the whole line love is invested with all the qualities flung out from the soundless collision of cold strength and delicate beauty. It is not merely that the mind is "fooled" by the sequence of the words, but that Swinburne has undermined sequence to

the extent that any word in a stanza may brush lightly against any other, "swift to fasten and swift to sever." The passage is the height of Paterian musicality, and a critic with a certain kind of literalist bias might call it meaningless. It is both beautiful and moving, though what it says is not strictly what its words say.

The largest equation in the passage is that of the alternative fates of the lovers, and in it lies the evidence that the *or* which structures the poetry of Swinburne, Tennyson, and Rossetti signals loss as surely as it strives for unity. Doubling is not only connection but negation. Side by side, possibilities cancel each other. Both of Swinburne's stories disappear into time, and in their annihilation is his exhilaration. Like Tennyson a death-artist, Swinburne finds freedom and power at the dead center of loss.

In his dedicatory epistle to his collected works, and without quite saying that he is categorizing poems, Swinburne depicts two realms of the mind. One is the seacoast, which he describes in terms of *contrasts*—the "glory of cliff and crag" versus "the dreary beauty, inhuman if not unearthly in its desolation, of the innumerable creeks and inlets" or "the sand-encumbered tides" wearing at the beaches versus, further offshore, "the ineffable fascination of . . . translucent depths of water and divers-coloured banks of submarine foliage and flowerage." In this landscape, what Lang calls "Swinburne's bone-bred antitheses (unity and division, pleasure and pain, desire and restraint, growth and stasis, etc.)" are both embodied and soothed. The second realm is unrelieved by such contrasts—and it is therefore, for Swinburne, unrelieving, an "oppression." It is "inland or woodland solitude—the splendid oppression of nature at noon which found utterance of old in words of such singular and everlasting significance as panic and nympholepsy." Swinburne's preference for scenic, stylistic, and thematic borderlines, for what Rosenberg calls "the moment when anything shades into its opposite or contraries fuse," is very close to psychic necessity. The shoreline, shifting and reshifting, is his mind in dynamic balance. When the undulant comforts of his landscape and rhythm are somehow thwarted or suspended, he writes near boredom and terror. In **"Neap-Tide,"** for example, the disappearance of the shoreline (both the sea and the land are "far") becomes an image of perilously low energy and personal decline:

> Far off is the sea, and the land is afar:
>   The low banks reach at the sky,
>   Seen hence, and are heavenward high;
> Though light for the leap of a boy they are,
>   And the far sea late was nigh.

"A Nympholept," with its "stress of sun" at noon, concerns another hour that refuses to pass. Stranded, Swinburne is eventually seized with panic in the original sense as his divisions cry out unsoothed. Postponed, his deepest necessities swell into the sense of "wrath scarce hushed and of imminent ill to be." **The Lake of Gaube** also begins in "strong compulsive silence of the sun," and its strange tensions must be released in a dive into a lake "Death-dark and delicious as death in the dream of a lover and dreamer."

The rarity in Tennyson and Swinburne of the glaring landscapes in which elegiac dissolution is thwarted hints at the dangers distanced by their normal styles. But part of the emotional complexity of Swinburne's poetry is that for him the drive toward dissolution is itself tainted and self-punishing. Loss becomes something internal and continuing, a hemorrhage of the spirit, not merely sadness but damage. Desire is a wasting disease. The very source of Swinburne's poetry is defiled, and the muse, as the hymns to Lucrezia Borgia suggest, can be as much poisoner as healer.

In this originates Swinburne's counterimpulse: to drive beyond elegiac dissolution to an antiself of cold clarity, strength, indifference, and restraint. This half of Swinburne normally finds its image in the sea, or in women with the indifferent strength of the sea. But these imagined purities, even in the moment of their imagining, are soiled with self and self-loathing. Nonhuman indifference becomes inhuman cruelty. Cold clarity becomes pain. **"The Triumph of Time"** swells with both the elegiac flux Swinburne's poetry most gratefully inhabits and his always ambivalent desire to engage its heroic antithesis. Swinburne seeks his image of otherness in the Yeatsian Lady of Pain:

> And still, through the sound and the straining stream,
> Through the coil and chafe, they gleam in a dream,
> The bright fine lips so cruelly curled,
>   And strange swift eyes where the soul sits free.
>
> Free, without pity, withheld from woe,
>   Ignorant; fair as the eyes are fair.
> Would I have you change now, change at a blow,
>   Startled and stricken, awake and aware?
> Yea, if I could, would I have you see
> My very love of you filling me,
> And know my soul to the quick, as I know
>   The likeness and look of your throat and hair?

Like the ocean, she is free, pitiless, strong, without tenderness, even without sentience. Her quality is, in a phrase Yeats used for the sea but meant for Maud Gonne, "murderous innocence." Like Yeats, Swinburne pursues his other self through love of his opposite. "Ignorant," as so often in Yeats, marks her pure otherness—if she were capable of understanding Swinburne's love, she would lose the purity of her indifference and no longer be the thing he loves. One may well find masochism in such an arrangement, but then one will also have to find it in Tennyson and Yeats. Nor is it very far from the perceptual disciplines of Hopkins's "stress" and "instress." That is, Swinburne's masochism is in one aspect a painfully high amplification of the normal need of humans in general, and of Victorian poets in particular, to love something that is not themselves, to find, beyond the dimmings of the self, a beauty that is strange and fresh and hard. Pater, as usual, is the best analyst of the Pre-Raphaelite tendency, here in the essay on Morris:

> The colouring is intricate and delirious, as of "scarlet lilies." The influence of summer is like a poison in one's blood, with a sudden bewildered sickening of life and all things. . . . A passion of which the outlets are

sealed, begets a tension of nerve, in which the sensible world comes to one with a reinforced brilliancy and relief—all redness is turned into blood, all water into tears. Hence a wild, convulsed sensuousness in the poetry of the Middle Age, in which the things of nature begin to play a strange, delirious part. Of the things of nature the mediaeval mind had a deep sense; but its sense of them was not objective, no real escape to the world without us. The aspects and motions of nature only reinforced its prevailing mood, and were in conspiracy with one's own brain against one. A single sentiment invaded the world; everything was infused with a motive drawn from the soul.

The combination of absolute self-enclosure and feverish intensity is more characteristic of Pre-Raphaelite medievalism than of the Middle Ages. [In the introduction to Pater's *Selected Writings*] Bloom finds Pater here "hinting that sadomasochistic yearnings and the anxiety of being a late representative of the tradition are closely related" and that "the heightened intensity of Morris and Rosetti (and of Pater)"—and of Swinburne—"compensates for a destructively excessive sexual self-consciousness." Swinburne's poetry is a straining within a dream. If it is trying to escape the pain of whatever "reality" is, it is also trying to escape from the unreality of our *automatic* escape, our imprisonment in ourselves. Pain and intensity are not only what it flees but also a part of its return, a part of its clarity.

> **Often severely beautiful as dew on steel, Swinburne's language is narrowed to invoke a world of clarity, purity, and violence.**
>
> **—James Richardson**

Swinburne is a poet of macroscopic abundance and microscopic restraint, a poet of vast passion in search of heroic silence. Often severely beautiful as dew on steel, his language is narrowed to invoke a world of clarity, purity, and violence. Surely no work depends more on the inherent deliberateness of monosyllables. *Cold, break, swift, strong, glad, keen, wild, sharp, clear* are Swinburne's words. And yet his momentary restraints are continually overwhelmed by the swing and swell of his undulant, expanding mood. Admitting that Swinburne's language is "not like the language of bad poetry, dead," T. S. Eliot calls it limited because it is not like "the language which is more important to us . . . which is struggling to digest new objects, new groups of objects, new feelings, new aspects." There is at least a half-truth visible here since Eliot's purpose is a not very surprising contrast with Conrad and Joyce, but reservations must be registered, since the implication of "important" is that Swinburne is somehow less "realistic," less relevant.

Molly Bloom's monologue at the end of *Ulysses,* for example, is a portrayal of the state of awareness slightly below the rationally discursive but above that of emotions. This tributary of the literary stream of consciousness flows from that mood in which we are divided into speaker and listener and, with a kind of insomniac fervor, explain ourselves to ourselves, but surely no one think it is somehow "essentially" or "really" thought. This state, because it is (though barely) articulate, we can remember, and thus it seems in retrospect to occupy more of our lives than it actually does, but Joyce is showing us as we function during only a small part of the day. And even then his monologue is more verbal than the mind. He must constantly invent linguistic devices to approximate both thoughts and discontinuities that, in the mind, never reach words.

Swinburne's meditations in **"The Triumph of Time,"** are apparently more literary and coherent, and they are certainly—determinedly—less "new" in Eliot's sense, but they are in at least one way more fundamental. He, too, is concerned with repetitive explanations and self-dramatizations, but his fewer, older, dimmer words ride on rhythmic and syntactical patterns that deprive them of their objectivity. They body forth the deeper emotional ebb and surge that, brought a little further into consciousness, might eventually attach itself to more particular self-explanations and drive the Browningesque or even the Joycean monologue. Swinburne's is a vaguer intuition—it may be essentially nonverbal. But only a narrowly enthusiastic definition of realism would deny its reality.

Secondly, one must qualify Eliot's remark about the "digestion" of experience. There is constant digestion in Swinburne and Rossetti and Tennyson, constant dissolution. What Eliot misses is the *effort* of digestion—what sometimes fails is the resistance, the particularity of the Victorian world. In this regard, the cruelty and pain Swinburne often sees as the cause of his failures are essential to his self-denying quest—they are part of his attempt to discover resistance. His apostrophe to Sade, "You are only a very serious St. Simeon Stylites in an inverted position," asserts the quasi asceticism of his fascination. For Swinburne, pain is almost an antielegiac sensuousness. But it, too, fails to clear the dimness, for like all Swinburne's contraries it is blurred—by pleasure, by fear, by guilt—so that it becomes poisonous, damaging, impure, full of the shameful taint of self. As with his "broken blossom" or his "green reeds shattered," Swinburne seems able to discover the hardness of things only in its failure. A passage from **"Anactoria"** encapsulates both the direction and dissolution of his quest:

> Him would I reach, him smite, him desecrate,
> Pierce the cold lips of God with human breath,
> And mix his immortality with death.

Both worship and hatred make Gods human, and the pathetic fallacy in Swinburne is the pathetic fatality. Once tainted with humanity, with self, even a cruel, insentient God dissolves helplessly in the elegiac flux.

There are other directions. Swinburne's genius for self-abasement was exceeded only (but greatly) by his inhuman power, and he threw himself at the feet of Mazzini,

like Tennyson before him and Yeats after attempting the antiself of the public poet. The goddess of liberty engaged him deeply, but not painfully, not often poetically. Liberty is perhaps not the ideal subject for a man who was highest, best, even most free, in the shackles of his own obsessions, and one of the few successful poems in his Italian era is **"Hertha,"** which with its hypnotic chant and its philosophical fusion of actor and object recalls Emerson's "Brahma" and the erotic closeness of his own earlier work:

> Love or unlove me,
>   Unknow me or know,
> I am that which unloves me and loves; I am stricken,
>   and I am the blow.

The most interesting of Swinburne's tendencies, however, evolves from his early fascination with sterility, and specifically with the "barren mother," the "mother maid," that sea which in Swinburne's various moods is nature, Sade, trance, Mary Gordon, Sappho, passion, utter insentience, freedom, pain. Browning had also discovered the desert seacoast and also knew as a great advantage its absence of easy pleasure and intrusive humanity:

> Well—and you know, and not since this one year,
> The quiet seaside country? So do I:
> Who like it, in a manner, just because
> Nothing is prominently likeable
> To vulgar eye without a soul behind.

For Browning, here in *Red Cotton Night-Cap Country,* it was the background, and antithesis, for a story of grotesque passion. It was Swinburne's *mind,* a symbolic landscape so long and fervently inhabited that it had subsided into nature and into second nature. The barren strength of the coast becomes the very sensibility of **"On the Cliffs," "Neap-Tide," "Evening on the Broads,"** and the endlessly fascinating **"By the North Sea,"** a virtual encyclopedia of Swinburne:

> A land that is lonelier than ruin;
>   A sea that is stranger than death:
> Far fields that a rose never blew in,
>   Wan waste where the winds lack breath;
> Waste endless and boundless and flowerless
>   But of marsh-blossoms fruitless as free:
> Where earth lies exhausted, as powerless
>   To strive with the sea.

"Stranger than death," past "ruin," this landscape stretches beyond the elegiac flux, out of the range of the self. In waste and exhaustion, Swinburne begins to find the otherness, the strangeness, he seeks. It is perverse to say that "Swinburne projects an inner sense of desolation on to the Suffolk landscape" when the poem, on the contrary, swells with the exhilaration, wonder, and grateful peace that only abundant energy would find in such neutral tones:

> Miles, and miles, and miles of desolation!
>   Leagues on leagues on leagues without a change!
> Sign or token of some eldest nation

Here would make the strange land not so strange.
Time-forgotten, yea since time's creation,
    Seem these borders where the sea-birds range.

Slowly, gladly, full of peace and wonder
    Grows his heart who journeys here alone.
Earth and all its thoughts of earth sink under
    Deep as deep in water sinks a stone.
Hardly knows it if the rollers thunder,
    Hardly whence the lonely wind is blown.

"Desolation" is not used here as an objective correlative. Rather the *purity* of barrenness balances the relentlessly elegiac pathetic fallacy—"Sign or token of some eldest nation / Here would make the strange land not so strange." It does not *express* Swinburne; it cleanses him with its momentary *refusals* to express him.

But this poem about divine barrenness, inhuman purity, is also full of defilement, pervaded, as David Riede points out [in *Swinburne: A Study in Romantic Mythmaking*, 1978] by Swinburne's eroticism. For the sea can also be Dolores: "For the heart of the waters is cruel, / And the kisses are dire of their lips," and Swinburne senses his irresistible humanization of the other—"the hunger that moans in her passion"—as a desecration:

The grime of her greed is upon her,
    The sign of her deed is her soil;
As the earth's is her own dishonour,
    And corruption the crown of her toil:
She hath spoiled and devoured, and her honour
Is this, to be shamed by her spoil.

Meeting himself, Swinburne recoils from his own closeness. Life-giving antitheses appear, are contaminated, dissolve, are cleansed, reappear. In the climactic passage, he presides over what must be described in Swinburnean terms as a final cleanliness. He watches with terrible joy as the ocean saps a graveyard. Here, even the "effort of digestion" is apparent in the sinew of the verse:

Naked, shamed, cast out of consecration,
    Corpse and coffin, yea the very graves,
Scoffed at, scattered, shaken from their station,
    Spurned and scourged of wind and sea like slaves,
Desolate beyond man's desolation,
    Shrink and sink into the waste of waves.

Tombs, with bare white piteous bones protruded,
    Shroudless, down the loose collapsing banks,
Crumble, from their constant place detruded,
    That the sea devours and gives not thanks.
Graves where hope and prayer and sorrow brooded
    Gape and slide and perish, ranks on ranks.

Rows on rows and line by line they crumble,
    They that thought for all time through to be.
Scarce a stone whereon a child might stumble
    Breaks the grim field paced alone of me.
Earth, and man, and all their gods wax humble
    Here, where Time brings pasture to the sea.

Even the metaphorical possibility of rest is seemingly denied, but the action, predictably, contains its opposite. Swinburne overwhelms the last human outpost—our sense of shock and shame—and, as in **"A Forsaken Garden,"** presides with ecstasy over the sea's painful destruction of the future possibility of pain. Erosion is the fleeting moment lengthened and magnified, time made visible and palpable, and it is the mode of Swinburne's poetry. With surge and countersurge, it accomplishes its slow, almost undetectable changes. It is variations on the theme of variation. Like the seabird he imagined himself, like the wind indistinguishable from the bird, Swinburne is full of an energy that "satiety never may stifle."

"Gape and slide and perish." Perhaps it is not surprising that Eliot recalled the poet dwelling "completely . . . among words" when he ruminated, in "Burnt Norton," on their shiftiness:

Words strain,
Crack, and sometimes break, under the burden,
Under the tension, slip, slide, perish.

But even in *The Waste Land,* where there are notes for such things, Eliot acknowledges no Victorian debts. So we are still vaguely under the impression that Chaucer is behind "April is the cruelest month," though Arnold's "The Buried Life" and Tennyson's "Is it, then, regret for buried time / That keenlier in sweet April wakes?" stand virtually in front of it. Nor is there, among the barely credible *Quellenforschung* of those notes any indication that "mixing / Memory and desire" might be somewhat similar to Swinburne's "as mist with sea / Mixed, or as memory with desire." No deception is of course implied. Poets can more easily articulate their gratitude to those they wish to become than their identity with those they already are. For Eliot, as for Yeats, Victorian poetry is the barely audible music under consciousness, a music not less but more important for being unacknowledgable.

L. M. Findlay (essay date 1990)

SOURCE: "The Art of Apostasy: Swinburne and the Emperor Julian," in *Victorian Poetry,* Vol. 28, No. 1, Spring, 1990, pp. 69-78.

[*In the following essay, Findlay explores Swinburne's attitude toward Christianity by examining his poems "The Hymn to Prosperpine" and "The Garden of Proserpine."*]

Apostasy in England in the nineteenth century gained special prominence in the wake of Keble's famous Assize sermon of 1833 on "National Apostasy," with its scathing analysis of those "omens and tokens" which mark the "fashionable liberality of this generation," the spread of indifferentism, and the loss of respect for the solemnity of oaths and the Apostolic status of Bishops. Earlier in the century, we find a more briskly sectarian understanding of the term as a means of berating paganism in, for example, Richard Sheil's *The Apostate: A Tragedy in Five Acts*

(1818), Sir Aubrey de Vere's *Julian, The Apostate* (1822), or H. H. Milman's *The Fall of Jerusalem* (1822). When Milman comes to deal explicitly with Julian two decades later, in the third volume of his *History of Christianity,* he is able to treat the Emperor fairly generously because he begins by insisting that "Julian has, perhaps, been somewhat unfairly branded with the ill-sounding name of Apostate." That name was sounding more and more ill all the time to English ears, as the conditions in contemporary England threatened to emulate those prevailing in the Roman Empire in the fourth century A.D. Julian is perceived as increasingly relevant to England's apostasy, and F. D. Maurice [in *Moral and Metaphysical Philosophy,* 1972] can thus lament the loss of some of his works which "might have enabled us to understand much better wherein lay the weakness of that society which he was seeking to undermine; what that strength was which prevailed against him." Apostasy is no longer a foreigner's problem such as had occasioned Newman's two octaves of revulsion off the coast of France in 1833 [*Verses on Various Occasions,* 1889]. Indeed, Newman himself is now very much part of the problem whose consequences will be seen in the *Edinburgh Review* in 1849 as stemming from the fact that "those who were contending for the corruptions of the fourth century could not possibly find footing there, but must inevitably seek their ultimate resting place in Rome." To study Julian and his times is to become a Catholic like Newman or a mytholater like Strauss, whose ambivalent and limited recognition of Christianity as historically inevitable in Julian's time has been almost immediately rewritten in England as an unconditional assertion of the "fact" that "the Galilean is the genius of the future!" The Newman option dominates discussion in the 1840s and 1850s, but by the end of the latter decade the forces of aesthetic paganism are beginning to assert themselves more noticeably, and the full-blown Swinburnian challenge to the Victorian public is anticipated in terms such as those favored by John Stuart Blackie in 1858: "The heroic young emperor Julian was certainly not a solitary example of a talented and well-educated ancient, at a time when hellenism was no longer possible, who cleaved to the dynasty of departing Olympians from the strong faith of a poetic instinct that such gods were too beautiful to be false." The time is ripe for poetry and pugnacity to come together in the name of the old gods and their most loyal adherents.

Swinburne's reaction against Christianity is well known but imperfectly understood. Nor can the subtlety and complexity of his evolving religious opinions be thoroughly investigated here. However, an examination of two of his poems with strong connections to the Apostate may convey some sense of the need for a revisionary reading of his work and of the cultural context which helped to shape it. The earlier of the two poems to be considered, **"The Hymn to Proserpine,"** appeared in the first series of *Poems and Ballads* (1866) despite the concerns expressed by some of his friends and family. It is not surprising that someone like Swinburne would be attracted to the figure of Julian, especially in a collection which is emphatically pagan in its predilections and treatment of Venus, Dolores, and a number of other female figures. The

Ceres/Proserpine (Demeter/Persephone) legend is treated from the point of view of Ceres in **"At Eleusis,"** where Swinburne reworks such details as were known of the Eleusinian mysteries (into which Julian was initiated) in the interests of a distinctive vision of society, poetry, and agriculture:

> I Demeter speak of this,
> Who am the mother and mate of things:
> For as ill men by drugs or singing words
> Shut the doors inward of the narrowed womb
> Like a lock bolted with round iron through,
> Thus I shut up the body and sweet mouth
> Of all soft pasture and the tender land,
> So that no seed can enter in by it
> Though one sow quickly, nor some grain get out
> Past the hard clods men cleave and bite with steel
> To widen the sealed lips of them for use.

Despite its strong sense of negative enclosure, this poem accommodates the privative as part of the seasonal cycle, and affirms the propriety of a "burden equable" in the cultivation of language, social institutions, and the earth itself. They are grounded in each other in a poetic instantiation of fertility myth which reconstitutes the Christian Logos in interanimating pagan terms.

"The Garden of Proserpine," in contrast, expresses more recessive sentiments from the point of view of a soul in Hades. Through her nursing of Triptolemus, the infant prince of Eleusis, Ceres keeps herself closely involved with vital processes and the larger picture, but her daughter's human devotee concentrates on the underground phase of a double life which is clearly preferred to renewal and reunion above ground by the speaker, as also by Proserpine herself when she "forgets the earth her mother." The poem takes pains to establish the reality of its own environment—"Here . . . Here . . . Here . . ."—and tries to enact its own enclosure in stanza three as it moves from "Here" to "here," before proceeding to describe itself as an act of "brief thanksgiving" for mortality and its impending consequence, "sleep eternal / In an eternal night." We are promised not so much transcendence and resurrection as abeyance and "Then" oblivion, the impending triumph of narcosis over time. Swinburne's version of the *hortus conclusus* permits a combination of voyeurism ("I watch") and languor ("I am tired . . . I am weary") to distance and discredit, so far as it can, the arduous inconclusiveness of human existence. This goddess is no longer the victim and pining abductee of tradition but mistress of a domain where terms like "neighbour . . . Pale . . . deadly" are given a new, neopagan twist designed to arrest a double process in a single phase independent of the supplement of renewal.

However, before we encounter this vision in *Poems and Ballads* we are prepared for its uncompromising deathwish by **"The Hymn to Proserpine."** There are a number of challenges issued by the title of this earlier poem, the subtitle (*After the Proclamation in Rome of the Christian Faith*), and the epigraph (*Vicisti Galilaee*). **"Hymn"** reminds us that, in a century when many of the most famous

Christian hymns were composed, the pagan heritage of *hymnos* was not entirely forgotten. The Latin forms and historical situation of the action guide us towards an appreciation of the poem as uttered sometime between 313 A.D. (when this Proclamation was made) and 363 A.D. (when Julian died) by a figure whom Swinburne describes in a letter to Lady Trevelyan as the "Last Pagan" (*Letters,* 1:141). But can we be more precise about the identity of the speaker in the poem? The use of "I" intimates from the outset that this is a private response to a public edict. The words so strongly identified with Julian function as an evocative epigraph, and are then reiterated with slight modification in line 35: "Thou hast conquered, O pale Galilean." However, this utterance does not necessarily mean that the speaker is Julian himself, intent on reflecting on the pro-Christian stance of his predecessor Constantius or on the efficacy of his own proclamation of religious toleration in the Empire in 362 A.D., and hence anticipating his death-bed concession as Vigny's Julian is made to do. After all, the speaker appropriates some famous words by another notable pagan, Epictetus, in the antepenultimate line of the poem: "A little soul for a little bears up this corpse which is man." The Greek of Epictetus (*Psucharion ei bastazon nekron*) is given in a postscript, a final intertextual tribute to the Graeco-Latin mix of late Roman civilization and the extravagantly allusive discourse of Julian and his sophistic contemporaries. The reciter of this hymn, a poet "sick of singing" (l. 9), would appear to be a symbolic figure rather than a factual portrait of the Poet-Emperor, a nameless poet who nevertheless uses words soon to be firmly linked (like some of Swinburne's own) with calumny. Swinburne does not, as one might expect, haul Christianity over the coals for fabricating and disseminating this lie about Julian's death-bed concession. Instead of leaping to the Emperor's defense as he had to Baudelaire's and Hugo's and would to Blake's, he counters theological with poetic license by means of a composite figure whose discourse recognizes the powerful resonance of official calumny even as it redeploys it. Swinburne's deconstruction will work best not by disputing the historical veracity of Theodoret's lie but by exposing the desires that dictated its invention and favorable reception. The exposure proceeds in fifty-five couplets carefully calculated to offend the Victorian Christian reader. With the opening quotation from *Macbeth* (V.iii.22: "I have lived long enough"), another cultural icon is used to extend the domain of memory forward in time from the persona's situation closer to that of his creator. Macbeth's words express an appropriate sense of disillusionment, suggest that such disillusionment has had good reason to persist throughout the entire Christian era, and help prepare for later heroic defiance in face of inevitable defeat: "I kneel not neither adore you, but standing, look to the end" (l. 46). The Christian trinity is displaced briefly by the triune Proserpine, "Goddess and maiden and queen," in an act of poetic resistance to the reality of pagan gods "dethroned and deceased, cast forth, wiped out in a day" (l. 13). This resistance avoids utter futility by opening into a distinctly Swinburnian explanation of the nature of the victory that the Galilean and his followers will enjoy. Swinburne interprets Theodoret's lie via the kind of allegorical ruse dear to Julian; and, in particular, he employs

the figures of Venus (as also in **"Laus Veneris"**) and Proserpine to create a consoling context of endurance and alternating hegemony. The erasure of paganism is depicted as certainly dramatic but neither total nor permanent. Its resurgence, promised in the parodic typology of the poet's crown of bay leaves becoming like a crown of thorns (l. 19), and of Venus "imperial, her foot on the sea" (l. 86), has been deferred rather than absolutely denied. Swinburne implies that calming the waters of the Sea of Galilee is far different from dealing with "the wave of the world" (l. 54), where Christian miracle must in time give way to pagan myth. And so it will be with the earth also. Proserpine embodies a primordial principle of chthonic death and resurrection which antedates and will succeed its Christian facsimile. The persona of the poem cannot directly, immediately profit from this situation except in the form of a fitting end for himself and his poetry in unfavorable times, but that is reason enough for dedicating this hymn to Proserpine.

However, the nature of Swinburne's personal stake in all of this can be more fully appreciated by returning to the Julianic connection. The most stinging rebuke to Christianity in the **"Hymn"** is contained in the couplet,

> Thou hast conquered, O pale Galilean; the world
>   has grown gray from thy breath;
> We have drunken of things Lethean, and fed on the
>   fullness of death.

The move from polytheism to monotheism has proved especially disastrous for the poetic imagination. The baleful influence of the Christian Word has expunged color and vitality from "the world," while its sacraments have been used to obliterate the pagan past in the interest of a morbid present. The poem turns reflexively on the fate of language and imagination, and the words misascribed to Julian have been inscribed in Western culture so deeply that his sense of Christianity as the depletion of discourse cannot be easily ignored by those who share (or dispute) that sense. The persona of the poem can act anachronistically because the words and sentiments of Julian are, as far as Swinburne is concerned, in almost every sense his own. He is expounding a text whose burden of belatedness and *anomie* expresses his own understanding of the true poet's predicament in mid-Victorian England. The poem uses allusion (as to Macbeth's sense of emptiness ["mouth-honor, breath"]) and ironic echo (as of the Lord's Prayer in "our daily breath" [l. 11]), to help record the end of breath as inspiration (*theopneustia*) with the spread of the Christian Logos. The Word made Flesh is the word made unpoetic; the doctrine of Real Presence marks the effective absence of nature poetically mediated by the pagan gods; and Christian fictions of the plenary fill Julian and those who share his aesthetic paganism only with a sense of emptiness and decay. They have lived long enough.

The **"Hymn"** is only one of a series of attempts by Swinburne to rehabilitate classical paganism. Some of these are more intent on debunking Christianity than in offering any serious alternative to it, but all can be construed as acts of doubling and exploration rather than the definitive expression of a monolithic orthodoxy or heresy. Swinburne comes increasingly to realize that the revitalizing of beliefs currently and for some time effectively defunct requires retrieval with a difference, adaptation and not restoration. Consistent with this realization is his return to a Julianic theme in **"The Last Oracle,"** which appeared in the second series of *Poems and Ballads* in 1878. Once again belatedness is much in evidence, as the speaker gives in Greek the text of the "answer sent to Julian from Delphi (A.D. 361) when he sent to consult the God and was told it was all up with Phoebus." Once again utter futility is avoided through the lyric creation of a consolatory context wherein Julian's predicament can be sympathetically reinterpreted.

Swinburne shows great concern for accuracy in the Greek text which provides the intertextual occasion of the poem, but he has no hesitation in bending the historical facts so that the oracle seems immediately to result in the death of the Emperor, thereby ignoring the two years that elapsed between the one event and the other:

> Since the sad last pilgrim left thy dark mid shrine.
> Dark the shrine and dumb the fount of song thence
>   welling,
>   Save for words more sad than tears of blood, that
>   said:
> *Tell the king, on earth has fallen the glorious dwelling,*
>   *And the watersprings that spake are quenched*
>   *and dead.*
> *Not a cell is left the God, no roof, no cover*
>   *In his hand the prophet laurel flowers no more.*
> And the great king's high sad heart, thy last true lover,
>   Felt thine answer pierce and cleave it to the core.
>   And he bowed down his hopeless head
>   In the drift of the wide world's tide,
>   And dying, *Thou hast conquered,* he said,
>   *Galilean;* he said it, and died.
>   And the world that was thine and was ours
>   When the Graces took hands with the Hours
>   Grew cold as a winter wave
>   In the wind from a wide-mouthed grave,
>   As a gulf wide open to swallow
>   The light that the world held dear.
>   O father of all of us, Paian, Apollo,
>   Destroyer and healer, hear!
>
>   (ll. 4-24)

Swinburne rewrites the final part of Julian's life, strengthening the bonds between poetry, paganism, and vitality, before reworking theogony and cosmology in line with his own evolving credo. The harmonious passage of time symbolized by the dance of Charites and Horae ends with the extinguishing of the true Light of the World. The Emperor-Poet personifies the marriage of beauty and power, and his death reduces the options of "song" to silence, elegy (as in **"The Hymn to Proserpine"**), or the current impassioned apostrophe. Oracular language is thus made to have an immediate and fatal consequence, but its notoriously enigmatic qualities allow for later recuperation of its positive force in a primal scene of language, light, and divinity.

Julian's hymns to "The Mother of the Gods" and "King Helios" were, in Gibbon's eyes, disfigured by mysticism. Swinburne, in moving from the earth mother to the sun god, is aware of the implications for his own art but is encouraged none the less by Julian's example:

> The poem . . . is not, you will doubtless be surprised to hear, a hymn in praise of the triumph of Christianity over false Gods, but of Apollo regarded not as the son of Zeus the son of Chronos, but as the spirit or influence informing the thought or the soul of man with inner light (of which the sun's is the physical type) and thence with song or articulate speech which is the creator of all Gods imagined by man to love or fear or honour, who are all born or die as surely as they are born at the bidding of the same spirit. Thus Apollo-Paian, destroyer and healer, and not the Galilean, is established as the Logos which was not *with* but *before* God in the beginning, and is even now beholding the collapse, eclipse, and flight into outer darkness, of the God or Gods who vainly thought to have ousted him from the world as well as from Delphi, leaving the said world such deadly glories in the way of song as the *Inferno* and the *Dies Irae* (which latter I have always considered the typical and capital poem of Christianity proper—and most splendid it is) in place of the living songs of old.

As these comments to Edwin Harrison make clear, Swinburne is still very much aware of the response of Christian readers to his work. His tone is still impenitently neopagan, but it is less combative and more realistic about ongoing struggle for hegemony. In another letter on this topic to John Morley, Swinburne concedes that his poem in paraphrase "sounds rather metaphysical," but he does not "think the verse is obscure or turbid." It is not the metaphysical per se but its frequent victim, lucidity, about which he is self-conscious. However, his aesthetic reappropriation of the metaphysical "(of which the sun is the physical type)" attempts to blend neo-Platonism (*tupos* as inferior impression left by an antecedent force) and Biblical typology (the type of the sun having its antitype in Apollo restored to Delphi and the world). Poetic clarity cannot conceal a syncretism whose harmony can be re-read as the mediation of desire between contending, residually incompatible elements. The very act of signifying *sign*—by the term "type" in this instance—attempts to accommodate both representation and emplotment in a personal metaphysic, but it cannot entirely suppress the inconvenient aspects of the physical production of the sign and the very different ways in which it has been received and reproduced. As in the case of Carlyle, for example, desire for transcendence reveals its links to the transitive and the material, links that Swinburne exposed and deplored in the case of the Eucharist but was unable to eliminate from his own creed.

Swinburne's metaphysical reconstruction employs also an argument from origins to antedate and account in Apollonian terms for the Book of Genesis and St. John's Gospel. However, this theory of origins looks to ground itself in history as well as mythopoeia and typology, and this leads to a moderation of the claims against Christianity as enemy of poetry and the aesthetic imagination. *The Divine Comedy* and the *Dies Irae* may be grudgingly, ironically endorsed as "deadly glories in the way of song," as the best that is produced "When for chant of Greeks the wail of Galileans / Made the whole world moan with hymns of wrath and wrong" (ll. 31-32), but these admissions of the continuous power of song point also (albeit reluctantly) to the polemical excesses of **"The Hymn to Proserpine"** and to the increased tolerance that attends Swinburne's efforts to construct an alternative to Christianity. The epistolary supplements to his poem help to clarify the difference between Julian as epitome of despair (the bitter fruit of apostasy) and Julian as epitome of fidelity. Admittedly, the difference is one of emphasis rather than essence, as desire articulates its own goals, its enemies, and the nature of its own vulnerability to deconstruction, but this shift does permit the updating of the most famous lines from **"The Hymn"**:

> They are conquered, they break, they are stricken,
> Whose might made the whole world pale;
> They are dust that shall rise not or quicken
> Though the world for their death's sake wail.
>
> (ll. 109-112)

Swinburne has lived long enough, it seems, to convince himself through Apollo's gift of "song or articulate speech," "The spirit of man and the breath" (l. 62), that Christianity has now run its course. However, he still cannot conjure his own god into presence but must instead faithfully reiterate and end with an unanswered, phonocentric appeal to an absent, double-natured deity: "Destroyer and healer, hear!"

In his poetic reworking of the Julian legend, Swinburne reopens the question of the victory of Christianity over paganism in order to show the superiority of the vanquished to the victors, and to establish who are the true friends of art. Julian's apocryphal last words are first appropriated by Swinburne in a bitterly polemical context, and later they are replaced by a neo-pagan desire which, whether as speech or writing, is itself disturbed by its own mixture of mysticism and materiality, by the invention of ultimate origins in a medium whose birthright appears to be difference and temporality and desire. As he continues to answer the question he first posed for himself in *Atalanta in Calydon*—"Who hath given man speech?"—Swinburne's interest in the art of apostasy has to make room for the linguistically determined realities of art as apostasy. No less than religious hypostasis, aesthetic apostasis bears witness to the need to stand somewhere and for something, and also to the ways in which logos complicates even as it facilitates all statements of belief.

Joseph E. Riehl (essay date 1990)

SOURCE: "Swinburne's Doublings: *Tristram of Lyonesse, The Sisters,* and *The Tale of Balen,*" in *Victorian Poetry,* Vol. 28, Nos. 3-4, Autumn-Winter, 1990, pp. 1-17.

[*In the following essay, Riehl addresses the artistic function of the doubling of characters and character names in three of Swinburne's poems.*]

Long regarded as deploring work, Swinburne's later verse has gradually won serious regard as great art from twentieth-century readers. [In *SAQ*, 1958] Paull F. Baum's study of **"A Nympholept"** (1958) paved the way for major revaluation of this body of Swinburne's poetry. [In *Victorian Poetry*, 1971] Kerry McSweeney echoed Baum's admiration for **"A Nympholept,"** and added **"The Lake of Gaube"** as its equal. [In *TSLL*, 1972] Benjamin Franklin Fisher IV demonstrated how the worksheets for *Tristram of Lyonesse* reveal an alert creative imagination maintaining amazing control over the composition of that long poem. Others have tended to swell the chorus of such acclaim. In his later poems, Swinburne's own misgivings about reconciling his image as public figure at the Pines with the private artist of rebellion are symbolized by a dramatic device, a Shakespearean "doubling" of characters. In *The Tale of Balen,* such doubling leads to the creation of one of his best, most mature poems.

[In *Swinburne: An Experiment in Criticism,* 1972] Jerome McGann has noted Swinburne's habit of grammatical doubling, that is, of using pairs of words like "rain and ruin" to gain poetic effect. He contends that these doublings are not mere rhetorical duplications, but rather "Swinburne's most elementary techniques for suggesting the unity of existence, no matter what its transformations. Inevitably, Swinburne pushes the technique of grammatical doubling into the active tensions of character. In narrative and dramatic works of the late period he doubles not only character names, but the characters themselves. Three long poems in particular, *Tristram of Lyonesse* (1882), *The Sisters: A Tragedy* (1892), and *The Tale of Balen* (1896), encompass pairs of characters who are either twins or who bear the same name. This remarkable mirroring of double names with double characters is first to be traced in *Tristram of Lyonesse,* with its two Iseults and two Tristrams. Similar doubling occurs in *The Sisters: A Tragedy*: two former schoolmates, Reginald and Frank, court twin sisters, Mabel and Anne. In *The Tale of Balen,* Balen and Balan are twins, and Balen's descriptive epithet is "the Knight with Two Swords." In each of these works, human relations are used as metaphors for psychic integration.

I *Tristram of Lyonesse*

The character doublings in this poem are, of course, found in the original Malory, and in *Tristram* Swinburne first seems to have become aware of the artistic possibilities of its doublings. The two Iseults represent the seemingly eternal dilemma for Tristram, an apparently Tennysonian choice between lovers who alternately embody order or passion. Tristram, bewitched by a love potion, chooses passion. Both of the Iseults, in soliloquys, impart opposing conceptions of God and of love, the apparent alternatives facing Tristram. Insoluble in life, his dilemma is resolvable only in death by an ambiguous union with his chosen Iseult of Cornwall. Iseult of Brittany, consumed by hate, scheming revenge—even Tristram's death cannot deprive him of this union. The sea destroys their burial chapel, erected by King Mark, but the story of their love has conferred on them an immortality unequalled by the surviving Iseult.

Yet, Tristram's choice plays little part in his fall. In fact, the second, "minor" Tristram of Britany causes the death of Tristram of Lyonesse more immediately than either of the two Iseults. The minor Tristram asks for help in recovering his kidnapped lady, an adventure in which Tristram of Lyonesse receives a mortal wound. The doubling of Tristram's name allegorically implies that Tristram brings about his own death. Despite all received impressions, Tristram's actual choice is, in some sense, a choice of himself, not a choice between two women.

Swinburne exploited the double names of the source to create the appearance of a psychological choice for Tristram between two types of love: the selfless love of Iseult of Cornwall, who wishes to give her soul as hostage to God so that Tristram might be spared, and the selfish attachment of Iseult of Brittany, who, shamed by Tristram's rejection of her, calls down God's vengeance on him. However, as a natural man, "Child of heroic earth and heavenly sea, / The flower of all men," Tristram does not, in fact cannot, choose between the two Iseults or their two tryannical Gods. He is fated, both by the potion the lovers share at the opening of the tale, and by his own integrity, which permits no other course of action.

In fact, the possibility of choice haunts only one minor character, King Mark:

> he
> Was rent in twain betwixt harsh love and hate
> With pain and passion half compassionate
> That yearned and labored to be quit of shame,
> And could not: and his life grew smouldering flame.
>
> (4:131)

But this paradoxical ambivalence is not shared by any of the principal characters. The poem concerns itself not with choice, but with Tristram's struggle with fate and his consequent assertion of selfhood. Tristram's choice, if it can be called a choice at all, is not between one lover and another—the potion makes that impossible—but between avoidance of fate or acceptance. Tristram chooses his namesake-self in a dying resolution of a dilemma insoluable on earth.

Though only partly successful, *Tristram* nevertheless attests to the philosophical importance which Swinburne invested in the trope of doubling. A solemn and passionate meditation on death, *Tristram* poses, then negates, two possible versions of immortality: that conferred by everlasting fame, and that of an ecstatic mingling with the elements. In a philosophical discussion with Iseult, Tristram expresses envy of Merlin's existence in passionate though static union with material creation and with Vivien:

> [He] knows that the soul that was his soul [is] at one
> With the ardent world's, and in the spirit of earth
> His spirit of life reborn to mightier birth
> And mixed with things of elder life than ours.
>
> (4:116)

Iseult, in answer, deflates Tristram's ardent speculation that they, too, might share a like fate. Not for her the Whitmanesque consolation that in death we mix with the elements of exalted nature: "yet to pass / More fleet than mirrored faces from the glass / Out of all pain and all delight." Tristram, undaunted, tries Stoic consolation, that they will gain eternal fame: "how shall death put out the fire at heart, / Quench in men's eyes the head's remembered light / That time shall set but higher in more men's sight?" Iseult answers witheringly, parodying Mark 8.36: "'Ah,' she said, / What shall it profit me, being praised and dead?'" (4:116-118). She rejects both the classical consolation of fame and the romantic one of dissolution into the elements of the material world; ironically, we know that the lovers have eternal fame and that their bones mingle at the sea bottom in the ruins of their burial chapel. To Swinburne, in *Tristram* as elsewhere, death remained an enigma, the blankest possible.

Though we can know nothing of what comes after death, the possibility remains that one may establish a true ground for living by meditating on death. Swinburne explores that possibility in the last section of *Tristram*, **"The Sailing of the Swan."** Fate, it seems, controls our destiny in the material world, "Fate, that of all things save the soul of man / Is lord and God since body and soul began" (4:150). Fate controls all things, but not man's inner life; standing against fate is man's hope, which is "trustier than the truth of day," because it confirms the existence of the soul. Only the human soul, "life's own inmost fire" creates true life in a dead, material universe. The desire of the soul as it yearns for eternity is proof of the existence of "Truth . . . Fountain of all things living" (4:152). Thought, man's rational power, cannot comprehend this life-force, though outlines of it can be seen through a "glass." One comes to a finite realization of the eternal truth by examining the self mirrored in the world. But as Iseult points out, after death we pass from the mirror. Because man cannot permanently apprehend truth, he never permanently reconciles the opposing forces of his life. Only death reconciles them, and its harmonies lie outside our knowledge.

II *The Sisters*

A less successful work than *Tristram of Lyonesse, The Sisters: A Tragedy* also employs the trope of doubling in an investigation of fate. Unfortunately, Swinburne attempted to write realistic dialogue in blank verse, and, though technically impressive, the attempt often looks merely silly. The plot is likewise contrived. Twin "co-heiresses" Anne and Mabel Dilston have grown up with cousins Frank Dilston and Reginald Clavering. Reginald has just returned a hero, wounded at Waterloo. Frank and Reginald pursue Mabel; Mabel and Anne pursue Reginald. When Mabel agrees to marry Reginald, Frank accepts his loss, but Anne plots to murder her twin. A poet, Reginald has written a play for the two couples to perform. Anne takes advantage of one of the props, a vial of real poison, to kill Mabel. But Reginald also unknowingly drinks; their deaths end the play. The eponymous sisters are not identical twins; and when he asks Reginald which of the women he prefers, Sir Arthur unknowingly touches on the fatal aspect of Reginald's situation: "Anne's chestnut shell, Mabel's golden fire—/ Her emerald eyes, or Anne's dark violets— eh? / You have them both (a happy hero you!)" (10:268). Reginald's tragic plight is that both women love him.

Though the twins, Anne and Mabel, are different, they are easily mistaken for each other. Swinburne reinforces this confusion of identities by means of an obvious literary parallel: when Reginald and Frank reminisce about how the two couples once acted *A Midsummer Night's Dream,* Reginald cannot recall which characters the girls played. Frank remembers that Mabel, like Helena, is blonde, while Anne, like Hermia, is dark. One of Helena's speeches in Shakespeare's play indicates the composite identity of the two women:

> We, Hermia, like two artificial gods,
> Have with our needles created both one flower,
> Both on one sampler, sitting on one cushion,
> Both warbling of one song, both in one key,
> As if our hands, our sides, voices and minds,
> Had been incorporate.
>
> (202-210)

The reference to Helena and Hermia recalls the ecstatic union proposed by Tristram to Iseult, but between the sisters it is only an illusion. Only Reginald and Mabel can achieve the heroic union of Tristram and Iseult.

Reginald, like Tristram, sees his lover as a reflection of himself. He notices only their affinity: "And you? A girl there was who loved the saddle as well as I, / And was not slower at breaking bounds" (10:268). Dazzled by love, he abases himself and identifies her with a sun-god: "I never was or could be fit for you / To glance on or to tread on. You, whose face / Was always all the light of all the world" (10:273). Reginald's ecstatic identification of self with other is so blinding that Reginald mistakes his own image, seen in Mabel, for a sun-god. The passage repeats the identification of sun-self-Truth found in *Tristram.*

The Sisters has long been recognized as autobiographical. Reginald shares Swinburne's love of Northumberland countryside, his hatred of the Irish, even his rather effeminate looks. Reginald is the wish-fulfillment of Swinburne's military ambition. Significantly, Swinburne wrote *The Sisters* just as he was renewing his relations with his early love, Mary Gordon, and she is the likely model for Mabel (Lang, p. 128). While these fantasies do mar the play, we should notice the appearance once again of the motif of apparent choice between twin alternatives. As in the much more worthy *Tristram,* fate and chance preclude any choice, and the characters draw consolation from ecstatic union in death. Edmund Wilson implies that the structure of the play is far more complex than can be accounted for on a mere autobiographical reading. However, Swinburne's reiteration of the trope of doubling explains the apparently unnecessary complexity; it indicates that he thought of himself as a double plagued by unresolved alienation.

Another indication of Swinburne's personal feeling of "doubleness" is indicated by Swinburne's rather mischievous parodies, including more than one of his own style,

written at about the time of *The Sisters,* particularly his private parody of his own celebratory ode on Eton, expressing ambivalence toward his old school. T. Earle Welby remarks on Swinburne's "curious duality," and he sees Swinburne's portrait of himself in *The Sisters* as "a boy destined never to come to full normal manhood" [*A Study of Swinburne,* 1926]. Certainly, Swinburne's preoccupation with the doubleness of self and circumstances is more often than necessary forced into his art as a compulsive doubling of character and circumstance, and, regrettably in this case, is not the source of powerful art.

The deaths of Mabel and Reginald, however, clarify Swinburne's belief that fate controls our olives and that our only freedom is in selecting our own highest version of self, a task symbolized by a loving union with another. As in *Tristram,* Reginald recognizes his own best self in a "darkened glass," externalizing it in the character of Mabel. At the moment of death, however, he no longer sees her as an external god but asserts, "I am one with her / And she forgives" (10:321). Sir Arthur's concluding line, "They could have lived no happier than they die," is a callous view alien to his character as a father. By approving of their deadly, ecstatic union, however, he functions not as a realistic character but as a choric commentary upon their union. He also demonstrates why Swinburne failed in his only attempt at realistic dialogue.

III *The Tale of Balen* and "The Altar of Righteousness"

When Swinburne published *The Tale of Balen* in 1896, he had also been writing "The Altar of Righteousness," describing it as "a lyric poem on all the religions of the world. A philosophical, antitheist poem, borrowing from Blake, "The Altar" locates the origins of all religions in human confusion. Swinburne advances the Gnostic position that before the existence of religions man knew good and evil by means of his transcendent connection with a spirit of truth associated metaphorically with the powers of nature. The sense of truth, however, has nothing to do with material nature, "Invisible: eye hath not seen it, and ear hath not heard as the spirit hath heard / From the shrine that is lit not of sunlight or starlight the sound of a limitless word" (6:217). Though the dynamic spirit of truth exists always in men, eventually a more static religion preempts it. In Swinburne's metaphor, religion covers the stone (or altar) of truth with images of an authoritarian godhead, but cannot change it or affect its underlying truth:

> The faces of gods on the face of it carven, or
>   gleaming behind and above,
> Star-glorified Uranus, thunderous Jehovah, for terror
>   or worship or love,
> Change, wither, and brighten as flowers that the
>   wind of eternity sheds upon time,
> All radiant and transient and awful and mortal, and
>   leave it unmarred and sublime.
> As the tides that return and recede are the fears
>   and the hopes of the centuries that roll,
> Requenched and rekindled: but strong as the sun is
>   the sense of it shrined in the soul.
>
> (6:219)

The word "shrined" suggests "shined," as if the sense of single Truth in the soul both is "enshrined" and is the source of radiant truth in the soul's life. In a passage reminiscent of Blake's psychic "spectres," Swinburne writes that man's religion originates in a deadening psychic projection outward of man's inner power onto nature, inverting human values as it does: "the God of his trust was the wraith of the soul or the ghost of it slain, . . . Earth shuddered with worship, and knew not if hell were not hot in her breath; / If birth were not sin, and the dew of the morning the sweat of her death" (6:220-221). As the soul understands the capriciousness of Fate, it pictures a female Nature giving birth to a male Tyrant, "the night / That conceived him and bore him had thunder for utterance and lightning for light" (6:220), and man mistakes this "thunder" for God's voice. This mother-night, creator of the world, has nothing to do with justice, yet man sees it as divine, and perverts his original, immediate apprehension of a unitary good and evil into a nature-centered religion, in which paradox prevails: "Strange horror and hope, strange faith and unfaith, were his boon and his bane" (6:220). Because man identifies a fate as God, he denies his own inner good, and, alienated from himself, he unconsciously inverts value; he is ironically, "Convicted of evil on earth by the grace of a God found good." Yet while all the world's religions grow and fade, the original source of man's truth continues, and he unconsciously makes and unmakes religions at will: "shadows that willed as he would, that were made and unmade by his word" (6:221). Man, unknowingly assumes the power of a God, then fears himself.

According to **"The Altar,"** the knowledge that man has God-like power, made clear by meditation on Christ's death, has been subverted and lost by submission to an external nature-god. Ironically, "Christ [is] by Paul cast out" (6:228). The Church confuses the human Christ with the tyrannical Father, whose representative is Paul. In brief, man is alienated from the inward source of truth and has mistakenly identified the godhead as a being external to himself, located in the natural world. Christ is man in full possession of himself, who tears away the parasitic power of the Old Testament imperatives of the thundering fire-god and establishes the universal existence of the divine life in himself and hence in all men: "Time, and truth his child, though terror set earth and heaven at odds / See the light of manhood rise on the twilight of the Gods" (6:232). When Swinburne wrote to Watts in August of 1895, remarking that he had begun working on lines "*in re* Aeschylus *v.* Moses" (6:85), he meant that **"The Altar of Righteousness"** embodied an opposition between Hebraism and Hellenism. Whereas in the Greek world view, nature is a divine but impersonal agency operating indifferently to personal human destiny, the Hebrew ethos sees nature as a direct instrument of divine justice influencing human destiny. Swinburne's view is, in this instance, Hellenic.

Because of its philosophical views, Swinburne thought that **"The Altar of Righteousness"** was the more important of the two poems on which he was working during early 1896. Of *The Tale of Balen,* he wrote to Mary Louisa Molesworth, in self-effacing mood:

> I fancy boys who read poetry of any sort will like [it], it is so full of fighting and adventure. You will say that it is a queer of poem for a man of my age to write. . . . The groundwork is an old tale of chivalry which I have closely followed in all its incidents, with but few additions or variations: so it is only for the treatment of it that any credit—or discredit—is due to me.

> (6:98)

Much of the criticism of *Balen* has been directed at Swinburne's admitted failure or refusal to alter Malory's tale greatly, or has attempted to read the significance of the few additions that he made. Yet in spite of its frequently close paraphrases of Malory, *Balen* is one of the finest achievements of Swinburne's career, early or late. Swinburne never denied his debt to Malory, acknowledging it privately, in his letter to Molesworth, and publicly in the **"Dedicatory Epistle,"** yet little attention has been given to the positive achievement of the poem.

From a biographical point of view, Malory's tale provides Swinburne with a two-fold occasion for returning to memories of childhood. As in *The Sisters,* the central character of Balen is, like Swinburne himself, Northumbrian, delighting in landscape of his native ground; and like Tristram, a "child of heroic earth and heavenly sea," Balen is "A northern child of earth and sea" (4:171). A more private motive for the composition of the poem was the death of Swinburne's brother in 1891. Algernon was not close to the respectable and stable Edward, but his passing caused Swinburne to think about spiritual brotherhood; he wrote to Watts, "I should have died as my poor dear brother has just died, if instead of the worst of wives I had not found the best of friends" (6:14). Beneath his smug response to Edward's death we apprehend Swinburne's understanding of the harsh inevitability of his own fate along with an inchoate sense of brotherhood and its ameliorative connection with fate and identity.

The composition of *Balen* was also partly a response to Tennyson's retelling of the story, published ten years before. Swinburne meant his tale to be more faithful to Malory, whose version, Swinburne implied in the **"Dedicatory Epistle,"** rivals Homer in its representation of the power of fate in human life. Swinburne's well-known private rivalry with and occasional derision of Tennyson surely accounted for some of Swinburne's desire to disabuse the public of its mistaken ideas about Malory's virtues. More importantly, he wished to rescue Malory's daring energies from Tennyson's domestication. His faithfulness in paraphrasing Malory, therefore, was not the result of inattention or imitation but of his perception that Malory's tale, with its heroic double knights, possesses the latent power to express a powerful understanding of fate.

Because *The Tale of Balen* closely follows Malory's telling, its episodic character first impresses the reader as disconnected or random. But seen in its totality, the tale of two brothers, often deceived and finally duped into killing one another, is a narrative of great power. Of all the knights in Arthur's court, only Balen "the Wild" can accomplish the task set by a strange lady, by removing the sword which she wears at her waist. When she asks for its return Balen's refusal evokes a vengeful prophecy: he will kill with it "The man best loved of thee, and lay / Thine own life down for his" (4:180). The subsequent series of random-seeming adventures, which immerse Balen in a welter of suicide and murder of knights and ladies, leaves him saddened but undaunted by the bloodshed in which he is implicated by fate. In the end, preparing for battle with an unknown knight, without apparent motive or necessity, Balen accepts from a stranger a newer, stronger shield in exchange for his own. Without his familial shield, he fulfills the prophecy. He is tricked into combat with his brother Balan, who cannot recognize his twin because of his new shield. Balen slays him and is himself mortally wounded. His earthly fate remains impenetrable.

Swinburne follows Tennyson in making Balen and Balan twin brothers, a point not clear in Malory, and both poets see in the story psychological symbols involving a split in the human soul. Yet Tennyson sees the idyll of Balin (so he spelled Malory's "Balyne") as an allegory in which Balin the Savage represents the uncontrollable urges which would destroy the Round Table. In Tennyson's version, Balin attempts to suppress his rages, but when he learns of Guenevere's infidelity, he destroys his shield and utters a wild cry which his brother Balan assumes is the bellow of a wood-devil. Unable to recognize his now shieldless brother, Balan and Balin mutually destroy each other. Rationality and primitive emotion join in battle, and both die. In his clear and rational retelling, Tennyson suppresses all supernatural elements in the story. He deletes the fatal invisibility of Pellam's evil brother Garlon, and transforms King Pellam's collection of relics into an impious and avaricious fraud. Tennyson's *Balin and Balan* is a Freudian allegory in which the struggle between the inborn violence of Balin and the reasoned propriety of Balan eventually destroys them both. No third party, supernatural or not, can intervene.

Given the Freudian dichotomy predicated of Tennyson's allegorical interpretation of the brothers as opposing forces, it does not require much perspicuity to see Swinburne's twin brothers as a Jungian *coincidentia oppositorum,* fortuitously engaged in a battle which brings about a complementary union of polar forces. So Swinburne's Balen is not as irrational as Tennyson's Balin. Swinburne emphasizes not his rashness but the incomprehensibility of his condition; his defiance of the world is valiant given the malignity of his fate. Further, Swinburne, in contrast to Tennyson, strongly underscores the complementary nature of the twins. When they are reunited for the first time in the poem, Swinburne echoes Shakespeare's description of Hermia and Helena who "with our needles created both one flower . . . Both warbling of one song, both in one key." The two brothers are "Twin flower of bright Northumberland, / Twin sea-bird of their loud sea-strand, / Twin song-bird of their morn" (4:193). When Balan says "we / Will cleave together, bound and free, / As brethren should, being twain and one" (4:194), Swin-

burne uses words which suggest some of the paradoxical quality he saw in their union. Elsewhere, Swinburne describes the lightning that "cleaves in twain the shadow of night," and reverses the meanings of both words. "Cleave" means both "to sunder" and "to join together with," and "twain" likewise implies "two, yet joined into one." The words suggest that Balen and Balan, the paradoxically divided halves of a single soul, cannot be wholly reunited in life. In this sort of wordplay Swinburne does not deal in ambiguities but suggests instead the prevalence of paradox: we are both united and separate.

The ironic circumstances of the two brothers' first meeting in the poem supports the implication that life cannot accommodate the paradoxical human ideal of lasting union. Immediately before the meeting, Balen kills the knight Lanceor, who wished to avenge Balen's earlier offense to Arthur. Lanceor's lady, seeing him dead, kills herself, accusing Balen of her murder: "Two bodies and one heart thou hast slain, / Two hearts within one body" (4:192). Their deaths echo the deaths of Tristram and Iseult, for Iseult had prayed for a similar union in death:

> Keep *not* in twain for ever heart and heart
> That once, albeit by *not* thy law, were one;
> Let this be *not* thy will, that this be done.
> Let all else, all thou wilt of evil, be,
> But *no* doom, *none,* dividing him and me.
>
> (4:103; emphases mine)

Because of her union with Tristram, Iseult's rhetoric inverts ordinary pieties about the deity, as does **"The Altar of Righteousness."** In an ironic echo of Christ's plea in the Garden of Gethsemane, she entreats her god in negatives, because she comprehends that her deity's designs on man are evil. Like Iseult, Lanceor's lady achieves union with her knight only in death, and in spite of fate.

The negative vision of God in Iseult's rhetoric, and of Jehovah in **"The Altar of Righteousness,"** reappears in Balen's depiction of God as a tyrant in the opening scene of *The Tale of Balen.* When the mysterious lady foretells his doom, his response is stoic: "What chance God sends, that chance I take" (4:180), identifying God's will with fate and thus with the brute life of force: "'God's will', quoth he, 'it is we know, / Wherewith our lives are bound'" (4:180).

The death of Lanceor's lady evokes from Swinburne another transvaluing irony: "she woke / And struck one swift and bitter stroke / That healed her, and she died" (4:192). The suggestion of these lines, that death brings wholeness to life, is never made in Malory, and makes absurd Swinburne's playful assertion that the poem was mostly for "boys." It reiterates the theme, implicit in *Tristram* and *The Sisters,* that the sacrifice of lovers united in death is a metaphor for health and integrity.

Like the doomed lovers of *The Sisters,* Balen and Balan also achieve a fleeting union in life. When the brothers meet for the first time in the poem, their union evokes images of their Northumbrian home. All of the accrued fears of a lifetime are dismissed, leaving a central core of truth:

Ah then from Balen passed away
All dread of night, all doubt of day,
All care what life or death might say,
All thought of all worse months than May:

. . . . .

For no man's life knows love more fair
　　And fruitful of memorial things
Than this the deep dear love that breaks
With sense of life on life, and makes
The sundawn sunnier as it wakes
　　Where morning round it rings.

(4:193)

The divesting of earthly fear to reveal authentic truth associated metaphorically with the sun complements **"The Altar of Righteousness,"** which contends that fear creates deceptive religion, subverting truth into lies.

Conversely, when, in combat with Pellam in his castle, Balen forgets about his "second sword" in the heat of battle, this indicates that separation from his psychic twin, Balan, and the resulting fears, deprive him of his full selfhood. Unaware of his own incompleteness, he fails to use his full resources and substitutes instead a religious relic, the Spear of Longinus. This recourse to an externally derived religion indicates Balen's distance from full integrated selfhood.

The second, fatal meeting of the two brothers, like the first, evokes a reminiscence of wholeness. The temporary wholeness of the first meeting is tragically duplicated as a doomed union in the second. After his brother's death, Balen lingers into the night. The bittersweet restoration of Balen's wholeness is again evoked in a lyric recursion to images from Swinburne's Northumbrian childhood:

And there low lying, as hour on hour
Fled, all his life in all its flower
Came back as in a sunlit shower
Of dreams,

. . . . .

The joy that lives at heart and home,
The joy to rest, the joy to roam,
The joy of crags and scaurs he clomb,
The rapture of the encountering foam
　　Embraced and breasted of the boy,
The first good steed his knees bestrode,
The first wild sound of songs that flowed
Through ears that thrilled and heart that glowed
　　Fulfilled his death with joy.

(4:244-245)

Both of these depictions of ecstatic union between Balan and Balen imply that the immediate authenticity and truth apprehended in childhood had been lost in Balen's journey to the southern court of Arthur. In Arthur's court, Balen has been forced into a bad bargain, exchanging his natural individualism for the entangling world of human society, and its projections of fear. Nonetheless, Swinburne assures us that Balen's eventual death is joyful, because he regains the truth "shrined within," symbolized by his reunion with Balan. To describe the social world of

Balen one need only repeat the outline of Balen's adventures. In war, united for once with his brother, he succeeds in a good cause, the most admired knight in the battle against King Ryon. But Balen becomes alienated in peaceful society; without Balan he is incomplete, and he unintentionally causes strife. The vengeful resonance of the past binds him in cycles of revenge and of despair in which good deeds inevitably lead to horrifying consequences. But Balen remains innocent, though he is a lightning-rod for evil vengeance. For instance, the deaths of Lanceor and his lady stem from Lanceor's vow to avenge on Balen the affront given to Arthur when Balen rightfully killed the Lady of the Lake in his court. Merlin informs us that the deaths of Lanceor and his lady bring down a curse on Balen, dooming him to smite King Pellam "a dolorous stroke and strange," which will cause twelve years of evil to three kingdoms. Balen's initial killing of the Lady of the Lake, revenging her murder of Balen's mother, brings on the death of Lanceor, and the destruction of Pellam's castle. Thus, in *Balen* fate only appears random; in reality it is a complex and inescapable pattern of obligation and revenge. Swinburne sees this weaving and binding of fate as an inevitable effect of the movement of time:

As wave smites wave to death and dies,
　　So chance on hurtling chance like steel
Strikes, flashes, and is quenched, ere fear
Can whisper hope, or hope can hear,
If sorrow or joy be far or near
　　For time to hurt or heal.

(4:196)

The passage reinforces Swinburne's depiction of Balen as uneasy with the will of an incomprehensible and tyrannical God, yet willing to plunge unreservedly into the stream of life: "What chance God sends, that chance I take." Further, because Balen has entered the society of Camelot, a world where blood is literally forced from the innocent to heal the powerful, he is enmeshed in a world far more hostile to human life than the natural world from which he had come.

But nature is not benign to man. The passage above, beginning fit V of *Balen* also forms a part of a larger pattern which Swinburne has embroidered in Malory's tale emphasizing nature's beautiful destructiveness. He has divided his poem into seven fits, each opening with a passionate description of the natural world. In each case, however, the opening stanzas are not merely naturalistic description, but meditations on the joyous indifference of nature to man's hopes. For instance, fit IV opens with the image of the morning, laughing "to watch his trophies won," unheeding that, as the sun brings victory to morning, it will eventually bring on its death in night:

Each day that slays its hours and dies
Weeps, laughs, and lightens on our eyes,
And sees and hears not . . .

. . . . .

As shadows flashing down a glass.

(4:189)

Nature is indifferent even to its own constant dying, and, no matter how lovely, it cannot aid man's transcendence of fate, nor, obviously, can vengeful human society as represented by Camelot. Only in man's disdain for fate can transcendence be glimpsed. The integrity of Balen's personality shows most clearly in his defiance of fate even as it defeats him. His wholeness is symbolized by his final reunion with his twin Balan, but it is earned through a sustained refusal to accept guilt for what fate has compelled him to do. When Merlin prophesies "the dolorous stroke," Balen replies valiantly that if he knew Merlin's prophecy to be true, "Then even to make a liar of thee / Would I too slay myself, and see / How death bids dead men fare" (4:197). His achievement lies in his heroic willingness to thwart an evil fate, not from mere egoism but from a consciousness of fate's dark and inhuman purposes.

That Balen is associated with Christ reminds us that Christ too proclaimed his own selfhood as well as mankind's and that, according to Swinburne, his legacy was also clouded by the processes of human fear described in **"The Altar of Righteousness."** Early in *Balen,* the lady with the sword warns Balen that he will "lay / Thine own life down" for the man he will kill, echoing the Gospel of St. John. Later, Balen metes out "the dolorous stroke" to Pellam with the lance that pierced the side of Christ. Forgetting his second sword, Balen takes up the relic "Spear of Longinus" of the Parsival legend, and wounds King Pellam, engendering cosmic repercussions. In the ensuing fight at Pellam's castle, an evocation of the myth of the Fisher King, Pellam and Balan join together as a single sacrificial victim, and as the king falls, the walls of the castle are "rent from base to crown," recalling the temple veil "rent from the top to the bottom" (Matthew 27.51) at Christ's death. Both men lie together for three days in "death's blind kingdom" (4:235), suggesting that they share in reenacting the three days Christ lay in the tomb. Afterward, Pellam's subjects unaccountably fear the risen liberator-savior Balen, who had cleansed the world of the murderously invisible Garlon, and name him as the cause of their distress, projecting upon him the hellish power of the lance, although he remains innocent of the cosmic evil which has befallen their kingdom. Balen the savior is identified with the tyrant he has slain. In this respect, Balen may not seem to be fully assimilated to Christ, who does not become a tyrant in scripture. However, this association of Balen with Christ is clarified in **"The Altar of Righteousness,"** where Christ, like Balen, emerges as a savior whose good news has been perverted by Pauline distortions which replace Christ with a tyrannical Jehovah. Balan's exploit is soteriological, ending Pellam's and Garlon's reign of terror, literally rending the temple apart, but his deliverance of the kingdom, misinterpreted by the people, becomes a source of evil. Likewise, in **"The Altar of Righteousness"** Swinburne asserts that after Christ's death, his followers merged his image with a projection of their fear, the old tyrant Jehovah, "The dark old God who had slain him grew one with the Christ he slew / And poison was rank in the grain that with growth of his gospel grew" (6:229); in other words, because of the Pauline spectres of his followers, evil mixes with the good which Christ engendered. Balen likewise involuntarily shares the fate of Pellam. Like other themes

in **"The Altar of Righteousness"** this reference to the merging of Christ and Jehovah seems inspired by Blake, who used a similar image to depict the corruption of Christianity in *Jerusalem*: "The wine of the Spirit & the vineyards of the Holy-One / Here: turn into poisonous stupor & deadly intoxication." In **"The Altar of Righteousness,"** Christ, like Balen, involuntarily causes an almost universal destruction because his followers mix his message with a lie. Only in recent years does man appear ready to cast off the old tyrant God (6:229).

A final association of Balen with Christ occurs when he glimpses the castle where he will meet his doom; there he sees that "all the stone / Glowed in the sun's glare even as though blood stained it from the crucified / Dead burden of one that there had died" (4:233). As Balen and Balan die, we learn that their deaths save many others and put an end to the "custom" which had pitted knights against one another. The final act of the brothers ends a corrupt cycle of revenge, and frees men from bondage to fate and evil "custom."

The lyrics which begin each fit of the poem suggest that nature offers no reliable source for truth, a suggestion consonant with the vision of the poem, which declares that Balen's destiny marks something far more profound than otiose deeds dictated by random circumstance. The energy of Balen's defiance of fate which Swinburne sought to rescue from Tennyson's pietism is connected with the energies of Blake's Los who must destroy in order to create. The solar imagery which Swinburne earlier identified with autonomous selfhood is here extended to the Gospel of St. John, and the Christocentric light of the sun.

The story of Balen appealed to Swinburne on personal grounds since *The Tale of Balen*, along with the other works in which doubling occurs, probably served to reconcile disparity between the public, didactic face of the later Swinburne, and his more private, aesthetic face. His rejection of London social relationships (though passive, it was not wholly involuntary) mirrors Balen's Northumbrian distaste for Arthur's realm; his active love of nature takes idealized form in Balen's character; his devotion to his more-than-brother Watts emerges in the brotherly Balen and Balan. Further, Swinburne was drawn to Malory's tale because it so entirely suited his convictions about fate, religion, life, and death; those who have found the poem defective because it closely emulates Malory do not consider how deftly Swinburne turned Malory's tale to his own account. Balan's determination to test fate suited Swinburne's philosophy of devotion to an ineffable truth which permits us to banish fear and to imitate Tristram who reconciled "wholly without fear or fitful breath / The face of life watched by the face of death" (4:80), or Balen:

> So, dying not as a coward that dies
> And dares not look in death's dim eyes
> Straight as stars on seas and skies
> Whence moon and sun recoil and rise
>   He looked on life and death, and slept.

(4:245)

James P. Carley (essay date 1990)

SOURCE: An introduction to *Algernon Charles Swinburne,* The Boydell Press, 1990, pp. 1-9.

[In the following essay, Carley discusses the defining characteristics of Swinburne's Arthurian poems.]

Algernon Charles Swinburne (1837-1909) was one of the large group of poets and artists who fell under the spell of the Arthurian legend in the mid nineteenth century. As he would later explain in *Under the Microscope* (1872)

> The story as it stood of old had in it something almost of Hellenic dignity and significance; in it as in the great Greek legends we could trace from a seemingly small root of evil the birth and growth of a calamitous fate, not sent by mere malevolence of heaven, yet in its awful weight and mystery of darkness apparently out of all due retributive proportion to the careless sin or folly of presumptuous weakness which first incurred its infliction; so that by mere hasty resistance and return of violence for violence a noble man may unwittingly bring on himself and all his house the curse denounced on parricide, by mere casual indulgence in light love and passing wantonness a hero king may unknowingly bring on himself and all his kingdom the doom imposed on incest.

For Swinburne, as for so many others, Sir Thomas Malory's great collection, the *Morte Darthur* (which had become widely available through two editions—one by the poet Robert Southey—earlier in the century) represented a major source of inspiration. Even earlier, however, Swinburne's firsthand acquaintance with the fine illuminated medieval manuscripts in the library of his uncle, the Earl of Ashburnham, exerted a formative influence; years later he told Edmund Gosse 'that the medieval and French sections of his uncle's famous collection had been a source of unfailing enjoyment to him.' As an undergraduate at Oxford, he became a disciple of William Morris and Dante Gabriel Rossetti and wrote the first poems of the complete Arthuriad he envisaged in conscious imitation of their renditions.

The early poems are all short and several remain unfinished. Although he knew the general outlines of the Tristram story both from Malory and from various medieval French versions, Swinburne's chief model in his **'Queen Yseult'** (an incomplete work of six cantos in irregular iambic tetrameter rhyming triplets, written in 1857-58) was Sir Walter Scott's edition of *Sir Tristrem.* The poem begins at the point when Tristram's mother, Blancheflour, takes Roland 'to paramour' and ends with Yseult of Ireland's lonely vigil in Cornwall after Tristram has married Yseult of the White Hands: 'So she saw days go and come, / And at night in the old room / Lay she gazing thro' the gloom.' **'Queen Yseult'** stands as a verbal portrait of Yseult in all her beauty, emblemized by 'her golden corn-ripe hair'; the poem is a kind of equivalent to the voluptuous paintings being produced by Morris, Rossetti and others. **'Joyeuse Garde'** (1859) describes a meeting between Tristram and Yseult at Lancelot's cas-

tle. Summer heat and stillness are evoked—'the noon outside them seem to throb and sink / Wrought in the quiet to a rounded rhyme'—and form a correlative to Yseult's fears of separation and of Mark's plottings. **'King Ban'** (written in 1857 and published posthumously in 1915), is a melancholic and introspective fragment, based loosely on an adventure in the *Morte Darthur.* Unlike the equivalent scene in Malory, however, Arthur, his will sapped by 'A pleasure sweet and sick as marsh-flowers', does not come to the rescue of Ban, who is besieged from without by Claudas and betrayed from within by his own seneschal. Like Christ Ban prays that he not be forsaken—but the poem ends with the stark realization that he is 'stricken among men' and that friendship is false: 'a snake's life to poison me'. In **'The Day Before the Trial'** (1857-58), Swinburne recasts the episode described by Morris in 'The Defence of Guenevere', as Arthur ponders his wife's adultery and her beauty. The Guenevere evoked—'For all these years she grew more fair / More sweet her low sweet speeches were, / More long and heavy grew her hair'— is clearly recognizable as the proud and defiant queen in Morris' poem. **'Lancelot'** (1858-60) tells of Lancelot's Grail quest, a quest which strongly contrasts with the successful adventures of his son as portrayed by Morris in 'Sir Galahad: A Christmas Mystery'. **'Lancelot'** also serves as a kind of dramatization of Rossetti's painting 'Launcelot at the Shrine of the Sanc Grael'. Even more strong is the evocation of the same close and oppressive, debilitating atmosphere as that in Morris' 'King Arthur's Tomb': 'Very long and hot it was, / The dry light on the dry grass, / The set noon on lakes of glass'. In both cases, Lancelot's quest is ultimately a failure: in **'King Arthur's Tomb'** Guenevere repudiates Lancelot and chooses Christ over her mortal lover; in **'Lancelot'** the image of Guenevere as she once was—not as now 'grey cheeks and waning hair'—is superimposed on his incipient vision of the Grail.

The immediate inspiration for Swinburne's major Arthurian poem *Tristram of Lyonesse*—the **'Prelude'** of which was published in 1871, the complete poem in 1882—was Tennyson. 'I am impelled', Swinburne wrote to Rossetti on 22 December, 1869

> to write on the instant to say how delighted I am to find the Tennysonian seed ('if seed it may be called that seed has none—distinguishable in member, joint or limb') bearing the same fruit in your mind as in mine. Having read a few pages of the 'Grail' I fell at once tooth and nail upon Tristram and Iseult and wrote at an overture of the poem projected, all yesterday. My first sustained attempt at a poetic narrative may not be as good as Gudrun—but if it doesn't lick the Morte d'Albert I hope I may not die without extreme unction.'

The whole poem can be read, as this letter indicates (in spite of all the ironic commentary on Tennyson), as a kind of musical elaboration of the love/fate theme presented in the **'Prelude'.** In an elegant, almost Huysmans-like conceit, Swinburne invokes a zodiac of heroines, all doomed through love, itself an eternally repetitive force: 'The spirit that for temporal veil has on / The souls of all men woven in unison'. Of these heroines Iseult is Swinburne's own 'birth-month star' and he promises therefore to 'give / Out of my life to make [her] dead life live / Some days of mine'. In the overture, then, we have love and doom combined in the procession of tragic figures, time and recurrence underlined in the configuration as zodiac. Death as peaceful resolution, too, figures strongly; the dead lovers are all 'Healed of our wound of living.'

If *Tristram of Lyonesse* took its origin as a direct rebuttal of Tennyson's Camelot as Swinburne reacted against it, so too does the poem stand in contrast to Matthew Arnold's version of the Tristram legend:

> But the only possible excuse for an English poet who has ventured, after you [Arnold], to rehandle the story of Tristram and Iseult must be that which I offer—namely, that the old legend was so radically altered in its main points by your conception and treatment of that subject, and especially of the circumstances which bring about the catastrophe in all the old French forms of the romance, that the field was really open to a new writer who might wish to work on the old lines.

Swinburne was, as his letter implicitly suggests, much more familiar with the medieval sources than Arnold—who had not read Malory or the great medieval French romances when he composed his *Tristram and Iseult* (published in 1852). On 4 November 1869, Swinburne wrote to Burne-Jones:

> With 1) Mallory, 2) Scott's chaos [Sir Tristrem] . . . and—if I can get it—3) Michel's collection of every metrical fragment on Tristram extant, published by old Pickering, I shall have enough stuff to build my poem on. Besides the French poem, there is one (written at Micklegarth) in medieval Greek of the canine dialect which is at least a good lark.

The resonances of this wide reading permeate the poem, giving it an intellectual depth which balances the static intensity of the lovers' passion—as in **'The Sailing of the Swallow'** episode when

> . . . Tristram spake of many a noble thing,
> High feast and storm of tournay round the king,
> Strange quest by perilous lands of marsh and brake
> And circling woods branch-knotted like a snake
> And places pale with sins that they had seen . . .

Speaker and poet are both, it is clear, familiar travellers in these 'perilous lands' of high adventure.

In a much more obvious contrast to Arnold's *Tristram and Iseult, Tristram of Lyonesse* makes use of the traditional motif of the black and white sails, which forms a key part of the plot. In Swinburne's poem Iseult has consistently yoked love and death as consummation in ecstasy and unity:

> But I—this end God send me, would I say,
> To die not of division and a heart

> Rent or with sword of severance cloven apart,
> But only when thou diest and only where thou art,
> O thou my soul and spirit and breath to me . . .

In the context of this *leitmotif,* Iseult of the White Hand's final victory through her misinformation about the colour of the sails is not negligible; it is a major achievement and cruel punishment, since she ultimately thwarts the lovers of the final transcendent union towards which they had for so long been moving. Her bitterness and hate are also extraordinarily intense in this poem: there are few resemblances to Arnold's mild neurasthenic heroine. In Swinburne's *Tristram of Lyonesse*—unlike Arnold's poem where there are two children—the marriage is one in name only and Iseult of the White Hands remains a virgin. (Swinburne uses a hawthorn flower rather than the traditional drop of water as the means for her to signal this fact to her brother.) Iseult's colour, white, ultimately shades into the yellow of jealousy, as she comes to realize that 'Me, me, the fullness of their joy drains dry, / Their fruitfulness makes barren'. 'White-handed', Iseult is consumed not by love but by 'A virgin lust for vengeance'. By the end, she sees herself as an agent of a just Old Testament God and sitting by Tristram's side she rejoices that 'I am death'. The ironies implicit in the shared name with her rival become deeply bitter in this scene: Tristram, calling for Iseult of Ireland, his life and death; Iseult of the White Hands, responding as agent of vengeance; Tristram's 'death-bell faint and clear' call for one Iseult and the other's calm cruel answer 'I am here.'

After the lovers' death the previously unattractive King Mark—'With black streaked beard and cold unquiet eyes, / Close-mouthed, gaunt-cheeked, wan as a morning moon'—becomes himself a sympathetic commentator and interprets the action. The tragedy, as it is revealed to him by the writing around the sword, was inevitable; it was not selfishness but a cruel doom which determined the actions of the lovers. Fate, as it must, triumphed and sorrow becomes the only appropriate emotion. Sin does not enter into it; in this respect the tragedy resembles the earlier unjust punishment of Queen Morgause:

> Great pity it is and strange it seems to me
> God could not do them so much right as we,
> Who slay not men for witless evil done;
> And these the noblest under God's glad sun
> For sin they knew not he that knew shall slay,
> And smite blind men for stumbling in fair day.

The chapel which Mark erects for the lovers is a powerful symbol for the story itself and ties in neatly with another *leitmotif*—borrowed from Arnold—which runs through the poem: the story of Merlin and Nimue. For the lovers, Merlin's enchantment—one to which he willingly assented—becomes a longed-for state, 'sleep as kind as death'. Change normally rules all things, which is why Iseult desires death at the moment of consummation. It is, so it appears, impossible for normal mortals to escape from the unending cycle, but Merlin's fate gives us an inkling of how this might be accomplished: '[He] knows the soul that was his soul at one / With the ardent world's'. When Tristram reminds Iseult of Merlin's doom at the point when they themselves are ecstatically but temporarily enclosed at Joyous Gard, she observes that 'some joy it were to be / Lost in the sun's light and the all-girdling sea, / Mixed with the winds and woodlands, and to bear / Part in the large life of the quickening air, / And the sweet earth's, our mother'. (The motif of the all-cleansing sea is quintessentially Swinburnian.) But Iseult also fears that she is no Nimue—Nimue here seems a combination of Venus and the medieval goddess Nature—and that she and Tristram will never attain this peace even through death. The legend of Lyonesse, sinking off the coast of Cornwall (and it is worth remembering that the poem has Lyonesse in its title) provides Swinburne with the metaphor to allow Tristram and Iseult finally to achieve the sleep of Merlin. The chapel which the repentant Mark erected was subject like all things of this earth to time's sway—'moon and sun / And change of stars'—but when it sank under the sea (the source of life, the achiever of peace, unlike the sun the quickener of life), then the lovers escaped from the cycle; they became another model of Merlin's triumph. ([In *The Victorian Newsletter,* 1987] Clifton Snider sees the parallel in Jungian terms and suggests that 'Merlin, through union with the anima [symboized by Nimue], achieves a wholeness emblematic of the wholeness Tristram achieves with Iseult.')

It is difficult to characterize *Tristram of Lyonesse.* Arnold complained of Swinburne's prolixity, that is his 'fatal habit of using a hundred words where one would suffice' and T. S. Eliot labelled him as 'diffuse'—quickly adding, however, that 'diffuseness is one of his glories'. Many modern critics see the poem fitting into an epic tradition—with specific links to Milton's *Paradise Lost*—although Swinburne himself tells us that the poem was written

> not in the epic or romantic form of sustained or continuous narrative, but mainly through a succession of dramatic scenes or pictures with descriptive settings or backgrounds . . .

Related to the development of these dramatic scenes and recurring motifs are the musical correspondences and Swinburne felt that his work related strongly to the Wagnerian tradition. Not surprisingly, balance and repetition are key factors: **'The Sailing of the Swallow'** matches **'The Sailing of the Swan'** with the closely parallel invocations to Love and Fate (carried to extreme lengths with the first thirty-eight lines of **'The Sailing of the Swan'** replicating the rhyme scheme of the **'Prelude',** until finally in lines 39 and 40 'hate' and 'fate' replace 'above' and 'love'); the bower in the forest has its equivalent at Joyous Gard; Iseult of the White Hands' 'I am here' response in **'The Maiden Marriage'** is contrasted to her identical statement in **'The Sailing of the Swan'**; the opening 'And their four lips became one burning mouth' becomes the final 'And their four lips became one silent mouth'.

Swinburne asserted that *Tristram of Lyonesse* was a 'moral history'; i.e., the example of Tristram and Iseult shows us the narrowness of conventional morality and the neces-

sity of repudiating society's repressive rules—this is reflected in the very structure of the poem with its proliferation of paradoxes, oxymorons and other rhetorical devices of discontinuity. In order to be fulfilled, to achieve one's destiny, one must accept the power of passion and follow the directions where it will lead. The poem is, as Nicolas Tredell tells us [in *Victorian Poetry,* 1982], 'radically subversive' on all levels: 'Language, like myth and symbol, is pushed to the frontiers of sense and creates itself anew there.' Tennyson's stern, duty-laden, Christianity is dismissed and Walter Pater's mediaevalism where 'religion shades into sensuous love and sensuous love into religion' is embraced:

> Here, under this strange complex of conditions, as in some medicated air, exotic flowers of sentiment expand, among people of a remote and unaccustomed beauty, somnambulistic, frail, androgynous, the light almost shining through them.'
>
> (*Westminster Review,* n.s. 34 [1868])

The last of Swinburne's Arthurian poems—*The Tale of Balen* (1895/96)—represents a structural departure from the earlier works as well as an alternative to Tennyson's 'Balin and Balan'. In *The Tale of Balen* Swinburne consciously attempts to adhere carefully to his source in all its detail rather than taking the events and transforming them into a new narrative: 'The groundwork is an old tale of chivalry which I have closely followed in all its incidents, with but few additions or variations: so it is only for the treatment of it that any credit—or discredit—is due to me.' The story itself is one of tragic inevitability, brother killing brother and rendering fate 'full at last'—at which point the children of 'one star-crossed mother's woful womb' can find peace 'within one grave pit's gloom'. For Swinburne the theme seemed a mythic one of Hellenic proportion; it also profoundly reflected his own views of the human condition: 'There is no episode in the cycle of Arthurian romance more genuinely Homeric in its sublime simplicty of submission to the masterdom of fate than that which I have rather reproduced than recast in *The Tale of Balen* . . .' In terms of treatment Swinburne's most obvious contribution is poetic. He had long felt that the ballad was a major literary form—'there must be no waste of a word or a minute in the course of its rapid and fiery motion'—and in this poem he uses a ballad-like nine-line iambic tetrameter stanza (a form with which he had experimented earlier) both to give a medieval atmosphere and to shape his narrative.

Although *The Tale of Balen* was immensely popular when it was first published, most modern critics—such as David Staines—have labelled it nothing more than a 'dramatic paraphrase' and a failure as a poetic entity. For many it is the form itself which finally palls: as Philip Henderson [in *Swinburne: Portrait of a Poet,* 1974] has observed 'a metre resembling **'The Lady of Shalott'** becomes almost unendurable when spun out to such a length.' There has, however, been some reaction against this view and Antony Harrison [in *Swinburne,* 1988] has recently praised the poem's energy, enthusiastically proclaiming it 'the last truly important Victorian mediaevalist poem'.

Allison Pease (essay date 1997)

SOURCE: "Questionable Figures: Swinburne's *Poems and Ballads*," in *Victorian Poetry*, Vol. 35, No. 1, Spring, 1997, pp. 43-56.

[*In the following essay, Pease examines the controversy surrounding the publication of Swinburne's* Poems and Ballads, *maintaining that the debate was not only about pornography, but also about "middle- and upper-class male privilege in a society whose rigid class boundaries were threatening to give way to a feminized underclass."*]

How does a society decide to call one naked body art and another pornography? Clearly context and the set of expectations brought to viewing the body are determining features. But such a notion raises the question of what a society wants and comes to expect from its art. This question becomes particularly interesting when posed against the Victorian backdrop of Swinburne's release of *Poems and Ballads*. For on August 4, 1866, the literary establishment of London was roused to great excitement over Algernon Charles Swinburne's latest poetic flourish. Reviewers from across the political spectrum declared the poetry, "a carnival of ugly shapes," "unclean for the mere sake of uncleanness," exhibiting "a mind all aflame with the feverish carnality of a schoolboy." On the surface it seems that what shocked these critics most of all was the open representation of physical sexuality in the poetry. But while the reviews focus on obscenity, they are coded in a language that reveals an even deeper anxiety about middle- and upper-class male privilege in a society whose rigid class boundaries were threatening to give way to a feminized underclass.

Boundaries play a central role in *Poems and Ballads* as well as in the critical debate between Swinburne and his critics. In their representation of what was perceived as masculine women and feminine men, Swinburne's poems threaten to destabilize the socially constructed norms of male and female behavior. Likewise, his ambiguous and metonymic treatment of the body, his failure to "dress" desiring bodies in the cloak of language presupposed by the literary mores of the time (it is no coincidence that the Victorians were masterfully elaborate dressers, literally and literarily) threatens to destabilize the boundary between obscenity and art. Within the debate over *Poems and Ballads* the margins constructed between civilization and nature, order and chaos, procreation and perversion, and male and female are all raised, deconstructed, and, I would argue, reconstructed by Swinburne in his heated public response to the critics to reformulate male and upper-class hegemony not as antithetical to the notions of his critics, but in fact as complementary to them.

In *The Archeology of Knowledge and the Discourse of Language,* Foucault writes that "in every society the production of discourse is at once controlled, selected, organised and redistributed according to a certain number of procedures, whose role it is to avert its powers and its dangers, to cope with chance events, to evade its ponderous, awesome materiality." Ideology, in this sense, serves to produce and justify a series of prohibitions which determine what may be spoken, when and where it may be spoken, and who may speak. It creates and upholds boundaries. That the boundaries of a certain Victorian aesthetic and class ideology had been exceeded and therefore threatened by *Poems and Ballads* was clear when its reviews appeared.

John Morley, known as an able journalist with liberal leanings, levelled what Edmund Gosse mistakenly believed to be a death blow to Swinburne in *The Saturday Review* [August 4, 1866]. Morley wrote, "He is so firmly and avowedly fixed in an attitude of revolt against the current notions of decency and dignity and social duty that to beg of him to become a little more decent, to fly a little less persistently and gleefully to the animal side of human nature, is simply to beg him to be something different from Mr. Swinburne." Coming seven years after the publication of Darwin's *On the Origin of Species by Means of Natural Selection or the Preservation of the Favoured Races in the Struggle for Life* (1859), the charge of pandering to humanity's animal side is a grave accusation. Within the newly created discourse of evolution and degeneration, to become mired within the animal was to enact a return to a previous state of evolution, to regress, to be weak. Such a regression was frequently associated with the female (and, I will show, the lower classes), who was believed to be a less evolved creature than the rational male. Notions of "decency and dignity and social duty" were concepts implicitly wrapped up in the project of "civilization," man's orderly realm categorized as separate from nature and the savage instincts. Distinct from bodies that could be traced to a lineage with beasts, civilization was dominated by the realm of the mind, the spiritual, and the rational. It was defined by its difference from the body, the physical, and the instinctual. [In *Sexuality in Victorian Fiction,* 1993] Dennis Allen has noted that the Victorians frequently troped the sexual as chaotic because it was associated with the disorder of nature and the bestial instincts rather than with an ordered culture framed within the mind. Allen writes: "The Victorians see sex and sexuality as chaotic not only in their essence but in their effects, as forces that continually threaten to shatter the distinction between civilized and savage or culture and nature." Thus when Morley bemoans the fact that Swinburne "would scorn to throw any veil over pictures which kindle, as these do, all the fires of his imagination in their intensest heat and glow," he suggests that it is the "naked" or bestial forms of sexuality which give offense. Had he "veiled" them with the cloak of metaphor, they would in effect have traversed the boundaries from obscenity to art. Making even more explicit his sense of the mind/body hierarchy by troping it in the language of monarchy, Morley writes, "It is a very bad and silly thing to try to set up the pleasures of sense in the seat of the reason they have dethroned." Morley's Hegelian image of sense dethroning reason resonates not just with the obvious hierarchy of culture over nature, but with the Marxist image of social rebellion that suggests a fear of the lower echelons taking over the higher ones. *The Communist Manifesto* had been published in Germany in 1847, only nineteen years before *Poems and Ballads.*

For a society that had managed to maintain a great deal of its class striation while the battle cries of democracy had erupted variously around it, the image of the lower forces deposing the higher forces was not one to be cherished by the upper and middle classes. Sexuality tended to erode social classification as Allen has noted in the following passage:

> Founded on the earlier assumption of the quasi-onto-logical difference between social strata, the class system reflected a sense that members of other social classes were fundamentally different by nature from members of one's own class, almost "another species." On the other hand, newer ideas of common humanity, of rank as a potentially mutable difference in degree, also underlie the Victorian class system. Sex and sexuality, which can be enacted across class boundaries, bring latter notions to the fore, posing a threat to Victorian belief in the validity of social classifications.

Of all public figures, the prostitute, described by Judith Walkowitz [in *Degeneration Amongst Londoners,* 1885] as the "permeable and transgressed border between classes and sexes . . . the carrier of physical and moral pollution," is the representation of this threat. Along with prostitutes, lower-class urban dwellers in general were viewed by the upper classes as degenerate. Such tracts as *The Danger of Deterioration of Race* (1866) and *Degeneration Amongst Londoners* (1885) chronicle instances of the deterioration of the race in the form of shrinking physical stature, effeminacy, and communicable diseases. These texts manifest a growing social paranoia during the latter half of the nineteenth century that the underclass would somehow drag the rest of civilization down with it into a sexually degenerate chaos. The unveiled sexuality of Swinburne's poems threatens not just because it renders the obscene, but because the obscene is inherently connected with the underclasses. The unrestrained and repetitive sexuality of the poems enacts a transgression by which all passions and all people become the same, and that sameness is reflected not in a spiritual, rational purity that has a claim on "civilization," but in a bestial, sensual chaos that tends to collapse carefully constructed taxonomies.

The defense of male and class hegemony is mounted in Robert Buchanan's review in the *Athenaeum* where he says, "We may safely affirm, in the face of many pages of brilliant writing, that such a man is either no poet at all, or a poet degraded from his high estate, and utterly and miserably lost to the Muses." The words "high estate" are coded with class implications. For the production and consumption of poetry was generally the preoccupation of those with "high estates," the gentry. To have sunk below that estate is to have joined the underclass. Further, to have lost oneself to the Muses is to have lost oneself to the influence of the feminine, for the muse is always gendered female. Buchanan goes on to remark that Swinburne is "quite the Absalom of modern bards,—long-ringleted, flippant-lipped, down-cheeked, amorous-lidded." Such a description clearly portrays Swinburne as a coquettish female. Sunken below his high estate and lost to the Muses, Swinburne becomes that transgressed border between class and sex, that carrier of moral and physical pollution, the streetwalker.

My hyperbole in equating Swinburne with the streetwalker is intended to expose the hysteria latent in the critical reaction to Swinburne's poems. To say he touched a nerve would be an understatement. His depictions of sexually enslaved, sexually ambiguous characters biting one another and sucking the blood from inflicted bruises were just the kind of thing that could bring a Victorian family's reading session in the parlor to an unfortunate and abrupt close. Sieburth notes that "even the prudish Ruskin was sensually ensnared by the aural seductions of the rapturous cadences of 'Faustine': 'It made me all hot,' he admitted to its author, 'like pies with the devil's fingers in them.'" Though other poets of the period, like Tennyson and Browning, were writing of unrequited love, Swinburne's central theme, they were doing so in a "veiled" manner. That is, they worked in a figurative language that was palatable to the Victorian sensibility. Somewhere in his depictions, then, Swinburne crossed the boundary between what was perceived as art and what was perceived as obscenity.

The classifications for making aesthetic judgments with which Victorian critics were armed had been secured about seventy-five years earlier by Kant in his discourse on the beautiful and the sublime in *The Critique of Judgement.* In the *Critique,* Kant distinguishes the beautiful from the sublime by the treatment of form: "The beautiful in nature is a question of the form of the object, and this consists in limitation, whereas the sublime is to be found in an object even devoid of form, so far as it immediately involves, or else by its presence provokes, a representation of limitlessness." Whereas the sentiment of beauty in Kant is predicated on a sense of the harmony between man and nature and the rationality and intelligibility of the world, the sublime is conceived of as a mixture of pleasure and pain that forces man to recognize the limits of reason. The sublime is presented in terms of excess, it cannot be framed.

Well in place by the time Swinburne was publishing poetry, this Kantian aesthetic has influenced the way art has been judged well into our own century. In trying to distinguish obscenity from art, art critics up to the last twenty or thirty years have distinguished the naked from the nude by an act of framing, an artistic reforming of the body from the actual to the ideal. While the experience of art is static and reflective, non-artistic forms such as pornography typically incite the viewer to action. Art critic Lynda Nead has clarified this distinction in saying, "The pure aesthetic experience is posed as a consolidation of individual subjectivity; it can be seen in terms of the framing of the subject. In contrast, the experience of pornography is described as a kind of disturbance; it presents the possibility of an undoing of identity" [*The Female Nude,* 1992]. Thus Ruskin's rise in temperature is not an idealized, aesthetic act of contemplation, but indeed a disturbance, a provocation that presents the possibility of the undoing of "the prudish Ruskin."

Though it would be naive to claim along with Morley that Swinburne's bodily representations are true instances of linguistic mimesis without figuration or metaphor, it seems clear that his poetic personae are representations of an unframed, sublime excess. Both in gender and in emotion, they cannot be framed or contained within the privileged Victorian ideology that seeks to reify itself in its artistic images. In **"Anactoria,"** Sappho's hyperbolic passion is aligned with the male in her repeated desire to penetrate (bite or scratch) Anactoria. In **"Dolores"** the speaker (presumed male) imagines breast-feeding Dolores. In these acts the speakers exceed frames of gender and enter into the sublime. My own language betrays the perceived action of this excess, however, by claiming that they enter "into" the sublime. For there is no containment, and the transgression away from the frame of civilization and its gender or emotional norms is the critical act whereby readers encounter the perverse. It is this ambiguity—this excess of pleasure, pain, and terror—that threatens to undo the identity of the reader.

In its very sublimity, **"Anactoria"** threatens to disrupt that most ideological of constructs, the female body. Sappho, the poet-narrator, draws the correlation between her poetic text and its ideological constructs when she says to her lover Anactoria, "thy body is the song" (l. 74). In his notes on the text, Cecil Lang writes [in *The Pre-Raphaelites and Their Circle,* 1975] "It is not English poetry's first indictment of the irreconcilability of good and the means to good, but it is the first time that the vehicle has been, straightforwardly, homosexual love (with glancing blows at cunnilingus), which was not, a century ago, a literary staple of this happy breed of men." Unknowingly, Lang hits at the aesthetic problem of the text. Besides the obvious difficulties a Victorian reader might have had with homosexuality, it is the physicality of it that destabilizes the category of art into a flirtation with the obscene. Lang's curious parenthetical phrase which highlights the physical, "glancing blows at cunnilingus," itself resonates with something of a peep-show mentality. It suggests the pornographic.

What sets **"Anactoria"** and many of Swinburne's other poems apart from so much Victorian work is their continual metonymic representation of the unclothed body. In *The Flesh Made Word* (1987), Helena Michie discusses how Victorian authors were obsessed with dressing their heroines, that is, describing their dress with as little reference to the body as possible, and cloaking them with clichéd metaphors in order to distract the reader from the heroine's body. In contrast, Swinburne wastes no time in setting out to describe the bodies of his (always female) love objects, as can be seen in the opening stanzas of **"Laus Veneris"** and **"Dolores"**:

> Asleep or waking is it? for her neck,
> Kissed over close, wears yet a purple speck
>   Wherein the pained blood falters and goes out;
> Soft, and stung softly—fairer for a fleck.
>
> But though my lips shut sucking on the place,
> There is no vein at work upon her face;

> Her eyelids are so peaceable, no doubt
> Deep sleep has warmed her blood through all its
>   ways.
>
> ("Laus Veneris," ll. 1-8)

> Cold eyelids that hide like a jewel
>   Hard eyes that grow soft for an hour;
> The heavy white limbs, and the cruel
>   Red mouth like a venomous flower;
> When these are gone by with their glories,
> What shall rest of thee then, what remain,
> O mystic and sombre Dolores,
>   Our Lady of Pain?
>
> ("Dolores," ll. 1-9)

These passages, with their sublime repetition of lips, limbs, and eyelids, frame women's bodies through the speakers' voices. What these narratives fail to do, however, is suspend or transform the sexual desire implicit in the gaze and naming of parts by the male narrator. For art, in order to induce aesthetic contemplation (according to the Kantian formula), must represent the sublimation or transformation of sexual drives. Pornography's primary aim, conversely, is to excite the sexual drives of its viewers, often by a specular representation of sexual desire in its protagonists. In fine art the female nude acts as a function of the pure, disinterested gaze and of the body transubstantiated. In pornography the naked female represents the realm of mass culture where sensual desires are stimulated and gratified. Thus again, art is ideologically linked to a socially privileged sphere that brings to it a self-fulfilling set of expectations, its own frame as it were, from which to judge it. The transgression of artistic boundaries represents a departure into the degenerate masses, a virtual contamination of Victorian upper- and middle-class ideology.

Swinburne's poems fall dangerously between the two poles of art and obscenity. For in order to represent the aesthetic of the beautiful, the female body must be framed and given form within the conventions of art. It must be static matter contained within a socially acceptable boundary (Millais' *Ophelia* comes to mind). But when these representations fail to contain the connotations of the female body as sexual body, the image is judged to have gone beyond the bounds of art. Thus Sappho's lines occupy a liminal space between the metaphorically mediated and the metonymically unmediated:

> I feel thy blood against my blood: my pain
> Pains thee, and lips bruise lips, and vein stings vein,
> Let fruit be crushed on fruit, let flower on flower,
> Breast kindle breast, and either burn one hour.
>
> ("Anactoria," ll. 11-14)

For she lists metonymically blood, lips, veins, and breasts, yet dangles between them the tropes of fruit and flower. The passage raises fractured images of female bodies in sexual contact, and then suspends those images through ambiguous tropology, leaving the reader in the position of actively completing the image through the imagination. What activates the fullest imagination may itself be as fragmentary and metonymic as blood, veins, and breasts, provided these images be remembered as parts of the whole they stand for. Mixing metonymy and metaphor may flesh out a whole body of memory and imagination, and in doing so actively create the pornographic image of two women making (that is, the representation of an action) love. In this way, the poetry affiliates itself once again with Kant's notion of the sublime in which "the mind feels itself *set in motion* in the representation of the sublime in nature; whereas in the aesthetic judgement upon what is beautiful therein it is in restful contemplation." The sublime is literally obscene in that it is beyond representation, beyond the framework of Victorian ideology.

In their representation of what was perceived as masculine women and feminine men, Swinburne's poems threaten to destabilize the socially constructed norms of male and female behavior.

—Allison Pease

Contributing to this sublimity is the poems' repetitive, metonymical excess. Almost every poem in the volume mentions hair, eyes, eyelids, lips, and breasts. In the racier poems, there is mention of feet and ankles, even girdles, empty and full. The endless repetition of these sexually suggestive body parts intimates both the sublime and the pornographic. This is further suggested by Swinburne's use of participial modifiers for almost every body part. Lips are not just static lips, they are "shuddering lips" or "stinging lips." They suggest action, movement, and in doing so, imply the sexual. Bodies are described in these poems not as physical artifacts, but rather as one great body of desire, a series of metonyms that incite a heated, repetitive tone from the poems' narrators (perhaps in an effort to stabilize one's identity in the face of an undoing). **"Anactoria"** is the best example of this, particularly because it repeats so many of the same tropes of other poems. The poem's beginning exclaims (in typically Swinburnian hyperbole), "thine eyes / Blind me, thy tresses burn me, thy sharp sighs / Divide my flesh" (ll. 1-3). Here metonymic representatives of the physical enact a disintegration of Sappho as narrator. Anactoria's disembodied parts threaten, perhaps because of a specularly formed identity, to divide the very flesh of the creator of such metonymies. This is similar to Tannhäuser's claim in **"Laus Veneris"** that while Venus' "eyelids" lay upon her eyes "like flower on flower," his "eyelids" lay upon his eyes "like fire on fire." The objects, Venus and Anactoria, embody classic figures of artistic stasis to be judged aesthetically, and yet the irony is that the narrators themselves enact a subjective, passionately imaginative, and arguably perverse (**"Fragoletta"**'s necrophiliac reverie was bound to upset many) mediation of these objects as opposed to the placid and impersonal judgement which Kant prescribes. Thus the sublime repetition of language combined with a sexually charged gaze onto female objects of contemplation makes for a dangerously pornographic combination of ingredients.

In making bodies semantically and physically ambiguous, Swinburne purposefully inscribes his poetic personae with indeterminate gender. He presents characters that transgress constructed notions of male and female in order to realize what he believed was an admirable state of androgyny. In defending his poem **"Hermaphroditus,"** Swinburne relays his knowledge of the ideal:

> How favourite and frequent a vision among the Greeks was this of the union of sexes in one body of perfect beauty, none need be told. In Plato the legend has fallen into a form coarse, hard, and absurd. The theory of God splitting in two the double archetype of man and woman, the original hermaphrodite which had to get itself bisected into female and male, is repulsive enough. But the idea thus incarnate, literal or symbolic, is merely beautiful.

When Swinburne refers to Plato's myth of the androgyne, which appears in the *Symposium,* he is referring to Aristophanes' tale that describes man's origin as from one self-sufficient, spherically shaped being equipped with one head, two faces, four ears, "two organs of generation and everything else to correspond." Attempting to climb to heaven, these beings were struck down and divided in half by the jealous god Zeus. Desire, then, is the result of this fall from a primal state of wholeness into division. Swinburne discusses this mythical being as an ideal, and yet it is ironic that he is defending his depiction of a later and importantly different myth.

The poem **"Hermaphroditus"** is a four-sonnet sequence written in tribute to the famous statue at the Louvre. Both the statue and the poem find their origin not in Plato, but in Ovid's *Metamorphoses,* where the myth of the fallen Hermaphroditus takes on a different emphasis from Plato's prelapsarian myth of the androgyne. Briefly, Ovid tells the story of Salmacis, a nymph who presides over a fountain, and Hermaphroditus, a beautiful youth who came to bathe himself in Salmacis' waters. Upon sight of Hermaphroditus, Salmacis could not wait "to hold him naked in her arms." Though at first rebuffed by him, the nymph tricked Hermaphroditus into believing she was gone. When he stripped and waded into the pool, she ran and jumped onto him, "surrounding him with arms, legs, lips, and hands." Mounted onto the struggling boy, Salmacis prayed to the gods that they never be separated, and her prayer was granted: "They grew one body . . . so two became nor boy nor girl." Kari Weil, in her book *Androgyny,* remarks that "Salmacis's body and name are totally effaced in the 'enfeebled' figure that emerges from the pond, 'but half a man.'" Traditional depictions of Hermaphroditus, including the statue on which Swinburne based his poem, figure a male with breasts. Weil notes, "Beginning as a story of female desire, Ovid's myth ends as a tale of the fall of man, a fall from clear sexual division into sexual confusion."

The two myths go some way toward explaining some of the outrage over Swinburne's androgynous/hermaphroditic representations. For while androgyny represents a pre-existent, mythic ideal of wholeness, hermaphroditism represents a fall from individual wholeness into lack, and specifically male lack, for the female is simply erased. The hermaphrodite occupies bodily space, while the androgyne is always more complete in his/her absence. Weil positions these concepts rhetorically when she says, "Androgyny, like figuration, is unmarked, an object of desire untainted by difference. The hermaphrodite, on the other hand, is positioned on the side of the representational; it is excessive, or lacking." Once again we find ourselves back at the reviewer Morley's complaint that Swinburne fails to "veil," to figure, his subjects, choosing instead to write representational poetry. Depicting characters that are "more than womanly" or "less than men," language that is itself coded with the notion that there is, as Foucault puts it, a "true sex," and that to transgress the barrier for women is to add to a diminutive and for men to diminish an amplitude, Swinburne (dis)covers the constantly shifting lines of difference that rhetoric alone maintains.

In the final lines of **"Hermaphroditus,"** Swinburne confirms the woman's erasure by addressing the boy within the hermaphrodite:

> Yea, sweet, I know; I saw in what swift wise
>   Beneath the woman's and the water's kiss
>   Thy moist limbs melted into Salmacis,
> And the large light turned tender in thine eyes,
> And all thy boy's breath softened into sighs;
>   But Love being blind, how should he know of
>   this?
>
> (ll. 51-56)

What the reader is left with is the image of the effeminate male, the male "turned tender." This is but one in a series of images in *Poems and Ballads* of gender transgression, many of which are motivated by female desire.

In **"Fragoletta"** the speaker addresses "Love" as the "son of grief begot by joy," but then troubles his own declaration of gender by asking, "Being sexless, wilt thou be / Maiden or boy?" Leaving Love aside, the speaker goes on to describe his female love object in ambiguous physical terms, for it seems here that his lady is dead, yet nevertheless quite alive to his desire. She has "strange lips" and "ambiguous blood," her "maiden's mouth is cold, / Her breast-blossoms are simply red." Yet oddly in the next stanza the speaker reverses his description, saying "Thy mouth is made of fire and wine, / Thy barren bosom takes my kiss." Here again Swinburne destabilizes the category of the body. He goes further in the following lines by declaring of this already indeterminate maiden:

> Thou hast a serpent in thine hair
> In all the curls that close and cling;
> And ah, thy breast-flower!
> Ah love, thy mouth too fair
> To kiss and sting!
>
> (ll. 51-55)

The maiden becomes a phallic woman, a gynander that is, in Bram Dijkstra's words [in *Idols of Perversity,* 1986], "the symbol of complete degeneration":

She was the predatory woman, the autoerotic or lesbian woman who consorted with males in a futile attempt to absorb or syphon off their masculine energies in order to "become masculinized," but who otherwise chose to conjoin herself only with other women in an orgy of degenerative, self-extinguishing regression into the absolute of femininity, a perverse journey back to the primordial earth.

Dijkstra's Darwinian language brings us back to the idea that what was at stake for many Victorian readers was finding within their fine literature the reification of the idea that their society was in fact progressing toward that ever elusive goal of civilization. Effeminate sensuality was viewed as regressive, the shameful remnant of a bestial heritage. In fact, Dijkstra comments that "in the everyday world one encountered them [remnants of a bestial heritage] as the lower classes, the workers and the vagabonds, the unintelligent 'fodder' of industrial civilization."

Thus a poem like **"Dolores"** epitomizes this threat in that it describes a phallic woman who is representational of the lower classes. Dolores threatens to disrupt categories both of class and gender. In her "garden where all men may dwell" (l. 18), and her "house not of gold but of gain" (l. 22), Dolores is painted as a prostitute figure. Her "cruel / Red mouth like a venomous flower" (ll. 3-4) is a *vagina dentata* where men simultaneously desire and fear their own demise. Delineating a peculiar transformation of genital tropes from male to female, Dolores' lips are described as "Curled snakes that are fed from my breast" (l. 26). And yet as Dolores becomes the phallic woman, the poem's speaker transforms himself into a female vessel, crying out, "feed me and fill me with pleasure, / Ere pain come in turn" (ll. 31-32). These lines reflect not simply a desire to transgress into the female, but also into the child, as the desire to be fed suggests. The longing of the male subject to become the object of the female, and in doing so to become a child, raises the unavoidable question of masochism in Swinburne's work.

In his book *Masochism,* Gilles Deleuze suggests that masochism is the result of a male subject's desire to identify with what he calls the oral mother, a figure associated with nurturing and death. In the longing to identify with the oral mother, the subject attempts to humiliate and erase the internalized image of the father, thus returning, in a sense, to a stage before sexual difference, the pre-Oedipal. An interesting parallel can be found here with the myth of androgyny. As Weil has discovered, "Psychoanalysis equates androgyny with a repressed desire to return to the imaginary wholeness and self-sufficiency associated with the pre-Oedipal phase before sexual difference. The fantasy of the phallic mother is one manifestation of this desire that says that sexual difference is not an originary difference, that originally sexes were the same—i.e., the same as man—and that woman became 'different' as the result of a cut, hence of castration." In this light, Swinburne's interest in androgyny and his fascination with masochism seem but two sides of the same coin, a longing for the pre-Oedipal and the denial of difference.

Yet the messy rantings and ravings of his poetic personae achieve anything but this ideal. They are representations of the physical, and in being so, embody the presence of lack. They achieve the hermaphroditic, not the androgynous. If the following passage from **"Dolores"** carries the wish to desecrate the image of the father and to deny one's own sexual difference in the dream of androgyny, it fails to do so because of its physical immediacy:

> By the ravenous teeth that have smitten
>   Through the kisses that blossom and bud,
> By the lips intertwisted and bitten
>   Till the foam has a savour of blood,
> By the pulse as it rises and falters,
>   By the hands as they slacken and strain,
> I adjure thee, respond from thine altars,
>   Our Lady of Pain.
>
> (ll. 112-120)

The physical result of hermaphroditism, as Swinburne's **"Hermaphroditus"** acknowledges, results in the excessive intensification of insatiable sexual passions. It transgresses the boundary from the procreative to the perverse. And in its perversion, sexual subjects are left "barren" and "fruitless," two words that appear in almost every poem of the 1866 volume.

Perversion and procreation, of course, bring us back to the question of evolution. For if procreation is that which allows for evolution, perversion is a sign of the regressive. All of this stood as a threat to the rational male's sense of civilization as based in difference, and progressing in a Platonic sense ever upward. [In *Contemporary Poetry,* 1871] Robert Buchanan's attempt to assert an appropriate sense of hierarchy in response to Pre-Raphaelite poetry including Swinburne's can be read in his review "The Fleshly School of Poetry":

> The fleshly gentlemen have bound themselves by solemn league and covenant to extol fleshliness as the distinct and supreme end of poetic and pictorial art; to aver that poetic expression is greater than poetic thought, and by inference that the body is greater than the soul, and sound superior to sense; and that the poet, properly to develop his poetic faculty, must be an intellectual hermaphrodite, to whom the very facts of day and night are lost in a whirl of aesthetic terminology.

Buchanan's binaries privilege thought over expression, sense over sound, and soul over body. In accusing the poets of being "intellectual hermaphrodites" he does not invoke the myth of wholeness and plenitude, but rather he uses the myth to accuse them of effeminacy, of being but half men. He is looking here for a way to legitimate and reify the "male" world of thought, sense, and soul, the aesthetic realm associated with Kant's disinterested gaze at the beautiful that rests in imposing a structure of domination over potentially uncontrollable forms. Thus this review, like the others, complains of the threat to the gentry and its concomitant male privilege.

Swinburne's response to his attackers is an interesting one because while it overtly refutes the points raised by critics, it inadvertently acknowledges the fears raised around questions of a gender and class hierarchy, and in fact serves to reify if not reappropriate his poetic material as belonging precisely to a privileged male sphere. To begin, Swinburne invokes his own class privilege by remarking that he has not studied in the same schools as those of the "professional pressman." Indeed his Eton and Oxford education have left him in such a state of privilege that he is able to boast, "I have never worked for praise *or pay,* but simply by impulse, and to please myself" (italics mine). Having firmly established his position as one of the upper classes, he takes the opportunity of attacking the bourgeois and what he sees as the effeminate concerns of his reviewers:

> It would seem as though to publish a book were equivalent to thrusting it with violence into the hands of every mother and nurse in the kingdom as fit and necessary food for female infancy. . . . No one wishes to force men's food down the throats of babes and sucklings.

> The question at issue is wider than any between a single writer and his critics, or it might well be allowed to drop. It is this: whether or not the first and last requisite of art is to give no offense; whether or not all that cannot be lisped in the nursery or fingered in the schoolroom is therefore to be cast out of the library; whether or not the domestic circle is to be for all men and writers the outer limit and extreme horizon of their world of work.

The sadistic image of force in the first passage serves to bolster Swinburne's image as a masculine one. Indeed, it appears that of all the charges made against him, the accusation of effeminacy was most taken to heart, for his project in this reply is to pioneer a male space beyond the "domestic circle" that reappropriates his excesses for the category of art. While his critics had accused him of going beyond boundaries, Swinburne's response seeks to reclaim the sphere beyond the boundaries as a privileged male discourse of the profane. He extends this argument with phallic imagery that is intended to castrate his critics:

> The office of adult art is neither puerile nor feminine, but virile . . . the press will be as impotent as the pulpit to dictate laws and remove the landmarks of art. . . . Then all accepted work will be noble and chaste in the wider masculine sense, not truncated and curtailed, but outspoken and full-grown.

The claim made for virile and outspoken art suggests a new way to figure bodies aesthetically as through the sexually charged, male eye. This "wider masculine sense" includes the territory pioneered in *Poems and Ballads*. By proclaiming the virility and masculinity of his poems, Swinburne not only defends himself from accusations made in the press, but further serves to reify the misogyny implicit in the myth of Hermaphroditus and his representations of sexually ambiguous personae. To the cry from critics that he had threatened the privileged male sphere Swinburne triumphantly responded that in fact he had done no such thing, but rather that he had broadened the category, pioneered new territory, and discovered a virile land that was ready to be populated by men of discerning tastes.

FURTHER READING

Bibliography

Beetz, Kirk H. *Algernon Charles Swinburne: A Bibliography of Secondary Works, 1861-1980.* Metuchen, N. J.: Scarecrow Press, 1982, 227 p.

Chronologically arranged annotated bibliography of criticism.

Biography

Henderson, Philip. *Swinburne: Portrait of a Poet.* New York: Macmillan Publishing Co., 1974, 305 p.

Critical biography.

Lafourcade, Georges. *Swinburne: A Literary Biography.* London: G. Bell and Sons, 1932, 314 p.

Concentrates on the circumstances surrounding the writing and publication of Swinburne's principal works.

Thomas, Donald. *Swinburne: The Poet in His World.* New York: Oxford University Press, 1979, 256 p.

Anecdotal biography detailing Swinburne's relationship with those people who most affected his life and work.

Criticism

Beach, Joseph Warren. "Swinburne." In his *The Concept of Nature in Nineteenth-Century English Poetry,* pp. 455-69. New York: Pageant Book Co., 1956.

Examines political, spiritual, and humanistic convictions underlying Swinburne's nature poetry.

Chew, Samuel C. *Swinburne.* Boston: Little, Brown, and Co., 1929, 335 p.

Critical study of Swinburne's prose and poetry.

Cochran, Rebecca. "Swinburne's Fated Lovers in *Tristram and Lyonesse.*" *Tristania* XIII, Nos. 1-2 (Autumn-Spring 1987-1988): 53-61.

Lists Swinburne's structural alterations and omissions in his poem based on the love story.

———. "Swinburne's 'Lancelot' and Pre-Raphaelite Medievalism." *Victorian Newsletter* 74 (Fall 1988): 58-62.

Determines the Pre-Raphaelite influence on Swinburne's Arthurian poem.

Drinkwater, John. *Swinburne: An Estimate.* London: J. M. Dent & Sons, 1913, 215 p.

Critical study of Swinburne's lyric poetry, dramas, and criticism.

Fisher, Benjamin Franklin IV. "Swinburne." *Victorian Poetry* 28, No. 2 (Summer 1990): 224-28.

Surveys recent critical reaction to Swinburne's work.

Greenberg, Robert A. "'Erotion,' 'Anactoria,' and the Sapphic Passion." *Victorian Poetry* 29, No. 1 (Spring 1991): 79-87.

Compares the treatment of Sapphic love in "Erotion" and "Anactoria."

Hargreaves, H. A. *Swinburne's Medievalism: A Study in Victorian Love Poetry.* Baton Rouge: Louisiana State University Press, 1988, 205 p.

Explores the influence of medieval literature of courtly love on Swinburne's poetry.

Harrison, Antony H. "'Love Strong as Death and Valour Strong as Love': Swinburne and Courtly Love." *Victorian Poetry* 18, No. 1 (Spring 1980): 61-73.

Discusses the "depth of the resemblance between courtly love doctrine and Swinburne's private mythology of love, even as we find it in his early, more visceral works."

———. "The Medievalism of Swinburne's *Poems and Ballads, First Series:* Historicity and Erotic Aestheticism." *Papers on Language & Literature* 21, No. 2 (Spring 1985): 129-51.

Explores the ways in which the radical ideology of Swinburne's poems evolve from interactions among his historicist, erotic, and formal concerns.

Hyder, Clyde Kenneth, ed. *Swinburne: The Critical Heritage.* London: Routledge & Kegan Paul, 1970, 255 p.

Reprints important reviews of Swinburne's major works through *Poems and Ballads: Second Series.*

McGann, Jerome J. *Swinburne: An Experiment in Criticism.* Chicago: University of Chicago Press, 1972, 321 p.

Critical commentary cast in the form of dialogue between several contemporaries and acquaintances of Swinburne.

Meyers, Terry L. "Two Poems by Swinburne: 'Milton' and On the Effect of Wagner's Music." *Victorian Poetry* 31, No. 2 (Summer 1993): 203-09.

Discovers Swinburne's unpublished poem "Milton," and discusses the circumstances under which it was written.

Nicolson, Harold. *Swinburne and Baudelaire.* Oxford: Oxford at the Clarendon Press, 1930, 21 p.

Assessment of both poets with some comparison of their work.

Raymond, Meredith B. *Swinburne's Poetics: Theory and Practice.* The Hague: Mouton, 1971, 202 p.

Posits an aesthetic basis which applies to both Swinburne's poetry and criticism.

Riede, David G. *Swinburne: A Study of Romantic Myth-making.* Charlottesville: University Press of Virginia, 1978, 227 p.

Maintains that "Swinburne's major works show a continuous grappling with the works of the earlier romantics, and his career shows a steady progression to a more and more truly imaginative mythopoetic mode, eventually culminating in a unique, personal, fully articulated myth."

Victorian Poetry 9, No. 1-2 (Spring-Summer 1971): 1-260. Special issue devoted to studies of Swinburne.

Wagner-Lawlor, Jennifer. "Metaphorical 'Indiscretion' and Literary Survival in Swinburne's 'Anactoria'." *SEL: Studies in English Literature* 36, No. 4 (Autumn 1996): 917-34.

Analyzes the use of metaphor, literary tradition, and the theme of survival in Swinburne's poem.

Zonana, Joyce. "Swinburne's Sappho: The Muse as Sister-Goddess." *Victorian Poetry* 28, No. 1 (Spring 1990): 39-50.

Contends that: "By identifying Sappho as a Muse—and ultimately, as we shall see, as the Muse, not only for him, but for all poets—Swinburne radically redefines the nature of poetic inspiration and the role of a female principle in art produced by men."

Additional coverage of Swinburne's life and career is contained in the following sources published by The Gale Group: *Twentieth-Century Literature Criticism,* **Vols. 8, 36;** *DISCovering Authors; DISCovering Authors: British; DISCovering Authors: Canadian; DISCovering Authors: Most-Studied Authors Module; DISCovering Authors: Poets Module; World Literature Criticism; Contemporary Authors,* **Vols. 105, 140;** *Dictionary of Literary Biography,* **Vols. 35, 57; and** *Concise Dictionary of British Literary Biography, 1832-1890.*

Poetry Criticism
INDEXES

Literary Criticism Series
Cumulative Author Index

Cumulative Nationality Index

Cumulative Title Index

How to Use This Index

The main references

Calvino, Italo
1923–1985 .... **CLC 5, 8, 11, 22, 33, 39,**
73; SSC 3

list all author entries in the following Gale Literary Criticism series:

BLC = *Black Literature Criticism*
CLC = *Contemporary Literary Criticism*
CLR = *Children's Literature Review*
CMLC = *Classical and Medieval Literature Criticism*
DA = *DISCovering Authors*
DAB = *DISCovering Authors: British*
DAC = *DISCovering Authors: Canadian*
DAM = *DISCovering Authors: Modules*
     DRAM: *Dramatists Module*; *MST*: *Most-Studied Authors Module*;
     MULT: *Multicultural Authors Module*; *NOV*: *Novelists Module*;
     POET: *Poets Module*; *POP*: *Popular Fiction and Genre Authors Module*
DC = *Drama Criticism*
HLC = *Hispanic Literature Criticism*
LC = *Literature Criticism from 1400 to 1800*
NCLC = *Nineteenth-Century Literature Criticism*
PC = *Poetry Criticism*
SSC = *Short Story Criticism*
TCLC = *Twentieth-Century Literary Criticism*
WLC = *World Literature Criticism, 1500 to the Present*

The cross-references

See also CANR 23; CA 85-88;
    obituary CA116

list all author entries in the following Gale biographical and literary sources:

AAYA = *Authors & Artists for Young Adults*
AITN = *Authors in the News*
BEST = *Bestsellers*
BW = *Black Writers*
CA = *Contemporary Authors*
CAAS = *Contemporary Authors Autobiography Series*
CABS = *Contemporary Authors Bibliographical Series*
CANR = *Contemporary Authors New Revision Series*
CAP = *Contemporary Authors Permanent Series*
CDALB = *Concise Dictionary of American Literary Biography*
CDBLB = *Concise Dictionary of British Literary Biography*
DLB = *Dictionary of Literary Biography*
DLBD = *Dictionary of Literary Biography Documentary Series*
DLBY = *Dictionary of Literary Biography Yearbook*
HW = *Hispanic Writers*
JRDA = *Junior DISCovering Authors*
MAICYA = *Major Authors and Illustrators for Children and Young Adults*
MTCW = *Major 20th-Century Writers*
NNAL = *Native North American Literature*
SAAS = *Something about the Author Autobiography Series*
SATA = *Something about the Author*
YABC = *Yesterday's Authors of Books for Children*

Literary Criticism Series
Cumulative Author Index

Andrews, Elton V.
See Pohl, Frederik
Andreyev, Leonid (Nikolaevich) 1871-1919
   TCLC 3
   See also CA 104
Andric, Ivo 1892-1975 .... **CLC 8**
   See also CA 81-84; 57-60; CANR 43, 60; DLB
   147; MTCW 1
Androvar
   See Prado (Calvo), Pedro
Angelique, Pierre
   See Bataille, Georges
Angell, Roger 1920- .... **CLC 26**
   See also CA 57-60; CANR 13, 44, 70; DLB 171,
   185
Angelou, Maya 1928- .. **CLC 12, 35, 64, 77;**
   BLC 1; DA; DAB; DAC; DAM MST,
   MULT, POET, POP; WLCS
   See also AAYA 7, 20; BW 2; CA 65-68; CANR
   19, 42, 65; CLR 53; DLB 38; MTCW 1; SATA
   49
Anna Comnena 1083-1153 .... **CMLC 25**
Annensky, Innokenty (Fyodorovich) 1856-1909
   TCLC 14
   See also CA 110; 155
Annunzio, Gabriele d'
   See D'Annunzio, Gabriele
Anodos
   See Coleridge, Mary E(lizabeth)
Anon, Charles Robert
   See Pessoa, Fernando (Antonio Nogueira)
Anouilh, Jean (Marie Lucien Pierre) 1910-1987
   CLC 1, 3, 8, 13, 40, 50; DAM DRAM; DC 8
   See also CA 17-20R; 123; CANR 32; MTCW 1
Anthony, Florence
   See Ai
Anthony, John
   See Ciardi, John (Anthony)
Anthony, Peter
   See Shaffer, Anthony (Joshua); Shaffer, Peter
   (Levin)
Anthony, Piers 1934- ...... **CLC 35; DAM POP**
   See also AAYA 11; CA 21-24R; CANR 28, 56;
   DLB 8; MTCW 1; SAAS 22; SATA 84
Anthony, Susan B(rownell) 1916-1991...**T C L C**
   84
   See also CA 89-92; 134
Antoine, Marc
   See Proust, (Valentin-Louis-George-Eugene-)
   Marcel
Antoninus, Brother
   See Everson, William (Oliver)
Antonioni, Michelangelo 1912- .... **CLC 20**
   See also CA 73-76; CANR 45
Antschel, Paul 1920-1970
   See Celan, Paul
   See also CA 85-88; CANR 33, 61; MTCW 1
Anwar, Chairil 1922-1949 .... **TCLC 22**
   See also CA 121
Apollinaire, Guillaume 1880-1918...**TCLC 3,**
   8, 51; DAM POET; PC 7
   See also Kostrowitzki, Wilhelm Apollinaris de
   See also CA 152
Appelfeld, Aharon 1932- .... **CLC 23, 47**
   See also CA 112; 133
Apple, Max (Isaac) 1941- .... **CLC 9, 33**
   See also CA 81-84; CANR 19, 54; DLB 130
Appleman, Philip (Dean) 1926- .... **CLC 51**
   See also CA 13-16R; CAAS 18; CANR 6, 29, 56
Appleton, Lawrence
   See Lovecraft, H(oward) P(hillips)
Apteryx
   See Eliot, T(homas) S(tearns)

Apuleius, (Lucius Madaurensis) 125(?)-175(?)
   CMLC 1
Aquin, Hubert 1929-1977 .... **CLC 15**
   See also CA 105; DLB 53
Aragon, Louis 1897-1982 ... **CLC 3, 22; DAM**
   NOV, POET
   See also CA 69-72; 108; CANR 28, 71; DLB 72;
   MTCW 1
Arany, Janos 1817-1882 .... **NCLC 34**
Arbuthnot, John 1667-1735 .... **LC 1**
   See also DLB 101
Archer, Herbert Winslow
   See Mencken, H(enry) L(ouis)
Archer, Jeffrey (Howard) 1940- .... **CLC 28;**
   DAM POP
   See also AAYA 16; BEST 89:3; CA 77-80;
   CANR 22, 52; INT CANR-22
Archer, Jules 1915- .... **CLC 12**
   See also CA 9-12R; CANR 6, 69; SAAS 5; SATA
   4, 85
Archer, Lee
   See Ellison, Harlan (Jay)
Arden, John 1930- ...... **CLC 6, 13, 15; DAM**
   DRAM
   See also CA 13-16R; CAAS 4; CANR 31, 65,
   67; DLB 13; MTCW 1
Arenas, Reinaldo 1943-1990 ... **CLC 41; DAM**
   MULT; HLC
   See also CA 124; 128; 133; DLB 145; HW
Arendt, Hannah 1906-1975 .... **CLC 66, 98**
   See also CA 17-20R; 61-64; CANR 26, 60;
   MTCW 1
Aretino, Pietro 1492-1556 .... **LC 12**
Arghezi, Tudor 1880-1967 .... **CLC 80**
   See also Theodorescu, Ion N.
   See also CA 167
Arguedas, Jose Maria 1911-1969...**CLC 10, 18**
   See also CA 89-92; DLB 113; HW
Argueta, Manlio 1936- .... **CLC 31**
   See also CA 131; DLB 145; HW
Ariosto, Ludovico 1474-1533 .... **LC 6**
Aristides
   See Epstein, Joseph
Aristophanes 450B.C.-385B.C. .... **CMLC 4;**
   DA; DAB; DAC; DAM DRAM, MST; DC
   2; WLCS
   See also DLB 176
Arlt, Roberto (Godofredo Christophersen)
   1900-1942...**TCLC 29; DAM MULT; HLC**
   See also CA 123; 131; CANR 67; HW
Armah, Ayi Kwei 1939- .... **CLC 5, 33; BLC 1;**
   DAM MULT, POET
   See also BW 1; CA 61-64; CANR 21, 64; DLB
   117; MTCW 1
Armatrading, Joan 1950- .... **CLC 17**
   See also CA 114
Arnette, Robert
   See Silverberg, Robert
Arnim, Achim von (Ludwig Joachim von Arnim)
   1781-1831 .... **NCLC 5; SSC 29**
   See also DLB 90
Arnim, Bettina von 1785-1859 .... **NCLC 38**
   See also DLB 90
Arnold, Matthew 1822-1888 .. **NCLC 6, 29;**
   DA; DAB; DAC; DAM MST, POET; PC 5;
   WLC
   See also CDBLB 1832-1890; DLB 32, 57
Arnold, Thomas 1795-1842 .... **NCLC 18**
   See also DLB 55
Arnow, Harriette (Louisa) Simpson 1908-1986
   CLC 2, 7, 18
   See also CA 9-12R; 118; CANR 14; DLB 6;
   MTCW 1; SATA 42; SATA-Obit 47

Arouet, Francois-Marie
   See Voltaire
Arp, Hans
   See Arp, Jean
Arp, Jean 1887-1966 .... **CLC 5**
   See also CA 81-84; 25-28R; CANR 42
Arrabal
   See Arrabal, Fernando
Arrabal, Fernando 1932- ...... **CLC 2, 9, 18, 58**
   See also CA 9-12R; CANR 15
Arrick, Fran .... **CLC 30**
   See also Gaberman, Judie Angell
Artaud, Antonin (Marie Joseph) 1896-1948
   TCLC 3, 36; DAM DRAM
   See also CA 104; 149
Arthur, Ruth M(abel) 1905-1979 .... **CLC 12**
   See also CA 9-12R; 85-88; CANR 4; SATA 7, 26
Artsybashev, Mikhail (Petrovich) 1878-1927
   TCLC 31
Arundel, Honor (Morfydd) 1919-1973...**CLC**
   17
   See also CA 21-22; 41-44R; CAP 2; CLR 35;
   SATA 4; SATA-Obit 24
Arzner, Dorothy 1897-1979 .... **CLC 98**
Asch, Sholem 1880-1957 .... **TCLC 3**
   See also CA 105
Ash, Shalom
   See Asch, Sholem
Ashbery, John (Lawrence) 1927-...**CLC 2, 3,**
   4, 6, 9, 13, 15, 25, 41, 77; DAM POET
   See also CA 5-8R; CANR 9, 37, 66; DLB 5, 165;
   DLBY 81; INT CANR-9; MTCW 1
Ashdown, Clifford
   See Freeman, R(ichard) Austin
Ashe, Gordon
   See Creasey, John
Ashton-Warner, Sylvia (Constance) 1908-1984
   CLC 19
   See also CA 69-72; 112; CANR 29; MTCW 1
Asimov, Isaac 1920-1992...**CLC 1, 3, 9, 19, 26,**
   76, 92; DAM POP
   See also AAYA 13; BEST 90:2; CA 1-4R; 137;
   CANR 2, 19, 36, 60; CLR 12; DLB 8; DLBY
   92; INT CANR-19; JRDA; MAICYA; MTCW
   1; SATA 1, 26, 74
Assis, Joaquim Maria Machado de
   See Machado de Assis, Joaquim Maria
Astley, Thea (Beatrice May) 1925-..... **CLC 41**
   See also CA 65-68; CANR 11, 43
Aston, James
   See White, T(erence) H(anbury)
Asturias, Miguel Angel 1899-1974...**CLC 3, 8,**
   13; DAM MULT, NOV; HLC
   See also CA 25-28; 49-52; CANR 32; CAP 2;
   DLB 113; HW; MTCW 1
Atares, Carlos Saura
   See Saura (Atares), Carlos
Atheling, William
   See Pound, Ezra (Weston Loomis)
Atheling, William, Jr.
   See Blish, James (Benjamin)
Atherton, Gertrude (Franklin Horn) 1857-1948
   TCLC 2
   See also CA 104; 155; DLB 9, 78, 186
Atherton, Lucius
   See Masters, Edgar Lee
Atkins, Jack
   See Harris, Mark
Atkinson, Kate .... **CLC 99**
   See also CA 166
Attaway, William (Alexander) 1911-1986 **C L C**
   92; BLC 1; DAM MULT
   See also BW 2; CA 143; DLB 76

Atticus
See Fleming, Ian (Lancaster); Wilson, (Thomas) Woodrow

Atwood, Margaret (Eleanor) 1939-...**CLC 2, 3, 4, 8, 13, 15, 25, 44, 84; DA; DAB; DAC; DAM MST, NOV, POET; PC 8; SSC 2; WLC**
See also AAYA 12; BEST 89:2; CA 49-52; CANR 3, 24, 33, 59; DLB 53; INT CANR-24; MTCW 1; SATA 50

Aubigny, Pierre d'
See Mencken, H(enry) L(ouis)

Aubin, Penelope 1685-1731(?) ....**LC 9**
See also DLB 39

Auchincloss, Louis (Stanton) 1917-...**CLC 4, 6, 9, 18, 45; DAM NOV; SSC 22**
See also CA 1-4R; CANR 6, 29, 55; DLB 2; DLBY 80; INT CANR-29; MTCW 1

Auden, W(ystan) H(ugh) 1907-1973...**CLC 1, 2, 3, 4, 6, 9, 11, 14, 43; DA; DAB; DAC; DAM DRAM, MST, POET; PC 1; WLC**
See also AAYA 18; CA 9-12R; 45-48; CANR 5, 61; CDBLB 1914-1945; DLB 10, 20; MTCW 1

Audiberti, Jacques 1900-1965...**CLC 38; DAM DRAM**
See also CA 25-28R

Audubon, John James 1785-1851 ... **NCLC 47**

Auel, Jean M(arie) 1936-...**CLC 31, 107; DAM POP**
See also AAYA 7; BEST 90:4; CA 103; CANR 21, 64; INT CANR-21; SATA 91

Auerbach, Erich 1892-1957 .... **TCLC 43**
See also CA 118; 155

Augier, Emile 1820-1889 .... **NCLC 31**
See also DLB 192

August, John
See De Voto, Bernard (Augustine)

Augustine, St. 354-430 .... **CMLC 6; DAB**

Aurelius
See Bourne, Randolph S(illiman)

Aurobindo, Sri
See Ghose, Aurabinda

Austen, Jane 1775-1817...**NCLC 1, 13, 19, 33, 51; DA; DAB; DAC; DAM MST, NOV; WLC**
See also AAYA 19; CDBLB 1789-1832; DLB 116

Auster, Paul 1947- .... **CLC 47**
See also CA 69-72; CANR 23, 52

Austin, Frank
See Faust, Frederick (Schiller)

Austin, Mary (Hunter) 1868-1934 .. **TCLC 25**
See also CA 109; DLB 9, 78

Autran Dourado, Waldomiro
See Dourado, (Waldomiro Freitas) Autran

Averroes 1126-1198 .... **CMLC 7**
See also DLB 115

Avicenna 980-1037 .... **CMLC 16**
See also DLB 115

Avison, Margaret 1918- ..**CLC 2, 4, 97; DAC; DAM POET**
See also CA 17-20R; DLB 53; MTCW 1

Axton, David
See Koontz, Dean R(ay)

Ayckbourn, Alan 1939-... **CLC 5, 8, 18, 33, 74; DAB; DAM DRAM**
See also CA 21-24R; CANR 31, 59; DLB 13; MTCW 1

Aydy, Catherine
See Tennant, Emma (Christina)

Ayme, Marcel (Andre) 1902-1967 ...... **CLC 11**
See also CA 89-92; CANR 67; CLR 25; DLB 72; SATA 91

Ayrton, Michael 1921-1975 .... **CLC 7**
See also CA 5-8R; 61-64; CANR 9, 21

Azorin .... **CLC 11**
See also Martinez Ruiz, Jose

Azuela, Mariano 1873-1952 .. **TCLC 3; DAM MULT; HLC**
See also CA 104; 131; HW; MTCW 1

Baastad, Babbis Friis
See Friis-Baastad, Babbis Ellinor

Bab
See Gilbert, W(illiam) S(chwenck)

Babbis, Eleanor
See Friis-Baastad, Babbis Ellinor

Babel, Isaac
See Babel, Isaak (Emmanuilovich)

Babel, Isaak (Emmanuilovich) 1894-1941(?) **TCLC 2, 13; SSC 16**
See also CA 104; 155

Babits, Mihaly 1883-1941 .... **TCLC 14**
See also CA 114

Babur 1483-1530 .... **LC 18**

Bacchelli, Riccardo 1891-1985 .... **CLC 19**
See also CA 29-32R; 117

Bach, Richard (David) 1936-.. **CLC 14; DAM NOV, POP**
See also AITN 1; BEST 89:2; CA 9-12R; CANR 18; MTCW 1; SATA 13

Bachman, Richard
See King, Stephen (Edwin)

Bachmann, Ingeborg 1926-1973 .... **CLC 69**
See also CA 93-96; 45-48; CANR 69; DLB 85

Bacon, Francis 1561-1626 .... **LC 18, 32**
See also CDBLB Before 1660; DLB 151

Bacon, Roger 1214(?)-1292 .... **CMLC 14**
See also DLB 115

Bacovia, George .... **TCLC 24**
See also Vasiliu, Gheorghe

Badanes, Jerome 1937- .... **CLC 59**

Bagehot, Walter 1826-1877 .... **NCLC 10**
See also DLB 55

Bagnold, Enid 1889-1981 .... **CLC 25; DAM DRAM**
See also CA 5-8R; 103; CANR 5, 40; DLB 13, 160, 191; MAICYA; SATA 1, 25

Bagritsky, Eduard 1895-1934 .... **TCLC 60**

Bagrjana, Elisaveta
See Belcheva, Elisaveta

Bagryana, Elisaveta .... **CLC 10**
See also Belcheva, Elisaveta
See also DLB 147

Bailey, Paul 1937- .... **CLC 45**
See also CA 21-24R; CANR 16, 62; DLB 14

Baillie, Joanna 1762-1851 .... **NCLC 71**
See also DLB 93

Bainbridge, Beryl (Margaret) 1933-...**CLC 4, 5, 8, 10, 14, 18, 22, 62; DAM NOV**
See also CA 21-24R; CANR 24, 55; DLB 14; MTCW 1

Baker, Elliott 1922- .... **CLC 8**
See also CA 45-48; CANR 2, 63

Baker, Jean H. .... **TCLC 3, 10**
See also Russell, George William

Baker, Nicholson 1957- .. **CLC 61; DAM POP**
See also CA 135; CANR 63

Baker, Ray Stannard 1870-1946 ..... **TCLC 47**
See also CA 118

Baker, Russell (Wayne) 1925 .... **CLC 31**
See also BEST 89:4; CA 57-60; CANR 11, 41, 59; MTCW 1

Bakhtin, M.
See Bakhtin, Mikhail Mikhailovich

Bakhtin, M. M.
See Bakhtin, Mikhail Mikhailovich

Bakhtin, Mikhail
See Bakhtin, Mikhail Mikhailovich

Bakhtin, Mikhail Mikhailovich 1895-1975 **CLC 83**
See also CA 128; 113

Bakshi, Ralph 1938(?)- .... **CLC 26**
See also CA 112; 138

Bakunin, Mikhail (Alexandrovich) 1814-1876 **NCLC 25, 58**

Baldwin, James (Arthur) 1924-1987...**CLC 1, 2, 3, 4, 5, 8, 13, 15, 17, 42, 50, 67, 90; BLC 1; DA; DAB; DAC; DAM MST, MULT, NOV, POP; DC 1; SSC 10; WLC**
See also AAYA 4; BW 1; CA 1-4R; 124; CABS 1; CANR 3, 24; CDALB 1941-1968; DLB 2, 7, 33; DLBY 87; MTCW 1; SATA 9; SATA-Obit 54

Ballard, J(ames) G(raham) 1930-...**CLC 3, 6, 14, 36; DAM NOV, POP; SSC 1**
See also AAYA 3; CA 5-8R; CANR 15, 39, 65; DLB 14; MTCW 1; SATA 93

Balmont, Konstantin (Dmitriyevich) 1867-1943 **TCLC 11**
See also CA 109; 155

Balzac, Honore de 1799-1850...**NCLC 5, 35, 53; DA; DAB; DAC; DAM MST, NOV; SSC 5; WLC**
See also DLB 119

Bambara, Toni Cade 1939-1995...**CLC 19, 88; BLC 1; DA; DAC; DAM MST, MULT; WLCS**
See also AAYA 5; BW 2; CA 29-32R; 150; CANR 24, 49; DLB 38; MTCW 1

Bamdad, A.
See Shamlu, Ahmad

Banat, D. R.
See Bradbury, Ray (Douglas)

Bancroft, Laura
See Baum, L(yman) Frank

Banim, John 1798-1842 .... **NCLC 13**
See also DLB 116, 158, 159

Banim, Michael 1796-1874 .... **NCLC 13**
See also DLB 158, 159

Banjo, The
See Paterson, A(ndrew) B(arton)

Banks, Iain
See Banks, Iain M(enzies)

Banks, Iain M(enzies) 1954- .... **CLC 34**
See also CA 123; 128; CANR 61; DLB 194; INT 128

Banks, Lynne Reid .... **CLC 23**
See also Reid Banks, Lynne
See also AAYA 6

Banks, Russell 1940- .... **CLC 37, 72**
See also CA 65-68; CAAS 15; CANR 19, 52; DLB 130

Banville, John 1945- .... **CLC 46**
See also CA 117; 128; DLB 14; INT 128

Banville, Theodore (Faullain) de 1832-1891 **NCLC 9**

Baraka, Amiri 1934-...**CLC 1, 2, 3, 5, 10, 14, 33; BLC 1; DA; DAC; DAM MST, MULT, POET, POP; DC 6; PC 4; WLCS**
See also Jones, LeRoi
See also BW 2; CA 21-24R; CABS 3; CANR 27, 38, 61; CDALB 1941-1968; DLB 5, 7, 16, 38; DLBD 8; MTCW 1

Barbauld, Anna Laetitia 1743-1825...**NCLC 50**
See also DLB 107, 109, 142, 158

Barbellion, W. N. P. .... **TCLC 24**
See also Cummings, Bruce F(rederick)

Barbera, Jack (Vincent) 1945- .... **CLC 44**
See also CA 110; CANR 45

Cheever, John 1912-1982...**CLC 3, 7, 8, 11, 15, 25, 64; DA; DAB; DAC; DAM MST, NOV, POP; SSC 1; WLC**
See also CA 5-8R; 106; CABS 1; CANR 5, 27; CDALB 1941-1968; DLB 2, 102; DLBY 80, 82; INT CANR-5; MTCW 1

Cheever, Susan 1943- ....**CLC 18, 48**
See also CA 103; CANR 27, 51; DLBY 82; INT CANR-27

Chekhonte, Antosha
See Chekhov, Anton (Pavlovich)

Chekhov, Anton (Pavlovich) 1860-1904
TCLC 3, 10, 31, 55; DA; DAB; DAC; DAM DRAM, MST; DC 9; SSC 2, 28; WLC
See also CA 104; 124; SATA 90

Chernyshevsky, Nikolay Gavrilovich 1828-1889
NCLC 1

Cherry, Carolyn Janice 1942-
See Cherryh, C. J.
See also CA 65-68; CANR 10

Cherryh, C. J. ....**CLC 35**
See also Cherry, Carolyn Janice
See also AAYA 24; DLBY 80; SATA 93

Chesnutt, Charles W(addell) 1858-1932
TCLC 5, 39; BLC 1; DAM MULT; SSC 7
See also BW 1; CA 106; 125; DLB 12, 50, 78; MTCW 1

Chester, Alfred 1929(?)-1971 ....**CLC 49**
See also CA 33-36R; DLB 130

Chesterton, G(ilbert) K(eith) 1874-1936
TCLC 1, 6, 64; DAM NOV, POET; SSC 1
See also CA 104; 132; CDBLB 1914-1945; DLB 10, 19, 34, 70, 98, 149, 178; MTCW 1; SATA 27

Chiang, Pin-chin 1904-1986
See Ding Ling
See also CA 118

Ch'ien Chung-shu 1910- ....**CLC 22**
See also CA 130; MTCW 1

Child, L. Maria
See Child, Lydia Maria

Child, Lydia Maria 1802-1880 ....**NCLC 6**
See also DLB 1, 74; SATA 67

Child, Mrs.
See Child, Lydia Maria

Child, Philip 1898-1978 ....**CLC 19, 68**
See also CA 13-14; CAP 1; SATA 47

Childers, (Robert) Erskine 1870-1922...**TCLC 65**
See also CA 113; 153; DLB 70

Childress, Alice 1920-1994...**CLC 12, 15, 86, 96; BLC 1; DAM DRAM, MULT, NOV; DC 4**
See also AAYA 8; BW 2; CA 45-48; 146; CANR 3, 27, 50; CLR 14; DLB 7, 38; JRDA; MAICYA; MTCW 1; SATA 7, 48, 81

Chin, Frank (Chew, Jr.) 1940- ....**DC 7**
See also CA 33-36R; CANR 71; DAM MULT

Chislett, (Margaret) Anne 1943- ....**CLC 34**
See also CA 151

Chitty, Thomas Willes 1926- ....**CLC 11**
See also Hinde, Thomas
See also CA 5-8R

Chivers, Thomas Holley 1809-1858...**NCLC 49**
See also DLB 3

Chomette, Rene Lucien 1898-1981
See Clair, Rene
See also CA 103

Chopin, Kate..TCLC 5, 14; DA; DAB; SSC 8; WLCS
See also Chopin, Katherine
See also CDALB 1865-1917; DLB 12, 78

Chopin, Katherine 1851-1904
See Chopin, Kate
See also CA 104; 122; DAC; DAM MST, NOV

Chretien de Troyes c. 12th cent. - ....**CMLC 10**

Christie
See Ichikawa, Kon

Christie, Agatha (Mary Clarissa) 1890-1976
CLC 1, 6, 8, 12, 39, 48, 110; DAB; DAC; DAM NOV
See also AAYA 9; AITN 1, 2; CA 17-20R; 61-64; CANR 10, 37; CDBLB 1914-1945; DLB 13, 77; MTCW 1; SATA 36

Christie, (Ann) Philippa
See Pearce, Philippa
See also CA 5-8R; CANR 4

Christine de Pizan 1365(?)-1431(?) ....**LC 9**

Chubb, Elmer
See Masters, Edgar Lee

Chulkov, Mikhail Dmitrievich 1743-1792
LC 2
See also DLB 150

Churchill, Caryl 1938- ....**CLC 31, 55; DC 5**
See also CA 102; CANR 22, 46; DLB 13; MTCW 1

Churchill, Charles 1731-1764 ....**LC 3**
See also DLB 109

Chute, Carolyn 1947- ....**CLC 39**
See also CA 123

Ciardi, John (Anthony) 1916-1986... **CLC 10, 40, 44; DAM POET**
See also CA 5-8R; 118; CAAS 2; CANR 5, 33; CLR 19; DLB 5; DLBY 86; INT CANR-5; MAICYA; MTCW 1; SAAS 26; SATA 1, 65; SATA-Obit 46

Cicero, Marcus Tullius 106B.C.-43B.C.
CMLC 3

Cimino, Michael 1943- ....**CLC 16**
See also CA 105

Cioran, E(mil) M. 1911-1995 ....**CLC 64**
See also CA 25-28R; 149

Cisneros, Sandra 1954- ....**CLC 69; DAM MULT; HLC; SSC 32**
See also AAYA 9; CA 131; CANR 64; DLB 122, 152; HW

Cixous, Helene 1937- ....**CLC 92**
See also CA 126; CANR 55; DLB 83; MTCW 1

Clair, Rene ....**CLC 20**
See also Chomette, Rene Lucien

Clampitt, Amy 1920-1994 ......**CLC 32; PC 19**
See also CA 110; 146; CANR 29; DLB 105

Clancy, Thomas L., Jr. 1947-
See Clancy, Tom
See also CA 125; 131; CANR 62; INT 131; MTCW 1

Clancy, Tom ... CLC 45, 112; DAM NOV, POP
See also Clancy, Thomas L., Jr.
See also AAYA 9; BEST 89:1, 90:1

Clare, John 1793-1864...**NCLC 9; DAB; DAM POET; PC 23**
See also DLB 55, 96

Clarin
See Alas (y Urena), Leopoldo (Enrique Garcia)

Clark, Al C.
See Goines, Donald

Clark, (Robert) Brian 1932- ....**CLC 29**
See also CA 41-44R; CANR 67

Clark, Curt
See Westlake, Donald E(dwin)

Clark, Eleanor 1913-1996 ....**CLC 5, 19**
See also CA 9-12R; 151; CANR 41; DLB 6

Clark, J. P.
See Clark, John Pepper
See also DLB 117

Clark, John Pepper 1935- .... **CLC 38; BLC 1; DAM DRAM, MULT; DC 5**
See also Clark, J. P.
See also BW 1; CA 65-68; CANR 16, 72

Clark, M. R.
See Clark, Mavis Thorpe

Clark, Mavis Thorpe 1909- ....**CLC 12**
See also CA 57-60; CANR 8, 37; CLR 30; MAICYA; SAAS 5; SATA 8, 74

Clark, Walter Van Tilburg 1909-1971...**CLC 28**
See also CA 9-12R; 33-36R; CANR 63; DLB 9; SATA 8

Clark Bekederemo, J(ohnson) P(epper)
See Clark, John Pepper

Clarke, Arthur C(harles) 1917-...**CLC 1, 4, 13, 18, 35; DAM POP; SSC 3**
See also AAYA 4; CA 1-4R; CANR 2, 28, 55; JRDA; MAICYA; MTCW 1; SATA 13, 70

Clarke, Austin 1896-1974 ..... **CLC 6, 9; DAM POET**
See also CA 29-32; 49-52; CAP 2; DLB 10, 20

Clarke, Austin C(hesterfield) 1934-...**CLC 8, 53; BLC 1; DAC; DAM MULT**
See also BW 1; CA 25-28R; CAAS 16; CANR 14, 32, 68; DLB 53, 125

Clarke, Gillian 1937- ....**CLC 61**
See also CA 106; DLB 40

Clarke, Marcus (Andrew Hislop) 1846-1881
NCLC 19

Clarke, Shirley 1925- ....**CLC 16**

Clash, The
See Headon, (Nicky) Topper; Jones, Mick; Simonon, Paul; Strummer, Joe

Claudel, Paul (Louis Charles Marie) 1868-1955
TCLC 2, 10
See also CA 104; 165; DLB 192

Clavell, James (duMaresq) 1925-1994...**CLC 6, 25, 87; DAM NOV, POP**
See also CA 25-28R; 146; CANR 26, 48; MTCW 1

Cleaver, (Leroy) Eldridge 1935-1998 ..**CLC 30; BLC 1; DAM MULT**
See also BW 1; CA 21-24R; 167; CANR 16

Cleese, John (Marwood) 1939- ....**CLC 21**
See also Monty Python
See also CA 112; 116; CANR 35; MTCW 1

Cleishbotham, Jebediah
See Scott, Walter

Cleland, John 1710-1789 ....**LC 2**
See also DLB 39

Clemens, Samuel Langhorne 1835-1910
See Twain, Mark
See also CA 104; 135; CDALB 1865-1917; DA; DAB; DAC; DAM MST, NOV; DLB 11, 12, 23, 64, 74, 186, 189; JRDA; MAICYA; SATA 100; YABC 2

Cleophil
See Congreve, William

Clerihew, E.
See Bentley, E(dmund) C(lerihew)

Clerk, N. W.
See Lewis, C(live) S(taples)

Cliff, Jimmy ....**CLC 21**
See also Chambers, James

Clifton, (Thelma) Lucille 1936-.. **CLC 19, 66; BLC 1; DAM MULT, POET; PC 17**
See also BW 2; CA 49-52; CANR 2, 24, 42; CLR 5; DLB 5, 41; MAICYA; MTCW 1; SATA 20, 69

Clinton, Dirk
See Silverberg, Robert

Clough, Arthur Hugh 1819-1861 ....**NCLC 27**
See also DLB 32

Clutha, Janet Paterson Frame 1924-
See Frame, Janet
See also CA 1-4R; CANR 2, 36; MTCW 1
Clyne, Terence
See Blatty, William Peter
Cobalt, Martin
See Mayne, William (James Carter)
Cobb, Irvin S. 1876-1944 .... **TCLC 77**
See also DLB 11, 25, 86
Cobbett, William 1763-1835 .... **NCLC 49**
See also DLB 43, 107, 158
Coburn, D(onald) L(ee) 1938- .... **CLC 10**
See also CA 89-92
Cocteau, Jean (Maurice Eugene Clement) 1889-
1963 .... **CLC 1, 8, 15, 16, 43; DA; DAB;
DAC; DAM DRAM, MST, NOV; WLC**
See also CA 25-28; CANR 40; CAP 2; DLB 65;
MTCW 1
Codrescu, Andrei 1946- ...... **CLC 46; DAM
POET**
See also CA 33-36R; CAAS 19; CANR 13, 34, 53
Coe, Max
See Bourne, Randolph S(illiman)
Coe, Tucker
See Westlake, Donald E(dwin)
Coen, Ethan 1958- .... **CLC 108**
See also CA 126
Coen, Joel 1955- .... **CLC 108**
See also CA 126
The Coen Brothers
See Coen, Ethan; Coen, Joel
Coetzee, J(ohn) M(ichael) 1940-...**CLC 23, 33,
66; DAM NOV**
See also CA 77-80; CANR 41, 54; MTCW 1
Coffey, Brian
See Koontz, Dean R(ay)
Cohan, George M(ichael) 1878-1942
TCLC 60
See also CA 157
Cohen, Arthur A(llen) 1928-1986 .. **CLC 7, 31**
See also CA 1-4R; 120; CANR 1, 17, 42; DLB
28
Cohen, Leonard (Norman) 1934-...**CLC 3, 38;
DAC; DAM MST**
See also CA 21-24R; CANR 14, 69; DLB 53;
MTCW 1
Cohen, Matt 1942- .... **CLC 19; DAC**
See also CA 61-64; CAAS 18; CANR 40; DLB 53
Cohen-Solal, Annie 19(?)- .... **CLC 50**
Colegate, Isabel 1931- .... **CLC 36**
See also CA 17-20R; CANR 8, 22; DLB 14; INT
CANR-22; MTCW 1
Coleman, Emmett
See Reed, Ishmael
Coleridge, M. E.
See Coleridge, Mary E(lizabeth)
Coleridge, Mary E(lizabeth) 1861-1907
TCLC 73
See also CA 116; 166; DLB 19, 98
Coleridge, Samuel Taylor 1772-1834
**NCLC 9, 54; DA; DAB; DAC; DAM MST,
POET; PC 11; WLC**
See also CDBLB 1789-1832; DLB 93, 107
Coleridge, Sara 1802-1852 .... **NCLC 31**
See also DLB 199
Coles, Don 1928- .... **CLC 46**
See also CA 115; CANR 38
Coles, Robert (Martin) 1929-........... **CLC 108**
See also CA 45-48; CANR 3, 32, 66, 70; INT
CANR-32; SATA 23
Colette, (Sidonie-Gabrielle) 1873-1954 **T C L C
1, 5, 16; DAM NOV; SSC 10**
See also CA 104; 131; DLB 65; MTCW 1

Collett, (Jacobine) Camilla (Wergeland) 1813-
1895 .... **NCLC 22**
Collier, Christopher 1930- .... **CLC 30**
See also AAYA 13; CA 33-36R; CANR 13, 33;
JRDA; MAICYA; SATA 16, 70
Collier, James L(incoln) 1928- ...... **CLC 30;
DAM POP**
See also AAYA 13; CA 9-12R; CANR 4, 33, 60;
CLR 3; JRDA; MAICYA; SAAS 21; SATA 8,
70
Collier, Jeremy 1650-1726 .... **LC 6**
Collier, John 1901-1980 .... **SSC 19**
See also CA 65-68; 97-100; CANR 10; DLB 77
Collingwood, R(obin) G(eorge) 1889(?)-1943
TCLC 67
See also CA 117; 155
Collins, Hunt
See Hunter, Evan
Collins, Linda 1931- .... **CLC 44**
See also CA 125
Collins, (William) Wilkie 1824-1889...**NCLC 1,
18**
See also CDBLB 1832-1890; DLB 18, 70, 159
Collins, William 1721-1759 .. **LC 4, 40; DAM
POET**
See also DLB 109
Collodi, Carlo 1826-1890 .... **NCLC 54**
See also Lorenzini, Carlo
See also CLR 5
Colman, George 1732-1794
See Glassco, John
Colt, Winchester Remington
See Hubbard, L(afayette) Ron(ald)
Colter, Cyrus 1910- .... **CLC 58**
See also BW 1; CA 65-68; CANR 10, 66; DLB
33
Colton, James
See Hansen, Joseph
Colum, Padraic 1881-1972 .... **CLC 28**
See also CA 73-76; 33-36R; CANR 35; CLR 36;
MAICYA; MTCW 1; SATA 15
Colvin, James
See Moorcock, Michael (John)
Colwin, Laurie (E.) 1944-1992..**CLC 5, 13,
23, 84**
See also CA 89-92; 139; CANR 20, 46; DLBY
80; MTCW 1
Comfort, Alex(ander) 1920- ....**CLC 7; DAM
POP**
See also CA 1-4R; CANR 1, 45
Comfort, Montgomery
See Campbell, (John) Ramsey
Compton-Burnett, I(vy) 1884(?)-1969...**CLC 1,
3, 10, 15, 34; DAM NOV**
See also CA 1-4R; 25-28R; CANR 4; DLB 36;
MTCW 1
Comstock, Anthony 1844-1915 .... **TCLC 13**
See also CA 110
Comte, Auguste 1798-1857 .... **NCLC 54**
Conan Doyle, Arthur
See Doyle, Arthur Conan
Conde, Maryse 1937- .... **CLC 52, 92; BLCS;
DAM MULT**
See also Boucolon, Maryse
See also BW 2
Condillac, Etienne Bonnot de 1714-1780
LC 26
Condon, Richard (Thomas) 1915-1996
CLC 4, 6, 8, 10, 45, 100; DAM NOV
See also BEST 90:3; CA 1-4R; 151; CAAS 1;
CANR 2, 23; INT CANR-23; MTCW 1
Confucius 551B.C.-479B.C. ... **CMLC 19; DA;
DAB; DAC; DAM MST; WLCS**

Congreve, William 1670-1729...**LC 5, 21; DA;
DAB; DAC; DAM DRAM, MST, POET;
DC 2; WLC**
See also CDBLB 1660-1789; DLB 39, 84
Connell, Evan S(helby), Jr. 1924-...**CLC 4, 6,
45; DAM NOV**
See also AAYA 7; CA 1-4R; CAAS 2; CANR 2,
39; DLB 2; DLBY 81; MTCW 1
Connelly, Marc(us Cook) 1890-1980 ... **CLC 7**
See also CA 85-88; 102; CANR 30; DLB 7;
DLBY 80; SATA-Obit 25
Connor, Ralph .... **TCLC 31**
See also Gordon, Charles William
See also DLB 92
Conrad, Joseph 1857-1924...**TCLC 1, 6, 13,
25, 43, 57; DA; DAB; DAC; DAM MST,
NOV; SSC 9; WLC**
See also AAYA 26; CA 104; 131; CANR 60;
CDBLB 1890-1914; DLB 10, 34, 98, 156;
MTCW 1; SATA 27
Conrad, Robert Arnold
See Hart, Moss
Conroy, Pat
See Conroy, (Donald) Pat(rick)
Conroy, (Donald) Pat(rick) 1945-...**CLC 30,
74; DAM NOV, POP**
See also AAYA 8; AITN 1; CA 85-88; CANR
24, 53; DLB 6; MTCW 1
Constant (de Rebecque), (Henri) Benjamin
1767-1830 .... **NCLC 6**
See also DLB 119
Conybeare, Charles Augustus
See Eliot, T(homas) S(tearns)
Cook, Michael 1933- .... **CLC 58**
See also CA 93-96; CANR 68; DLB 53
Cook, Robin 1940- .... **CLC 14; DAM POP**
See also BEST 90:2; CA 108; 111; CANR 41;
INT 111
Cook, Roy
See Silverberg, Robert
Cooke, Elizabeth 1948- .... **CLC 55**
See also CA 129
Cooke, John Esten 1830-1886 .... **NCLC 5**
See also DLB 3
Cooke, John Estes
See Baum, L(yman) Frank
Cooke, M. E.
See Creasey, John
Cooke, Margaret
See Creasey, John
Cook-Lynn, Elizabeth 1930- ... **CLC 93; DAM
MULT**
See also CA 133; DLB 175; NNAL
Cooney, Ray .... **CLC 62**
Cooper, Douglas 1960- .... **CLC 86**
Cooper, Henry St. John
See Creasey, John
Cooper, J(oan) California ....**CLC 56; DAM
MULT**
See also AAYA 12; BW 1; CA 125; CANR 55
Cooper, James Fenimore 1789-1851...**NCLC 1,
27, 54**
See also AAYA 22; CDALB 1640-1865; DLB 3;
SATA 19
Coover, Robert (Lowell) 1932-...**CLC 3, 7, 15,
32, 46, 87; DAM NOV; SSC 15**
See also CA 45-48; CANR 3, 37, 58; DLB 2;
DLBY 81; MTCW 1
Copeland, Stewart (Armstrong) 1952-...**CLC 26**
Copernicus, Nicolaus 1473-1543 .... **LC 45**
Coppard, A(lfred) E(dgar) 1878-1957
TCLC 5; SSC 21
See also CA 114; 167; DLB 162; YABC 1

De Ferrari, Gabriella 1941- .... **CLC 65**
See also CA 146
Defoe, Daniel 1660(?)-1731 ..... **LC 1; DA;**
DAB; DAC; DAM MST, NOV; WLC
See also AAYA 27; CDBLB 1660-1789; DLB
39, 95, 101; JRDA; MAICYA; SATA 22
de Gourmont, Remy(-Marie-Charles)
See Gourmont, Remy (-Marie-Charles) de
de Hartog, Jan 1914- .... **CLC 19**
See also CA 1-4R; CANR 1
de Hostos, E. M.
See Hostos (y Bonilla), Eugenio Maria de
de Hostos, Eugenio M.
See Hostos (y Bonilla), Eugenio Maria de
Deighton, Len .... **CLC 4, 7, 22, 46**
See also Deighton, Leonard Cyril
See also AAYA 6; BEST 89:2; CDBLB 1960 to
Present; DLB 87
Deighton, Leonard Cyril 1929-
See Deighton, Len
See also CA 9-12R; CANR 19, 33, 68; DAM
NOV, POP; MTCW 1
Dekker, Thomas 1572(?)-1632 ... **LC 22; DAM**
DRAM
See also CDBLB Before 1660; DLB 62, 172
de la Cruz, (Sor)Juana Ines 1648-1695 .. **LC 5**
Delafield, E. M. 1890-1943 .... **TCLC 61**
See also Dashwood, Edmee Elizabeth Monica de
la Pasture
See also DLB 34
de la Mare, Walter (John) 1873-1956
TCLC 4, 53; DAB; DAC; DAM MST,
POET; SSC 14; WLC
See also CA 163; CDBLB 1914-1945; CLR 23;
DLB 162; SATA 16
Delaney, Franey
See O'Hara, John (Henry)
Delaney, Shelagh 1939- .... **CLC 29; DAM**
DRAM
See also CA 17-20R; CANR 30, 67; CDBLB
1960 to Present; DLB 13; MTCW 1
Delany, Mary (Granville Pendarves) 1700-1788
LC 12
Delany, Samuel R(ay, Jr.) 1942-...**CLC 8, 14,**
38; BLC 1; DAM MULT
See also AAYA 24; BW 2; CA 81-84; CANR 27,
43; DLB 8, 33; MTCW 1
De La Ramee, (Marie) Louise 1839-1908
See Ouida
See also SATA 20
de la Roche, Mazo 1879-1961 .... **CLC 14**
See also CA 85-88; CANR 30; DLB 68; SATA
64
De La Salle, Innocent
See Hartmann, Sadakichi
Delbanco, Nicholas (Franklin) 1942-...**CLC 6,**
13
See also CA 17-20R; CAAS 2; CANR 29, 55;
DLB 6
del Castillo, Michel 1933- .... **CLC 38**
See also CA 109
Deledda, Grazia (Cosima) 1875(?)-1936
TCLC 23
See also CA 123
Delibes, Miguel .... **CLC 8, 18**
See also Delibes Setien, Miguel
Delibes Setien, Miguel 1920-
See Delibes, Miguel
See also CA 45-48; CANR 1, 32; HW; MTCW 1
DeLillo, Don 1936-...**CLC 8, 10, 13, 27, 39, 54,**
76; DAM NOV, POP
See also BEST 89:1; CA 81-84; CANR 21; DLB
6, 173; MTCW 1

de Lisser, H. G.
See De Lisser, H(erbert) G(eorge)
See also DLB 117
De Lisser, H(erbert) G(eorge) 1878-1944
TCLC 12
See also de Lisser, H. G.
See also BW 2; CA 109; 152
Deloney, Thomas (?)-1600 .... **LC 41**
See also DLB 167
Deloria, Vine (Victor), Jr. 1933-...... **CLC 21;**
DAM MULT
See also CA 53-56; CANR 5, 20, 48; DLB 175;
MTCW 1; NNAL; SATA 21
Del Vecchio, John M(ichael) 1947- .... **CLC 29**
See also CA 110; DLBD 9
de Man, Paul (Adolph Michel) 1919-1983
CLC 55
See also CA 128; 111; CANR 61; DLB 67;
MTCW 1
De Marinis, Rick 1934- .... **CLC 54**
See also CA 57-60; CAAS 24; CANR 9, 25,
50
Dembry, R. Emmet
See Murfree, Mary Noailles
Demby, William 1922-..... **CLC 53; BLC 1;**
DAM MULT
See also BW 1; CA 81-84; DLB 33
de Menton, Francisco
See Chin, Frank (Chew, Jr.)
Demijohn, Thom
See Disch, Thomas M(ichael)
de Montherlant, Henry (Milon)
See Montherlant, Henry (Milon) de
Demosthenes 384B.C.-322B.C. .... **CMLC 13**
See also DLB 176
de Natale, Francine
See Malzberg, Barry N(athaniel)
Denby, Edwin (Orr) 1903-1983 .... **CLC 48**
See also CA 138; 110
Denis, Julio
See Cortazar, Julio
Denmark, Harrison
See Zelazny, Roger (Joseph)
Dennis, John 1658-1734 .... **LC 11**
See also DLB 101
Dennis, Nigel (Forbes) 1912-1989 .... **CLC 8**
See also CA 25-28R; 129; DLB 13, 15; MTCW
1
Dent, Lester 1904(?)-1959 .... **TCLC 72**
See also CA 112; 161
De Palma, Brian (Russell) 1940- .... **CLC 20**
See also CA 109
de Pizan, Christine 1365-1431 .... **LC 9**
De Quincey, Thomas 1785-1859 .... **NCLC 4**
See also CDBLB 1789-1832; DLB 110;
144
Deren, Eleanora 1908(?)-1961
See Deren, Maya
See also CA 111
Deren, Maya 1917-1961 .... **CLC 16, 102**
See also Deren, Eleanora
Derleth, August (William) 1909-1971...**CLC 31**
See also CA 1-4R; 29-32R; CANR 4; DLB 9;
DLBD 17; SATA 5
Der Nister 1884-1950 .... **TCLC 56**
de Routisie, Albert
See Aragon, Louis
Derrida, Jacques 1930- .... **CLC 24, 87**
See also CA 124; 127
Derry Down Derry
See Lear, Edward
Dersonnes, Jacques
See Simenon, Georges (Jacques Christian)

Desai, Anita 1937- .... **CLC 19, 37, 97; DAB;**
DAM NOV
See also CA 81-84; CANR 33, 53; MTCW 1;
SATA 63
de Saint-Luc, Jean
See Glassco, John
de Saint Roman, Arnaud
See Aragon, Louis
Descartes, Rene 1596-1650 .... **LC 20, 35**
De Sica, Vittorio 1901(?)-1974 .... **CLC 20**
See also CA 117
Desnos, Robert 1900-1945 .... **TCLC 22**
See also CA 121; 151
Destouches, Louis-Ferdinand 1894-1961
CLC 9, 15
See also Celine, Louis-Ferdinand
See also CA 85-88; CANR 28; MTCW 1
de Tolignac, Gaston
See Griffith, D(avid Lewelyn) W(ark)
Deutsch, Babette 1895-1982 .... **CLC 18**
See also CA 1-4R; 108; CANR 4; DLB 45; SATA
1; SATA-Obit 33
Devenant, William 1606-1649 .... **LC 13**
Devkota, Laxmiprasad 1909-1959 .. **TCLC 23**
See also CA 123
De Voto, Bernard (Augustine) 1897-1955
TCLC 29
See also CA 113; 160; DLB 9
De Vries, Peter 1910-1993...**CLC 1, 2, 3, 7, 10,**
28, 46; DAM NOV
See also CA 17-20R; 142; CANR 41; DLB 6;
DLBY 82; MTCW 1
Dexter, John
See Bradley, Marion Zimmer
Dexter, Martin
See Faust, Frederick (Schiller)
Dexter, Pete 1943- .... **CLC 34, 55; DAM POP**
See also BEST 89:2; CA 127; 131; INT 131;
MTCW 1
Diamano, Silmang
See Senghor, Leopold Sedar
Diamond, Neil 1941- .... **CLC 30**
See also CA 108
Diaz del Castillo, Bernal 1496-1584 ..... **LC 31**
di Bassetto, Corno
See Shaw, George Bernard
Dick, Philip K(indred) 1928-1982...**CLC 10,**
30, 72; DAM NOV, POP
See also AAYA 24; CA 49-52; 106; CANR 2,
16; DLB 8; MTCW 1
Dickens, Charles (John Huffam) 1812-1870
NCLC 3, 8, 18, 26, 37, 50; DA; DAB; DAC;
DAM MST, NOV; SSC 17; WLC
See also AAYA 23; CDBLB 1832-1890; DLB
21, 55, 70, 159, 166; JRDA; MAICYA; SATA
15
Dickey, James (Lafayette) 1923-1997...**CLC 1,**
2, 4, 7, 10, 15, 47, 109; DAM NOV, POET,
POP
See also AITN 1, 2; CA 9-12R; 156; CABS 2;
CANR 10, 48, 61; CDALB 1968-1988; DLB
5, 193; DLBD 7; DLBY 82, 93, 96, 97; INT
CANR-10; MTCW 1
Dickey, William 1928-1994 .... **CLC 3, 28**
See also CA 9-12R; 145; CANR 24; DLB 5
Dickinson, Charles 1951- .... **CLC 49**
See also CA 128
Dickinson, Emily (Elizabeth) 1830-1886
NCLC 21; DA; DAB; DAC; DAM MST,
POET; PC 1; WLC
See also AAYA 22; CDALB 1865-1917; DLB 1;
SATA 29

Drayham, James
 See Mencken, H(enry) L(ouis)
Drayton, Michael 1563-1631 ..... **LC 8; DAM POET**
 See also DLB 121
Dreadstone, Carl
 See Campbell, (John) Ramsey
Dreiser, Theodore (Herman Albert) 1871-1945
 TCLC 10, 18, 35, 83; DA; DAC; DAM MST, NOV; SSC 30; WLC
 See also CA 106; 132; CDALB 1865-1917; DLB 9, 12, 102, 137; DLBD 1; MTCW 1
Drexler, Rosalyn 1926- .... **CLC 2, 6**
 See also CA 81-84; CANR 68
Dreyer, Carl Theodor 1889-1968 .... **CLC 16**
 See also CA 116
Drieu la Rochelle, Pierre(-Eugene) 1893-1945
 TCLC 21
 See also CA 117; DLB 72
Drinkwater, John 1882-1937 .... **TCLC 57**
 See also CA 109; 149; DLB 10, 19, 149
Drop Shot
 See Cable, George Washington
Droste-Hulshoff, Annette Freiin von 1797-1848
 NCLC 3
 See also DLB 133
Drummond, Walter
 See Silverberg, Robert
Drummond, William Henry 1854-1907
 TCLC 25
 See also CA 160; DLB 92
Drummond de Andrade, Carlos 1902-1987
 CLC 18
 See also Andrade, Carlos Drummond de
 See also CA 132; 123
Drury, Allen (Stuart) 1918- .... **CLC 37**
 See also CA 57-60; CANR 18, 52; INT CANR-18
Dryden, John 1631-1700 .... **LC 3, 21; DA; DAB; DAC; DAM DRAM, MST, POET; DC 3; WLC**
 See also CDBLB 1660-1789; DLB 80, 101, 131
Duberman, Martin (Bauml) 1930- .... **CLC 8**
 See also CA 1-4R; CANR 2, 63
Dubie, Norman (Evans) 1945- .... **CLC 36**
 See also CA 69-72; CANR 12; DLB 120
Du Bois, W(illiam) E(dward) B(urghardt) 1868-1963 ... **CLC 1, 2, 13, 64, 96; BLC 1; DA; DAC; DAM MST, MULT, NOV; WLC**
 See also BW 1; CA 85-88; CANR 34; CDALB 1865-1917; DLB 47, 50, 91; MTCW 1; SATA 42
Dubus, Andre 1936- . **CLC 13, 36, 97; SSC 15**
 See also CA 21-24R; CANR 17; DLB 130; INT CANR-17
Duca Minimo
 See D'Annunzio, Gabriele
Ducharme, Rejean 1941- .... **CLC 74**
 See also CA 165; DLB 60
Duclos, Charles Pinot 1704-1772 .... **LC 1**
Dudek, Louis 1918- .... **CLC 11, 19**
 See also CA 45-48; CAAS 14; CANR 1; DLB 88
Duerrenmatt, Friedrich 1921-1990...**CLC 1, 4, 8, 11, 15, 43, 102; DAM DRAM**
 See also CA 17-20R; CANR 33; DLB 69, 124; MTCW 1
Duffy, Bruce (?)- .... **CLC 50**
Duffy, Maureen 1933- .... **CLC 37**
 See also CA 25-28R; CANR 33, 68; DLB 14; MTCW 1
Dugan, Alan 1923- .... **CLC 2, 6**
 See also CA 81-84; DLB 5

du Gard, Roger Martin
 See Martin du Gard, Roger
Duhamel, Georges 1884-1966 .... **CLC 8**
 See also CA 81-84; 25-28R; CANR 35; DLB 65; MTCW 1
Dujardin, Edouard (Emile Louis) 1861-1949
 TCLC 13
 See also CA 109; DLB 123
Dulles, John Foster 1888-1959 .... **TCLC 72**
 See also CA 115; 149
Dumas, Alexandre (pere)
 See Dumas, Alexandre (Davy de la Pailleterie)
Dumas, Alexandre (Davy de la Pailleterie) 1802-1870 .. **NCLC 11; DA; DAB; DAC; DAM MST, NOV; WLC**
 See also DLB 119, 192; SATA 18
Dumas, Alexandre (fils) 1824-1895 ..**NCLC 71; DC 1**
 See also AAYA 22; DLB 192
Dumas, Claudine
 See Malzberg, Barry N(athaniel)
Dumas, Henry L. 1934-1968 .... **CLC 6, 62**
 See also BW 1; CA 85-88; DLB 41
du Maurier, Daphne 1907-1989...**CLC 6, 11, 59; DAB; DAC; DAM MST, POP; SSC 18**
 See also CA 5-8R; 128; CANR 6, 55; DLB 191; MTCW 1; SATA 27; SATA-Obit 60
Dunbar, Paul Laurence 1872-1906...**TCLC 2, 12; BLC 1; DA; DAC; DAM MST, MULT, POET; PC 5; SSC 8; WLC**
 See also BW 1; CA 104; 124; CDALB 1865-1917; DLB 50, 54, 78; SATA 34
Dunbar, William 1460(?)-1530(?) .... **LC 20**
 See also DLB 132, 146
Duncan, Dora Angela
 See Duncan, Isadora
Duncan, Isadora 1877(?)-1927 .... **TCLC 68**
 See also CA 118; 149
Duncan, Lois 1934- .... **CLC 26**
 See also AAYA 4; CA 1-4R; CANR 2, 23, 36; CLR 29; JRDA; MAICYA; SAAS 2; SATA 1, 36, 75
Duncan, Robert (Edward) 1919-1988...**CLC 1, 2, 4, 7, 15, 41, 55; DAM POET; PC 2**
 See also CA 9-12R; 124; CANR 28, 62; DLB 5, 16, 193; MTCW 1
Duncan, Sara Jeannette 1861-1922...**TCLC 60**
 See also CA 157; DLB 92
Dunlap, William 1766-1839 .... **NCLC 2**
 See also DLB 30, 37, 59
Dunn, Douglas (Eaglesham) 1942-...**CLC 6, 40**
 See also CA 45-48; CANR 2, 33; DLB 40; MTCW 1
Dunn, Katherine (Karen) 1945- .... **CLC 71**
 See also CA 33-36R; CANR 72
Dunn, Stephen 1939- .... **CLC 36**
 See also CA 33-36R; CANR 12, 48, 53; DLB 105
Dunne, Finley Peter 1867-1936 .... **TCLC 28**
 See also CA 108; DLB 11, 23
Dunne, John Gregory 1932- .... **CLC 28**
 See also CA 25-28R; CANR 14, 50; DLBY 80
Dunsany, Edward John Moreton Drax Plunkett 1878-1957
 See Dunsany, Lord
 See also CA 104; 148; DLB 10
Dunsany, Lord .... **TCLC 2, 59**
 See also Dunsany, Edward John Moreton Drax Plunkett
 See also DLB 77, 153, 156
du Perry, Jean
 See Simenon, Georges (Jacques Christian)

Durang, Christopher (Ferdinand) 1949-
 CLC 27, 38
 See also CA 105; CANR 50
Duras, Marguerite 1914-1996...**CLC 3, 6, 11, 20, 34, 40, 68, 100**
 See also CA 25-28R; 151; CANR 50; DLB 83; MTCW 1
Durban, (Rosa) Pam 1947- .... **CLC 39**
 See also CA 123
Durcan, Paul 1944- .... **CLC 43, 70; DAM POET**
 See also CA 134
Durkheim, Emile 1858-1917 .... **TCLC 55**
Durrell, Lawrence (George) 1912-1990
 CLC 1, 4, 6, 8, 13, 27, 41; DAM NOV
 See also CA 9-12R; 132; CANR 40; CDBLB 1945-1960; DLB 15, 27; DLBY 90; MTCW 1
Durrenmatt, Friedrich
 See Duerrenmatt, Friedrich
Dutt, Toru 1856-1877 .... **NCLC 29**
Dwight, Timothy 1752-1817 .... **NCLC 13**
 See also DLB 37
Dworkin, Andrea 1946- .... **CLC 43**
 See also CA 77-80; CAAS 21; CANR 16, 39; INT CANR-16; MTCW 1
Dwyer, Deanna
 See Koontz, Dean R(ay)
Dwyer, K. R.
 See Koontz, Dean R(ay)
Dwyer, Thomas A. 1923- .... **CLC 114**
 See also CA 115
Dye, Richard
 See De Voto, Bernard (Augustine)
Dylan, Bob 1941- .... **CLC 3, 4, 6, 12, 77**
 See also CA 41-44R; DLB 16
Eagleton, Terence (Francis) 1943-
 See Eagleton, Terry
 See also CA 57-60; CANR 7, 23, 68; MTCW 1
Eagleton, Terry .... **CLC 63**
 See also Eagleton, Terence (Francis)
Early, Jack
 See Scoppettone, Sandra
East, Michael
 See West, Morris L(anglo)
Eastaway, Edward
 See Thomas, (Philip) Edward
Eastlake, William (Derry) 1917-1997 .. **CLC 8**
 See also CA 5-8R; 158; CAAS 1; CANR 5, 63; DLB 6; INT CANR-5
Eastman, Charles A(lexander) 1858-1939
 TCLC 55; DAM MULT
 See also DLB 175; NNAL; YABC 1
Eberhart, Richard (Ghormley) 1904-...**CLC 3, 11, 19, 56; DAM POET**
 See also CA 1-4R; CANR 2; CDALB 1941-1968; DLB 48; MTCW 1
Eberstadt, Fernanda 1960- .... **CLC 39**
 See also CA 136; CANR 69
Echegaray (y Eizaguirre), Jose (Maria Waldo) 1832-1916 .... **TCLC 4**
 See also CA 104; CANR 32; HW; MTCW 1
Echeverria, (Jose) Esteban (Antonino) 1805-1851 .... **NCLC 18**
Echo
 See Proust, (Valentin-Louis-George-Eugene-) Marcel
Eckert, Allan W. 1931- .... **CLC 17**
 See also AAYA 18; CA 13-16R; CANR 14, 45; INT CANR-14; SAAS 21; SATA 29, 91; SATA-Brief 27
Eckhart, Meister 1260(?)-1328(?) .... **CMLC 9**
 See also DLB 115

Author Index

Fellini, Federico 1920-1993 .... **CLC 16, 85**
    See also CA 65-68; 143; CANR 33
Felsen, Henry Gregor 1916- .... **CLC 17**
    See also CA 1-4R; CANR 1; SAAS 2; SATA 1
Fenno, Jack
    See Calisher, Hortense
Fenton, James Martin 1949- .... **CLC 32**
    See also CA 102; DLB 40
Ferber, Edna 1887-1968 .... **CLC 18, 93**
    See also AITN 1; CA 5-8R; 25-28R; CANR 68;
    DLB 9, 28, 86; MTCW 1; SATA 7
Ferguson, Helen
    See Kavan, Anna
Ferguson, Samuel 1810-1886 .... **NCLC 33**
    See also DLB 32
Fergusson, Robert 1750-1774 .... **LC 29**
    See also DLB 109
Ferling, Lawrence
    See Ferlinghetti, Lawrence (Monsanto)
Ferlinghetti, Lawrence (Monsanto) 1919(?)-
    CLC 2, 6, 10, 27, 111; DAM POET; PC 1
    See also CA 5-8R; CANR 3, 41; CDALB 1941-
    1968; DLB 5, 16; MTCW 1
Fernandez, Vicente Garcia Huidobro
    See Huidobro Fernandez, Vicente Garcia
Ferrer, Gabriel (Francisco Victor) Miro
    See Miro (Ferrer), Gabriel (Francisco Victor)
Ferrier, Susan (Edmonstone) 1782-1854
    NCLC 8
    See also DLB 116
Ferrigno, Robert 1948(?)- .... **CLC 65**
    See also CA 140
Ferron, Jacques 1921-1985 ..... **CLC 94; DAC**
    See also CA 117; 129; DLB 60
Feuchtwanger, Lion 1884-1958 .... **TCLC 3**
    See also CA 104; DLB 66
Feuillet, Octave 1821-1890 .... **NCLC 45**
    See also DLB 192
Feydeau, Georges (Leon Jules Marie) 1862-1921
    TCLC 22; DAM DRAM
    See also CA 113; 152; DLB 192
Fichte, Johann Gottlieb 1762-1814...**NCLC 62**
    See also DLB 90
Ficino, Marsilio 1433-1499 .... **LC 12**
Fiedeler, Hans
    See Doeblin, Alfred
Fiedler, Leslie A(aron) 1917- .... **CLC 4, 13, 24**
    See also CA 9-12R; CANR 7, 63; DLB 28, 67;
    MTCW 1
Field, Andrew 1938- .... **CLC 44**
    See also CA 97-100; CANR 25
Field, Eugene 1850-1895 .... **NCLC 3**
    See also DLB 23, 42, 140; DLBD 13; MAICYA;
    SATA 16
Field, Gans T.
    See Wellman, Manly Wade
Field, Michael 1915-1971 .... **TCLC 43**
    See also CA 29-32R
Field, Peter
    See Hobson, Laura Z(ametkin)
Fielding, Henry 1707-1754 .. **LC 1; DA; DAB;
    DAC; DAM DRAM, MST, NOV; WLC**
    See also CDBLB 1660-1789; DLB 39, 84,
    101
Fielding, Sarah 1710-1768 .... **LC 1, 44**
    See also DLB 39
Fields, W. C. 1880-1946 .... **TCLC 80**
    See also DLB 44
Fierstein, Harvey (Forbes) 1954- ..... **CLC 33;
    DAM DRAM, POP**
    See also CA 123; 129
Figes, Eva 1932- .... **CLC 31**
    See also CA 53-56; CANR 4, 44; DLB 14

Finch, Anne 1661-1720 .... **LC 3; PC 21**
    See also DLB 95
Finch, Robert (Duer Claydon) 1900-...**CLC 18**
    See also CA 57-60; CANR 9, 24, 49; DLB 88
Findley, Timothy 1930- .. **CLC 27, 102; DAC;
    DAM MST**
    See also CA 25-28R; CANR 12, 42, 69; DLB 53
Fink, William
    See Mencken, H(enry) L(ouis)
Firbank, Louis 1942-
    See Reed, Lou
    See also CA 117
Firbank, (Arthur Annesley) Ronald 1886-1926
    TCLC 1
    See also CA 104; DLB 36
Fisher, M(ary) F(rances) K(ennedy) 1908-1992
    CLC 76, 87
    See also CA 77-80; 138; CANR 44
Fisher, Roy 1930- .... **CLC 25**
    See also CA 81-84; CAAS 10; CANR 16; DLB
    40
Fisher, Rudolph 1897-1934...**TCLC 11; BLC 2;
    DAM MULT; SSC 25**
    See also BW 1; CA 107; 124; DLB 51, 102
Fisher, Vardis (Alvero) 1895-1968 .... **CLC 7**
    See also CA 5-8R; 25-28R; CANR 68; DLB 9
Fiske, Tarleton
    See Bloch, Robert (Albert)
Fitch, Clarke
    See Sinclair, Upton (Beall)
Fitch, John IV
    See Cormier, Robert (Edmund)
Fitzgerald, Captain Hugh
    See Baum, L(yman) Frank
FitzGerald, Edward 1809-1883 .... **NCLC 9**
    See also DLB 32
Fitzgerald, F(rancis) Scott (Key) 1896-1940
    **TCLC 1, 6, 14, 28, 55; DA; DAB; DAC;
    DAM MST, NOV; SSC 6, 31; WLC**
    See also AAYA 24; AITN 1; CA 110; 123;
    CDALB 1917-1929; DLB 4, 9, 86; DLBD 1,
    15, 16; DLBY 81, 96; MTCW 1
Fitzgerald, Penelope 1916- ..... **CLC 19, 51, 61**
    See also CA 85-88; CAAS 10; CANR 56; DLB
    14, 194
Fitzgerald, Robert (Stuart) 1910-1985
    CLC 39
    See also CA 1-4R; 114; CANR 1; DLBY 80
FitzGerald, Robert D(avid) 1902-1987
    CLC 19
    See also CA 17-20R
Fitzgerald, Zelda (Sayre) 1900-1948..**TCLC 52**
    See also CA 117; 126; DLBY 84
Flanagan, Thomas (James Bonner) 1923-
    CLC 25, 52
    See also CA 108; CANR 55; DLBY 80; INT 108;
    MTCW 1
Flaubert, Gustave 1821-1880...**NCLC 2, 10,
    19, 62, 66; DA; DAB; DAC; DAM MST,
    NOV; SSC 11; WLC**
    See also DLB 119
Flecker, Herman Elroy
    See Flecker, (Herman) James Elroy
Flecker, (Herman) James Elroy 1884-1915
    TCLC 43
    See also CA 109; 150; DLB 10, 19
Fleming, Ian (Lancaster) 1908-1964...**CLC 3,
    30; DAM POP**
    See also AAYA 26; CA 5-8R; CANR 59; CDBLB
    1945-1960; DLB 87, 201; MTCW 1; SATA 9
Fleming, Thomas (James) 1927- .... **CLC 37**
    See also CA 5-8R; CANR 10; INT CANR-10;
    SATA 8

Fletcher, John 1579-1625 .... **LC 33; DC 6**
    See also CDBLB Before 1660; DLB 58
Fletcher, John Gould 1886-1950 ..... **TCLC 35**
    See also CA 107; 167; DLB 4, 45
Fleur, Paul
    See Pohl, Frederik
Flooglebuckle, Al
    See Spiegelman, Art
Flying Officer X
    See Bates, H(erbert) E(rnest)
Fo, Dario 1926-...**CLC 32, 109; DAM DRAM**
    See also CA 116; 128; CANR 68; DLBY 97;
    MTCW 1
Fogarty, Jonathan Titulescu Esq.
    See Farrell, James T(homas)
Folke, Will
    See Bloch, Robert (Albert)
Follett, Ken(neth Martin) 1949- ..... **CLC 18;
    DAM NOV, POP**
    See also AAYA 6; BEST 89:4; CA 81-84; CANR
    13, 33, 54; DLB 87; DLBY 81; INT CANR-
    33; MTCW 1
Fontane, Theodor 1819-1898 .... **NCLC 26**
    See also DLB 129
Foote, Horton 1916- .... **CLC 51, 91; DAM
    DRAM**
    See also CA 73-76; CANR 34, 51; DLB 26; INT
    CANR-34
Foote, Shelby 1916-... **CLC 75; DAM NOV,
    POP**
    See also CA 5-8R; CANR 3, 45; DLB 2, 17
Forbes, Esther 1891-1967 .... **CLC 12**
    See also AAYA 17; CA 13-14; 25-28R; CAP 1;
    CLR 27; DLB 22; JRDA; MAICYA; SATA 2,
    100
Forche, Carolyn (Louise) 1950-...**CLC 25, 83,
    86; DAM POET; PC 10**
    See also CA 109; 117; CANR 50; DLB 5, 193;
    INT 117
Ford, Elbur
    See Hibbert, Eleanor Alice Burford
Ford, Ford Madox 1873-1939...**TCLC 1, 15,
    39, 57; DAM NOV**
    See also CA 104; 132; CDBLB 1914-1945; DLB
    162; MTCW 1
Ford, Henry 1863-1947 .... **TCLC 73**
    See also CA 115; 148
Ford, John 1586-(?)............................... **DC 8**
    See also CDBLB Before 1660; DAM DRAM;
    DLB 58
Ford, John 1895-1973 .... **CLC 16**
    See also CA 45-48
Ford, Richard 1944-...................... **CLC 46, 99**
    See also CA 69-72; CANR 11, 47
Ford, Webster
    See Masters, Edgar Lee
Foreman, Richard 1937-..................... **CLC 50**
    See also CA 65-68; CANR 32, 63
Forester, C(ecil) S(cott) 1899-1966 .... **CLC 35**
    See also CA 73-76; 25-28R; DLB 191; SATA 13
Forez
    See Mauriac, Francois (Charles)
Forman, James Douglas 1932- .... **CLC 21**
    See also AAYA 17; CA 9-12R; CANR 4, 19, 42;
    JRDA; MAICYA; SATA 8, 70
Fornes, Maria Irene 1930- .... **CLC 39, 61**
    See also CA 25-28R; CANR 28; DLB 7; HW;
    INT CANR-28; MTCW 1
Forrest, Leon (Richard) 1937-1997 ... **CLC 4;
    BLCS**
    See also BW 2; CA 89-92; 162; CAAS 7; CANR
    25, 52; DLB 33

Gregory, Isabella Augusta (Persse) 1852-1932
TCLC 1
See also CA 104; DLB 10
Gregory, J. Dennis
See Williams, John A(lfred)
Grendon, Stephen
See Derleth, August (William)
Grenville, Kate 1950- .... **CLC 61**
See also CA 118; CANR 53
Grenville, Pelham
See Wodehouse, P(elham) G(renville)
Greve, Felix Paul (Berthold Friedrich) 1879-
1948
See Grove, Frederick Philip
See also CA 104; 141; DAC; DAM MST
Grey, Zane 1872-1939 ... **TCLC 6; DAM POP**
See also CA 104; 132; DLB 9; MTCW 1
Grieg, (Johan) Nordahl (Brun) 1902-1943
TCLC 10
See also CA 107
Grieve, C(hristopher) M(urray) 1892-1978
CLC 11, 19; DAM POET
See also MacDiarmid, Hugh; Pteleon
See also CA 5-8R; 85-88; CANR 33; MTCW 1
Griffin, Gerald 1803-1840 .... **NCLC 7**
See also DLB 159
Griffin, John Howard 1920-1980 .... **CLC 68**
See also AITN 1; CA 1-4R; 101; CANR 2
Griffin, Peter 1942- .... **CLC 39**
See also CA 136
Griffith, D(avid Lewelyn) W(ark) 1875(?)-1948
TCLC 68
See also CA 119; 150
Griffith, Lawrence
See Griffith, D(avid Lewelyn) W(ark)
Griffiths, Trevor 1935- .... **CLC 13, 52**
See also CA 97-100; CANR 45; DLB 13
Griggs, Sutton Elbert 1872-1930(?)...**TCLC 77**
See also CA 123; DLB 50
Grigson, Geoffrey (Edward Harvey) 1905-1985
CLC 7, 39
See also CA 25-28R; 118; CANR 20, 33; DLB
27; MTCW 1
Grillparzer, Franz 1791-1872 .... **NCLC 1**
See also DLB 133
Grimble, Reverend Charles James
See Eliot, T(homas) S(tearns)
Grimke, Charlotte L(ottie) Forten 1837(?)-1914
See Forten, Charlotte L.
See also BW 1; CA 117; 124; DAM MULT, POET
Grimm, Jacob Ludwig Karl 1785-1863
NCLC 3
See also DLB 90; MAICYA; SATA 22
Grimm, Wilhelm Karl 1786-1859 ..... **NCLC 3**
See also DLB 90; MAICYA; SATA 22
Grimmelshausen, Johann Jakob Christoffel von
1621-1676 ....**LC 6**
See also DLB 168
Grindel, Eugene 1895-1952
See Eluard, Paul
See also CA 104
Grisham, John 1955- ...... **CLC 84; DAM POP**
See also AAYA 14; CA 138; CANR 47, 69
Grossman, David 1954- .... **CLC 67**
See also CA 138
Grossman, Vasily (Semenovich) 1905-1964
CLC 41
See also CA 124; 130; MTCW 1
Grove, Frederick Philip .... **TCLC 4**
See also Greve, Felix Paul (Berthold Friedrich)
See also DLB 92
Grubb
See Crumb, R(obert)

Grumbach, Doris (Isaac) 1918-...**CLC 13, 22,**
64
See also CA 5-8R; CAAS 2; CANR 9, 42, 70;
INT CANR-9
Grundtvig, Nicolai Frederik Severin 1783-1872
NCLC 1
Grunge
See Crumb, R(obert)
Grunwald, Lisa 1959- .... **CLC 44**
See also CA 120
Guare, John 1938- ... **CLC 8, 14, 29, 67; DAM**
DRAM
See also CA 73-76; CANR 21, 69; DLB 7;
MTCW 1
Gudjonsson, Halldor Kiljan 1902-1998
See Laxness, Halldor
See also CA 103; 164
Guenter, Erich
See Eich, Guenter
Guest, Barbara 1920- .... **CLC 34**
See also CA 25-28R; CANR 11, 44; DLB 5, 193
Guest, Judith (Ann) 1936- .. **CLC 8, 30; DAM**
NOV, POP
See also AAYA 7; CA 77-80; CANR 15; INT
CANR-15; MTCW 1
Guevara, Che .... **CLC 87; HLC**
See also Guevara (Serna), Ernesto
Guevara (Serna), Ernesto 1928-1967
See Guevara, Che
See also CA 127; 111; CANR 56; DAM MULT; HW
Guild, Nicholas M. 1944- .... **CLC 33**
See also CA 93-96
Guillemin, Jacques
See Sartre, Jean-Paul
Guillen, Jorge 1893-1984 .... **CLC 11; DAM**
MULT, POET
See also CA 89-92; 112; DLB 108; HW
Guillen, Nicolas (Cristobal) 1902-1989
CLC 48, 79; BLC 2; DAM MST, MULT,
POET; HLC; PC 23
See also BW 2; CA 116; 125; 129; HW
Guillevic, (Eugene) 1907- .... **CLC 33**
See also CA 93-96
Guillois
See Desnos, Robert
Guillois, Valentin
See Desnos, Robert
Guiney, Louise Imogen 1861-1920 .. **TCLC 41**
See also CA 160; DLB 54
Guiraldes, Ricardo (Guillermo) 1886-1927
TCLC 39
See also CA 131; HW; MTCW 1
Gumilev, Nikolai (Stepanovich) 1886-1921
TCLC 60
See also CA 165
Gunesekera, Romesh 1954- .... **CLC 91**
See also CA 159
Gunn, Bill .... **CLC 5**
See also Gunn, William Harrison
See also DLB 38
Gunn, Thom(son William) 1929-...**CLC 3, 6,**
18, 32, 81; DAM POET
See also CA 17-20R; CANR 9, 33; CDBLB 1960
to Present; DLB 27; INT CANR-33; MTCW 1
Gunn, William Harrison 1934(?)-1989
See Gunn, Bill
See also AITN 1; BW 1; CA 13-16R; 128; CANR
12, 25
Gunnars, Kristjana 1948- .... **CLC 69**
See also CA 113; DLB 60
Gurdjieff, G(eorgei) I(vanovich) 1877(?)-1949
TCLC 71
See also CA 157

Gurganus, Allan 1947- ... **CLC 70; DAM POP**
See also BEST 90:1; CA 135
Gurney, A(lbert) R(amsdell), Jr. 1930-
CLC 32, 50, 54; DAM DRAM
See also CA 77-80; CANR 32, 64
Gurney, Ivor (Bertie) 1890-1937 .... **TCLC 33**
See also CA 167
Gurney, Peter
See Gurney, A(lbert) R(amsdell), Jr.
Guro, Elena 1877-1913 .... **TCLC 56**
Gustafson, James M(oody) 1925-..... **CLC 100**
See also CA 25-28R; CANR 37
Gustafson, Ralph (Barker) 1909- .... **CLC 36**
See also CA 21-24R; CANR 8, 45; DLB 88
Gut, Gom
See Simenon, Georges (Jacques Christian)
Guterson, David 1956- .... **CLC 91**
See also CA 132
Guthrie, A(lfred) B(ertram), Jr. 1901-1991
CLC 23
See also CA 57-60; 134; CANR 24; DLB 6;
SATA 62; SATA-Obit 67
Guthrie, Isobel
See Grieve, C(hristopher) M(urray)
Guthrie, Woodrow Wilson 1912-1967
See Guthrie, Woody
See also CA 113; 93-96
Guthrie, Woody .... **CLC 35**
See also Guthrie, Woodrow Wilson
Guy, Rosa (Cuthbert) 1928- .... **CLC 26**
See also AAYA 4; BW 2; CA 17-20R; CANR
14, 34; CLR 13; DLB 33; JRDA; MAICYA;
SATA 14, 62
Gwendolyn
See Bennett, (Enoch) Arnold
H. D. .... **CLC 3, 8, 14, 31, 34, 73; PC 5**
See also Doolittle, Hilda
H. de V.
See Buchan, John
Haavikko, Paavo Juhani 1931-..... **CLC 18, 34**
See also CA 106
Habbema, Koos
See Heijermans, Herman
Habermas, Juergen 1929- .... **CLC 104**
See also CA 109
Habermas, Jurgen
See Habermas, Juergen
Hacker, Marilyn 1942- .. **CLC 5, 9, 23, 72, 91;**
DAM POET
See also CA 77-80; CANR 68; DLB 120
Haeckel, Ernst Heinrich (Philipp August) 1834-
1919 .... **TCLC 83**
See also CA 157
Haggard, H(enry) Rider 1856-1925...**TCLC 11**
See also CA 108; 148; DLB 70, 156, 174, 178;
SATA 16
Hagiosy, L.
See Larbaud, Valery (Nicolas)
Hagiwara Sakutaro 1886-1942...**TCLC 60; PC**
18
Haig, Fenil
See Ford, Ford Madox
Haig-Brown, Roderick (Langmere) 1908-1976
CLC 21
See also CA 5-8R; 69-72; CANR 4, 38; CLR 31;
DLB 88; MAICYA; SATA 12
Hailey, Arthur 1920-... **CLC 5; DAM NOV,**
POP
See also AITN 2; BEST 90:3; CA 1-4R; CANR
2, 36; DLB 88; DLBY 82; MTCW 1
Hailey, Elizabeth Forsythe 1938- .... **CLC 40**
See also CA 93-96; CAAS 1; CANR 15, 48; INT
CANR-15

Hasek, Jaroslav (Matej Frantisek) 1883-1923 **TCLC 4**
See also CA 104; 129; MTCW 1

Hass, Robert 1941- ..... **CLC 18, 39, 99; PC 16**
See also CA 111; CANR 30, 50, 71; DLB 105; SATA 94

Hastings, Hudson
See Kuttner, Henry

Hastings, Selina .... **CLC 44**

Hathorne, John 1641-1717 .... **LC 38**

Hatteras, Amelia
See Mencken, H(enry) L(ouis)

Hatteras, Owen .... **TCLC 18**
See also Mencken, H(enry) L(ouis); Nathan, George Jean

Hauptmann, Gerhart (Johann Robert) 1862-1946 .... **TCLC 4; DAM DRAM**
See also CA 104; 153; DLB 66, 118

Havel, Vaclav 1936- ..... **CLC 25, 58, 65; DAM DRAM; DC 6**
See also CA 104; CANR 36, 63; MTCW 1

Haviaras, Stratis .... **CLC 33**
See also Chaviaras, Strates

Hawes, Stephen 1475(?)-1523(?) .... **LC 17**
See also DLB 132

Hawkes, John (Clendennin Burne, Jr.) 1925-1998 .... **CLC 1, 2, 3, 4, 7, 9, 14, 15, 27, 49**
See also CA 1-4R; 167; CANR 2, 47, 64; DLB 2, 7; DLBY 80; MTCW 1

Hawking, S. W.
See Hawking, Stephen W(illiam)

Hawking, Stephen W(illiam) 1942- . **CLC 63, 105**
See also AAYA 13; BEST 89:1; CA 126; 129; CANR 48

Hawkins, Anthony Hope
See Hope, Anthony

Hawthorne, Julian 1846-1934 .... **TCLC 25**
See also CA 165

Hawthorne, Nathaniel 1804-1864 . **NCLC 39; DA; DAB; DAC; DAM MST, NOV; SSC 3, 29; WLC**
See also AAYA 18; CDALB 1640-1865; DLB 1, 74; YABC 2

Haxton, Josephine Ayres 1921-
See Douglas, Ellen
See also CA 115; CANR 41

Hayaseca y Eizaguirre, Jorge
See Echegaray (y Eizaguirre), Jose (Maria Waldo)

Hayashi, Fumiko 1904-1951 .... **TCLC 27**
See also CA 161; DLB 180

Haycraft, Anna
See Ellis, Alice Thomas
See also CA 122

Hayden, Robert E(arl) 1913-1980...**CLC 5, 9, 14, 37; BLC 2; DA; DAC; DAM MST, MULT, POET; PC 6**
See also BW 1; CA 69-72; 97-100; CABS 2; CANR 24; CDALB 1941-1968; DLB 5, 76; MTCW 1; SATA 19; SATA-Obit 26

Hayford, J(oseph) E(phraim) Casely
See Casely-Hayford, J(oseph) E(phraim)

Hayman, Ronald 1932- .... **CLC 44**
See also CA 25-28R; CANR 18, 50; DLB 155

Haywood, Eliza 1693(?)-1756 .... **LC 44**
See also DLB 39

Haywood, Eliza (Fowler) 1693(?)-1756...**LC 1, 44**

Hazlitt, William 1778-1830 .... **NCLC 29**
See also DLB 110, 158

Hazzard, Shirley 1931- .... **CLC 18**
See also CA 9-12R; CANR 4, 70; DLBY 82; MTCW 1

Head, Bessie 1937-1986...**CLC 25, 67; BLC 2; DAM MULT**
See also BW 2; CA 29-32R; 119; CANR 25; DLB 117; MTCW 1

Headon, (Nicky) Topper 1956(?)- .... **CLC 30**

Heaney, Seamus (Justin) 1939-...**CLC 5, 7, 14, 25, 37, 74, 91; DAB; DAM POET; PC 18; WLCS**
See also CA 85-88; CANR 25, 48; CDBLB 1960 to Present; DLB 40; DLBY 95; MTCW 1

Hearn, (Patricio) Lafcadio (Tessima Carlos) 1850-1904 .... **TCLC 9**
See also CA 105; 166; DLB 12, 78

Hearne, Vicki 1946- .... **CLC 56**
See also CA 139

Hearon, Shelby 1931- .... **CLC 63**
See also AITN 2; CA 25-28R; CANR 18, 48

Heat-Moon, William Least .... **CLC 29**
See also Trogdon, William (Lewis)
See also AAYA 9

Hebbel, Friedrich 1813-1863 .....**NCLC 43; DAM DRAM**
See also DLB 129

Hebert, Anne 1916-.... **CLC 4, 13, 29; DAC; DAM MST, POET**
See also CA 85-88; CANR 69; DLB 68; MTCW 1

Hecht, Anthony (Evan) 1923-. **CLC 8, 13, 19; DAM POET**
See also CA 9-12R; CANR 6; DLB 5, 169

Hecht, Ben 1894-1964 .... **CLC 8**
See also CA 85-88; DLB 7, 9, 25, 26, 28, 86

Hedayat, Sadeq 1903-1951 .... **TCLC 21**
See also CA 120

Hegel, Georg Wilhelm Friedrich 1770-1831 **NCLC 46**
See also DLB 90

Heidegger, Martin 1889-1976 .... **CLC 24**
See also CA 81-84; 65-68; CANR 34; MTCW 1

Heidenstam, (Carl Gustaf) Verner von 1859-1940 .... **TCLC 5**
See also CA 104

Heifner, Jack 1946- .... **CLC 11**
See also CA 105; CANR 47

Heijermans, Herman 1864-1924 ..... **TCLC 24**
See also CA 123

Heilbrun, Carolyn G(old) 1926- .... **CLC 25**
See also CA 45-48; CANR 1, 28, 58

Heine, Heinrich 1797-1856 .... **NCLC 4, 54**
See also DLB 90

Heinemann, Larry (Curtiss) 1944- .... **CLC 50**
See also CA 110; CAAS 21; CANR 31; DLBD 9; INT CANR-31

Heiney, Donald (William) 1921-1993
See Harris, MacDonald
See also CA 1-4R; 142; CANR 3, 58

Heinlein, Robert A(nson) 1907-1988...**CLC 1, 3, 8, 14, 26, 55; DAM POP**
See also AAYA 17; CA 1-4R; 125; CANR 1, 20, 53; DLB 8; JRDA; MAICYA; MTCW 1; SATA 9, 69; SATA-Obit 56

Helforth, John
See Doolittle, Hilda

Hellenhofferu, Vojtech Kapristian z
See Hasek, Jaroslav (Matej Frantisek)

Heller, Joseph 1923-...**CLC 1, 3, 5, 8, 11, 36, 63; DA; DAB; DAC; DAM MST, NOV, POP; WLC**
See also AAYA 24; AITN 1; CA 5-8R; CABS 1; CANR 8, 42, 66; DLB 2, 28; DLBY 80; INT CANR-8; MTCW 1

Hellman, Lillian (Florence) 1906-1984 **CLC 2, 4, 8, 14, 18, 34, 44, 52; DAM DRAM; DC 1**
See also AITN 1, 2; CA 13-16R; 112; CANR 33; DLB 7; DLBY 84; MTCW 1

Helprin, Mark 1947- .... **CLC 7, 10, 22, 32; DAM NOV, POP**
See also CA 81-84; CANR 47, 64; DLBY 85; MTCW 1

Helvetius, Claude-Adrien 1715-1771 ... **LC 26**

Helyar, Jane Penelope Josephine 1933-
See Poole, Josephine
See also CA 21-24R; CANR 10, 26; SATA 82

Hemans, Felicia 1793-1835 .... **NCLC 71**
See also DLB 96

Hemingway, Ernest (Miller) 1899-1961 **CLC 1, 3, 6, 8, 10, 13, 19, 30, 34, 39, 41, 44, 50, 61, 80; DA; DAB; DAC; DAM MST, NOV; SSC 1, 25; WLC**
See also AAYA 19; CA 77-80; CANR 34; CDALB 1917-1929; DLB 4, 9, 102; DLBD 1, 15, 16; DLBY 81, 87, 96; MTCW 1

Hempel, Amy 1951- .... **CLC 39**
See also CA 118; 137; CANR 70

Henderson, F. C.
See Mencken, H(enry) L(ouis)

Henderson, Sylvia
See Ashton-Warner, Sylvia (Constance)

Henderson, Zenna (Chlarson) 1917-1983 **SSC 29**
See also CA 1-4R; 133; CANR 1; DLB 8; SATA 5

Henley, Beth .... **CLC 23; DC 6**
See also Henley, Elizabeth Becker
See also CABS 3; DLBY 86

Henley, Elizabeth Becker 1952-
See Henley, Beth
See also CA 107; CANR 32; DAM DRAM, MST; MTCW 1

Henley, William Ernest 1849-1903 ... **TCLC 8**
See also CA 105; DLB 19

Hennissart, Martha
See Lathen, Emma
See also CA 85-88; CANR 64

Henry, O. .... **TCLC 1, 19; SSC 5; WLC**
See also Porter, William Sydney

Henry, Patrick 1736-1799 .... **LC 25**

Henryson, Robert 1430(?)-1506(?) ...... **LC 20**
See also DLB 146

Henry VIII 1491-1547 .... **LC 10**

Henschke, Alfred
See Klabund

Hentoff, Nat(han Irving) 1925- .... **CLC 26**
See also AAYA 4; CA 1-4R; CAAS 6; CANR 5, 25; CLR 1, 52; INT CANR-25; JRDA; MAICYA; SATA 42, 69; SATA-Brief 27

Heppenstall, (John) Rayner 1911-1981 **CLC 10**
See also CA 1-4R; 103; CANR 29

Heraclitus c. 540B.C.-c. 450B.C. ..... **CMLC 22**
See also DLB 176

Herbert, Frank (Patrick) 1920-1986...**CLC 12, 23, 35, 44, 85**
See also AAYA 21; CA 53-56; 118; CANR 5, 43; DLB 8; INT CANR-5; MTCW 1; SATA 9, 37; SATA-Obit 47

Herbert, George 1593-1633 .... **LC 24; DAB; DAM POET; PC 4**
See also CDBLB Before 1660; DLB 126

Herbert, Zbigniew 1924- .... **CLC 9, 43; DAM POET**
See also CA 89-92; CANR 36; MTCW 1

Herbst, Josephine (Frey) 1897-1969..**CLC 34**
See also CA 5-8R; 25-28R; DLB 9

Jones, David Robert 1947-
See Bowie, David
See also CA 103
Jones, Diana Wynne 1934- .... **CLC 26**
See also AAYA 12; CA 49-52; CANR 4, 26, 56;
CLR 23; DLB 161; JRDA; MAICYA; SAAS
7; SATA 9, 70
Jones, Edward P. 1950- .... **CLC 76**
See also BW 2; CA 142
Jones, Gayl 1949- ..... **CLC 6, 9; BLC 2; DAM
MULT**
See also BW 2; CA 77-80; CANR 27, 66; DLB
33; MTCW 1
Jones, James 1921-1977 .... **CLC 1, 3, 10, 39**
See also AITN 1, 2; CA 1-4R; 69-72; CANR 6;
DLB 2, 143; DLBD 17; MTCW 1
Jones, John J.
See Lovecraft, H(oward) P(hillips)
Jones, LeRoi .... **CLC 1, 2, 3, 5, 10, 14**
See also Baraka, Amiri
Jones, Louis B. .... **CLC 65**
See also CA 141
Jones, Madison (Percy, Jr.) 1925- .... **CLC 4**
See also CA 13-16R; CAAS 11; CANR 7, 54;
DLB 152
Jones, Mervyn 1922- .... **CLC 10, 52**
See also CA 45-48; CAAS 5; CANR 1; MTCW
1
Jones, Mick 1956(?)- .... **CLC 30**
Jones, Nettie (Pearl) 1941- .... **CLC 34**
See also BW 2; CA 137; CAAS 20
Jones, Preston 1936-1979 .... **CLC 10**
See also CA 73-76; 89-92; DLB 7
Jones, Robert F(rancis) 1934- .... **CLC 7**
See also CA 49-52; CANR 2, 61
Jones, Rod 1953- .... **CLC 50**
See also CA 128
Jones, Terence Graham Parry 1942-...**CLC 21**
See also Jones, Terry; Monty Python
See also CA 112; 116; CANR 35; INT 116
Jones, Terry
See Jones, Terence Graham Parry
See also SATA 67; SATA-Brief 51
Jones, Thom 1945(?)- .... **CLC 81**
See also CA 157
Jong, Erica 1942- .... **CLC 4, 6, 8, 18, 83;
DAM NOV, POP**
See also AITN 1; BEST 90:2; CA 73-76; CANR
26, 52; DLB 2, 5, 28, 152; INT CANR-26;
MTCW 1
Jonson, Ben(jamin) 1572(?)-1637 .. **LC 6, 33;
DA; DAB; DAC; DAM DRAM, MST,
POET; DC 4; PC 17; WLC**
See also CDBLB Before 1660; DLB 62, 121
Jordan, June 1936- ..... **CLC 5, 11, 23, 114;
BLCS; DAM MULT, POET**
See also AAYA 2; BW 2; CA 33-36R; CANR
25, 70; CLR 10; DLB 38; MAICYA; MTCW
1; SATA 4
Jordan, Neil (Patrick) 1950- .... **CLC 110**
See also CA 124; 130; CANR 54; INT 130
Jordan, Pat(rick M.) 1941- .... **CLC 37**
See also CA 33-36R
Jorgensen, Ivar
See Ellison, Harlan (Jay)
Jorgenson, Ivar
See Silverberg, Robert
Josephus, Flavius c. 37-100 .... **CMLC 13**
Josipovici, Gabriel 1940- .... **CLC 6, 43**
See also CA 37-40R; CAAS 8; CANR 47; DLB 14
Joubert, Joseph 1754-1824 .... **NCLC 9**
Jouve, Pierre Jean 1887-1976 .... **CLC 47**
See also CA 65-68

Jovine, Francesco 1902-1950 .... **TCLC 79**
Joyce, James (Augustine Aloysius) 1882-1941
**TCLC 3, 8, 16, 35, 52; DA; DAB; DAC;
DAM MST, NOV, POET; PC 22; SSC 3, 26;
WLC**
See also CA 104; 126; CDBLB 1914-1945; DLB
10, 19, 36, 162; MTCW 1
Jozsef, Attila 1905-1937 .... **TCLC 22**
See also CA 116
Juana Ines de la Cruz 1651(?)-1695 . **LC 5;
PC 24**
Judd, Cyril
See Kornbluth, C(yril) M.; Pohl, Frederik
Julian of Norwich 1342(?)-1416(?) .... **LC 6**
See also DLB 146
Junger, Sebastian 1962- .... **CLC 109**
See also CA 165
Juniper, Alex
See Hospital, Janette Turner
Junius
See Luxemburg, Rosa
Just, Ward (Swift) 1935- .... **CLC 4, 27**
See also CA 25-28R; CANR 32; INT CANR-32
Justice, Donald (Rodney) 1925- .. **CLC 6, 19,
102; DAM POET**
See also CA 5-8R; CANR 26, 54; DLBY 83; INT
CANR-26
Juvenal .... **CMLC 8**
See also Juvenalis, Decimus Junius
Juvenalis, Decimus Junius 55(?)-c. 127(?)
See Juvenal
Juvenis
See Bourne, Randolph S(illiman)
Kacew, Romain 1914-1980
See Gary, Romain
See also CA 108; 102
Kadare, Ismail 1936- .... **CLC 52**
See also CA 161
Kadohata, Cynthia .... **CLC 59**
See also CA 140
Kafka, Franz 1883-1924...**TCLC 2, 6, 13, 29, 47,
53; DA; DAB; DAC; DAM MST, NOV; SSC
5, 29; WLC**
See also CA 105; 126; DLB 81; MTCW 1
Kahanovitsch, Pinkhes
See Der Nister
Kahn, Roger 1927- .... **CLC 30**
See also CA 25-28R; CANR 44, 69; DLB 171;
SATA 37
Kain, Saul
See Sassoon, Siegfried (Lorraine)
Kaiser, Georg 1878-1945 .... **TCLC 9**
See also CA 106; DLB 124
Kaletski, Alexander 1946- .... **CLC 39**
See also CA 118; 143
Kalidasa fl. c. 400- .... **CMLC 9; PC 22**
Kallman, Chester (Simon) 1921-1975 . **CLC 2**
See also CA 45-48; 53-56; CANR 3
Kaminsky, Melvin 1926-
See Brooks, Mel
See also CA 65-68; CANR 16
Kaminsky, Stuart M(elvin) 1934- .... **CLC 59**
See also CA 73-76; CANR 29, 53
Kane, Francis
See Robbins, Harold
Kane, Paul
See Simon, Paul (Frederick)
Kane, Wilson
See Bloch, Robert (Albert)
Kanin, Garson 1912- .... **CLC 22**
See also AITN 1; CA 5-8R; CANR 7; DLB 7
Kaniuk, Yoram 1930- .... **CLC 19**
See also CA 134

Kant, Immanuel 1724-1804 .... **NCLC 27, 67**
See also DLB 94
Kantor, MacKinlay 1904-1977 .... **CLC 7**
See also CA 61-64; 73-76; CANR 60, 63; DLB
9, 102
Kaplan, David Michael 1946- .... **CLC 50**
Kaplan, James 1951- .... **CLC 59**
See also CA 135
Karageorge, Michael
See Anderson, Poul (William)
Karamzin, Nikolai Mikhailovich 1766-1826
NCLC 3
See also DLB 150
Karapanou, Margarita 1946- .... **CLC 13**
See also CA 101
Karinthy, Frigyes 1887-1938 .... **TCLC 47**
Karl, Frederick R(obert) 1927- .... **CLC 34**
See also CA 5-8R; CANR 3, 44
Kastel, Warren
See Silverberg, Robert
Kataev, Evgeny Petrovich 1903-1942
See Petrov, Evgeny
See also CA 120
Kataphusin
See Ruskin, John
Katz, Steve 1935- .... **CLC 47**
See also CA 25-28R; CAAS 14, 64; CANR 12;
DLBY 83
Kauffman, Janet 1945- .... **CLC 42**
See also CA 117; CANR 43; DLBY 86
Kaufman, Bob (Garnell) 1925-1986 ..**CLC 49**
See also BW 1; CA 41-44R; 118; CANR 22; DLB
16, 41
Kaufman, George S. 1889-1961 ..... **CLC 38;
DAM DRAM**
See also CA 108; 93-96; DLB 7; INT 108
Kaufman, Sue .... **CLC 3, 8**
See also Barondess, Sue K(aufman)
Kavafis, Konstantinos Petrou 1863-1933
See Cavafy, C(onstantine) P(eter)
See also CA 104
Kavan, Anna 1901-1968 .... **CLC 5, 13, 82**
See also CA 5-8R; CANR 6, 57; MTCW 1
Kavanagh, Dan
See Barnes, Julian (Patrick)
Kavanagh, Patrick (Joseph) 1904-1967
CLC 22
See also CA 123; 25-28R; DLB 15, 20; MTCW 1
Kawabata, Yasunari 1899-1972... **CLC 2, 5, 9,
18, 107; DAM MULT; SSC 17**
See also CA 93-96; 33-36R; DLB 180
Kaye, M(ary) M(argaret) 1909- .... **CLC 28**
See also CA 89-92; CANR 24, 60; MTCW 1;
SATA 62
Kaye, Mollie
See Kaye, M(ary) M(argaret)
Kaye-Smith, Sheila 1887-1956 .... **TCLC 20**
See also CA 118; DLB 36
Kaymor, Patrice Maguilene
See Senghor, Leopold Sedar
Kazan, Elia 1909- .... **CLC 6, 16, 63**
See also CA 21-24R; CANR 32
Kazantzakis, Nikos 1883(?)-1957...**TCLC 2, 5,
33**
See also CA 105; 132; MTCW 1
Kazin, Alfred 1915- .... **CLC 34, 38**
See also CA 1-4R; CAAS 7; CANR 1, 45; DLB 67
Keane, Mary Nesta (Skrine) 1904-1996
See Keane, Molly
See also CA 108; 114; 151
Keane, Molly .... **CLC 31**
See also Keane, Mary Nesta (Skrine)
See also INT 114

Manley, (Mary) Delariviere 1672(?)-1724
LC 1
See also DLB 39, 80
Mann, Abel
See Creasey, John
Mann, Emily 1952- .... **DC 7**
See also CA 130; CANR 55
Mann, (Luiz) Heinrich 1871-1950 .... **TCLC 9**
See also CA 106; 164; DLB 66
Mann, (Paul) Thomas 1875-1955...**TCLC 2, 8,
14, 21, 35, 44, 60; DA; DAB; DAC; DAM
MST, NOV; SSC 5; WLC**
See also CA 104; 128; DLB 66; MTCW 1
Mannheim, Karl 1893-1947 .... **TCLC 65**
Manning, David
See Faust, Frederick (Schiller)
Manning, Frederic 1887(?)-1935 .... **TCLC 25**
See also CA 124
Manning, Olivia 1915-1980 .... **CLC 5, 19**
See also CA 5-8R; 101; CANR 29; MTCW 1
Mano, D. Keith 1942- .... **CLC 2, 10**
See also CA 25-28R; CAAS 6; CANR 26, 57;
DLB 6
Mansfield, Katherine ...... **TCLC 2, 8, 39;
DAB; SSC 9, 23; WLC**
See also Beauchamp, Kathleen Mansfield
See also DLB 162
Manso, Peter 1940- .... **CLC 39**
See also CA 29-32R; CANR 44
Mantecon, Juan Jimenez
See Jimenez (Mantecon), Juan Ramon
Manton, Peter
See Creasey, John
Man Without a Spleen, A
See Chekhov, Anton (Pavlovich)
Manzoni, Alessandro 1785-1873 ..... **NCLC 29**
Mapu, Abraham (ben Jekutiel) 1808-1867
NCLC 18
Mara, Sally
See Queneau, Raymond
Marat, Jean Paul 1743-1793 .... **LC 10**
Marcel, Gabriel Honore 1889-1973 ... **CLC 15**
See also CA 102; 45-48; MTCW 1
Marchbanks, Samuel
See Davies, (William) Robertson
Marchi, Giacomo
See Bassani, Giorgio
Margulies, Donald .... **CLC 76**
Marie de France c. 12th cent. -...**CMLC 8;
PC 22**
Marie de l'Incarnation 1599-1672 .... **LC 10**
Marier, Captain Victor
See Griffith, D(avid Lewelyn) W(ark)
Mariner, Scott
See Pohl, Frederik
Marinetti, Filippo Tommaso 1876-1944
TCLC 10
See also CA 107; DLB 114
Marivaux, Pierre Carlet de Chamblain de 1688-
1763 .... **LC 4; DC 7**
Markandaya, Kamala .... **CLC 8, 38**
See also Taylor, Kamala (Purnaiya)
Markfield, Wallace 1926- .... **CLC 8**
See also CA 69-72; CAAS 3; DLB 2, 28
Markham, Edwin 1852-1940 .... **TCLC 47**
See also CA 160; DLB 54, 186
Markham, Robert
See Amis, Kingsley (William)
Marks, J
See Highwater, Jamake (Mamake)
Marks-Highwater, J
See Highwater, Jamake (Mamake)

Markson, David M(errill) 1927- .... **CLC 67**
See also CA 49-52; CANR 1
Marley, Bob .... **CLC 17**
See also Marley, Robert Nesta
Marley, Robert Nesta 1945-1981
See Marley, Bob
See also CA 107; 103
Marlowe, Christopher 1564-1593 ...**LC 22;
DA; DAB; DAC; DAM DRAM, MST; DC
1; WLC**
See also CDBLB Before 1660; DLB 62
Marlowe, Stephen 1928-
See Queen, Ellery
See also CA 13-16R; CANR 6, 55
Marmontel, Jean-Francois 1723-1799 ...**LC 2**
Marquand, John P(hillips) 1893-1960
CLC 2, 10
See also CA 85-88; DLB 9, 102
Marques, Rene 1919-1979 ...... **CLC 96; DAM
MULT; HLC**
See also CA 97-100; 85-88; DLB 113; HW
Marquez, Gabriel (Jose) Garcia
See Garcia Marquez, Gabriel (Jose)
Marquis, Don(ald Robert Perry) 1878-1937
TCLC 7
See also CA 104; 166; DLB 11, 25
Marric, J. J.
See Creasey, John
Marryat, Frederick 1792-1848 .... **NCLC 3**
See also DLB 21, 163
Marsden, James
See Creasey, John
Marsh, (Edith) Ngaio 1899-1982 . **CLC 7, 53;
DAM POP**
See also CA 9-12R; CANR 6, 58; DLB 77;
MTCW 1
Marshall, Garry 1934- .... **CLC 17**
See also AAYA 3; CA 111; SATA 60
Marshall, Paule 1929- .... **CLC 27, 72; BLC 3;
DAM MULT; SSC 3**
See also BW 2; CA 77-80; CANR 25; DLB 157;
MTCW 1
Marshallik
See Zangwill, Israel
Marsten, Richard
See Hunter, Evan
Marston, John 1576-1634 .... **LC 33; DAM
DRAM**
See also DLB 58, 172
Martha, Henry
See Harris, Mark
Marti, Jose 1853-1895 .... **NCLC 63; DAM
MULT; HLC**
Martial c. 40-c. 104 .... **PC 10**
Martin, Ken
See Hubbard, L(afayette) Ron(ald)
Martin, Richard
See Creasey, John
Martin, Steve 1945- .... **CLC 30**
See also CA 97-100; CANR 30; MTCW 1
Martin, Valerie 1948- .... **CLC 89**
See also BEST 90:2; CA 85-88; CANR 49
Martin, Violet Florence 1862-1915...**TCLC 51**
Martin, Webber
See Silverberg, Robert
Martindale, Patrick Victor
See White, Patrick (Victor Martindale)
Martin du Gard, Roger 1881-1958 . **TCLC 24**
See also CA 118; DLB 65
Martineau, Harriet 1802-1876 .... **NCLC 26**
See also DLB 21, 55, 159, 163, 166, 190; YABC 2
Martines, Julia
See O'Faolain, Julia

Martinez, Enrique Gonzalez
See Gonzalez Martinez, Enrique
Martinez, Jacinto Benavente y
See Benavente (y Martinez), Jacinto
Martinez Ruiz, Jose 1873-1967
See Azorin; Ruiz, Jose Martinez
See also CA 93-96; HW
Martinez Sierra, Gregorio 1881-1947..**TCLC 6**
See also CA 115
Martinez Sierra, Maria (de la O'LeJarraga)
1874-1974 .... **TCLC 6**
See also CA 115
Martinsen, Martin
See Follett, Ken(neth Martin)
Martinson, Harry (Edmund) 1904-1978
CLC 14
See also CA 77-80; CANR 34
Marut, Ret
See Traven, B.
Marut, Robert
See Traven, B.
Marvell, Andrew 1621-1678 .... **LC 4, 43; DA;
DAB; DAC; DAM MST, POET; PC 10;
WLC**
See also CDBLB 1660-1789; DLB 131
Marx, Karl (Heinrich) 1818-1883 ... **NCLC 17**
See also DLB 129
Masaoka Shiki .... **TCLC 18**
See also Masaoka Tsunenori
Masaoka Tsunenori 1867-1902
See Masaoka Shiki
See also CA 117
Masefield, John (Edward) 1878-1967
CLC 11, 47; DAM POET
See also CA 19-20; 25-28R; CANR 33; CAP 2;
CDBLB 1890-1914; DLB 10, 19, 153, 160;
MTCW 1; SATA 19
Maso, Carole 19(?)- .... **CLC 44**
Mason, Bobbie Ann 1940-.. **CLC 28, 43, 82;
SSC 4**
See also AAYA 5; CA 53-56; CANR 11, 31, 58;
DLB 173; DLBY 87; INT CANR-31; MTCW
1
Mason, Ernst
See Pohl, Frederik
Mason, Lee W.
See Malzberg, Barry N(athaniel)
Mason, Nick 1945- .... **CLC 35**
Mason, Tally
See Derleth, August (William)
Mass, William
See Gibson, William
Master Lao
See Lao Tzu
Masters, Edgar Lee 1868-1950...**TCLC 2, 25;
DA; DAC; DAM MST, POET; PC 1;
WLCS**
See also CA 104; 133; CDALB 1865-1917; DLB
54; MTCW 1
Masters, Hilary 1928- .... **CLC 48**
See also CA 25-28R; CANR 13, 47
Mastrosimone, William 19(?)- .... **CLC 36**
Mathe, Albert
See Camus, Albert
Mather, Cotton 1663-1728 .... **LC 38**
See also CDALB 1640-1865; DLB 24, 30,
140
Mather, Increase 1639-1723 .... **LC 38**
See also DLB 24
Matheson, Richard Burton 1926- ...... **CLC 37**
See also CA 97-100; DLB 8, 44; INT 97-100
Mathews, Harry 1930- .... **CLC 6, 52**
See also CA 21-24R; CAAS 6; CANR 18, 40

McNeile, Herman Cyril 1888-1937
See Sapper
See also DLB 77
McNickle, (William) D'Arcy 1904-1977
CLC 89; DAM MULT
See also CA 9-12R; 85-88; CANR 5, 45; DLB
175; NNAL; SATA-Obit 22
McPhee, John (Angus) 1931- .... CLC 36
See also BEST 90:1; CA 65-68; CANR 20, 46,
64, 69; DLB 185; MTCW 1
McPherson, James Alan 1943- ... CLC 19, 77;
BLCS
See also BW 1; CA 25-28R; CAAS 17; CANR
24; DLB 38; MTCW 1
McPherson, William (Alexander) 1933-
CLC 34
See also CA 69-72; CANR 28; INT CANR-28
Mead, Margaret 1901-1978 .... CLC 37
See also AITN 1; CA 1-4R; 81-84; CANR 4;
MTCW 1; SATA-Obit 20
Meaker, Marijane (Agnes) 1927-
See Kerr, M. E.
See also CA 107; CANR 37, 63; INT 107; JRDA;
MAICYA; MTCW 1; SATA 20, 61, 99
Medoff, Mark (Howard) 1940- .... CLC 6, 23;
DAM DRAM
See also AITN 1; CA 53-56; CANR 5; DLB 7;
INT CANR-5
Medvedev, P. N.
See Bakhtin, Mikhail Mikhailovich
Meged, Aharon
See Megged, Aharon
Meged, Aron
See Megged, Aharon
Megged, Aharon 1920- .... CLC 9
See also CA 49-52; CAAS 13; CANR 1
Mehta, Ved (Parkash) 1934- .... CLC 37
See also CA 1-4R; CANR 2, 23, 69; MTCW 1
Melanter
See Blackmore, R(ichard) D(oddridge)
Melies, Georges 1861-1938 .... TCLC 81
Melikow, Loris
See Hofmannsthal, Hugo von
Melmoth, Sebastian
See Wilde, Oscar (Fingal O'Flahertie Wills)
Meltzer, Milton 1915- .... CLC 26
See also AAYA 8; CA 13-16R; CANR 38; CLR
13; DLB 61; JRDA; MAICYA; SAAS 1;
SATA 1, 50, 80
Melville, Herman 1819-1891...NCLC 3, 12, 29,
45, 49; DA; DAB; DAC; DAM MST, NOV;
SSC 1, 17; WLC
See also AAYA 25; CDALB 1640-1865; DLB 3,
74; SATA 59
Menander c. 342B.C.-c. 292B.C. ...... CMLC 9;
DAM DRAM; DC 3
See also DLB 176
Mencken, H(enry) L(ouis) 1880-1956
TCLC 13
See also CA 105; 125; CDALB 1917-1929; DLB
11, 29, 63, 137; MTCW 1
Mendelsohn, Jane 1965(?)- .... CLC 99
See also CA 154
Mercer, David 1928-1980 .... CLC 5; DAM
DRAM
See also CA 9-12R; 102; CANR 23; DLB 13;
MTCW 1
Merchant, Paul
See Ellison, Harlan (Jay)
Meredith, George 1828-1909 ... TCLC 17, 43;
DAM POET
See also CA 117; 153; CDBLB 1832-1890; DLB
18, 35, 57, 159

Meredith, William (Morris) 1919-...CLC 4, 13,
22, 55; DAM POET
See also CA 9-12R; CAAS 14; CANR 6, 40; DLB
5
Merezhkovsky, Dmitry Sergeyevich 1865-1941
TCLC 29
Merimee, Prosper 1803-1870 ... NCLC 6, 65;
SSC 7
See also DLB 119, 192
Merkin, Daphne 1954- .... CLC 44
See also CA 123
Merlin, Arthur
See Blish, James (Benjamin)
Merrill, James (Ingram) 1926-1995...CLC 2, 3,
6, 8, 13, 18, 34, 91; DAM POET
See also CA 13-16R; 147; CANR 10, 49, 63;
DLB 5, 165; DLBY 85; INT CANR-10;
MTCW 1
Merriman, Alex
See Silverberg, Robert
Merriman, Brian 1747-1805 .... NCLC 70
Merritt, E. B.
See Waddington, Miriam
Merton, Thomas 1915-1968...CLC 1, 3, 11, 34,
83; PC 10
See also CA 5-8R; 25-28R; CANR 22, 53; DLB
48; DLBY 81; MTCW 1
Merwin, W(illiam) S(tanley) 1927-...CLC 1, 2,
3, 5, 8, 13, 18, 45, 88; DAM POET
See also CA 13-16R; CANR 15, 51; DLB 5, 169;
INT CANR-15; MTCW 1
Metcalf, John 1938- .... CLC 37
See also CA 113; DLB 60
Metcalf, Suzanne
See Baum, L(yman) Frank
Mew, Charlotte (Mary) 1870-1928 ... TCLC 8
See also CA 105; DLB 19, 135
Mewshaw, Michael 1943- .... CLC 9
See also CA 53-56; CANR 7, 47; DLBY 80
Meyer, June
See Jordan, June
Meyer, Lynn
See Slavitt, David R(ytman)
Meyer-Meyrink, Gustav 1868-1932
See Meyrink, Gustav
See also CA 117
Meyers, Jeffrey 1939- .... CLC 39
See also CA 73-76; CANR 54; DLB 111
Meynell, Alice (Christina Gertrude Thompson)
1847-1922 .... TCLC 6
See also CA 104; DLB 19, 98
Meyrink, Gustav .... TCLC 21
See also Meyer-Meyrink, Gustav
See also DLB 81
Michaels, Leonard 1933-...CLC 6, 25; SSC 16
See also CA 61-64; CANR 21, 62; DLB 130;
MTCW 1
Michaux, Henri 1899-1984 .... CLC 8, 19
See also CA 85-88; 114
Micheaux, Oscar 1884-1951 .... TCLC 76
See also DLB 50
Michelangelo 1475-1564 .... LC 12
Michelet, Jules 1798-1874 .... NCLC 31
Michener, James A(lbert) 1907(?)-1997
CLC 1, 5, 11, 29, 60, 109; DAM NOV, POP
See also AAYA 27; AITN 1; BEST 90:1; CA 5-
8R; 161; CANR 21, 45, 68; DLB 6; MTCW 1
Mickiewicz, Adam 1798-1855 .... NCLC 3
Middleton, Christopher 1926- .... CLC 13
See also CA 13-16R; CANR 29, 54; DLB 40
Middleton, Richard (Barham) 1882-1911
TCLC 56
See also DLB 156

Middleton, Stanley 1919- .... CLC 7, 38
See also CA 25-28R; CAAS 23; CANR 21, 46;
DLB 14
Middleton, Thomas 1580-1627 . LC 33; DAM
DRAM, MST; DC 5
See also DLB 58
Migueis, Jose Rodrigues 1901- .... CLC 10
Mikszath, Kalman 1847-1910 .... TCLC 31
Miles, Jack .... CLC 100
Miles, Josephine (Louise) 1911-1985CLC 1, 2,
14, 34, 39; DAM POET
See also CA 1-4R; 116; CANR 2, 55; DLB 48
Militant
See Sandburg, Carl (August)
Mill, John Stuart 1806-1873 ..... NCLC 11, 58
See also CDBLB 1832-1890; DLB 55, 190
Millar, Kenneth 1915-1983 ....CLC 14; DAM
POP
See also Macdonald, Ross
See also CA 9-12R; 110; CANR 16, 63; DLB 2;
DLBD 6; DLBY 83; MTCW 1
Millay, E. Vincent
See Millay, Edna St. Vincent
Millay, Edna St. Vincent 1892-1950
TCLC 4, 49; DA; DAB; DAC; DAM MST,
POET; PC 6; WLCS
See also CA 104; 130; CDALB 1917-1929; DLB
45; MTCW 1
Miller, Arthur 1915-... CLC 1, 2, 6, 10, 15, 26,
47, 78; DA; DAB; DAC; DAM DRAM,
MST; DC 1; WLC
See also AAYA 15; AITN 1; CA 1-4R; CABS 3;
CANR 2, 30, 54; CDALB 1941-1968; DLB
7; MTCW 1
Miller, Henry (Valentine) 1891-1980... CLC 1,
2, 4, 9, 14, 43, 84; DA; DAB; DAC; DAM
MST, NOV; WLC
See also CA 9-12R; 97-100; CANR 33, 64;
CDALB 1929-1941; DLB 4, 9; DLBY 80;
MTCW 1
Miller, Jason 1939(?)- .... CLC 2
See also AITN 1; CA 73-76; DLB 7
Miller, Sue 1943- .... CLC 44; DAM POP
See also BEST 90:3; CA 139; CANR 59; DLB
143
Miller, Walter M(ichael, Jr.) 1923-...CLC 4, 30
See also CA 85-88; DLB 8
Millett, Kate 1934- .... CLC 67
See also AITN 1; CA 73-76; CANR 32, 53;
MTCW 1
Millhauser, Steven (Lewis) 1943- CLC 21, 54,
109
See also CA 110; 111; CANR 63; DLB 2
Millin, Sarah Gertrude 1889-1968 ..... CLC 49
See also CA 102; 93-96
Milne, A(lan) A(lexander) 1882-1956
TCLC 6; DAB; DAC; DAM MST
See also CA 104; 133; CLR 1, 26; DLB 10, 77,
100, 160; MAICYA; MTCW 1; SATA 100;
YABC 1
Milner, Ron(ald) 1938- .... CLC 56; BLC 3;
DAM MULT
See also AITN 1; BW 1; CA 73-76; CANR 24;
DLB 38; MTCW 1
Milnes, Richard Monckton 1809-1885
NCLC 61
See also DLB 32, 184
Milosz, Czeslaw 1911-...CLC 5, 11, 22, 31, 56,
82; DAM MST, POET; PC 8; WLCS
See also CA 81-84; CANR 23, 51; MTCW 1
Milton, John 1608-1674 ... LC 9, 43; DA; DAB;
DAC; DAM MST, POET; PC 19; WLC
See also CDBLB 1660-1789; DLB 131, 151

Nash, (Fredric) Ogden 1902-1971 .. **CLC 23;
    DAM POET; PC 21**
    See also CA 13-14; 29-32R; CANR 34, 61; CAP
    1; DLB 11; MAICYA; MTCW 1; SATA 2, 46
Nashe, Thomas 1567-1601(?) .... **LC 41**
    See also DLB 167
Nashe, Thomas 1567-1601 .... **LC 41**
Nathan, Daniel
    See Dannay, Frederic
Nathan, George Jean 1882-1958 ..... **TCLC 18**
    See also Hatteras, Owen
    See also CA 114; DLB 137
Natsume, Kinnosuke 1867-1916
    See Natsume, Soseki
    See also CA 104
Natsume, Soseki 1867-1916 .... **TCLC 2, 10**
    See also Natsume, Kinnosuke
    See also DLB 180
Natti, (Mary) Lee 1919-
    See Kingman, Lee
    See also CA 5-8R; CANR 2
Naylor, Gloria 1950- .. **CLC 28, 52; BLC 3;
    DA; DAC; DAM MST, MULT, NOV, POP;
    WLCS**
    See also AAYA 6; BW 2; CA 107; CANR 27,
    51; DLB 173; MTCW 1
Neihardt, John Gneisenau 1881-1973...**CLC 32**
    See also CA 13-14; CANR 65; CAP 1; DLB 9,
    54
Nekrasov, Nikolai Alekseevich 1821-1878
    NCLC 11
Nelligan, Emile 1879-1941 .... **TCLC 14**
    See also CA 114; DLB 92
Nelson, Willie 1933- .... **CLC 17**
    See also CA 107
Nemerov, Howard (Stanley) 1920-1991
    CLC 2, 6, 9, 36; DAM POET; PC 24
    See also CA 1-4R; 134; CABS 2; CANR 1, 27,
    53; DLB 5, 6; DLBY 83; INT CANR-27;
    MTCW 1
Neruda, Pablo 1904-1973...**CLC 1, 2, 5, 7, 9, 28,
    62; DA; DAB; DAC; DAM MST, MULT,
    POET; HLC; PC 4; WLC**
    See also CA 19-20; 45-48; CAP 2; HW; MTCW
    1
Nerval, Gerard de 1808-1855 ..**NCLC 1, 67;
    PC 13; SSC 18**
Nervo, (Jose) Amado (Ruiz de) 1870-1919
    TCLC 11
    See also CA 109; 131; HW
Nessi, Pio Baroja y
    See Baroja (y Nessi), Pio
Nestroy, Johann 1801-1862 .... **NCLC 42**
    See also DLB 133
Netterville, Luke
    See O'Grady, Standish (James)
Neufeld, John (Arthur) 1938-............. **CLC 17**
    See also AAYA 11; CA 25-28R; CANR 11, 37,
    56; CLR 52; MAICYA; SAAS 3; SATA 6, 81
Neville, Emily Cheney 1919- .... **CLC 12**
    See also CA 5-8R; CANR 3, 37; JRDA;
    MAICYA; SAAS 2; SATA 1
Newbound, Bernard Slade 1930-
    See Slade, Bernard
    See also CA 81-84; CANR 49; DAM DRAM
Newby, P(ercy) H(oward) 1918-1997 .. **CLC 2,
    13; DAM NOV**
    See also CA 5-8R; 161; CANR 32, 67; DLB 15;
    MTCW 1
Newlove, Donald 1928- .... **CLC 6**
    See also CA 29-32R; CANR 25
Newlove, John (Herbert) 1938-.......... **CLC 14**
    See also CA 21-24R; CANR 9, 25

Newman, Charles 1938- .... **CLC 2, 8**
    See also CA 21-24R
Newman, Edwin (Harold) 1919- .... **CLC 14**
    See also AITN 1; CA 69-72; CANR 5
Newman, John Henry 1801-1890 .... **NCLC 38**
    See also DLB 18, 32, 55
Newton, Suzanne 1936- .... **CLC 35**
    See also CA 41-44R; CANR 14; JRDA; SATA 5, 77
Nexo, Martin Andersen 1869-1954...**TCLC 43**
Nezval, Vitezslav 1900-1958 .... **TCLC 44**
    See also CA 123
Ng, Fae Myenne 1957(?)- .... **CLC 81**
    See also CA 146
Ngema, Mbongeni 1955- .... **CLC 57**
    See also BW 2; CA 143
Ngugi, James T(hiong'o) .... **CLC 3, 7, 13**
    See also Ngugi wa Thiong'o
Ngugi wa Thiong'o 1938-..... **CLC 36; BLC 3;
    DAM MULT, NOV**
    See also Ngugi, James T(hiong'o)
    See also BW 2; CA 81-84; CANR 27, 58; DLB
    125; MTCW 1
Nichol, B(arrie) P(hillip) 1944-1988 .. **CLC 18**
    See also CA 53-56; DLB 53; SATA 66
Nichols, John (Treadwell) 1940- .... **CLC 38**
    See also CA 9-12R; CAAS 2; CANR 6, 70;
    DLBY 82
Nichols, Leigh
    See Koontz, Dean R(ay)
Nichols, Peter (Richard) 1927-...**CLC 5, 36, 65**
    See also CA 104; CANR 33; DLB 13; MTCW 1
Nicolas, F. R. E.
    See Freeling, Nicolas
Niedecker, Lorine 1903-1970 .... **CLC 10, 42;
    DAM POET**
    See also CA 25-28; CAP 2; DLB 48
Nietzsche, Friedrich (Wilhelm) 1844-1900
    TCLC 10, 18, 55
    See also CA 107; 121; DLB 129
Nievo, Ippolito 1831-1861 .... **NCLC 22**
Nightingale, Anne Redmon 1943-
    See Redmon, Anne
    See also CA 103
Nightingale, Florence 1820-1910 .... **TCLC 85**
    See also DLB 166
Nik. T. O.
    See Annensky, Innokenty (Fyodorovich)
Nin, Anais 1903-1977...**CLC 1, 4, 8, 11, 14, 60;
    DAM NOV, POP; SSC 10**
    See also AITN 2; CA 13-16R; 69-72; CANR 22,
    53; DLB 2, 4, 152; MTCW 1
Nishida, Kitaro 1870-1945 .... **TCLC 83**
Nishiwaki, Junzaburo 1894-1982 .... **PC 15**
    See also CA 107
Nissenson, Hugh 1933-...................... **CLC 4, 9**
    See also CA 17-20R; CANR 27; DLB 28
Niven, Larry .... **CLC 8**
    See also Niven, Laurence Van Cott
    See also AAYA 27; DLB 8
Niven, Laurence Van Cott 1938-
    See Niven, Larry
    See also CA 21-24R; CAAS 12; CANR 14, 44,
    66; DAM POP; MTCW 1; SATA 95
Nixon, Agnes Eckhardt 1927-............. **CLC 21**
    See also CA 110
Nizan, Paul 1905-1940 .... **TCLC 40**
    See also CA 161; DLB 72
Nkosi, Lewis 1936- .... **CLC 45; BLC 3; DAM
    MULT**
    See also BW 1; CA 65-68; CANR 27; DLB 157
Nodier, (Jean) Charles (Emmanuel) 1780-1844
    NCLC 19
    See also DLB 119

Noguchi, Yone 1875-1947 .... **TCLC 80**
Nolan, Christopher 1965- .... **CLC 58**
    See also CA 111
Noon, Jeff 1957- .... **CLC 91**
    See also CA 148
Norden, Charles
    See Durrell, Lawrence (George)
Nordhoff, Charles (Bernard) 1887-1947
    TCLC 23
    See also CA 108; DLB 9; SATA 23
Norfolk, Lawrence 1963- .... **CLC 76**
    See also CA 144
Norman, Marsha 1947- .... **CLC 28; DAM
    DRAM; DC 8**
    See also CA 105; CABS 3; CANR 41; DLBY 84
Normyx
    See Douglas, (George) Norman
Norris, Frank 1870-1902 .... **SSC 28**
    See also Norris, (Benjamin) Frank(lin, Jr.)
    See also CDALB 1865-1917; DLB 12, 71, 186
Norris, (Benjamin) Frank(lin, Jr.) 1870-1902
    TCLC 24
    See also Norris, Frank
    See also CA 110; 160
Norris, Leslie 1921-............................. **CLC 14**
    See also CA 11-12; CANR 14; CAP 1; DLB 27
North, Andrew
    See Norton, Andre
North, Anthony
    See Koontz, Dean R(ay)
North, Captain George
    See Stevenson, Robert Louis (Balfour)
North, Milou
    See Erdrich, Louise
Northrup, B. A.
    See Hubbard, L(afayette) Ron(ald)
North Staffs
    See Hulme, T(homas) E(rnest)
Norton, Alice Mary
    See Norton, Andre
    See also MAICYA; SATA 1, 43
Norton, Andre 1912- .... **CLC 12**
    See also Norton, Alice Mary
    See also AAYA 14; CA 1-4R; CANR 68; CLR
    50; DLB 8, 52; JRDA; MTCW 1; SATA 91
Norton, Caroline 1808-1877 .... **NCLC 47**
    See also DLB 21, 159, 199
Norway, Nevil Shute 1899-1960
    See Shute, Nevil
    See also CA 102; 93-96
Norwid, Cyprian Kamil 1821-1883...**NCLC 17**
Nosille, Nabrah
    See Ellison, Harlan (Jay)
Nossack, Hans Erich 1901-1978 .... **CLC 6**
    See also CA 93-96; 85-88; DLB 69
Nostradamus 1503-1566 .... **LC 27**
Nosu, Chuji
    See Ozu, Yasujiro
Notenburg, Eleanora (Genrikhovna) von
    See Guro, Elena
Nova, Craig 1945- .... **CLC 7, 31**
    See also CA 45-48; CANR 2, 53
Novak, Joseph
    See Kosinski, Jerzy (Nikodem)
Novalis 1772-1801 .... **NCLC 13**
    See also DLB 90
Novis, Emile
    See Weil, Simone (Adolphine)
Nowlan, Alden (Albert) 1933-1983 .. **CLC 15;
    DAC; DAM MST**
    See also CA 9-12R; CANR 5; DLB 53
Noyes, Alfred 1880-1958 .... **TCLC 7**
    See also CA 104; DLB 20

p'Bitek, Okot 1931-1982 .... **CLC 96; BLC 3; DAM MULT**
See also BW 2; CA 124; 107; DLB 125; MTCW 1

Peacock, Molly 1947- .... **CLC 60**
See also CA 103; CAAS 21; CANR 52; DLB 120

Peacock, Thomas Love 1785-1866 .. **NCLC 22**
See also DLB 96, 116

Peake, Mervyn 1911-1968 .... **CLC 7, 54**
See also CA 5-8R; 25-28R; CANR 3; DLB 15, 160; MTCW 1; SATA 23

Pearce, Philippa .... **CLC 21**
See also Christie, (Ann) Philippa
See also CLR 9; DLB 161; MAICYA; SATA 1, 67

Pearl, Eric
See Elman, Richard (Martin)

Pearson, T(homas) R(eid) 1956- .... **CLC 39**
See also CA 120; 130; INT 130

Peck, Dale 1967- .... **CLC 81**
See also CA 146; CANR 72

Peck, John 1941- .... **CLC 3**
See also CA 49-52; CANR 3

Peck, Richard (Wayne) 1934- .... **CLC 21**
See also AAYA 1, 24; CA 85-88; CANR 19, 38; CLR 15; INT CANR-19; JRDA; MAICYA; SAAS 2; SATA 18, 55, 97

Peck, Robert Newton 1928- ..... **CLC 17; DA; DAC; DAM MST**
See also AAYA 3; CA 81-84; CANR 31, 63; CLR 45; JRDA; MAICYA; SAAS 1; SATA 21, 62

Peckinpah, (David) Sam(uel) 1925-1984 **C L C 20**
See also CA 109; 114

Pedersen, Knut 1859-1952
See Hamsun, Knut
See also CA 104; 119; CANR 63; MTCW 1

Peeslake, Gaffer
See Durrell, Lawrence (George)

Peguy, Charles Pierre 1873-1914 .... **TCLC 10**
See also CA 107

Peirce, Charles Sanders 1839-1914...**TCLC 81**

Pena, Ramon del Valle y
See Valle-Inclan, Ramon (Maria) del

Pendennis, Arthur Esquir
See Thackeray, William Makepeace

Penn, William 1644-1718 .... **LC 25**
See also DLB 24

PEPECE
See Prado (Calvo), Pedro

Pepys, Samuel 1633-1703 .. **LC 11; DA; DAB; DAC; DAM MST; WLC**
See also CDBLB 1660-1789; DLB 101

Percy, Walker 1916-1990... **CLC 2, 3, 6, 8, 14, 18, 47, 65; DAM NOV, POP**
See also CA 1-4R; 131; CANR 1, 23, 64; DLB 2; DLBY 80, 90; MTCW 1

Percy, William Alexander 1885-1942 **TCLC 84**
See also CA 163

Perec, Georges 1936-1982 .... **CLC 56**
See also CA 141; DLB 83

Pereda (y Sanchez de Porrua), Jose Maria de 1833-1906................................. **TCLC 16**
See also CA 117

Pereda y Porrua, Jose Maria de
See Pereda (y Sanchez de Porrua), Jose Maria de

Peregoy, George Weems
See Mencken, H(enry) L(ouis)

Perelman, S(idney) J(oseph) 1904-1979 **CLC 3, 5, 9, 15, 23, 44, 49; DAM DRAM; SSC 32**
See also AITN 1, 2; CA 73-76; 89-92; CANR 18; DLB 11, 44; MTCW 1

Peret, Benjamin 1899-1959 .... **TCLC 20**
See also CA 117

Peretz, Isaac Loeb 1851(?)-1915 .. **TCLC 16; SSC 26**
See also CA 109

Peretz, Yitzhhok Leibush
See Peretz, Isaac Loeb

Perez Galdos, Benito 1843-1920 ..... **TCLC 27**
See also CA 125; 153; HW

Perrault, Charles 1628-1703 .... **LC 2**
See also MAICYA; SATA 25

Perry, Brighton
See Sherwood, Robert E(mmet)

Perse, St.-John
See Leger, (Marie-Rene Auguste) Alexis Saint-Leger

Perutz, Leo 1882-1957 .... **TCLC 60**
See also DLB 81

Peseenz, Tulio F.
See Lopez y Fuentes, Gregorio

Pesetsky, Bette 1932-......................... **CLC 28**
See also CA 133; DLB 130

Peshkov, Alexei Maximovich 1868-1936
See Gorky, Maxim
See also CA 105; 141; DA; DAC; DAM DRAM, MST, NOV

Pessoa, Fernando (Antonio Nogueira) 1898-1935 **TCLC 27; HLC; PC 20**
See also CA 125

Peterkin, Julia Mood 1880-1961 .... **CLC 31**
See also CA 102; DLB 9

Peters, Joan K(aren) 1945-................. **CLC 39**
See also CA 158

Peters, Robert L(ouis) 1924- .... **CLC 7**
See also CA 13-16R; CAAS 8; DLB 105

Petofi, Sandor 1823-1849 .... **NCLC 21**

Petrakis, Harry Mark 1923-................. **CLC 3**
See also CA 9-12R; CANR 4, 30

Petrarch 1304-1374 .... **CMLC 20; DAM POET; PC 8**

Petrov, Evgeny .... **TCLC 21**
See also Kataev, Evgeny Petrovich

Petry, Ann (Lane) 1908-1997 ..... **CLC 1, 7, 18**
See also BW 1; CA 5-8R; 157; CAAS 6; CANR 4, 46; CLR 12; DLB 76; JRDA; MAICYA; MTCW 1; SATA 5; SATA-Obit 94

Petursson, Halligrimur 1614-1674 .... **LC 8**

Peychinovich
See Vazov, Ivan (Minchov)

Phaedrus 18(?)B.C.-55(?) .... **CMLC 25**

Philips, Katherine 1632-1664 .... **LC 30**
See also DLB 131

Philipson, Morris H. 1926- .... **CLC 53**
See also CA 1-4R; CANR 4

Phillips, Caryl 1958-... **CLC 96; BLCS; DAM MULT**
See also BW 2; CA 141; CANR 63; DLB 157

Phillips, David Graham 1867-1911 . **TCLC 44**
See also CA 108; DLB 9, 12

Phillips, Jack
See Sandburg, Carl (August)

Phillips, Jayne Anne 1952-...**CLC 15, 33; SSC 16**
See also CA 101; CANR 24, 50; DLBY 80; INT CANR-24; MTCW 1

Phillips, Richard
See Dick, Philip K(indred)

Phillips, Robert (Schaeffer) 1938- ..... **CLC 28**
See also CA 17-20R; CAAS 13; CANR 8; DLB 105

Phillips, Ward
See Lovecraft, H(oward) P(hillips)

Piccolo, Lucio 1901-1969 .... **CLC 13**
See also CA 97-100; DLB 114

Pickthall, Marjorie L(owry) C(hristie) 1883-1922 .... **TCLC 21**
See also CA 107; DLB 92

Pico della Mirandola, Giovanni 1463-1494 **LC 15**

Piercy, Marge 1936-..**CLC 3, 6, 14, 18, 27, 62**
See also CA 21-24R; CAAS 1; CANR 13, 43, 66; DLB 120; MTCW 1

Piers, Robert
See Anthony, Piers

Pieyre de Mandiargues, Andre 1909-1991
See Mandiargues, Andre Pieyre de
See also CA 103; 136; CANR 22

Pilnyak, Boris .... **TCLC 23**
See also Vogau, Boris Andreyevich

Pincherle, Alberto 1907-1990..... **CLC 11, 18; DAM NOV**
See also Moravia, Alberto
See also CA 25-28R; 132; CANR 33, 63; MTCW 1

Pinckney, Darryl 1953- .... **CLC 76**
See also BW 2; CA 143

Pindar 518B.C.-446B.C. ...... **CMLC 12; PC 19**
See also DLB 176

Pineda, Cecile 1942- .... **CLC 39**
See also CA 118

Pinero, Arthur Wing 1855-1934 .... **TCLC 32; DAM DRAM**
See also CA 110; 153; DLB 10

Pinero, Miguel (Antonio Gomez) 1946-1988 **CLC 4, 55**
See also CA 61-64; 125; CANR 29; HW

Pinget, Robert 1919-1997 .... **CLC 7, 13, 37**
See also CA 85-88; 160; DLB 83

Pink Floyd
See Barrett, (Roger) Syd; Gilmour, David; Mason, Nick; Waters, Roger; Wright, Rick

Pinkney, Edward 1802-1828 .... **NCLC 31**

Pinkwater, Daniel Manus 1941- .... **CLC 35**
See also Pinkwater, Manus
See also AAYA 1; CA 29-32R; CANR 12, 38; CLR 4; JRDA; MAICYA; SAAS 3; SATA 46, 76

Pinkwater, Manus
See Pinkwater, Daniel Manus
See also SATA 8

Pinsky, Robert 1940-..... **CLC 9, 19, 38, 94; DAM POET**
See also CA 29-32R; CAAS 4; CANR 58; DLBY 82

Pinta, Harold
See Pinter, Harold

Pinter, Harold 1930-...**CLC 1, 3, 6, 9, 11, 15, 27, 58, 73; DA; DAB; DAC; DAM DRAM, MST; WLC**
See also CA 5-8R; CANR 33, 65; CDBLB 1960 to Present; DLB 13; MTCW 1

Piozzi, Hester Lynch (Thrale) 1741-1821 **NCLC 57**
See also DLB 104, 142

Pirandello, Luigi 1867-1936 .. **TCLC 4, 29; DA; DAB; DAC; DAM DRAM, MST; DC 5; SSC 22; WLC**
See also CA 104; 153

Pirsig, Robert M(aynard) 1928 ...**CLC 4, 6, 73; DAM POP**
See also CA 53-56; CANR 42; MTCW 1; SATA 39

Pisarev, Dmitry Ivanovich 1840-1868 **NCLC 25**

Pix, Mary (Griffith) 1666-1709 .... **LC 8**
See also DLB 80

Pixerecourt, (Rene Charles) Guilbert de 1773-1844 .... **NCLC 39**
See also DLB 192
Plaatje, Sol(omon) T(shekisho) 1876-1932
TCLC 73; BLCS
See also BW 2; CA 141
Plaidy, Jean
See Hibbert, Eleanor Alice Burford
Planche, James Robinson 1796-1880
NCLC 42
Plant, Robert 1948- .... **CLC 12**
Plante, David (Robert) 1940- . **CLC 7, 23, 38;**
DAM NOV
See also CA 37-40R; CANR 12, 36, 58; DLBY 83; INT CANR-12; MTCW 1
Plath, Sylvia 1932-1963...**CLC 1, 2, 3, 5, 9, 11, 14, 17, 50, 51, 62, 111; DA; DAB; DAC; DAM MST, POET; PC 1; WLC**
See also AAYA 13; CA 19-20; CANR 34; CAP 2; CDALB 1941-1968; DLB 5, 6, 152; MTCW 1; SATA 96
Plato 428(?)B.C.-348(?)B.C. .... **CMLC 8; DA; DAB; DAC; DAM MST; WLCS**
See also DLB 176
Platonov, Andrei .... **TCLC 14**
See also Klimentov, Andrei Platonovich
Platt, Kin 1911-................................... **CLC 26**
See also AAYA 11; CA 17-20R; CANR 11; JRDA; SAAS 17; SATA 21, 86
Plautus c. 251B.C.-184B.C. .. **CMLC 24; DC 6**
Plick et Plock
See Simenon, Georges (Jacques Christian)
Plimpton, George (Ames) 1927- .... **CLC 36**
See also AITN 1; CA 21-24R; CANR 32, 70; DLB 185; MTCW 1; SATA 10
Pliny the Elder c. 23-79 .... **CMLC 23**
Plomer, William Charles Franklin 1903-1973
CLC 4, 8
See also CA 21-22; CANR 34; CAP 2; DLB 20, 162, 191; MTCW 1; SATA 24
Plowman, Piers
See Kavanagh, Patrick (Joseph)
Plum, J.
See Wodehouse, P(elham) G(renville)
Plumly, Stanley (Ross) 1939- .... **CLC 33**
See also CA 108; 110; DLB 5, 193; INT 110
Plumpe, Friedrich Wilhelm 1888-1931
TCLC 53
See also CA 112
Po Chu-i 772-846 .... **CMLC 24**
Poe, Edgar Allan 1809-1849...**NCLC 1, 16, 55; DA; DAB; DAC; DAM MST, POET; PC 1; SSC 1, 22; WLC**
See also AAYA 14; CDALB 1640-1865; DLB 3, 59, 73, 74; SATA 23
Poet of Titchfield Street, The
See Pound, Ezra (Weston Loomis)
Pohl, Frederik 1919- .... **CLC 18; SSC 25**
See also AAYA 24; CA 61-64; CAAS 1; CANR 11, 37; DLB 8; INT CANR-11; MTCW 1; SATA 24
Poirier, Louis 1910-
See Gracq, Julien
See also CA 122; 126
Poitier, Sidney 1927- .... **CLC 26**
See also BW 1; CA 117
Polanski, Roman 1933- .... **CLC 16**
See also CA 77-80
Poliakoff, Stephen 1952- .... **CLC 38**
See also CA 106; DLB 13
Police, The
See Copeland, Stewart (Armstrong); Summers, Andrew James; Sumner, Gordon Matthew

Polidori, John William 1795-1821 .. **NCLC 51**
See also DLB 116
Pollitt, Katha 1949- .... **CLC 28**
See also CA 120; 122; CANR 66; MTCW 1
Pollock, (Mary) Sharon 1936- .... **CLC 50; DAC; DAM DRAM, MST**
See also CA 141; DLB 60
Polo, Marco 1254-1324 .... **CMLC 15**
Polonsky, Abraham (Lincoln) 1910- .. **CLC 92**
See also CA 104; DLB 26; INT 104
Polybius c. 200B.C.-c. 118B.C. .... **CMLC 17**
See also DLB 176
Pomerance, Bernard 1940-..... **CLC 13; DAM DRAM**
See also CA 101; CANR 49
Ponge, Francis (Jean Gaston Alfred) 1899-1988
CLC 6, 18; DAM POET
See also CA 85-88; 126; CANR 40
Pontoppidan, Henrik 1857-1943 ..... **TCLC 29**
Poole, Josephine .... **CLC 17**
See also Helyar, Jane Penelope Josephine
See also SAAS 2; SATA 5
Popa, Vasko 1922-1991 .... **CLC 19**
See also CA 112; 148; DLB 181
Pope, Alexander 1688-1744 ...... **LC 3; DA; DAB; DAC; DAM MST, POET; WLC**
See also CDBLB 1660-1789; DLB 95, 101
Porter, Connie (Rose) 1959(?)- .... **CLC 70**
See also BW 2; CA 142; SATA 81
Porter, Gene(va Grace) Stratton 1863(?)-1924
TCLC 21
See also CA 112
Porter, Katherine Anne 1890-1980...**CLC 1, 3, 7, 10, 13, 15, 27, 101; DA; DAB; DAC; DAM MST, NOV; SSC 4, 31**
See also AITN 2; CA 1-4R; 101; CANR 1, 65; DLB 4, 9, 102; DLBD 12; DLBY 80; MTCW 1; SATA 39; SATA-Obit 23
Porter, Peter (Neville Frederick) 1929-
CLC 5, 13, 33
See also CA 85-88; DLB 40
Porter, William Sydney 1862-1910
See Henry, O.
See also CA 104; 131; CDALB 1865-1917; DA; DAB; DAC; DAM MST; DLB 12, 78, 79; MTCW 1; YABC 2
Portillo (y Pacheco), Jose Lopez
See Lopez Portillo (y Pacheco), Jose
Post, Melville Davisson 1869-1930 . **TCLC 39**
See also CA 110
Potok, Chaim 1929- .... **CLC 2, 7, 14, 26, 112; DAM NOV**
See also AAYA 15; AITN 1, 2; CA 17-20R; CANR 19, 35, 64; DLB 28, 152; INT CANR-19; MTCW 1; SATA 33
Potter, (Helen) Beatrix 1866-1943
See Webb, (Martha) Beatrice (Potter)
See also MAICYA
Potter, Dennis (Christopher George) 1935-1994
CLC 58, 86
See also CA 107; 145; CANR 33, 61; MTCW 1
Pound, Ezra (Weston Loomis) 1885-1972
CLC 1, 2, 3, 4, 5, 7, 10, 13, 18, 34, 48, 50, 112; DA; DAB; DAC; DAM MST, POET; PC 4; WLC
See also CA 5-8R; 37-40R; CANR 40; CDALB 1917-1929; DLB 4, 45, 63; DLBD 15; MTCW 1
Povod, Reinaldo 1959-1994 .... **CLC 44**
See also CA 136; 146
Powell, Adam Clayton, Jr. 1908-1972
CLC 89; BLC 3; DAM MULT
See also BW 1; CA 102; 33-36R

Powell, Anthony (Dymoke) 1905-...**CLC 1, 3, 7, 9, 10, 31**
See also CA 1-4R; CANR 1, 32, 62; CDBLB 1945-1960; DLB 15; MTCW 1
Powell, Dawn 1897-1965 .... **CLC 66**
See also CA 5-8R; DLBY 97
Powell, Padgett 1952- .... **CLC 34**
See also CA 126; CANR 63
Power, Susan 1961-.............................. **CLC 91**
Powers, J(ames) F(arl) 1917-...**CLC 1, 4, 8, 57; SSC 4**
See also CA 1-4R; CANR 2, 61; DLB 130; MTCW 1
Powers, John J(ames) 1945-
See Powers, John R.
See also CA 69-72
Powers, John R. .... **CLC 66**
See also Powers, John J(ames)
Powers, Richard (S.) 1957- .... **CLC 93**
See also CA 148
Pownall, David 1938- .... **CLC 10**
See also CA 89-92; CAAS 18; CANR 49; DLB 14
Powys, John Cowper 1872-1963...**CLC 7, 9, 15, 46**
See also CA 85-88; DLB 15; MTCW 1
Powys, T(heodore) F(rancis) 1875-1953
TCLC 9
See also CA 106; DLB 36, 162
Prado (Calvo), Pedro 1886-1952 ..... **TCLC 75**
See also CA 131; HW
Prager, Emily 1952- .... **CLC 56**
Pratt, E(dwin) J(ohn) 1883(?)-1964 . **CLC 19; DAC; DAM POET**
See also CA 141; 93-96; DLB 92
Premchand .... **TCLC 21**
See also Srivastava, Dhanpat Rai
Preussler, Otfried 1923-...................... **CLC 17**
See also CA 77-80; SATA 24
Prevert, Jacques (Henri Marie) 1900-1977
CLC 15
See also CA 77-80; 69-72; CANR 29, 61; MTCW 1; SATA-Obit 30
Prevost, Abbe (Antoine Francois) 1697-1763
LC 1
Price, (Edward) Reynolds 1933-...**CLC 3, 6, 13, 43, 50, 63; DAM NOV; SSC 22**
See also CA 1-4R; CANR 1, 37, 57; DLB 2; INT CANR-37
Price, Richard 1949- .... **CLC 6, 12**
See also CA 49-52; CANR 3; DLBY 81
Prichard, Katharine Susannah 1883-1969
CLC 46
See also CA 11-12; CANR 33; CAP 1; MTCW 1; SATA 66
Priestley, J(ohn) B(oynton) 1894-1984
CLC 2, 5, 9, 34; DAM DRAM, NOV
See also CA 9-12R; 113; CANR 33; CDBLB 1914-1945; DLB 10, 34, 77, 100, 139; DLBY 84; MTCW 1
Prince 1958(?)- .... **CLC 35**
Prince, F(rank) T(empleton) 1912- .... **CLC 22**
See also CA 101; CANR 43; DLB 20
Prince Kropotkin
See Kropotkin, Peter (Aleksieevich)
Prior, Matthew 1664-1721 .... **LC 4**
See also DLB 95
Prishvin, Mikhail 1873-1954 .... **TCLC 75**
Pritchard, William H(arrison) 1932-
CLC 34
See also CA 65-68; CANR 23; DLB 111

Pritchett, V(ictor) S(awdon) 1900-1997
   CLC 5, 13, 15, 41; DAM NOV; SSC 14
   See also CA 61-64; 157; CANR 31, 63; DLB 15,
   139; MTCW 1
Private 19022
   See Manning, Frederic
Probst, Mark 1925- ....**CLC 59**
   See also CA 130
Prokosch, Frederic 1908-1989 ....**CLC 4, 48**
   See also CA 73-76; 128; DLB 48
Prophet, The
   See Dreiser, Theodore (Herman Albert)
Prose, Francine 1947- ....**CLC 45**
   See also CA 109; 112; CANR 46; SATA 101
Proudhon
   See Cunha, Euclides (Rodrigues Pimenta) da
Proulx, Annie
   See Proulx, E(dna) Annie
Proulx, E(dna) Annie 1935- ...**CLC 81; DAM
   POP**
   See also CA 145; CANR 65
**Proust, (Valentin-Louis-George-Eugene-)
   Marcel** 1871-1922 ..**TCLC 7, 13, 33;
   DA; DAB; DAC; DAM MST, NOV; WLC**
   See also CA 104; 120; DLB 65; MTCW 1
Prowler, Harley
   See Masters, Edgar Lee
Prus, Boleslaw 1845-1912 ....**TCLC 48**
Pryor, Richard (Franklin Lenox Thomas) 1940-
   CLC 26
   See also CA 122
Przybyszewski, Stanislaw 1868-1927
   TCLC 36
   See also CA 160; DLB 66
Pteleon
   See Grieve, C(hristopher) M(urray)
   See also DAM POET
Puckett, Lute
   See Masters, Edgar Lee
Puig, Manuel 1932-1990...**CLC 3, 5, 10, 28, 65;
   DAM MULT; HLC**
   See also CA 45-48; CANR 2, 32, 63; DLB 113;
   HW; MTCW 1
Pulitzer, Joseph 1847-1911 ....**TCLC 76**
   See also CA 114; DLB 23
Purdy, A(lfred) W(ellington) 1918-...**CLC 3, 6,
   14, 50; DAC; DAM MST, POET**
   See also CA 81-84; CAAS 17; CANR 42, 66;
   DLB 88
Purdy, James (Amos) 1923-...**CLC 2, 4, 10, 28,
   52**
   See also CA 33-36R; CAAS 1; CANR 19, 51;
   DLB 2; INT CANR-19; MTCW 1
Pure, Simon
   See Swinnerton, Frank Arthur
Pushkin, Alexander (Sergeyevich) 1799-1837
   **NCLC 3, 27; DA; DAB; DAC; DAM
   DRAM, MST, POET; PC 10; SSC 27; WLC**
   See also SATA 61
P'u Sung-ling 1640-1715 ....**LC 3; SSC 31**
Putnam, Arthur Lee
   See Alger, Horatio, Jr.
Puzo, Mario 1920- ... **CLC 1, 2, 6, 36, 107;
   DAM NOV, POP**
   See also CA 65-68; CANR 4, 42, 65; DLB 6;
   MTCW 1
Pygge, Edward
   See Barnes, Julian (Patrick)
Pyle, Ernest Taylor 1900-1945
   See Pyle, Ernie
   See also CA 115; 160

Pyle, Ernie 1900-1945 ....**TCLC 75**
   See also Pyle, Ernest Taylor
   See also DLB 29
Pyle, Howard 1853-1911 ....**TCLC 81**
   See also CA 109; 137; CLR 22; DLB 42, 188;
   DLBD 13; MAICYA; SATA 16, 100
Pym, Barbara (Mary Crampton) 1913-1980
   CLC 13, 19, 37, 111
   See also CA 13-14; 97-100; CANR 13, 34; CAP
   1; DLB 14; DLBY 87; MTCW 1
Pynchon, Thomas (Ruggles, Jr.) 1937-
   **CLC 2, 3, 6, 9, 11, 18, 33, 62, 72; DA; DAB;
   DAC; DAM MST, NOV, POP; SSC 14;
   WLC**
   See also BEST 90:2; CA 17-20R; CANR 22, 46;
   DLB 2, 173; MTCW 1
Pythagoras c. 570B.C.-c. 500B.C. ... **CMLC 22**
   See also DLB 176
Q
   See Quiller-Couch, SirArthur (Thomas)
Qian Zhongshu
   See Ch'ien Chung-shu
Qroll
   See Dagerman, Stig (Halvard)
Quarrington, Paul (Lewis) 1953- ....**CLC 65**
   See also CA 129; CANR 62
Quasimodo, Salvatore 1901-1968 ......**CLC 10**
   See also CA 13-16; 25-28R; CAP 1; DLB 114;
   MTCW 1
Quay, Stephen 1947- ....**CLC 95**
Quay, Timothy 1947- ....**CLC 95**
Queen, Ellery ....**CLC 3, 11**
   See also Dannay, Frederic; Davidson, Avram; Lee,
   Manfred B(ennington); Marlowe, Stephen;
   Sturgeon, Theodore (Hamilton); Vance, John
   Holbrook
Queen, Ellery, Jr.
   See Dannay, Frederic; Lee, Manfred B(ennington)
Queneau, Raymond 1903-1976...**CLC 2, 5, 10,
   42**
   See also CA 77-80; 69-72; CANR 32; DLB 72;
   MTCW 1
Quevedo, Francisco de 1580-1645 ....**LC 23**
Quiller-Couch, SirArthur (Thomas) 1863-1944
   TCLC 53
   See also CA 118; 166; DLB 135, 153, 190
Quin, Ann (Marie) 1936-1973 ....**CLC 6**
   See also CA 9-12R; 45-48; DLB 14
Quinn, Martin
   See Smith, Martin Cruz
Quinn, Peter 1947- ....**CLC 91**
Quinn, Simon
   See Smith, Martin Cruz
Quiroga, Horacio (Sylvestre) 1878-1937
   TCLC 20; DAM MULT; HLC
   See also CA 117; 131; HW; MTCW 1
Quoirez, Francoise 1935-......................**CLC 9**
   See also Sagan, Francoise
   See also CA 49-52; CANR 6, 39; MTCW 1
Raabe, Wilhelm (Karl) 1831-1910 .. **TCLC 45**
   See also CA 167; DLB 129
Rabe, David (William) 1940- .... **CLC 4, 8, 33;
   DAM DRAM**
   See also CA 85-88; CABS 3; CANR 59; DLB 7
Rabelais, Francois 1483-1553 .....**LC 5; DA;
   DAB; DAC; DAM MST; WLC**
Rabinovitch, Sholem 1859-1916
   See Aleichem, Sholom
   See also CA 104
Rachilde 1860-1953 ....**TCLC 67**
   See also DLB 123, 192
Racine, Jean 1639-1699 .. **LC 28; DAB; DAM
   MST**

Radcliffe, Ann (Ward) 1764-1823...**NCLC 6, 55**
   See also DLB 39, 178
Radiguet, Raymond 1903-1923 .... **TCLC 29**
   See also CA 162; DLB 65
Radnoti, Miklos 1909-1944 .... **TCLC 16**
   See also CA 118
Rado, James 1939- ....**CLC 17**
   See also CA 105
Radvanyi, Netty 1900-1983
   See Seghers, Anna
   See also CA 85-88; 110
Rae, Ben
   See Griffiths, Trevor
Raeburn, John (Hay) 1941- ....**CLC 34**
   See also CA 57-60
Ragni, Gerome 1942-1991 ....**CLC 17**
   See also CA 105; 134
Rahv, Philip 1908-1973 ....**CLC 24**
   See also Greenberg, Ivan
   See also DLB 137
Raimund, Ferdinand Jakob 1790-1836
   NCLC 69
   See also DLB 90
Raine, Craig 1944- ....**CLC 32, 103**
   See also CA 108; CANR 29, 51; DLB 40
Raine, Kathleen (Jessie) 1908- ....**CLC 7, 45**
   See also CA 85-88; CANR 46; DLB 20; MTCW
   1
Rainis, Janis 1865-1929 ....**TCLC 29**
Rakosi, Carl 1903-..............................**CLC 47**
   See also Rawley, Callman
   See also CAAS 5; DLB 193
Raleigh, Richard
   See Lovecraft, H(oward) P(hillips)
Raleigh, Sir Walter 1554(?)-1618... **LC 31, 39**
   See also CDBLB Before 1660; DLB 172
Rallentando, H. P.
   See Sayers, Dorothy L(eigh)
Ramal, Walter
   See de la Mare, Walter (John)
Ramana Maharshi 1879-1950 .... **TCLC 84**
Ramon, Juan
   See Jimenez (Mantecon), Juan Ramon
Ramos, Graciliano 1892-1953 .... **TCLC 32**
   See also CA 167
Rampersad, Arnold 1941- ....**CLC 44**
   See also BW 2; CA 127; 133; DLB 111; INT
   133
Rampling, Anne
   See Rice, Anne
Ramsay, Allan 1684(?)-1758 ....**LC 29**
   See also DLB 95
Ramuz, Charles-Ferdinand 1878-1947
   TCLC 33
   See also CA 165
Rand, Ayn 1905-1982...**CLC 3, 30, 44, 79; DA;
   DAC; DAM MST, NOV, POP; WLC**
   See also AAYA 10; CA 13-16R; 105; CANR 27;
   MTCW 1
Randall, Dudley (Felker) 1914- .....**CLC 1;
   BLC 3; DAM MULT**
   See also BW 1; CA 25-28R; CANR 23; DLB
   41
Randall, Robert
   See Silverberg, Robert
Ranger, Ken
   See Creasey, John
Ransom, John Crowe 1888-1974...**CLC 2, 4, 5,
   11, 24; DAM POET**
   See also CA 5-8R; 49-52; CANR 6, 34; DLB 45,
   63; MTCW 1
Rao, Raja 1909- ....**CLC 25, 56; DAM NOV**
   See also CA 73-76; CANR 51; MTCW 1

Raphael, Frederic (Michael) 1931-...**CLC 2, 14**
   See also CA 1-4R; CANR 1; DLB 14
Ratcliffe, James P.
   See Mencken, H(enry) L(ouis)
Rathbone, Julian 1935- .... **CLC 41**
   See also CA 101; CANR 34
Rattigan, Terence (Mervyn) 1911-1977
   CLC 7; DAM DRAM
   See also CA 85-88; 73-76; CDBLB 1945-1960;
     DLB 13; MTCW 1
Ratushinskaya, Irina 1954- .... **CLC 54**
   See also CA 129; CANR 68
Raven, Simon (Arthur Noel) 1927- .... **CLC 14**
   See also CA 81-84
Ravenna, Michael
   See Welty, Eudora
Rawley, Callman 1903-
   See Rakosi, Carl
   See also CA 21-24R; CANR 12, 32
Rawlings, Marjorie Kinnan 1896-1953
   TCLC 4
   See also AAYA 20; CA 104; 137; DLB 9, 22,
     102; DLBD 17; JRDA; MAICYA; SATA 100;
     YABC 1
Ray, Satyajit 1921-1992 .... **CLC 16, 76; DAM**
   MULT
   See also CA 114; 137
Read, Herbert Edward 1893-1968 .... **CLC 4**
   See also CA 85-88; 25-28R; DLB 20, 149
Read, Piers Paul 1941- .... **CLC 4, 10, 25**
   See also CA 21-24R; CANR 38; DLB 14; SATA
     21
Reade, Charles 1814-1884 .... **NCLC 2**
   See also DLB 21
Reade, Hamish
   See Gray, Simon (James Holliday)
Reading, Peter 1946- .... **CLC 47**
   See also CA 103; CANR 46; DLB 40
Reaney, James 1926- ...**CLC 13; DAC; DAM**
   MST
   See also CA 41-44R; CAAS 15; CANR 42; DLB
     68; SATA 43
Rebreanu, Liviu 1885-1944 .... **TCLC 28**
   See also CA 165
Rechy, John (Francisco) 1934-...**CLC 1, 7, 14,**
   18, 107; DAM MULT; HLC
   See also CA 5-8R; CAAS 4; CANR 6, 32, 64;
     DLB 122; DLBY 82; HW; INT CANR-6
Redcam, Tom 1870-1933 .... **TCLC 25**
Reddin, Keith .... **CLC 67**
Redgrove, Peter (William) 1932- ...**CLC 6, 41**
   See also CA 1-4R; CANR 3, 39; DLB 40
Redmon, Anne .... **CLC 22**
   See also Nightingale, Anne Redmon
   See also DLBY 86

Reed, Eliot
   See Ambler, Eric

Reed, Ishmael 1938-...**CLC 2, 3, 5, 6, 13, 32, 60;**
   BLC 3; DAM MULT
   See also BW 2; CA 21-24R; CANR 25, 48; DLB
     2, 5, 33, 169; DLBD 8; MTCW 1
Reed, John (Silas) 1887-1920 .... **TCLC 9**
   See also CA 106
Reed, Lou .... **CLC 21**
   See also Firbank, Louis
Reeve, Clara 1729-1807 .... **NCLC 19**
   See also DLB 39
Reich, Wilhelm 1897-1957 .... **TCLC 57**
Reid, Christopher (John) 1949- .... **CLC 33**
   See also CA 140; DLB 40
Reid, Desmond
   See Moorcock, Michael (John)

Reid Banks, Lynne 1929-
   See Banks, Lynne Reid
   See also CA 1-4R; CANR 6, 22, 38; CLR 24;
     JRDA; MAICYA; SATA 22, 75
Reilly, William K.
   See Creasey, John
Reiner, Max
   See Caldwell, (Janet Miriam) Taylor (Holland)
Reis, Ricardo
   See Pessoa, Fernando (Antonio Nogueira)
Remarque, Erich Maria 1898-1970 . **CLC 21;**
   DA; DAB; DAC; DAM MST, NOV
   See also AAYA 27; CA 77-80; 29-32R; DLB 56;
     MTCW 1
Remizov, A.
   See Remizov, Aleksei (Mikhailovich)
Remizov, A. M.
   See Remizov, Aleksei (Mikhailovich)
Remizov, Aleksei (Mikhailovich) 1877-1957
   TCLC 27
   See also CA 125; 133
Renan, Joseph Ernest 1823-1892 .... **NCLC 26**
Renard, Jules 1864-1910 .... **TCLC 17**
   See also CA 117
Renault, Mary .... **CLC 3, 11, 17**
   See also Challans, Mary
   See also DLBY 83
Rendell, Ruth (Barbara) 1930-... **CLC 28, 48;**
   DAM POP
   See also Vine, Barbara
   See also CA 109; CANR 32, 52; DLB 87; INT
     CANR-32; MTCW 1
Renoir, Jean 1894-1979 .... **CLC 20**
   See also CA 129; 85-88
Resnais, Alain 1922- .... **CLC 16**
Reverdy, Pierre 1889-1960 .... **CLC 53**
   See also CA 97-100; 89-92
Rexroth, Kenneth 1905-1982...**CLC 1, 2, 6, 11,**
   22, 49, 112; DAM POET; PC 20
   See also CA 5-8R; 107; CANR 14, 34, 63;
     CDALB 1941-1968; DLB 16, 48, 165; DLBY
     82; INT CANR-14; MTCW 1
Reyes, Alfonso 1889-1959 .... **TCLC 33**
   See also CA 131; HW
Reyes y Basoalto, Ricardo Eliecer Neftali
   See Neruda, Pablo
Reymont, Wladyslaw (Stanislaw) 1868(?)-1925
   TCLC 5
   See also CA 104
Reynolds, Jonathan 1942- .... **CLC 6, 38**
   See also CA 65-68; CANR 28
Reynolds, Joshua 1723-1792 .... **LC 15**
   See also DLB 104
Reynolds, Michael Shane 1937- .... **CLC 44**
   See also CA 65-68; CANR 9
Reznikoff, Charles 1894-1976 .... **CLC 9**
   See also CA 33-36; 61-64; CAP 2; DLB 28, 45
Rezzori (d'Arezzo), Gregor von 1914-1998
   CLC 25
   See also CA 122; 136; 167
Rhine, Richard
   See Silverstein, Alvin
Rhodes, Eugene Manlove 1869-1934
   TCLC 53
Rhodius, Apollonius c. 3rd cent. B.C.-**CMLC 28**
   See also DLB 176
R'hoone
   See Balzac, Honore de
Rhys, Jean 1890(?)-1979...**CLC 2, 4, 6, 14, 19,**
   51; DAM NOV; SSC 21
   See also CA 25-28R; 85-88; CANR 35, 62;
     CDBLB 1945-1960; DLB 36, 117, 162;
     MTCW 1

Ribeiro, Darcy 1922-1997 .... **CLC 34**
   See also CA 33-36R; 156
Ribeiro, Joao Ubaldo (Osorio Pimentel) 1941-
   CLC 10, 67
   See also CA 81-84
Ribman, Ronald (Burt) 1932- .... **CLC 7**
   See also CA 21-24R; CANR 46
Ricci, Nino 1959- .... **CLC 70**
   See also CA 137
Rice, Anne 1941- .... **CLC 41; DAM POP**
   See also AAYA 9; BEST 89:2; CA 65-68; CANR
     12, 36, 53
Rice, Elmer (Leopold) 1892-1967...**CLC 7, 49;**
   DAM DRAM
   See also CA 21-22; 25-28R; CAP 2; DLB 4, 7;
     MTCW 1
Rice, Tim(othy Miles Bindon) 1944- .. **CLC 21**
   See also CA 103; CANR 46
Rich, Adrienne (Cecile) 1929-...**CLC 3, 6, 7, 11,**
   18, 36, 73, 76; DAM POET; PC 5
   See also CA 9-12R; CANR 20, 53; DLB 5, 67;
     MTCW 1
Rich, Barbara
   See Graves, Robert (von Ranke)
Rich, Robert
   See Trumbo, Dalton
Richard, Keith .... **CLC 17**
   See also Richards, Keith
Richards, David Adams 1950-...**CLC 59; DAC**
   See also CA 93-96; CANR 60; DLB 53
Richards, I(vor) A(rmstrong) 1893-1979
   CLC 14, 24
   See also CA 41-44R; 89-92; CANR 34; DLB 27
Richards, Keith 1943-
   See Richard, Keith
   See also CA 107
Richardson, Anne
   See Roiphe, Anne (Richardson)
Richardson, Dorothy Miller 1873-1957
   TCLC 3
   See also CA 104; DLB 36
Richardson, Ethel Florence (Lindesay) 1870-
   1946
   See Richardson, Henry Handel
   See also CA 105
Richardson, Henry Handel .... **TCLC 4**
   See also Richardson, Ethel Florence (Lindesay)
   See also DLB 197
Richardson, John 1796-1852...**NCLC 55; DAC**
   See also DLB 99
Richardson, Samuel 1689-1761...**LC 1, 44; DA;**
   DAB; DAC; DAM MST, NOV; WLC
   See also CDBLB 1660-1789; DLB 39
Richler, Mordecai 1931-... **CLC 3, 5, 9, 13, 18,**
   46, 70; DAC; DAM MST, NOV
   See also AITN 1; CA 65-68; CANR 31, 62; CLR
     17; DLB 53; MAICYA; MTCW 1; SATA 44,
     98; SATA-Brief 27
Richter, Conrad (Michael) 1890-1968
   CLC 30
   See also AAYA 21; CA 5-8R; 25-28R; CANR
     23; DLB 9; MTCW 1; SATA 3
Ricostranza, Tom
   See Ellis, Trey
Riddell, Charlotte 1832-1906 .... **TCLC 40**
   See also CA 165; DLB 156
Riding, Laura .... **CLC 3, 7**
   See also Jackson, Laura (Riding)
Riefenstahl, Berta Helene Amalia 1902-
   See Riefenstahl, Leni
   See also CA 108
Riefenstahl, Leni .... **CLC 16**
   See also Riefenstahl, Berta Helene Amalia

Salinas, Luis Omar 1937- .... **CLC 90; DAM MULT; HLC**
See also CA 131; DLB 82; HW

Salinas (y Serrano), Pedro 1891(?)-1951 **TCLC 17**
See also CA 117; DLB 134

Salinger, J(erome) D(avid) 1919-...**CLC 1, 3, 8, 12, 55, 56; DA; DAB; DAC; DAM MST, NOV, POP; SSC 2, 28; WLC**
See also AAYA 2; CA 5-8R; CANR 39; CDALB 1941-1968; CLR 18; DLB 2, 102, 173; MAICYA; MTCW 1; SATA 67

Salisbury, John
See Caute, (John) David

Salter, James 1925- .... **CLC 7, 52, 59**
See also CA 73-76; DLB 130

Saltus, Edgar (Everton) 1855-1921 .. **TCLC 8**
See also CA 105; DLB 202

Saltykov, Mikhail Evgrafovich 1826-1889 **NCLC 16**

Samarakis, Antonis 1919- .... **CLC 5**
See also CA 25-28R; CAAS 16; CANR 36

Sanchez, Florencio 1875-1910 .... **TCLC 37**
See also CA 153; HW

Sanchez, Luis Rafael 1936- .... **CLC 23**
See also CA 128; DLB 145; HW

Sanchez, Sonia 1934-... **CLC 5; BLC 3; DAM MULT; PC 9**
See also BW 2; CA 33-36R; CANR 24, 49; CLR 18; DLB 41; DLBD 8; MAICYA; MTCW 1; SATA 22

Sand, George 1804-1876 ..**NCLC 2, 42, 57; DA; DAB; DAC; DAM MST, NOV; WLC**
See also DLB 119, 192

Sandburg, Carl (August) 1878-1967...**CLC 1, 4, 10, 15, 35; DA; DAB; DAC; DAM MST, POET; PC 2; WLC**
See also AAYA 24; CA 5-8R; 25-28R; CANR 35; CDALB 1865-1917; DLB 17, 54; MAICYA; MTCW 1; SATA 8

Sandburg, Charles
See Sandburg, Carl (August)

Sandburg, Charles A.
See Sandburg, Carl (August)

Sanders, (James) Ed(ward) 1939- ...... **CLC 53**
See also CA 13-16R; CAAS 21; CANR 13, 44; DLB 16

Sanders, Lawrence 1920-1998 ...... **CLC 41; DAM POP**
See also BEST 89:4; CA 81-84; 165; CANR 33, 62; MTCW 1

Sanders, Noah
See Blount, Roy (Alton), Jr.

Sanders, Winston P.
See Anderson, Poul (William)

Sandoz, Mari(e Susette) 1896-1966 ... **CLC 28**
See also CA 1-4R; 25-28R; CANR 17, 64; DLB 9; MTCW 1; SATA 5

Saner, Reg(inald Anthony) 1931- .... **CLC 9**
See also CA 65-68

Sannazaro, Jacopo 1456(?)-1530 .... **LC 8**

Sansom, William 1912-1976 ..... **CLC 2, 6; DAM NOV; SSC 21**
See also CA 5-8R; 65-68; CANR 42; DLB 139; MTCW 1

Santayana, George 1863-1952 .... **TCLC 40**
See also CA 115; DLB 54, 71; DLBD 13

Santiago, Danny ....**CLC 33**
See also James, Daniel (Lewis)
See also DLB 122

Santmyer, Helen Hoover 1895-1986 ..**CLC 33**
See also CA 1-4R; 118; CANR 15, 33; DLBY 84; MTCW 1

Santoka, Taneda 1882-1940 .... **TCLC 72**

Santos, Bienvenido N(uqui) 1911-1996 **CLC 22; DAM MULT**
See also CA 101; 151; CANR 19, 46

Sapper .... **TCLC 44**
See also McNeile, Herman Cyril

Sapphire 1950-....................................... **CLC 99**

Sappho fl. 6th cent. B.C.-....... **CMLC 3; DAM POET; PC 5**
See also DLB 176

Sarduy, Severo 1937-1993 .... **CLC 6, 97**
See also CA 89-92; 142; CANR 58; DLB 113; HW

Sargeson, Frank 1903-1982 .... **CLC 31**
See also CA 25-28R; 106; CANR 38

Sarmiento, Felix Ruben Garcia
See Dario, Ruben

Saro-Wiwa, Ken(ule Beeson) 1941-1995 **CLC 114**
See also BW 2; CA 142; 150; CANR 60; DLB 157

Saroyan, William 1908-1981...**CLC 1, 8, 10, 29, 34, 56; DA; DAB; DAC; DAM DRAM, MST, NOV; SSC 21; WLC**
See also CA 5-8R; 103; CANR 30; DLB 7, 9, 86; DLBY 81; MTCW 1; SATA 23; SATA-Obit 24

Sarraute, Nathalie 1900-...**CLC 1, 2, 4, 8, 10, 31, 80**
See also CA 9-12R; CANR 23, 66; DLB 83; MTCW 1

Sarton, (Eleanor) May 1912-1995...**CLC 4, 14, 49, 91; DAM POET**
See also CA 1-4R; 149; CANR 1, 34, 55; DLB 48; DLBY 81; INT CANR-34; MTCW 1; SATA 36; SATA-Obit 86

Sartre, Jean-Paul 1905-1980... **CLC 1, 4, 7, 9, 13, 18, 24, 44, 50, 52; DA; DAB; DAC; DAM DRAM, MST, NOV; DC 3; SSC 32; WLC**
See also CA 9-12R; 97-100; CANR 21; DLB 72; MTCW 1

Sassoon, Siegfried (Lorraine) 1886-1967 **CLC 36; DAB; DAM MST, NOV, POET; PC 12**
See also CA 104; 25-28R; CANR 36; DLB 20, 191; DLBD 18; MTCW 1

Satterfield, Charles
See Pohl, Frederik

Saul, John (W. III) 1942- .... **CLC 46; DAM NOV, POP**
See also AAYA 10; BEST 90:4; CA 81-84; CANR 16, 40; SATA 98

Saunders, Caleb
See Heinlein, Robert A(nson)

Saura (Atares), Carlos 1932- .... **CLC 20**
See also CA 114; 131; HW

Sauser-Hall, Frederic 1887-1961 .... **CLC 18**
See also Cendrars, Blaise
See also CA 102; 93-96; CANR 36, 62; MTCW 1

Saussure, Ferdinand de 1857-1913 . **TCLC 49**

Savage, Catharine
See Brosman, Catharine Savage

Savage, Thomas 1915- .... **CLC 40**
See also CA 126; 132; CAAS 15; INT 132

Savan, Glenn 19(?)- .... **CLC 50**

Sayers, Dorothy L(eigh) 1893-1957 . **TCLC 2, 15; DAM POP**
See also CA 104; 119; CANR 60; CDBLB 1914-1945; DLB 10, 36, 77, 100; MTCW 1

Sayers, Valerie 1952- .... **CLC 50**
See also CA 134; CANR 61

Sayles, John (Thomas) 1950- .... **CLC 7, 10, 14**
See also CA 57-60; CANR 41; DLB 44

Scammell, Michael 1935- .... **CLC 34**
See also CA 156

Scannell, Vernon 1922- .... **CLC 49**
See also CA 5-8R; CANR 8, 24, 57; DLB 27; SATA 59

Scarlett, Susan
See Streatfeild, (Mary) Noel

Schaeffer, Susan Fromberg 1941-...**CLC 6, 11, 22**
See also CA 49-52; CANR 18, 65; DLB 28; MTCW 1; SATA 22

Schary, Jill
See Robinson, Jill

Schell, Jonathan 1943- .... **CLC 35**
See also CA 73-76; CANR 12

Schelling, Friedrich Wilhelm Joseph von 1775-1854 .... **NCLC 30**
See also DLB 90

Schendel, Arthur van 1874-1946 .... **TCLC 56**

Scherer, Jean-Marie Maurice 1920-
See Rohmer, Eric
See also CA 110

Schevill, James (Erwin) 1920- .... **CLC 7**
See also CA 5-8R; CAAS 12

Schiller, Friedrich 1759-1805 .. **NCLC 39, 69; DAM DRAM**
See also DLB 94

Schisgal, Murray (Joseph) 1926- .... **CLC 6**
See also CA 21-24R; CANR 48

Schlee, Ann 1934- .... **CLC 35**
See also CA 101; CANR 29; SATA 44; SATA-Brief 36

Schlegel, August Wilhelm von 1767-1845 **NCLC 15**
See also DLB 94

Schlegel, Friedrich 1772-1829 .... **NCLC 45**
See also DLB 90

Schlegel, Johann Elias (von) 1719(?)-1749 **LC 5**

Schlesinger, Arthur M(eier), Jr. 1917- **CLC 84**
See also AITN 1; CA 1-4R; CANR 1, 28, 58; DLB 17; INT CANR-28; MTCW 1; SATA 61

Schmidt, Arno (Otto) 1914-1979 .... **CLC 56**
See also CA 128; 109; DLB 69

Schmitz, Aron Hector 1861-1928
See Svevo, Italo
See also CA 104; 122; MTCW 1

Schnackenberg, Gjertrud 1953- .... **CLC 40**
See also CA 116; DLB 120

Schneider, Leonard Alfred 1925-1966
See Bruce, Lenny
See also CA 89-92

Schnitzler, Arthur 1862-1931...**TCLC 4; SSC 15**
See also CA 104; DLB 81, 118

Schoenberg, Arnold 1874-1951 .... **TCLC 75**
See also CA 109

Schonberg, Arnold
See Schoenberg, Arnold

Schopenhauer, Arthur 1788-1860 ... **NCLC 51**
See also DLB 90

Schor, Sandra (M.) 1932(?)-1990 .... **CLC 65**
See also CA 132

Schorer, Mark 1908-1977 .... **CLC 9**
See also CA 5-8R; 73-76; CANR 7; DLB 103

Schrader, Paul (Joseph) 1946-............ **CLC 26**
See also CA 37-40R; CANR 41; DLB 44

Schreiner, Olive (Emilie Albertina) 1855-1920 **TCLC 9**
See also CA 105; 154; DLB 18, 156, 190

Schulberg, Budd (Wilson) 1914- .... **CLC 7, 48**
See also CA 25-28R; CANR 19; DLB 6, 26, 28; DLBY 81

Schulz, Bruno 1892-1942...**TCLC 5, 51; SSC 13**
See also CA 115; 123
Schulz, Charles M(onroe) 1922- .... **CLC 12**
See also CA 9-12R; CANR 6; INT CANR-6;
SATA 10
Schumacher, E(rnst) F(riedrich) 1911-1977
CLC 80
See also CA 81-84; 73-76; CANR 34
Schuyler, James Marcus 1923-1991.... **CLC 5,
23; DAM POET**
See also CA 101; 134; DLB 5, 169; INT 101
Schwartz, Delmore (David) 1913-1966
CLC 2, 4, 10, 45, 87; PC 8
See also CA 17-18; 25-28R; CANR 35; CAP 2;
DLB 28, 48; MTCW 1
Schwartz, Ernst
See Ozu, Yasujiro
Schwartz, John Burnham 1965- .... **CLC 59**
See also CA 132
Schwartz, Lynne Sharon 1939- .... **CLC 31**
See also CA 103; CANR 44
Schwartz, Muriel A.
See Eliot, T(homas) S(tearns)
Schwarz-Bart, Andre 1928- .... **CLC 2, 4**
See also CA 89-92
Schwarz-Bart, Simone 1938- ... **CLC 7; BLCS**
See also BW 2; CA 97-100
Schwob, Marcel (Mayer Andre) 1867-1905
TCLC 20
See also CA 117; 168; DLB 123
Sciascia, Leonardo 1921-1989 .... **CLC 8, 9, 41**
See also CA 85-88; 130; CANR 35; DLB 177;
MTCW 1
Scoppettone, Sandra 1936- .... **CLC 26**
See also AAYA 11; CA 5-8R; CANR 41; SATA
9, 92
Scorsese, Martin 1942- .... **CLC 20, 89**
See also CA 110; 114; CANR 46
Scotland, Jay
See Jakes, John (William)
Scott, Duncan Campbell 1862-1947
TCLC 6; DAC
See also CA 104; 153; DLB 92
Scott, Evelyn 1893-1963 .... **CLC 43**
See also CA 104; 112; CANR 64; DLB 9, 48
Scott, F(rancis) R(eginald) 1899-1985..**CLC 22**
See also CA 101; 114; DLB 88; INT 101
Scott, Frank
See Scott, F(rancis) R(eginald)
Scott, Joanna 1960- .... **CLC 50**
See also CA 126; CANR 53
Scott, Paul (Mark) 1920-1978 .... **CLC 9, 60**
See also CA 81-84; 77-80; CANR 33; DLB 14;
MTCW 1
Scott, Sarah 1723-1795 .... **LC 44**
See also DLB 39
Scott, Walter 1771-1832 .. **NCLC 15, 69; DA;
DAB; DAC; DAM MST, NOV, POET; PC
13; SSC 32; WLC**
See also AAYA 22; CDBLB 1789-1832; DLB
93, 107, 116, 144, 159; YABC 2
Scribe, (Augustin) Eugene 1791-1861
NCLC 16; DAM DRAM; DC 5
See also DLB 192
Scrum, R.
See Crumb, R(obert)
Scudery, Madeleine de 1607-1701 .... **LC 2**
Scum
See Crumb, R(obert)
Scumbag, Little Bobby
See Crumb, R(obert)
Seabrook, John
See Hubbard, L(afayette) Ron(ald)

Sealy, I. Allan 1951- .... **CLC 55**
Search, Alexander
See Pessoa, Fernando (Antonio Nogueira)
Sebastian, Lee
See Silverberg, Robert
Sebastian Owl
See Thompson, Hunter S(tockton)
Sebestyen, Ouida 1924- .... **CLC 30**
See also AAYA 8; CA 107; CANR 40; CLR 17;
JRDA; MAICYA; SAAS 10; SATA 39
Secundus, H. Scriblerus
See Fielding, Henry
Sedges, John
See Buck, Pearl S(ydenstricker)
Sedgwick, Catharine Maria 1789-1867
NCLC 19
See also DLB 1, 74
Seelye, John (Douglas) 1931- .... **CLC 7**
See also CA 97-100; CANR 70; INT 97-100
Seferiades, Giorgos Stylianou 1900-1971
See Seferis, George
See also CA 5-8R; 33-36R; CANR 5, 36; MTCW
1
Seferis, George .... **CLC 5, 11**
See also Seferiades, Giorgos Stylianou
Segal, Erich (Wolf) 1937-.. **CLC 3, 10; DAM
POP**
See also BEST 89:1; CA 25-28R; CANR 20, 36,
65; DLBY 86; INT CANR-20; MTCW 1
Seger, Bob 1945- .... **CLC 35**
Seghers, Anna .... **CLC 7**
See also Radvanyi, Netty
See also DLB 69
Seidel, Frederick (Lewis) 1936- .... **CLC 18**
See also CA 13-16R; CANR 8; DLBY 84
Seifert, Jaroslav 1901-1986 .... **CLC 34, 44, 93**
See also CA 127; MTCW 1
Sei Shonagon c. 966-1017(?) .... **CMLC 6**
Selby, Hubert, Jr. 1928- . **CLC 1, 2, 4, 8;
SSC 20**
See also CA 13-16R; CANR 33; DLB 2
Selzer, Richard 1928- .... **CLC 74**
See also CA 65-68; CANR 14
Sembene, Ousmane
See Ousmane, Sembene
Senancour, Etienne Pivert de 1770-1846
NCLC 16
See also DLB 119
Sender, Ramon (Jose) 1902-1982 ...... **CLC 8;
DAM MULT; HLC**
See also CA 5-8R; 105; CANR 8; HW; MTCW
1
Seneca, Lucius Annaeus 4B.C.-65 ...**CMLC 6;
DAM DRAM; DC 5**
Senghor, Leopold Sedar 1906-...**CLC 54; BLC
3; DAM MULT, POET**
See also BW 2; CA 116; 125; CANR 47; MTCW 1
Serling, (Edward) Rod(man) 1924-1975
CLC 30
See also AAYA 14; AITN 1; CA 162; 57-60; DLB
26
Serna, Ramon Gomez de la
See Gomez de la Serna, Ramon
Serpieres
See Guillevic, (Eugene)
Service, Robert
See Service, Robert W(illiam)
See also DAB; DLB 92
Service, Robert W(illiam) 1874(?)-1958
**TCLC 15; DA; DAC; DAM MST, POET;
WLC**
See also Service, Robert
See also CA 115; 140; SATA 20

Seth, Vikram 1952-...**CLC 43, 90; DAM MULT**
See also CA 121; 127; CANR 50; DLB 120
Seton, Cynthia Propper 1926-1982 .... **CLC 27**
See also CA 5-8R; 108; CANR 7
Seton, Ernest (Evan) Thompson 1860-1946
TCLC 31
See also CA 109; DLB 92; DLBD 13; JRDA;
SATA 18
Seton-Thompson, Ernest
See Seton, Ernest (Evan) Thompson
Settle, Mary Lee 1918-.................. **CLC 19, 61**
See also CA 89-92; CAAS 1; CANR 44; DLB 6;
INT 89-92
Seuphor, Michel
See Arp, Jean
**Sevigne, Marie (de Rabutin-Chantal) Marquise
de** 1626-1696 .... **LC 11**
Sewall, Samuel 1652-1730 .... **LC 38**
See also DLB 24
Sexton, Anne (Harvey) 1928-1974... **CLC 2, 4,
6, 8, 10, 15, 53; DA; DAB; DAC; DAM
MST, POET; PC 2; WLC**
See also CA 1-4R; 53-56; CABS 2; CANR 3, 36;
CDALB 1941-1968; DLB 5, 169; MTCW 1;
SATA 10
Shaara, Michael (Joseph, Jr.) 1929-1988
CLC 15; DAM POP
See also AITN 1; CA 102; 125; CANR 52;
DLBY 83
Shackleton, C. C.
See Aldiss, Brian W(ilson)
Shacochis, Bob .... **CLC 39**
See also Shacochis, Robert G.
Shacochis, Robert G. 1951-
See Shacochis, Bob
See also CA 119; 124; INT 124
Shaffer, Anthony (Joshua) 1926- .... **CLC 19;
DAM DRAM**
See also CA 110; 116; DLB 13
Shaffer, Peter (Levin) 1926-**CLC 5, 14, 18, 37,
60; DAB; DAM DRAM, MST; DC 7**
See also CA 25-28R; CANR 25, 47; CDBLB
1960 to Present; DLB 13; MTCW 1
Shakey, Bernard
See Young, Neil
Shalamov, Varlam (Tikhonovich) 1907(?)-1982
CLC 18
See also CA 129; 105
Shamlu, Ahmad 1925- .... **CLC 10**
Shammas, Anton 1951- .... **CLC 55**
Shange, Ntozake 1948- ... **CLC 8, 25, 38, 74;
BLC 3; DAM DRAM, MULT; DC 3**
See also AAYA 9; BW 2; CA 85-88; CABS 3;
CANR 27, 48; DLB 38; MTCW 1
Shanley, John Patrick 1950- .... **CLC 75**
See also CA 128; 133
Shapcott, Thomas W(illiam) 1935- .... **CLC 38**
See also CA 69-72; CANR 49
Shapiro, Jane .... **CLC 76**
Shapiro, Karl (Jay) 1913- ..... **CLC 4, 8, 15, 53**
See also CA 1-4R; CAAS 6; CANR 1, 36, 66;
DLB 48; MTCW 1
Sharp, William 1855-1905 .... **TCLC 39**
See also CA 160; DLB 156
Sharpe, Thomas Ridley 1928-
See Sharpe, Tom
See also CA 114; 122; INT 122
Sharpe, Tom .... **CLC 36**
See also Sharpe, Thomas Ridley
See also DLB 14
Shaw, Bernard .... **TCLC 45**
See also Shaw, George Bernard
See also BW 1

Shaw, G. Bernard
See Shaw, George Bernard
Shaw, George Bernard 1856-1950...**TCLC 3, 9, 21; DA; DAB; DAC; DAM DRAM, MST; WLC**
See also Shaw, Bernard
See also CA 104; 128; CDBLB 1914-1945; DLB 10, 57, 190; MTCW 1
Shaw, Henry Wheeler 1818-1885 .... **NCLC 15**
See also DLB 11
Shaw, Irwin 1913-1984 .. **CLC 7, 23, 34; DAM DRAM, POP**
See also AITN 1; CA 13-16R; 112; CANR 21; CDALB 1941-1968; DLB 6, 102; DLBY 84; MTCW 1
Shaw, Robert 1927-1978 .... **CLC 5**
See also AITN 1; CA 1-4R; 81-84; CANR 4; DLB 13, 14
Shaw, T. E.
See Lawrence, T(homas) E(dward)
Shawn, Wallace 1943- .... **CLC 41**
See also CA 112
Shea, Lisa 1953- .... **CLC 86**
See also CA 147
Sheed, Wilfrid (John Joseph) 1930-...**CLC 2, 4, 10, 53**
See also CA 65-68; CANR 30, 66; DLB 6; MTCW 1
Sheldon, Alice Hastings Bradley 1915(?)-1987
See Tiptree, James, Jr.
See also CA 108; 122; CANR 34; INT 108; MTCW 1
Sheldon, John
See Bloch, Robert (Albert)
Shelley, Mary Wollstonecraft (Godwin) 1797-1851**NCLC 14, 59; DA; DAB; DAC; DAM MST, NOV; WLC**
See also AAYA 20; CDBLB 1789-1832; DLB 110, 116, 159, 178; SATA 29
Shelley, Percy Bysshe 1792-1822... **NCLC 18; DA; DAB; DAC; DAM MST, POET; PC 14; WLC**
See also CDBLB 1789-1832; DLB 96, 110, 158
Shepard, Jim 1956- .... **CLC 36**
See also CA 137; CANR 59; SATA 90
Shepard, Lucius 1947- .... **CLC 34**
See also CA 128; 141
Shepard, Sam 1943-...**CLC 4, 6, 17, 34, 41, 44; DAM DRAM; DC 5**
See also AAYA 1; CA 69-72; CABS 3; CANR 22; DLB 7; MTCW 1
Shepherd, Michael
See Ludlum, Robert
Sherburne, Zoa (Morin) 1912- .... **CLC 30**
See also AAYA 13; CA 1-4R; CANR 3, 37; MAICYA; SAAS 18; SATA 3
Sheridan, Frances 1724-1766 .... **LC 7**
See also DLB 39, 84
Sheridan, Richard Brinsley 1751-1816
NCLC 5; DA; DAB; DAC; DAM DRAM, MST; DC 1; WLC
See also CDBLB 1660-1789; DLB 89
Sherman, Jonathan Marc .... **CLC 55**
Sherman, Martin 1941(?)- .... **CLC 19**
See also CA 116; 123
Sherwin, Judith Johnson 1936- ...... **CLC 7, 15**
See also CA 25-28R; CANR 34
Sherwood, Frances 1940- .... **CLC 81**
See also CA 146
Sherwood, Robert E(mmet) 1896-1955
TCLC 3; DAM DRAM
See also CA 104; 153; DLB 7, 26
Shestov, Lev 1866-1938 .... **TCLC 56**

Shevchenko, Taras 1814-1861 .... **NCLC 54**
Shiel, M(atthew) P(hipps) 1865-1947...**TCLC 8**
See also Holmes, Gordon
See also CA 106; 160; DLB 153
Shields, Carol 1935- .... **CLC 91, 113; DAC**
See also CA 81-84; CANR 51
Shields, David 1956- .... **CLC 97**
See also CA 124; CANR 48
Shiga, Naoya 1883-1971 .... **CLC 33; SSC 23**
See also CA 101; 33-36R; DLB 180
Shilts, Randy 1951-1994 .... **CLC 85**
See also AAYA 19; CA 115; 127; 144; CANR 45; INT 127
Shimazaki, Haruki 1872-1943
See Shimazaki Toson
See also CA 105; 134
Shimazaki Toson 1872-1943 .... **TCLC 5**
See also Shimazaki, Haruki
See also DLB 180
Sholokhov, Mikhail (Aleksandrovich) 1905-1984
CLC 7, 15
See also CA 101; 112; MTCW 1; SATA-Obit 36
Shone, Patric
See Hanley, James
Shreve, Susan Richards 1939- .... **CLC 23**
See also CA 49-52; CAAS 5; CANR 5, 38, 69; MAICYA; SATA 46, 95; SATA-Brief 41
Shue, Larry 1946-1985 .... **CLC 52; DAM DRAM**
See also CA 145; 117
Shu-Jen, Chou 1881-1936
See Lu Hsun
See also CA 104
Shulman, Alix Kates 1932- .... **CLC 2, 10**
See also CA 29-32R; CANR 43; SATA 7
Shuster, Joe 1914- .... **CLC 21**
Shute, Nevil .... **CLC 30**
See also Norway, Nevil Shute
Shuttle, Penelope (Diane) 1947- .... **CLC 7**
See also CA 93-96; CANR 39; DLB 14, 40
Sidney, Mary 1561-1621 .... **LC 19, 39**
Sidney, Sir Philip 1554-1586 .. **LC 19, 39; DA; DAB; DAC; DAM MST, POET**
See also CDBLB Before 1660; DLB 167
Siegel, Jerome 1914-1996 .... **CLC 21**
See also CA 116; 151
Siegel, Jerry
See Siegel, Jerome
Sienkiewicz, Henryk (Adam Alexander Pius) 1846-1916 .... **TCLC 3**
See also CA 104; 134
Sierra, Gregorio Martinez
See Martinez Sierra, Gregorio
Sierra, Maria (de la O'LeJarraga) Martinez
See Martinez Sierra, Maria (de la O'LeJarraga)
Sigal, Clancy 1926- .... **CLC 7**
See also CA 1-4R
Sigourney, Lydia Howard (Huntley) 1791-1865
NCLC 21
See also DLB 1, 42, 73
Siguenza y Gongora, Carlos de 1645-1700
LC 8
Sigurjonsson, Johann 1880-1919 .... **TCLC 27**
Sikelianos, Angelos 1884-1951 .... **TCLC 39**
Silkin, Jon 1930- .... **CLC 2, 6, 43**
See also CA 5-8R; CAAS 5; DLB 27
Silko, Leslie (Marmon) 1948- **CLC 23, 74, 114; DA; DAC; DAM MST, MULT, POP; WLCS**
See also AAYA 14; CA 115; 122; CANR 45, 65; DLB 143, 175; NNAL
Sillanpaa, Frans Eemil 1888-1964 ..... **CLC 19**
See also CA 129; 93-96; MTCW 1

Sillitoe, Alan 1928- ......**CLC 1, 3, 6, 10, 19, 57**
See also AITN 1; CA 9-12R; CAAS 2; CANR 8, 26, 55; CDBLB 1960 to Present; DLB 14, 139; MTCW 1; SATA 61
Silone, Ignazio 1900-1978 .... **CLC 4**
See also CA 25-28; 81-84; CANR 34; CAP 2; MTCW 1
Silver, Joan Micklin 1935- .... **CLC 20**
See also CA 114; 121; INT 121
Silver, Nicholas
See Faust, Frederick (Schiller)
Silverberg, Robert 1935-...**CLC 7; DAM POP**
See also AAYA 24; CA 1-4R; CAAS 3; CANR 1, 20, 36; DLB 8; INT CANR-20; MAICYA; MTCW 1; SATA 13, 91
Silverstein, Alvin 1933- .... **CLC 17**
See also CA 49-52; CANR 2; CLR 25; JRDA; MAICYA; SATA 8, 69
Silverstein, Virginia B(arbara Opshelor) 1937-
CLC 17
See also CA 49-52; CANR 2; CLR 25; JRDA; MAICYA; SATA 8, 69
Sim, Georges
See Simenon, Georges (Jacques Christian)
Simak, Clifford D(onald) 1904-1988... **CLC 1, 55**
See also CA 1-4R; 125; CANR 1, 35; DLB 8; MTCW 1; SATA-Obit 56
Simenon, Georges (Jacques Christian) 1903-1989 ... **CLC 1, 2, 3, 8, 18, 47; DAM POP**
See also CA 85-88; 129; CANR 35; DLB 72; DLBY 89; MTCW 1
Simic, Charles 1938- ... **CLC 6, 9, 22, 49, 68; DAM POET**
See also CA 29-32R; CAAS 4; CANR 12, 33, 52, 61; DLB 105
Simmel, Georg 1858-1918 .... **TCLC 64**
See also CA 157
Simmons, Charles (Paul) 1924- .... **CLC 57**
See also CA 89-92; INT 89-92
Simmons, Dan 1948- ...... **CLC 44; DAM POP**
See also AAYA 16; CA 138; CANR 53
Simmons, James (Stewart Alexander) 1933-
CLC 43
See also CA 105; CAAS 21; DLB 40
Simms, William Gilmore 1806-1870...**NCLC 3**
See also DLB 3, 30, 59, 73
Simon, Carly 1945- .... **CLC 26**
See also CA 105
Simon, Claude 1913-1984 ... **CLC 4, 9, 15, 39; DAM NOV**
See also CA 89-92; CANR 33; DLB 83; MTCW 1
Simon, (Marvin) Neil 1927-...**CLC 6, 11, 31, 39, 70; DAM DRAM**
See also AITN 1; CA 21-24R; CANR 26, 54; DLB 7; MTCW 1
Simon, Paul (Frederick) 1941(?)- .... **CLC 17**
See also CA 116; 153
Simonon, Paul 1956(?)- .... **CLC 30**
Simpson, Harriette
See Arnow, Harriette (Louisa) Simpson
Simpson, Louis (Aston Marantz) 1923-
CLC 4, 7, 9, 32; DAM POET
See also CA 1-4R; CAAS 4; CANR 1, 61; DLB 5; MTCW 1
Simpson, Mona (Elizabeth) 1957- ...... **CLC 44**
See also CA 122; 135; CANR 68
Simpson, N(orman) F(rederick) 1919-..**CLC 29**
See also CA 13-16R; DLB 13
Sinclair, Andrew (Annandale) 1935-..**CLC 2, 14**
See also CA 9-12R; CAAS 5; CANR 14, 38; DLB 14; MTCW 1

Sinclair, Emil
See Hesse, Hermann
Sinclair, Iain 1943- .... **CLC 76**
See also CA 132
Sinclair, Iain MacGregor
See Sinclair, Iain
Sinclair, Irene
See Griffith, D(avid Lewelyn) W(ark)
Sinclair, Mary Amelia St. Clair 1865(?)-1946
See Sinclair, May
See also CA 104
Sinclair, May 1863-1946 .... **TCLC 3, 11**
See also Sinclair, Mary Amelia St. Clair
See also CA 166; DLB 36, 135
Sinclair, Roy
See Griffith, D(avid Lewelyn) W(ark)
Sinclair, Upton (Beall) 1878-1968...**CLC 1, 11,**
15, 63; DA; DAB; DAC; DAM MST, NOV;
WLC
See also CA 5-8R; 25-28R; CANR 7; CDALB
1929-1941; DLB 9; INT CANR-7; MTCW
1; SATA 9
Singer, Isaac
See Singer, Isaac Bashevis
Singer, Isaac Bashevis 1904-1991...**CLC 1, 3, 6,**
9, 11, 15, 23, 38, 69, 111; DA; DAB; DAC;
DAM MST, NOV; SSC 3; WLC
See also AITN 1, 2; CA 1-4R; CANR 1, 39;
CDALB 1941-1968; CLR 1; DLB 6, 28, 52;
DLBY 91; JRDA; MAICYA; MTCW 1; SATA
3, 27; SATA-Obit 68
Singer, Israel Joshua 1893-1944 ..... **TCLC 33**
Singh, Khushwant 1915- .... **CLC 11**
See also CA 9-12R; CAAS 9; CANR 6
Singleton, Ann
See Benedict, Ruth (Fulton)
Sinjohn, John
See Galsworthy, John
Sinyavsky, Andrei (Donatevich) 1925-1997
CLC 8
See also CA 85-88; 159
Sirin, V.
See Nabokov, Vladimir (Vladimirovich)
Sissman, L(ouis) E(dward) 1928-1976
CLC 9, 18
See also CA 21-24R; 65-68; CANR 13; DLB 5
Sisson, C(harles) H(ubert) 1914- .... **CLC 8**
See also CA 1-4R; CAAS 3; CANR 3, 48; DLB
27
Sitwell, Dame Edith 1887-1964...**CLC 2, 9, 67;**
DAM POET; PC 3
See also CA 9-12R; CANR 35; CDBLB 1945-
1960; DLB 20; MTCW 1
Siwaarmill, H. P.
See Sharp, William
Sjoewall, Maj 1935-............................ **CLC 7**
See also CA 65-68
Sjowall, Maj
See Sjoewall, Maj
Skelton, Robin 1925-1997 .... **CLC 13**
See also AITN 2; CA 5-8R; 160; CAAS 5; CANR
28; DLB 27, 53
Skolimowski, Jerzy 1938- .... **CLC 20**
See also CA 128
Skram, Amalie (Bertha) 1847-1905...**TCLC 25**
See also CA 165
Skvorecky, Josef (Vaclav) 1924-...**CLC 15, 39,**
69; DAC; DAM NOV
See also CA 61-64; CAAS 1; CANR 10, 34, 63;
MTCW 1
Slade, Bernard .... **CLC 11, 46**
See also Newbound, Bernard Slade
See also CAAS 9; DLB 53

Slaughter, Carolyn 1946- .... **CLC 56**
See also CA 85-88
Slaughter, Frank G(ill) 1908- .... **CLC 29**
See also AITN 2; CA 5-8R; CANR 5; INT
CANR-5
Slavitt, David R(ytman) 1935-........ **CLC 5, 14**
See also CA 21-24R; CAAS 3; CANR 41; DLB
5, 6
Slesinger, Tess 1905-1945 .... **TCLC 10**
See also CA 107; DLB 102
Slessor, Kenneth 1901-1971 .... **CLC 14**
See also CA 102; 89-92
Slowacki, Juliusz 1809-1849 .... **NCLC 15**
Smart, Christopher 1722-1771 ... **LC 3; DAM**
POET; PC 13
See also DLB 109
Smart, Elizabeth 1913-1986 .... **CLC 54**
See also CA 81-84; 118; DLB 88
Smiley, Jane (Graves) 1949-.... **CLC 53, 76;**
DAM POP
See also CA 104; CANR 30, 50; INT CANR-30
Smith, A(rthur) J(ames) M(arshall) 1902-1980
CLC 15; DAC
See also CA 1-4R; 102; CANR 4; DLB 88
Smith, Adam 1723-1790 .... **LC 36**
See also DLB 104
Smith, Alexander 1829-1867 .... **NCLC 59**
See also DLB 32, 55
Smith, Anna Deavere 1950- .... **CLC 86**
See also CA 133
Smith, Betty (Wehner) 1896-1972 ...... **CLC 19**
See also CA 5-8R; 33-36R; DLBY 82; SATA 6
Smith, Charlotte (Turner) 1749-1806
NCLC 23
See also DLB 39, 109
Smith, Clark Ashton 1893-1961 .... **CLC 43**
See also CA 143
Smith, Dave .... **CLC 22, 42**
See also Smith, David (Jeddie)
See also CAAS 7; DLB 5
Smith, David (Jeddie) 1942-
See Smith, Dave
See also CA 49-52; CANR 1, 59; DAM POET
Smith, Florence Margaret 1902-1971
See Smith, Stevie
See also CA 17-18; 29-32R; CANR 35; CAP 2;
DAM POET; MTCW 1
Smith, Iain Crichton 1928- .... **CLC 64**
See also CA 21-24R; DLB 40, 139
Smith, John 1580(?)-1631 .... **LC 9**
See also DLB 24, 30
Smith, Johnston
See Crane, Stephen (Townley)
Smith, Joseph, Jr. 1805-1844 .... **NCLC 53**
Smith, Lee 1944- .... **CLC 25, 73**
See also CA 114; 119; CANR 46; DLB 143;
DLBY 83; INT 119
Smith, Martin
See Smith, Martin Cruz
Smith, Martin Cruz 1942- ...... **CLC 25; DAM**
MULT, POP
See also BEST 89:4; CA 85-88; CANR 6, 23,
43, 65; INT CANR-23; NNAL
Smith, Mary-Ann Tirone 1944- .... **CLC 39**
See also CA 118; 136
Smith, Patti 1946- .... **CLC 12**
See also CA 93-96; CANR 63
Smith, Pauline (Urmson) 1882-1959...**TCLC 25**
Smith, Rosamond
See Oates, Joyce Carol
Smith, Sheila Kaye
See Kaye-Smith, Sheila

Smith, Stevie .... **CLC 3, 8, 25, 44; PC 12**
See also Smith, Florence Margaret
See also DLB 20
Smith, Wilbur (Addison) 1933- .... **CLC 33**
See also CA 13-16R; CANR 7, 46, 66; MTCW 1
Smith, William Jay 1918- .... **CLC 6**
See also CA 5-8R; CANR 44; DLB 5; MAICYA;
SAAS 22; SATA 2, 68
Smith, Woodrow Wilson
See Kuttner, Henry
Smolenskin, Peretz 1842-1885 .... **NCLC 30**
Smollett, Tobias (George) 1721-1771 ..... **LC 2**
See also CDBLB 1660-1789; DLB 39, 104
Snodgrass, W(illiam) D(e Witt) 1926-...**CLC 2,**
6, 10, 18, 68; DAM POET
See also CA 1-4R; CANR 6, 36, 65; DLB 5;
MTCW 1
Snow, C(harles) P(ercy) 1905-1980...**CLC 1, 4,**
6, 9, 13, 19; DAM NOV
See also CA 5-8R; 101; CANR 28; CDBLB 1945-
1960; DLB 15, 77; DLBD 17; MTCW 1
Snow, Frances Compton
See Adams, Henry (Brooks)
Snyder, Gary (Sherman) 1930-...**CLC 1, 2, 5, 9,**
32; DAM POET; PC 21
See also CA 17-20R; CANR 30, 60; DLB 5, 16,
165
Snyder, Zilpha Keatley 1927- .... **CLC 17**
See also AAYA 15; CA 9-12R; CANR 38; CLR
31; JRDA; MAICYA; SAAS 2; SATA 1, 28, 75
Soares, Bernardo
See Pessoa, Fernando (Antonio Nogueira)
Sobh, A.
See Shamlu, Ahmad
Sobol, Joshua .... **CLC 60**
Socrates 469B.C.-399B.C. .... **CMLC 27**
Soderberg, Hjalmar 1869-1941 ...... **TCLC 39**
Sodergran, Edith (Irene)
See Soedergran, Edith (Irene)
Soedergran, Edith (Irene) 1892-1923
TCLC 31
Softly, Edgar
See Lovecraft, H(oward) P(hillips)
Softly, Edward
See Lovecraft, H(oward) P(hillips)
Sokolov, Raymond 1941- .... **CLC 7**
See also CA 85-88
Solo, Jay
See Ellison, Harlan (Jay)
Sologub, Fyodor .... **TCLC 9**
See also Teternikov, Fyodor Kuzmich
Solomons, Ikey Esquir
See Thackeray, William Makepeace
Solomos, Dionysios 1798-1857 .... **NCLC 15**
Solwoska, Mara
See French, Marilyn
Solzhenitsyn, Aleksandr I(sayevich) 1918-
CLC 1, 2, 4, 7, 9, 10, 18, 26, 34, 78; DA;
DAB; DAC; DAM MST, NOV; SSC 32;
WLC
See also AITN 1; CA 69-72; CANR 40, 65;
MTCW 1
Somers, Jane
See Lessing, Doris (May)
Somerville, Edith 1858-1949 .... **TCLC 51**
See also DLB 135
Somerville & Ross
See Martin, Violet Florence; Somerville, Edith
Sommer, Scott 1951- .... **CLC 25**
See also CA 106
Sondheim, Stephen (Joshua) 1930-... **CLC 30,**
39; DAM DRAM
See also AAYA 11; CA 103; CANR 47, 68

Song, Cathy 1955- .... **PC 21**
> See also CA 154; DLB 169

Sontag, Susan 1933-...**CLC 1, 2, 10, 13, 31, 105;
DAM POP**
> See also CA 17-20R; CANR 25, 51; DLB 2, 67;
> MTCW 1

Sophocles 496(?)B.C.-406(?)B.C. .. **CMLC 2;
DA; DAB; DAC; DAM DRAM, MST; DC
1; WLCS**
> See also DLB 176

Sordello 1189-1269 .... **CMLC 15**
Sorel, Julia
> See Drexler, Rosalyn

Sorrentino, Gilbert 1929-...**CLC 3, 7, 14, 22, 40**
> See also CA 77-80; CANR 14, 33; DLB 5, 173;
> DLBY 80; INT CANR-14

Soto, Gary 1952-.. **CLC 32, 80; DAM MULT;
HLC**
> See also AAYA 10; CA 119; 125; CANR 50; CLR
> 38; DLB 82; HW; INT 125; JRDA; SATA 80

Soupault, Philippe 1897-1990 .... **CLC 68**
> See also CA 116; 147; 131

Souster, (Holmes) Raymond 1921-...**CLC 5, 14;
DAC; DAM POET**
> See also CA 13-16R; CAAS 14; CANR 13, 29,
> 53; DLB 88; SATA 63

Southern, Terry 1924(?)-1995 .... **CLC 7**
> See also CA 1-4R; 150; CANR 1, 55; DLB 2

Southey, Robert 1774-1843 .... **NCLC 8**
> See also DLB 93, 107, 142; SATA 54

Southworth, Emma Dorothy Eliza Nevitte 1819-
> 1899 .... **NCLC 26**

Souza, Ernest
> See Scott, Evelyn

Soyinka, Wole 1934-...**CLC 3, 5, 14, 36, 44;
BLC 3; DA; DAB; DAC; DAM DRAM,
MST, MULT; DC 2; WLC**
> See also BW 2; CA 13-16R; CANR 27, 39; DLB
> 125; MTCW 1

Spackman, W(illiam) M(ode) 1905-1990
CLC 46
> See also CA 81-84; 132

Spacks, Barry (Bernard) 1931- .... **CLC 14**
> See also CA 154; CANR 33; DLB 105

Spanidou, Irini 1946- .... **CLC 44**
Spark, Muriel (Sarah) 1918-**CLC 2, 3, 5, 8, 13,
18, 40, 94; DAB; DAC; DAM MST, NOV;
SSC 10**
> See also CA 5-8R; CANR 12, 36; CDBLB 1945-
> 1960; DLB 15, 139; INT CANR-12; MTCW 1

Spaulding, Douglas
> See Bradbury, Ray (Douglas)

Spaulding, Leonard
> See Bradbury, Ray (Douglas)

Spence, J. A. D.
> See Eliot, T(homas) S(tearns)

Spencer, Elizabeth 1921- .... **CLC 22**
> See also CA 13-16R; CANR 32, 65; DLB 6;
> MTCW 1; SATA 14

Spencer, Leonard G.
> See Silverberg, Robert

Spencer, Scott 1945- .... **CLC 30**
> See also CA 113; CANR 51; DLBY 86

Spender, Stephen (Harold) 1909-1995...**CLC 1,
2, 5, 10, 41, 91; DAM POET**
> See also CA 9-12R; 149; CANR 31, 54; CDBLB
> 1945-1960; DLB 20; MTCW 1

Spengler, Oswald (Arnold Gottfried) 1880-1936
TCLC 25
> See also CA 118

Spenser, Edmund 1552(?)-1599...**LC 5, 39; DA;
DAB; DAC; DAM MST, POET; PC 8; WLC**
> See also CDBLB Before 1660; DLB 167

Spicer, Jack 1925-1965 ..... **CLC 8, 18, 72;
DAM POET**
> See also CA 85-88; DLB 5, 16, 193

Spiegelman, Art 1948- .... **CLC 76**
> See also AAYA 10; CA 125; CANR 41, 55

Spielberg, Peter 1929-.......................... **CLC 6**
> See also CA 5-8R; CANR 4, 48; DLBY 81

Spielberg, Steven 1947- .... **CLC 20**
> See also AAYA 8, 24; CA 77-80; CANR 32;
> SATA 32

Spillane, Frank Morrison 1918-
> See Spillane, Mickey
> See also CA 25-28R; CANR 28, 63; MTCW 1;
> SATA 66

Spillane, Mickey .... **CLC 3, 13**
> See also Spillane, Frank Morrison

Spinoza, Benedictus de 1632-1677 .... **LC 9**
Spinrad, Norman (Richard) 1940- ..... **CLC 46**
> See also CA 37-40R; CAAS 19; CANR 20; DLB
> 8; INT CANR-20

Spitteler, Carl (Friedrich Georg) 1845-1924
TCLC 12
> See also CA 109; DLB 129

Spivack, Kathleen (Romola Drucker) 1938-
CLC 6
> See also CA 49-52

Spoto, Donald 1941- .... **CLC 39**
> See also CA 65-68; CANR 11, 57

Springsteen, Bruce (F.) 1949- .... **CLC 17**
> See also CA 111

Spurling, Hilary 1940- .... **CLC 34**
> See also CA 104; CANR 25, 52

Spyker, John Howland
> See Elman, Richard (Martin)

Squires, (James) Radcliffe 1917-1993...**CLC 51**
> See also CA 1-4R; 140; CANR 6, 21

Srivastava, Dhanpat Rai 1880(?)-1936
> See Premchand
> See also CA 118

Stacy, Donald
> See Pohl, Frederik

Stael, Germaine de 1766-1817
> See Stael-Holstein, Anne Louise Germaine
> Necker Baronn
> See also DLB 119

**Stael-Holstein, Anne Louise Germaine Necker
Baronn** 1766-1817 .... **NCLC 3**
> See also Stael, Germaine de
> See also DLB 192

Stafford, Jean 1915-1979...**CLC 4, 7, 19, 68;
SSC 26**
> See also CA 1-4R; 85-88; CANR 3, 65; DLB 2,
> 173; MTCW 1; SATA-Obit 22

Stafford, William (Edgar) 1914-1993...**CLC 4,
7, 29; DAM POET**
> See also CA 5-8R; 142; CAAS 3; CANR 5, 22;
> DLB 5; INT CANR-22

Stagnelius, Eric Johan 1793-1823 ... **NCLC 61**
Staines, Trevor
> See Brunner, John (Kilian Houston)

Stairs, Gordon
> See Austin, Mary (Hunter)

Stannard, Martin 1947- .... **CLC 44**
> See also CA 142; DLB 155

Stanton, Elizabeth Cady 1815-1902...**TCLC 73**
> See also DLB 79

Stanton, Maura 1946- .... **CLC 9**
> See also CA 89-92; CANR 15; DLB 120

Stanton, Schuyler
> See Baum, L(yman) Frank

Stapledon, (William) Olaf 1886-1950
TCLC 22
> See also CA 111; 162; DLB 15

Starbuck, George (Edwin) 1931-1996
CLC 53; DAM POET
> See also CA 21-24R; 153; CANR 23

Stark, Richard
> See Westlake, Donald E(dwin)

Staunton, Schuyler
> See Baum, L(yman) Frank

Stead, Christina (Ellen) 1902-1983...**CLC 2, 5,
8, 32, 80**
> See also CA 13-16R; 109; CANR 33, 40; MTCW
> 1

Stead, William Thomas 1849-1912
TCLC 48
> See also CA 167

Steele, Richard 1672-1729 .... **LC 18**
> See also CDBLB 1660-1789; DLB 84, 101

Steele, Timothy (Reid) 1948- .... **CLC 45**
> See also CA 93-96; CANR 16, 50; DLB 120

Steffens, (Joseph) Lincoln 1866-1936
TCLC 20
> See also CA 117

Stegner, Wallace (Earle) 1909-1993.... **CLC 9,
49, 81; DAM NOV; SSC 27**
> See also AITN 1; BEST 90:3; CA 1-4R; 141;
> CAAS 9; CANR 1, 21, 46; DLB 9; DLBY 93;
> MTCW 1

Stein, Gertrude 1874-1946...**TCLC 1, 6, 28, 48;
DA; DAB; DAC; DAM MST, NOV, POET;
PC 18; WLC**
> See also CA 104; 132; CDALB 1917-1929; DLB
> 4, 54, 86; DLBD 15; MTCW 1

Steinbeck, John (Ernst) 1902-1968...**CLC 1, 5,
9, 13, 21, 34, 45, 75; DA; DAB; DAC; DAM
DRAM, MST, NOV; SSC 11; WLC**
> See also AAYA 12; CA 1-4R; 25-28R; CANR 1,
> 35; CDALB 1929-1941; DLB 7, 9; DLBD 2;
> MTCW 1; SATA 9

Steinem, Gloria 1934- .... **CLC 63**
> See also CA 53-56; CANR 28, 51; MTCW 1

Steiner, George 1929-.... **CLC 24; DAM NOV**
> See also CA 73-76; CANR 31, 67; DLB 67;
> MTCW 1; SATA 62

Steiner, K. Leslie
> See Delany, Samuel R(ay, Jr.)

Steiner, Rudolf 1861-1925 .... **TCLC 13**
> See also CA 107

Stendhal 1783-1842 ..... **NCLC 23, 46; DA;
DAB; DAC; DAM MST, NOV; SSC 27;
WLC**
> See also DLB 119

Stephen, Adeline Virginia
> See Woolf, (Adeline) Virginia

Stephen, SirLeslie 1832-1904 .... **TCLC 23**
> See also CA 123; DLB 57, 144, 190

Stephen, Sir Leslie
> See Stephen, SirLeslie

Stephen, Virginia
> See Woolf, (Adeline) Virginia

Stephens, James 1882(?)-1950 .... **TCLC 4**
> See also CA 104; DLB 19, 153, 162

Stephens, Reed
> See Donaldson, Stephen R.

Steptoe, Lydia
> See Barnes, Djuna

Sterchi, Beat 1949- .... **CLC 65**
Sterling, Brett
> See Bradbury, Ray (Douglas); Hamilton, Edmond

Sterling, Bruce 1954- .... **CLC 72**
> See also CA 119; CANR 44

Sterling, George 1869-1926 .... **TCLC 20**
> See also CA 117; 165; DLB 54

Stern, Gerald 1925- .... **CLC 40, 100**
> See also CA 81-84; CANR 28; DLB 105

Stern, Richard (Gustave) 1928- ..... **CLC 4, 39**
See also CA 1-4R; CANR 1, 25, 52; DLBY 87;
INT CANR-25

Sternberg, Josef von 1894-1969 .... **CLC 20**
See also CA 81-84

Sterne, Laurence 1713-1768 .... **LC 2; DA;
DAB; DAC; DAM MST, NOV; WLC**
See also CDBLB 1660-1789; DLB 39

Sternheim, (William Adolf) Carl 1878-1942
TCLC 8
See also CA 105; DLB 56, 118

Stevens, Mark 1951- .... **CLC 34**
See also CA 122

Stevens, Wallace 1879-1955...**TCLC 3, 12, 45;
DA; DAB; DAC; DAM MST, POET; PC 6;
WLC**
See also CA 104; 124; CDALB 1929-1941; DLB
54; MTCW 1

Stevenson, Anne (Katharine) 1933-...**CLC 7, 33**
See also CA 17-20R; CAAS 9; CANR 9, 33; DLB
40; MTCW 1

Stevenson, Robert Louis (Balfour) 1850-1894
**NCLC 5, 14, 63; DA; DAB; DAC; DAM
MST, NOV; SSC 11; WLC**
See also AAYA 24; CDBLB 1890-1914; CLR 10,
11; DLB 18, 57, 141, 156, 174; DLBD 13;
JRDA; MAICYA; SATA 100; YABC 2

Stewart, J(ohn) I(nnes) M(ackintosh) 1906-1994
CLC 7, 14, 32
See also CA 85-88; 147; CAAS 3; CANR 47;
MTCW 1

Stewart, Mary (Florence Elinor) 1916-
CLC 7, 35; DAB
See also CA 1-4R; CANR 1, 59; SATA 12

Stewart, Mary Rainbow
See Stewart, Mary (Florence Elinor)

Stifle, June
See Campbell, Maria

Stifter, Adalbert 1805-1868...**NCLC 41; SSC 28**
See also DLB 133

Still, James 1906- .... **CLC 49**
See also CA 65-68; CAAS 17; CANR 10, 26;
DLB 9; SATA 29

Sting 1951-
See Sumner, Gordon Matthew
See also CA 167

Stirling, Arthur
See Sinclair, Upton (Beall)

Stitt, Milan 1941- .... **CLC 29**
See also CA 69-72

Stockton, Francis Richard 1834-1902
See Stockton, Frank R.
See also CA 108; 137; MAICYA; SATA 44

Stockton, Frank R. .... **TCLC 47**
See also Stockton, Francis Richard
See also DLB 42, 74; DLBD 13; SATA-Brief 32

Stoddard, Charles
See Kuttner, Henry

Stoker, Abraham 1847-1912
See Stoker, Bram
See also CA 105; 150; DA; DAC; DAM MST,
NOV; SATA 29

Stoker, Bram 1847-1912...**TCLC 8; DAB; WLC**
See also Stoker, Abraham
See also AAYA 23; CDBLB 1890-1914; DLB
36, 70, 178

Stolz, Mary (Slattery) 1920- .... **CLC 12**
See also AAYA 8; AITN 1; CA 5-8R; CANR 13,
41; JRDA; MAICYA; SAAS 3; SATA 10, 71

Stone, Irving 1903-1989 .. **CLC 7; DAM POP**
See also AITN 1; CA 1-4R; 129; CAAS 3; CANR
1, 23; INT CANR-23; MTCW 1; SATA 3;
SATA-Obit 64

Stone, Oliver (William) 1946- .... **CLC 73**
See also AAYA 15; CA 110; CANR 55

Stone, Robert (Anthony) 1937-...**CLC 5, 23, 42**
See also CA 85-88; CANR 23, 66; DLB 152; INT
CANR-23; MTCW 1

Stone, Zachary
See Follett, Ken(neth Martin)

Stoppard, Tom 1937-...**CLC 1, 3, 4, 5, 8, 15, 29,
34, 63, 91; DA; DAB; DAC; DAM DRAM,
MST; DC 6; WLC**
See also CA 81-84; CANR 39, 67; CDBLB 1960
to Present; DLB 13; DLBY 85; MTCW 1

Storey, David (Malcolm) 1933-...**CLC 2, 4, 5, 8;
DAM DRAM**
See also CA 81-84; CANR 36; DLB 13, 14;
MTCW 1

Storm, Hyemeyohsts 1935- .... **CLC 3; DAM
MULT**
See also CA 81-84; CANR 45; NNAL

Storm, (Hans) Theodor (Woldsen) 1817-1888
NCLC 1; SSC 27
See also DLB 129

Storni, Alfonsina 1892-1938 .. **TCLC 5; DAM
MULT; HLC**
See also CA 104; 131; HW

Stoughton, William 1631-1701 .... **LC 38**
See also DLB 24

Stout, Rex (Todhunter) 1886-1975 ...... **CLC 3**
See also AITN 2; CA 61-64; CANR 71

Stow, (Julian) Randolph 1935- ..... **CLC 23, 48**
See also CA 13-16R; CANR 33; MTCW 1

Stowe, Harriet (Elizabeth) Beecher 1811-1896
**NCLC 3, 50; DA; DAB; DAC; DAM MST,
NOV; WLC**
See also CDALB 1865-1917; DLB 1, 12, 42, 74,
189; JRDA; MAICYA; YABC 1

Strachey, (Giles) Lytton 1880-1932...**TCLC 12**
See also CA 110; DLB 149; DLBD 10

Strand, Mark 1934- .... **CLC 6, 18, 41, 71;
DAM POET**
See also CA 21-24R; CANR 40, 65; DLB 5;
SATA 41

Straub, Peter (Francis) 1943-... **CLC 28, 107;
DAM POP**
See also BEST 89:1; CA 85-88; CANR 28, 65;
DLBY 84; MTCW 1

Strauss, Botho 1944- .... **CLC 22**
See also CA 157; DLB 124

Streatfeild, (Mary) Noel 1895(?)-1986..**CLC 21**
See also CA 81-84; 120; CANR 31; CLR 17;
DLB 160; MAICYA; SATA 20; SATA-Obit 48

Stribling, T(homas) S(igismund) 1881-1965
CLC 23
See also CA 107; DLB 9

Strindberg, (Johan) August 1849-1912
**TCLC 1, 8, 21, 47; DA; DAB; DAC; DAM
DRAM, MST; WLC**
See also CA 104; 135

Stringer, Arthur 1874-1950 .... **TCLC 37**
See also CA 161; DLB 92

Stringer, David
See Roberts, Keith (John Kingston)

Stroheim, Erich von 1885-1957 ...... **TCLC 71**

Strugatskii, Arkadii (Natanovich) 1925-1991
CLC 27
See also CA 106; 135

Strugatskii, Boris (Natanovich) 1933-...**CLC 27**
See also CA 106

Strummer, Joe 1953(?)- .... **CLC 30**

Stuart, Don A.
See Campbell, John W(ood, Jr.)

Stuart, Ian
See MacLean, Alistair (Stuart)

Stuart, Jesse (Hilton) 1906-1984...**CLC 1, 8, 11,
14, 34; SSC 31**
See also CA 5-8R; 112; CANR 31; DLB 9, 48,
102; DLBY 84; SATA 2; SATA-Obit 36

Sturgeon, Theodore (Hamilton) 1918-1985
CLC 22, 39
See also Queen, Ellery
See also CA 81-84; 116; CANR 32; DLB 8;
DLBY 85; MTCW 1

Sturges, Preston 1898-1959 .... **TCLC 48**
See also CA 114; 149; DLB 26

Styron, William 1925-...**CLC 1, 3, 5, 11, 15, 60;
DAM NOV, POP; SSC 25**
See also BEST 90:4; CA 5-8R; CANR 6, 33;
CDALB 1968-1988; DLB 2, 143; DLBY 80;
INT CANR-6; MTCW 1

Su, Chien 1884-1918
See Su Man-shu
See also CA 123

Suarez Lynch, B.
See Bioy Casares, Adolfo; Borges, Jorge Luis

Suckow, Ruth 1892-1960 .... **SSC 18**
See also CA 113; DLB 9, 102

Sudermann, Hermann 1857-1928 ... **TCLC 15**
See also CA 107; DLB 118

Sue, Eugene 1804-1857 .... **NCLC 1**
See also DLB 119

Sueskind, Patrick 1949- .... **CLC 44**
See also Suskind, Patrick

Sukenick, Ronald 1932- .... **CLC 3, 4, 6, 48**
See also CA 25-28R; CAAS 8; CANR 32; DLB
173; DLBY 81

Suknaski, Andrew 1942- .... **CLC 19**
See also CA 101; DLB 53

Sullivan, Vernon
See Vian, Boris

Sully Prudhomme 1839-1907 .... **TCLC 31**

Su Man-shu .... **TCLC 24**
See also Su, Chien

Summerforest, Ivy B.
See Kirkup, James

Summers, Andrew James 1942- .... **CLC 26**

Summers, Andy
See Summers, Andrew James

Summers, Hollis (Spurgeon, Jr.) 1916-
CLC 10
See also CA 5-8R; CANR 3; DLB 6

**Summers, (Alphonsus Joseph-Mary Augustus)
Montague** 1880-1948 .... **TCLC 16**
See also CA 118; 163

Sumner, Gordon Matthew .... **CLC 26**
See also Sting

Surtees, Robert Smith 1803-1864 ... **NCLC 14**
See also DLB 21

Susann, Jacqueline 1921-1974 .... **CLC 3**
See also AITN 1; CA 65-68; 53-56; MTCW 1

Su Shih 1036-1101 .... **CMLC 15**

Suskind, Patrick
See Sueskind, Patrick
See also CA 145

Sutcliff, Rosemary 1920-1992...**CLC 26; DAB;
DAC; DAM MST, POP**
See also AAYA 10; CA 5-8R; 139; CANR 37;
CLR 1, 37; JRDA; MAICYA; SATA 6, 44, 78;
SATA-Obit 73

Sutro, Alfred 1863-1933 .... **TCLC 6**
See also CA 105; DLB 10

Sutton, Henry
See Slavitt, David R(ytman)

Svevo, Italo 1861-1928 .. **TCLC 2, 35; SSC 25**
See also Schmitz, Aron Hector

Swados, Elizabeth (A.) 1951- .... **CLC 12**
See also CA 97-100; CANR 49; INT 97-100

Wahloo, Per 1926-1975 ....**CLC 7**
See also CA 61-64

Wahloo, Peter
See Wahloo, Per

Wain, John (Barrington) 1925-1994... **CLC 2, 11, 15, 46**
See also CA 5-8R; 145; CAAS 4; CANR 23, 54; CDBLB 1960 to Present; DLB 15, 27, 139, 155; MTCW 1

Wajda, Andrzej 1926- ....**CLC 16**
See also CA 102

Wakefield, Dan 1932- ....**CLC 7**
See also CA 21-24R; CAAS 7

Wakoski, Diane 1937-...**CLC 2, 4, 7, 9, 11, 40; DAM POET; PC 15**
See also CA 13-16R; CAAS 1; CANR 9, 60; DLB 5; INT CANR-9

Wakoski-Sherbell, Diane
See Wakoski, Diane

Walcott, Derek (Alton) 1930-...**CLC 2, 4, 9, 14, 25, 42, 67, 76; BLC 3; DAB; DAC; DAM MST, MULT, POET; DC 7**
See also BW 2; CA 89-92; CANR 26, 47; DLB 117; DLBY 81; MTCW 1

Waldman, Anne (Lesley) 1945- ....**CLC 7**
See also CA 37-40R; CAAS 17; CANR 34, 69; DLB 16

Waldo, E. Hunter
See Sturgeon, Theodore (Hamilton)

Waldo, Edward Hamilton
See Sturgeon, Theodore (Hamilton)

Walker, Alice (Malsenior) 1944-...**CLC 5, 6, 9, 19, 27, 46, 58, 103; BLC 3; DA; DAB; DAC; DAM MST, MULT, NOV, POET, POP; SSC 5; WLCS**
See also AAYA 3; BEST 89:4; BW 2; CA 37-40R; CANR 9, 27, 49, 66; CDALB 1968-1988; DLB 6, 33, 143; INT CANR-27; MTCW 1; SATA 31

Walker, David Harry 1911-1992 ....**CLC 14**
See also CA 1-4R; 137; CANR 1; SATA 8; SATA-Obit 71

Walker, Edward Joseph 1934-
See Walker, Ted
See also CA 21-24R; CANR 12, 28, 53

Walker, George F. 1947- ... **CLC 44, 61; DAB; DAC; DAM MST**
See also CA 103; CANR 21, 43, 59; DLB 60

Walker, Joseph A. 1935-.........**CLC 19; DAM DRAM, MST**
See also BW 1; CA 89-92; CANR 26; DLB 38

Walker, Margaret (Abigail) 1915-.. **CLC 1, 6; BLC; DAM MULT; PC 20**
See also BW 2; CA 73-76; CANR 26, 54; DLB 76, 152; MTCW 1

Walker, Ted ....**CLC 13**
See also Walker, Edward Joseph
See also DLB 40

Wallace, David Foster 1962-....... **CLC 50, 114**
See also CA 132; CANR 59

Wallace, Dexter
See Masters, Edgar Lee

Wallace, (Richard Horatio) Edgar 1875-1932 **TCLC 57**
See also CA 115; DLB 70

Wallace, Irving 1916-1990 .. **CLC 7, 13; DAM NOV, POP**
See also AITN 1; CA 1-4R; 132; CAAS 1; CANR 1, 27; INT CANR-27; MTCW 1

Wallant, Edward Lewis 1926-1962...**CLC 5, 10**
See also CA 1-4R; CANR 22; DLB 2, 28, 143; MTCW 1

Walley, Byron
See Card, Orson Scott

Walpole, Horace 1717-1797 ....**LC 2**
See also DLB 39, 104

Walpole, Hugh (Seymour) 1884-1941...**TCLC 5**
See also CA 104; 165; DLB 34

Walser, Martin 1927- ....**CLC 27**
See also CA 57-60; CANR 8, 46; DLB 75, 124

Walser, Robert 1878-1956...**TCLC 18; SSC 20**
See also CA 118; 165; DLB 66

Walsh, Jill Paton ....**CLC 35**
See also Paton Walsh, Gillian
See also AAYA 11; CLR 2; DLB 161; SAAS 3

Walter, Villiam Christian
See Andersen, Hans Christian

Wambaugh, Joseph (Aloysius, Jr.) 1937- **CLC 3, 18; DAM NOV, POP**
See also AITN 1; BEST 89:3; CA 33-36R; CANR 42, 65; DLB 6; DLBY 83; MTCW 1

Wang Wei 699(?)-761(?) ....**PC 18**

Ward, Arthur Henry Sarsfield 1883-1959
See Rohmer, Sax
See also CA 108

Ward, Douglas Turner 1930- ....**CLC 19**
See also BW 1; CA 81-84; CANR 27; DLB 7, 38

Ward, Mary Augusta
See Ward, Mrs. Humphry

Ward, Mrs. Humphry 1851-1920 ... **TCLC 55**
See also DLB 18

Ward, Peter
See Faust, Frederick (Schiller)

Warhol, Andy 1928(?)-1987 ....**CLC 20**
See also AAYA 12; BEST 89:4; CA 89-92; 121; CANR 34

Warner, Francis (Robert le Plastrier) 1937- **CLC 14**
See also CA 53-56; CANR 11

Warner, Marina 1946- ....**CLC 59**
See also CA 65-68; CANR 21, 55; DLB 194

Warner, Rex (Ernest) 1905-1986 ....**CLC 45**
See also CA 89-92; 119; DLB 15

Warner, Susan (Bogert) 1819-1885...**NCLC 31**
See also DLB 3, 42

Warner, Sylvia (Constance) Ashton
See Ashton-Warner, Sylvia (Constance)

Warner, Sylvia Townsend 1893-1978 ..**CLC 7, 19; SSC 23**
See also CA 61-64; 77-80; CANR 16, 60; DLB 34, 139; MTCW 1

Warren, Mercy Otis 1728-1814 ......**NCLC 13**
See also DLB 31, 200

Warren, Robert Penn 1905-1989...**CLC 1, 4, 6, 8, 10, 13, 18, 39, 53, 59; DA; DAB; DAC; DAM MST, NOV, POET; SSC 4; WLC**
See also AITN 1; CA 13-16R; 129; CANR 10, 47; CDALB 1968-1988; DLB 2, 48, 152; DLBY 80, 89; INT CANR-10; MTCW 1; SATA 46; SATA-Obit 63

Warshofsky, Isaac
See Singer, Isaac Bashevis

Warton, Thomas 1728-1790 ......**LC 15; DAM POET**
See also DLB 104, 109

Waruk, Kona
See Harris, (Theodore) Wilson

Warung, Price 1855-1911 ....**TCLC 45**

Warwick, Jarvis
See Garner, Hugh

Washington, Alex
See Harris, Mark

Washington, Booker T(aliaferro) 1856-1915 **TCLC 10; BLC 3; DAM MULT**
See also BW 1; CA 114; 125; SATA 28

Washington, George 1732-1799 ....**LC 25**
See also DLB 31

Wassermann, (Karl) Jakob 1873-1934 **TCLC 6**
See also CA 104; DLB 66

Wasserstein, Wendy 1950- .... **CLC 32, 59, 90; DAM DRAM; DC 4**
See also CA 121; 129; CABS 3; CANR 53; INT 129; SATA 94

Waterhouse, Keith (Spencer) 1929- ... **CLC 47**
See also CA 5-8R; CANR 38, 67; DLB 13, 15; MTCW 1

Waters, Frank (Joseph) 1902-1995 ....**CLC 88**
See also CA 5-8R; 149; CAAS 13; CANR 3, 18, 63; DLBY 86

Waters, Roger 1944- ....**CLC 35**

Watkins, Frances Ellen
See Harper, Frances Ellen Watkins

Watkins, Gerrold
See Malzberg, Barry N(athaniel)

Watkins, Gloria 1955(?)-
See hooks, bell
See also BW 2; CA 143

Watkins, Paul 1964-.............................**CLC 55**
See also CA 132; CANR 62

Watkins, Vernon Phillips 1906-1967 ..**CLC 43**
See also CA 9-10; 25-28R; CAP 1; DLB 20

Watson, Irving S.
See Mencken, H(enry) L(ouis)

Watson, John H.
See Farmer, Philip Jose

Watson, Richard F.
See Silverberg, Robert

Waugh, Auberon (Alexander) 1939- ....**CLC 7**
See also CA 45-48; CANR 6, 22; DLB 14, 194

Waugh, Evelyn (Arthur St. John) 1903-1966 **CLC 1, 3, 8, 13, 19, 27, 44, 107; DA; DAB; DAC; DAM MST, NOV, POP; WLC**
See also CA 85-88; 25-28R; CANR 22; CDBLB 1914-1945; DLB 15, 162, 195; MTCW 1

Waugh, Harriet 1944- ....**CLC 6**
See also CA 85-88; CANR 22

Ways, C. R.
See Blount, Roy (Alton), Jr.

Waystaff, Simon
See Swift, Jonathan

Webb, (Martha) Beatrice (Potter) 1858-1943 **TCLC 22**
See also Potter, (Helen) Beatrix
See also CA 117

Webb, Charles (Richard) 1939- ....**CLC 7**
See also CA 25-28R

Webb, James H(enry), Jr. 1946- ....**CLC 22**
See also CA 81-84

Webb, Mary (Gladys Meredith) 1881-1927 **TCLC 24**
See also CA 123; DLB 34

Webb, Mrs. Sidney
See Webb, (Martha) Beatrice (Potter)

Webb, Phyllis 1927- ....**CLC 18**
See also CA 104; CANR 23; DLB 53

Webb, Sidney (James) 1859-1947 ... **TCLC 22**
See also CA 117; 163; DLB 190

Webber, Andrew Lloyd ....**CLC 21**
See also Lloyd Webber, Andrew

Weber, Lenora Mattingly 1895-1971...**CLC 12**
See also CA 19-20; 29-32R; CAP 1; SATA 2, 26

Weber, Max 1864-1920 ....**TCLC 69**
See also CA 109

Webster, John 1579(?)-1634(?).... **LC 33; DA; DAB; DAC; DAM DRAM, MST; DC 2; WLC**
See also CDBLB Before 1660; DLB 58

Poetry Criticism
Cumulative Nationality Index

PC Cumulative Title Index

Title Index

Title Index

Title Index

ISBN 0-7876-2015-7

90000

9 780787 620158